College Accounting

DISCARD

College Accounting

A PRACTICAL APPROACH

CANADIAN SEVENTH EDITION

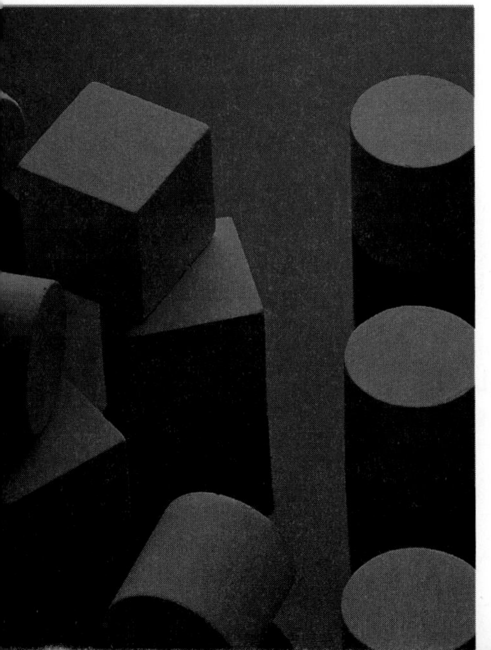

Jeffrey Slater

North Shore Community College

Beverly, Massachusetts

Brian Zwicker

Grant MacEwan Community College

Edmonton, Alberta

Prentice Hall Canada Inc., Toronto, Ontario

Canadian Cataloguing in Publication Data

Slater, Jeffrey, 1947–
College accounting: a practical approach

Canadian 7th ed.
Includes index
ISBN 0-13-020471-4

1. Accounting. I. Zwicker, Brian, 1944– . II. Title.

HF5635.S49 2000 657'.044 C99-930094-6

© 2000, 1996, 1993, 1991 Prentice-Hall Canada Inc., Toronto, Ontario
Pearson Education

ALL RIGHTS RESERVED

No part of this book may be reproduced in any form without permission in writing from the publisher.

Prentice-Hall, Inc., Upper Saddle River, New Jersey
Prentice-Hall International (UK) Limited, London
Prentice-Hall of Australia, Pty. Limited, Sydney
Prentice-Hall Hispanoamericana, S.A., Mexico City
Prentice-Hall of India Private Limited, New Delhi
Prentice-Hall of Japan, Inc., Tokyo
Simon & Schuster Southeast Asia Private Limited, Singapore
Editora Prentice-Hall do Brasil, Ltda., Rio de Janeiro

ISBN 0-13-020471-4

Vice-President and Editorial Director: Patrick Ferrier
Developmental Editor: Anita Smale, CA
Senior Marketing Manager: Ann Byford
Production Editor: Nicole Mellow
Copy Editor: Carol Fordyce
Production Coordinator: Jane Schell
Art Director: Mary Opper
Cover and Interior Design: Sarah Battersby
Cover Image: Superstock
Page Layout: Debbie Kumpf/Hermia Chung

Original American edition published by Prentice-Hall, Inc., Upper Saddle River, New Jersey
Copyright © 1999, 1996, 1993, 1992, 1989

3 4 5 03 02 01

Printed and bound in the United States of America.

Visit the Prentice Hall Canada Web site! Send us your comments, browse our catalogues, and more at **www.phcanada.com**. Or reach us through e-mail at **phcinfo_pubcanada@prenhall.com**

Simply Accounting® is a registered trademark of ACCPAC INTERNATIONAL INC.

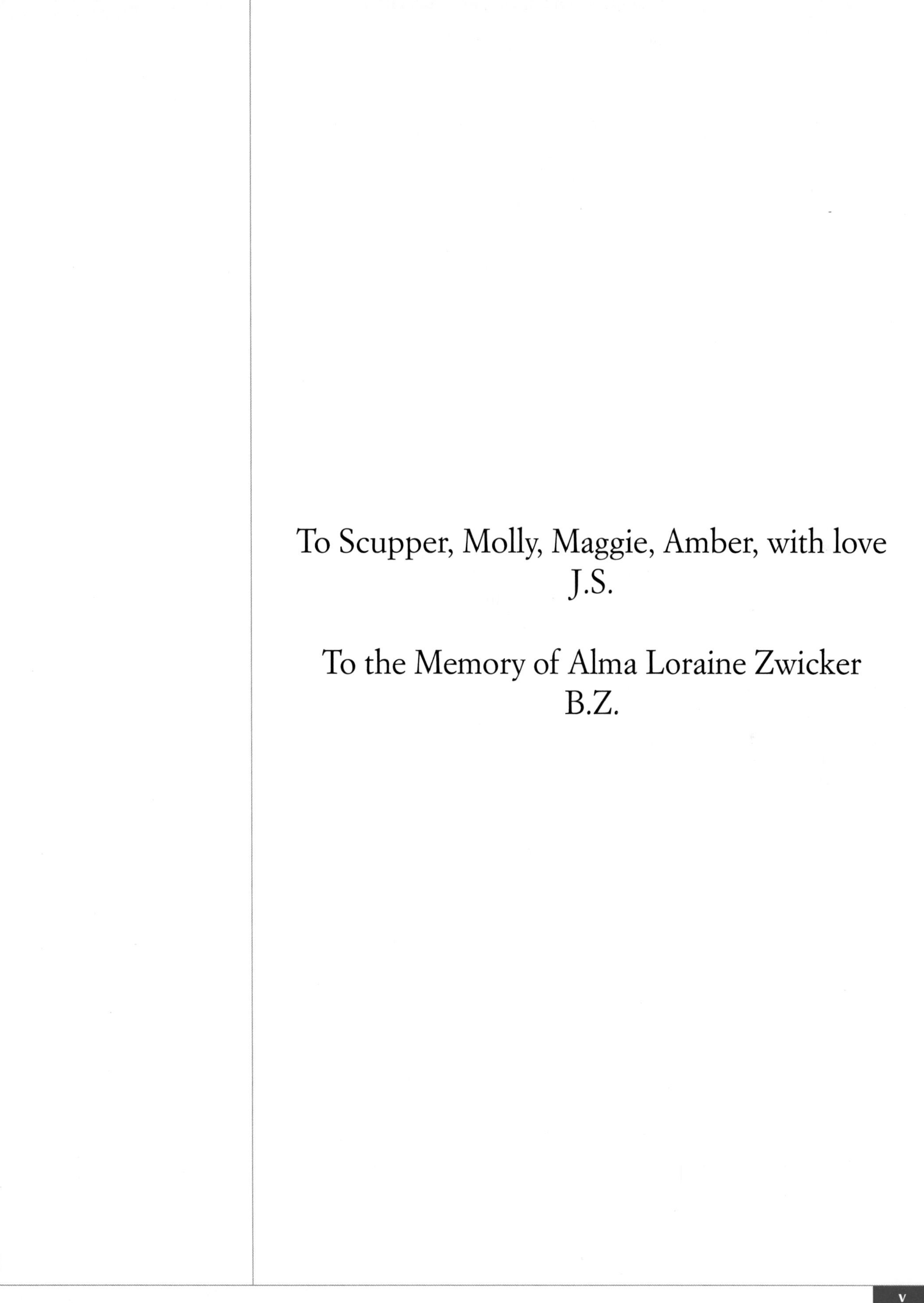

To Scupper, Molly, Maggie, Amber, with love
J.S.

To the Memory of Alma Loraine Zwicker
B.Z.

Brief Contents

Contents

Tejal Govande

CHAPTER 10 SPECIAL JOURNALS: PURCHASES AND CASH PAYMENTS 407

CHAPTER 11 THE SYNOPTIC (COMBINED) JOURNAL 467

CHAPTER 12 PREPARING A WORKSHEET FOR A MERCHANDISING COMPANY 497

CHAPTER 13 COMPLETION OF THE ACCOUNTING CYCLE FOR A MERCHANDISING COMPANY 531

CHAPTER 14 ACCOUNTING FOR BAD DEBTS 576

Preface

TO THE STUDENT

College Accounting: A Practical Approach, Canadian Seventh Edition, was written to introduce you to accounting, a dynamic tool of business. What is accounting and why will you find it useful? Accounting is a planned and orderly way of keeping records for the purpose of seeing how a business is performing. It answers such questions as: Is the business profitable or is it losing money? Which business activities are contributing most to profits and which to losses? Which resources are well employed and which are being wasted? Who owes the business money, and how much? What does the business owe? Accounting is also important for regulatory and tax purposes. You will be surprised at how often your understanding of accounting will work for you on the job.

Learning accounting means familiarizing yourself with many new terms and concepts. Don't be tempted to cut corners and take shortcuts; you will get the most out of your study of accounting if you follow the detailed, step-by-step directions provided in this text. Once you have learned the basic terms and concepts, the rest will quickly fall into place.

We have set up each chapter according to a special format that time has proven makes it easier to learn and remember the material in the chapter. Let's look at each component of a chapter and see why it was set up that way:

- *The Big Picture.* To provide a conceptual overview of topics that will be discussed, each chapter now opens with a short vignette called The Big Picture. The scenarios come from the experience of Tony Freedman, who started his own business (Eldorado Computer Centre) upon graduation from a local community college. Tony keeps his own books, and shares with students how he uses accounting procedures to run a successful and growing business. A Continuing Problem involving Eldorado Computer Centre ends each chapter, covering accounting procedures for an entire business cycle.
- *Broad objectives with page references to introduce the chapter.* These objectives allow you to see where you're headed; they set the stage for the more specific objectives to be found later in the chapter. Page references are given where the material for each objective can be found.
- *Chapters broken down into learning units.* Students continually tell us that they learn best when material is broken into small, manageable units. This way, if a question comes up it can be identified and solved immediately without waiting until the whole chapter is read. And, in this way, you can test yourself on smaller amounts of material to be sure that you've mastered each bit before going on to the next.
- *Objectives with page references follow each unit.* After you have read the unit, the objectives give you a chance to recap what you've read. Stop to see if you can answer the objective—if not, go back to the page referred to and review the material.
- *Self-review quiz follows each unit.* This is a chance to test yourself on what you've just learned and try some hands-on applications of the theory just covered. The forms for the quizzes are in your *Study Guide with Working Papers*. The

solution to the quiz follows right after the quiz in the text. Don't worry if you get something wrong in the quiz—these quizzes are for you, not for your professor. If you do have trouble with the quiz, go back to the problem area in the unit and review it before going on to the next unit.

- *Dunkin' Donuts boxes* More than half the chapters now contain realistic descriptions of how accounting is used at both franchise stores and corporate headquarters of this very successful, internationally known company. These descriptions show you how the skills you learn in class are applied in realistic ways. All boxes are based on interviews with members of the accounting department at corporate headquarters of this well-known company.
- *Discussion questions at the end of the chapter.* These questions relate to the theory covered in the chapter. It is important to make sure you can answer them before going on to the next chapter.
- *Exercises and mini exercises at the end of the chapter.* Exercises review specific topics covered in the chapter. Notes in the margin identify the topic covered by each exercise—if you know you need more work on a certain topic that you feel uncertain about, seek out those exercises that deal with that topic.
- *Problems at the end of the chapter.* There are Groups A, B, and C problems in the text; forms for the problems are provided in your *Study Guide with Working Papers*. As with the exercises, notes in the margin identify the topic(s) covered by each problem.
- *Practical accounting applications at the end of the chapter.* These give you a way to test your accounting knowledge in a situation that might occur on the job. They're challenging and fun.
- *Ethical case sections.* These allow students to formulate a position on a number of realistic situations which they may someday find themselves in. These are most useful for stimulating classroom discussion.
- *Practice problems follow certain chapters.* These problems, called Mini Practice Sets, give a list of transactions and other information needed to perform certain tasks in accounting covered by a set of chapters. At the end of Chapter 5 is a problem that reviews the accounting cycle; in this problem you go through the accounting cycle twice to give you a more complete idea of the procedures involved at the end of each month. At the end of Chapter 8 there is a summary of payroll procedures. After Chapter 13 there is a problem that deals with transactions in a sole proprietorship merchandising company. These problems help put all the theory together in a practical way. Forms for completing the problems are provided in your *Study Guide with Working Papers*.
- *Cumulative review quizzes with page references at the end of the chapter.* Since accounting builds from one chapter to another, it is important to review vocabulary and accounting applications. At the end of each chapter you will find a cumulative review quiz. Each quiz, with page references, will have three parts: vocabulary review, accounting theory, and application problems. The forms for these quizzes, along with the worked-out solutions, will be found in your *Study Guide with Working Papers*.
- *Computer workshops at the end of some chapters.* Computer-based simulations are provided at various points in the text. The almost universal reliance upon computer processing in accounting makes it essential for accounting students to have a good exposure to the subject. Since most educational institutions in Canada already own copies of *Simply Accounting*®, this program from Computer Associates has been selected as the program of choice. Data diskettes are supplied to adopting institutions who wish to use the computer-based simulations. The purpose of the data diskettes is to relieve students of the task of creating their own sets of data. Not only would that be time-consuming, but also it could lead to a number of errors. This way, all students begin with the same accurate data and

can proceed quickly to learn the essentials. We believe that the accounting program chosen, *Simply Accounting for Windows* (Version 6.0A), is used by the majority of postsecondary educational institutions in Canada. However, there may be a small number who do not use it. For those institutions, it is recommended that the simulations be used, but data diskettes will not be available.

If you follow this chapter layout carefully, you will find that you learn the basic terms and concepts easily and remember them better, and that the many chances to apply them in a practical way help you to remember them.

TO THE INSTRUCTOR

Genesis

College Accounting: A Practical Approach, Canadian Seventh Edition, is the result of years of teaching and writing experience in accounting. Our intention in writing this book was to create a vehicle to help maximize student mastery of accounting concepts and procedures.

The needs of students who are not, at this time, considering a career in accounting are unique. It has been our goal in the Canadianization of this text to preserve all the quality features of the US edition and to insert high-quality Canadian material in order to present the best possible resource for students.

Our approach is based on tried and proven learning techniques, and these techniques have, in turn, been reinforced and shaped by in-class experience with students. We have listened to a number of concerns from instructors, and this edition continues to feature the Type C problems. This material should greatly benefit the many institutions that have multiple sections and will provide increased choices for all adopters. We have increased the length and complexity of the Type C problems slightly, but have also tried to be faithful to the text's original purpose—to present accounting for students who are not currently planning a career in the field. A number of other significant features are also incorporated, including integrating GST and HST into Chapters 9, 10, and 11. Most of those reviewers who were approached found this preferable to adding another appendix. We have, however, tried to compartmentalize the presentation intelligently so as not to get in the way of any instructor who may choose to de-emphasize the topic of GST/HST.

The most significant inclusion in this edition is the extension to the computer accounting content. Computers are nowadays involved in accounting to a large extent. While it is still true, we believe, that students best learn practical accounting in traditional ways, it is no longer appropriate to leave students with no knowledge of the ways in which computers can interface with accounting. Accordingly, we have added several excellent computer workshops to those that were available in the previous edition, and have revised Appendix B. These changes, taken together, should afford students a unique and valuable learning experience.

Specifically, new computer workshops have been developed and added at the end of Chapter 6 (with emphasis on bank reconciliations), Chapter 9 (to illustrate the sales journal), and Chapter 15 (to introduce the inventory module). We feel that this new material is useful in extending students' experience and education in today's business environment, which increasingly relies upon computers. However, the material is evolutionary in nature, and does not get in the way of more traditional approaches to mastering the topics in each chapter.

There were many options to consider carefully in selecting the software we felt would be most effective in meeting students' needs. Our basic premise was that all, or almost all, institutions which intend to offer computer accounting components in their courses already own (or license) accounting software, and most of these depend upon *Simply Accounting*. We have therefore elected to supply data diskettes in this format. One advantage of this program is the important option to keep the data sets updated for newer versions of the software, should demand warrant.

The data sets are based upon the latest version of *Simply Accounting* (Version 6.0A) available at the time of writing. The data should be automatically upgraded by future versions of the software.

If our decision does not match your institution's needs, please let your Prentice Hall representative know. The marketplace in this area is very dynamic; we intend to revise and enlarge our data sets continually to meet your needs better.

There are a number of other useful changes made to the Seventh Edition which are designed to facilitate the learning process. While it is not deemed appropriate to include more problems in the text itself, new Type D problems (complete with solutions) have been added to the *Instructor's Resource Guide*. These new problems may be used to help students in various ways, including extra practice, quizzes, examinations, or classroom demonstrations. We feel that this is a major change that is being implemented for the right reasons.

Another valuable change is the extension of material on bank reconciliations. Responses to our market survey suggested that this material (already the most realistic available) could be expanded, so that change was implemented. You will find a new section in Chapter 6 describing and illustrating a realistic bank reconciliation simulation, and two new problems which students can use to demonstrate their mastery of the material. The previous question remains intact, and, of course, a computer workshop has been added to illustrate how *Simply Accounting* handles this aspect of accounting.

The end result is, we believe, a clear, accurate, up-to-date, pedagogically effective text, accompanied by a fully articulated package. The text and its ancillaries offer a full range of teaching and learning tools from which the instructor can choose. It's our hope that the Canadian Seventh Edition will continue to be a positive experience for students and instructors alike.

About the Book

College Accounting: A Practical Approach, Canadian Seventh Edition, is set up so that students have small, manageable units of material to learn, followed by immediate feedback through the self-review quizzes at the end of each unit. Each chapter is divided into learning units, and is organized in the following way.

The Big Picture To provide a conceptual overview of topics that will be discussed, each chapter now opens with a short vignette called The Big Picture. The scenarios come from the experience of Tony Freedman, who started his own business (Eldorado Computer Centre) upon graduation from a local community college. Tony keeps his own books, and shares with students how he uses accounting procedures to run a successful and growing business. A Continuing Problem involving Eldorado Computer Centre ends each chapter, covering accounting procedures for an entire business cycle.

Broad objectives with page references to introduce the chapter These objectives allow students to see where they're headed; they set the stage for the more specific objectives to be found later in the chapter. Page references are given so that the material for each objective can be found easily.

Chapters broken down into learning units Students constantly tell us that they learn best when material is broken into small, manageable units. This way, if a question comes up it can be identified and solved immediately without waiting until the whole chapter is read. And, in this way, students can test themselves on smaller amounts of material to be sure that they've mastered each bit before going on.

Objectives with page references follow each unit At the end of each unit, the objectives are reiterated, giving students a chance to recap what they've read. If they can't respond to an objective, they can go back to the page referred to and review the material.

Self-review quiz follows each unit This is a chance for students to test themselves on what they've just learned and try some hands-on applications of the theory just covered. The forms for the quiz are in the *Study Guide with Working Papers*. The solution to the quiz immediately follows the quiz in the text. If students have trouble with the quiz, they can go back to the problem area in the unit and review it before going on to the next unit.

Summary of key points and key terms at the end of the chapter The material covered in the chapter is reviewed by unit at the end of the chapter. The key points of the summary provide one more chance to review and to point out any weakness in understanding the chapter. Accounting as a discipline is full of new vocabulary. The trick to learning this new vocabulary is to take it slowly and review it often. The terms introduced in the chapter are listed and defined at the end of the chapter so that students can review them and make sure they know what they mean and how they are used in the chapter.

Blueprint at the end of the chapter Some people learn better by seeing something in chart or diagram form rather than reading about it. And we all remember things better if we learn them several different ways. The goal of the blueprint is to review visually the key concepts or procedures in the chapter. It is like a road map, showing students in simple steps what they have just been through in the chapter.

Dunkin' Donuts boxes More than half the chapters now contain realistic descriptions of how accounting is used at both franchise stores and corporate headquarters of this very successful, internationally known company. By reading about how useful the worksheet is to a small business owner (Chapter 4) or how state-of-the-art point-of-sale terminals help store owners manage cash efficiently and effectively (Chapter 6), students are better able to see how the skills they learn in class are applied in realistic ways. All boxes are based on interviews with members of the accounting department at corporate headquarters of this well-known company.

Discussion questions at the end of the chapter These questions review the theory covered in the chapter. Students should make sure they can answer them before going on to the next chapter.

Exercises and mini exercises at the end of the chapter These exercises review specific topics covered in the chapter. Notes in the margin identify the topic covered by each exercise—students who know they need more work on a certain topic can seek out those exercises that deal with the topic.

Problems at the end of the chapter There are Groups A, B, and C problems in the text and a completely new set (the D problems) in the *Instructor's Resource Guide*. Forms to be used to answer them are provided in the *Study Guide with Working Papers*. As with the exercises, notes in the margin identify the topic covered by each problem and, new with this edition, check figures are provided for all problems in the text.

Practical accounting applications at the end of the chapter These are a way to test accounting knowledge in a situation that might occur on the job. They're fun and challenging.

Ethical issues A critical thinking/ethical case is introduced at the end of each chapter. Designed to provoke discussion during class periods, these exercises allow students to grapple with real issues such as those they may face when they enter the workplace.

Practice problems following certain chapters These problems, called Mini Practice Sets, give a list of transactions and information needed to perform certain tasks in accounting covered by a set of chapters. At the end of Chapter 5 is a problem that reviews the accounting cycle; in this problem, students go through the accounting cycle twice to get a more complete idea of the procedures involved at the end of each month. At the end of Chapter 8, there is a summary of payroll procedures.

After Chapter 13 there is a problem that deals with transactions of a sole proprietorship merchandising company. This project covers a three-month period. These problems help put all the theory together in a practical way. Forms for completing the problem are provided in the *Study Guide with Working Papers*. The Mini Practice Sets after Chapters 8 and 13 have been fully revised, and include GST and HST where appropriate.

Computer workshops At appropriate points in the text, special workshops make the learning of computer accounting effective, efficient, and as painless as possible. Use of one of Canada's top programs ensures that most students gain familiarity with this vital learning component.

Canadian Seventh Edition Highlights

The following are some key features that make this text and its supplements more current and supportive of classroom and homework activities.

Payroll updated Chapters 7 and 8 have been rewritten where necessary to reflect the latest laws in effect in Canada.

GST and HST accounting These taxes are a reality in Canada. The essential details of how to account for GST and HST are covered, beginning in Chapter 9. Chapters 9 and 10 have been designed to accommodate instructors who choose either to emphasize or to de-emphasize this topic, and problem material using HST has been introduced.

Chapter on inventory expanded In Chapter 15, students are provided with theory, practice, and applications regarding inventory costing methods and practices. Emphasis is placed on the perpetual inventory method for those who choose to stress it.

Accounting Recall: A cumulative approach At the end of each chapter, students get a chance to recall cumulatively what they've learned in past chapters. The recall is broken into three parts: vocabulary, theory, and practical applications (a page reference is provided for each question). The *Study Guide with Working Papers* contains the forms as well as solutions for the Accounting Recall materials. It's a great review before beginning the next chapter.

Old Chapter 15 eliminated Based on a survey of users, it was decided to reduce the chapter count slightly to make way for the several innovations noted elsewhere. The least used of all chapters was the chapter on notes receivable and notes payable.

Problem material expanded As in previous editions, the A and B sets of problems are designed to reinforce concepts introduced in the chapters. Instructors may also choose from a C set of problems, created to permit a wider choice for institutions which offer multiple sections. These problems are a bit more rigorous than the A and B sets, and will require students to stretch somewhat. New type D problems are included in the *Instructor's Resource Manual* which can add greatly to the classroom experience.

Focus on realistic business-world concepts Several new features address this concern. Whether it be The Big Picture (a small business is described and grows from chapter to chapter); the Continuing Problem (based on the same company as in The Big Picture); newly-designed computer workshops (for instance, Chapter 6 now covers how *Simply Accounting* helps to reconcile bank statements); or the Dunkin' Donuts boxes, no effort has been spared to add to each student's experience the realism that today's business education demands.

Expanded computer workshop coverage While the basic goal of the package has not changed (to facilitate the learning of the basics of accounting), it is appropriate to introduce all students to the realities of the workplace. Hence, we have carefully conceived and integrated three additional computer accounting workshops into the text. Provision of data sets on diskette allows all students to acquire computer accounting skills in an effective and efficient way. Additionally, when these workshops are used as assignments, instructors can count on all students beginning with identical data—an important consideration when grades are to be assigned. Appendix B, which explains the *Simply Accounting* program, has also been revised to cover the latest version available—Version 6.0A.

The Slater/Zwicker Package

The text is just the starting point. Because the needs of Canadian instructors are very high on our priority list, we have taken certain other steps designed to maximize instructor effectiveness and efficiency. These steps include the provision of an *Instructor's Resource Manual*, a Test Item File and PH Test Manager (a computerized test bank on CD-ROM). Another significant change is the complete Canadianization of the *Study Guide with Working Papers* and the *Solutions Manual*. We have invested a great many hours into ensuring the highest quality possible, and we hope it shows in increased clarity, accuracy, and consistency. Let's look at some of the support systems included in Slater/Zwicker package.

Learning Aids to Support the Slater/Zwicker System

Instructor's Resource Manual Newly expanded for this edition is the *Instructor's Resource Manual*. It is intended to bring together between two covers all of the materials that act to facilitate and augment each instructor's own special skills, strengths, and experience. *The Instructor's Resource Manual* includes:

- **Type D problems** Like the C-type problems in the text, these new problems are very slightly more challenging than the A or B problems. Solutions are provided (also in the *Instructor's Resource Manual*) so these new problems can be used in interesting ways—such as for extra-challenge work for students, or on quizzes or examinations. The headings for most of the C-type problems in the *Study Guide with Working Papers* have been deliberately left off (at the request of a number of instructors), and this means these forms can be used for the D-type problems as well, if that is convenient.
- **Class quizzes** Short exercises or review questions designed to reinforce aspects of the chapter coverage
- **Class activities** Something the whole class can take part in to review and reinforce key points
- **Lesson outlines** Chapter material is designed for a variety of classroom situations. There is probably a style that closely fits most educational institutions' scheduling preferences.
- **Typical student misconceptions** This identification of common errors gathered from more than 35 years combined of accounting teaching experience may be valuable—especially to those instructors who are just beginning their careers.
- **Teaching tips** Valuable suggestions that help students remember and assimilate the material
- **Business-world notes** Deals with what actually happens in accounting in the real world and takes students beyond the textbook.
- **Lecture notes** While not intended to replace an appropriate lesson plan, these notes may be very useful as a check that nothing critical is overlooked.

Simply Accounting Data Disk and **Solutions Disk**, and **Electronic Transparencies in PowerPoint** on disk are packaged with the *Instructor's Resource Manual*. (These items are also available in the password-protected Instructor Resources section of *College Accounting's* Companion Website.)

Study Guide with Working Papers This has undergone all necessary revision and enhancement. It contains forms for the quiz at the end of each learning unit in the chapter, for all exercises and mini exercises, for the problems (A, B, and C) at the end of each chapter, and for the practice-set problems that follow Chapters 5, 8, and 13. In addition, all worksheets are now treated as foldouts—a significant enhancement. At the end of each chapter of the *Study Guide with Working Papers*, there is a summary practice test designed to prepare students for in-class exams. It consists of fill-in-the-blank questions, a matching question, and true/false questions. In addition, the forms and solutions for the end-of-chapter Accounting Recalls in the text help students review the concepts covered in each chapter before going on to the next. The answers to the tests are at the end of each chapter of the *Study Guide with Working Papers*. As with the previous editions, the *Study Guide with Working Papers* is a completely Canadian publication. Many changes have been made to help ensure that each student's experience is as effective and efficient as possible.

Solutions Manual This manual provides answers to discussion questions and solutions to exercises, mini exercises, problems, practice problems, practical accounting applications, and ethical cases.

In the front of the *Solutions Manual* is a grid of all problems showing level of difficulty and estimated time needed for completion.

To ensure accurate solutions, each page of the *Solutions Manual* was carefully reviewed by Laurence P. Hanchard, CA. His exacting review will be appreciated by all instructors using this package.

Test Item File Now containing more than 800 questions, the *Test Item File* has been substantially revised and expanded. Every chapter contains multiple-choice, true/false, and problem/essay questions. Each question is coded by degree of difficulty (easy, moderate, or difficult). We have ensured that topics of special concern to Canadians, such as GST, HST, CPP contributions, and Canadian tax procedures, are appropriately covered.

PH Test Manager (Windows CD-ROM) Prentice Hall's computerized test files uses a state-of-the-art software program that provides fast, simple, and error-free test generation. Entire tests can be previewed on-screen before printing. *PH Test Manager* can print multiple variations of the same test, scrambling the order of questions and multiple-choice answers. Tests can be saved in ASCII format and revised in your word-processing system.

Transparency Masters When producing a text with such a rich support package as *College Accounting*, it is important that we consider the environmental and production costs that result when instructors use only a few transparencies. In response to concerns about these costs, we are offering a special package that contains the *Solutions Manual* and a supply of clear acetates. Thus, instructors who adopt the text are provided with the opportunity to produce transparencies for the specific solutions that they choose to show in their classrooms. We hope you find this a creative response to concerns about waste and the environment. New in this edition is the fact that all solutions have been generated with projection needs in mind. Special high-resolution printing combined with boldface fonts ensure maximum clarity in all situations.

Companion Website with online Study Guide and Simply Accounting data sets Our exciting new website includes a comprehensive online study guide that presents students with numerous review exercises and research tools. There is a detailed review of key concepts for every chapter, and practice tests with true/false and multiple choice questions, completion exercises, and accounting problems. Students obtain instant feedback for questions and exercises, and they may view full solutions to problems. A page reference to the text is supplied with every answer, while destinations and search tools facilitate further research into key organizations and topics discussed in the text. The companion website also provides the data sets for the computer workshops in the text, as well as a syllabus builder for instructors and more. See www.prenticehall.ca/slater and explore.

Accounting's Greatest Hits Website Prentice Hall is proud to present *Accounting's Greatest Hits*—the websites on the Internet that provide the best accounting information for students, instructors, accountants, researchers, and anyone interested in the latest from the world of accounting.

Beginning on Accounting's Greatest Hits home page, you can link to over 80 websites that will, in turn, provide links to hundreds more. The accounting sites are grouped into the following broad categories: International, Careers, Firms, Resources, Tax, Software, and Humour. Regular updates to this site ensure that you have access to the newest accounting sites on the Internet, providing accounting information that is as current as possible. You can access this site by clicking on the Accounting's Greatest Hits button on the *College Accounting* companion website. Be sure to bookmark this site for future visits.

Look for the Accounting's Greatest Hits icon when you need accounting information on the Internet. The icon is your assurance that you have accessed one of the most comprehensive collections of accounting resources available on the web. These are truly Accounting's Greatest Hits!

ACKNOWLEDGMENTS

The task of publishing a Canadian edition of any textbook is a challenging venture. In this case it helped to be working from an outstanding original and with an outstanding team.

Thanks are certainly due to the many helpful folks at Prentice Hall Canada Inc., including Vice-President and Editorial Director Pat Ferrier, Developmental Editor Anita Smale, and Production Editor Nicole Mellow. And special thanks to copy editor Carol Fordyce for her diligence and hard work.

Thanks are also due to the reviewers for their valuable feedback: Richard F. Barnes, The Career Academy; Robert Dearden, Red River Community College; Augusta Ford, College of the North Atlantic; Dianne Girard, Sprott-Shaw Community College; Vita Nielsen, Northern Alberta Institute of Technology; A. Guy Penney, College of the North Atlantic; Doug Ringrose, Grant MacEwan Community College; Ray Rodda, Cambrian College; Penny Shaw, Malaspina University College; and Dr. J.T. Walton, Northern Alberta Institute of Technology.

Special recognition is due to Larry Knechtel and Doug Ringrose from Grant MacEwan Community College, who have used portions of the text in their classes and shared their thoughts and experiences. Thanks to Eric Saemisch at Revenue Canada and David Younie from the Canadian Employment Centre for their able assistance in obtaining most of the government forms. Mary Watson of Computer Associates provided her usual sterling assistance in matters relating to her company's computer software.

The *Study Guide with Working Papers* and the *Solutions Manual* were created with able assistance by Pat Leslie, who helped with other tasks as well.

Certain of the data sets were created by Chenelle Beck, who also reviewed all of the computer workshop material.

My final thanks go to Laurie Hanchard who not only carried out his assigned duties of reviewing both the *Study Guide with Working Papers* and the *Solutions Manual* with remarkable care and attention, but also took it as a personal goal to add substantial value to the overall package. The text—indeed, all aspects of this project—is much improved because of Laurie's efforts.

Despite the best efforts of so many talented people, it is inevitable that a few errors will persist. I accept responsibility for them and would appreciate your help in identifying them so that they can be totally eliminated in future printings.

Brian Zwicker
Edmonton, Alberta

Testimonial

As requested, I have read the first pass pages of *College Accounting*, Canadian Seventh Edition, by Slater and Zwicker, Chapters 1–15. I have also read the pages of the *Study Guide with Working Papers* and the *Solutions Manual* for *College Accounting*. I checked the arithmetic and logic in all three books with respect to the worked examples and exhibits in the proofed copies. I also ensured that the references to these examples and exhibits within the text were accurate.

Laurence P. Hanchard, C.A.

The Prentice Hall Canada companion Website...

Your Internet companion to the most exciting, state-of-the-art educational tools on the Web!

The Prentice Hall Canada Companion Website is easy to navigate and is organized to correspond to the chapters in this textbook. The Companion Website is comprised of four distinct, functional features:

1) **Customized Online Resources**

2) **Online Study Guide**

3) **Reference Material**

4) **Communication**

Explore the four areas in this Companion Website. Students and distance learners will discover resources for indepth study, research, and communication, empowering them in their quest for greater knowledge and maximizing their potential for success in the course.

A NEW WAY TO DELIVER EDUCATIONAL CONTENT

1) Customized Online Resources

Our Companion Websites provide instructors and students with a range of options to access, view, and exchange content.

- **Syllabus Builder** provides *instructors* with the option to create online classes and construct an online syllabus linked to specific modules in the Companion Website.
- **Mailing lists** enable *instructors* and *students* to receive customized promotional literature.
- **Preferences** enable *students* to customize the sending of results to various recipients, and also to customize how the material is sent, e.g., as html, text, or as an attachment.
- **Help** includes an evaluation of the user's system and a tune-up area that makes updating browsers and plug-ins easier. This new feature will enhance the user's experience with Companion Websites.

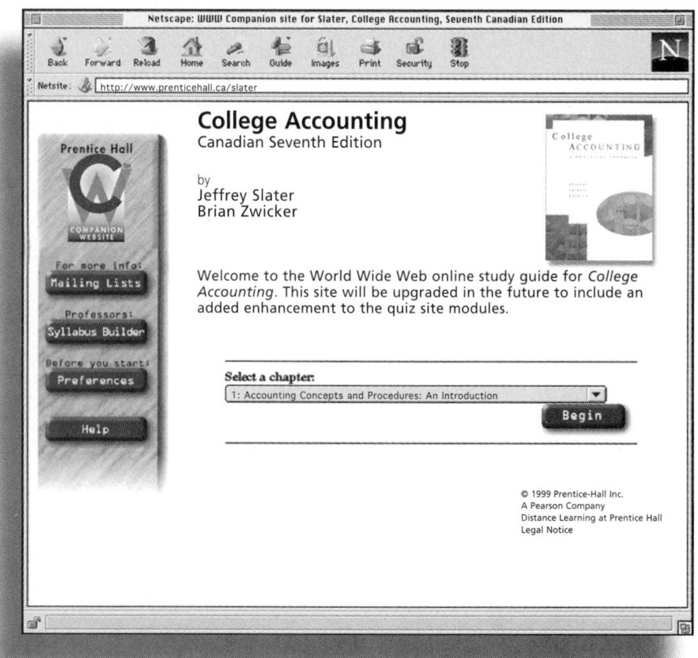

www.prenticehall.ca/slater

Prentice Hall COMPANION WEBSITE™

2) Online Study Guide

Interactive Study Guide modules form the core of the student learning experience in the Companion Website. These modules are categorized according to their functionality:

• Quizzes • Multiple Choice • True-False • Matching • Problems

The Homework Quizzes, Multiple Choice, True-False, and Matching modules provide students with the ability to send answers to our grader and receive instant feedback on their progress through our Results Reporter. Coaching comments and references back to the textbook ensure that students take advantage of all resources available to enhance their learning experience.

3) Reference Material

Reference material broadens text coverage with up-to-date resources for learning. **Accounting's Greatest Hits** supplies links to hundreds of accounting Web sites. **Web Destinations** provides a directory of Web sites relevant to the subject matter in each chapter. **Net News (Internet Newsgroups)** are a fundamental source of information about a discipline, containing a wealth of brief, opinionated postings. **Net Search** simplifies key term searches using Internet search engines.

4) Communication

Companion Websites contain the communication tools necessary to deliver courses in a **Distance Learning** environment. **Message Board** allows users to post messages and check back periodically for responses. **Live Chat** allows users to discuss course topics in real time, and enables professors to host online classes.

Communication facilities of Companion Websites provide a key element for distributed learning environments. There are two types of communication facilities currently in use in Companion Websites:

- **Message Board** – this module takes advantage of browser technology, providing the users of each Companion Website with a national newsgroup to post and reply to relevant course topics.
- **Live Chat** – enables instructor-led group activities in real time. Using our chat client, instructors can display Website content while students participate in the discussion.

Companion Websites are currently available for:

- Horngren: Introduction to Financial Accounting
- Horngren: Cost Accounting
- Horngren: Management Accounting
- Starke: Contemporary Management in Canada
- Kotler: Principles of Marketing
- Evans: Marketing Essentials

Note: CW content will vary slightly from site to site depending on discipline requirements.

The Companion Websites can be found at:

www.prenticehall.ca/slater

PRENTICE HALL CANADA
1870 Birchmount Road
Scarborough, Ontario M1P 2J7

To order:
Call: 1-800-567-3800
Fax: 1-800-263-7733

For samples:
Call: 1-800-850-5813
Fax: (416) 299-2539
E-mail: phcinfo_pubcanada@prenhall.com

Accounting Concepts and Procedures

1

AN INTRODUCTION

THE BIG PICTURE

◆

People start businesses for many reasons: to be their own boss; to be a success; to build their own financial empire; to bring a great idea to the market. But all businesses share one goal—to increase in value.

Tony Freedman, a graduate of his local community college, decided that he wanted to use his acquired skills as a computer technician and build his own business, Eldorado Computer Centre. His technical skills would provide the services his customers needed, and his knowledge of accounting would show how his business was doing. He would provide added value to his customers and to his business at the same time. As he thought about his business, he asked these questions:

- What type of business organization shall I form?
- How much money will I need to start, and where will it come from?
- What will I charge my customers?
- What will my projected revenue and expenses be?

Tony had learned that accounting is the language of business because it helps translate events into numbers that show how a company is doing. He used this language to answer his questions and to write a business plan to open a sole proprietorship on July 2.

To the student

A business must have a way to track its financial activities. Accounting is the process of gathering, processing, reporting, and communicating this information. "The Big Picture" introduces each chapter by connecting accounting to the real world of business. At the end of each chapter, you will find the "Continuing Problem," which asks you to apply what you have learned in the chapter to a real business situation.

Chapter Objectives

- **Defining and listing the functions of accounting (p. 4)**
- **Recording transactions in the basic accounting equation (p. 7)**
- **Seeing how revenue, expenses, and withdrawals expand the basic accounting equation (p. 12)**
- **Preparing an income statement, a statement of owner's equity, and a balance sheet (p. 18)**

Accounting is the language of business; it provides information to managers, owners, investors, governmental agencies, and others inside and outside the organization. Accounting provides answers and insights to questions like these:

- Is Subway's cash balance sufficient?
- Should McDonald's expand its product line?
- Can Canadian Airlines International pay its debt obligations?
- What percentage of IBM's marketing budget is for television advertisement? How does this compare with the competition? What is the overall financial condition of IBM?

Smaller businesses also need answers to their financial questions:

- Did business increase enough over the last year to warrant hiring a new assistant?
- Should we spend more money to design, produce, and send out new brochures in an effort to create more business?

Acounting is as important to individuals as it is to businesses; it answers questions like:

- Should I take out a loan for a new car or wait until I can afford to pay cash?
- Would my money work better in a chartered bank or in a credit union savings plan?

Accounting is the process that analyzes, records, classifies, summarizes, reports, and interprets financial information for decision makers—whether individuals, small businesses, large corporations, or governmental agencies—in a timely fashion. It is important that students understand the "whys" of the accounting process. Just knowing the mechanics is not enough.

CATEGORIES OF BUSINESS ORGANIZATION

There are three main categories of business organization: (1) sole proprietorship, (2) partnership, and (3) corporation. Let's define each of them and look at their advantages and disadvantages. This information also appears in Table 1-1.

Sole Proprietorship

A **sole proprietorship** is a business that has one owner. That person is both the owner and the manager of the business. One advantage of a sole proprietorship is that the owner makes all the decisions for the business. One disadvantage is that, if the business cannot pay its obligations, the business owner must pay them. This means that the owner could lose some of his personal assets (e.g., his house or his savings).

Sole proprietorships are easy to form. They end if the business closes or when the owner dies.

TABLE 1-1 Types of Business Organization

	Sole Proprietorship	Partnership	Corporation
Ownership	Business owned by one person	Business owned by more than one person	Business owned by shareholders
Formation	Easy to form	Easy to form	More difficult to form
Liability	Owner could lose personal assets to meet obligations of business.	Partners could lose personal assets to meet obligations of partnership.	Limited personal risk Shareholders' loss is usually limited to their investment in the company.
Closing	Ends with death of owner or closing of business	Ends with death of a partner or exit of a partner	Can continue indefinitely

Partnership

A **partnership** is a form of business ownership that has at least two owners (partners). Each partner acts as an owner of the company. This is an advantage because the partners can share the decision-making and the risks of the business. A disadvantage is that, as in a sole proprietorship, the partners' personal assets could be lost if the partnership cannot meet its obligations.

Partnerships are easy to form. They end when a partner dies or leaves the partnership.

Corporation

Disney is an example of a corporation.

A **corporation** is a business owned by shareholders. The corporation may have only a few shareholders or it may have many shareholders. The shareholders are not personally liable for the corporation's debts, and they usually do not have input into the business decisions.

Corporations are more difficult to form than sole proprietorships or partnerships. Corporations can exist indefinitely.

Classifying Organizations by Activity

Whether we are looking at a sole proprietorship, a partnership, or a corporation, the business can be classified by what the business does to earn money. Companies are categorized as service, merchandising, or manufacturing businesses.

A local cab company is a good example of a **service company** because it provides a service. The first part of this book focusses on service businesses.

TABLE 1-2 Examples of Service, Merchandising, and Manufacturing Businesses

Service Businesses	Merchandising Businesses	Manufacturing Businesses
Pete's Taxi Service	Sears	Mattel
Jane's Painting Co.	Eddie Bauer	General Motors
Dr. Wheeler, M.D.	The Bay	Toro
H&R Block	Eaton's	Bombardier

Stores like Sears and Eddie Bauer sell products. They are called merchandising companies. **Merchandising companies** can either make and sell their own products or sell products that are made by other suppliers. Companies like Mattel and General Motors that only make products are called **manufacturers.**

Definition of Accounting

Accounting (also called the **accounting process**) is a system that measures the activities of a business in financial terms. It provides reports and financial statements that show how the various transactions the business undertook (e.g., buying and selling goods) affected the business. It does this by performing the following functions:

- **Analyzing:** Looking at what happened and how the business was affected
- **Recording:** Putting the information into the accounting system
- **Classifying:** Grouping all of the same activities (e.g., all purchases) together

There are many career opportunities in accounting. They vary according to the amount of education and experience required. You should note that, while a lot of routine accounting work is now done using computers, this has not lessened the need for all kinds of accounting personnel.

Accounting Clerks: Accounting clerks perform most of a business's recordkeeping functions. Sometimes, accounting clerks perform specific functions and are given a title that relates to these functions. Payroll clerk and accounts payable clerk are examples of such titles. Accounting clerks may perform their work manually or by computer.

Accounting clerks generally are required to have completed at least a one-semester accounting course.

Bookkeepers: Bookkeepers are sometimes called "general bookkeepers" or "full-charge bookkeepers." That is because they do general accounting work, perform some summarizing and analyzing of accounting information, and supervise the accounting clerks. In some companies, they also may help managers and owners interpret accounting information. The size of the company determines the bookkeeper's responsibility.

Usually, bookkeepers need one or two years of accounting training and experience as an accounting clerk. Some computer knowledge may be helpful, too.

Accountants: Accountants plan, summarize, analyze, report, and interpret accounting information. Other responsibilities include assisting the owners and managers of the business in making financial decisions and supervising other accounting personnel.

Generally, accountants need a college diploma in accounting. They also may need additional professional credentials.

Accountants fall into three general classifications: public accountants, private accountants, and not-for-profit accountants. The opportunities in these categories are discussed opposite:

- **Summarizing:** Creating totals by category and/or date which are used in the next two functions
- **Reporting:** Issuing the reports that tell the results of the previous functions
- **Interpreting:** Examining the reports to determine how the various pieces of information they contain relate to each other

The system communicates the reports and financial statements to people who are interested in the information, such as the business's decision-makers, investors, creditors, governmental agencies (e.g., Revenue Canada), and so on.

As you can see, a lot of people use these reports. A set of procedures and guidelines exists to make sure that everyone prepares and interprets them the same way. These guidelines are known as **generally accepted accounting principles (GAAP).**

Now let's look at the difference between bookkeeping and accounting. Keep in mind that we will use the terms "accounting" and "the accounting process" interchangeably.

Public Accountants: Public accountants provide services to clients for a fee. They may work alone or work for an accounting firm. Two professional accounting bodies are chiefly concerned with public accounting in Canada: the Certified General Accountants Association and the Canadian Institute of Chartered Accountants. (All professional groups have provincial identities as well.) Membership is restricted to those who have passed a challenging set of qualifying examinations and who have served a period of training in various accounting positions. These professional accountants perform many accounting tasks, but they also provide advice on taxation, perform audits, and consult on many aspects of business operations.

Private Accountants (Managerial Accountants): The main difference between public accountants and private accountants is that most private accountants work for a single business. A business may employ one accountant, or it may have many.

Private accountants who pass an examination prepared by the Society of Management Accountants of Canada can become Certified Management Accountants (CMAs). Those who pass the exam given by the Institute of Internal Auditors can become Certified Internal Auditors (CIAs).

There are many opportunities in private accounting. Private accountants may manage the accounting system, prepare reports and financial statements, prepare budgets, or determine certain costs (e.g., the cost of producing a new product). Some large firms have their own tax accountants and internal auditors.

Non-profit (Governmental) Accountants: Non-profit accounting is used by governmental agencies and non-profit agencies such as religious organizations, hospitals, and charitable organizations. These entities use accountants to prepare budgets and to keep records.

It is important to know that some non-profit agencies do make money. These agencies can keep their non-profit classifications if they keep the profit in the agency. Also, accounting procedures are similar to—but not quite the same as—procedures for profit-making businesses.

Difference between Bookkeeping and Accounting

Confusion often arises concerning the difference between bookkeeping and accounting. **Bookkeeping** is the recording (record-keeping) function of the accounting process; a bookkeeper enters accounting information in the company's books. An accountant takes that information and prepares the financial reports that are used to analyze the company's financial position. *Accounting* involves many complex activities. Often, it includes the preparation of tax and financial reports, budgeting, and analyses of financial information.

Today, computers are used for routine bookkeeping operations that used to take weeks or months to complete. This text takes this into consideration by explaining how the advantages of the computer can be applied to a manual accounting system by using hands-on knowledge of how accounting works. Basic accounting knowledge is needed even though computers can help with routine tasks.

LEARNING UNIT 1-1
The Accounting Equation

ASSETS, LIABILITIES, AND EQUITIES

Let's begin our study of accounting concepts and procedures by looking at a small business: Catherine Hall's law practice. Catherine decided to open her practice at the end of August. She consulted her accountant before she made her decision. The accountant told her some important things before she made this decision. First, he told her the new business would be considered a separate **business entity** whose finances had to be kept separate and distinct from Catherine's personal finances. The accountant went on to say that all transactions can be analyzed using the basic accounting equation: Assets = Liabilities + Owner's Equity.

Catherine had never heard of the basic accounting equation. She listened carefully as the accountant explained the terms used in the equation and how the equation works.

Assets

Cash, land, supplies, office equipment, buildings, and other properties of value *owned* by a firm are called **assets.**

Equities

The rights or financial claim to the assets are called **equities.** Equities belong to those who supply the assets. If you are the only person to supply assets to the firm, you have the sole right or financial claim to them. For example, if you supply the law firm with \$4,000 in cash and \$3,000 in office equipment, your equity in the firm is \$7,000.

Relationship between Assets and Equities

The relationship between assets and equities is

Assets	=	**Equities**
(Total value of items *owned* by a business)		(Total claims against the assets)

The total dollar value of the assets of your law firm will be equal to the total dollar value of the financial claims to those assets, that is, equal to the total dollar value of the equities.

The total dollar value is broken down on the left-hand side of the equation to show the specific items of value owned by the business and on the right-hand side to show the types of claims against the assets owned.

Liabilities

A firm may have to borrow money to buy more assets; when this occurs it means the firm is *buying assets on account* (buy now, pay later). Suppose the law firm purchases a desk for $400 on account from Joe's Stationery, and the store is willing to wait 10 days for payment. The law firm has created a **liability:** an obligation to pay which comes due in the future. Joe's Stationery is called the **creditor.** This liability—the amount owed to Joe's Stationery—gives the store the right, or the financial claim, to $400 of the law firm's assets. When Joe's Stationery is paid, the store's rights to the assets of the law firm will end, since the obligation has been paid off.

Basic Accounting Equation

Elements of the basic accounting equation

To understand better the various claims to a business's assets, accountants divide equities into two parts. The claims of creditors—outside persons or businesses—are labelled *liabilities*. The claims of the business's owner are labelled **owner's equity**. Let's see how the accounting equation looks now. It can be rewritten as follows:

Assets = **Equities**

1. Liabilities: rights of creditors
2. Owner's equity: rights of owner

Assets = Liabilities + Owner's Equity

The total value of all the assets of a firm equals the combined total value of the financial claims of the creditors (liabilities) and the claims of the owner (owner's equity). This is known as the **basic accounting equation.** The basic accounting equation provides a basis for understanding the conventional accounting system of a business. The equation records business transactions in a logical and orderly way that shows their impact on the company's assets, liabilities, and owner's equity.

The purpose of the accounting equation

Importance of Creditors

Assets
− Liabilities
= Owner's Equity

Another way of presenting the basic accounting equation is:

Assets − Liabilities = Owner's Equity

This form of the equation stresses the importance of creditors. The owner's rights to the business's assets are determined after the rights of the creditors are subtracted. In other words, creditors have first claim on assets. If a firm has no liabilities—and therefore no creditors—the owner has the total rights to assets. Another term for the owner's current investment, or equity, in the business's assets is **capital.**

In accounting, capital does not mean cash. Capital is the owner's current investment, or equity, in the assets of the business.

The term *cash* in accounting includes currency and cheques on hand and bank accounts also. In this textbook, the term *cash* will usually mean the balance in the company's bank account.

As Catherine Hall's law firm engages in business transactions (paying bills, serving clients, and so on), changes will take place in the assets, liabilities, and owner's equity (capital). Let's analyze some of these transactions.

Transaction A: **Aug. 28: Catherine invests $7,000 in cash and $800 worth of office equipment in the business.**

On August 28, Catherine withdraws $7,000 from her personal bank account and deposits the money in the law firm's newly opened bank account. She also invests $800 worth of office equipment in the business. She plans to be open for business on

September 1. With the help of her accountant, Catherine begins to prepare the accounting records for the business. We put this information into the basic accounting equation as follows:

In our analyses, assume that any number without a sign in front of it is a + amount.

ASSETS			=	LIABILITIES	+ OWNER'S EQUITY
Cash	**+**	**Office Equipment**	**=**		**C. Hall, Capital**
$7,000	**+**	**$800**	=		**$7,800**
		$7,800	=	$7,800	

Note that the total value of the assets, cash, and office equipment—$7,800—is equal to the combined total value of liabilities (none, so far) and owner's equity ($7,800). Remember, Catherine Hall has supplied all the cash and office equipment, so she has the sole financial claim to the assets. Note that the heading "C. Hall, Capital" is written under the owner's equity heading. The $7,800 is Catherine's investment, or equity, in the firm's assets.

Note: **Capital is part of owner's equity; it is not an asset.**

Transaction B: **Aug. 29: Law practice buys office equipment for cash, $900.**

From the initial investment of $7,000 cash, the law firm buys $900 worth of office equipment (such as a desk). **Equipment** lasts a long time, while **supplies** (such as pens) tend to be used up relatively quickly.

	ASSETS			=	LIABILITIES	+ OWNER'S EQUITY
	Cash	+	Office Equipment	=		C. Hall, Capital
BEGINNING BALANCE	$7,000	+	$800	=		$7,800
TRANSACTION	−900	+	900			
ENDING BALANCE	6,100	+	$1,700	=		$7,800
			$7,800	=	$7,800	

Shift in Assets

As a result of the last transaction, the law office has less cash but has increased its amount of office equipment. This is called a **shift in assets**—the makeup of the assets has changed, but the total of the assets remains the same.

Suppose you go food shopping at the supermarket with $100 and spend $60. Now you have two assets, food and money. The composition of the assets has been *shifted*—you have more food and less money than you did—but the *total* of the assets has not increased or decreased. The total value of the food, $60, plus the cash, $40, is still $100. When you borrow money from the bank, on the other hand, you have an increase in cash (an asset) and an increase in liabilities; overall there is an increase in assets, not just a shift.

An accounting equation can remain in balance even if only one side is affected. The key point to remember is that the left-hand-side total of assets must always equal the right-hand-side total of liabilities and owner's equity.

Transaction C: **Aug. 30: Business buys additional office equipment on account, $400.**

The law firm purchases an additional $400 worth of chairs and desks from Wilmington Company. Instead of demanding cash right away, Wilmington agrees to deliver the equipment and to allow up to 60 days for the law practice to pay the invoice (bill).

This liability, or obligation to pay in the future, has some interesting effects on the basic accounting equation. Wilmington Company has accepted as payment a partial claim against the assets of the law practice. This claim exists until the law firm pays the bill. This unwritten promise to pay the creditor is a liability called **accounts payable.**

	ASSETS			=	LIABILITIES	+	OWNER'S EQUITY
	Cash	+	**Office Equipment**	=	**Accounts Payable**		**C. Hall, Capital**
BALANCE FORWARD	$6,100	+	$1,700	=			$7,800
TRANSACTION			+400	=	+400		
ENDING BALANCE	6,100	+	$2,100	=	$ 400		$7,800
			$8,200	=	$8,200		

When this information is analyzed, we can see that the law practice has increased what it owes (accounts payable) as well as what it owns (office equipment) by $400. The law practice gains $400 in an asset but has an obligation to pay Wilmington Company at a future date.

The owner's equity remains unchanged. This transaction results in an increase of total assets from $7,800 to $8,200.

Finally, note that after each transaction the basic accounting equation remains in balance.

LEARNING UNIT 1-1 REVIEW

AT THIS POINT you should be able to:

- List the functions of accounting. (pp. 2, 4–5)
- Define and explain the differences between sole proprietorships, partnerships, and corporations. (pp. 2–3)
- Compare and contrast bookkeeping and accounting. (p. 6)
- Explain the role of the computer as an accounting tool. (p. 6)
- State the purpose of the accounting equation. (p. 6)
- Explain the difference between liabilities and owner's equity. (p. 7)
- Define capital. (p. 7)
- Explain the difference between a shift in assets and an increase in assets. (p. 8)

To test your understanding of this material, complete Self-Review Quiz 1-1. The blank forms you need are in the *Study Guide with Working Papers* for Chapter 1. The solution to the quiz follows the quiz here in the text. If you have difficulty doing the problems, review Learning Unit 1-1 and the solution to the quiz.

Keep in mind that learning accounting is like learning to type—the more you practice, the better you become. You will not be an expert in one day. Be patient. It will all come together.

SELF-REVIEW QUIZ 1-1

(The blank forms you need are on page 1-1 of the *Study Guide with Working Papers.*)

Record the following transactions in the basic accounting equation:

1. Pete O'Brien invests $14,000 to begin a real estate office.
2. The real estate office buys $600 worth of computer equipment for cash.
3. The real estate company buys $500 worth of additional computer equipment on account.

Solution to Self-Review Quiz 1-1

	ASSETS		=	LIABILITIES	+	OWNER'S EQUITY
	Cash	+ Computer Equipment	=	Accounts Payable	+	Pete O'Brien, Capital
1.	+$14,000					+$14,000
BALANCE	14,000		=			14,000
2.	−600	+$600				
BALANCE	13,400 +	600	=			14,000
3.		500		+$500		
ENDING BALANCE	$13,400	+ $ 1,100	=	$500	+	$14,000
		$14,500	=	$14,500		

Quiz Tip

Note that transaction 2 is a shift in assets while transaction 3 is an increase in assets. Keep asking yourself *what did the business get* and *who supplied it to the business.* Remember, capital is not cash. Cash is an asset while capital is part of owner's equity.

LEARNING UNIT 1-2

The Balance Sheet

The balance sheet shows the company's financial position as of a particular date. (In our example, that date is at the end of August.)

In the first learning unit, the transactions for Catherine Hall's law office were recorded in the accounting equation. The transactions we recorded occurred before the law firm opened for business. A report, called a **balance sheet** or **statement of financial position**, can show the position of the company before it started operating. The balance sheet is a formal report that presents the information from the ending balances of both sides of the accounting equation. Think of the balance sheet as a snapshot of the business's financial position as of a particular date.

Let's look at the balance sheet of Catherine Hall's law practice for August 31, 2001, shown in Figure 1-1. The figures in the balance sheet come from the ending balances of the accounting equation for the law practice as shown in Learning Unit 1-1.

Note in Figure 1-1 that the assets owned by the law practice appear on the left-hand side and that liabilities and owner's equity appear on the right-hand side. Both sides equal $8,200. This *balance* between left and right gives the balance sheet its name. In later chapters we will be looking at other ways to set up a balance sheet.

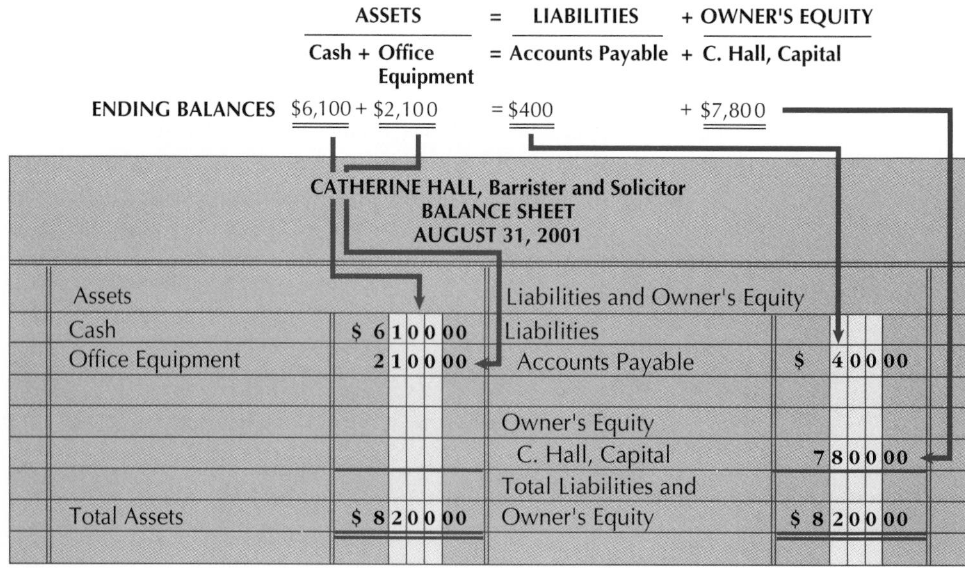

FIGURE 1-1
The Balance Sheet

Do you remember the three elements that make up a balance sheet?

Assets, liabilities, and owner's equity

Points to Remember in Preparing a Balance Sheet

The Heading

The heading of the balance sheet provides the following information:

- The company name: Catherine Hall, Barrister and Solicitor
- The name of the report: Balance Sheet
- The date for which the report is prepared: August 31, 2001

Use of the Dollar Sign

Note that the dollar sign is not repeated every time a figure appears. As shown in the balance sheet for Catherine Hall's law practice, it is usually placed to the left of each column's top figure and to the left of the column's total.

Distinguishing the Total

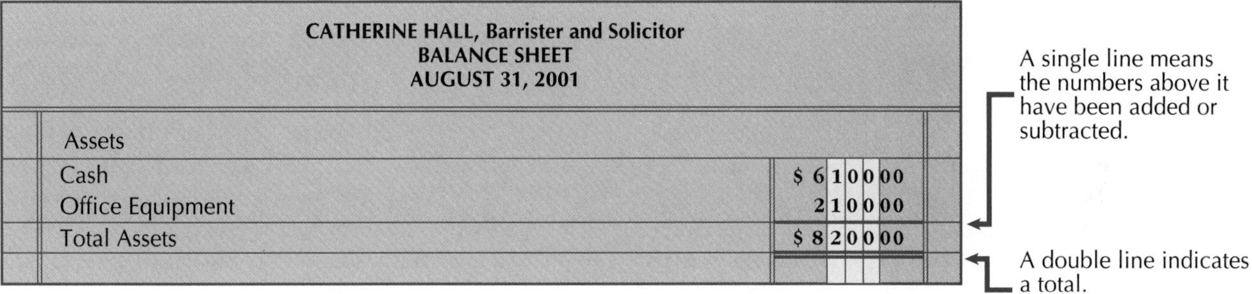

CATHERINE HALL, Barrister and Solicitor
BALANCE SHEET
AUGUST 31, 2001

Assets	
Cash	$ 6100 00
Office Equipment	2100 00
Total Assets	$ 8200 00

A single line means the numbers above it have been added or subtracted.
A double line indicates a total.

When adding numbers down a column, use a single line before the total and a double line beneath it. A single line means that the numbers above it have been added or subtracted. A double line indicates a total. It is important to align the numbers in the column; many errors occur because these figures are not lined up. These rules are the same for all accounting reports.

This balance sheet gives Catherine the information she needs to see the law firm's financial position before it opens for business. This information does not tell her, however, whether the firm will make a profit.

LEARNING UNIT 1-2 REVIEW

AT THIS POINT you should be able to:

- Define and state the purpose of a balance sheet. (p. 10)
- Identify and define the elements making up a balance sheet. (p. 10)
- Show the relationship between the accounting equation and the balance sheet. (p. 10)
- Prepare a balance sheet in proper form from information provided. (p. 10)
- Place dollar signs correctly in a formal report. (p. 11)

SELF-REVIEW QUIZ 1-2

(The blank forms you need are on page 1-2 of the *Study Guide with Working Papers.*)

The date is November 30, 2001. Use the following information to prepare in proper form a balance sheet for Janning Company:

Accounts Payable	$30,000
Cash	8,000
A. Janning, Capital	9,000
Office Equipment	31,000

Quiz Tip

The heading of a balance sheet answers the questions *Who, What, and When.* November 30, 2001, is the particular date.

Solution to Self-Review Quiz 1-2

JANNING COMPANY
BALANCE SHEET
NOVEMBER 30, 2001

Assets		Liabilities and Owner's Equity	
Cash	$ 8 000 00	Liabilities	
Office Equipment	$ 31 000 00	Accounts Payable	$ 30 000 00
		Owner's Equity	
		A. Janning, Capital	9 000 00
		Total Liabilities and	
Total Assets	$ 39 000 00	Owner's Equity	$ 39 000 00

Capital does not mean cash. The capital amount is the owner's current investment of assets in the business.

LEARNING UNIT 1-3

The Accounting Equation Expanded: Revenue, Expenses, and Withdrawals

As soon as Catherine Hall's office opened, she began performing legal services for her clients and earning revenue for the business. At the same time, as a part of doing business, she incurred various expenses, such as rent.

When Catherine asked her accountant how these transactions fitted into the accounting equation, he began by defining some terms.

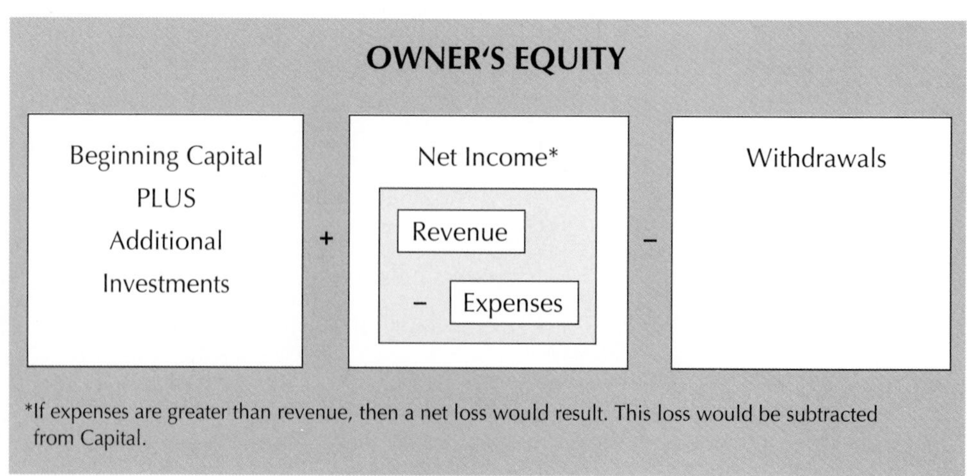

FIGURE 1-2
Owner's Equity

When revenue is earned, it is recorded as an increase in owner's equity and an increase in assets.

Accounts receivable is an asset. The law firm expects to be able to receive amounts owed from clients at a later date.

Remember: Accounts receivable results from earning revenue even when cash is not yet received.

Record an expense when it is incurred, whether it is paid then or is to be paid later.

Key terms in the accounting equation

Revenue A service company earns **revenue** when it provides services to its clients. Catherine's law firm earned revenue when she provided legal services to her clients for legal fees. When revenue is earned, owner's equity is increased. In effect, revenue is a subdivision of owner's equity.

Assets are increased. The increase is in the form of cash if the client pays right away. If the client promises to pay in the future, the increase is called **accounts receivable.** When revenue is earned, the transaction is recorded as an increase in revenue and an increase in assets (either as cash and/or as accounts receivable, depending on whether it was paid right away or will be paid in the future).

Expenses A business's **expenses** are the costs the company incurs in carrying on operations in its effort to create revenue. Expenses are also a subdivision of owner's equity; when expenses are incurred, they *decrease* owner's equity. Expenses can be paid for in cash or they can be charged.

Net Income/Net Loss When revenue totals more than expenses, **net income** is the result; when expenses total more than revenue, **net loss** is the result.

Withdrawals At some point Catherine Hall may need to withdraw cash or other assets from the business to pay living or other personal expenses that do not relate to the business. We will record these transactions in an account called **withdrawals.** Sometimes this account is called the *owner's drawing account.* The withdrawals account is a subdivision of owner's equity that records personal expenses not related to the business. Withdrawals decrease owner's equity.

It is important to remember the difference between expenses and withdrawals. Expenses relate to business operations; withdrawals are the result of personal needs outside the normal operations of the business.

Now let's analyze the September transactions for Catherine Hall's law firm using an **expanded accounting equation** that includes withdrawals, revenues, and expenses.

Expanded accounting equation

Transaction D: **Sept. 1–30: Provided legal services for cash, $3,000.**

Transactions A, B, and C were discussed earlier, when the law office was being formed in August. See Learning Unit 1-1.

In the law firm's first month of operation a total of $3,000 in cash was received for legal services performed. In the accounting equation the asset Cash is increased by $3,000. Revenue is also increased by $3,000, resulting in an increase in owner's equity.

	ASSETS			= LIABILITIES	+		OWNER'S EQUITY		
	Cash	+ Accts. Rec.	+ Office Equip.	=	Accts. Pay.	+ C. Hall, Capital	− C. Hall, Withdr.	+ Revenue	− Expenses
BAL. FWD.	$6,100		+$ 2,100	=	$ 400	+$7,800			
TRANS.	+3,000							+ $3,000	
END. BAL.	$9,100		+$ 2,100	=	$ 400	+$7,800		+ $3,000	
			$11,200	=	$11,200				

A revenue column was added to the basic accounting equation. Amounts are recorded in the revenue column when they are earned. They are also recorded in the assets columns, under Cash and/or under Accounts Receivable. Do not think of revenue as an asset. It is part of owner's equity. It is the revenue that creates an inward flow of cash and accounts receivable.

Transaction E: **Sept. 1–30: Provided legal services on account, $4,000.**

	ASSETS			= LIABILITIES +	OWNER'S EQUITY			
	Cash	+ Accts. Rec.	+ Office Equip.	= Accts. Pay.	+ C. Hall, Capital	– C. Hall, Withdr.	+ Revenue	– Expenses
BAL. FWD.	$9,100		+ $ 2,100	= $ 400	+ $7,800		+ $3,000	
TRANS.		$+4,000					+4,000	
END. BAL.	$9,100	+ $4,000	+ $ 2,100	= $ 400	+ $7,800		+ $7,000	
			$15,200	= $15,200				

Catherine's law practice performed legal work on account for $4,000. The firm did not receive the cash for these earned legal fees; it accepted an unwritten promise from these clients that payment would be received in the future.

Transaction F: **Sept. 1–30: Received $700 cash as partial payment from previous services performed on account.**

During September some of Catherine's clients who had received services and promised to pay in the future decided to reduce what they owed the practice by $700 when their bills came due. This is shown as follows on the expanded accounting equation.

	ASSETS			= LIABILITIES +	OWNER'S EQUITY			
	Cash	+ Accts. Rec.	+ Office Equip.	= Accts. Pay.	+ C. Hall, Capital	– C. Hall, Withdr.	+ Revenue	– Expenses
BAL. FWD.	$9,100	+ $4,000	+ $2,100	= $ 400	+$7,800		+ $7,000	
TRANS.	+700	−700						
END. BAL.	$9,800	+ $3,300	+ $2,100	= $ 400	+$7,800		+ $7,000	
			$15,200	= $15,200				

The law firm increased the asset Cash by $700 and reduced another asset, Accounts Receivable, by $700. The *total* of assets does not change. The right-hand side of the expanded accounting equation has not been touched because the total on the left-hand side of the equation has not changed. The revenue was recorded when it was earned, and the *same revenue cannot be recorded twice.* This transaction analyzes the situation *after* the revenue has been previously earned and recorded. Transaction F shows a shift in assets—increased cash and reduced accounts receivable.

Transaction G: **Sept. 1–30: Paid salaries expense, $600.**

	ASSETS			=	LIABILITIES +	OWNER'S EQUITY			
	Cash	+ Accts. Rec.	+ Office Equip.	=	Accts. Pay.	+ C. Hall, Capital	− C. Hall, Withdr.	+ Revenue	− Expenses
BAL. FWD.	$9,800	+ $3,300	+ $ 2,100	=	$ 400	+$7,800		+ $7,000	
TRANS.	−600								+600
END. BAL.	$9,200	+ $3,300	+ $ 2,100	=	$ 400	+$7,800		+ $7,000	−$600
			$14,600	=	$14,600				

As expenses increase, they decrease owner's equity. This incurred expense of $600 reduces the cash by $600. Although the expense was paid, the total of our expenses to date has *increased* by $600. Keep in mind that owner's equity decreases as expenses increase, so the accounting equation remains in balance.

Transaction H: **Sept. 1–30: Paid rent expense, $700.**

	ASSETS			=	LIABILITIES +	OWNER'S EQUITY			
	Cash	+ Accts. Rec.	+ Office Equip.	=	Accts. Pay.	+ C. Hall, Capital	− C. Hall, Withdr.	+ Revenue	− Expenses
BAL. FWD.	$9,200	+ $3,300	+ $2,100	=	$400	+$7,800		+ $7,000	− $ 600
TRANS.	−700								+700
END. BAL.	$8,500	+ $3,300	+ $2,100	=	$400	+$7,800		+ $7,000	− $1,300
			+ $13,900	=	$13,900				

During September the practice incurred rent expenses of $700. This rent was not paid in advance; it was paid when it came due. The payment of rent reduces the asset Cash by $700 and increases the expenses of the firm, resulting in a decrease in owner's equity. The firm's expenses are now $1,300.

Transaction I: **Sept. 1–30: Incurred advertising expenses of $300, to be paid next month.**

	ASSETS			=	LIABILITIES +	OWNER'S EQUITY			
	Cash	+ Accts. Rec.	+ Office Equip.	=	Accts. Pay.	+ C. Hall, Capital	− C. Hall, Withdr.	+ Revenue	− Expenses
BAL. FWD.	$8,500	+ $3,300	+ $2,100	=	$400	+$7,800		+ $7,000	− $1,300
TRANS.					+300				+300
END. BAL.	$8,500	+ $3,300	+ $2,100	=	$700	+$7,800		+ $7,000	− $1,600
			$13,900	=	$13,900				

Catherine ran an ad in the local newspaper and incurred an expense of $300. This increase in expenses caused a corresponding decrease in owner's equity. Since Catherine has not paid the newspaper for the advertising yet, her firm owes $300. Thus the firm's liabilities (Accounts Payable) increase by $300. Eventually, when the bill comes in and is paid, both Cash and Accounts Payable will be decreased.

Transaction J: **Sept. 1–30: Catherine withdrew $200 for personal use.**

	ASSETS			=	LIABILITIES +	OWNER'S EQUITY			
	Cash	+ Accts. Rec.	+ Office Equip.	=	Accts. Pay.	+ C. Hall, Capital	− C. Hall, Withdr.	+ Revenue	− Expenses
BAL. FWD.	$8,500	+ $3,300	+ $ 2,100	=	$700	+ $7,800		+ $7,000	− $1,600
TRANS.	−200						+200		
END. BAL.	$8,300	+ $3,300	+ $ 2,100	=	$700	+ $7,800	− $200	+ $7,000	− $1,600
			$13,700	=	$13,700				

By taking $200 for personal use, Catherine has *increased* her withdrawals from the business by $200 and decreased the asset Cash by $200. Note that, as withdrawals increase, the owner's equity will *decrease*. Keep in mind that a withdrawal is *not* a business expense. It is a subdivision of owner's equity that records money or other assets an owner withdraws from the business for *personal* use.

Subdivision of Owner's Equity

Take a moment to review the subdivisions of owner's equity:

- As capital increases, owner's equity increases (see transaction A).
- As withdrawals increase, owner's equity decreases (see transaction J).
- As revenue increases, owner's equity increases (see transaction D).
- As expenses increase, owner's equity decreases (see transaction G).

Catherine Hall's Expanded Accounting Equation

The following is a summary of the expanded accounting equation for Catherine Hall's law firm. The + or – sign in front of a transaction indicates whether the account is increased or decreased by that transaction.

Catherine Hall
Barrister and Solicitor
Expanded Accounting Equation: A Summary

	ASSETS			=	LIABILITIES +	OWNER'S EQUITY			
	Cash	+ Accts. Rec.	+ Office Equip.	=	Accts. Pay.	+ C. Hall, Capital	− C. Hall, Withdr.	+ Revenue	− Expenses
A.	$7,000		+ $800	=		+$7,800			
BALANCE	7,000	+	800	=		7,800			
B.	−900		+900						
BALANCE	6,100		+ 1,700	=		7,800			
C.			+400		+$400				
BALANCE	6,100		+ 2,100	=	400	+ 7,800			
D.	+3,000							+$3,000	
BALANCE	9,100		+ 2,100	=	400	+ 7,800		+ 3,000	
E.		+$4,000						+4,000	
BALANCE	9,100	+ 4,000	+ 2,100	=	400	+ 7,800		+ 7,000	
F.	+700	−700							
BALANCE	9,800	+ 3,300	+ 2,100	=	400	+ 7,800		+ 7,000	
G.	−600								+$600
BALANCE	9,200	+ 3,300	+ 2,100	=	400	+ 7,800		+ 7,000	− 600
H.	−700								+700
BALANCE	8,500	+ 3,300	+ 2,100	=	400	+ 7,800		+ 7,000	− 1,300
I.					+300				+300
BALANCE	8,500	+ 3,300	+ 2,100	=	700	+ 7,800		+ 7,000	− 1,600
J.	−200						+$200		
END. BAL.	$8,300	+$3,300	+ $2,100	=	$700	+ $7,800	− $200	+ $7,000	− $1,600

LEARNING UNIT 1-3 REVIEW

AT THIS POINT you should be able to:

- Define and explain the difference between revenue and expenses. (p. 13)
- Define and explain the difference between net income and net loss. (p. 13)
- Explain the subdivision of owner's equity. (pp. 14–16)
- Explain the effects of withdrawals, revenue, and expenses on owner's equity. (pp. 15–16)
- Record transactions in an expanded accounting equation and balance the basic accounting equation as a means of checking the accuracy of your calculations. (p. 16)

SELF-REVIEW QUIZ 1-3

(The blank forms you need are on page 1-2 of the *Study Guide with Working Papers.*)

Quiz Tip

Think of expenses and withdrawals as *increasing.* As they increase, they will reduce the owner's rights. For example, in transaction 4 withdrawals increased by $500, resulting in total withdrawals increasing from $800 to $1,300. This represents a decrease in Owner's Equity.

Record the following transactions in the expanded accounting equation for the Bing Company. Note that all titles have a beginning balance.

1. Received cash revenue, $3,000.
2. Billed customers for services rendered, $6,000.
3. Received a bill for telephone expenses (to be paid next month), $125.
4. Bob Bing withdrew cash for personal use, $500.
5. Received $1,000 from customers in partial payment for services performed in transaction 2.

Solution to Self-Review Quiz 1-3

	ASSETS			=	LIABILITIES +	OWNER'S EQUITY			
	Cash	+ Accts. Rec.	+ Cleaning Equip.	=	Accts. Pay.	+ B. Bing, Capital	− B. Bing, Withdr.	+ Revenue	− Expenses
BEG. BAL.	$10,000	+ $ 2,500	+ $6,500	=	$1,000	+ $11,800	− $ 800	+ $ 9,000	− $2,000
1.	+3,000							+3,000	
BALANCE	13,000	+ 2,500	+ 6,500	=	1,000	+ 11,800	− 800	+ 12,000	− 2,000
2.		+6,000						+6,000	
BALANCE	13,000	+ 8,500	+ 6,500	=	1,000	+ 11,800	− 800	+ 18,000	− 2,000
3.					+125				+125
BALANCE	13,000	+ 8,500	+ 6,500	=	1,125	+ 11,800	− 800	+ 18,000	− 2,125
4.	−500						+500		
BALANCE	12,500	+ 8,500	+ 6,500	=	1,125	+ 11,800	− 1,300	+ 18,000	− 2,125
5.	+1,000	−1,000							
END. BAL.	$13,500	+ $ 7,500	+ $6,500	=	$1,125	+ $11,800	− $ 1,300	+ $18,000	− $2,125
		$27,500		=			$27,500		

LEARNING UNIT 1-4

Preparing Financial Reports

Catherine Hall would like to be able to find out whether her firm is making a profit, so she asks her accountant whether he can measure the firm's financial performance on a monthly basis. Her accountant replies that there are a number of financial reports that he can prepare, such as the income statement which shows how well the law firm has performed over a specific period of time. The accountant can use the information in the income statement to prepare other reports.

THE INCOME STATEMENT

The income statement is prepared from data found in the revenue and expense columns of the expanded accounting equation.

An **income statement** is an accounting report that shows business results in terms of revenue and expenses. If revenues are greater than expenses, the report shows net income. If expenses are greater than revenues, the report shows net loss. An income statement can cover any number of months up to 12. It does not usually cover more than one year. The report shows the result of all revenues and expenses throughout the entire period and not just as of a specific date. The income statement for Catherine Hall's law firm is shown in Figure 1-3.

FIGURE 1-3
The Income Statement

CATHERINE HALL, Barrister and Solicitor INCOME STATEMENT FOR MONTH ENDED SEPTEMBER 30, 2001		
Revenue:		
Legal Fees		$7 000 00
Operating Expenses:		
Salaries Expense	$600 00	
Rent Expense	700 00	
Advertising Expense	300 00	
Total Operating Expenses		1 600 00
Net Income		$5 400 00

Points to Remember in Preparing an Income Statement

Heading The heading of an income statement tells the same three things as all other accounting reports: the company's name, the name of the report, and the period of time the report covers (or the date prepared).

The inside column of numbers ($600, $700, $300) is used to subtotal all expenses ($1,600) before subtracting them from revenue.

The Set-Up As you can see on the income statement, the inside column of numbers ($600, $700, and $300) is used to subtotal all expenses ($1,600) before subtracting them from revenue ($7,000 − $1,600 = $5,400).

Operating expenses may be listed in alphabetical order, in order of largest amounts to smallest, or in a set order established by the accountant.

THE STATEMENT OF OWNER'S EQUITY

As we said, the income statement is a business report that shows business results in terms of revenue and expenses. But how does net income or net loss affect owner's equity? To find that out we have to look at a second type of report, the statement of owner's equity.

If this statement of owner's equity is omitted, the information will be included in the owner's equity section of the balance sheet.

The **statement of owner's equity** shows for a certain period of time what changes occurred in Catherine Hall, Capital. The statement of owner's equity is shown in Figure 1-4.

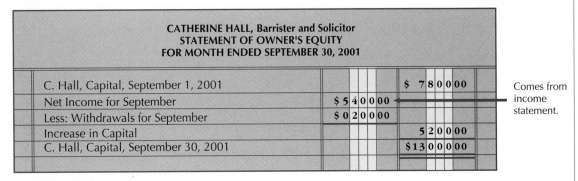

CATHERINE HALL, Barrister and Solicitor STATEMENT OF OWNER'S EQUITY FOR MONTH ENDED SEPTEMBER 30, 2001		
C. Hall, Capital, September 1, 2001		$ 7800 00
Net Income for September	$ 5400 00	
Less: Withdrawals for September	$ 0200 00	
Increase in Capital		5200 00
C. Hall, Capital, September 30, 2001		$13000 00

Comes from income statement.

FIGURE 1-4 Statement of Owner's Equity

The capital of Catherine Hall can be

Increased by: Owner Investment
Net Income (Revenue − Expenses)

Decreased by: Owner Withdrawals
Net Loss (Expenses greater than Revenue)

Remember, a withdrawal is *not* a business expense and thus is not involved in the calculation of net income or net loss on the income statement. It appears on the statement of owner's equity. The statement of owner's equity summarizes the effects of all the subdivisions of owner's equity (revenue, expenses, withdrawals) on beginning capital. The ending capital figure ($13,000) will be the beginning figure in the next statement of owner's equity.

Suppose that Catherine's law firm had operated at a loss in the month of September. Suppose instead of net income there was a net loss, and an additional investment of $700 was made on September 15. This is how the statement would look if this had happened.

CATHERINE HALL, Barrister and Solicitor STATEMENT OF OWNER'S EQUITY FOR MONTH ENDED SEPTEMBER 30, 2001		
C. Hall, Capital, September 1, 2001		$7800 00
Additional Investment, September 15, 2001		700 00
		$8500 00
Less: Net Loss for September	$400 00	
Withdrawals for September	100 00	
Decrease in Capital		500 00
C. Hall, Capital, September 30, 2001		$8000 00

THE BALANCE SHEET

Now let's look at how to prepare a balance sheet from the expanded accounting equation (see Figure 1-5). As you can see, the asset accounts (Cash, Accounts Receivable, and Office Equipment) appear on the left side of the balance sheet. Accounts Payable and C. Hall, Capital, appear on the right side. Notice that the $13,000 of capital can be calculated within the accounting equation, or read from the statement of owner's equity.

FIGURE 1-5 The Balance Sheet and the Accounting Equation

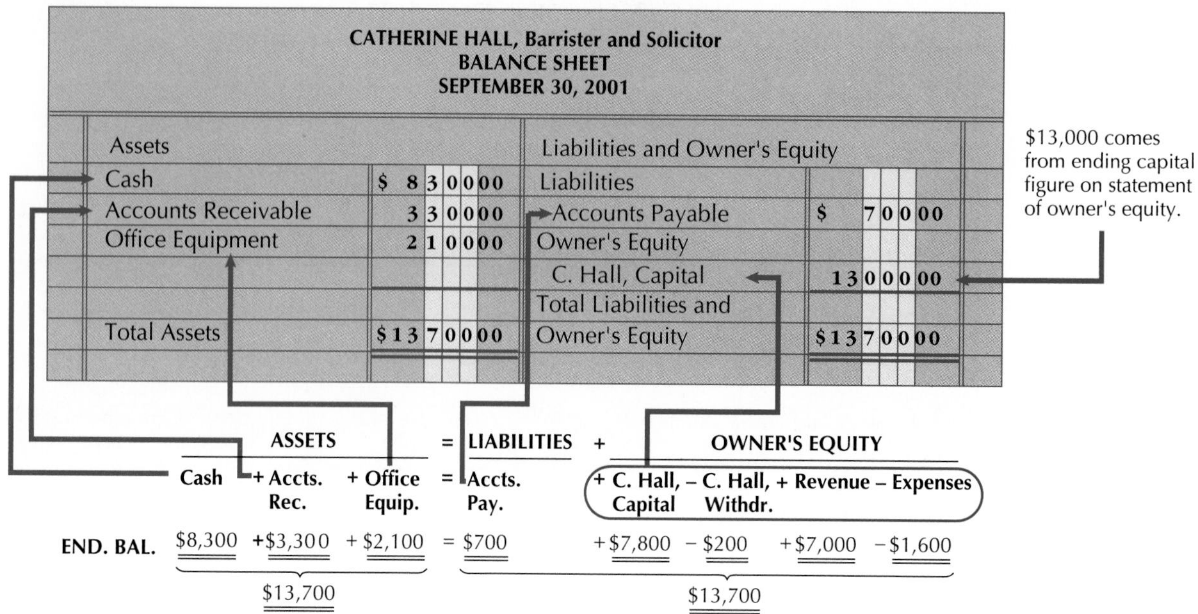

CATHERINE HALL, Barrister and Solicitor
BALANCE SHEET
SEPTEMBER 30, 2001
Assets
Cash
Accounts Receivable
Office Equipment
Total Assets
$ 8 3 0 0 00
3 3 0 0 00
2 1 0 0 00
$ 1 3 7 0 0 00
Liabilities and Owner's Equity
Liabilities
Accounts Payable
Owner's Equity
C. Hall, Capital
Total Liabilities and Owner's Equity
$ 7 0 0 00
1 3 0 0 0 00
$ 1 3 7 0 0 00
$13,000 comes from ending capital figure on statement of owner's equity.
ASSETS = LIABILITIES + OWNER'S EQUITY
Cash + Accts. Rec. + Office Equip. = Accts. Pay.
+ C. Hall, Capital – C. Hall, Withdr. + Revenue – Expenses
END. BAL. $8,300 +$3,300 + $2,100 = $700 +$7,800 – $200 +$7,000 –$1,600
$13,700
$13,700

MAIN ELEMENTS OF THE INCOME STATEMENT, THE STATEMENT OF OWNER'S EQUITY, AND THE BALANCE SHEET

In this chapter we have discussed three financial reports: the income statement, the statement of owner's equity, and the balance sheet. (There is a fourth report, called the statement of cash flows, that is not covered in this textbook.) Let us review what elements of the expanded accounting equation go into each report, and the usual order in which the reports are prepared. Figure 1-5 presents a diagram of the accounting equation and the balance sheet. Table 1-3 summarizes the points below the table.

TABLE 1-3 WHAT GOES ON EACH FINANCIAL REPORT

	Income Statement	Statement of Owner's Equity	Balance Sheet
Assets			X
Liabilities			X
Capital* (beginning)		X	
Capital (ending)		X	X
Withdrawals		X	
Revenues	X		
Expenses	X		
Net Income (Loss)	X	X	

* **Note:** Additional investments go on the statement of owner's equity.

- The income statement is prepared first; it includes revenues and expenses and shows net income or net loss. This net income or net loss is used to update the next report, the statement of owner's equity.
- The statement of owner's equity is prepared second; it includes beginning capital and any additional investments, the net income or net loss shown on the income statement, withdrawals, and the total, which is the **ending capital.**
- The balance sheet is prepared last; it includes the final balances of each of the elements listed in the accounting equation under Assets and Liabilities. The balance in Capital comes from the statement of owner's equity.

LEARNING UNIT 1-4 REVIEW

AT THIS POINT you should be able to:

- Define and state the purpose of the income statement, the statement of owner's equity, and the balance sheet. (pp. 18–19)
- Discuss why the income statement should be prepared first. (p. 20)
- Compare and contrast these three financial reports. (p. 20)
- Calculate a new figure for capital on the statement of owner's equity and balance sheet. (p. 19)
- Show what happens on a statement of owner's equity if there is a net loss. (p. 19)

SELF-REVIEW QUIZ 1-4

(The blank forms you need are on pages 1-3 and 1-4 of the *Study Guide with Working Papers.*)

From the following balances for Rusty Realty prepare:

1. Income statement for month ended November 30, 2002
2. Statement of owner's equity for the month ended November 30, 2002
3. Balance sheet as of November 30, 2002

Cash	$4,000
Accounts Receivable	1,370
Store Furniture	1,490
Accounts Payable	900
R. Rusty, Capital, November 1, 2002	$5,000
R. Rusty, Withdrawals	100
Commissions Earned	1,500
Rent Expense	200
Advertising Expense	150
Salaries Expense	90

Solution to Self-Review Quiz 1-4

Quiz Tip

Note that the inside column is used only for subtotalling.

RUSTY REALTY
INCOME STATEMENT
FOR MONTH ENDED NOVEMBER 30, 2002

Revenue:		
Commissions Earned		$ 1500 00
Operating Expenses:		
Rent Expense	$ 200 00	
Advertising Expense	150 00	
Salaries Expense	90 00	
Total Operating Expenses		440 00
Net Income		$ 1060 00

Quiz Tip

The Net Income from the Income Statement is used to help build the Statement of Owner's Equity.

RUSTY REALTY
STATEMENT OF OWNER'S EQUITY
FOR MONTH ENDED NOVEMBER 30, 2002

R. Rusty, Capital, November 1, 2002		$ 5000 00
Net Income for November	$ 1060 00	
Less: Withdrawals for November	100 00	
Increase in Capital		960 00
R. Rusty, Capital, November 30, 2002		$ 5960 00

Quiz Tip

The new figure for Capital, from the Statement of Owner's Equity, is used as the Capital figure on the Balance Sheet.

RUSTY REALTY
BALANCE SHEET
NOVEMBER 30, 2002

Assets		Liabilities and Owner's Equity	
Cash	$ 4000 00	Liabilities	
Accounts Receivable	1370 00	Accounts Payable	$ 900 00
Store Furniture	1490 00		
		Owner's Equity	
		R. Rusty, Capital	5960 00
		Total Liabilities and	
Total Assets	$ 6860 00	Owner's Equity	$ 6860 00

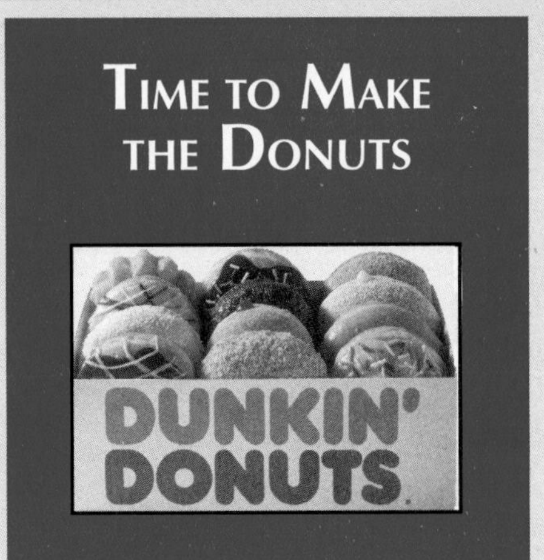

Time to Make the Donuts

Remember the TV ad in which Fred the Baker stumbles out of bed in the dark and drives to work—stopping only to wake up a rooster on the way? Fred is dedicated to making doughnuts (and the coffee and the bagels) fresh for the early morning customers at his Dunkin' Donuts store. Fred Baker, one of Dunkin' Donuts newest shop owners, smiled as he thought of this commercial while he drove to work early one morning. Fred's name had been the source of lots of jokes—thousands of them—about his choice of companies, since it was also the name of the character in Dunkin' Donuts long-running ad campaign. Like everyone else, Fred Baker was fond of Fred the Baker.

So what has this to do with accounting? Plenty, as it turns out. As one of Dunkin' Donuts shop owners, Fred Baker wears two hats—his baker's cap and an accountant's green eyeshade. He makes the donuts, and he manages the accounts for his store. To learn how to do his job, Fred attended Dunkin' Donuts University. We'll share the financial lessons he learned there with you. The baking lessons—NO.

When you look at Fred's store, you are really seeing two businesses. Fred is the owner of his store, and he is a sole proprietor. He operates under an agreement with Dunkin' Donuts Inc. of Randolph, Massachusetts. Dunkin' Donuts Inc. supplies the business know-how and support (like training, national advertising, and recipes). Fred supplies capital (his investment) and his baking, management, and effort. Dunkin' Donuts Inc. and Fred operate interdependent businesses and both rely on accounting information for their success.

Dunkin' Donuts Inc., in business since 1950, has grown dramatically over the years, to the point that it now has stores in 43 states, 8 provinces, and 20 countries. To manage this enormous service business requires very careful control of each of its 4,139 stores. At Dunkin' Donuts headquarters, Dwayne Goulding, Business Consultant for Fred's zone, monitors Fred's reports closely. It is his job to see that Fred makes money at making donuts, which in turn results in Dunkin' Donuts Inc. making money too.

Why does headquarters require accounting reports? Accounting reports give the information both Fred and the company need to make business decisions in a number of vital areas. For example:

1. Before Fred could buy his Dunkin' Donuts store, the company needed to know how much cash Fred had and his assets and liabilities. Fred prepared a personal balance sheet to give them this information.
2. Fred needs to know if his store is making a profit. He prepares an income statement to tell him that.
3. Dwayne needs to know if Fred's store is profitable and well run, compared with other shops in the zone. He compares the income statements of all shops to learn this. He also looks at competing businesses.
4. Fred must have the right amount of supplies on hand. If he has too little, he can't make the doughnuts. If he has too much, some may spoil. The Balance Sheet tells him what supplies are on hand. It also alerts Dwayne to potential problems Fred may have.
5. How often do Dunkin' Donuts stores report accounting information? Fred prepares a monthly income statement and balance sheet. He also prepares a daily sales report, which he summarizes every Saturday and sends to national headquarters. In addition, Fred does a weekly payroll report, which Dwayne reviews.

Discussion Questions

1. What makes Fred a sole proprietor?
2. Why are Fred and Dunkin' Donuts interdependent businesses?
3. Why did Fred have to share his personal balance sheet with Dunkin' Donuts? Do you think most interdependent businesses do this?
4. What does Dunkin' Donuts learn from Fred's company income statement and balance sheet?

Chapter Review

Comprehensive Demonstration Problem with Solution Tips

(The blank forms you need are on pages 1-5 and 1-6 of the *Study Guide with Working Papers.*)

Michael Brown opened his law office on June 1, 2000. During the first month of operations Michael conducted the following transactions:

1. Invested $5,000 in cash in the law practice.
2. Paid $600 for office equipment purchased.
3. Purchased additional office equipment on account, $1,000.
4. Performed legal services for clients, receiving cash, $2,000.
5. Paid salaries, $800.
6. Performed legal services for clients on account, $1,000.
7. Paid rent, $1,200.
8. Withdrew $500 from his law practice for personal use.
9. Received $500 from customers in partial payment for legal services performed, transaction 6.

Assignment

a. Record these transactions in the expanded accounting equation.

b. Prepare the financial statements at June 30 for Michael Brown, Barrister and Solicitor.

Solution to Comprehensive Demonstration Problem

a. Expanded Accounting Equation

	ASSETS			= LIABILITIES +		OWNER'S EQUITY		
	Cash	+ Accts. Rec.	+ Office Equip.	= Accts. Pay.	+ M. Brown, Capital	− M. Brown, Withdr.	+ Revenue	− Expenses
1.	+$5,000				+$5,000			
BAL.	5,000			=	5,000			
2.	−600		+$600					
BAL.	4,400		+ 600	=	5,000			
3.			+1,000	+$1,000				
BAL.	4,400		+ 1,600	= 1,000	+ 5,000			
4.	+2,000						+$2,000	
BAL.	6,400		+ 1,600	= 1,000	+ 5,000		+ 2,000	
5.	−800							+$800
BAL.	5,600		+ 1,600	= 1,000	+ 5,000		+ 2,000	− 800
6.		+$1,000					+1,000	
BAL.	5,600	+ 1,000	+ 1,600	= 1,000	+ 5,000		+ 3,000	− 800
7.	−1,200							+1,200
BAL.	4,400	+ 1,000	+ 1,600	= 1,000	+ 5,000		+ 3,000	− 2,000
8.	−500					+$500		
BAL.	3,900	+ 1,000	+ 1,600	= 1,000	+ 5,000	− 500	+ 3,000	− 2,000
9.	+500	−500						
END. BAL.	$4,400	+ $500	+ $1,600	= $1,000	+ $5,000	− $500	+ $3,000	− $2,000
			$6,500	= $6,500				

Solution Tips to Expanded Accounting Equation

- **Transaction 1:** The business increased its cash by $5,000. Owner's Equity (Capital) increased when Michael supplied the cash to the business.
- **Transaction 2:** There was a shift in assets when the equipment was purchased. The business lowered its cash by $600, and a new column—Office Equipment—was introduced for the $600 worth of equipment that was bought. The amount of capital was not altered because the owner did not supply any new funds.
- **Transaction 3:** When creditors supplied $1,000 worth of additional equipment, the business's Accounts Payable showed the debt. The business had increased what it *owed* the creditors.
- **Transaction 4:** Legal Fees, a revenue account and a subdivision of owner's equity, was increased when the law firm provided a service even if no money was received. The service provided an inward flow of $2,000 cash, an asset. Remember, legal fees are *not* an asset. As legal fees increase, owner's equity increases.
- **Transaction 5:** The salary paid by Michael showed as an $800 increase in expenses, and a corresponding decrease in cash.
- **Transaction 6:** Michael did the work and earned the $1,000. That $1,000 was recorded as revenue. This time the legal fees created an inward flow of assets, called Accounts Receivable, of $1,000. Remember, legal fees are *not* an asset. They are a subdivision of owner's equity.
- **Transaction 7:** The $1,200 rent expense reduced owner's equity as well as cash.
- **Transaction 8:** Withdrawals are for personal use. Here, business cash decreased by $500 while Michael's Withdrawals account increased $500. Withdrawals decrease the owner's equity.
- **Transaction 9:** This transaction did not reflect new revenue in the form of legal fees. It was only a shift in assets: more cash and reduced accounts receivable.

b. Financial Statements

Michael Brown, Barrister and Solicitor
Income Statement
for Month Ended June 30, 2000

Revenue:		
Legal Fees		$3,000
Operating Expenses:		
Salaries Expense	$ 800	
Rent Expense	1,200	
Total Operating Expenses		2,000
Net Income		$1,000

Michael Brown, Barrister and Solicitor
Statement of Owner's Equity
for Month Ended June 30, 2000

Michael Brown, Capital, June 1, 2000		$5,000
Net Income for June	$1,000	
Less: Withdrawals for June	500	
Increase in Capital		500
Michael Brown, Capital, June 30, 2000		$5,500

Michael Brown, Barrister and Solicitor
Balance Sheet
June 30, 2000

Assets		*Liabilities and Owner's Equity*	
Cash	$4,400	Liabilities	
Accounts Receivable	500	Accounts Payable	$1,000
Office Equipment	1,600	Owner's Equity	
		M. Brown, Capital	5,500
Total Assets	$6,500	Total Liabilities and Owner's Equity	$6,500

Solution Tips to Financial Reports

- **Income statement:** This statement lists only Revenues and Expenses for a specified period of time. Inside column is for subtotalling. Withdrawals are not listed here.
- **Statement of Owner's Equity:** The statement of owner's equity takes the net income figure of $1,000 and adds it to Beginning Capital less any withdrawals. This new capital figure of $5,500 will go on the balance sheet. This report shows changes in Capital for a specified period of time.
- **Balance Sheet:** The $4,400, $500, $1,600, and $1,000 came from the totals of the expanded accounting equation. The Capital figure of $5,500 came from the statement of owner's equity. This balance sheet reports Assets, Liabilities, and a new figure for Capital at a specific date.

Summary of Key Points

Learning Unit 1-1

1. The functions of accounting involve analyzing, recording, classifying, summarizing, reporting, and interpreting financial information.
2. A sole proprietorship is a business owned by one person. A partnership is a business owned by two or more persons. A corporation is a business owned by shareholders.
3. Bookkeeping is the recording part of accounting.
4. The computer is a tool to use in the accounting process.
5. Assets = Liabilities + Owner's Equity is the basic accounting equation that helps in analyzing business transactions.
6. Liabilities represent amounts owed to creditors, while capital represents what is invested by the owner.
7. Capital does not mean cash. Capital is the owner's current investment. The owner could have invested equipment that was purchased before the new business was started.
8. In a shift of assets, the composition of assets changes, but the total value of assets does not change. For example, if a bill is paid by a customer, the firm increases cash (an asset) but decreases accounts receivable (an asset), so there is no overall increase in assets; total assets remain the same. When you borrow money from a bank, you have an increase in cash (an asset) and an increase in liabilities; overall there is an increase in assets, not just a shift.

Learning Unit 1-2

1. The balance sheet is a report written as of a particular date. It lists the assets, liabilities, and owner's equity of a business. The heading of the balance sheet answers the questions *Who, What,* and *When* (as of a specific date).
2. The balance sheet is a formal report of a financial position.

Learning Unit 1-3

1. Revenue generates an inward flow of assets. Expenses generate an outward flow of assets or a potential outward flow. Revenue and expenses are subdivisions of owner's equity. Revenue is not an asset.
2. When revenue totals more than expenses, net income is the result; when expenses total more than revenue, net loss is the result.
3. Owner's equity can be subdivided into four elements: capital, withdrawals, revenue, and expenses.
4. Withdrawals decrease owner's equity; revenue increases owner's equity; expenses decrease owner's equity. A withdrawal is not a business expense; it is for personal use.

Learning Unit 1-4

1. The income statement is a report written for a specific period of time that lists earned revenue and expenses incurred to produce the earned revenue. The net income or net loss will be used in the statement of owner's equity.
2. The statement of owner's equity reveals the causes of a change in capital. This report lists additional investments in the company, net income (or net loss), and withdrawals. The ending figure for capital will be used on the balance sheet.
3. The balance sheet uses the ending balances of assets and liabilities from the accounting equation and the capital from the statement of owner's equity.
4. The income statement should be prepared first because the information on it related to net income or net loss is used to prepare the statement of owner's equity, which in turn provides information about capital for the balance sheet. In this way one builds upon the next, and it begins with the income statement.

Key Terms

Accounting A system that measures a business's activities in financial terms, provides written reports and financial statements about those activities, and communicates these reports to decision makers and others (p. 4)

Accounting process See **Accounting.** (p. 4)

Accounts payable Amounts owed to creditors that result from the purchase of goods or services on account; a liability (p. 9)

Accounts receivable Amounts to be paid by customers resulting from sales of goods and/or services; an asset (p. 13)

Assets Properties (resources) of value owned by a business (cash, supplies, equipment, land, and so on) (p. 6)

Balance sheet A report, as of a particular date, that shows the amount of assets owned by a business as well as the amount of claims (liabilities and owner's equity) against these assets (p. 10)

Basic accounting equation Assets = Liabilities + Owner's Equity (p. 7)

Bookkeeping The recording function of the accounting process (p. 6)

Business entity In accounting it is assumed that a business is separate and distinct from the personal assets of the owner. Each unit or entity requires separate accounting functions. (p. 6)

Capital The owner's investment of equity in the company (p. 7)

Corporation A type of business organization that is owned by shareholders. Usually, shareholders are not personally liable for the corporation's debts. (p. 3)

Creditor Someone who has a claim to assets (p. 7)

Ending capital Beginning Capital + Additional Investments + Net Income − Withdrawals = Ending Capital. *Or:* Beginning Capital + Additional Investments − Net Loss − Withdrawals = Ending Capital (p. 20)

Equipment Assets acquired to be used in business activities, usually with an expected life of from two to ten years (p. 8)

Equities The financial claim of creditors (liabilities) and owners (owner's equity) who supply the assets to a firm (p. 6)

Expanded accounting equation Assets = Liabilities + Capital − Withdrawals + Revenue − Expenses (p. 13)

Expense A cost incurred in running a business by consuming goods or services in producing revenue; a subdivision of owner's equity. When expenses increase, there is a decrease in owner's equity. (p. 13)

Generally accepted accounting principles (GAAP) The procedures and guidelines that must be followed during the accounting process (p. 5)

Income statement An accounting report that details the performance of a firm (revenue minus expenses) for a specific period of time (p. 18)

Liabilities Obligations that come due in the future. Liabilities result in increasing the financial rights or claims of creditors to assets. (p. 7)

Manufacturing company Business that makes a product and sells it to its customers. It may also make and sell its own products. (p. 4)

Merchandising company Business that buys a product from a manufacturing company, distributor, or wholesaler to sell to its customers (p. 4)

Net income When revenue totals more than expenses, the result is net income. (p. 13)

Net loss When expenses total more than revenue, the result is net loss. (p. 13)

Owner's equity Rights or financial claims to the assets of a business by the owner (in the accounting equation, assets minus liabilities) (p. 7)

Partnership A form of business organization that has at least two owners. The partners are usually personally liable for the partnership's debts. (p. 3)

Revenue An amount earned by performing services for customers or selling goods to customers. Revenue can be in the form of cash and/or accounts receivable. It is a subdivision of owner's equity—as revenue increases, owner's equity increases. (p. 13)

Service company Business that provides a service (p. 3)

Shift in assets A shift that occurs when the composition of the assets has changed, but the total of the assets remains the same (p. 8)

Sole proprietorship A type of business ownership that has one owner. The owner is personally liable for paying the business's debts. (p. 2)

Statement of financial position Another name for a balance sheet (p. 10)

Statement of owner's equity A financial report that reveals the change in capital. The ending figure for capital is then placed on the balance sheet. (p. 19)

Supplies One type of asset acquired by a firm. A supply item has a much shorter life than equipment, and its acquisition is usually treated as an expense. Sometimes it is treated as an asset—both treatments are possible. (p. 8)

Withdrawals A subdivision of owner's equity that records money or other assets an owner withdraws from a business for personal use (p. 13)

Blueprint of Financial Reports

❶ Income Statement
Measuring performance

Revenue		XXX
Less: Operating expenses		
Expense 1	XXX	
Expense 2	XX	
Expense 3	XX	XXX
Net Income		XXX

❷ Statement of Owner's Equity
Calculating new figure for Capital

Beginning Capital		XXX
Additional Investments		XXX
Total Investments		XXX
Net Income (or Loss)	XXX	
Less: Withdrawals	XXX	
Change in Capital		XXX
Ending Capital		XXX

❸ Balance Sheet
Showing where we now stand

Assets		Liabilities and Owner's Equity	
	XXX	Liabilities	XXX
	XXX	Owner's Equity	
	XXX	Ending Capital	XXX
Total Assets	XXX	Total Liabilities +	
		Owner's Equity	XXX

Questions, Mini Exercises, Exercises, and Problems

Discussion Questions

1. What are the functions of accounting?
2. Define, compare, and contrast sole proprietorships, partnerships, and corporations.
3. How are businesses classified?
4. What is the relationship of bookkeeping to accounting?
5. List the three elements of the basic accounting equation.
6. Define capital.
7. The total of the left-hand side of the accounting equation must equal the total of the right-hand side. True or false? Please explain.
8. A balance sheet tells a company where it is going and how well it will perform. True or false? Please explain.

9. Revenue is an asset. True or false? Please explain.
10. Into what categories is owner's equity subdivided?
11. A withdrawal is a business expense. True or false? Please explain.
12. As expenses increase they cause owner's equity to increase. Defend or reject.
13. What does an income statement show?
14. The statement of owner's equity calculates only ending withdrawals. True or false? Please explain.

Mini Exercises

(The blank forms you need are on page 1-7 of the *Study Guide with Working Papers.*)

Classifying Accounts

1. Classify each of the following items, as an asset (A), liability (L), or part of owner's equity (OE).
   - **a.** Land ______
   - **b.** Accounts Payable ______
   - **c.** P. Jean, Capital ______
   - **d.** Supplies on hand ______
   - **e.** Cash ______
   - **f.** Computer Equipment ______

The Accounting Equation

2. Complete:
   - **a.** A(n) __________ __________ __________ results when the total of the assets remain the same but the makeup of the assets has changed.
   - **b.** Assets − __________ = Owner's Equity.
   - **c.** Capital does not mean __________.

Shift versus Increase in Assets

3. Identify which transaction below results in a shift in assets (S) and which transaction causes an increase in assets (I).
   - **a.** Ace Jewellery bought computer equipment for cash. __________
   - **b.** Jake's Appliances bought office equipment on account. __________

The Balance Sheet

4. From the following, calculate what would be the total of assets on the balance sheet.

G. Hanna, Capital	$8,000
Word Processing Equipment	600
Accounts payable	2,000
Cash	9,400

The Accounting Equation Expanded

5. Identify with a ✓ which of the following are subdivisions of owner's equity.
   a. Land ________
   b. B. Flynn, Capital ________
   c. Accounts Receivable ________
   d. B. Flynn, Withdrawals ________
   e. Accounts Payable ________
   f. Rent Expense ________
   g. Office Equipment ________
   h. Hair Salon Fees Earned ________

Identifying Assets

6. Identify with a ✓ which of the following are *not* assets.
   a. Supplies on Hand ________
   b. Accounts Payable ________
   c. Legal Fees Earned ________
   d. Accounts Receivable ________

The Accounting Equation Expanded

7. Which of the following statements are false?
   a. ______ Revenue is an asset.
   b. ______ Revenue is a subdivision of owner's equity.
   c. ______ Revenue provides an inward flow of cash and/or accounts receivable.
   d. ______ Withdrawals are part of total assets.

Preparing Financial Reports

8. Indicate whether the following items would appear on the income statement (IS), statement of owner's equity (OE), or balance sheet (BS).
   a. ______ B. Clo, Withdrawals
   b. ______ Supplies on Hand
   c. ______ Accounts Payable
   d. ______ Computer Equipment
   e. ______ Commission Fees Earned
   f. ______ Salaries Expense
   g. ______ B. Clo, Capital (Beginning)
   h. ______ Accounts Receivable

Preparing Financial Reports

9. Indicate next to each statement whether it refers to the Income Statement (IS), statement of owner's equity (OE), or balance sheet (BS).
   a. ______ Calculate new figure for Capital.
   b. ______ Prepared as of a particular date
   c. ______ Statement that is prepared first
   d. ______ Report listing revenues and expenses

Exercises

(The forms you need are on pages 1-8 and 1-9 of the *Study Guide with Working Papers.*)

The accounting equation

1-1. Complete the following table:

ASSETS = LIABILITIES + OWNER'S EQUITY

	ASSETS	=	LIABILITIES	+	OWNER'S EQUITY
a.	$7,000	=	?	+	$2,000
b.	?	=	$6,000	+	$8,000
c.	$10,000	=	$4,000	+	?

Recording transactions in the accounting equation

1-2. Record the following transactions in the basic accounting equation:

ASSETS = LIABILITIES + OWNER'S EQUITY

Treat each transaction separately.

a. Jim invests $60,000 in his company.
b. He buys equipment for cash, $600.
c. He buys equipment on account, $900.

Preparing a balance sheet

1-3. From the following, prepare a balance sheet for Ann's Cleaners at the end of November 2001: Cash, $30,000; Cleaning Equipment, $8,000; Accounts Payable, $9,000; A. Bright, Capital, ?.

Recording transactions in the expanded accounting equation

1-4. Record the following transactions in the expanded accounting equation. The running balance may be omitted for simplicity.

ASSETS			= LIABILITIES +	OWNER'S EQUITY			
Cash	+ Accounts Receivable	+ Computer Equipment	= Accounts Payable	+ B. Wong, Capital	− B. Wong, Withdrawals	+ Revenue	− Expenses

a. Bill Wong invested $60,000 in a computer company.
b. Bought computer equipment on account, $7,000.
c. Paid personal telephone bill from company bank account, $200.
d. Received cash for services rendered, $14,000.
e. Billed customers for services rendered for the month, $30,000.
f. Paid current rent expense, $4,000.
g. Paid supplies expense, $1,500.

Preparing the income statement, statement of owner's equity, and balance sheet

1-5. From the following account balances for June, prepare in proper form (a) an income statement, (b) a statement of owner's equity, and (c) a balance sheet for French Realty.

Cash	$3,310
Accounts Receivable	1,490
Office Equipment	6,700
Accounts Payable	2,000
S. French, Capital, June 1	8,000
S. French, Withdrawals	40
Professional Fees	2,900
Salaries Expense	500
Utilities Expense	360
Rent Expense	500

Group A Problems

(The forms you need are on pages 1-10 to 1-16 of the *Study Guide with Working Papers.*)

The accounting equation

Check Figure

Total Assets $16,600

1A-1. Maggie Kay decided to open Kay's Realty. Maggie completed the following transactions:

a. Invested $16,000 cash from her personal bank account into the business.
b. Bought equipment for cash, $4,000.
c. Bought additional equipment on account, $1,000.
d. Paid $400 cash to reduce what was owed from the transaction in **(c)**.

Based on the above information, record these transactions in the basic accounting equation.

Preparing a balance sheet

Check Figure

Total Assets $59,000

1A-2. Joyce Hill is the accountant for Green's Advertising Service. From the following information, her task is to construct a balance sheet as of September 30, 2002, in proper form. Could you help her?

Building	$35,000
Accounts Payable	30,000
R. Green, Capital	29,000
Cash	10,000
Equipment	14,000

Recording transactions in the expanded accounting equation

Check Figure

Total Assets $15,640

1A-3. At the end of November, Rick Fox decided to open his own typing service. Analyze the following transactions he completed by recording their effects in the expanded accounting equation.

a. Invested $10,000 in his typing service.
b. Bought new office equipment on account, $4,000.
c. Received cash for typing services rendered, $500.
d. Performed typing services on account, $2,100.
e. Paid secretary's salary, $350.
f. Paid office supplies expense for the month, $210.
g. Rent expenses for office were due but not yet paid, $900.
h. Rick Fox withdrew cash for personal use, $400.

Preparing the income statement, statement of owner's equity, and balance sheet

Check Figure

Total Assets, $3,385

1A-4. Jane West, owner of West's Stencilling Service, has requested that you prepare from the following balances (a) an income statement for June 2002, (b) a statement of owner's equity for June, and (c) a balance sheet as of June 30, 2002.

Cash	$2,300
Accounts Receivable	400
Equipment	685
Accounts Payable	310
J. West, Capital, June 1, 2002	1,200
J. West, Withdrawals	300
Stencilling Fees	3,000
Advertising Expense	110
Repair Expense	25
Travel Expense	250
Supplies Expense	190
Rent Expense	250

Comprehensive problem

1A-5. John, a retired army officer, opened Tobey's Catering Service. As his accountant, analyze the transactions listed below and present in proper form:

1. The analysis of the transactions by utilizing the expanded accounting equation
2. A balance sheet showing the position of the firm before opening on November 1, 2001
3. An income statement for the month of November
4. A statement of owner's equity for November
5. A balance sheet as of November 30, 2001

Check Figure
Total Assets, Nov. 30 $24,060

2001
Oct. 25 John Tobey invested $20,000 in the catering business from his personal savings account.
27 Bought equipment for cash from Munroe Co., $700.
28 Bought additional equipment on account from Ryan Co., $1,000.
29 Paid $600 to Ryan Co. as partial payment of the October 28 transaction.

(You should now prepare your balance sheet as of October 31, 2001.)

Nov. 1 Catered a graduation and immediately collected cash, $2,400.
5 Paid salaries of employees, $690.
8 Prepared desserts for customers on account, $300.
10 Received $100 cash as partial payment of November 8 transaction.
15 Paid telephone bill, $60.
17 John paid his home electricity bill from the company's bank account, $90.
20 Catered a wedding and received cash, $1,800.
25 Bought additional equipment on account, $400.
28 Rent expense due but not yet paid, $600
30 Paid supplies expense, $400.

Group B Problems

(The forms you need are on pages 1-10 to 1-16 of the *Study Guide with Working Papers.*)

The accounting equation

1B-1. Maggie Kay began a new business called Kay's Realty. The following transactions resulted:

a. Maggie invested $17,000 cash from her personal bank account into the realty company.
b. Bought equipment on account, $1,800.
c. Paid $800 cash to reduce what was owed from transaction **b**.
d. Purchased additional equipment for cash, $3,000.

Record these transactions in the basic accounting equation.

Check Figure
Total Assets, $18,000

Preparing a balance sheet

1B-2. Joyce Hill has asked you to prepare a balance sheet as of September 30, 2002, for Green's Advertising Service. Could you assist Joyce?

R. Green, Capital	$19,000
Accounts Payable	70,000
Equipment	41,000
Building	16,000
Cash	32,000

Check Figure
Total Assets, $89,000

Recording transactions in the expanded accounting equation

Check Figure

Total Assets, $14,820

1B-3. Rick Fox decided to open his own typing service company at the end of November. Analyze the following transactions by recording their effects in the expanded accounting equation.

a. Rick Fox invested $9,000 in the typing service.
b. Purchased new office equipment on account, $3,000.
c. Received cash for typing services rendered, $1,290.
d. Paid secretary's salary, $310.
e. Billed customers for typing services rendered, $2,690.
f. Paid rent expense for the month, $500.
g. Rick withdrew cash for personal use, $350.
h. Advertising expense due but not yet paid, $100

Preparing an income statement, statement of owner's equity, and balance sheet

Check Figure

Total Assets, $3,723

1B-4. Jane West, owner of West's Stencilling Service, has requested that you prepare from the following balances (a) an income statement for June 2002, (b) a statement of owner's equity for June, and (c) a balance sheet as of June 30, 2002.

Cash	$2,043
Accounts Receivable	1,140
Equipment	540
Accounts Payable	45
J. West, Capital, June 1, 2002	3,720
J. West, Withdrawals	360
Stencilling Fees	1,098
Advertising Expense	135
Repair Expense	45
Travel Expense	90
Supplies Expense	270
Rent Expense	240

Comprehensive problem

Check Figure

Total Assets, Nov. 30 $25,005

1B-5. John Tobey, a retired army officer, opened Tobey's Catering Service. As his accountant, analyze the transactions listed below and present the following information in proper form:

1. The analysis of the transactions by utilizing the expanded accounting equation
2. A balance sheet showing the financial position of the firm before opening on November 1, 2001
3. An income statement for the month of November
4. A statement of owner's equity for November
5. A balance sheet as of November 30, 2001

2001
Oct. 25 John Tobey invested $17,500 in the catering business.
27 Bought equipment on account from Munroe Co., $900.
28 Bought equipment for cash from Ryan Co., $1,500.
29 Paid $300 to Munroe Co. as partial payment of the October 27 transaction.

Nov. 1 Catered a business luncheon and immediately collected cash, $2,000.
5 Paid salaries of employees, $350.
8 Provided catering services to Northwest Community College on account, $4,500.
10 Received from Northwest Community College $1,000 cash as partial payment of November 8 transaction.

15 Paid telephone bill, $95.
17 Tobey paid his home mortgage with a company cheque, $650.
20 Provided catering services and received cash, $1,800.
25 Bought additional equipment on account, $300.
28 Rent expense due but not yet paid, $750
30 Paid supplies expense, $600.

Group C Problems

(The forms you need are on pages 1-17 to 1-23 of the *Study Guide with Working Papers.*)

The accounting equation

1C-1. Brenda Tobert began a new business called Tobert's Graphics. The following transactions resulted:

Transaction A: Brenda invested $21,000 cash from her personal bank account in the graphics company.

Check Figure
Total Assets, $24,000

Transaction B: Bought computer equipment on account, $5,000.

Transaction C: Paid $2,000 cash to reduce what was owed from Transaction B.

Transaction D: Purchased office equipment for cash, $3,000.

Record these transactions in the basic accounting equation.

Preparing a balance sheet

1C-2. George Fontaine has asked you to prepare a balance sheet as of April 30, 2001, for Fontaine Database Service. Could you assist him?

Check Figure
Total Assets, $68,000

George Fontaine, Capital	$41,000
Accounts Payable	27,000
Equipment	18,000
Building	39,000
Cash	11,000

Recording transactions in the expanded accounting equation

1C-3. Ray Owens decided to open his own training services company at the end of October. Analyze the following transactions by recording their effects in the expanded accounting equation.

Check Figure
Total Assets, $22,908

Transaction A: Ray invested $15,000 in the company.
Transaction B: Purchased new office equipment on account, $4,500.
Transaction C: Received cash for services rendered, $2,350.
Transaction D: Paid secretary's salary, $800.
Transaction E: Billed customers for training services rendered, $3,650.
Transaction F: Paid rent expense for the month, $600.
Transaction G: Ray withdrew cash for personal use, $1,000.
Transaction H: Advertising expense was due but as yet unpaid, $400.
Transaction I: Repair to office equipment paid, $192.

Preparing an income statement, statement of owner's equity, and balance sheet

1C-4. Jennifer Pace, owner of Jennifer's Fashion Service, has requested that you prepare from the following balances: (a) an income statement for July 2001; (b) a statement of owner's equity for July; and (c) a balance sheet as of July 31, 2001.

Check Figure
Total Assets $8,776

Cash	$1,524
Accounts Receivable	3,672
Equipment	3,580
Accounts Payable	1,830

Jennifer Pace, Capital, July 1, 2001	6,430
Jennifer Pace, Withdrawals	710
Consulting Fees Earned	4,815
Advertising Expense	635
Repair Expense	387
Travel Expense	1,690
Supplies Expense	262
Rent Expense	440
Office Expenses	175

Comprehensive problem

1C-5. Jean Vende opened First City Surveying Service. As his accountant, analyze the transactions listed and present to Mr. Vende the following information, in proper form:

1. The analysis of the transactions by utilizing the expanded accounting equation

2. A balance sheet showing the financial position of the firm before opening on May 1, 2001

3. An income statement for the month of May

4. A statement of owner's equity for May

5. A balance sheet as of May 31, 2001

Check Figure

Total Assets May 31 $30,447

April	25	Jean invested $20,000 in the surveying business.
	27	Bought equipment on account from Chapman & Co., $4,100.
	28	Bought equipment for cash from Majestic Co., $2,895.
	29	Paid $2,000 to Chapman & Co. as partial payment of the April 27 transaction.
May	1	Surveyed a new business location and immediately collected cash, $2,350.
	5	Paid salaries of employees, $975.
	8	Provided surveying services to City Community College on account, $4,950.
	10	Received from City Community College $2,500 cash as partial payment of May 8 transaction.
	15	Paid telephone bill, $104.
	17	Jean paid his home mortgage from the company's bank account, $1,043.
	20	Provided surveying services and received cash, $1,825.
	25	Bought additional equipment on account from Jensen Bros., $2,415.
	28	Paid rent expense for the month, $825.
	30	Paid supplies expense, $246.
	31	Advertising bill received but not yet paid, $410

REAL WORLD APPLICATIONS

(The forms you need are on pages 1-24 to 1-25 of the *Study Guide with Working Papers.*)

1R-1.

You have just been hired to prepare, if possible, an income statement for the year ended December 31, 2003, for Logan's Window Washing Company. The problem is that Bill Logan kept only the following records (on the back of a piece of cardboard).

Money in:

Window cleaning	*$11,376*
My investment	*1,200*
Loan from brother-in-law	*4,000*

Money out:

Salaries	*$5,080*
Withdrawals	*6,200*
Supplies expense	*1,400*

What I owe or they owe me

A. People that work for me but I still owe salaries to $1,800
B. Owe bank interest of $300
C. Work done but clients still owe me $2,900
D. Advertising bill due but not paid $95

Assume that Logan's Window Washing Company records all revenues when earned and all expenses when incurred.

You feel that it is part of your job to tell Bill how to organize his records better. What would you tell him?

1R-2.

While Jon Lune was on a business trip, he asked Abby Slowe, the bookkeeper for Lune Co., to try to complete a balance sheet for the year ended December 31, 2001. Abby, who had been on the job only two months, submitted the following:

LUNE CO.
FOR THE YEAR ENDED DECEMBER 31, 2001

Building	$446 000 00	Accounts Payable	$127 604 00
Land	72 935 00	Accounts Receivable	104 337 00
Notes Payable	75 328 00	Auto	14 268 00
Cash	10 016 00	Desks	6 825 00
J. Lune, Capital	?	Total Equity	$250 034 00

1. Could you help Abby fix as well as complete the balance sheet?
2. What written recommendations would you make about the bookkeeper? Should she be retained?
3. Suppose that (a) Jon Lune invested an additional $20,000 in cash as well as additional desks with a value of $8,000 and (b) Lune Co. bought an auto for $6,000 that was originally marked $8,000, paying $2,000 down and issuing a note for the balance. Could you prepare an updated balance sheet? Assume that these two transactions occurred on January 4.

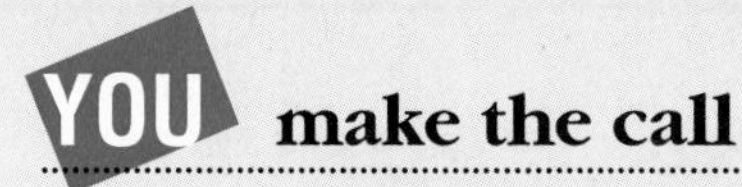

make the call

Critical Thinking/Ethical Case

(The forms you need are on page 1-26 of the *Study Guide with Working Papers.*)

1R-3.
Paul Kloss, Accountant for Lowe & Co., travelled to Vancouver on company business. His total expenses came to $350. Paul felt that since the trip extended over the weekend he could "pad" his expense account with an additional $100 of expenses. After all, weekends represent his own time, not the company's. What would you do? Write your specific recommendations to Paul.

ACCOUNTING RECALL
A CUMULATIVE APPROACH

THIS EXAMINATION REVIEWS CHAPTER 1.

Your *Study Guide with Working Papers* has forms on pages 1-27 to 1-29 to complete this exam, as well as worked-out solutions. The page reference next to each question identifies the page in this text to turn back to for review if you answer the question incorrectly.

PART I Vocabulary Review

Match the terms in the left column below with the appropriate definition or phrase in the right-hand column.

Page Ref.			
(7)	1. Capital	A.	Prepared as of a particular date
(13)	2. Accounts receivable	B.	A liability
(2)	3. Sole proprietorship	C.	For personal use
(13)	4. Expense	D.	Provides an inward flow of assets
(10)	5. Balance sheet	E.	Company owned and managed by one person
(13)	6. Revenue	F.	Amount owed by customers
(13)	7. Withdrawals	G.	Owner's investment
(18)	8. Income statement	H.	A cost of running a business
(9)	9. Accounts payable	I.	Broken into four subdivisions
(7)	10. Owner's equity	J.	Prepared for specific period of time

PART II True or False (Accounting Theory)

(13) 11. Revenue is an asset.

(12) 12. The four subdivisions of owner's equity are capital, withdrawals, revenue, and expenses.

(13) 13. As expenses increase, owner's equity increases.

(18) 14. Accounts receivable goes on the income statement.

(19) 15. The statement of owner's equity calculates a new figure for capital.

Continuing Problem

The following problem will continue from one chapter to the next, carrying the balances forward from month to month. Each chapter will focus on the learning experience of the chapter and add additional information as the business grows. The necessary forms are provided on pages 1-28 to 1-30 of the *Study Guide with Working Papers.*

Tony Freedman decided to begin his own computer service business on July 2, 2001. He named the business the Eldorado Computer Centre. During the first month Tony conducted the following business transactions:

(a) Invested $4,500 of his savings into the business
(b) Paid $1,200 (cheque #201) for a computer from Multi Systems, Inc.
(c) Paid $500 (cheque #202) for office equipment from Office Furniture, Inc.
(d) Set up a new account with Office Depot and purchased $250 in office supplies on credit
(e) Paid July rent, $400 (cheque #203)
(f) Repaired a system for a customer; collected $250
(g) Collected $200 for system upgrade labour charge from a customer
(h) Electric bill due but unpaid, $85
(i) Received $1,200 for services performed on Taylor Golf computers
(j) Tony withdrew $100 (cheque #204) to take his wife Carol out in celebration of opening the new business. *Note:* The business is too small to worry about GST (or HST).

Assignment

1. Set up an expanded accounting equation spreadsheet using the following accounts:

Assets	**Liabilities**	**Owner's Equity**
Cash	Accounts Payable	T. Freedman, Capital
Supplies		T. Freedman, Withdrawals
Computer Shop		Service Revenue
Equipment		Expenses (notate type)
Office Equipment		

2. Analyze and record each transaction in the expanded accounting equation.
3. Prepare the financial statements for Eldorado Computer Centre for the period ending July 31.

Debits and Credits

2

ANALYZING AND RECORDING BUSINESS TRANSACTIONS

THE BIG PICTURE

◆

As the owner of Eldorado Computer Centre, Tony Freedman spends most of his time interacting with customers and performing services for them. Only some of Freedman's activities, however, are business transactions. In a business transaction an exchange takes place. Cash is paid for services. Credit is given to customers. Rent is paid for the use of space. Each transaction must be recorded in the accounts of Freedman's business.

In this chapter you will see how every transaction must affect at least two accounts. As you learned in Chapter 1, every account is categorized under a heading from the accounting equation: assets, liabilities, or owner's equity. When you analyze a transaction, you decide not only which accounts change in value, but also whether they increase or decrease. Remember that the accounting equation must always be kept in balance, and the key to recording every transaction is the interpretation of what happened.

To analyze transactions accurately and to keep the accounting equation in balance, you will use T accounts and a system of debits and credits. The T account lets us write the value of a transaction as a credit or debit in a standard format. A T account can be easily totalled at any time. The rules for debits and credits assure us that if debits equal credits in every transaction then the accounting equation will always balance. Whether you use a manual or a computerized accounting system, you must analyze transactions correctly to get correct results.

At the end of each monthly accounting period, Freedman prepares a trial balance, a test of the equality of debits and credits in all his accounts. He can then use the account balances to generate financial statements that he can compare from month to month.

Chapter Objectives

- Setting up and organizing a chart of accounts (p. 46)
- Recording transactions in T accounts according to the rules of debit and credit (p. 47)
- Preparing a trial balance (p. 56)
- Preparing financial reports from a trial balance (pp. 56–57)

In Chapter 1, we used the expanded accounting equation to document the financial transactions performed by Catherine Hall's law firm. Remember how long it was: The cash column had a long list of pluses and minuses, and there was no quick system of recording and summarizing the increases and decreases of cash or other items. Can you imagine the problem Canadian Tire or Tim Horton's would have if they used the expanded accounting equation to track the thousands of business transactions they do each day?

LEARNING UNIT 2-1

The T Account

Let's look at the problem a little more closely. Every business transaction is recorded in the accounting equation under a specific **account.** There are different accounts for each of the subdivisions of the accounting equation—there are asset accounts, liability accounts, expense accounts, revenue accounts, and so on. What is needed is a way to record the increases and decreases in specific account *categories* and yet keep them together in one place. The answer is the **standard account** form (see Figure 2-1). A standard account is a formal account that includes columns for date, explanation, posting reference, debit, and credit. Each account has a separate form and all transactions affecting that account are recorded on the form. All the business's account forms (which often are referred to as *ledger accounts*) are then placed in a **ledger.** Each page of the ledger contains one account. The ledger may be in the form of a bound or a loose-leaf book. If computers are used, the ledger may be part of a computer printout. For simplicity's sake, in this chapter we will use the **T account** form. This form got its name because it looks like the letter T. Generally, T accounts are used for demonstration purposes.

FIGURE 2-1
The Standard Account Form

The standard account form is the source of the T account's shape.

Account Title							Account No.
Date	Item	PR	Debit	Date	Item	PR	Credit

Each T account contains three basic parts:

	1 Title of Account	
2	Left side | Right side	3

All T accounts have this structure. In accounting, the left side of any T account is called the **debit** side.

Debit defined

1. The *left* side of any T account
2. An amount entered on the left side of any account is said to be *debited* to an account.

Left side Dr. (debit)	

At this point, for you the word *debit* in accounting means a position, the left side of an account. Don't think of it as good (+) or bad (−).

Amounts entered on the left side of any account are said to be *debited* to an account. The word *debit* is from the Latin *debere*; the abbreviation for debit is Dr.

The right side of any T account is called the **credit** side.

Credit defined

1. The *right* side of any T account
2. An amount entered on the right side of an account is said to be *credited* to an account.

	Right side Cr. (credit)

Amounts entered on the right side of an account are said to be *credited* to an account. The word *credit* is from the Latin *credere;* the abbreviation for credit is Cr.

At this point, do not associate the definitions of debit and credit with the words *increase* and *decrease.* Think of debit or credit as only indicating a *position* (left side or right side) of a T account.

Balancing an Account

Dollar signs are not used in standard accounts or T accounts. However, dollar signs are used in formal financial reports.

No matter which individual account is being balanced, the procedure used to balance it will be the same.

	Dr.	Cr.
Entries →	3,000	300
	500	400
Footings →	3,500	700
Balance →	2,800	

In the "real" world, the T account would also include the date of the transaction. The date would appear to the left of the entry:

		Dr.	Cr.	
	4/2	3,000	4/3	300
	4/20	500	4/25	400
Footings		3,500		700
Balance		2,800		

Footings aid in balancing an account. The ending balance is the difference between the footings.

If the balance were greater on the credit side, that is the side the ending balance would be on.

Note that on the debit (left) side the amounts add up to $3,500. On the credit (right) side the amounts add up $700. The $3,500 and the $700 written in small type are called footings. Footings help in calculating the new (or ending) balance. The **ending balance** ($2,800) is placed on the debit or left side, since the balance of the debit side is greater than that of the credit side.

Remember, the ending balance does not tell us anything about increase or decrease. It only tells us that we have an ending balance of $2,800 on the debit side.

LEARNING UNIT 2-1 REVIEW

AT THIS POINT you should be able to:

- Define ledger. (p. 42)
- State the purpose of a T account. (p. 42)
- Identify the three parts of a T account. (p. 43)
- Define debit. (p. 43)
- Define credit. (p. 43)
- Explain footings and calculate the balance of an account. (p. 43)

SELF-REVIEW QUIZ 2-1

(The blank forms you need are on page 2-1 of the *Study Guide with Working Papers.*)

Respond True or False to the following:

1.

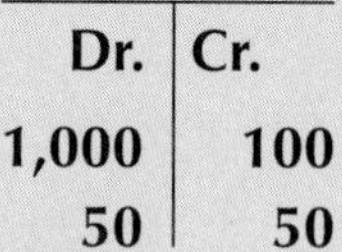

Dr.	Cr.
1,000	100
50	50

The balance of the account is $900 Cr.

2. A credit always means increase.
3. A debit is the left side of any account.
4. A ledger can be prepared manually or by computer.
5. Footings replace the need for debits and credits.

Quiz Tip

Dr. + Dr. ⟶ Add to get Dr. balance.

Cr. + Cr. ⟶ Add to get Cr. balance.

Dr. – Cr. ⟶ Subtract to get balance for the larger side.

Solutions to Self-Review Quiz 2-1

1. False **2.** False **3.** True **4.** True **5.** False

LEARNING UNIT 2-2

Recording Business Transactions: Debits and Credits

Can you get a queen in checkers? In a baseball game does a runner rounding first base skip second base and run over the pitcher's mound to get to third? No—most of us don't do such things because we follow the rules of the game. Usually we learn the rules first and reflect on the reasons for them afterward. The same is true in accounting.

Instead of first trying to understand all the rules of debit and credit and how they were developed in accounting, it will be easier to learn the rules by "playing the game."

T ACCOUNT ENTRIES FOR ACCOUNTING IN THE ACCOUNTING EQUATION

Have patience. Learning the rules of debit and credit is like learning to play any game—the more you play, the easier it becomes. Table 2-1 shows the rules for the side on which you enter an increase or a decrease for each of the separate accounts in the accounting equation. For example, an increase is entered on the debit side in the asset account, but on the credit side for a liability account.

It might be easier to visualize these rules of debit and credit if we look at them in the T account form, using + to show increase and − to show decrease.

ASSETS		= LIABILITIES +		OWNER'S EQUITY							
				+ Capital		− Withdrawals +		Revenue		− Expenses	
Dr.	Cr.	Dr.	Cr.	Dr.	Cr.	Dr.	Cr.	Dr.	Cr.	Dr.	Cr.
+	−	−	+	−	+	+	−	−	+	+	−

Rules for Assets Work in the Opposite Direction to Those for Liabilities When you look at the equation you can see that the rules for assets work in the opposite direction to those for liabilities. That is, for assets the increases appear on the debit side and the decreases are shown on the credit side; the opposite is true for liabilities. As for owner's equity, the rules for withdrawals and expenses, which *decrease* owner's equity, work in the opposite direction to the rules for capital and revenue, which *increase* owner's equity.

Assets		+ Withdrawals +		Expenses		= Liabilities		+ Capital		+ Revenue	
Dr.	Cr.	Dr.	Cr.	Dr.	Cr.	Dr.	Cr.	Dr.	Cr.	Dr.	Cr.
+	−	+	−	+	−	−	+	−	+	−	+

Normal Balance	
Dr.	**Cr.**
Assets	Liabilities
Expenses	Capital
Withdrawals	Revenue

This setup may help you understand that the rules for withdrawals and expenses are just the opposite of the rules for capital and revenue.

A **normal balance of an account** is the side that increases by the rules of debit and credit. For example, the balance of cash is a debit balance, because an asset is increased by a debit. We will discuss normal balances further in Chapter 3.

Balancing the Equation It is important to remember that any amount(s) entered on the debit side of a T account or accounts also must be on the credit side of another T account or accounts. This ensures that the total amount added to the debit side will equal the total amount added to the credit side, thereby keeping the accounting equation in balance.

Be sure to follow the rules of debit and credits when recording accounts. They were designed to keep the accounting equation in balance.

TABLE 2-1 RULES OF DEBIT AND CREDIT

Account Category	Increase (Normal Balance)	Decrease
Assets	Debit	Credit
Liabilities	Credit	Debit
Owner's Equity		
Capital	Credit	Debit
Withdrawals	Debit	Credit
Revenue	Credit	Debit
Expenses	Debit	Credit

The chart of accounts aids in locating and identifying accounts quickly.

Large companies may have up to four digits assigned to each title, and sometimes up to 24 digits (e.g., Exxon).

Chart of Accounts Our job is to analyze Catherine Hall's business transactions—the transactions we looked at in Chapter 1—using a system of accounts guided by the rules of debits and credits that will summarize increases and decreases of individual accounts in the ledger. The goal is to prepare an income statement, statement of owner's equity, and balance sheet for Catherine Hall. Sound familiar? If this system works, the rules of debits and credits and the use of accounts will give us the same answers as in Chapter 1, but with greater ease.

Catherine's accountant developed what is called a **chart of accounts.** The chart of accounts is a numbered list of all of the business's accounts. It allows accounts to be located quickly. In Catherine's business, for example, 100s are assets, 200s are liabilities, and so on. As you see in Table 2-2, each separate asset and liability has its own number. Note that the chart may be expanded as the business grows.

TABLE 2-2 CHART OF ACCOUNTS FOR CATHERINE HALL, BARRISTER AND SOLICITOR

Balance Sheet Accounts	
Assets	**Liabilities**
111 Cash	211 Accounts Payable
112 Accounts Receivable	
121 Office Equipment	**Owner's Equity**
	311 Catherine Hall, Capital
	312 Catherine Hall, Withdrawals
Income Statement Accounts	
Revenue	**Expenses**
411 Legal Fees	511 Salaries Expense
	512 Rent Expense
	513 Advertising Expense

THE ACCOUNTING ANALYSIS: FIVE STEPS

Steps to analyze and record transactions. Steps 1 and 2 will come from the chart of accounts.

Remember the rules of debit and credit tell us only on which side to place information. Whether the debit or credit represents increases or decreases depends on the account category:

- Assets, Expenses, and Withdrawals, which are increased with a debit
- Liabilities, Owner's Equity, and Revenue, which are increased with a credit

Think of a business transaction as an exchange—you get something and you give or part with something.

We will analyze the transactions in Catherine Hall's law firm using a teaching device called a *transaction analysis chart* to record these five steps. (Keep in mind that the transaction analysis chart is not a part of any formal accounting system.) There are five steps in analyzing each business transaction:

Step 1: Determine which accounts are affected. Example: cash, accounts payable, rent expense. A transaction always affects at least two accounts.

Step 2: Determine which categories the accounts belong to—assets, liabilities, capital, withdrawals, revenue, or expenses. Example: Cash is an asset.

Step 3: Determine whether the accounts increase or decrease. Example: If you receive cash, that account is increasing.

Step 4: What do the rules of debits and credits say (Table 2-1)?

Step 5: What does the T account look like? Place amounts in accounts, on either the left or right side depending on the rules in Table 2-1.

This is how the five-step analysis looks in chart form:

1 Accounts Affected	2 Category	3 ↓ or ↑ (decrease) (increase)	4 Rules of Dr. and Cr.	5 Appearance of T Accounts

Let us emphasize a major point: *Do not try to debit or credit an account until you have gone through the first four steps of the transaction analysis.*

Note that in column 3 of the chart there can be any combination of arrows, as long as the sum of the debits equals the sum of the credits in the T accounts in column 5.

Applying the Transaction Analysis to Catherine Hall's Law Practice

Transaction A: Aug. 28: Catherine Hall invests $7,000 cash and $800 worth of office equipment in the business.

1 Accounts Affected	2 Category	3 ↓ ↑	4 Rules of Dr. and Cr.	5 Appearance of T Accounts
Cash	Asset	↑	Dr.	Cash 111: (A) 7,000 (debit side)
Office Equipment	Asset	↑	Dr.	Office Equipment 121: (A) 800 (debit side)
C. Hall, Capital	Owner's Equity	↑	Cr.	C. Hall, Capital 311: 7,800 (A) (credit side)

Note again that every transaction affects at least two T accounts, and that the total amount added to the debit side(s) must equal the total amount added to the credit side(s) of the T accounts of each transaction.

Analysis of Transaction A

Step 1: Which accounts are affected? The law firm receives cash and office equipment, so three accounts are involved: cash, office equipment, and C. Hall, Capital. These account titles come from the chart of accounts.

Step 2: Which categories do these accounts belong to? Cash and office equipment are assets; C. Hall, Capital, is owner's equity.

Step 3: Are the accounts increasing or decreasing? The cash and office equipment, both assets, are increasing in the business. The rights or claims of C. Hall, Capital, are also increasing, since Catherine invested money and office equipment in the business.

Step 4: What do the rules say? According to the rules of debit and credit, an increase in assets (cash and office equipment) is a debit. An increase in capital is a credit. Note that the total dollar amount of debits will equal the total dollar amount of credits when the T accounts are updated in column 5.

Step 5: What does the T account look like? The amount for cash and office equipment is entered on the debit side. The amount for C. Hall, Capital, goes on the credit side.

A transaction that involves more than one credit or more than one debit is called a **compound entry.** This first transaction of Catherine Hall's law firm is a compound entry; it involves a debit of $7,000 to Cash and a debit of $800 to Office Equipment (as well as a credit of $7,800 to C. Hall, Capital).

There is a name for this double-entry analysis of transactions, where two or more accounts are affected and the total of debits equals the total of credits. It is called **double-entry bookkeeping**. This double-entry system helps in checking the recording of business transactions.

Double-entry bookkeeping system

The total of all debits is equal to the total of all credits.

As we continue, the explanations will be brief, but do not forget to apply the five steps in analyzing and recording each business transaction.

Transaction B: Aug. 29: Law practice bought office equipment for cash, $900.

1 Accounts Affected	2 Category	3 ↓ ↑	4 Rules of Dr. and Cr.	5 T-Account Update
Office Equipment	Asset	↑	Dr.	Office Equipment 121: (A) 800; (B) 900 (debit side)
Cash	Asset	↓	Cr.	Cash 111: (A) 7,000 (debit side) / 900 (B) (credit side)

Analysis of Transaction B

Step 1: The law firm paid cash for the office equipment it received. The accounts involved in the transaction are Cash and Office Equipment.

Step 2: The accounts belong to these categories: Office Equipment is an asset account; Cash is an asset account.

Step 3: The asset account Office Equipment is increasing. The asset account Cash is decreasing—it is being reduced in order to buy the office equipment.

Step 4: An increase in the asset account Office Equipment is a debit; a decrease in the asset account Cash is a credit.

Step 5: When the amounts are placed in the T accounts, the amount for office equipment goes on the debit side and the amount for cash on the credit side.

Transaction C: Aug. 30: Bought more office equipment on account, $400.

1 Accounts Affected	2 Category	3 ↓ ↑	4 Rules of Dr. and Cr.	5 T-Account Update
Office Equipment	Asset	↑	Dr.	Office Equipment 121: (A) 800; (B) 900; (C) 400 (debit side)
Accounts Payable	Liability	↑	Cr.	Accounts Payable 211: 400 (C) (credit side)

Analysis of Transaction C

Step 1: The law firm receives office equipment by promising to pay in the future. An obligation or liability account, Accounts Payable, is created.

Step 2: Office Equipment is an asset. Accounts Payable is a liability.

Step 3: The asset account Office Equipment is increasing; the liability account Accounts Payable is increasing because the law firm is increasing what it owes.

Step 4: An increase in the asset account Office Equipment is a debit. An increase in the liability account Accounts Payable is a credit.

Step 5: Enter the amount for office equipment on the debit side of the T account. The amount for accounts payable goes on the credit side.

Transaction D: Sept. 1–30: Provided legal services for cash, $3,000.

1 Accounts Affected	2 Category	3 ↓ ↑	4 Rules of Dr. and Cr.	5 T-Account Update
Cash	Asset	↑	Dr.	Cash 111 (A) 7,000 | 900 (B) (D) 3,000 |
Legal Fees	Revenue	↑	Cr.	Legal Fees 411 | 3,000 (D)

Analysis of Transaction D

Step 1: The firm has earned revenue from legal services and receives $3,000 in cash.

Step 2: Cash is an asset account. Legal fees are revenue.

Step 3: Cash, an asset account, is increasing. Legal fees, or revenue, is also increasing.

Step 4: An increase in cash, an asset, is debited. An increase in legal fees, or revenue, is credited.

Step 5: Enter the amount for cash on the debit side of the T account. Enter the amount for legal fees on the credit side.

Transaction E: Sept. 1–30: Provided legal services on account, $4,000.

1 Accounts Affected	2 Category	3 ↓ ↑	4 Rules of Dr. and Cr.	5 T-Account Update
Accounts Receivable	Asset	↑	Dr.	Accounts Receivable 112 (E) 4,000 |
Legal Fees	Revenue	↑	Cr.	Legal Fees 411 | 3,000 (D) | 4,000 (E)

Analysis of Transaction E

Step 1: The law practice has earned revenue but has not yet received payment (cash). The amounts owed by these clients are called *accounts receivable.* Revenue is earned at the time the legal services are provided, whether payment is received then or will be received sometime in the future.

Step 2: Accounts Receivable is an asset account. Legal Fees is a revenue account.

Step 3: The Accounts Receivable account is increasing because the law practice has increased the amount owed to it for legal fees that have been earned but not paid. The Legal Fees account, or revenue, is increasing.

Step 4: An increase in the asset account Accounts Receivable is a debit. An increase in revenue is a credit.

Step 5: Enter the amount for Accounts Receivable on the debit side of the T account. The amount for Legal Fees goes on the credit side.

Transaction F: Sept. 1–30: Received $700 cash from clients for services rendered previously on account.

1 Accounts Affected	2 Category	3 ↓ ↑	4 Rules of Dr. and Cr.	5 T-Account Update
Cash	Asset	↑	Dr.	Cash 111: Dr. (A) 7,000; (D) 3,000; (F) 700 — Cr. 900 (B)
Accounts Receivable	Asset	↓	Cr.	Accounts Receivable 112: Dr. (E) 4,000 — Cr. 700 (F)

Analysis of Transaction F

Step 1: The law firm collects $700 in cash from previous revenue earned. Since the revenue is recorded at the time it is earned, and not when the payment is made, in this transaction we are concerned only with the payment, which affects the Cash and Accounts Receivable accounts.

Step 2: Cash is an asset account. Accounts Receivable is an asset account.

Step 3: Since clients are paying what is owed, cash (asset) is increasing and the amount owed (accounts receivable) is decreasing (the total amount owed by clients to Hall is going down). This transaction results in a shift in assets, more cash for less accounts receivable.

Step 4: An increase in the Cash account, an asset, is a debit. A decrease in the Accounts Receivable account, an asset, is a credit.

Step 5: Enter the amount for Cash on the debit side of the T account. The amount for Accounts Receivable goes on the credit side.

Transaction G: Sept. 1–30: Paid salaries expense, $600.

1 Accounts Affected	2 Category	3 ↓ ↑	4 Rules of Dr. and Cr.	5 T-Account Update
Salaries Expense	Expense	↑	Dr.	Salaries Expense 511: Dr. (G) 600
Cash	Asset	↓	Cr.	Cash 111: Dr. (A) 7,000; (D) 3,000; (F) 700 — Cr. 900 (B); 600 (G)

Analysis of Transaction G

Step 1: The law firm pays $600 worth of salaries expense by cash.

Step 2: Salaries Expense is an expense account. Cash is an asset account.

Step 3: The salaries expense of the law firm is increasing, which results in a decrease in cash available.

Step 4: An increase in Salaries Expense, an expense account, is a debit. A decrease in Cash, an asset account, is a credit.

Step 5: Enter the amount for Salaries Expense on the debit side of the T account. The amount for Cash goes on the credit side.

Transaction H: Sept. 1–30: Paid rent expense, $700.

1 Accounts Affected	2 Category	3 ↓ ↑	4 Rules of Dr. and Cr.	5 T-Account Update
Rent Expense	Expense	↑	Dr.	Rent Expense 512: Dr. (H) 700
Cash	Asset	↓	Cr.	Cash 111: Dr. (A) 7,000; (D) 3,000; (F) 700 — Cr. 900 (B); 600 (G); 700 (H)

Analysis of Transaction H

Step 1: The law firm's rent expenses are paid in cash.

Step 2: Rent is an expense. Cash is an asset.

Step 3: The rent expense increases the expenses, and the payment for the rent expense decreases the cash.

Step 4: An increase in Rent Expense, an expense account, is a debit. A decrease in Cash, an asset account, is a credit.

Step 5: Enter the amount for Rent Expense on the debit side of the T account. Place the amount for Cash on the credit side.

Transaction I: Sept. 1–30: Received a bill for Advertising Expense (to be paid next month), $300.

1 Accounts Affected	2 Category	3 ↓ ↑	4 Rules of Dr. and Cr.	5 T-Account Update
Advertising Expense	Expense	↑	Dr.	Advertising Expense 513: Dr. (I) 300
Accounts Payable	Liability	↑	Cr.	Accounts Payable 211: Cr. 400 (C); 300 (I)

Analysis of Transaction I

Step 1: The advertising bill has come in and payment is due but has not yet been made. Therefore the accounts involved here are Advertising Expense and Accounts Payable; the expense has created a liability.

Step 2: Advertising Expense is an expense account. Accounts Payable is a liability account.

Step 3: Both the expense and the liability are increasing.

Step 4: An increase in an expense is a debit. An increase in a liability is a credit.

Step 5: Enter the amount for the Advertising Expense account on the debit side of the T account. Enter the amount for the Accounts Payable account on the credit side.

Transaction J: Sept. 1–30: Hall withdrew cash for personal use, $200.

1 Accounts Affected	2 Category	3 ↓ ↑	4 Rules of Dr. and Cr.	5 T-Account Update
C. Hall, Withdrawals	Owner's Equity (Withdrawals)*	↓	Dr.	C. Hall, Withdrawals 312 Dr.: (J) 200
Cash	Asset	↓	Cr.	Cash 111 Dr.: (A) 7,000; (D) 3,000; (F) 700 Cr.: 900 (B); 600 (G); 700 (H); 200 (J)

*Withdrawals are actually a sub-category of Owner's Equity and act as a contra account—that is, as the Withdrawals account increases the Owner's Equity account decreases.

Analysis of Transaction J

Step 1: Catherine Hall withdraws cash from the business for *personal* use. This withdrawal is not a business expense.

Step 2: This transaction affects the Withdrawals and Cash accounts.

Step 3: Catherine has increased what she has withdrawn from the business for personal use. The business cash has been decreased.

Step 4: An increase in withdrawals is a debit. A decrease in cash is a credit. (*Remember:* Withdrawals go on the statement of owner's equity; expenses go on the income statement.)

Step 5: Enter the amount for C. Hall, Withdrawals on the debit side of the T account. The amount for Cash goes on the credit side.

ASSETS = LIABILITIES + CAPITAL − WITHDRAWALS + REVENUE − EXPENSES

Cash 111 = Accounts Payable 211 + C. Hall, Capital 311 − C. Hall, Withdrawals 312 + Legal Fees 411 − Salaries Expense 511

Cash 111	
(A) 7,000	900 (B)
(D) 3,000	600 (G)
(F) 700	700 (H)
	200 (J)

Accounts Payable 211	
	400 (C)
	300 (I)

C. Hall, Capital 311	
	7,800 (A)

C. Hall, Withdrawals 312	
(J) 200	

Legal Fees 411	
	3,000 (D)
	4,000 (E)

Salaries Expense 511	
(G) 600	

Accounts Receivable 112	
(E) 4,000	700 (F)

− Rent Expense 512	
(H) 700	

Office Equipment 121	
(A) 800	
(B) 900	
(C) 400	

− Advertising Expense 513	
(I) 300	

LEARNING UNIT 2-2 REVIEW

AT THIS POINT you should be able to:

- State the rules of debit and credit. (p. 43)
- List the five steps of a transaction analysis. (p. 46)
- Show how to fill out a transaction analysis chart. (p. 47)
- Explain double-entry bookkeeping. (p. 47)

SELF-REVIEW QUIZ 2-2

(The blank forms you need are on pages 2-1 and 2-2 of the *Study Guide with Working Papers.*)

O'Malley Company uses the following accounts from its chart of accounts: Cash (111), Accounts Receivable (112), Equipment (121), Accounts Payable (211), Bill O'Malley, Capital (311), Bill O'Malley, Withdrawals (312), Professional Fees (411), Utilities Expense (511), and Salaries Expense (512).

Record the following transactions in transaction analysis charts.

A. Bill O'Malley invested in the business $900 cash and equipment worth $600 from his personal assets.

B. Billed clients for services rendered, $9,000.

C. Utilities bill due but as yet unpaid, $125

D. Bill O'Malley withdrew cash for personal use, $120.

E. Paid salaries expense, $250.

Solution to Self-Review Quiz 2-2

Quiz Tip

Column 1 titles must come from the chart of accounts. The order doesn't matter as long as the total of all debits equals the total of all credits.

A.

1 Accounts Affected	2 Category	3 ↓ ↑	4 Rules of Dr. and Cr.	5 T-Account Update
Cash	Asset	↑	Dr.	Cash 111: (A) 900 |
Equipment	Asset	↑	Dr.	Equipment 121: (A) 600 |
Bill O'Malley, Capital	Capital	↑	Cr.	Bill O'Malley, Capital 311: | 1,500 (A)

When a buiness bills a client, it increases an asset.

B.

1 Accounts Affected	2 Category	3 ↓ ↑	4 Rules of Dr. and Cr.	5 T-Account Update
Accounts Receivable	Asset	↑	Dr.	Accounts Receivable 112: (B) 9,000 |
Professional Fees	Revenue	↑	Cr.	Professional Fees 411: | 9,000 (B)

Record an expense when it happens, whether or not it is paid.

C.

1 Accounts Affected	2 Category	3 ↓ ↑	4 Rules of Dr. and Cr.	5 T-Account Update
Utilities Expense	Expense	↑	Dr.	Utilities Expense 511: (C) 125 |
Accounts Payable	Liability	↑	Cr.	Accounts Payable 211: | 125 (C)

Think of withdrawals as a subcategory of owner's equity.

D.

1 Accounts Affected	2 Category	3 ↓ ↑	4 Rules of Dr. and Cr.	5 T-Account Update
Bill O'Malley, Withdrawals	Owner's Equity (Withdrawals)	↓	Dr.	Bill O'Malley, Withdrawals 312: (D) 120 |
Cash	Asset	↓	Cr.	Cash 111: (A) 900 | 120 (D)

Think of expenses as always increasing.

E.

1 Accounts Affected	2 Category	3 ↓ ↑	4 Rules of Dr. and Cr.	5 T-Account Update
Salaries Expense	Expense	↑	Dr.	Salaries Expense 512: (E) 250 |
Cash	Asset	↓	Cr.	Cash 111: (A) 900 | 120 (D), 250 (E)

LEARNING UNIT 2-3

The Trial Balance and Preparation of Financial Reports

Let us look at all the transactions we have discussed for Catherine Hall's business, arranged by T account and recorded using the rules of debit and credit.

ASSETS = LIABILITIES + CAPITAL − WITHDRAWALS + REVENUE − EXPENSES

Cash 111 = **Accounts Payable 211** + **C. Hall, Capital 311** − **C. Hall, Withdrawals 312** + **Legal Fees 411** − **Salaries Expense 511**

Cash 111 Dr.	Cash 111 Cr.	Accounts Payable 211 Dr.	Accounts Payable 211 Cr.	C. Hall, Capital 311 Dr.	C. Hall, Capital 311 Cr.	C. Hall, Withdrawals 312 Dr.	C. Hall, Withdrawals 312 Cr.	Legal Fees 411 Dr.	Legal Fees 411 Cr.	Salaries Expense 511 Dr.	Salaries Expense 511 Cr.
(A) 7,000	900 (B)		400 (C)		7,800 (A)	(J) 200			3,000 (D)	(G) 600	
(D) 3,000	600 (G)		300 (I)						4,000 (E)		
(F) 700	700 (H)		700						7,000		
	200 (J)										
10,700	2,400										
8,300											

Accounts Receivable 112

Dr.	Cr.
(E) 4,000	700 (F)
3,300	

− **Rent Expense 512**

Dr.	Cr.
(H) 700	

Office Equipment 121

Dr.	Cr.
(A) 800	
(B) 900	
(C) 400	
2,100	

− **Advertising Expense 513**

Dr.	Cr.
(I) 300	

This grouping of accounts is much easier to use than the expanded accounting equation because all of the transactions that affect a particular account are in one place.

As we saw in Learning Unit 2-2, when all the transactions are recorded in the accounts, the total of all the debits should be equal to the total of all the credits. (If it is not, the accountant must go back and find the error by checking the numbers and adding every column again.)

THE TRIAL BALANCE

Footings are used to indicate or obtain the balance of any T account. They are not needed if there is only one entry in the account.

Footings are used to indicate or obtain the balance of any T account which has more than one entry. If all entries in the account are on one side, the total *is* the footing. If there are entries on both sides of the account, the balance is obtained by subtracting the smaller total (footing) from the larger. For example, look at the Cash account on page 55. The footing for the debit side is $10,700 and the footing for the credit side is $2,400. Since the debit side is larger, we subtract $2,400 from $10,700 to arrive at an *ending balance* of $8,300. Now look at the Rent Expense account. There is no need for a footing because there is only one entry. The amount itself is the ending balance. When the ending balance has been found for every account, we should be able to show that the total of all debits equals the total of all credits.

As mentioned earlier, the ending balance of cash, $8,300, is a *normal balance* because it is on the side that increases the asset account.

Only the ending balance of each account is listed.

The ending balances are used to prepare a **trial balance.** The trial balance is not a financial report, although it is used to prepare financial reports. The trial balance lists all of the accounts with their balances in the same order as they appear in the chart of accounts. It proves the accuracy of the ledger.

In the ideal situation, businesses would take a trial balance every day. The large number of transactions most businesses conduct each day makes this impractical. Instead, trial balances are prepared periodically.

Keep in mind that the figure for capital might not be the beginning figure if any additional investment has taken place during the period. You can tell this by looking at the capital account in the ledger.

A more detailed discussion of the trial balance will be provided in the next chapter. For now, notice the heading, how the accounts are listed, the debits in the left column, the credits in the right, and the fact that the total of debits is equal to the total of credits.

A trial balance for Catherine Hall's firm's accounts is shown in Figure 2-2.

FIGURE 2-2
Trial Blance for Catherine Hall's Law Firm

Since this is not a formal report, there is no need to use dollar signs; however, the single and double lines under subtotals and final totals are still used for clarity.

CATHERINE HALL, Barrister and Solicitor
TRIAL BALANCE
SEPTEMBER 30, 2001

	Dr.	Cr.
Cash	8 300 00	
Accounts Receivable	3 300 00	
Office Equipment	2 100 00	
Accounts Payable		700 00
C. Hall, Capital		7 800 00
C. Hall, Withdrawals	200 00	
Legal Fees		7 000 00
Salaries Expense	600 00	
Rent Expense	700 00	
Advertising Expense	300 00	
Totals	15 500 00	15 500 00

PREPARING FINANCIAL REPORTS

The trial balance is used to prepare the financial reports. The diagram in Figure 2-3 shows how financial reports can be prepared from a trial balance. Remember, financial reports do not have debit or credit columns. The left column in the income statement and the statement of owner's equity is used only to subtotal numbers. If there were more than one liability, we would have two columns on the right-hand side of the balance sheet, one to subtotal the liabilities (inside column) and the total of the liabilities in the right column.

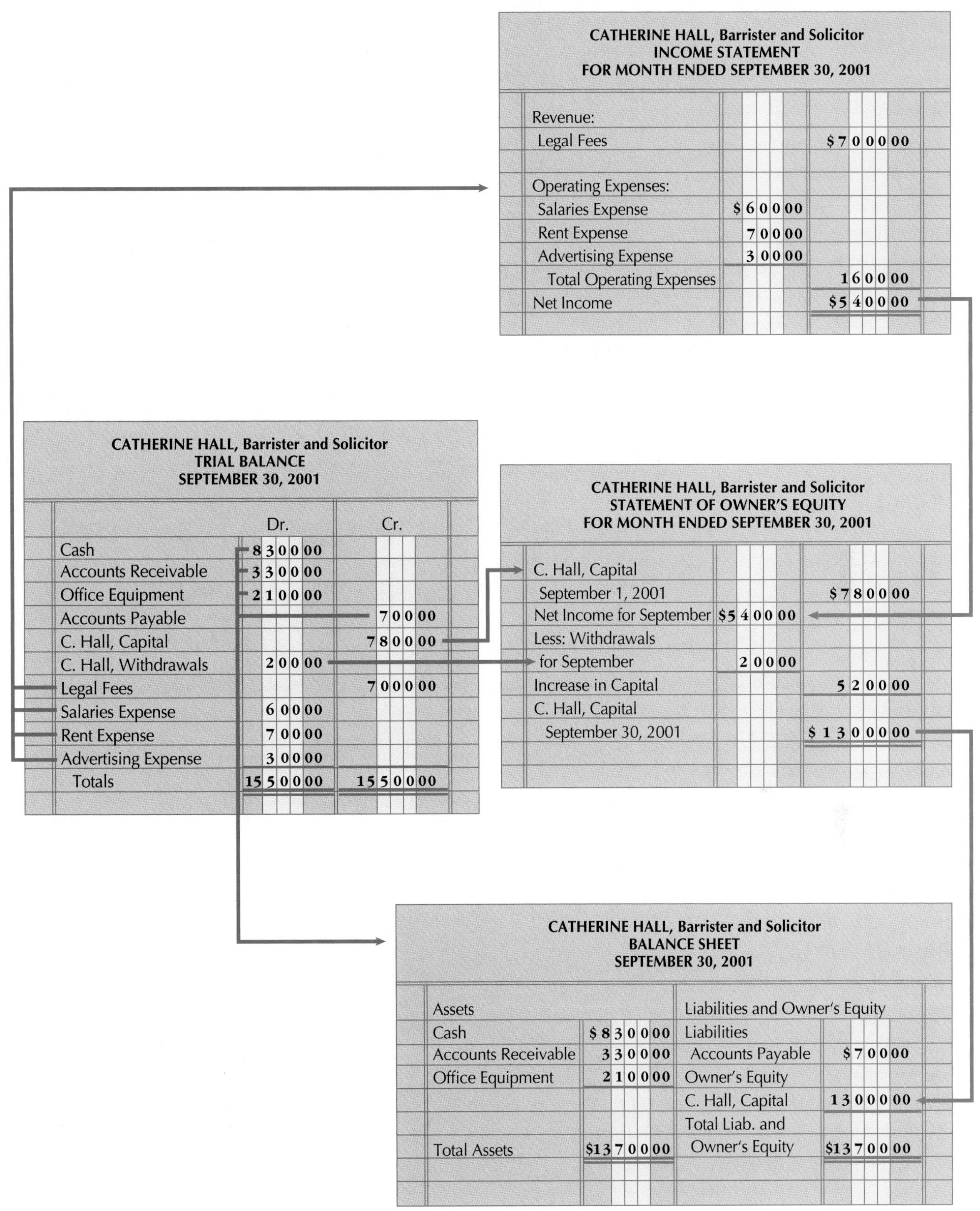

CATHERINE HALL, Barrister and Solicitor
INCOME STATEMENT
FOR MONTH ENDED SEPTEMBER 30, 2001

Revenue:		
Legal Fees		$7 000 00
Operating Expenses:		
Salaries Expense	$600 00	
Rent Expense	700 00	
Advertising Expense	300 00	
Total Operating Expenses		1 600 00
Net Income		$5 400 00

CATHERINE HALL, Barrister and Solicitor
TRIAL BALANCE
SEPTEMBER 30, 2001

	Dr.	Cr.
Cash	8 300 00	
Accounts Receivable	3 300 00	
Office Equipment	2 100 00	
Accounts Payable		700 00
C. Hall, Capital		7 800 00
C. Hall, Withdrawals	200 00	
Legal Fees		7 000 00
Salaries Expense	600 00	
Rent Expense	700 00	
Advertising Expense	300 00	
Totals	15 500 00	15 500 00

CATHERINE HALL, Barrister and Solicitor
STATEMENT OF OWNER'S EQUITY
FOR MONTH ENDED SEPTEMBER 30, 2001

C. Hall, Capital		
September 1, 2001		$7 800 00
Net Income for September	$5 400 00	
Less: Withdrawals		
for September	200 00	
Increase in Capital		5 200 00
C. Hall, Capital		
September 30, 2001		$13 000 00

CATHERINE HALL, Barrister and Solicitor
BALANCE SHEET
SEPTEMBER 30, 2001

Assets		Liabilities and Owner's Equity	
Cash	$8 300 00	Liabilities	
Accounts Receivable	3 300 00	Accounts Payable	$700 00
Office Equipment	2 100 00	Owner's Equity	
		C. Hall, Capital	13 000 00
		Total Liab. and	
Total Assets	$13 700 00	Owner's Equity	$13 700 00

FIGURE 2-3 Steps in Preparing Financial Reports from a Trial Balance

LEARNING UNIT 2-3 REVIEW

AT THIS POINT you should be able to:

- Explain the role of footings. (p. 56)
- Prepare a trial balance from a set of accounts. (p. 56)
- Prepare financial reports from a trial balance. (p. 56)

SELF-REVIEW QUIZ 2-3

(The blank forms you need are on pages 2-2 to 2-4 of the *Study Guide with Working Papers.*)

As the bookkeeper of Pam's Hair Salon you are to prepare from the following accounts on June 30, 2002: (1) a trial balance as of June 30; (2) an income statement for the month ended June 30; (3) a statement of owner's equity for the month ended June 30; and (4) a balance sheet as of June 30, 2002.

Cash 111

Dr.	Cr.
4,500	300
2,000	100
1,000	1,200
300	1,300
	2,600

Accounts Payable 211

Dr.	Cr.
300	700

Salon Fees 411

Dr.	Cr.
	3,500
	1,000

Accounts Receivable 121

Dr.	Cr.
1,000	300

Pam Jay, Capital 311

Dr.	Cr.
	4,000 *

Rent Expense 511

Dr.	Cr.
1,200	

Salon Equipment 131

Dr.	Cr.
700	

Pam Jay, Withdrawals 321

Dr.	Cr.
100	

Salon Supplies Expense 521

Dr.	Cr.
1,300	

Salaries Expense 531

Dr.	Cr.
2,600	

* No additional investments.

Solution to Self-Review Quiz 2-3

❶

PAM'S HAIR SALON
TRIAL BALANCE
JUNE 30, 2002

	Dr.	Cr.
Cash	2 3 0 0 00	
Accounts Receivable	7 0 0 00	
Salon Equipment	7 0 0 00	
Accounts Payable		4 0 0 00
Pam Jay, Capital		4 0 0 0 00
Pam Jay, Withdrawals	1 0 0 00	
Salon Fees		4 5 0 0 00
Rent Expense	1 2 0 0 00	
Salon Supplies Expense	1 3 0 0 00	
Salaries Expense	2 6 0 0 00	
Totals	8 9 0 0 00	8 9 0 0 00

❷

PAM'S HAIR SALON
INCOME STATEMENT
FOR MONTH ENDED JUNE 30, 2002

Revenue:		
Salon Fees		$ 4 5 0 0 00
Operating Expenses:		
Rent Expense	$ 1 2 0 0 00	
Salon Supplies Expense	1 3 0 0 00	
Salaries Expense	2 6 0 0 00	
Total Operating Expenses		5 1 0 0 00
Net Loss		$ 6 0 0 00

❸

PAM'S HAIR SALON
STATEMENT OF OWNER'S EQUITY
FOR MONTH ENDED JUNE 30, 2002

Pam Jay, Capital		
June 1, 2002		$ 4 0 0 0 00
Less: Net Loss for June	$ 6 0 0 00	
Withdrawals for June	1 0 0 00	
Decrease in Capital		7 0 0 00
Pam Jay, Capital		
June 30, 2002		$ 3 3 0 0 00

Note: The net loss results in a decrease in Capital.

❹

PAM'S HAIR SALON
BALANCE SHEET
JUNE 30, 2002

Assets		Liabilities and Owner's Equity	
Cash	$ 2 3 0 0 00	Liabilities	
Accounts Receivable	7 0 0 00	Accounts Payable	$ 4 0 0 00
Salon Equipment	7 0 0 00		
		Owner's Equity	
		Pam Jay, Capital	3 3 0 0 00
		Total Liab. and	
Total Assets	$ 3 7 0 0 00	Owner's Equity	$ 3 7 0 0 00

Quiz Tip

Financial reports have no debts or credits. The inside columns are used to subtotal the numbers.

TIME TO PUT DEBITS ON THE LEFT . . .
DUNKIN'
DONUTS

Dunkin' Donuts shop owners have many accounts to deal with: food costs, payroll, rent, utilities, supplies, advertising, promotion, and—biggest of all—cash. It's critical for them to keep debits and credits straight. If not, both they and Dunkin' Donuts Inc. could lose a lot of money—fast.

Many of Dunkin' Donuts smaller shop owners keep their own accounts, while most of the larger shops use accountants. In some areas of the country, some accountants actually specialize in handling Dunkin' Donuts accounts for individual shop owners. But many shop owners, especially those with just one shop, handle the books themselves, both to save money and to keep a finger on the pulse of their business.

The balance sheet for each shop must be submitted to the zone's business consultant on the last Saturday of each month at noon. Fred had once been late in sending the balance sheet because he mistakenly debited both cash and supplies when he paid for an order of paper cups. Fred had been angry with himself for having made such a basic error. Dwayne had been understanding, but had encouraged him to review the rules for recording debits and credits.

"It's only going to get harder, Fred," Dwayne had said. "Once you computerize your accounts, debits and credits are not as visible as they are with your paper system. You will only enter the payables, and the computer does the other side of the balance sheet. So a thorough knowledge of debits and credits is critical to understanding the computerized system. And the way you're building up the business, it won't be long before you'll want to switch to the computer."

Discussion Questions

1. Why is the cash account so important in Fred's business?
2. Why do you think that most of the larger shops use accountants to do their books instead of doing them themselves?
3. Is the difference between debits and credits important to shop owners who don't do their own books?

Chapter Review

Comprehensive Demonstration Problem with Solution Tips

(The blank forms you need are on pages 2-5 to 2-7 of the *Study Guide with Working Papers.*)

The chart of accounts of Mel's Delivery Service includes the following: Cash, 111; Accounts Receivable, 112; Office Equipment, 121; Delivery Trucks, 122; Accounts Payable, 211; Mel Free, Capital, 311; Mel Free, Withdrawals, 312; Delivery Fees Earned, 411; Advertising Expense, 511; Gas Expense, 512; Salaries Expense, 513; and Telephone Expense, 514. The following transactions occurred for Mel's Delivery Service during the month of July:

Transaction A: Mel invested $10,000 in the business from his personal savings account.
Transaction B: Bought delivery trucks on account, $17,000.
Transaction C: Received but did not yet pay advertising bill, $700.
Transaction D: Bought office equipment for cash, $1,200.
Transaction E: Received cash for delivery services rendered, $15,000.
Transaction F: Paid salaries expense, $3,000.
Transaction G: Paid gas expense for company trucks, $1,250.
Transaction H: Billed customers for delivery services rendered, $4,000.
Transaction I: Paid telephone bill, $300.
Transaction J: Received $3,000 as partial payment of transaction H.
Transaction K: Mel paid home telephone bill from the company bank account, $150.

As Mel's newly employed accountant, you must do the following:

1. Set up T accounts in a ledger.
2. Record transactions in the T accounts. (Place the letter of the transaction next to the entry.)
3. Foot the T accounts where appropriate.
4. Prepare a trial balance at the end of July.
5. Prepare from the trial balance, in proper form, (a) an income statement for the month of July, (b) a statement of owner's equity, and (c) a balance sheet as of July 31, 2001.

Solution to Comprehensive Demonstration Problem

1, 2, 3. GENERAL LEDGER

Cash 111

Debit	Credit
(A) 10,000	1,200 (D)
(E) 15,000	3,000 (F)
(J) 3,000	1,250 (G)
	300 (I)
	150 (K)
28,000	5,900
22,100	

Accounts Payable 211

Debit	Credit
	17,000 (B)
	700 (C)
	17,700

Advertising Expense 511

Debit	Credit
(C) 700	

Accounts Receivable 112

Dr.	Cr.
(H) 4,000	3,000 (J)
1,000	

Mel Free, Capital 311

Dr.	Cr.
	10,000 (A)

Gas Expense 512

Dr.	Cr.
(G) 1,250	

Office Equipment 121

Dr.	Cr.
(D) 1,200	

Mel Free, Withdrawals 312

Dr.	Cr.
(K) 150	

Salaries Expense 513

Dr.	Cr.
(F) 3,000	

Delivery Trucks 122

Dr.	Cr.
(B) 17,000	

Delivery Fees Earned 411

Dr.	Cr.
	15,000 (E)
	4,000 (H)
	19,000

Telephone Expense 514

Dr.	Cr.
(I) 300	

Solution Tips to Recording Transactions

A.	Cash	A	↑	Dr.
	Mel Free, Capital	OE	↑	Cr.

B.	Delivery Trucks	A	↑	Dr.
	Accounts Payable	L	↑	Cr.

C.	Advertising Expense	Exp.	↑	Dr.
	Accounts Payable	L	↑	Cr.

D.	Office Equipment	A	↑	Dr.
	Cash	A	↓	Cr.

E.	Cash	A	↑	Dr.
	Del. Fees Earned	Rev.	↑	Cr.

F.	Salaries Expense	Exp.	↑	Dr.
	Cash	A	↓	Cr.

G.	Gas Expense	Exp.	↑	Dr.
	Cash	A	↓	Cr.

H.	Accts. Receivable	A	↑	Dr.
	Del. Fees Earned	Rev.	↑	Cr.

I.	Tel. Expense	Exp.	↑	Dr.
	Cash	A	↓	Cr.

J.	Cash	A	↑	Dr.
	Accts. Receivable	A	↓	Cr.

K.	Mel Free, Withdr.	OE	↓	Dr.
	Cash	A	↓	Cr.

Solution Tips to Footings

3. Footings:

Cash	Add left side $28,000.
	Add right side $5,900.
	Take difference $22,100 and place on side which is larger.
Accounts Payable	Add $17,000 + $700 and leave on same side. Total is $17,700.

Solution Tips to Preparation of a Trial Balance

4. Trial balance is a list of the ledger's ending balances. The list is in the same order as the chart of accounts. Each title has only one amount listed, either as a debit or credit balance.

Mel's Delivery Service
Trial Balance
July 31, 2001

	Dr.	Cr.
Cash	22,100	
Accounts Receivable	1,000	
Office Equipment	1,200	
Delivery Trucks	17,000	
Accounts Payable		17,700
Mel Free, Capital		10,000
Mel Free, Withdrawals	150	
Delivery Fees Earned		19,000
Advertising Expense	700	
Gas Expense	1,250	
Salaries Expense	3,000	
Telephone Expense	300	
TOTALS	46,700	46,700

5.

(a)

Mel's Delivery Service
Income Statement
for Month Ended July 31, 2001

Revenue:		
Delivery Fees Earned		$19,000
Operating Expenses:		
Advertising Expense	$ 700	
Gas Expense	1,250	
Salaries Expense	3,000	
Telephone Expense	300	
Total Operating Expenses		5,250
Net Income		$13,750

(b)

Mel's Delivery Service
Statement of Owner's Equity
for Month Ended July 31, 2001

Mel Free, Capital, July 1, 2001		$10,000
Net Income for July	$13,750	
Less: Withdrawals for July	150	
Increase in Capital		13,600
Mel Free, Capital, July 31, 2001		$23,600

(c)

Mel's Delivery Service
Balance Sheet
July 31, 2001

Assets		**Liabilities and Owner's Equity**	
Cash	22,100	Liabilities	
Accounts Receivable	1,000	Accounts Payable	$17,700
Office Equipment	1,200		
Delivery Trucks	17,000	Owner's Equity	
		Mel Free, Capital	23,600
Total Assets	**$41,300**	**Total Liabilities and Owner's Equity**	**$41,300**

Solution Tips for Preparing Financial Reports from a Trial Balance

		Trial Balance Dr.	Trial Balance Cr.
Balance Sheet	Assets	X	
	Liabilities		X
Statement of Equity	Capital		X
	Withdrawals	X	
Income Statement	Revenues		X
	Expenses	X	
		XX	XX

Net income on the income statement of $13,750 goes on the statement of owner's equity.

Ending capital of $23,600 on the statement of owner's equity goes on the balance sheet as the new figure for capital.

Note: There are no debits or credits on Financial Reports. The inside column is used for subtotalling.

Summary of Key Points

Learning Unit 2-1

1. A T account is a simplified version of a standard account.
2. A ledger is a group of accounts.
3. A debit is the left-hand position (side) of an account and a credit is the right-hand position (side) of an account.

4. A footing is the total of one side of an account: the ending balance is the difference between the footings on the left and right sides.

Learning Unit 2-2

1. A chart of accounts for a company lists the account titles and their numbers.
2. The transaction analysis chart is a teaching device, not to be confused with standard accounting procedures.
3. A compound entry is a transaction involving more than one debit or credit.

Learning Unit 2-3

1. In double-entry bookkeeping, the recording of each business transaction affects two or more accounts, and the total of debits equals the total of credits.
2. A trial balance is a list of the ending balances of all accounts, listed in the same order as on the chart of accounts.
3. Any additional investments during the period will result in having a figure for capital in the trial balance different from the beginning figure for capital in the statement of owner's equity.
4. There are *no* debit or credit columns on the three financial reports.

KEY TERMS

Account An accounting device used in bookkeeping to record increases and decreases of business transactions relating to individual assets, liabilities, capital, withdrawals, revenue, expenses, and so on (p. 42)

Chart of accounts A numbering system of accounts that lists the account titles and account numbers to be used by a company (p. 46)

Compound entry A transaction involving more than one debit or credit (p. 47)

Credit The right-hand side of any account. A number entered on the right side of any account is said to be credited to an account. (p. 43)

Debit The left-hand side of any account. A number entered on the left side of any account is said to be debited to an account. (p. 43)

Double-entry bookkeeping An accounting system in which the recording of each transaction affects two or more accounts, and the total of the debits is equal to the total of the credits (p. 47)

Ending balance The difference between footings in a T account (p. 43)

Footings The totals of the two sides of a T account (p. 56)

Ledger A group of accounts that records data from business transactions (p. 42).

Normal balance of an account The side of an account that increases by the rules of debit and credit (p. 45)

Standard account A formal account that includes columns for date, explanation, posting reference, debit, and credit (p. 42)

T account A skeleton version of a standard account, used for demonstration purposes (p. 42)

Trial balance A list of the ending balances of all the accounts in a ledger. The total of the debits should equal the total of the credits. (p. 56)

Blueprint for Preparing Financial Reports from a Trial Balance

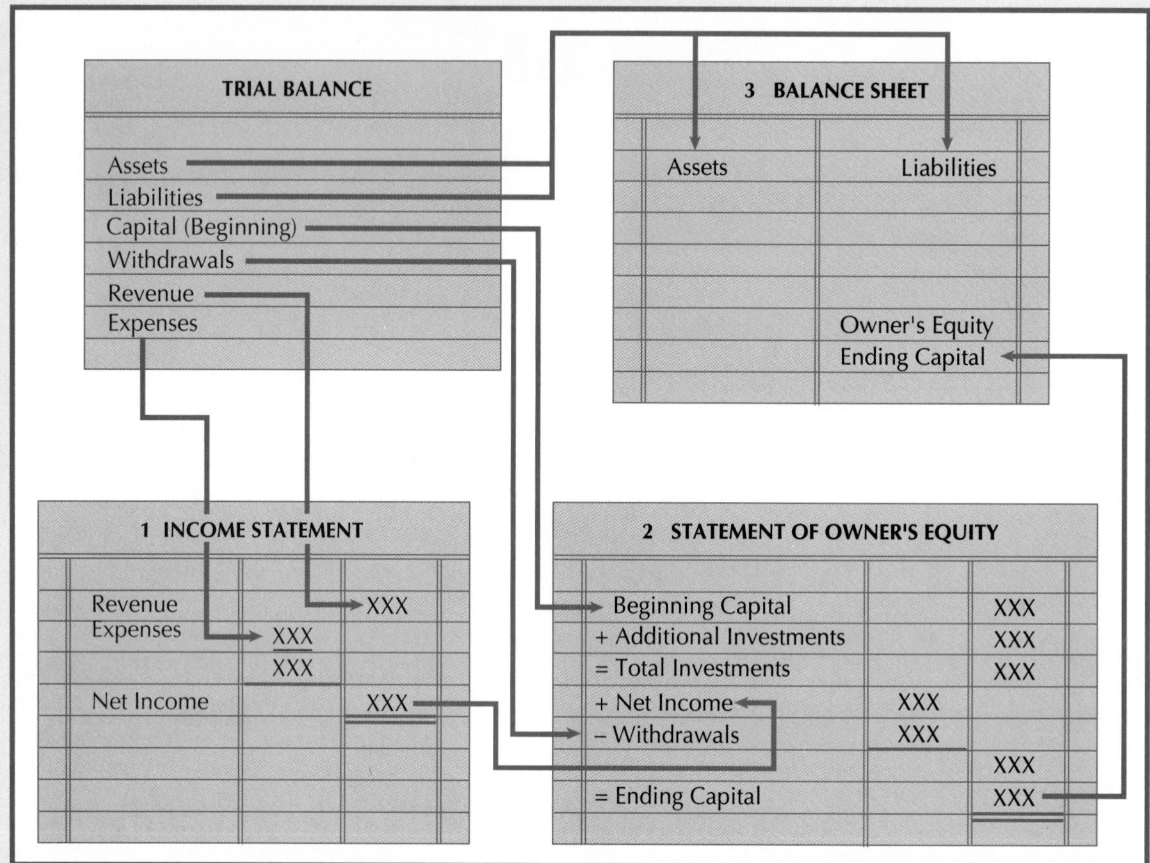

Questions, Mini Exercises, Exercises, and Problems

Discussion Questions

1. Define a ledger.
2. Why is the left-hand side of an account called a debit?
3. Footings are used in balancing all accounts. True or false? Please explain.
4. What is the end product of the accounting process?
5. What do we mean when we say that a transaction analysis chart is a teaching device?
6. What are the five steps of the transaction analysis chart?
7. Explain the concept of double-entry bookkeeping.
8. A trial balance is a formal report. True or false? Please explain.
9. Why are there no debit or credit columns on financial reports?
10. Compare the financial statements prepared from the expanded accounting equation with those prepared from a trial balance.

Mini Exercises

(The blank forms you need are on page 2-8 in the *Study Guide with Working Papers.*)

The T Account

1. For the following, foot and balance each account.

Cash 110			
4/8	2,000	4/14	2,000
4/12	6,000		

R. Rich, Capital 311			
		5,000	3/1
		3,000	4/14
		6,000	4/15

Transaction Analysis

2. Complete the following:

Account	Category	↑	↓	Normal Balance
A. Cash	Asset	Dr.	Cr.	Dr.
B. Prepaid Rent				
C. Accounts Payable				
D. B. Block, Capital				
E. B. Block, Withdrawals				
F. Legal Fees Earned				
G. Salary Expense				

Transaction Analysis

3. Record the following transaction in the transaction analysis chart: Provided legal services for $4,000, receiving $3,000 cash with the remainder to be paid next month.

Accounts Affected	Category	↓ ↑	Rules of Dr. and Cr.	T Accounts

Trial Balance

4. Rearrange the following titles in the order in which they would appear in a trial balance:

Selling Expense
Accounts Receivable
Accounts Payable
D. Cope, Capital
Computer Equipment
Legal Fees Earned
D. Cope, Withdrawals
Rent Expense
Advertising Expense
Cash

Trial Balance/Financial Reports

5. For the following trial balance, identify the report in the following list in which each title will appear:

- Income Statement (IS)
- Statement of Owner's Equity (OE)
- Balance Sheet (BS)

Logan Co.
Trial Balance
September 30, 2000

		Dr.	Cr.
A. ______	Cash	390	
B. ______	Supplies	100	
C. ______	Office Equipment	200	
D. ______	Accounts Payable		100
E. ______	D. Heath, Capital		450
F. ______	D. Heath, Withdrawals	160	
G. ______	Fees Earned		290
H. ______	Hair Salon Fees		300
I. ______	Salaries Expense	130	
J. ______	Rent Expense	120	
K. ______	Advertising Expense	40	
	TOTALS	1,140	1,140

Exercises

(The blank forms you need are on pages 2-9 and 2-10 in the *Study Guide with Working Papers.*)

Preparing a chart of accounts

2-1. From the following account titles, prepare a chart of accounts, using the same numbering system as used in this chapter.

Word Processing Equipment	Professional Fees
Rent Expense	A. Sting, Capital
Accounts Payable	Cash
Accounts Receivable	Salaries Expense
Repair Expense	A. Sting, Withdrawals

Preparing a transaction analysis chart

2-2. Record the following transaction in the transaction analysis chart: Heather Reese bought a new piece of office equipment for $11,000, paying $2,000 down and charging the rest.

2-3. Complete the table on page 69. For each account listed on the left, indicate the category to which it belongs, whether increases and decreases in the account are marked on the debit or credit side, and in which financial report the account appears. A sample is provided.

Accounts, categories, rules, and the reports on which they appear

Accounts Affected	Category	↑	↓	Appears on Which Financial Report
Supplies	Asset	Dr.	Cr.	Balance Sheet
Legal Fees Earned				
D. Long, Withdrawals				
Accounts Payable				
Salaries Expense				
Auto				

Rules of debits and credits

2-4. Given the following accounts, complete the table by inserting the appropriate number next to each individual transaction to indicate which account is debited and which account is credited.

1. Cash
2. Accounts Receivable
3. Equipment
4. Accounts Payable
5. B. Baker, Capital
6. B. Baker, Withdrawals
7. Plumbing Fees Earned
8. Salaries Expense
9. Advertising Expense
10. Supplies Expense

Transaction	Rules Dr.	Rules Cr.
A. Paid salaries expense.	8	1
B. Bob paid personal utilities bill from company bank account.		
C. Advertising bill was received but not yet paid.		
D. Received cash from plumbing fees.		
E. Paid supplies expense.		
F. Bob invested additional equipment in the business.		
G. Billed customers for plumbing services rendered.		
H. Received one-half the balance from transaction G.		
I. Bought equipment on account.		

Preparing financial reports

2-5. From the following trial balance of Hall's Cleaners, prepare the following:

- Income statement
- Statement of owner's equity
- Balance sheet

HALL'S CLEANERS TRIAL BALANCE JULY 31, 2003		
	Dr.	Cr.
Cash	550 00	
Equipment	692 00	
Accounts Payable		455 00
J. Hall, Capital		800 00
J. Hall, Withdrawals	198 00	
Cleaning Fees		458 00
Salaries Expense	160 00	
Utilities Expense	113 00	
Totals	1713 00	1713 00

Group A Problems

(The forms you need are on pages 2-11 to 2-16 of the *Study Guide with Working Papers.*)

Using a transaction analysis chart

2A-1. The following transactions occurred in the opening and operation of Ted's Bookkeeping Service.

a. Ted Williams opened his bookkeeping service by investing $6,000 from his personal savings account.

b. Purchased store equipment on account, $3,000.

c. Rent expense was due but unpaid, $600.

d. Received cash for bookkeeping services rendered, $800.

e. Billed a client on account, $500.

f. Ted Williams withdrew cash for personal use, $200.

Complete the transaction analysis chart in the *Study Guide with Working Papers.* The chart of accounts includes Cash; Accounts Receivable; Store Equipment; Accounts Payable; Ted Williams, Capital; Ted Williams, Withdrawals; Bookkeeping Fees Earned; and Rent Expense.

Check Figure

Cash	
6,000	200
800	

Recording transactions in ledger accounts

2A-2. Lee White opened a travel agency, and the following transactions resulted:

a. Lee White invested $20,000 in the travel agency.

b. Bought office equipment on account, $4,000.

c. Agency received cash for travel arrangements that it completed for a client, $3,000.

d. Lee White paid a personal bill from the company bank account, $50.

e. Paid advertising expense for the month, $700.

f. Rent expense for the month was due but not yet paid, $900.

g. Paid $800 as partial payment of what was owed from the transaction in **b.**

As Lee White's accountant, analyze and record the transactions in T-account form. Set up the T accounts on the basis of the chart of accounts on page 71. Enter each transaction in the appropriate T account and label it with the letter of the transaction.

Check Figure

	Cash		
(a)	20,000	50	(d)
(c)	3,000	700	(e)
		800	(g)

Chart of Accounts

Assets	Revenue
Cash 111	Travel Fees Earned 411
Office Equipment 121	
	Expenses
Liabilities	Advertising Expense 511
Accounts Payable 211	Rent Expense 512
Owner's Equity	
L. White, Capital 311	
L. White, Withdrawals 312	

Preparing a trial balance from the T accounts

2A-3. From the following T accounts of Mike's Window Washing Service, (a) record and foot the balances on the appropriate pages in the *Study Guide with Working Papers*, and (b) prepare a trial balance in proper form for May 31, 2001.

Check Figure
Trial Balance Total $12,700

Cash 111

Dr.	Cr.
(A) 5,000	100 (D)
(G) 3,500	200 (E)
	400 (F)
	200 (H)
	900 (I)

Accounts Payable 211

Dr.	Cr.
(D) 100	1,300 (C)

Fees Earned 411

Dr.	Cr.
	6,500 (B)

Accounts Receivable 112

Dr.	Cr.
(B) 6,500	3,500 (G)

Mike Frank, Capital 311

Dr.	Cr.
	5,000 (A)

Rent Expense 511

Dr.	Cr.
(F) 400	

Office Equipment 121

Dr.	Cr.
(C) 1,300	
(H) 200	

Mike Frank, Withdrawals 312

Dr.	Cr.
(I) 900	

Utilities Expense 512

Dr.	Cr.
(E) 200	

Preparing financial reports from the trial balance

2A-4. From the trial balance of Grace Lantz, Barrister and Solicitor, prepare (a) an income statement for the month of May, (b) a statement of owner's equity for the month ended May 31, and (c) a balance sheet as of May 31, 2002.

Check Figure
Total Assets $6,400

GRACE LANTZ, Barrister and Solicitor
TRIAL BALANCE
MAY 31, 2002

	Dr.	Cr.
Cash	5000 00	
Accounts Receivable	650 00	
Office Equipment	750 00	
Accounts Payable		4300 00
Salaries Payable		675 00
G. Lantz, Capital		1275 00
G. Lantz, Withdrawals	300 00	
Revenue from Legal Fees		1350 00
Utilities Expense	300 00	
Rent Expense	450 00	
Salaries Expense	150 00	
Totals	7600 00	7600 00

Comprehensive problem

2A-5. The chart of accounts for Angel's Delivery Service is as follows:

Chart of Accounts	
Assets	**Revenue**
Cash 111	Delivery Fees Earned 411
Accounts Receivable 112	
Office Equipment 121	**Expenses**
Delivery Trucks 122	Advertising Expense 511
	Gas Expense 512
Liabilities	Salaries Expense 513
Accounts Payable 211	Telephone Expense 514
Owner's Equity	
Alice Angel, Capital 311	
Alice Angel, Withdrawals 312	

Check Figure

Total Trial Balance $38,100

Angel's Delivery Service completed the following transactions during the month of March:

Transaction A: Alice Angel invested $16,000 in the delivery service from her personal savings account.
Transaction B: Bought delivery trucks on account, $18,000.
Transaction C: Bought office equipment for cash, $600.
Transaction D: Paid advertising expense, $250.
Transaction E: Collected cash for delivery services rendered, $2,600.
Transaction F: Paid drivers' salaries, $900.
Transaction G: Paid gas expense for trucks, $1,200.
Transaction H: Performed delivery services for a customer on account, $800.
Transaction I: Telephone expense was due but not yet paid, $700.
Transaction J: Received $300 as partial payment of transaction H.
Transaction K: Alice Angel withdrew cash for personal use, $300.

As Alice's newly employed accountant, you must:

1. Set up T accounts in a ledger.
2. Record transactions in the T accounts. (Place the letter of the transaction next to the entry.)
3. Foot the T accounts where appropriate.
4. Prepare a trial balance at the end of March.
5. Prepare from the trial balance, in proper form, (a) an income statement for the month of March, (b) a statement of owner's equity for the month of March and (c) a balance sheet as of March 31, 2000.

Group B Problems

(The forms you need are on pages 2-11 to 2-16 of the *Study Guide with Working Papers.*)

Using a transaction analysis chart

2B-1. Ted Williams decided to open a bookkeeping service. Record the following transactions in the transaction analysis charts:

Transaction A: Ted invested $1,500 in the bookkeeping service from his personal savings account.

Check Figure

Cash	
1,500	275
1,200	

Transaction B: Purchased store equipment on account, $900.
Transaction C: Rent expense was due but unpaid, $250.
Transaction D: Performed bookkeeping services for cash, $1,200.
Transaction E: Billed clients for bookkeeping services rendered, $700.
Transaction F: Ted paid his home heating bill using a company cheque, $275.

The chart of accounts for the shop includes Cash; Accounts Receivable; Store Equipment; Accounts Payable; Ted Williams, Capital; Ted Williams, Withdrawals; Bookkeeping Fees Earned; and Rent Expense.

Recording transactions in ledger accounts

2B-2. Lee White established a new travel agency. Record the following transactions for Lee in T-account form. Label each entry with the letter of the transaction.

Transaction A: Lee White invested $18,000 in the travel agency from her personal bank account.
Transaction B: Bought office equipment on account, $6,000.
Transaction C: Travel agency rendered service to Jensen Corp. and received cash, $1,200.
Transaction D: Lee White withdrew cash for personal use, $200.
Transaction E: Paid advertising expense, $600.
Transaction F: Rent expense was due but not yet paid, $500.
Transaction G: Paid $400 in partial payment of transaction B.

The chart of accounts includes Cash, 111; Office Equipment, 121; Accounts Payable, 211; L. White, Capital, 311; L. White, Withdrawals, 312; Travel Fees Earned, 411; Advertising Expense, 511; and Rent Expense, 512.

Check Figure

Cash			
(A)	18,000	200	(D)
(C)	1,200	600	(E)
		400	(G)

Preparing a trial balance from the T accounts

2B-3. From the following T accounts of Mike's Window Washing Service, (a) record and foot the balances on the appropriate pages in the *Study Guide with Working Papers,* and (b) prepare a trial balance for May 31, 2001.

Cash 111	
(A) 10,000	4,000 (C)
(F) 4,000	310 (D)
(G) 2,000	50 (E)
	600 (H)

Accounts Receivable 112	
(G) 2,000	

Office Equipment 121	
(B) 2,000	
(C) 4,000	

Accounts Payable 211	
	2,000 (B)

Mike Frank, Capital 311	
	10,000 (A)

Mike Frank, Withdrawals 312	
(H) 600	

Fees Earned 411	
	4,000 (F)
	4,000 (G)

Rent Expense 511	
(D) 310	

Utilities Expense 512	
(E) 50	

Check Figure
Trial Balance Total $20,000

Preparing financial reports from the trial balance

2B-4. From the trial balance of Grace Lantz, Barrister and Solicitor, prepare (a) an income statement for the month of May, (b) a statement of owner's equity for the month ended May 31, and (c) a balance sheet as of May 31, 2002.

Check Figure

Total Assets $10,800

GRACE LANTZ, Barrister and Solicitor
TRIAL BALANCE
MAY 31, 2002

	Debit	Credit
Cash	6 000 00	
Accounts Receivable	2 400 00	
Office Equipment	2 400 00	
Accounts Payable		200 00
Salaries Payable		600 00
G. Lantz, Capital		4 000 00
G. Lantz, Withdrawals	2 000 00	
Revenue from Legal Fees		8 800 00
Utilities Expense	100 00	
Rent Expense	300 00	
Salaries Expense	400 00	
Totals	13 600 00	13 600 00

Comprehensive problem

Check Figure

Trial Balance Total $84,300

2B-5. The chart of accounts of Angel's Delivery Service includes the following: Cash, 111; Accounts Receivable, 112; Office Equipment, 121; Delivery Trucks, 122; Accounts Payable, 211; Alice Angel, Capital, 311; Alice Angel, Withdrawals, 312; Delivery Fees Earned, 411; Advertising Expense, 511; Gas Expense, 512; Salaries Expense, 513; and Telephone Expense, 514. The following transactions resulted for Angel's Delivery Service during the month of March:

Transaction A: Alice invested $40,000 in the business from her personal savings account.

Transaction B: Bought delivery trucks on account, $25,000.

Transaction C: Advertising bill was received but not yet paid, $800.

Transaction D: Bought office equipment for cash, $2,500.

Transaction E: Received cash for delivery services rendered, $13,000.

Transaction F: Paid salaries expense, $1,850.

Transaction G: Paid gas expense for company trucks, $750.

Transaction H: Billed customers for delivery services rendered, $5,500.

Transaction I: Paid telephone bill, $400.

Transaction J: Received $1,600 as partial payment of transaction H.

Transaction K: Alice paid home telephone bill with a company cheque, $88.

As Alice's newly employed accountant, you must:

1. Set up T accounts in a ledger.
2. Record transactions in the T accounts. (Place the letter of the transaction next to the entry.)
3. Foot the T accounts where appropriate.
4. Prepare a trial balance at the end of March.
5. Prepare from the trial balance, in proper form, (a) an income statement for the month of March, (b) a statement of owner's equity for the month ended March 31, and (c) a balance sheet as of March 31, 2000.

Group C Problems

(The forms you need are on pages 2-17 to 2-21 of the *Study Guide with Working Papers*.)

Using a transaction analysis chart

2C-1. Sheila Cronkite decided to open a bookkeeping service. Record the following transactions in the transaction analysis charts:

Transaction A: Sheila invested $3,500 in the bookkeeping service from her personal savings account.

Transaction B: Purchased office equipment on account, $1,900.

Transaction C: Rent expense was due but not yet paid, $425.

Transaction D: Performed bookkeeping services for cash, $2,500.

Transaction E: Billed clients for bookkeeping services rendered, $1,500.

Transaction F: Sheila paid a home repair bill from the company bank account, $215.

The chart of accounts for the shop includes Cash; Accounts Receivable; Office Equipment; Accounts Payable; Sheila Cronkite, Capital; Sheila Cronkite, Withdrawals; Bookkeeping Fees Earned; and Rent Expense.

Check Figure

Cash	
3,500	215
2,500	

Recording transactions in ledger accounts

2C-2. Bernie Quinlan established an editing company. Record the following transactions for Bernie in T-account form. Label each entry with the letter of the transaction.

Transaction A: Bernie Quinlan invested $32,000 in the business from his personal bank account.

Transaction B: Bought office equipment on account, $9,600.

Transaction C: Business rendered service to Portias Corp. and received cash, $3,400.

Transaction D: Bernie Quinlan withdrew cash for personal use, $800.

Transaction E: Paid advertising expense, $725.

Transaction F: Rent expense was due but not yet paid, $800.

Transaction G: Paid $2,600 in partial payment of Transaction B.

The chart of accounts includes Cash, 111; Office Equipment, 121; Accounts Payable, 211; Bernie Quinlan, Capital, 311; Bernie Quinlan, Withdrawals, 312; Editing Fees Earned, 411; Advertising Expense, 511; and Rent Expense, 512.

Check Figure

Cash			
(A)	32,000	800	(D)
(C)	3,400	725	(E)
		2,600	(G)

Preparing a trial balance from the T accounts

2C-3. From the following T accounts of Ricky's Small Engine Repair Service, (a) record and foot the balances on the appropriate pages in the *Study Guide with Working Papers*, and (b) prepare a trial balance for October 31, 2002.

Check Figure

Trial Balance Total $16,000

Cash 111

Dr.	Cr.
(A) 6,000	4,000 (C)
(F) 4,000	340 (D)
(G) 3,000	150 (E)
	600 (I)

Accounts Receivable 112

Dr.	Cr.
(G) 1,000	

Office Equipment 121

Dr.	Cr.
(B) 2,000	
(C) 4,000	

Accounts Payable 211

Dr.	Cr.
	2,000 (B)

Ricky Cheung, Capital 311

Dr.	Cr.
	6,000 (A)

Ricky Cheung, Withdrawals 312

Dr.	Cr.
(I) 600	

Fees Earned 411

Dr.	Cr.
	4,000 (F)
	4,000 (G)

Rent Expense 511

Dr.	Cr.
(D) 340	

Utilities Expense 512

Dr.	Cr.
(E) 150	

Preparing financial reports from the trial balance

2C-4. From the trial balance of Adrian Shaver, Architect, shown below, prepare (a) an income statement for the month of June, (b) a statement of owner's equity for the month ended June 30, and (c) a balance sheet as of June 30, 2002.

Check Figure

Total Assets $9,740

ADRIAN SHAVER, Architect
TRIAL BALANCE
JUNE 30, 2002

	Dr.	Cr.
Cash in Bank	2 4 0 0 00	
Accounts Receivable	8 7 5 00	
Supplies	2 6 5 00	
Equipment	6 2 0 0 00	
Accounts Payable		6 2 0 00
Andrian Shaver, Capital		5 8 0 0 00
Andrian Shaver, Withdrawals	9 5 0 00	
Fees Earned		6 5 1 5 00
Rent Expense	1 2 0 0 00	
Advertising Expense	4 8 0 00	
Utilities Expense	5 6 5 00	
Totals	1 2 9 3 5 00	1 2 9 3 5 00

Comprehensive problem

Check Figure

Trial Balance Total $57,450

2C-5. The chart of accounts of Clara's Design Service includes the following: Cash, 111; Accounts Receivable, 112; Office Equipment, 121; Design Equipment, 122; Accounts Payable, 211; Clara Dean, Capital, 311; Clara Dean, Withdrawals, 312; Design Fees Earned, 411; Advertising Expense, 511; Repair Expense, 512; Salaries Expense, 513; and Telephone Expense, 514. The following transactions occurred for Clara's Design Service during the month of March:

Transaction A: Clara invested $33,000 in the business from her personal savings account.
Transaction B: Bought design equipment on account, $14,000.
Transaction C: Advertising bill was received but not yet paid, $750.
Transaction D: Bought office equipment for cash, $3,300.
Transaction E: Received cash for design services rendered, $5,900.
Transaction F: Paid salaries expense, $1,720.
Transaction G:. Paid repair expense for design equipment, $320.
Transaction H: Billed customers for design services rendered, $4,300.
Transaction I: Paid telephone bill, $150.
Transaction J: Received $2,000 as partial payment of Transaction H.
Transaction K: Clara paid home telephone bill from company bank account, $66.
Transaction L: Paid $500 on the bill received in Transaction C.

As Clara's newly employed accountant, your task is to:

1. Set up T accounts in a ledger.
2. Record transactions in the T accounts. (Place the letter of the transaction next to the entry.)
3. Foot the T accounts where appropriate.
4. Prepare a trial balance for the end of March.
5. Prepare from the trial balance, in proper form, (a) an income statement for the month of March, (b) a statement of owner's equity for the month ended March 31, and (c) a balance sheet as of March 31, 2000.

REAL WORLD APPLICATIONS

(The forms you need are on pages 2-22 and 2-23 of the *Study Guide with Working Papers.*)

2R-1.

Andy Leaf is a careless bookkeeper. He is having a terrible time getting his trial balance to balance. Andy has asked for your assistance in preparing a correct trial balance. The following is the incorrect trial balance.

RANCH COMPANY
TRIAL BALANCE
JUNE 30, 2002

	Dr.	Cr.
Cash	510 00	
Accounts Receivable		635 00
Office Equipment	360 00	
Accounts Payable	110 00	
Wages Payable	10 00	
H. Clo, Capital	635 00	
H. Clo, Withdrawals	1440 00	
Professional Fees		2240 00
Rent Expense		240 00
Advertising Expense	25 00	
Totals	3090 00	3115 00

Facts you have discovered:

- Debits to the Cash account were $2,640; credits to the Cash account were $2,150.
- Amy Hall paid $15 but this was not updated in Accounts Receivable.
- A purchase of office equipment for $5 on account was never recorded in the ledger.
- Revenue was understated in the ledger by $180.

Explain how these errors affected the ending balances for the accounts involved, and show how the trial balance will indeed balance once they are corrected.

Tell Ranch Company how it can avoid this problem in the future. Write out your recommendations.

2R-2.

Alice Groove, owner of Lonton Company, asked her bookkeeper how each of the following situations will affect the totals of the trial balance and individual ledger accounts.

- An $850 payment for a desk was recorded as a debit to Office Equipment, $85, and a credit to Cash, $85.
- A payment of $300 to a creditor was recorded as a debit to Accounts Payable, $300, and a credit to Cash, $100.
- An Accounts Receivable collection of $400 was recorded as a debit to Cash, $400, and a credit to J. Ray, Capital, $400.
- The payment of a liability of $400 was recorded as a debit to Accounts Payable, $40, and a credit to Supplies, $40.
- A purchase of equipment for $800 was recorded as a debit to Supplies, $800, and a credit to Cash, $800.
- A payment of $95 to a creditor was recorded as a debit to Accounts Payable, $95, and a credit to Cash, $59.

What did the bookkeeper tell her? Which accounts were overstated and which understated? Which were correct? Explain in writing how mistakes can be avoided in the future.

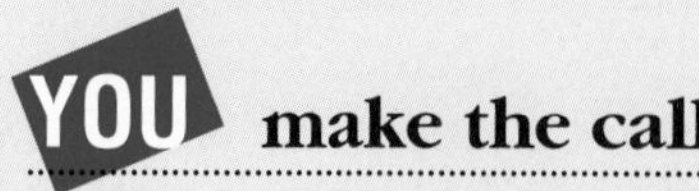

Critical Thinking/Ethical Case

2R-3.

Audrey Flet, the bookkeeper of ALN Co., was scheduled to leave on a three-week vacation at 5 o'clock on Friday. She couldn't get the company's trial balance to balance. At 4:30, she decided to put in fictitious figures to make it balance. Audrey told herself she would fix it when she got back from her vacation. Was Audrey right or wrong to do this? Why?

ACCOUNTING RECALL

A CUMULATIVE APPROACH

THIS EXAMINATION REVIEWS CHAPTERS 1 AND 2.

Your *Study Guide with Working Papers* (page 2-24) has forms to complete this exam, as well as worked-out solutions. The page reference next to each question identifies the page to turn back to if you answer the question incorrectly.

PART I Vocabulary Review

Match each term on the left side with the appropriate definition or phrase in the right-hand column.

Page Ref.		
(56)	1. Trial balance	A. Total remains the same.
(43)	2. Debit	B. Entering numbers on right side
(45)	3. Normal balance	C. Subdivisions of owner's equity
(13)	4. Revenue	D. Group of accounts
(43)	5. Crediting	E. Numbering system
(10)	6. Balance sheet	F. Left side of an account
(8)	7. Shift in assets	G. Prepared as of a particular date
(46)	8. Chart of accounts	H. Not an asset
(42)	9. Ledger	I. Side of account that increases it
(16)	10. Capital, withdrawals, revenue, expenses	J. List of the ledger balances

PART II True or False (Accounting Theory)

(43) 11. A debit always means increase.

(56) 12. There are no debit or credit columns on financial reports.

(56) 13. The trial balance lists only the ending figure for capital that goes on the balance sheet.

(45) 14. An increase in a withdrawal is a credit.

(56) 15. The trial balance is not a formal report.

CONTINUING PROBLEM

The Eldorado Computer Centre created its chart of accounts as follows:

Chart of Accounts
as of June 1, 2001

Assets
1000 Cash
1020 Accounts Receivable
1025 Prepaid Rent
1030 Supplies
1080 Computer Shop Equipment
1090 Office Equipment

Liabilities
2000 Accounts Payable

Owner's Equity
3000 T. Freedman, Capital
3010 T. Freedman, Withdrawals

Revenue
4000 Service Revenue

Expenses
5010 Advertising Expense
5020 Rent Expense
5030 Utilities Expense
5040 Phone Expense
5050 Supplies Expense
5060 Insurance Expense
5070 Postage Expense

You will use this chart of accounts to complete the Continuing Problem.

The following problem continues from Chapter 1. The balances as of July 31 have been brought forward in your *Study Guide with Working Papers* on pages 2-25 to 2-26. Additional transactions were:

(k) Received the phone bill for the month of July, $155
(l) Paid $150 (cheque #205) for insurance for the month
(m) Paid $200 (cheque #206) of the amount due from transaction (d) in Chapter 1
(n) Paid advertising expense for the month, $1,400 (cheque #207)
(o) Billed a client (Jeannine Sparks) for services rendered, $850
(p) Collected $900 for services rendered
(q) Paid the electric bill in full for the month of July [cheque #208—transaction (h), Chapter 1]
(r) Paid cash (cheque #209) for $50 in stamps
(s) Purchased $200 worth of supplies from Computer Connection on account

Assignment

1. Set up T accounts in a ledger.
2. Record the transactions (k) through (s) in the appropriate T accounts.
3. Foot the T accounts where appropriate.
4. Prepare a trial balance at the end of August.
5. Prepare from the trial balance an income statement, statement of owner's equity, and a balance sheet for the two months ending August 31, 2001.

Beginning the Accounting Cycle

3

Journalizing, Posting, and the Trial Balance

The Big Picture

◆

At Eldorado Computer Centre, Tony Freedman uses the standard accounting practice of keeping a journal. Later, he copies (or "posts") transactions to a ledger, where each account is separate so that it can be totalled.

Like a personal diary, an accounting journal lets you capture information as it happens. You first analyze each transaction to determine which ledger accounts will be affected. Then you record your analysis—along with descriptive notes—in the journal.

Eldorado's journal lets Freedman look up transactions easily. He can also check his analysis at any time. If an error is discovered when he prepares the trial balance, he can trace his steps back to the original transaction and make corrections.

The Eldorado Computer Centre deals with many different source documents, such as cheques, calculator tapes, receipts, invoices, purchase orders, and deposit slips. When customers enter Tony's store, they complete a repair order authorizing the centre to do the work. Once the work is completed, Tony issues a bill or "invoice." The customer may pay in cash, or Tony may extend credit. Either way, Tony records the invoice as a business transaction.

Of course, people make mistakes in accounting records. Nonetheless, these records are kept in ink, not pencil. Corrections are shown clearly and initialled. This record shows a complete and reliable record of events.

Chapter Objectives

- ◆ Journalizing—analyzing and recording business transactions into a journal (p. 81)
- ◆ Posting—transferring information from a journal to a ledger (p. 90)
- ◆ Preparing a trial balance (p. 97)

The normal accounting procedures that are performed over a period of time are called the **accounting cycle.** The accounting cycle takes place in a period of time called an **accounting period.** An accounting period is the period of time covered by the income statement. Although it can be any time period up to one year (e.g., one month or three months), most businesses use a one-year accounting period. The year can be either a **calendar year** (January 1 through December 31) or a fiscal year.

A **fiscal year** is an accounting period that runs for any 12 consecutive months, so it can be the same as a calendar year. A business can choose any fiscal year that is convenient. For example, some retailers may decide to end their fiscal year when inventories and business activity are at a low point, such as after the Christmas season. This is called a **natural business year.** Using a natural business year allows the business to count its year-end inventory when it is easiest to do so.

Businesses would not be able to operate successfully if they prepared financial reports only at the end of their calendar or fiscal year. That is why most businesses prepare **interim reports** on a monthly, quarterly, or semiannual basis.

This chapter covers steps 1 to 4 of the accounting cycle (see Table 3-1, page 82).

In this chapter, as well as in Chapters 4 and 5, we will follow Brenda Clark's new business, Clark's Word Processing Services. We will follow the normal accounting procedures that the business performs over a period of time. Clark has chosen to use a fiscal period of January 1 to December 31, which also is the calendar year.

Table 3-1 lists the steps in the business accounting cycle, both for a manual system and for a computerized system. This table should be used as a reference table. By the end of Chapter 5, every step will have been explained and illustrated in the manual accounting system.

LEARNING UNIT 3-1

Analyzing and Recording Business Transactions in a Journal: Steps 1 and 2 of the Accounting Cycle

The General Journal

A business uses a journal to record transactions in chronological order. A ledger accumulates information from a journal. The journal and the ledger are in two different books.

Chapter 2 taught us how to analyze and record business transactions in T accounts, or ledger accounts. However, recording a debit in an account on one page of the ledger and recording the corresponding credit on a different page of the ledger can make it difficult to find errors. It would be much easier if all of the business's transactions were located in the same place. That is the function of the **journal** or **general journal.** Transactions are entered in the journal in chronological order (January 1, 8, 15, etc.), and then this recorded information is used to update the ledger accounts. In computerized accounting, a journal may be recorded on disk or tape.

We will use a general journal, the simplest form of a journal, to record the transactions of Clark's Word Processing Services. A transaction (debit[s] + credit[s])

TABLE 3-1 STEPS OF THE ACCOUNTING CYCLE

STEPS OF THE ACCOUNTING CYCLE

Manual Accounting System	Computerized Accounting System
1. Business transactions occur and generate source documents.	1. Business transactions occur and generate source documents.
2. Analyze and record business transactions in a journal.	2. Analyze and record business transactions in a computerized journal.
3. Post or transfer information from journal to ledger.	3. Computer automatically posts information from journal to ledger.
4. Prepare a trial balance.	4. Trial balance is prepared automatically.
5. Prepare a worksheet.	5. No worksheet is necessary.
6. Prepare financial statements.	6. Record adjusting entries in a computerized journal; posting is automatic.
7. Journalize and post adjusting entries.	7. Financial statements are prepared automatically.
8. Journalize and post closing entries.	8. Closing procedures are usually completed automatically.
9. Prepare a post-closing trial balance.	9. Trial balance is prepared automatically.

Use the above table as a reference in your study of Chapters 3, 4, and 5.

Journal—book of original entry
Ledger—book of final entry

that has been analyzed and recorded in a journal is called a **journal entry.** The process of recording the journal entry in the journal is called **journalizing.**

The journal is called the **book of original entry,** since it contains the first formal information about the business transactions. The ledger is known as the **book of final entry,** because the information it contains has been transferred from the journal. Like the ledger, the journal may be a bound or loose-leaf book. Each of the journal pages looks like the one in Figure 3-1. The pages of the journal are numbered consecutively from page 1. Keep in mind that the journal and the ledger are separate books. Also note that both journals and ledgers exist in computerized accounting, although they may look different from the manual formats.

Relationship between the Journal and the Chart of Accounts

The accountant must refer to the business's chart of accounts for the account name that is to be used in the journal. Every company has its own "unique" chart of accounts.

The chart of accounts for Clark's Word Processing Services appears on page 83. By the end of Chapter 5, we will have discussed each of these accounts.

CLARK'S WORD PROCESSING SERVICES GENERAL JOURNAL						
						Page 1
Date		Account Titles and Description	PR	Dr.	Cr.	

FIGURE 3-1
The General Journal

Note that we will continue to use transaction analysis charts as a teaching aid in the journalizing process.

Clark's Word Processing Services
Chart of Accounts

Assets (100–199)
111 Cash
112 Accounts Receivable
114 Office Supplies
115 Prepaid Rent
121 Word Processing Equipment
122 Accumulated Amortization, Word Processing Equipment

Liabilities (200–299)
211 Accounts Payable
212 Salaries Payable

Owner's Equity (300–399)
311 Brenda Clark, Capital
312 Brenda Clark, Withdrawals
313 Income Summary

Revenue (400–499)
411 Word Processing Fees

Expenses (500–599)
511 Office Salaries Expense
512 Advertising Expense
513 Telephone Expense
514 Office Supplies Expense
515 Rent Expense
516 Amortization Expense, Word Processing Equipment

Journalizing the Transactions of Clark's Word Processing Services

Certain formalities must be followed in making journal entries:

- The debit portion of the transaction always is recorded first.
- The credit portion of a transaction is indented about 1 cm and placed below the debit portion.
- The explanation of the journal entry follows immediately after the credit and about 2 cm from the date column.
- A one-line space follows each transaction and explanation. This makes the journal easier to read, and there is less chance of mixing transactions.
- Finally, as always, the total amount of debits must equal the total amount of credits. The same format is used for each of the entries in the journal.

May 1, 2001: Brenda Clark began the business by investing $10,000 in cash.

1 Accounts Affected	2 Category	3 ↑ ↓	4 Rules of Dr. and Cr.
Cash	Asset	↑	Dr.
Brenda Clark, Capital	Owner's Equity	↑	Cr.

CLARK'S WORD PROCESSING SERVICES
GENERAL JOURNAL

Page 1

Date		Account Titles and Description	PR	Dr.	Cr.
2001 May	1	Cash		1000000	
		Brenda Clark, Capital			1000000
		Initial investment of cash by owner			

For now the PR (posting reference) column is blank; we will discuss it later.

Let's now look at the structure of this journal entry. The entry contains the following information:

1. Year of the journal entry	2001
2. Month of the journal entry	May
3. Day of the journal entry	1
4. Name(s) of account(s) debited	Cash
5. Name(s) of account(s) credited	Brenda Clark, Capital
6. Explanation of transaction	Investment of cash
7. Amount of debit(s)	$10,000
8. Amount of credit(s)	$10,000

May 1: Purchased word processing equipment from Ben Co. for $6,000, paying $1,000 and promising to pay the balance within 30 days.

1 Accounts Affected	2 Category	3 ↑ ↓	4 Rules of Dr. and Cr.
Word Processing Equipment	Asset	↑	Dr.
Cash	Asset	↓	Cr.
Accounts Payable	Liability	↑	Cr.

Note that in this compound entry we have one debit and two credits—but the total amount of debits equals the total amount of credits.

This transaction affects three accounts. When a journal entry has more than two accounts, it is called a **compound journal entry.**

A journal entry that includes three or more accounts is called a compound journal entry.

		Date		PR	Dr.	Cr.
		1	Word Processing Equipment		6 0 0 0 00	
			Cash			1 0 0 0 00
			Accounts Payable			5 0 0 0 00
			Purchase of equipment from Ben Co.			

In this entry, only the day is entered in the date column. That is because the year and month were entered at the top of the page from the first transaction. There is no need to repeat this information until a new page is needed or a change of month occurs.

May 1: Rented office space, paying $1,200 in advance for the first three months.

1 Accounts Affected	2 Category	3 ↑ ↓	4 Rules of Dr. and Cr.
Prepaid Rent	Asset	↑	Dr.
Cash	Asset	↓	Cr.

Rent paid in advance is an asset.

In this transaction Clark gains an asset called prepaid rent and gives up an asset, cash. The prepaid rent does not become an expense until it expires.

		Date		PR	Dr.	Cr.
		1	Prepaid Rent		1 2 0 0 00	
			Cash			1 2 0 0 00
			Rent paid in advance (3 months)			

May 3: Purchased office supplies from Norris Co. on account, $600.

1 Accounts Affected	2 Category	3 ↑ ↓	4 Rules of Dr. and Cr.
Office Supplies	Asset	↑	Dr.
Accounts Payable	Liability	↑	Cr.

Supplies become an expense when used up.

Remember, supplies are an asset when they are purchased. Once they are used up or consumed in the operation of business, they become an expense.

		Date		PR	Dr.	Cr.
		3	Office Supplies		6 0 0 00	
			Accounts Payable			6 0 0 00
			Purchase of supplies on account			
			from Norris Co.			

May 7: Completed sales promotion pieces for a client and immediately collected $3,000.

1 Accounts Affected	2 Category	3 ↑ ↓	4 Rules of Dr. and Cr.
Cash	Asset	↑	Dr.
Word Processing Fees	Revenue	↑	Cr.

7	Cash		3 000 00	
	Word Processing Fees			3 000 00
	Cash received for services rendered			

May 11: Paid office salaries, $650.

1 Accounts Affected	2 Category	3 ↑ ↓	4 Rules of Dr. and Cr.
Office Salaries Expense	Expense	↑	Dr.
Cash	Asset	↓	Cr.

11	Office Salaries Expense		650 00	
	Cash			650 00
	Payment of office salaries			

Remember, expenses are recorded when they are incurred, no matter when they are paid.

May 18: Advertising bill from Al's News Co. comes in but is not paid, $250.

1 Accounts Affected	2 Category	3 ↑ ↓	4 Rules of Dr. and Cr.
Advertising Expense	Expense	↑	Dr.
Accounts Payable	Liability	↑	Cr.

18	Advertising Expense		250 00	
	Accounts Payable			250 00
	Bill in but not paid from Al's News Co.			

Keep in mind that, as withdrawals *increase,* owner's equity *decreases.*

May 20: Brenda Clark wrote a cheque on the bank account of the business to pay her home mortgage payment of $625.

1 Accounts Affected	2 Category	3 ↑ ↓	4 Rules of Dr. and Cr.
Brenda Clark, Withdrawals	Owner's Equity (Withdrawals)	↓	Dr.
Cash	Asset	↓	Cr.

20	Brenda Clark, Withdrawals		625 00	
	Cash			625 00
	Personal withdrawal of cash			

Reminder: Revenue is recorded when it is earned, no matter when the cash is actually received.

May 22: Billed Morris Company for a sophisticated word processing job, $5,000.

1 Accounts Affected	2 Category	3 ↑ ↓	4 Rules of Dr. and Cr.
Accounts Receivable	Asset	↑	Dr.
Word Processing Fees	Revenue	↑	Cr.

22	Accounts Receivable		5000 00	
	Word Processing Fees			5000 00
	Billed Morris Co. for fees earned			

May 25: Paid office salaries, $650.

1 Accounts Affected	2 Category	3 ↑ ↓	4 Rules of Dr. and Cr.
Office Salaries Expense	Expense	↑	Dr.
Cash	Asset	↓	Cr.

***Note:* Since we are on page 2 of the journal, the year and month are repeated.**

CLARK'S WORD PROCESSING SERVICES
GENERAL JOURNAL

Page 2

Date		Account Titles and Description	PR	Dr.	Cr.
2001 May	25	Office Salaries Expense		650 00	
		Cash			650 00
		Payment of office salaries			

May 28: Paid half the amount owed for word processing equipment purchased May 1 from Ben Co., $2,500.

1 Accounts Affected	2 Category	3 ↑ ↓	4 Rules of Dr. and Cr.
Accounts Payable	Liability	↓	Dr.
Cash	Asset	↓	Cr.

	28	Accounts Payable		2500 00	
		Cash			2500 00
		Paid half the amount owed Ben Co.			

May 29: Received and paid telephone bill, $220.

1 Accounts Affected	2 Category	3 ↑ ↓	4 Rules of Dr. and Cr.
Telephone Expense	Expense	↑	Dr.
Cash	Asset	↓	Cr.

	29	Telephone Expense		220 00	
		Cash			220 00
		Paid telephone bill			

This concludes the journal transactions of Clark's Word Processing Services. (See pages 93 and 94 for a summary of all the transactions.)

LEARNING UNIT 3-1 REVIEW

AT THIS POINT you should be able to:

- Explain the purpose of the accounting cycle. (p. 81)
- Define and explain the relationship of the accounting period to the income statement. (p. 81)
- Compare and contrast a calendar year and a fiscal year. (p. 81)
- Explain the term "natural business year." (p. 81)
- Explain the function of interim reports. (p. 81)
- Define and state the purpose of a journal. (p. 81)
- Compare and contrast a book of original entry and a book of final entry. (p. 82)
- Differentiate between a chart of accounts and a journal. (p. 82)
- Explain a compound entry. (p. 84)
- Journalize business transactions. (p. 83)

SELF-REVIEW QUIZ 3-1

(The blank forms you need are on pages 3-1 and 3-2 of the *Study Guide with Working Papers.*)

The following are the transactions of Lowe's Repair Service. Journalize the transactions in proper form. The chart of accounts includes Cash; Accounts Receivable; Prepaid Rent; Repair Supplies; Repair Equipment; Accounts Payable; A. Lowe, Capital; A. Lowe, Withdrawals; Repair Fees Earned; Salaries Expense; Advertising Expense; and Supplies Expense.

2000

June 1 A. Lowe invested $6,000 cash and $4,000 worth of repair equipment in the business.

1 Paid two months' rent in advance, $1,200.

4 Bought repair supplies from Melvin Co. on account, $600. (These supplies have not yet been consumed or used up.)

15 Performed repair work, received $600 in cash, and had to bill Doe Co. for remaining balance of $300.

18 A. Lowe paid his home telephone bill, $50, using a company cheque.

20 Advertising bill for $400 from Jones Co. was received but payment was not due yet. (Advertising has already appeared in the newspaper.)

24 Paid salaries, $1,400.

Quiz Tip

All titles for the debits and credits come from the chart of accounts. Debits are against the date column and credits are indented. The description is indented further. The PR column is left blank in the journalizing process.

Solution to Self-Review Quiz 3-1

LOWE'S REPAIR SERVICE
GENERAL JOURNAL

Page 1

Date		Account Titles and Description	PR	Dr.	Cr.
2000 June	1	Cash		600000	
		Repair Equipment		400000	
		A. Lowe, Capital			1000000
		Owner investment			
	1	Prepaid Rent		120000	
		Cash			120000
		Rent paid in advance			
	4	Repair Supplies		60000	
		Accounts Payable			60000
		Purchase of supplies on account			
	15	Cash		60000	
		Accounts Receivable		30000	
		Repair Fees Earned			90000
		Performed repairs			
	18	A. Lowe, Withdrawals		5000	
		Cash			5000
		Personal withdrawal			
	20	Advertising Expense		40000	
		Accounts Payable			40000
		Advertising bill			
	24	Salaries Expense		140000	
		Cash			140000
		Paid salaries			

*Note that the PR column is left blank in the journalizing process.

LEARNING UNIT 3-2

Posting to the Ledger: Step 3 of the Accounting Cycle

The general journal serves a particular purpose; it puts every transaction that the business makes in one place. There are things it cannot do, however. For example, if you were asked to find the balance of the cash account from the general journal, you would have to go through the entire journal and look for only the cash entries. Then you would have to add up the debits and the credits for the cash account (separately) and determine the difference between the two totals.

What we really need to do to find balances of accounts is transfer the information from the journal to the general ledger. This is called **posting.** In the general ledger we will accumulate an ending balance for each account so that we can prepare financial statements.

Posting

Footings are not needed in three-column accounts.

In Chapter 2, we used the T-account form to make our ledger entries. T accounts are very simple, but they are not used in the real business world. They are used only for demonstration purposes. In practice, accountants often use a **three-column account** form that includes a column for each account's running balance. Figure 3-2 shows a standard three-column account (all the details are made up). We will use that format in the text from now on to illustrate general ledger accounts.

FIGURE 3-2
Three-Column Account

GENERAL LEDGER

Accounts Payable — Account No. 211

Date 2000		Explanation	Post. Ref.	Debit	Credit	DR or CR	Balance
May	1		GJ1		6 000 00	CR	6 000 00
	3		GJ1		400 00	CR	6 400 00
	18		GJ1		175 00	CR	6 575 00
	28		GJ2	3 000 00		CR	3 575 00

Now let's look at how to post the transactions of Clark's Word Processing Services from its journal. The diagram in Figure 3-3 (page 92) shows how to post the cash line from the journal to the ledger. The steps in the posting process are numbered and illustrated in the figure.

Step 1: In the Cash account in the ledger, record the date (May 1, 2001) and the amount of the entry ($10,000).

Step 2: Record the page number of the journal "GJ1" in the posting reference (PR) column of the Cash account.

Step 3: Calculate the new balance of the account. You keep a running balance in each account as you would in your chequebook. To do this you take the present balance in the account on the previous line and add or subtract the transaction as necessary to arrive at your new balance.

Step 4: Record the account number of Cash (111) in the posting reference (PR) column of the journal. This is called **cross-referencing.**

The same sequence of steps occurs for each line in the journal. In a manual system like Clark's, the debits and credits in the journal may be posted in the order in which they were recorded, or all the debits may be posted first and then all the credits. If Clark used a computer system, the program would post at the press of a menu button.

Using Posting References

The posting references are very helpful. In the journal, the PR column tells us which transactions have or have not been posted and also to which accounts they were posted. In the ledger, the posting reference leads us back to the original transaction in its entirety, so that we can see why the debit or credit was recorded and what other accounts were affected. (It leads us back to the original transaction by identifying the journal and the page in the journal from which the information came.)

FIGURE 3-3
How to Post from Journal to Ledger

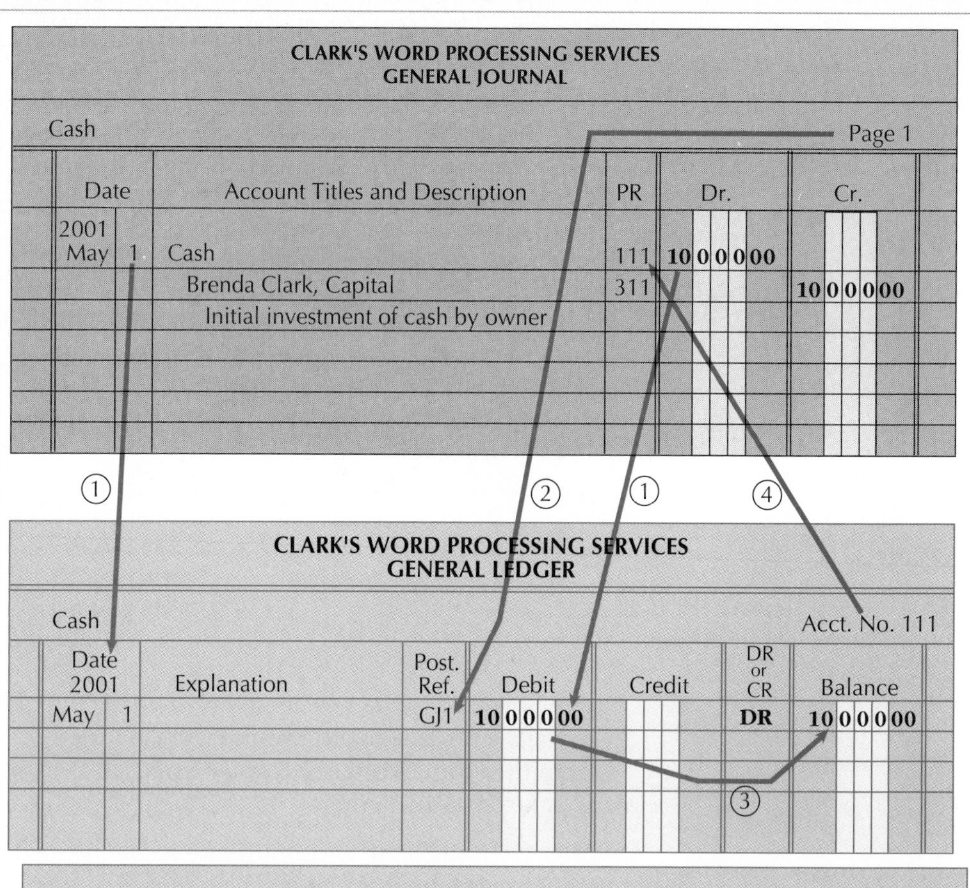

CLARK'S WORD PROCESSING SERVICES
GENERAL JOURNAL

Cash — Page 1

Date		Account Titles and Description	PR	Dr.	Cr.
2001					
May	1	Cash	111	10 0 0 0 00	
		Brenda Clark, Capital	311		10 0 0 0 00
		Initial investment of cash by owner			

CLARK'S WORD PROCESSING SERVICES
GENERAL LEDGER

Cash — Acct. No. 111

Date 2001		Explanation	Post. Ref.	Debit	Credit	DR or CR	Balance
May	1		GJ1	10 0 0 0 00		DR	10 0 0 0 00

Brenda Clark, Capital — Acct. No. 311

Date 2001		Explanation	Post. Ref.	Debit	Credit	DR or CR	Balance
May	1		GJ1		10 0 0 0 00	CR	10 0 0 0 00

LEARNING UNIT 3-2 REVIEW

AT THIS POINT you should be able to:

- State the purpose of posting. (p. 90)
- Discuss the advantages of the three-column account. (p. 91)
- Identify the elements to be posted. (p. 92)
- From journalized transactions, post to the general ledger. (p. 92)

SELF-REVIEW QUIZ 3-2

(The forms you need are on pages 3-3 to 3-6 of the *Study Guide with Working Papers.*)

The following are the journalized transactions of Clark's Word Processing Services. Your task is to post information to the ledger. The ledger in your workbook has all the account titles and numbers that were used from the chart of accounts.

CLARK'S WORD PROCESSING SERVICES
GENERAL JOURNAL

Page 1

Date		Account Titles and Description	PR	Dr.	Cr.
2001 May	1	Cash		10 000 00	
		Brenda Clark, Capital			10 000 00
		Initial investment of cash by owner			
	1	Word Processing Equipment		6 000 00	
		Cash			1 000 00
		Accounts Payable			5 000 00
		Purchase of equipment from Ben Co.			
	1	Prepaid Rent		1 200 00	
		Cash			1 200 00
		Rent paid in advance (3 months)			
	3	Office Supplies		600 00	
		Accounts Payable			600 00
		Purchase of supplies on account from			
		Norris Co.			
	7	Cash		3 000 00	
		Word Processing Fees			3 000 00
		Cash received for services rendered			
	11	Office Salaries Expense		650 00	
		Cash			650 00
		Payment of office salaries			
	18	Advertising Expense		250 00	
		Accounts Payable			250 00
		Bill received but not paid from			
		Al's News Co.			
	20	Brenda Clark, Withdrawals		625 00	
		Cash			625 00
		Personal withdrawal of cash			
	22	Accounts Receivable		5 000 00	
		Word Processing Fees			5 000 00
		Billed Morris Co. for fees earned			

CLARK'S WORD PROCESSING SERVICES
GENERAL JOURNAL

Page 2

Date		Account Titles and Description	PR	Dr.	Cr.
2001 May	25	Office Salaries Expense		650 00	
		Cash			650 00
		Payment of office salaries			
	28	Accounts Payable		2500 00	
		Cash			2500 00
		Paid half the amount owed Ben Co.			
	29	Telephone Expense		220 00	
		Cash			220 00
		Paid telephone bill			

Solution to Self-Review Quiz 3-2

Posting references

Remember, the PR column remains empty until the entries have been posted.

CLARK'S WORD PROCESSING SERVICES
GENERAL JOURNAL

Page 1

Date		Account Titles and Description	PR	Dr.	Cr.
2001 May	1	Cash	111	10000 00	
		Brenda Clark, Capital	311		10000 00
		Initial investment of cash by owner			
	1	Word Processing Equipment	121	6000 00	
		Cash	111		1000 00
		Accounts Payable	211		5000 00
		Purchase of equipment from Ben Co.			
	1	Prepaid Rent	115	1200 00	
		Cash	111		1200 00
		Rent paid in advance (3 months)			
	3	Office Supplies	114	600 00	
		Accounts Payable	211		600 00
		Purchase of supplies on accounting from Norris Co.			
	7	Cash	111	3000 00	
		Word Processing Fees	411		3000 00
		Cash received for services rendered			
	11	Office Salaries Expense	511	650 00	
		Cash	111		650 00
		Payment of office salaries			

(cont.)

			Account Titles and Description	PR	Dr.	Cr.
		18	Advertising Expense	512	250 00	
			Accounts Payable	211		250 00
			Bill received but not paid from			
			Al's News Co.			
		20	Brenda Clark, Withdrawals	312	625 00	
			Cash	111		625 00
			Personal withdrawal of cash			
		22	Accounts Receivable	112	5000 00	
			Word Processing Fees	411		5000 00
			Billed Morris Co. for fees earned			

CLARK'S WORD PROCESSING SERVICES
GENERAL JOURNAL

Page 2

Date		Account Titles and Description	PR	Dr.	Cr.
2001 May	25	Office Salaries Expense	511	650 00	
		Cash	111		650 00
		Payment of office salaries			
	28	Accounts Payable	211	2500 00	
		Cash	111		2500 00
		Paid half the amount owed Ben Co.			
	29	Telephone Expense	513	220 00	
		Cash	111		220 00
		Paid telephone bill			

Posting to ledger accounts

CLARK'S WORD PROCESSING SERVICES
PARTIAL GENERAL LEDGER

Cash — Acct. No. 111

Date 2001		Explanation	Post. Ref.	Debit	Credit	DR or CR	Balance
May	1		GJ1	10000 00		DR	10000 00
	1		GJ1		1000 00	DR	9000 00
	1		GJ1		1200 00	DR	7800 00
	7		GJ1	3000 00		DR	10800 00
	15		GJ1		650 00	DR	10150 00
	20		GJ1		625 00	DR	9525 00
	27		GJ2		650 00	DR	8875 00
	28		GJ2		2500 00	DR	6375 00
	29		GJ2		220 00	DR	6155 00

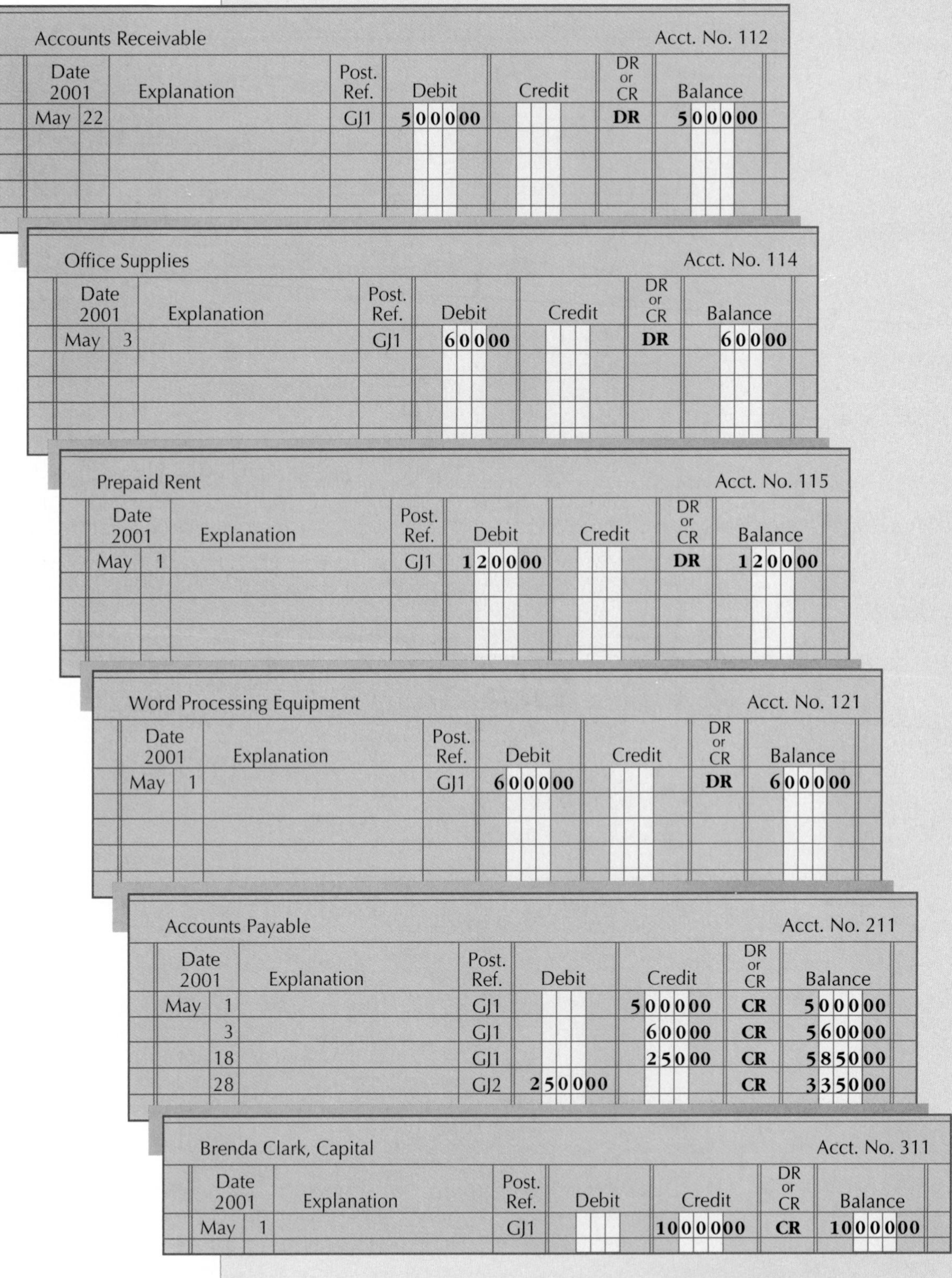

Accounts Receivable — Acct. No. 112

Date 2001		Explanation	Post. Ref.	Debit	Credit	DR or CR	Balance
May	22		GJ1	5000 00		DR	5000 00

Office Supplies — Acct. No. 114

Date 2001		Explanation	Post. Ref.	Debit	Credit	DR or CR	Balance
May	3		GJ1	600 00		DR	600 00

Prepaid Rent — Acct. No. 115

Date 2001		Explanation	Post. Ref.	Debit	Credit	DR or CR	Balance
May	1		GJ1	1200 00		DR	1200 00

Word Processing Equipment — Acct. No. 121

Date 2001		Explanation	Post. Ref.	Debit	Credit	DR or CR	Balance
May	1		GJ1	6000 00		DR	6000 00

Accounts Payable — Acct. No. 211

Date 2001		Explanation	Post. Ref.	Debit	Credit	DR or CR	Balance
May	1		GJ1		5000 00	CR	5000 00
	3		GJ1		600 00	CR	5600 00
	18		GJ1		250 00	CR	5850 00
	28		GJ2	2500 00		CR	3350 00

Brenda Clark, Capital — Acct. No. 311

Date 2001		Explanation	Post. Ref.	Debit	Credit	DR or CR	Balance
May	1		GJ1		10000 00	CR	10000 00

Brenda Clark, Withdrawals							Acct. No. 312
Date 2001		Explanation	Post. Ref.	Debit	Credit	DR or CR	Balance
May	20		GJ1	625 00		DR	625 00

Word Processing Fees							Acct. No. 411
Date 2001		Explanation	Post. Ref.	Debit	Credit	DR or CR	Balance
May	7		GJ1		3000 00	CR	3000 00
	22		GJ1		5000 00	CR	8000 00

Office Salaries Expense							Acct. No. 511
Date 2001		Explanation	Post. Ref.	Debit	Credit	DR or CR	Balance
May	11		GJ1	650 00		DR	650 00
	25		GJ2	650 00		DR	1300 00

Advertising Expense							Acct. No. 512
Date 2001		Explanation	Post. Ref.	Debit	Credit	DR or CR	Balance
May	18		GJ1	250 00		DR	250 00

Telephone Expense							Acct. No. 513
Date 2001		Explanation	Post. Ref.	Debit	Credit	DR or CR	Balance
May	29		GJ2	220 00		DR	220 00

Quiz Tip

The Post. Ref. column in the ledger tells from which part of the journal the information came. The PR column in the journal (the last to be filled in) tells to what account number in the ledger the information was posted.

LEARNING UNIT 3-3

Preparing the Trial Balance: Step 4 of the Accounting Cycle

Did you notice in Self-Review Quiz 3-2 that each account had a running balance figure? Did you know the normal balance of each account in Clark's ledger? As we discussed in Chapter 2, the list of the individual accounts with their balances taken from the ledger is called a **trial balance.**

The trial balance shown in Figure 3-4 (page 98) was developed from the ledger accounts of Clark's Word Processing Services that were posted and balanced in Self-Review Quiz 3-2. If the information is journalized or posted incorrectly, the trial balance will not be correct.

There are some things the trial balance will not show:

The totals of a trial balance can balance and yet be incorrect.

- The capital figure on the trial balance may not be the beginning capital figure. For instance, if Brenda Clark had made additional investments during the period, the additional investment would have been journalized and posted to the capital account. The only way to tell if the capital balance on the trial balance is the original balance is to check the ledger capital account to see whether any additional investments were made. This will be important when we make financial reports.

CLARK'S WORD PROCESSING SERVICES
TRIAL BALANCE
MAY 31, 2001

	Debit	Credit
Cash	6 1 5 5 00	
Accounts Receivable	5 0 0 0 00	
Office Supplies	6 0 0 00	
Prepaid Rent	1 2 0 0 00	
Word Processing Equipment	6 0 0 0 00	
Accounts Payable		3 3 5 0 00
Brenda Clark, Capital		10 0 0 0 00
Brenda Clark, Withdrawals	6 2 5 00	
Word Processing Fees		8 0 0 0 00
Office Salaries Expense	1 3 0 0 00	
Advertising Expense	2 5 0 00	
Telephone Expense	2 2 0 00	
Totals	21 3 5 0 00	21 3 5 0 00

The trial balance lists the accounts in the same order as in the ledger. The $6,155 figure for cash came from the ledger.

FIGURE 3-4 The Trial Balance

- There is no guarantee that transactions have been properly recorded. For example, the following errors would remain undetected: (1) a transaction that may have been omitted in the journalizing process; (2) a transaction incorrectly analyzed and recorded in the journal; (3) a journal entry journalized or posted twice.

What to do if a trial balance doesn't balance

The trial balance of Clark's Word Processing Services shows that the total of debits is equal to the total of credits. But what happens if the trial balance is in balance, but the correct amount is not recorded in each ledger account? Accuracy in the journalizing and posting process will help ensure that no errors are made.

Even if there is an error, the first rule is "Don't panic." Everyone makes mistakes, and there are accepted ways of correcting them. Once an entry has been made in ink, correcting an error must always show that the entry has been changed and who changed it. Sometimes the change has to be explained.

Some common mistakes

Correcting the trial balance: What to do if your trial balance doesn't balance

If the trial balance does not balance, the cause could be something relatively simple. Here are some common errors and how they can be fixed:

- If the difference (the amount you are off) is 10, 100, 1,000, etc., there probably is a mathematical error.

Did you clear your adding machine?

- If the difference is equal to an individual account balance in the ledger, the amount could have been omitted. It is also possible that the figure was not posted from the general journal.
- Divide the difference by 2; then check to see if a debit should have been a credit and vice versa in the ledger or trial balance. Example: $150 difference ÷ 2 = $75. This means you may have placed $75 as a debit to an account instead of a credit or vice versa.
- If the difference is evenly divisible by 9, a slide or a transposition may have occurred. A **slide** is an error resulting from adding or deleting zeros in writing numbers. For example, $4,175.00 may have been copied as $41.75. A **transposition** is the accidental rearrangement of the digits of a number. For example, $4,175 might have been accidentally written as $4,157.

- Compare the balances in the trial balance with the ledger accounts to check for copying errors.
- Recompute balances in each ledger account.
- Trace all postings from journal to ledger.

If you cannot find the error after you have done all of this, take a coffee break. Then start all over again.

MAKING A CORRECTION BEFORE POSTING

Before posting, error correction is straightforward. Simply draw a line through the incorrect entry in the journal, write the correct information above the line, and write your initials near the change.

Correcting an Error in an Account Title The following illustration shows an error and its correction in an account title:

		Description	P.R.	Debit	Credit
	1	Word Processing Equipment		6000 00	
		Cash			1000 00
		Accounts Payable amp ~~Accounts Receivable~~			5000 00
		Purchase of equipment from Ben Co.			

Correcting a Numerical Error Numbers are handled the same way as account titles, as the next change, from 520 to 250, shows:

		Description	P.R.	Debit	Credit
	18	Advertising Expense		250 00	
		Accounts Payable			amp 250 00 ~~520 00~~
		Bill from Al's News			

Correcting an Entry Error If a number has been entered in the wrong column, a straight line is drawn through it, and the number is then written in the correct column:

		Description	P.R.	Debit	Credit
	1	Word Processing Equipment		6000 00	
		Cash			1000 00
		Accounts Payable	amp	~~5000 00~~	5000 00
		Purchase of equipment from Ben Co.			

MAKING A CORRECTION AFTER POSTING

It is also possible to correct an amount that is properly entered in the journal but posted incorrectly to the proper account in the ledger. The first step is to draw a line through the error and write the correct figure above it. The next step is changing the running balance to reflect the corrected posting. Here, too, a line is drawn through the balance and the corrected balance is written above it. Both changes must be initialled.

Word Processing Fees							Acct. No. 411
Date 2001		Explanation	Post. Ref.	Debit	Credit	DR or CR	Balance
May	7		GJ1		2,500.00	CR	2,500.00
	22		GJ1		~~100.00~~ 4,100.00 amp	CR	~~2,600.00~~ 6,600.00 amp

CORRECTING AN ENTRY POSTED TO THE WRONG ACCOUNT

Drawing a line through an error and writing the correction above it is possible when a mistake has occurred within the proper account, but when an error involves a posting to the wrong account the journal must include a correction accompanied by an explanation. In addition, the correct information must be posted to the appropriate ledger accounts.

Suppose, for example, that as a result of tracing postings from journal entries to ledger accounts you find that a $180 telephone bill was incorrectly debited as an advertising expense. The following illustration shows how this is done.

Step 1: The error is corrected by making a new entry in the journal, dated with the date when the correction is entered, and the correction is explained.

GENERAL JOURNAL					Page 3
Date 2001		Account Titles and Description	PR	Dr.	Cr.
May	29	Telephone Expense	513	180.00	
		Advertising Expense	512		180.00
		To correct error in which			
		Advertising Expense was debited			
		for charges to Telephone Expense			

Step 2: The Advertising Expense ledger account is also corrected, by posting the new entry.

Advertising Expense							Acct. No. 512
Date 2001		Explanation	Post. Ref.	Debit	Credit	DR or CR	Balance
May	18		GJ1	175.00		DR	175.00
	23		GJ1	180.00		DR	355.00
	29	*Correcting entry*	GJ3		180.00	DR	175.00

Step 3: The Telephone Expense ledger is corrected.

Telephone Expense							Acct. No. 513
Date 2001		Explanation	Post. Ref.	Debit	Credit	DR or CR	Balance
May	29		GJ3	180.00		DR	180.00

LEARNING UNIT 3-3 REVIEW

AT THIS POINT you should be able to:

- Prepare a trial balance from a ledger, which uses three-column accounts. (p. 97)
- Analyze and correct a trial balance that doesn't balance. (p. 98)
- Correct journal and posting errors. (p. 99)

SELF-REVIEW QUIZ 3-3

(The blank forms you need are on page 3-7 of the *Study Guide with Working Papers.*)

1.

Interoffice Memo

TO: Al Vincent

FROM: Professor Jones

RE: Trial Balance

You have submitted to me an incorrect trial balance. Could you please rework and turn it in to me before next Friday?

Note: Individual amounts look OK.

A. RICE
TRIAL BALANCE
OCTOBER 31, 2002

	Dr.	Cr.
Cash		806000
Operating Expenses		170000
A. Rice, Withdrawals		40000
Service Revenue		540000
Equipment	500000	
Accounts Receivable	354000	
Accounts Payable	200000	
Supplies	30000	
A. Rice, Capital		1160000

2. A $7,000 debit to office equipment was mistakenly journalized and posted on June 9, 2002, to office supplies. Prepare the appropriate journal entry to correct this error.

Quiz Tip

Items in a trial balance are listed in the same order as in the ledger or the chart of accounts. Expect each account to have its normal balance (either debit or credit).

Solution to Self-Review Quiz 3-3

1.

A. RICE
TRIAL BALANCE
OCTOBER 31,2002

	Dr.	Cr.
Cash	806000	
Accounts Receivable	354000	
Supplies	30000	
Equipment	500000	
Accounts Payable		200000
A. Rice, Capital		1160000
A. Rice, Withdrawals	40000	
Service Revenue		540000
Operating Expenses	170000	
Totals	1900000	1900000

2.

GENERAL JOURNAL — Page 4

Date		Account Titles and Description	PR	Dr.	Cr.
2002 June	9	Office Equipment		700000	
		Office Supplies			700000
		To correct error in which office supplies			
		were debited for purchase of			
		office equipment			

Chapter Review

COMPREHENSIVE DEMONSTRATION PROBLEM WITH SOLUTION TIPS

(The blank forms you need are on pages 3-8 to 3-10 in the *Study Guide with Working Papers.*)

In March, Abby's Employment Agency had the following transactions:

2001

March	1	Abby Todd invested $5,000 in the new employment agency.
	4	Bought equipment for cash, $800.
	5	Earned employment fee commission, $200, but payment from Blue Co. will not be received until June.
	6	Paid wages expense, $300.
	7	Abby Todd paid her home utility bill from the company bank account, $75.
	9	Placed Rick Wool at VCR Corporation, receiving $1,200 cash.
	15	Paid cash for supplies, $600.
	28	Telephone bill was received but not yet paid, $180.
	29	Advertising bill was received but not yet paid, $400.

The chart of accounts includes: Cash, 111; Accounts Receivable, 112; Supplies, 131; Equipment, 141; Accounts Payable, 211; A. Todd, Capital, 311; A. Todd, Withdrawals, 321; Employment Fees Earned, 411; Wages Expense, 511; Telephone Expense, 521; Advertising Expense, 531.

Required

a. Set up a ledger based on the chart of accounts.

b. Journalize (all page 1) and post transactions.

c. Prepare a trial balance for March 31.

Solution to Comprehensive Demonstration Problem

a. See solution to **b**, General Ledger on page 105.

b. Journalizing

ABBY'S EMPLOYMENT AGENCY
GENERAL JOURNAL

Page 1

Date		Account Titles and Description	PR	Dr.	Cr.
2001 Mar.	1	Cash	111	5 0 0 0 00	
		A. Todd, Capital	311		5 0 0 0 00
		Owner investment			
	4	Equipment	141	8 0 0 00	
		Cash	111		8 0 0 00
		Bought equipment for cash			
	5	Accounts Receivable	112	2 0 0 00	
		Employment Fees Earned	411		2 0 0 00
		Fees on account from Blue Co.			
	6	Wages Expense	511	3 0 0 00	
		Cash	111		3 0 0 00
		Paid wages			
	7	A. Todd, Withdrawals	321	7 5 00	
		Cash	111		7 5 00
		Personal withdrawals			
	9	Cash	111	1 2 0 0 00	
		Employment Fees Earned	411		1 2 0 0 00
		Cash fees			
	15	Supplies	131	6 0 0 00	
		Cash	111		6 0 0 00
		Bought supplies for cash			
	28	Telephone Expense	521	1 8 0 00	
		Accounts Payable	211		1 8 0 00
		Telephone bill owed			
	29	Advertising Expense	531	4 0 0 00	
		Accounts Payable	211		4 0 0 00
		Advertising bill received			

c. Posting

GENERAL LEDGER

Cash — Acct. No. 111

Date 2001		Explanation	Post. Ref.	Debit	Credit	DR or CR	Balance
Mar.	1		GJ1	500000		DR.	500000
	4		GJ1		80000	DR.	420000
	6		GJ1		30000	DR.	390000
	7		G1		7500	DR.	382500
	9		GJ1	120000		DR.	502500
	15		GJ1		60000	DR.	442500

A. Todd, Capital — Acct. No. 311

Date 2001		Explanation	Post. Ref.	Debit	Credit	DR or CR	Balance
Mar.	1		GJ1		500000	CR.	500000

A. Todd Withdrawals — Acct. No. 321

Date 2001		Explanation	Post. Ref.	Debit	Credit	DR or CR	Balance
Mar.	7		GJ1	7500		DR.	7500

Accounts Receivable — Acct. No. 112

Date 2001		Explanation	Post. Ref.	Debit	Credit	DR or CR	Balance
Mar.	5		GJ1	20000		DR.	20000

Employment Fees Earned — Acct. No. 411

Date 2001		Explanation	Post. Ref.	Debit	Credit	DR or CR	Balance
Mar.	5		GJ1		20000	CR.	20000
Mar.	9		GJ1		120000	CR.	140000

Supplies — Acct. No. 131

Date 2001		Explanation	Post. Ref.	Debit	Credit	DR or CR	Balance
Mar.	15		GJ1	60000		DR.	60000

Wages Expense — Acct. No. 511

Date 2001		Explanation	Post. Ref.	Debit	Credit	DR or CR	Balance
Mar.	6		GJ1	30000		DR.	30000

Equipment — Acct. No. 141

Date 2001		Explanation	Post. Ref.	Debit	Credit	DR or CR	Balance
Mar.	4		GJ1	80000		DR.	80000

Telephone Expense — Acct. No. 521

Date 2001		Explanation	Post. Ref.	Debit	Credit	DR or CR	Balance
Mar.	28		GJ1	18000		DR.	18000

Accounts Payable — Acct. No. 211

Date 2001		Explanation	Post. Ref.	Debit	Credit	DR or CR	Balance
Mar.	28		GJ1		18000	CR.	18000
	29		GJ1		40000	CR.	58000

Advertising Expense — Acct. No. 531

Date 2001		Explanation	Post. Ref.	Debit	Credit	DR or CR	Balance
Mar.	29		GJ1	40000		DR.	40000

Solution Tips to Journalizing

1. When journalizing, the PR column is not filled in.
2. Write the name of the debit against the date column. Indent credits and list them below debits. Be sure total debits for each transaction equal total credits.
3. Skip a line after each transaction.

The Analysis of the Journal Entries

March 1	Cash	A	↑	Dr.	$5,000
	A. Todd, Capital	O.E.	↑	Cr.	$5,000

4	Equipment	A	↑	Dr.	$ 800
	Cash	A	↓	Cr.	$ 800

5	Accts. Receivable	A	↑	Dr.	$ 200
	Empl. Fees Earned	Rev.	↑	Cr.	$ 200

6	Wage Expense	Exp.	↑	Dr.	$ 300
	Cash	A	↓	Cr.	$ 300

7	A. Todd, Withdrawals	O.E. (Withdrawals)	↓	Dr.	$ 75
	Cash	A	↓	Cr.	$ 75

9	Cash	A	↑	Dr.	$1,200
	Empl. Fees Earned	Rev.	↑	Cr.	$1,200

15	Supplies	A	↑	Dr.	$ 600
	Cash	A	↓	Cr.	$ 600

28	Telephone Expense	Exp.	↑	Dr.	$ 180
	Accounts Payable	L	↑	Cr.	$ 180

29	Advertising Expense	Exp.	↑	Dr.	$ 400
	Accounts Payable	L	↑	Cr.	$ 400

Solution Tips to Posting

The Post. Ref. column in the ledger cash account tells you from which page in the general journal the information came (page 1). After the ledger cash account is posted, account number "111" is put in the PR column of the journal. (This is called cross-referencing.)

Note that we keep a running balance in the cash account. A $5,000 Dr. balance and a $200 credit entry result in a new debit balance of $4,800.

c. Trial balance

Abby's Employment Agency
Trial Balance
March 31, 2001

	Dr.	Cr.
Cash	4,425	
Accounts Receivable	200	
Supplies	600	
Equipment	800	
Accounts Payable		580
A. Todd, Capital		5,000
A. Todd, Withdrawals	75	
Employment Fees Earned		1,400
Wage Expense	300	
Telephone Expense	180	
Advertising Expense	400	
Totals	**6,980**	**6,980**

Solution Tip to Trial Balance

The trial balance lists the ending balance of each account, with the accounts in the order in which they appear in the ledger. The total of $6,980 on the left equals $6,980 on the right.

SUMMARY OF KEY POINTS

Learning Unit 3-1

1. The accounting cycle is a sequence of accounting procedures that are usually performed during an accounting period.
2. An accounting period is the time period for which the income statement is prepared. The time period can be any period up to one year.
3. A calendar year is from January 1 to December 31. The fiscal year is any 12-month period. A fiscal year could be a calendar year but does not have to be.
4. Interim reports are statements that are usually prepared for a portion of the business's calendar or fiscal year (e.g., a month or a quarter).
5. A general journal is a book that records transactions in chronological order. Here debits and credits are shown together on one page. It is the book of original entry.
6. The ledger is a collection of accounts where information is accumulated from the postings of the journal. The ledger is the book of final entry.
7. Journalizing is the process of recording journal entries.
8. The chart of accounts provides the specific titles of accounts to be entered in the journal.
9. When journalizing, the posting reference (PR) column is left blank.
10. A compound journal entry occurs when more than two accounts are affected in the journalizing process of a business transaction.

Learning Unit 3-2

1. Posting is the process of transferring information from the journal to the ledger.
2. The journal and ledger contain the same information but in a different form.
3. The three-column account aids in keeping a running balance of an account.
4. The normal balance of an account will be located on the side that increases according to the rules of debits and credits. For example, the normal balances of liabilities occur on the credit side.
5. The mechanical process of posting requires care in accurately transferring dates, posting references, titles, and amounts.

Learning Unit 3-3

1. A trial balance can balance but be incorrect. For example, an entire journal entry may not have been posted.
2. If a trial balance doesn't balance, check for errors in addition, omission of postings, slides, transpositions, copying errors, and so on.
3. Specific procedures should be followed in making corrections in journals and ledgers.

KEY TERMS

Accounting cycle For each accounting period, the process that begins with the recording of business transactions or procedures into a journal and ends with the completion of a post-closing trial balance (p. 81)

Accounting period The period of time for which an income statement is prepared (p. 81)

Book of final entry A ledger that receives information about business transactions from a book of original entry (a journal) (p. 82)

Book of original entry Book that records the first formal information about business transactions—a journal (p. 82)

Calendar year January 1 to December 31 (p. 81)

Compound journal entry A journal entry that affects more than two accounts (p. 84)

Cross-referencing Adding to the PR column of the journal the account number of the ledger account that was updated from the journal, and inserting the journal page on the ledger account (p. 91)

Fiscal year The 12-month period a business chooses for its accounting year (p. 81)

General journal The simplest form of a journal, which records information from transactions in chronological order as they occur. This journal links the debit and credit parts of transactions. (p. 81)

General ledger A collection of accounts which includes all those needed to contain the individual balances which show up on any of the financial statements (asset accounts, liability and equity accounts, revenue accounts, and expense accounts, plus a few others) (p. 90)

Interim reports Financial reports that are prepared for a month, quarter, or some other portion of the fiscal year (p. 81)

Journal A listing of business transactions in chronological order. The journal links on one page the debit and credit parts of transactions (p. 81)

Journal entry The transaction (debits and credits) that is recorded in a journal once it is analyzed (p. 82)

Journalizing The process of recording a transaction entry in the journal (p. 82)

Natural business year A business's fiscal year that ends at the same time as a slow seasonal period begins (p. 81)

Posting The transferring, copying, or recording of information from a journal to a ledger (p. 90)

Slide The error of adding or deleting zeros in the writing of a number; example: 79,200→7,920 (p. 98)

Three-column account A running balance account that records debits and credits and has a column for an ending balance (debit or credit), and which replaces the standard two-column account we used earlier (p. 91)

Transposition The accidental rearrangement of the digits of a number; example: 152→125 (p. 98)

Trial balance An informal listing of the ledger accounts and their balances that aids in proving the equality of debits and credits (p. 97)

Blueprint of First Four Steps of the Accounting Cycle

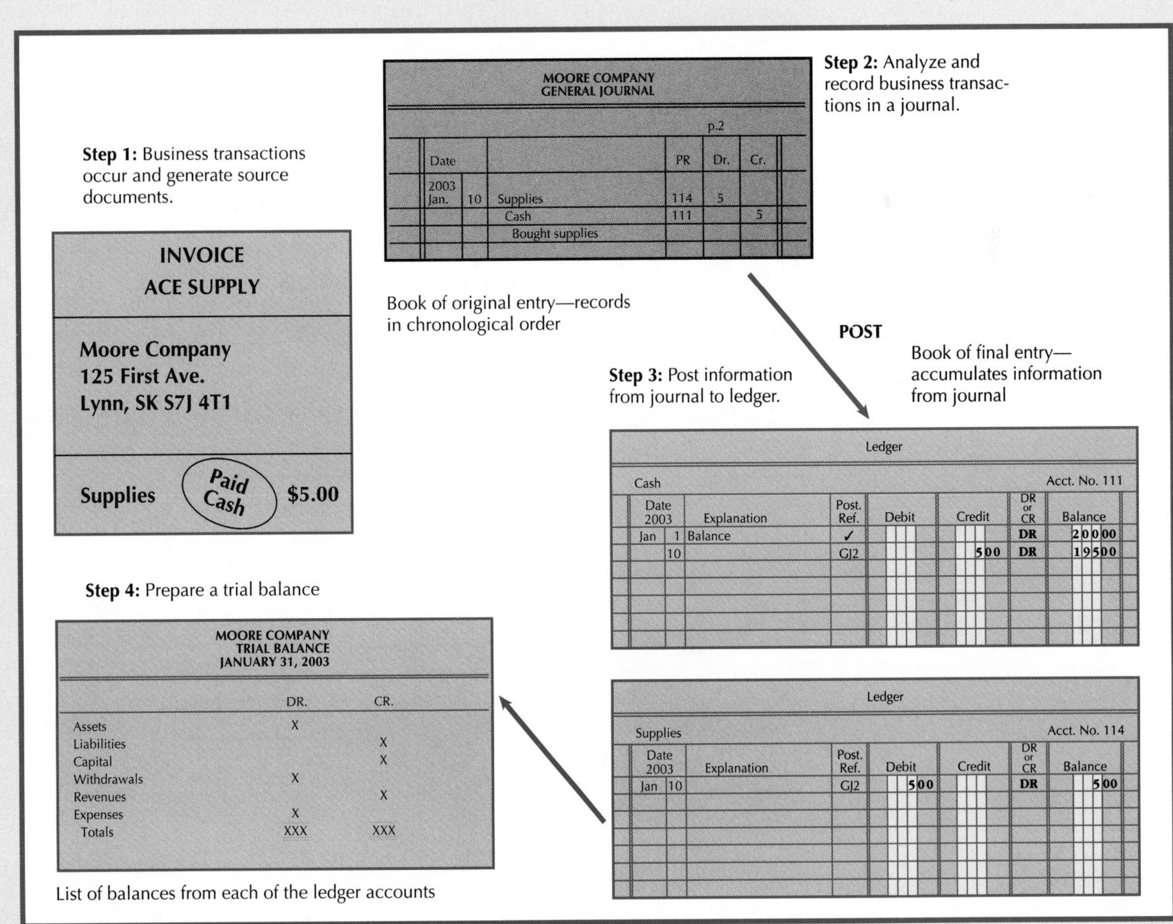

List of balances from each of the ledger accounts

QUESTIONS, MINI EXERCISES, EXERCISES, AND PROBLEMS

Discussion Questions

1. Explain the concept of the accounting cycle.
2. An accounting period is based on the balance sheet. Agree or disagree.
3. Compare and contrast a calendar year versus a fiscal year.
4. What are interim reports?
5. Why is the ledger called the book of final entry?
6. How do transactions get "linked" in a general journal?
7. What is the relationship of the chart of accounts to the general journal?
8. What is a compound journal entry?
9. Posting means updating the journal. Agree or disagree. Please comment.
10. The side that decreases an account is the normal balance. True or false?
11. The PR column of a general journal is the last item to be filled in during the posting process. Agree or disagree.
12. Discuss the concept of cross-referencing.
13. What is the difference between a transposition and a slide?

Mini Exercises

(The blank forms you need are on page 3-11 of the *Study Guide with Working Papers.*)

General Journal

1. Complete the following from the general journal of Ranger Company.

RANGER COMPANY
GENERAL JOURNAL
Page 1

Date		Account Titles and Descriptions	PR	Dr.	Cr.
2000 Aug.	18	Cash		7 0 0 0 00	
		Equipment		2 0 0 00	
		B. Ranger, Capital			7 2 0 0 00
		Initial investment by owner			

a. Year of journal entry ________
b. Month of journal entry ________
c. Day of journal entry ________
d. Name(s) of account(s) debited ________
e. Name(s) of account(s) credited ________
f. Explanation of transaction ________
g. Amount of debit(s) ________
h. Amount of credit(s) ________
i. Page of journal ________

General Journal

2. Provide the explanation for each of these general journal entries.

GENERAL JOURNAL — Page 4

Date		Account Titles and Descriptions	PR	Debit	Credit
2000 July	9	Cash		7 0 0 0 00	
		Office Equipment		5 0 0 0 00	
		A. Rye, Capital			1 2 0 0 0 00
		(A)			
	15	Cash		3 0 00	
		Accounts Receivable		6 0 00	
		Hair Fees Earned			9 0 00
		(B)			
	20	Advertising Expense		4 0 00	
		Accounts Payable			4 0 00
		(C)			

Posting and Balancing

3. Balance this three-column account. What function does the PR column serve? When will Account 111 be used in the journalizing and posting process?

Name: Cash — Account No. 111

Date 2000		Explanation	Post. Ref.	Debit	Credit	DR or CR	Balance
June	4		GJ1	15 00			
	5		GJ1	6 00			
	9		GJ2		4 00		
	10		GJ3	1 00			

The Trial Balance

4. The following trial balance was prepared *incorrectly*.

a. Rearrange the accounts in proper order.

b. Calculate the total of the trial balance. (Small numbers are used intentionally so you can do the calculations in your head.) Assume each account has a normal balance.

Larkin Company
Trial Balance
October 31, 2002

	Dr.	Cr.
B. Larkin, Capital	14	
Equipment	9	
Rent Expense		4
Advertising Expense		3
Accounts Payable		8
Taxi Fare Income	16	
Cash	17	
B. Larkin, Withdrawals		5
Totals	**56**	**20**

Correcting Entry

5. On May 1, 2002, a telephone expense for $180 was debited to Repair Expense. On June 12, 2002, this error was found. Prepare the correcting journal entry. When would a correcting entry *not* be needed?

Exercises

Preparing journal entries

(The forms you need are on pages 3-12 to 3-16 of the *Study Guide with Working Papers.*)

3-1. Prepare journal entries for the following transactions that occurred during November:

2002
Nov. 1 Ann Carter invested $20,000 cash and $2,000 worth of equipment in her new business.
3 Purchased building for $60,000 on account.
12 Purchased a truck from Lange Co. for $18,000 cash.
18 Bought supplies from Green Co. on account, $700.

Preparing journal entries

3-2. Record the following in the general journal of Fay's Repair Shop.

2001
Jan. 2 Fay Hope invested $15,000 cash in the repair shop.
5 Paid $7,000 for shop equipment.
8 Bought from Lowell Co. shop equipment for $6,000 on account.
14 Received $900 for repair fees earned.
18 Billed Sullivan Co. $900 for services rendered.
20 Fay withdrew $300 for personal use.

Posting

3-3. Post the following transactions to the ledger of King Company. The partial ledger of King Company includes Cash, 111; Equipment, 121; Accounts Payable, 211; and A. King, Capital, 311. Please use three-column accounts in the posting process.

Page 4

Date 2000			PR	Dr.	Cr.
April	6	Cash		1500000	
		A. King, Capital			1500000
		Cash investment			
	14	Equipment		900000	
		Cash			400000
		Accounts Payable			500000
		Purchase of equipment			

Journalizing, posting, and preparing a trial balance

3-4. From the following transactions for Lowe Company for the month of July, (a) prepare journal entries (assume that it is page 1 of the journal), (b) post to the ledger (use three-column account style), and (c) prepare a trial balance.

2002
July 1 Joan Lowe invested $6,000 in the business.
4 Bought from Lax Co. equipment on account, $800.

15 Billed Friend Co. for services rendered, $4,000.
18 Received $5,000 cash for services rendered.
24 Paid salaries expense, $1,800.
28 Joan withdrew $400 for personal use.

Chart of accounts includes: Cash, 111; Accounts Receivable, 112; Equipment, 121; Accounts Payable, 211; J. Lowe, Capital, 311; J. Lowe, Withdrawals, 312; Fees Earned, 411; Salaries Expense, 511.

Correcting the trial balance

3-5. You have been hired to correct the following trial balance that has been recorded improperly from the ledger to the trial balance.

SUNG CO. TRIAL BALANCE MARCH 31, 2003		
	Dr.	Cr.
Accounts Payable	200000	
A. Sung, Capital		650000
A. Sung, Withdrawals		30000
Services Earned		470000
Concessions Earned	250000	
Rent Expense	40000	
Salaries Expense	250000	
Miscellaneous Expense		130000
Cash	1000000	
Accounts Receivable		120000
Totals	1740000	1400000

Correcting entry

3-6. On February 6, 2001, Mike Sullivan made the following journal entry to record the purchase on account of office equipment priced at $1,400.00. This transaction had not yet been posted when the error was discovered. Make the appropriate correction.

GENERAL JOURNAL					
Date		Account Titles and Description	PR	Dr.	Cr.
2001 Feb.	6	Office Equipment		90000	
		Accounts Payable			90000
		Purchase of office equipment on account			

Group A Problems

(The forms you need are on pages 3-17 to 3-26 of the *Study Guide with Working Papers.*)

Journalizing

3A-1. Sue Vance operates Vance's Dog Grooming Centre. As the bookkeeper, you have been requested to journalize the following transactions:

2001
July 1 Paid rent for two months in advance, $3,000.
3 Purchased grooming equipment on account from Leek's Supply House, $2,500.

Check Figure
July 21
Dr. Advertising Expense $120
Cr. Accounts Payable $120

10 Purchased grooming supplies from Angel's Wholesale for $600 cash.
12 Received $1,400 cash from grooming fees earned.
20 Sue withdrew $400 for her personal use.
21 Advertising bill was received from *Daily Sun* but was still unpaid, $120.
25 Paid cleaning expense, $90.
28 Paid salaries expense, $500.
29 Performed grooming work for $1,700; however, payment will not be received from Rick's Kennel until August.
30 Paid Leek's Supply House half the amount owed from July 3 transaction.

Your task is to journalize the above transactions. The chart of accounts for Vance's Dog Grooming Centre is as follows:

Chart of Accounts

Assets	Owner's Equity
111 Cash	311 Sue Vance, Capital
112 Accounts Receivable	312 Sue Vance, Withdrawals
114 Prepaid Rent	
116 Grooming Supplies	**Revenue**
121 Grooming Equipment	411 Grooming Fees Earned
Liabilities	**Expenses**
211 Accounts Payable	511 Advertising Expense
	512 Salaries Expense
	514 Cleaning Expense

Comprehensive problem: journalizing, posting, and preparing a trial balance

3A-2. On June 1, 2002, Molly Taylor opened Taylor's Dance Studio. The following transactions occurred in June:

2002
June
1 Molly Taylor invested $8,000 in the dance studio.
1 Paid three months' rent in advance, $1,000.
3 Purchased $700 worth of equipment from Astor Co. on account.
5 Received $900 cash for fitness training workshop for dancers.
8 Purchased $300 worth of supplies for cash.
9 Billed Lester Co. $2,100 for group dance lesson for its employees.
10 Paid salaries of assistants, $400.
15 Molly Taylor withdrew $150 from the business for her personal use.
28 Paid electrical expense, $125.
29 Paid telephone bill for June, $190.

Check Figure
Trial Balance Total $11,700

Required

a. Set up the ledger based on the charts of accounts on page 115.
b. Journalize (using journal page 1) and post the June transactions.
c. Prepare a trial balance as of June 30, 2002.

The chart of accounts for Taylor's Dance Studio is as follows:

Chart of Accounts

Assets
111 Cash
112 Accounts Receivable
114 Prepaid Rent
121 Supplies
131 Equipment

Liabilities
211 Accounts Payable

Owner's Equity
311 Molly Taylor, Capital
312 Molly Taylor, Withdrawals

Revenue
411 Fees Earned

Expenses
511 Electrical Expense
512 Salaries Expense
531 Telephone Expense

Comprehensive problem: journalizing, posting, and preparing a trial balance

Check Figure

Trial Balance Total $14,600

3A-3. The following transactions occurred in June 2003 for A. French Placement Agency:

2003
June 1 A. French invested $9,000 cash in the placement agency.
1 Bought equipment on account from Hook Co., $2,000.
3 Earned placement fees of $1,600, but payment will not be received until July.
5 A. French withdrew $100 for his personal use.
7 Paid wages expense, $300.
9 Placed a client on a local TV show, receiving $600 cash.
15 Bought supplies on account from Lyon Co., $500.
28 Paid telephone bill for June, $160.
29 Advertising bill from Shale Co. was received but not yet paid, $900.

The chart of accounts for A. French Placement Agency is as follows:

Chart of Accounts

Assets
111 Cash
112 Accounts Receivable
131 Supplies
141 Equipment

Liabilities
211 Accounts Payable

Owner's Equity
311 A. French, Capital
321 A. French, Withdrawals

Revenue
411 Placement Fees Earned

Expenses
511 Wages Expense
521 Telephone Expense
531 Advertising Expense

Required

a. Set up the ledger based on the chart of accounts.

b. Journalize (page 1) and post the June transactions.

c. Prepare a trial balance as of June 30, 2003.

Group B Problems

(The forms you need are on pages 3-17 to 3-26 of the *Study Guide with Working Papers.*)

Journalizing

3B-1. In April 2001, Sue Vance opened a new dog grooming centre. Please assist her by journalizing the following business transactions:

Check Figure

April 21
Dr. Advertising Expense $75
Cr. Accounts Payable $75

2001

April
1 Sue Vance invested $4,000 worth of grooming equipment as well as $6,000 cash in the new business.
3 Purchased grooming supplies on account from Rex Co., $500.
10 Purchased office equipment on account from Ross Stationery, $400.
12 Sue paid her home telephone bill from the company bank account, $60.
20 Received $600 cash for grooming services performed.
21 Advertising bill was received but not yet paid, $75.
25 Cleaning bill was received but not yet paid, $90.
28 Performed grooming work for Jay Kennels, $700; however, payment will not be received until May.
29 Paid salaries expense, $400.
30 Paid Ross Stationery half the amount owed from April 10 transaction.

The chart of accounts for Vance's Dog Grooming Centre includes: Cash, 111; Accounts Receivable, 112; Prepaid Rent, 114; Grooming Supplies, 116; Office Equipment, 120; Grooming Equipment, 121; Accounts Payable, 211; Sue Vance, Capital, 311; Sue Vance, Withdrawals, 312; Grooming Fees Earned, 411; Advertising Expense, 511; Salaries Expense, 512; and Cleaning Expense, 514.

Comprehensive problem: journalizing, posting, and preparing a trial balance

3B-2. In June the following transactions occurred for Taylor's Dance Studio:

Check Figure

Trial Balance Total $9,620

2002

June
1 Molly Taylor invested $6,000 in the dance studio:
1 Paid four months' rent in advance, $1,200.
3 Purchased supplies on account from A.J.K., $700.
5 Purchased equipment on account from Reese Company, $900.
8 Received $1,300 cash for dance training program provided to Northwest Junior College.
9 Billed Long Co. for dance lessons provided, $600.
10 Molly withdrew $400 from the dance studio to buy a new saw for her home.
15 Paid salaries expense, $400.
28 Paid telephone bill, $118.
29 Electricity bill was received but not yet paid, $120.

Required

a. Set up a ledger.

b. Journalize (all page 1) and post the June transactions.

c. Prepare a trial balance as of June 30, 2002.

Chart of accounts includes: Cash, 111; Accounts Receivable, 112; Prepaid Rent, 114; Supplies, 121; Equipment, 131; Accounts Payable, 211; Molly Taylor, Capital, 311; Molly Taylor, Withdrawals, 321; Fees Earned, 411; Electrical Expense, 511; Salaries Expense, 521; Telephone Expense, 531.

Comprehensive problem: journalizing, posting, and preparing a trial balance

3B-3. In June, A. French Placement Agency had the following transactions:

2003

June
1 A. French invested $6,000 in the new placement agency.
2 Bought equipment for cash, $350.

Check Figure

Trial Balance Total $9,385

3 Earned placement fee commission, $2,100, but payment from Avon Co. will not be received until July.
5 Paid wages expense, $400.
7 A. French paid his home utility bill using a company cheque, $69.
9 Placed Jay Diamond on a national TV show, receiving $900 cash.
15 Paid cash for supplies, $350.
28 Telephone bill was received but not yet paid, $185.
29 Advertising bill was received but not yet paid, $200.

The chart of accounts includes: Cash, 111; Accounts Receivable, 112; Supplies, 131; Equipment, 141; Accounts Payable, 211; A. French, Capital, 311; A. French, Withdrawals, 321; Placement Fees Earned, 411; Wage Expense, 511; Telephone Expense, 521; Advertising Expense, 531.

Required

a. Set up a ledger based on the chart of accounts.
b. Journalize (all page 1) and post transactions.
c. Prepare a trial balance for June 30, 2003.

Group C Problems

(The forms you need are on pages 3-27 to 3-36 of the *Study Guide with Working Papers.*)

Journalizing

3C-1. In August, Leo Barth opened a personal financial planning centre. Please assist him by journalizing the following business transactions:

Check Figure

Aug 21
Dr. Advertising Expense $310
Cr. Accounts Payable $310

2003
Aug. 1 Leo Barth invested $5,000 worth of computer equipment as well as $9,000 cash in the new business.
3 Purchased computer supplies on account from Kent Co., $360.
10 Purchased office equipment on account from Apex Stationery, $1,650.
12 Leo paid his home telephone bill from the company bank account, $41.
20 Received $930 cash for financial planning services performed.
21 Advertising bill was received but not yet paid, $310.
25 Cleaning bill was received but not yet paid, $79.
28 Performed financial planning services for Franklin Corp., $2,400; however, payment will not be received until September.
29 Paid salaries expense, $950.
30 Paid Apex Stationery half the amount owed from August 10 transaction, $825.
31 Received bill for repairs on equipment, $295—not yet paid.

The chart of accounts for the company includes: Cash, 111; Accounts Receivable, 112; Prepaid Rent, 114; Computer Supplies, 116; Office Equipment, 120; Computer Equipment, 121; Accounts Payable, 211; Leo Barth, Capital, 311; Leo Barth, Withdrawals, 312; Planning Fees Earned, 411; Advertising Expense, 511; Salaries Expense, 512; Repairs Expense, 513; and Cleaning Expense, 514.

Comprehensive problem: journalizing, posting, and preparing a trial balance

Check Figure

Trial Balance Total $14,292

3C-2. In July the following transactions occurred for Mary's Aerobic Studio.

2002
July 2 Mary Steeper invested $7,300 in the studio.
2 Paid three months' rent in advance, $1,500.
3 Purchased supplies on account from Marlin Supplies, $480.
5 Purchased equipment on account from Brinkley Company, $2,750.
8 Received $1,800 cash for aerobic training program provided to Anne Webber Dance Group.

9 Billed Short Co. for aerobic lessons provided, $1,500.
10 Mary withdrew $975 from the aerobics studio to buy a new sofa for her apartment.
15 Paid salaries expense, $1,220.
28 Paid telephone bill for studio, $160.
28 Electricity bill was received but not yet paid, $172.
31 Advertising bill was received from City Newspaper, $290.

Required

a. Set up a ledger.
b. Journalize (all page 1) and post the July transactions.
c. Prepare a trial balance as of July 31, 2002.

Chart of accounts includes: Cash, 111; Accounts Receivable, 112; Prepaid Rent, 114; Supplies, 121; Equipment, 131; Accounts Payable, 211; Mary Steeper, Capital, 311; Mary Steeper, Withdrawals, 321; Fees Earned, 411; Advertising Expense, 511; Electrical Expense, 515; Salaries Expense, 521; Telephone Expense, 531.

Comprehensive problem: journalizing, posting, and preparing a trial balance

Check Figure

Trial Balance Total $22,830

3C-3. In June, Matt Nepoose Investigative Agency had the following transactions:

2001
June 1 Matt Nepoose invested $18,000 in the new agency.
2 Bought equipment for cash, $5,100.
3 Earned investigative fee, $3,200, but payment from client will not be received until later.
5 Paid wages expense, $1,100.
7 Matt paid his home water and gas bill from the company bank account, $107.
9 Located missing spouse, receiving $975 cash.
15 Paid cash for supplies, $270.
25 Received half of the fee earned on June 3, $1,600.
28 Telephone bill was received but not yet paid, $130.
29 Advertising bill was received but not yet paid, $525.

The chart of accounts includes: Cash, 111; Accounts Receivable, 112; Supplies, 131; Equipment, 141; Accounts Payable, 211; M. Nepoose, Capital, 311; M. Nepoose, Withdrawals, 321; Investigative Fees Earned, 411; Wage Expense, 511; Telephone Expense, 521; Advertising Expense, 531.

Required

a. Set up a ledger based on the chart of accounts.
b. Journalize (all page 1) and post transactions.
c. Prepare a trial balance for June 30, 2001.

REAL WORLD APPLICATIONS

(The forms you need are on pages 3-37 to 3-38 of the *Study Guide with Working Papers.*)

3R-1.
Paul Regan, bookkeeper of Hampton Co., has been up half the night trying to get his trial balance to balance. Here are his results:

HAMPTON CO. TRIAL BALANCE JUNE 30, 2001		
	Dr.	Cr.
Office Sales		5 720 00
Cash in Bank	3 260 00	
Accounts Receivable	5 660 00	
Office Equipment	8 400 00	
Accounts Payable		4 160 00
D. Hole, Capital		11 560 00
D. Hole, Withdrawals		700 00
Wages Expense	2 600 00	
Rent Expense	940 00	
Utilities Expense	26 00	
Office Supplies	120 00	
Prepaid Rent	180 00	

Ken Small, the accountant, compared Paul's amounts in the trial balance with those in the ledger, recomputed each account balance, and compared postings. Ken found the following errors:

1. A $200 debit to D. Hole, Withdrawals, was posted as a credit.
2. D. Hole, Withdrawals, was listed on the trial balance as a credit.
3. A Note Payable account with a credit balance of $2,400 was not listed on the trial balance.
4. The pencilled footings for Accounts Payable were debits of $5,320 and credits of $8,800.
5. A debit of $180 to Prepaid Rent was not posted.
6. The entry for office supplies bought for $60 was posted as a credit to Supplies.
7. A debit of $120 to Accounts Receivable was not posted.
8. A cash payment of $420 was credited to Cash for $240.
9. The pencilled footing of the credits to Cash was overstated by $400.
10. The Utilities Expense of $260 was listed in the trial balance as $26.

Assist Paul Regan by preparing a correct trial balance. What advice could you give Ken about Paul? Can you explain the situation to Paul? Put your answers in writing.

3R-2.

Lauren Oliver, an accountancy lab tutor, is having a debate with some of her assistants. They are trying to find out how each of the following five unrelated situations would affect the trial balance:

1. A $5 debit to cash in the ledger was not posted.
2. A $10 debit to Computer Supplies was debited to Computer Equipment.
3. An $8 debit to Wages Expense was debited twice to the account.
4. A $4 debit to Computer Supplies was debited to Computer Sales.
5. A $35 credit to Accounts Payable was posted as a $53 credit.

Could you indicate to Lauren the effect that each situation will have on the trial balance? If a situation will have no effect, indicate that fact. Put in writing how each of these situations could be avoided in the future.

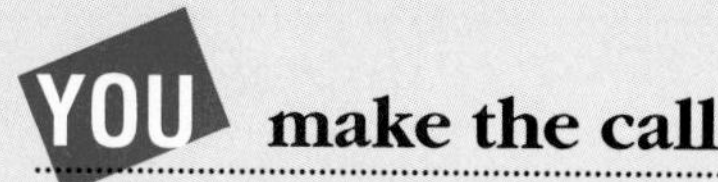

make the call

Critical Thinking/Ethical Case

3R-3.

Jay Simons, the accountant of See Co., wanted to buy a new computer software package for his general ledger. He couldn't do it because all funds were frozen for the rest of the fiscal period. Jay called his friend at Joor Industries and asked whether he could copy their software. Why should or shouldn't Jay have done that?

ACCOUNTING RECALL

A CUMULATIVE APPROACH

THIS EXAMINATION REVIEWS CHAPTERS 1 THROUGH 3.

Your *Study Guide and Working Papers* has forms (pages 3-39 to 3-43) to complete this exam, as well as worked-out solutions. The page reference next to each question identifies the page to turn back to if you answer the question incorrectly.

PART I Vocabulary Review

Match each term on the left side with the related definition or phrase on the right.

Page Ref.	Term		Definition
(46)	1. Chart of accounts	A.	Process of recording transactions in a journal
(81)	2. Ledger	B.	Rearrangement of digits
(98)	3. Slide	C.	Book of original entry
(81)	4. Calendar year	D.	Running balance
(98)	5. Transposition	E.	Transferring information
(91)	6. Three-column account	F.	January 1 to December 31
(82)	7. Journalizing	G.	Adding or deleting numbers
(84)	8. Compound entry	H.	Numbering system
(90)	9. Posting	I.	More than two accounts
(81)	10. Journal	J.	Book of final entry

PART II True or False (Accounting Theory)

(82) 11. The ledger is located in the same book as the journal.

(91) 12. The PR column of a general journal is completed after the posting to the ledger is complete.

(99) 13. Correcting errors in journalizing can be done only before posting.

(81) 14. A calendar year could be a fiscal year.

(98) 15. A trial balance could balance but be incorrect.

Continuing Problem

Tony's computer centre is picking up in business, so he has decided to expand his bookkeeping system to a general journal/ledger system. The balances from August have been forwarded to the ledger accounts. The forms are in the *Study Guide with Working Papers*, pages 3-40 to 3-45.

Assignment

1. Use the chart of accounts provided in Chapter 2 (page 79) to record the transactions illustrated by the following documents.

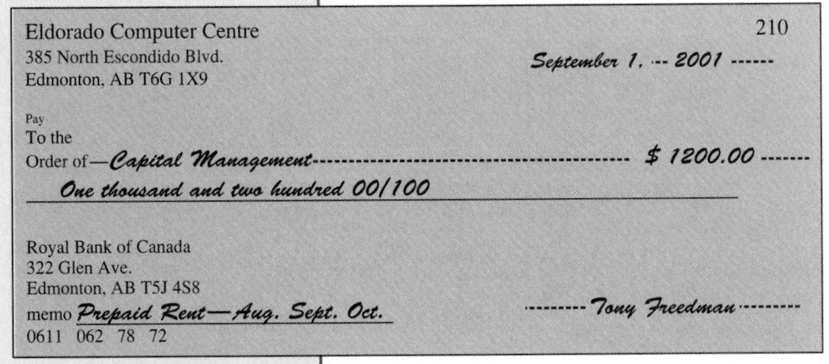

Eldorado Computer Centre 210
385 North Escondido Blvd.
Edmonton, AB T6G 1X9
September 1, -- 2001 ------

Pay
To the
Order of—*Capital Management*------------------------ *$ 1200.00* -------
One thousand and two hundred 00/100

Royal Bank of Canada
322 Glen Ave.
Edmonton, AB T5J 4S8
memo *Prepaid Rent—Aug. Sept. Oct.* --------*Tony Freedman*--------
0611 062 78 72

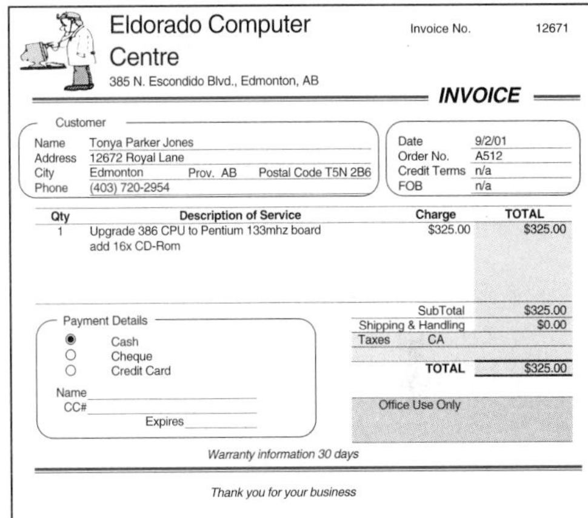

Eldorado Computer Centre
385 N. Escondido Blvd., Edmonton, AB
Invoice No. 12671
INVOICE

Customer
Name Tonya Parker Jones
Address 12672 Royal Lane
City Edmonton Prov. AB Postal Code T5N 2B6
Phone (403) 720-2954

Date 9/2/01
Order No. A512
Credit Terms n/a
FOB n/a

Qty	Description of Service	Charge	TOTAL
1	Upgrade 386 CPU to Pentium 133mhz board add 16x CD-Rom	$325.00	$325.00

Payment Details
◉ Cash
○ Cheque
○ Credit Card
Name
CC#
Expires

SubTotal $325.00
Shipping & Handling $0.00
Taxes CA
TOTAL $325.00

Office Use Only

Warranty information 30 days

Thank you for your business

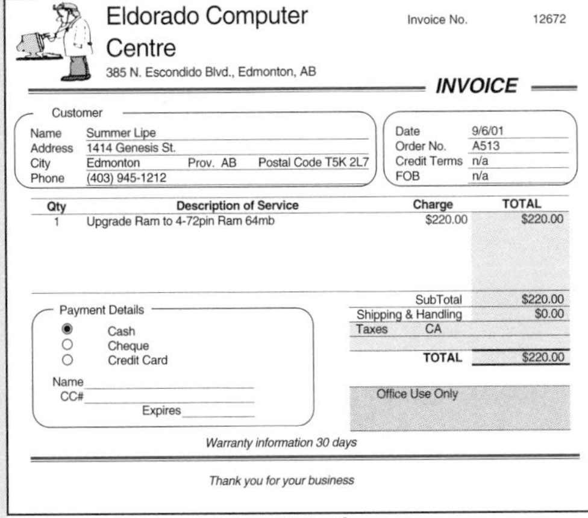

Eldorado Computer Centre
385 N. Escondido Blvd., Edmonton, AB
Invoice No. 12672
INVOICE

Customer
Name Summer Lipe
Address 1414 Genesis St.
City Edmonton Prov. AB Postal Code T5K 2L7
Phone (403) 945-1212

Date 9/6/01
Order No. A513
Credit Terms n/a
FOB n/a

Qty	Description of Service	Charge	TOTAL
1	Upgrade Ram to 4-72pin Ram 64mb	$220.00	$220.00

Payment Details
◉ Cash
○ Cheque
○ Credit Card
Name
CC#
Expires

SubTotal $220.00
Shipping & Handling $0.00
Taxes CA
TOTAL $220.00

Office Use Only

Warranty information 30 days

Thank you for your business

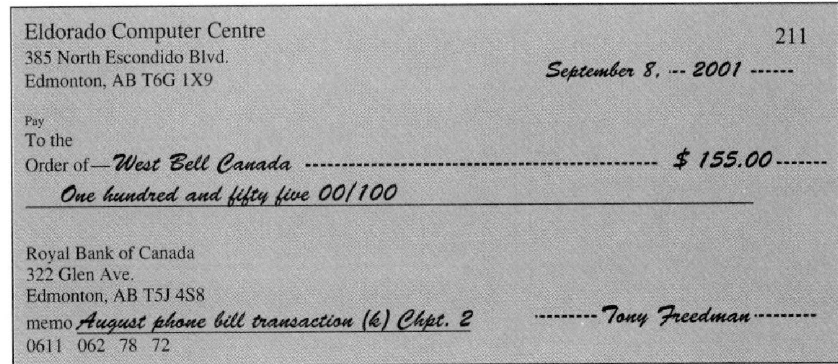

Eldorado Computer Centre 211
385 North Escondido Blvd.
Edmonton, AB T6G 1X9
September 8, -- 2001 ------

Pay
To the
Order of—*West Bell Canada* ------------------------ *$ 155.00*-------
One hundred and fifty five 00/100

Royal Bank of Canada
322 Glen Ave.
Edmonton, AB T5J 4S8
memo *August phone bill transaction (k) Chpt. 2* --------*Tony Freedman*--------
0611 062 78 72

Refer back to Chapter 2, transaction (k).

Jeannine Sparks 251
1919 Sierra St.
Edmonton, AB T6H 3J5
September 12, -- 2001 ------

Pay
To the
Order of—*Eldorado Computer Centre* ------------------------ *$ 850.00*-------
Eight Hundred and Fifty dollars 00/100

First National Bank
322 Cardiff Ave.
Edmonton, AB T5J 3E6
memo *Computer Fixed, Transaction (o) Chpt. 2* --------*Jeannine Sparks*--------
0611 062 78 72

Refer back to Chapter 2, transaction (o).

Eldorado Computer Centre 212
385 North Escondido Blvd.
Edmonton, AB T6G 1X9
September 15, -- 2001 ------

Pay
To the
Order of—*Computer Connection* ------------------------ *$ 200.00*-------
Two hundred dollars and 00/100

Royal Bank of Canada
322 Glen Ave.
Edmonton, AB T5J 4S8
memo *Account due from transaction (s) Chpt. 2* --------*Tony Freedman*--------
0611 062 78 72

Refer back to Chapter 2, transaction (s).

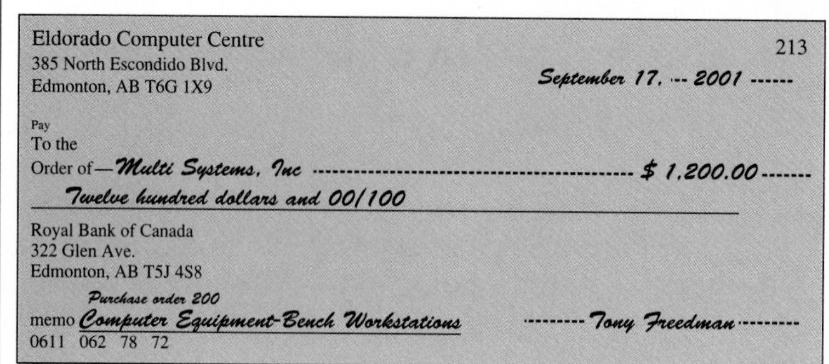

Eldorado Computer Centre
385 North Escondido Blvd.
Edmonton, AB T6G 1X9

213

September 17, --- 2001 ------

Pay
To the
Order of—Multi Systems, Inc -- $ 1,200.00 -------

Twelve hundred dollars and 00/100

Royal Bank of Canada
322 Glen Ave.
Edmonton, AB T5J 4S8

Purchase order 200
memo Computer Equipment-Bench Workstations

-------- Tony Freedman --------

0611 062 78 72

Purchased computer shop equipment.

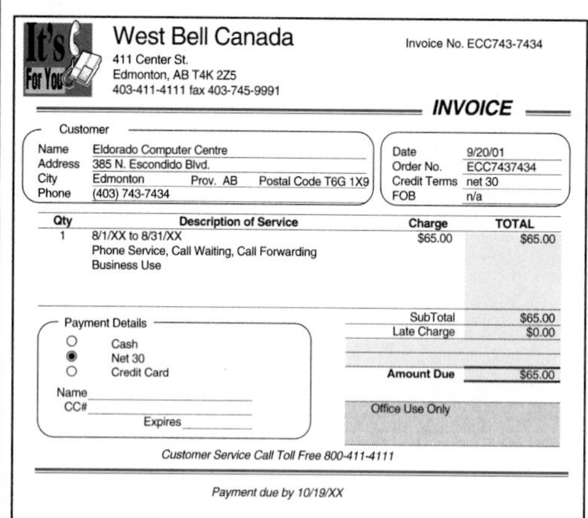

West Bell Canada
411 Center St.
Edmonton, AB T4K 2Z5
403-411-4111 fax 403-745-9991

Invoice No. ECC743-7434

INVOICE

Customer
Name: Eldorado Computer Centre
Address: 385 N. Escondido Blvd.
City: Edmonton Prov. AB Postal Code T6G 1X9
Phone: (403) 743-7434

Date: 9/20/01
Order No.: ECC7437434
Credit Terms: net 30
FOB: n/a

Qty	Description of Service	Charge	TOTAL
1	8/1/XX to 8/31/XX Phone Service, Call Waiting, Call Forwarding Business Use	$65.00	$65.00

Payment Details: ○ Cash ◉ Net 30 ○ Credit Card
Name
CC#
Expires

SubTotal	$65.00
Late Charge	$0.00
Amount Due	$65.00

Office Use Only

Customer Service Call Toll Free 800-411-4111

Payment due by 10/19/XX

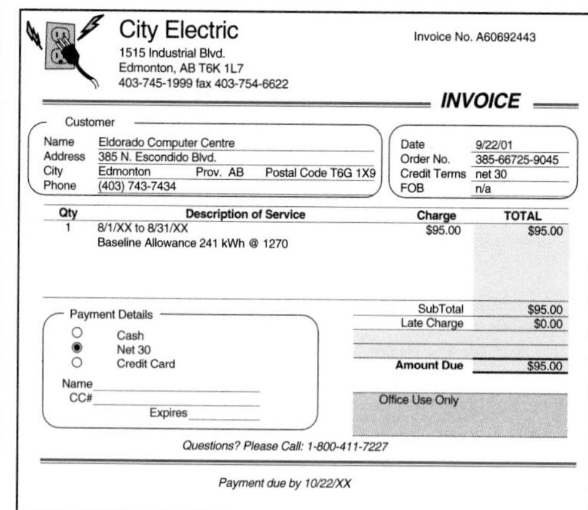

City Electric
1515 Industrial Blvd.
Edmonton, AB T6K 1L7
403-745-1999 fax 403-754-6622

Invoice No. A60692443

INVOICE

Customer
Name: Eldorado Computer Centre
Address: 385 N. Escondido Blvd.
City: Edmonton Prov. AB Postal Code T6G 1X9
Phone: (403) 743-7434

Date: 9/22/01
Order No.: 385-66725-9045
Credit Terms: net 30
FOB: n/a

Qty	Description of Service	Charge	TOTAL
1	8/1/XX to 8/31/XX Baseline Allowance 241 kWh @ 1270	$95.00	$95.00

Payment Details: ○ Cash ◉ Net 30 ○ Credit Card
Name
CC#
Expires

SubTotal	$95.00
Late Charge	$0.00
Amount Due	$95.00

Office Use Only

Questions? Please Call: 1-800-411-7227

Payment due by 10/22/XX

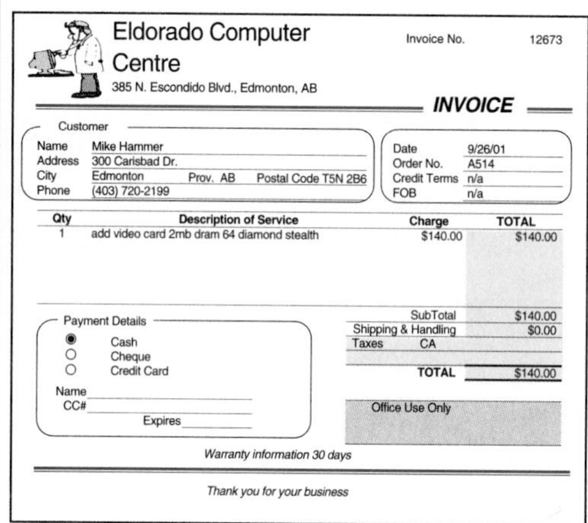

Eldorado Computer Centre
385 N. Escondido Blvd., Edmonton, AB

Invoice No. 12673

INVOICE

Customer
Name: Mike Hammer
Address: 300 Carisbad Dr.
City: Edmonton Prov. AB Postal Code T5N 2B6
Phone: (403) 720-2199

Date: 9/26/01
Order No.: A514
Credit Terms: n/a
FOB: n/a

Qty	Description of Service	Charge	TOTAL
1	add video card 2mb dram 64 diamond stealth	$140.00	$140.00

Payment Details: ◉ Cash ○ Cheque ○ Credit Card
Name
CC#
Expires

SubTotal	$140.00
Shipping & Handling	$0.00
Taxes CA	
TOTAL	$140.00

Office Use Only

Warranty information 30 days

Thank you for your business

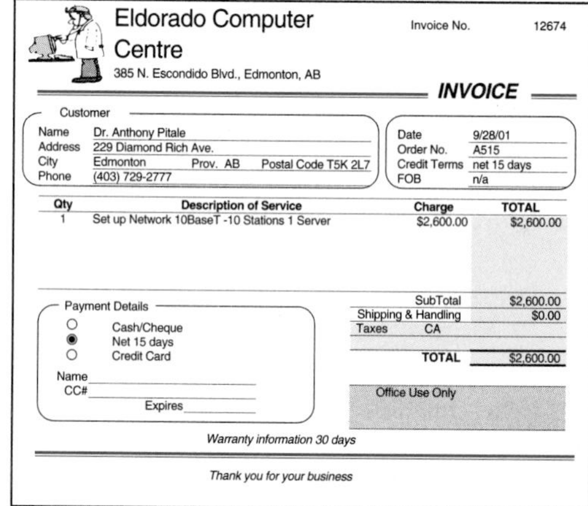

Eldorado Computer Centre
385 N. Escondido Blvd., Edmonton, AB

Invoice No. 12674

INVOICE

Customer
Name: Dr. Anthony Pitale
Address: 229 Diamond Rich Ave.
City: Edmonton Prov. AB Postal Code T5K 2L7
Phone: (403) 729-2777

Date: 9/28/01
Order No.: A515
Credit Terms: net 15 days
FOB: n/a

Qty	Description of Service	Charge	TOTAL
1	Set up Network 10BaseT -10 Stations 1 Server	$2,600.00	$2,600.00

Payment Details: ○ Cash/Cheque ◉ Net 15 days ○ Credit Card
Name
CC#
Expires

SubTotal	$2,600.00
Shipping & Handling	$0.00
Taxes CA	
TOTAL	$2,600.00

Office Use Only

Warranty information 30 days

Thank you for your business

2. Post all transactions to the general ledger accounts (the Prepaid Rent account #1025 has been added to the chart of accounts).
3. Prepare a trial balance for September 30, 2001.
4. Prepare the financial statements for the three months ended September 30, 2001.

COMPUTER WORKSHOP

Computerized Accounting Application for Chapter 3

Journalizing, Posting, General Ledger, Trial Balance, and Chart of Accounts

Before starting on this assignment, read and complete the tasks discussed in Parts A, B, and F of Appendix B: Computerized Accounting at the back of this book.

How to open the company data files

1. Click on the **Start** button. Point to Programs; point to Simply Accounting; then click on Simply Accounting in the final menu presented.
2. The *Simply Accounting®* copyright screen will appear briefly; then the Simply Accounting Open File dialogue box will appear. Insert your Student Data Files disk into disk drive A. Enter the following path into the **File name** text box: `A:\student\atlas.asc.`
3. Click on the **Open** button. The program will respond with a request for the **Session** date. The **Session** date is the date associated with the current work session. Once the **Session** date is advanced, it cannot be turned back to an earlier date.
4. Enter 12/31/01 into the **Session** text box; then click on the **OK** button. Click on the **OK** button in response to the message "The date entered is more than one week past your previous **Session** date of 12/01/01." When you start *Simply Accounting*, the file name for the company's data files (in this case Atlas) will appear in the title bar at the top of the Company Window. Your screen will look like this:

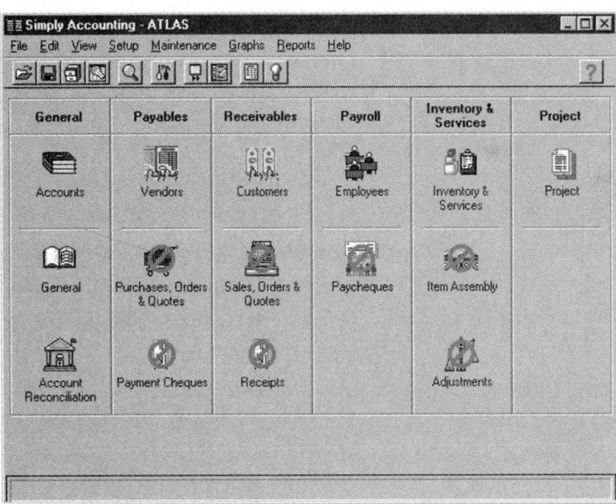

Note that the icons for Purchases, Payments, Sales, Receipts, Payroll, Transfers, and Adjustments Journals are shown with the no-entry symbol. The General Journal has no symbol. The Atlas Company will be using only the General Journal to record transactions.

How to add your name to the company name

5. It is important for you to be able to identify the specific reports that you print for each assignment as your own, particularly if you are using a computer that shares a printer with other computers. *Simply Accounting* prints the name of the company you are working with at the top of each report. To personalize your reports so that you can identify both the company and your printed reports, the company name needs to be modified to include your name:

a. Click on the **Setup** menu; then click on Company Information. The Company Information dialogue box will appear.

b. In the Company Information dialogue box use the mouse to position the insertion point immediately before "Your Name" in the **Name** text box; drag through the "Your Name" text to highlight the text; then type your name. Your screen will look similar to the one shown below:

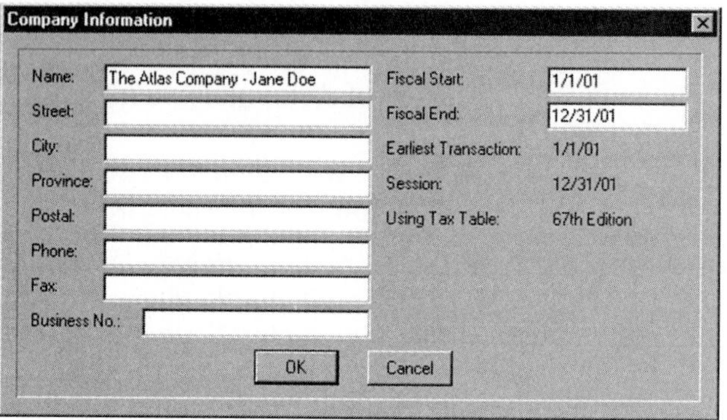

c. Click on the **OK** button to return to the Company Window.

How to record a general journal entry

6. The owner of The Atlas Company has invested $10,000 in the business. Double-click on the General icon to open the General Journal dialogue box. Enter the word "Memo" into the **Source** text box; press the TAB key; enter 12/01/01 into the **Date** text box; press the TAB key; enter "Initial investment of cash by owner" into the **Comment** text box; then press the TAB key.

   The Source text box can be used for any reference number or notation you wish to associate with a general journal entry and the source document that authorizes the entry. The Date text box is used to record the date when the transaction occurred. The Comment text box can be used for comments related to the journal entry in much the same way as an explanation is used when journal entries are recorded in a manual accounting system. Note that a flashing insertion point is positioned in the Account text box.

7. With the flashing insertion point positioned in the **Account** text box, press the ENTER key. The Select Account dialogue box will appear. Double-click on 1110 Cash. The program will enter the account number and name into the **Account** text box, and the flashing insertion point will move to the **Debits** text box.

8. Enter 10000 into the **Debits** text box; then press the TAB key. Dollar amounts can be entered in several ways. For example, to enter $50.00, type 50, or 50., or 50.00. Do not enter commas. To enter an amount containing a decimal point, type the decimal point as part of the amount. For example, enter five dollars and twenty-five cents as 5.25. The flashing insertion point will move to the **Account** text box ready for the selection of the account to be credited for this entry.

9. With the flashing insertion point positioned in the **Account** text box, press the ENTER key to bring up the Select Account dialogue box. Click on the down-arrow button on the scroll bar to the right of the Select account listing to advance the display until 3110 Owner's Capital appears. Double-click on 3110 Owner's Capital. The program will offer the same amount as the Debits portion of the entry as a default amount in the **Credits** text box. The Credits amount remains highlighted.

10. Press the TAB key to accept the default Credits amount. This completes the data you need to enter into the General Journal dialogue box to record the journal entry for the initial investment of cash by the owner. Your screen should look like this:

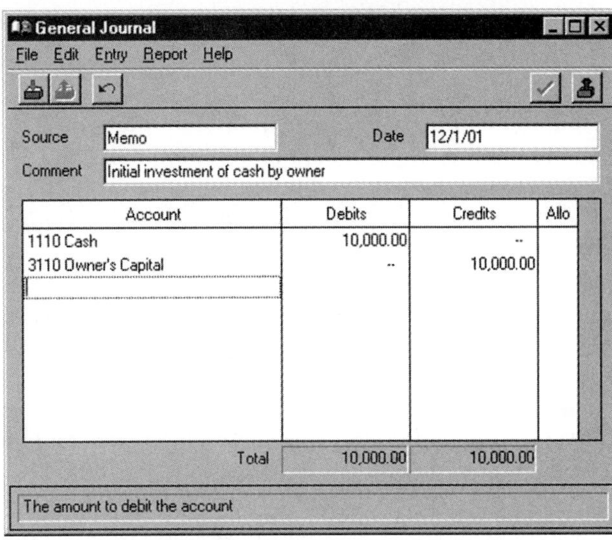

How to review a journal entry

11. Before posting this transaction, you need to verify that the transaction data are correct by reviewing the journal entry. To review the entry, click on the **General Journal Report** menu; then click on Display General Journal Entry. The journal entry representing the data you have recorded in the General Journal dialogue box is displayed. Review the journal entry for accuracy, noting any errors.

How to edit an entry prior to posting

12. Close the General Journal Entry window by clicking on the **Close** button. If you have made an error, use the following editing techniques to correct the error.

Editing a General Journal Entry

- Move to the text box that contains the error by pressing either the TAB key to move forward through each text box or the SHIFT and TAB keys together to move to a previous text box. This will highlight the selected text box information so that you can change it. Alternatively, you can use the mouse to point to a text box and drag through the incorrect information to highlight it.
- Type the correct information; then press the TAB key to enter it.
- Note that when editing a dollar amount entered into the **Debits** or **Credits** text box, the program does not automatically change the corresponding Debits or Credits amount to agree with the new amount you have entered.
- If you have associated a transaction with an incorrect account, double-click on the incorrect account; then select the correct account from the Select Account dialogue box. This will replace the incorrect account with the correct account.
- Note that the Post icon will be dimmed (unavailable) until the journal entry is in balance.
- To discard an entry and start over, click on the **Close** button. Click on the **Yes** button in response to the question "Are you sure you want to discard this journal entry?"
- Review the journal entry for accuracy after any editing corrections.

Note this point carefully!

- **It is important to note that the only way to edit a journal entry after it is posted is to reverse the entry and enter the correct journal entry.** To correct journal entries posted in error, see "Reversing an Entry Made in the General Journal Dialogue Box" in Part C of Appendix B: Computerized Accounting.

How to post an entry

13. After verifying that the journal entry is correct, click on the Post icon to post this transaction. A blank General Journal dialogue box is displayed, ready for additional General Journal transactions to be recorded.

Recording additional transactions

14. Record the following additional journal entries (enter `Memo` into the **Source** text box for each transaction; then enter the date listed for each transaction):

2001

Dec.	1	Paid rent for two months in advance, $400.
	3	Purchased office supplies on account, $100.
	9	Billed a customer for fees earned, $1,500.
	13	Paid telephone bill, $180.
	20	Owner withdrew $500 from the business.
	27	Received $450 for fees earned.
	31	Paid salaries expense, $700.

15. After you have posted the additional journal entries, click on the **Close** button to close the General Journal dialogue box. This will restore the Company Window screen, and the General Journal icon will remain highlighted.

How to display and print a general journal

16. In the Company Window, click on Reports in the menu bar; then point to Journal Entries, and click on General Journal. The General Journal Options dialogue box will appear, asking you to define the information you want displayed. Leave the **Current Year** and **By Posting Date** options buttons selected; leave the **All Ledger Entries** check box checked; enter 12/01/01 into the **Start** text box; leave the **Finish** text box date set at 12/31/01; then click on the **OK** button. The following General Journal Display will appear on your screen:

General Journal Display

File Help

12/1/01 to 12/31/01			Debits	Credits
12/1/01	J1	Memo, Initial investment of cash by owner		
		1110 Cash	10,000.00	-
		3110 Owner's Capital	-	10,000.00
12/1/01	J2	Memo, Rent paid in advance for two months		
		1140 Prepaid Rent	400.00	-
		1110 Cash	-	400.00
12/3/01	J3	Memo, Purchased office supplies on account		
		1150 Office Supplies	100.00	-
		2110 Accounts Payable	-	100.00
12/9/01	J4	Memo, Billed customers for fees earned		
		1120 Accounts Receivable	1,500.00	-
		4110 Fees Earned	-	1,500.00
12/13/01	J5	Memo, Paid telephone bill		
		5150 Telephone Expense	180.00	-
		1110 Cash	-	180.00
12/20/01	J6	Memo, Owner's personal withdrawal		
		3120 Owner's Withdrawal	500.00	-
		1110 Cash	-	500.00

Double-click to display Vendor or Customer Aged Report or Employee Report

17. The scroll bars can be used to advance the display to view other portions of the report. ***Note:*** You may display the entire General Journal Display window by clicking on the maximize icon.

18. Click on the General Journal Display **File** menu; then click on Print to print the General Journal. If you experience any difficulties with your printer (for example, the type size is too small), refer to Part F of Appendix B: Computerized Accounting for information on how to adjust the print and display settings.

What to do if you posted an incorrect entry

19. Review your printed General Journal. If you have made an error in a posted journal entry, see "Reversing an Entry Made in the General Journal Dialogue Box" in Part C of Appendix B: Computerized Accounting at the back of this book for information on how to correct the error.

How to display and print a general ledger report

20. Click on the **Close** button to close the General Journal Display window; click on the Company Window **Reports** menu; point to Financials; then click on General Ledger. The General Ledger Report Options dialogue box will appear. Leave the Current Year option button selected. Enter 12/01/01 into the **Start** text box; leave the **Finish** text box date set at 12/31/01; click on the **Select All** button; then click on the **OK** button. Your screen will look like this:

General Ledger Report

File Help

12/1/01 to 12/31/01				Debits	Credits	E
1110 Cash						
12/1/01	Initial investment of cash by o...	Memo	J1	10,000.00	-	10
12/1/01	Rent paid in advance for two ...	Memo	J2	-	400.00	9
12/13/01	Paid telephone bill	Memo	J5	-	180.00	9
12/20/01	Owner's personal withdrawal	Memo	J6	-	500.00	8
12/27/01	Received for fees earned	Memo	J7	450.00	-	9
12/31/01	Paid salaries expense	Memo	J8	-	700.00	8
				10,450.00	1,780.00	
1120 Accounts Receivable						
12/9/01	Billed customers for fees earn...	Memo	J4	1,500.00	-	1
				1,500.00	0.00	
1140 Prepaid Rent						
12/1/01	Rent paid in advance for two ...	Memo	J2	400.00	-	

Double-click to display Transaction details for current entry.

21. The scroll bars can be used to advance the display to view other portions of the report.
22. In the General Ledger Report screen, click on the **File** menu; then click on Print to print the General Ledger Report.

How to display and print a trial balance

23. Click on the **Close** button to close the General Ledger Report window; click on the Company Window **Reports** menu; point to Financials; then click on Trial Balance. The Trial Balance Options dialogue box will appear. Leave the **Select a Report** text box set at Current Year. Leave the **As at** date set at 12/31/01; then click on the **OK** button. Your screen will look like this:

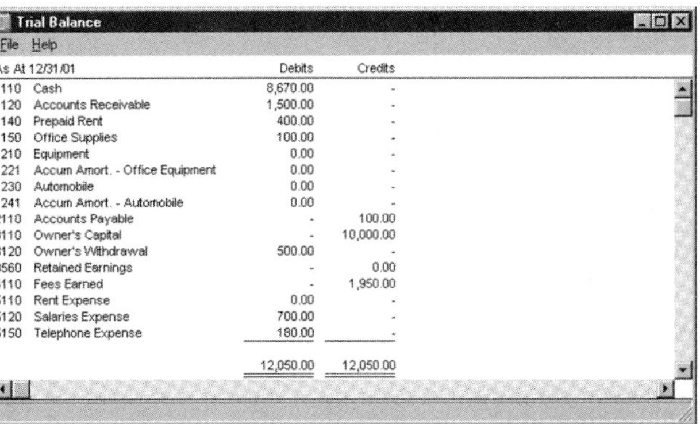

Trial Balance

File Help

As At 12/31/01		Debits	Credits
1110	Cash	8,670.00	-
1120	Accounts Receivable	1,500.00	-
1140	Prepaid Rent	400.00	-
1150	Office Supplies	100.00	-
1210	Equipment	0.00	-
1221	Accum Amort. - Office Equipment	0.00	-
1230	Automobile	0.00	-
1241	Accum Amort. - Automobile	0.00	-
2110	Accounts Payable	-	100.00
3110	Owner's Capital	-	10,000.00
3120	Owner's Withdrawal	500.00	-
3560	Retained Earnings	-	0.00
4110	Fees Earned	-	1,950.00
5110	Rent Expense	0.00	-
5120	Salaries Expense	700.00	-
5150	Telephone Expense	180.00	-
		12,050.00	12,050.00

24. The scroll bar can be used to advance the display to view other portions of the report.
25. Click on the Trial Balance **File** menu; then click on Print to print the Trial Balance.

How to display and print a chart of accounts

26. Click on the **Close** button to close the Trial Balance window; click on the Accounts icon under the General Module column in the Company Window; click the Display icon to display the Chart of Accounts.* The Chart of Accounts window will appear. Move the mouse pointer just to the right of the Cash account. The mouse pointer will appear as a magnifying glass and the **Status Bar** will indicate that you can "Double-click to display All Transactions Report for current account." Your screen will look like this:

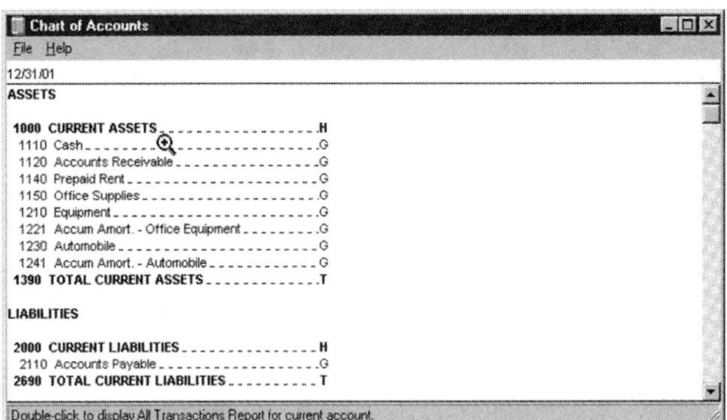

Chart of Accounts

File Help

12/31/01

ASSETS

1000 CURRENT ASSETS .... H
1110 Cash .... G
1120 Accounts Receivable .... G
1140 Prepaid Rent .... G
1150 Office Supplies .... G
1210 Equipment .... G
1221 Accum Amort. - Office Equipment .... G
1230 Automobile .... G
1241 Accum Amort. - Automobile .... G
1390 TOTAL CURRENT ASSETS .... T

LIABILITIES

2000 CURRENT LIABILITIES .... H
2110 Accounts Payable .... G
2690 TOTAL CURRENT LIABILITIES .... T

Double-click to display All Transactions Report for current account.

*You can also obtain a chart of accounts display by clicking on Reports/List in the menu bar, then clicking on Chart of Accounts.

27. Double-click with your mouse. Your screen will look like this:

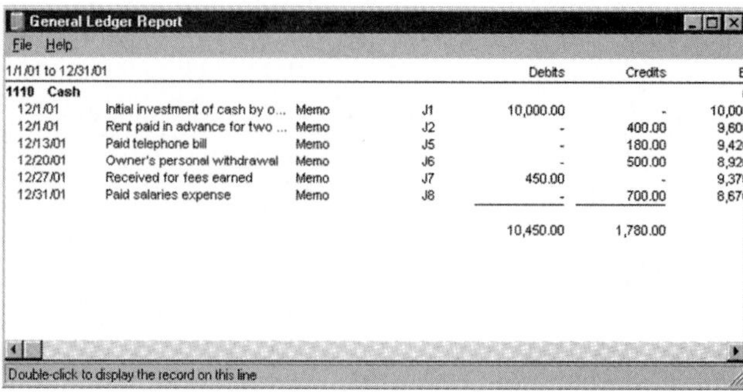

1/1/01 to 12/31/01				Debits	Credits	B
1110 Cash						
12/1/01	Initial investment of cash by o...	Memo	J1	10,000.00	-	10,00
12/1/01	Rent paid in advance for two ...	Memo	J2	-	400.00	9,60
12/13/01	Paid telephone bill	Memo	J5	-	180.00	9,42
12/20/01	Owner's personal withdrawal	Memo	J6	-	500.00	8,92
12/27/01	Received for fees earned	Memo	J7	450.00	-	9,37
12/31/01	Paid salaries expense	Memo	J8	-	700.00	8,67
				10,450.00	1,780.00	

Simply Accounting's drill-down feature

28. Going deeper into the detail that supports a report in this manner is called "drilling-down." You can drill-down to detailed supporting information on any Simply Accounting report where the mouse pointer changes to a magnifying glass. The **Status Bar** will tell you what information will appear when you double-click on an item in a report.

29. Click on the **Close** button to close the General Ledger Report window: click on the Chart of Accounts **File** menu; then click on Print to print the Chart of Accounts.

30. Click on the **Close** button to close the Chart of Accounts window and return to the Company Window.

How to exit from the program

31. Click on the Company Window **File** menu; then click on Exit to end the current work session and return to your Windows desktop. Your work will automatically be saved to your Student Data Files disk.

32. You can exit from *Simply Accounting* at any time during a current work session. Click on the Company Window **File** menu; then click on Exit. To resume working on an assignment, open the company data files; then leave the **Session** date set at the default date offered.

How to save your work during a current work session

33. To save your work during a lengthy current work session, click on the Company Window **File** menu. Click on Save; then continue with your current work session. It is a good practice to save your work about every 10 minutes or so when you are involved in a lengthy work session.

34. Your instructor may ask you to make a special backup using the Save As command in the File menu. By giving your data set a different name, you wind up with two versions of your data and can restore from an earlier copy if that is helpful.

35. A Quick Reference Guide is in Appendix B: Computerized Accounting at the back of this textbook. You will find this guide useful for locating the page number on which frequently used *Simply Accounting* procedures are explained in detail.

Completing the report transmittal

36. Complete The Atlas Company Report Transmittal located in Appendix A in your *Study Guide with Working Papers.*

The Accounting Cycle Continued

4

Preparing Worksheets and Financial Reports

The Big Picture

◆

Revenue is increasing at Eldorado Computer Centre. Tony Freedman can see the receipts from day to day. He has increased store hours, and now he's busier than ever making sure his customers are satisfied—so busy, in fact, that he was surprised when the fiscal year ended. "How well is the business doing?" Freedman wondered.

To answer that question he will have to prepare financial reports. But to prepare those reports he'll first have to gather information from his records and then make adjustments to be sure that he follows *GAAP*, "generally accepted accounting principles." Using the accrual method of accounting, GAAP's "revenue recognition principle" requires that revenue be recorded in the period in which it is earned. The GAAP "matching principle" require that expenses be matched against the revenue generated. For instance, rental and utility expenses are recorded as they are used, not necessarily when they are paid.

Following these principles sometimes requires *adjustments*, actions that bring accounts up to date. They are internal transactions that do not involve an outside party. Adjusting entries usually are made at the end of the accounting period, but some businesses make them more frequently. Accounts commonly adjusted include: prepaid accounts, supplies, long-term assets (which depreciate, or lose value, over time), interest, salaries, and taxes.

In this chapter you will learn to use a 10-column worksheet to help organize and check data in a trial balance. You'll make adjustments, adjust the trial balance, and complete the income-statement section and balance-sheet section of the worksheet. Using your worksheet, you will then prepare financial statements. These financial reports give a better picture of "how well the business is doing" than day-to-day receipts.

Chapter Objectives

- Adjustments: prepaid rent, office supplies, amortization on equipment, and accrued salaries (p.131)
- Preparation of adjusted trial balance on the worksheet (p. 137)
- The income statement and balance sheet sections of the worksheet (p. 140)
- Preparing financial reports from the worksheet (p. 143)

The accompanying diagram shows the steps of the accounting cycle that were completed for Clark's Word Processing Services in the last chapter. This chapter continues the cycle with the preparation of a worksheet and the three financial reports.

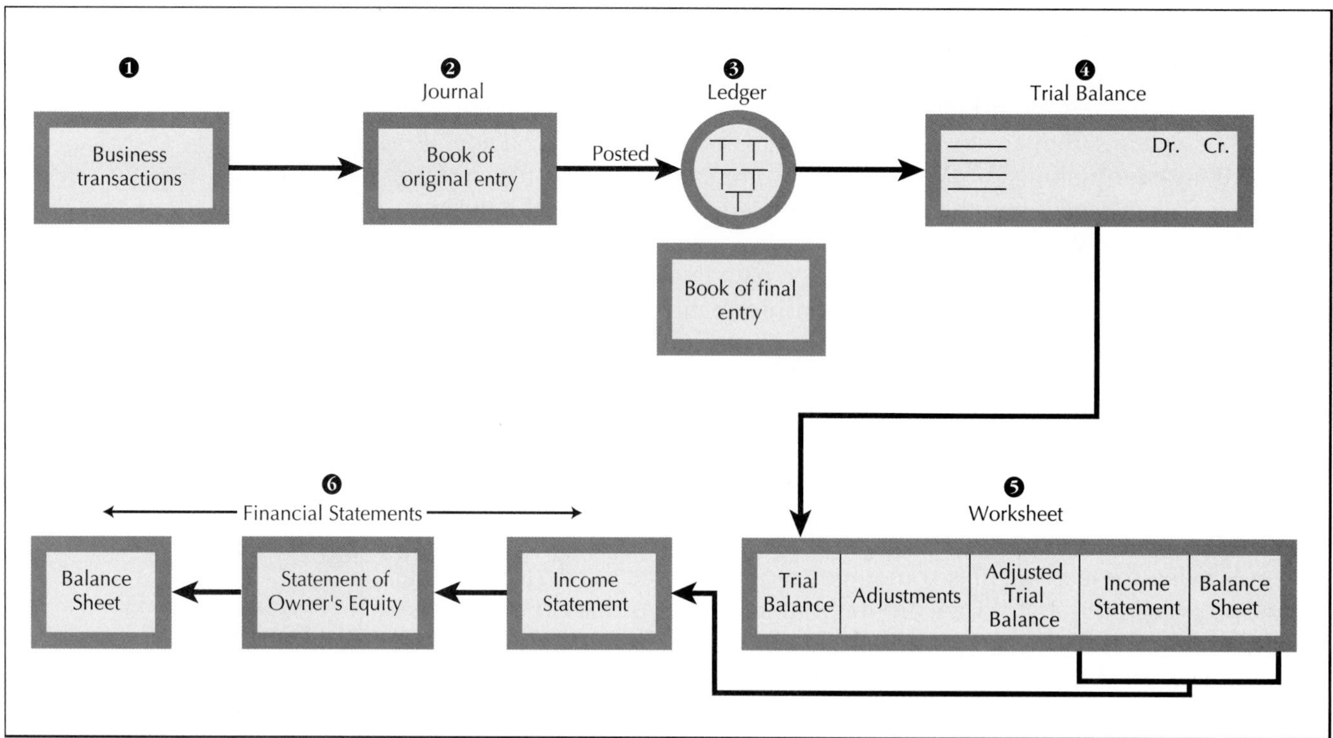

LEARNING UNIT 4-1

Step 5 of the Accounting Cycle: Preparing a Worksheet

The worksheet is not a formal report, so no dollar signs appear on it. Because it is a ruled form, there are no commas, either.

As is true for all accounting reports, the heading includes the name of the company, the name of the report, the date, and the accounting period covered.

An accountant uses a **worksheet** to organize and check data before preparing financial reports necessary to complete the accounting cycle. The most important function of the worksheet is to allow the accountant to find and correct errors before financial statements are prepared. In a way, a worksheet acts as the accountant's scratch pad. No one sees the worksheet once the formal reports are prepared. A sample worksheet is shown in Figure 4-1.

The accounts listed on the far left of the worksheet are taken from the ledger. The rest of the worksheet has five sections: trial balance, adjustments, adjusted trial balance, income statement, and balance sheet. Each of these sections is divided into debit and credit columns. Refer often to the special overlays in Figure 4-5 (following page 140b) as you study this learning unit. The transparencies illustrating the completion of a worksheet can be very useful to your understanding of the process.

CLARK'S WORD PROCESSING SERVICES
WORKSHEET
FOR MONTH ENDING MAY 31, 2001

Account Titles	Trial Balance Dr.	Trial Balance Cr.	Adjustments Dr.	Adjustments Cr.	Adjusted Trial Balance Dr.	Adjusted Trial Balance Cr.	Income Statement Dr.	Income Statement Cr.
Cash	6155 00							
Accounts Receivable	5000 00							
Office Supplies	600 00							
Prepaid Rent	1200 00							
Word Processing Equipment	6000 00							
Accounts Payable		3350 00						
Brenda Clark, Capital		10000 00						
Brenda Clark, Withdrawals	625 00							
Word Processing Fees		8000 00						
Office Salaries Expense	1300 00							
Advertising Expense	250 00							
Telephone Expense	220 00							
	21350 00	21350 00						

FIGURE 4-1
Sample Worksheet

THE TRIAL BALANCE SECTION

We discussed how to prepare a trial balance in Chapter 3. Some companies prepare a separate trial balance; others, such as Clark's Word Processing Services, prepare the trial balance directly on the worksheet. Every account in the ledger that has a balance is entered in the trial balance. Additional titles from the ledger are added as they are needed. (We will show this later.)

THE ADJUSTMENTS SECTION

Chapters 1 to 3 discussed transactions that occurred with outside suppliers and companies. In a real business, inside transactions also occur during the accounting cycle. These transactions must be recorded, too. At the end of the worksheet process, the accountant will have all of the business's accounts up to date and ready to be used to prepare the formal financial reports. By analyzing each of Clark's accounts on the worksheet, the accountant will be able to identify specific accounts that must be **adjusted** to bring them up to date. The accountant for Clark's Word Processing Services needs to adjust the following accounts:

Adjusting is like fine-tuning your TV set.

- Office Supplies
- Prepaid Rent
- Word Processing Equipment
- Office Salaries Expense

Let's look at how to analyze and adjust each of these accounts.

Adjusting the Office Supplies Account

On May 31, the accountant found out that the company had only $100 worth of office supplies on hand. When the company originally purchased the $600 worth of office supplies, they were considered an asset. But as the supplies were used up they became an expense.

The adjustment for supplies deals with the amount of supplies used up.

- Office supplies available, $600
- Office supplies left or on hand as of May 31, $100
- Office supplies used up in the operation of the business for the month of May, $500

Adjustments affect both the income statement and the balance sheet.

Office Supplies Expense 514

500	

This is supplies used up.

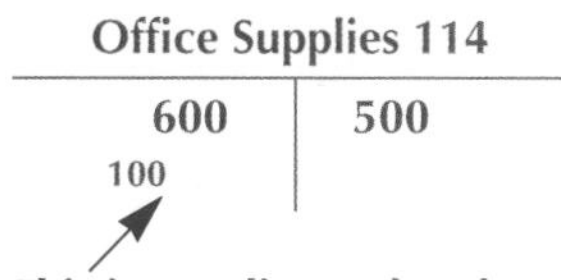

This is supplies on hand.

As a result, the asset Office Supplies is too high on the trial balance (it should be $100, not $600). At the same time, if we don't show the additional expense of supplies used, the company's *net income* will be too high.

If Clark's accountant does not adjust the trial balance to reflect the change, the company's net income would be too high on the income statement and both sides (assets and owner's equity) of the balance sheet also would be too high.

Now let's look at the adjustment for office supplies in terms of the transaction analysis chart.

Will go on income statement.

Accounts Affected	Category	↑ ↓	Rules
Office Supplies Expense	Expense	↑	Dr.
Office Supplies	Asset	↓	Cr.

Will go on balance sheet.

For our discussion, the letter A is used to code the Office Supplies adjustment because it is the first account to be adjusted.

Note:* All accounts listed below the trial balance will be *increasing.

The Office Supplies Expense account comes from the Chart of Accounts on page 83. Since it is not listed in the trial balance account titles, it must be listed below the trial balance. Let's see how we enter this adjustment on the worksheet.

Place $500 in the debit column of the adjustments section on the same line as Office Supplies Expense. Place $500 in the credit column of the adjustments section on the same line as Office Supplies. The numbers in the adjustment column show what is used, *not* what is on hand.

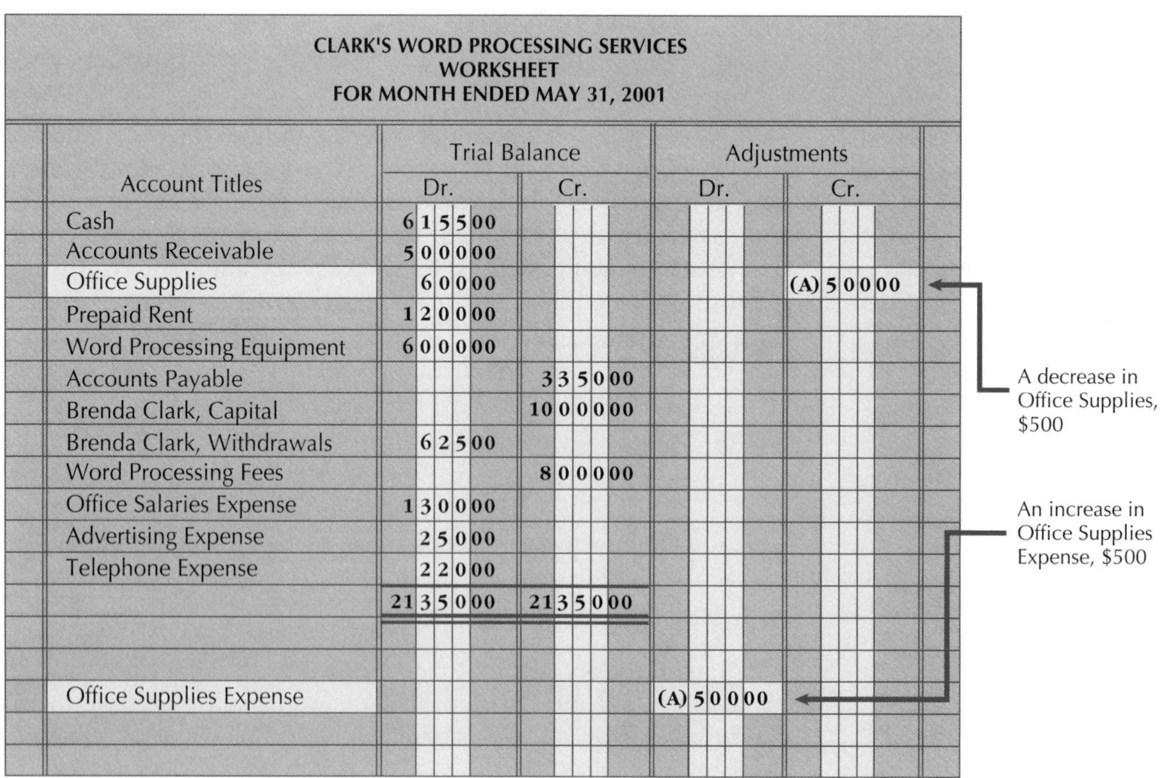

CLARK'S WORD PROCESSING SERVICES
WORKSHEET
FOR MONTH ENDED MAY 31, 2001

Account Titles	Trial Balance Dr.	Trial Balance Cr.	Adjustments Dr.	Adjustments Cr.
Cash	6155 00			
Accounts Receivable	5000 00			
Office Supplies	600 00			(A) 500 00
Prepaid Rent	1200 00			
Word Processing Equipment	6000 00			
Accounts Payable		3350 00		
Brenda Clark, Capital		10000 00		
Brenda Clark, Withdrawals	625 00			
Word Processing Fees		8000 00		
Office Salaries Expense	1300 00			
Advertising Expense	250 00			
Telephone Expense	220 00			
	21350 00	21350 00		
Office Supplies Expense			(A) 500 00	

The Office Supplies Expense account indicates the amount of supplies used up. It is listed below other trial balance accounts, since it was not on the original trial balance.

A debit will increase the account Office Supplies Expense; a credit will reduce the asset account Office Supplies.

Adjusting Prepaid Rent: On page 98 the trial balance showed a figure for Prepaid Rent of $1,200. The amount of rent *expired* is the adjustment figure used to update Prepaid Rent and Rent Expense.

Rent Expense 515

Dr.	Cr.
400	

Prepaid Rent 115

Dr.	Cr.
1,200	400 Adj.
800	

Take this one slowly.

Original cost of $6,000 for word processing equipment remains *unchanged* after adjustments.

Adjusting the Prepaid Rent Account

Back on May 1, Clark's Word Processing Services paid three months' rent in advance. The accountant realized that the rent expense would be $400 per month ($1,200 ÷ 3 months = $400).

Remember, when rent expense is paid in advance, it is considered an asset called *prepaid rent.* When the asset, prepaid rent, begins to expire or be used up it becomes an expense. Now it is May 31, and one month's prepaid rent has become an expense.

How is this handled? Should the account be $1,200, or is there really only $800 of prepaid rent left as of May 31? What do we need to do to bring prepaid rent to the "true" balance? The answer is that we must increase Rent Expense by $400 and decrease Prepaid Rent by $400.

Without this adjustment, the expenses for Clark's Word Processing Services for May will be too low, and the asset Prepaid Rent will be too high. If unadjusted amounts were used in the formal reports, the net income shown on the income statement would be too high, and both sides (assets and owner's equity) would be too high on the balance sheet.

In terms of our transaction analysis chart, the adjustment would look like this:

Accounts Affected	Category	↑ ↓	Rules
Rent Expense	Expense	↑	Dr.
Prepaid Rent	Asset	↓	Cr.

Will go on income statement. (Dr.)

Will go on balance sheet. (Cr.)

Like the Office Supplies Expense account, the Rent Expense account comes from the chart of accounts on page 83.

The worksheet on page 134 shows how to enter an adjustment to Prepaid Rent.

Adjusting the Word Processing Equipment Account for Amortization

The life of the asset affects how it is adjusted. The two accounts we discussed above, Office Supplies and Prepaid Rent, involved things that are used up relatively quickly. Equipment—like word processing equipment—is expected to last much longer. Also, it is expected to help produce revenue over a longer period. That is why accountants treat it differently. The balance sheet reports the **historical cost,** or original cost, of the equipment. The original cost also is reflected in the ledger. The adjustment shows how the cost of the equipment is allocated (spread) over its expected useful life. This spreading is called **amortization.** To amortize the equipment, we have to figure out how much its value goes down each month. Then we have to keep a running total of how that amortization mounts up over time. Revenue Canada has a specific set of rules (called Capital Cost Allowance rules) which tell how businesses in Canada may amortize their assets for tax purposes. For accounting reports, however, different methods can be used to calculate amortization. We will use the simplest method—straight-line amortization—to calculate the amortization of Clark's Word Processing Services' equipment. Under the straight-line method, equal amounts are taken over successive periods of time.

The Rent Expense is the second account to be adjusted. We label it B as a reference for our discussion.

Rent expense is listed below other trial balance accounts, since it was not on the original trial balance.

Again, note that accounts listed below the trial balance are always increasing.

CLARK'S WORD PROCESSING SERVICES
WORKSHEET
FOR MONTH ENDED MAY 31, 2001

Account Titles	Trial Balance Dr.	Trial Balance Cr.	Adjustments Dr.	Adjustments Cr.
Cash	6 1 5 5 00			
Accounts Receivable	5 0 0 0 00			
Office Supplies	6 0 0 00			(A) 5 0 0 00
Prepaid Rent	1 2 0 0 00			(B) 4 0 0 00
Word Processing Equipment	6 0 0 0 00			
Accounts Payable		3 3 5 0 00		
Brenda Clark, Capital		10 0 0 0 00		
Brenda Clark, Withdrawals	6 2 5 00			
Word Processing Fees		8 0 0 0 00		
Office Salaries Expense	1 3 0 0 00			
Advertising Expense	2 5 0 00			
Telephone Expense	2 2 0 00			
	21 3 5 0 00	21 3 5 0 00		
Office Supplies Expense			(A) 5 0 0 00	
Rent Expense			(B) 4 0 0 00	

A decrease in Prepaid Rent, $400

An increase in Rent Expense, $400

The calculation of amortization for the year for Clark's Word Processing Services is as follows:

$$\frac{\text{Cost of Equipment} - \text{Residual Value}}{\text{Estimated Years of Usefulness}}$$

Assume equipment has a 5-year life.

Word processing equipment has an expected life of approximately five years. At the end of that time, the property's value is called its "residual value." Think of **residual value** as the estimated value of the equipment at the end of the fifth year. For Clark, the equipment has an estimated residual value of $1,200.

Clark's will record $960 of amortization each year.

$$\frac{\$6{,}000 - \$1{,}200}{5 \text{ Years}} = \frac{\$4{,}800}{5} = \$960 \text{ Amortization per year}$$

Our trial balance is for one month, so we must determine the adjustment for that month:

Amortization is an expense reported on the income statement.

$$\frac{\$960}{12 \text{ Months}} = \$80 \text{ Amortization per month}$$

This $80 is known as *Amortization Expense* and will be shown on the income statement.

Next, we have to create a new account that can keep a running total of the amortization amount apart from the original cost of the equipment. That account is called **Accumulated Amortization.**

Accumulated Amortization

Dr.	Cr.
–	+

is a contra-asset account found on the balance sheet.

The Accumulated Amortization account shows the relationship between the original cost of the equipment and the amount of amortization that has been taken or accumulated over a period of time. This is a **contra-asset account**; it has a normal balance opposite that of an asset such as equipment. Accumulated Amortization will summarize, accumulate, or build up the amount of amortization that is taken on the word processing equipment over its estimated useful life.

At the end of June the accumulated amortization will be $160, but historical cost will stay at $6,000.

Remember, book value is not the same as market value.

This is how this would look on a partial balance sheet of Clark's Word Processing Services.

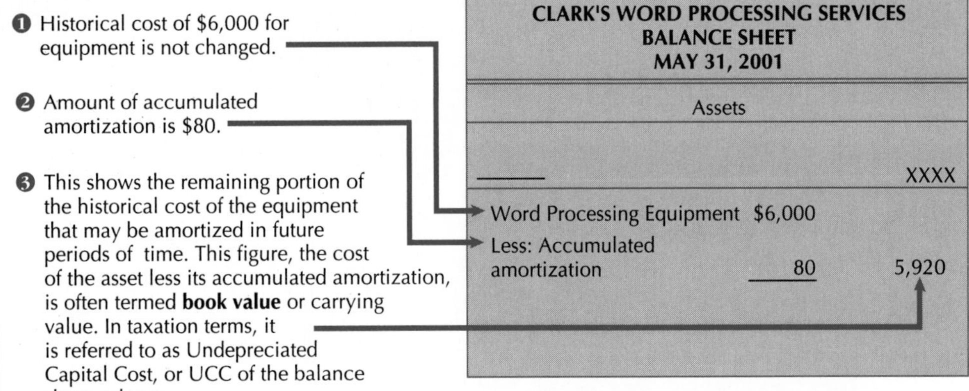

❶ Historical cost of $6,000 for equipment is not changed.
❷ Amount of accumulated amortization is $80.
❸ This shows the remaining portion of the historical cost of the equipment that may be amortized in future periods of time. This figure, the cost of the asset less its accumulated amortization, is often termed book value or carrying value. In taxation terms, it is referred to as Undepreciated Capital Cost, or UCC of the balance sheet column.
CLARK'S WORD PROCESSING SERVICES
BALANCE SHEET
MAY 31, 2001
Assets
XXXX
Word Processing Equipment $6,000
Less: Accumulated amortization 80 5,920

Recording amortization as an expense does not mean that there is any current payment of cash.

Let's summarize the key points before going on to enter the adjustment on the worksheet:

1. Amortization Expense goes on the income statement, which results in:
   a. An increase in total expenses
   b. A decrease in net income
2. Accumulated amortization is a contra-asset account found on the balance sheet next to its related equipment account.
3. The original cost of equipment is not reduced; it stays the same until the equipment is sold or removed.
4. Each month the amount in the Accumulated Amortization account grows larger, while the cost of the equipment remains the same.
5. Businesses may reduce their income tax expense by deducting Capital Cost Allowance (CCA). This CCA is similar to amortization, and some smaller businesses may use CCA values for their amortization expense.

Now, let's analyze the adjustment on the transaction analysis chart.

Amortization Expense Word Processing Equipment 516

Dr.	Cr.
80	

Accumulated Amortization Word Processing Equipment 122

Dr.	Cr.
80	

Will go on income statement.

Accounts Affected	Category	↑ ↓	Rules
Amortization Expense, Word Processing Equipment	Expense	↑	Dr.
Accumulated Amortization, Word Processing Equipment	Asset (Contra)	↑	Cr.

Will go on balance sheet.

Note that the original cost of the equipment on the worksheet has *not* been changed ($6,000).

Remember, the original cost of the equipment never changes: (1) The equipment account is not included among the affected accounts because the original cost of equipment remains the same; and (2) the original cost does not change. When the Accumulated Amortization increases (as a credit), the equipment's **book value** decreases.

The worksheet on page 136 shows how we enter the adjustment for amortization of word processing equipment.

CLARK'S WORD PROCESSING SERVICES
WORKSHEET
FOR MONTH ENDED MAY 31, 2001

Account Titles	Trial Balance Dr.	Trial Balance Cr.	Adjustments Dr.	Adjustments Cr.
Cash	6 1 5 5 00			
Accounts Receivable	5 0 0 0 00			
Office Supplies	6 0 0 00			(A) 5 0 0 00
Prepaid Rent	1 2 0 0 00			(B) 4 0 0 00
Word Processing Equipment	6 0 0 0 00			
Accounts Payable		3 3 5 0 00		
Brenda Clark, Capital		10 0 0 0 00		
Brenda Clark, Withdrawals	6 2 5 00			
Word Processing Fees		8 0 0 0 00		
Office Salaries Expense	1 3 0 0 00			
Advertising Expense	2 5 0 00			
Telephone Expense	2 2 0 00			
	21 3 5 0 00	21 3 5 0 00		
Office Supplies Expense			(A) 5 0 0 00	
Rent Expense			(B) 4 0 0 00	
Amortization Exp., W.P. Equip.			(C) 8 0 00	
Acc. Amortization, W.P. Equip.				(C) 8 0 00

An increase in Amortization Expense, Word Processing Equipment

An increase in Accumulated Amortization, Word Processing Equipment

The third account to be adjusted is assigned the letter C.

Because this is a new business, neither account had a previous balance. Therefore, neither is listed in the account titles of the trial balance. We need to list both accounts below Rent Expense in the account titles section. On the worksheet, put $80 in the debit column of the adjustments section on the same line as Amortization Expense, W. P. Equipment, and put $80 in the credit column of the adjustments section on the same line as Accumulated Amortization, W. P. Equipment.

Next month (June in our example), accumulated amortization will appear listed in the original trial balance.

Next month, on June 30, a further $80 would be entered under Amortization Expense, and Accumulated Amortization would show a balance of $160. Remember, in May Clark's was a new company, so no previous amortization was taken.

Now let's look at the last adjustment for Clark's Word Processing Services.

Accumulated Amortization	
Dr.	Cr.
	History of amount of amortization taken to date

Adjusting the Salaries Payable Account

Clark's Word Processing Services paid $1,300 in Office Salaries Expense (see the trial balance of any previous worksheet in this chapter). The last salary cheques for the month were paid on May 25. How can we update this account to show the salary expense as of May 31?

Adjusting salaries

John Murray worked for Clark's on May 28, 29, 30, and 31, but his next paycheque is not due until June 8. John earned $350 for these four days. Is the $350 an expense to Clark's in May, when it was earned, or in June when it is due and is paid?

May

S	M	T	W	T	F	S
		1	2	3	4	5
6	7	8	9	10	11	12
13	14	15	16	17	18	19
20	21	22	23	24	25	26
27	28	29	30	31		

An expense can be incurred without being paid as long as it has helped in creating earned revenue for a period of time.

Think back to Chapter 1, when we first discussed revenue and expenses. We noted then that revenue is recorded when it is earned, not when the payment is received, and expenses are recorded when they are incurred, not when they are actually paid. This principle will be discussed further in a later chapter; for now it is enough to remember that we record revenue and expenses when they occur, because we want to match earned revenue with the expenses that resulted in earning those revenues. In this case, by working those four days, John Murray created some revenue for Clark's in May. Therefore, the office salaries expense must be shown in May—the month in which the revenue was earned.

The results are:

- Office Salaries Expense is increased by $350. This unpaid and unrecorded expense for salaries for which payment is not yet due is called **accrued salaries.** In effect, we now show the true expense for salaries ($1,650 instead of $1,300):

Office Salaries Expense	
1,300	
350	

- The second result is that salaries payable is increased by $350. Clark's has created a liability called Salaries Payable, meaning that the firm owes money for salaries. When the firm pays John Murray, it will reduce its liability, Salaries Payable, as well as decrease its cash.

In terms of the transaction analysis chart, the following would be done:

Office Salaries Expense 511	
1,300	
350	

Salaries Payable 212	
	350

Accounts Affected	Category	↑ ↓	Rules
Office Salaries Expense	Expense	↑	Dr.
Salaries Payable	Liability	↑	Cr.

How the adjustment for accrued salaries is entered on the worksheet is shown at the top of page 138.

The account Office Salaries Expense is already listed in the account titles, so $350 is placed in the debit column of the adjustments section on the same line as Office Salaries Expense. However, because the Salaries Payable is not listed in the account titles, the account title Salaries Payable is added below the trial balance, below Accumulated Amortization, W. P. Equipment. Also, $350 is placed in the credit column of the adjustments section on the same line as Salaries Payable.

Now that we have finished all the adjustments that we intended to make, we total the adjustments section, as shown in Figure 4-2 (page 138).

THE ADJUSTED TRIAL BALANCE SECTION

The adjusted trial balance is the next section on the worksheet. To fill it out, we must summarize the information in the trial balance and adjustments sections, as shown in Figure 4-3 (page 139).

Note that, when the numbers are brought across from the trial balance to the adjusted trial balance, two debits will be added together and two credits will be added together. If the numbers include a debit and a credit, take the difference between the two and place it on the side which had the larger figure.

Now that we have completed the adjustments and adjusted trial balance sections of the worksheet, it is time to move on to the income statement and the balance sheet sections. Before we do that, however, look at the chart shown in Table 4-1 (page 140). This table should be used as a reference to help you in filling out the next two sections of the worksheet.

The Salaries Payable account is coded D because it is the fourth account to be added.

Remember, all accounts added below the trial balance are increasing.

CLARK'S WORD PROCESSING SERVICES
WORKSHEET
FOR MONTH ENDED MAY 31, 2001

Account Titles	Trial Balance Dr.	Trial Balance Cr.	Adjustments Dr.	Adjustments Cr.
Cash	6 155 00			
Accounts Receivable	5 000 00			
Office Supplies	600 00			(A) 500 00
Prepaid Rent	1 200 00			(B) 400 00
Word Processing Equipment	6 000 00			
Accounts Payable		3 350 00		
Brenda Clark, Capital		10 000 00		
Brenda Clark, Withdrawals	625 00			
Word Processing Fees		8 000 00		
Office Salaries Expense	1 300 00		(D) 350 00	
Advertising Expense	250 00			
Telephone Expense	220 00			
	21 350 00	21 350 00		
Office Supplies Expense			(A) 500 00	
Rent Expense			(B) 400 00	
Amortization Exp., W.P. Equip.			(C) 80 00	
Accumulated Amort., W.P. Equip.				(C) 80 00
Salaries Payable				(D) 350 00

An increase in Office Salaries Expense, $350

An increase in Salaries Payable, $350

FIGURE 4-2
The Adjustments Section of The Worksheet

CLARK'S WORD PROCESSING SERVICES
WORKSHEET
FOR MONTH ENDED MAY 31, 2001

Account Titles	Trial Balance Dr.	Trial Balance Cr.	Adjustments Dr.	Adjustments Cr.
Cash	6 155 00			
Accounts Receivable	5 000 00			
Office Supplies	600 00			(A) 500 00
Prepaid Rent	1 200 00			(B) 400 00
Word Processing Equipment	6 000 00			
Accounts Payable		3 350 00		
Brenda Clark, Capital		10 000 00		
Brenda Clark, Withdrawals	625 00			
Word Processing Fees		8 000 00		
Office Salaries Expense	1 300 00		(D) 350 00	
Advertising Expense	250 00			
Telephone Expense	220 00			
	21 350 00	21 350 00		
Office Supplies Expense			(A) 500 00	
Rent Expense			(B) 400 00	
Amortization Expense, W.P. Equip.			(C) 80 00	
Accum. Amort., W.P. Equip.				(C) 80 00
Salaries Payable				(D) 350 00
			1 330 00	1 330 00

FIGURE 4-3 The Adjusted Trial Balance Section of the Worksheet

CLARK'S WORD PROCESSING SERVICES
WORKSHEET
FOR MONTH ENDED MAY 31, 2001

Account Titles	Trial Balance Dr.	Trial Balance Cr.	Adjustments Dr.	Adjustments Cr.	Adjusted Trial Balance Dr.	Adjusted Trial Balance Cr.
Cash	6 1 5 5 00				6 1 5 5 00	
Accounts Receivable	5 0 0 0 00				5 0 0 0 00	
Office Supplies	6 0 0 00			(A) 5 0 0 00	1 0 0 00	
Prepaid Rent	1 2 0 0 00			(B) 4 0 0 00	8 0 0 00	
Word Processing Equipment	6 0 0 0 00				6 0 0 0 00	
Accounts Payable		3 3 5 0 00				3 3 5 0 00
Brenda Clark, Capital		10 0 0 0 00				10 0 0 0 00
Brenda Clark, Withdrawals	6 2 5 00				6 2 5 00	
Word Processing Fees		8 0 0 0 00				8 0 0 0 00
Office Salaries Expense	1 3 0 0 00		(D) 3 5 0 00		1 6 5 0 00	
Advertising Expense	2 5 0 00				2 5 0 00	
Telephone Expense	2 2 0 00				2 2 0 00	
	21 3 5 0 00	21 3 5 0 00				
Office Supplies Expense			(A) 5 0 0 00		5 0 0 00	
Rent Expense			(B) 4 0 0 00		4 0 0 00	
Amortization Exp., W.P. Equip.			(C) 8 0 00		8 0 00	
Accum. Amort., W.P. Equip.				(C) 8 0 00		8 0 00
Salaries Payable				(D) 3 5 0 00		3 5 0 00
			1 3 3 0 00	1 3 3 0 00	21 7 8 0 00	21 7 8 0 00

If no adjustment is made, just carry over amount from trial balance on same side.

Supplies were $600 but we used up $500, leaving us with a $100 balance in supplies. *Note:* If there are a debit and a credit, take the *difference* between the two and place it on the side which had the larger figure.

Note: Equipment is *not* adjusted here.

Two debits are added together. If two credits, they also would have been added together.

Carry these amounts over to adjusted trial balance in the same positions.

Note: The total of the left (debit) must equal the total of the right (credit) ($21,780).

TABLE 4-1 NORMAL BALANCES AND ACCOUNT CATEGORIES

Account Title	Category	Normal Balance on Adjusted Trial Balance	Income Statement Dr.	Income Statement Cr.	Balance Sheet Dr.	Balance Sheet Cr.
Cash	Asset	Dr.			X	
Accounts Receivable	Asset	Dr.			X	
Office Supplies	Asset	Dr.			X	
Prepaid Rent	Asset	Dr.			X	
Word Processing Equipment	Asset	Dr.			X	
Accounts Payable	Liability	Cr.				X
Brenda Clark, Capital	Owner's Equity	Cr.				X
Brenda Clark, Withdrawals	Owner's Equity	Dr.			X	
Word Processing Fees	Revenue	Cr.		X		
Office Salaries Expense	Expense	Dr.	X			
Advertising Expense	Expense	Dr.	X			
Telephone Expense	Expense	Dr.	X			
Office Supplies Expense	Expense	Dr.	X			
Rent Expense	Expense	Dr.	X			
Amortization Expense, W. P. Equipment	Expense	Dr.	X			
Accumulated Amortization, W. P. Equipment	Asset (Contra)	Cr.				X
Salaries Payable	Liability	Cr.				X

Keep in mind that the numbers from the adjusted trial balance are carried over to one of the last four columns of the worksheet before the bottom section is completed.

THE INCOME STATEMENT SECTION

In the worksheet, net income is placed in the debit column of the income statement. Net loss goes in the credit column.

As shown in Figure 4-4 , the income statement section lists only revenue and expenses from the adjusted trial balance. Note that Accumulated Amortization and Salaries Payable do not go on the income statement. Accumulated Amortization is a contra-asset account found on the balance sheet. Salaries Payable is a liability account found on the balance sheet.

The revenue ($8,000) and all the individual expenses are listed in the income statement section. The revenue is placed in the credit column of the income statement section because it has a credit balance. The expenses have debit balances, so they are placed in the debit column of the income statement section. The following steps must be taken after the debits and credits are placed in the correct columns:

The difference between $3,100 Dr. and $8,000 Cr. indicates a net income of $4,900. Do not think of the Net Income as a Dr. or Cr. The $4,900 is placed in the debit column to balance the two columns at $8,000. Actually, the credit side is larger by $4,900.

Step 1: Total the debits and the credits.

Step 2: Calculate the difference between the totals of the debit and credit columns and place this difference on the side with the smaller total.

Step 3: Total the two columns again.

The worksheet in Figure 4-4 shows that the label "Net Income" is added in the account title column on the same line as $4,900. When there is a net income, it will be placed in the debit column of the income statement section of the worksheet. If there is a net loss, it is placed in the credit column. The $8,000 total indicates that the two columns are in balance.

CLARK'S WORD PROCESSING SERVICES
WORKSHEET
FOR MONTH ENDED MAY 31, 2001

Account Titles	Adjusted Trial Balance Dr.	Adjusted Trial Balance Cr.	Income Statement Dr.	Income Statement Cr.
Cash	6155 00			
Accounts Receivable	5000 00			
Office Supplies	100 00			
Prepaid Rent	800 00			
Word Processing Equipment	6000 00			
Accounts Payable		3350 00		
Brenda Clark, Capital		10000 00		
Brenda Clark, Withdrawals	625 00			
Word Processing Fees		8000 00		8000 00
Office Salaries Expense	1650 00		1650 00	
Advertising Expense	250 00		250 00	
Telephone Expense	220 00		220 00	
Office Supplies Expense	500 00		500 00	
Rent Expense	400 00		400 00	
Amortization Expense, W.P. Equipment	80 00		80 00	
Accumulated Amortization, W.P. Equipment		80 00		
Salaries Payable		350 00		
	21780 00	21780 00	3100 00	8000 00
Net Income			4900 00	
			8000 00	8000 00

FIGURE 4-4 The Income Statement Section of the Worksheet

Remember: The ending figure for capital is *not* on the worksheet.

To see whether additional investments occurred for the period you must check the capital account in the ledger.

The amounts come from the adjusted trial balance, except the $4,900, which was carried over from the income statement section.

THE BALANCE SHEET SECTION

To fill out the balance sheet section of the worksheet, the following are carried over from the adjusted trial balance section: assets, contra-assets, liabilities, capital, and withdrawals. Because the beginning figure for capital is used on the worksheet, the net income is brought over to the credit column of the balance sheet so the two columns balance.

Let's now look at the completed worksheet in Figure 4-5 to see how the balance sheet section is completed. The base worksheet here provides the trial balance. When Overlay No. 1 is placed over the base worksheet, we can see all the adjustments and the adjusted trial balance. Overlay No. 2 provides the income statement items and also the balance sheet items. Finally, Overlay No. 3 totals the income statement and balance sheet columns, determines the difference, enters the difference appropriately in each statement, and totals the columns again. Note how the net income of $4,900 is brought over to the credit column of the worksheet. The figure for capital is also in the credit column, while the figure for withdrawals is in the debit column. By placing the net income in the credit column both sides total $18,680. If a net loss were to occur, it would be placed in the debit column of the balance sheet column.

CLARK'S WORD PROCESSING SERVICES
WORKSHEET
FOR MONTH ENDED MAY 31, 2001

Account Titles	Trial Balance		Adjustments		Adjusted Trial Balance		Income Statement		Balance Sheet	
	Dr.	Cr.	Dr.	Cr.	Dr.	Cr.	Dr.	Cr.	Dr.	Cr.
Cash	6155 00									
Accounts Receivable	5000 00									
Office Supplies	600 00									
Prepaid Rent	1200 00									
Word Processing Equipment	6000 00									
Accounts Payable		3350 00								
Brenda Clark, Capital		10000 00								
Brenda Clark, Withdrawals	625 00									
Word Processing Fees		8000 00								
Office Salaries Expense	1300 00									
Advertising Expense	250 00									
Telephone Expense	220 00									
	21350 00	21350 00								

FIGURE 4-5 Sample Worksheet

Flip to Overlay No. 1 — Adjustments A, B, C, and D

Now that we have completed the worksheet, we can go on to the three financial reports. But first let's summarize our progress.

LEARNING UNIT 4-1 REVIEW

AT THIS POINT you should be able to:

- Define and explain the purpose of a worksheet. (p. 130)
- Explain the need as well as the process for adjustments. (p. 131)
- Explain the concept of amortization. (p. 133)
- Explain the difference between amortization expense and accumulated amortization. (p. 135)
- Prepare a worksheet from a trial balance and adjustment data. (p. 137)

SELF-REVIEW QUIZ 4-1

From the accompanying trial balance and adjustment data, complete a worksheet for P. Logan Company for the month ended December 31, 2003. (You can use a blank foldout worksheet located at the end of the *Study Guide with Working Papers.*)

Note: The numbers used in this quiz may seem impossibly small, but we have done that on purpose, so that at this point you don't have to worry about arithmetic, just about preparing the worksheet correctly.

P. LOGAN COMPANY
TRIAL BALANCE
DECEMBER 31, 2003

	Dr.	Cr.
Cash	15 00	
Accounts Receivable	3 00	
Prepaid Insurance	3 00	
Store Supplies	5 00	
Store Equipment	6 00	
Accumulated Amortization, Store Equipment		4 00
Accounts Payable		2 00
P. Logan, Capital		14 00
P. Logan, Withdrawals	3 00	
Revenue from Clients		25 00
Rent Expense	2 00	
Salaries Expense	8 00	
	45 00	45 00

Adjustment Data

a. Amortization Expense, Store Equipment, $1
b. Insurance Expired, $2
c. Supplies on hand, $1
d. Salaries owed but not paid to employees, $3

Solution to Self-Review Quiz 4-1

Don't adjust this line! Store Equipment always contains the historical cost.

P. LOGAN COMPANY
WORKSHEET
FOR MONTH ENDED DECEMBER 31, 2003

Account Titles	Trial Balance Dr.	Trial Balance Cr.	Adjustments Dr.	Adjustments Cr.	Adjusted Trial Balance Dr.	Adjusted Trial Balance Cr.	Income Statement Dr.	Income Statement Cr.	Balance Sheet Dr.	Balance Sheet Cr.
Cash	15 00				15 00				15 00	
Accounts Receivable	3 00				3 00				3 00	
Prepaid Insurance	3 00			(B) 2 00	1 00				1 00	
Store Supplies	5 00			(C) 4 00	1 00				1 00	
Store Equipment	6 00				6 00				6 00	
Accumulated Amortization, Store Equipment		4 00		(A) 1 00		5 00				5 00
Accounts Payable		2 00				2 00				2 00
P. Logan, Capital		14 00				14 00				14 00
P. Logan, Withdrawals	3 00				3 00				3 00	
Revenue from Clients		25 00				25 00		25 00		
Rent Expense	2 00				2 00		2 00			
Salaries Expense	8 00		(D) 3 00		11 00		11 00			
	45 00	45 00								
Amortization Expense, Store Equipment			(A) 1 00		1 00		1 00			
Insurance Expense			(B) 2 00		2 00		2 00			
Supplies Expense			(C) 4 00		4 00		4 00			
Salaries Payable				(D) 3 00		3 00				3 00
			10 00	10 00	49 00	49 00	20 00	25 00	29 00	24 00
Net Income							5 00			5 00
							25 00	25 00	29 00	29 00

Note that Accumulated Amortization is listed in trial balance, since this is not a new company. Store Equipment has already been amortized $4 from an earlier period.

Quiz Tip

The adjustment for supplies worth $4 represents the amount *used up*. The *on hand* amount of $1 ends up on the adjusted trial balance.

LEARNING UNIT 4-2

Step 6 of the Accounting Cycle: Preparing the Financial Statements from the Worksheet

The formal financial reports can be prepared from the worksheet completed in Learning Unit 4-1. Before beginning, we must check that the entries on the worksheet are correct and in balance. To do this, we have to be sure that (1) all entries are recorded in the appropriate columns, (2) the correct amounts are entered in the proper places, (3) the addition is correct across the columns (i.e., from the trial balance to the adjusted trial balance to the financial reports), and (4) the columns are added correctly.

PREPARING THE INCOME STATEMENT

The first report to be prepared for Clark's Word Processing Services is the income statement. When preparing the income statement, it is important to remember that:

1. Every figure on the formal report is on the worksheet. Figure 4-6 (page 144) shows where each of these figures goes on the income statement.
2. There are no debit or credit columns on the formal report.
3. The inside column on financial reports is used for subtotalling.
4. Withdrawals do not go on the income statement; they go on the statement of owner's equity.

Take a moment to look at the income statement in Figure 4-6. Note which items go where from the income statement section of the worksheet onto the formal report.

PREPARING THE STATEMENT OF OWNER'S EQUITY

Figure 4-7 (page 144) is the statement of owner's equity for Clark's. The figure shows from where on the worksheet the information comes. It is important to remember that, if there were additional investments, the figure on the worksheet for capital would not be the beginning figure for capital. Checking the ledger account for capital will tell you whether the amount is correct. Note how net income and withdrawals aid in calculating the new figure for capital.

PREPARING THE BALANCE SHEET

In preparing the balance sheet (page 145), remember that the balance sheet section totals on the worksheet ($18,680) do *not* usually match the totals on the formal balance sheet ($17,975). This is because information is grouped differently on the formal report. First, in the formal report, Accumulated Amortization ($80) is subtracted from Word Processing Equipment, reducing the balance. Second, Withdrawals ($625) are subtracted from Owner's Equity, reducing the balance further. These two reductions (–$80 + [–$625] = –$705) represent the difference between the worksheet and the formal version of the balance sheet ($17,975 – $18,680 = –$705). Figure 4-8 (page 145) shows how to prepare the balance sheet from the worksheet.

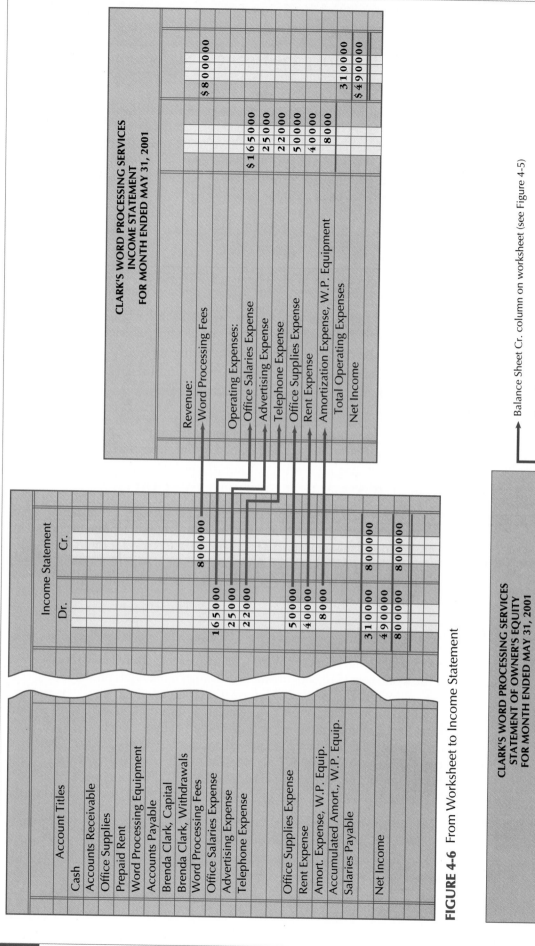

Account Titles	Income Statement Dr.	Income Statement Cr.
Cash		
Accounts Receivable		
Office Supplies		
Prepaid Rent		
Word Processing Equipment		
Accounts Payable		
Brenda Clark, Capital		
Brenda Clark, Withdrawals		
Word Processing Fees		800000
Office Salaries Expense	165000	
Advertising Expense	25000	
Telephone Expense	22000	
Office Supplies Expense	50000	
Rent Expense	40000	
Amort. Expense, W.P. Equip.	8000	
Accumulated Amort., W.P. Equip.		
Salaries Payable		
	310000	800000
Net Income	490000	
	800000	800000

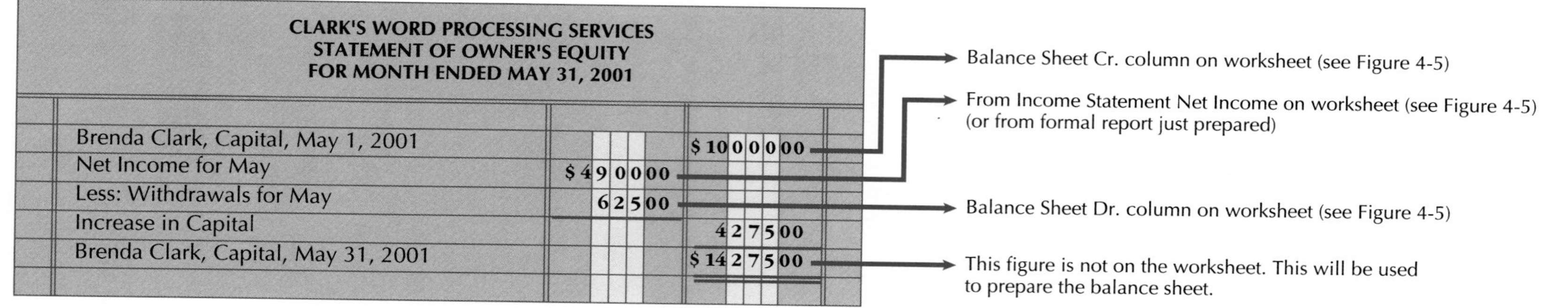

CLARK'S WORD PROCESSING SERVICES
INCOME STATEMENT
FOR MONTH ENDED MAY 31, 2001

Revenue:		
Word Processing Fees		$800000
Operating Expenses:		
Office Salaries Expense	$165000	
Advertising Expense	25000	
Telephone Expense	22000	
Office Supplies Expense	50000	
Rent Expense	40000	
Amortization Expense, W.P. Equipment	8000	
Total Operating Expenses		310000
Net Income		$490000

FIGURE 4-6 From Worksheet to Income Statement

CLARK'S WORD PROCESSING SERVICES
STATEMENT OF OWNER'S EQUITY
FOR MONTH ENDED MAY 31, 2001

Brenda Clark, Capital, May 1, 2001		$1000000
Net Income for May	$490000	
Less: Withdrawals for May	62500	
Increase in Capital		427500
Brenda Clark, Capital, May 31, 2001		$1427500

Balance Sheet Cr. column on worksheet (see Figure 4-5)

From Income Statement Net Income on worksheet (see Figure 4-5) (or from formal report just prepared)

Balance Sheet Dr. column on worksheet (see Figure 4-5)

This figure is not on the worksheet. This will be used to prepare the balance sheet.

FIGURE 4-7 Completing a Statement of Owner's Equity

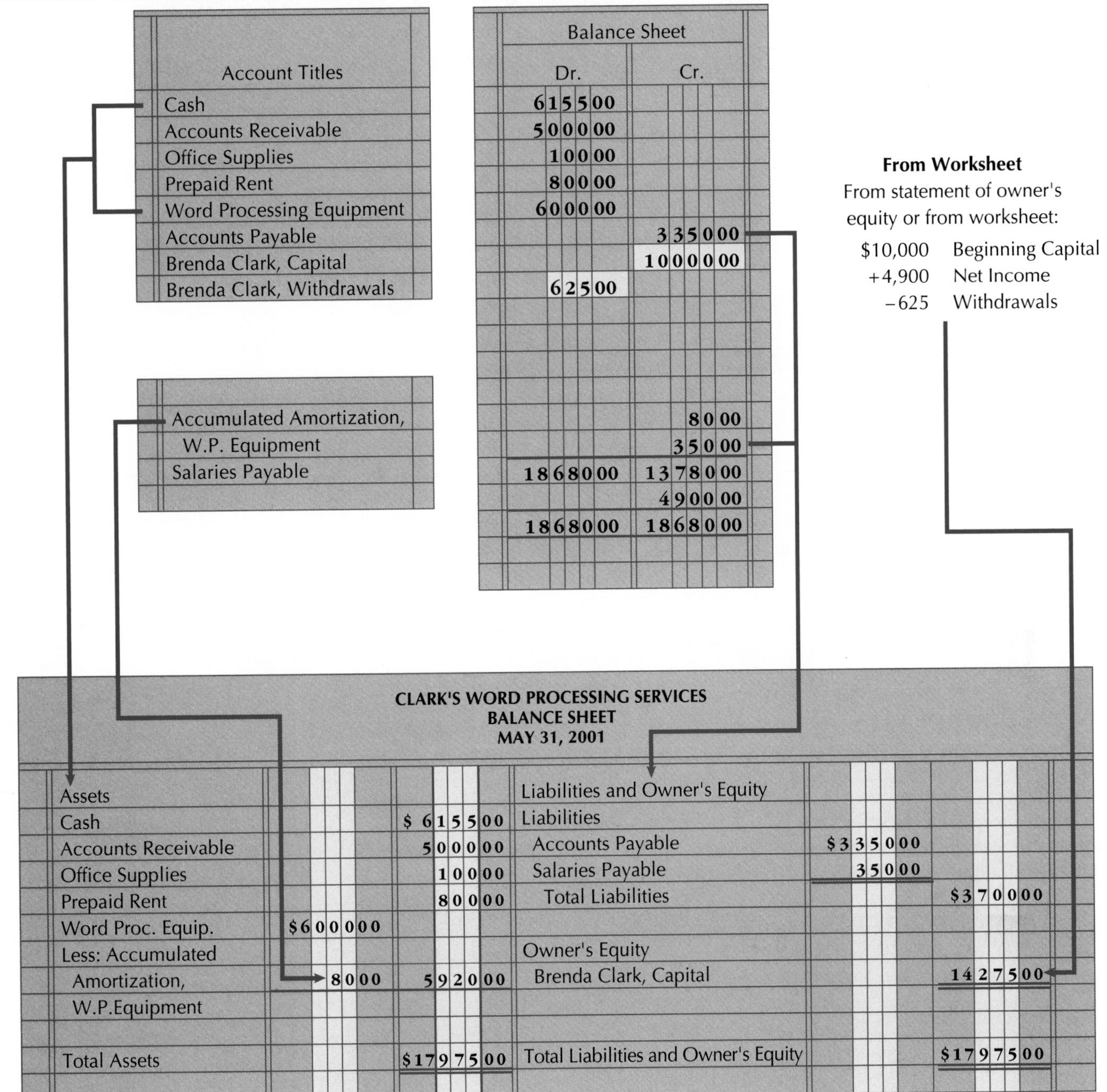

FIGURE 4-8 From Worksheet to Balance Sheet

LEARNING UNIT 4-2 REVIEW

AT THIS POINT you should be able to:

- Prepare the three financial reports from a worksheet. (p. 143)
- Explain why totals of the formal balance sheet don't match totals of balance sheet columns on the worksheet. (p. 143)

SELF-REVIEW QUIZ 4-2

(The forms you need are located on pages 4-2 and 4-3 of the *Study Guide with Working Papers.*)

From the worksheet on page 142 for P. Logan, prepare (1) an income statement for December; (2) a statement of owner's equity; and (3) a balance sheet for December 31, 2003. No additional investments took place during the period.

Solution to Self-Review Quiz 4-2

Quiz Tip

The income statement is made up of revenue and expenses. Use the inside column for subtotalling.

P. LOGAN COMPANY
INCOME STATEMENT
FOR THE MONTH ENDED DECEMBER 31, 2003

Revenue:		
Revenue from clients		$2500
Operating Expenses:		
Rent Expense	$200	
Salaries Expense	1100	
Amortization Expense, Store Equipment	100	
Insurance Expense	200	
Supplies Expense	400	
Total Operating Expenses		2000
Net Income		$500

Quiz Tip

The $5 on the income statement is used to update the statement of owner's equity.

P. LOGAN COMPANY
STATEMENT OF OWNER'S EQUITY
FOR THE MONTH ENDED DECEMBER 31, 2003

P. Logan, Capital, December 1, 2003		$1400
Net Income for December	$500	
Less: Withdrawals for December	300	
Increase in Capital		200
P. Logan, Capital, December 31, 2003		$1600

Quiz Tip

The ending capital figure on the statement of owner's equity ($16) is used as the capital figure on the balance sheet.

P. LOGAN COMPANY
BALANCE SHEET
DECEMBER 31, 2003

Assets			Liabilities and Owner's Equity		
Cash		$1500	Liabilities		
Accounts Receivable		300	Accounts Payable	$200	
Prepaid Insurance		100	Salaries Payable	300	
Store Supplies		100	Total Liabilities		$500
Store Equipment	$600		Owner's Equity		
Less Accumulated Amortization, Store Equipment	500	100	P. Logan, Capital		1600
			Total Liabilities and Owner's Equity		
Total Assets		$2100			$2100

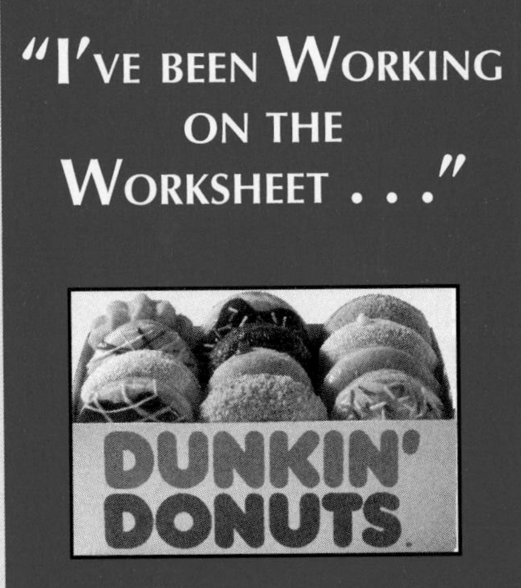

"I'VE BEEN WORKING ON THE WORKSHEET . . ."
DUNKIN'
DONUTS

Fred has dreams. Big ones. He wants to develop his business to the point where he can start another Dunkin' Donuts shop. To do that, Fred realizes that he will have to manage his current shop more efficiently. His doughnuts and muffins are widely praised, and his bagel line is so successful that he has hired more help. But along with this success has come more paperwork. Fred now spends hours on his accounts.

Dunkin' Donuts' business consultant, Dwayne Goulding, knows that Fred needs to reduce the time he spends handling his accounts. Dwayne has suggested that Fred hire an accountant, or that he switch to a computerized accounting system, as many owners have done recently. Fred has been hesitant to do either, because he wants to control the finances himself. And save money. And he fears computers. What to do?

Seeing Fred's dilemma, Dwayne encourages him to contact his zone's Advisory Council. This Advisory Council, like hundreds across the country, offers fellow Dunkin' Donuts shop owners from the same zone a chance to get together to share ways to improve their operations and discuss common problems. They work with Dwayne and the rest of the Dunkin' Donuts managerial team to keep their interdependent businesses running smoothly and profitably.

When Fred approaches the Council, they are very supportive. "I've been there, Fred, so I know how you feel," says Joe Franklin, from two towns away. "First, you're on the right track when you prepare a worksheet. It's too easy to mess up if you try to skip this step. Next, you might want to try keeping a clean copy of last month's worksheet. Even though you don't have to submit it to Dwayne, you frequently have to go back and refer to it when questions come up on your income statement or balance sheet. When your worksheet is all crossed out and doodled on, like this one is, you can't find info fast. Also, you may need your worksheets at tax time. I sure found that out the hard way!"

Discussion Questions

1. What is an Advisory Council? Why do you think that Dwayne recommended that Fred seek their advice?
2. Why do you think that some small business owners fear computerization and equate it with a loss of financial control?
3. Why is a clean worksheet helpful even after that month's statements have been prepared?

Chapter Review

COMPREHENSIVE DEMONSTRATION PROBLEM WITH SOLUTION TIPS

(The blank forms you need are on pages 4-4 and 4-5 of the *Study Guide with Working Papers.*)

From the following trial balance and additional data, (1) complete a worksheet and (2) prepare the three financial reports (numbers are intentionally small so you may concentrate on the theory).

Frost Company
Trial Balance
December 31, 2002

	Dr.	*Cr.*
Cash	14	
Accounts Receivable	4	
Prepaid Insurance	5	
Plumbing Supplies	3	
Plumbing Equipment	7	
Accumulated Amortization, Plumbing Equipment		5
Accounts Payable		1
J. Frost, Capital		12
J. Frost, Withdrawals	3	
Plumbing Fees		27
Rent Expense	4	
Salaries Expense	5	
Totals	45	45

Adjustment Data

a. Insurance expired $3
b. Plumbing supplies on hand $1
c. Amortization Expense, Plumbing Equipment $1
d. Salaries owed but not paid to employees $2

Solution Tips for Building a Worksheet

1. Adjustments

a.

Insurance Expense	**Expense**	↑	**Dr.**	**$3**
Prepaid Insurance	**Asset**	↓	**Cr.**	**$3**

Expired means used up.

b.

Plumbing Supplies Expense	**Expense**	↑	**Dr.**	**$2**
Plumbing Supplies	**Asset**	↓	**Cr.**	**$2**

$3 − $1 on hand = $2 *used up!*

FROST COMPANY
WORKSHEET
FOR MONTH ENDED DECEMBER 31, 2002

Account Titles	Trial Balance		Adjustments		Adjusted Trial Balance		Income Statement		Balance Sheet	
	Dr.	Cr.	Dr.	Cr.	Dr.	Cr.	Dr.	Cr.	Dr.	Cr.
Cash	1400				1400				1400	
Accounts Receivable	400				400				400	
Prepaid Insurance	500			(A) 300	200				200	
Plumbing Supplies	300			(B) 200	100				100	
Plumbing Equipment	700				700				700	
Accumulated Amortization, Plumbing Equipment		500		(C) 100		600				600
Accounts Payable		100				100				100
J. Frost, Capital		1200				1200				1200
J. Frost, Withdrawals	300				300				300	
Plumbing Fees		2700				2700		2700		
Rent Expense	400				400		400			
Salaries Expense	500		(D) 200		700		700			
	4500	4500								
Insurance Expense			(A) 300		300		300			
Plumbing Supplies Expense			(B) 200		200		200			
Amortization Expense Plumbing Equipment			(C) 100		100		100			
Salaries Payable				(D) 200		200				200
			800	800	4800	4800	1700	2700	3100	2100
Net Income							1000			1000
							2700	2700	3100	3100

c.

Amortization Expense, Plumbing Equipment	Expense	↑	Dr.	$1
Accumulated Amortization, Plumbing Equipment	Asset (Contra)	↑	Cr.	$1

The original cost of equipment of $7 is not "touched."

d.

Salaries Expense	Expense	↑	Dr.	$2
Salaries Payable	Liability	↑	Cr.	$2

2. Last four columns of worksheet are prepared from adjusted trial balance.
3. Capital of $12 is the old figure. Net income of $10 (revenue − expenses) is brought over to same side as capital on the balance sheet Cr. column to balance columns.

Frost Company
Income Statement
for Month Ended December 31, 2002

Revenue:		
Plumbing Fees		$27
Operating Expenses:		
Rent Expense	$4	
Salaries Expense	7	
Insurance Expense	3	
Plumbing Supplies Expense	2	
Amortization Expense, Plumbing Equipment	1	
Total Operating Expenses		17
Net Income		$10

Frost Company
Statement of Owner's Equity
for Month ended December 31, 2002

J. Frost, Capital, December 1, 2002		$12
Net Income for December	$10	
Less: Withdrawals for December	3	
Increase in Capital		7
J. Frost, Capital, December 31, 2002		$19

Frost Company
Balance Sheet
December 31, 2002

Assets			Liabilities and Owner's Equity		
Cash		$14	Liabilities:		
Accounts Receivable		4	Accounts Payable	$1	
Prepaid Insurance		2	Salaries Payable	2	
Plumbing Supplies		1	Total Liabilities		$3
Plumbing Equipment	$7				
Less: Accum. Amort.	6	1	Owner's Equity:		
			J. Frost, Capital		19
Total Assets		$22	Total Liabilities and Owner's Equity		$22

Solution Tips for Preparing Financial Reports from a Worksheet

The inside columns of the three financial reports are used for subtotalling. There are no debits or credits on the formal reports.

Report	
Income statement	From income statement columns of worksheet for revenue and expenses
Statement of owner's equity	From balance sheet Cr. column for old figure for Capital; Net Income from income statement; from balance sheet Dr. column for Withdrawals figure
Balance sheet	From balance sheet Dr. column for assets; from balance sheet Cr. column for Liabilities and Accumulated Amortization; new figure for Capital from statement of owner's equity

Note how Plumbing Equipment $7 and Accumulated Amortization $6 are rearranged on the formal balance sheet. The total assets figure of $22 is not on the worksheet. Remember that there are no debits or credits on formal reports.

Summary of Key Points

Learning Unit 4-1

1. The worksheet is not a formal report.
2. Adjustments update certain accounts so that they will be up to their latest balance before financial reports are prepared. Adjustments are the result of internal transactions.
3. Adjustments will affect both the income statement and the balance sheet.
4. Accounts listed *below* the account titles on the trial balance of the worksheet are *increasing*.
5. The original cost of a piece of equipment is not adjusted; historical cost is not lost.
6. Amortization is the process of spreading the original cost of the asset over its expected useful life.
7. Accumulated amortization is a contra-asset on the balance sheet that summarizes, accumulates, or builds up the amount of amortization that an asset has accumulated.
8. Book value is the original cost less accumulated amortization.
9. Accrued salaries are unpaid and unrecorded expenses that are accumulating but for which payment is not yet due.
10. Revenue and expenses go on income statement sections of the worksheet. Assets, contra-assets, liabilities, capital, and withdrawals go on balance sheet sections of the worksheet.

Learning Unit 4-2

1. The formal reports prepared from a worksheet do not have debit or credit columns.

2. Revenue and expenses go on the income statement. Beginning capital plus net income less withdrawals (or beginning capital minus net loss, less withdrawals) goes on the statement of owner's equity. Be sure to check the capital account in the ledger to see if any additional investments took place. Assets, contra-assets, liabilities, and the new figure for capital go on the balance sheet.

KEY TERMS

Accrued salaries Salaries that are earned by employees but unpaid and unrecorded during the period (and thus need to be recorded by an adjustment) and will not come due for payment until the next accounting period (p. 137)

Accumulated amortization A contra-asset account that summarizes or accumulates the amount of amortization that has been taken on an asset (p. 134)

Adjusting The process of calculating the latest up-to-date balance of each account at the end of an accounting period (p. 131)

Amortization The allocation (spreading) of the cost of an asset (such as an auto or equipment) over its expected useful life (p. 133)

Book value Cost of equipment less accumulated amortization (p. 135)

Contra-asset account An account which causes another, related account to be restated or revalued. Its normal balance is a credit, which reduces the net asset value (p. 134)

Historical cost The actual cost of an asset at time of purchase (p. 133)

Residual value Book value of an asset after all the allowable amortization has been deducted (p. 134)

Worksheet A columnar device used by accountants to aid them in completing the accounting cycle. It is not a formal report (p. 130)

Blueprint of Steps 5 and 6 of the Accounting Cycle

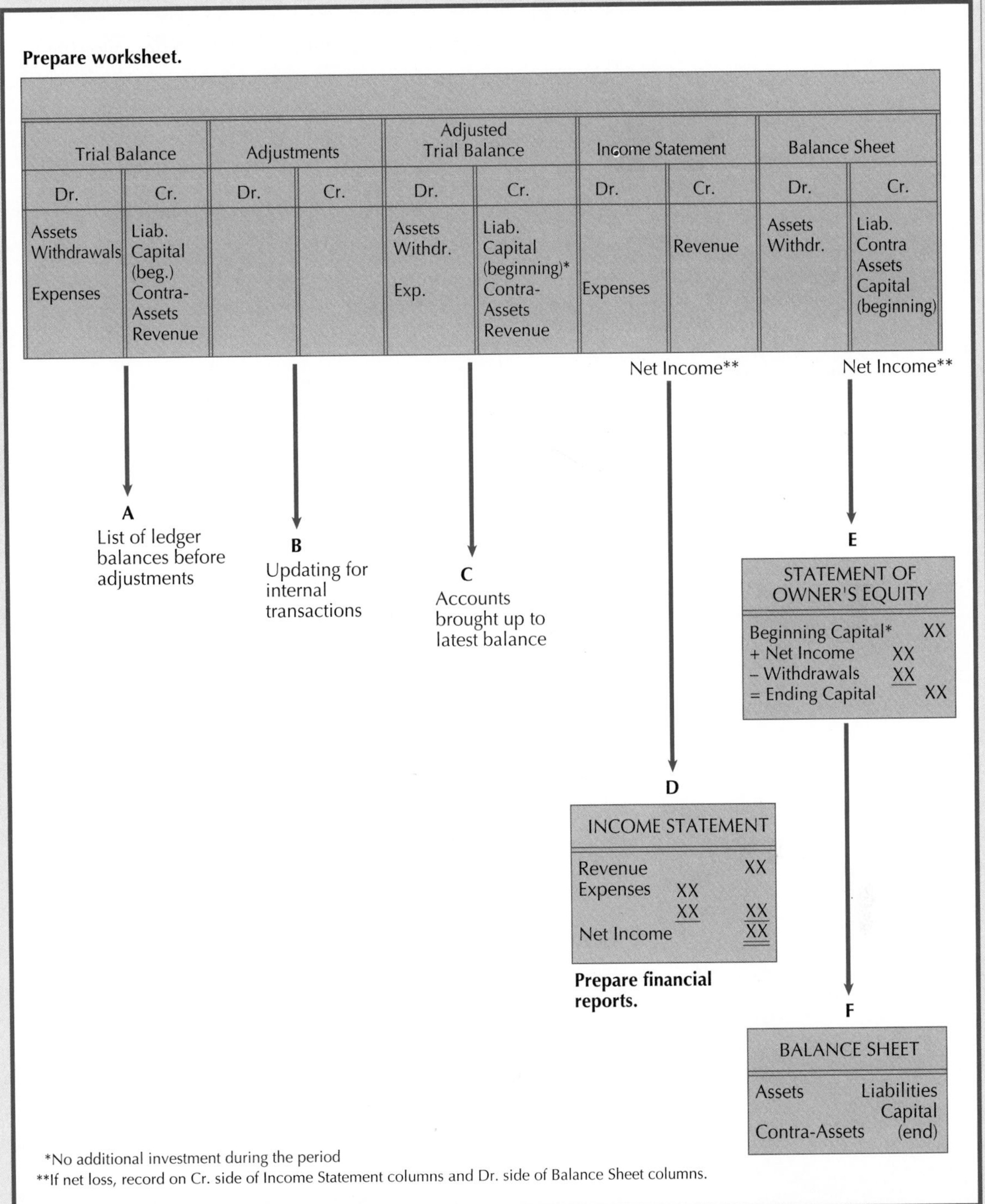

Questions, Mini Exercises, Exercises, and Problems

Discussion Questions

1. Worksheets are required in every company's accounting cycle. Please agree or disagree and explain why.
2. What is the purpose of adjusting accounts?

3. What is the relationship of internal transactions to the adjusting process?
4. Explain how an adjustment can affect both the income statement and balance sheet. Please give an example.
5. Why do we need the accumulated amortization account?
6. Amortization expense goes on the balance sheet. True or false? Why?
7. Each month the cost of accumulated amortization grows while the cost of equipment goes up. Agree or disagree. Defend your position.
8. Define accrued salaries.
9. Why don't the formal financial reports contain debit or credit columns?
10. Explain how the financial reports are prepared from the worksheet.

Mini Exercises

(The blank forms you need are on pages 4-6 and 4-7 of the *Study Guide with Working Papers.*)

Adjustment for Supplies

1. Before Adjustment:

Supplies		Supplies Expense	
400			

Given

At year-end an inventory of supplies shows $50.

Required

a. How much is the adjustment for supplies?
b. Draw a transaction analysis box for this adjustment.
c. What will the balance of supplies be on the adjusted trial balance?

Adjustment for Prepaid Rent

2. Before Adjustment:

Prepaid Rent		Rent Expense	
700			

Given

At year-end rent expired is $300.

Required

a. How much is the adjustment for Prepaid Rent?
b. Draw a transaction analysis box for this adjustment.
c. What will be the balance of Prepaid Rent on the adjusted trial balance?

Adjustment for Amortization

3. Before Adjustment:

Equipment		Accumulated Amortization, Equipment		Amortization Expense, Equipment	
6,000			1,000		

Given

At year-end, amortization on equipment is $1,000.

Required

a. Which of the three T accounts above is not affected?

b. Which title is a contra-asset?

c. Draw a transaction analysis box for this adjustment.

d. What will be the balance of each of these three accounts on the adjusted trial balance?

Adjustment for Accrued Salaries

4. Before Adjustment:

Salaries Expense		Salaries Payable	
900			

Given

Accrued Salaries, $200

Required

a. Draw a transaction analysis box for this adjustment.

b. What will be the balances of these two accounts on the adjusted trial balance?

Worksheet

5. From the following adjusted trial balance titles on a worksheet, identify in which column each account will be listed in the last four columns of the worksheet.

(ID) Income statement Dr. column

(IC) Income statement Cr. column

(BD) Balance sheet Dr. column

(BC) Balance sheet Cr. column

ATB	ID	IC	BD	BC
a. Supplies	______	______	______	______
b. Accounts Receivable	______	______	______	______
c. Cash	______	______	______	______
d. Prepaid Rent	______	______	______	______
e. Equipment	______	______	______	______
f. Accumulated Amortization	______	______	______	______
g. B., Capital	______	______	______	______
h. B., Withdrawals	______	______	______	______
i. Taxi Fare Income	______	______	______	______
j. Advertising Expense	______	______	______	______
k. Office Supplies Expense	______	______	______	______
l. Rent Expense	______	______	______	______
m. Amortization Expense	______	______	______	______
n. Salaries Payable	______	______	______	______

6. From the following balance sheet (which was made from the worksheet and other financial reports) explain why the lettered numbers were not found on the worksheet. *Hint:* There are no debits or credits on the formal financial reports.

H. Wells
Balance Sheet
December 31, 2000

Assets			*Liabilities and Owner's Equity*			
Cash		$6	Liabilities			
Accounts Receivable		2	Accounts Payable	$2		
Supplies		2	Salaries Payable	1		
Equipment	$10		Total Liabilities		$3	(B)
Less: Accumulated			Owner's Equity			
Amortization	4	6	H. Wells, Capital		13	(C)
Total Assets		$16 (A)	Total Liabilities and Owner's Equity		$16	(D)

Exercises

(The blank forms you need are on pages 4-8 and 4-9 of the *Study Guide with Working Papers.*)

Categorizing accounts

4-1. Complete the following table.

Account	Category	Normal Balance	On Which Financial Report(s) Found
Salary Expense			
Prepaid Insurance			
Equipment			
Accumulated Depreciation			
A. Jax, Capital			
A. Jax, Withdrawals			
Salaries Payable			
Amortization Expense			

Reviewing adjustments and the transaction analysis charts

4-2. Use transaction analysis charts to analyze the following adjustments:
a. Amortization on equipment, $500
b. Rent expired, $200

Recording adjusting entries

4-3. From the following adjustment data, calculate the adjustment amount and record appropriate debits or credits:
a. Supplies purchased, $600
Supplies on hand, $200
b. Store equipment, $10,000
Accumulated amortization before adjustment, $900
Amortization expense, $100

Preparing a worksheet

4-4. From the following trial balance and adjustment data, complete a worksheet for J. Trent as of December 31, 2002:
a. Amortization expense, equipment $2.00
b. Insurance expired $1.00
c. Store supplies on hand $4.00
d. Wages owed, but not paid, $5.00 (they are an expense in the old year)

J. TRENT TRIAL BALANCE DECEMBER 31, 2002		
	Dr.	Cr.
Cash	900	
Accounts Receivable	200	
Prepaid Insurance	700	
Store Supplies	600	
Store Equipment	700	
Accumulated Amortization, Equipment		200
Accounts Payable		400
J. Trent, Capital		1700
J. Trent, Withdrawals	600	
Revenue from Clients		2400
Rent Expense	400	
Wage Expense	600	
	4700	4700

Preparing financial reports from a worksheet

4-5. From the completed worksheet in Exercise 4-4, prepare:

a. An income statement for December

b. A statement of owner's equity for December

c. A balance sheet as of December 31, 2002

Group A Problems

(The blank forms you need are on pages 4-10 and 4-11 of the *Study Guide with Working Papers.*)

Completing a partial worksheet up to the adjusted trial balance

4A-1. The following is the trial balance for Silver's Fitness Centre for December 31, 2001.

Check Figure

Total, Adjusted Trial Balance $26,550

SILVER'S FITNESS CENTRE TRIAL BALANCE DECEMBER 31, 2001		
	Debit	Credit
Cash in Bank	410000	
Accounts Receivable	500000	
Gym Supplies	540000	
Gym Equipment	720000	
Accumulated Amortization , Gym Equipment		375000
J. Silver, Capital		1070000
J. Silver, Withdrawals	300000	
Gym Fees		1130000
Rent Expense	90000	
Advertising Expense	15000	
	2575000	2575000

Given

The following adjustment data on December 31:

a. Gym supplies on hand, $1,500

b. Amortization taken on gym equipment, $800

Complete a partial worksheet up to the adjusted trial balance.

Completing a worksheet

Check Figure

Net Income $804

4A-2. Below is the trial balance for Fred's Plumbing Service for December 31, 2003.

FRED'S PLUMBING SERVICE
TRIAL BALANCE
DECEMBER 31, 2003

	Dr.	Cr.
Cash in Bank	3 6 0 6 00	
Accounts Receivable	7 0 0 00	
Prepaid Rent	8 0 0 00	
Plumbing Supplies	7 4 2 00	
Plumbing Equipment	1 4 0 0 00	
Accumulated Amortization, Plumbing Equipment		1 0 6 0 00
Accounts Payable		4 4 2 00
Fred Jack, Capital		3 2 5 0 00
Plumbing Revenue		4 3 5 6 00
Heat Expense	4 0 0 00	
Advertising Expense	2 0 0 00	
Wages Expense	1 2 6 0 00	
	9 1 0 8 00	9 1 0 8 00

Adjustment data to update the trial balance:

a. Rent expired, $500

b. Plumbing supplies on hand (remaining), $100

c. Amortization expense, plumbing equipment, $200

d. Wages earned by workers but not paid and not due until January, $350

Required

Prepare a worksheet for Fred's Plumbing Service for the month of December.

Comprehensive problem

Check Figure

Net Income $2,140

4A-3. The following is the trial balance for Kevin's Moving Co.

KEVIN'S MOVING CO.
TRIAL BALANCE
OCTOBER 31, 2002

	Dr.	Cr.
Cash	5 0 0 0 00	
Prepaid Insurance	2 5 0 0 00	
Moving Supplies	1 2 0 0 00	
Moving Truck	1 1 0 0 0 00	
Accumulated Amortization, Moving Truck		9 0 0 0 00
Accounts Payable		2 7 6 8 00
K. Hoff, Capital		5 4 4 2 00
K. Hoff, Withdrawals	1 4 0 0 00	
Revenue from Moving		9 0 0 0 00
Wages Expense	3 7 1 2 00	
Rent Expense	1 0 8 0 00	
Advertising Expense	3 1 8 00	
	2 6 2 1 0 00	2 6 2 1 0 00

Adjustment data to update trial balance:

a. Insurance expired, $700

b. Moving supplies on hand, $900

c. Amortization on moving truck, $500

d. Wages earned but unpaid, $250

Required

1. Complete a worksheet for Kevin's Moving Co. for the month of October.

2. Prepare an income statement for October, a statement of owner's equity for October, and a balance sheet as of October 31, 2002.

Comprehensive problem

4A-4. The following is a trial balance for Dick's Repair Service.

Check Figure

Net Income $1,830

DICK'S REPAIR SERVICE
TRIAL BALANCE
NOVEMBER 30, 2001

	Dr.	Cr.
Cash	3 2 0 0 00	
Prepaid Insurance	4 0 0 0 00	
Repair Supplies	4 6 0 0 00	
Repair Equipment	3 0 0 0 00	
Accumulated Amortization, Repair Equipment		7 0 0 00
Accounts Payable		5 5 7 0 00
D. Horn, Capital		3 8 0 0 00
Revenue from Repairs		7 0 0 0 00
Wages Expense	1 8 0 0 00	
Rent Expense	3 6 0 00	
Advertising Expense	1 1 0 00	
	17 0 7 0 00	17 0 7 0 00

Adjustment data to update the trial balance:

a. Insurance expired, $700

b. Repair supplies on hand, $3,000

c. Amortization on repair equipment, $200

d. Wages earned but not yet paid, $400

Required

1. Complete a worksheet for Dick's Repair Service for the month of November.

2. Prepare an income statement for November, a statement of owner's equity for November, and a balance sheet as of November 30, 2001.

Group B Problems

(The blank forms you need are on pages 4-10 and 4-11 of the *Study Guide with Working Papers.*)

Completing a partial worksheet up to adjusted trial balance

4B-1. Please complete a partial worksheet up to the adjusted trial balance using the following adjustment data and trial balance:

a. Gym supplies on hand, $2,600

b. Amortization taken on gym equipment, $500

SILVER'S FITNESS CENTRE TRIAL BALANCE DECEMBER 31, 2001		
	Dr.	Cr.
Cash in Bank	200000	
Accounts Receivable	200000	
Gym Supplies	420000	
Gym Equipment	800000	
Accumulated Amortization, Gym Equipment		570000
J. Silver, Capital		1100000
J. Silver, Withdrawals	100000	
Gym Fees		140000
Rent Expense	80000	
Advertising Expense	10000	
	1810000	1810000

Check Figure

Total, Adjusted Trial Balance $18,600

Completing a worksheet

4B-2. Given the following trial balance and adjustment data of Fred's Plumbing Service, prepare a worksheet for the month of December.

FRED'S PLUMBING SERVICE TRIAL BALANCE DECEMBER 31, 2003		
	Dr.	Cr.
Cash in Bank	39600	
Accounts Receivable	28400	
Prepaid Rent	40000	
Plumbing Supplies	31000	
Plumbing Equipment	100000	
Accumulated Amortization, Plumbing Equipment		20000
Accounts Payable		34600
Fred Jack, Capital		45600
Plumbing Revenue		468000
Heat Expense	63200	
Advertising Expense	120000	
Wages Expense	146000	
Total	568200	568200

Check Figure

Net Income $673

Adjustment Data

a. Plumbing supplies on hand, $60

b. Rent expired, $150

c. Amortization on plumbing equipment, $200

d. Wages earned but unpaid, $115

Comprehensive problem

4B-3. Using the following trial balance and adjustment data for Kevin's Moving Co., prepare:

1. A worksheet for the month of October
2. An income statement for October, a statement of owner's equity for October, and a balance sheet as of October 31, 2002

Adjustment Data

a. Insurance expired $600

b. Moving supplies on hand $310

Check Figure

Net Loss $1,628

KEVIN'S MOVING CO. TRIAL BALANCE OCTOBER 31, 2002		
	Dr.	Cr.
Cash	3 9 2 0 00	
Prepaid Insurance	3 2 8 8 00	
Moving Supplies	1 4 0 0 00	
Moving Truck	10 6 5 8 00	
Accumulated Amortization, Moving Truck		3 6 6 0 00
Accounts Payable		1 3 1 2 00
K. Hoff, Capital		17 4 8 2 00
K. Hoff, Withdrawals	4 2 4 0 00	
Revenue from Moving		8 1 6 2 00
Wages Expense	5 7 1 2 00	
Rent Expense	1 0 8 0 00	
Advertising Expense	3 1 8 00	
	30 6 1 6 00	30 6 1 6 00

c. Amortization on moving truck $580

d. Wages earned but unpaid $410

Comprehensive problem

4B-4. As the bookkeeper of Dick's Repair Service, use the information that follows to prepare:

1. A worksheet for the month of November
2. An income statement for November, a statement of owner's equity for November, and a balance sheet as of November 30, 2001

Check Figure

Net Income $1,012

DICK'S REPAIR SERVICE TRIAL BALANCE NOVEMBER 30, 2001		
	Dr.	Cr.
Cash	3 2 0 4 00	
Prepaid Insurance	4 0 0 0 00	
Repair Supplies	7 7 0 00	
Repair Equipment	3 1 0 6 00	
Accumulated Amortization, Repair Equipment		6 5 0 00
Accounts Payable		1 9 0 4 00
D. Horn, Capital		6 2 5 8 00
Revenue from Repairs		5 6 3 4 00
Wages Expense	1 6 0 0 00	
Rent Expense	1 5 6 0 00	
Advertising Expense	2 0 6 00	
	14 4 4 6 00	14 4 4 6 00

Adjustment Data

a. Insurance expired $300

b. Repair supplies on hand $170

c. Amortization on repair equipment $250

d. Wages earned but unpaid $106

Group C Problems

(The forms you need are on pages 4-12 and 4-13 of the *Study Guide with working Papers.*)

Completing a partial worksheet up to adjusted trial balance

4C-1. Please complete a partial worksheet up to the adjusted trial balance for Neil's Gallery and Art Supplies using the following adjustment data and trial balance:

a. Art supplies on hand, $840

b. Amortization taken on equipment, $435

Check Figure

Total, Adjusted Trial Balance $11,461

NEIL'S GALLERY AND ART SUPPLIES
TRIAL BALANCE
DECEMBER 31, 2002

	Dr.	Cr.
Cash in Bank	141000	
Accounts Receivable	92000	
Art Supplies	217000	
Equipment	395000	
Accumulated Amortization, Equipment		217500
Neil Lightning, Capital		560100
Neil Lightning, Withdrawals	85000	
Fees Earned		325000
Rent Expense	90000	
Advertising Expense	37000	
Utilities Expense	45600	
Totals	1102600	1102600

Completing a worksheet

4C-2. Given the following trial balance and adjustment data for Sun-Yo's Carpentry Service, your task is to prepare a worksheet for the month of November.

Check Figure

Net Loss $243

SUN-YO'S CARPENTRY SERVICE
TRIAL BALANCE
NOVEMBER 30, 2003

	Dr.	Cr.
Cash in Bank	92400	
Accounts Receivable	82000	
Prepaid Rent	70000	
Carpentry Supplies	74200	
Carpentry Equipment	392500	
Accumulated Amortization, Carpentry Equipment		245000
Accounts Payable		38400
Sun-Yo Kwon, Capital		274800
Carpentry Service Revenue		447700
Advertising Expense	51000	
Utilities Expense	67800	
Wages Expense	176000	
Totals	1005900	1005900

Adjustment Data

a. Carpentry supplies on hand, $320

b. Rent expired, $350

c. Amortization on carpentry equipment, $755
d. Wages earned but unpaid, $245

Comprehensive problem

4C-3. Using the following trial balance and adjustment data of Farro's Repair Co., prepare:

1. A worksheet for the month of October
2. An income statement for October, a statement of owner's equity for October, and a balance sheet as of October 31, 2001

Adjustment Data

a. Insurance expired, $463
b. Repair supplies on hand, $805
c. Amortization on repair equipment, $702
d. Amortization on building, $540
e. Wages earned but unpaid, $966

Check Figure
Net Income $5,028

FARRO'S REPAIR CO. TRIAL BALANCE OCTOBER 31, 2001		
	Dr.	Cr.
Cash in Bank	132600	
Prepaid Insurance	138900	
Repair Supplies	114800	
Repair Equipment	846000	
Building	5000000	
Accumulated Amortization, Repair Equipment		395200
Accumulated Amortization, Building		1492000
Accounts Payable		72400
Patricia Farro, Capital		4308500
Patricia Farro, Withdrawals	840000	
Repair Fees Revenue		1626500
Wages Expense	589000	
Utilities Expense	84100	
Advertising Expense	149200	
Totals	7894600	7894600

Comprehensive problem

4C-4. As the bookkeeper of Northwest Internet Access Service, use the information that follows to prepare:

1. A worksheet for the month of August
2. An income statement for August, a statement of owner's equity for August, and a balance sheet as of August 31, 2000

Adjustment Data

a. Insurance expired, $421
b. Computer supplies on hand, $215
c. Amortization on computer equipment, $826
d. Wages earned but unpaid, $680
e. Advertising bill received, not yet paid, $185

Check Figure

Net Income $4,892

NORTHWEST INTERNET ACCESS TRIAL BALANCE AUGUST 31, 2000		
	Dr.	Cr.
Cash in Bank	228 00	
Prepaid Insurance	1020 00	
Computer Supplies	426 00	
Computer Equipment	11480 00	
Accumulated Amortization, Computer Equipment		4152 00
Accounts Payable		840 00
Lucy Northwest, Capital		2357 00
Lucy Northwest, Withdrawals	1410 00	
Revenue from Services Provided		14385 00
Wages Expense	4760 00	
Rent Expense	1485 00	
Advertising Expense	925 00	
Totals	21734 00	21734 00

REAL WORLD APPLICATIONS

(The blank form you need is on page 4-14 of the *Study Guide with Working Papers.*)

4R-1.

To: Hal Hogan, Bookkeeper

From: Pete Tennant, V. P.

Re: Adjustments for year ended December 31, 2001

Hal, here is the information you requested. Please supply me with the adjustments needed ASAP. Also, please put in writing why we need to do these adjustments.

Thanks

Attached to memo:

a. Insurance data:

Policy No.	*Date of Policy Purchase*	*Policy Length*	*Cost*
100	November 1 of previous year	4 years	$480
200	May 1 of current year	2 years	600
300	September 1 of current year	1 year	240

b. Rent data: Prepaid rent had a $500 balance at beginning of year. An additional $400 of rent was paid in advance in June. At year-end, $200 of rent had expired.

c. Revenue data: Accrued storage fees of $500 were earned but uncollected and unrecorded at year end.

4R-2.

Hint: Unearned Rent is a liability on the balance sheet.

On Friday, Harry Swag's boss asks him to prepare a special report, due on Monday at 8 a.m. Harry gathers the following material in his briefcase:

		December 31	
		2001	*2002*
Prepaid Advertising		$300	$600
Interest Payable		150	350
Unearned Rent		500	300
Cash paid for: Advertising	$1,900		
Interest	1,500		
Cash received for: Rent	2,300		

As his best friend, could you help Harry show the amounts that are to be reported on the 2002 income statement for (a) Advertising Expense, (b) Interest Expense, and (c) Rent Fees Earned. Please explain in writing why unearned rent is considered a liability.

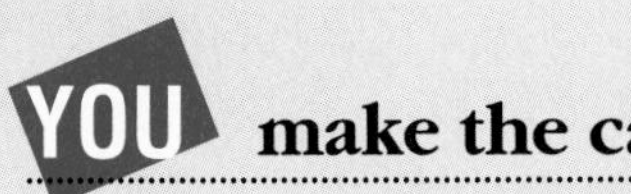

make the call

Critical Thinking/Ethical Case

4R-3.

Janet Fox, President of Angel Co., went to a tax seminar. One of the speakers at the seminar advised the audience to put off showing expenses until next year because doing so would allow them to take advantage of a new tax law. When Janet returned to the office, she called in her accountant, Frieda O'Riley. She told Frieda to forget about making any adjustments for salaries in the old year so more expenses could be shown in the new year. Frieda told her that putting off these expenses would not follow generally accepted accounting principles. Janet said she should do it anyway. You make the call. Write your specific recommendations to Frieda.

ACCOUNTING RECALL

A CUMULATIVE APPROACH

THIS EXAMINATION REVIEWS CHAPTERS 1 THROUGH 4.

Pages 4-15 and 4-18 of the *Study Guide with Working Papers* have the forms to complete this exam, as well as worked-out solutions. The page reference next to each question identifies the page to turn back to if you answer the question incorrectly.

PART I Vocabulary Review

Match each term on the left side with the appropriate definition or phrase on the right.

Page Ref.		
(133)	1. Prepaid rent	A. Estimated value of an asset after all amortization has been taken
(137)	2. Accrued salaries	B. Earned but unpaid
(133)	3. Amortization expense	C. Actual cost at time of purchase
(133)	4. Accumulated amortization	D. Columnar device
(137)	5. Normal balance	

(134)	6. Residual value	E. Rent paid in advance
(131)	7. An asset	F. Cost – accumulated amortization
(130)	8. Worksheet	G. Supplies
(135)	9. Book value	H. Shown on the income statement
(133)	10. Historical cost	I. Side of an account that increases
		J. Contra-asset

PART II True or False (Accounting Theory)

(131) 11. Adjustments are the result of external transactions.
(132) 12. Adjustments affect only the balance sheet.
(135) 13. Accumulated amortization and equipment will both go on the balance sheet.
(134) 14. The normal balance of accumulated amortization is a debit.
(143) 15. All financial reports could be prepared from a worksheet.

Continuing Problem

At the end of September, Tony took a complete inventory of his supplies and found the following:

5 dozen 1/40 screws at a cost of $8.00 a dozen
2 dozen 1/20 screws at a cost of $5.00 a dozen
2 cartons of computer inventory paper at a cost of $14 a carton
3 feet of coaxial cable at a cost of $4.00 per foot

After speaking to his accountant, he found that a reasonable amortization amount for each of his long-term assets is as follows:

Computer purchased July 5, 2001	Amortization $33 a month
Office Equipment purchased July 17, 2001	Amortization $10 a month
Computer Workstations purchased September 17, 2001	Amortization $20 a month

Tony uses the straight-line method of amortization and declares no salvage value for any of the assets. If any long-term asset is purchased in the first fifteen days of the month, he will charge amortization for the full month. If an asset is purchased on the sixteenth of the month, or later, he will not charge amortization in the month it was purchased.

August and September's rent has now expired.

Assignment

Use your trial balance from the completed problem in Chapter 3 and the above adjusting information to complete the worksheet for the three months ended September 30, 2001. From the worksheets prepare the financial statements. (See pages 4-16 to 4-19 in your *Study Guide with Working Papers.*)

COMPUTER WORKSHOP

COMPUTERIZED ACCOUNTING APPLICATION FOR CHAPTER 4

PART A: Compound Journal Entries, Adjusting Entries, and Financial Reports

PART B: Backup Procedures

Before starting on this assignment, read and complete the tasks discussed in Parts A, B, and F of Appendix B: Computerized Accounting at the back of this book, and complete the Computerized Accounting Application assignment at the end of Chapter 3.

PART A Compound Journal Entries, Adjusting Entries, and Financial Reports

Open the company data files

1. Click on the **Start** button. Point to Programs; point to Simply Accounting; then click on Simply Accounting in the final menu presented. The Simply Accounting Open File dialogue box will appear.
2. Insert your Student Data Files disk into disk drive A. Enter the following path into the **File name** text box: `A:\student\zell.asc`
3. Click on the **Open** button; enter 12/31/02 into the **Session** date text box; then click on the **OK** button. Click on the **OK** button in response to the message "The date entered is more than one week past your previous Using date of 12/01/02." The Company Window for Zell will appear.

Add your name to the company name

4. Click on the Company Window Setup menu; then click on Company Information. The Company Information dialogue box will appear. Insert your name in place of the text "Your Name" in the **Name** text box. Click on the **OK** button to return to the Company Window.

How to record a compound journal entry

5. In the Computerized Accounting Application assignment in Chapter 3 you learned how to record journal entries in the General Journal dialogue box. Compound journal entries can also be recorded in the General Journal dialogue box. The owner of The Zell Company has made an investment in the business consisting of $5,000 in cash and an automobile valued at $12,000. Open the General Journal dialogue box. Enter the word `Memo` into the **Source** text box; press the TAB key; enter 12/01/02 into the **Date** text box; press the TAB key; enter `Initial investment by owner` into the **Comment** text box; then press the TAB key. The flashing insertion point will be positioned in the **Account** text box.
6. With the flashing insertion point positioned in the **Account** text box, press the ENTER key. The Select Account dialogue box will appear. Double-click on 1110 Cash; enter 5000 into the **Debits** text box; then press the TAB key.
7. Press the ENTER key to bring up the Select Account dialogue box. Double-click on 1230 Automobile. The program will offer 5000.00 as a default amount in the **Credits** text box. The Credits amount remains highlighted. You do not want to accept the default. To override the default, enter − 12000 (Be sure to enter the minus sign!); then press the TAB key. The 12000.00 amount will move to the **Debits** text box.
8. Press the ENTER key to bring up the Select Account dialogue box; then double-click on 3110 Owner's Capital. The program will offer the total of the Debits portion of the compound journal entry (17000.00) as a default amount in the **Credits** text box. The Credits amount remains highlighted. Press the TAB key to

accept the default Credits amount. This completes the data you need to enter into the General Journal dialogue box to record the compound journal entry for the initial investment by the owner. Your screen should look like this:

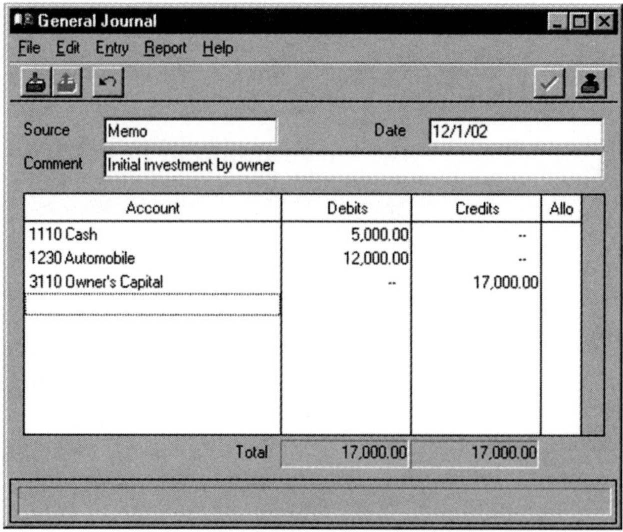

Review the compound journal entry

9. Click on the General Journal **Report** menu; then click on Display General Journal Entry. Review the compound journal entry for accuracy, noting any errors.
10. Close the General Journal Entry window; then make any editing corrections required.

Post the entry

11. After verifying that the compound journal entry is correct, click on the Post icon to post this transaction.

Record additional transactions

12. Record the following additional journal entries (enter `Memo` into the **Source** text box for each transaction; then enter the date listed for each transaction):

2002		
Dec.	1	Paid rent for two months in advance, $500.
	3	Purchased office supplies ($200) and office equipment ($1,100), both on account.
	9	Billed a customer for fees earned, $2,000.
	13	Paid telephone bill, $150.
	20	Owner withdrew $475 from the business for personal use.
	27	Received $600 for fees earned.
	30	Paid salaries expense, $800.

Display and print a general journal and trial balance

13. After you have posted the additional journal entries, close the General Journal; then print the following reports:
    a. General Journal (By posting date, All ledger entries, Start: 12/01/02, Finish: 12/31/02).
    b. Trial Balance as at 12/31/02.
14. Review your printed reports. If you have made an error in a posted journal entry, see "Reversing an Entry Made in the General Journal Dialogue Box" in Part C of Appendix B: Computerized Accounting for information on how to correct the error.

How to record adjusting journal entries

15. Open the General Journal; then record adjusting journal entries based on the following adjustment data (*Source:* Memo; *Date:* 12/31/02; *Comment:* Adjusting entry):
    a. One month's rent has expired.
    b. An inventory shows $25 worth of office supplies remaining.
    c. Amortization on office equipment, $50
    d. Amortization on automobile, $150

How to display and print a general journal, general ledger, and trial balance

16. After you have posted the adjusting journal entries, close the General Journal; then print the following reports:
    a. General Journal (By posting date, All ledger entries, Start: 12/31/02, Finish: 12/31/02).
    b. General Ledger Report (Start: 12/01/02, Finish: 12/31/02, select All).
    c. Trial Balance As at 12/31/02.
17. Review your printed reports. If you have made an error in a posted journal entry, see "Reversing an Entry Made in the General Journal Dialogue Box" in Part C of Appendix B: Computerized Accounting for information on how to correct the error.

How to display and print an income statement

18. Click on the Company Window **Reports** menu; point to Financials; then click on Income Statement. The Income Statement Options dialogue box will appear, asking you to define the information you want displayed. Leave the **Select a Report** text box set at Current Year. Leave the **Start** text box date set at 12/01/02; leave the **Finish** text box date set at 12/31/02; then click on the **OK** button. Your screen will look like this:

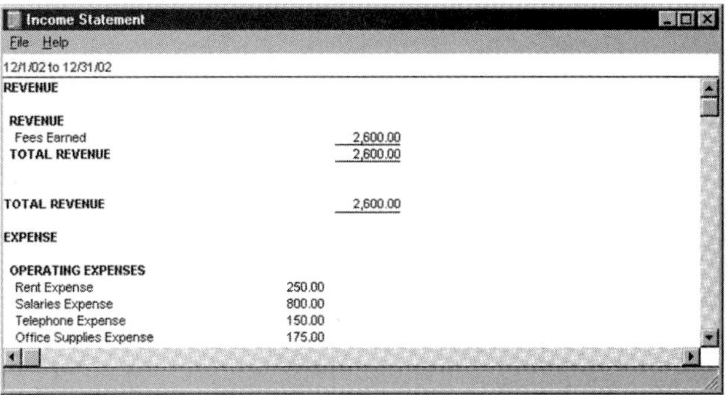

19. The scroll bar can be used to advance the display to view other portions of the report.
20. Click on the Income Statement **File** menu; then click on Print to print the Income Statement.

How to display and print a balance sheet

21. Close the Income Statement window; click on the Company Window **Reports** menu; point to Financials; then click on Balance Sheet. The Balance Sheet Options dialogue box will appear, asking you to define the information you want displayed. Leave the **Select a Report** text box set at Current Year. Leave the **As at** date set as 12/31/02; then click on the **OK** button. Your screen will look like this:

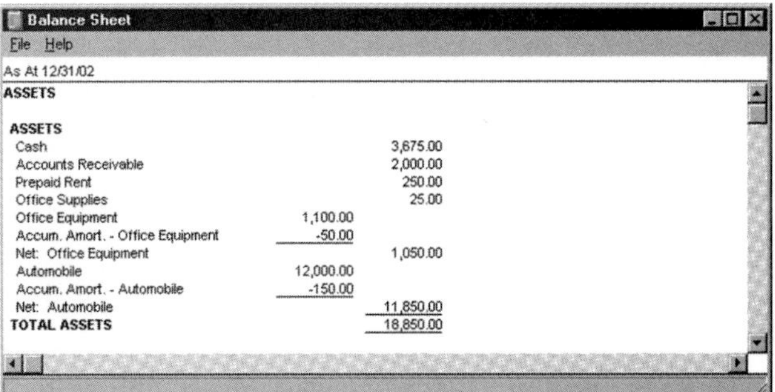

22. Use the scroll bar to advance the display to the Owner's Equity section of the Balance Sheet. Note that the program has included the Statement of Owner's Equity information directly in the Owner's Equity section of the Balance Sheet.
23. Click on the Balance Sheet **File** menu; click on Print to print the Balance Sheet; then close the Balance Sheet window to return to the Company Window.

Exit from the program

24. Click on the Company Window **File** menu; then click on Exit to end the current work session and return to your Windows desktop.

PART B Backup Procedures

Companies that use computerized accounting systems make frequent backup copies of their accounting data for two major reasons:

1. To ensure that they have a copy of the accounting data in case the current data becomes damaged.
2. To permit the printing of historical reports after the Using date has been advanced to a new month.

The methods used to make backup copies of company data files vary greatly. Large companies may back up daily using sophisticated high-speed tape backup devices while small companies may back up weekly on floppy diskettes or one of the many larger-capacity removable disks such as those used with a Zip drive or the Imation L5120.

Normally, all backup copies of a company's data files are stored on a secondary storage medium separate from the original data files in case the original storage medium becomes damaged. However, for the purposes of this introduction to computerized accounting systems, you will be using the working copy of your Student Data Files disk to store backup copies of a company's data files. You will be using a backup method known as the Save As method.

How to make a backup copy of a company's data files

1. Click on the **Start** button. Point to Programs; point to Simply Accounting; then click on Simply Accounting in the final menu presented. The Simply Accounting Open File dialogue box will appear.
2. Insert your Student Data Files disk into disk drive A. Enter the following path into the **File name** text box: `A:\student\zell.asc`
3. Click on the **Open** button; leave the **Session** date set at 12/31/02; then click on the **OK** button. The Company Window for Zell will appear on your screen.
4. Click on the Company Window **File** menu; then click on Save As. The Save As dialogue box will appear. Enter the following new file name into the **File name** text box: `A:\student\zelldec.asc`
5. Click on the **Save** button. Note that the company name in the Company Window has changed from Zell to Zelldec. Click on the Company Window **File** menu again; then click on Save As. Enter the following new file name into the **File name** text box: `A:\student\zell.asc`
6. Click on the **Save** button. Click on the **Yes** button to confirm that you want to replace the existing file. Note that the company name in the Company Window has changed back from Zelldec to Zell.
7. You now have two sets of company data files for The Zell Company on your Student Data Files disk. The current data is stored under the file name zell.asc. The backup data for December is stored under the file name zelldec.asc.

Exit from the program

8. Click on the Company Window **File** menu; then click on Exit to end the current work session and return to your Windows desktop.

Complete the report transmittal

9. For information on when you might want to use the backup copy of a company's data files, see Part E of Appendix B: Computerized Accounting in the back of this book.
10. Complete The Zell Company Report Transmittal located in Appendix A in your *Study Guide and Working Papers.*

The Accounting Cycle Completed

5

ADJUSTING, CLOSING, AND POST-CLOSING TRIAL BALANCE

THE BIG PICTURE

◆

As Tony Freedman began to prepare for his busiest season, he thought it might be a good time to end the fiscal year for Eldorado Computer Centre and record the adjusting entries before closing the books.

Under GAAP, every business is required to complete an accounting cycle within 12 months of starting business. Freedman had chosen to end his cycle using a fiscal-year date of September 30. He chose this date because it was a good time to complete inventory and take time to analyze his books. As Christmas gets closer he knows there will be a lot of potential new business because it's the "giving" season.

Adjusting entries must be recorded and posted to the permanent books to reflect the changes. This will bring each ledger account up to date with the balances reflected on the financial statements.

The final step ends with closing the books. This process closes the temporary accounts (revenue, expenses, and withdrawals) into the permanent account (capital). Remember that owner's equity is made up with several temporary accounts that reflect how the business is doing. Profits (when revenue exceeds expenses) from the business increase the worth of a business. On the other hand, a net loss will decrease the worth of a business. Similarly, when an owner personally withdraws assets from the business, that too will decrease the value of the business. Closing the books is simply a process of moving the temporary account balances to the permanent account.

Chapter Objectives	◆ **Journalizing and posting adjusting entries (p. 172)** ◆ **Journalizing and posting closing entries (p. 176)** ◆ **Preparing a post-closing trial balance (p. 186)**

In Chapters 3 and 4 we completed these steps of the manual accounting cycle for Clark's Word Processing Services:

Remember, for ease of presentation we are using a month as the accounting cycle for Clark's. In the "real" world, the cycle can be any time period that does not exceed one year.

Step 1: Business transactions occurred and generated source documents.
Step 2: Business transactions were analyzed and recorded in a journal.
Step 3: Information was posted or transferred from journal to ledger.
Step 4: A trial balance was prepared.
Step 5: A worksheet was completed.
Step 6: Financial statements were prepared.

This chapter covers the following steps, which will complete Clark's accounting cycle for the month of May:

Step 7: Journalizing and posting adjusting entries
Step 8: Journalizing and posting closing entries
Step 9: Preparing a post-closing trial balance

LEARNING UNIT 5-1

Journalizing and Posting Adjusting Entries: Step 7 of the Accounting Cycle

Recording Journal Entries from the Worksheet

At this point, many ledger accounts are *not up to date.*

Purpose of adjusting entries.

The information in the worksheet is up to date. The financial reports prepared from that information can give the business's management and other interested parties a good idea of where the business stands as of a particular date. The problem is that the worksheet is an informal report. The information concerning the adjustments has not been placed in the journal, or posted to the ledger accounts. This means that the books are not up to date and ready for the next accounting cycle to begin. For example, the ledger shows $1,200 of prepaid rent (page 96), but the balance sheet we prepared in Chapter 4 shows an $800 balance. Essentially, the worksheet is a tool for preparing financial reports. Now we must use the adjustment columns of the worksheet as a basis for bringing the ledger up to date. We do this by **adjusting journal entries** (see Figure 5-2). Again, the updating must be done before the next accounting period starts. For Clark's Word Processing Services, the next period begins on June 1.

Figure 5-2 shows the adjusting journal entries for Clark's taken from the adjustments section of the worksheet (see Figure 5-1). Once the adjusting journal entries are posted to the ledger, the accounts making up the financial statements that were prepared from the worksheet will correspond with the updated ledger. (Keep in mind that this is the same journal we have been using.) Let's look at some simplified T accounts to show how Clark's ledger looked before and after the adjustments were posted (see adjustments A to D on page 174).

FIGURE 5-1
Journalizing and Posting Adjustments from the Adjustments Section of the Worksheet

Account Titles	Trial Balance Dr.	Trial Balance Cr.	Adjustments Dr.	Adjustments Cr.
Cash	6 1 5 5 00			
Accounts Receivable	5 0 0 0 00			
Office Supplies	6 0 0 00			(A) 5 0 0 00
Prepaid Rent	1 2 0 0 00			(B) 4 0 0 00
Word Processing Equipment	6 0 0 0 00			
Accounts Payable		3 3 5 0 00		
Brenda Clark, Capital		10 0 0 0 00		
Brenda Clark, Withdrawals	6 2 5 00			
Word Processing Fees		8 0 0 0 00		
Office Salaries Expense	1 3 0 0 00		(D) 3 5 0 00	
Advertising Expense	2 5 0 00			
Telephone Expense	2 2 0 00			
	21 3 5 0 00	21 3 5 0 00		
Office Supplies Expense			(A) 5 0 0 00	
Rent Expense			(B) 4 0 0 00	
Amortization Expense, W.P. Equipment			(C) 8 0 00	
Accumulated Amortization, W.P. Equipment				(C) 8 0 00
Salaries Payable				(D) 3 5 0 00
			1 3 3 0 00	1 3 3 0 00

FIGURE 5-2
Adjusting Journal Entries

CLARK'S WORD PROCESSING SERVICES
GENERAL JOURNAL

Page 2

Date		Account Titles and Description	PR	Dr.	Cr.
		Adjusting Entries			
May	31	Office Supplies Expense	514	5 0 0 00	
		Office Supplies	114		5 0 0 00
		Office Supplies used up			
	31	Rent Expense	515	4 0 0 00	
		Prepaid Rent	115		4 0 0 00
		Rent expired			
	31	Amortization Expense, W.P. Equipment	516	8 0 00	
		Accumulated Amortization, W.P. Equipment	122		8 0 00
		Estimated amortization of asset			
	31	Office Salaries Expense	511	3 5 0 00	
		Salaries Payable	212		3 5 0 00
		Accrued salary to May 31			

Adjustments A to D in the adjustments section of the worksheet must be recorded in the journal and posted to the ledger.

Adjustment A

Before posting:

Office Supplies 114	
600	

Office Supplies Expense 514	

After posting:

Office Supplies 114	
600	500

Office Supplies Expense 514	
500	

Adjustment B

Before posting:

Prepaid Rent 115	
1,200	

Rent Expense 515	

After posting:

Prepaid Rent 115	
1,200	400

Rent Expense 515	
400	

Adjustment C

Before posting:

Word Processing Equipment 121	
6,000	

Amortization Expense, W. P. Equipment 516	

Accumulated Amortization, W. P. Equipment 122	

After posting:

Word Processing Equipment 121	
6,000	

Amortization Expense, W. P. Equipment 516	
80	

Accumulated Amortization, W. P. Equipment 122	
	80

This last adjustment shows the same balances for Amortization Expense and Accumulated Amortization. However, in subsequent adjustments the Accumulated Amortization balance will keep getting larger, but the debit to Amortization Expense and the credit to Accumulated Amortization will be the same. We will see why in a moment.

Adjustment D

Before posting:

Office Salaries Expense 511	
650	
650	

Salaries Payable 212	

After posting:

Office Salaries Expense 511	
650	
650	
350	

Salaries Payable 212	
	350

LEARNING UNIT 5-1 REVIEW

AT THIS POINT you should be able to:

- Define and state the purpose of adjusting entries. (p. 172)
- Journalize adjusting entries from the worksheet. (p. 173)
- Post journalized adjusting entries to the ledger. (p. 174)
- Compare specific ledger accounts before and after posting of the journalized adjusting entries. (p. 174)

SELF-REVIEW QUIZ 5-1

(The blank forms you need are on pages 5-1 and 5-2 of the *Study Guide with Working Papers.*)

Turn to the worksheet of P. Logan Company (p. 142) and (1) journalize and post the adjusting entries and (2) compare the adjusted ledger accounts before and after the adjustments are posted. T accounts with beginning balances are provided in your *Study Guide*.

Solution to Self-Review Quiz 5-1

Quiz Tip

These journal entries come from the adjustments column of the worksheet.

Page 2

Date		Account Titles and Description	PR	Dr.	Cr.
		Adjusting Entries			
Dec.	31	Amortization Expense, Store Equipment	511	1 00	
		Accumulated Amortization, Store Equipment	122		1 00
		Estimated amortization of equipment			
	31	Insurance Expense	516	2 00	
		Prepaid Insurance	116		2 00
		Insurance expired			
	31	Supplies Expense	514	4 00	
		Store Supplies	114		4 00
		Store Supplies used			
	31	Salaries Expense	512	3 00	
		Salaries Payable	212		3 00
		Accrued salaries payable			

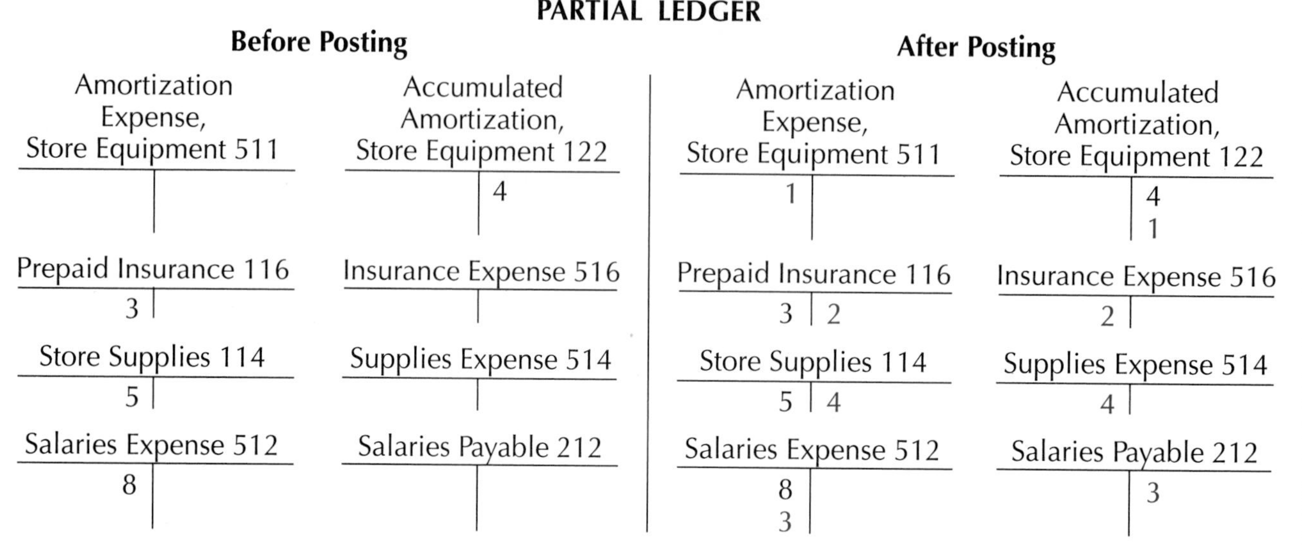

LEARNING UNIT 5-2

Journalizing and Posting Closing Entries: Step 8 of the Accounting Cycle

To make recording of the next fiscal year's transactions easier, a mechanical step, called **closing,** is taken by the accountant at Clark's. Closing is used to end—or close off—the revenue, expense, and withdrawal accounts at the end of the fiscal year. The information needed to complete closing entries will be found in the income statement and balance sheet sections of the worksheet.

To make it easier to understand this process, we will first look at the difference between temporary (nominal) accounts and permanent (real) accounts.

Here is the expanded accounting equation we used in an earlier chapter:

Assets = Liabilities + Capital − Withdrawals + Revenues − Expenses

Permanent accounts are found on the balance sheet.

Three of the items in that equation—assets, liabilities, and capital—are known as **real** or **permanent accounts**, because their balances are carried over from one fiscal year to another. The other three items—withdrawals, revenue, and expenses—are called **nominal** or **temporary accounts,** because their balances are not carried over from one fiscal year to another. Instead, their balances are set at zero at the beginning of each fiscal year. This allows us to accumulate new data about revenue, expenses, and withdrawals in the new fiscal year. The process of closing summarizes the effects of the temporary accounts on capital for that period by using **closing journal entries** and by posting them to the ledger. When the closing process is complete, the accounting equation will be reduced to:

Assets = Liabilities + Ending Capital

After all closing entries are journalized and posted to the ledger, all temporary accounts have a zero balance in the ledger. Closing is a step-by-step process.

If you look back at page 144 in Chapter 4, you will see that we have calculated the new capital on the balance sheet for Clark's Word Processing Services to be $14,275. But before the mechanical closing procedures are journalized and posted, the capital account of Brenda Clark in the ledger is only $10,000 (Chapter 3, page 96). Let's look now at how to journalize and post closing entries.

How to journalize closing entries

There are four steps to be performed in journalizing closing entries:

Step 1: Clear the revenue balances and transfer them to Income Summary. **Income Summary** is a temporary account in the ledger needed for closing. At the end of the closing process there will be no balance in Income Summary.

Revenue → Income Summary

Step 2: Clear the individual expense balances and transfer them to Income Summary.

Expenses → Income Summary

Step 3: Clear the balance in Income Summary and transfer it to Capital.

Income Summary → Capital

Step 4: Clear the balance in Withdrawals and transfer it to Capital.

Withdrawals → Capital

Figure 5-3 is a visual representation of these four steps. Keep in mind that this information must first be journalized and then posted to the appropriate ledger accounts. The worksheet presented in Figure 5-4 contains all the figures we will need for the closing process.

An Income Summary is a temporary account located in the chart of accounts under Owner's Equity. It does not have a normal balance of a debit or a credit.

Sometimes, closing the accounts is referred to as "clearing the accounts."

Don't forget two goals of closing:

1. Clear all temporary accounts in the ledger.
2. Update Capital to a new balance that reflects a summary of all the temporary accounts.

All numbers used in the closing process can be found on the worksheet in Figure 5-4 (page 178). Note that the *account* Income Summary is *not* on the worksheet.

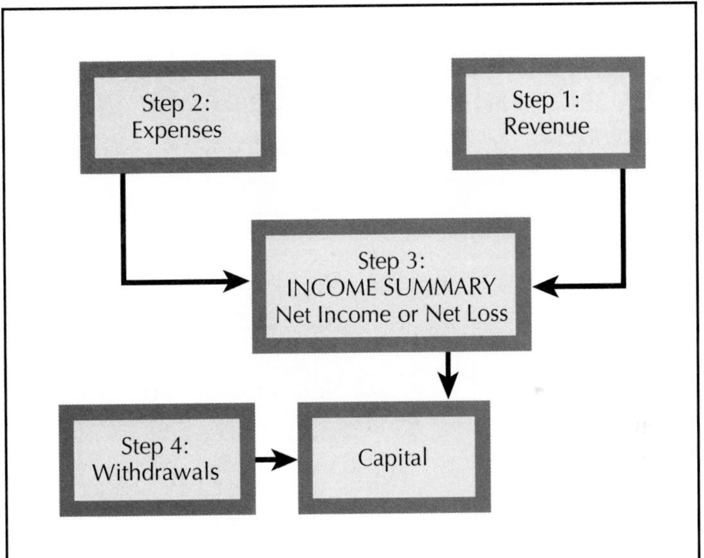

FIGURE 5-3
Four Steps in Journalizing Closing Entries

Step 1: Clear Revenue Balances and Transfer to Income Summary

Here is what is in the ledger before closing entries are journalized and posted:

Word Processing Fees 411		Income Summary 313	
	8,000		

The income statement section on the worksheet on page 178 shows that the Word Processing Fees have a credit balance of $8,000. To close or clear this to zero in the ledger, a debit of $8,000 is needed. But if we add an amount to the debit side, we must also add a credit—so we add $8,000 on the credit side of the Income Summary account.

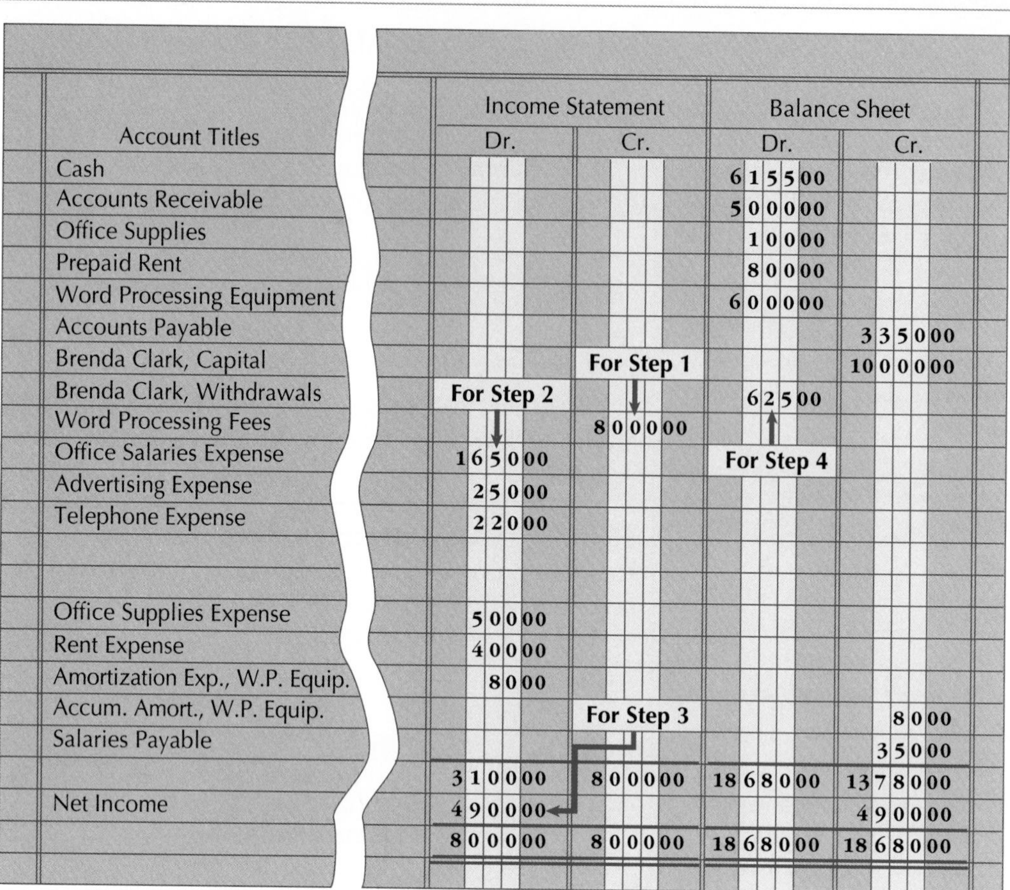

Account Titles	Income Statement Dr.	Income Statement Cr.	Balance Sheet Dr.	Balance Sheet Cr.
Cash			6155 00	
Accounts Receivable			5000 00	
Office Supplies			100 00	
Prepaid Rent			800 00	
Word Processing Equipment			6000 00	
Accounts Payable				3350 00
Brenda Clark, Capital				10000 00
Brenda Clark, Withdrawals			625 00	
Word Processing Fees		8000 00		
Office Salaries Expense	1650 00			
Advertising Expense	250 00			
Telephone Expense	220 00			
Office Supplies Expense	500 00			
Rent Expense	400 00			
Amortization Exp., W.P. Equip.	80 00			
Accum. Amort., W.P. Equip.				80 00
Salaries Payable				350 00
	3100 00	8000 00	18680 00	13780 00
Net Income	4900 00			4900 00
	8000 00	8000 00	18680 00	18680 00

FIGURE 5-4
Closing Figures on the Worksheet

The following is the journalized closing entry for step 1:

				Dr.	Cr.
May	31	Word Processing Fees	411	8000 00	
		Income Summary	313		8000 00
		To close income account			

This is what Word Processing Fees and Income Summary should look like in the ledger after step 1 closing entries are journalized and posted:

Word Processing Fees 411	
8,000 Closing	8,000 Revenue

Income Summary 313	
	8,000 Revenue

Note that the revenue balance is cleared to zero and transferred to Income Summary, a temporary account also located in the ledger.

Step 2: Clear Individual Expense Balances and Transfer the Total to Income Summary

Here is what is in the ledger for each expense before step 2 closing entries are journalized and posted. Each expense is listed on the worksheet in the debit column of the income statement section as above.

Office Salaries Expense 511	
650	
650	
350	

Advertising Expense 512	
250	

Telephone Expense 513	
220	

Office Supplies Expense 514	
500	

Rent Expense 515	
400	

Amortization Expense, W. P. Equipment 516	
80	

The income statement section of the worksheet lists all the expenses as debits. If we want to reduce each expense to zero, each one must be credited.

The following is the journalized closing entry for step 2:

The $3,100 is the total of the expenses on the worksheet.

31	Income Summary	313	3 100 00	
	Office Salaries Expense	511		1 650 00
	Advertising Expense	512		250 00
	Telephone Expense	513		220 00
	Office Supplies Expense	514		500 00
	Rent Expense	515		400 00
	Amortization Expense, W.P.Equipment	516		80 00
	To close expense accounts			

This is what individual expense accounts and the Income Summary should look like in the ledger after step 2 closing entries are journalized and posted:

Office Salaries Expense 511	
650	Closing 1,650
650	
350	

Advertising Expense 512	
250	Closing 250

Telephone Expense 513	
220	Closing 220

Office Supplies Expense 514	
500	Closing 500

Rent Expense 515	
400	Closing 400

Amortization Expense 516	
80	Closing 80

Income Summary 313	
Expenses	Revenue
Step 2 3,100	8,000 Step 1

Remember, the worksheet is a tool. The accountant realizes that the information about the total of the expenses will be transferred to Income Summary.

Step 3: Clear Balance in Income Summary (Net Income) and Transfer It to Capital

This is how the Income Summary and Brenda Clark, Capital, accounts look before step 3:

Income Summary 313	
3,100	8,000
	4,900

Brenda Clark, Capital 311	
	10,000

Note that the balance of Income Summary (Revenue minus Expenses or $8,000 – $3,100) is $4,900. That is the amount we must clear from the Income Summary account and transfer to the Brenda Clark, Capital, account.

The opposite would take place if the business had a net loss.

In order to transfer the balance of $4,900 from Income Summary (check the bottom of the debit column of the income statement section on the worksheet; see Figure 5-4) to Capital, it will be necessary to debit Income Summary for $4,900 (the difference between the revenue and expenses) and credit or increase Capital of Brenda Clark with $4,900.

This is the journalized closing entry for step 3:

	31	Income Summary	313	4900 00	
		Brenda Clark, Capital	311		4900 00
		Transfer profit for period to Capital acct.			

At the end of these three steps, Income Summary has a zero balance. If we had a net loss the end result would be to decrease capital. The entry would be to debit Capital and credit Income Summary for the loss.

This is what the Income Summary and Brenda Clark, Capital, accounts will look like in the ledger after step 3 closing entries are journalized and posted:

	Income Summary 313		
Total of Expenses →	3,100	8,000	← **Revenue**
Debit to close account →	4,900	4,900	← **Net income**

Brenda Clark, Capital 311		
	10,000	
	4,900	**Net income**

Step 4: Clear the Withdrawals Balance and Transfer It to Capital

Next, we must close the Withdrawals account. The Brenda Clark, Withdrawals, and Brenda Clark, Capital, accounts now look like this:

Brenda Clark, Withdrawals 312	
625	

Brenda Clark, Capital 311	
	10,000
	4,900

To bring the Withdrawals account to a zero balance, and summarize its effect on Capital, we must credit Withdrawals and debit Capital.

Remember, withdrawals are a non-business expense and thus not transferred to Income Summary. The closing entry is journalized as follows:

	31	Brenda Clark, Capital	311	625 00	
		Brenda Clark, Withdrawals	312		625 00
		Transfer withdrawals to Capital account			

Note that the $10,000 is a beginning balance since no additional investments were made during the period.

At this point the Brenda Clark, Withdrawals, and Brenda Clark, Capital, accounts would look like this in the ledger.

Brenda Clark, Withdrawals 312	
625	Closing 625

Brenda Clark, Capital 311	
Withdrawals → 625	10,000 ← **Beginning balance**
	4,900 ← **Net income**

CLARK'S WORD PROCESSING SERVICES GENERAL JOURNAL					
Date 2001		Account Title and Description	Post. Ref.	Dr.	Cr.
May	31	Word Processing Fees	411	8 000 00	
		Income Summary	313		8 000 00
		To close income account			
	31	Income Summary	313	3 100 00	
		Office Salaries Expense	511		1 650 00
		Advertising Expense	512		250 00
		Telephone Expense	513		220 00
		Office Supplies Expense	514		500 00
		Rent Expense	515		400 00
		Amortization Expense, WP Equipment	516		80 00
		To close expense accounts			
	31	Income Summary	313	4 900 00	
		Brenda Clark, Capital	311		4 900 00
		Transfer profit to capital			
	31	Brenda Clark, Capital	311	625 00	
		Brenda Clark, Withdrawals	312		625 00
		Transfer withdrawals to capital			

Now let's look at a summary of the closing entries. The complete ledger for Clark's Word Processing Services is shown in Figure 5-5 beginning on this page. Note that the word "adjusting" or "closing" is written in the explanation column of individual ledgers, as for example in the one for Office Supplies. If the goals of closing have been achieved, only permanent accounts will have balances carried to the next fiscal year. All temporary accounts should have zero balances.

FIGURE 5-5
Complete Ledger

CLARK'S WORD PROCESSING SERVICES
GENERAL LEDGER

Cash — Account No. 111

Date 2001		Explanation	Post. Ref.	Debit	Credit	DR or CR	Balance
May	1		GJ1	10 000 00		DR	10 000 00
	1		GJ1		1 000 00	DR	9 000 00
	1		GJ1		1 200 00	DR	7 800 00
	7		GJ1	3 000 00		DR	10 800 00
	11		GJ1		650 00	DR	10 150 00
	20		GJ1		625 00	DR	9 525 00
	25		GJ2		650 00	DR	8 875 00
	28		GJ2		2 500 00	DR	6 375 00
	29		GJ2		220 00	DR	6 155 00

(**FIGURE 5-5** cont.)

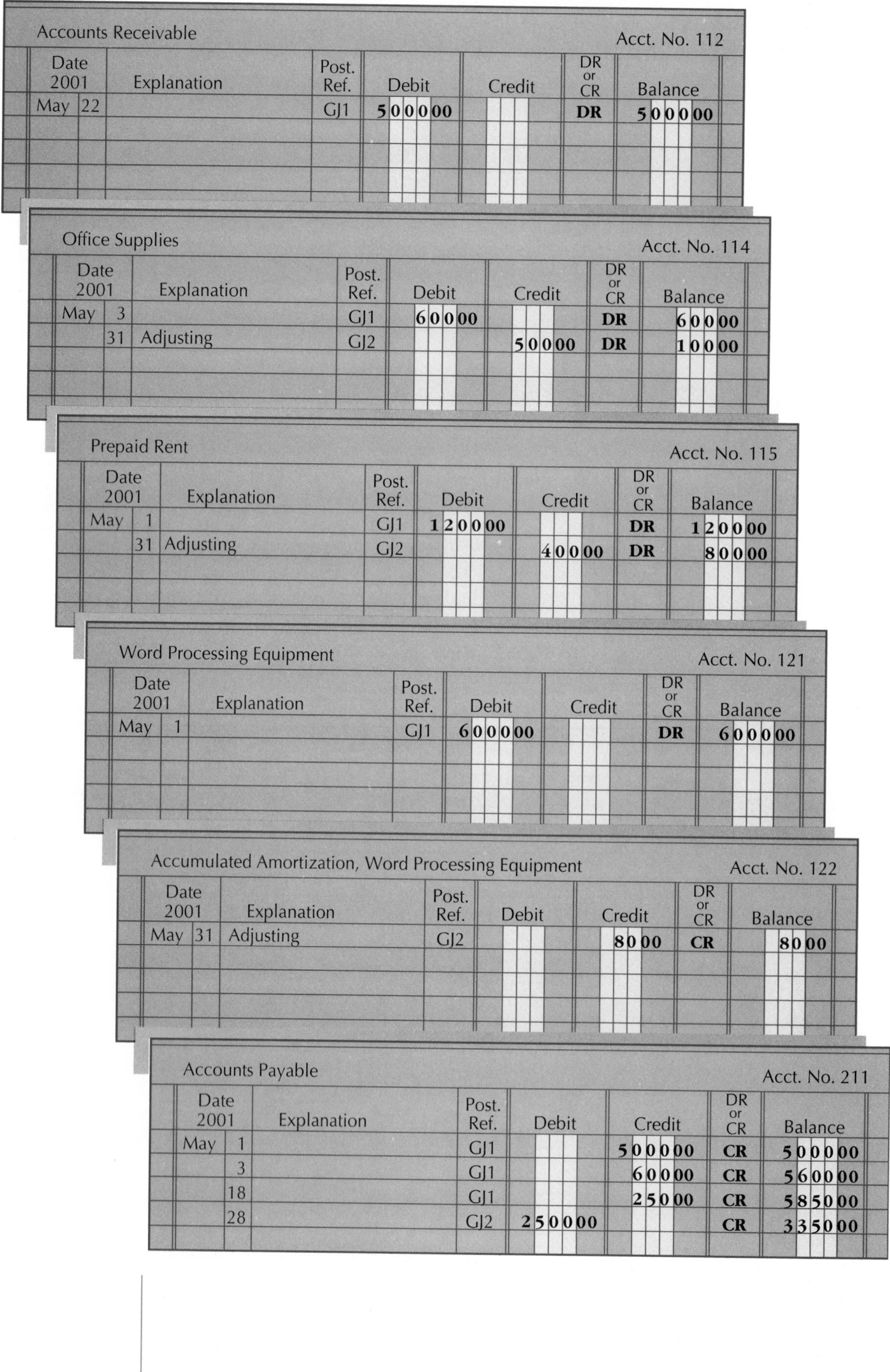

Accounts Receivable — Acct. No. 112

Date 2001		Explanation	Post. Ref.	Debit	Credit	DR or CR	Balance
May	22		GJ1	5,000.00		DR	5,000.00

Office Supplies — Acct. No. 114

Date 2001		Explanation	Post. Ref.	Debit	Credit	DR or CR	Balance
May	3		GJ1	600.00		DR	600.00
	31	Adjusting	GJ2		500.00	DR	100.00

Prepaid Rent — Acct. No. 115

Date 2001		Explanation	Post. Ref.	Debit	Credit	DR or CR	Balance
May	1		GJ1	1,200.00		DR	1,200.00
	31	Adjusting	GJ2		400.00	DR	800.00

Word Processing Equipment — Acct. No. 121

Date 2001		Explanation	Post. Ref.	Debit	Credit	DR or CR	Balance
May	1		GJ1	6,000.00		DR	6,000.00

Accumulated Amortization, Word Processing Equipment — Acct. No. 122

Date 2001		Explanation	Post. Ref.	Debit	Credit	DR or CR	Balance
May	31	Adjusting	GJ2		80.00	CR	80.00

Accounts Payable — Acct. No. 211

Date 2001		Explanation	Post. Ref.	Debit	Credit	DR or CR	Balance
May	1		GJ1		5,000.00	CR	5,000.00
	3		GJ1		600.00	CR	5,600.00
	18		GJ1		250.00	CR	5,850.00
	28		GJ2	2,500.00		CR	3,350.00

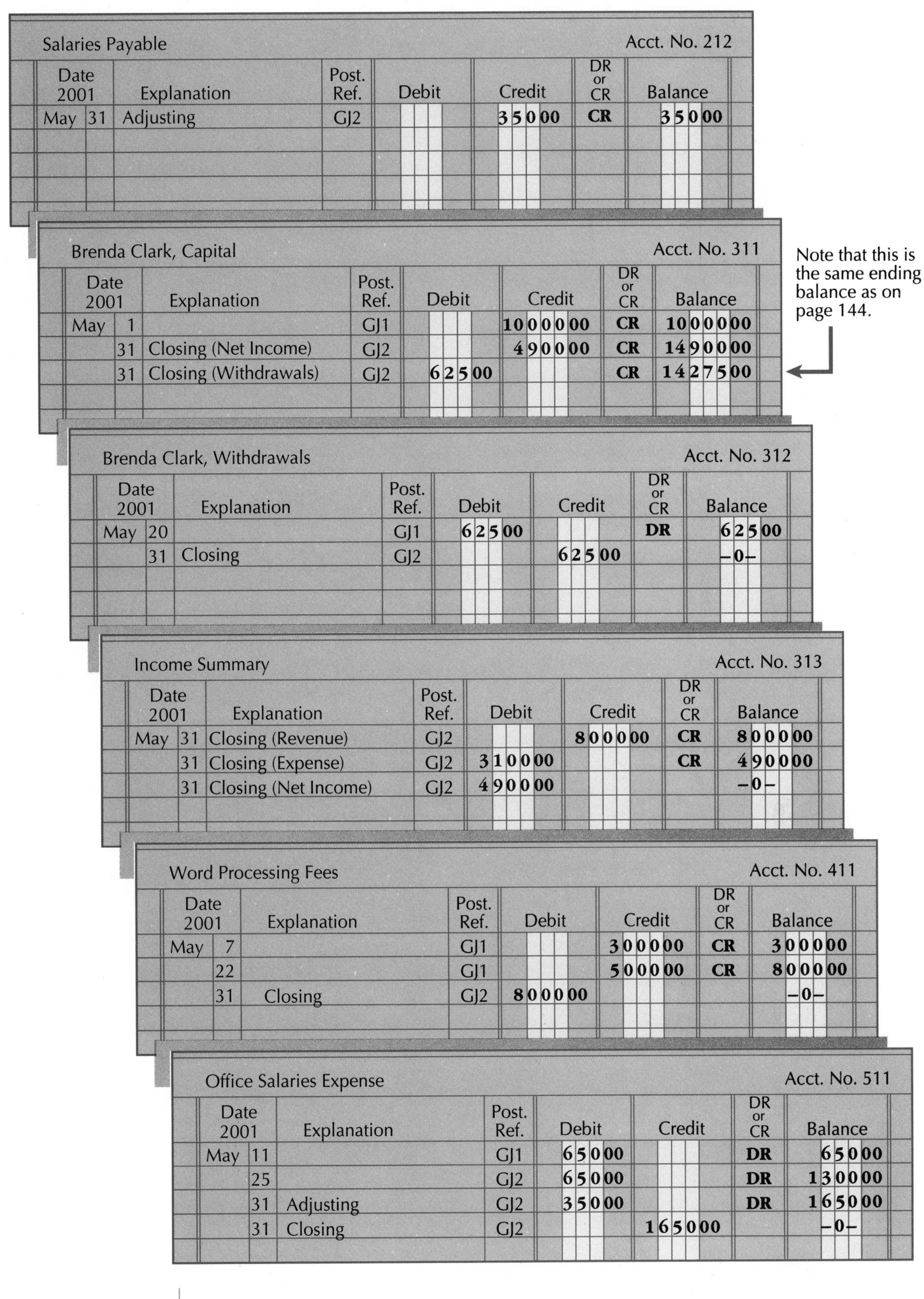

Salaries Payable — Acct. No. 212

Date 2001		Explanation	Post. Ref.	Debit	Credit	DR or CR	Balance
May	31	Adjusting	GJ2		350 00	CR	350 00

Brenda Clark, Capital — Acct. No. 311

Date 2001		Explanation	Post. Ref.	Debit	Credit	DR or CR	Balance
May	1		GJ1		10000 00	CR	10000 00
	31	Closing (Net Income)	GJ2		4900 00	CR	14900 00
	31	Closing (Withdrawals)	GJ2	625 00		CR	14275 00

Note that this is the same ending balance as on page 144.

Brenda Clark, Withdrawals — Acct. No. 312

Date 2001		Explanation	Post. Ref.	Debit	Credit	DR or CR	Balance
May	20		GJ1	625 00		DR	625 00
	31	Closing	GJ2		625 00		–0–

Income Summary — Acct. No. 313

Date 2001		Explanation	Post. Ref.	Debit	Credit	DR or CR	Balance
May	31	Closing (Revenue)	GJ2		8000 00	CR	8000 00
	31	Closing (Expense)	GJ2	3100 00		CR	4900 00
	31	Closing (Net Income)	GJ2	4900 00			–0–

Word Processing Fees — Acct. No. 411

Date 2001		Explanation	Post. Ref.	Debit	Credit	DR or CR	Balance
May	7		GJ1		3000 00	CR	3000 00
	22		GJ1		5000 00	CR	8000 00
	31	Closing	GJ2	8000 00			–0–

Office Salaries Expense — Acct. No. 511

Date 2001		Explanation	Post. Ref.	Debit	Credit	DR or CR	Balance
May	11		GJ1	650 00		DR	650 00
	25		GJ2	650 00		DR	1300 00
	31	Adjusting	GJ2	350 00		DR	1650 00
	31	Closing	GJ2		1650 00		–0–

(**FIGURE 5-5** cont.)

Advertising Expense — Acct. No. 512

Date 2001		Explanation	Post. Ref.	Debit	Credit	DR or CR	Balance
May	18		GJ1	250 00		DR	250 00
	31	Closing	GJ2		250 00		–0–

Telephone Expense — Acct. No. 513

Date 2001		Explanation	Post. Ref.	Debit	Credit	DR or CR	Balance
May	29		GJ2	220 00		DR	220 00
	31	Closing	GJ2		220 00		–0–

Office Supplies Expense — Acct. No. 514

Date 2001		Explanation	Post. Ref.	Debit	Credit	DR or CR	Balance
May	31	Adjusting	GJ2	500 00		DR	500 00
	31	Closing	GJ2		500 00		–0–

Rent Expense — Acct. No. 515

Date 2001		Explanation	Post. Ref.	Debit	Credit	DR or CR	Balance
May	31	Adjusting	GJ2	400 00		DR	400 00
	31	Closing	GJ2		400 00		–0–

Amortization Expense, Word Processing Equipment — Acct. No. 516

Date 2001		Explanation	Post. Ref.	Debit	Credit	DR or CR	Balance
May	31	Adjusting	GJ2	80 00		DR	80 00
		Closing	GJ2		80 00		–0–

LEARNING UNIT 5-2 REVIEW

AT THIS POINT you should be able to:

- Define closing. (p. 176)
- Differentiate between temporary (nominal) and permanent (real) accounts. (p. 176)
- List the four mechanical steps of closing. (p. 177)
- Explain the role of the Income Summary account. (p. 177)
- Explain the role of the worksheet in the closing process. (p. 177)

SELF-REVIEW QUIZ 5-2

(The blank forms you need are on pages 5-2 and 5-3 of the *Study Guide with Working Papers.*)

Go to the worksheet for P. Logan on page 142. Then (1) journalize and post the closing entries and (2) calculate the new balance for P. Logan, Capital.

Solution to Self-Review Quiz 5-2

Date		Account Titles and Description	PR	Dr.	Cr.
		Closing Entries			
Dec.	31	Revenue from Clients	410	25 00	
		Income Summary	312		25 00
		To close income account			
	31	Income Summary	312	20 00	
		Rent Expense	518		2 00
		Salaries Expense	512		11 00
		Amortization Expense, Store Equipment	510		1 00
		Insurance Expense	516		2 00
		Supplies Expense	514		4 00
		To close expense accounts			
	31	Income Summary	312	5 00	
		P. Logan, Capital	310		5 00
		Transfer net income to Capital accounts			
	31	P. Logan, Capital	310	3 00	
		P. Logan, Withdrawals	311		3 00
		Transfer withdrawals to Capital accounts			

PARTIAL LEDGER

P. Logan, Capital 310

Dr.	Cr.
3	14
	5
	16

Revenue from Clients 410

Dr.	Cr.
25	25

Supplies Expense 514

Dr.	Cr.
4	4

P. Logan, Withdrawals 311

Dr.	Cr.
3	3

Amortization Expense, Store Equipment. 510

Dr.	Cr.
1	1

Insurance Expense 516

Dr.	Cr.
2	2

Income Summary 312		Salaries Expense 512		Rent Expense 518	
20	25	11	11	2	2
5					

Quiz Tip

No calculations are needed in the closing process. All numbers come from the worksheet. Income summary is a temporary account in the ledger.

P. Logan, Capital		$14
Net Income	$5	
Less: Withdrawals	3	
Increase in Capital		2
P. Logan, Capital (ending)		$16

LEARNING UNIT 5-3

The Post-Closing Trial Balance: Step 9 of the Accounting Cycle and the Accounting Cycle Reviewed

The post-closing trial balance helps prove the accuracy of the adjusting and closing process. It contains the true ending figure for capital.

PREPARING A POST-CLOSING TRIAL BALANCE

The last step in the accounting cycle is the preparation of a **post-closing trial balance** (sometimes called an opening trial balance) which lists only permanent accounts in the ledger and their balances after adjusting and closing entries have been posted. This post-closing trial balance aids in checking whether the ledger is in balance. It is important to do this checking because so many new postings go to the ledger from the adjusting and closing process.

The procedure for taking a post-closing trial balance is the same as for a trial balance, except that, since closing entries have closed all temporary accounts, the post-closing trial balance will contain only permanent accounts (balance sheet). Keep in mind, however, that adjustments have occurred.

THE ACCOUNTING CYCLE REVIEWED

Table 5-1 lists the steps we completed in the manual accounting cycle for Clark's Word Processing Services for the month of May.

Insight: Most companies journalize and post adjusting and closing entries only at the end of their fiscal year. A company that prepares interim reports may complete only the first six steps of the cycle. Worksheets allow the preparation of interim reports without the formal adjusting and closing of the books.

Insight: To prepare a financial report for April, the data needed can be obtained by subtracting the worksheet accumulated totals for the end of March from the worksheet prepared at the end of April. In this chapter, we chose a month that would show the completion of an entire cycle for Clark's Word Processing Services.

TABLE 5-1 STEPS OF THE MANUAL ACCOUNTING CYCLE

Step	Explanation
1. Business transactions occur and generate source documents.	Source documents are cash register tapes, sales tickets, bills, cheques, payroll cards, etc.
↓	↓
2. Analyze and record business transactions into a journal.	Called journalizing
↓	↓
3. Post or transfer information from journal to ledger.	Copying the debits and credits of the journal entries into the ledger accounts
↓	↓
4. Prepare a trial balance.	Summarizing each individual ledger account and listing these accounts and their balances to test for mathematical accuracy in recording transactions
↓	↓
5. Prepare a worksheet.	A multicolumn form that summarizes accounting information to complete the accounting cycle
↓	↓
6. Prepare financial statements.	Income statement, statement of owner's equity, and balance sheet
↓	↓
7. Journalize and post adjusting entries.	Use figures in the adjustment columns of worksheet.
↓	↓
8. Journalize and post closing entries.	Use figures in the income statement and balance sheet sections of worksheet.
↓	↓
9. Prepare a post-closing trial balance.	Prove the mathematical accuracy of the adjusting and closing process of the accounting cycle.

LEARNING UNIT 5-3 REVIEW

AT THIS POINT you should be able to:

- Prepare a post-closing trial balance. (p. 186)
- Explain the relationship of interim reports to the accounting cycle. (p. 186)

SELF-REVIEW QUIZ 5-3

(The blank forms you need are on page 5-3 of the *Study Guide with Working Papers.*)

From the ledger on pages 181 to 184, prepare a post-closing trial balance.

Solution to Self-Review Quiz 5-3

CLARK'S WORD PROCESSING SERVICES POST-CLOSING TRIAL BALANCE MAY 31, 2001		
	Dr.	Cr.
Cash	6 1 5 5 00	
Accounts Receivable	5 0 0 0 00	
Office Supplies	1 0 0 00	
Prepaid Rent	8 0 0 00	
Word Processing Equipment	6 0 0 0 00	
Accumulated Amortization, Word Processing Equipment		8 0 00
Accounts Payable		3 3 5 0 00
Salaries Payable		3 5 0 00
Brenda Clark, Capital		14 2 7 5 00
Totals	18 0 5 5 00	18 0 5 5 00

The post-closing trial balance contains only permanent accounts because all temporary accounts have been closed. All temporary accounts are summarized in the capital account.

Closing Time

The doorbell rang at 1 a.m. "The cavalry has arrived!" said the giant in the doorway.

"You're a real friend in need, Lou," said Fred gratefully, as he opened the door. "I've been over and over this, and I can't get it to balance. And my monthly closing is due to Dwayne at noon tomorrow! I hate to bother you so late, but . . ." Fred had called Lou Jacobs, his roommate at Dunkin' Donuts University. Lou had ridden hard to the rescue—one and a half hours on the expressway.

"You look as if you haven't slept in days, Fred," interrupted Lou. "This is what friends are for. Let me at those accounts! You put a pot of coffee on. I'll start with payroll, because you hired someone this month."

Dunkin' Donuts company policy calls for a closing every month, on the last Saturday, before noon. This way comparisons between shops are most valid. Dunkin' Donuts University stresses to all shop owners that the monthly closing grows more difficult as the year progresses. Errors get harder to find, and accuracy becomes ever more critical. There is, unfortunately, no set way to find errors, and even no set place to start. Lou chose payroll because it is one of the largest expenses and because of the new hire.

At 2:45 a.m. Lou woke Fred, who was dozing. "I think I've got it, Fred! It looks like you messed up on adjusting the Salaries Expense account. I looked at the Payroll Register and compared the total to the Salaries Payable account. It didn't match! Remember, you hired Maria Sanchez on the 26th, so you have to increase both the Salaries Expense and the Salaries Payable lines, because she has accrued wages. Salaries Expense is a debit and Salaries Payable is a credit. You skipped the payable. Now, If you make this adjusting entry in the General Journal, the worksheet will balance."

Fred's sigh of relief turned into a big yawn, and they both laughed. "Thank heavens you stayed awake in Accounting class!" said Fred, with another huge yawn.

Discussion Questions

1. How would the adjustment be made if Maria Sanchez received $6.50 per hour and worked 25 hours? Where would you place her accrued wages?
2. Fred bought six new uniforms for Maria Sanchez for $72 each, but forgot to post this to the Uniforms account. How much will the closing balance be off? In what way will it be off?
3. Why does Dunkin' Donuts require a monthly closing from each shop, no matter how much—or little—business each does?

Chapter Review

Comprehensive demonstration problem with solution tips

(The blank forms you need are on pages 5-4 to 5-10 of the *Study Guide with Working Papers.*)

From the following transactions for Rolo Company, complete the entire accounting cycle. The chart of accounts includes:

Assets
111 Cash
112 Accounts Receivable
114 Prepaid Rent
115 Office Supplies
121 Office Equipment
122 Accumulated Amortization, Office Equipment

Liabilities
211 Accounts Payable
212 Salaries Payable

Owner's Equity
311 Rolo Kern, Capital
312 Rolo Kern, Withdrawals
313 Income Summary

Revenue
411 Fees Earned

Expenses
511 Salaries Expense
512 Advertising Expense
513 Rent Expense
514 Office Supplies Expense
515 Amortization Expense, Office Equipment

We will use unusually small numbers to simplify calculation and emphasize the theory.

2001
Jan. 2 Rolo Kern invested $1,200 cash and $100 worth of office equipment to open Rolo Co.
2 Paid rent for three months in advance, $300.
4 Purchased office equipment on account, $50.
6 Bought office supplies for cash, $40.
8 Collected $400 for services rendered.
12 Rolo paid his home electric bill from the company bank account, $20.
14 Provided $100 worth of services to clients who will not pay until next month.
16 Paid salaries, $60.
18 Advertising bill for $70 was received but will not be paid until next month.

Adjustment Data on January 31

a. Supplies on Hand	$6
b. Rent Expired	$100
c. Amortization, Office Equipment	$20
d. Salaries Accrued	$50

Journalizing Transactions and Posting to Ledger, Rolo Company

General Journal — Page 1

Date		Account Titles and Description	PR	Dr.	Cr.
2001 Jan.	2	Cash	111	1200 00	
		Office Equipment	121	100 00	
		R. Kern, Capital	311		1300 00
		Initial investment			
	2	Prepaid Rent	114	300 00	
		Cash	111		300 00
		Rent paid in advance—3 months			
	4	Office Equipment	121	50 00	
		Accounts Payable	211		50 00
		Purchased equipment on account			
	6	Office Supplies	115	40 00	
		Cash	111		40 00
		Supplies purchased for cash			
	8	Cash	111	400 00	
		Fees Earned	411		400 00
		Services rendered			
	12	R. Kern, Withdrawals	312	20 00	
		Cash	111		20 00
		Personal payment of a bill			
	14	Accounts Receivable	112	100 00	
		Fees Earned	411		100 00
		Services rendered on account			
	16	Salaries Expense	511	60 00	
		Cash	111		60 00
		Paid salaries			
	18	Advertising Expense	512	70 00	
		Accounts Payable	211		70 00
		Advertising bill, but not paid			

Solution Tips to Journalizing and Posting Transactions

Jan. **2**

Cash	**Asset**	↑	**Dr.**	**$1,200**
Office Equipment	**Asset**	↑	**Dr.**	**$ 100**
R. Kern, Capital	**Capital**	↑	**Cr.**	**$1,300**

Jan. **2**

Prepaid Rent	**Asset**	↑	**Dr.**	**$ 300**
Cash	**Asset**	↓	**Cr.**	**$ 300**

Jan. 4	Office Equipment Accounts Payable	Asset Liability	↑ ↑	Dr. Cr.	$ 50 $ 50
Jan. 6	Office Supplies Cash	Asset Asset	↑ ↓	Dr. Cr.	$ 40 $ 40
Jan. 8	Cash Fees Earned	Asset Revenue	↑ ↑	Dr. Cr.	$ 400 $ 400
Jan. 12	R. Kern, Withdrawals Cash	Owner's Equity (Withdr.) Asset	↓ ↓	Dr. Cr.	$ 20 $ 20
Jan. 14	Accounts Receivable Fees Earned	Asset Revenue	↑ ↑	Dr. Cr.	$ 100 $ 100
Jan.16	Salaries Expense Cash	Expense Asset	↑ ↓	Dr. Cr.	$ 60 $ 60
Jan. 18	Advertising Expense Accounts Payable	Expense Liability	↑ ↑	Dr. Cr.	$ 70 $ 70

Note: All account titles come from the chart of accounts. When journalizing, the PR column of the general journal is blank. It is in the posting process that we update the ledger. The Post. Ref. column in the ledger accounts tells us from which journal page the information came. After posting to the account in the ledger, we fill in the PR column of the journal, telling us to what account number the information was transferred.

COMPLETING THE WORKSHEET

See the worksheet on page 192.

Solution Tips to the Trial Balance and Completion of the Worksheet

After the posting process is complete from the journal to the ledger, we take the ending balance in each account and prepare a trial balance on the worksheet. If an account title has no balance, it is not listed on the trial balance. New titles on the worksheet will be added below the trial balance as needed.

ROLO COMPANY
WORKSHEET
FOR MONTH ENDED JANUARY 31, 2001

Account Titles	Trial Balance Dr.	Trial Balance Cr.	Adjustments Dr.	Adjustments Cr.	Adjusted Trial Balance Dr.	Adjusted Trial Balance Cr.	Income Statement Dr.	Income Statement Cr.	Balance Sheet Dr.	Balance Sheet Cr.
Cash	1180 00				1180 00				1180 00	
Accounts Receivable	100 00				100 00				100 00	
Prepaid Rent	300 00			(B) 100 00	200 00				200 00	
Office Supplies	40 00			(A) 34 00	6 00				6 00	
Office Equipment	150 00				150 00				150 00	
Accounts Payable		120 00				120 00				120 00
R. Kern, Capital		1300 00				1300 00				1300 00
R. Kern, Withdrawals	20 00				20 00				20 00	
Fees Earned		500 00				500 00		500 00		
Salaries Expense	60 00		(D) 50 00		110 00		110 00			
Advertising Expense	70 00				70 00		70 00			
	1920 00	1920 00								
Office Supplies Expense			(A) 34 00		34 00		34 00			
Rent Expense			(B) 100 00		100 00		100 00			
Amort. Expense, Office Equip.			(C) 20 00		20 00		20 00			
Accum. Amort., Office Equip.				(C) 20 00		20 00				20 00
Salaries Payable				(D) 50 00		50 00				50 00
			204 00	204 00	1990 00	1990 00	334 00	500 00	1656 00	1490 00
Net Income							166 00			166 00
							500 00	500 00	1656 00	1656 00

ADJUSTMENTS

The amount of office supplies on hand ($6) is *not* the adjustment. Need to calculate amount used up.

Office Supplies Expense	**Expense**	↑	**Dr.**	**$ 34**	**($40 − $6)**
Office Supplies	**Asset**	↓	**Cr.**	**$ 34**	

Expired

Rent Expense	**Expense**	↑	**Dr.**	**$100**	
Prepaid Rent	**Asset**	↓	**Cr.**	**$100**	

Do not touch original cost of equipment.

Amort. Exp., Office Equip.	**Expense**	↑	**Dr.**	**$ 20**	
Accum. Amort., Office Equip.	**Asset (Contra)**	↓	**Cr.**	**$ 20**	

Owed but not paid

Salaries Expense	**Expense**	↑	**Dr.**	**$ 50**	
Salaries Payable	**Liability**	↑	**Cr.**	**$ 50**	

Note: This information is on the worksheet but has *not* been updated in the ledger. (This will happen when we journalize and post adjustments at end of cycle.)

Note that the last four columns of the worksheet come from numbers on the adjusted trial balance.

We move Net Income of $166 to the balance sheet credit column, since the capital figure is the old one on the worksheet.

PREPARING THE FORMAL FINANCIAL REPORTS

ROLO COMPANY
INCOME STATEMENT
FOR MONTH ENDED JANUARY 31, 2001

Revenue:		
Fees Earned		$500 00
Operating Expenses:		
Salaries Expense	$110 00	
Advertising Expense	70 00	
Office Supplies Expense	34 00	
Rent Expense	100 00	
Amortization Expense, Office Equipment	20 00	
Total Operating Expenses		334 00
Net Income		$166 00

ROLO COMPANY
STATEMENT OF OWNER'S EQUITY
FOR MONTH ENDED JANUARY 31, 2001

R. Kern, Capital, January 1, 2001		$1300 00
Net Income for January	$166 00	
Less: Withdrawals for January	20 00	
Increase in Capital		146 00
R. Kern, Capital, January 31, 2001		$1446 00

ROLO COMPANY
BALANCE SHEET
JANUARY 31, 2001

Assets			Liabilities and Owner's Equity		
Cash		$1 180 00	Liabilities:		
Accounts Receivable		100 00	Accounts Payable	$ 120 00	
Prepaid Rent		200 00	Salaries Payable	50 00	
Office Supplies		6 00	Total Liabilities		$ 170 00
Office Equipment	$ 150 00		Owner's Equity:		
Less: Acc. Amort.	20 00	130 00	R. Kern, Capital		1 446 00
			Total Liabilities and		
Total Assets		$1 616 00	Owner's Equity		$1 616 00

Solution Tips to Preparing the Financial Reports

The reports are prepared from the worksheet. (Many of the ledger accounts are not up to date.) The income statement lists revenue and expenses. The net income figure of $166 is used to update the statement of owner's equity. The statement of owner's equity calculates a new figure for Capital, $1,446 (Beginning Capital + Net Income − Withdrawals). This new figure is then listed on the balance sheet (Assets, Liabilities, and a new figure for Capital).

JOURNALIZING AND POSTING ADJUSTING AND CLOSING ENTRIES

See the journal at the top of page 195.

Solution Tips to Journalizing and Posting Adjusting and Closing Entries

ADJUSTMENTS

The adjustments from the worksheet are journalized (same journal) and posted to the ledger. Now ledger accounts will be brought up to date. Remember, we have already prepared the financial reports from the worksheet. Our goal now is to get the ledger up to date.

CLOSING

Note: Income Summary is a temporary account located in the ledger.

Goals

Where do I get my information for closing?

1. Adjust all temporary accounts in the ledger to zero balances.
2. Determine a new figure for capital in the ledger.

	General Journal					Page 2
	Date		Account Titles and Description	PR	Dr.	Cr.
			Adjusting Entries			
	Jan.	31	Office Supplies Expense	514	3400	
			Office Supplies	115		3400
			Supplies used			
		31	Rent Expense	513	10000	
			Prepaid Rent	114		10000
			Rent expired			
		31	Amortization Expense, Office Equipment	515	2000	
			Accumulated Amortization, Office Equip.	122		2000
			Estimated Amortization			
		31	Salaries Expense	511	5000	
			Salaries Payable	212		5000
			Accrued salaries			
			Closing Entries			
Closing: Step 1 ►		31	Fees Earned	411	50000	
			Income Summary	313		50000
			To close income accounts			
Closing: Step 2 ►		31	Income Summary	313	33400	
			Salaries Expense	511		11000
			Advertising Expense	512		7000
			Office Supplies Expense	514		3400
			Rent Expense	513		10000
			Amortization Expense, Office Equipment	515		2000
			To close expense accounts			
Closing: Step 3 ►		31	Income Summary	313	16600	
			R. Kern, Capital	311		16600
			Transfer profit to Capital			
Closing: Step 4 ►		31	R. Kern, Capital	311	2000	
			R. Kern, Withdrawals	312		2000
			Transfer withdrawals to Capital			

Steps in the Closing Process

Step 1: Close revenue to Income Summary.

Step 2: Close individual expenses to Income Summary.

Step 3: Close balance of Income Summary to Capital. (This really is the net income figure on the worksheet.)

Step 4: Close balance of Withdrawals to Capital.

All the journal closing entries are posted. (No new calculations are needed, since all figures are on the worksheet.) The result in the ledger is that all temporary accounts have a zero balance.

GENERAL LEDGER

Cash — Acct. No. 111

Date 2001		Explanation	Post. Ref.	Debit	Credit	DR or CR	Balance
Jan.	2		GJ1	1200 00		DR.	1200 00
	2		GJ1		300 00	DR.	900 00
	6		GJ1		40 00	DR.	860 00
	8		G1	400 00		DR.	1260 00
	12		GJ1		20 00	DR.	1240 00
	16		GJ1		60 00	DR.	1180 00

Accounts Receivable — Acct. No. 112

Date 2001		Explanation	Post. Ref.	Debit	Credit	DR or CR	Balance
Jan.	14		GJ1	100 00		DR.	100 00

Prepaid Rent — Acct. No. 114

Date 2001		Explanation	Post. Ref.	Debit	Credit	DR or CR	Balance
Jan.	2		GJ1	300 00		DR.	300 00
	31	Adjustment	GJ1		100 00	DR.	200 00

Office Supplies — Acct. No. 115

Date 2001		Explanation	Post. Ref.	Debit	Credit	DR or CR	Balance
Jan.	6		GJ1	40 00		DR.	40 00
	31	Adjustment	GJ2		34 00	DR.	6 00

Office Equipment — Acct. No. 121

Date 2001		Explanation	Post. Ref.	Debit	Credit	DR. CR.	Balance
Jan.	2		GJ1	100 00		DR.	100 00
	4		GJ1	50 00		DR.	150 00

Accumulated Amortization, Office Equipment — Acct. No. 122

Date 2001		Explanation	Post. Ref.	Debit	Credit	DR or CR	Balance
Jan.	31	Adjustment	GJ2		20 00	CR.	20 00

Accounts Payable — Acct. No. 211

Date 2001		Explanation	Post. Ref.	Debit	Credit	DR or CR	Balance
Jan.	4		GJ1		50 00	CR.	50 00
	18		GJ1		70 00	CR.	120 00

Salaries Payable — Acct. No. 212

Date 2001		Explanation	Post. Ref.	Debit	Credit	DR or CR	Balance
Jan.	31	Adjustment	GJ2		50 00	CR.	50 00

Rolo Kern, Capital — Acct. No. 311

Date 2001		Explanation	Post. Ref.	Debit	Credit	DR or CR	Balance
Jan.	2		GJ1		1300 00	CR.	1300 00
	31	Closing	GJ2		166 00	CR.	1466 00
	31	Closing	GJ2	20 00		CR.	1446 00

Rolo Kern, Withdrawals — Acct. No. 312

Date 2001		Explanation	Post. Ref.	Debit	Credit	DR or CR	Balance
Jan.	12		GJ1	20 00		DR.	20 00
	31	Closing	GJ2		20 00		–0–

Income Summary — Acct. No. 313

Date 2001		Explanation	Post. Ref.	Debit	Credit	DR or CR	Balance
Jan.	31	Closing	GJ2		500 00	CR.	500 00
	31	Closing	GJ2	334 00		CR.	166 00
	31	Closing	GJ2	166 00			–0–

Fees Earned — Acct. No. 411

Date 2001		Explanation	Post. Ref.	Debit	Credit	DR. CR.	Balance
Jan.	8		GJ1		400 00	CR.	400 00
	14		GJ1		100 00	CR.	500 00
	31	Closing	GJ2	500 00			–0–

Salaries Expense — Acct. No. 511

Date 2001		Explanation	Post. Ref.	Debit	Credit	DR. CR.	Balance
Jan.	16	Closing	GJ1	60 00		DR.	60 00
	31	Adjusting	GJ2	50 00		DR.	110 00
	31	Closing	GJ2		110 00		–0–

Advertising Expense — Acct. No. 512

Date 2001		Explanation	Post. Ref.	Debit	Credit	DR. CR.	Balance
Jan.	18		GJ1	70 00		DR.	70 00
	31	Closing	GJ2		70 00		–0–

Rent Expense — Acct. No. 513

Date 2001		Explanation	Post. Ref.	Debit	Credit	DR. CR.	Balance
Jan.	31	Adjusting	GJ2	100 00		DR.	100 00
	31	Closing	GJ2		100 00		–0–

Office Supplies Expense — Acct. No. 514

Date 2001		Explanation	Post. Ref.	Debit	Credit	DR. CR.	Balance
Jan.	31	Adjusting	GJ2	34 00		DR.	34 00
	31	Closing	GJ2		34 00		–0–

Amortization Expense, Office Equipment — Acct. No. 515

Date 2001		Explanation	Post. Ref.	Debit	Credit	DR. CR.	Balance
Jan.	31	Adjusting	GJ2	20 00		DR.	20 00
	31	Closing	GJ2		20 00		–0–

These are all permanent accounts.

ROLO CO. POST-CLOSING TRIAL BALANCE JANUARY 31, 2001		
	Dr.	Cr.
Cash	1 1 8 0 00	
Accounts Receivable	1 0 0 00	
Prepaid Rent	2 0 0 00	
Office Supplies	6 00	
Office Equipment	1 5 0 00	
Accumulated Amortization, Office Equipment		2 0 00
Accounts Payable		1 2 0 00
Salaries Payable		5 0 00
R. Kern, Capital		1 4 4 6 00
Total	1 6 3 6 00	1 6 3 6 00

Solution Tips for the Post-Closing Trial Balance

The post-closing trial balance is a list of the ledger *after* adjusting and closing entries have been completed. Note the figure for capital $1,446 is the new figure.

Beginning Capital	$1,300
+ Net Income	166
− Withdrawals	20
= Ending Capital	$1,446

Next accounting period we will enter new amounts in the Revenues, Expenses, and Withdrawals accounts. For now, the post-closing trial balance is made up only of permanent accounts.

Summary of Key Points

Learning Unit 5-1

1. After formal financial reports have been prepared, the ledger has still not been brought up to date.
2. Information for journalizing adjusting entries comes from the adjustments section of the worksheet.

Learning Unit 5-2

1. Closing is a mechanical process that is completed before the accountant can record transactions for the next fiscal year.
2. Assets, Liabilities, and Capital are permanent (real) accounts; their balances are carried over from one fiscal year to another. Withdrawals, Revenue, and Expenses are nominal (temporary) accounts; their balances are *not* carried over from one fiscal year to another.
3. Income Summary is a temporary account in the general ledger and does not have a normal balance. It will summarize revenue and expenses and transfer the balance to capital. Withdrawals do not go into Income Summary because they are *not* business expenses.
4. All information for closing can be obtained from the worksheet.

5. When closing is complete, all temporary accounts in the ledger will have a zero balance, and all this information will be updated in the Capital account.
6. Closing entries are usually done only at year-end. Interim reports can be prepared from worksheets that are prepared monthly, quarterly, etc.

Learning Unit 5-3

1. The post-closing trial balance is prepared from the ledger accounts after the adjusting and closing entries have been posted.
2. The accounts on the post-closing trial balance are all permanent accounts.

Key terms

Adjusting journal entries Journal entries that are needed in order to update specific ledger accounts to reflect correct balances at the end of an accounting period (p. 172)

Closing The process of bringing the balances of all revenue, expense, and withdrawal accounts to zero, ready for a new fiscal year (p. 176)

Closing journal entries Journal entries that are prepared to (a) reduce or clear all temporary accounts to a zero balance or (b) update capital to a new closing balance (p. 176)

Income Summary A temporary account in the ledger that summarizes revenue and expenses and transfers its balance (net income or net loss) to capital. It does not have a normal balance. (p. 177)

Nominal accounts See **Temporary accounts** (p. 176)

Permanent accounts Accounts whose balances are carried over to the next fiscal year; examples: assets, liabilities, capital (p. 176)

Post-closing trial balance The final step in the accounting cycle that lists only permanent accounts in the ledger and their balances after adjusting and closing entries have been posted (p. 186)

Real accounts See **Permanent accounts** (p. 176)

Temporary accounts Accounts whose balances at end of a fiscal year are not carried over to the next fiscal year. These accounts—Revenue, Expenses, Withdrawals—help to provide a new or ending figure for capital to begin the next fiscal year. Keep in mind that Income Summary is also a temporary account. (p. 176)

Blueprint of the Closing Process from the Worksheet

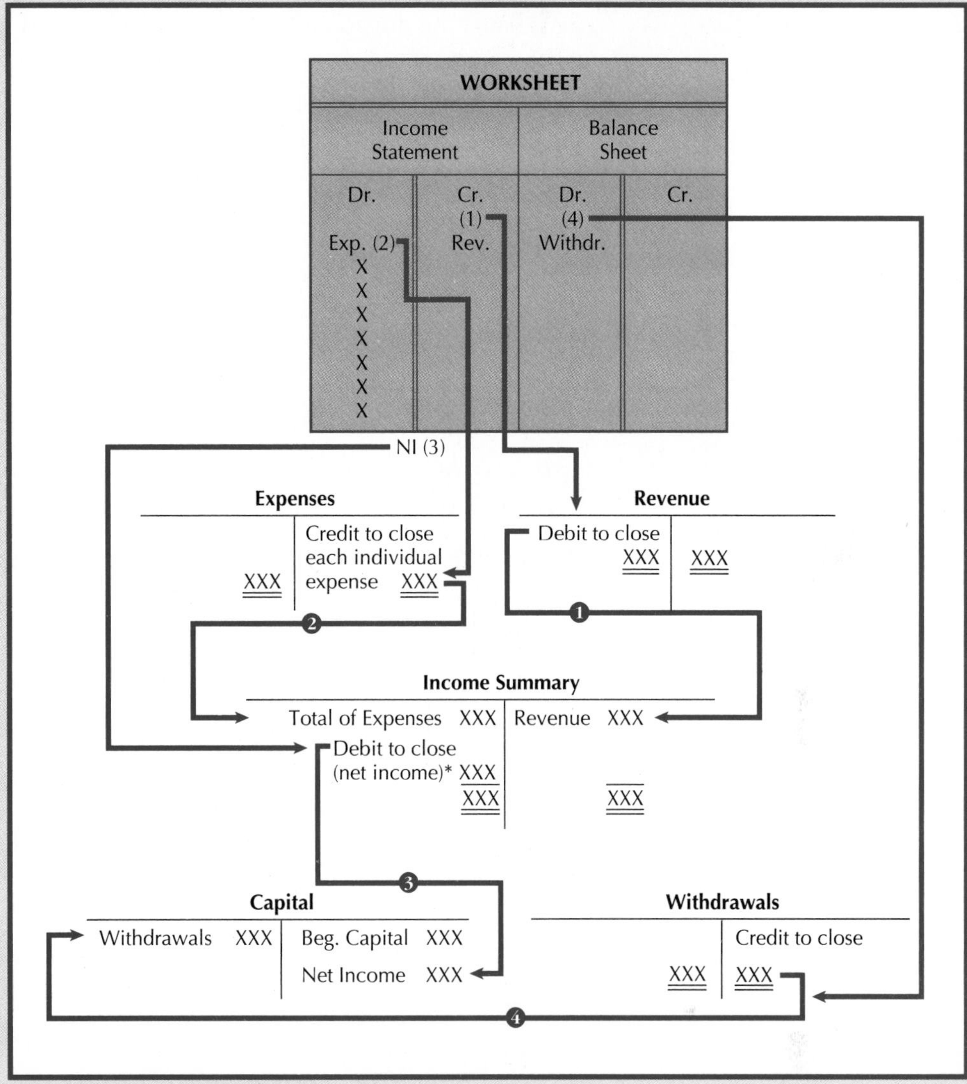

*If a net loss, it would require a credit to close.

The Closing Steps

1. Close revenue balances to Income Summary.
2. Close each *individual* expense and transfer the *total* of all expenses to Income Summary.
3. Transfer the balance in Income Summary (Net Income or Net Loss) to Capital.
4. Close Withdrawals to Capital.

Questions, Mini Exercises, Exercises, and Problems

Discussion Questions

1. When a worksheet is completed, what balances are found in the general ledger?
2. Why must adjusting entries be journalized even though the formal reports have already been prepared?
3. "Closing slows down the recording of next year's transactions." Defend or reject this statement with supporting evidence.
4. What is the difference between temporary and permanent accounts?

5. What are the two major goals of the closing process?
6. List the four steps in closing.
7. What is the purpose of Income Summary and where is it located?
8. How can a worksheet aid the closing process?
9. What accounts are usually listed on a post-closing trial balance?
10. Closing entries are always prepared once a month. Agree or disagree. Why?

Mini Exercises

(The blank forms you need are on pages 5-11 and 5-12 of the *Study Guide with Working Papers.*)

Journalizing and Posting Adjusting Entries

1. Post the following adjusting entries (be sure to cross-reference back to the journal) that came from the Adjustment columns of the worksheet.

General Journal — Page 3

Date		Account Titles and Description	PR	Dr.	Cr.
Dec.	31	Insurance Expense		6 00	
		Prepaid Insurance			6 00
		Insurance expired			
	31	Supplies Expense		3 00	
		Store Supplies			3 00
		Supplies used			
	31	Amortization Expense, Store Equipment		7 00	
		Accum. Amortization, Store Equipment			7 00
		Estimated amortization			
	31	Salaries Expense		4 00	
		Salaries Payable			4 00
		Accrued salaries			

LEDGER ACCOUNTS BEFORE ADJUSTING ENTRIES POSTED

Prepaid Insurance 115	
10	

Insurance Expense 510	

Store Supplies 116	
15	

Amortization Expense, Store Equipment 512	

Accumulated Amortization, Store Equipment 119	
	12

Supplies Expense 514	

Salaries Payable 210	

Salaries Expense 516	
7	

Closing Steps and Journalizing Closing Entries

2.

Worksheet			
IS		BS	
Dr.	Cr.	Dr.	Cr.
(2) EXPENSES	Revenue (1)	Withdrawals	(4)
NI (3)			

Goals of Closing

1. Temporary accounts in the ledger should have a zero balance.
2. New figure for capital is determined in closing.

Note: All closing can be done from the worksheet. Income Summary is a temporary account in the ledger.

From the above worksheet explain the four steps of closing. Keep in mind that each *individual* expense normally would be listed in the closing process.

Journalizing Closing Entries

3. From the following accounts, journalize the closing entries (assume that December 31 is the closing date).

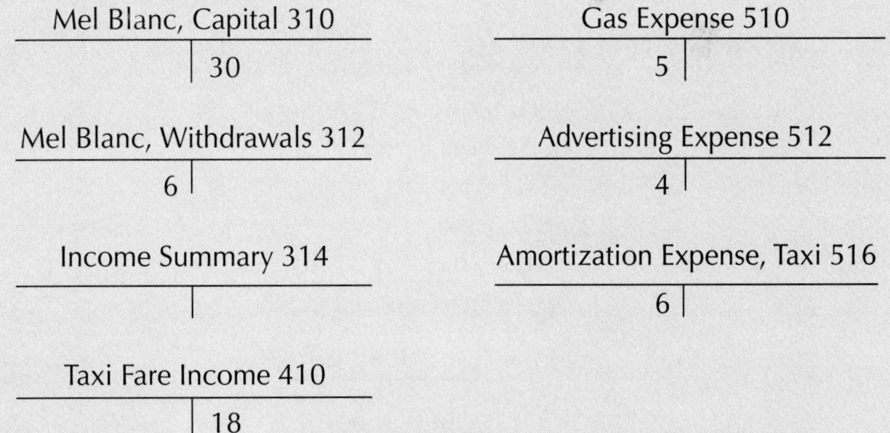

Posting to Income Summary

4. Draw a T account of Income Summary and post to it all entries from question 3 that affect it. Is Income Summary a temporary or permanent account?

Posting to Capital

5. Draw a T account for Mel Blanc, Capital, and post to it all entries from question 3 that affect it. What is the final balance of the capital account?

Exercises

(The blank forms you need are on pages 5-13 and 5-14 of the *Study Guide with Working Papers.*)

Journalizing adjusting entries

5-1. From the adjustments section of a worksheet presented here, prepare adjusting journal entries for the end of December.

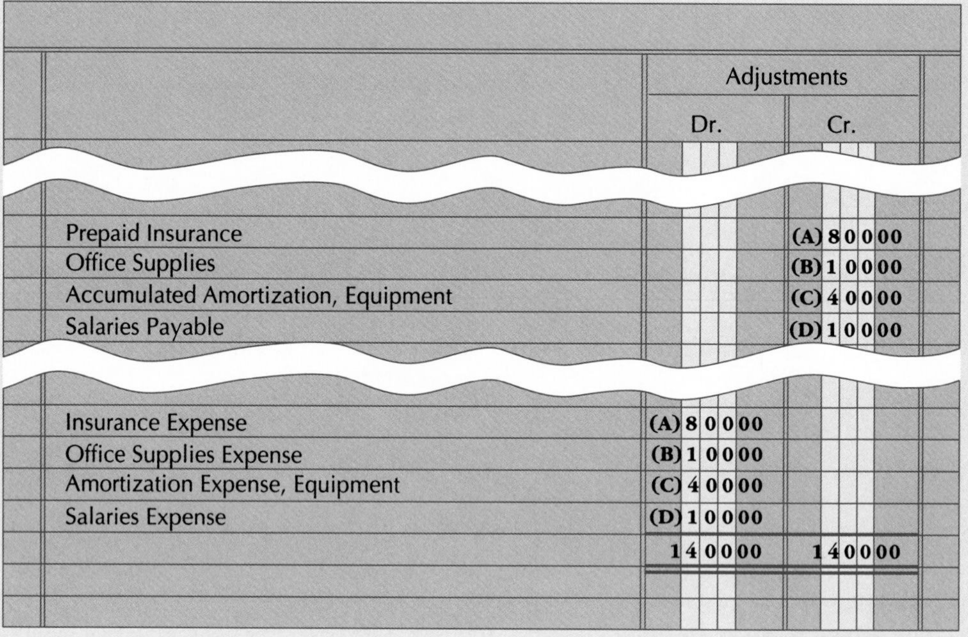

	Adjustments Dr.	Adjustments Cr.
Prepaid Insurance		(A) 800 00
Office Supplies		(B) 100 00
Accumulated Amortization, Equipment		(C) 400 00
Salaries Payable		(D) 100 00
Insurance Expense	(A) 800 00	
Office Supplies Expense	(B) 100 00	
Amortization Expense, Equipment	(C) 400 00	
Salaries Expense	(D) 100 00	
	1400 00	1400 00

Temporary versus permanent accounts

5-2. Complete this table by placing an X in the correct column for each item.

	Temporary	*Permanent*	*Will Be Closed*
Example: **Accounts Receivable**		X	
1. Income Summary			
2. A. Rose, Capital			
3. Salary Expense			
4. A. Rose, Withdrawals			
5. Fees Earned			
6. Accounts Payable			
7. Cash			

Closing entries

5-3. From the following T accounts, journalize the four closing entries on December 31, 2000.

J. King, Capital	
	14,000

Rent Expense	
5,000	

J. King, Withdrawals	
4,000	

Wages Expense	
7,000	

Income Summary	

Insurance Expense	
1,200	

Fees Earned	
	33,000

Amortization Expense, Office Equipment	
900	

Reconstructing closing entries

5-4. From the following posted T accounts, reconstruct the closing journal entries for December 31, 2002.

M. Foster, Capital

Dr.	Cr.
Withdrawals 100	2,000 (Dec. 1)
	700 Net Income

Insurance Expense

Dr.	Cr.
50	Closing 50

M. Foster, Withdrawals

Dr.	Cr.
100	Closing 100

Wages Expense

Dr.	Cr.
100	Closing 100

Income Summary

Dr.	Cr.
Expenses 600	Revenue 1,300
700	

Rent Expense

Dr.	Cr.
200	Closing 200

Salon Fees

Dr.	Cr.
Closing 1,300	1,300

Amortization Expense, Equipment

Dr.	Cr.
250	Closing 250

Post-closing trial balance

5-5. From the following accounts (not in order), prepare a post-closing trial balance for Wey Co. on December 31, 2003. ***Note:*** These balances are ***before*** closing.

Accounts Receivable	18,875
Legal Library	14,250
Office Equipment	59,700
Repair Expense	2,850
Salaries Expense	1,275
P. Wey, Capital	63,450
P. Wey, Withdrawals	1,500
Legal Fees Earned	$12,000
Accounts Payable	45,000
Cash	22,000

Group A Problems

(The blank forms you need are on pages 5-15 to 5-30 of the *Study Guide with Working Papers.*)

Review of preparing a worksheet and journalizing adjusting and closing entries

Check Figure

Net Income $4,780

5A-1. The following data are given for Marc's Consulting Service:

MARC'S CONSULTING SERVICE
TRIAL BALANCE
JUNE 30, 2002

	Dr.	Cr.
Cash	1800000	
Accounts Receivable	600000	
Prepaid Insurance	40000	
Supplies	150000	
Equipment	300000	
Accumulated Amortization, Equipment		90000
Accounts Payable		1000000
M. Key, Capital		1230000
M. Key, Withdrawals	30000	
Consulting Fees Earned		900000
Salaries Expense	140000	
Telephone Expense	100000	
Advertising Expense	60000	
	3220000	3220000

Adjustment Data

a. Insurance expired, $300
b. Supplies on hand, $800
c. Amortization on equipment, $100
d. Salaries earned by employees but not to be paid until July, $200

Required

1. Prepare a worksheet.
2. Journalize adjusting and closing entries.

Journalizing and posting adjusting and closing entries, and preparing a post-closing trial balance

Check Figure

Post-Closing Trial Balance $3,504

5A-2. Enter the beginning balance in each account in your working papers from the trial balance columns of the worksheet on page 205. Then (1) journalize and post adjusting and closing entries and (2) prepare from the ledger a post-closing trial balance for the month of March.

Comprehensive review of the entire accounting cycle, Chapters 1–5

Check Figure

Net Income $15, 780

5A-3. As the bookkeeper of Pete's Plowing, you have been asked to complete the entire accounting cycle for Pete from the following information:

2000

Jan.	1	Pete invested $7,000 cash and $6,000 worth of snow equipment in the plowing company.
	1	Paid rent in advance for garage space, $2,000.
	4	Purchased office equipment on account from Ling Corp., $7,200.
	6	Purchased snow supplies for $700 cash.
	8	Collected $15,000 from plowing local shopping centres.
	12	Pete Mack withdrew $1,000 from the business for personal use.
	20	Plowed North East Co. parking lots, payment not to be received until March, $5,000.
	26	Paid salaries to employees, $1,800.

POTTER CLEANING SERVICE
WORKSHEET
FOR MONTH ENDED MARCH 31, 2001

Account Titles	Trial Balance Dr.	Trial Balance Cr.	Adjustments Dr.	Adjustments Cr.	Adjusted Trial Balance Dr.	Adjusted Trial Balance Cr.	Income Statement Dr.	Income Statement Cr.	Balance Sheet Dr.	Balance Sheet Cr.
Cash	400 00				400 00				400 00	
Prepaid Insurance	520 00			(A) 180 00	340 00				340 00	
Cleaning Supplies	144 00			(B) 100 00	44 00				44 00	
Auto	2720 00				2720 00				2720 00	
Accum. Amortization Auto		860 00		(C) 150 00		1010 00				1010 00
Accounts Payable		224 00				224 00				224 00
B. Potter, Capital		540 00				540 00				540 00
B. Potter, Withdrawals	460 00				460 00				460 00	
Cleaning Fees		4680 00				4680 00		4680 00		
Salaries Expense	1440 00		(D) 160 00		1600 00		1600 00			
Telephone Expense	264 00				264 00		264 00			
Advertising Expense	196 00				196 00		196 00			
Gas Expense	160 00				160 00		160 00			
	6304 00	6304 00								
Insurance Expense			(A) 180 00		180 00		180 00			
Cleaning Supplies Expense			(B) 100 00		100 00		100 00			
Amortization Expense, Auto			(C) 150 00		150 00		150 00			
Salaries Payable				(D) 160 00		160 00				160 00
			590 00	590 00	6614 00	6614 00	2650 00	4680 00	3964 00	1934 00
Net Income							2030 00			2030 00
							4680 00	4680 00	3964 00	3964 00

28 Paid Ling Corp. one-half amount owed for office equipment.
29 Advertising bill was received from Bush Co. but will not be paid until March, $900.
30 Paid telephone bill, $210.

Adjustment Data

a. Snow supplies on hand, $400
b. Rent expired, $600
c. Amortization on office equipment, $120
($7,200 ÷ 5 yr. ➜ $1,440/12 mo.= $120)
d. Amortization on snow equipment, $100
($6,000 ÷ 5 yr. ➜ $1,200/12 mo. = $100)
e. Accrued salaries, $190

Chart of Accounts

Assets
111 Cash
112 Accounts Receivable
114 Prepaid Rent
115 Snow Supplies
121 Office Equipment
122 Accumulated Amortization, Office Equipment
123 Snow Equipment
124 Accumulated Amortization, Snow Equipment

Liabilities
211 Accounts Payable
212 Salaries Payable

Owner's Equity
311 Pete Mack, Capital
312 Pete Mack, Withdrawals
313 Income Summary

Revenue
411 Plowing Fees

Expenses
511 Salaries Expense
512 Advertising Expense
513 Telephone Expense
514 Rent Expense
515 Snow Supplies Expense
516 Amortization Expense, Office Equipment
517 Amortization Expense, Snow Equipment

Group B Problems

(The blank forms you need are on pages 5-15 to 5-30 of the *Study Guide with Working Papers.*)

5B-1.

Review of preparing a worksheet, and journalizing and closing entries

To: Ron Ear
From: Sue French
Re: Accounting Needs

Please prepare ASAP from the following information (attached) (1) a worksheet along with (2) journalized adjusting and closing entries.

Check Figure

Net Income $3,530

MARC'S CONSULTING SERVICE TRIAL BALANCE JUNE 30, 2002		
	Dr.	Cr.
Cash	10 150 00	
Accounts Receivable	5 000 00	
Prepaid Insurance	700 00	
Supplies	300 00	
Equipment	12 950 00	
Accumulated Amortization, Equipment		4 000 00
Accounts Payable		5 750 00
M. Key, Capital		15 150 00
M. Key, Withdrawals	400 00	
Consulting Fees Earned		5 200 00
Salaries Expense	450 00	
Telephone Expense	70 00	
Advertising Expense	80 00	
	30 100 00	30 100 00

Adjustment Data

a. Insurance expired, $100

b. Supplies on hand, $20

c. Amortization on equipment, $200

d. Salaries earned by employees but not due to be paid until July, $490

Journalizing and posting adjusting and closing entries, and preparing a post-closing trial balance

Check Figure

Post-Closing Trial Balance $3,294

5B-2. Enter the beginning balance in each account in your working papers from the trial balance columns of the worksheet on page 208. Then (1) journalize and post adjusting and closing entries and (2) prepare from the ledger a post-closing trial balance for the end of March.

Comprehensive review of entire accounting cycle, Chapters 1–5

Check Figure

Net Income $9,610

5B-3. From the following transactions as well as additional data, complete the entire accounting cycle for Pete's Plowing (use the chart of accounts on page 206).

2000

Jan.	1	To open the business, Pete invested $8,000 cash and $9,600 worth of snow equipment.
	1	Paid rent for five months in advance, $3,000.
	4	Purchased office equipment on account from Russell Co., $6,000.
	6	Bought snow supplies, $350.
	8	Collected $7,000 for plowing during winter storm emergency.
	12	Pete paid his home telephone bill using a company cheque, $70.
	20	Billed Eastern Freight Co. for plowing fees earned but not to be received until March, $6,500.
	24	Advertising bill was received from Jones Co. but will not be paid until next month, $350.
	26	Paid salaries to employees, $1,800.
	28	Paid Russell Co. one-half of amount owed for office equipment.
	29	Paid telephone bill of company, $165.

Adjustment Data

a. Snow supplies on hand, $200

b. Rent expired, $600

POTTER CLEANING SERVICE
WORKSHEET
FOR MONTH ENDED MARCH 31, 2001

Account Titles	Trial Balance		Adjustments		Adjusted Trial Balance		Income Statement		Balance Sheet	
	Dr.	Cr.	Dr.	Cr.	Dr.	Cr.	Dr.	Cr.	Dr.	Cr.
Cash	1,724.00				1,724.00				1,724.00	
Prepaid Insurance	350.00			(A) 200.00	150.00				150.00	
Cleaning Supplies	800.00			(B) 600.00	200.00				200.00	
Auto	1,220.00				1,220.00				1,220.00	
Accumulated Amortization, Auto		660.00		(C) 150.00		810.00				810.00
Accounts Payable		674.00				674.00				674.00
B. Potter, Capital		2,480.00				2,480.00				2,480.00
B. Potter, Withdrawals	600.00				600.00				600.00	
Cleaning Fees		3,700.00				3,700.00		3,700.00		
Salaries Expense	2,000.00		(D) 175.00		2,175.00		2,175.00			
Telephone Expense	284.00				284.00		284.00			
Advertising Expense	276.00				276.00		276.00			
Gas Expense	260.00				260.00		260.00			
	7,514.00	7,514.00								
Insurance Expense			(A) 200.00		200.00		200.00			
Cleaning Supplies Expense			(B) 600.00		600.00		600.00			
Amortization Expense, Auto			(C) 150.00		150.00		150.00			
Salaries Payable				(D) 175.00		175.00				175.00
			1,125.00	1,125.00	7,839.00	7,839.00	3,945.00	3,700.00	3,894.00	4,139.00
Net Loss								245.00	245.00	
							3,945.00	3,945.00	4,139.00	4,139.00

c. Amortization on office equipment ($6,000 ÷ 4 yr. → $1,500 ÷ 12 = $125), $125

d. Amortization on snow equipment ($9,600 ÷ 2 yr. → $4,800 ÷ 12 = $400), $400

e. Salaries accrued, $300

Group C Problems

(The forms you need are on pages 5-31 to 5-47 of the *Study Guide with Working Papers*.)

Review of preparing a worksheet, and journalizing adjusting and closing entries

Check Figure

Net Income $4,081

5C-1.

> To: Max Vleeming
>
> From: Grace Friesen
>
> Re: Accounting Procedures
>
> Please prepare from the following information (attached) (1) a worksheet along with (2) journalized adjusting and closing entries for the period ending May 31, 2002.

Adjustment Data

a. Insurance expired, $298

b. Supplies on hand, $782

c. Amortization on storage equipment, $720

d. Amortization on building, $975

e. Wages earned by employees but not due to be paid until June, $1,648

GRACE STORAGE COMPANY
TRIAL BALANCE
MAY 31, 2002

	Debit	Credit
Cash in Bank	2 6 6 0 00	
Prepaid Insurance	6 8 1 00	
Storage Supplies	1 7 4 2 00	
Storage Equipment	9 7 4 0 00	
Accumulated Amortization, Storage Equipment		4 2 1 8 00
Building	58 0 0 0 00	
Accumulated Amortization, Building		21 4 7 0 00
Accounts Payable		2 8 6 0 00
Grace Friesen, Capital		41 3 3 5 00
Grace Friesen, Withdrawals	5 7 4 2 00	
Storage Fees Revenue		18 7 2 0 00
Wages Expense	8 2 4 0 00	
Utilities Expense	9 2 6 00	
Advertising Expense	8 7 2 00	
Totals	88 6 0 3 00	88 6 0 3 00

Journalizing and posting adjusting and closing entries, and preparing a post-closing trial balance

Check Figure

Post-Closing Trial Balance $29,505.71

5C-2. Refer to the worksheet for Olson Computer Repair Service on page 210. The balances (from the trial balance column) in each account are already entered in your working papers. (1) Journalize and post adjusting and closing entries to each account in the ledger, and (2) prepare from the ledger a post-closing trial balance at the end of November.

OLSON COMPUTER REPAIR SERVICE
WORKSHEET
NOVEMBER 30, 2000

Account Titles	Trial Balance Dr.	Trial Balance Cr.	Adjustments Dr.	Adjustments Cr.	Adjusted Trial Balance Dr.	Adjusted Trial Balance Cr.	Income Statement Dr.	Income Statement Cr.	Balance Sheet Dr.	Balance Sheet Cr.
Cash	136648			(A) 4827	131821				131821	
Prepaid Insurance	71456			(C) 23455	48001				48001	
Accounts Receivable	527742				527742				527742	
Repair Parts and Supplies	159747			(D) 84240	75507				75507	
Van	2167500				2167500				2167500	
Accumulated Amortization, Van		810365		(B) 61875		872240				872240
Accounts Payable		377260		(F) 24300		401560				401560
Sylvia Olson, Capital		1266358				1266358				1266358
Sylvia Olson, Withdrawals	260000				260000				260000	
Repair Revenue		1645870				1645870		1645870		
Advertising Expense	71438		(F) 24300		95738		95738			
Automotive Expense	234551				234551		234551			
Cleaning Expense	37500				37500		37500			
Miscellaneous Expense	17814				17814		17814			
Postage and Office Expense	28417				28417		28417			
Salaries Expense	387040		(E) 42000		429040		429040			
	4099853	4099853								
Insurance Expense			(C) 23455		23455		23455			
Bank Charges Expense			(A) 4827		4827		4827			
Amortization Expense, Van			(B) 61875		61875		61875			
Salaries Payable				(E) 42000		42000				42000
Supplies Expense			(D) 84240		84240		84240			
			240697	240697	4228028	4228028	1017457	1645870	3210571	2582158
Net Income							628413			628413
							1645870	1645870	3210571	3210571

Comprehensive review of the entire accounting cycle, Chapters 1–5

Check Figure

Net Income $7,850.67

5C-3. From the following transactions as well as additional data, please complete the entire accounting cycle for Martin's Plumbing (use a chart of accounts similar to the one on page 206).

2001		
May	1	To open the business, Martin Atherton invested $12,000 cash and $5,400 worth of plumbing equipment.
	1	Paid rent for four months in advance, $2,400.
	4	Purchased office equipment on account from MacKenzie Co., $4,100.
	6	Bought plumbing supplies, $870.
	8	Collected $3,600 for plumbing services provided.
	9	Martin paid his home utility bill with a company cheque, $122.
	10	Billed Western Construction Co. for plumbing fees earned but not to be received until later, $9,600.
	14	Advertising bill was received from ABCD Radio Co. but is not to be paid until next month, $420.
	21	Received cheque from Western Construction Co. in partial payment on transaction dated May 10, $4,800.
	26	Paid salaries to employees, $2,650.
	28	Paid MacKenzie Co. one-half of amount owed for office equipment, $2,050.
	29	Paid telephone bill of company, $184.
	31	Received bill from George's Cleaning to be paid in June, $215.

Adjusting Data

a. Plumbing supplies on hand, $328

b. Rent expired, $600

c. Amortization on office equipment, $68.33
($4,100 ÷ 5 yr. → $820 ÷ 12 = $68.33)

d. Amortization on plumbing equipment, $150
($5,400 ÷ 3 yr. → $1,800 ÷ 12 = $150)

e. Salaries accrued, $520

REAL WORLD APPLICATIONS

(The forms you need are on page 5-48 of the *Study Guide with Working Papers.*)

5R-1.

Ann Humphrey needs a loan from the Charles Bank to help finance her business. She has submitted to the Charles Bank the following unadjusted trial balance. As the loan officer, you will be meeting with Ann tomorrow. Could you make some specific written suggestions to Ann regarding her loan report?

Cash in Bank	770	
Accounts Receivable	1,480	
Office Supplies	3,310	
Equipment	7,606	
Accounts Payable		684
A. Humphrey, Capital		8,000
Service Fees		17,350
Salaries	11,240	
Utilities Expense	842	
Rent Expense	360	
Insurance Expense	280	
Advertising Expense	146	
Totals	26,034	26,034

5R-2.

Janet Smothey is the new bookkeeper who replaced Dick Burns, owing to his sudden illness. Janet finds on her desk a note requesting that she close the books and supply the ending capital figure. Janet is upset, since she can find only the following:

a. Revenue and expense accounts were all zero balance.

b. Income Summary

14,360	19,300

c. Owner withdrew $8,000.

d. Owner's beginning capital was $34,400.

Could you help Janet accomplish her assignment? What written suggestions should Janet make to her supervisor so that this situation will not happen again?

make the call

Critical Thinking/Ethical Case

5R-3.

Todd Silver is the purchasing agent for Moore Company. One of his suppliers, Gem Company, offers Todd a free vacation to France if he buys at least 75 percent of Moore's supplies from Gem Company. Todd, who is angry because Moore Company has not given him a raise in over a year, is considering the offer. Write out your recommendation to Todd.

ACCOUNTING RECALL

A CUMULATIVE APPROACH

THIS EXAMINATION REVIEWS CHAPTERS 1 THROUGH 5.

Page 5-49 of the *Study Guide with Working Papers* has forms to complete this exam, as well as worked-out solutions. The page reference next to each question identifies the page to turn back to if you answer the question incorrectly.

PART I Vocabulary Review

Match each term on the left side with the appropriate definition or phrase in the right-hand column.

Page Ref.	Term		Definition
(176)	1. Closing entries	A.	Updates specific ledger accounts
(135)	2. Book value	B.	A temporary account with debit balance
(177)	3. Income summary	C.	A permanent account
(134)	4. Contra-asset	D.	Lists only permanent accounts
(132)	5. Supplies	E.	Clears all temporary accounts
(81)	6. Journal	F.	Book of original entry
(186)	7. Post-closing trial balance	G.	A temporary account in the ledger
(172)	8. Adjusting journal entries		

(42) 9. Ledger

(13) 10. Withdrawals

H. Cost – accumulated amortization

I. Book of final entry

J. Accumulated amortization

PART II True or False (Accounting Theory)

(177) 11. Income summary has a normal balance of a debit.

(176) 12. After closing, all temporary accounts will be cleared to zero balance.

(176) 13. Closing entries cannot be made from a worksheet.

(137) 14. The worksheet shows the beginning figure for capital.

(187) 15. Financial reports are prepared after journalizing and posting adjusting and closing entries.

Continuing Problem

Tony has decided to end the Eldorado Computer Centre's first year as of September 30, 2001. Below is an updated chart of accounts.

Assets

1000 Cash

1020 Accounts Receivable

1025 Prepaid Rent

1030 Supplies

1080 Computer Shop Equipment

1081 Accumulated Amortization Computer Shop Equipment

1090 Office Equipment

1091 Accumulated Amortization Office Equipment

Liabilities

2000 Accounts Payable

Owner's Equity

3000 T. Freedman, Capital

3010 T. Freedman, Withdrawals

3020 Income Summary

Revenue

4000 Service Revenue

Expenses

5010 Advertising Expense

5020 Rent Expense

5030 Utilities Expense

5040 Phone Expense

5050 Supplies Expense

5060 Insurance Expense

5070 Postage Expense

5080 Amortization Expense, Computer Shop Equipment

5090 Amortization Expense, Office Equipment

Assignment

(See pages 5-50 to 5-55 in your *Study Guide with Working Papers.*)

1. Journalize the adjusting entries from Chapter 4.
2. Post the adjusting entries to the ledger.
3. Journalize the closing entries.
4. Post the closing entries to the ledger.
5. Prepare a post-closing trial balance.

MINI PRACTICE SET

Valdez Realty

Reviewing the Accounting Cycle Twice

This comprehensive review problem requires you to complete the accounting cycle for Valdez Realty twice. This will allow you to review Chapters 1 to 5 while reinforcing the relationships among all parts of the accounting cycle. By completing two cycles, you will see how the ending June balances in the ledger are used to accumulate data in July. (The blank forms you need are on pages 5-59 to 5-75 of the *Study Guide with Working Papers.*)

The following chart shows the steps of the accounting cycle and the page in the text where each step is covered. You can use it to review the accounting cycle before you start and as a reference while you are working.

Steps in the Accounting Cycle	Page in Text Where Covered
1. Business transactions occur and generate source documents. ↓	**1.** page 81
2. Analyze and record business transactions into a journal. ↓	**2.** page 83
3. Post or transfer information from journal to ledger. ↓	**3.** page 91
4. Prepare a trial balance. ↓	**4.** page 97
5. Prepare a worksheet. ↓	**5.** page 130
6. Prepare financial statements. ↓	**6.** page 143
7. Journalize and post adjusting entries. ↓	**7.** page 172
8. Journalize and post closing entries. ↓	**8.** page 176
9. Prepare a post-closing trial balance.	**9.** page 186

First, let's look at the chart of accounts for Valdez Realty (top of page 215).

On June 1 Juan Valdez opened a real estate office called Valdez Realty. The following transactions were completed for the month of June:

2001

June 1 Juan Valdez invested $7,000 cash in the real estate agency along with $3,000 worth of office equipment.

1 Rented office space and paid three months rent in advance, $2,100.

Valdez Realty
Chart of Accounts

Assets		Revenue	
111	Cash	411	Commissions Earned
112	Accounts Receivable		
114	Prepaid Rent	**Expenses**	
115	Office Supplies	511	Rent Expense
121	Office Equipment	512	Salaries Expense
122	Accumulated Amortization, Office Equipment	513	Gas Expense
		514	Repairs Expense
123	Automobile	515	Telephone Expense
124	Accumulated Amortization, Automobile	516	Advertising Expense
		517	Office Supplies Expense
		518	Amortization Expense, Office Equipment
Liabilities			
211	Accounts Payable	519	Amortization Expense, Automobile
212	Salaries Payable		
		524	Miscellaneous Expense
Owner's Equity			
311	Juan Valdez, Capital		
312	Juan Valdez, Withdrawals		
313	Income Summary		

2001

June	1	Bought an automobile on account, $12,000.
	4	Purchased office supplies for cash, $300.
	5	Purchased additional office supplies on account, $150.
	6	Sold a house and collected a $6,000 commission.
	8	Paid gas bill, $22.
	15	Paid the salary of the part-time office secretary, $350.
	17	Sold a building lot and earned a commission, $6,500. Payment is to be received on July 8.
	20	Juan Valdez withdrew $1,000 from the business to pay personal expenses.
	21	Sold a house and collected a $3,500 commission.
	22	Paid gas bill, $25.
	24	Paid $600 to repair automobile.
	30	Paid the salary of the part-time office secretary, $350.
	30	Paid the June telephone bill, $510.
	30	Received advertising bill for June, $1,200. The bill is to be paid on July 2.

Required Work for June

1. Journalize transactions and post to ledger accounts.
2. Prepare a trial balance in the first two columns of the worksheet and complete the worksheet using the following adjustment data:
   - **a.** One month's rent had expired.
   - **b.** An inventory shows $50 worth of office supplies remaining.
   - **c.** Amortization on office equipment, $100
   - **d.** Amortization on automobile, $200
3. Prepare a June income statement, statement of owner's equity, and balance sheet.

4. From the worksheet, journalize and post adjusting and closing entries (page 3 of journal).
5. Prepare a post-closing trial balance.

During July, Valdez Realty completed these transactions:

2001		
July	1	Paid for June office supplies purchased on account, $150.
	1	Purchased additional office supplies on account, $700.
	2	Paid advertising bill for June.
	3	Sold a house and collected a commission, $6,600.
	6	Paid for gas expense, $29.
	8	Collected commission from sale of building lot on June 17.
	9	Paid $2,000 of the balance owing on automobile purchased June 1.
	12	Paid $300 to send employees to realtor's workshop.
	15	Paid the salary of the part-time office secretary, $350.
	17	Sold a house and earned a commission of $2,400. Commission to be received on August 10.
	18	Sold a building lot and collected a commission of $7,000.
	22	Sent a cheque for $40 to help sponsor a local road race to aid the poor. (This is not to be considered an advertising expense, but it is a business expense.)
	24	Paid for repairs to automobile, $590.
	28	Juan Valdez withdrew $1,800 from the business to pay personal expenses.
	30	Paid the salary of the part-time office secretary, $350.
	30	Paid the July telephone bill, $590.
	30	Advertising bill for July was received, $1,400. The bill is to be paid on August 2.

Required Work for July

1. Journalize transactions in a general journal (pages 4 and 5) and post to ledger accounts.
2. Prepare a trial balance in the first two columns of the worksheet and complete the worksheet using the following adjustment data:
   a. One month's rent had expired.
   b. An inventory shows $90 worth of office supplies remaining.
   c. Amortization on office equipment, $100
   d. Amortization on automobile, $200
3. Prepare a July income statement, statement of owner's equity, and balance sheet.
4. From the worksheet, journalize and post adjusting and closing entries (page 6 of journal).
5. Prepare a post-closing trial balance.

COMPUTER WORKSHOP

Computerized Accounting Application for Valdez Realty Mini Practice Set (Chapter 5)

Closing Process and Post-Closing Trial Balance

Before starting on this assignment, read and complete the tasks discussed in Parts A, B, and F of Appendix B: Computerized Accounting at the back of this book and complete the Computerized Accounting Application assignments at the ends of Chapters 3 and 4.

This comprehensive review problem requires you to complete the accounting cycle for Valdez Realty twice. This will allow you to review Chapters 1 to 5 while reinforcing the relationships among all parts of the accounting cycle. By completing two cycles, you will see how the ending June balances in the ledger are used to accumulate data in July.

PART A The June Accounting Cycle

On June 1, Juan Valdez opened a real estate office called Valdez Realty.

Open the company data files

1. Click on the **Start** button. Point to Programs; point to Simply Accounting; then click on Simply Accounting in the final menu presented. The Simply Accounting Open File dialogue box will appear.
2. Insert your Student Data Files disk into disk drive A. Enter the following path into the **File name** text box: `A:\student\valdez.asc`
3. Click on the **Open** button, enter 06/30/03 into the **Session** text box; then click on the **OK** button. Click on the **OK** button in response to the message "The date entered is more than one week past your previous **Session** date of 06/01/03." The Company Window for Valdez will appear.

Add your name to the company name

4. Click on the Company Window **Setup** menu; then click on Company Information. The Company Information dialogue box will appear. Insert your name in place of the text "Your Name" in the **Name** text box. Click on the **OK** button to return to the Company Window. Your instructor may suggest you do a **File**: **Save As** procedure here (using a different file name) to make it easier to start over if a mistake is made later on.

Record June transactions

5. Open the General Journal dialogue box; then record the following journal entries (enter `Memo` into the **Source** text box for each transaction; then enter the date listed for each transaction):

2003

June 1 Juan Valdez invested $7,000 cash in the real estate agency along with $3,000 in office equipment.
1 Rented office space and paid three months rent in advance, $2,100.
1 Bought an automobile on account, $12,000.
4 Purchased office supplies for cash, $300.
5 Purchased additional office supplies on account, $150.
6 Sold a house and collected a $6,000 commission.
8 Paid gas bill, $22.
15 Paid the salary of the part-time office secretary, $350.
17 Sold a building lot and earned a commission, $6,500. Expected receipt of commission 07/08/03.

20 Juan Valdez withdrew $1,000 from the business to pay personal expenses.
21 Sold a house and collected a $3,500 commission.
22 Paid gas bill, $25.
24 Paid $600 to repair automobile.
30 Paid the salary of the part-time office secretary, $350.
30 Paid the June telephone bill, $510.
30 Received advertising bill for June, $1,200. The bill is to be paid on 07/02/03.

Print reports.

6. After you have posted the journal entries, close the General Journal; then print the following reports:
   a. General Journal (By posting date, All ledger entries, Start: 06/01/03, Finish: 06/30/03).
   b. Trial Balance As at 06/30/03.

   Review your printed reports. If you have made an error in a posted journal entry, see "Reversing an Entry Made in the General Journal Dialogue Box" in Part C of Appendix B: Computerized Accounting for information on how to correct the error.

Record June adjusting entries.

7. Open the General Journal; then record adjusting journal entries based on the following adjustment data (*Source:* Memo; *Date:* 06/30/03; *Comment:* Adjusting entry):
   a. One month's rent has expired.
   b. An inventory shows $50 worth of office supplies remaining.
   c. Amortization on office equipment, $100
   d. Amortization on automobile, $200

Print reports.

8. After you have posted the adjusting journal entries, close the General Journal; then print the following reports:
   a. General Journal (By posting date, All ledger entries, Start: 06/01/03, Finish: 06/30/03)
   b. Trial Balance As at 06/30/03
   c. General Ledger Report (Start: 06/01/03, Finish: 06/30/03, Select All)
   d. Income Statement (Start: 06/01/03, Finish: 06/30/03)
   e. Balance Sheet As at 06/30/03

   Review your printed reports. If you have made an error in a posted journal entry, see "Reversing an Entry Made in the General Journal Dialogue Box" in Part C of Appendix B: Computerized Accounting for information on how to correct the error.

How to close the accounting records

9. *Simply Accounting* has the capability to perform the first three steps of the closing process automatically.

Done automatically by the program

Step 1: Clear Revenue balance and transfer to Income Summary.

Step 2: Clear individual expense balances and transfer the total to Income Summary.

Step 3: Clear balance in Income Summary and transfer it to Capital.

It does not have the capability of performing the fourth step of the closing process automatically, so you will need to record this closing journal entry.

You need to record this closing entry.

Step 4: Clear the Withdrawals balance and transfer it to Capital.

Record entry to close Withdrawals account.

10. Open the General Journal; then record the closing journal entry for Juan Valdez's Withdrawals account.
11. After you have posted the closing entry for Juan Valdez's Withdrawals account, close the General Journal to return to the Company Window.

Make a backup copy of June accounting records.

12. Click on the **Company Window File** menu; click on **Save As**; then enter the following new file name into the **File name** text box: `A:\student\valdjune.asc`
13. Click on the **Save** button. Note that the company name in the Company Window has changed from Valdez to Valdjune. Click on the **Company Window File** menu again; then click on Save As. Enter the following new file name into the **File name** text box: `A:\student\valdez.asc`
14. Click on the **Save** button. Click on the **Yes** button to confirm that you want to replace the existing file. Note that the company name in the Company Window has changed back from Valdjune to Valdez.
15. You now have two sets of company data files for Valdez Realty on your Student Data Files disk. The current data is stored under the file name valdez.asc. The backup data for June is stored under the file name valdjune.asc.

Important information about the closing process

16. The next instruction will ask you to advance the **Session** date to a new month. It is this procedure that instructs the program to complete the first three steps in the closing process. It is important that you make a backup copy of a company's data files prior to advancing the **Session** date to a new month. When you advance the **Session** date to the first new month of a new fiscal year, the program will permanently remove all journal entries from all Journals and all individual postings of journal entries to the general ledger accounts. You will not be able to display or print a General Journal or General Ledger report based on dates in the prior month, nor will you be able to record journal entries for dates in the prior month. If for some reason you need to print a General Journal or General Ledger, or record a transaction that occurred in the prior month, you can do so by using the backup copy of the company's data files that you created prior to advancing the **Session** date. See Part E of Appendix B: Computerized Accounting at the end of this book for information on how and when to use a backup copy of a company's data files.

How to advance the using date

17. Click on the Company Window **Maintenance** menu; then click on Advance Using Date. Click on the **No** button in response to the question "Would you like to backup now?" Enter 07/01/03 into the **New Session** text box; then click on the **OK** button. Click on the **OK** button in response to the message "You have entered both a new calendar quarter and a new fiscal year. If you proceed, the program will zero all employees' quarter-to-date payroll information, move the current year's data into last year, close all Revenue and Expense account balances into the Retained Earnings integration account, and set the new fiscal year's dates. Print all employee reports and make a backup before proceeding."
18. The warning message stated that the revenue and expense accounts would be closed to an account titled Retained Earnings. This is the account that corporations use to accumulate earnings. Valdez Realty is a sole proprietorship, and the program will correctly close the revenue and expense accounts to Income Summary and close Income Summary to the Juan Valdez, Capital, account even though the message used a different account name. The backup you created using the Save As method will serve as the backup suggested in the warning message.

Exit from the program.

19. Print a post-closing Trial Balance As at 07/01/03.

Print a Post-closing Trial Balance.

20. Click on the Company Window **File** menu; then click on Exit to end the current work session and return to your Windows desktop.

Complete the report transmittal.

21. Complete the Valdez Realty Report Transmittal for June located in Appendix A of your *Study Guide with Working Papers.*

PART B The July Accounting Cycle

Open the company data files.

1. Click on the **Start** button. Point to Programs: point to Simply Accounting; then click on Simply Accounting in the final menu presented. The Simply Accounting Open File dialogue box will appear.
2. Insert your Student Data Files disk into disk drive A. Enter the following path into the **File name** text box: `A:\student\valdez.asc`
3. Click on the **Open** button; enter 07/31/03 into the **Session** text box; then click on the **OK** button. Click on the **OK** button in response to the message "The date entered is more than one week past your previous **Session** date of 07/01/03." The Company Window for Valdez Realty will appear.

Modify the Fiscal End date.

4. Click on the Company Window **Setup** menu; then click on Company Information. The Company Information dialogue box will appear. Enter 07/31/03 as the new Fiscal End date; then click on the **OK** button.

Record July transactions.

5. Open the General Journal dialogue box; then record the following journal entries (enter `Memo` into the **Source** text box for each transaction; then enter the date listed for each transaction):

2003

July	1	Paid for June office supplies purchased on account, $150.
	1	Purchased additional office supplies on account, $700.
	2	Paid advertising bill for June.
	3	Sold a house and collected a commission, $6,600.
	6	Paid for gas expense, $29.
	8	Collected commission from sale of building lot on 06/17/03.
	9	Paid $2,000 of the balance owing on automobile purchased June 1.
	12	Paid $300 to send employees to realtor's workshop.
	15	Paid the salary of the part-time office secretary, $350.
	17	Sold a house and earned a commission of $2,400. Expected receipt of commission 08/10/03.
	18	Sold a building lot and collected a commission of $7,000.
	22	Sent a cheque for $40 to help sponsor a local road race to aid the poor. (This is not to be considered an advertising expense, but it is a business expense.)
	24	Paid for repairs to automobile, $590.
	28	Juan Valdez withdrew $1,800 from the business to pay personal expenses.
	30	Paid the salary of the part-time office secretary, $350.
	30	Paid the July telephone bill, $590.
	30	Advertising bill for July was $1,400. The bill is to be paid on 08/02/03.

Print reports.

6. After you have posted the journal entries, close the General Journal; then print the following reports:
   - **a.** General Journal (By posting date, All ledger entries, Start: 07/01/03, Finish: 07/31/03).
   - **b.** Trial Balance As at 07/31/03.

   Review your reports. If you have made an error in a posted journal entry, see "Reversing an Entry Made in the General Journal Dialogue Box" in Part C of Appendix B: Computerized Accounting for information on how to correct the error.

Record July adjusting entries.

7. Open the General Journal; then record adjusting journal entries based on the following adjustment data (*Source:* Memo; *Date:* 7/31/03; *Comment:* Adjusting entry):
   a. One month's rent has expired.
   b. An inventory shows $90 worth of office supplies remaining.
   c. Amortization on office equipment, $100
   d. Amortization on automobile, $200

Print reports.

8. After you have posted the adjusting journal entries, close the General Journal; then print the following reports:
   a. General Journal (By posting date, All ledger entries, Start: 07/01/03, Finish: 07/31/03)
   b. Trial Balance As at 07/31/03
   c. General Ledger Report (Start: 07/01/03, Finish: 07/31/03, Select All)
   d. Income Statement (Start: 07/01/03, Finish: 07/31/03)
   e. Balance Sheet As at 07/31/03

   Review your reports. If you have made an error in a posted journal entry, see "Reversing an Entry Made in the General Journal Dialogue Box" in Part C of Appendix B: Computerized Accounting for information on how to correct the error.

Record entry to close Withdrawals account.

9. Record the closing journal entry for Juan Valdez's Withdrawals account.
10. After you have posted the closing entry for Juan Valdez's Withdrawals account, close the General Journal to return to the Company Window.

Make a backup copy of July accounting records.

11. Click on the Company Window **File** menu; click on Save As; then enter the following new file name in the **File name** text box:
    `A:\student\valdjuly.asc`
12. Click on the **Save** button. Note that the company name in the Company Window has changed from Valdez to Valdjuly. Click on the Company Window File menu again; then click on Save As. Enter the following new file name into the **File name** text box: `A:\student\valdez.asc`
13. Click on the **Save** button. Click on the **Yes** button in response to the question "Replace existing file?" Note that the company name in the Company Window has changed back from Valdjuly to Valdez.
14. You now have three sets of company data files for Valdez Realty on your Student Data Files disk. The current data is stored under the file name valdez.asc. The backup data for June is stored under the file name valdjune.asc, and the backup data for July is stored under the file name valdjuly.asc.

Advance the Using Date.

15. Click on the Company Window **Maintenance** menu; then click on Advance Session Date. Click on the **No** button in response to the question "Would you like to backup now?" Enter 08/01/03 into the **New Session Date** text box; then click on the **OK** button. Click on the **OK** button in response to the warning message. The backup you created using the Save As method will serve as the backup suggested in the warning message.

Print a Post-closing Trial Balance. 16. Print a Post-closing Trial Balance As at 08/01/03.

Exit from the program. 17. Click on the Company Window **File** menu; then click on Exit to end the current work session and return to your Windows desktop.

Complete the Report Transmittal. 18. Complete the Valdez Realty Report Transmittal for July located in Appendix A of your *Study Guide with Working Papers.*

Banking Procedures and Control of Cash

6

THE BIG PICTURE

As Tony Freedman planned for the upcoming months, he thought about the problems he'd had managing cash. In particular, he often ran short of change and frequently lost track of small cash purchases. Eldorado Computer Centre was currently using one chequing account for paying bills and making deposits. Maybe new banking technology was the solution, Tony thought; so he prepared some questions to ask of a customer service representative at his bank:

- Should I have an ATM card for my business versus a small cash account kept on site?
- Is there an advantage to having an on-line machine for ATM or credit card transactions for my customers?
- Is there a benefit to banking on line?

The bank's customer service representative responded:

> Using an ATM card certainly has advantages when you want to make deposits or withdraw cash outside banking hours, and it beats standing in long teller lines during banking hours. However, an ATM card will not solve your problem of making change for customers at your place of business, or small cash expenditures on an as-needed basis.
>
> There is an advantage to having an on-line debit machine for your business. For a small monthly expense, your customers can make payments from their accounts without writing a cheque. The bank will clear the transaction only if the funds are available, which eliminates your possible expense of accepting non- (or not-) sufficient-funds cheques. Some of our customers choose to handle their banking transactions via the computer. They like not having to leave their homes or their offices for most banking transactions—although there are still some security measures to be concerned with.

Even though technology offered some new options that Tony might make use of in the future, he decided that basic accounting was the answer to his current cash control woes. First he would reconcile his cash ledger accounts for the past four months with his bank statements. He also decided that it would be necessary to establish a petty cash fund.

Chapter Objectives

- Depositing, writing, and endorsing cheques for a chequing account (pp. 224 to 227)
- Reconciling a bank statement (p. 227)
- Establishing and replenishing a petty cash fund; setting up an auxiliary petty cash record (pp. 239 to 242)
- Establishing and replenishing a change fund (p. 242)
- Handling transactions involving cash short and over (pp. 243 and 244)

The internal control policies of a company will depend on things such as number of employees, company size, sources of cash, and so on.

In this chapter we introduce Art's Wholesale Clothing Company. As Art Newner finds his business increasing, he is becoming quite concerned about developing a system of procedures and records for close control over the cash receipts and cash payments of the business. This is called **internal control** and includes control over the store's assets as well as a way of monitoring the company's operations. (Certain details of the journalizing process used in Art's company are covered in detail in Chapters 9 and 10. Some instructors may take a few minutes from coverage of Chapter 6 material to cover briefly the essentials of special journals, while others may take up Chapter 6 following Chapter 10.)

Art, his accountant, and a consultant studied the situation and developed the following company policies:

1. Responsibilities and duties of employees will be assigned so that, for example, the person receiving the cash, whether at the register or by opening the mail, will not record this information in the accounting records. The accountant, on the other hand, will not be handling the cash receipts.
2. All cash receipts of Art's Wholesale will be deposited in the bank the same day they arrive.
3. All payments will be made by cheque (except petty cash items, which will be discussed later in this chapter).
4. Employees will be rotated among jobs. This allows workers to become acquainted with the work of others as well as to prepare for a possible changeover of jobs.
5. Art Newner will sign all cheques after receiving authorization to pay from the departments concerned.
6. At time of payment, all supporting invoices or documents will be stamped paid. That will show when the invoice or document is paid as well as the number of the cheque used.
7. All cheques will be prenumbered. This will control the use of cheques and make it difficult to use a cheque fraudulently without its being revealed at some point.

Let's now look at the chequing account of Art's Wholesale, along with specific bank procedures.

LEARNING UNIT 6-1

Bank Procedures, Chequing Accounts, and Bank Reconciliations

Before Art's Wholesale opened on April 1, Art had a meeting at the Royal Bank to discuss the steps for opening and using a chequing account for the company.

Opening a chequing account

Purpose of a signature card

The manager of the bank gave Art a signature card to fill out. The signature card includes space for signature(s), business and home addresses, references, type of account, and so on. The manager explained that this was for Art to sign (since he would be signing cheques for the company) so that the bank could check and validate his signature when cheques were presented for payment. The signature card would be kept in the bank's files so that possible forgeries could be spotted.

Art also received preprinted **deposit slips** and a set of cheques. The deposit slips are to be used when Art's Wholesale receives cash or cheques from any source and deposits them in the chequing account. One copy of the deposit slip stays with the bank and a duplicate copy is date stamped by the bank and remains with the company. Thus it can be verified that items in the cash receipts journal that make up the deposit have actually been deposited correctly.

When a bank credits your account, it is increasing the balance.

Notice on the deposit slip in Figure 6-1 (page 226) that much of the information is preprinted. This saves time as well as labour in processing the deposit. If the bank is closed Art will place a locked bag (provided by the bank) in a night depository so that the deposit bag is in a safe place overnight. The bank will credit (increase) his account balance when the deposit is processed on the next banking day.

Types of cheque endorsement

Endorsements can be made by using a rubber stamp instead of a handwritten signature.

Before any cheque can be deposited or cashed, the bank requires that it be *endorsed*. **Endorsement** is the signing of one's name on the *back* of the cheque. This process transfers ownership to the bank, which can collect the money from the person or company that issued the cheque. Figure 6-2 (page 227) shows several common types of endorsement that Art's Wholesale could use.

Now let's look at Art's chequebook to see how payments will be recorded.

The chequebook

***Drawer*—one who writes the cheque**

***Drawee*—bank which pays money to payee**

***Payee*—one to whom cheque is payable**

Figure 6-3 (page 228) is an example of the type of cheque used by Art's Wholesale. This **cheque** is a written order signed by Art Newner (the **drawer** or one who writes the cheque) instructing Royal Bank (the **drawee**) to pay a specific sum of money to Joe Francis Company, the **payee**, the one to whom the cheque is payable. Note some of the following key points:

1. The number of the cheque is preprinted, along with the company's address.
2. The cheque stub is filled out first. The stub will be used in recording transactions as well as for future reference. Note here that the beginning balance was $7,100; a deposit of $784 brought the balance to $7,884 before the cheque for $4,000 was written, leaving an ending balance of $3,884.
3. The dashed line before and after XX/100 is meant to fill up space on the cheque so that changes cannot easily be made in the amount.
4. When the cheque is handwritten, the amount written in words should start on the far left and should use only one "and" to signify the decimal position, as in "one hundred seventeen dollars *and* 42/100."

If the written amount on the cheque doesn't match the amount expressed in figures, Royal Bank will pay the amount written in words, or will return the cheque unpaid, or will check with the drawer to see which amount is correct.

Many companies use cheque-writing machines, which impress the amount of the cheque in figures and words on the cheque itself. This prevents anyone from making fraudulent changes by hand on the cheque.

Now let's turn our attention to looking at the transactions of Art's Wholesale that affect the chequing account.

FIGURE 6-1 A Deposit Slip

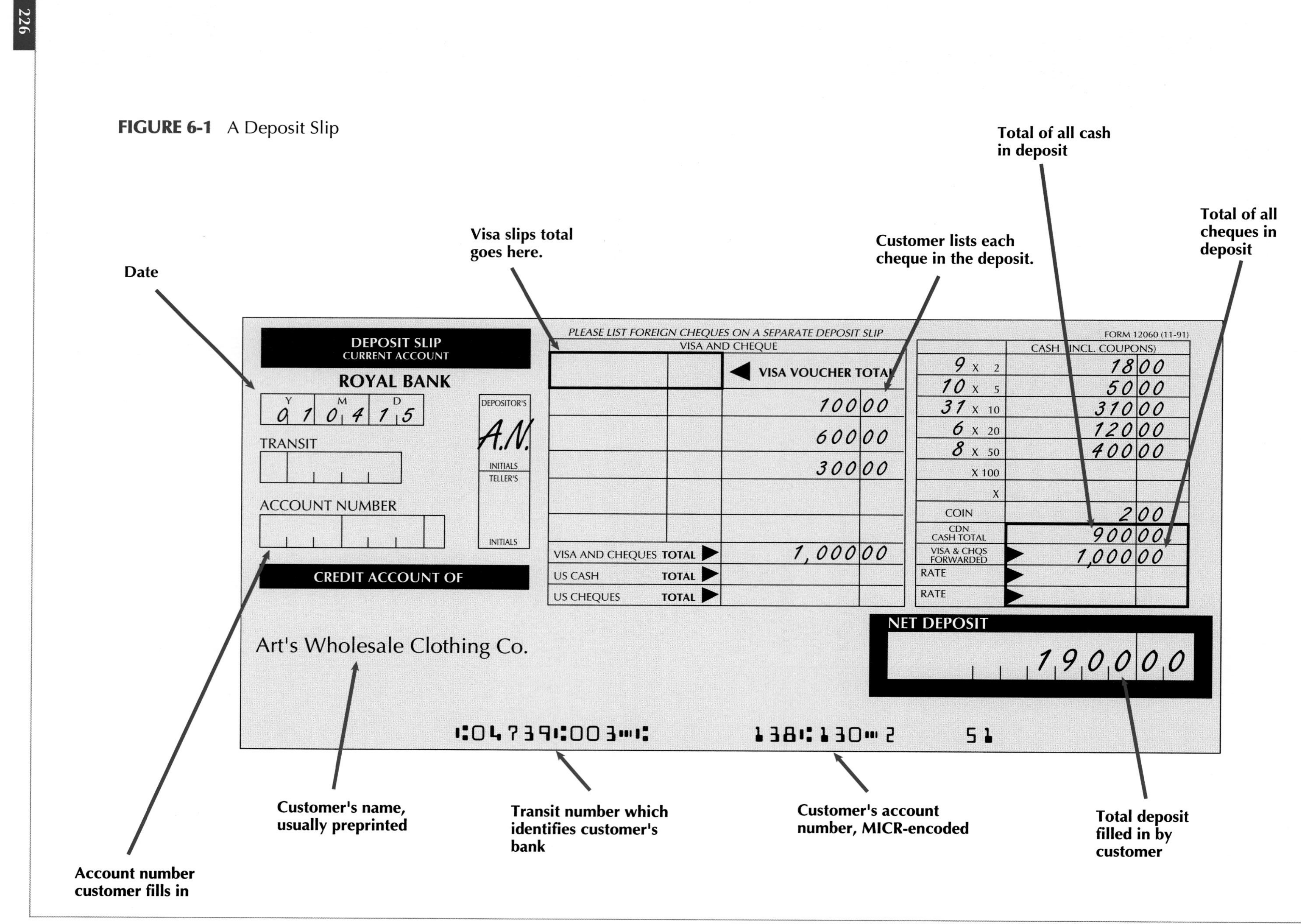

FIGURE 6-2
Types of Cheque Endorsement

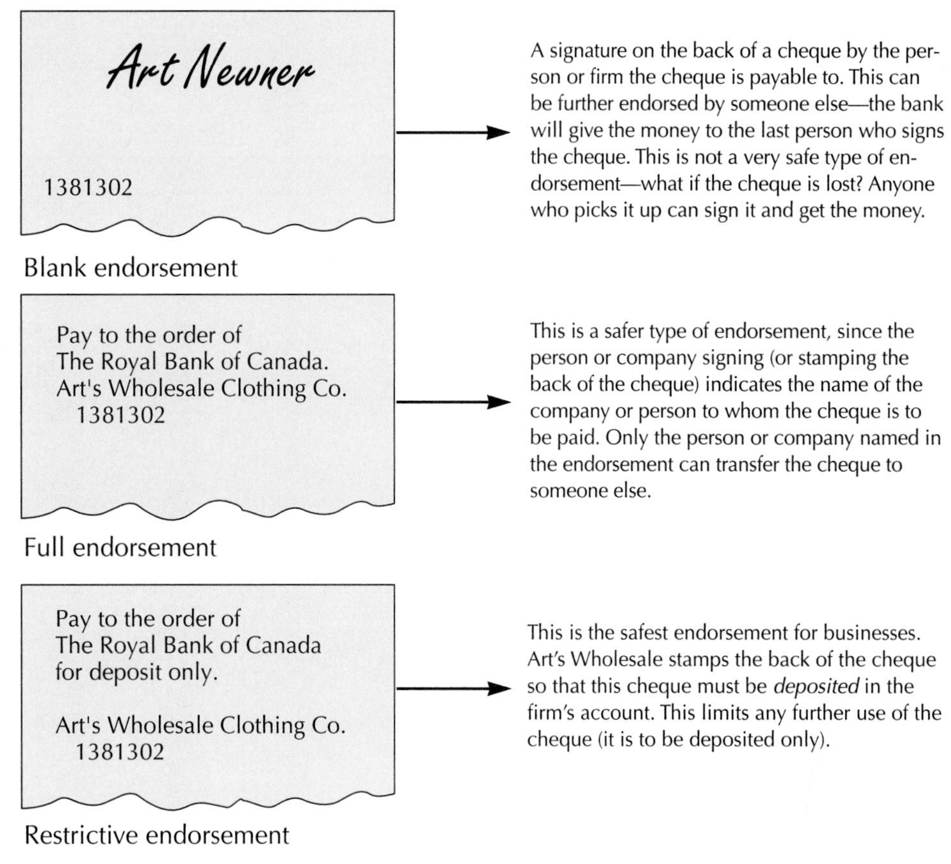

Art Newner
1381302
A signature on the back of a cheque by the person or firm the cheque is payable to. This can be further endorsed by someone else—the bank will give the money to the last person who signs the cheque. This is not a very safe type of endorsement—what if the cheque is lost? Anyone who picks it up can sign it and get the money.
Blank endorsement
Pay to the order of
The Royal Bank of Canada.
Art's Wholesale Clothing Co.
1381302
This is a safer type of endorsement, since the person or company signing (or stamping the back of the cheque) indicates the name of the company or person to whom the cheque is to be paid. Only the person or company named in the endorsement can transfer the cheque to someone else.
Full endorsement
Pay to the order of
The Royal Bank of Canada
for deposit only.
Art's Wholesale Clothing Co.
1381302
This is the safest endorsement for businesses. Art's Wholesale stamps the back of the cheque so that this cheque must be deposited in the firm's account. This limits any further use of the cheque (it is to be deposited only).
Restrictive endorsement

TRANSACTIONS AFFECTING THE CHEQUEBOOK

The figures used for deposits in this chapter differ from the figures to be used in Chapter 9 mainly because of the GST—to be covered in Chapters 9 and 10.

The transactions of Art's Wholesale for the month of April that affect the chequing account (Figure 6-4, page 229) are the same transactions that will be shown in Chapters 9 and 10 in the cash receipts and cash payments journal. Remember, all payments of money are by written cheque (except petty cash), and all money (cheques) received is deposited in the bank account.

Today some chequing accounts earn interest. The type of chequing account used by Art's Wholesale has a monthly service charge, but we assume that there is no individual charge for each cheque written, and the account does not pay interest.

Differences may result because of timing considerations.

Note in Figure 6-4 that the bank deposits ($15,324) minus the cheques written ($6,994) give an ending chequebook balance of $8,330.

At the end of April the bank sends Art a statement that the balance of the cash account is $7,919. How can this be? The following section discusses how this occurs and how it should be handled. Let's now look at the process to reconcile the difference between the bank and chequebook balances.

THE BANK RECONCILIATION PROCESS

The bank statement or report (see Figure 6-5, page 230) shows the beginning balance of the bank account at the start of the month, along with the cheques the bank has paid and any deposits received. Any other charges or additions to the bank balance are indicated by codes found on the statement. All cheques that have been paid by the bank are sent back to Art's Wholesale. These are called **cancelled cheques** because they have been processed by the bank and are no longer negotiable.

The problem is that this ending bank balance of $7,919 does not agree with the amount in Art's chequebook, $8,330, or the balance in the cash account in the ledger, $8,330. Such differences are caused partly by the time it takes to process a company's

FIGURE 6-3 A Typical Cheque and Cheque Stub

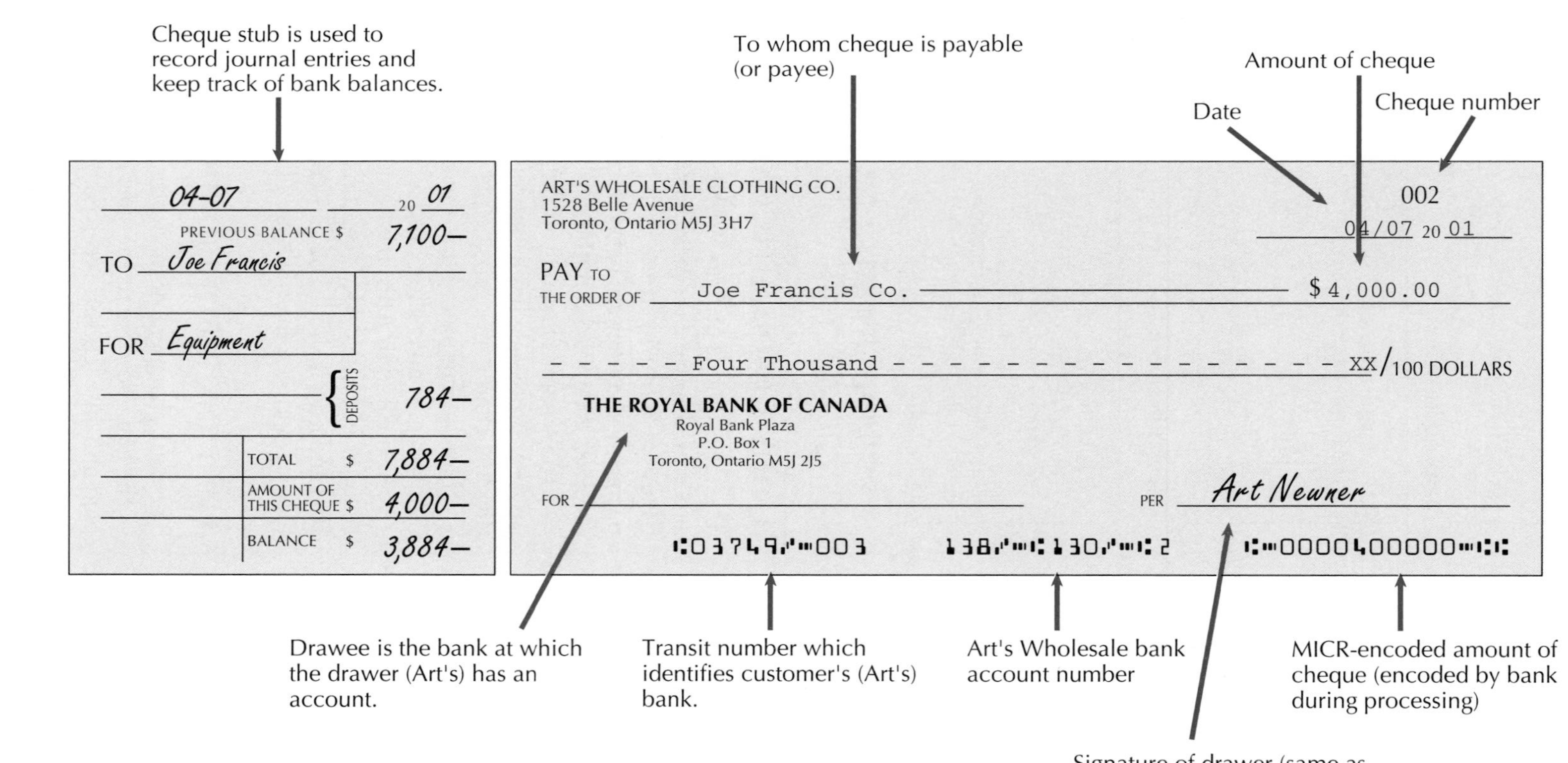
Cheque stub is used to record journal entries and keep track of bank balances.
To whom cheque is payable (or payee)
Amount of cheque
Date
Cheque number
04-07
20 01
PREVIOUS BALANCE $ 7,100—
TO Joe Francis
FOR Equipment
DEPOSITS 784—
TOTAL $ 7,884—
AMOUNT OF THIS CHEQUE $ 4,000—
BALANCE $ 3,884—
ART'S WHOLESALE CLOTHING CO.
1528 Belle Avenue
Toronto, Ontario M5J 3H7
002
04/07 20 01
PAY TO THE ORDER OF Joe Francis Co.
$ 4,000.00
- - - - - Four Thousand - - - - - - - - - - - - - - - - XX/100 DOLLARS
THE ROYAL BANK OF CANADA
Royal Bank Plaza
P.O. Box 1
Toronto, Ontario M5J 2J5
FOR
PER Art Newner
Drawee is the bank at which the drawer (Art's) has an account.
Transit number which identifies customer's (Art's) bank.
Art's Wholesale bank account number
MICR-encoded amount of cheque (encoded by bank during processing)
Signature of drawer (same as on the signature card), or one who orders the bank to pay a sum of money

FIGURE 6-4
Transactions Affecting Chequebook Balance

Bank Deposits Made for April

Date of Deposit	*Amount*	*Received from*
April 1	$8,000	Art Newner, Capital
4	784	Cheque—Hal's Clothing
16	2,880	Cash sales/Cheque—Bevans Company
22	1,960	Cheque—Roe Company
27	500	Sale of equipment
30	1,200	Cash sales
Total deposits for month	$15,324	

Cheques Written for Month of April

Date	*Cheque No.*	*Payment to*	*Amount*	*Description*
April 2	1	Peter Blum	$ 900	Insurance paid in advance
7	2	Joe Francis Company	4,000	Paid for equipment
9	3	Rick Flo Co.	800	Cash purchases
12	4	Thorpe Company	594	Paid for purchases
28	5	Payroll	700	Salaries
		Total amount of cheques written	$ 6,994	

Cash/cheque	$15,324
Cheques paid	- 6,994
Balance in company chequebook	$ 8,330

transactions. A company records a transaction when it occurs. A bank cannot record a deposit until it receives the funds. It cannot pay a cheque until the cheque is presented by the payee. In addition, the bank statement will report fees and transactions that the company did not know about.

Art's accountant has to find out why there is a difference between the balances and how the records can be brought into balance. The process of reconciling the bank balance on the bank statement versus the company's chequebook balance is called a **bank reconciliation**, which must be done monthly. To prepare the bank reconciliation Art's accountant takes a number of steps.

Deposits in Transit

Relationship of cash receipts journal to bank reconciliation

Deposits in transit: These unrecorded deposits could result if a deposit were placed in a night depository on the last day of the month.

In comparing the list of deposits received by the bank with those shown in the cash receipts journal* (Figure 6-6, page 230), the accountant notices that the two deposits made on April 27 and 30 for $500 and $1,200 are not on the bank's statement. The accountant realizes that in order to prepare this statement the bank included information about Art's Wholesale only up to April 25. These two deposits made by Art were not shown on the monthly bank statement, since they arrived at the bank after the statement was printed. This timing becomes a consideration in the reconciliation process. The deposits not yet added to the bank balance are called **deposits in transit**. These two deposits need to be added to the bank balance shown on the bank statement.

Art's Wholesale's chequebook is not affected, since the two deposits have already been added to its balance. The bank has no way of knowing that the deposits are coming until they are received.

*To be covered in detail in Chapter 9.

ROYAL BANK PLAZA BRANCH
P.O. BOX 1
TORONTO, ONTARIO
M5J 2J5

03749

ART'S WHOLESALE CLOTHING CO.
1528 BELLE AVENUE
TORONTO, ONTARIO
M5J 3H7

Account Statement

Account No.	
138 130 2	
Period From	To
Apr 01/01	Apr 25/01
Enclosures	Page
3	1

Date	Transaction Description		Cheques & Debits	Deposits & Credits	Balance
Apr 01	Balance Forward				.00
Apr 01	Deposit			8,000.00	8,000.00
Apr 02	Cheque -	001	900.00		7,100.00
Apr 04	Deposit			784.00	7,884.00
Apr 07	Cheque -	002	4,000.00		3,884.00
Apr 09	Cheque -	003	800.00		3,084.00
Apr 16	Deposit			2,880.00	5,964.00
Apr 22	Deposit			1,960.00	7,924.00
Apr 25	SERVICE CHARGE		5.00		7,919.00

No. of Debits	Total Amount	No. of Credits	Total Amount
4	5,705.00	4	13,624.00

FIGURE 6-5 Bank Statement

Outstanding Cheques

Relationship of cash payments journal to bank reconciliation

The accountant places the cheques returned by the bank in numerical order (1, 2, 3, etc.). He opens the cash payments journal* (Figure 6-7) and places a checkmark (✓) next to each payment cheque that was returned by the bank. This indicates that the amount shown in the cash payments journal has been paid and the bank has

FIGURE 6-6 Cash Receipts Journal

ART'S WHOLESALE CLOTHING COMPANY
CASH RECEIPTS JOURNAL

Page 1

Date 2001		Cash Dr.	Sales Discounts Dr.	Accounts Receivable Cr.	Sales Cr.	Sundry Account Name	Post. Ref.	Amount Cr.
April	1	✓8 000 00				Art Newner, Capital	311	8 000 00
	4	✓ 784 00	16 00	800 00		Hal's Clothing	✓	
	16	✓1 900 00			1 900 00	Cash Sales	✗	
	16	✓ 980 00	20 00	1 000 00		Bevans Company	✓	
	22	✓1 960 00	40 00	2 000 00		Roe Company	✓	
	27	500 00				Store Equipment	121	500 00
	30	1 200 00			1 200 00	Cash Sales	✗	
	30	15 324 00	76 00	3 800 00	3 100 00			8 500 00
		(111)	(413)	(113)	(411)			(X)

*To be covered in detail in Chapter 10.

FIGURE 6-7
Cash Payments Journal

ART'S WHOLESALE CLOTHING COMPANY
CASH PAYMENTS JOURNAL

Page 1

Date 2001		Chq. No.	Account Debited	Post. Ref.	Sundry Payable Dr.	Accounts Payable Dr.	Purchases Discount Cr.	Cash Cr.	
April	2	1	Prepaid Insurance	116	900 00			900 00	✔
	7	2	Joe Francis Company	✔		4000 00		4000 00	✔
	9	3	Purchases, Thor. Co.	511	800 00			800 00	✔
	12	4	Thorpe Company	✔		600 00	6 00	594 00	
	28	5	Salaries Expense, ABH	611	700 00			700 00	
	30				2400 00	4600 00	6 00	6994 00	
					(X)	(211)	(512)	(111)	

returned the cheques processed (or cancelled after payment). The accountant notices in the cash payments journal that two payments were not made by the bank and that these cheques, Nos. 4 and 5, were not returned by the bank. On Art's Wholesale's books these two cheques have been deducted from the chequebook balance; therefore, these **outstanding cheques**, or cheques that have not been presented to the bank for payment, need to be deducted from the bank balance. At some point these cheques will reach the bank. Keep in mind that the chequebook balance has already subtracted the amount of these two cheques; it is the *bank* that has no idea that these cheques have been written. When they are presented for payment, then the bank will reduce the amount of the balance.

Cheques Nos. 4 and 5 are outstanding.

Cheques outstanding: Cheques which have been drawn by the payor but have not yet reached the bank for payment

The accountant also notices a bank service charge of $5. This means that Art's Wholesale's chequebook balance should be lowered by $5.

Note in Figure 6-6 that the $500 and $1,200 are not checked off, since they did not appear on the bank statement.

The accountant is continually on the lookout for **NSF (non-sufficient funds)** cheques. This means that, when the company deposits a cheque, occasionally it will be returned because of the customer's lack of sufficient funds. If this happens, it will result in Art's Wholesale's having less money than was thought and thus having to (1) lower the chequebook balance and (2) try to collect the amount from the customer. The bank would notify Art's Wholesale of an NSF cheque (or other deductions) by a **debit memorandum**. Think of a debit memorandum as a deduction from the depositor's balance. Since, to a bank, a customer's account represents a liability (the bank must pay out funds if the customer so directs), any reduction in the fund balance requires a debit—hence the term "debit memorandum." Of course, a debit memorandum is recorded by a credit (to cash) on the books of the customer.

Debit memorandum: Deduct from balance

If the bank acts as a collecting agent for Art's Wholesale, say in collecting notes, it will charge Art a small fee, and the net amount collected will be added to the bank balance. The bank will send to Art a **credit memorandum** verifying the increase in the depositor's balance. This would be recorded by a debit in the company's books as the bank account (an asset) is increasing.

Credit memorandum: Add to balance

A bank reconciliation can be done on the back of the bank statement (see Figure 6-8). Note that the chequebook balance of $8,330 less the $5 service charge will in fact equal the adjusted balance.

A journal entry is also needed to bring the ledger accounts of Cash and Service Charge Expense up to date. Any adjustment to the chequebook balance results in a journal entry. The following entry was made to accomplish this:

Adjustments to the chequebook balance must be journalized and posted. This keeps the depositor's ledger accounts (especially cash) up to date.

April	30	Service Charge Expense*		5 00	
		Cash			5 00

* Could be recorded as miscellaneous expense, or bank charges expense.

FIGURE 6-8
Bank Reconciliation Using Back of Bank Statement

HOW TO BALANCE THIS STATEMENT WITH YOUR RECORD OF DEPOSITS AND WITHDRAWALS

1. Mark off on your account record all deposits and withdrawals appearing on the front of this account statement.
2. Enter any deposits and withdrawals not recorded in your account record (i.e., bank interest or fees).
3. Complete the worksheet below. If we can be of assistance to you, please contact us.

ACCOUNT RECONCILIATION WORKSHEET

ENTER the closing balance shown on the front of this account statement:				7,919.00
ADD all deposits/credits which do not appear on this account statement:			500.00	
			1,200.00	
TOTAL additions:			> +	1,700.00
SUB-TOTAL:				9,619.00
SUBTRACT all withdrawals/debits which do not appear on this account statement:		4	594.00	
		5	700.00	
TOTAL subtractions:			> −	1,294.00
This balance should agree with your record of deposits and withdrawals:				8,325.00

Example of a More Comprehensive Bank Reconciliation

Keep in mind that both the bank and the depositor can make mistakes that will not be discovered until the reconciliation process.

The bank reconciliation of Art's Wholesale, which we have just prepared, was not as complicated as it might have been for many other companies. Let's take a moment to look at the bank reconciliation for Monroe Company, which is based on the following:

1. Chequebook balance: $6,105
2. Balance reported by bank: $5,230
3. Recorded in journal cheque No. 108 for $54 *more* than should have been when store equipment was purchased
4. Bank charged interest of $137 on bank loan
5. A bounced cheque for $252 (NSF) has to be covered by Monroe. The bank has lowered Monroe's balance by $252 (see Figure 6-9)
6. Bank service charge of $10
7. Deposits in transit, $1,084

FIGURE 6-9
Bank Reconciliation of Monroe Company

MONROE COMPANY
BANK RECONCILIATION AS OF JUNE 30, 2001

Chequebook Balance			Balance per Bank		
Ending Chequebook Balance		$6105	Bank Statement Balance		$5,230
Add:			Add:		
Error in recording			Deposits in Transit		1,084
Cheque No. 108		54			$6,314
		$6,159			
			Deduct:		
Deduct:			Cheque no.	191..$204	
NSF Cheque	$252			198.. 250	
Bank Service Charge	10			201.. 100	
Bank loan interest	137	399			554
Reconciled Balance		$5,760	Reconciled Balance		$5,760

DM: Remember, a debit memorandum is sent by the bank indicating a reduction in depositor's balance. Examples: NSF cheque, cheque printing

CM: A credit memorandum is sent by a bank indicating an increase in depositor's balance.

Remember: If Monroe Company's chequing account were the type that earned interest, it would have increased the chequebook balance.

8. Interest charged on bank loan, $137
9. Cheques not yet processed by the bank:

Cheque	*Amount*
191	$204
198	250
201	100

Note the following journal entries needed to update Monroe Company's books. *Every time an adjustment is made in the reconciliation process to the chequebook balance, a journal entry will be needed.*

Date		Account	PR	Debit	Credit
2001 June	30	Bank Interest Expense		137.00	
		Cash			137.00
	30	Cash		54.00	
		Store Equipment			54.00
	30	Accounts Receivable, Alvin Sooth		252.00	
		Cash			252.00
	30	Miscellaneous Expense		10.00	
		Cash			10.00
		To reconcile bank balance			

Bank Reconciliations—A Realistic Example

To better illustrate the business world approach to reconciling bank accounts, we present below some data for The Fabulous Fudge Warehouse for the month of October 2001. The "initial data" consists of three things:

1. A bank reconciliation, as of September 30, 2001
2. A listing of all transactions recorded in the company's general ledger for October
3. A "simulated" bank statement for October

THE FABULOUS FUDGE WAREHOUSE
BANK RECONCILIATION
SEPTEMBER 30, 2001

Balance per Bank Statement			$4,300.24
Add: Deposit in Transit			647.92
			4,948.16
Less: Outstanding Cheques:			
	Chq 224	500.98	
	Chq 241	240.00	
	Chq 242	836.36	
	Chq 243	127.67	
	Chq 244	550.29	2,255.30
			$2,692.86
Balance per General Ledger			$2,710.36
Less Bank Charges			17.50
			$2,692.86

Date: November 10, 2001 9:40 am
G/L Listing 1100

THE FABULOUS FUDGE WAREHOUSE

General Ledger Listing as of October 31, 2001

Page: 1

Period	Source	Date	Description	Reference	Posting Entry	Batch Entry	Debits	Credits	Net Change/ Balance
	1100 Royal Bank - Chequing								2,710.36
10	GL-GJ	01-Oct-01	MELNYK PROPERTIES LTD.	CHQ 245	10 - 1	10 - 1		1,105.00	1,605.36
10	GL-GJ	01-Oct-01	CONFECTION EXPORTS - Deposit	1709F	10 - 2	10 - 2	1,449.00		3,054.36
10	GL-GJ	01-Oct-01	JULIAN'S DEPT. STORE - Deposit	1711F	10 - 3	10 - 3	767.68		3,822.04
10	GL-GJ	02-Oct-01	FUDGE FEASTS OF LONDON - Deposit	1712F	10 - 4	10 - 4	344.54		4,166.58
10	GL-GJ	02-Oct-01	ONTARIO SUGAR C0-OP	CHQ 246	10 - 5	10 - 5		1,000.87	3,165.71
10	GL-GJ	05-Oct-01	THE CHOCOLATE MOUNTAIN - Deposit	1713F	10 - 6	10 - 6	428.00		3,593.71
10	GL-GJ	05-Oct-01	CHOCOLATES GALORE - Deposit	1714F	10 - 7	10 - 7	498.98		4,092.69
10	GL-GJ	05-Oct-01	CANADA POST	CHQ 247	10 - 8	10 - 8		322.04	3,770.65
10	GL-GJ	09-Oct-01	CANDY AND ROSES - Deposit	1715F	10 - 9	10 - 9	187.50		3,958.15
10	GL-GJ	09-Oct-01	THE EASTONIA - Deposit	1716F	10 - 10	10 - 10	527.87		4,486.02
10	GL-GJ	10-Oct-01	BANK SERVICE CHARGES	ADJ126	10 - 11	10 - 11		17.50	4,468.52
10	GL-GJ	12-Oct-01	HOTEL ON THE LAKE - Deposit	1717F	10 - 12	10 - 12	804.23		5,272.75
10	GL-GJ	15-Oct-01	CANADA ADVERTISING CO.	CHQ 248	10 - 13	10 - 13		652.00	4,620.75
10	GL-GJ	15-Oct-01	THE PHONE COMPANY	CHQ 249	10 - 14	10 - 14		204.93	4,415.82
10	GL-GJ	15-Oct-01	CITY UTILITY	CHQ 250	10 - 15	10 - 15		300.15	4,115.67
10	GL-GJ	16-Oct-01	BC IMPORTS - Deposit	1720F	10 - 16	10 - 16	1,727.69		5,843.36
10	GL-GJ	16-Oct-01	ANDERSON PLASTICS	CHQ 251	10 - 17	10 - 17		565.55	5,277.81
10	GL-GJ	17-Oct-01	NAILA'S CONFECTIONARY - Deposit	1721F	10 - 18	10 - 18	226.00		5,503.81
10	GL-GJ	19-Oct-01	THE NUT HOUSE - Deposit	1724F	10 - 19	10 - 19	585.04		6,088.85
10	GL-GJ	22-Oct-01	KINGSTON MALL CANDY - Deposit	1722F	10 - 20	10 - 20	151.31		6,240.16
10	GL-GJ	23-Oct-01	CONFECTION EXPORTS - Deposit	1725F	10 - 21	10 - 21	1,350.00		7,590.16
10	GL-GJ	24-Oct-01	FARGO'S MALL ORDER CO. - Deposit	1726F	10 - 22	10 - 22	950.00		8,540.16
10	GL-GJ	26-Oct-01	MOUNTAIN INN - Deposit	1727F	10 - 23	10 - 23	500.00		9,040.16
10	GL-GJ	26-Oct-01	ECUADOR COCOA BEAN CO.	CHQ 252	10 - 24	10 - 24		975.00	8,065.16
10	GL-GJ	26-Oct-01	ZOE'S DAIRY FARM	CHQ 253	10 - 25	10 - 25		1,023.00	7,042.16
10	GL-GJ	29-Oct-01	BETTY FIELD - Salary	CHQ 254	10 - 26	10 - 26		1,200.00	5,842.16
10	GL-GJ	29-Oct-01	LEONARD FIELD - Salary	CHQ 255	10 - 27	10 - 27		1,100.00	4,742.16
10	GL-GJ	29-Oct-01	MARY JACOBSON - Salary	CHQ 256	10 - 28	10 - 28		1,200.00	3,542.16
10	GL-GJ	29-Oct-01	MORGAN COAST - Salary	CHQ 257	10 - 29	10 - 29		2,350.00	1,192.16
10	GL-GJ	30-Oct-01	RBC - Loan Repayment	10 - 28	10 - 30	10 - 30		500.00	692.16
10	GL-GJ	30-Oct-01	NEW YORK VARIETY STORES - Deposit	1728F	10 - 31	10 - 31	1,124.00		1,816.16
10	GL-GJ	30-Oct-01	MICHIGAN FUDGE - Deposit	1729F	10 - 32	10 - 32	824.00		2,640.16
10	GL-GJ	31-Oct-01	BANFF BOXED CHOCOLATES - Deposit	1730F	10 - 33	10 - 33	792.11		3,432.27

ROYAL BANK OF CANADA
NORTHWEST BRANCH
109 NORTH BEND ROAD
MISTAYA, ONTARIO
M1P 1Y1

Account Statement

Account No.	
254-292-8	
Period	
From	To
Sep. 30/01	Oct. 30/01
Enclosures	Page
14	1

THE FABULOUS FUDGE WAREHOUSE
404 NORTH BEND ROAD
MISTAYA, ONTARIO
M1P 4Y1

Date	Transaction Description		Cheques & Debits	Deposits & Credits	Balance
	Balance Forward				4,300.24
Sep 30	Deposit			647.92	4,948.16
	Loan Proceeds			10,000.00	14,948.16
	Cheque	245	1,105.00		13,843.16
	Cheque	242	836.36		13,006.80
Oct 01	Deposit			1,449.00	14,455.80
Oct 01	Deposit			767.68	15,223.48
Oct 02	Deposit			344.54	15,568.02
	Cheque	243	127.67		15,440.35
	Cheque	244	550.29		14,890.06
Oct 05	Deposit			428.00	15,318.06
Oct 05	Deposit			498.98	15,817.04
	Cheque	246	1,000.87		14,816.17
	Cheque	241	240.00		14,576.17
Oct 09	Deposit			187.50	14,763.67
Oct 09	Deposit			527.87	15.291.54
Oct 12	Deposit			804.23	16,095.77
	Cheque	247	322.04		15,773.73
	Cheque	250	300.15		15,473.58
	Cheque	249	204.93		15,268.65
Oct 16	Deposit			1,727.69	16,996.34
Oct 17	Deposit			226.00	17,222.34
Oct 19	Deposit			585.04	17,807.38
Oct 22	Deposit			151.31	17,958.69
	Cheque	248	652.00		17,306.69
Oct 23	Deposit			1,350.00	18,656.69
Oct 24	Deposit			950.00	19,606.69
Oct 25	Bank Service Charges		18.75		19,587.94
Oct 26	Deposit			500.00	20,087.94
	Cheque	254	1,200.00		18,887.94
	Cheque	257	2,350.00		16,537.94
	Cheque	255	1,100.00		15,437.94
Oct 27	Loan Payment—Principal		500.00		14,937.94
	Loan Interest Payment		115.30		14,822.64
	Cheque	251	565.55		14,257.09
Oct 28	Interest Earned			84.60	14,341.69
Oct 29	Deposit			1,124.00	15,465.69
Oct 30	Deposit			824.00	16,289.69

No. of Debits	16	Total Amount Debits	11,188.91	Total Fees	18.75
No. of Credits	19	Total Amount Credits	23,178.36	Interest Paid	0.00

To do a bank reconciliation for this period, note that there are two figures which must be brought into agreement:

- The G/L listing shows a balance of $3,432.27.
- The bank statement shows a balance of $16,289.69.

Before we begin, there are two important points to note:

1. In the business world, the bank statement would have with it the cancelled cheques (and other documentation such as debit memos, etc.). It is not possible to include these in a textbook, but the bank statement shows enough information for our purposes (especially note that the cheque numbers are shown).
2. It is highly recommended that each student take the time to actually perform the following steps. (You may use a pencil if you wish to preserve the resale value of your textbook.)

Here are the steps to follow to reconcile this bank account for October:

Step 1: Examine the previous bank reconciliation, and "check-off" (on the reconciliation, the bank statement, or the G/L Listing, as appropriate) the items which are shown there. In particular, check off:

- The outstanding deposit: It shows up as the first deposit in October. Put a checkmark (✓) beside this on the statement, and also put a checkmark beside this figure on the September reconciliation. This signifies that the amounts are "cleared."
- The five outstanding cheques: Put a checkmark, on both the bank statement and the September 30 reconciliation, beside each cheque which "cleared" the bank in October. Note that only the last four cheques cleared the bank (do not put a checkmark beside Cheque 224 on the reconciliation).
- The bank charges of $17.50: Although these showed up on the September bank statement, they were entered in the accounting records in October (see the G/L listing and put a checkmark there).

Step 2: Compare the deposits recorded in the G/L listing with those shown on the bank statement, placing a checkmark beside those which are shown in both places with the same amount. Observe that the final deposit shown in the G/L listing for $792.11 does not show up and is not checked. Also note that the amount of $84.60 on the bank statement is not checked, and the bank loan proceeds of $10,000.00 have not been entered in the G/L listing.

Step 3: Compare the cheques entered on the G/L listing with the cheques listed on the bank statement. Put a checkmark, on the statement and on the G/L listing, beside those which show up in both places. Notice that three of the October cheques did not "clear" the bank in October.

Step 4: Look for any unchecked items on the G/L listing and on the bank statement. Note the service charges for October of $18.75 as well as loan interest of $115.30.

Step 5: Prepare the bank reconciliation by following a "standard" procedure:

a. Start with Balance per Bank Statement, $16,289.69.
b. Add any outstanding (unchecked) deposits (there is only one).
c. Subtract any outstanding (unchecked) cheques (there are three new ones, plus one from September).
d. Generate a subtotal.
e. Start a second "calculation" with Balance per General Ledger, $3,432.27.
f. Add any amount(s) which have been added to the bank account (by the bank) and will be entered in the company's ledger accounts in November ($86.40 + $10,000.00).
g. Subtract any amount(s) which have been deducted from the bank account (by the bank) and will be entered in the company's ledger accounts in November ($18.75 + $115.30).

When you have finished, your reconciliation at the end of October 2001, should look like this:

THE FABULOUS FUDGE WAREHOUSE
BANK RECONCILIATION
OCTOBER 31, 2001

Balance per Bank Statement			$16,289.69
Add: Deposit in Transit			792.11
			17,081.80
Less: Outstanding Cheques:			
	Chq 224	500.98	
	Chq 252	975.00	
	Chq 253	1,023.00	
	Chq 256	1,200.00	3,698.98
Reconciled Balance			**13,382.82**
Balance per GL—Unadjusted			3,432.27
Add: Interest Income*			84.60
Loan Proceeds*			10,000.00
			13,516.87
Less: Service Charges*			18.75
Loan Interest*			115.30
Reconciled Balance			**13,382.82**

*To be entered in November, 2001

Reconciling a bank account is an important task and should be done promptly each month. Often the work is performed by reasonably junior accounting clerks and then reviewed by a supervisor. Not all reconciliations look exactly like those shown here, but any differences will be cosmetic—the underlying principles are the same.

Before summing up this unit, let's look at two interesting trends in the banking field.

New trends in banking

Electronic Funds Transfer

Many financial institutions have developed or are developing a way to transfer funds among parties electronically, without the use of paper cheques. The system that does this is called **electronic funds transfer (EFT)**. Let's look at an example.

Grant MacEwan Community College, with appropriate authorization from its employees, deposits payroll cheques directly into each employee's bank account, rather than issuing paper cheques. The bank, on receiving computer-coded payroll data, adds each employee's payroll amount to his or her account. This saves time and the possible loss or theft of payroll cheques.

Another good example is the **automatic teller machine (ATM)**. Expect to see these machines used for more transactions than simple banking chores. The sale of stamps, bus passes, and similar items through ATMs is a real possibility. We now also see bank cards used in supermarkets, fast food chains, and other retail establishments (the term *debit card* is used in connection with these transactions as a substitute for cash).

We may also see increased use of "smart cards" where the amount of cash is electronically embedded in the card itself and is read by an electronic device at a checkout to pay for purchases.

Cheque Truncation (Safekeeping)

Some banks do not return cancelled cheques to the depositor but use a procedure called **cheque truncation** or **safekeeping**. What this means is that the bank holds a cancelled cheque for a specific period of time (usually 90 days) and then keeps a microfilm copy handy. The original cheque is destroyed. What happens if a copy of a cheque is needed? For a small fee the bank provides the depositor with the cheque or a photocopy. (Photocopies will be accepted as evidence by Revenue Canada for tax returns and audits.)

Truncation cuts down on the amount of "paper" that is returned to customers and thus provides substantial cost savings. It is estimated that over five million cheques are written each day in Canada.

LEARNING UNIT 6-1 REVIEW

AT THIS POINT you should be able to:

- Define and explain the need for deposit slips. (p. 225)
- Explain where the bank's transit number is located on the cheque and what its purpose is. (p. 226)
- List and compare and contrast the three common types of cheque endorsement. (p. 227)
- Explain the structure of a cheque. (p. 228)
- Define and state the purpose of a bank statement. (p. 227)
- Explain the relationship of special journals to the bank reconciliation process. (pp. 230–231)
- Explain deposits in transit, cheques outstanding, service charge, and NSF cheques. (pp. 229–231)
- Explain the difference between a debit memorandum and a credit memorandum. (p. 231)
- Explain how to do a bank reconciliation. (p. 233–237)
- Explain electronic funds transfer and cheque truncation. (p. 237)

SELF-REVIEW QUIZ 6-1

(The blank forms you need are on page 6-1 of the *Study Guide with Working Papers.*)

Indicate, by placing an X under it, the heading that describes the appropriate action for each of the following situations:

Situation	Add to Bank Balance	Deduct from Bank Balance	Add to Chequebook Balance	Deduct from Chequebook Balance
1. Bank service charge				
2. Deposits in transit				
3. NSF cheque				
4. A $50 cheque written and recorded by the company as $60				
5. Proceeds of a note collected by the bank				
6. Cheque outstanding				

Quiz Tip

Deposits in transit are added to the bank balance while cheques outstanding are subtracted from the bank balance.

Solution to Self-Review Quiz 6-1

Situation	Add to Bank Balance	Deduct from Bank Balance	Add to Chequebook Balance	Deduct from Chequebook Balance
1				X
2	X			
3				X
4			X	
5			X	
6		X		

LEARNING UNIT 6-2

The Establishment of Petty Cash and Change Funds

Petty Cash is an asset on the balance sheet.

Art realized how time-consuming and expensive it would be to write cheques for small amounts to pay for postage, small supplies, delivery charges, and so on. What was needed was a **petty cash fund**. It was estimated that, for any given month, Art's Wholesale would need a fund of $60 to cover small expenditures. A cheque payable to the order of the custodian (one of Art's employees responsible for overseeing the fund) was drawn and cashed to establish the fund. The cash was placed in a small metal box with a simple lock which gave control of the fund to the custodian. Payments out of the fund were made only when a receipt or other supporting documentation was presented by the person requesting the money.

Similarly, Art established a change fund to make cash transactions with customers more convenient. This unit will explain how to manage petty cash and change funds.

SETTING UP THE PETTY CASH FUND

Petty Cash is an asset which is established by drawing a new cheque. The Petty Cash account is debited only when established unless the amount of the petty cash fund is changed.

Shown here is the transaction analysis chart for the establishment of a $60 petty cash fund, which would be entered in the general journal on May 1, 2001, as shown below.

1 Accounts Affected	2 Category	3 ↑↓	4 Rules
Petty Cash	Asset	↑	Dr.
Cash (cheques)	Asset	↓	Cr.

GENERAL JOURNAL — Page 1

Date		Account Title and Description	PR	Dr.	Cr.
2001 May	1	Petty Cash		6000	
		Cash			6000
		Establishment of Petty Cash Fund			

Note the new asset called *Petty Cash*; this new asset was created by writing cheque No. 6, thereby reducing the asset Cash. In reality, the total assets stay the same; what has occurred is a shift from the asset Cash (cheque No. 6) to a new asset account called Petty Cash.

The cheque for $60 is made payable to the custodian, John Sullivan, who endorses the cheque, cashes it, and uses the cash to operate the petty cash fund.

The Petty Cash account is not debited or credited again if the size of the fund is not changed. If the $60 fund is used up very quickly, the fund should be increased. If the fund is too large, the Petty Cash account should be reduced.

But who is responsible for controlling the petty cash fund? Art gives his office manager, John Sullivan, the responsibility and the authority to make payments from the petty cash fund. In other companies the cashier or secretary may be in charge of petty cash.

Making payments from the petty cash fund

John Sullivan has the responsibility for filling out a **petty cash voucher** for each cash payment made from the petty cash fund.

Note that the voucher (shown in Figure 6-10) when completed will include:

1. The voucher number (which will be in sequence): 1
2. The date: May 2
3. The person or organization to whom the payment was made: Al's Cleaners
4. The amount of payment: $3.00
5. The reason for payment: cleaning
6. The signature of the person who approved the payment: John Sullivan
7. The signature of the person who received the payment from petty cash: Art Newner
8. The account to which the expense will be charged

Vouchers in box
+ Cash in box
= Original amount placed in petty cash

The completed vouchers are placed in the petty cash box. No matter how many vouchers John Sullivan fills out, *the total of (1) the vouchers in the box and (2) the cash on hand should equal the original amount of petty cash with which the fund was established ($60).*

Assume that at the end of May the following items are documented by petty cash vouchers in the petty cash box as having been paid by John Sullivan:

2001
May 2 Cleaning package, $3.00
5 Postage stamps, $9.00
8 First aid supplies, $15.00
9 Delivery expense, $6.00
14 Delivery expense, $15.00
27 Postage stamps, $6.00

Think of the auxiliary petty cash record as a worksheet that gathers information for the journal entry.

John records this information in the **auxiliary petty cash record** shown in Figure 6-11. It is not a special journal, but an aid to John—an auxiliary record that is not essential but is quite helpful as part of the petty cash system. You may want to think of the

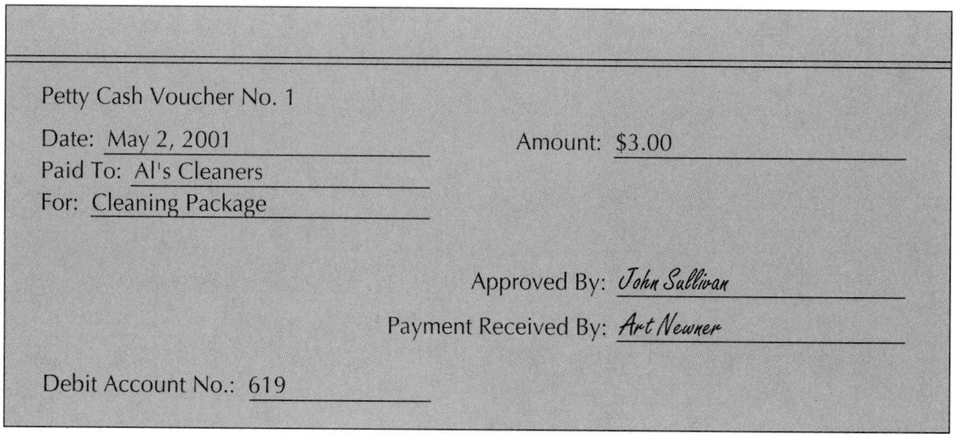

Petty Cash Voucher No. 1

Date: May 2, 2001 Amount: $3.00
Paid To: Al's Cleaners
For: Cleaning Package

Approved By: John Sullivan
Payment Received By: Art Newner

Debit Account No.: 619

FIGURE 6-10
Petty Cash Voucher

Date 2001		Voucher No.	Description	Receipts	Payments	Category of Payments: Postage Expense	Delivery Expense	Sundry: Account	Amount
May	1		Establishment	60 00					
	2	1	Cleaning		3 00			Cleaning	3 00
	5	2	Postage		9 00	9 00			
	8	3	First Aid		15 00			Misc.	15 00
	9	4	Delivery		6 00		6 00		
	14	5	Delivery		15 00		15 00		
	27	6	Postage		6 00	6 00			
			Total	60 00	54 00	15 00	21 00		18 00

FIGURE 6-11 Auxiliary Petty Cash Record

auxiliary petty cash record as an optional worksheet. Let's look at how to replenish the petty cash fund.

How to replenish the petty cash fund

No postings will be done from the auxiliary book; it is not a journal. At some point the summarized information found in the auxiliary petty cash record will be used as a basis for a journal entry in the cash payments journal and eventually posted to appropriate ledger accounts to reflect up-to-date balances.

The expenses of $54 (see Figure 6-11) are recorded in the general journal, debited to the appropriate accounts (Figure 6-12), and a new cheque, No. 17, for $54 is cashed and the proceeds given to John Sullivan for the petty cash fund. The petty cash box once again holds $60 cash. The old vouchers that were used are stamped to indicate that they have been processed and the fund replenished. The expenses recorded in the general journal to cover the replenishment of the petty cash fund will subsequently be posted to the ledger.

Note that in the replenishment process the debits in the cash payments journal (Figure 6-12) are a summary of the totals (except sundry) of expenses or other items from the auxiliary petty cash record. Posting of these specific expenses will ensure that the expenses will not be understated on the income statement. The credit to cash allows us to draw a cheque for $54 to put money back in the petty cash box. The $60 in the box now agrees with the petty cash account balance. *The end result is that*

FIGURE 6-12 Establishment and Replenishment of Petty Cash Fund

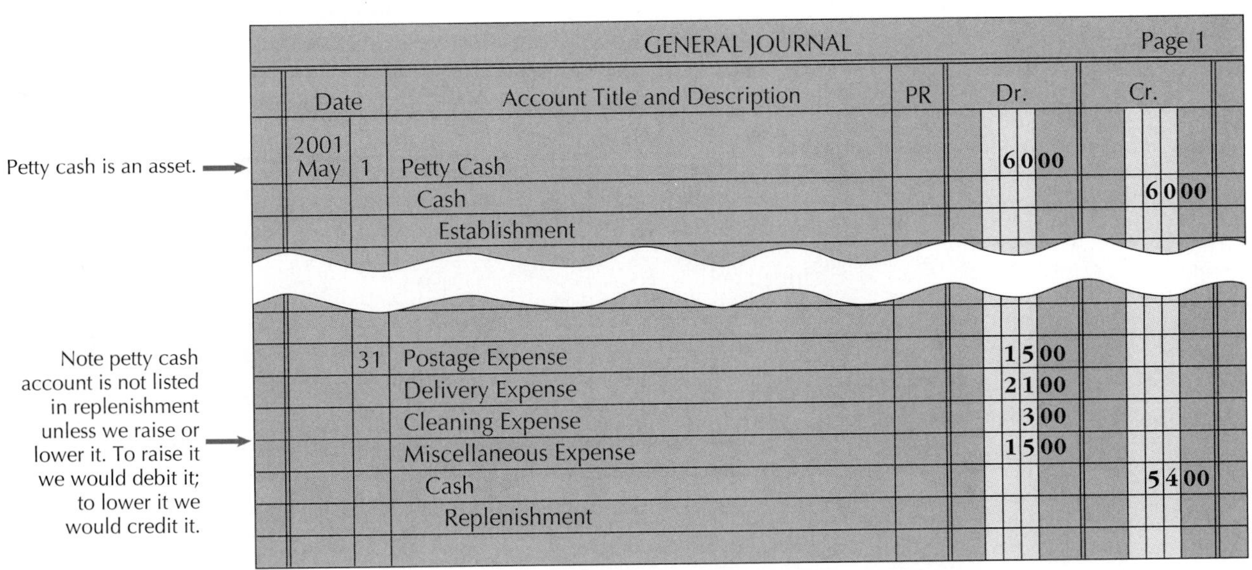

Petty cash is an asset.
Note petty cash account is not listed in replenishment unless we raise or lower it. To raise it we would debit it; to lower it we would credit it.

GENERAL JOURNAL — Page 1

Date		Account Title and Description	PR	Dr.	Cr.
2001 May	1	Petty Cash		60 00	
		Cash			60 00
		Establishment			
	31	Postage Expense		15 00	
		Delivery Expense		21 00	
		Cleaning Expense		3 00	
		Miscellaneous Expense		15 00	
		Cash			54 00
		Replenishment			

AUXILIARY PETTY CASH RECORD

Date 2001		Voucher No.	Description	Receipts	Payments	Category of Payments: Postage Expense	Delivery Expense	Sundry: Account	Amount
May	1		Establishment	60 00					
	2	1	Cleaning		3 00			Cleaning	3 00
	5	2	Postage		9 00	9 00			
	8	3	First Aid		15 00			Misc.	15 00
	9	4	Delivery		6 00		6 00		
	14	5	Delivery		15 00		15 00		
	27	6	Postage		6 00	6 00			
			Totals	60 00	54 00	15 00	21 00		18 00
			Ending Balance		6 00				
				60 00	60 00				
			Ending Balance	6 00					
	31		Replenishment	54 00					
	31		Balance (New)	60 00					

FIGURE 6-13
Recording Replenishment in the Petty Cash Record

our petty cash box is filled, and we have justified which accounts the petty cash money was spent for. Think of replenishment as a single, summarizing entry.

A new cheque is written in the replenishment process, which is payable to the custodian, cashed by Sullivan, and the cash placed in the petty cash box.

Remember, if at some point the petty cash fund is to be greater than $60, a cheque can be written that will increase Petty Cash and decrease Cash. If the Petty Cash account balance is to be reduced, we can credit or reduce Petty Cash. But for our present purpose Petty Cash will remain at $60.

The auxiliary petty cash record after replenishment would look as in Figure 6-13. (Keep in mind that no postings are made from the auxiliary book.)

Figure 6-14 may help you put the sequence together.

Before concluding this unit, let's look at how Art will handle setting up a change fund and at problems with cash shortages and overages.

SETTING UP A CHANGE FUND AND INSIGHT INTO CASH SHORT AND OVER

Change Fund is an asset on the balance sheet.

If a company like Art's Wholesale expects to have many cash transactions occurring, it may be a good idea to establish a **change fund** or float. This is a fund that is placed in the cash register drawer and used to make change for customers who pay cash. Art decides to put $120 in the change fund, made up of various denominations of bills and coins. Let's look at a transaction analysis chart for this sort of procedure.

1 Accounts Affected	2 Category	3 ↑↓	4 Dr./Cr.
Change Fund	Asset	↑	Dr.
Cash	Asset	↓	Cr.

At the close of the business day, Art will place the balance of the change fund back in the safe in the office. He will set up the change fund (the same amount of $120) in the appropriate denominations for the next business day. He will deposit in the bank the *remainder* of the cash taken in for the day.

Date 2001		Description	New Cheque Written	Recorded in Cash Payments Journal	Petty Cash Voucher Prepared	Recorded in Auxiliary Petty Cash Record
May	1	Establishment of petty cash for $60	X	X		X
	2	Paid salaries, $2,000	X	X		
	13	Paid $10 from petty cash for bandages			X	X
	19	Paid $8 from petty cash for postage			X	X
	24	Paid light bill, $200	X	X		
	29	Replenishment of petty cash to $60	X	X		X

Have nothing to do with petty cash (amounts too great) → 2

In this step, the old expenses are listed in the cash payments journal and a new cheque is written to replenish the fund. All old vouchers are removed from the petty cash box. → 29

May 1: Dr. Petty Cash, Cr. Cash

May 13 and 19: No journal entries

May 29: Dr. Individual expenses, Cr. Cash

FIGURE 6-14 Steps Involving Petty Cash

Now let's look at how to record errors that are made in making change, called *cash short and over.*

Cash Short and Over

Beginning change fund
+ Cash register total
= Cash should have on hand
– Counted cash
= Shortage or overage of cash

In a local pizza shop the total sales for the day did not match the amount of cash on hand. Errors often happen in making change. To record and summarize the differences in cash, an account called **Cash Short and Over** is used. This account will record both overages (too much money) and shortages (not enough money). Let's first look at the account (in T-account form).

Cash Short and Over	
Dr.	Cr.
Shortage	Overage

All shortages will be recorded as debits and all overages will be recorded as credits. This account is temporary. If the ending balance of the account is a debit (a shortage) it is considered a miscellaneous expense that would be reported on the income statement. If the balance of the account is a credit (an overage) it is considered as other income reported on the income statement. Let's look at how the Cash Short and Over account could be used to record shortages or overages in sales as well as in the petty cash process.

Example 1: Shortages and Overages in Sales

On December 5, the pizza shop rang up sales of $560 for the day but had only $530 in cash.

1 Accounts Affected	2 Category	3 ↑↓	4 Dr./Cr.
Cash	**Asset**	↑	**Debit $530**
Cash Short and Over	**Expense**	↑	**Debit $30**
Sales	**Revenue**	↑	**Credit $560**

The journal entry would be as follows:

Date		Account	Dr.	Cr.
Dec.	5	Cash	530 00	
		Cash Short and Over	30 00	
		Sales		560 00
		Cash shortage		

Note that the shortage of $30 is a debit and would be recorded on the income statement as a miscellaneous expense.

What would the entry look like if the pizza shop showed a $50 overage?

1 Accounts Affected	2 Category	3 ↑↓	4 Dr./Cr.
Cash	**Asset**	↑	**Debit $610**
Cash Short and Over	**Expense**	↑	**Debit $50**
Sales	**Revenue**	↑	**Credit $560**

The journal entry would be as follows:

Date		Account	Dr.	Cr.
Dec.	5	Cash	610 00	
		Cash Short and Over		50 00
		Sales		560 00
		Cash overage		

Note that the Cash Short and Over account would be reported as other income on the income statement. Now let's look at how to use this Cash Short and Over account to record petty cash transactions.

Example 2: Cash Short and Over in Petty Cash

A local computer company had established a $200 petty cash fund. Today, November 30, the petty cash box had $160 in vouchers as well as $32 in coin and currency. What would be the journal entry to replenish petty cash?

Assume the vouchers were made up of $90 for postage and $70 for supplies expense. If you add up the vouchers and cash in the box, cash is short by $8.

1 Accounts Affected	2 Category	3 ↑↓	4 Dr./Cr.
Postage Expense	**Expense**	↑	**Debit $90**
Supplies Expense	**Expense**	↑	**Debit $70**
Cash Short and Over	**Expense**	↑	**Debit $8**
Cash	**Asset**	↓	**Credit $168**

The journal entry would be as follows:

Date		Account	Dr.	Cr.
Nov.	8	Postage Expense	90 00	
		Supplies Expense	70 00	
		Cash Short and Over	8 00	
		Cash		168 00
		Replenish petty cash		

If there had been an overage, the cash short and over would be a credit as other income. If an auxiliary petty cash record is used to record the cash short and over, it would be recorded as a payment of $8 under the category of payments in the sundry column. The Solution in Self-Review Quiz 6-2 shows how a fund shortage would be recorded in the auxiliary record.

LEARNING UNIT 6-2 REVIEW

AT THIS POINT you should be able to:

- State the purpose of a petty cash fund. (p. 239)
- Prepare a journal entry to establish a petty cash fund. (p. 239)
- Prepare a petty cash voucher. (p. 240)
- Explain the relationship of the auxiliary petty cash record to the petty cash process. (p. 240)
- Prepare a journal entry to replenish Petty Cash to its original amount. (p. 244)
- Explain why individual expenses are debited in the replenishment process. (p. 241)
- Explain how a change fund is established. (p. 242)
- Explain how Cash Short and Over could be a miscellaneous expense. (p. 241)

SELF-REVIEW QUIZ 6-2

(The blank forms you need are on pages 6-1 and 6-2 of the *Study Guide with Working Papers.*)

As the custodian of the petty cash fund, it is your task to prepare entries to establish the fund on October 1, as well as to replenish the fund on October 31. Please keep an auxiliary petty cash record.

2001		
Oct.	1	Establish petty cash fund for $90, cheque No. 8.
	5	Voucher 1, delivery expense, $21
	9	Voucher 2, delivery expense, $15
	10	Voucher 3, office repair expense, $24
	17	Voucher 4, general expense, $12
	30	Replenishment of petty cash fund, $78, cheque No. 108 (Cheque would be payable to the custodian.)

Cheques to establish and replenish Petty Cash would be made out to the custodian.

Solution to Self-Review Quiz 6-2

GENERAL JOURNAL — Page 6

Date		Account Title and Description	PR	Dr.	Cr.
2001 Oct.	1	Petty Cash		90 00	
		Cash			90 00
		Establishment, Check 8			
	31	Delivery Expense		36 00	
		General Expense		12 00	
		Office Repair Expense		24 00	
		Cash Short and Over		6 00	
		Cash			78 00
		Replenishment, Check 108			

AUXILIARY PETTY CASH RECORD

Date 2001		Voucher No.	Description	Receipts	Payments	Category of Payments: Delivery Expense	General Expense	Sundry: Account	Sundry: Amount
Oct.	1		Establishment	90 00					
	5	1	Delivery		21 00	21 00			
	9	2	Delivery		15 00	15 00			
	10	3	Repairs		24 00			Office Repairs	24 00
	17	4	General		12 00		12 00	Cash Short	
	25	5	Fund shortage		6 00			and Over	6 00
			Totals	90 00	78 00	36 00	12 00		30 00
			Ending Balance		12 00				
				90 00	90 00				
	30		Ending Balance	12 00					
	31		Replenishment	78 00					
Nov.	1		Balance (New)	90 00					

Quiz Tip

How to calculate shortage:

\$21 + \$15 + \$24 +\$12 = \$72

in vouchers replenished with \$78 cheque; thus had a \$6 shortage.

Note that the amount for cash short and over was entered into the Auxiliary Petty Cash Record.

Dunkin' Donuts is urging its shop owners to get rid of their cash registers and switch to a new IBM point-of-sale terminal. With these new machines, clerks just use a touch screen to punch in the number and type of items bought. This is faster than using the old cash registers and easier to learn. Training staff to handle cash is a critical component of a cash business like Dunkin' Donuts. Every sale must be recorded—and recorded correctly. Cash control is built into the new IBM system, which also provides the owners with information that will help them spot problems and track trends.

Fred was pleased when he heard about the new system at the company's annual convention in Orlando, Florida. Register training was a recurring problem for him and for most store owners. Now the terminals in the store would be easier to learn. They would be linked, so he would be able to see consolidated data quickly. But the chore of closing out the cash drawer at the end of a shift remained. And it was still a critical control point.

"I gotta remember that," said Fred, thinking back to the convention, "when I explain how to close out her cash register drawer to Sally again. Even though she messes up my Cash Summary almost every day, getting mad sure hasn't helped. Maybe if I go through it with her step-by-step." Fred had spent hours figuring out a discrepancy between the cash in the drawer and the register tape. Sally had forgotten to void a mistaken entry for $99.99. Fred had first suspected that Sally had made a huge error in counting change.

Nodding happily to himself, Fred treated himself to one of his glazed doughnuts. Doing the daily Cash Summary normally gave Fred a sense of accomplishment (when Sally wasn't working). And the monthly chore of reconciling the shop's bank account had been no problem. The cash on the monthly financials that he submitted to Dwayne were right on the money.

Discussion Questions

1. How would Fred catch a discrepancy in the cash account?
2. How would Fred record a loss?
3. Why is cash register training so important to a service business like Fred's?
4. Why does Dunkin' Donuts invest time, money, and effort in investigating new cash handling systems like the IBM point-of-sale terminals?

Chapter Review

Summary of key points

Learning Unit 6-1

1. Restrictive endorsement limits any further negotiation of a cheque.
2. Cheque stubs are filled out first before a cheque is written.
3. The payee is the person to whom the cheque is payable. The drawer is the one who orders the bank to pay a sum of money. The drawee is the bank where the drawer has an account.
4. The process of reconciling the bank balance with the company's cash balance is called bank reconciliation. The timing of deposits, when the bank statement was issued, and other factors often result in differences between the bank balance and the chequebook balance.
5. Deposits in transit are added to the bank balance.
6. Cheques outstanding are subtracted from the bank balance.
7. NSF means that an account has insufficient funds to pay a cheque; therefore the amount is not included in the recipient's bank balance and the chequing account balance is lowered.
8. When a bank debits your account, an amount is deducted from your balance. A credit to the account is an increase in your balance.
9. All adjustments to the chequebook balance require journal entries.

Learning Unit 6-2

1. Petty Cash is an asset found on the balance sheet.
2. The Auxiliary Petty Cash Record is an auxiliary book; thus no postings are done from this book. Think of it as an optional worksheet.
3. When a petty cash fund is established, the amount is entered as a debit to Petty Cash and a credit to Cash in the cash payments journal.
4. At the time of replenishment of the petty cash fund, all expenses are debited (by category) and a credit to Cash (a new cheque) results. This replenishment, when journalized and posted, updates the ledger from the journal.
5. The only time the Petty Cash account is used is to establish the fund to begin with or to bring the fund to a higher or lower level. If the petty cash level is deemed sufficient, all replenishments will debit specific expenses and credit Cash, and a new cheque will be written. The asset Petty Cash account balance will remain unchanged.
6. A change fund is an asset that is used to make change for customers on cash sales.
7. Cash Short and Over is an account that is either a miscellaneous expense or miscellaneous income, depending on whether the ending balance is a shortage or an overage.

Key terms

ATM Automatic teller machine (p. 237)

Auxiliary petty cash record A supplementary record for summarizing petty cash information (p. 240)

Bank reconciliation The process of reconciling the chequebook balance with the bank balance given on the bank statement (p. 229)

Bank statement A report sent by a bank to a customer indicating the previous balance, individual cheques processed, individual deposits received, service charges, and ending bank balance (p. 230)

Cancelled cheque A cheque that has been processed by a bank and is no longer negotiable (p. 227)

Cash Short and Over The account that records cash shortages and overages. If ending balance is a debit, it is recorded on the income statement as a miscellaneous expense; if it is a credit, it is recorded as miscellaneous income. (p. 243)

Change fund A fund made up of various denominations of bills and coins that is used to make change to customers (p. 242)

Cheque A form used to indicate a specific amount of money that is to be paid by the bank to a named person or company (p. 225)

Cheque truncation (safekeeping) Procedure whereby cheques are not returned to the drawer with the bank statement but are instead kept at the bank for a certain amount of time before being first transferred to microfilm and then destroyed (p. 237)

Credit memorandum Increase in depositor's balance (p. 231)

Debit memorandum Decrease in depositor's balance (p. 231)

Deposits in transit Deposits that were made by customers of a bank but did not reach, or were not processed by, the bank before the preparation of the bank statement (p. 229)

Deposit slip A form provided by a bank for use in recording deposits of money or cheques into a bank account (p. 225)

Drawee Bank with which the drawer has an account (p. 225)

Drawer Person who writes a cheque (p. 225)

Endorsement *Blank*—could be further endorsed. *Full*—restricts further endorsement to only the person or company named. *Restrictive*—restricts any further endorsement (p. 225)

EFT (electronic funds transfer) An electronic system that transfers funds without use of paper cheques (p. 237)

Internal control A system of procedures and methods to control a firm's assets as well as monitor its operations (p. 224)

NSF (Non-sufficient Funds) Notation indicating that a cheque has been written on an account that lacks sufficient funds to back it up (p. 231)

Outstanding cheques Cheques written by a company or person that were not received or not processed by the bank before the preparation of the bank statement (p. 231)

Payee The person or company the cheque is payable to (p. 225)

Petty cash fund A fund (source) that allows payment of small amounts without the writing of cheques (p. 239)

Petty cash voucher A petty cash form to be completed when money is taken out of petty cash (p. 240)

Blueprint of a Bank Reconciliation

Ending Balance per Books		$XXX
Add:		
Recording of errors that understate balance	XXX	
Proceeds of notes collected by bank or other items credited (added) by bank but not yet updated in chequebook	XXX	
		XXX
Deduct:		
Recording of errors that overstate balance	XXX	
Service charges	XXX	
Printing charges	XXX	
NSF cheque, etc., or other items debited (charged) by bank but not yet updated in chequebook	XXX	
		XXX
Reconciled Balance (Adjusted Balance)		$XXX

Balance per Bank		
Ending Bank Statement Balance (last figure on bank statement)		$XXX
Add:		
Deposits in transit (amount not yet credited by bank)	XXX	
Bank errors	XXX	
		XXX
Deduct:		
List of outstanding cheques (amount not yet debited by bank)	XXX	
Bank errors	XXX	
		XXX
Reconciled Balance (Adjusted Balance)		$XXX

Questions, Mini Exercises, Exercises, and Problems

Discussion Questions

1. What is the purpose of internal control?
2. What is the advantage of having preprinted deposit slips?
3. Explain the difference between a blank endorsement and a restrictive endorsement.
4. Explain the difference between payee, drawer, and drawee.
5. Why should cheque stubs be filled out first, before the cheque itself is written?
6. "A bank statement is sent twice a month." True or false? Please explain.
7. Explain the end product of a bank reconciliation.
8. Why are cheques outstanding subtracted from the bank balance?
9. "An NSF results in a bank's issuing the depositor a credit memorandum." Agree or disagree. Please support your response.
10. Why do adjustments to the chequebook balance in the reconciliation process need to be journalized?
11. What is EFT?
12. What is meant by cheque truncation or safekeeping?
13. "Petty cash is a liability." Accept or reject.

14. Explain the relationship of the auxiliary petty cash record to the cash payments journal.
15. At time of replenishment, why are the totals of individual expenses debited?
16. Explain the purpose of a change fund.
17. Explain how Cash Short and Over can be a miscellaneous expense.

Mini Exercises

(The blank forms you need are on page 6-3 in the *Study Guide with Working Papers.*)

Bank Reconciliation

1. Indicate which of the actions (**1** through **4**) listed below must be taken when doing a bank reconciliation for each of the six situations (**a** through **f**) described below.

   1. Add to bank balance
   2. Deduct from bank balance
   3. Add to chequebook balance
   4. Deduct from chequebook balance

   ____ **a.** $5 bank service charge
   ____ **b.** $100 deposit in transit
   ____ **c.** $30 NSF cheque
   ____ **d.** A $15 cheque was written and recorded as $25.
   ____ **e.** Bank collected a $1,000 note less $50 collection fee.
   ____ **f.** Cheque No. 111 was outstanding for $55.

Journal Entries in Reconciliation Process

2. Which of the transactions in question 1 above would require a journal entry?

Bank Reconciliation

3. From the following, construct a bank reconciliation for Woody Co. as of May 31, 2001.

Chequebook balance	$10
Bank statement balance	15
Deposits in transit	5
Outstanding cheques	15
Bank service charge	5

Petty Cash

4. Indicate which of the actions (**1** through **4**) listed below would be necessary for each of the situations (**a** through **f**) described at the top of page 252.

   1. New cheque written
   2. Recorded in general journal
   3. Petty cash voucher prepared
   4. Recorded in auxiliary petty cash record.

____ a. Established petty cash
____ b. Paid $1,000 bill
____ c. Paid $2 for band-aids from petty cash
____ d. Paid $30.00 for stamps from petty cash
____ e. Paid electricity bill, $250
____ f. Replenished petty cash

Replenishment of Petty Cash

5. Petty cash was originally established with $20. During the month $5 was paid out for band-aids and $6 for stamps. During replenishment, the custodian discovered that the balance in petty cash was $8. Record, using a general journal entry, the replenishment of petty cash back to $20.

Increasing Petty Cash

6. In question 5 above, if the custodian decided to raise the level of petty cash to $30, what would be the journal entry to replenish (use a general journal entry)?

Exercises

Bank reconciliation

(The blank forms you need are on pages 6-4 and 6-5 of the *Study Guide with Working Papers.*)

6-1. From the following information, construct a bank reconciliation for Norry Co. as of July 31, 2001. Then prepare journal entries if needed.

Ending chequebook balance	$420
Ending bank statement balance	300
Deposits (in transit)	200
Outstanding cheques	95
Bank service charge (debit memo)	15

Establishing and replenishing petty cash

6-2. In general journal form, prepare journal entries to establish a petty cash fund on July 2 and replenish it on July 31.

2000		
July	2	A $40 petty cash fund is established.
	31	At end of month $12 cash plus the following paid vouchers exist: donations expense, $10; postage expense, $7; office supplies expense, $7; miscellaneous expense, $4.

Cash shortage in replenishment

6-3. If, in Exercise 6-2, cash on hand was $11, prepare the entry to replenish the petty cash on July 31.

Cash overage in replenishment

6-4. If, in Exercise 6-2, cash on hand was $13, prepare the entry to replenish the petty cash on July 31.

Calculating cash shortage in a change fund

6-5. At the end of the day, the clerk for Pete's Variety Shop noticed an error in the amount of cash he had. Total cash sales from the sales tape were $1,100, while the total cash in the till was $1,066. Pete also keeps a $30 change fund in his shop. Prepare an appropriate general journal entry to record the cash sales as well as reveal the cash shortage.

Group A Problems

(The blank forms you need are on pages 6-6 to 6-11 of the *Study Guide with Working Papers.*)

Preparing a bank reconciliation, including collection of a note

Check Figure

Reconciled Balance $6,498

6A-1. Rose Company received a bank statement from TD Bank indicating a bank balance of $7,013. Based on Rose's cheque stubs, the ending chequebook balance was $5,840. Your task is to prepare a bank reconciliation for Rose Company as of July 31, 2002, from the following information (please journalize entries as needed):

a. Cheques outstanding: No. 124, $620; No. 126, $870

b. Deposits in transit, $975

c. Bank service charge, $14

d. TD Bank collected a note for Rose, $680, less an $8 collection fee.

Preparing a bank reconciliation with an NSF cheque, using the back of a bank statement.

Check Figure

Reconciled Balance $4,415

6A-2. From the bank statement on the next page and the items below, please (1) complete the bank reconciliation for Rick's Deli found on the reverse of the bank statement and (2) journalize the appropriate entries as needed.

a. A deposit of $2,000 is in transit

b. Rick's Deli has an ending chequebook balance of $4,845.

c. Cheques outstanding: No. 111, $725; No. 119, $1,100; No. 121, $360

d. Jim Rice's cheque for $400 bounced because of lack of sufficient funds.

Establishing and replenishing of petty cash

Relationship to auxiliary petty cash record

Check Figure

Cash replenishment $38

6A-3. The following transactions occurred in April and were related to the general journal and petty cash fund of Merry Co.:

2001		
April	1	Issued cheque No. 14 for $75 to establish a petty cash fund.
	5	Paid $5 from petty cash for postage, voucher No. 1.
	8	Paid $10 from petty cash for office supplies, voucher No. 2.
	17	Paid $8 from petty cash for office supplies, voucher No. 3.
	24	Paid $6 from petty cash for postage, voucher No. 4.
	26	Paid $9 from petty cash for local church donation, voucher No. 5 (this is a miscellaneous payment).
	28	Issued cheque No. 15 to Roy Kloon to pay for office equipment, $700.

The chart of accounts includes Cash, 100; Petty Cash, 120; Office Equipment, 130; Postage Expense, 610; Office Supplies Expense, 620; Miscellaneous Expense, 630. The headings of the auxiliary petty cash records are as follows:

AUXILIARY PETTY CASH RECORD

					Category of Payments			
							Sundry	
Date 2001	Voucher No.	Description	Receipts	Payments	Postage Expense	Office Supplies Expense	Account	Amount

Required

1. Record the appropriate entries in the general journal as well as in the auxiliary petty cash record as needed.
2. Be sure to replenish the petty cash fund on April 30 (cheque No. 16).

BANK OF SASKATCHEWAN
10050 - 101 Street
Regina, Saskatchewan
S4J 6E2

03749

RICK'S DELI
8811 - 102 Street
Regina, SA
S4S 3G6

Account Statement

Account No.	
241 673 6	
Period	
From	To
Feb 01/03	Feb 28/03
Enclosures	Page
2	1

Date	Transaction Description		Cheques & Debits	Deposits & Credits	Balance
Feb 01	Balance Forward				5,200.00
Feb 02	Cheque -	108	90.00		
Feb 03	Cheque -	114	210.00		4,900.00
Feb 10	Deposit			300.00	
Feb 10	Cheque -	116	150.00		5,050.00
Feb 14	Deposit			600.00	5,650.00
Feb 15	Cheque -	113	600.00		5,050.00
Feb 20	Deposit			400.00	
Feb 20	NSF Returned Item		400.00		5,050.00
Feb 22	Deposit			1,200.00	6,250.00
Feb 24	Cheque -	117	1,200.00		5,050.00
Feb 26	Deposit			180.00	5,230.00
Feb 28	Cheque -	120	600.00		
Feb 28	Service Charge		30.00		4,600.00

No. of Debits	Total Amount	No. of Credits	Total Amount
8	3,280.00	5	2,680.00

Establishing and replenishing petty cash, including handling a cash shortage

6A-4. From the following, record the transactions in Logan's auxiliary petty cash record and general journal.

Check Figure
Cash replenishment $90

2000

Oct.	1	A cheque was drawn (No. 444) payable to Roberta Floss, petty cashier, to establish a $150 petty cash fund.
	5	Paid $24 for postage stamps, voucher No. 1.
	9	Paid $15 for delivery charges on goods for resale, voucher No. 2.
	12	Paid $10 for donation to a mission (Miscellaneous Expense), voucher No. 3.
	14	Paid $12 for postage stamps, voucher No. 4.
	17	Paid $10 for delivery charges on goods for resale, voucher No. 5.
	27	Purchased computer supplies from petty cash for $11, voucher No. 6.
	28	Paid $6 for postage, voucher No. 7.
	29	Drew cheque No. 618 to replenish petty cash and cover a $2 shortage.

Group B Problems

(The blank forms you need are on pages 6-6 to 6-11 of the *Study Guide with Working Papers.*)

Preparing a bank reconciliation, including collection of a note

Check Figure

Reconciled Balance $6,569

6B-1. As the bookkeeper of Rose Company you received the bank statement from TD Bank indicating a balance of $5,344. The ending chequebook balance was $4,835. Prepare the bank reconciliation for Rose Company as of July 31, 2002, and prepare journal entries as needed based on the following:

a. Deposits in transit, $2,850

b. Bank service charges, $24

c. Cheques outstanding: No. 111, $478; No. 115, $1,147

d. TD Bank collected a note for Rose, $1,770, less a $12 collection fee.

Preparing a bank reconciliation with an NSF cheque, using the back side of a bank statement.

Check Figure

Reconciled Balance $922

6B-2. Based on the following, please (1) complete the bank reconciliation for Rick's Deli found on the reverse of the bank statement below, and (2) journalize the appropriate entries as needed.

a. Cheques outstanding: No. 110, $92; No. 116, $140; No. 118, $76

b. A deposit of $420 is in transit.

c. The chequebook balance of Rick's Deli shows an ending balance of $976.

d. Jim Rice's cheque for $50 bounced because of lack of sufficient funds.

BANK OF SASKATCHEWAN
10050 - 101 Street
Regina, Saskatchewan
S4J 6E2

03749

RICK'S DELI
8811 - 102 Street
Regina, SA
S3A 3G6

Account Statement

Account No.	
241 673 6	
Period	
From	To
Apr 01/03	Apr 30/03
Enclosures	Page
2	1

Date	Transaction Description		Cheques & Debits	Deposits & Credits	Balance
Apr 01	Balance Forward				898.00
Apr 02	Cheque -	108	12.00		
Apr 03	Cheque -	114	36.00		850.00
Apr 10	Deposit			40.00	
Apr 10	Cheque -	115	20.00		870.00
Apr 14	Deposit			80.00	950.00
Apr 15	Cheque -	113	80.00		870.00
Apr 20	Deposit			50.00	
Apr 20	NSF Returned Item		50.00		870.00
Apr 22	Deposit			160.00	1030.00
Apr 24	Cheque -	117	160.00		870.00
Apr 26	Deposit			24.00	894.00
Apr 28	Cheque -	109	80.00		
Apr 28	Service Charge		4.00		810.00

No. of Debits	Total Amount	No. of Credits	Total Amount
8	442.00	5	354.00

Establishment and replenishment of petty cash

Relationship to auxiliary petty cash record

Check Figure

Cash replenishment $48

6B-3. From the following transactions, (1) record the entries as needed in the general journal of Merry Co. as well as the auxiliary petty cash record, and (2) replenish the petty cash fund on April 30 (cheque No. 6).

2001		
April	1	Issued cheque No. 4 for $80 to establish a petty cash fund.
	5	Paid $9 from petty cash for postage, voucher No. 1.
	8	Paid $12 from petty cash for office supplies, voucher No. 2.
	17	Paid $9 from petty cash for office supplies, voucher No. 3.
	24	Paid $6 from petty cash for postage, voucher No. 4.
	26	Paid $12 from petty cash for local church donation, voucher No. 5 (this is a miscellaneous payment).
	28	Issued cheque No. 5 to Roy Kloon to pay for office equipment, $800.

Chart of accounts includes: Cash, 100; Petty Cash, 120; Office Equipment, 130; Postage Expense, 610; Office Supplies Expense, 620; Miscellaneous Expense, 630. Use the same headings as in Problem 6A-3.

Establishing and replenishing petty cash, and covering a cash shortage

Check Figure

Cash replenishment $73

6B-4. From the following, record the transactions in Logan's auxiliary petty cash record and general journal:

2000		
Oct.	1	Roberta Floss, the petty cashier, cashed a cheque, No. 444, to establish a $100 petty cash fund.
	5	Paid $18 for postage stamps, voucher No. 1.
	9	Paid $12 for delivery charges on goods for resale, voucher No. 2.
	12	Paid $10 for donation to a church (Miscellaneous Expense), voucher No. 3.
	14	Paid $14 for postage stamps, voucher No. 4.
	17	Paid $5 for delivery charges on goods for resale, voucher No. 5.
	27	Purchased computer supplies from petty cash for $7, voucher No. 6.
	28	Paid $4 for postage, voucher No. 7.
	29	Drew cheque No. 618 to replenish petty cash and cover a $3 shortage.

Group C Problems

Preparing a bank reconciliation, including collection of a note

(The blank forms you need are on pages 6-12 to 6-18 of the *Study Guide with Working Papers*.)

Check Figure

Reconciled Balance $4,677

6C-1. Graham Company received a bank statement from Royal Bank indicating a bank balance of $4,789. Based on Graham's cheque stubs, the ending chequebook balance was $4,147. Your task is to prepare a bank reconciliation for Graham Company as of May 31, 2001, from the following information (please journalize entries as needed):

a. Cheques outstanding: No. 354, $297; No. 356, $512; No. 347, $684

b. Deposits in transit, $1,381

c. Bank service charge, $39

d. Royal Bank collected a note for Graham, $734, less a $14 collection fee.

e. Notice was received that a cheque from Harry Pride, a customer, was returned NSF, $151.

Preparing a bank reconciliation with an NSF cheque, using the back of a bank statement

Check Figure

Reconciled Balance $4,847

6C-2. From the following July 28, 2002, bank statement, please (1) complete a bank reconciliation for The Fresh Flower Shop and (2) journalize the appropriate entries as needed.

a. A deposit of $2,122 is in transit.

b. The Fresh Flower Shop has an ending chequebook balance of $5,111.

c. Cheques outstanding: No. 231, $298; No. 245, $509; No. 246, $76; No 247, $237.

d. Jane Yate's cheque for $225 bounced because of non-sufficient funds.

e. Cheque No. 241 for utilities expense was entered in the cash payments journal as $358.

f. The cheque for $607 shown by the bank as paid on July 28 was actually a cheque of the Active Automotive Repair. This error will be corrected by the bank next month. The bank apologized for the error.

BANK OF INDUSTRY AND COMMERCE
48 JAMES STREET
HALIFAX, NOVA SCOTIA
B4T 2L0

08179

Account Statement

Account No.
914 817 2

Period
From Jun 29/02 To Jul 28/02

Enclosures 2 Page 1

THE FRESH FLOWER SHOP
121 SPRING GARDEN ROAD
HALIFAX, NS
B5H 3E6

Date	Transaction Description		Cheques & Debits	Deposits & Credits	Balance
Jul 01	Balance Forward				2,824.00
Jul 02	Cheque -	241	385.00		2,439.00
Jul 03	Cheque -	240	410.00		2,029.00
Jul 10	Deposit			1,712.00	
Jul 10	Cheque -	243	250.00		3,491.00
Jul 14	Deposit			950.00	4,441.00
Jul 15	Cheque -	242	1,214.00		3,227.00
Jul 16	Deposit			225.00	3,452.00
Jul 20	NSF Returned Item		225.00		3,227.00
Jul 22	Deposit			1,260.00	4,487.00
Jul 24	Cheque -	248	1,410.00		3,077.00
Jul 26	Deposit			780.00	3,857.00
Jul 28	Cheque -	1126	607.00		
Jul 28	Service Charge		12.00		3,238.00

No. of Debits	Total Amount	No. of Credits	Total Amount
8	4,513.00	5	4,927.00

Establishment and replenishment of petty cash

Relationship to auxiliary petty cash record

Check Figure

Cash replenishment $178

6C-3. The following transactions occurred in March and were related to the general journal and petty cash fund of Samuel & Co.:

2001		
March	1	Issued cheque No. 314 for $200 to establish a petty cash fund.
	5	Paid $45 from petty cash for postage, voucher No. 1.
	8	Paid $39 from petty cash for office supplies, voucher No. 2.
	17	Paid $27 from petty cash for office supplies, voucher No. 3.

24 Paid $47 from petty cash for postage, voucher No. 4.
26 Paid $20 from petty cash for local church donation, voucher No. 5 (this is a miscellaneous payment).
28 Issued cheque No. 315 to Klondike Office Equipment to pay for office equipment, $1,890.

The chart of accounts includes Cash, 100; Petty Cash, 105; Office Equipment, 170; Postage Expense, 645; Office Supplies Expense, 640; Miscellaneous Expense, 630. The headings of the auxiliary petty cash records are the same as for 6A-3.

Required

1. Record the appropriate entries in the general journal and the auxiliary petty cash record as needed.
2. Be sure to replenish the petty cash fund on March 31 (cheque No. 316).

Establishing and replenishing petty cash and covering a cash shortage

Check Figure

Cash replenishment $212

6C-4. From the following, record the transactions in Caron Co.'s auxiliary petty cash record and general journal.

2000
Oct. 1 A cheque was drawn (No. 772) payable to Herb Kiriak, petty cashier, to establish a $250 petty cash fund.
5 Paid $41 for postage stamps, voucher No. 1.
9 Paid $16 for delivery charges on goods for resale, voucher No. 2.
12 Gave $30 donation to a church (Miscellaneous Expense), voucher No. 3.
14 Paid $57 for postage stamps, voucher No. 4.
17 Paid $13 for delivery charges on goods for resale, voucher No. 5.
27 Purchased computer supplies from petty cash for $19, voucher No. 6.
28 Paid $32 for postage, voucher No. 7.
29 Drew cheque No. 813 to replenish petty cash (a $4 shortage was apparent when the cash was balanced).

Realistic bank reconciliation scenarios

Check Figure

Reconciled Balance $10,912.45

6C-5. Shown below are the following for Wagstaff Energy Consulting:

a. Bank reconciliation completed, as of March 31, 2002
b. General Ledger listing for April 2002
c. Bank statement for March 29 to April 28, 2002

WAGSTAFF ENERGY CONSULTING
BANK RECONCILIATION
MARCH 31, 2002

Balance per Bank Statement			11,635.79
Add: Deposit in Transit		750.00	
		1,070.00	1,820.00
			13,455.79
Less: Outstanding cheques:			
	Chq 0435	109.14	
	Chq 0436	1,200.00	
	Chq 0437	80.27	
	Chq 0438	1,050.00	
	Chq 0439	475.00	2,914.41
Balance per General Ledger			**10,541.38**

Date: May 12, 2002 2:12 pm
G/L Listing for account 1100

WAGSTAFF ENERGY CONSULTING

General Ledger Listing as of April 30, 2002

Page: 1

Period	Source	Date	Description	Reference	Posting Entry	Batch Entry	Debits	Credits	Net Balance
	1100 Bank of Alberta - Chequing								10,541.38
4	GL-GJ	01-Apr-02	ALBERTA PHONE CO.	CHQ 0440	4 - 1	4 - 1		153.29	10,388.09
4	GL-GJ	01-Apr-02	MAXIM OFFICE SUPPLIES	CHQ 0441	4 - 2	4 - 2		85.29	10,302.80
4	GL-GJ	02-Apr-02	CANADA POST	CHQ 0442	4 - 3	4 - 3		275.54	10,027.26
4	GL-GJ	02-Apr-02	HANDI PRINT AND GRAPHICS	CHQ 0443	4 - 4	4 - 4		475.00	9,552.26
4	GL-GJ	05-Apr-02	CITY TRUCK STOPS - Deposit	LT504	4 - 5	4 - 5	1,664.00		11,216.26
4	GL-GJ	08-Apr-02	PERFORMANCE OIL CHANGE - Deposit	LT498	4 - 6	4 - 6	535.00		11,751.26
4	GL-GJ	08-Apr-02	AUTO ROW SALES & SERVICE - Deposit	LT499	4 - 7	4 - 7	750.00		12,501.26
4	GL-GJ	08-Apr-02	SINCLAIR UTILITY	CHQ 0444	4 - 8	4 - 8		175.83	12,325.43
4	GL-GJ	08-Apr-02	KENYA COFFEE COMPANY	CHQ 0445	4 - 9	4 - 9		50.24	12,275.19
4	GL-GJ	09-Apr-02	THE CO-OPS OF MONTANA - Deposit	LT500	4 - 10	4 - 10	984.61		13,259.80
4	GL-GJ	09-Apr-02	RED'S GAS BAR - Deposit	LT503	4 - 11	4 - 11	125.91		13,385.71
4	GL-GJ	15-Apr-02	W. CANADA TRUCK STOPS - Deposit	LT496	4 - 12	4 - 12	377.73		13,763.44
4	GL-GJ	15-Apr-02	CITY NEWSPAPER	CHQ 0446	4 - 13	4 - 13		352.45	13,410.99
4	GL-GJ	15-Apr-02	REVENUE CANADA -GST	CHQ 0447	4 - 14	4 - 14		2,870.00	10,540.99
4	GL-GJ	15-Apr-02	REVENUE CANADA	CHQ 0448	4 - 15	4 - 15		1,794.10	8,746.89
4	GL-GJ	16-Apr-02	SUPER SAVE SERVICE - Deposit	LT490	4 - 16	4 - 16	521.82		9,268.71
4	GL-GJ	17-Apr-02	CARLY'S TRUCK WASH - Deposit	LT501	4 - 17	4 - 17	475.24		9,743.95
4	GL-GJ	17-Apr-02	APRIL'S MART - Deposit	LT502	4 - 18	4 - 18	125.91		9,869.86
4	GL-GJ	18-Apr-02	ELDORADO PETROLEUM - Deposit	LT495	4 - 19	4 - 19	2,140.00		12,009.86
4	GL-GJ	23-Apr-02	WEYBURN REFINERY	CHQ 0449	4 - 20	4 - 20		1,095.00	10,914.86
4	GL-GJ	23-Apr-02	TRI-CITY GAS - Deposit	LT505	4 - 21	4 - 21	704.19		11,619.05
4	GL-GJ	25-Apr-02	BENNY'S AUTO REPAIR - Deposit	LT506	4 - 22	4 - 22	1,151.97		12,771.02
4	GL-GJ	26-Apr-02	B OF A LOAN PAYMENT	4 - 23	4 - 23	4 - 23		203.38	12,567.64
4	GL-GJ	26-Apr-02	B OF A LOAN INTEREST	4 - 24	4 - 24	4 - 24		40.00	12,527.64
4	GL-GJ	26-Apr-02	LESLEY TRIPP - Salary	CHQ 0450	4 - 25	4 - 25		1,200.00	11,327.64
4	GL-GJ	26-Apr-02	ANDREW GOINGS - Salary	CHQ 0451	4 - 26	4 - 26		1,050.00	10,277.64
4	GL-GJ	29-Apr-02	EDISON TUNE-UPS ALBERTA - Deposit	LT507	4 - 27	4 - 27	1,145.99		11,423.63

BANK OF ALBERTA
105 STREET BRANCH
SINCLAIR, ALBERTA
T1Y 4P8

Account Statement

Account No.	
2361-445-99	
Period From	To
Mar 29/02	Apr 29/02
Enclosures	Page
14	50

WAGSTAFF ENERGY CONSULTING
5024–103 STREET
SINCLAIR, ALBERTA
T1J 2E2

Date	Transaction Description		Cheques & Debits	Deposits & Credits	Balance
	Balance Forward				11,635.79
Mar 29	Error Correction		750.00		10,885.79
	Loan Proceeds			750.00	11,635.79
	Deposit			750.00	12,385.79
Apr 01	Deposit			1,070.00	13,455.79
	Cheque	0439	475.00		12,980.79
	Cheque	0435	109.14		12,871.65
	Cheque	0437	80.27		12,791.38
	Cheque	0440	153.29		12,638.09
	Cheque	0442	275.54		12,362.55
	NSF Returned	0493	550.29		11,812.26
Apr 05	NSF Charge		15.00		11,797.26
Apr 05	Deposit			1,664.00	13,461.26
	Cheque	0438	1,050.00		12,411.26
	Cheque	0441	85.29		12,325.97
Apr 08	Deposit			535.00	12,860.97
Apr 08	Deposit			750.00	13,610.97
Apr 09	Deposit			984.61	14,595.58
	Cheque	0436	1,200.00		13,395.58
	Cheque	0443	475.00		12,920.58
	Cheque	0444	175.83		12,744.75
Apr 09	Deposit			125.91	12,870.66
	Cheque	0447	2,870.00		10,000.66
	Cheque	0448	1,794.10		8,206.56
Apr 15	Deposit			377.73	8,584.29
Apr 16	Deposit			521.82	9,106.11
Apr 17	Deposit			475.24	9,581.35
Apr 17	Deposit			125.91	9,707.26
Apr 18	Deposit			2,140.00	11,847.26
	Cheque	0445	50.24		11,797.02
Apr 19	Bank Service Charge		15.66		11,781.36
Apr 23	Deposit			704.19	12,485.55
Apr 25	Deposit			1,151.97	13,637.52
Apr 26	Loan Interest		40.00		13,597.52
	Loan Payment		203.38		13,394.14
	Cheque	0446	352.45		13,041.69
Apr 27	Interest Earned			69.77	13,111.46

No. of Debits	20	Total Amount Debits	10,720.48	Total Fees	15.66
No. of Credits	16	Total Amount Credits	12,196.15	Interest Paid	69.77

Required:

Reconcile the Balance per Bank Statement ($13,111.46) with the Balance per General Ledger of $11,423.63.

REAL WORLD APPLICATIONS

(The blank forms you need are on pages 6-19 to 6-20 of the *Study Guide with Working Papers.*)

6R-1.

Karen Johnson, the bookkeeper of Hoop Co., has appointed Jim Pool as the petty cash custodian. The following transactions occurred in November:

2001	
Nov. 25	Cheque No. 441 was written and cashed to establish a $50 petty cash fund.
27	Paid $8.50 delivery charge for goods purchased for resale.
29	Purchased office supplies for $12 from petty cash.
30	Purchased postage stamps for $15 from petty cash.

On December 3 Jim received the following internal memo:

TO: Jim Pool

FROM: Karen Johnson

RE: Petty Cash

Jim, I'll need $5 for postage stamps. By the way, I noticed that our petty cash account seems to be too low. Let's increase its size to $100.

Could you help Jim replenish petty cash on December 3 by providing him with a general journal entry? Support your answer and indicate whether Karen was correct.

6R-2.

Ginger Company has a policy of depositing all receipts and making all payments by cheque. On receiving the bank statement, Bill Free, a new bookkeeper, is quite upset that the balance in cash in the ledger is $4,209.50 while the ending bank balance is $4,440.50. Bill is convinced the bank has made an error. Based on the following facts, is Bill's concern warranted? What other suggestions could you offer Bill in the bank reconciliation process?

a. The November 30 cash receipts, $611, had been placed in the bank's night depository after banking hours and consequently did not appear on the bank statement as a deposit.

b. Two debit memoranda and a credit memorandum were included with the returned cheque. None of the memoranda had been recorded at the time of the reconciliation. The first debit memorandum covered a $130 NSF cheque written by Abby Ellen. The second was a $6.50 debit memorandum for service charges. The credit memorandum was for $494 and represented the proceeds less a $6 collection fee from a $500 non-interest-bearing note collected for Ginger Company by the bank.

c. It was also found that cheques No. 942 for $71.50 and No. 947 for $206.50, both written and recorded on November 28, were not among the cancelled cheques returned.

d. Bill found that cheque No. 899 was correctly drawn for $1,094, in payment for a new cash register. However, this cheque had been recorded as though it were for $1,148.

e. The October bank reconciliation showed two cheques outstanding on September 30, No. 621 for $152.50 and No. 630 for $179.30. Cheque No. 630 was returned with the November bank statement, but cheque No. 621 was not.

6R-3.
On March 2, 2001, the accountant for Bergen Carpet Co. was injured in a skiing accident and was advised not to return to work for six weeks. The owners of the company are anxious to ensure that the company's bank account statement is reconciled and have asked you to perform this task. You are presented with the following information:

a. Bank reconciliation prepared by the regular accountant at January 31, 2001:

Bergen Carpet Co.
Bank Reconciliation
January 31, 2001

Balance per Bank Statement			$ 8,364.02
Add: Deposit in Transit			2,576.03
			10,940.05
Less: Outstanding Cheques			
	No. 417	$ 28.30	
	419	1,043.25	
	423	1,722.30	2,793.85
Balance per General Ledger			$ 8,146.20

b. General ledger listing of Bank Account (#110) for the month of February (see p. 263)

c. Bank statement from the Royal Bank for the month ending February 26, 2001 (see p. 264)

Required

Prepare the necessary reconciliation and any journal entries needed at February 28, 2001.

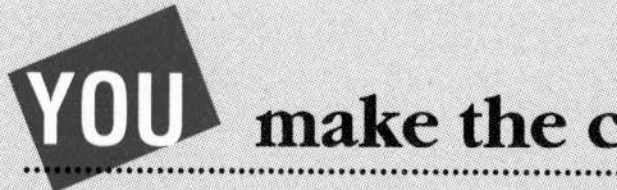

make the call

Critical Thinking/Ethical Case

6R-4.
Jerry Ary, the bookkeeper of Logan Co., received a bank statement from Ajax Bank. Jerry noticed a $200 mistake made by the bank in the company's favour. Jerry called his supervisor, who said that, as long as it benefits the company, he should not tell the bank about the error. You make the call. Write your specific recommendations to Jerry.

Date: 11 Mar. 01 11:06 am
G/L Listing

BERGEN CARPET CO.

General Ledger Listing as of 28 Feb 01

Page: 1

G/L listing for account [110] to [110]
for department [ ] to [222],
for fiscal period [2] 0 [2] ,
sorted by [Account] .

Last posting sequence number: 4

Acct. Dept.

Pd	Srce	Date	Description	Reference	Posting Entry	Batch Entry	Debits	Credits	Net Change/ Balance
	110	Bank							8,146.20
2	GL-GJ	01 Feb 01	KING PROPERTY	CHQ 404	2 - 1	2 - 1		974.15	
2	GL-GJ	01 Feb 01	SANDRA SMYTHE - Deposit	1007	2 - 2	2 - 2	8,145.38		
2	GL-GJ	02 Feb 01	INGRID LUNDREN - Deposit	1008	2 - 3	2 - 3	909.50		
2	GL-GJ	02 Feb 01	CAMPUS COPY SHOPPE	CHQ 424	2 - 4	2 - 4		133.75	
2	GL-GJ	02 Feb 01	BENJAMIN YEE	02 - 05	2 - 5	2 - 5	4,381.65		
2	GL-GJ	05 Feb 01	LITEMORE NEON SIGNS	CHQ 425	2 - 6	2 - 6		80.25	
2	GL-GJ	05 Feb 01	NORM & JANET TAYLOR - Deposit	1009	2 - 7	2 - 7	969.01		
2	GL-GJ	06 Feb 01	NAME - IT!	CHQ 426	2 - 9	2 - 9		240.75	
2	GL-GJ	07 Feb 01	JERRY SIMON - Deposit	1011	2 - 10	2 - 10	2,782.00		
2	GL-GJ	07 Feb 01	SAXONY WOOL MILLS	CHQ 427	2 - 11	2 - 11		4,559.11	
2	GL-GJ	07 Feb 01	QUALITY CARPET COMPANY	CHQ 428	2 - 12	2 - 12		6,829.28	
2	GL-GJ	07 Feb 01	JODY ARCHER	CHQ 429	2 - 13	2 - 13		25.00	
2	GL-GJ	08 Feb 01	CITY PHONE COMPANY	CHQ 430	2 - 14	2 - 14		121.75	
2	GL-GJ	08 Feb 01	CITY UTILITY COMPANY	CHQ 431	2 - 15	2 - 15		111.14	
2	GL-GJ	08 Feb 01	JOE'S GAS BAR	CHQ 432	2 - 16	2 - 16		94.66	
2	GL-GJ	08 Feb 01	WOOD'S STATIONERY	CHQ 433	2 - 17	2 - 17		1,091.40	
2	GL-GJ	02 Feb 01	CASH	CHQ 434	2 - 18	2 - 18		100.00	
2	GL-GJ	09 Feb 01	IVY LEUNG - Deposit	1012	2 - 19	2 - 19	2,169.96		
2	GL-GJ	09 Feb 01	EMILY BERGEN - Salary	CHQ 435	2 - 20	2 - 20		697.35	
2	GL-GJ	09 Feb 01	JAMES BERGEN - Salary	CHQ 436	2 - 21	2 - 21		697.35	
2	GL-GJ	09 Feb 01	RBC/TERMPLAN LOAN PAYMENT	02 - 22	2 - 22	2 - 22		601.87	
2	GL-GJ	09 Feb 01	RBC/DEMAND LOAN INTEREST	02 - 23	2 - 23	2 - 23		695.20	
2	GL-GJ	13 Feb 01	PAT HARPER - Deposit	1013	2 - 27	2 - 27	404.46		
2	GL-GJ	15 Feb 01	CITY LIGHTING	CHQ 437	2 - 29	2 - 29		112.50	
2	GL-GJ	15 Feb 01	FREDDY DUNCAN	CHQ 438	2 - 30	2 - 30		2,010.40	
2	GL-GJ	15 Feb 01	RECEIVER GENERAL FOR CANADA	CHQ 439	2 - 31	2 - 31		993.04	
2	GL-GJ	15 Feb 01	VOID	CHQ 440	2 - 32	2 - 32	0.00		
2	GL-GJ	16 Feb 01	WILSON INSURANCE AGENCY	CHQ 441	2 - 33	2 - 33		802.50	
2	GL-GJ	16 Feb 01	COMMUNITY CALENDAR	CHQ 442	2 - 34	2 - 34		246.10	
2	GL-GJ	16 Feb 01	STANDARD NEWS	CHQ 443	2 - 35	2 - 35		909.50	
2	GL-GJ	16 Feb 01	T C CHURCHILL - Deposit	1015	2 - 36	2 - 36	3,610.18		
2	GL-GJ	16 Feb 01	RBC/LOAN PROCESSING CHARGE	02 - 37	2 - 37	2 - 37		40.00	
2	GL-GJ	19 Feb 01	BEATRICE DAY - Deposit	1016	2 - 38	2 - 38	4,068.68		
2	GL-GJ	22 Feb 01	JOAN ANDERSON - Deposit	02 - 44	2 - 44	2 - 44	2,569.07		
2	GL-GJ	23 Feb 01	EMILY BERGEN - Salary	CHQ 444	2 - 46	2 - 46		697.35	
2	GL-GJ	23 Feb 01	JAMES BERGEN - Salary	CHQ 445	2 - 47	2 - 47		697.35	
2	GL-GJ	24 Feb 01	BOB JONES	CHQ 446	2 - 49	2 - 49		240.00	
2	GL-GJ	26 Feb 01	MICHEL ROBICHAUD - Deposit	02 - 53	2 - 53	2 - 53	3,456.10		
2	GL-GJ	26 Feb 01	JUDY CARMICHAEL - Deposit	1022	2 - 54	2 - 54	1,218.20		
2	GL-GJ	28 Feb 01	DMJ CONSTRUCTION - Deposit	02 - 55	2 - 55	2 - 55	1,786.90		
2	GL-GJ	28 Feb 01	FREDDY DUNCAN	CHQ 447	2 - 56	2 - 56		1,950.90	
2	GL-GJ	28 Feb 01	GEORGE BETTS	CHQ 448	2 - 57	2 - 57		1,213.20	
2	GL-GJ	28 Feb 01	GREENBRIAR RESTAURANT	CHQ 449	2 - 58	2 - 58		76.15	9,429.09
			Acct 110 - Balance, Feb 28, 2001						17,575.29

ROYAL BANK
MAIN BRANCH
10107 JASPER AVENUE
EDMONTON ALTA
T5J 1W9 03749

Account Statement

Account No.	
124-629-7	
Period From	To
Jan 27/01	Feb 26/01
Enclosures	Page
	1

BERGEN CARPET CO
BAY 215
10620 - 104 AVENUE
EDMONTON AB
T5J 3G2

Date	Transaction Description		Cheques & Debits	Deposits & Credits	Balance
	Balance Forward				8,364.02
Jan 27	Deposit			2,576.03	10,940.05
Jan 28	Cheque -	404	974.15		
	Cheque -	419	1,043.25		8,922.65
Jan 29	Cheque -	423	1,722.30		7,200.35
Jan 30	Cheque -	424	133.75		7,066.60
Feb 01	Deposit			8,145.38	15,211.98
Feb 02	Deposit			5,291.15	
	Cheque -	434	100.00		20,403.13
Feb 03	Deposit			969.01	21,372.14
Feb 06	Deposit			2,782.00	
	Cheque -	425	80.25		
	Loan Payment - Principal		601.87		
	Loan Interest		695.20		22,776.82
Feb 07	Cheque -	430	121.75		
	Cheque -	436	697.35		
	Cheque -	435	697.35		21,260.37
Feb 08	Deposit			2,169.96	
	Cheque -	431	111.14		23,319.19
Feb 10	Cheque -	433	1,091.40		
	Cheque -	432	94.66		
	Cheque -	428	6,829.28		
	Cheque -	426	240.75		15,063.10
Feb 13	Deposit			404.46	
	Loan Management Fee		40.00		
	Cheque -	438	2,010.40		
	Cheque -	427	4,559.11		
	Cheque -	437	112.50		8,745.55
Feb 14	Deposit			3,610.18	12,355.73
Feb 15	Deposit			4,068.68	
	Cheque -	429	25.00		16,399.41
Feb 17	Cheque -	441	802.50		15,596.91
Feb 20	Cheque -	442	246.10		
	NSF Returned		404.46		14,946.35
Feb 21	NSF Charge		15.00		14,931.35
Feb 24	Cheque -	444	697.35		
	Cheque -	445	697.35		13,536.65
Feb 25	Deposit			2,569.07	
	Cheque -	439	993.04		15,112.68
Feb 26	Deposit			4,674.30	
	Cheque -	446	240.00		
	Service Charge		18.45		19,528.53

No. of Debits	Total Amount	No. of Credits	Total Amount
30	26,095.71	11	37,260.22

ACCOUNTING RECALL
A CUMULATIVE APPROACH

THIS EXAMINATION REVIEWS CHAPTERS 1 THROUGH 6.

Your *Study Guide with Working Papers*, page 6-21, has forms to complete this exam, as well as worked-out solutions. The page reference next to each question identifies the page to turn back to if you answer the question incorrectly.

PART I Vocabulary Review

Match each term on the left side to the appropriate definition or phrase on the right.

Page Ref.			
(243)	1. Cash short and over	A.	A supplementary record
(227)	2. Blank endorsement	B.	Person who writes a cheque
(225)	3. Payee	C.	A process of reconciling
(225)	4. Drawer	D.	Recorded on the income statement
(231)	5. Outstanding cheques	E.	Person or company to whom the cheque is payable
(229)	6. Bank reconciliation	F.	Lacks sufficient funds
(240)	7. Auxiliary petty cash record	G.	Cheque truncation
(237)	8. Safekeeping	H.	Add to bank balance
(229)	9. Deposits in transit	I.	Cheques written but not processed by bank
(231)	10. NSF	J.	Could be further endorsed

PART II True or False (Accounting Theory)

(239) 11. Petty cash is a liability.

(240) 12. The auxiliary petty cash record is a special journal.

(227) 13. Restrictive endorsements limit any further negotiation of a cheque.

(231) 14. NSF cheques result in lowering the bank balance in the reconciliation process.

(241) 15. In replenishment, the old expenses are shown and a new cheque is written.

CONTINUING PROBLEM

The books have been closed for the first year-end for Eldorado Computer Centre. The company ended up with a marginal profit for the first three months in operation. Tony expects faster growth as he enters into a busy season.

Following is a list of transactions for the month of October. Petty Cash Account #1010 and Miscellaneous Expense Account #5100 have been added to the chart of accounts.

Assignment

(See pages 6-22 to 6-29 in your *Study Guide with Working Papers.*)

1. Record the transactions in general journal or petty cash format.
2. Post the transactions to the general ledger accounts.
3. Prepare a trial balance.

Oct. 1 Paid rent for November, December, and January, $1,200 (cheque #214).
2 Established a petty cash fund for $100.
4 Collected $3,600 from a cash customer for building three systems.
5 Collected $2,600, the amount due from A. Pitale, an Accounts Receibale customer, on invoice #12674.
6 Purchased $25 worth of stamps, using petty cash voucher #101.
7 Withdrew $2,000 (cheque #215) for personal use.
8 Purchased $22 worth of supplies, using petty cash voucher #102.
12 Paid the newspaper carrier $10, using petty cash voucher #103.
16 Paid the amount due on the September phone bill, $65 (cheque #216).
17 Paid the amount due on the September electric bill, $95 (cheque #217).
22 Performed computer services for Taylor Golf; billed the client $4,200 (invoice #12675).
23 Paid $20 for computer paper, using petty cash voucher #104.
30 Took $15 out of petty cash for lunch, voucher #105.
31 Replenished the petty cash. Coin and currency in drawer $8.00.

Since Tony was so busy trying to close his books, he forgot to reconcile his last three months of bank statements. What follows on pages 267 and 268 is a list of all deposits and cheques written for the past three months (each entry is identified by chapter, transaction date, or transaction letter) and bank statements for July through September. The statement for October won't arrive until the first week of November.

Eldorado Computer Centre Summary of Deposits and Cheques

Chapter	Transaction	Payor/Payee	Amount
		DEPOSITS	
1	(a)	Tony Freedman	$4,500
1	(f)	Cash customer	250
1	(g)	Cash customer	200
1	(i)	Taylor Golf	1200
2	(p)	Cash customer	900
3	Sept. 2	Tonya Parker Jones	325
3	Sept. 6	Summer Lipe	220
3	Sept. 12	Jeannine Sparks	850
3	Sept. 26	Mike Hammer	140

Chapter	Transaction	Cheque #	Payor/Payee	Amount
			CHEQUES	
1	(b)	201	Multi Systems	$1200
1	(c)	202	Office Furniture, Inc.	600
1	(e)	203	Capital Management	400
1	(j)	204	Tony Freedman	100
2	(l)	205	Insurance Protection, Inc.	150
2	(m)	206	Office Depot	200
2	(n)	207	Computer Edge Magazine	1400
2	(q)	208	City Electric	85
2	(r)	209	Canada Post	50
3	Sept. 1	210	Capital Management	1200
3	Sept. 8	211	West Bell Canada	155
3	Sept. 15	212	Computer Connection	200
3	Sept. 17	213	Multi Systems, Inc.	1200

BANK STATEMENT
Royal Bank of Canada 322 Glen Avenue, Edmonton, AB T5P 2T9

Eldorado Computer Centre Statement Date: July 22 , 2001

Cheques Paid:			***Deposits and Credits:***	
Date paid	***Number***	***Amount***	***Date received***	***Amount***
7-4	*201*	*1200.00*	*7-1*	*4500.00*
7-7	*202*	*600.00*	*7-10*	*250.00*
7-15	*203*	*400.00*	*7-20*	*1200.00*
			7-21	*200.00*
Total 3 cheques paid for $2,200.00			***Total Deposits***	***$6,150.00***

Ending Balance on July 22—$3,950.00

Received Statement July 29, 2001.

BANK STATEMENT
Royal Bank of Canada 322 Glen Avenue, Edmonton, AB T5P 2T9

Eldorado Computer Centre Statement Date: August 21, 2001

Cheques Paid:			***Deposits and Credits:***	
Date paid	***Number***	***Amount***	***Date received***	***Amount***
8-2	*204*	*100.00*	*8-12*	*900.00*
8-3	*205*	*150.00*		
8-10	*206*	*200.00*		
8-15	*207*	*1400.00*		
8-20	*208*	*85.00*	***Total Deposits***	***$900.00***

Total 5 cheques paid for $1935.00

Beginning balance on July 22—$3,950.00 Ending balance on August 21—$2,915.00

Received statement August 27, 2001.

BANK STATEMENT
Royal Bank of Canada 322 Glen Avenue, Edmonton, AB T5P 2T9

Eldorado Computer Centre ***Statement Date: September 20 , 2001***

Cheques Paid:			*Deposits and Credits:*	
Date paid	*Number*	*Amount*	*Date received*	*Amount*
9-2	*209*	*50.00*	*9-4*	*325.00*
9-6	*210*	*1200.00*	*9-7*	*220.00*
9-12	*211*	*155.00*	*9-14*	*850.00*
Total 3 cheques paid for $1405.00			*Total Deposits*	*$1,395.00*
Beginning balance on August 21 $2,915.00			*Ending balance on September 20 $2,905.00*	

Received Statement September 29, 2001.

Assignment

1. Compare the Computer Centre's deposits and cheques with the bank statements, and complete a bank reconciliation as of September 30.

COMPUTER WORKSHOP

Computerized Accounting Application for Mike's Management Consulting (Chapter 6)

Bank Reconciliation

Before starting on this assignment, read and complete the tasks discussed in Parts A, B, and F of Appendix B: Computerized Accounting at the back of this book and complete the Computerized Accounting Application assignments at the ends of Chapters 3 and 4.

1. Start Windows. Insert your Student Data Files disk into drive A or B; then double-click on the CA-Simply Accounting icon.
2. Select **Open Existing Company**; then enter the following path:
   - `a:\mike.asc` (if you are storing your student data files on the disk in drive A)
3. Enter 08/31/2001 into the **Session** text box; then click on the **OK** button. Click on the **OK** button in response to the message "The date entered is more than one week past your previous using date of 07/31/2001." The Company Window for Mike's Management Consulting will appear.
4. Click on the Company Window **Setup** menu, then click on Company Information. The Company Information dialogue box will appear. Insert your name in place of the text Your Name in the **Name** text box. Click on the **OK** button to return to the Company Window.
5. Open the General Journal dialogue box; then record the following journal entries (enter the cheque or deposit number listed into the Source text box; then enter the date listed for each transaction):

2001		
Aug	1	Paid August's rent, $500 (cheque No. 110)
	1	Purchased office supplies, $150 (cheque No. 111)
	2	Paid for office furniture bought on account, $400 (cheque No. 112)
	3	Received consulting fee, $1,500 (deposit No. 4)
	4	Paid for newspaper advertisement, $110 (cheque No. 113)
	10	Received payment for Accounts Receivable, $1,050 (deposit No. 5)
	13	Purchased computer, $1,300 (cheque No. 114)
	15	Paid part-time secretary's salary, $425 (cheque No. 115)
	17	Paid utility bill, $120 (cheque No. 116)
	18	Provided consulting service on account, $1,150 (invoice No. I-104)
	25	Received consulting fee, $1,675 (deposit No. 6)
	30	Paid phone bill, $95 (cheque No. 117)
	31	Received payment for Accounts Receivable $1,150 (deposit No. 7)
	31	Paid part-time secretary's salary, $425 (cheque No. 118)
	31	Owner withdrew cash for personal use, $1,200 (cheque No. 119)
	31	One month insurance expired, $50

6. After you have posted the journal entries, close the General Journal; then print a Trial Balance. Make sure the current book balance is $9,620.00.
7. Click on the Company Window **File** menu. Click on Save As, then enter the following new file name into the **Save File As** text box: `a:\mikeaug.asc`
8. Click on the Save button. Note that the Company Name in the Company Window has changed from mike to mikeaug. Click on the Company Window **File** menu again; then click on Save As. Enter the following new file name into the Save File As text box: `a:mike.asc`

9. Click on the **Save** button. Click on the **Yes** button in response to the question "Replace existing data files with the same name?" Note that the Company Name in the Company Window has changed back from mikeaug to mike.

10. You now have two sets of company data files for Mike's Management Consulting for your Student Data files disk. The current data is stored under the file name mike.asc. The August backup data is stored under the file name mikeaug.asc.

11. Below is the August 29, 2001, bank statement for Mike's Management Consulting. You will use this statement to prepare the bank reconciliation for the month of August. Note that the Account Reconciliation feature of the program has already been set up and integrated for this assignment. For information on setting up this feature, look under Help in the Company Window.

Bank Statement
August 29, 2001

		Debits	**Credits**	**Balance**
July 29	Balance Forward			9,865.00
July 30	Cheque #107	95.00		
July 31	Deposit		625.00	
	Charges for New Cheques	85.00		
	Cheque #108	425.00		
	Cheque #109	1,000.00		
August 01	Cheque #110	500.00		
	Cheque #111	150.00		
August 02	Cheque #112	400.00		
August 03	Deposit		1,500.00	
August 05	Cheque #113	110.00		
August 10	Deposit		1,050.00	
August 13	Cheque #114	1,300.00		
	Charge to Certify Cheque	20.00		
August 15	Cheque #115	425.00		
August 17	Cheque #116	120.00		
August 25	Deposit		1,675.00	
August 29	Interest Earned		75.00	
	Service Charge	15.00		
	Balance			10,145.00
		4,645.00	4,925.00	
		Total Debits	Total Credits	

12. To begin to reconcile the account, open the Account Reconciliation Journal by double-clicking the **Account Reconciliation** button in the Company Window. The following screen should appear:

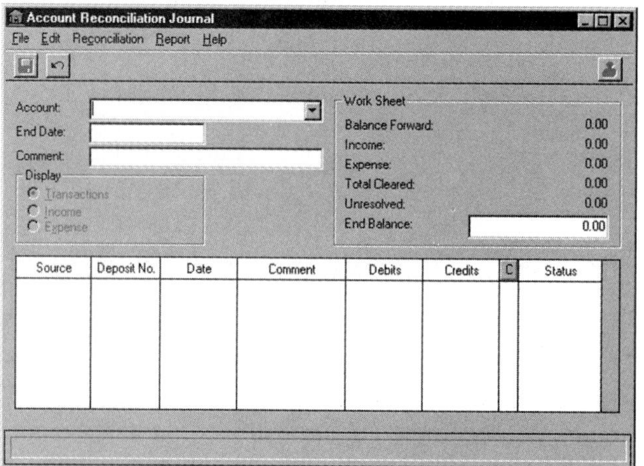

13. Choose the account you wish to reconcile by clicking on the arrow next to the Account field and highlighting the appropriate account from the drop-down list. In this case, there is only one account set up for reconciliation. Accept this account, then press the TAB key. Type `08/31/2001` in the End Date field. Press TAB again to place the cursor in the Comment field; then type `August Bank Reconciliation`. Select **Transactions** from the Display options and enter the end balance from the August bank statement into the End Balance field. Your screen should look like this:

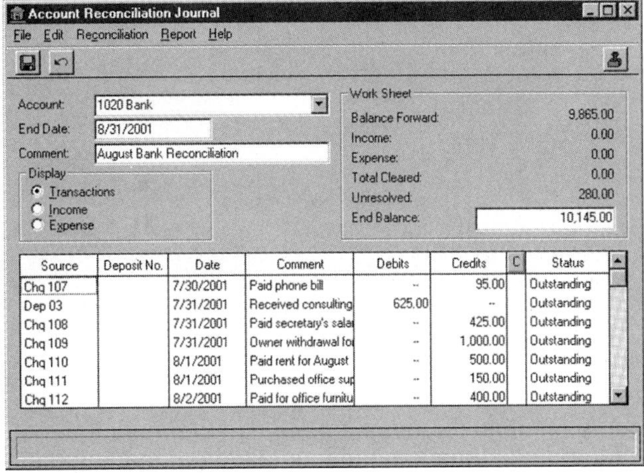

14. You are now able to change the status of any of the transactions listed. To change the status of a transaction from outstanding to cleared, click in the **C** column next to the transaction you want to change. A check mark will appear in the **C** column and you will notice that the status of the transaction will change to cleared. If you wish to change the status of a transaction back to outstanding, click in the **C** column again. The check mark will disappear and the status will change back to outstanding.

15. Check off all the transactions which appear on the August 29, 2001, bank statement. Your screen should look like this:

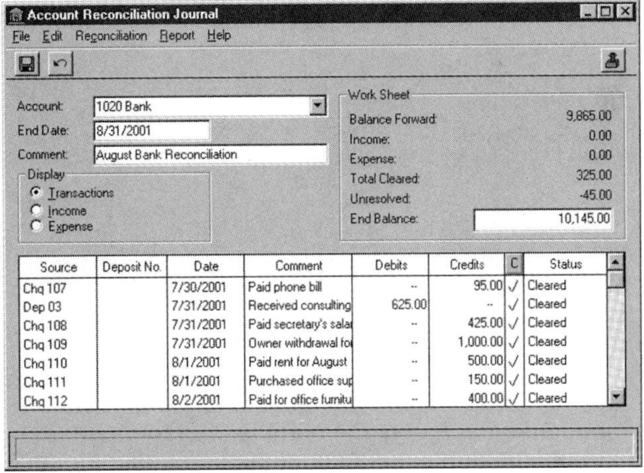

16. The next step in the reconciliation process is to enter those amounts which appear on the bank statement but have not yet been recorded in Mike's accounting records.

17. To enter Income items such as interest, select Income from the Display options in the Account Reconciliation Journal to view the following dialogue box:

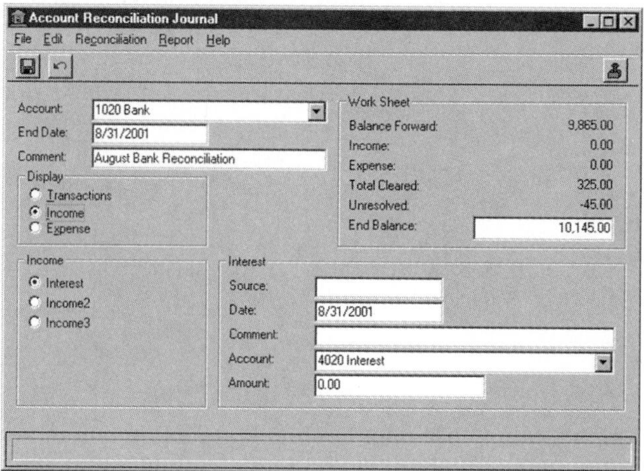

18. Type `Aug Bank Stmt` in the Source field; then press the TAB key. Accept the date in the Date field. Press the TAB key again and enter `August Interest` in the Comment field. Accept the default account listed and then enter the amount of interest earned for August 2001 (`$75`) in the Amount field.

19. Expense items are dealt with in a manner similar to that used for Income items. Select **Expenses** under the Display options in the Account Reconciliation Journal to view the following dialogue box:

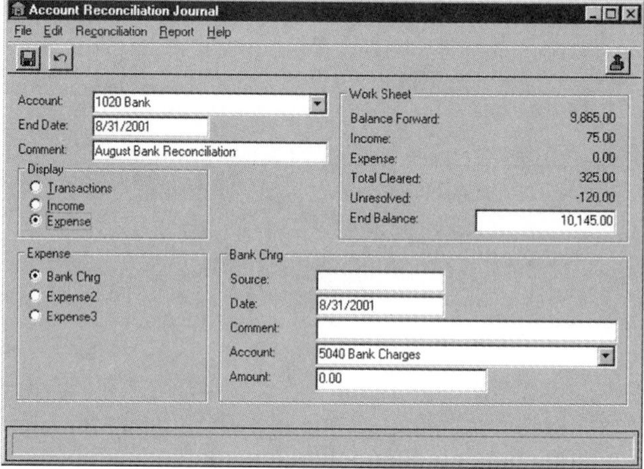

20. Type `Aug Bank Stmt` in the Source field; then press the TAB key. Accept the date shown in the Date field. Press the TAB key again and enter `August Bank Charges` in the Comment field. Accept the default account listed and then enter the amount of the bank charges for August 2001 (`$120`) in the Amount field.

21. The above steps record the entries in the Account Reconciliation Journal, but do not post them. Before posting, you should review the entries to make sure they are correct. Select **Report** from the top menu bar in the Account Reconciliation Journal; then select **Display Account Reconciliation Transaction Detail**. Your screen should look like this:

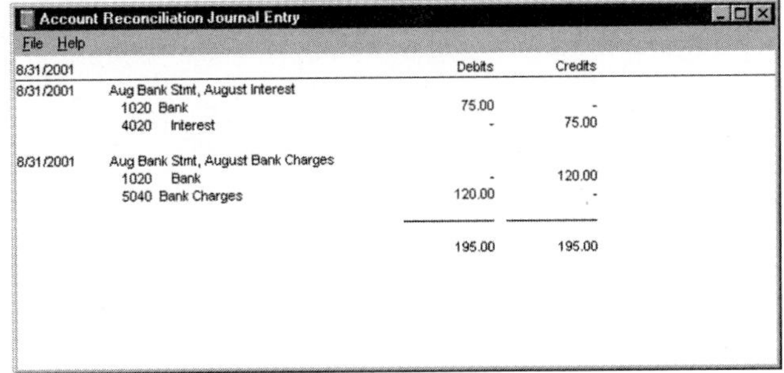

		Debits	Credits
8/31/2001			
8/31/2001	Aug Bank Stmt, August Interest		
	1020 Bank	75.00	-
	4020 Interest	-	75.00
8/31/2001	Aug Bank Stmt, August Bank Charges		
	1020 Bank	-	120.00
	5040 Bank Charges	120.00	-
		195.00	195.00

22. When you are sure the entries are correct, return to the Account Reconciliation Journal and select the **Post** icon.
23. Exit from the Account Reconciliation Journal and print the following reports:
    a. Account Reconciliation Journal
    b. Account Reconciliation Detail Report
    c. Account Reconciliation Summary Report
24. To view the Account Reconciliation Journal, click on the Reports icon while the **Account Reconciliation** button is highlighted. The Account Reconciliation Journal Options dialogue box will appear. The Account Reconciliation Journal can be displayed either by Date or by Journal Number. Select date; then select 07/01/2001 as the Start Date and accept 08/31/2001 as the End Date. Click on **OK** and the Account Reconciliation Journal Display screen will be shown. To print the report, click on the **File** menu and select **Print**. Close the Account Reconciliation Journal Display to return to the Company Window.
25. To view the Account Reconciliation Detail Report, select **Account Reconciliation** under Reports in the Company Window. Make sure to click on **Detail**, then select the account for which you want the report. Accept the default dates given (07/01/2001 and 08/31/2001) as well as the default settings. Click **OK** and the Account Reconciliation Detail Report will be shown. To print the report, click on the File menu and select Print. Close the Account Reconciliation Detail Report to return to the Company Window.
26. To review the Account Reconciliation Summary Report, select **Account Reconciliation** under Reports in the Company Window. Click on **Summary**, then select the account for which you want the report. Accept the default dates given; then click **OK**. The Account Reconciliation Summary Report will be shown. To print the report, click on the **File** menu and select **Print**. Close the Account Reconciliation Summary Report to return to the Company Window.
27. Click on the Company Window **File** menu. Click on **Save As**; then enter the following new file name into the Save File As text box: `a:/mikerec.asc`
28. Click on the **Save** button. Note that the Company Name in the Company Window has changed from mike to mikerec. Click on the Company Window **File** menu again; then click on **Save As**. Enter the following new file name into the Save File as text box: `a:/mike.asc`
29. Click on the **Save** button. Click on the **Yes** button in response to the question "Replace existing data files with the same name?" Note that the Company Name in the Company Window has changed back from mikerec to mike.
30. You now have three sets of company data for Mike's Management Consulting. The current data is stored under the file name mike.asc. The backup data for August is stored under the file name mikeaug.asc and the backup data for the reconciliation is stored under the file name mikerec.asc.
31. Click on the Company Window **File** menu; then click on **Exit** to end the current work session and return to your Windows desktop.

Payroll Concepts and Procedures

7

EMPLOYEE TAXES

THE BIG PICTURE

The Eldorado Computer Centre ended its first year so successfully that owner Tony Freedman decided to hire two employees. He would pay them based on an hourly wage, using time cards to track the hours they worked. Freedman knew that this would involve significant expense and effort. In many companies the cost of payroll is more than half of total expenses. Beyond the cost of wages, however, a business becomes responsible for complying with rules that govern payroll deductions.

In addition to paying wages on time, the business must deduct taxes and other amounts. It must account for this money very strictly and pass it on to the proper agency according to government rules and regulations. These regulations are constantly changing, and the person handling payroll must be aware of all changes in order to stay in compliance with the law.

Some companies choose an outside service to prepare the payroll and issue the cheques. Much of the work is done with computer accounting payroll software. Since Freedman will have only two employees (in addition to himself), he has decided to take on the task himself to save the expense of hiring an outside service.

In this chapter you will learn how to calculate hourly wages and overtime. You will also learn the basic rules and procedure for making payroll deductions, withholding taxes, and paying taxes withheld.

Chapter Objectives

- ◆ How to calculate gross pay, routine deductions, and net pay for an employee (p. 276)
- ◆ How to prepare a company's payroll summary (p. 282)
- ◆ How to record a typical payroll from a summary (p. 284)
- ◆ How to maintain an individual's earnings record (p. 286)

Becoming an expert in the subject of payroll and related issues can take a long time. This is because:

1. There are many federal and provincial laws which affect payroll, and they change periodically.
2. Sometimes employers and employees view each other with suspicion in matters concerning payroll. This requires special care to get the figures correct.
3. The actual computation and payment of a payroll is quite detailed, leaving room for a number of mistakes to occur.

In Canada today a company has two common alternatives for processing a payroll manually:

- ◆ Use a microcomputer with appropriate software, such as *Simply Accounting.*
- ◆ Contract with a payroll service (either an independent service or one connected with a chartered bank).

Either alternative is attractive to medium- or large-sized companies. Many smaller companies continue to process their payroll manually, thus avoiding the costs of the more sophisticated alternatives. Programs like *Simply Accounting* also can help in processing a payroll for smaller companies with simple payroll needs.

In this chapter we will examine the details of a payroll for ABC Company Ltd. for the first week in March. We will stress those things which affect individual employees. The next chapter examines the same subject from the employer's point of view.

In this chapter and the next, many deductions, maximum amounts, and minimum amounts are obtained from recently published figures from Revenue Canada. Students should be aware that these will change at least annually. Your instructor may supply you with the most up-to-date figures, but remember that you should concentrate on learning the principles involved, not on matching the exact figures illustrated in this chapter and the next.

The tables which are included in the appendices at the end of this chapter for CPP and EI have been somewhat condensed to save space. If you use these condensed tables, your figures will differ by a few cents from the "official" tables. This is not a problem for classroom use, but you should not use the textbook tables for any real-world payroll taxes.

Learning Unit 7-1

Important Laws and How They Affect Payroll

A number of laws and regulations at the federal and provincial levels govern payroll. We will look at several of them here.

Minimum wage laws

Every province has a law which sets the lowest hourly wage that can legally be paid to an employee. The actual **minimum wage** varies somewhat from province to province and has a very small effect on the subject of payroll.

However, such laws also set out the maximum number of hours an employee can be asked to work per day and per week before an *overtime* premium must be paid. A typical requirement (and the one we shall adopt) is that employees who work more than 8 hours on any day or 40 hours in a week must be paid at time-and-a-half for the overtime hours. If Janet Johnson worked 4 hours on Monday, 8 hours on Tuesday, 11 hours on Wednesday, 8 hours on Friday, and 4 hours on Saturday, she would have worked only 35 hours during the week but would have earned 3 hours of overtime premium because she worked 11 hours on Wednesday.

Now suppose that Janet worked the following hours during a sample week:

Monday	7 hours	
Tuesday	8 hours	
Wednesday	11 hours	
Thursday	8 hours	
Friday	7 hours	
Saturday	4 hours	
Total	45 hours	for the week

If Janet's hourly rate were $10 per hour, her gross wages for the week would be computed as follows:

Regular time	40 h @ $10.00/h	$400
Overtime	5 h @ $15.00/h	75
Total earnings		$475

Note that the three hours of overtime worked on Wednesday are included in the total overtime of five hours.

Sometimes employers arrive at the same total by a slightly different calculation:

Regular rate	45 h @ $10.00/h	$450
Overtime rate (or premium)	5 h @ $5.00/h	25
Total earnings		$475

This second approach stresses the cost of overtime. A manager can more easily recognize the added cost of asking employees to work longer hours. We will use the first approach in this chapter, since it reflects the point of view of the employee.

Federal and provincial income tax

The federal and provincial governments each require employees to pay a tax based on the income they earn. The details of our **income tax** system are not covered here, but we need to know a few essentials:

1. Taxes are *calculated* once a year: Employees must file a tax return by April 30 for the year ended on the previous December 31. However, the tax is *collected* from employees by payroll deductions each pay period.
2. The federal government and the provincial governments (except Quebec) cooperate by having a single payroll tax deduction which is then divided up according to a legal formula. The amount of income tax an employee must pay is determined by a large number of factors such as number of dependents, level of earnings, other sources of income, permitted deductions, and so on. The amount of income tax deducted from an employee's pay for a week is found by

Payroll periods can be:
Weekly: 52 pay periods/year
Biweekly: 26 pay periods/year
Semimonthly: 24 pay periods/year
Monthly: 12 pay periods/year

consulting the tables in a booklet called *Payroll Deductions Tables (T4032)*, which is provided by Revenue Canada Taxation. These tables vary somewhat from province to province, but the example shown (based on the province of Ontario) is typical (see Appendix 7-1 at the end of this chapter). The ranges of earnings per week are shown on the left and the figures in the 11 columns of deductions shown across the page get smaller as they go from left to right. These figures correspond to increasing levels of exemptions claimed by an employee on a form called a **TD1** (Figure 7-1). In our example, Janet Johnson is claiming the normal deduction for a single person, **claim code 1**. Actually, she may be divorced, separated, or married to a husband who is also earning income, thus making him ineligible as a dependent.

The employer is not responsible for verifying the claims made by employees on their TD1 forms

Notice that the procedure for deducting income tax is not very precise. The actual tax that Janet will have to pay for the year will depend on dozens of factors, some of them quite personal (such as whether she has paid any deductible tuition fees during the taxation year, or whether she has charitable donations to claim). The purpose of the deduction tables is to ensure that wage earners pay about as much tax as they would owe on their earnings for the week. Sometimes employees have to pay extra tax when they file their annual tax returns, but usually they get a refund. This is because the tables tend to ignore many allowable tax deductions.

In our example, Janet Johnson will have $82.25 in tax deducted from her pay this week. Refer to Appendix 7-1 and be sure you see where this figure is obtained.

Canada or Quebec Pension Plan

About 30 years ago the **Canada and Quebec Pension Plans** were introduced. Their purpose was to provide a pension benefit (as well as certain other benefits) for Canadians at retirement. The law requires a deduction of 3.2 percent from the earnings of each taxpayer in Canada who is at least 18 years of age but not 70 years or older and who is not in receipt of a disability or retirement pension from CPP. (The first $67.31 of earnings in a week are not subject to this deduction. Likewise, earnings in excess of $36,900 per year are not subject to the 3.2 percent levy.) The rate is in the process of being gradually increased, to reach just over 4 percent. This increase is necessary to ensure that funds are available to meet the requirements of Canadians who will be claiming benefits early in the next century.

Recently, the government has been sending a summary of CPP contributions made to each worker in Canada.

In an effort to conserve resources, the government has begun to publish the various tables of deductions in computer-readable format. Your instructor may arrange to supply you with a copy, or make a copy available for the duration of the course.

It is possible to compute the necessary deduction for the Canada Pension Plan (CPP) for each employee, but the federal government has provided detailed tables in the booklet *Payroll Deductions Tables (T4032)* to make this unnecessary (see Appendix 7-2 and Learning Unit 7-2). As you can see, Janet Johnson will have a CPP deduction of $13.03—($475 – $67.31) × 0.032—made from her wages this pay period. The federal government maintains a precise record of the CPP payments made by each Canadian because the benefits we will receive are related to the contributions we make plus the amounts contributed by our employers on our behalf—by law, the same amount as is deducted. There are more details on this in the next chapter.

Employment Insurance Plan

It is a requirement for virtually all employees, regardless of age, to participate in Canada's **employment insurance (EI) plan**. (There are a number of exceptions.) This plan entitles workers to a certain level of income if they become unemployed. The details are very complex and a full discussion of the plan is beyond the scope of this text.

FIGURE 7-1
TD1 Form

Revenue Canada Revenu Canada

PERSONAL TAX CREDITS RETURN

Instructions

Complete this return if you have a new employer or payer, and you will receive one or more of the following types of income:

- salary, wages, commissions, pensions, or any other remuneration; or
- Employment Insurance benefits.

You **do not** have to file a new return every year unless your marital status changes or you expect a change in your personal credits for that year. Complete a new return no later than seven days after the change. It is an offence to file a false return.

If you make regular spousal support payments, or if you regularly contribute to a registered retirement savings plan (RRSP) during the year, you can reduce the amount of tax to be withheld from your income. To make this request, you have to write to your tax services office for a letter of authority.

You do not need a letter of authority if your employer deducts RRSP contributions from your salary.

If you receive non-employment income, such as a pension or Old Age Security, and you want to have extra tax deducted at source, you can complete Form TD3, *Request for Income Tax Deduction on Non-Employment Income.*

If you need help, ask your employer or payer, or call your tax services office or tax centre. You can find the telephone numbers listed under "Revenue Canada" in the Government of Canada section of your telephone book.

TD1 E (98) **Confidential calculation on back – Employee's copy**

Employer's or payer's copy

Revenue Canada Revenu Canada

PERSONAL TAX CREDITS RETURN

After you complete this return, give it to your employer or payer.

Last name (capital letters)	Usual first name and initials	Employee number
JOHNSON	JANET	N/A
Address	For non-residents only – country of permanent residence	Social insurance number
123 Main Street		123456789
Any City, Province — Postal code: X1X 1X1		Date of birth (Year / Month / Day): 1966 / 03 / 12

1. Basic personal amount

Everyone can claim **$6,456** as the basic personal amount. **Credit claimed** $ 6,456

- If you choose to claim this amount, **enter $6,456.**
- If you choose not to claim this amount (e.g., when you have more than one employer or payer and you have already claimed the basic personal amount), **enter 0** in box A on the other side of this return. Do not complete sections 2 to 8. You may want to complete sections 10 to 12.
- If you are a non-resident, and you are including 90% or more of your annual world income when determining your taxable income in Canada, you can claim certain personal amounts. If you are including less than 90% of your annual world income, **enter 0** in box A on the other side of this return. If you are not sure about your non-resident status, or need more information, call your tax services office or tax centre.

2. Spousal amount

You can claim an amount for supporting your spouse if you are **married or have a common-law spouse.**

Generally, a common-law spouse is a person of the opposite sex with whom you live in a common-law relationship for any continuous period of at least 12 months, including any period of separation (due to a breakdown in the relationship) of less than 90 days. It can also be a person of the opposite sex with whom you live in a common-law relationship and who is the natural or adoptive parent of your child. If you are not sure about your status, or need more information, call your tax services office or tax centre.

Equivalent-to-spouse amount

You can claim an equivalent-to-spouse amount if you are **single, divorced, separated, or widowed,** and you support a dependant who is:

- under 18, your parent or grandparent, or mentally or physically infirm;
- related to you by blood, marriage, or adoption; and
- living with you, in Canada, in a home that you maintain; (a dependant may live away from home while attending school.)

Calculating the amount

If you marry during the year, your spouse's net income includes the income earned before and during the marriage.
If the net income for the year of your spouse or dependant will be:

- more than $5,918, **enter 0;**
- $538 or less, **enter $5,380;** or
- more than $538, complete calculation 2 on the back of this return and **enter** the result as credit claimed. **Credit claimed** $

If your equivalent-to-spouse claim is for an infirm dependant age 18 or older, you may be able to claim an amount in section 3. Otherwise, any person you claim here cannot be claimed again in section 3.

3. Amount for infirm dependants age 18 or older

You can claim an amount for each infirm dependant age 18 or older who is your or your spouse's:

- child or grandchild, and has a physical or mental infirmity; or
- parent, grandparent, brother, sister, aunt, uncle, niece, or nephew, who resides in Canada, and has a physical or mental infirmity.

Calculating the amount

If your dependant's net income for the year will be:

- $4,103 or less, **enter $2,353;** or
- more than $4,103, complete calculation 3 on the back of this return and **enter** the result as credit claimed.

You can claim an amount for each infirm dependant you have. **Credit claimed** $

4. Amount for eligible pension income

Eligible pension income includes pension payments received from a pension plan or fund as a life annuity, and foreign pension payments. It does not include payments from the Canada Pension Plan or Quebec Pension Plan, Old Age Security, guaranteed supplements, or lump-sum withdrawals from a pension fund.

If you receive an eligible pension income, you can claim your eligible pension income or $1,000, whichever amount is **less.** **Credit claimed** $

5. Age amount

If you will be 65 or older at the end of the year and your estimated net income from all sources for the year will be:

- $25,921 or less, **enter $3,482;**
- more than $25,921, but less than $49,134.33, complete calculation 5 on the back of this return and **enter** the result as credit claimed; or
- more than $49,134.33, **enter $0.** **Credit claimed** $

TD1 E (98) (Ce formulaire existe aussi en français.) 0500 Canada

FIGURE 7-1
(cont.)

Calculation 2: net income more than $538, calculate: .... $ 5,918
Minus: net income of spouse or dependant ....
Total ....
Report the total in section 2 as a credit claimed.

Calculation 3: net income more than $4,103, calculate: $ 6,456
Minus: dependant's net income ....
If more than $2,353, enter $2,353 ....
Minus: equivalent-to-spouse amount claimed in section 2 ....
Total: If negative, **enter 0** ....
Report the total in section 3 as a credit claimed.

Calculation 5: net income over $25,921, but less than $49,134.33, calculate basic age amount :...... $ 3,482 A
Reduced by:
1. Annual estimated net income $ ________
2. Less base amount ....$ − 25,921
3. Line 1 minus line 2 ....$ ________
4. Multiply line 3 ________ by 15% .... ________ B
Total: A minus B. If negative, **enter 0** .... $
Report the total in section 5 as a credit claimed.

Claim Codes	
Total claim amount	**Claim codes**
No claim amount	0
Minimum $ 6,456	1
$ 6,456.01 - 8,037	2
8,037.01 - 9,619	3
9,619.01 - 11,202	4
11,202.01 - 12,783	5
12,783.01 - 14,364	6
14,364.01 - 15,946	7
15,946.01 - 17,527	8
17,527.01 - 19,109	9
19,109.01 - 20,693	10
$ 20,693.01 - and over Manual calculation required by employer	X
No tax withholding required	E

---

6. Tuition fees and education amount

Enter your tuition fees, for courses you will take in the year, to attend a university, college, or an institution that the Minister of Human Resources Development has certified ....

Add $200 for each month in the year that you will be enrolled full-time in a qualifying educational program at a university, college, or a school offering job retraining courses or correspondence courses ....

Subtotal ....

Subtract any scholarships, fellowships, or bursaries you will receive in the year (do not report the first $500) ....

Enter the total amount claimed. If the amount is negative, **enter 0**. .... **Credit claimed** $

7. Disability amount

You can claim $4,233 if you are severely impaired, mentally or physically, and are claiming the disability amount by using Form T2201, *Disability Tax Credit Certificate*.
Such an impairment has to markedly restrict your daily living activities. The impairment has to last, or be expected to last, for a continuous period of at least 12 months.

Enter the total amount claimed .... **Credit claimed** $

8. Amounts transferred from your spouse, or dependants

You can transfer any of the following amounts that your spouse, or dependants do not need to reduce their federal income tax to zero.

Age amount – If your spouse will be 65 or older this year, you can claim any unused balance of the age amount to a maximum of **$3,482** ....

Pension income amount – If your spouse receives eligible pension income, you can claim any unused balance of the eligible pension amount to a maximum of **$1,000** ....

Disability amount – If your spouse or dependant is disabled, you can claim the unused balance of their disability amount, to a maximum of **$4,233** for each person ....

Tuition fees and education amount – If you are supporting a spouse, child or grandchild attending a university, college, or a certified educational institution, you can claim the unused balance of their tuition fees and education amounts to a maximum of **$5,000** for each person ....

Enter the total amount calculated .... **Credit claimed** $

9. Total all your personal tax credit amounts from sections 1 to 8 .... **Total of credits** $6,456

See the claim codes at the top of this page to determine which claim code applies to you. Enter this code in box **A**.
If the total of your tax credits is more than your total employment income from all sources for the year, your claim code is "E." [1] **A**

Additional information

10. Additional tax to be deducted

If you receive other income, you may want to have more tax deducted from each pay. By doing this, you may not have to pay as much tax when you file your income tax return. To choose this option, state the amount of additional tax you want to have deducted from each pay. To change this deduction later, you have to complete a new TD1 return. $

11. Deduction for living in a prescribed zone (e.g., Yukon Territory, or Northwest Territories)

If you live in the Yukon Territory, Northwest Territories, or another prescribed zone for more than six months in a row, beginning or ending this year, you can claim:

- $7.50 for each day that you live in the prescribed zone; or
- $15 for each day that you live in the prescribed zone, if during that time you live in a dwelling that you maintain, and you are the only person living in that dwelling who is claiming this deduction. $
  For more information, get Form T2222 and the publication, *Northern Residents Deductions – Places in Prescribed Zones*, which you can get from any tax services office or tax centre.

12. If you live in **Ontario, Manitoba, Saskatchewan,** or **British Columbia** enter the number of your dependants under 18 years old at the end of the year.

For **Ontario, Manitoba,** and **Saskatchewan** residents, only the spouse with the higher net income can enter an amount.
If you live in **Ontario, Manitoba,** or **British Columbia,** do not include a child claimed for the equivalent-to-spouse amount in section 2.

I certify that the information given in this return is, to the best of my knowledge, correct and complete.

Signature *Janet Johnson* Date *Jan. 7, 2001*

Printed in Canada

Source: Revenue Canada. Reproduced with permission of the Minister of Public Works and Government Services Canada, 1999.

The EI deduction rate is subject to change from year to year. However, the $39,000 maximum insurable earnings is fixed until the year 2000.

In each pay period an amount of 2.70 percent is deducted from an employee's wages. This deduction applies only to the first $39,000 per year. Fortunately, the deductions are rather straightforward for most employees and can be found in the same booklet as the CPP deductions (see Appendix 7-3 at the end of this chapter). In Janet Johnson's case, she will have an EI deduction of $12.80 (approximately $475.00 × 0.027) made from her wages for this week.

CPP and EI: Some additional information

Students should be aware that unique CPP deduction tables are supplied for weekly, biweekly, semimonthly, and monthly pay periods. In calculating the CPP deduction per pay period, there is no maximum contribution per period—just an annual upper limit ($1,068.80 for 1998).

The EI deduction, however, is different. A single table is used for all pay periods. As can be seen from the bottom of any EI table, there is a maximum deduction for each annual period. Since the maximum insurable earning is $39,000, the annual maximum premium is $1,053 ($39,000 × 0.027).

Workers' compensation plans

In all provinces, workers' incomes are protected in the event of an injury which occurs on the job. Since the cost of this protection is typically paid by the employer, no deductions are made from employees' wages. We will not pursue this matter further in this chapter.

Various union agreements

Most unions operate under laws which are enacted provincially or federally. In many businesses, workers have been organized into bargaining units, or unions. Normally, the union and the employer agree that **union dues** are to be deducted from the employees' wages and forwarded to the union treasurer, usually monthly. In our example, the ABC Company Ltd. does not have unionized employees and therefore no deductions are shown.

Other deductions

Other deductions are sometimes made from an employee's earnings. Details will vary from one employer to another but the following deductions are common in Canada:

1. Medical and dental insurance premiums
2. Company pension plan—current service
3. Company pension plan—past service
4. Charitable donations
5. Canada Savings Bonds instalments
6. Parking charges
7. Social fund charges
8. Repayment of loans or advances
9. Long-term income replacement premiums
10. Life insurance premiums
11. Garnishees

LEARNING UNIT 7-1 REVIEW

AT THIS POINT you should be able to:

- Calculate regular and overtime earnings. (p. 276)
- Explain the purpose of a TD1 form. (p. 277)
- Determine income tax deductions given a completed TD1 form and total earnings. (p. 277)
- Determine a deduction for CPP from tables supplied. (p. 277)
- Determine a deduction for EI from tables supplied. (p. 280)
- Explain the operation of maximum deductions for both CPP and EI. (p. 280)
- Describe in general terms the nature of certain other routine deductions. (p. 280)

SELF-REVIEW QUIZ 7-1

Using the tables in Appendices 7-1, 7-2, and 7-3, determine the gross pay and deductions for income tax, CPP, and EI for Peter Black, a single taxpayer who worked 42 hours last week at a wage rate of $10 per hour.

Solution to Self-Review Quiz 7-1

Gross pay:		
40 h @ $10/h		$400.00
2 h @ $15/h (overtime)		30.00
Gross pay		$430.00
Deductions:		
Income tax (from Appendix 7-1)	$71.35	
CPP (from Appendix 7-2)	11.59	
EI (from Appendix 7-3)	11.61	
Total deductions		94.55
Net pay ($430 – $94.55)		$335.45

LEARNING UNIT 7-2

A Typical Payroll

The ABC Company Ltd. has six employees to be paid for the first week of March. They are listed below, together with the number of hours each worked and their rates of pay:

To keep things simple, we assume no carry-forward balances into the month of March. In reality there would usually be such balances (tax, CPP, and EI payable, for example).

Name	*Hours*	*Rate*
Janet Johnson	45	$10/h
Peter Black	42	10/h
John Chernochan	44	8/h
Tony Chui	40	11/h
Beth Madora	35	8/h
Elaine Dumont, Manager	40	800/wk

ABC Company Ltd. Payroll Summary Sheet for the Week Ending March 7, 2001						
Employee Name	Claim Code	Rate of Pay	Hours Worked	Earnings		
				Regular	Overtime	Gross Pay
Janet Johnson	1	10/h	45	400 00	75 00	475 00
Peter Black	1	10/h	42	400 00	30 00	430 00
John Chernochan	4	8/h	44	320 00	48 00	368 00
Tony Chui	1	11/h	40	440 00		440 00
Beth Madora	1	8/h	35	280 00		280 00
Elaine Dumont	3	800/wk	40	800 00		800 00
				2 640 00	153 00	2 793 00
	(A)	(B)	(C)	(D)	(E)	(F)

FIGURE 7-2
Payroll Summary

Employees are paid weekly at the ABC Company Ltd. The **payroll summary** above (Figure 7-2) has been prepared based upon tables and calculations covered earlier in this chapter. Don't worry if the summary appears a bit complicated—we will deal with each column in turn.

THE PAYROLL SUMMARY IN DETAIL

Many medium- to large-sized companies use a computer to help prepare their payroll. The data output from a computerized payroll is often remarkably similar to the illustrations in this chapter.

Claim Code 0 is used for non-resident taxpayers.

A. Claim Code Employers require employees to complete and sign a TD1 exemption form at the beginning of employment and whenever there is a change in the employee's circumstances. As can be seen from Figure 7-1, this form allows employees to specify their exemption status so that an appropriate amount of income tax can be deducted. The claim code for each employee is shown in this column. You can see that four of the employees are claiming a claim code of 1, resulting in the maximum income tax deduction at their earnings level. The other two employees (John and Elaine) presumably have dependents which allow them to specify a higher claim code, with a lower income tax deduction at their earnings level. A new TD1 can be filed at any time, and until a new form is filed the old claim code continues. If a form is not filed, each employee is treated as if he or she has a claim code of 1.

B. Rate of Pay The rates of pay are as set out above. Notice that all employees except Elaine are paid on an hourly basis. Elaine, as manager, receives a weekly salary.

C. Hours Worked Each employee may work a different number of hours in each week. Remember that *overtime rates* will apply to hours in excess of 40 per week or 8 in one day. Notice also that Elaine's hours are shown even though she is not paid according to the number of hours she worked. It is typical to record daily the hours worked by each employee. A weekly total is then transferred to this column in the payroll summary.

D. Regular Earnings Regular earnings are computed based upon regular hours per week—or, as in Elaine's case, a salary.

E. Overtime Earnings The segregation of overtime earnings helps the owners of ABC Company Ltd. to control this expensive use of employees' time. A common practice is to hire an additional employee when this figure becomes too high.

F. Gross Pay Each employee earns a total amount per week. It is this figure which governs the legally required deductions.

FIGURE 7-2 (cont.)

Deductions IT	CPP	EI	Medical	Charitable	Net Pay	Chq. No.
82 25	13 03	12 80		2 00	364 92	1407
71 35	11 59	11 61	9 00	2 00	324 45	1408
37 05	9 61	9 94	17 00	2 00	292 40	1409
73 25	11 91	11 88		2 00	340 96	1410
35 35	6 79	7 55	9 00	2 00	219 31	1411
177 90	23 41	21 56	17 00	2 00	558 13	1412
477 15	76 34	75 34	52 00	12 00	2100 17	
(G)	(H)	(I)	(J)	(K)	(L)	(M)

G. Income Tax Deduction From Appendix 7-1 we have already seen that Janet's income tax deduction is $82.25. Make sure that you can find the amounts deducted for the other employees in Appendix 7-1.

H. CPP Deduction Appendix 7-2 is the source for these CPP deductions.

I. EI Deduction See Appendix 7-3 to trace each employee's EI deduction.

J. Medical Deduction The law regarding medical deductions varies from one province to another. Some provinces do not require a deduction for provincial health care plans. In our example, a deduction is required for each household. This explains why no deductions are made from Janet's and Tony's wages. We may assume that they are covered by their spouses' deductions.

K. Charitable Deduction Each employee has agreed to a weekly deduction to support a charitable cause—perhaps Operation Eyesight.

L. Net Pay This is each employee's gross pay less all deductions, often known as **take-home pay**.

M. Cheque Number A cheque is issued to each employee for the exact amount due. When the cheques are issued, their numbers are written here.

LEARNING UNIT 7-2 REVIEW

AT THIS POINT you should be able to:

- Calculate earnings, deductions, and net pay for an employee. (pp. 282–283)
- Describe the preparation of a payroll summary. (pp. 281–282)
- Explain the purpose of each column in a payroll summary. (pp. 282–283)

SELF-REVIEW QUIZ 7-2

If a new employee, Robert Meade, begins employment next week, calculate his gross and net pay assuming a TD1 claim code of 3, 40 hours worked, a wage of $8/h, and no medical or charitable deduction.

Solution to Self-Review Quiz 7-2

Did you calculate a net pay of $269.94? Details are:

Gross pay: 40 h @ $8/h		$320.00
Deductions:		
Income tax (from Appendix 7-1)	$33.35	
CPP (from Appendix 7-2)	8.07	
EI (from Appendix 7-3)	8.64	
Medical	0.00	
Charitable	0.00	
Total deductions		50.06
Net pay ($320.00 – $50.06)		$269.94

LEARNING UNIT 7-3

Recording and Payment

The details in Figure 7-2 are used to make the journal entry shown below which records the payroll for the first week in March for the ABC Company Ltd.:

March	7	Salaries and Wages Expense	279300	
"		Income Taxes Payable		47715
"		CPP Payable		7634
"		EI Payable		7534
"		Medical Plan Payable		5200
"		Charitable Contributions Payable		1200
"		Salaries and Wages Payable		210017
"		To record payroll for first week in March		

Some companies keep track of different salary or wage expenses separately. For instance, it is useful to separate Elaine's salary from the wages of the other workers. The owners can then separate the cost of management from the cost of labour. It is also useful to further break down the labour cost into more detail. Consider the additional information available to the owners if we assume that Tony and Beth are sales personnel. The debit to **Sales Wages Expense** would be $720 ($440 + $280). Instead of the single debit of $2,793 to an account called **Salaries and Wages Expense**, we would now have three debits:

March	7	Management Salaries Expense	80000	
"		Sales Wages Expense	72000	
"		Wages Expense	127300	

(The credit side of the entry would not change.)

If we assume that the ABC Company Ltd. uses this more detailed method, then the entry would be posted to the ledger accounts as summarized below (opening balances are ignored):

Management Salaries Expense	
800.00	

Expense on the Income Statement

Sales Wages Expense	
720.00	

Expense on the Income Statement

Wages Expense	
1,273.00	

Expense on the Income Statement

Income Taxes Payable	
	477.15

Liability on the Balance Sheet

CPP Payable	
	76.34

Liability on the Balance Sheet

EI Payable	
	75.34

Liability on the Balance Sheet

Medical Plan Payable	
	52.00

Liability on the Balance Sheet

Charitable Donations Payable	
	12.00

Liability on the Balance Sheet

Salaries and Wages Payable	
	2,100.17

Liability on the Balance Sheet

Figure 7-3 summarizes the main elements of the payroll process.

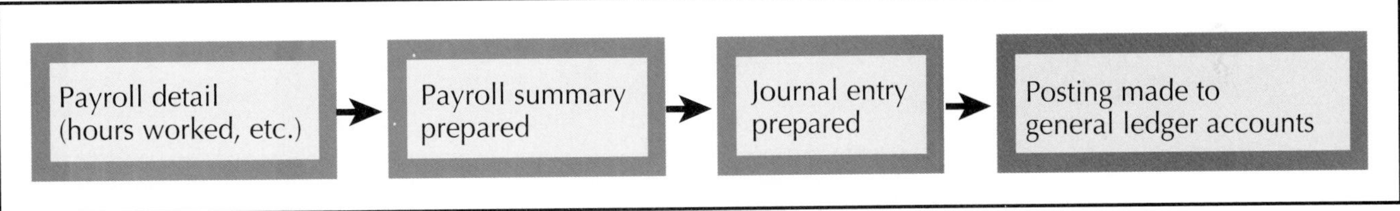

FIGURE 7-3 The Payroll Recording and Posting Process

LAST STEP DIRECTLY AFFECTING EMPLOYEES

From the employees' point of view, the best part of the payroll process is receiving their net pay each week. The ABC Company Ltd. writes a cheque to each employee in payment of his or her weekly **take-home pay** (see columns L and M, Figure 7-2). As each cheque is written, it is recorded in the **cash disbursements journal,** as shown in Figure 7-4, below. The cash disbursements journal is explained more fully in Chapter 10. For now, it is acceptable to imagine that each cheque is recorded individually in the general journal (not illustrated).

CASH DISBURSEMENTS JOURNAL

Date 2001		Chq. No.	Accounts Payment To:	PR	Sundry Dr.	Accounts Payable Dr.	Salaries and Wages Payable Dr.	Purchases Discount Cr.	Cash Cr.
Mar.	9	1407	Janet Johnson				364 92		364 92
	"	1408	Peter Black				324 45		324 45
	"	1409	John Chernochan				292 40		292 40
	"	1410	Tony Chui				340 96		340 96
	"	1411	Beth Madora				219 31		219 31
	"	1412	Elaine Dumont				558 13		558 13

FIGURE 7-4 Cash Disbursements Journal

When the cash disbursements journal is posted, the balance in the Salaries and Wages Payable account will be reduced to zero. This is as it should be, since the amount recorded as payable, $2,100.17, has been paid by cheques 1407–1412 and the amount remaining to be paid is nil. Please remember that the cash disbursements journal is posted at the end of the month. It is only after the cheques have been issued, recorded, and posted that the balance in the Salaries and Wages Payable account will be zero.

Most companies pay their employees by cheque, although in a very few cases companies pay out actual cash. Many large companies transfer wages directly to their employees' bank accounts. Some companies have a separate bank account on which they issue their payroll cheques. The main reason for this practice is to simplify the payment process and reconciliation of bank accounts, especially when the number of employees is large.

Employee Earnings Record

In order to meet legal requirements, the ABC Company Ltd. must keep a separate record of each employee's earnings. This **employee earnings record** is essential for the following reasons:

1. Every year (by February 28), ABC Company Ltd. must prepare and deliver to each employee a summary of the previous calendar year's earnings and related deductions. This form is known as a **T4** (or **T4A** slip or **T4 Supplementary**). Refer to Figure 7-5 for a sample of this form. Notice that in order to complete this form accurately a detailed record of each employee's earnings and deductions must be kept.

FIGURE 7-5
T4 Slip

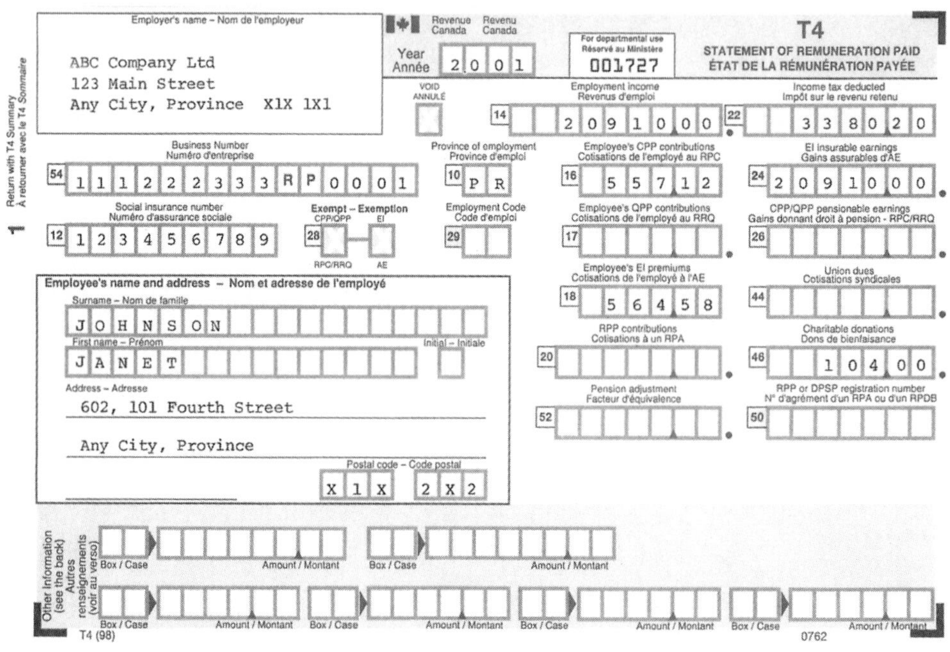

1 Return with T4 Summary / À retourner avec le T4 Sommaire

Revenue Canada / Revenu Canada

T4
STATEMENT OF REMUNERATION PAID
ÉTAT DE LA RÉMUNÉRATION PAYÉE

Employer's name – Nom de l'employeur:
ABC Company Ltd
123 Main Street
Any City, Province X1X 1X1

Year / Année: 2001

For departmental use / Réservé au Ministère: 001727

VOID / ANNULÉ

14	Employment income / Revenus d'emploi	20910.00
22	Income tax deducted / Impôt sur le revenu retenu	3380.20
54	Business Number / Numéro d'entreprise	111222333RP0001
10	Province of employment / Province d'emploi	PR
16	Employee's CPP contributions / Cotisations de l'employé au RPC	557.12
24	EI insurable earnings / Gains assurables d'AE	20910.00
12	Social insurance number / Numéro d'assurance sociale	123456789
28	Exempt – Exemption: CPP/QPP (RPC/RRQ), EI (AE)	
29	Employment Code / Code d'emploi	
17	Employee's QPP contributions / Cotisations de l'employé au RRQ	
26	CPP/QPP pensionable earnings / Gains donnant droit à pension - RPC/RRQ	
18	Employee's EI premiums / Cotisations de l'employé à l'AE	564.58
44	Union dues / Cotisations syndicales	
20	RPP contributions / Cotisations à un RPA	
46	Charitable donations / Dons de bienfaisance	104.00
52	Pension adjustment / Facteur d'équivalence	
50	RPP or DPSP registration number / N° d'agrément d'un RPA ou d'un RPDB	

Employee's name and address – Nom et adresse de l'employé
Surname – Nom de famille: JOHNSON
First name – Prénom: JANET
Initial – Initiale:
Address – Adresse: 602, 101 Fourth Street
Any City, Province
Postal code – Code postal: X1X 2X2

Other information (see the back) / Autres renseignements (voir au verso): Box / Case — Amount / Montant

T4 (98) 0762

Source: Revenue Canada. Reproduced with permission of the Minister of Public Works and Government Services Canada, 1999.

2. When an employee leaves his or her employment for any reason, a special form is required to comply with the employment insurance laws. This form, called a **Record of Employment**, is shown in Figure 7-6.
3. In deducting CPP, it is necessary to keep deducting only as long as an employee's earnings are below a certain level. CPP is payable up to a maximum of $1,068.80 for 1998. Therefore it is necessary to stop making deductions when this amount is reached. For EI there is no maximum per pay period, but the total per year cannot exceed $1,053.00.

Figure 7-7 shows a partial employee earnings record for Janet Johnson for the latest year.

Human Resources Development Canada / Développement des ressources humaines Canada

IF COMPLETING THIS FORM BY HAND, USE A PEN AND PRESS FIRMLY

EMPLOYER: THE GUIDE - HOW TO COMPLETE THE RECORD OF EMPLOYMENT, PROVIDES DETAILED INSTRUCTIONS.

Protected when completed - B

RECORD OF EMPLOYMENT (ROE)

1 SERIAL NO.

2 SERIAL NO. OF ROE AMENDED OR REPLACED

3 EMPLOYER'S PAYROLL REFERENCE NO.

4 EMPLOYER'S NAME AND ADDRESS

5 REVENUE CANADA BUSINESS NO. (BN)

6 PAY PERIOD TYPE

7 POSTAL CODE

8 SOCIAL INSURANCE NO.

9 EMPLOYEE'S NAME AND ADDRESS

10 FIRST DAY WORKED — D M Y

11 LAST DAY FOR WHICH PAID — D M Y

12 FINAL PAY PERIOD ENDING DATE — D M Y

13 OCCUPATION

14 EXPECTED DATE OF RECALL — ☐ UNKNOWN ☐ NOT RETURNING — D M Y

15A TOTAL INSURABLE HOURS ACCORDING TO CHART ON REVERSE

16 REASON FOR ISSUING THIS ROE ▶ ENTER CODE

FOR FURTHER INFORMATION, CONTACT

TELEPHONE NO. ▶ ( )

15B TOTAL INSURABLE EARNINGS ACCORDING TO CHART ON REVERSE — $

15C **ONLY COMPLETE IF** THERE HAS BEEN A PAY PERIOD WITH NO INSURABLE EARNINGS. COMPLETE ACCORDING TO CHART ON REVERSE.

P.P.	INSURABLE EARNINGS	P.P.	INSURABLE EARNINGS	P.P.	INSURABLE EARNINGS
1		2		3	
4		5		6	
7		8		9	
10		11		12	
13		14		15	
16		17		18	
19		20		21	
22		23		24	
25		26		27	

17 **ONLY COMPLETE IF** PAYMENTS OR BENEFITS (OTHER THAN REGULAR PAY) PAID IN OR IN ANTICIPATION OF THE FINAL PAY PERIOD OR PAYABLE AT A LATER DATE.

A - VACATION PAY — $

B - STATUTORY HOLIDAY PAY FOR — D M Y — $ / $ / $

C - OTHER MONIES (SPECIFY) — $ / $ / $

18 **COMMENTS**

19 **ONLY COMPLETE IF** PAID SICK/MATERNITY/PARENTAL LEAVE OR GROUP WAGE LOSS INDEMNITY PAYMENT (AFTER THE LAST DAY WORKED).

PAYMENT START DATE — D M Y

AMOUNT — $ — **PER DAY** ☐ **PER WEEK** ☐

20 COMMUNICATION PREFERRED IN — ☐ ENGLISH ☐ FRENCH

21 TELEPHONE NO. ( )

22 I AM AWARE THAT IT IS AN OFFENCE TO MAKE FALSE ENTRIES AND HEREBY CERTIFY THAT ALL STATEMENTS ON THIS FORM ARE TRUE.

SIGNATURE OF ISSUER — NAME OF ISSUER (please print) — DATE D M Y

INS-2106-09-98E

Canada

NOTE TO EMPLOYEE :THIS IS A VALUABLE DOCUMENT. KEEP IT IN A SAFE PLACE.
IF YOU INTEND TO FILE A CLAIM FOR E.I. INCOME BENEFITS YOU SHOULD DO SO IMMEDIATELY.
THE REVERSE OF PART 1 CONTAINS IMPORTANT INFORMATION.

EMPLOYEE'S COPY PART 1

Ce formulaire est également disponible en français.

ENTER CODE

- A SHORTAGE OF WORK
- B STRIKE OR LOCKOUT
- C RETURN TO SCHOOL
- D ILLNESS OR INJURY
- E QUIT
- F PREGNANCY PARENTAL
- G RETIREMENT
- H WORK SHARING
- J APPRENTICE TRAINING
- M DISMISSAL
- N LEAVE OF ABSENCE
- K OTHER EXPLAIN IN THE COMMENTS SECTION

PART 2 (BLUE) MUST BE SENT TO HUMAN RESOURCES DEVELOPMENT CANADA P.O. BOX 9000 BATHURST, N.B. E2A 4T3

FIGURE 7-6 Record of Employment

Source: Revenue Canada. Reproduced with permission of the Minister of Public Works and Government Services Canada, 1999.

Name of Employee	Janet Johnson	ABC Company Ltd.	Employee Address:
Social Insurance Number	123 456 789	Employee Earnings Record	123 Main Street
Date of Birth	03/12/72	for the Calendar Year 2001	Any City, Province
			A1B 1C1

Week	Claim Code	Rate of Pay	Hours Worked	Earnings			Deductions						
				Regular	Overtime	Gross Pay	IT	CPP	EI	Medical	Charitable	Net Pay	Chq. No.
1	1	10/h	40	400 00		400 00	63 75	10 63	10 80	0 00	2 00	312 82	1061
2			40	400 00		400 00	63 75	10 63	10 80	0 00	2 00	312 82	1102
3			42	400 00	30 00	430 00	71 35	11 59	11 61	0 00	2 00	333 45	1150
4			40	400 00		400 00	63 75	10 63	10 80	0 00	2 00	312 82	1194
5			40	400 00		400 00	63 75	10 63	10 80	0 00	2 00	312 82	1237
6			36	360 00		360 00	54 30	9 35	9 72	0 00	2 00	284 63	1291
7			40	400 00		400 00	63 75	10 63	10 80	0 00	2 00	312 82	1322
8			41	400 00	15 00	415 00	67 55	11 11	11 18	0 00	2 00	323 16	1368
9			45	400 00	75 00	475 00	82 25	13 03	12 80	0 00	2 00	364 92	1407
10			40	400 00		400 00	63 75	10 63	10 80	0 00	2 00	312 82	1451
11			40	400 00		400 00	63 75	10 63	10 80	0 00	2 00	312 82	1490
49		11/h	46	440 00	99 00	539 00	97 40	15 09	14 53	0 00	2 00	409 98	3021
50			40	440 00		440 00	73 25	11 91	11 88	0 00	2 00	340 96	3191
51			38	418 00		418 00	68 50	11 21	11 29	0 00	2 00	325 00	3154
52			40	440 00		440 00	73 25	11 91	11 88	0 00	2 00	340 96	3214
Totals for the Year				20280 00	630 00	20910 00	3380 20	557 12	564 58	0 00	104 00	15922 10	

FIGURE 7-7 Employee Earnings Record

LEARNING UNIT 7-3 REVIEW

AT THIS POINT you should be able to:

- Record a payroll from a payroll summary. (p. 284)
- Break down gross wages into more detail. (p. 284)
- Post the entry recording the payroll into appropriate ledger accounts. (p. 285)
- Demonstrate the payment of net pay to employees by cheque. (p. 285)
- Record the cheques to employees in the Cash Disbursements Journal. (p. 285)
- Illustrate the employee's earnings record. (p. 288)
- Describe the Record of Employment form. (pp. 286–287)
- State the upper limit of EI and CPP deductions. (p. 286)

SELF-REVIEW QUIZ 7-3

Indicate whether the following statements are true or false:

1. All payroll registers are special journals. This means no payroll entry is ever needed.
2. Income Tax Payable is a liability on the balance sheet.
3. Salaries and Wages Expense has a normal balance of a debit.
4. Employee earnings records are optional for an employer.
5. The Record of Employment form must be completed annually for each employee.
6. All wages must be paid by cheque.
7. Cheques paying wages must be recorded in the cash disbursements journal.

Solution to Self-Review Quiz 7-3

1. False
2. True
3. True
4. False
5. False. The Record of Employment is required only when an employee leaves.
6. False. Cash or automatic bank transfers are also normal.
7. True, in general, although other possibilities exist, such as special payroll journals, or even the general journal (for very small companies).

Time After Time: Stuck on Payroll Records

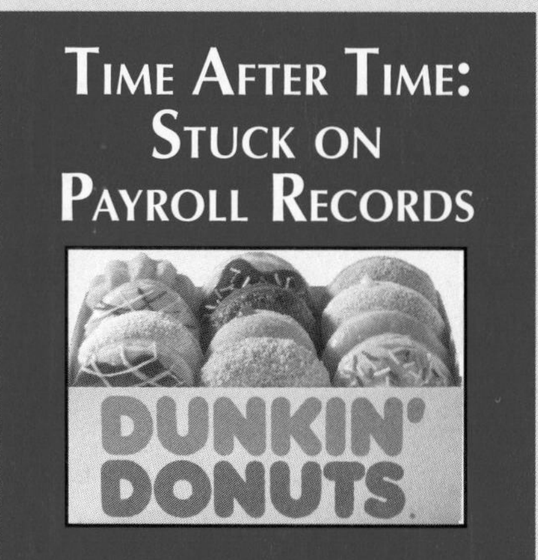

All Dunkin' Donuts shops keep a master file of employee information, containing every employee's name, address, telephone number, social insurance number, rate of pay, hours worked per week, and TD1 form. Different shop owners offer different rates of pay, depending on local conditions. They offer different benefits as well. They employ mostly part-time workers, usually with a core of full-timers. Fred, for example, pays clerks with less than one year's experience the minimum wage. He offers health and dental insurance. Some of the bigger shop owners also offer profit sharing to employees with a minimum of five years of service. The frequency of pay varies by province, and sometimes by city. So, of course, do tax rates.

All this information must be recorded and reported to the various provincial, local, and federal authorities—and to Dunkin' Donuts headquarters, through the zone's business consultant.

Scheduling workers and keeping payroll records are Fred's least-favourite jobs. He was pleased to hear Dwayne announce at an Advisory Council meeting that the company's new IBM terminals would offer an electronic scheduling package.

"Wow! That will really help, Dwayne!" said Fred joyously. "No more different colours of ink just to keep track of who will work when! Now we can plan around the exam schedules of the part-timers without a hassle! Scheduling will be my favourite module in the new system!"

"Sure," said Molly Harris, another shop owner. "Now you can concentrate on payroll records. What fun!"

Fred groaned.

Discussion Questions

1. What payroll records does Fred need to keep for his doughnut shop?
2. What other information might Fred want in order to schedule working hours for each employee?
3. How does the payroll register help Fred prepare the payroll? Consult the process outlined on page 285.

Chapter Review

Summary of Key Points

Learning Unit 7-1

1. The minimum wage law sets the lowest hourly wage that can be paid to an employee and establishes the maximum number of hours per day and per week that an employee may work before an overtime premium must be paid.
2. Employers may calculate overtime pay separately from regular pay in order to highlight the cost of having employees work overtime.
3. Each pay period, employees are required to pay income tax and to contribute to the Canada Pension Plan and the Employment Insurance Plan according to their level of earnings. The amount to be deducted for each is found in tables published by the federal government.
4. A TD1 form specifies the claim code for each employee. This in turn governs the income tax deducted each pay period.
5. CPP and EI have a maximum contribution of $1,068.80 per year and $1,053.00 per year respectively. (These maximums will change annually.)
6. Other deductions (for example, union dues or company-related matters) may also be made from an employee's earnings.

Learning Unit 7-2

1. Each pay period a payroll summary is prepared. It includes the following information for each employee: claim code; rate of pay; hours worked; regular earnings; overtime earnings; gross pay; income tax deduction; CPP deduction; EI deduction; other deductions such as medical and charitable; net pay; and cheque number.
2. Gross pay determines the level of deductions.
3. Gross pay less deductions equals net, or "take-home," pay.

Learning Unit 7-3

1. The payroll register is completed each pay period and provides basic data for recording the payroll.
2. The Salaries and Wages Expense entry is made and posted to ledger accounts. In addition to summarizing the deductions payable, the ledger accounts are used to classify wage expenses by type.
3. Each payroll cheque written is recorded in the cash disbursements journal (or the general journal). Journal amounts or totals are posted to the general ledger monthly.
4. Employers must maintain an employee earnings record for each employee. The source of the information summarized here is the payroll register.
5. Each year employers must prepare and deliver to each employee a T4 or T4A form which summarizes the employee's earnings and deductions for the calendar year.
6. When an employee leaves, is laid off, or is terminated, the employer must complete a Record of Employment form.

KEY TERMS

Canada (or Quebec) Pension Plan Provides a retirement benefit for all Canadians who contribute to the plan during their employment years. Requires a payroll deduction from each employee until a yearly maximum is reached. (The maximum we are using is $1,068.80, but a new maximum is used each year.) (p. 277)

Claim code A number from 0 to 10 which determines the amount of income tax deducted each pay period. The appropriate claim code is based on information provided by the employee when completing a TD1 form. (p. 277)

Employee earnings record A page, or sheet, or computer file which records and totals the details concerning an employee's earnings, deductions, net pay, and identification details for a calendar year. Used in preparing T4 slips. (p. 286)

Employment insurance plan A plan to which all employees must contribute and which provides a certain level of income for those workers who are unemployed. Contributions are made up to a maximum of $1,053 per year (based on 2.7 percent of the maximum insurable earnings of $39,000). (p. 277)

Income tax deductions Amounts withheld from employees' wages each period and sent (on behalf of the employees) to the federal government. The amount of the deduction is determined by tables published by the federal government, customized for each province. (p. 283)

Minimum wage laws Laws which govern the lowest wage legally payable in a province. Such a law also states the province's rules about overtime premiums and maximum weekly working hours. (p. 276)

Other deductions Most employees have a variety of items for which a deduction is required. The exact type and amount of these deductions will vary a great deal from one employer to another. Common examples are union dues and provincial health care premiums. (p. 280)

Payroll summary Sometimes known as the payroll journal or payroll register, this document lists in considerable detail the income, deductions, net pay, and other information for each employee for a given pay period. A total for all employees per category is always shown. This summary forms the basis for posting to appropriate ledger accounts. (p. 282)

Record of Employment Special form to be completed for each employee at the end of his or her employment. Used in helping to determine the level of unemployment insurance payments a taxpayer is eligible for. (p. 287)

TD1 form A form completed by an employee upon commencement of employment (and periodically thereafter) which sets out the deductions claimed by the employee. A claim code determined by this form affects the amount of income tax deducted. (pp. 277–279)

T4 slip or T4 Supplementary A special form issued annually to each employee summarizing annual earnings and deductions and used by an employee as a basic document in filing an annual income tax return. (p. 286)

Blueprint for Recording, Posting, and Paying the Payroll

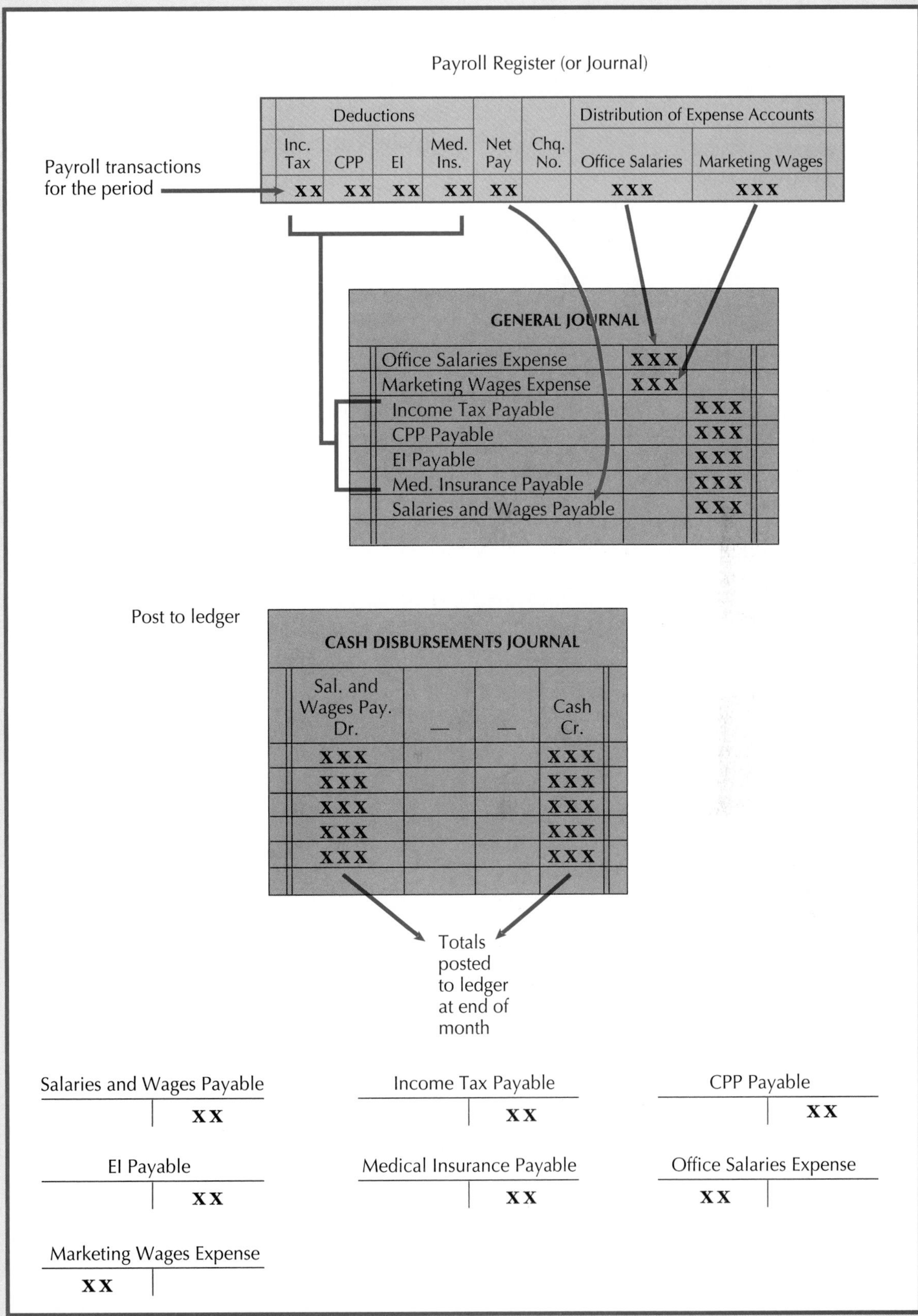

QUESTIONS, MINI EXERCISES, EXERCISES, AND PROBLEMS

Discussion Questions

1. Explain how overtime is usually calculated.
2. Define and state the purpose of completing a T4 Supplementary.
3. Usually, claiming more credits on a TD1 results in receiving more money per paycheque. Please comment.
4. All payroll registers must be special journals. True or false?
5. Define and state the purpose of the Canada and the Quebec Pension Plans.
6. The employer doesn't have to contribute to the Canada Pension Plan. Agree or disagree.
7. Explain how federal and provincial income tax withholdings are determined.
8. What is a calendar year?
9. Define the purpose of an income tax deduction.
10. What purposes does the employee earnings record serve?
11. Explain the differences in determining CPP and EI deductions.
12. Draw a diagram showing how the following relate: (a) weekly payroll; (b) payroll register; (c) individual earnings; (d) journal entries; (e) cash disbursements journal.
13. If you earned $80,000 this year, you would pay more CPP than your brother, who earned $60,000. Agree or disagree? Explain.

Mini Exercises

(The forms you need are on page 7-2 of the *Study Guide with Working Papers*.)

Calculating Gross Earnings

1. Calculate the total wages earned (assume an overtime rate of time-and-a-half over 40 hours):

Employee	*Hourly Rate*	*No. of Hours Worked*
A. Dawn Slowic	$10	37
B. Jill Jones	12	50

CPP and EI

2. Pete Martin, married but claiming code 1, has cumulative earnings before this weekly pay period of $41,500. Assuming he is paid $1,200 this week, what will his deduction be for CPP and EI?

Net Pay

3. Calculate Pete's net pay from question 2 above. Income tax is $410 and health insurance is $40.

Payroll Register

4. For each of the six items listed below, indicate which of these three descriptions applies:

   (1) Total of gross pay—comes from distribution of expense accounts

   (2) A deduction

(3) Net pay

____ **A.** Office Salaries Expense and Wages Expense
____ **B.** CPP Payable
____ **C.** EI Payable
____ **D.** Federal Income Tax Payable
____ **E.** Medical Insurance Payable
____ **F.** Salaries and Wages Payable

Payroll Account

5. Indicate for each of the accounts listed below which of the following applies:

(1) An asset
(2) A liability
(3) An expense
(4) Appears in the income statement
(5) Appears on the balance sheet

____ **A.** CPP Payable
____ **B.** Office Salaries Expense
____ **C.** Federal Income Tax Payable
____ **D.** EI Payable
____ **E.** Salaries and Wages Payable

Exercises

(The forms you need are on page 7-3 of the *Study Guide with Working Papers.*)

Calculating wages with overtime

7-1. Calculate the total wages earned for each employee (assume an overtime rate of time-and-a-half over 40 hours):

Employee	*Hourly Rate*	*Hours Worked*
Jean Knott	$11.20	36
Abe Janzen	13.00	44
Mike Toth	14.00	46

Calculating net pay

7-2. Compute the net pay for each employee for the first week of February, using the tables in the text.

Employee	*Status*	*Claim Code*	*This Week's Pay*
Abe Smith	Married	4	$610
May Cheung	Single	1	420

The only deductions are for income tax, CPP, and EI.

Categorizing accounts

7-3. Complete the table.

	Category	*Dr./Cr.*	*Financial Report on Which Account Appears*
CPP Payable			
Income Tax Payable			
Medical Insurance Payable			
Wages and Salaries Payable			
Office Salaries Expense			
Marketing Wages Expense			

Payroll register and the journal entry

7-4. The following weekly payroll journal entry was prepared by Moore Co. Explain from which columns of the payroll register the data have come?

			Debit	Credit
Jan.	7	Shop Expense	600000	
		Factory Wages Expense	400000	
		CPP Payable		31500
		EI Payable		270000
		Income Tax Payable		27000
		Union Dues Payable		21000
		Salaries and Wages Payable		650500

Paying the payroll

7-5. From Exercise 4, prepare the general ledger entry to record payment of the payroll, given the following data for January 9:

Employee	*Employee's Net Pay*	*Cheque No.*
Nina Smith	$2,930	111
Jean Logan	1,200	112
Fred Singer	2,375	113

Group A Problems

(The forms you need are on pages 7-4 to 7-10 of the *Study Guide with Working Papers.*)

Calculating gross earnings with overtime

Check Figure

Tony Lee Gross Earnings $728.00

7A-1. From the following information, please complete the chart for gross earnings for the week. (Assume an overtime rate of time-and-a-half over 40 hours.)

Employee	*Hourly Rate*	*Number of Hours Worked*	*Gross Earnings*
Jane Reynolds	$ 8.00	44	
Pete Duncan	11.50	36	
Maria Cardinal	12.00	42	
Tony Lee	14.00	48	

Completing a payroll register

Check Figure

Net Pay $2,295.72

7A-2. Montana Company has five salaried employees. Your task is to record the following information for the last week of March in a payroll register.

Employee	*Department*	*Claim Code*	*Weekly Salary*
Jenny Quan	Sales	3	$725
Frank Sloan	Sales	1	420
Alberta Nobel	Office	2	980
Jeremy Gold	Office	4	605
Nancy James	Sales	1	435

Assume that each employee contributes $10 per week for union dues.

Check Figure

Net Pay $1,525.01

7A-3. The bookkeeper for Pinto Co. gathered the following data from employee earnings records as well as daily time cards. Your task is (1) to complete a payroll register on November 4 and (2) to journalize the appropriate entry to record the payroll.

Group C Problems

(The forms you need are on pages 7-11 to 7-20 of the *Study Guide with Working Papers.*)

7C-1. From the following data, calculate the gross earnings for each of the five employees, who are entitled to time-and-a-half for any hours exceeding 40 for the week or 8 in any given day.

Calculating gross earnings with overtime

Employee	*M*	*T*	*W*	*T*	*F*	*S*	*Total Hours*	*Hourly Rate*
A. Fran Sorter	6	8	8	10	8	6	46	$12.00
B. Barb Frank	6	7	8	8	7	5	41	15.00
C. Amos Ng	8	7	8	10	8	—	41	10.00
D. Carl Holdman	9	6	8	11	7	6	47	16.00
E. Erika Hance	8	7	9	13	8	6	51	14.00

Check Figure
Erika Hance Gross Earnings $791.00

7C-2. The employees mentioned in problem 7C-1 work for the Waylon Corporation Ltd. Complete a payroll register for the second week of February, using the gross earnings you obtained in answering 7C-1. Assume the following additional information:

Completing the payroll register

Employee	*Claim Code*	*Union Dues*	*Medical Plan*
A	2	$16	$32.00
B	1	16	48.00
C	3	16	32.00
D	4	16	32.00
E	1	16	48.00

Check Figure
Net Pay $2,130.29

7C-3. (Alternative to 7C-2) Assume the following gross earnings for the employees of Waylon Corporation Ltd. for the third week of February. Other information remains the same as in 7C-2. Complete the payroll register for the third week of February.

Completing the payroll register (alternative problem)

Employee	*Gross Earnings*
A	$478.00
B	567.00
C	431.00
D	792.00
E	558.00

Check Figure
Net Pay $1,888.46

Recording the payroll entry

7C-4. Refer to the payroll register you completed in 7C-2. Prepare the journal entry necessary to record the payroll for the second week of February.

Recording the payroll entry (alternative problem)

7C-5. (Alternative to 7C-4) Refer to the payroll register you completed in 7C-3. Prepare the journal entry necessary to record the payroll for the third week of February.

Completing the payroll register and journalizing the payroll entry

7C-6. The payroll clerk for the Marlin Company Ltd. has assembled the following data for the company's five employees, before suddenly becoming quite ill. You have been approached to complete the payroll register so that the employees can receive their cheques in a timely fashion. You must (1) complete the payroll register for the week ending October 20 and (2) prepare the entry necessary to record the payroll. Hours in excess of 40 in any given week are paid at time-and-a-half.

Check Figure
Net Pay $2,542.09

Employee	Claim Code	M	T	W	T	F	S	Rate	Dept.	CPP to Date	Union Dues	Medical
		Daily Time										
Fred Mora	2	—	8	8	10	12	5	$14.00	Sales	$1057.10	$8	$22
Pat Samuels	1	9	—	7	10	7	8	12.00	Sales	684.10	8	40
Emilia Leung	3	8	9	8	9	8	6	10.50	Admin.	486.70	8	22
Keith Jones	5	8	8	8	8	8	—	16.00	Admin.	227.40	8	40
David Jarvic*	1	9	8	7	11	8	8	1,400.00*	Mgr.	1068.80	-	40

* Weekly salary. This employee has already earned $40,600 so far this year.

Comprehensive payroll problem—completing payroll registers, journalizing payrolls, and recording cheques issued

Check Figure

Net Pay $4,709.15

7C-7. Comet Engineering Inc. is a consulting firm which employs four professional staff, two casual clerks, and you as office manager (accountant). Everyone except the clerks is paid a weekly salary. The clerks are paid an hourly rate and receive time-and-a-half for hours worked in excess of 8 per day or 40 per week. Using the information below, complete the payroll register for the week ending August 21, make the necessary entry to record the payroll for that week, and record the issuance of cheques to each employee. Daily hours for the clerks are shown at the end.

Employee	Claim Code	Rate or Salary	Life Ins.	Disab.	Med.	Donations	CPP to Date	Chq. No.
Donna Alvarez	3	$1,540.00	$19	$32	$36.00	$25.00	$1,068.80	574
Joan Kemp	4	1,390.00	12	28	36.00	25.00	1,052.70	575
John Harper	1	1,290.00	10	24	18.00	18.00	947.60	576
Tim Culver	2	1,340.00	8	25	36.00	18.00	484.37	577
May Silver	1	14.00	—	—	18.00	—	245.23	578
Joe Polemko	4	12.00	—	—	36.00	5.00	428.64	579
Yourself	2	875.00	6	18	18.00	5.00	548.75	580

Hourly employees worked:

	M	T	W	T	F	S	Total
May Silver	8	8	9	10	5	8	48
Joe Polemko	10	8	12	8	5	—	43

Hourly workers receive 1.5 × rate for more than 40 hours in a week, or more than 8 hours in any given day. None of the employees will reach the EI maximum this pay period, except Donna Alvarez, who reached the limit of $39,000 two pay periods ago.

REAL WORLD APPLICATIONS

(The forms you need are on page 7-21 of the *Study Guide with Working Papers.*)

7R-1.

Small Co., a sole proprietorship, has two employees, Jim Roy and Janice Alter. The owner of Small Co. is Bert Ryan. During the current pay period, Jim has worked 48 hours and Janice 56. The reason for these extra hours is that both Jim and Janice worked their regular 40-hour work week, plus Jim worked 8 extra hours on Sunday while Janice worked 8 extra hours on Saturday as well as Sunday. Their contract with Small Co. is that they are each paid an hourly rate of $8 per hour with all hours over 40 per week to be at time-and-a-half and overtime hours on Sunday, that is, hours over eight, to be paid at double time. Bert the owner feels he is also entitled to a salary, since he works many hours. He plans to pay himself $425 per week.

As the accountant of Small Co., could you calculate the gross pay for Jim and Janice and offer some advice to Bert regarding his salary?

7R-2.

Marcy Moore recently moved to your city from another large Canadian centre. She was employed as an engineer by a large oil company and was rather well paid. She now works as a senior engineer for a newly established consulting firm. When she moved in October, Marcy had contributed the yearly maximum CPP premiums of $1,068.80 as well as the limit of $1,053.00 for EI while employed at the oil company, and feels it is unfair of her new employer to continue to deduct CPP and EI from her salary. She has heard that you are taking an accounting course, and has asked you for your opinion.

What advice can you give her?

make the call

Critical Thinking/Ethical Case

7R-3.

Russ Todd works for a delicatessen. As the bookkeeper Russ has been asked by the owner to keep two separate books for sales tax. The owner has asked Todd to hire someone on the weekends to punch in false tapes that can be submitted to the province. These tapes would show low sales and thus less liability for sales tax payments. You make the call. Write down your specific recommendations to Russ.

ACCOUNTING RECALL

A CUMULATIVE APPROACH

THIS EXAMINATION REVIEWS CHAPTERS 1 THROUGH 7.

Your *Study Guide with Working Papers* (page 7-22) has forms to complete this exam, as well as worked-out solutions. The page reference next to each question identifies the page to turn back to if you answer the question incorrectly.

PART I Vocabulary Review

Match each term on the left side with the appropriate definition or related phrase in the right-hand column.

Page Ref.		
(282)	1. Total earnings columns	A. Gross pay less deductions
(239)	2. Petty cash	B. Records gross payroll
(286)	3. T4 slip	C. A pension plan for most employees
(277)	4. Tax deductions	D. An asset
(286)	5. Calendar year	E. National insurance plan
(277)	6. TD1 form	F. Found in tables organized by province
(277)	7. EI	G. Basis for determining tax deductions
(283)	8. Net pay	H. An annual summary of payroll amounts
(286)	9. Employee earnings record	I. January 1 to December 31
(277)	10. CPP	J. Updated each pay period

PART II True or False (Accounting Theory)

(276) 11. A biweekly pay period results in 24 payrolls each year.

(282) 12. A payroll register is considered a special journal.

(282) 13. The total earnings column of a payroll register shows earnings that are subject to income tax.

(284) 14. Wages and Salaries Payable records gross pay.

(291) 15. The employee earnings record is updated from the payroll register.

Continuing Problem

In preparing for next year, Tony Freedman has hired two employees to work on an hourly basis, assisting with some troubleshooting and repair work. Assume the following details:

- **a.** The following accounts have been added to the chart of accounts: Wage Expense #5110; Income Taxes Payable #2020; CPP Payable #2030; EI Payable #2040; and Wages Payable #2010.
- **b.** CPP is deducted according to the tables in Appendix 7-2 to this chapter.
- **c.** EI is deducted according to Appendix 7-3 to this chapter.
- **d.** Both employees have claim codes of 1.
- **e.** Each employee earns $10 an hour and is paid time-and-one-half for hours worked in excess of 40 weekly.

Assignment

(See pages 7-23 to 7-31 in your *Study Guide with Working Papers.*)

1. Record the transactions listed below in general journal format, and post to the general ledger.
2. Prepare a payroll register.
3. Prepare a trial balance as of November 30, 2001.

Nov. 1 Billed Vita Needle Company $6,800; invoice No. 12676, for services rendered.

3 Billed Accu Pac, Inc. $3,900; invoice No. 12677, for services rendered.

5 Purchased new shop benches $1,400 on account from System Design Furniture (their invoice No. 8771).

7 Paid the two employees wages: Lance Kumm, 38 hours, and Aurelle Hall, 42 hours (cheques No. 220 and No. 221).

9 Received the phone bill, $150.

12 Collected $500 of the amount due from Taylor Golf.

14 Paid the two employees wages: Lance Kumm, 25 hours, and Aurelle Hall, 36 hours (cheques No. 222 and No. 223).

18 Collected $800 of the amount due from Taylor Golf.

20 Purchased a fax machine for the office from Multi Systems on credit, $450 (their invoice No. 1784).

21 Paid the two employees wages: Lance Kumm, 26 hours, and Aurelle Hall, 35 hours (cheques No. 224 and 225).

26 Collected half of the amount due from Vita Needle Company re Nov. 1 transaction.

28 Paid the two employees wages: Lance Kumm, 38 hours, and Aurelle Hall, 44 hours (cheques No. 226 and No. 227).

Employee Payroll Deductions (Extracted): Income Tax, CPP, EI

Appendix 7-1—Ontario Tax Tables

Ontario — **Ontario**

Federal and Provincial Tax Deductions — **Retenues d'impôt fédéral et provincial**

Weekly (52 pay periods a year) — **Hebdomadaire (52 périodes de paie par année)**

Pay / Rémunération		If the employee's claim code from the TD1(E) form is / Si le code de demande de l'employé selon le formulaire TD1(F) est										
		0	1	2	3	4	5	6	7	8	9	10
From / De	Less than / Moins de	Deduct from each pay / Retenez sur chaque paie										
237.-	241.	57.15	25.90	22.05	12.60	4.70						
241.-	245.	58.05	26.85	23.00	13.85	5.35	.05					
245.-	249.	59.00	27.80	23.95	15.05	6.00	.70					
249.-	253.	59.95	28.75	24.90	16.30	6.70	1.35					
253.-	257.	60.90	29.70	25.85	17.55	7.55	2.00					
257.-	261.	61.85	30.60	26.80	18.80	8.80	2.65					
261.-	265.	62.80	31.55	27.75	20.00	10.05	3.35					
265.-	269.	63.75	32.50	28.70	21.05	11.25	4.00					
269.-	273.	64.70	33.45	29.65	22.00	12.50	4.65					
273.-	277.	65.65	34.40	30.60	22.95	13.75	5.30					
277.-	281.	66.60	35.35	31.55	23.90	14.95	5.95	.65				
281.-	285.	67.55	36.30	32.50	24.85	16.20	6.60	1.30				
285.-	289.	68.50	37.25	33.45	25.80	17.45	7.45	1.95				
289.-	293.	69.45	38.20	34.40	26.70	18.65	8.70	2.60				
293.-	297.	70.40	39.15	35.30	27.65	19.90	9.95	3.30				
297.-	301.	71.35	40.10	36.25	28.60	20.95	11.15	3.95				
301.-	305.	72.30	41.05	37.20	29.55	21.90	12.40	4.60				
305.-	309.	73.25	42.00	38.15	30.50	22.85	13.65	5.25				
309.-	313.	74.15	42.95	39.10	31.45	23.80	14.85	5.90	.60			
313.-	317.	75.10	43.90	40.05	32.40	24.75	16.10	6.55	1.25			
317.-	321.	76.05	44.85	41.00	33.35	25.70	17.35	7.35	1.90			
321.-	325.	77.00	45.80	41.95	34.30	26.65	18.55	8.60	2.55			
325.-	329.	77.95	46.70	42.90	35.25	27.60	19.80	9.85	3.25			
329.-	333.	78.90	47.65	43.85	36.20	28.55	20.90	11.05	3.90			
333.-	337.	79.85	48.60	44.80	37.15	29.50	21.85	12.30	4.55			
337.-	341.	80.80	49.55	45.75	38.10	30.45	22.80	13.55	5.20			
341.-	345.	81.75	50.50	46.70	39.05	31.40	23.70	14.75	5.85	.55		
345.-	349.	82.70	51.45	47.65	40.00	32.35	24.65	16.00	6.50	1.20		
349.-	353.	83.65	52.40	48.60	40.95	33.25	25.60	17.25	7.25	1.85		
353.-	357.	84.60	53.35	49.55	41.90	34.20	26.55	18.45	8.50	2.50		
357.-	361.	85.55	54.30	50.45	42.80	35.15	27.50	19.70	9.75	3.15		
361.-	365.	86.50	55.25	51.40	43.75	36.10	28.45	20.80	10.95	3.85		
365.-	369.	87.45	56.20	52.35	44.70	37.05	29.40	21.75	12.20	4.50		
369.-	373.	88.40	57.15	53.30	45.65	38.00	30.35	22.70	13.45	5.15		
373.-	377.	89.30	58.10	54.25	46.60	38.95	31.30	23.65	14.65	5.80	.50	
377.-	381.	90.25	59.05	55.20	47.55	39.90	32.25	24.60	15.90	6.45	1.15	
381.-	385.	91.20	60.00	56.15	48.50	40.85	33.20	25.55	17.15	7.15	1.80	
385.-	389.	92.15	60.95	57.10	49.45	41.80	34.15	26.50	18.40	8.40	2.45	
389.-	393.	93.10	61.90	58.05	50.40	42.75	35.10	27.45	19.60	9.65	3.10	
393.-	397.	94.05	62.80	59.00	51.35	43.70	36.05	28.40	20.75	10.85	3.80	
397.-	401.	95.00	63.75	59.95	52.30	44.65	37.00	29.35	21.70	12.10	4.45	
401.-	405.	95.95	64.70	60.90	53.25	45.60	37.95	30.30	22.65	13.35	5.10	
405.-	409.	96.90	65.65	61.85	54.20	46.55	38.90	31.25	23.55	14.55	5.75	.45
409.-	413.	97.85	66.60	62.80	55.15	47.50	39.80	32.15	24.50	15.80	6.40	1.10
413.-	417.	98.80	67.55	63.75	56.10	48.40	40.75	33.10	25.45	17.05	7.05	1.75
417.-	421.	99.75	68.50	64.70	57.05	49.35	41.70	34.05	26.40	18.30	8.30	2.40
421.-	425.	100.70	69.45	65.65	58.00	50.30	42.65	35.00	27.35	19.50	9.55	3.05
425.-	429.	101.65	70.40	66.55	58.90	51.25	43.60	35.95	28.30	20.65	10.75	3.70
429.-	433.	102.60	71.35	67.50	59.85	52.20	44.55	36.90	29.25	21.60	12.00	4.40
433.-	437.	103.55	72.30	68.45	60.80	53.15	45.50	37.85	30.20	22.55	13.25	5.05
437.-	441.	104.50	73.25	69.40	61.75	54.10	46.45	38.80	31.15	23.50	14.45	5.70
441.-	445.	105.40	74.20	70.35	62.70	55.05	47.40	39.75	32.10	24.45	15.70	6.35
445.-	449.	106.35	75.15	71.30	63.65	56.00	48.35	40.70	33.05	25.40	16.95	7.00
449.-	453.	107.30	76.10	72.25	64.60	56.95	49.30	41.65	34.00	26.35	18.20	8.20
453.-	457.	108.25	77.05	73.20	65.55	57.90	50.25	42.60	34.95	27.30	19.40	9.40

D-2 **This table is available on diskette (TOD). Vous pouvez obtenir cette table sur disquette (TSD).**

Source: Revenue Canada. Reproduced with permission of the Minister of Public Works and Government Services Canada, 1999.

Ontario
Federal and Provincial Tax Deductions
Weekly (52 pay periods a year)

Ontario
Retenues d'impôt fédéral et provincial
Hebdomadaire (52 périodes de paie par année)

Pay / Rémunération From / De	Less than / Moins de	If the employee's claim code from the TD1(E) form is / Si le code de demande de l'employé selon le formulaire TD1(F) est: 0	1	2	3	4	5	6	7	8	9	10
			Deduct from each pay / Retenez sur chaque paie									
457.-	465.	109.70	78.45	74.60	66.95	59.30	51.65	44.00	36.35	28.70	21.05	11.30
465.-	473.	111.60	80.35	76.50	68.85	61.20	53.55	45.90	38.25	30.60	22.95	13.75
473.-	481.	113.45	82.25	78.40	70.75	63.10	55.45	47.80	40.15	32.50	24.85	16.20
481.-	489.	115.35	84.15	80.30	72.65	65.00	57.35	49.70	42.05	34.40	26.75	18.70
489.-	497.	117.25	86.05	82.20	74.55	66.90	59.25	51.60	43.95	36.30	28.65	20.95
497.-	505.	119.15	87.90	84.10	76.45	68.80	61.15	53.50	45.85	38.20	30.55	22.85
505.-	513.	121.05	89.80	86.00	78.35	70.70	63.00	55.40	47.70	40.05	32.40	24.75
513.-	521.	122.95	91.70	87.90	80.25	72.55	64.90	57.25	49.60	41.95	34.30	26.65
521.-	529.	124.85	93.60	89.80	82.10	74.45	66.80	59.15	51.50	43.85	36.20	28.55
529.-	537.	126.75	95.50	91.65	84.00	76.35	68.70	61.05	53.40	45.75	38.10	30.45
537.-	545.	128.65	97.40	93.55	85.90	78.25	70.60	62.95	55.30	47.65	40.00	32.35
545.-	553.	130.50	99.30	95.45	87.80	80.15	72.50	64.85	57.20	49.55	41.90	34.25
553.-	561.	132.40	101.20	97.35	89.70	82.05	74.40	66.75	59.10	51.45	43.80	36.10
561.-	569.	134.30	103.05	99.25	91.60	83.95	76.30	68.65	61.00	53.35	45.70	38.00
569.-	577.	136.75	105.50	101.65	94.00	86.35	78.70	71.05	63.40	55.75	48.10	40.45
577.-	585.	139.70	108.45	104.65	97.00	89.30	81.65	74.00	66.35	58.70	51.05	43.40
585.-	593.	142.65	111.40	107.60	99.95	92.30	84.65	77.00	69.35	61.65	54.00	46.35
593.-	601.	145.60	114.40	110.55	102.90	95.25	87.60	79.95	72.30	64.65	57.00	49.30
601.-	609.	148.55	117.35	113.50	105.85	98.20	90.55	82.90	75.25	67.60	59.95	52.30
609.-	617.	151.55	120.30	116.45	108.80	101.15	93.50	85.85	78.20	70.55	62.90	55.25
617.-	625.	154.50	123.25	119.45	111.80	104.10	96.45	88.80	81.15	73.50	65.85	58.20
625.-	633.	157.45	126.20	122.40	114.75	107.10	99.45	91.80	84.10	76.45	68.80	61.15
633.-	641.	160.40	129.15	125.35	117.70	110.05	102.40	94.75	87.10	79.45	71.80	64.10
641.-	649.	163.35	132.15	128.30	120.65	113.00	105.35	97.70	90.05	82.40	74.75	67.10
649.-	657.	166.35	135.10	131.25	123.60	115.95	108.30	100.65	93.00	85.35	77.70	70.05
657.-	665.	169.30	138.05	134.25	126.60	118.90	111.25	103.60	95.95	88.30	80.65	73.00
665.-	673.	172.25	141.00	137.20	129.55	121.90	114.20	106.55	98.90	91.25	83.60	75.95
673.-	681.	175.20	143.95	140.15	132.50	124.85	117.20	109.55	101.90	94.25	86.60	78.90
681.-	689.	178.15	146.95	143.10	135.45	127.80	120.15	112.50	104.85	97.20	89.55	81.90
689.-	697.	181.15	149.90	146.05	138.40	130.75	123.10	115.45	107.80	100.15	92.50	84.85
697.-	705.	184.10	152.85	149.05	141.35	133.70	126.05	118.40	110.75	103.10	95.45	87.80
705.-	713.	187.05	155.80	152.00	144.35	136.70	129.00	121.35	113.70	106.05	98.40	90.75
713.-	721.	190.05	158.85	155.00	147.35	139.70	132.05	124.40	116.75	109.10	101.45	93.80
721.-	729.	193.10	161.85	158.05	150.40	142.70	135.05	127.40	119.75	112.10	104.45	96.80
729.-	737.	196.10	164.90	161.05	153.40	145.75	138.10	130.45	122.80	115.15	107.50	99.80
737.-	745.	199.15	167.90	164.10	156.40	148.75	141.10	133.45	125.80	118.15	110.50	102.85
745.-	753.	202.15	170.95	167.10	159.45	151.80	144.15	136.50	128.85	121.20	113.55	105.85
753.-	761.	205.25	174.00	170.15	162.50	154.85	147.20	139.55	131.90	124.25	116.60	108.95
761.-	769.	208.30	177.10	173.25	165.60	157.95	150.30	142.65	135.00	127.35	119.70	112.00
769.-	777.	211.40	180.15	176.35	168.70	161.00	153.35	145.70	138.05	130.40	122.75	115.10
777.-	785.	214.45	183.25	179.40	171.75	164.10	156.45	148.80	141.15	133.50	125.85	118.20
785.-	793.	217.55	186.30	182.50	174.85	167.20	159.50	151.85	144.20	136.55	128.90	121.25
793.-	801.	220.65	189.40	185.55	177.90	170.25	162.60	154.95	147.30	139.65	132.00	124.35
801.-	809.	223.70	192.45	188.65	181.00	173.35	165.70	158.05	150.40	142.75	135.05	127.40
809.-	817.	226.80	195.55	191.70	184.05	176.40	168.75	161.10	153.45	145.80	138.15	130.50
817.-	825.	229.85	198.60	194.80	187.15	179.50	171.85	164.20	156.55	148.90	141.25	133.55
825.-	833.	232.95	201.70	197.90	190.25	182.55	174.90	167.25	159.60	151.95	144.30	136.65
833.-	841.	236.00	204.80	200.95	193.30	185.65	178.00	170.35	162.70	155.05	147.40	139.75
841.-	849.	239.10	207.85	204.05	196.40	188.75	181.05	173.40	165.75	158.10	150.45	142.80
849.-	857.	242.15	210.95	207.10	199.45	191.80	184.15	176.50	168.85	161.20	153.55	145.90
857.-	865.	245.25	214.00	210.20	202.55	194.90	187.25	179.60	171.95	164.25	156.60	148.95
865.-	873.	248.35	217.10	213.25	205.60	197.95	190.30	182.65	175.00	167.35	159.70	152.05
873.-	881.	251.40	220.15	216.35	208.70	201.05	193.40	185.75	178.10	170.45	162.80	155.10
881.-	889.	254.50	223.25	219.45	211.75	204.10	196.45	188.80	181.15	173.50	165.85	158.20
889.-	897.	257.55	226.35	222.50	214.85	207.20	199.55	191.90	184.25	176.60	168.95	161.30

This table is available on diskette (TOD). Vous pouvez obtenir cette table sur disquette (TSD). D-3

Ontario

Federal and Provincial Tax Deductions
Weekly (52 pay periods a year)

Ontario

Retenues d'impôt fédéral et provincial
Hebdomadaire (52 périodes de paie par année)

Pay / Rémunération		If the employee's claim code from the TD1(E) form is / Si le code de demande de l'employé selon le formulaire TD1(F) est										
		0	1	2	3	4	5	6	7	8	9	10
From / De	Less than / Moins de		Deduct from each pay / Retenez sur chaque paie									
897.-	909.	261.40	230.20	226.35	218.70	211.05	203.40	195.75	188.10	180.45	172.80	165.10
909.-	921.	266.05	234.80	230.95	223.30	215.65	208.00	200.35	192.70	185.05	177.40	169.75
921.-	933.	270.70	239.40	235.60	227.95	220.30	212.60	204.95	197.30	189.65	182.00	174.35
933.-	945.	275.60	244.05	240.20	232.55	224.90	217.25	209.60	201.95	194.30	186.65	179.00
945.-	957.	280.50	248.65	244.80	237.15	229.50	221.85	214.20	206.55	198.90	191.25	183.60
957.-	969.	285.40	253.25	249.45	241.80	234.15	226.50	218.85	211.20	203.50	195.85	188.20
969.-	981.	290.30	257.90	254.05	246.40	238.75	231.10	223.45	215.80	208.15	200.50	192.85
981.-	993.	295.20	262.50	258.70	251.00	243.35	235.70	228.05	220.40	212.75	205.10	197.45
993.-	1005.	300.10	267.10	263.30	255.65	248.00	240.35	232.70	225.05	217.40	209.70	202.05
1005.-	1017.	304.95	271.85	267.90	260.25	252.60	244.95	237.30	229.65	222.00	214.35	206.70
1017.-	1029.	309.85	276.75	272.70	264.90	257.20	249.55	241.90	234.25	226.60	218.95	211.30
1029.-	1041.	314.75	281.65	277.60	269.50	261.85	254.20	246.55	238.90	231.25	223.60	215.90
1041.-	1053.	319.65	286.55	282.50	274.35	266.45	258.80	251.15	243.50	235.85	228.20	220.55
1053.-	1065.	324.55	291.45	287.35	279.25	271.15	263.40	255.75	248.10	240.45	232.80	225.15
1065.-	1077.	329.45	296.35	292.25	284.15	276.05	268.05	260.40	252.75	245.10	237.45	229.75
1077.-	1089.	334.35	301.25	297.15	289.05	280.95	272.80	265.00	257.35	249.70	242.05	234.40
1089.-	1101.	339.25	306.15	302.05	293.95	285.85	277.70	269.60	261.95	254.30	246.65	239.00
1101.-	1113.	344.15	311.00	306.95	298.85	290.75	282.60	274.50	266.60	258.95	251.30	243.60
1113.-	1125.	349.05	315.90	311.85	303.75	295.65	287.50	279.40	271.25	263.55	255.90	248.25
1125.-	1137.	353.95	320.80	316.75	308.65	300.50	292.40	284.30	276.15	268.15	260.50	252.85
1137.-	1149.	359.10	325.95	321.90	313.80	305.65	297.55	289.45	281.30	273.20	265.35	257.70
1149.-	1161.	364.95	331.45	327.35	319.25	311.15	303.00	294.90	286.80	278.65	270.55	262.85
1161.-	1173.	371.05	336.90	332.85	324.70	316.60	308.45	300.35	292.25	284.10	276.00	268.00
1173.-	1185.	377.15	342.35	338.30	330.20	322.05	313.95	305.80	297.70	289.60	281.45	273.35
1185.-	1197.	383.25	347.80	343.75	335.65	327.50	319.40	311.30	303.15	295.05	286.95	278.80
1197.-	1209.	389.35	353.30	349.20	341.10	333.00	324.85	316.75	308.65	300.50	292.40	284.25
1209.-	1221.	395.45	358.75	354.70	346.55	338.45	330.35	322.20	314.10	306.00	297.85	289.75
1221.-	1233.	401.55	364.55	360.15	352.05	343.90	335.80	327.70	319.55	311.45	303.35	295.20
1233.-	1245.	407.70	370.65	366.10	357.50	349.40	341.25	333.15	325.00	316.90	308.80	300.65
1245.-	1257.	413.80	376.75	372.20	363.15	354.85	346.70	338.60	330.50	322.35	314.25	306.15
1257.-	1269.	419.90	382.85	378.30	369.25	360.30	352.20	344.05	335.95	327.85	319.70	311.60
1269.-	1281.	426.00	388.95	384.45	375.35	366.25	357.65	349.55	341.40	333.30	325.20	317.05
1281.-	1293.	432.10	395.05	390.55	381.45	372.40	363.30	355.00	346.90	338.75	330.65	322.50
1293.-	1305.	438.20	401.20	396.65	387.55	378.50	369.40	360.45	352.35	344.20	336.10	328.00
1305.-	1317.	444.30	407.30	402.75	393.65	384.60	375.50	366.45	357.80	349.70	341.55	333.45
1317.-	1329.	450.45	413.40	408.85	399.80	390.70	381.65	372.55	363.50	355.15	347.05	338.90
1329.-	1341.	456.55	419.50	414.95	405.90	396.80	387.75	378.65	369.60	360.60	352.50	344.35
1341.-	1353.	462.65	425.60	421.05	412.00	402.90	393.85	384.75	375.70	366.60	357.95	349.85
1353.-	1365.	468.75	431.70	427.20	418.10	409.00	399.95	390.90	381.80	372.75	363.65	355.30
1365.-	1377.	474.85	437.80	433.30	424.20	415.15	406.05	397.00	387.90	378.85	369.75	360.75
1377.-	1389.	480.95	443.95	439.40	430.30	421.25	412.15	403.10	394.00	384.95	375.85	366.80
1389.-	1401.	487.10	450.05	445.50	436.45	427.35	418.25	409.20	400.10	391.05	382.00	372.90
1401.-	1413.	493.20	456.15	451.60	442.55	433.45	424.40	415.30	406.25	397.15	388.10	379.00
1413.-	1425.	499.30	462.25	457.70	448.65	439.55	430.50	421.40	412.35	403.25	394.20	385.10
1425.-	1437.	505.40	468.35	463.80	454.75	445.65	436.60	427.50	418.45	409.35	400.30	391.20
1437.-	1449.	511.50	474.45	469.95	460.85	451.80	442.70	433.65	424.55	415.50	406.40	397.30
1449.-	1461.	517.60	480.55	476.05	466.95	457.90	448.80	439.75	430.65	421.60	412.50	403.45
1461.-	1473.	523.70	486.70	482.15	473.05	464.00	454.90	445.85	436.75	427.70	418.60	409.55
1473.-	1485.	529.85	492.80	488.25	479.20	470.10	461.00	451.95	442.90	433.80	424.75	415.65
1485.-	1497.	535.95	498.90	494.35	485.30	476.20	467.15	458.05	449.00	439.90	430.85	421.75
1497.-	1509.	542.05	505.00	500.45	491.40	482.30	473.25	464.15	455.10	446.00	436.95	427.85
1509.-	1521.	548.15	511.10	506.55	497.50	488.40	479.35	470.25	461.20	452.10	443.05	433.95
1521.-	1533.	554.25	517.20	512.70	503.60	494.55	485.45	476.40	467.30	458.25	449.15	440.10
1533.-	1545.	560.35	523.30	518.80	509.70	500.65	491.55	482.50	473.40	464.35	455.25	446.20
1545.-	1557.	566.45	529.45	524.90	515.80	506.75	497.65	488.60	479.50	470.45	461.35	452.30

D-4 **This table is available on diskette (TOD). Vous pouvez obtenir cette table sur disquette (TSD).**

Simulated Canada Pension Plan Contributions

Weekly (52 Pay periods a year)

Students are advised to use this table for classroom purposes only. Although accurate, it has fewer categories of pay amounts than the real table.

Pay From	To	CPP	Pay From	To	CPP	Pay From	To	CPP	Pay From	To	CPP	Pay From	To	CPP
-	67.30	-	134.01	135.00	2.15	206.01	207.00	4.45	278.01	279.00	6.76	350.01	351.00	9.06
67.31	67.83	0.01	135.01	136.00	2.18	207.01	208.00	4.49	279.01	280.00	6.79	351.01	352.00	9.09
67.84	68.19	0.02	136.01	137.00	2.21	208.01	209.00	4.52	280.01	281.00	6.82	352.01	353.00	9.13
68.20	68.54	0.03	137.01	138.00	2.25	209.01	210.00	4.55	281.01	282.00	6.85	353.01	354.00	9.16
68.55	68.90	0.05	138.01	139.00	2.28	210.01	211.00	4.58	282.01	283.00	6.89	354.01	355.00	9.19
68.91	69.26	0.06	139.01	140.00	2.31	211.01	212.00	4.61	283.01	284.00	6.92	355.01	356.00	9.22
69.27	69.62	0.07	140.01	141.00	2.34	212.01	213.00	4.65	284.01	285.00	6.95	356.01	357.00	9.25
69.63	69.99	0.08	141.01	142.00	2.37	213.01	214.00	4.68	285.01	286.00	6.98	357.01	358.00	9.29
70.00	71.00	0.10	142.01	143.00	2.41	214.01	215.00	4.71	286.01	287.00	7.01	358.01	359.00	9.32
71.01	72.00	0.13	143.01	144.00	2.44	215.01	216.00	4.74	287.01	288.00	7.05	359.01	360.00	9.35
72.01	73.00	0.17	144.01	145.00	2.47	216.01	217.00	4.77	288.01	289.00	7.08	360.01	361.00	9.38
73.01	74.00	0.20	145.01	146.00	2.50	217.01	218.00	4.81	289.01	290.00	7.11	361.01	362.00	9.41
74.01	75.00	0.23	146.01	147.00	2.53	218.01	219.00	4.84	290.01	291.00	7.14	362.01	363.00	9.45
75.01	76.00	0.26	147.01	148.00	2.57	219.01	220.00	4.87	291.01	292.00	7.17	363.01	364.00	9.48
76.01	77.00	0.29	148.01	149.00	2.60	220.01	221.00	4.90	292.01	293.00	7.21	364.01	365.00	9.51
77.01	78.00	0.33	149.01	150.00	2.63	221.01	222.00	4.93	293.01	294.00	7.24	365.01	366.00	9.54
78.01	79.00	0.36	150.01	151.00	2.66	222.01	223.00	4.97	294.01	295.00	7.27	366.01	367.00	9.57
79.01	80.00	0.39	151.01	152.00	2.69	223.01	224.00	5.00	295.01	296.00	7.30	367.01	368.00	9.61
80.01	81.00	0.42	152.01	153.00	2.73	224.01	225.00	5.03	296.01	297.00	7.33	368.01	369.00	9.64
81.01	82.00	0.45	153.01	154.00	2.76	225.01	226.00	5.06	297.01	298.00	7.37	369.01	370.00	9.67
82.01	83.00	0.49	154.01	155.00	2.79	226.01	227.00	5.09	298.01	299.00	7.40	370.01	371.00	9.70
83.01	84.00	0.52	155.01	156.00	2.82	227.01	228.00	5.13	299.01	300.00	7.43	371.01	372.00	9.73
84.01	85.00	0.55	156.01	157.00	2.85	228.01	229.00	5.16	300.01	301.00	7.46	372.01	373.00	9.77
85.01	86.00	0.58	157.01	158.00	2.89	229.01	230.00	5.19	301.01	302.00	7.49	373.01	374.00	9.80
86.01	87.00	0.61	158.01	159.00	2.92	230.01	231.00	5.22	302.01	303.00	7.53	374.01	375.00	9.83
87.01	88.00	0.65	159.01	160.00	2.95	231.01	232.00	5.25	303.01	304.00	7.56	375.01	376.00	9.86
88.01	89.00	0.68	160.01	161.00	2.98	232.01	233.00	5.29	304.01	305.00	7.59	376.01	377.00	9.89
89.01	90.00	0.71	161.01	162.00	3.01	233.01	234.00	5.32	305.01	306.00	7.62	377.01	378.00	9.93
90.01	91.00	0.74	162.01	163.00	3.05	234.01	235.00	5.35	306.01	307.00	7.65	378.01	379.00	9.96
91.01	92.00	0.77	163.01	164.00	3.08	235.01	236.00	5.38	307.01	308.00	7.69	379.01	380.00	9.99
92.01	93.00	0.81	164.01	165.00	3.11	236.01	237.00	5.41	308.01	309.00	7.72	380.01	381.00	10.02
93.01	94.00	0.84	165.01	166.00	3.14	237.01	238.00	5.45	309.01	310.00	7.75	381.01	382.00	10.05
94.01	95.00	0.87	166.01	167.00	3.17	238.01	239.00	5.48	310.01	311.00	7.78	382.01	383.00	10.09
95.01	96.00	0.90	167.01	168.00	3.21	239.01	240.00	5.51	311.01	312.00	7.81	383.01	384.00	10.12
96.01	97.00	0.93	168.01	169.00	3.24	240.01	241.00	5.54	312.01	313.00	7.85	384.01	385.00	10.15
97.01	98.00	0.97	169.01	170.00	3.27	241.01	242.00	5.57	313.01	314.00	7.88	385.01	386.00	10.18
98.01	99.00	1.00	170.01	171.00	3.30	242.01	243.00	5.61	314.01	315.00	7.91	386.01	387.00	10.21
99.01	100.00	1.03	171.01	172.00	3.33	243.01	244.00	5.64	315.01	316.00	7.94	387.01	388.00	10.25
100.01	101.00	1.06	172.01	173.00	3.37	244.01	245.00	5.67	316.01	317.00	7.97	388.01	389.00	10.28
101.01	102.00	1.09	173.01	174.00	3.40	245.01	246.00	5.70	317.01	318.00	8.01	389.01	390.00	10.31
102.01	103.00	1.13	174.01	175.00	3.43	246.01	247.00	5.73	318.01	319.00	8.04	390.01	391.00	10.34
103.01	104.00	1.16	175.01	176.00	3.46	247.01	248.00	5.77	319.01	320.00	8.07	391.01	392.00	10.37
104.01	105.00	1.19	176.01	177.00	3.49	248.01	249.00	5.80	320.01	321.00	8.10	392.01	393.00	10.41
105.01	106.00	1.22	177.01	178.00	3.53	249.01	250.00	5.83	321.01	322.00	8.13	393.01	394.00	10.44
106.01	107.00	1.25	178.01	179.00	3.56	250.01	251.00	5.86	322.01	323.00	8.17	394.01	395.00	10.47
107.01	108.00	1.29	179.01	180.00	3.59	251.01	252.00	5.89	323.01	324.00	8.20	395.01	396.00	10.50
108.01	109.00	1.32	180.01	181.00	3.62	252.01	253.00	5.93	324.01	325.00	8.23	396.01	397.00	10.53
109.01	110.00	1.35	181.01	182.00	3.65	253.01	254.00	5.96	325.01	326.00	8.26	397.01	398.00	10.57
110.01	111.00	1.38	182.01	183.00	3.69	254.01	255.00	5.99	326.01	327.00	8.29	398.01	399.00	10.60
111.01	112.00	1.41	183.01	184.00	3.72	255.01	256.00	6.02	327.01	328.00	8.33	399.01	400.00	10.63
112.01	113.00	1.45	184.01	185.00	3.75	256.01	257.00	6.05	328.01	329.00	8.36	400.01	401.00	10.66
113.01	114.00	1.48	185.01	186.00	3.78	257.01	258.00	6.09	329.01	330.00	8.39	401.01	402.00	10.69
114.01	115.00	1.51	186.01	187.00	3.81	258.01	259.00	6.12	330.01	331.00	8.42	402.01	403.00	10.73
115.01	116.00	1.54	187.01	188.00	3.85	259.01	260.00	6.15	331.01	332.00	8.45	403.01	404.00	10.76
116.01	117.00	1.57	188.01	189.00	3.88	260.01	261.00	6.18	332.01	333.00	8.49	404.01	405.00	10.79
117.01	118.00	1.61	189.01	190.00	3.91	261.01	262.00	6.21	333.01	334.00	8.52	405.01	406.00	10.82
118.01	119.00	1.64	190.01	191.00	3.94	262.01	263.00	6.25	334.01	335.00	8.55	406.01	407.00	10.85
119.01	120.00	1.67	191.01	192.00	3.97	263.01	264.00	6.28	335.01	336.00	8.58	407.01	408.00	10.89
120.01	121.00	1.70	192.01	193.00	4.01	264.01	265.00	6.31	336.01	337.00	8.61	408.01	409.00	10.92
121.01	122.00	1.73	193.01	194.00	4.04	265.01	266.00	6.34	337.01	338.00	8.65	409.01	410.00	10.95
122.01	123.00	1.77	194.01	195.00	4.07	266.01	267.00	6.37	338.01	339.00	8.68	410.01	411.00	10.98
123.01	124.00	1.80	195.01	196.00	4.10	267.01	268.00	6.41	339.01	340.00	8.71	411.01	412.00	11.01
124.01	125.00	1.83	196.01	197.00	4.13	268.01	269.00	6.44	340.01	341.00	8.74	412.01	413.00	11.05
125.01	126.00	1.86	197.01	198.00	4.17	269.01	270.00	6.47	341.01	342.00	8.77	413.01	414.00	11.08
126.01	127.00	1.89	198.01	199.00	4.20	270.01	271.00	6.50	342.01	343.00	8.81	414.01	415.00	11.11
127.01	128.00	1.93	199.01	200.00	4.23	271.01	272.00	6.53	343.01	344.00	8.84	415.01	416.00	11.14
128.01	129.00	1.96	200.01	201.00	4.26	272.01	273.00	6.57	344.01	345.00	8.87	416.01	417.00	11.17
129.01	130.00	1.99	201.01	202.00	4.29	273.01	274.00	6.60	345.01	346.00	8.90	417.01	418.00	11.21
130.01	131.00	2.02	202.01	203.00	4.33	274.01	275.00	6.63	346.01	347.00	8.93	418.01	419.00	11.24
131.01	132.00	2.05	203.01	204.00	4.36	275.01	276.00	6.66	347.01	348.00	8.97	419.01	420.00	11.27
132.01	133.00	2.09	204.01	205.00	4.39	276.01	277.00	6.69	348.01	349.00	9.00	420.01	421.00	11.30
133.01	134.00	2.12	205.01	206.00	4.42	277.01	278.00	6.73	349.01	350.00	9.03	421.01	422.00	11.33

Simulated Canada Pension Plan Contributions

Weekly (52 Pay periods a year)

Students are advised to use this table for classroom purposes only. Although accurate, it has fewer categories of pay amounts than the real table.

Pay From	Pay To	CPP	Pay From	Pay To	CPP	Pay From	Pay To	CPP	Pay From	Pay To	CPP	Pay From	Pay To	CPP
422.01	423.00	11.37	495.01	496.00	13.70	636.01	638.00	18.23	782.01	784.00	22.90	1,120.01	1,125.00	33.77
423.01	424.00	11.40	496.01	497.00	13.73	638.01	640.00	18.29	784.01	786.00	22.97	1,125.01	1,130.00	33.93
424.01	425.00	11.43	497.01	498.00	13.77	640.01	642.00	18.36	786.01	788.00	23.03	1,130.01	1,135.00	34.09
425.01	426.00	11.46	498.01	499.00	13.80	642.01	644.00	18.42	788.01	790.00	23.09	1,135.01	1,140.00	34.25
426.01	427.00	11.49	499.01	500.00	13.83	644.01	646.00	18.49	790.01	792.00	23.16	1,140.01	1,145.00	34.41
427.01	428.00	11.53	500.01	502.00	13.88	646.01	648.00	18.55	792.01	794.00	23.22	1,145.01	1,150.00	34.57
428.01	429.00	11.56	502.01	504.00	13.94	648.01	650.00	18.61	794.01	796.00	23.29	1,150.01	1,155.00	34.73
429.01	430.00	11.59	504.01	506.00	14.01	650.01	652.00	18.68	796.01	798.00	23.35	1,155.01	1,160.00	34.89
430.01	431.00	11.62	506.01	508.00	14.07	652.01	654.00	18.74	798.01	800.00	23.41	1,160.01	1,165.00	35.05
431.01	432.00	11.65	508.01	510.00	14.13	654.01	656.00	18.81	800.01	805.00	23.53	1,165.01	1,170.00	35.21
432.01	433.00	11.69	510.01	512.00	14.20	656.01	658.00	18.87	805.01	810.00	23.69	1,170.01	1,175.00	35.37
433.01	434.00	11.72	512.01	514.00	14.26	658.01	660.00	18.93	810.01	815.00	23.85	1,175.01	1,180.00	35.53
434.01	435.00	11.75	514.01	516.00	14.33	660.01	662.00	19.00	815.01	820.00	24.01	1,180.01	1,185.00	35.69
435.01	436.00	11.78	516.01	518.00	14.39	662.01	664.00	19.06	820.01	825.00	24.17	1,185.01	1,190.00	35.85
436.01	437.00	11.81	518.01	520.00	14.45	664.01	666.00	19.13	825.01	830.00	24.33	1,190.01	1,195.00	36.01
437.01	438.00	11.85	520.01	522.00	14.52	666.01	668.00	19.19	830.01	835.00	24.49	1,195.01	1,200.00	36.17
438.01	439.00	11.88	522.01	524.00	14.58	668.01	670.00	19.25	835.01	840.00	24.65	1,200.01	1,205.00	36.33
439.01	440.00	11.91	524.01	526.00	14.65	670.01	672.00	19.32	840.01	845.00	24.81	1,205.01	1,210.00	36.49
440.01	441.00	11.94	526.01	528.00	14.71	672.01	674.00	19.38	845.01	850.00	24.97	1,210.01	1,215.00	36.65
441.01	442.00	11.97	528.01	530.00	14.77	674.01	676.00	19.45	850.01	855.00	25.13	1,215.01	1,220.00	36.81
442.01	443.00	12.01	530.01	532.00	14.84	676.01	678.00	19.51	855.01	860.00	25.29	1,220.01	1,225.00	36.97
443.01	444.00	12.04	532.01	534.00	14.90	678.01	680.00	19.57	860.01	865.00	25.45	1,225.01	1,230.00	37.13
444.01	445.00	12.07	534.01	536.00	14.97	680.01	682.00	19.64	865.01	870.00	25.61	1,230.01	1,235.00	37.29
445.01	446.00	12.10	536.01	538.00	15.03	682.01	684.00	19.70	870.01	875.00	25.77	1,235.01	1,240.00	37.45
446.01	447.00	12.13	538.01	540.00	15.09	684.01	686.00	19.77	875.01	880.00	25.93	1,240.01	1,245.00	37.61
447.01	448.00	12.17	540.01	542.00	15.16	686.01	688.00	19.83	880.01	885.00	26.09	1,245.01	1,250.00	37.77
448.01	449.00	12.20	542.01	544.00	15.22	688.01	690.00	19.89	885.01	890.00	26.25	1,250.01	1,255.00	37.93
449.01	450.00	12.23	544.01	546.00	15.29	690.01	692.00	19.96	890.01	895.00	26.41	1,255.01	1,260.00	38.09
450.01	451.00	12.26	546.01	548.00	15.35	692.01	694.00	20.02	895.01	900.00	26.57	1,260.01	1,265.00	38.25
451.01	452.00	12.29	548.01	550.00	15.41	694.01	696.00	20.09	900.01	905.00	26.73	1,265.01	1,270.00	38.41
452.01	453.00	12.33	550.01	552.00	15.48	696.01	698.00	20.15	905.01	910.00	26.89	1,270.01	1,275.00	38.57
453.01	454.00	12.36	552.01	554.00	15.54	698.01	700.00	20.21	910.01	915.00	27.05	1,275.01	1,280.00	38.73
454.01	455.00	12.39	554.01	556.00	15.61	700.01	702.00	20.28	915.01	920.00	27.21	1,280.01	1,285.00	38.89
455.01	456.00	12.42	556.01	558.00	15.67	702.01	704.00	20.34	920.01	925.00	27.37	1,285.01	1,290.00	39.05
456.01	457.00	12.45	558.01	560.00	15.73	704.01	706.00	20.41	925.01	930.00	27.53	1,290.01	1,295.00	39.21
457.01	458.00	12.49	560.01	562.00	15.80	706.01	708.00	20.47	930.01	935.00	27.69	1,295.01	1,300.00	39.37
458.01	459.00	12.52	562.01	564.00	15.86	708.01	710.00	20.53	935.01	940.00	27.85	1,300.01	1,305.00	39.53
459.01	460.00	12.55	564.01	566.00	15.93	710.01	712.00	20.60	940.01	945.00	28.01	1,305.01	1,310.00	39.69
460.01	461.00	12.58	566.01	568.00	15.99	712.01	714.00	20.66	945.01	950.00	28.17	1,310.01	1,315.00	39.85
461.01	462.00	12.61	568.01	570.00	16.05	714.01	716.00	20.73	950.01	955.00	28.33	1,315.01	1,320.00	40.01
462.01	463.00	12.65	570.01	572.00	16.12	716.01	718.00	20.79	955.01	960.00	28.49	1,320.01	1,325.00	40.17
463.01	464.00	12.68	572.01	574.00	16.18	718.01	720.00	20.85	960.01	965.00	28.65	1,325.01	1,330.00	40.33
464.01	465.00	12.71	574.01	576.00	16.25	720.01	722.00	20.92	965.01	970.00	28.81	1,330.01	1,335.00	40.49
465.01	466.00	12.74	576.01	578.00	16.31	722.01	724.00	20.98	970.01	975.00	28.97	1,335.01	1,340.00	40.65
466.01	467.00	12.77	578.01	580.00	16.37	724.01	726.00	21.05	975.01	980.00	29.13	1,340.01	1,345.00	40.81
467.01	468.00	12.81	580.01	582.00	16.44	726.01	728.00	21.11	980.01	985.00	29.29	1,345.01	1,350.00	40.97
468.01	469.00	12.84	582.01	584.00	16.50	728.01	730.00	21.17	985.01	990.00	29.45	1,350.01	1,355.00	41.13
469.01	470.00	12.87	584.01	586.00	16.57	730.01	732.00	21.24	990.01	995.00	29.61	1,355.01	1,360.00	41.29
470.01	471.00	12.90	586.01	588.00	16.63	732.01	734.00	21.30	995.01	1,000.00	29.77	1,360.01	1,365.00	41.45
471.01	472.00	12.93	588.01	590.00	16.69	734.01	736.00	21.37	1,000.01	1,005.00	29.93	1,365.01	1,370.00	41.61
472.01	473.00	12.97	590.01	592.00	16.76	736.01	738.00	21.43	1,005.01	1,010.00	30.09	1,370.01	1,375.00	41.77
473.01	474.00	13.00	592.01	594.00	16.82	738.01	740.00	21.49	1,010.01	1,015.00	30.25	1,375.01	1,380.00	41.93
474.01	475.00	13.03	594.01	596.00	16.89	740.01	742.00	21.56	1,015.01	1,020.00	30.41	1,380.01	1,385.00	42.09
475.01	476.00	13.06	596.01	598.00	16.95	742.01	744.00	21.62	1,020.01	1,025.00	30.57	1,385.01	1,390.00	42.25
476.01	477.00	13.09	598.01	600.00	17.01	744.01	746.00	21.69	1,025.01	1,030.00	30.73	1,390.01	1,395.00	42.41
477.01	478.00	13.13	600.01	602.00	17.08	746.01	748.00	21.75	1,030.01	1,035.00	30.89	1,395.01	1,400.00	42.57
478.01	479.00	13.16	602.01	604.00	17.14	748.01	750.00	21.81	1,035.01	1,040.00	31.05	1,400.01	1,405.00	42.73
479.01	480.00	13.19	604.01	606.00	17.21	750.01	752.00	21.88	1,040.01	1,045.00	31.21	1,405.01	1,410.00	42.89
480.01	481.00	13.22	606.01	608.00	17.27	752.01	754.00	21.94	1,045.01	1,050.00	31.37	1,410.01	1,415.00	43.05
481.01	482.00	13.25	608.01	610.00	17.33	754.01	756.00	22.01	1,050.01	1,055.00	31.53	1,415.01	1,420.00	43.21
482.01	483.00	13.29	610.01	612.00	17.40	756.01	758.00	22.07	1,055.01	1,060.00	31.69	1,420.01	1,425.00	43.37
483.01	484.00	13.32	612.01	614.00	17.46	758.01	760.00	22.13	1,060.01	1,065.00	31.85	1,425.01	1,430.00	43.53
484.01	485.00	13.35	614.01	616.00	17.53	760.01	762.00	22.20	1,065.01	1,070.00	32.01	1,430.01	1,435.00	43.69
485.01	486.00	13.38	616.01	618.00	17.59	762.01	764.00	22.26	1,070.01	1,075.00	32.17	1,435.01	1,440.00	43.85
486.01	487.00	13.41	618.01	620.00	17.65	764.01	766.00	22.33	1,075.01	1,080.00	32.33	1,440.01	1,445.00	44.01
487.01	488.00	13.45	620.01	622.00	17.72	766.01	768.00	22.39	1,080.01	1,085.00	32.49	1,445.01	1,450.00	44.17
488.01	489.00	13.48	622.01	624.00	17.78	768.01	770.00	22.45	1,085.01	1,090.00	32.65	1,450.01	1,455.00	44.33
489.01	490.00	13.51	624.01	626.00	17.85	770.01	772.00	22.52	1,090.01	1,095.00	32.81	1,455.01	1,460.00	44.49
490.01	491.00	13.54	626.01	628.00	17.91	772.01	774.00	22.58	1,095.01	1,100.00	32.97	1,460.01	1,465.00	44.65
491.01	492.00	13.57	628.01	630.00	17.97	774.01	776.00	22.65	1,100.01	1,105.00	33.13	1,465.01	1,470.00	44.81
492.01	493.00	13.61	630.01	632.00	18.04	776.01	778.00	22.71	1,105.01	1,110.00	33.29	1,470.01	1,475.00	44.97
493.01	494.00	13.64	632.01	634.00	18.10	778.01	780.00	22.77	1,110.01	1,115.00	33.45	1,475.01	1,480.00	45.13
494.01	495.00	13.67	634.01	636.00	18.17	780.01	782.00	22.84	1,115.01	1,120.00	33.61	1,480.01	1,485.00	45.29

Simulated Employment Insurance Premiums

Any number of pay periods a year

Students are advised to use this table for classroom purposes only. Although accurate, it has fewer categories of pay amounts than the real table.

Insurable Earnings From	To	EI remiu	Insurable Earnings From	To	EI remiu	Insurable Earnings From	To	EI remiu	Insurable Earnings From	To	EI remiu	Insurable Earnings From	To	EI remium
-	0.55	0.01	26.83	27.83	0.74	98.84	100.00	2.68	171.01	172.00	4.63	246.01	247.00	6.66
0.56	0.92	0.02	27.84	28.83	0.77	100.01	101.00	2.71	172.01	173.00	4.66	247.01	248.00	6.68
0.93	1.29	0.03	28.84	29.83	0.79	101.01	102.00	2.74	173.01	174.00	4.68	248.01	249.00	6.71
1.30	1.66	0.04	29.84	30.83	0.82	102.01	103.00	2.77	174.01	175.00	4.71	249.01	250.00	6.74
1.67	2.03	0.05	30.84	31.83	0.85	103.01	104.00	2.79	175.01	176.00	4.74	250.01	251.00	6.76
2.04	2.40	0.06	31.84	32.83	0.87	104.01	105.00	2.82	176.01	177.00	4.77	251.01	252.00	6.79
2.41	2.77	0.07	32.84	33.83	0.90	105.01	106.00	2.85	177.01	178.00	4.79	252.01	253.00	6.82
2.78	3.14	0.08	33.84	34.83	0.93	106.01	107.00	2.88	178.01	179.00	4.82	253.01	254.00	6.84
3.15	3.51	0.09	34.84	35.83	0.95	107.01	108.00	2.90	179.01	180.00	4.85	254.01	255.00	6.87
3.52	3.88	0.10	35.84	36.83	0.98	108.01	109.00	2.93	180.01	181.00	4.87	255.01	256.00	6.90
3.89	4.25	0.11	36.84	37.83	1.01	109.01	110.00	2.96	181.01	182.00	4.90	256.01	257.00	6.93
4.26	4.62	0.12	37.84	38.83	1.04	110.01	111.00	2.98	182.01	183.00	4.93	257.01	258.00	6.95
4.63	4.99	0.13	38.84	39.83	1.06	111.01	112.00	3.01	183.01	184.00	4.95	258.01	259.00	6.98
5.00	5.36	0.14	39.84	40.83	1.09	112.01	113.00	3.04	184.01	185.00	4.98	259.01	260.00	7.01
5.37	5.73	0.15	40.84	41.83	1.12	113.01	114.00	3.06	185.01	186.00	5.01	260.01	261.00	7.03
5.74	6.10	0.16	41.84	42.83	1.14	114.01	115.00	3.09	186.01	187.00	5.04	261.01	262.00	7.06
6.11	6.47	0.17	42.84	43.83	1.17	115.01	116.00	3.12	187.01	188.00	5.06	262.01	263.00	7.09
6.48	6.84	0.18	43.84	44.83	1.20	116.01	117.00	3.15	188.01	189.00	5.09	263.01	264.00	7.11
6.85	7.21	0.19	44.84	45.83	1.22	117.01	118.00	3.17	189.01	190.00	5.12	264.01	265.00	7.14
7.22	7.58	0.20	45.84	46.83	1.25	118.01	119.00	3.20	190.01	191.00	5.14	265.01	266.00	7.17
7.59	7.95	0.21	46.84	47.83	1.28	119.01	120.00	3.23	191.01	192.00	5.17	266.01	267.00	7.20
7.96	8.32	0.22	47.84	48.83	1.31	120.01	121.00	3.25	192.01	193.00	5.20	267.01	268.00	7.22
8.33	8.69	0.23	48.84	49.83	1.33	121.01	122.00	3.28	193.01	194.00	5.22	268.01	269.00	7.25
8.70	9.06	0.24	49.84	50.83	1.36	122.01	123.00	3.31	194.01	195.00	5.25	269.01	270.00	7.28
9.07	9.43	0.25	50.84	51.83	1.39	123.01	124.00	3.33	195.01	196.00	5.28	270.01	271.00	7.30
9.44	9.80	0.26	51.84	52.83	1.41	124.01	125.00	3.36	196.01	197.00	5.31	271.01	272.00	7.33
9.81	10.17	0.27	52.84	53.83	1.44	125.01	126.00	3.39	197.01	198.00	5.33	272.01	273.00	7.36
10.18	10.54	0.28	53.84	54.83	1.47	126.01	127.00	3.42	198.01	199.00	5.36	273.01	274.00	7.38
10.55	10.91	0.29	54.84	55.83	1.49	127.01	128.00	3.44	199.01	200.00	5.39	274.01	275.00	7.41
10.92	11.28	0.30	55.84	56.83	1.52	128.01	129.00	3.47	200.01	201.00	5.41	275.01	276.00	7.44
11.29	11.65	0.31	56.84	57.83	1.55	129.01	130.00	3.50	201.01	202.00	5.44	276.01	277.00	7.47
11.66	12.02	0.32	57.84	58.83	1.58	130.01	131.00	3.52	202.01	203.00	5.47	277.01	278.00	7.49
12.03	12.39	0.33	58.84	59.83	1.60	131.01	132.00	3.55	203.01	204.00	5.49	278.01	279.00	7.52
12.40	12.76	0.34	59.84	60.83	1.63	132.01	133.00	3.58	204.01	205.00	5.52	279.01	280.00	7.55
12.77	13.13	0.35	60.84	61.83	1.66	133.01	134.00	3.60	205.01	206.00	5.55	280.01	281.00	7.57
13.14	13.50	0.36	61.84	62.83	1.68	134.01	135.00	3.63	206.01	207.00	5.58	281.01	282.00	7.60
13.51	13.87	0.37	62.84	63.83	1.71	135.01	136.00	3.66	207.01	208.00	5.60	282.01	283.00	7.63
13.88	14.24	0.38	63.84	64.83	1.74	136.01	137.00	3.69	208.01	209.00	5.63	283.01	284.00	7.65
14.25	14.61	0.39	64.84	65.83	1.76	137.01	138.00	3.71	209.01	210.00	5.66	284.01	285.00	7.68
14.62	14.98	0.40	65.84	66.83	1.79	138.01	139.00	3.74	210.01	211.00	5.68	285.01	286.00	7.71
14.99	15.35	0.41	66.84	67.83	1.82	139.01	140.00	3.77	211.01	212.00	5.71	286.01	287.00	7.74
15.36	15.72	0.42	67.84	68.83	1.85	140.01	141.00	3.79	212.01	213.00	5.74	287.01	288.00	7.76
15.73	16.09	0.43	68.84	69.83	1.87	141.01	142.00	3.82	213.01	214.00	5.76	288.01	289.00	7.79
16.10	16.46	0.44	69.84	70.83	1.90	142.01	143.00	3.85	214.01	215.00	5.79	289.01	290.00	7.82
16.47	16.83	0.45	70.84	71.83	1.93	143.01	144.00	3.87	215.01	216.00	5.82	290.01	291.00	7.84
16.84	17.20	0.46	71.84	72.83	1.95	144.01	145.00	3.90	216.01	217.00	5.85	291.01	292.00	7.87
17.21	17.57	0.47	72.84	73.83	1.98	145.01	146.00	3.93	217.01	218.00	5.87	292.01	293.00	7.90
17.58	17.94	0.48	73.84	74.83	2.01	146.01	147.00	3.96	218.01	219.00	5.90	293.01	294.00	7.92
17.95	18.31	0.49	74.84	75.83	2.03	147.01	148.00	3.98	219.01	220.00	5.93	294.01	295.00	7.95
18.32	18.68	0.50	75.84	76.83	2.06	148.01	149.00	4.01	220.01	221.00	5.95	295.01	296.00	7.98
18.69	19.05	0.51	76.84	77.83	2.09	149.01	150.00	4.04	221.01	222.00	5.98	296.01	297.00	8.01
19.06	19.42	0.52	77.84	78.83	2.12	150.01	151.00	4.06	222.01	223.00	6.01	297.01	298.00	8.03
19.43	19.79	0.53	78.84	79.83	2.14	151.01	152.00	4.09	223.01	224.00	6.03	298.01	299.00	8.06
19.80	20.16	0.54	79.84	80.83	2.17	152.01	153.00	4.12	224.01	225.00	6.06	299.01	300.00	8.09
20.17	20.53	0.55	80.84	81.83	2.20	153.01	154.00	4.14	225.01	226.00	6.09	300.01	301.00	8.11
20.54	20.90	0.56	81.84	82.83	2.22	154.01	155.00	4.17	226.01	227.00	6.12	301.01	302.00	8.14
20.91	21.27	0.57	82.84	83.83	2.25	155.01	156.00	4.20	227.01	228.00	6.14	302.01	303.00	8.17
21.28	21.64	0.58	83.84	84.83	2.28	156.01	157.00	4.23	228.01	229.00	6.17	303.01	304.00	8.19
21.65	22.01	0.59	84.84	85.83	2.30	157.01	158.00	4.25	229.01	230.00	6.20	304.01	305.00	8.22
22.02	22.38	0.60	85.84	86.83	2.33	158.01	159.00	4.28	230.01	231.00	6.22	305.01	306.00	8.25
22.39	22.75	0.61	86.84	87.83	2.36	159.01	160.00	4.31	231.01	232.00	6.25	306.01	307.00	8.28
22.76	23.12	0.62	87.84	88.83	2.39	160.01	161.00	4.33	232.01	233.00	6.28	307.01	308.00	8.30
23.13	23.49	0.63	88.84	89.83	2.41	161.01	162.00	4.36	233.01	234.00	6.30	308.01	309.00	8.33
23.50	23.86	0.64	89.84	90.83	2.44	162.01	163.00	4.39	234.01	235.00	6.33	309.01	310.00	8.36
23.87	24.23	0.65	90.84	91.83	2.47	163.01	164.00	4.41	235.01	236.00	6.36	310.01	311.00	8.38
24.24	24.60	0.66	91.84	92.83	2.49	164.01	165.00	4.44	236.01	237.00	6.39	311.01	312.00	8.41
24.61	24.97	0.67	92.84	93.83	2.52	165.01	166.00	4.47	237.01	238.00	6.41	312.01	313.00	8.44
24.98	25.34	0.68	93.84	94.83	2.55	166.01	167.00	4.50	238.01	239.00	6.44	313.01	314.00	8.46
25.35	25.71	0.69	94.84	95.83	2.57	167.01	168.00	4.52	239.01	240.00	6.47	314.01	315.00	8.49
25.72	26.08	0.70	95.84	96.83	2.60	168.01	169.00	4.55	240.01	241.00	6.49	315.01	316.00	8.52
26.09	26.45	0.71	96.84	97.83	2.63	169.01	170.00	4.58	241.01	242.00	6.52	316.01	317.00	8.55
26.46	26.82	0.72	97.84	98.83	2.66	170.01	171.00	4.60	242.01	243.00	6.55	317.01	318.00	8.57

Simulated Employment Insurance Premiums

Any number of pay periods a year

Students are advised to use this table for classroom purposes only. Although accurate, it has fewer categories of pay amounts than the real table.

Insurable Earnings From		Insurable Earnings To	EI remiu
318.01	~	319.00	8.60
319.01	~	321.00	8.64
321.01	~	323.00	8.69
323.01	~	325.00	8.75
325.01	~	327.00	8.80
327.01	~	329.00	8.86
329.01	~	331.00	8.91
331.01	~	333.00	8.96
333.01	~	335.00	9.02
335.01	~	337.00	9.07
337.01	~	339.00	9.13
339.01	~	341.00	9.18
341.01	~	343.00	9.23
343.01	~	345.00	9.29
345.01	~	347.00	9.34
347.01	~	349.00	9.40
349.01	~	351.00	9.45
351.01	~	353.00	9.50
353.01	~	355.00	9.56
355.01	~	357.00	9.61
357.01	~	359.00	9.67
359.01	~	361.00	9.72
361.01	~	363.00	9.77
363.01	~	365.00	9.83
365.01	~	367.00	9.88
367.01	~	369.00	9.94
369.01	~	371.00	9.99
371.01	~	373.00	10.04
373.01	~	375.00	10.10
375.01	~	377.00	10.15
377.01	~	379.00	10.21
379.01	~	381.00	10.26
381.01	~	383.00	10.31
383.01	~	385.00	10.37
385.01	~	387.00	10.42
387.01	~	389.00	10.48
389.01	~	391.00	10.53
391.01	~	393.00	10.58
393.01	~	395.00	10.64
395.01	~	397.00	10.69
397.01	~	399.00	10.75
399.01	~	401.00	10.80
401.01	~	403.00	10.85
403.01	~	405.00	10.91
405.01	~	407.00	10.96
407.01	~	409.00	11.02
409.01	~	411.00	11.07
411.01	~	413.00	11.12
413.01	~	415.00	11.18
415.01	~	417.00	11.23
417.01	~	419.00	11.29
419.01	~	421.00	11.34
421.01	~	423.00	11.39
423.01	~	425.00	11.45
425.01	~	427.00	11.50
427.01	~	429.00	11.56
429.01	~	431.00	11.61
431.01	~	433.00	11.66
433.01	~	435.00	11.72
435.01	~	437.00	11.77
437.01	~	439.00	11.83
439.01	~	441.00	11.88
441.01	~	443.00	11.93
443.01	~	445.00	11.99
445.01	~	447.00	12.04
447.01	~	449.00	12.10
449.01	~	451.00	12.15
451.01	~	453.00	12.20
453.01	~	455.00	12.26
455.01	~	457.00	12.31
457.01	~	459.00	12.37
459.01	~	461.00	12.42
461.01	~	463.00	12.47

Insurable Earnings From		Insurable Earnings To	EI remiu
463.01	~	465.00	12.53
465.01	~	467.00	12.58
467.01	~	469.00	12.64
469.01	~	471.00	12.69
471.01	~	473.00	12.74
473.01	~	475.00	12.80
475.01	~	477.00	12.85
477.01	~	479.00	12.91
479.01	~	481.00	12.96
481.01	~	483.00	13.01
483.01	~	485.00	13.07
485.01	~	487.00	13.12
487.01	~	489.00	13.18
489.01	~	491.00	13.23
491.01	~	493.00	13.28
493.01	~	495.00	13.34
495.01	~	497.00	13.39
497.01	~	499.00	13.45
499.01	~	501.00	13.50
501.01	~	503.00	13.55
503.01	~	505.00	13.61
505.01	~	507.00	13.66
507.01	~	509.00	13.72
509.01	~	511.00	13.77
511.01	~	513.00	13.82
513.01	~	515.00	13.88
515.01	~	517.00	13.93
517.01	~	519.00	13.99
519.01	~	521.00	14.04
521.01	~	523.00	14.09
523.01	~	525.00	14.15
525.01	~	527.00	14.20
527.01	~	529.00	14.26
529.01	~	531.00	14.31
531.01	~	533.00	14.36
533.01	~	535.00	14.42
535.01	~	537.00	14.47
537.01	~	539.00	14.53
539.01	~	541.00	14.58
541.01	~	543.00	14.63
543.01	~	545.00	14.69
545.01	~	547.00	14.74
547.01	~	549.00	14.80
549.01	~	551.00	14.85
551.01	~	553.00	14.90
553.01	~	555.00	14.96
555.01	~	557.00	15.01
557.01	~	559.00	15.07
559.01	~	561.00	15.12
561.01	~	563.00	15.17
563.01	~	565.00	15.23
565.01	~	567.00	15.28
567.01	~	569.00	15.34
569.01	~	571.00	15.39
571.01	~	573.00	15.44
573.01	~	575.00	15.50
575.01	~	577.00	15.55
577.01	~	579.00	15.61
579.01	~	581.00	15.66
581.01	~	583.00	15.71
583.01	~	585.00	15.77
585.01	~	587.00	15.82
587.01	~	589.00	15.88
589.01	~	591.00	15.93
591.01	~	593.00	15.98
593.01	~	595.00	16.04
595.01	~	597.00	16.09
597.01	~	599.00	16.15
599.01	~	601.00	16.20
601.01	~	603.00	16.25
603.01	~	605.00	16.31
605.01	~	607.00	16.36
607.01	~	609.00	16.42

Insurable Earnings From		Insurable Earnings To	EI remiu
609.01	~	611.00	16.47
611.01	~	613.00	16.52
613.01	~	615.00	16.58
615.01	~	617.00	16.63
617.01	~	619.00	16.69
619.01	~	621.00	16.74
621.01	~	623.00	16.79
623.01	~	625.00	16.85
625.01	~	627.00	16.90
627.01	~	629.00	16.96
629.01	~	631.00	17.01
631.01	~	633.00	17.06
633.01	~	635.00	17.12
635.01	~	637.00	17.17
637.01	~	639.00	17.23
639.01	~	641.00	17.28
641.01	~	643.00	17.33
643.01	~	645.00	17.39
645.01	~	647.00	17.44
647.01	~	649.00	17.50
649.01	~	651.00	17.55
651.01	~	653.00	17.60
653.01	~	655.00	17.56
655.01	~	657.00	17.71
657.01	~	659.00	17.77
659.01	~	661.00	17.82
661.01	~	663.00	17.87
663.01	~	665.00	17.93
665.01	~	667.00	17.98
667.01	~	669.00	18.04
669.01	~	671.00	18.09
671.01	~	673.00	18.14
673.01	~	675.00	18.20
675.01	~	677.00	18.25
677.01	~	679.00	18.31
679.01	~	681.00	18.36
681.01	~	683.00	18.41
683.01	~	685.00	18.47
685.01	~	687.00	18.52
687.01	~	689.00	18.58
689.01	~	691.00	18.63
691.01	~	693.00	18.68
693.01	~	695.00	18.74
695.01	~	697.00	18.79
697.01	~	699.00	18.85
699.01	~	701.00	18.90
701.01	~	703.00	18.95
703.01	~	705.00	19.01
705.01	~	707.00	19.06
707.01	~	709.00	19.12
709.01	~	711.00	19.17
711.01	~	713.00	19.22
713.01	~	715.00	19.28
715.01	~	717.00	19.33
717.01	~	719.00	19.39
719.01	~	721.00	19.44
721.01	~	723.00	19.49
723.01	~	725.00	19.55
725.01	~	727.00	19.60
727.01	~	729.00	19.66
729.01	~	731.00	19.71
731.01	~	733.00	19.76
733.01	~	735.00	19.82
735.01	~	737.00	19.87
737.01	~	739.00	19.93
739.01	~	741.00	19.98
741.01	~	743.00	20.03
743.01	~	745.00	20.09
745.01	~	747.00	20.14
747.01	~	749.00	20.20
749.01	~	751.00	20.25
751.01	~	753.00	20.30
753.01	~	755.00	20.36

Insurable Earnings From		Insurable Earnings To	EI remiu
755.01	~	758.00	20.43
758.01	~	761.00	20.51
761.01	~	764.00	20.59
764.01	~	767.00	20.67
767.01	~	770.00	20.75
770.01	~	773.00	20.83
773.01	~	776.00	20.91
776.01	~	779.00	20.99
779.01	~	782.00	21.07
782.01	~	785.00	21.15
785.01	~	788.00	21.24
788.01	~	791.00	21.32
791.01	~	794.00	21.40
794.01	~	797.00	21.48
797.01	~	800.00	21.56
800.01	~	803.00	21.64
803.01	~	806.00	21.72
806.01	~	809.00	21.80
809.01	~	812.00	21.88
812.01	~	815.00	21.96
815.01	~	818.00	22.05
818.01	~	821.00	22.13
821.01	~	824.00	22.21
824.01	~	827.00	22.29
827.01	~	830.00	22.37
830.01	~	833.00	22.45
833.01	~	836.00	22.53
836.01	~	839.00	22.61
839.01	~	842.00	22.69
842.01	~	845.00	22.77
845.01	~	848.00	22.86
848.01	~	851.00	22.94
851.01	~	854.00	23.02
854.01	~	857.00	23.10
857.01	~	860.00	23.18
860.01	~	863.00	23.26
863.01	~	866.00	23.34
866.01	~	869.00	23.42
869.01	~	872.00	23.50
872.01	~	875.00	23.58
875.01	~	878.00	23.67
878.01	~	881.00	23.75
881.01	~	884.00	23.83
884.01	~	887.00	23.91
887.01	~	890.00	23.99
890.01	~	893.00	24.07
893.01	~	896.00	24.15
896.01	~	899.00	24.23
899.01	~	902.00	24.31
902.01	~	905.00	24.39
905.01	~	908.00	24.48
908.01	~	911.00	24.56
911.01	~	914.00	24.64
914.01	~	917.00	24.72
917.01	~	920.00	24.80
920.01	~	923.00	24.88
923.01	~	926.00	24.96
926.01	~	929.00	25.04
929.01	~	932.00	25.12
932.01	~	935.00	25.20
935.01	~	938.00	25.29
938.01	~	941.00	25.37
941.01	~	944.00	25.45
944.01	~	947.00	25.53
947.01	~	950.00	25.61
950.01	~	953.00	25.69
953.01	~	956.00	25.77
956.01	~	959.00	25.85
959.01	~	962.00	25.93
962.01	~	965.00	26.01
965.01	~	968.00	26.10
968.01	~	971.00	26.18
971.01	~	974.00	26.26

Insurable Earnings From		Insurable Earnings To	EI remium
974.01	~	979.00	26.37
979.01	~	984.00	26.50
984.01	~	989.00	26.64
989.01	~	994.00	26.77
994.01	~	999.00	26.91
999.01	~	1,004.00	27.04
1,004.01	~	1,009.00	27.18
1,009.01	~	1,014.00	27.31
1,014.01	~	1,019.00	27.45
1,019.01	~	1,024.00	27.58
1,024.01	~	1,029.00	27.72
1,029.01	~	1,034.00	27.85
1,034.01	~	1,039.00	27.99
1,039.01	~	1,044.00	28.12
1,044.01	~	1,049.00	28.26
1,049.01	~	1,054.00	28.39
1,054.01	~	1,059.00	28.53
1,059.01	~	1,064.00	28.66
1,064.01	~	1,069.00	28.80
1,069.01	~	1,074.00	28.93
1,074.01	~	1,079.00	29.07
1,079.01	~	1,084.00	29.20
1,084.01	~	1,089.00	29.34
1,089.01	~	1,094.00	29.47
1,094.01	~	1,099.00	29.61
1,099.01	~	1,104.00	29.74
1,104.01	~	1,109.00	29.88
1,109.01	~	1,114.00	30.01
1,114.01	~	1,119.00	30.15
1,119.01	~	1,124.00	30.28
1,124.01	~	1,129.00	30.42
1,129.01	~	1,134.00	30.55
1,134.01	~	1,139.00	30.69
1,139.01	~	1,144.00	30.82
1,144.01	~	1,149.00	30.96
1,149.01	~	1,154.00	31.09
1,154.01	~	1,159.00	31.23
1,159.01	~	1,164.00	31.36
1,164.01	~	1,169.00	31.50
1,169.01	~	1,174.00	31.63
1,174.01	~	1,179.00	31.77
1,179.01	~	1,184.00	31.90
1,184.01	~	1,189.00	32.04
1,189.01	~	1,194.00	32.17
1,194.01	~	1,199.00	32.31
1,199.01	~	1,204.00	32.44
1,204.01	~	1,210.00	32.59
1,210.01	~	1,220.00	32.81
1,220.01	~	1,230.00	33.08
1,230.01	~	1,240.00	33.35
1,240.01	~	1,250.00	33.62
1,250.01	~	1,260.00	33.89
1,260.01	~	1,270.00	34.16
1,270.01	~	1,280.00	34.43
1,280.01	~	1,290.00	34.70
1,290.01	~	1,300.00	34.97
1,300.01	~	1,310.00	35.24
1,310.01	~	1,320.00	35.51
1,320.01	~	1,330.00	35.78
1,330.01	~	1,340.00	36.05
1,340.01	~	1,350.00	36.32
1,350.01	~	1,360.00	36.59
1,360.01	~	1,370.00	36.86
1,370.01	~	1,380.00	37.13
1,380.01	~	1,390.00	37.40
1,390.01	~	1,400.00	37.67
1,400.01	~	1,410.00	37.94
1,410.01	~	1,420.00	38.21
1,420.01	~	1,430.00	38.48
1,430.01	~	1,440.00	38.75
1,440.01	~	1,450.00	39.02
1,450.01	~	1,460.00	39.29
1,460.01	~	1,470.00	39.56

To obtain deductions for amounts in excess of $1470.00, multiply the earnings amount by **.027**

Note - Yearly maximum employee premiums are $1,053.00

The Employer's Tax Responsibilities

8

PRINCIPLES

AND

PROCEDURES

THE BIG PICTURE

The goals for Eldorado Computer Centre this year are to increase earnings, to expand into additional locations, and to increase revenue by 30 percent. Freedman realizes that company growth will eventually mean hiring more people. Therefore, although his revenue will increase, his operating expenses will also increase because of the additional payroll expenses he will incur.

After studying Chapter 8, you will understand these extra expenses. They include employer payroll taxes and worker's compensation insurance, which the law requires the employer to pay. Although Freedman is not offering benefits to his part-time employees at this time, he realizes that this too could become an additional operating expense.

Annual federal tax-related returns must be prepared and submitted, in addition to the monthly forms which report the various amounts connected with payroll, such as CPP and employment insurance as well as federal and provincial income tax deductions.

Chapter Objectives

- How to calculate and record the employer's expenses associated with payroll (p. 312)
- How employers remit and record their employees' deductions to Revenue Canada (p. 316)
- Employers' annual responsibilities for filing the T4 Summary form (p. 320)

In the previous chapter we examined how ABC Company Ltd. calculates its weekly payroll and maintains a record of each employee's earnings. In Canada, many employers must remit monthly to the government the totals deducted from their employees in the previous month. Certain employers (those who have more than $15,000 to remit monthly) must send in their withholdings more often, while some very small employers may now remit only every quarter (only if there are withholdings of less than $1000 per month). In the balance of this chapter we will assume a smaller employer who remits monthly.

An important fact in our country is that employers share with their employees the total cost of CPP and EI. The employer's share of these payments is considered an expense of doing business and is accounted for as such. In this chapter we will examine how this expense is calculated and illustrate the forms that need to be completed (and sent to the government) as part of the payroll process. We will also examine the accounting procedures which must be followed.

LEARNING UNIT 8-1

Employer's Expenses Associated with Payroll

If you take over another employer's business, you must still obtain a new identification number (unless the business is a corporation).

Employers must apply for a remittance number in order to handle their responsibilities for payroll correctly. A special form called a Request for a **Business Number** [Form RC1(E)] must be submitted which asks the employer to answer several questions about the business's operations.* Once this form is processed, the employer is issued a permanent unique identification number. This number is used to ensure that the amounts of money sent (we often say *remitted*) to the government each month are recorded correctly, that is, in the right company's account. It is also used for GST remittances and other purposes.

The actual amount sent to the government each month depends on three deductions taken from employees' wages:

1. Income tax
2. Canada (or Quebec) Pension Plan
3. Employment insurance

A simple **remittance formula** can be used to ensure that the correct figure is remitted each period:

Notice that the income tax amount is sent by the employer, but is not an expense, as the employees are paying it.

Income tax deducted × 1.0	= XXX.XX
CPP deducted × 2.0	= XXX.XX
EI deducted × 2.4	= XXX.XX
Total	= $XXX.XX

*The same form is also used to obtain a Business Number for GST and other purposes.

We will soon see in more detail how this formula works. Before we look at the details, however, a word of caution: The employer should ensure that the required remittance is made by the due date (usually the 15th day of the month following the payroll deductions). Failure to remit on time usually results in a penalty of 10 percent of the amount due over $500.00. This penalty is harsh and should be avoided. Not only is the amount high, but also it is not deductible as a business expense for tax purposes.

How to calculate employer's remittance

Income Tax

Some provinces levy higher tax rates than others. Except in Quebec, this provincial tax is calculated as a percentage of the federal tax. Basic provincial tax rates may resemble these:

Alberta 45.5%

Ontario 45%

(both for the 1998 tax year)

In Quebec, provincial income tax is calculated as a percentage of taxable income.

Remember that all employees pay an amount of income tax based upon their level of earnings. We saw in Chapter 7 that the ABC Company Ltd. deducted income tax from each employee's earnings. This amount must now be sent to the government. Notice that the amount sent is exactly the same as the amount deducted, since the employer does not contribute to the employee's tax. This part of the required remittance is therefore quite simple: Each month employers must send in the exact amount of income tax deducted from employees in the previous month. In our simple formula that is why we multiply by 1.0—the result is exactly the amount deducted.

Canada (Quebec) Pension Plan

Every employee also contributes an amount every pay period to CPP (at least until the maximum is reached). In Canada, the employer must match the employee's contribution to CPP. This means that the amount of CPP remitted is exactly double the amount deducted. In our simple formula, that is why we multiply by 2.0—the result is double the amount deducted.

If an employee commences a job with a new employer partway through a calendar year, the deduction of CPP is calculated without regard to the CPP already paid while employed by the former company. If the employee pays more than the yearly maximum, then a refund of CPP contributions can be claimed by the individual when he or she files an income tax return for the year. The employer's share is not refundable and cannot be recovered.

Employment Insurance

Recall that employees contribute an amount every pay period for employment insurance. Employers also contribute to EI by paying an amount which is 140 percent of the deductions made from employees' wages. The effect is that the employer must remit 2.4 times the amount deducted from the employees. In our simple formula, that is why we multiply by 2.4—1.0 for the employees' deduction, plus 1.4 for the employer's share. This 1.4 employer's portion can be reduced if the employer has an approved wage-loss replacement plan, but in this chapter we are assuming no reduction. Also note that the rules for overpayment of EI are almost exactly the same as for CPP: The employee can recover his or her overpayment at tax time, while there is no refund to an employer.

In Chapter 7, the employer made the following journal entry for the payroll in the first week in March:

GENERAL JOURNAL

Date		Account Titles and Description	PR	Dr.	Cr.
Mar	7	Management Salaries Expense		800 00	
		Sales Wages Expense		720 00	
		Wages Expense		1 273 00	
		Income Taxes Payable			477 15
		CPP Payable			76 34
		EI Payable			75 34
		Medical Plan Payable			52 00
		Charitable Contributions Payable			12 00
		Salaries and Wages Payable			2 100 17
		To record payroll for the first week in March			

ABC Company Ltd. must now make the following additional entry to record its liability correctly:

GENERAL JOURNAL

Date		Account Titles and Description	PR	Dr.	Cr.
Mar	7	Employee Benefits Expense		181 82	
		CPP Payable (1 × 76.34)			76 34
		EI Payable (1.4 × 75.34)			105 48
		To record employer portion of CPP and			
		EI for week 1, March			

Note: This expense—employee benefits expense—is also known by many different names—payroll taxes expense, for example. Some employers separate it into EI and CPP portions, but this is not usually necessary.

After the above entry is posted, the following T accounts would be changed as shown:

Employee Benefits Expense

Dr.	Cr.
181.82*	

Expense on the Income Statement

CPP Payable

Dr.	Cr.
	76.34**
	76.34*

Liability on the Balance Sheet

EI Payable

Dr.	Cr.
	75.34**
	105.48*

Liability on the Balance Sheet

—

* New entry made above

** Original entry from Chapter 7

As a final note, students should be aware that employers sometimes share, or pay entirely for, the cost of other employee benefits, such as extended health care, long-term disability insurance, and dental plans. These costs would also be recorded by journal entry at the same time CPP and EI are recorded. For example, if ABC Company agreed that they would charge their employees only half the cost of health care, they would make the following entry instead of the one illustrated previously:

GENERAL JOURNAL

Page 4

Date		Account Titles and Description	PR	Dr.	Cr.
Mar	7	Employee Benefits Expense		233 82	
		CPP Payable			76 34
		EI Payable			105 48
		Medical Plan payable			52 00
		To record employer's portion of CPP, EI,			
		and medical insurance for week 1, March			

LEARNING UNIT 8-1 REVIEW

AT THIS POINT you should be able to:

- Explain one purpose of form RC1(E). (p. 311)
- Calculate the employer's share of CPP and EI. (p. 311)
- Explain when employee deductions must be remitted. (p. 312)
- Journalize the employer's employee benefits expense. (p. 313)
- Post the above journal entry to appropriate ledger accounts (p. 313)

SELF-REVIEW QUIZ 8-1

(The forms you need are on page 8-1 of the *Study Guide with Working Papers.*)

Given the following journal entry for the payroll totals for the second week in March, prepare the entry to record ABC Company Ltd.'s portion of CPP and EI:

GENERAL JOURNAL

Date		Account Titles and Description	PR	Dr.	Cr.
Mar	14	Salaries and Wages Expense		2805 00	
		Income Taxes Payable			481 25
		CPP Payable			76 72
		EI Payable			75 74
		Medical Plan Payable			52 00
		Charitable Contributions Payable			12 00
		Salaries and Wages Payable			2107 29
		To record payroll for week 2 in March			

Solution to Self-Review Quiz 8-1

GENERAL JOURNAL

Date		Account Titles and Description	PR	Dr.	Cr.
Mar	14	Employee Benefits Expense		182 76	
		CPP Payable (1×.76.72)			76 72
		EI Payable (1.4 × 75.74)			106 04
		To record employer portion of CPP and			
		EI for week 2, March			

LEARNING UNIT 8-2

Completing the Monthly Remittance Form

Income tax × 1
+ CPP × 2
+ UI × 2.4 = Amount

CPP × 1
+ UI × 1.4 = Employer's expense

Most smaller companies are required to remit the total amounts due with respect to their payrolls each month by the 15th of the following month. Payment may be made at most financial institutions in Canada, or a cheque can be mailed as long as it reaches the government by the appropriate deadline.

We have already seen the ABC Company Ltd.'s entries for the first two weeks in March. Let us assume the following payroll data for the third and fourth weeks:

GENERAL JOURNAL

Date		Account Titles and Description	Post. Ref.	Dr.	Cr.
Mar	21	Salaries and Wages Expense		2781 00	
		Income Taxes Payable			473 45
		CPP Payable			75 95
		EI Payable			75 09
		Medical Plan Payable			52 00
		Charitable Contributions Payable			12 00
		Salaries and Wages Payable			2092 51
		To record payroll for week 3, March—new data			

GENERAL JOURNAL

Date		Account Titles and Description	Post. Ref.	Dr.	Cr.
Mar	28	Salaries and Wages Expense		2856 00	
		Income Taxes Payable			502 20
		CPP Payable			78 35
		EI Payable			77 11
		Medical Plan Payable			52 00
		Charitable Contributions Payable			12 00
		Salaries and Wages Payable			2134 34
		To record payroll for week 4, March—new data			

* See Self-Review Quiz 8-1.

GENERAL JOURNAL

Date		Account Titles and Description	Post. Ref.	Dr.	Cr.
Mar	21	Employee Benefits Expense		181 08	
		CPP Payable (1 × 75.95)			75 95
		EI Payable (1.4 × 75.09)			105 13
		To record employer portion of CPP and			
		EI for the third week of March—new data			

GENERAL JOURNAL

Date		Account Titles and Description	Post. Ref.	Dr.	Cr.
Mar	28	Employee Benefits Expense		186 30	
		CPP Payable (1 × 78.35)			78 35
		EI Payable (1.4 × 77.11)			107 95
		To record employer portion of CPP and			
		EI for the fourth week of March—new data			

After posting, the relevant liability T-accounts would appear as shown:

		Income Taxes Payable	CPP Payable	UI Payable
Week 1:	Employees	477.15*	76.34*	75.34*
	Employer		76.34**	105.48**
Week 2:	Employees	481.25*	76.72*	75.74*
	Employer		76.72**	106.04**
Week 3:	Employees	473.45*	75.95*	75.09*
	Employer		75.95**	105.13**
Week 4:	Employees	502.20*	78.35*	77.11*
	Employer		78.35**	107.95**
Balance (March)		1,934.05	614.72	727.88

* Original payroll entry
** Benefits entry

Since these liability accounts contain the total amounts due, ABC Company Ltd. can complete the required **Remittance Form (PD7A)** as shown in Figure 8-1.

Revenue Canada / Revenu Canada

STATEMENT OF ACCOUNT FOR CURRENT SOURCE DEDUCTIONS PD7A(E)Rev.4/96

1

Statement of account as of 03/23/01 Account number 111222333RP Employer name ABC COMPANY LTD

You can make your payment where you bank or to:

Balances on last statement		Current balances	
Amount paid for	Assessed amount owing	Amount paid for	Assessed amount owing
3,146.20		3,276.65	

EXPLANATION OF CHANGES

Date	Description		Amount
22 Mar	Payment Feb 2001	Date Recd 15 Mar 2001	3,146.20CR

Thank you for your payment.
Please use Part 2 to make your next remittance or explain on the back, Part 3, why you will not be remitting.

Pierre Gravelle, Q.C.
Deputy Minister of National Revenue

2 Revenue Canada / Revenu Canada

CURRENT SOURCE DEDUCTIONS REMITTANCE VOUCHER **PD7A(E)** Rev.4/96

6

Account number: 111222333RP

For departmental use only

ABC COMPANY LTD.
123 PINE ROAD
ANY CITY, PR X1X 1X1

Amount of payment 3 2 7 6 6 5

Month for which deductions were withheld — Year Month

Gross monthly payroll (dollars only) 1 1 2 3 5 0 0

Number of employees in last pay period 6

⑆0 2000⑈ 117⑆ 96

FIGURE 8-1 Remittance Form, page 1 (Reverse side not shown): Section 1 shows the statement returned to the employer from the bank which has deposited the remittance. Section 2 shows the remittance form, which is filled out and sent to the Receiver General.

Source: Revenue Canada. Reproduced with permission of the Minister of Public Works and Government Services Canada, 1999.

ABC Company Ltd. will issue a cheque for $3,276.65 dated April 15, payable to the Receiver General for Canada. This cheque will be entered in the cash disbursements journal in April. When this cheque is entered, the following accounts will be affected:

GENERAL JOURNAL

Date		Account Titles and Description	Post. Ref.	Dr.	Cr.
April	15	Income Taxes Payable		1934 05	
		CPP Payable		614 72	
		EI Payable		727 88	
		Cash			3276 65
		To record payment of withholdings			

After these amounts are posted, the liability accounts will all have zero balances.

Remember that by April 15 there will be two new weekly payrolls (in April) to contend with, so the ledger accounts may not ever have a balance of exactly zero. The amount payable at the end of any month, however, will be accurate when all postings have been made.

So far in these chapters we have been illustrating the use of three separate liability accounts, as is obvious from the journal entry above. Many companies prefer to operate a single account called, not surprisingly, Due to Receiver General. While some detail may be obscured by using just one account, it is true that a single cheque is written each month, so this practice is justified.

Students will recall that employers sometimes pay part or all of the cost of other benefits. These costs are not sent to the Receiver General; instead, they are remitted (usually monthly) to the provincial health care plan and/or private insurance companies which provide the benefits. These details of payroll are handled in a manner similar to the remittance to the Receiver General and are not dealt with further in this text.

LEARNING UNIT 8-2 REVIEW

AT THIS POINT you should be able to:

- Explain the balances in the following ledger accounts before the monthly remittance to the Receiver General is made. (p. 316)
  - **a.** Income tax payable
  - **b.** CPP payable
  - **c.** EI payable
- Complete form PD7A for a typical company. (p. 317)
- Issue and record the cheque which would accompany form PD7A. (p. 228)
- Explain how the balances in the ledger accounts listed in **a.** to **c.** above would change after posting the remittance cheque. (p. 318)

SELF-REVIEW QUIZ 8-2

(The forms you need are on pages 8-1 and 8-2 of the *Study Guide with Working Papers.*)

Given the two semimonthly payrolls summarized by the journal entries opposite, answer the following:

1. What journal entries would be made to record the employer's share of CPP and EI for the month?
2. Post the original entries and the entries you suggested in question 1 to the T accounts shown. (Not all T accounts are shown; please ignore the ones not shown.)
3. What amount would the employer remit to the Receiver General by the 15th of the following month?

Here are the semimonthly journal entries:

GENERAL JOURNAL

Date	Account Titles and Description	Post. Ref.	Dr.	Cr.
	Sales Salaries		2850 00	
	Office Salaries		3240 00	
	Income Taxes Payable			1560 00
	CPP Payable			122 40
	EI Payable			164 43
	Salaries and Wages Payable			4243 17
	To record payroll data for the first half of the month			

GENERAL JOURNAL

Date	Account Titles and Description	Post. Ref.	Dr.	Cr.
	Sales Salaries		2850 00	
	Office Salaries		3175 00	
	Income Taxes Payable			1445 00
	CPP Payable			121 80
	EI Payable			162 68
	Salaries and Wages Payable			4295 52
	To record payroll data for the second half of the month			

Here are the T accounts to use in question 2 of the Self-Review Quiz (opening balances are ignored):

Income Tax Payable **CPP Payable** **EI Payable**

Solutions to Self-Review Quiz 8-2

1.

GENERAL JOURNAL

Date		Account Titles and Description	Post. Ref.	Dr.	Cr.
		Employee Benefits Expense		36062	
		CPP Payable			11240
		EI Payable (164.43 × 1.4)			24822
		To record benefits expense for the			
		second half of the month			

GENERAL JOURNAL

Date		Account Titles and Description	Post. Ref.	Dr.	Cr.
		Employee Benefits Expense		34955	
		CPP Payable			12180
		EI Payable (162.68 × 1.4)			22775
		To record benefits expense for the			
		second half of the month			

2. Your T accounts should appear as follows:

Income Tax Payable

Dr.	Cr.
	1,560.00
	1,445.00
	3,005.00 Balance

CPP Payable

Dr.	Cr.
	122.40
	122.40
	121.80
	121.80
	488.40 Balance

UI Payable

Dr.	Cr.
	164.43
	230.20
	162.68
	227.75
	785.06 Balance

3. The employer would remit $4,278.46, calculated as follows:

Income Tax Payable (balance)	$3,005.00
CPP Payable (balance)	488.40
EI Payable (balance)	785.06
	$4,278.46

LEARNING UNIT 8-3

Employer's Annual T4 Summary

Every year, employers are required to file an annual return called a **T4 Summary** (see Figure 8-2). This return summarizes the information provided to employees on their T4 forms (see Chapter 7, Figure 7-5).

Revenue Canada / Revenu Canada

For the year ending December 31, / Pour l'année se terminant le 31 décembre **2001**

For departmental use / Réservé au Ministère: 0505 001743

T4 Summary / Sommaire

SUMMARY OF REMUNERATION PAID / SOMMAIRE DE LA RÉMUNÉRATION PAYÉE

Important — See the information on the back of this form. / Lisez les renseignements donnés au verso de ce formulaire.

Business Number – Numéro d'entreprise: 111223333 RP0001

Name and address of employer – Nom et adresse de l'employeur:

ABC Company Ltd
123 Pine Road
Any City, Province
X1X 1X1

You have to file the T4 return on or before **February 28, 1999.** Vous devez produire votre déclaration T4 au plus tard le **28 février 1999.**

88	Total number of T4 slips filed – Nombre total de feuillets T4 produits	10
14	Employment income – Revenus d'emploi	1556705.0
20	Registered pension plan (RPP) contributions / Cotisations à un régime de pension agréé (RPA)	
52	Pension adjustment – Facteur d'équivalence	
24	EI insurable earnings – Gains assurables d'AE	
16	Employee's CPP contributions – Cotisations de l'employé au RPC	4197.46
27	Employer's CPP contributions – Cotisations de l'employeur au RPC	4197.46
18	Employee's EI premiums – Cotisations de l'employé à l'AE	4203.09
19	Employer's EI premiums – Cotisations de l'employeur à l'AE	5884.33
22	Income tax deducted – Impôt sur le revenu retenu	25350.80
80	Total deductions reported (16 + 27 + 18 + 19 + 22) / Total des retenues déclarées (16 + 27 + 18 + 19 + 22)	43833.14
82	Minus: remittances – Moins : versements	43833.14
	Subtotal – Total partiel	
83	New Hires Program refund / Remboursement selon le programme pour l'embauche de nouveaux travailleurs	
	Difference – Différence	

We do not charge or refund a difference of less than $2. / Nous n'exigeons et ne remboursons pas une différence inférieure à 2 $.

84 Overpayment – Paiement en trop	86 Balance due – Solde à payer	Amount enclosed – Somme jointe

For departmental use – Réservé au Ministère

Last to current / Précédente à courante: 90 1 — Other / Autre: 3

Pro Forma: 91 2

93 Y – A / D – J

PD15-1: 94 — NHPR RENT: 95

POF PSF: 96 — NLFP APPT: 97

Memo – Note

Prepared by – Établi par

Date

SIN of the proprietor(s) or principal owner(s) – NAS du ou des propriétaires

Canadian-controlled private corporations or unincorporated employers / Sociétés privées sous contrôle canadien ou employeurs non constitués: 74 ______ 75 ______

Person to contact about this return – Personne avec qui communiquer au sujet de cette déclaration: 76 ELAINE DUMONT

Area code / Indicatif régional: 78 900 — Telephone number / Numéro de téléphone: 123 4567 — Extension / Poste:

Certification – Attestation

I, / Je, ELAINE DUMONT (Name in capital letters – Nom en lettres majuscules), certify that the information given in this T4 return (T4 Summary and related T4 slips) is, to the best of my knowledge, correct and complete. / atteste que les renseignements fournis dans cette déclaration T4 (la déclaration T4 *Sommaire* et les feuillets T4 *connexes*) sont, à ma connaissance, exacts et complets.

Date	Signature of authorized person – Signature d'une personne autorisée	Position or office – Titre ou poste
February 22, 2002	Elaine Dumont	Manager

Privacy Act, personal information bank number RCT/P-PU-005
Loi sur la protection des renseignements personnels, fichier de renseignements personnels numéro RCT/P-PU-005

T4 Summary - Sommaire (98) 2873 Canada

FIGURE 8-2 Summary of Remuneration Paid

Source: Revenue Canada. Reproduced with permission of the Minister of Public Works and Government Services Canada, 1999.

Careful, accurate work helps ensure that the filing of the T4-T4A Summary is not an unpleasant task.

Employee Name	Total Wages	Deductions: Income Tax	CPP	EI
Janet Johnson	$ 20,910.00	3,380.20	557.12	564.58
Peter Black	20,875.00	3,364.40	556.00	563.61
John Chernochan	19,462.00	2,034.80	510.79	525.47
Tony Chui	22,147.00	3,666.00	596.70	597.97
Beth Madora	18,256.50	2,724.00	472.21	492.93
Elaine Dumont	38,400.00	8,101.40	1,116.80	1,036.80
Casual employees (Total)	15,620.00	2,080.00	387.84	421.73
Totals	$155,670.50	25,350.80	4,197.46	4,203.09

It is important to note that the form illustrated in Figure 8-2 is completed for a calendar year. Even if the fiscal year ends on September 30, the T4 Summary must be filed for the calendar year (January 1 to December 31). The deadline for submitting this form to the government and the T4 forms to the employees is February 28 each year for the calendar year ended the previous December 31.

The completion of this form can be a difficult task, because any errors made during the year in completing the payroll register, and any errors made in preparing the employees' individual T4 slips, will be discovered in this final step. The totals shown for CPP, EI, and income tax as illustrated in the table above must also agree with the totals remitted according to the monthly PD7A form or any deficiency remitted (see Figure 8-1).

It is not unusual to find intelligent, hard-working, successful employers who find this aspect of payroll processing to be very difficult. Some computer firms selling payroll software are successful because they promise employers relief from the manual balancing procedures each February 28. In actual fact, the task is not too difficult—provided the payroll register is completed with neatness and accuracy and all subsequent steps are done with care.

LEARNING UNIT 8-3 REVIEW

AT THIS POINT you should be able to:

- Describe the process of filing an annual T4 Summary. (p. 320)
- Illustrate the completion of the T4 Summary. (p. 321)

SELF-REVIEW QUIZ 8-3

(The form you need is on page 8-2 of the *Study Guide with Working Papers.*)

Respond true or false to the following:

1. A T4 Summary must be filed each year by February 28.
2. A T4 Summary is sent to each employee by February 28 each year.
3. The completion of the T4 forms can be a difficult task.
4. The total of the individual amounts on all T4 Supplementary forms must equal the totals on the T4 Summary.

Solutions to Self-Review Quiz 8-3

1. True **2.** False **3.** True **4.** True

A Taxing Time

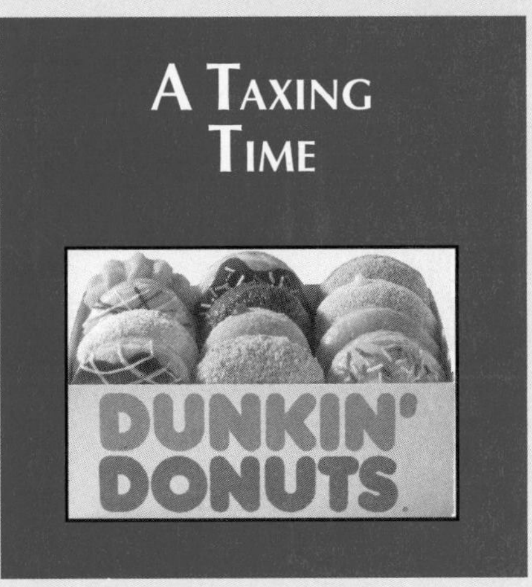

"As an employer, Fred, what are your tax responsibilities?" asked George Olsen, president of the local Kiwanis club. They were at one of the luncheons sponsored by the club every month. Fred had been asked to join a panel discussion on *The Role of Small Business in Our Local Economy*. Luckily, George had told the panelists the questions in advance, so Fred had his answers ready.

"Well, of course, I pay income taxes myself. I also have to send in federal taxes withheld for each of my employees. I have to withhold employment taxes, as well as CPP for each of them. I pay workers' compensation, too," said Fred quickly.

"That's funny," said a voice from the audience. "My brother-in-law has a Dunkin' Donuts shop in the US and he pays city taxes too. What's going on here?"

"Naturally, the situation is slightly different for Dunkin' Donuts shop owners in different cities and countries," said Fred confidently. "No Canadian cities have city income taxes. Different provinces have different regulations about workers' compensation, as well."

"Oh, right," said the voice, sounding embarrassed.

"What happens at the corporate level at Dunkin' Donuts, Fred?" asked George Olsen, shifting the topic diplomatically.

"That's a really big operation, as you can imagine," said Fred. "We have corporate employees in many provinces, states, and countries, so a portion of the payroll function is not handled in-house. Instead it is outsourced to ADP, an international payroll processing service. They generate the cheques and handle the tax reporting to the various tax authorities. The corporate employees manage all the other aspects of the payroll process, from collecting information on hours worked to analysis of the labour dollars."

"Thanks, Fred," said George. "Now, let's move on to Eva Jonet who is going to tell us about advertising her new nail salon."

Fred nodded and breathed a sign of relief as Eva took the microphone from him. He much preferred baking to public speaking!

Discussion Questions

1. George had warned Fred not to use technical language in preparing his remarks, so Fred didn't mention any payroll forms by name or number. List three government forms connected with payroll and explain briefly the purpose of each.
2. Fred is a monthly depositor of payroll taxes. Why? What other options are there?
3. Assume that Fred owed $2,679.90 in payroll withholdings for November. When would it be due? What would happen if that day were a holiday?

Chapter Review

SUMMARY OF KEY POINTS

Learning Unit 8-1

1. The employer's remittance to the Receiver General includes (a) income tax (employees' deductions), (b) CPP (both employees' and employer's shares), and (c) EI (again both employees' and employer's shares).
2. The payroll tax expense is made up of both CPP (same amount as deducted from employees) and EI (1.4 times the amount deducted from employees).
3. Journal entries are made to record the payroll and then to record the employer's share of CPP and EI.
4. Employers sometimes share, or pay entirely for, the cost of other employee benefits (health care, insurance, etc.). These costs would also be recorded by journal entry at the same time as CPP and EI.

Learning Unit 8-2

1. Employers must complete form PD7A and submit it with their remittance to the Receiver General for Canada by the 15th day of the month following the month in which the salary payment was made. (Larger employers remit more often.)
2. A significant penalty is paid by any employer remitting after the due date.
3. Employers sometimes pay part or all of the cost of health care, insurance plans, etc., on behalf of their employees. These costs are not sent to the Receiver General; instead, they are remitted (usually monthly) to the provincial health care plan and/or private companies which provide the benefits.

Learning Unit 8-3

1. Once every year, by February 28, employers must file an annual T4. Summary (for the previous calendar year) with the federal government.
2. On or before the same date, each employee must be given a copy of his or her individual earnings summary form (T4 Supplementary). This form summarizes all relevant payroll information for each employee for the previous calendar year.
3. Unless care is taken in preparing the payroll records throughout the year, the completion of the T4 forms can be a challenging task.

KEY TERMS

Business number A number given by the federal government which uniquely identifies each employer who is required to forward deductions made from employees. Used to keep track of the exact remittance each employer sends on behalf of its employees. (p. 311)

(Monthly) Remittance Form (PD7A) A form used to identify the employer and the amounts of money sent to the Receiver General for Canada periodically on behalf of employees (p. 316)

Remittance formula A formula which can be used to double-check the amount of money being sent in each month on behalf of the employees. (p. 311) Computed as:

Income tax deducted × 1.0	=	XXX.XX
CPP deducted × 2.0	=	XX.XX
EI deducted × 2.4	=	XX.XX
Total		XXX.XX

T4 Summary A form sent to the federal government once each year showing the totals of income tax, CPP, and EI deducted from all employees during the last calendar year. The totals on this form must agree exactly with the totals submitted on the various T4 Supplementary forms described below. (p. 320)

T4 Supplementary A form given to each employee by February 28 every year which gives the totals of wages earned, income tax, CPP, and EI deducted, and other similar information for the past calendar year. Total of all T4 Supplementary slips must agree with the totals reported on the T4 Summary (see above). (p. 286)

Blueprint of the Tax Calendar

A Sampling of Dates Involving Employer's Tax Responsibilities

January 15 (and the 15th of each month)	PD7A form	Remit the monthly amount to the Receiver General for Canada. Remember the formula: 1 × tax deducted + 2 × CPP deducted + 2.4 × EI deducted = Total amount to be remitted
February 28	T4 form	Complete these forms and send or deliver them to all persons employed during the year.
February 28	T4 Summary	Send this form, together with copies of the individual T4 forms, to the government. The totals on this form must match the sum of all individual T4 slips, and, as well, must agree with the employer's accounting records.

Certain other forms may be required throughout the year, although they are not subject to an exact timetable:

	RC1 form	Every employer needs to obtain a permanent number which permits the government to keep an accurate record of funds remitted. Since this number is permanent, employers will need to submit this form only once.
	Record of Employment	Whenever an employee ceases his or her employment, this form must be completed and a copy given to the former employee within one week. A copy goes to the government to assist in the fair and efficient administration of the Employment Insurance Act.

QUESTIONS, MINI EXERCISES, EXERCISES, AND PROBLEMS

Discussion Questions

1. What makes up employee benefits expense?
2. All employers must remit their payroll deductions once a month (by the 15th of the following month). Please comment.
3. The only payroll-related costs borne by employers are CPP and EI. Please comment.
4. An RC1 form must be submitted annually by all employers. True or false?
5. Why could failure to remit employees' deductions on time be costly?
6. Each employer doubles the amount of income tax deducted from employees each month when remitting to the Receiver General for Canada. True or false?
7. Which of the following accurately summarizes the correct formula for determining the monthly remittance to the Receiver General? (IT = income tax.)
   a. (2 × IT) + (2.4 × CPP) + (2 × EI)
   b. (1 × IT) + (2 × CPP) + (2.4 × EI)
   c. (1 × IT) + (2.4 × CPP) + (2 × EI)
   d. (2 × IT) + (2 × CPP) + (2.4 × EI)
8. A remittance form (PD7A) must be sent to the federal government once every pay period. True or false?
9. Why do some computer firms do good business selling payroll software to employers?
10. Employers must complete their T4 Summaries no later than two months after the end of their fiscal year. True or false?

Mini Exercises

(The forms you need are on page 8-3 of the *Study Guide with Working Papers*.)

1. The Fisher Company had two employees for the week ended July 23. On the basis of the following information, prepare a general journal entry to record the employee benefits expense for that payroll.

		Deductions			
Employee	*Salary*	*IT*	*CPP*	*EI*	*Net Pay*
Brett Pym	900	230	27	24	619
Carmen Flynn	1000	268	30	27	675

2. Assume that the Fisher Company (see above) had five payrolls in the month of July, all identical to the one shown above. What amount would the company send to the Receiver General in August to meet its legal obligation for payroll remittance?
3. For the payroll week ending on September 30 (the 39th payroll period of the year), the three employees shown below had gross earnings as indicated. Each had been employed at the same salary since January 1:

Beth Hudson	$1,000
John Wong	925
Ida Hastings	850

Without using tables, compute the amount of CPP and EI to be deducted from each employee for payroll number 39.

4. Fred Blake has agreed to work for the Cummings Foundation at a total annual salary of $42,000. He is uncertain whether he should be paid biweekly or semi-monthly, and has asked for your assistance. Calculate the typical deductions for CPP and EI that must be taken from Fred's salary under either alternative. Will the choice affect the total EI or CPP Fred pays during the year?

Exercises

(The forms you need are on page 8-4 of the *Study Guide with Working Papers.*)

Recording employee benefits expense

8-1. From the following information, prepare a general journal entry to record the employee benefits expense for Jones Company for the weekly payroll of July 9:

Employee	*Total Salary*	*Deductions* *Tax*	*CPP*	*EI*	*Net Pay*
Troy Ness	900	211	27	24	638
Jay Young	600	114	17	16	453
Tim Wyatt	800	185	23	22	570

Recording employee benefits expense

8-2. From the following information, prepare a general journal entry to record the employee benefits expense for Windsor Company for the monthly payroll for July:

Employee	*Total Salary*	*Deductions* *Tax*	*CPP*	*EI*	*Net Pay*
Bert Lamont	2,500	467	71	68	1,894
Joan Quan	2,300	413	64	62	1,761
Mark Totem	1,700	270	45	46	1,339
Jean Dzurko	1,800	292	48	49	1,411

Remittance calculation

8-3. What amount will the Windsor Company send to the Receiver General in the month of August (for the July payroll)? See Exercise 2 above.

Recording payroll tax expense, stage 1

8-4. For the first two weeks of March, the Star Company had payroll details as shown below:

Employee	*Hours*	*Rate*	*Total Pay*	*Deductions* *Tax*	*CPP*	*EI*	*Net Pay*
Pam Tifford	80	16	1,280	259	37	34	950
Isaac Gold	70	17	1,190	229	34	32	895
Bob Boudreau	80	14	1,120	203	32	30	855

Prepare the general journal entry to record the employee benefits expense for the two-week period.

Recording employee benefits expense, stage 2

8-5. For the last two weeks in March, the Star Company had payroll details as shown below:

Employee	*Hours*	*Rate*	*Total Pay*	*Deductions* *Tax*	*CPP*	*EI*	*Net Pay*
Pam Tifford	75	16	1,200	229	34	32	905
Isaac Gold	85	17	1,445	324	42	39	1,040
Jim Francis	80	14	1,120	195	32	30	863

Prepare the general journal entry to record the employee benefits expense for the last two-week period.

Calculating a remittance—multiple periods

8-6. There are only four payroll weeks in March. Calculate the total remittance that Star Company would make to the Receiver General in the month of April based on its March payroll activities. Refer to Exercises 4 and 5 above.

Group A Problems

(The forms you need are on pages 8-5 to 8-9 of the *Study Guide with Working Papers*.)

Check Figure

Employee Benefits Expense $799.60

8A-1. The payroll register for Rice Company is summarized below for the month of April:

		Deductions						
Employee	*Total Salary*	*Tax*	*CPP*	*UI*	*Medical*	*Union Dues*	*Net Pay*	*Chq. No.*
Bob Roberts	2,700	526	77	73	22	21	1,981	474
Robin Case	2,600	505	74	70	44	21	1,886	475
Bailey Tropp	2,200	306	61	59	44	21	1,709	476
Ishma Blumen	2,300	413	64	62	44	21	1,696	477

Recording employee benefits expense, and subsequent entries

The union dues are remitted to the treasurer of the union by the 10th day of the next month. Rice Company matches its employees' contributions to the medical plan. Assume that the information in the above table has been recorded as cheques 474 to 477 were issued.

Required

a. Record the company's benefits expense, assuming no such entry was made when cheques 474 to 477 were recorded.

b. In May, the Rice Company issued the following three cheques:
1. May 10, 2000, to the Employees' Union, cheque No. 495.
2. May 15, 2000, to the Receiver General, cheque No. 502.
3. May 20, 2000, to the Provincial Health Care Insurance Company, cheque No. 531.

How much was each cheque for?

c. What journal entries would be made to record the three cheques in **b** above?

Recording employee benefits expense, and subsequent calculations

8A-2. Gibraltor Inc. recorded the following details in its payroll journal for March:

		Deductions							
Employee	*Total Salary*	*Tax*	*CPP*	*EI*	*LTD*	*Medical*	*Union Dues*	*Net Pay*	*Chq. No.*
Fred Jones	2,700	543	77	73	29	20	28	1,930	716
May George	2,300	413	64	62	46	40	28	1,647	717
Brendan May	2,400	421	67	65	46	20	28	1,753	718
Joyce Fisher	2,200	389	61	59	29	–	28	1,401	719
Pat Sail	1,900	317	51	51	29	20	28	1,404	720

Union dues are remitted by the end of the following month to the employees' union treasurer. Employees pay 100 percent of the long term disability (LTD). Gibraltor Inc. matches its employees' contributions to the medical plan and remits by the 20th of the following month.

Check Figure

Employee Benefits Expense $854.00

Required

a. Assume that there was no employee benefits expense recognized as the payroll register was recorded. Give the general journal entry necessary to record this employee benefits expense for March.

b. List the cheques, together with their amounts and dates, which Gibraltar Inc. would issue in April with respect to the above payroll data.

8A-3. The Candy Co. pays its workers twice each month. Data for the two pay periods in June is shown below:

Check Figure

Employee Benefits Expense, June 30 $435.00

First half of June:

				Deductions						
Employee	*Hours*	*Rate*	*Total Pay*	*Tax*	*CPP*	*EI*	*Union*	*Chari-table*	*Net Pay*	*Chq. No.*
Ann Wyatt	90	15	1,350	265	39	36	14	10	986	312
Jim Elliot	95	14	1,330	259	38	36	14	10	973	313
Bren Stairs	85	13	1,105	187	31	30	14	10	833	314
Becky Holmes	92	14	1,288	221	37	35	14	10	971	315

Second half of June:

				Deductions						
Employee	*Hours*	*Rate*	*Total Pay*	*Tax*	*CPP*	*EI*	*Union*	*Chari-table*	*Net Pay*	*Chq. No.*
Ann Wyatt	94	15	1,410	292	40	38	14	10	1,016	387
Jim Elliot	95	14	1,330	259	38	36	14	10	973	388
Bren Stairs	90	13	1,170	202	33	32	14	10	879	389
Becky Holmes	96	15	1,440	274	41	39	14	10	1,062	390

Recording employee benefits expense—a more comprehensive example

Union dues must be remitted to the union treasurer by the 15th of the following month. Candy Co. matches the employees' charitable contributions to Save the Children Canada on a 2-to-1 basis. Donations are mailed to this organization semi-annually. Deductions from all employees to May 31 this year have totalled $425. A cheque will be sent for the first half of the year on July 5, 2001.

Required

a. Assuming that the payroll register has been posted, but no entries have been made for employee benefits expense for June, make the two journal entries that are necessary to record this expense for Candy Co. for June.

b. Give details of the various cheques which will be issued in July based on Candy Co.'s payroll activities for the year so far.

8A-4. The Ripcord Parachute Club employs three people and pays them on a weekly basis. Payroll data for the four weeks in February are given below:

Week 1—February

		Deductions							
Employee	*Sal.*	*Tax*	*CPP*	*EI*	*LTD*	*Pen.*	*Med.*	*Net Pay*	*Chq. No.*
Phil May	700	153	20	19	15	38	16	439	205
Linda Barry	700	153	20	19	15	35	10	448	206
Howard Post	800	189	23	22	15	41	16	494	207

Week 2—February

Employee	*Sal.*	*Tax*	*CPP*	*EI*	*LTD*	*Pen.*	*Med.*	*Net Pay*	*Chq. No.*
		Deductions							
Phil May	800	189	23	22	15	41	16	494	216
Linda Barry	700	153	20	19	15	35	10	448	217
Howard Post	800	189	23	22	15	41	16	494	218

Week 3—February

Employee	*Sal.*	*Tax*	*CPP*	*EI*	*LTD*	*Pen.*	*Med.*	*Net Pay*	*Chq. No.*
		Deductions							
Phil May	800	189	23	22	15	41	16	494	221
Linda Barry	700	153	20	19	15	35	10	448	222
Howard Post	800	189	23	22	15	41	16	494	223

Week 4—February

Employee	*Sal.*	*Tax*	*CPP*	*EI*	*LTD*	*Pen.*	*Med.*	*Net Pay*	*Chq. No.*
		Deductions							
Phil May	800	189	23	22	15	41	16	494	244
Linda Barry	700	153	20	19	15	35	10	448	245
Howard Post	850	211	25	23	15	44	16	513	246

Assumptions

Check Figure

Cheque to Receiver General for Canada $3,236.00

Employees pay 100 percent of the cost of long term disability (LTD). Employees contribute just over 5 percent of their salary to the pension plan; the employer contributes 6 percent of the employees' salary to the plan. Medical cost is split 50/50 by employees and employer. All payroll-related deductions are paid on the 15th of March.

Required

Recording employee benefits expense—multiple periods

a. In recording in the payroll journal in February, the bookkeeper for the Ripcord Parachute Club did not record any expense for employee benefits. Give the four journal entries which should be made for the month to record this expense.

Posting routine entries for a monthly period

b. Post the entries from the payroll journal and the entries in **a** above to the T accounts shown below. (You may ignore the accounts which are not shown.)

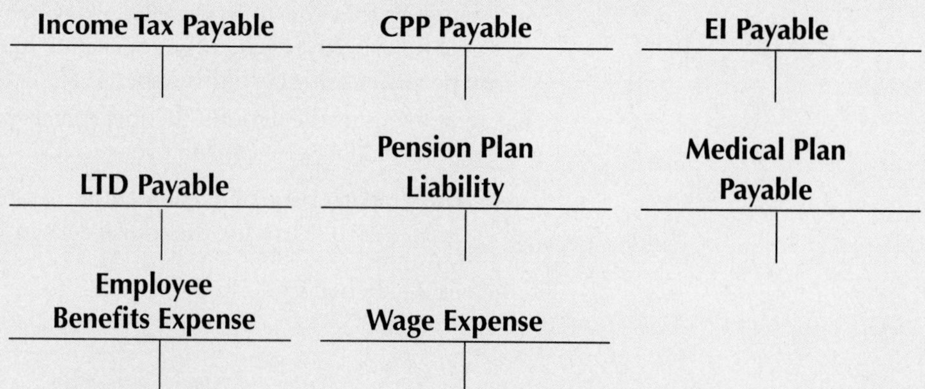

Calculating remittances

c. List the cheques and the amounts of the cheques which will be issued on March 15 for the February payroll.

Group B Problems

(The forms you need are on pages 8-5 to 8-9 of the *Study Guide with Working Papers.*)

Check Figure
Employee Benefits Expense
$842.40

8B-1. The payroll register for Rice Company is summarized below for the month of April:

Employee	*Total Salary*	*Tax*	*CPP*	*EI*	*Medical*	*Union Dues*	*Net Pay*	*Chq. No.*
		Deductions						
Bob Roberts	2,800	580	80	76	24	23	2,017	662
Robin Case	2,700	526	77	73	48	23	1,953	663
Bailey Tropp	2,300	413	64	62	48	23	1,690	664
Ishma Blumen	2,400	421	67	65	48	23	1,776	665

Recording employee benefits expense, and subsequent entries

The union dues are remitted to the treasurer of the union by the 10th day of the next month. Rice Company matches its employees' contributions to the medical plan. Assume that the information in the above table has been recorded as cheques 662 to 665 were issued.

Required

a. Record the company's benefits expense, assuming no such entry was made when cheques 662 to 665 were recorded.

b. In May, Rice Company issued the following three cheques:
1. May 10, 2000, to the Employees' Union, cheque No. 681.
2. May 15, 2000, to the Receiver General, cheque No. 698.
3. May 20, 2000, to the Provincial Health Care Insurance Company, cheque No. 713.

How much was each cheque for?

c. What entries would be made to record the three cheques in **b** above?

Check Figure
Employee Benefits Expense
$946.00

8B-2. Gibraltor Inc. recorded the following details in its payroll journal for March:

Employee	*Total Salary*	*Tax*	*CPP*	*EI*	*LTD*	*Medical*	*Union Dues*	*Net Pay*	*Chq. No.*
		Deductions							
Fred Jones	2,800	531	80	76	25	22	30	2,036	833
May George	2,400	421	67	65	48	44	30	1,725	834
Brendan May	2,500	467	71	68	25	22	30	1,817	835
Joyce Fisher	2,300	413	64	68	48	44	30	1,544	836
Pat Sail	2,000	341	55	54	25	22	30	1,473	837

Recording employee benefits expense, and subsequent calculations

Union dues are remitted by the end of the following month to the employees' union treasurer. Employees pay 100 percent of the long term disability (LTD). Gibraltor Inc. matches its employees' contributions to the medical plan and remits by the 20th of the following month.

Required

a. Assume that there was no employees' benefit expense recognized as the payroll register was recorded. Give the general journal entry necessary to record this employee benefits expense for March.

b. List the cheques, together with their amounts and dates, which Gibraltor Inc. would issue in April with respect to the above payroll data.

8B-3. The Candy Co. pays its workers twice each month. Data for the two pay periods in June are shown below:

First half of June:

				Deductions						
Employee	*Hours*	*Rate*	*Total Pay*	*Tax*	*CPP*	*EI*	*Union*	*Chari-table*	*Net Pay*	*Chq. No.*
Ann Wyatt	85	16	1,360	272	39	37	18	6	988	318
Jim Elliot	100	14	1,400	285	40	38	18	6	1,013	319
Bren Stairs	85	13	1,105	187	31	30	18	6	833	320
Becky Holmes	92	14	1,288	221	37	35	18	6	971	321

Check Figure

Employee Benefits Expense June 30 $413.60

Second half of June:

				Deductions						
Employee	*Hours*	*Rate*	*Total Pay*	*Tax*	*CPP*	*EI*	*Union*	*Chari-table*	*Net Pay*	*Chq. No.*
Ann Wyatt	99	16	1,584	352	46	43	18	6	1,119	343
Jim Elliot	95	14	1,330	259	38	36	18	6	973	344
Bren Stairs	96	13	1,248	224	35	34	18	6	931	345
Becky Holmes	88	15	1,320	234	38	36	18	6	988	346

Recording employee benefits expense—a more comprehensive example

Union dues must be remitted to the union treasurer by the 15th of the following month. Candy Co. matches the employees' charitable contributions to Save the Children Canada on a 2-to-1 basis. Donations are mailed to this organization semi-annually. Deductions from all employees to May 31 this year have totalled $280. A cheque will be sent for the first half of the year on July 5, 2001.

Required

a. Assuming that the payroll register has been posted, but no entries have been made for employee benefits expense for June, make the two journal entries that are necessary to record this expense for Candy Co. for June.

b. Give details of the various cheques which will be issued in July based on Candy Co.'s payroll activities for the year so far.

8B-4. The Ripcord Parachute Club employs three people and pays them on a weekly basis. Payroll data for the four weeks in February are given below:

Week 1—February

		Deductions							
Employee	*Sal.*	*Tax*	*CPP*	*EI*	*LTD*	*Pen.*	*Med.*	*Net Pay*	*Chq. No.*
Phil May	850	211	25	23	12	44	18	517	318
Linda Barry	800	189	23	22	12	41	12	501	319
Howard Post	900	230	27	24	12	46	18	543	320

Check Figure

Cheque to Receiver General for Canada $3,877.20

Week 2—February

		Deductions							
Employee	*Sal.*	*Tax*	*CPP*	*EI*	*LTD*	*Pen.*	*Med.*	*Net Pay*	*Chq. No.*
Phil May	900	230	27	24	12	46	18	543	334
Linda Barry	800	189	23	22	12	41	12	501	335
Howard Post	900	230	27	24	12	46	18	543	336

Week 3—February

Employee	*Sal.*	*Tax*	*CPP*	*EI*	*LTD*	*Pen.*	*Med.*	*Net Pay*	*Chq. No.*
		Deductions							
Phil May	900	230	27	24	12	46	18	543	356
Linda Barry	800	189	23	22	12	41	12	501	357
Howard Post	900	230	27	24	12	46	18	543	358

Week 4—February

Employee	*Sal.*	*Tax*	*CPP*	*EI*	*LTD*	*Pen.*	*Med.*	*Net Pay*	*Chq. No.*
		Deductions							
Phil May	900	230	27	24	12	46	18	543	377
Linda Barry	800	189	23	22	12	41	12	501	378
Howard Post	950	249	28	26	12	49	18	568	379

Assumptions

Employees pay 100 percent of the cost of long term disability (LTD). Employees contribute just over 5 percent of their salary to the pension plan; the employer contributes 6 percent of the employees' salary to the plan. Medical cost is split 50/50 by employees and employer. All payroll-related deductions are paid on the 15th of March.

Required

Recording employee benefits expense—multiple periods

a. In recording the payroll journal in February, the bookkeeper for the Ripcord Parachute Club did not record any expense for employee benefits. Give the four journal entries which should be made for the month to record this expense.

Posting routine entries for a monthly period

b. Post the entries from the payroll journal and the entries in **a** above to the T accounts shown below. (You may ignore the accounts which are not shown.)

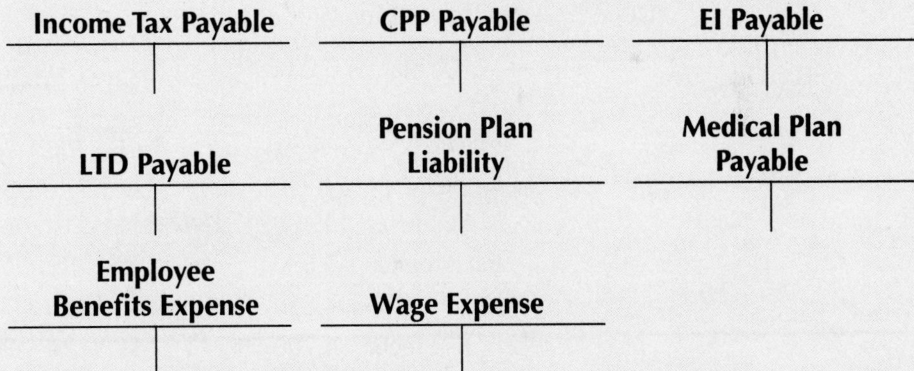

c. List the cheques and the amounts of the cheques which will be issued on March 15 for the February payroll.

Group C Problems

(The forms you need are on pages 8-10 to 8-15 of the *Study Guide with Working Papers.*)

8C-1. The payroll register for Bawlf Hardware Ltd. for the month of May is shown at the top of page 334:

Check Figure

Payroll Tax Expense $829.20

Employee	Salary	Deductions IT	CPP	EI	Health	LTD	Union	Net Pay	Chq. No.
Jake Jacobson	2,300	413	64	62	25	35	24	1,677	514
Mary Hind	1,950	330	53	53	42	30	24	1,418	515
Kyle George	1,800	292	48	49	25	31	24	1,331	516
Lily Chau	2,400	437	67	65	42	37	24	1,728	517
Roy Verhagen	1,800	292	48	49	42	27	24	1,318	518
	10,250	1,764	280	278	176	160	120	7,472	

Recording benefits expense and computing and entering cheques issued re payroll

Union dues must be submitted to the treasurer of the union by the 20th day of the next month. Bawlf Hardware matches the employees' contributions to the long term disability plan and the total must be sent to the insurance company by the 10th of the month following the payroll. Assume that all payroll information except benefits has been recorded as the cheques 514 to 518 were issued.

Required

a. Record Bawlf's benefits expense for the month of May.

b. In June, Bawlf Hardware issued the following three cheques:

1. Cheque 543, June 10, to ABC Insurance Company for the LTD
2. Cheque 551, June 15, to the Receiver General for Canada for employee deductions
3. Cheque 567, June 15, to the Hardware Employees Union, Local 471, for union dues

How much was each cheque for?

c. What entry would be made in the general journal to record each cheque in **b** above?

8C-2. Counterpoint Counselling Inc. recorded the following details in its Professional Payroll Journal for July:

Check Figure

Payroll Tax Expense $2,079.40

Employee	Salary	Deductions IT	CPP	EI	Char.	Life Ins.	Assn. Dues	Health	Net Pay	Chq. No.
Paula Amer	3,950	988	117	107	50	40	42	78	2,528	582
Mike Steves	4,400	1,185	131	119	60	45	42	78	2,740	583
Pat McIvor	3,680	902	108	99	50	40	42	46	2,393	584
Debbie Chan	4,850	1,376	146	131	70	50	42	78	2,957	585
Boris Hecht	4,700	1,313	141	127	70	50	42	46	2,911	586
Ken Gere	4,000	1,024	119	108	50	40	42	78	2,539	587
	25,580	6,788	762	691	350	265	252	404	16,068	

Recording benefits expense and liabilities; calculating dates and amounts of cheques to be issued

Counterpoint matches the charitable donation of each employee and forwards the total on the 25th of each month to the Canadian Centre for Counselling Research. Association dues are sent to the Provincial Counsellors Society on the 20th of each month. Life insurance premiums are remitted to ABCD Insurance Company Ltd. by the 20th day of the following month. Health insurance premiums are remitted to the Provincial Health Care Organization by the 15th of the next month, at the same time as the employee deductions are sent to the Receiver General for Canada.

Required

a. Give the general journal entry necessary to complete the recording of this payroll, assuming no entry was made for benefits or related expenses when the payroll was recorded.

b. List the cheques, along with their amounts and dates, which Counterpoint would issue in the month of August, with respect to this payroll.

8C-3. Refer to Problem 7C-2.

Required

Check Figure

Payroll Taxes Espense $214.51

a. Give the general journal entry necessary to recognize all payroll benefits expense arising from that payroll, given the entry you made in Chapter 7.

8C-4. Refer to Problem 7C-3 (page 299).

Required

Recording benefits expense and liabilities

a. Give the general journal entry necessary to recognize all payroll benefits expenses arising from that payroll, given the entry you made in Problem 7C-3.

Check Figure

Payroll Taxes Expense $186.35

Recording benefits expense and liabilities

8C-5. Munchkin Bakery Ltd. pays its employees every two weeks (26 pay periods per year). There are two pay periods in the month of March, and details of each follow:

Check Figure

Payroll Taxes Expense $548.40

March 12 Payroll

		Deductions						
Employee	*Salary*	*IT*	*CPP*	*EI*	*Health*	*Union*	*Net Pay*	*Chq. No.*
Holly Wilson	1,700	422	50	46	22	8	1,152	358
Reg Black	1,025	180	28	28	22	8	759	359
Amos Troy	1,150	211	32	31	38	8	830	360
Bernie Dyck	975	169	27	26	38	8	707	361
Cindy Nishimura	1,210	235	34	33	22	8	878	362
Totals	6,060	1,217	171	164	142	40	4,326	

March 26 Payroll

		Deductions						
Employee	*Salary*	*IT*	*CPP*	*EI*	*Health*	*Union*	*Net Pay*	*Chq. No.*
Holly Wilson	1,700	422	50	46	22	8	1,152	386
Reg Black	1,050	187	29	28	22	8	776	387
Amos Troy	1,100	199	31	30	38	8	794	388
Bernie Dyck	1,025	180	28	28	38	8	743	389
Cindy Nishimura	1,246	247	36	34	22	8	899	390
Totals	6,121	1,235	174	166	142	40	4,364	

Union dues must be remitted to the union treasurer by the 28th of the following month, while health premiums are matched by Munchkin and remitted to the provincial treasurer by the 10th of the month following. A cheque is sent to the Receiver General by the 15th of each following month as well.

Recording benefits expense and related liabilities for two pay periods, plus calculating details of payroll benefits cheques to be issued

Required

a. Assuming that the payroll register has been journalized but no other related entries made, prepare the two journal entries necessary to record the benefits expense for March.

b. Give the details of all cheques which Munchkin will issue in April with respect to payroll deductions.

Check Figure

Cheque to Receiver General for Canada $7,146.62

Recording benefits expense and related liabilities for five pay periods in a month, plus calculating details of payroll benefits cheques to be issued

8C-6. The Grierson Auto Repair Company pays each of its employees weekly each Friday. During the month of May there were five pay periods, which are detailed below. (Note that employees pay 100 percent of the cost of health and dental plans.)

Week 1

		Deductions							
Employee	*Weekly Earnings*	*IT*	*CPP*	*EI*	*Union Dues*	*Health Plan*	*Dental Plan*	*Net Pay*	*Chq. No.*
Hal Dyer	740.00	167.90	21.49	19.98	7.00	13.20	9.75	500.68	1475
Carol James	785.00	186.30	22.97	21.15	7.00	9.20	9.75	528.63	1476
LeRoy Cohen	866.00	217.10	25.61	23.34	7.00	9.20	9.75	574.00	1477
Peter Tsui	900.00	230.20	26.57	24.31	7.00	13.20	9.75	588.97	1478
Wendy Sage	725.00	161.85	21.05	19.55	7.00	13.20	9.75	492.60	1479
Weekly Totals	4,016.00	963.35	117.69	108.33	35.00	58.00	48.75	2,684.88	

Week 2

		Deductions							
Employee	*Weekly Earnings*	*IT*	*CPP*	*EI*	*Union Dues*	*Health Plan*	*Dental Plan*	*Net Pay*	*Chq. No.*
Hal Dyer	718.00	158.85	20.79	19.39	7.00	13.20	9.75	489.02	1512
Carol James	738.00	167.90	21.43	19.93	7.00	9.20	9.75	502.79	1513
LeRoy Cohen	884.00	223.25	26.09	23.83	7.00	9.20	9.75	584.88	1514
Peter Tsui	892.00	226.35	26.41	24.07	7.00	13.20	9.75	585.22	1515
Wendy Sage	705.00	155.80	20.41	19.01	7.00	13.20	9.75	479.83	1516
Weekly Totals	3,937.00	932.15	115.13	106.23	35.00	58.00	48.75	2,641.74	

Week 3

		Deductions							
Employee	*Weekly Earnings*	*IT*	*CPP*	*EI*	*Union Dues*	*Health Plan*	*Dental Plan*	*Net Pay*	*Chq. No.*
Hal Dyer	765.00	177.10	22.33	20.67	7.00	13.20	9.75	514.95	1577
Carol James	714.00	158.85	20.66	19.28	7.00	9.20	9.75	489.26	1578
LeRoy Cohen	832.00	201.70	24.49	22.45	7.00	9.20	9.75	557.41	1579
Peter Tsui	916.00	234.80	27.21	24.72	7.00	13.20	9.75	599.32	1580
Wendy Sage	725.00	161.85	21.05	19.55	7.00	13.20	9.75	492.60	1581
Weekly Totals	3,952.00	934.30	115.74	106.67	35.00	58.00	48.75	2,653.54	

Week 4

Employee	Weekly Earnings	Deductions IT	CPP	EI	Union Dues	Health Plan	Dental Plan	Net Pay	Chq. No.
Hal Dyer	810.00	195.55	23.69	21.88	7.00	13.20	10.50	538.18	1604
Carol James	736.00	164.90	21.37	19.87	7.00	9.20	10.50	503.16	1605
LeRoy Cohen	884.00	223.25	26.09	23.83	7.00	9.20	10.50	584.13	1606
Peter Tsui	815.00	195.55	23.85	21.96	7.00	13.20	10.50	542.94	1607
Wendy Sage	725.00	161.85	21.05	19.55	7.00	13.20	10.50	491.85	1608
Weekly Totals	3,970.00	941.10	116.05	107.09	35.00	58.00	52.50	2,660.26	

Week 5

Employee	Weekly Earnings	Deductions IT	CPP	EI	Union Dues	Health Plan	Dental Plan	Net Pay	Chq. No.
Hal Dyer	731.00	164.90	21.24	19.71	7.00	13.20	10.50	494.45	1638
Carol James	714.00	158.85	20.66	19.28	7.00	9.20	10.50	488.51	1639
LeRoy Cohen	866.00	217.10	25.61	23.34	7.00	9.20	10.50	573.25	1640
Peter Tsui	904.00	230.20	26.73	24.39	7.00	13.20	10.50	591.98	1641
Wendy Sage	725.00	161.85	21.05	19.55	7.00	13.20	10.50	491.85	1642
Weekly Totals	3,940.00	932.90	115.29	106.27	35.00	58.00	52.50	2,640.04	

Required

a. Assuming that the payroll register has been journalized but no other related entries have been made, prepare the five journal entries necessary to record the benefits expense for May 2002.

b. Give the details of all cheques which Grierson will issue in June 2002 with respect to payroll deductions.

REAL WORLD APPLICATIONS

(The forms you need are on page 8-16 of the *Study Guide with Working Papers.*)

8R-1.
The Tidy Tax Return Co. employs 50 extra people for the period February 1 through April 30 each year in order to process a large volume of tax returns. Each employee receives $10 per hour and works 40 hours a week (for 14 weeks). Early in May, all 50 additional workers are laid off.

A personnel service has offered to supply the needed 50 workers at a cost of $12 per hour. The managers of Tidy Tax Return Co. are not sure whether to accept the new offer.

Please prepare a memo to the management outlining the advantages of using the personnel service bureau and also the advantages of continuing with the present arrangement. Do not restrict your answer to financial considerations only.

make the call

Critical Thinking/Ethical Case

8R-2.
Abby Ross works in the Payroll Department for Lange Co. as a junior accountant. Abby also is going to school for an advanced degree in accounting. After work each day

she uses the company's photocopy machine to make extra copies of her assignments. Should she be photocopying personal material on a company machine? You make the call. Write down your specific recommendations to Abby.

ACCOUNTING RECALL

A CUMULATIVE APPROACH

THIS EXAMINATION REVIEWS CHAPTERS 1 THROUGH 8.

Your *Study Guide with Working Papers* (pages 8-17 to 8-18) has forms to complete this exam, as well as worked-out solutions. The page reference next to each question identifies the page to turn back to if you answer the question incorrectly.

PART I Vocabulary Review

Match the terms to the appropriate definition or phrase.

Page Ref.	Term		Definition
(316)	1. PD7A	A.	A liability account
(313)	2. Payroll tax expense	B.	Form used to obtain a Business Number
(280)	3. Union dues	C.	Makes two differing amounts agree.
(322)	4. Fiscal year	D.	Rarely an expense
(320)	5. T4 Summary	E.	Form sent with remittance
(227)	6. Bank reconciliation	F.	Employer's share of benefits
(286)	7. Record of employment	G.	Any 52-week period
(280)	8. Medical plan payable	H.	Filled out only when an employee leaves
(311)	9. RC1(E)	I.	Form summarizing calendar year events in the payroll

PART II True or False (Accounting Theory)

(312) 10. Income tax deductions are part of the payroll tax expense.

(311) 11. Remittances are sent to the Receiver General each quarter.

(277) 12. Employees often must pay more income tax than has been deducted from their paycheques.

(286) 13. Employers are required by law to file a record of employment form for each employee annually.

(311) 14. Each employer must obtain a unique identification number from the federal government to permit employee deductions to be tracked accurately.

Continuing Problem

Because it is the end of the calendar year, Tony Freedman knows that, in addition to recording the normal entries for December, he will need to complete certain tasks which relate to payroll. Specifically, he will need to prepare T4 slips for his two employees, then complete the T4 Summary for the year (remember that he has had employees for only two months).

Assignment

(See pages 8-19 to 8-31 in your *Study Guide with Working Papers.*)

Dec. 1 Record the employer's share of payroll benefits for the previous month. Refer to the work you completed for the end of November (Chapter 7) for the details you need to complete this task.

5 Paid the two employees their wages: L. Kumm, 43 hours, and A. Hall, 34 hours (cheques No. 228 and No. 229).

7 Received the balance of the amount due from Vita Needle Company, November 1, 2001, invoice No. 12676.

9 Received invoice No. 4668 from City Newspaper re advertising seasonal specials, terms 2% 10 days, net 30 days, $480.

10 Received December telephone bill, $165.

12 Paid the two employees their wages: L. Kumm, 40 hours, and A. Hall, 42 hours (cheques No. 230 and No. 231).

13 Paid telephone bill received November 9, $150 (cheque No. 232).

14 Collected amount owing by Accu Pac, Inc., re November 3 invoice No. 12677.

15 Purchased for cash the remaining inventory of a friend's computer sales operation, $7,000 (cheque No. 233).

15 Paid amount due to Receiver General re November wages, $768.84 (cheque No. 234).

16 Paid amount due to System Design Furniture re November 5 purchase (their invoice No. 8771), $1,400 (cheque No. 235).

17 Paid amount due to Multi Systems for November 20 purchase (their invoice No. 1784), $450 (cheque No. 236).

18 Purchased on account from Alpha Office Co., supplies totalling $318, their invoice No. 8161, terms net 30 Days.

19 Paid the two employees their wages: L. Kumm, 34 hours, and A. Hall, 36 hours (cheques No. 237 and No. 238).

20 Billed new customer, Carson Engineering Corp., for major project involving 28 of their computers, $8,750. Invoice No. 12678.

21 Paid overdue utilities bill for November and December, $486.00, to City Electric (cheque No. 239).

24 Paid the two employees their wages to noon today: L. Kumm, 32 hours, and A. Hall, 38 hours (cheques No. 240 and No. 241). Because of seasonal factors, these are their final cheques this calendar year (office closed until January 2, 2002).

31 Record the employer's share of payroll benefits for the month of December. Refer to the details of your payroll journal in order to complete this task.

Pete's Market

Completing Payroll Requirements

This Mini Practice Set will aid in putting the pieces of payroll together. In this project, you are the bookkeeper and will have the responsibility of recording payroll in the payroll register, paying the payroll, recording the employer's tax responsibilities, and making payment according to the Receiver General's requirements.

Pete's Market, owned by Pete Reel, is located at 33 Riel Drive, Your Town, Alberta T5C 1L2. His Business Number is 12345 6789 RP. The following are the employees of Pete's Market, along with their salaries, exemptions, etc.

Weekly Salaries

Date	*Name*	*Claim Code*	*Weekly Salary*
Oct. 4, 2001	Fred Flynn	1	$900
Oct. 11, 2001	Fred Flynn	1	900
Oct. 18, 2001	Fred Flynn	1	950
Oct. 25, 2001	Fred Flynn	1	950

Note: Fred Flynn receives a salary increase October 12, 2001.

Date	*Name*	*Claim Code*	*Weekly Salary*
Oct. 4, 2001	Mary Jones	1	$850
Oct. 11, 2001	Mary Jones	1	850
Oct. 18, 2001	Mary Jones	1	850
Oct. 25, 2001	Mary Jones	1	850

Note: On October 11, 2001, Mary reaches her CPP maximum of $1,068.80. Deduct only $2.31 CPP for Mary in that payroll, then no further CPP in October.

Date	*Name*	*Claim Code*	*Weekly Salary*
Oct. 4, 2001	Lilly Vron	1	$700
Oct. 11, 2001	Lilly Vron	1	700
Oct. 18, 2001	Lilly Vron	1	700
Oct. 25, 2001	Lilly Vron	1	700

Source deductions payable at September 30, 2001 (employer portion already recorded):

CPP Payable	*EI Payable*	*Income Taxes Payable*
$503.68	$623.12	$2,427.52

Required

(The forms you need are on pages 8-34 to 8-36 of the *Study Guide with Working Papers.*)

Using the general journal and payroll register provided, complete the following for the month of October 2001:

2001

Oct. 4 Complete payroll register for October 4 payroll, journal payroll entry, and journalize entry for employer's CPP and EI expense.

4 Transfer cash for October 4 payroll net pay from operating account to payroll account.

11 Process payroll (follow same procedures as for October 4 payroll above).

11 Transfer cash for October 11 payroll net pay from operating account to payroll account.

15 Pay Receiver General for prior month's source deductions payable.

18 Process payroll for October 18. Note change in Fred Flynn's salary.

18 Transfer cash for October 18 payroll net pay from operating account to payroll account.

25 Process payroll for October 25.

25 Transfer cash for October 25 payroll net pay from operating account to payroll account.

Computerized Accounting Application for Pete's Market Mini Practice Set (Chapter 8)

Completing Payroll and Miscellaneous Other Requirements

Before starting on this assignment, read and complete the tasks discussed in Parts A, B, and F of Appendix B at the end of this book and complete the Computer Workshop assignments for Chapter 3, Chapter 4, and the Valdez Realty Mini Practice Set (Chapter 5).

Pete's Market, owned by Pete Reel, is located at 33 Riel Drive, Your Town, Alberta T5C 1L2. His Business No. is 12345 6789 RP. The data set for *CA-Simply Accounting for Windows* packaged with this text uses the 1998 federal and provincial tax laws, and these are calculated automatically by the program. If your version of the program uses a different set of tax laws, your figures may vary a bit from the figures provided, but they should be reasonably similar.

The Payroll Journal in *CA-Simply Accounting for Windows* is designed to work with the General Ledger module in an integrated fashion. When transactions are recorded in the Payroll Journal, the program automatically updates the Payroll Register, records the journal entry, and posts to all accounts affected in the General Ledger. The following are the employees of Pete's Market and their weekly wages for the month of October:

	Fred Flynn	*Mary Jones*	*Lilly Vron*
Oct. 4	900	850	700
Oct. 11	900	850	700
Oct. 18	950	850	700
Oct. 25	950	850	700

The claim code for all employees is 1, except that Mary Jones changes to code 4 on October 25 (you will need to make this change). The personal exemption is $6,456 for code 1 and $11,202 for code 4.

On October 12, Fred Flynn received a raise of $50 per week. Mary will reach the maximum CPP contribution for the year as outlined by Revenue Canada during the month, and you will need to manage this situation correctly. The maximum CPP payable in the current year is $1,068.80.

Here is the trial balance for Pete's Market as at 30/09/2003 provided in the data set:

1010	Operating Account	$30,451.14	—
1020	Payroll Account	529.24	—
1050	GST Paid	3,897.12	—
1110	Computer Equipment	3,500.00	—
1210	Furniture and Fixtures	2,750.00	—
2010	Accounts Payable		$2,086.50
2270	EI Payable		635.04
2280	CPP Payable		575.60
2290	Income Taxes Payable		2,326.24
2395	GST Collected		9,601.56

2450	Loan Payable		$ 950.00
3600	Pete Reel, Capital		10,000.00
4005	Sales		$158,403.94
5040	Purchases	66,713.95	—
5520	Accounting and Legal	825.00	—
5530	Advertising	387.24	—
5535	Bank Charges and Interest	35.00	—
5545	Office	200.00	—
5555	Telephone	242.04	—
5560	Wages	69,600.00	—
5565	EI Expense	2,630.85	—
5570	CPP Expense	2,042.30	—
5585	Courses	775.00	—
	Totals	$184,578.88	$184,578.88

1. Start Windows; insert your Student Data Files disk into drive A or B; then double-click on the CA-Simply Accounting icon. The CA-Simply Accounting Open File dialogue box will appear.
2. Enter the following path into the **Open File name** text box:
   - ◆ `a:\pete:asc` (if you are storing your student data files on the disk in drive A).
3. Click on the **OK** button; enter "10/04/2003" into the **Session** text box; then click on the **OK** button. The Company Window for Pete will appear.
4. Click on the Company Window **Setup** Menu; then click on Company Information. The Company Information dialogue box will appear. Insert your name in place of the text "Name" in the **Name** text box. Click on the **OK** button to return to the Company Window.
5. Double-click on the Payroll Journal icon. The Payroll Journal dialogue box will appear.
6. Click on the arrow button to the right of the **To the Order of** text box. Click on Fred Flynn's name; then press the TAB key.
7. Accept the default cheque number; click on the **TAB** key, enter date, click again on the TAB key; click on the **Salary** text box; enter "900"; then press the TAB key. This completes the data you need to enter into the Payroll Journal dialogue box to record the payroll journal entry for Fred Flynn's October 4 weekly payroll. Your screen should look like this:

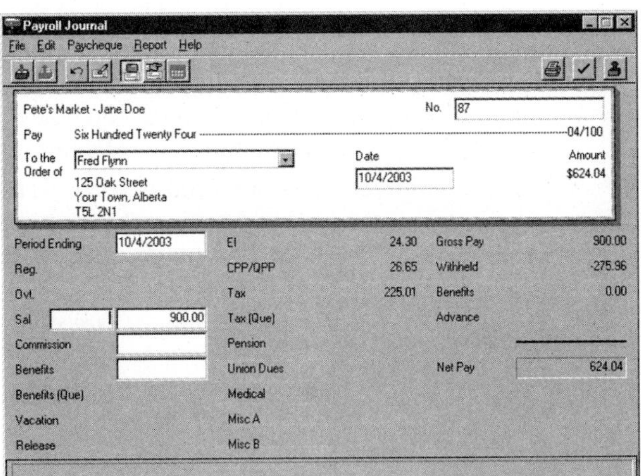

8. Before posting this transaction, you need to verify that the transaction data are correct by reviewing the Payroll Journal entry. To review the entry, click on the Payroll Journal **Report** menu; then click on Display Payroll Journal Entry. The journal entry representing the data you have recorded in the Payroll Journal dialogue box is displayed.
9. Note that the program has combined the journal entry to record and pay the payroll with the journal entry to record the employer's payroll tax expenses into a single compound journal entry. Also note that the program uses three individual payroll tax expense accounts (CPP, EI, and Tax Expense) in place of a single Payroll Tax Expense account. Review the payroll entry for accuracy, noting any errors.
10. Close the Payroll Journal Entry window by double-clicking on the **Control** menu box. If you have made an error, use the following editing techniques to correct it:

Editing a Payroll Journal Entry

- Move to the text box that contains the error by pressing either the TAB key to move forward through each text box or the SHIFT and TAB keys together to move to a previous text box. This will highlight the selected text box information so that you can change it. Alternatively, you can use the mouse to point to a text box and drag through the incorrect information to highlight it.
- Type the correct information; then press the TAB key to enter it.
- If you have associated the transaction with an incorrect employee, reselect the correct employee from the employee list display after clicking on the arrow button to the right of the **To the Order of** text box.
- To discard an entry and start over, double-click on the **Control** menu box. Click on the **Yes** button in response to the question "Are you sure you want to discard this journal entry?"
- Review the journal entry for accuracy after editing corrections.
- It is important to note that the only way to edit a payroll journal entry after it is posted is to reverse the entry and input the correct entry. To correct payroll journal entries posted in error, see Part C of Appendix B.

11. After verifying that the payroll journal entry is correct, click on the Post icon to post this transaction. A blank Payroll Journal dialogue box is displayed, ready for additional Payroll Journal transactions to be recorded.
12. Record the October 4 payroll journal for Mary Jones and Lilly Vron in a manner similar to your recording of Fred Flynn. Close the Payroll Journal.
13. Using the General Journal, record a transfer to the payroll bank account from the general bank account for the exact amount of the net pay for the three employees, as determined in the payroll entries you have just completed. You may find it handy to view or print the payroll journal to assist you with this task. Date this entry 10/04/03 (so there is no need to adjust the **Session** date) and use TSF-40 for the source.
14. Click on the Company Window **Maintenance** menu; then click on Advance Session Date. Click on No in response to the question "You have never backed up your data. Would you like to backup now?" Enter "10/10/03" into the **New session date** text box; then click on the **OK** button.
15. Using the General Journal, record the transactions below. Before entering these, create a new account, Office Supplies (number 1040). Make this a right account so that it will add in with other current asset accounts.

    Oct. 9 — Paid for office supplies, $202 to T&G Office Supplies Co. Use cheque number 43 for the operating account.

    Oct. 10 — Purchased products from Market Distributions on account, $2,165.
16. Click on the Company Window **Maintenance** menu; then click on Advance Session Date. Enter "10/11/03" into the **New session date** text box; then click on the **OK** button.
17. Record the October 11 payroll for Fred Flynn, Mary Jones, and Lilly Vron. Close the Payroll Journal.

18. Using the General Journal, record a transfer to the payroll bank account from the general bank account for the exact amount of the net pay for the three employees, as determined in the October 11 payroll entries you just completed.

19. Advance **Session** date to 10/13/03. Record the following general journal entry after setting up the new account described:

    Oct. 13 Pete Reel withdraws $3,000 from the business general account for personal use. Use the cheque number 44. You must set up a new account in the ledger to handle this withdrawal. Use account number 3710. See Appendix A if assistance is needed in setting up accounts.

20. Advance **Session** date to 10/15/03. Record the following general journal entry:

    Oct. 15 Record the compound journal entry for the payment of source deductions to the Receiver General for Canada from last month's payroll. The figures you need are on the trial balance (see above). Use cheque number 45 from the operating bank account.

21. Advance **Session** date to 10/17/03. Record the following general journal entry:

    Oct. 17 Purchased a new office desk from Office Warehouse on account, $450. Use a logical cheque number.

22. Close the General Journal. In the Company Window, click on **Maintenance**; then advance **Session** date to 10/18/03.

    Note that Fred Flynn's salary increased from $900 to $950. You will need to make this change before recording the October 18 payroll. In the Company Window, click on **Employee Ledger** and change the salary per pay period from $900 to $950.

23. Record the October 18 payroll for Fred Flynn, Mary Jones, and Lilly Vron.

24. After you have posted the payroll journal entries, double-click on the **Control** menu box to close the Payroll Journal dialogue box. This will restore the Company Window screen.

25. Using the General Journal, record a transfer to the payroll bank account from the general bank account for the exact amount of the net pay for the three employees, as determined in the October 18 payroll entries you just completed.

26. Change the **Session** date to 10/25/03 and record the 10/25/03 payroll journal entries for Fred Flynn and Lilly Vron.

    Note that Mary Jones's claim code changed from 1 to 4. To make this change double-click on her **Employee Ledger** from the Company Window and enter "11,202" as her total claim amount in the **Federal Claim** box. Record Mary Jones's payroll for 10/25/03.

    Notice also that the program automatically adjusted Mary's CPP deduction toward the end of October. Since she reached the maximum for the year ($1,068.80 as this book is written), no additional deduction is necessary after this point is reached.

    Remember to transfer funds to the payroll bank account.

27. Click on the Company Window **Report** menu; then click on Employee. The Employee Report Options dialogue box will appear. Click on the **Employee Summary** option button; click on the **Select All** button; then click **OK**. From the **File** menu option, select Print to print the report. Close this window and open the General Journal.

28. Using the General Journal, and a **Session** date of 10/30/03, record the following transactions (use logical cheque numbers in all cases):

    Oct. 26 Payment to JR Accounting Services, $625

    Oct. 27 Payment to Campus Telephone, $82.15

    Oct. 30 Deposit to general account. Sales for the month were $8,878.50.

29. Record the accrued salaries payable ($2000) as of October 31, 2003. You will need to create a new account (Accrued Salaries Payable, number 2398) before making this adjusting entry in the General Journal as of 10/31/03. If you need help in creating a new account, see Appendix A.

30. The program can display and print separate journal reports that list transactions recorded in a specific journal (General, Purchases, Payments, Sales, Receipts, Payroll, Transfers, or Adjustments). The program can also generate a single General Journal

Report that lists transactions recorded in all journals. To display or print such a report, check the **All ledger entries** check box.

31. Print the following reports:
    a. Employee Summary (Select All).
    b. General Journal (By posting date, All ledger entries, Start 10/01/03, finish 10/31/03).
    c. Trial Balance as of 10/31/03.
    d. Financial statements (if required by your instructor).
32. Review your printed reports. If you have made an error in a posted journal entry, see Part C of Appendix B for information on how to correct the error.
33. Click on the Company Window **File** menu; click on Save As; then enter the new file name into the **Save file as** text box:
    - `a:\peteoct.asc` (if you are storing your student data files on the disk in drive A).
34. Click on the **Save** button. Note that the company name in the Company Window has changed from Pete to Peteoct. Click on the Company Window **File** menu again; then click on Save As. Enter the following new file name into the **Save file as** text box:
    - `a:\pete.asc` (if you are storing your student data files on the disk in drive A).
35. Click on the **Save** button. Click on the **Yes** button in response to the question "Replace existing data files with the same name?" Note that the company name in the Company Window has changed back from Peteoct to Pete.
36. You now have two sets of company data files for Pete's Market on your Student Data Files disk. The current data is stored under the file name pete.asc. The October backup data is stored under the file name peteoct.asc.

Special Journals

9

Sales and

Cash

Receipts

The Big Picture

◆

In reviewing the records last month for the Eldorado Computer Centre, Tony Freedman discovered that his retail business had increased his revenue and profits. He also discovered that it is important to keep accurate detailed records of sales transactions. He decided to experiment with some specialized journals to track his sales activity and receipt of cash payments.

The cash receipts journal will assist Freedman in trimming down the number of entries he has to post daily for the business. Since controlling cash is one of the most important things a business must do in order to avoid financial difficulty, cash transactions must be posted accurately. The retail side of his business has increased the cash inflow, and also, by its very nature, the increased potential of loss or theft. Protecting this cash requires implementing some internal control procedures to avoid loss or theft.

The other specialized journal Tony has decided to experiment with is the sales journal. This journal will allow him to keep track of his sales to customers on credit. Freedman has extended more credit to his customers, and he wants to keep a closer look at his sales on account. He wants to know how he is collecting from those sales.

In this chapter you will learn the importance of protecting your cash and collecting your accounts receivable from credit customers. The schedule of accounts receivable prepared at the end of the month will give you details of what dollar amount is owed by each customer. The ease of posting from specialized journals will help reduce the potential for errors when you have a lot of repetitive transactions.

Chapter Objectives

- Journalizing sales on account in a sales journal (p. 354)
- Posting from a sales journal to the general ledger (p. 354)
- Recording in the accounts receivable ledger from a sales journal (p. 354)
- Preparing, journalizing, recording, and posting a credit memorandum (p. 358)
- Recording PST and GST (and HST) in the sales journal as well as with a credit memorandum (pp. 356–359)
- Journalizing and posting transactions using a cash receipts journal, as well as recording to the accounts receivable ledger (pp. 370–371)
- Preparing a schedule of accounts receivable (p. 373)

In Chapters 9 and 10 we will take a look at how merchandising companies operate. Chapter 9 focusses on sellers of goods; Chapter 10 discusses buyers. Let's first look at Chou's Toy Shop to get an overview of merchandise terms and journal entries. After that, we will take an in-depth look at how Art's Wholesale Clothing Company keeps its books.

LEARNING UNIT 9-1

Chou's Toy Shop: Seller's View of a Merchandising Company

Chou's Toy Shop is a **retailer.** It buys toys, games, bikes, etc., from manufacturers and **wholesalers** and resells these goods (or **merchandise**) to its customers. The shelving, display cases, and so on are called "fixtures" or "equipment." These items are not for resale.

Gross sales

Gross sales: revenue earned from the sale of merchandise to customers

Each cash or charge sale made at Chou's Toy Shop is rung up at the cash register. Suppose the shop had $3,000 in sales on July 18. Of that amount, sales worth $1,800 were cash sales and $1,200 worth of sales were charged. This is how the account that recorded those sales would look:

Sales (Gross)	
Dr.	Cr.
	3,000 ← Revenue account with a credit balance

This account is a revenue account with a credit balance and will be found on the income statement. Here is the journal entry for the day. ***Note:*** We will talk about provincial sales tax and GST later.

Accounts Affected	Category	↑↓	Rules	T Account Update
Cash	Asset	↑	Dr.	Cash: Dr. 1,800
Accounts Receivable	Asset	↑	Dr.	Accounts Receivable: Dr. 1,200
Sales	Revenue	↑	Cr.	Sales: Cr. 3,000

July	18	Cash		1800 00		
		Accounts Receivable		1200 00		
		Sales			3000 00	
		Sales for July 18				

SALES RETURNS AND ALLOWANCES

It would be great for Chou if all the customers were completely satisfied, but that is rarely the case. On July 19, Michelle Reese brought back a doll she bought on account for $50. She told Chou that the doll was defective and she wanted either a price reduction or a new doll. They agreed on a $10 price reduction. Michelle now owes Chou $40. The account called **Sales Returns and Allowances** would record this information.

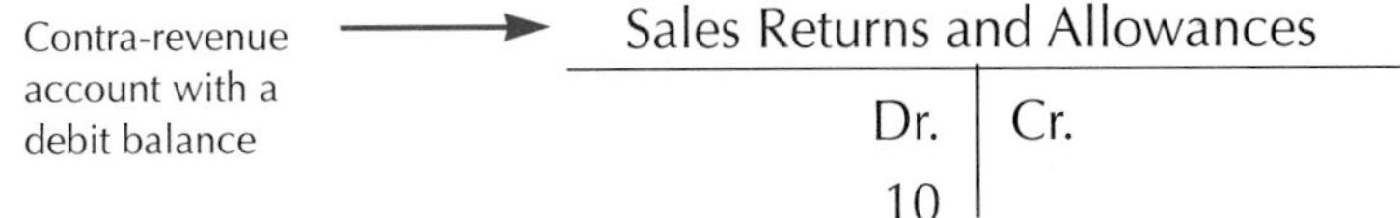

This account is a contra-revenue account with a debit balance. It will be recorded on the income statement. This is how the journal entry would look:

Accounts Affected	Category	↑↓	Rules	T Account Update
Sales Returns and Allowances	**Revenue (Contra)**	↓	**Dr.**	**Sales Returns & Allowances** Dr. 10 | Cr.
Accounts Receivable, Michelle Reese	**Asset**	↓	**Cr.**	**Accounts Receivable** Dr. 1,200 | Cr. 10

Look at how the sales returns and allowances increase.

July	19	Sales Returns and Allowances		10 00		
		Accounts Receivable, Michelle Reese			10 00	
		Issued credit memorandum				

SALES DISCOUNT

Chou gives a 2 percent **sales discount** to customers who pay their bills early. He wanted his customers to know about this policy, so he posted the following sign at the cash register:

Sales Discount Policy

2/10, n/30	2% discount is allowed off price on bill if paid within the first 10 days, or full amount is due within 30 days.
n/10, EOM	No discount, and full amount of bill is due within 10 days after the end of the month.

Note that the **discount period** is the time during which a discount is granted. The discount period is shorter than the **credit period,** which is the length of time allowed to pay the amount owed on the bill.

If Michelle pays her $40 bill early, she will get an $0.80 discount. This is the account that records this information:

Contra-revenue account with a debit balance → Sales Discount

Dr.	Cr.
0.80	

This is how Michelle's discount is calculated:

$$0.02 \times \$40 = \$0.80$$

Michelle pays her bill on July 24. She is entitled to the discount because she paid her bill within 10 days. Let's look at how Chou would record this on the company's books.

Gross sales
− Sales discounts
− SRA
= Net sales

Accounts Affected	Category	↑↓	Rules	T Account Update
Cash	Asset	↑	Dr.	Cash — Dr. 39.20 | Cr.
Sales Discounts	Revenue (Contra)	↓	Dr.	Sales Discounts — Dr. 0.80 | Cr.
Accounts Receivable	Asset	↓	Cr.	Accounts Receivable — Dr. 1,200 | Cr. 10, 40

			Dr.	Cr.
July	24	Cash	39 20	
		Sales Discounts	80	
		Accounts Receivable, Michelle Reese		40 00

Although Michelle pays $39.20, her Accounts Receivable is credited for the full amount, $40. ***Note:*** The actual or **net sales** for Chou would be gross sales less sales returns and allowances and less any sales discounts.

In the examples so far we have not shown any transactions with provincial sales tax. Let's look at how Chou would record monthly sales if provincial sales tax were charged.

Provincial sales tax payable

None of the examples above show provincial sales tax. Still, like it or not, Chou must collect that tax from his customers and send it to the province. Sales tax represents a liability to Chou's business.

Assume that Chou's business is located in a province that charges a 5 percent sales tax. Remember, Chou's sales on July 18 were $3,000. Chou must figure out the provincial sales tax on the sales. For this purpose, let's assume that there were only two sales on that date: the cash sale ($1,800) and the charge sale ($1,200).

The provincial sales tax on the cash sale is calculated as follows:

$$\$1,800 \times 0.05 = \$90 \text{ tax}$$

$$\$1,800 + \$90 \text{ tax} = \$1,890 \text{ cash}$$

Here is how the provincial sales tax on the charge sale is computed:

$$\$1,200 \times 0.05 = \$60 \text{ tax} + \$1,200 \text{ charge} = \$1,260 \text{ Accounts Receivable}$$

This is how it would be recorded:

Accounts Affected	Category	↑↓	Rules	T Account Update
Cash	Asset	↑	Dr.	Cash — Dr. 1,890 | Cr.
Accounts Receivable	Asset	↑	Dr.	Accounts Receivable — Dr. 1,260 | Cr.
Sales Tax Payable	Liability	↑	Cr.	Sales Tax Payable — Dr. | Cr. 90, 60
Sales	Revenue	↑	Cr.	Sales — Dr. | Cr. 3,000

Date		Account Titles and Description	PR	Dr.	Cr.
July	18	Cash		1 8 9 0 00	
		Accounts Receivable		1 2 6 0 00	
		Sales Tax Payable			1 5 0 00
		Sales			3 0 0 0 00
		July 18 Sales			

In a later unit in this chapter, we will show you how to record a credit memorandum with sales tax. Notice that in either case (cash or credit) it is the customer who pays the provincial sales tax, not Chou's business.

LEARNING UNIT 9-1 REVIEW

AT THIS POINT you should be able to:

- Explain the purpose of a contra-revenue account. (p. 349)
- Explain how to calculate net sales. (p. 350)
- Define, journalize, and explain gross sales, sales returns and allowances, and sales discounts. (pp. 348–350)
- Journalize an entry for sales tax payable. (p. 351)

SELF-REVIEW QUIZ 9-1

(The forms you need can be found on page 9-1 of the *Study Guide with Working Papers.*)

Which of the following statements are false?

1. Sales Returns and Allowances is a contra-asset account.
2. Sales Discounts has a normal balance of a debit.
3. Sales Tax Payable is a liability.
4. Sales Discounts is a contra-asset.
5. Credit terms are standard in all industries.

Quiz Tip

Sales	Revenue	↑ Cr.
Sales Returns and Allowances	Revenue (Contra)	↑ Dr.
Sales Discounts	Revenue (Contra)	↑ Dr.

Solution to Self-Review Quiz 9-1

Numbers 1, 4, and 5 are false.

LEARNING UNIT 9-2

The Sales Journal and Accounts Receivable Subsidary Ledger

SPECIAL JOURNALS

Now let's examine how Art's Wholesale Clothing Company keeps its books. Art's business conducts many transactions. The following partial general journal shows the journal entries Art's must make for these sales on account transactions.

ART'S WHOLESALE CLOTHING COMPANY GENERAL JOURNAL					
April	3	Accounts Receivable, Hal's		80000	
		Sales			80000
		Sales on account			
	6	Accounts Receivable, Bevans		160000	
		Sales			160000
		Sales on account			
	18	Accounts Receivable, Roe		200000	
		Sales			200000
		Sales on account			

This method is not very efficient. However, if Art's Wholesale Clothing Company kept a **special journal** for each type of transaction conducted, the number of postings and recordings required for each transaction would be reduced. After carefully looking at the situation with his accountant, Art has decided to use the following special journals:

For a discussion of recording of credit cards in special journals see Appendix A.

Special Journal Type	*What It Records*	
Sales journal	Sale of merchandise on account	Covered in this chapter
Cash receipts journal	Receiving cash from any source	

Purchases journal	Buying merchandise or other items on account	Covered in next chapter
Cash payments journal (cash disbursements journal)	Payment of cash for any purpose	

SUBSIDIARY LEDGERS

In the same way that Art's Wholesale Clothing Company needs more than just a general journal, the business needs more than just a general ledger. For example, so far in this text, the only title we have used for recording amounts owed to the seller has been Accounts Receivable. Art could have replaced the Accounts Receivable title in the general ledger with the following list of customers who owe him money:

- Accounts Receivable, Bevans Company
- Accounts Receivable, Hal's Clothing
- Accounts Receivable, Mel's Department Store
- Accounts Receivable, Roe Company

As you can see, this would not be manageable if Art had 1,000 credit customers. To solve this problem, Art sets up a separate **accounts receivable subsidiary ledger.** Such a special ledger, often simply called a **subsidiary ledger,** contains a single type of account, such as "on account" customers. A page is opened for each customer and the pages are usually arranged alphabetically by customer name.

The diagram in Figure 9-1 shows how the accounts receivable subsidiary ledger fits in with the general ledger. To clarify the difference in updating the general ledger versus the subsidiary ledger, we will *post* to the general ledger and *record* in the subsidiary ledger. The word "post" refers to information that is moved from the journal to the general ledger; the word "record" refers to information that is transferred from the journal into the individual customer's account in the subsidiary ledger.

The general ledger is *not* in the same book as the accounts receivable subsidiary ledger.

The accounts receivable subsidiary ledger, or any other subsidiary ledger, can be in the form of a card file, a binder notebook, or computer tapes or disks. It probably will not have page numbers. The accounts receivable subsidiary ledger is

Proving: At the end of the month, the sum of the accounts receivable subsidiary ledger will equal the ending balance in accounts receivable, the controlling account in the general ledger.

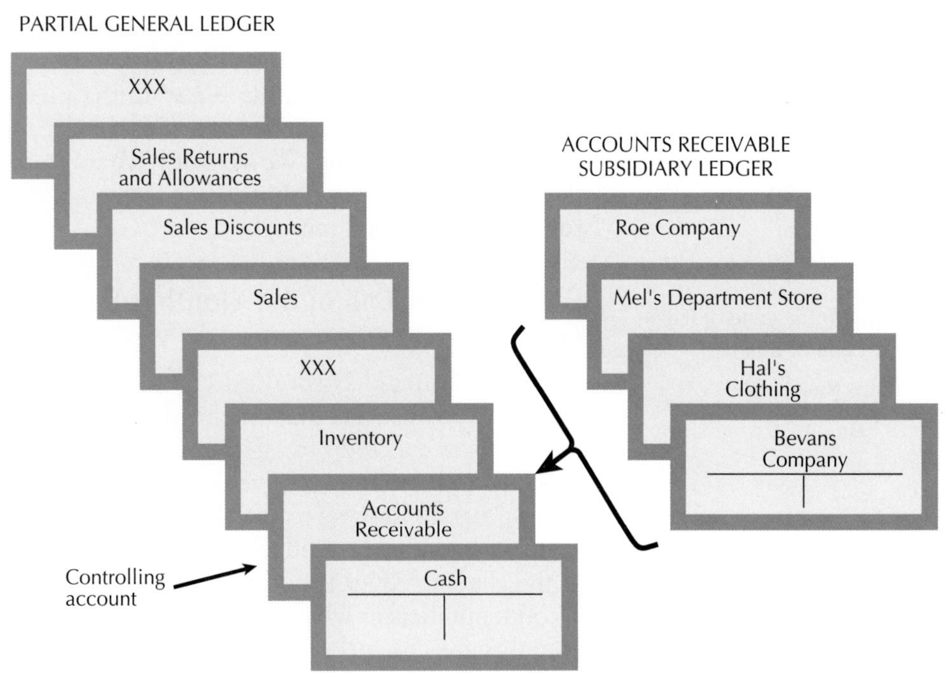

FIGURE 9-1
Partial General Ledger and Accounts Receivable Subsidiary Ledger of Art's Wholesale Clothing Company

organized alphabetically by customer name and address; new customers can be added and inactive customers deleted.

When using an accounts receivable subsidiary ledger, the Accounts Receivable in the general ledger is called the **controlling account,** since it summarizes or controls the accounts receivable subsidiary ledger. At the end of the month the total of the individual accounts in the accounts receivable ledger must equal the ending balance in Accounts Receivable in the general ledger.

Art's Wholesale Clothing Company will use the following subsidiary ledgers:

Accounts receivable subsidiary ledger	Records money owed by credit customers	Covered in this chapter
Accounts payable subsidiary ledger	Records money owed to creditors	Covered in next chapter

Let's now look more closely at the sales journal, general ledger, and subsidiary ledger for Art's Wholesale Clothing Company to see how transactions are updated in the special journal as well as posted and recorded to specific titles.

THE SALES JOURNAL

The **sales journal** for Art's Wholesale Clothing Company records all sales made on account to customers. Figure 9-2 shows the sales journal at the end of the first month in operation, along with the recordings in the accounts receivable ledger and posting to the general ledger. Keep in mind that the reason the balances in the accounts receivable subsidiary ledger are *debit* balances is that the customers listed *owe* Art's Wholesale money. For some companies, a sales journal might have multiple revenue account columns.

Look at the first transaction listed in the sales journal. It shows that on April 3 Art's Wholesale Clothing Company sold merchandise on account to Hal's Clothing for $800. The bill or **sales invoice** for this sale is shown in Figure 9-3 on page 356.

Recording from the Sales Journal to the Accounts Receivable Subsidiary Ledger

Recording in the accounts receivable subsidiary ledger occurs daily.

Hal's Clothing

Dr.	Cr.
4/3 SJ1 800	

✓ in the journal means accounts receivable ledger has been updated.

As shown on the first line of the sales journal in Figure 9-2, the information on the invoice is recorded in the sales journal. However, *the PR column is left blank.* As soon as possible we now update the accounts receivable subsidiary ledger. To do this, we pull out the Hal's Clothing file card and update it: The debit side must show the $800 he owes Art along with the date (April 3) and page of the sales journal (SJ1). Once that is done, place a ✔ in the posting-reference column of the sales journal.The accounts receivable subsidiary ledger shows us Hal's outstanding balance at any moment in time. We do not have to go through all the invoices. Note that the sales journal needs only one line instead of the three lines that would have been required in a general journal.

Posting at the End of the Month from the Sales Journal to the General Ledger

Recording to the general ledger occurs at end of month.

Accounts Receivable 113

Dr.	Cr.
4/30 SJ1 6,500	

Sales 411

Dr.	Cr.
	6,500 4/30 SJ1

The sales journal is totalled ($6,500) at the end of the month. Looking at page 355, you can see that one heading of Art's sales journal is a debit to accounts receivable and a credit to sales. Therefore, at the end of the month the $6,500 total is posted to Accounts Receivable (debit) *and* to Sales (credit) in the general ledger. In the general ledger we record the date (4/30), the initials of the journal (SJ), the page of the sales journal (1), and the appropriate debit or credit ($6,500). Once the account in the general ledger is updated, we place below the totals in the sales journal the account numbers to which the information was posted (as in Figure 9-4, where these accounts are 113 and 411).

FIGURE 9-2
Sales Journal Recording and Postings

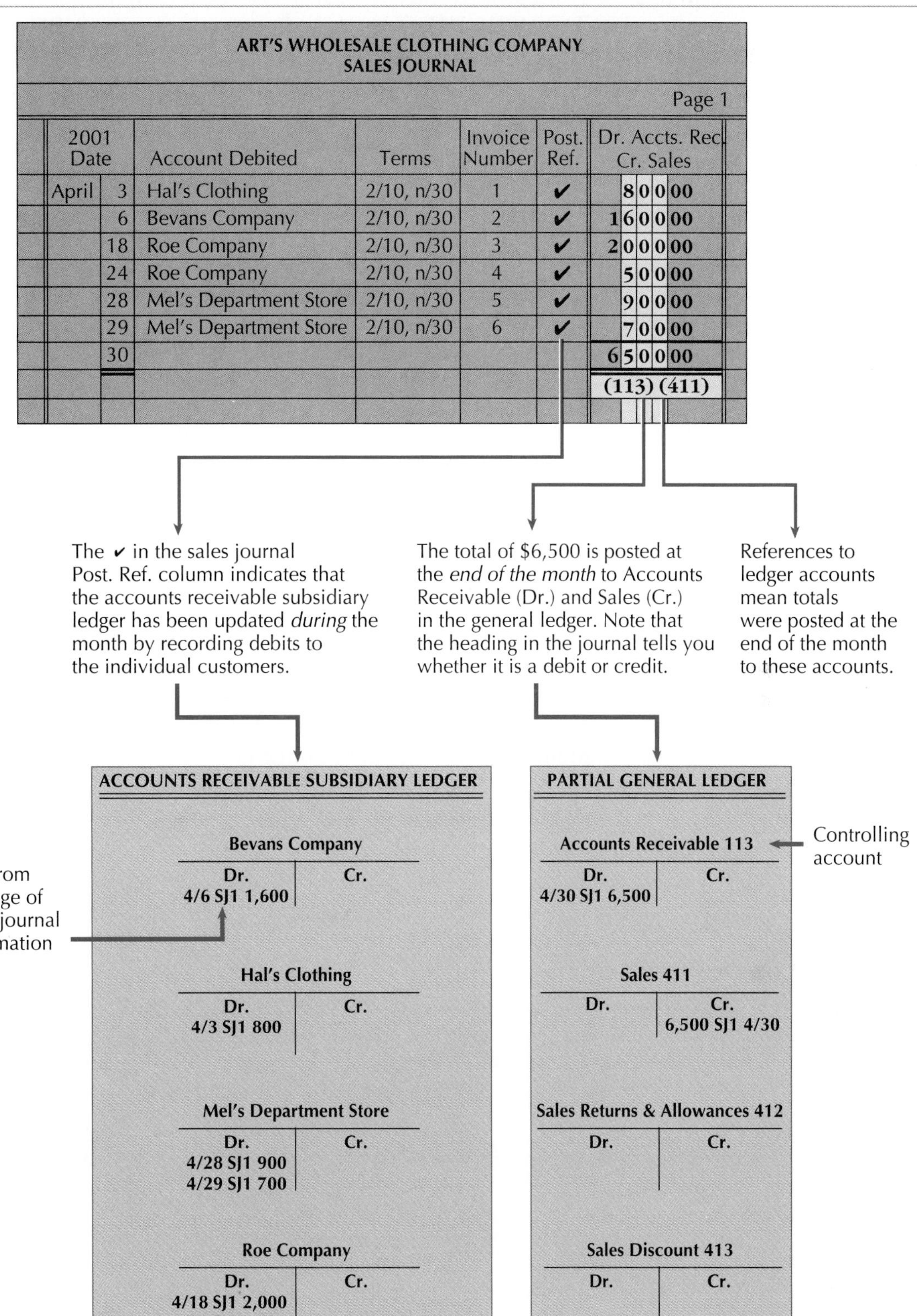

ART'S WHOLESALE CLOTHING COMPANY
SALES JOURNAL

Page 1

2001 Date		Account Debited	Terms	Invoice Number	Post. Ref.	Dr. Accts. Rec. Cr. Sales
April	3	Hal's Clothing	2/10, n/30	1	✔	800 00
	6	Bevans Company	2/10, n/30	2	✔	1600 00
	18	Roe Company	2/10, n/30	3	✔	2000 00
	24	Roe Company	2/10, n/30	4	✔	500 00
	28	Mel's Department Store	2/10, n/30	5	✔	900 00
	29	Mel's Department Store	2/10, n/30	6	✔	700 00
	30					6500 00
						(113) (411)

The ✔ in the sales journal Post. Ref. column indicates that the accounts receivable subsidiary ledger has been updated *during* the month by recording debits to the individual customers.
The total of $6,500 is posted at the *end of the month* to Accounts Receivable (Dr.) and Sales (Cr.) in the general ledger. Note that the heading in the journal tells you whether it is a debit or credit.
References to ledger accounts mean totals were posted at the end of the month to these accounts.
ACCOUNTS RECEIVABLE SUBSIDIARY LEDGER
Bevans Company
Dr. Cr.
4/6 SJ1 1,600
Hal's Clothing
Dr. Cr.
4/3 SJ1 800
Mel's Department Store
Dr. Cr.
4/28 SJ1 900
4/29 SJ1 700
Roe Company
Dr. Cr.
4/18 SJ1 2,000
4/24 SJ1 500
PARTIAL GENERAL LEDGER
Accounts Receivable 113
Dr. Cr.
4/30 SJ1 6,500
Sales 411
Dr. Cr.
6,500 SJ1 4/30
Sales Returns & Allowances 412
Dr. Cr.
Sales Discount 413
Dr. Cr.
Controlling account
Tells us from which page of the sales journal the information comes.

Provincial Sales Tax

Art's Wholesale Clothing Company does not have to deal with provincial sales tax because it sells goods wholesale. However, if Art's were a retail company, it would have to collect and remit provincial sales tax.

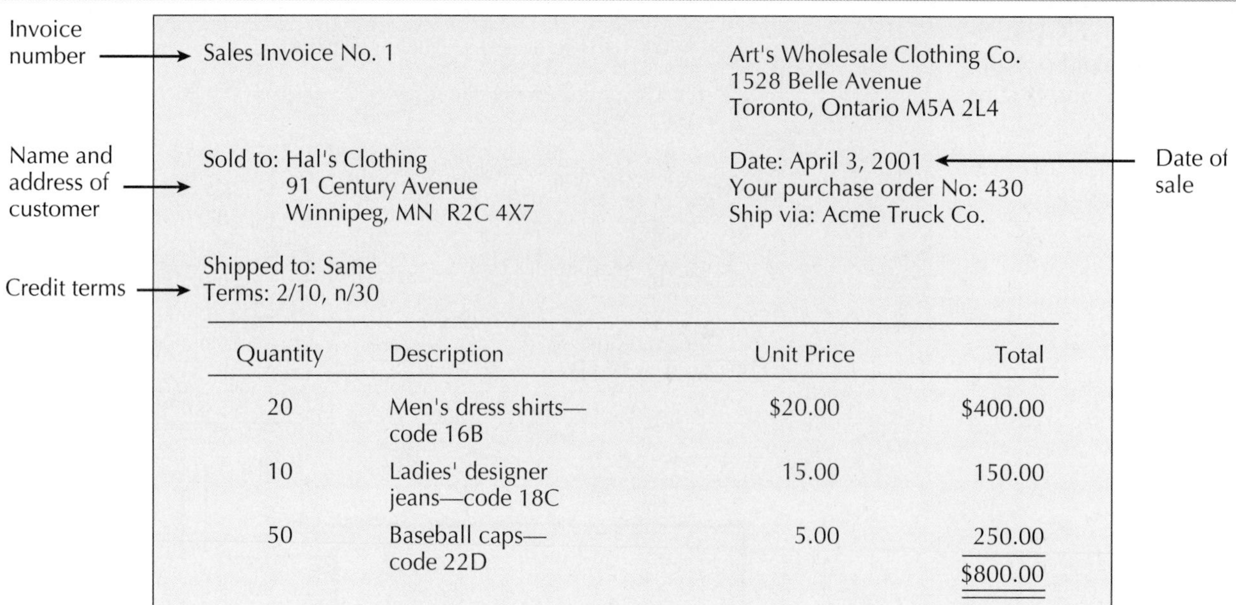

Sales Invoice No. 1

Art's Wholesale Clothing Co.
1528 Belle Avenue
Toronto, Ontario M5A 2L4

Sold to: Hal's Clothing
91 Century Avenue
Winnipeg, MN R2C 4X7

Date: April 3, 2001
Your purchase order No: 430
Ship via: Acme Truck Co.

Shipped to: Same
Terms: 2/10, n/30

Quantity	Description	Unit Price	Total
20	Men's dress shirts—code 16B	$20.00	$400.00
10	Ladies' designer jeans—code 18C	15.00	150.00
50	Baseball caps—code 22D	5.00	250.00
			$800.00

FIGURE 9-3 Sales Invoice

Sales Tax Payable

	XXX

A liability in general ledger

Let's look at how Munroe Menswear Company, a retailer, handles provincial sales tax on a sale made to Jones Company. Figure 9-4 shows Munroe's Sales Journal.

Also, a new account, **Provincial Sales Tax Payable,** must be created. That account is a liability account in the general ledger with a credit balance. The customer owes Munroe the sale amount plus the tax.

Keep in mind that if sales discounts are available they are not normally calculated on the sales tax. The discount is on the selling price less any returns before the tax. For example, if Jones receives a 2 percent discount, he pays the following:

	$5,250	Total owed (tax is $250)
$5,000 × 0.02 = $100 savings →	− 100	Savings (discount)
	$5,150	Amount paid

FIGURE 9-4
Munroe Sales Journal

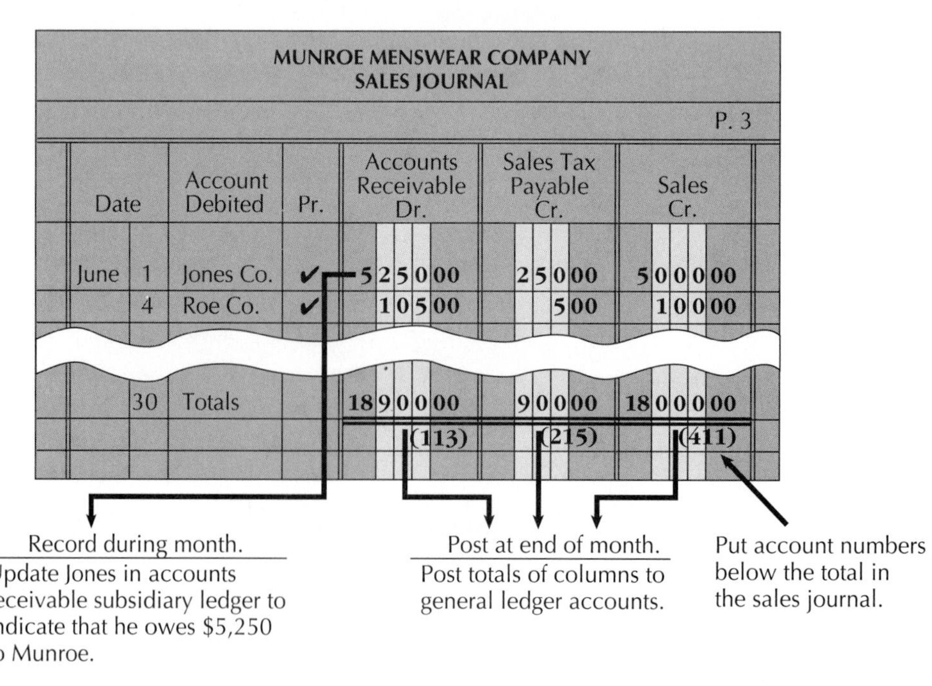

MUNROE MENSWEAR COMPANY
SALES JOURNAL

P. 3

Date		Account Debited	Pr.	Accounts Receivable Dr.	Sales Tax Payable Cr.	Sales Cr.
June	1	Jones Co.	✓	5 2 5 0 00	2 5 0 00	5 0 0 0 00
	4	Roe Co.	✓	1 0 5 00	5 00	1 0 0 00
	30	Totals		18 9 0 0 00	9 0 0 00	18 0 0 0 00
				(113)	(215)	(411)

Record during month.
Update Jones in accounts receivable subsidiary ledger to indicate that he owes $5,250 to Munroe.
Post at end of month.
Post totals of columns to general ledger accounts.
Put account numbers below the total in the sales journal.

LEARNING UNIT 9-2 REVIEW

AT THIS POINT you should be able to:

- Define and state the purposes of special journals. (p. 352)
- Define and state the purposes of the accounts receivable subsidiary ledger. (p. 353)
- Define and state the purpose of the controlling account, Accounts Receivable. (p. 354)
- Journalize, record, and post sales on account to a sales journal and its related accounts receivable and general ledgers. (p. 354)

SELF-REVIEW QUIZ 9-2

(The forms you need are on page 9-1 of the *Study Guide with Working Papers.*)

Which of the following statements are false?

1. Special journals completely replace the general journal.
2. Special journals aid the division of labour.
3. The subsidiary ledger makes the general ledger less manageable.
4. The subsidiary ledger is separate from the general ledger.
5. The controlling account is located in the accounts receivable subsidiary ledger.
6. The total(s) of a sales journal is(are) posted to the general ledger at the end of the month.
7. The accounts receivable subsidiary ledger is arranged in alphabetical order.
8. Transactions recorded into a sales journal are recorded only weekly to the accounts receivable subsidiary ledger.

Quiz Tip

The normal balance of the Accounts Receivable subsidiary ledger is a debit.

Solution to Self-Review Quiz 9-2

Numbers 1, 3, 5, and 8 are false.

LEARNING UNIT 9-3

The Credit Memorandum

At the beginning of this chapter we introduced the Sales Returns and Allowances account. Merchandising businesses often use this account to handle transactions involving goods that have already been sold. For example, if a customer returns the goods he has bought, his account will be credited for the amount charged for the goods returned; if a customer gets an allowance because the goods he purchased were damaged, his account will be credited for the amount of the allowance. In both of these examples, the company's net sales revenue decreases. That is why the account is called a contra-revenue account: The sales revenue decreases and its normal balance is a debit.

A credit memorandum *reduces* accounts receivable.

Companies usually handle sales returns and allowances by means of a **credit memorandum.** Credit memoranda inform customers that the amount of the goods returned or the amount allowed for damaged goods has been subtracted from (credited to) the customer's ongoing account with the company.

End result is that Bevan owes Art's Wholesale less money.

Art's Wholesale Clothing Co.
1528 Belle Avenue
Toronto, ON M5A 2L4

Credit Memorandum No. 1

Date: April 12, 2001

Credit to: Bevans Company
110 Aster Road
Amherst, NS B4H 3A5

We credit your account as follows:
Merchandise returned 60 model 8B men's dress gloves—$600

FIGURE 9-5
Credit Memorandum

Remember, no provincial sales tax was involved because Art's is a wholesale company.

A sample credit memorandum from Art's Wholesale Clothing Company appears in Figure 9-5. It shows that on April 12 credit memo No. 1 was issued to Bevans Company for defective merchandise that had been returned. (Figure 9-2 shows that Art's Wholesale Clothing Company sold Bevans Company $1,600 worth of merchandise on April 6.)

Sales Returns and Allowances

Dr.	Cr.
+	−

A contra-revenue account

Let's assume that Art's Wholesale has high-quality goods and does not expect many sales returns and allowances. On this assumption, no special journal for sales returns and allowances will be needed. Instead, any returns and allowances will be recorded in the general journal, and all postings and recordings will be done when journalized. Let's look at a transaction analysis chart before we journalize, record, and post this transaction.

Note that the Sales Returns and Allowances account is increasing, which in turn reduces sales revenue and reduces the amount owed by the customer (accounts receivable).

Accounts Affected	Category	↑↓	Rules
Sales Returns and Allowances	Revenue (Contra)	↓	Dr.
Accounts Receivable, Bevans Co.	Asset	↓	Cr.

JOURNALIZING, RECORDING, AND POSTING THE CREDIT MEMORANDUM

The credit memorandum results in two postings to the general ledger and one recording in the accounts receivable subsidiary ledger (see Figure 9-6).

FIGURE 9-6
Postings and Recordings for the Credit Memorandum in the Subsidiary and General Ledgers

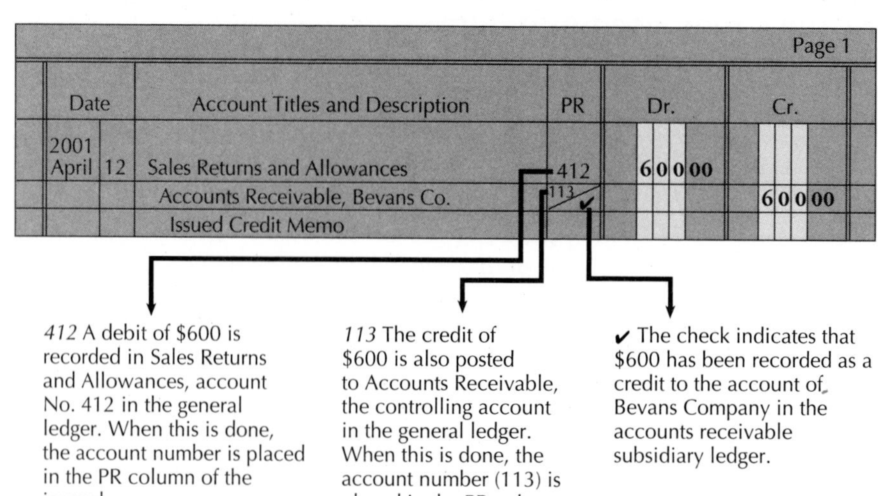
Page 1

Date		Account Titles and Description	PR	Dr.	Cr.
2001 April	12	Sales Returns and Allowances	412	600 00	
		Accounts Receivable, Bevans Co.	113/✓		600 00
		Issued Credit Memo			

412 A debit of $600 is recorded in Sales Returns and Allowances, account No. 412 in the general ledger. When this is done, the account number is placed in the PR column of the journal.
113 The credit of $600 is also posted to Accounts Receivable, the controlling account in the general ledger. When this is done, the account number (113) is placed in the PR column of the journal.
✓ The check indicates that $600 has been recorded as a credit to the account of Bevans Company in the accounts receivable subsidiary ledger.

Remember, sales discounts are *not* taken on returns.

Note in the PR column next to Accounts Receivable, Bevans Co., that there is a diagonal line with the account number 113 above and a ✔ below. This is to show that the amount of $600 has been credited to Accounts Receivable, the controlling account in the general ledger, *and* credited to the account of Bevans Company in the accounts receivable subsidiary ledger.

If the accountant for Art's Wholesale Clothing Company decided to develop a special journal for sales allowances and returns, the entry for a credit memorandum such as the one we've been discussing would look like this:

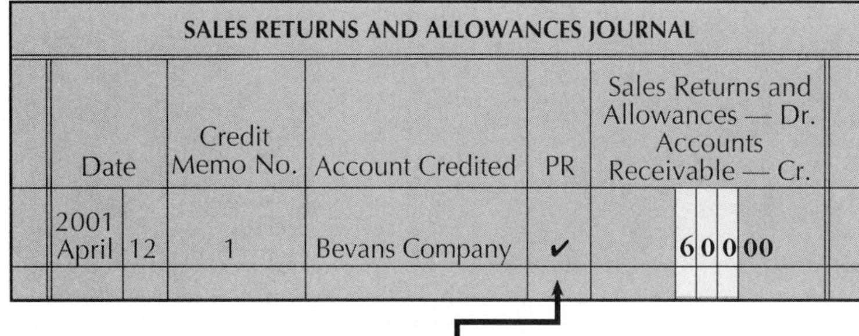

SALES RETURNS AND ALLOWANCES JOURNAL

Date		Credit Memo No.	Account Credited	PR	Sales Returns and Allowances — Dr. Accounts Receivable — Cr.
2001 April	12	1	Bevans Company	✔	600 00

During the month, the subsidiary ledger is updated.

THE CREDIT MEMORANDUM WITH PROVINCIAL SALES TAX (PST)

Figure 9-4 shows the sales journal for Munroe Menswear Company. Remember, since Munroe is a retail company, its customers must pay provincial sales tax if they are in a province which charges PST. Let's assume that on June 8 Roe returns $50 worth of the $100 worth of merchandise he bought earlier in the month. Let's analyze and journalize the credit memo that Munroe issued. Keep in mind that the customer is no longer responsible for paying for either the returned merchandise or the tax on it.

Accounts Affected	Category	↑↓	Rules	T Account Update
Sales Returns and Allowances	Revenue (Contra)	↓	Dr.	Sales Returns and Allowances: Dr. 50 | Cr.
Provincial Sales Tax Payable ($5 tax on $100) ($2.50 tax on $50)	Liability	↓	Dr.	Provincial Sales Tax Payable: Dr. 2.50 | Cr.
Accounts Receivable, Roe	Asset	↓	Cr.	Accounts Receivable: Dr. | Cr. 52.50; Roe Co.: Dr. 105 | Cr. 52.50

Date		Account	PR	Dr.	Cr.
June	8	Sales Returns and Allowances		50 00	
		Provincial Sales Tax Payable		2 50	
		Accounts Receivable, Roe Co.			52 50
		Issued credit memo			

This journal entry requires three postings to the general ledger and one recording for Roe in the accounts receivable subsidiary ledger. Note that since Roe returned half of his merchandise he was able to reduce what he pays for provincial sales tax by half (from $5 to $2.50).

LEARNING UNIT 9-3 REVIEW

AT THIS POINT you should be able to:

- Explain Provincial Sales Tax Payable in relation to Sales Discount. (p. 356)
- Explain, journalize, post, and record a credit memorandum with or without provincial sales tax. (pp. 359–360)

SELF-REVIEW QUIZ 9-3

(The forms you need are on pages 9-1 to 9-3 of the *Study Guide with Working Papers.*)

Journalize the following transactions in the sales journal or general journal for Moss Co. Record in the accounts receivable subsidiary ledger and post to general ledger accounts as appropriate. Use the same journal headings that we used for Art's Wholesale Clothing Company. (All sales carry credit terms of 2/10, n/30.) There is no provincial sales tax.

2000
May 1 Sold merchandise on account to Jane Company, invoice No. 1, $600.
5 Sold merchandise on account to Ralph Company, invoice No. 2, $2,500.
20 Issued credit memo No. 1 to Jane Company for $200 for defective merchandise returned.

Solution to Self-Review Quiz 9-3

Quiz Tip

Total of accounts receivable subsidiary ledger, $400 + $2,500, does indeed equal the balance in the controlling account, accounts receivable, $2,900, at the end of the month, in the general ledger.

MOSS COMPANY
SALES JOURNAL

Page 1

Date		Account Debited	Terms	Invoice No.	Post. Ref.	Dr. Accts. Rec. Cr. Sales
2000 May	1	Jane Company	2/10, n/30	1	✔	600 00
	5	Ralph Company	2/10, n/30	2	✔	2 500 00
	31					3 100 00
						(112) (411)

MOSS COMPANY
GENERAL JOURNAL

Page 1

Date		Account Titles and Description	PR	Dr.	Cr.
2000 May	20	Sales Returns and Allowances	412	200 00	
		Accounts Receivable, Jane Company	112/✔		200 00
		Issued credit memo #1			

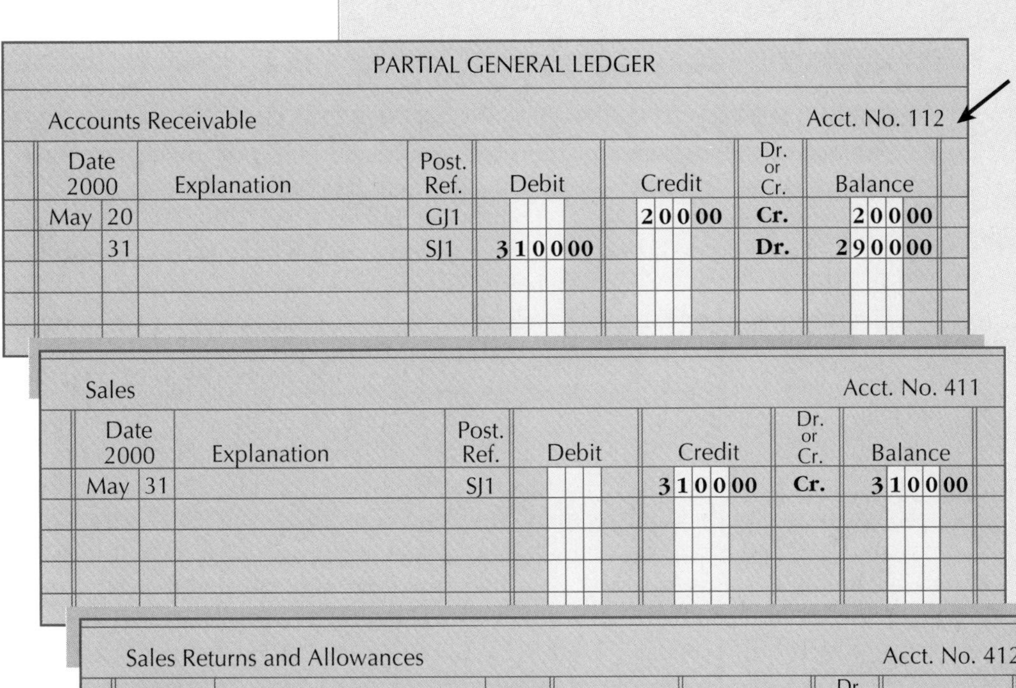

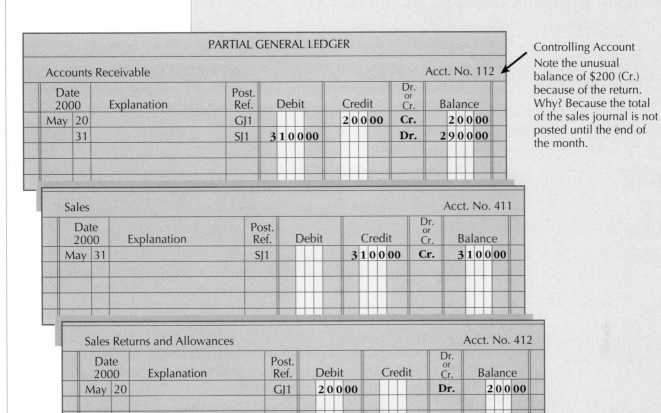

PARTIAL GENERAL LEDGER

Accounts Receivable — Acct. No. 112

Date 2000		Explanation	Post. Ref.	Debit	Credit	Dr. or Cr.	Balance
May	20		GJ1		200 00	Cr.	200 00
	31		SJ1	3 100 00		Dr.	2 900 00

Sales — Acct. No. 411

Date 2000		Explanation	Post. Ref.	Debit	Credit	Dr. or Cr.	Balance
May	31		SJ1		3 100 00	Cr.	3 100 00

Sales Returns and Allowances — Acct. No. 412

Date 2000		Explanation	Post. Ref.	Debit	Credit	Dr. or Cr.	Balance
May	20		GJ1	200 00		Dr.	200 00

Controlling Account

Note the unusual balance of $200 (Cr.) because of the return. Why? Because the total of the sales journal is not posted until the end of the month.

ACCOUNTS RECEIVABLE LEDGER

NAME Jane Company
ADDRESS 1218 Broadview Avenue, Toronto, ON M5X 2A1

Date 2000		Explanation	Post. Ref.	Debit	Credit	Dr. Balance
May	1		SJ1	600 00		600 00
	20		GJ1		200 00	400 00

The customer owes Moss money and thus has a debit balance.

NAME Ralph Company
ADDRESS 1300 Marine Drive, West Vancouver, BC V6P 9B6

Date 2000		Explanation	Post. Ref.	Debit	Credit	Dr. Balance
May	5		SJ1	2 500 00		2 500 00

LEARNING UNIT 9-4

How Companies Record GST and HST

All Canadians must pay either GST (7%) or HST (15%) on the majority of things they buy. The Goods and Services Tax (GST) was introduced in 1991, while the Harmonized Sales Tax (HST) went into effect in 1997. The HST is now collected in Nova Scotia, New Brunswick, and Newfoundland (and may be implemented in other provinces as well by the time you read this). It is designed to eliminate PST in those provinces by combining PST and GST into one tax—the HST. In all three provinces, the HST rate is lower than the previous combination of PST and GST, but it does apply to most services, whereas PST generally did not.

The rules for sharing the HST collected have been agreed to by the provincial and federal governments (the federal government keeps 7 percent and 8 percent goes to the relevant province). It is very important to realize that the rules for GST and HST are identical and, apart from the obvious difference in rates, the accounting procedures are the same. In this textbook, we have elected to illustrate GST (at 7 percent) because the majority of Canadians are faced with this tax. We have included a problem in each of the three sections (A, B, and C problems) which is designed to illustrate HST, and instructors may assign these if appropriate for their students.

Similarities and differences between PST and GST

Before illustrating the normal accounting treatment of the GST/HST, notice that there are both similarities and differences between the GST and provincial sales taxes (covered in Learning Unit 9-3). Like the provincial sales tax (PST), the GST/HST is added to the total of each invoice prepared for a customer. And, like the PST, the GST/HST must be remitted to the appropriate taxing authority periodically.

However, there are also a few notable differences:

1. GST/HST applies to services as well as goods (for example, a lawyer will add 7 (or 15) percent to each invoice for professional services).
2. GST/HST applies at all levels in the economy—not just the retail level as in the case of PST.
3. GST/HST is paid by businesses to their suppliers as well as collected by them from their customers. The difference between the tax collected from customers and the tax paid to suppliers is the amount sent to the federal government each period.
4. GST/HST might result in a business's receiving a refund in some periods. Since GST/HST is payable on large asset purchases (a delivery van, for example), a business may claim this amount against the GST/HST they owe. In the long run, if a business is successful, it should remit more GST/HST than it receives as a refund; however in a particular period it may be eligible to receive a refund.

GST/HST COLLECTED ON SALES

To illustrate the basic accounting treatment for **GST/HST collected**, we will refer to an example you have already seen. Figure 9-3 (sales invoice) showed what an invoice would look like before GST/HST. Figure 9-7 shows the same invoice with GST added.

Note: There are more similarities with than differences from the bookkeeping procedures described previously.

You should notice two things about this invoice. First, GST is added at 7 percent (HST would be added at 15 percent) of the total price of the goods. Second, the invoice shows a registration (or business) number. Each business in Canada (*except very small ones*) must be registered for GST/HST by the federal government and use the number in all their dealings with the federal government. (It is the same number illustrated in the previous chapter with respect to payroll remittances, but with a different suffix.)

FIGURE 9-7
Sales Invoice with GST

Sales Invoice No. 1

Art's Wholesale
Clothing Co.
1528 Belle Avenue
Toronto, Ontario, M5A 2L4

Sold to: Hal's Clothing
91 Century Avenue
Winnipeg, MN R2C 4X7

Date: April 3, 2001
Your purchase order No: 430
Ship via: Acme Truck Co.

Shipped to: Same
Terms: 2/10, n/30

Quantity	Description	Unit Price	Total
20	Men's dress shirts—code 16B	$20.00	$400.00
10	Ladies' designer jeans—code 18C	15.00	150.00
50	Baseball caps—code 22D	5.00	250.00
		Subtotal	$800.00
	Add:	GST	56.00
		TOTAL	$856.00

Business No. 109309799

This invoice is recorded in the sales journal of Art's Wholesale Clothing Company. The main difference is that now the bookkeeping task is made slightly longer because of the need to keep track of the GST. Figure 9-2 showed the sales journal before GST. Figure 9-8 shows how this new invoice, and some others not illustrated individually, are recorded with GST. Posting to the various ledger accounts is also illustrated.

The total invoice amounts are posted during the month to the individual customers' accounts in the accounts receivable ledger. This process is identical to the pre-GST/HST method except that the totals are higher.

At the end of the month, instead of posting a single amount as *both* a credit (to Sales) and a debit (to Accounts Receivable), there are three totals to post. A new account is now required—GST collected, #212. This is a liability account in the general ledger with a credit balance. Notice that the totals of the two credits (Sales and GST) equal the single debit (Accounts Receivable).

GST/HST AND THE CREDIT MEMORANDUM

The credit memorandum with GST is very similar to an invoice with GST except that the amounts are opposite in meaning and effect, and often smaller.

As you already know, occasionally a business finds it necessary to issue to a customer a credit memorandum (often called a credit note). The pre-GST form of a credit memorandum is shown in Figure 9-5. The new form of credit memorandum is shown in Figure 9-9 (page 365).

As before, we will assume that the volume of credit notes is low and that Art's Wholesale uses the general journal to record these. The journal entry will appear as shown in Figure 9-10 (page 365).

Remember that the $42 debit posting will reduce the amount of GST owing to the federal government and must be taken into account when preparing a cheque for the amount owing at period-end. The customer, Bevans Company, now receives a credit totalling $642. This includes the extra 7 percent for GST. Since the original invoice included this 7 percent tax as an addition, it is proper that any refund for returned or damaged goods also include the 7 percent tax. The amount owing to Art's Wholesale by Bevans Company is reduced by $642.

PROVINCIAL SALES TAX WITH GST/HST

In most provinces (not in Nova Scotia, New Brunswick, Newfoundland, or Alberta), when a sale is made to a customer at the retail level, provincial sales tax is added to

ART'S WHOLESALE CLOTHING COMPANY
SALES JOURNAL

Page 1

Date 2001		Account Debited	Terms	Invoice Number	Post. Ref.	DR Accts. Rec.	CR GST Collected	Cr. Sales
April	3	Hal's Clothing	2/10, n/30	1	✔	856 00	56 00	800 00
	6	Bevans Company	2/10, n/30	2	✔	1 712 00	112 00	1 600 00
	18	Roe Company	2/10, n/30	3	✔	2 140 00	140 00	2 000 00
	24	Roe Company	2/10, n/30	4	✔	535 00	35 00	500 00
	28	Mel's Dept. Store	2/10, n/30	5	✔	963 00	63 00	900 00
	29	Mel's Dept Store	2/10, n/30	6	✔	749 00	49 00	700 00
	30					6 955 00	455 00	6 500 00
						(113)	(212)	(411)

The ✔ in the sales Journal Post. Ref. column indicates that the accounts receivable subsidiary ledger has been updated *during* the month by recording debits to the individual customers.

References to ledger accounts mean totals were posted at the end of the month to these accounts.

The total of $6,500 is posted at the end of the month to Sales (Cr.) in the general ledger.

ACCOUNTS RECEIVABLE LEDGER

Bevans Company

Dr.	Cr.
4/6 SJ1 1,712	

Hal's Clothing

Dr.	Cr.
4/3 SJ1 856	

Mel's Department Store

Dr.	Cr.
4/28 SJ1 963	
4/29 SJ1 749	

Roe Company

Dr.	Cr.
4/18 SJ1 2,140	
4/24 SJ1 535	

PARTIAL GENERAL LEDGER

Accounts Receivable 113

Dr.	Cr.
4/30 SJ1 6,955	

Sales 411

Dr.	Cr.
	6,500 SJ1 4/30

GST Collected 212

Dr.	Cr.
	455 SJ1 4/30

FIGURE 9-8
Sales Journal and Postings with GST

the invoice. Since 1991, it has been necessary also to add GST to these invoices. A typical invoice in a province with a 9 percent provincial sales tax might look like Figure 9-11 (page 366).

In provinces which charge HST, the invoice would look like Figure 9-7, except HST at 15 percent would replace GST at 7 percent.

Sales Invoice with PST and GST/HST

The Munroe Menswear Company would record this invoice along with other invoices for June 2002 in their sales journal. This recording and posting process is illustrated

FIGURE 9-9
Credit Memorandum with GST

Art's Wholesale Clothing Co.
1528 Belle Aveune
Toronto, ON M5A 2L4

Credit Memorandum No. 1

Date: April 12, 2001

Credit to: Bevans Company
110 Aster Road
Amherst, NS B4H 3A5

We credit your account as follows:

Merchandise returned 60 model 8B men's dress gloves—	$600.00
Plus GST	42.00
Total Credit	$642.00

Business No. 109309799

No sales discount is taken on GST/HST or PST amounts because the monies are collected on behalf of the government.

in Figure 9-12. Note that, apart from the addition of one more column (for the GST), this is similar to the illustration shown in Figure 9-8.

Also worthy of repetition is the point that if sales discounts are available, they are usually taken on the *sales amount only*, not the GST/HST or PST. If Jones Co. receives a 2 percent discount on invoice No. 1420 (see Figure 9-11), they would pay the following amount:

Original sales amount of invoice No. 1420	$1,500
Less: 2% Discount	30
	1,470
Plus: PST as originally computed	135
Plus: GST as originally computed	105
Amount paid	$1,710

FIGURE 9-10
Postings for the Credit Memorandum with GST

ART'S WHOLESALE CLOTHING CO.
GENERAL JOURNAL

Page 1

Date		Account Titles and Descriptions	PR	Debit	Credit
2001 April	12	GST Collected	212	42 00	
		Sales Returns and Allowances	412	600 00	
		Accounts Receivable, Bevans Co.	113/✓		642 00

212 A debit of $42 is recorded in the GST Collected account 212 in the general ledger. When this is done, the account number is placed in the PR column of the journal.

412 A debit of $600 is recorded in Sales Returns and Allowances, account 412 in the general ledger. When this is done, the account number is placed in the PR column of the journal.

113 The credit of $642 is also posted to Accounts Receivable, the controlling account in the general ledger. When this is done, the account number (113) is placed in the PR column of the journal, above the /.

✓ The check indicates that $642 has been recorded as a credit in the account of Bevans Company in the accounts receivable ledger.

FIGURE 9-11
Sales Invoice with PST and GST

Munroe Menswear Company
147 Main Street
Saskatoon, Saskatchewan
S8A 2G7

To: Jones Company
228 Market Street
Saskatoon, Saskatchewan
S8J 2P2

Invoice # 1420
June 01, 2002

10 Company Blazers with logo @ $150.00 each		$1,500.00
	PST @ 9%	135.00
		1,635.00
	GST @ 7%	105.00
	Total	$1,740.00

Business No. 142716491

Credit Memorandum with PST and GST/HST

The credit memorandum with PST and GST is very similar to an invoice with PST and GST except that the amounts are opposite in meaning and effect, and often smaller.

Let us assume that Jones Co. receives permission to return some of the goods billed on invoice No.1420 (Figure 9-11). This results in a credit memorandum (or credit note) being prepared by Munroe Menswear Company. This credit memo would appear as shown in Figure 9-13.

The credit memo would be recorded by Munroe Company in their general journal (unless there was a large number of returns, in which case a special journal could be used). The entry to record credit note No. 104 is as shown in Figure 9-14.

This entry is posted in a similar fashion to the entry in Figure 9-10. The only change is that there is also a posting of a debit to PST Payable (account number 210) as well as to GST Collected (account number 212).

FIGURE 9-12
Munroe's Sales Journal with GST

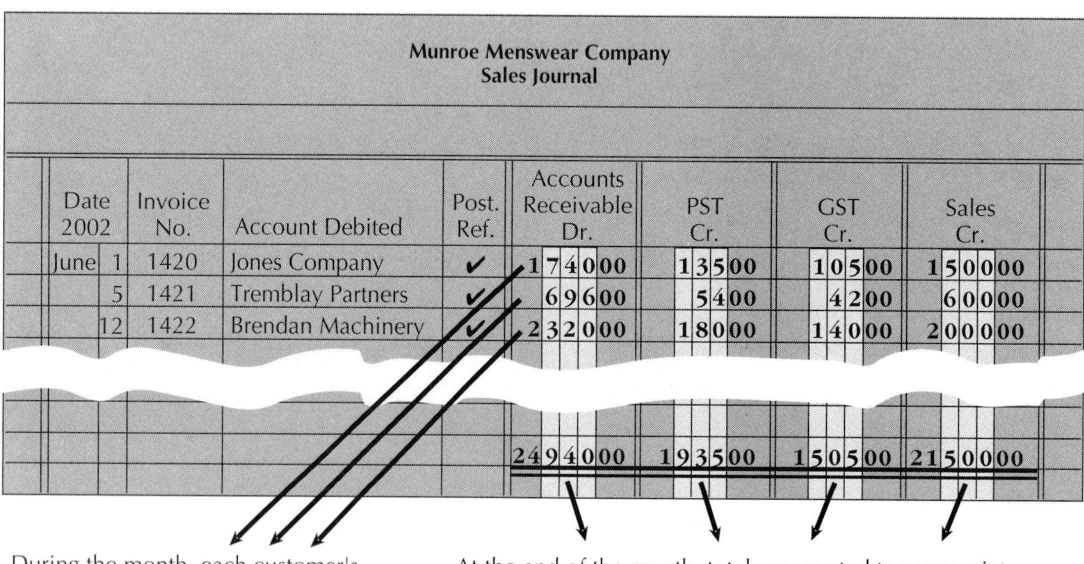

Munroe Menswear Company
Sales Journal

Date 2002		Invoice No.	Account Debited	Post. Ref.	Accounts Receivable Dr.	PST Cr.	GST Cr.	Sales Cr.
June	1	1420	Jones Company	✔	1740 00	135 00	105 00	1500 00
	5	1421	Tremblay Partners	✔	696 00	54 00	42 00	600 00
	12	1422	Brendan Machinery	✔	2320 00	180 00	140 00	2000 00
					24940 00	1935 00	1505 00	21500 00

During the month, each customer's account in the accounts receivable ledger is recorded to update the amount owed. Note that these figures include the PST and GST.

At the end of the month, totals are posted to appropriate accounts in the general ledger. Note that Dr. total to Accounts Receivable ($24,940) equals the total of the three Cr. postings to PST, GST, and Sales ($1935 + $1505 + $21,500 = $24,940).

FIGURE 9-13
Credit Memo with PST and GST

Munroe Menswear Company
147 Main Street
Saskatoon, Saskatchewan
S8A 2G7

To: Jones Company
228 Market Street
Saskatoon, Saskatchewan
S8J 2P2

Credit Memo # 104
July 15, 2002

Returned 2 Blazers—Ref. Invoice 1420, June 1, 2002—@ $150.00 each

	$300.00
PST @ 9%	27.00
	327.00
GST @ 7%	21.00
Total	$348.00

Business No. 142716491

FIGURE 9-14
Recording Credit Memo with PST and GST

MUNROE MENSWEAR COMPANY
GENERAL JOURNAL

Page 1

Date		Account Titles and Descriptions	PR	Debit	Credit
2002 July	15	Sales Returns and Allowances	412	300 00	
		GST Collected	212	21 00	
		PST Payable	210	27 00	
		Accounts Receivable, Jones Co.	113/✓		348 00
		To record credit memo number 104			

LEARNING UNIT 9-4 REVIEW

AT THIS POINT you should be able to:

1. Explain the basics of GST/HST added to sales invoices in Canada. (p. 362)
2. Explain, journalize, and post an invoice which includes both GST and PST. (pp. 362–364)
3. Explain, journalize, and post a credit memorandum which includes both GST and PST. (pp. 363–365)

SELF-REVIEW QUIZ 9-4

(The forms you need are on pages 9-3 and 9-4 of the *Study Guide with Working Papers.*)

Journalize the following transactions in the sales journal or the general journal for Moss Company. Post to the accounts receivable and general ledger accounts as appropriate. Use the same journal headings and general ledger account numbers that were used in Figures 9-12 and 9-14.

2000

May 1 Sold merchandise to Jane Company, invoice No. 101—$400 plus PST $36 plus GST $28—total $464.00. Terms 2/10, n/30

5 Sold merchandise to Ralph Company, invoice No. 102—$3000 plus PST $270 plus GST $210—total $3,480.00. Terms 2/10, n/30

21 Issued credit memorandum to Ralph Company, CM #4—$500 plus PST $45 plus GST $35—total $580.00. Reason—defective goods

Solution to Self-Review Quiz 9-4

MOSS COMPANY
SALES JOURNAL

Page 1

Date 2000		Account Debited	Invoice Number	Post. Ref.	Dr. Accts. Rec.	Cr. PST Collected	Cr. GST Collected	Cr. Sales
May	1	Jane Company	101	✔	46400	3600	2800	40000
	5	Ralph Company	102	✔	348000	27000	21000	300000
					394400	30600	23800	340000
					(112)	(210)	(212)	(411)

MOSS COMPANY
GENERAL JOURNAL

Date		Account Titles and Descriptions	Post. Ref.	Debit	Credit
2000 May	21	Sales Returns and Allowances	412	50000	
		GST Collected	212	3500	
		PST Payable	210	4500	
		Accounts Receivable, Ralph Co.	112/✔		58000
		To record credit memo No. 4			

PARTIAL GENERAL LEDGER

NAME: Accounts Receivable — Acct. No. 112

Date 2000		Explanation	Post. Ref.	Debit	Credit	Dr. or Cr.	Balance
May	21		GJ		580.00	Dr.	3 364.00
May	31		SJ1	3 944.00		Cr.	3 944.00

NAME: PST Payable — Acct. No. 210

Date 2000		Explanation	Post. Ref.	Debit	Credit	Dr. or Cr.	Balance
May	21		GJ1	45.00		Dr.	45.00
	31		SJ1		306.00	Cr.	261.00

NAME: GST Collected — Acct. No. 212

Date 2000		Explanation	Post. Ref.	Debit	Credit	Dr. or Cr.	Balance
May	21		GJ1	35.00		Dr.	35.00
	31		SJ1		238.00	Cr.	203.00

NAME: Sales — Acct. No. 411

Date 2000		Explanation	Post. Ref.	Debit	Credit	Dr. or Cr.	Balance
May	31		SJ1		3 400.00	Cr.	3 400.00

NAME: Sales Returns and Allowances — Acct. No. 412

Date 2000		Explanation	Post. Ref.	Debit	Credit	Dr. or Cr.	Balance
May	21		GJ1	500.00		Dr.	500.00

PARTIAL ACCOUNTS RECEIVABLE LEDGER

NAME Jane Company
ADDRESS 1218 Broadview Avenue, Toronto, ON M5X 2A1

Date 2000		Explanation	Post. Ref.	Debit	Credit	Dr. Balance
May	1		SJ1	464.00		464.00

NAME Ralph Company
ADDRESS 1300 Marine Drive, West Vancouver, BC V6P 9B6

Date 2000		Explanation	Post. Ref.	Debit	Credit	Dr. Balance
May	5		SJ1	3 480.00		3 480.00
	21		GJ1		580.00	2 900.00

LEARNING UNIT 9-5

Cash Receipts Journal and Schedule of Accounts Receivable

Besides the sales journal, another special journal often used in a merchandising operation is the cash receipts journal. The **cash receipts journal** records the receipt of cash (or cheques) from any source. The number of columns a cash receipts journal will have depends on how frequently certain types of transaction occur. For example, in the cash receipts journal for Art's Wholesale the accountant has developed the headings shown in Figure 9-15. Note that a column for GST (on cash sales only) has been included. GST on credit sales is recorded in the sales journal as already described. Below each heading is a description of the purpose of that column and when to update the accounts receivable ledger as well as general ledger.

The following transactions occurred in April for Art's Wholesale and affected the cash receipts journal:

2001

April 1 Art Newner invested $8,000 in the business.

4 Received cheque from Hal's Clothing for payment of invoice No. 1 less discount.

15 Cash sales for first half of April, $900 plus GST

16 Received cheque from Bevans Company in settlement of invoice No. 2 less returns and discount.

22 Received cheque from Roe Company for payment of invoice No. 3 less discount.

27 Sold store equipment, $500.

30 Cash sales for second half of April, $1,200 plus GST

FIGURE 9-15
Cash Receipts Journal with GST

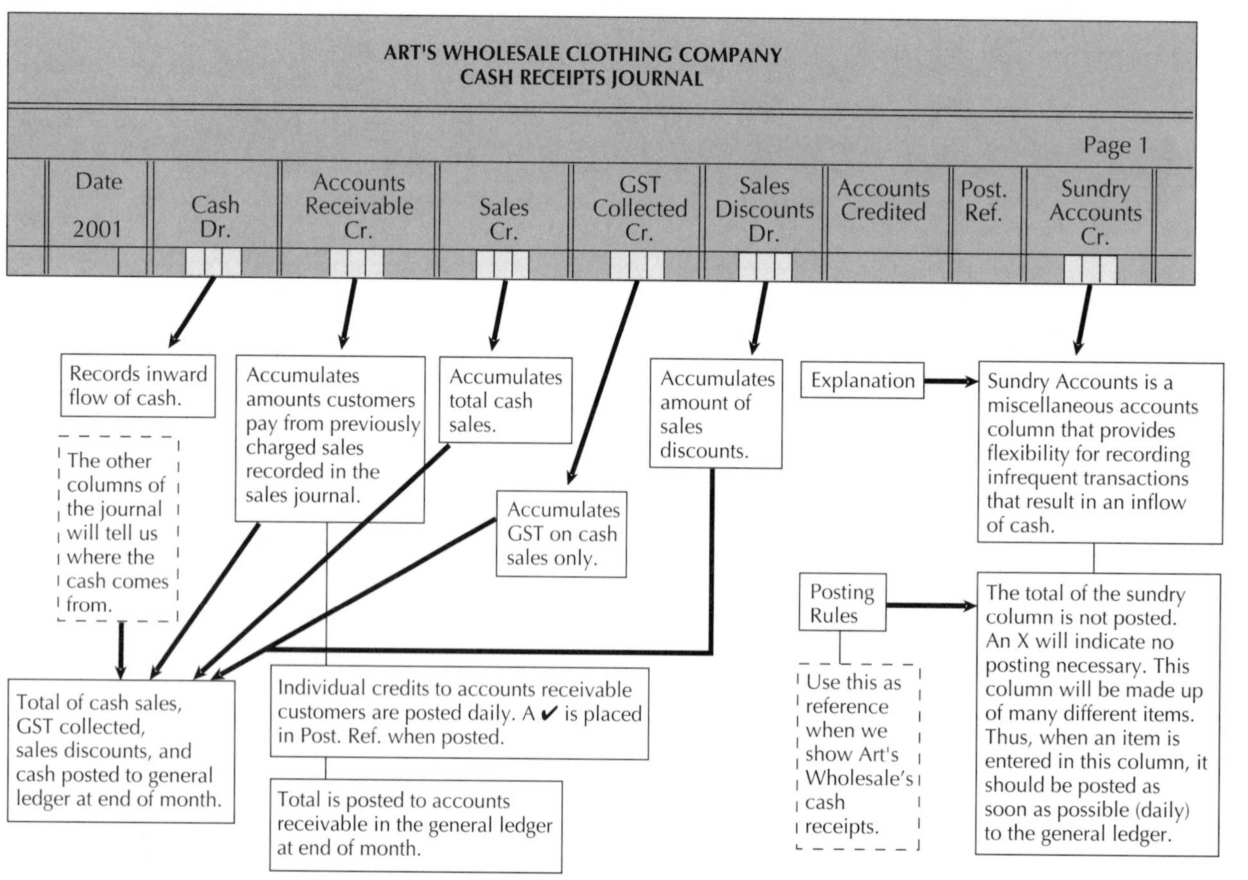

FIGURE 9-16
Cash Receipts Journal and Posting with GST

Figure 9-16 shows the cash receipts journal for the end of April along with the recordings to the accounts receivable ledger and posting to the general ledger. Study the diagram; we will review it in a moment.

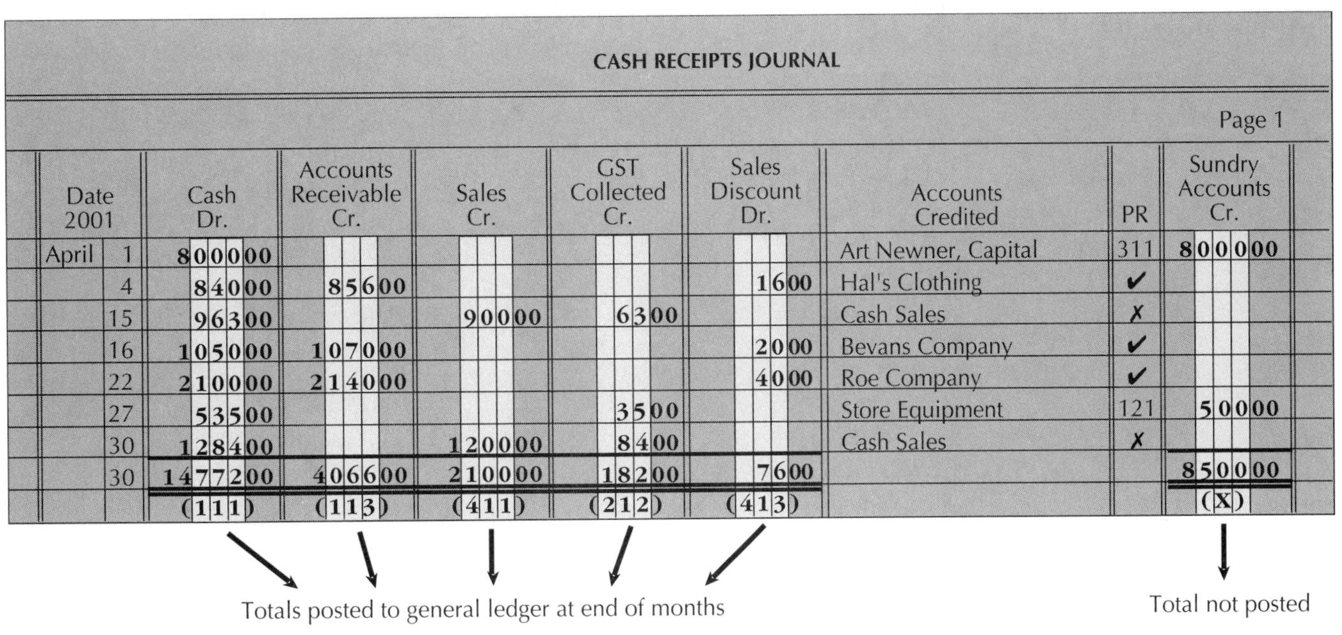

CASH RECEIPTS JOURNAL

Page 1

Date 2001		Cash Dr.	Accounts Receivable Cr.	Sales Cr.	GST Collected Cr.	Sales Discount Dr.	Accounts Credited	PR	Sundry Accounts Cr.
April	1	800000					Art Newner, Capital	311	800000
	4	84000	85600			1600	Hal's Clothing	✔	
	15	96300		90000	6300		Cash Sales	✗	
	16	105000	107000			2000	Bevans Company	✔	
	22	210000	214000			4000	Roe Company	✔	
	27	53500			3500		Store Equipment	121	50000
	30	128400		120000	8400		Cash Sales	✗	
	30	1477200	406600	210000	18200	7600			850000
		(111)	(113)	(411)	(212)	(413)			(X)

ACCOUNTS RECEIVABLE LEDGER

NAME Bevans Company
ADDRESS 110 Aster Road, Amherst, NS B4H 3A5

Date 2001		Explanation	Post. Ref.	Debit	Credit	Dr. Balance
April	6		SJ1	171200		171200
	12		GJ1		64200	107000
	16		CRJ1		107000	-0-

NAME Hal's Clothing
ADDRESS 91 Century Avenue, Winnipeg, MN R2C 4X7

Date 2001		Explanation	Post. Ref.	Debit	Credit	Dr. Balance
April	3		SJ1	85600		85600
	4		CRJ1		85600	-0-

NAME Mel's Department Store
ADDRESS 181 Foss Road, Fredericton, NB E3A 2N8

Date 2001		Explanation	Post. Ref.	Debit	Credit	Dr. Balance
April	28		SJ1	96300		96300
	29		SJ1	74900		171200

NAME Roe Company
ADDRESS 18 Rantool Street, Regina, SK S4P 3J7

Date 2001		Explanation	Post. Ref.	Debit	Credit	Dr. Balance
April	18		SJ1	214000		214000
	22		CRJ1		214000	-0-
	24		SJ1	53500		53500

Note on accounts receivable: Very occasionally (due to an error, such as when a customer pays twice for the same invoice) a credit balance may be called for. Credit balances are opposite to the normal debit balance and are signified by placing the balance in brackets. For example, suppose that Hal's Clothing (see above) mistakenly paid its invoice twice. Their account would then appear as follows:

NAME Hal's Clothing
ADDRESS 91 Century Avenue, Winnipeg, MN R2C 4X7

Date 2001		Explanation	Post. Ref.	Debit	Credit	Dr. Balance
April	3		SJ1	85600		85600
	4		CRJ1		85600	-0-
	10		CRJ1		85600	(85600)

PARTIAL GENERAL LEDGER

Cash — Acct. No. 111

Date 2001		Explanation	Post. Ref.	Debit	Credit	DR or CR	Balance
April	30		CRJ1	1477200		DR.	1477200

Accounts Receivable — Acct. No. 113

Date 2001		Explanation	Post. Ref.	Debit	Credit	DR or CR	Balance
April	12		GJ1		64200	CR.	64200
	30		SJ1	695500		DR.	631300
	30		CRJ1		406600	DR.	224700

Store Equipment — Acct. No. 121

Date 2001		Explanation	Post. Ref.	Debit	Credit	DR or CR	Balance
April	1	Balance				DR.	400000
	27		CRJ1		50000	DR.	350000

GST Collected — Acct. No. 212

Date 2001		Explanation	Post. Ref.	Debit	Credit	DR or CR	Balance
April	12		GJ1	4200		DR.	4200
	30		SJ1		45500	CR.	41300
	30		CRJ1		18200	CR.	59500

Art Newner, Capital — Acct. No. 311

Date 2001		Explanation	Post. Ref.	Debit	Credit	DR or CR	Balance
April	1		CRJ1		800000	CR.	800000

Sales — Acct. No. 411

Date 2001		Explanation	Post. Ref.	Debit	Credit	DR or CR	Balance
April	30		SJ1		650000	CR.	650000
	30		CRJ1		210000	CR.	860000

NAME Sales Returns and Allowances — Acct. No. 412

Date 2001		Explanation	Post. Ref.	Debit	Credit	DR or CR	Balance
April	12		GJ1	60000		DR.	60000

Sales Discounts — Acct. No. 413

Date 2001		Explanation	Post. Ref.	Debit	Credit	DR or CR	Balance
April	30		CRJ1	7600		DR.	7600

JOURNALIZING, RECORDING, AND POSTING FROM THE CASH RECEIPTS JOURNAL

On April 4 Art's Wholesale received a cheque from Hal's Clothing for payment of invoice No. 1 less discount. Remember, it was in the sales journal that this transaction was first recorded (Figure 9-8). At that time we updated the accounts receivable ledger, indicating that Hal's Clothing owed Art $856. Since Hal's Clothing is paying within the 10-day discount period, Art's Wholesale offers a $16 sales discount ($800 × 0.02). (Remember, all credit sales carried terms of 2/10, n/30.)

Now, when payment is received, Art's Wholesale updates the cash receipts journal (see page 371) by entering the date (April 4), cash debit of $840, sales discounts debit of $16, credit to accounts receivable of $856, and which account name (Hal's Clothing) is to be credited. The terms of sale indicate that Hal's Clothing is entitled to the discount and no longer owes Art's Wholesale the $856 balance. *As soon as this line is entered into the cash receipts journal, Art's Wholesale will update the ledger account of Hal's Clothing.* Note in the accounts receivable ledger of Hal's Clothing how the date (April 4), posting reference (CRJ1), and credit amount ($856) are recorded. The balance in the accounts receivable ledger is zero. The last step of this transaction is to go back to the cash receipts journal and put a ✔ in the posting reference column.

In studying this cash receipts journal, note that:

The last step is to put a checkmark in the PR of the cash receipts journal to show the accounts receivable ledger is up to date.

1. All totals of cash receipts in the journal columns except sundry were posted to the general ledger at the end of the month.
2. Art Newner, Capital, and Store Equipment were posted to the general ledger when entered in the sundry column. It is assumed that the equipment account had a beginning balance of $4,000 in the general ledger. There is no GST on the owner's capital contribution.
3. The cash sales were not posted when entered (thus the X to show no posting is needed). The sales and cash totals are posted at the end of the month.
4. A ✔ means information was recorded daily to the accounts receivable ledger.
5. The Description of Receipt column describes each transaction.

We can prove the accuracy of recording transactions of the cash receipts journal by totalling the columns with debit balances and the columns with credit balances. This process, called **cross-footing**, is done before the totals are posted. Also, if a bookkeeper were using more than one page for the cash receipts journal, the balances on the bottom of one page would be brought forward to the top of the next page. This verifying of totals would result in less work when trying to find journalizing or posting errors at a later date. Let's see how to cross-foot the cash receipts journal of Art's Wholesale (Figure 9-16).

Proving the cash receipts journal

Debit Columns	=	**Credit Columns**
Cash + Sales Discounts	=	**Accounts Receivable + Sales + Sundry + GST**
$14,772 + $76	=	**$4,066 + $2,100 + $8,500 + $182**
$14,848	=	**$14,848**

Now let's take a moment to see what PST would look like in the cash receipts journal of a business that would need to record sales tax as well as GST. A typical cash receipts journal might look as follows:

CASH RECEIPTS JOURNAL

Page 1

Date 2001	Cash Dr.	Accounts Receivable Cr.	Sales Cr.	PST Collected Cr.	GST Collected Cr.	Sales Discounts Dr.	Accounts Credited	Post. Ref.	Sundry Accounts Cr.

The total of the sales tax as a result of cash sales would be posted to Sales Tax Payable in the general ledger at the end of the month. It represents a liability of the merchant to forward the tax to the provincial government. Remember, no cash discounts are taken on the sales tax (or GST).

Now let's prove the accounts receivable ledger to the controlling account—Accounts Receivable—at the end of April for Art's Wholesale Clothing Company.

SCHEDULE OF ACCOUNTS RECEIVABLE

The total of sales tax payable would be posted to Sales Tax Payable in the general ledger at the end of the month.

From Figure 9-16 let's list the customers that have an ending balance in the accounts receivable ledger of Art's Wholesale. This listing is called a **schedule of accounts receivable**. The balance of the controlling account, Accounts Receivable ($2,247), in the general ledger (see p. 371) does indeed equal the sum of the individual customer balances in the accounts receivable ledger ($2,247) as shown below in the schedule of accounts receivable. The schedule of accounts receivable can help forecast potential cash inflows as well as possible credit and collection decisions.

Art's Wholesale Clothing Company
Schedule of Accounts Receivable
April 30, 2001

Mel's Department Store	$1,712.00
Roe Company	535.00
Total Accounts Receivable	$2,247.00

LEARNING UNIT 9-5 REVIEW

AT THIS POINT you should be able to:

1. Journalize, record, and post transactions with or without sales tax using a cash receipts journal. (pp. 372–373)
2. Prepare a schedule of accounts receivable. (p. 373)

SELF-REVIEW QUIZ 9-5

(The forms you need are on pages 9-5 to 9-7 of the *Study Guide with Working Papers*.)

Journalize, cross-foot, record, and post when appropriate the following transactions into the cash receipts journal of Moore Co. Use the same headings as for Art's Wholesale.

Accounts Receivable Ledger

Name	*Balance*	*Invoice No.*
Irene Welch	$535	1
Chantel Simard	214	2

Partial General Ledger

Account	*Account No.*	*Balance*
Cash	110	$600
Accounts Receivable	120	749
Store Equipment	130	600
GST Collected	212	49
Sales	410	700
Sales Discounts	420	—

2001
May 1 Received cheque from Irene Welch for invoice No. 1 less 2 percent discount.
8 Cash sales collected, $400 plus GST of $28
15 Received cheque from Chantel Simard for invoice No. 2 less 2 percent discount.
19 Sold store equipment at cost, $300 (plus GST).

Solution to Self-Review Quiz 9-5

MOORE COMPANY
CASH RECEIPTS JOURNAL

Page 2

Date 2001		Cash Dr.	Accounts Receivable Cr.	Sales Cr.	GST Collected Cr.	Sales Discounts Dr.	Description of Receipt	Post. Ref.	Sundry Accounts Cr.
May	1	525 00	535 00			10 00	Irene Welch	✔	
	8	428 00		400 00	28 00		Cash Sales	✗	
	15	210 00	214 00			4 00	Chantel Simard	✔	
	19	321 00			21 00		Store Equipment	130	300 00
	31	1484 00	749 00	400 00	49 00	14 00			300 00
		(110)	(120)	(410)	(212)	(420)			(X)

Cross-footing: $1,498.00 = $1,498.00

Quiz Tip

Sum of all debits equals sum of all credits.

Quiz Tip

The total of the Sundry column is not posted; only individual amounts are posted to the general ledger.

PARTIAL GENERAL LEDGER

Cash — Acct. No. 110

Date 2001		Explanation	Post. Ref.	Debit	Credit	DR or CR	Balance
May	1	Balance	✔			DR.	600 00
	31		CRJ2	1484 00		DR.	2084 00

Accounts Receivable — Acct. No. 120

Date 2001		Explanation	Post. Ref.	Debit	Credit	DR or CR	Balance
May	1	Balance	✔			DR.	749 00
	31		CRJ2		749 00		-0-

Store Equipment — Acct. No. 130

Date 2001		Explanation	Post. Ref.	Debit	Credit	DR or CR	Balance
May	1	Balance	✔			DR.	600 00
	19		CRJ2		300 00	DR.	300 00

PARTIAL GENERAL LEDGER (Cont.)

GST Collected — Acct. No. 212

Date 2001		Explanation	Post. Ref.	Debit	Credit	DR or CR	Balance
May	1	Balance	✔			CR.	4900
	31		CRJ2		4900	CR.	9800

Sales — Acct. No. 410

Date 2001		Explanation	Post. Ref.	Debit	Credit	DR or CR	Balance
May	1	Balance	✔			CR.	70000
	31		CRJ2		40000	CR.	110000

Sales Discounts — Acct. No. 420

Date 2001		Explanation	Post. Ref.	Debit	Credit	DR or CR	Balance
May	31		CRJ2	1400		DR.	1400

ACCOUNTS RECEIVABLE LEDGER

NAME Irene Welch
ADDRESS 10 Rong Road, Timmins, ON P4N 4M3

Date 2001		Explanation	Post. Ref.	Debit	Credit	Dr. Balance
May	1	Balance	✔			53500
	1		CRJ2		53500	–0–

NAME Chantel Simard
ADDRESS 9017 Robitaille Road, Montreal, PQ H1K 4R3

Date 2001		Explanation	Post. Ref.	Debit	Credit	Dr. Balance
May	1	Balance	✔			21400
	15		CRJ2		21400	–0–

Chapter Review

COMPREHENSIVE DEMONSTRATION PROBLEM WITH SOLUTION TIPS

(The forms you need are on pages 9-8 to 9-10 of the *Study Guide with Working Papers.*)

a. Journalize, record, and post as needed the following transactions to the sales, cash receipts, and general journals. All terms are 2/10, n/30.

b. Prepare a schedule of accounts receivable.

Ignore GST and PST.

Solution Tips to Journalizing

	2001		
CRJ	July	2	Walter Lantz invested $2,000 in the business.
SJ		2	Sold merchandise on account to Panda Co., invoice No. 1—$300.
SJ		2	Sold merchandise on account to Buzzard Co., invoice No. 2—$600.
CRJ		3	Cash sale—$400
GJ		9	Issued credit memorandum No. 1 to Panda Co. for defective merchandise—$100.
CRJ		10	Received cheque from Panda Co. for invoice No. 1 less returns and discount.
CRJ		16	Cash sale—$500
SJ		19	Sold merchandise on account to Panda Co.—$550, invoice No. 3.

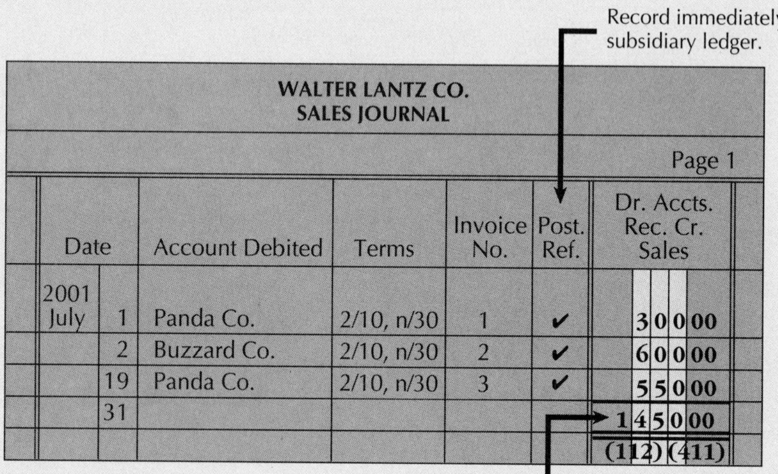

WALTER LANTZ CO.
SALES JOURNAL

Page 1

Date		Account Debited	Terms	Invoice No.	Post. Ref.	Dr. Accts. Rec. Cr. Sales
2001 July	1	Panda Co.	2/10, n/30	1	✔	300 00
	2	Buzzard Co.	2/10, n/30	2	✔	600 00
	19	Panda Co.	2/10, n/30	3	✔	550 00
	31					1450 00
						(112) (411)

Record immediately in subsidiary ledger.
Total posted at end of month to general ledger accounts.

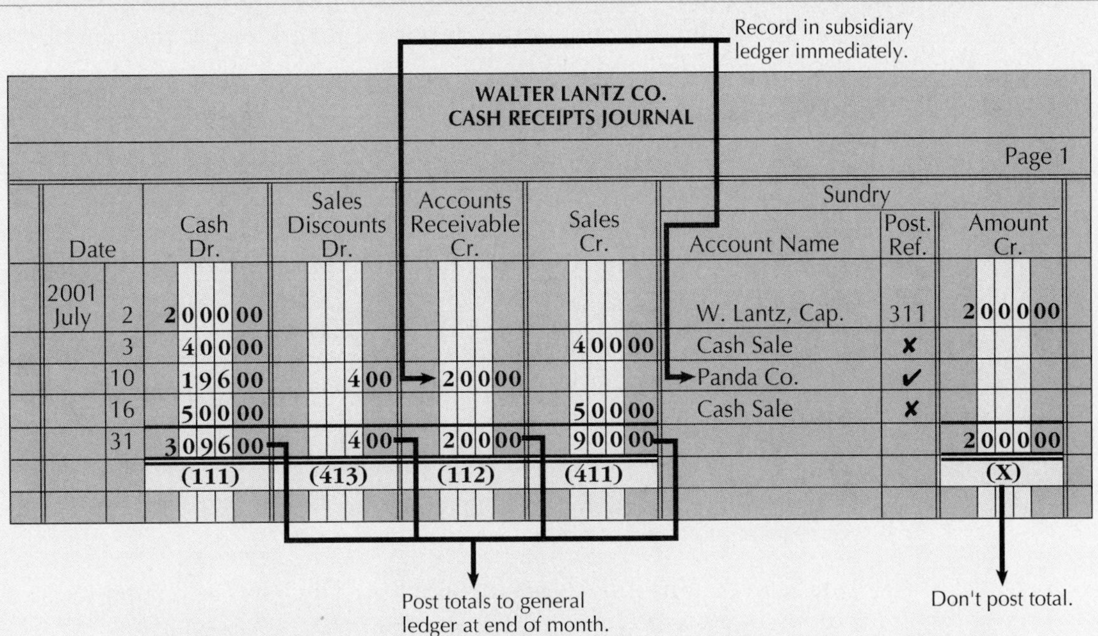

Record in subsidiary ledger immediately.
Post totals to general ledger at end of month.
Don't post total.

WALTER LANTZ CO.
CASH RECEIPTS JOURNAL

Page 1

Date		Cash Dr.	Sales Discounts Dr.	Accounts Receivable Cr.	Sales Cr.	Sundry Account Name	Sundry Post. Ref.	Sundry Amount Cr.
2001 July	2	2 000 00				W. Lantz, Cap.	311	2 000 00
	3	400 00			400 00	Cash Sale	✗	
	10	196 00	4 00	200 00		Panda Co.	✔	
	16	500 00			500 00	Cash Sale	✗	
	31	3 096 00	4 00	200 00	900 00			2 000 00
		(111)	(413)	(112)	(411)			(X)

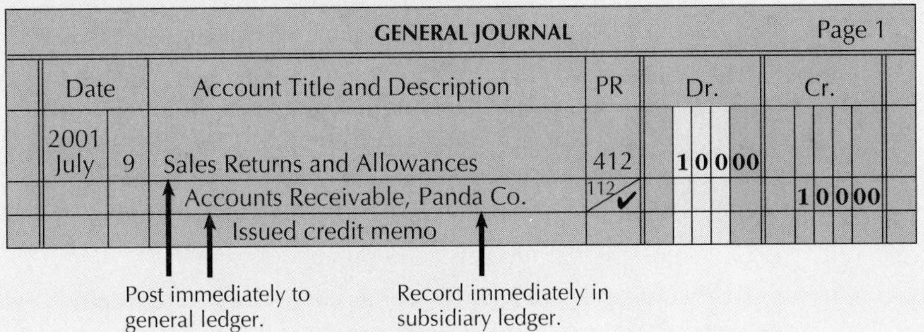

Post immediately to general ledger.
Record immediately in subsidiary ledger.

GENERAL JOURNAL Page 1

Date		Account Title and Description	PR	Dr.	Cr.
2001 July	9	Sales Returns and Allowances	412	100 00	
		Accounts Receivable, Panda Co.	112/✔		100 00
		Issued credit memo			

Accounts receivable subsidiary ledger is usually a debit balance.

Accounts Receivable Subsidiary Ledger

Buzzard Co.

Date		PR	Debit	Credit	Dr. Balance
2001 July	2	SJ1	600 00		600 00

Panda Co.

Date		PR	Debit	Credit	Dr. Balance
2001 July	1	SJ1	300 00		300 00
	9	GJ1		100 00	200 00
	10	CRJ1		200 00	–0–
	19	SJ1	550 00		550 00

General Ledger

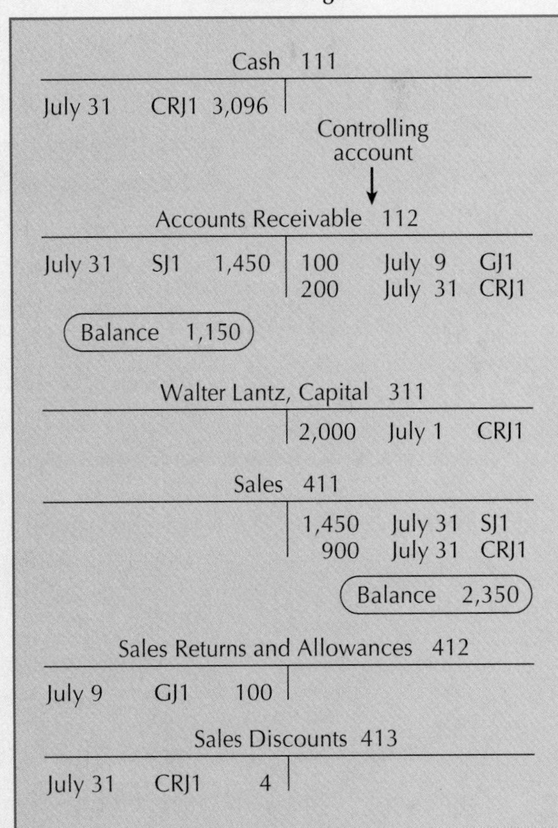

Cash 111

July 31 CRJ1 3,096 |

Controlling account

Accounts Receivable 112

Debit	Credit
July 31 SJ1 1,450	100 July 9 GJ1
	200 July 31 CRJ1

Balance 1,150

Walter Lantz, Capital 311

| 2,000 July 1 CRJ1

Sales 411

Debit	Credit
	1,450 July 31 SJ1
	900 July 31 CRJ1

Balance 2,350

Sales Returns and Allowances 412

July 9 GJ1 100 |

Sales Discounts 413

July 31 CRJ1 4 |

The controlling account at the end of the month equals the sum of the accounts receivable subsidiary ledger.

LANTZ CO. SCHEDULE OF ACCOUNTS RECEIVABLE JULY 31, 2001	
Buzzard Co.	$ 600 00
Panda Co.	550 00
Total Accounts Receivable	$1 150 00

SUMMARY OF KEY POINTS

Learning Unit 9-1

1. Sales Returns and Allowances and Sales Discounts are contra-revenue accounts.
2. Net Sales = Gross Sales − Sales Returns and Allowances − Sales Discounts.
3. Discounts are not taken on sales tax, freight, or goods returned. The discount period is shorter than the credit period.

Learning Unit 9-2

1. A general journal is still used with special journals.
2. A sales journal records sales on account.
3. The accounts receivable subsidiary ledger, organized in alphabetical order, is not in the same book as Accounts Receivable, the controlling account in the general ledger.
4. At the end of the month the total of all customers' ending balances in the accounts receivable subsidiary ledger should be equal to the ending balance in Accounts Receivable, the controlling account in the general ledger.

Learning Unit 9-3

1. The ✔ in the posting-reference column of the sales journal means a customer's account in the accounts receivable ledger (or the accounts receivable subsidiary ledger) has been updated (or recorded) during the month.
2. At the end of the month the totals of the sales journal are posted to general ledger accounts.
3. Provincial Sales Tax Payable is a liability found in the general ledger.
4. When a credit memorandum is issued, the result is that Sales Returns and Allowances is increasing, and Accounts Receivable is decreasing. When we record this in a general journal we assume that all parts of the transaction will be posted to the general ledger and recorded in the subsidiary ledger when the entry is journalized.

Learning Unit 9-4

1. Recording GST/HST in the sales journal requires the addition of one new column. Other procedures are not changed.

2. Often both PST and GST will appear on the same invoice. Recording this in the sales journal requires the use of two extra columns but again the basic procedures are little changed.
3. When a sales discount is allowed, it is taken on the pre-PST and pre-GST/HST amount only, not on the total invoice.
4. Recording a credit memorandum with PST and GST/HST requires an extra line in the general journal for each. The credit to the customer's account includes the invoice amount plus PST and GST/HST.

Learning Unit 9-5

1. The cash receipts journal records receipt of cash from any source.
2. The Sundry column records the credit part of a transaction that does not occur frequently. Never post the *total* of sundry. Post items in sundry column to the general ledger when entered.
3. A ✔ in the posting reference column of the cash receipts journal means that the accounts receivable subsidiary ledger has been updated (recorded) with a credit.
4. A ✔ in the cash receipts journal posting-reference column means no posting was necessary, since the totals of these columns will be posted at the end of the month.
5. Cross-footing means proving that the total of debits and the total of credits are equal in the special journal, thus verifying the accuracy of recording.
6. A schedule of accounts receivable is a listing of the ending balances of customers in the accounts receivable subsidiary ledger. This total should be the same balance as found in the controlling account, Accounts Receivable, in the general ledger.

Key terms

Accounts receivable subsidiary ledger A book or file that contains the individual records of amounts owed by various credit customers, usually in alphabetical order (p. 353)

Cash receipts journal A special journal that records all transactions involving the receipt of cash from any source (p. 370)

Controlling account—Accounts Receivable The Accounts Receivable account in the general ledger, after postings are complete, shows the total amount of money owed to a firm. This figure is broken down in the accounts receivable subsidiary ledger, where it indicates specifically who owes the money. (p. 354)

Credit memorandum A piece of paper sent by the seller to a customer who has returned merchandise previously purchased on credit. The credit memorandum indicates to the customer that the seller is reducing the amount owed by the customer. (p. 357)

Credit period Length of time allowed for payment of goods sold on account (p. 350)

Cross-footing The process of proving that the total debit columns of a special journal are equal to the total credit columns of a special journal (p. 372)

Discount period A period during which a customer can take a cash discount to encourage early payment of bills. The discount period is shorter than the credit period. (p. 350)

Goods and Services Tax (GST) A "value added" tax introduced in Canada in 1991. It is added to most sales of goods and services. Currently it is calculated at 7 percent. (p. 362)

Gross sales The revenue earned from the sale of merchandise to customers (p. 348)

GST Collected account The tax amount billed to customers and due to be sent to the federal government. It is a liability account with a credit balance. See also the next chapter for a fuller explanation of the net amount payable. (p. 362)

Harmonized Sales Tax (HST) A new 15 percent tax identical to GST, collected in Nova Scotia, New Brunswick, and Newfoundland. It replaces both the PST and GST in those three provinces. (p. 362)

Merchandise Goods brought into a store for resale to customers (p. 348)

Net sales Gross sales less sales returns and allowances less sales discounts (p. 350)

Provincial Sales Tax (PST) Payable account An account in the general ledger that accumulates the amount of provincial sales tax owed. It has a credit balance. (p. 350)

Retailers Merchants who buy goods from wholesalers or manufacturers for resale to customers (p. 348)

Sales discounts Cash discounts granted to customers for payments made within a specific period of time. A contra-revenue account is used to record sales discounts granted. (p. 349)

Sales invoice A bill sent to customer(s) reflecting a sale, usually on credit (p. 354)

Sales journal A special journal used to record only sales made on account. It may have multiple colums if GST/HST or PST is involved. (p. 354)

Sales Returns and Allowances account A contra-revenue account that records price adjustments and allowances granted on merchandise that is defective and has been returned (p. 349)

Schedule of accounts receivable A list of the customers, in alphabetical order, that have an outstanding balance in the accounts receivable subsidiary ledger. This total should be equal to the balance of the Accounts Receivable controlling account in the general ledger at the end of the month (p. 373)

Special journal A journal used to record similar groups of transactions. *Example:* the sales journal, which records all sales on account (p. 352)

Subsidiary ledger A ledger that contains accounts of a single type. *Example:* the accounts receivable subsidiary ledger, which records all customers that purchase goods on account (p. 353)

Sundry Miscellaneous accounts column(s) in a special journal, which records transactions that do not occur too often. (p. 370)

Wholesalers Those who buy goods from suppliers and manufacturers for sale to retailers (p. 348)

Blueprint of Sales and Cash Receipts Journals

Summary of How to Post and Record Single-Column Sales Journal

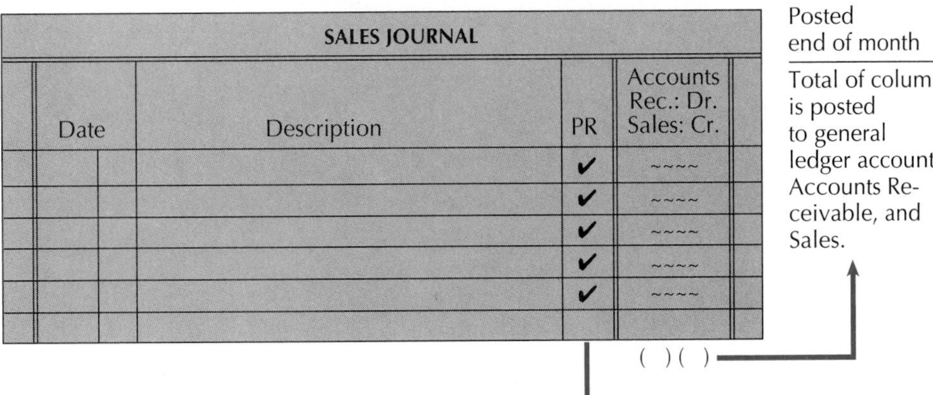

SALES JOURNAL
Date
Description
PR
Accounts Rec.: Dr. Sales: Cr.
( )( )

Posted end of month

Total of column is posted to general ledger accounts, Accounts Receivable, and Sales.

Recorded during the month

Accounts receivable subsidiary ledger is updated as soon as transaction is entered in sales journal. A ✔ indicates that recording is complete to the accounts receivable ledger customer account.

Posting and Recording: Multicolumn Sales Journal

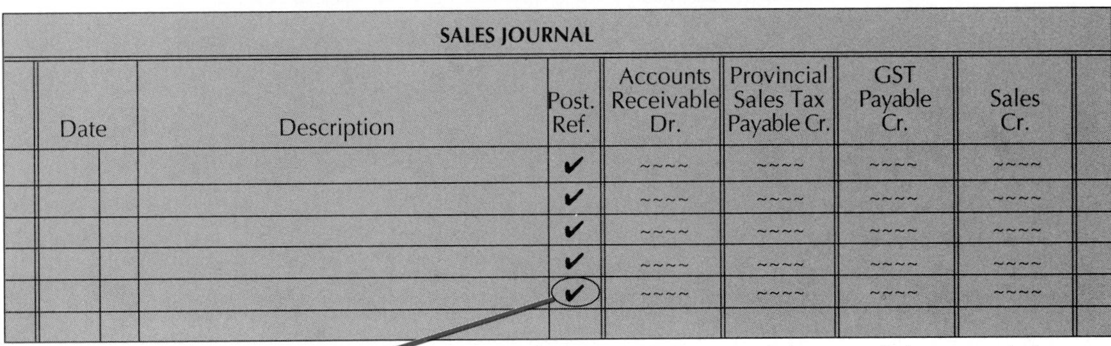

SALES JOURNAL
Date
Description
Post. Ref.
Accounts Receivable Dr.
Provincial Sales Tax Payable Cr.
GST Payable Cr.
Sales Cr.
( ) ( ) ( ) ( )

During the month the accounts receivable ledger is updated as soon as transactions are entered in the journal. A check mark indicates that posting is completed to the customer's account in the accounts receivable subledger.

End of month total is posted to Accounts Receivable control account in the general ledger.

End of month totals of both taxes payable accounts are posted to their respective accounts in the general ledger

End of month total of sales is posted to the general ledger.

Recording a Credit Memo without Sales Tax or GST in a General Journal

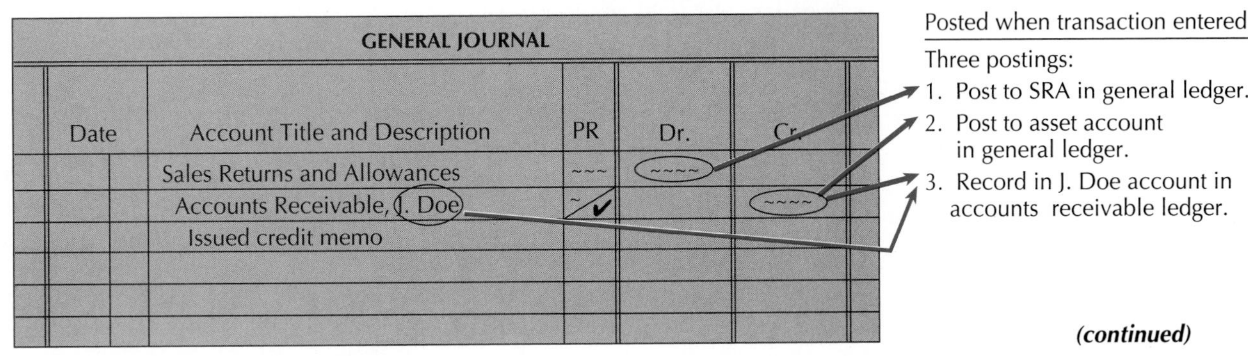

GENERAL JOURNAL
Date
Account Title and Description
PR
Dr.
Cr.
Sales Returns and Allowances
Accounts Receivable, J. Doe
Issued credit memo

Posted when transaction entered

Three postings:

1. Post to SRA in general ledger.
2. Post to asset account in general ledger.
3. Record in J. Doe account in accounts receivable ledger.

(continued)

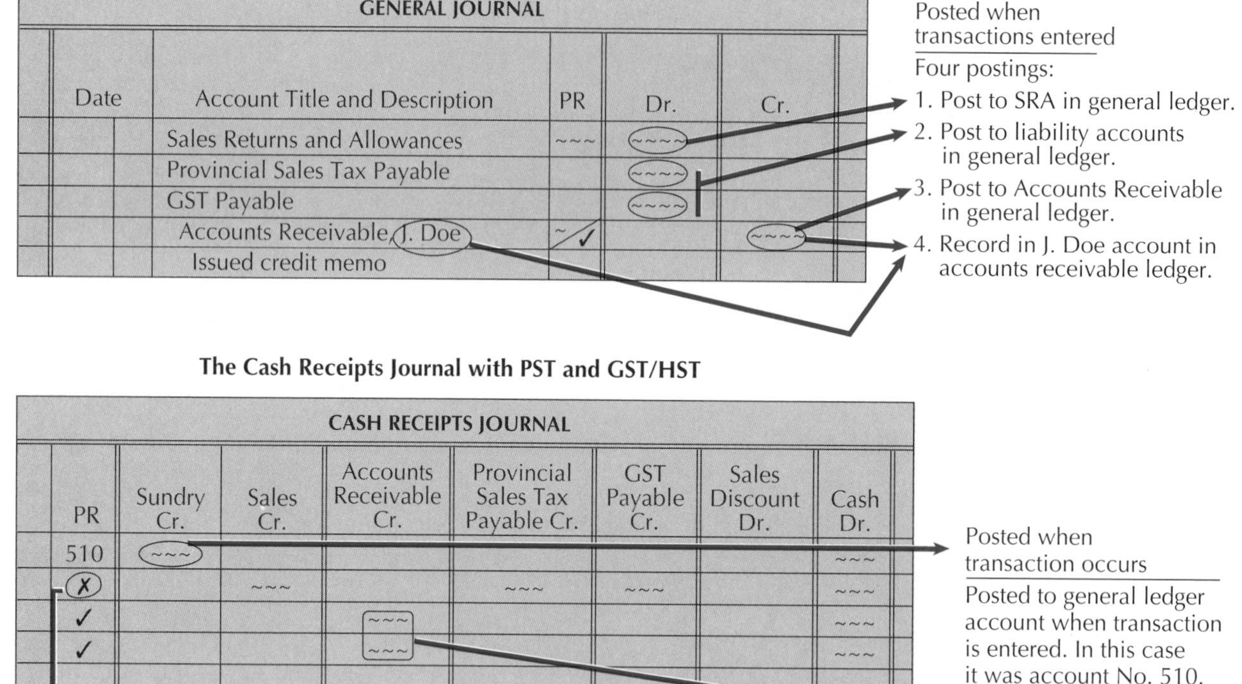

Questions, Mini Exercises, Exercises, and Problems

Discussion Questions

1. Explain the purpose of a contra-revenue account.
2. What is the normal balance of sales discounts?
3. Give two examples of contra-revenue accounts.
4. What is the difference between a discount period and a credit period?
5. Explain the terms (a) 2/10, n/30; (b) n/10, EOM.
6. If special journals are used, what purpose will a general journal serve?
7. Compare and contrast the controlling account Accounts Receivable with the accounts receivable subsidiary ledger.
8. Why is the accounts receivable subsidiary ledger organized in alphabetical order?
9. When is a sales journal used?
10. What is an invoice? What purpose does it serve?

11. Why is provincial sales tax a liability to the business?
12. Sales discounts are taken on sales tax. Agree or disagree and tell why.
13. When a seller issues a credit memorandum (assume no provincial sales tax), what accounts will be affected?
14. Explain the function of a cash receipts journal.
15. When is the Sundry column of the cash receipts journal posted?
16. Explain the purpose of a schedule of accounts receivable.

Mini Exercises

(The forms you need are on pages 9-11 and 9-12 of the *Study Guide with Working Papers.*)

Overview

1. Complete the following table for Sales, Sales Returns and Allowances, and Sales Discounts.

	Category	↑ ↓	Rules	Temporary or Permanent

Calculating Net Sales

2. Given the following, calculate net sales:

Gross sales	$20
Sales returns and allowances	2
Sales discounts	1

Sales Journal and General Journal

3. Beside each of the three transactions below the box, enter the number of any of the following five treatments which apply. (More than one number can be used.)

> 1. Journalize into sales journal.
> 2. Record immediately to subsidiary ledger.
> 3. Post totals from sales journal at end of month to general ledger.
> 4. Journalize in general journal.
> 5. Record and post immediately to subsidiary and general ledger.

a. ________ Sold merchandise on account to Ree Co., invoice No. 1—$50.
b. ________ Sold merchandise on account to Flynn Co., invoice No. 2—$100.
c. ________ Issued credit memorandum No. 1 to Flynn Co. for defective merchandise—$25.

Credit Memorandum

4. Draw a transaction analysis box for the following credit memorandum: Issued credit memorandum to Bob Corp. for defective merchandise—$50.

Sales and Cash Receipts Journal

5. Beside each of the three transactions below the box, enter the number of any of the following six treatments which apply. (A number can be used more than once.)

> **1.** Journalize into sales journal.
> **2.** Journalize into cash receipts journal.
> **3.** Record immediately to subsidiary ledger.
> **4.** Totals of special journals will be posted at end of month (except Sundry column).
> **5.** Post to general ledger immediately.
> **6.** Journalize into general journal.

a. ________ Sold merchandise on account to Ally Co., invoice No. 10—$40.
b. ________ Received cheque from Moore Co.—$100 less 2 percent discount.
c. ________ Cash Sales—$100.
d. ________ Issued credit memorandum No. 2 to Ally Co. for defective merchandise—$20.

6. From the following, prepare a schedule of accounts receivable for Blue Co., for May 31, 2000.

Accounts Receivable Subsidiary Ledger

Bon Co.

5/6 SJ1 100	

Peke Co.

5/20 SJ1 30	5/27 CRJ1 10

Green Co.

5/9 SJ1 10	

General Ledger

Accounts Receivable

5/31 SJ1 140	5/31 CRJ1 10

Exercises

(The forms you need are on pages 9-13 to 9-15 of the *Study Guide with Working Papers.*)

Recording to accounts receivable ledger and posting to general ledger

9-1. From the following sales journal, record in the accounts receivable subsidiary ledger and post to the general ledger accounts as appropriate.

SALES JOURNAL

P. 1

Date		Account Debited	Invoice No.	PR	Dr. Accts. Receivable Cr. Sales
2001 April	18	Kevin Stone Co.	1		400 00
	19	Bill Valley Co.	2		600 00

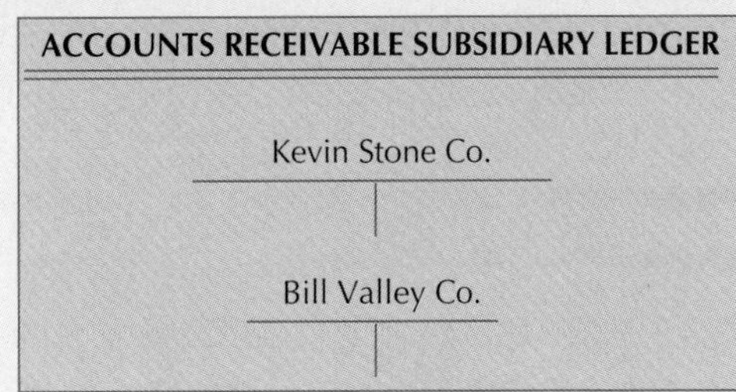

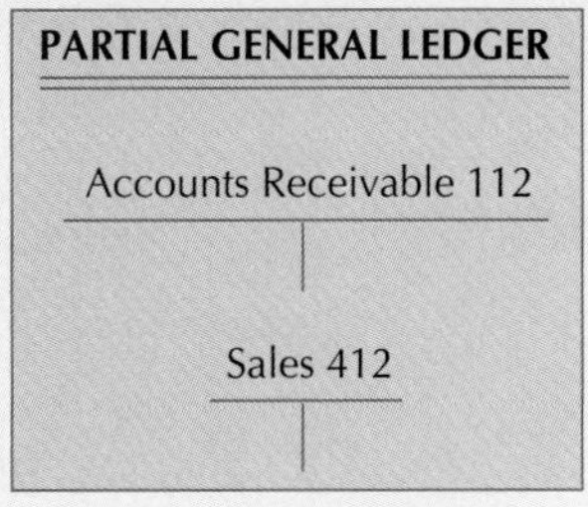

Journalizing, recording, and posting that includes credit memorandum.

9-2. Journalize, record, and post when appropriate the following transactions into the sales journal (same headings as Exercise 9-1) and general journal (page 1) (all sales carry terms of 2/10, n/30):

2001
May 16 Sold merchandise on account to Ronald Co., invoice No. 1, $1,000.
18 Sold merchandise on account to Bass Co., invoice No. 2, $1,700.
20 Issued credit memorandum No. 1 to Bass Co. for defective merchandise, $700.

Use the following account numbers: Accounts Receivable, 112; Sales, 411; Sales Returns and Allowances, 412.

Journalizing transaction into cash receipts journal.

9-3. From Exercise 9-2, journalize in the cash receipts journal the receipt of a cheque from Ronald Co. for payment of invoice No. 1 on May 24. Use the same headings as for Walter Lantz Co. (on p. 377).

Journalizing, recording, and posting sales and cash receipts journal; schedule of accounts receivable.

9-4. From the following transactions for Edna Co., when appropriate, journalize, record, post, and prepare a schedule of accounts receivable. Use the same journal headings (all page 1) and chart of accounts that Art's Wholesale Clothing used in the text (use Edna Cares, Capital). You will have to set up your own accounts receivable subsidiary ledger and partial general ledger as needed. All sales terms are 2/10, n/30.

2002
June 1 Edna Cares invested $3,000 in the business.
1 Sold merchandise on account to Boston Co., invoice No. 1, $700.
2 Sold merchandise on account to Gary Co., invoice No. 2, $900.
3 Cash sale, $200
8 Issued credit memorandum No. 1 to Boston for defective merchandise, $200.
10 Received cheque from Boston for invoice No. 1 less returns and discount.
15 Cash sale, $400
18 Sold merchandise on account to Boston Co., invoice No. 3, $600.

9-5. From the following facts calculate what Ann Frost must pay Blue Co. for the purchase of a dining-room set. Sale terms are 2/10, n/30.

a. Sales ticket price before tax, $4,000—dated April 5

b. Provincial sales tax, 8 percent, GST, 7 percent

c. Returned one defective chair for credit of $400 before any taxes on April 8.

d. Paid bill on April 13.

9-6. Peter Rockford purchased eight stereo speakers from Waverly Electronics for his restaurant. The price before any taxes was $400.00 each. Terms were 2/10, n/30, and PST of 10 percent was added to the total before GST of 7 percent was included. What amount will Rockford pay, given the following:

a. Sale was dated June 11, 2003.

b. Returned two speakers because of defective sound on June 15, 2003.

c. Credit of $400 each plus all applicable taxes was received on June 15.

d. Full payment was made on June 20, 2003.

Group A Problems

(The forms you need are on pages 9-16 to 9-38 of the *Study Guide with Working Papers.*)

Multicolumn journal: journalizing and posting to general ledger and recording to accounts receivable subsidiary ledger and preparing a schedule of accounts receivable

Check Figure

Schedule of Accounts Receivable $3,210.00

9A-1. Jill Blue has opened Max Co., a wholesale grocery and pizza company. The following transactions occurred in June:

2001

June 1 Sold grocery merchandise to Joe Kase Co. on account, $400, invoice No. 1.

4 Sold pizza merchandise to Sue Moore Co. on account, $600, invoice No. 2.

8 Sold grocery merchandise to Long Co. on account, $700, invoice No. 3.

10 Issued credit memorandum No. 1 to Joe Kase for $150 worth of grocery merchandise returned because of spoilage.

15 Sold pizza merchandise to Sue Moore Co. on account, $160, invoice No. 4.

19 Sold grocery merchandise to Long Co. on account, $300, invoice No. 5.

25 Sold pizza merchandise to Joe Kase Co. on account, $1,200, invoice No. 6.

Required

1. Journalize the transactions in the appropriate journals.
2. Record in the accounts receivable subsidiary ledger and post to the general ledger as appropriate.
3. Prepare a schedule of accounts receivable.

Multicolumn sales journal: Use of sales tax; journalizing and posting to general ledger and recording to accounts receivable subsidiary ledger; and preparing a schedule of accounts receivable

Check Figure

Schedule of Accounts Receivable $13,045.00

9A-2. The following transactions of Ted's Auto Supply occurred in November (your working papers have balances as of November 1 for certain general ledger and accounts receivable ledger accounts):

2000

Nov. 1 Sold auto parts merchandise to R. Volan on account, $1,000, invoice No. 60, plus 5 percent PST.

5 Sold auto parts merchandise to J. Seth on account, $800, invoice No. 61, plus 5 percent PST.

8 Sold auto parts merchandise to Lance Corner on account, $9,000, invoice No. 62, plus 5 percent PST.

10 Issued credit memorandum No. 12 to R. Volan for $500 for defective auto parts merchandise returned from November 1 transaction. (Be careful to record the reduction in sales tax payable as well.)

12 Sold auto parts merchandise to J. Seth on account, $600, invoice No. 63, plus 5 percent PST.

Required

1. Journalize the transactions in the appropriate journals.
2. Record in the accounts receivable subsidiary ledger and post to the general ledger as appropriate.
3. Prepare a schedule of accounts receivable.

9A-3. Mark Peaker owns Peaker's Sneaker Shop. (In your working papers, balances as of May 1 are provided for the accounts receivable and general ledger accounts.) The following transactions occurred in May:

Comprehensive problem: recording transactions in sales, cash receipts, and general journals; recording in accounts receivable subsidiary ledger and posting to general ledger; preparing a schedule of accounts receivable

(No GST or PST applied)

Check Figure

Schedule of Accounts Receivable $5,700.00

2003

May 1 Mark Peaker invested an additional $12,000 in the sneaker store.
3 Sold $700 worth of merchandise on account to B. Dale, sales invoice No. 60, terms 1/10, n/30.
4 Sold $500 worth of merchandise on account to Ron Lester, sales invoice No. 61, terms 1/10, n/30.
9 Sold $200 worth of merchandise on account to Jim Zon, sales invoice No. 62, terms 1/10, n/30.
10 Received cash from B. Dale in payment of May 3 transaction, sales invoice No. 60, less discount.
20 Sold $3,000 worth of merchandise on account to Pam Pry, sales invoice No. 63, terms 1/10, n/30.
22 Received cash payment from Ron Lester in payment of May 4 transaction, sales invoice No. 61.
23 Collected cash sales, $3,000.
24 Issued credit memorandum No. 1 to Pam Pry for $2,000 worth of merchandise returned from May 20 sales on account.
26 Received cash from Pam Pry in payment of May 20 sales invoice No. 63. (Don't forget about the credit memo and discount.)
28 Collected cash sales, $7,000.
30 Sold sneaker rack equipment for $300 cash. (Beware.)
30 Sold merchandise, priced at $4,000, on account to Ron Lester, sales invoice No. 64, terms 1/10, n/30.
31 Issued credit memorandum No. 2 to Ron Lester for $700 worth of merchandise returned from May 30 transaction, sales invoice No. 64.

Required

1. Journalize the transactions.
2. Record in the accounts receivable subsidiary ledger and post to general ledger as needed.
3. Prepare a schedule of accounts receivable.

9A-4. Bill Murray opened Bill's Cosmetic Market on April 1. There are 8 percent PST and 7 percent GST charged on all cosmetic sales. Bill offers no sales discounts. The following transactions occurred in April:

Comprehensive problem: using GST and PST in recording transactions in sales, cash receipts, and general journals; recording in accounts receivable subsidiary ledger and posting to general ledger; cross-footing and preparing a schedule of accounts receivable

Check Figure

Schedule of Accounts Receivable $1,782.50

2001

April 1 Bill Murray invested $8,000 in the Cosmetic Market from his personal savings account.
5 From the cash register tapes, lipstick cash sales were $5,000 plus taxes.
5 From the cash register tapes, eye shadow cash sales were $2,000 plus taxes.
8 Sold lipstick on account to Alice Koy Co., $300, sales invoice No. 1, plus taxes.
9 Sold eye shadow on account to Marika Sanchez Co., $1,000, sales invoice No. 2, plus taxes.
15 Issued credit memorandum No. 1 to Alice Koy Co. for $150 for lipstick returned. (Be sure to reduce taxes payable for Bill's.)
19 Marika Sanchez Co. paid half the amount owed from sales invoice No. 2, dated April 9.
21 Sold lipstick on account to Jeff Tong Co., $300, sales invoice No. 3, plus taxes.
24 Sold eye shadow on account to Rusty Neal Co., $800, sales invoice No. 4, plus taxes.
25 Issued credit memorandum No. 2 to Jeff Tong Co. for $200 (plus taxes) for lipstick returned from sales invoice No. 3, dated April 21.

29 Cash sales taken from the cash register tape showed:
1. Lipstick—$1,000 + taxes
2. Eye shadow—$3,000 + taxes

29 Sold lipstick on account to Marika Sanchez Co., $400, sales invoice No. 5, plus taxes.

30 Received payment from Marika Sanchez Co. of sales invoice No. 5, dated April 29.

Required

1. Journalize the above in the sales journal, cash receipts journal, or general journal.
2. Record in the accounts receivable subsidiary ledger and post to the general ledger when appropriate.
3. Prepare a schedule of accounts receivable for the end of April.

Comprehensive problem: using HST in recording transactions in sales, cash receipts, and general journals; recording in accounts receivable and posting to general ledger; cross-footing and preparing a schedule of accounts receivable

Check Figure

Schedule of Accounts Receivable $4,926.19

9A-5. Mary Parker owns Parker's SCUBA Shop. (In your working papers, balances as of April 1 are provided for the accounts receivable and general ledger accounts.) In Mary's province it is necessary to add HST of 15 percent to arrive at the final invoice amount. The following transactions occurred in April:

2002

April 1 Mary Parker invested an additional $17,000 in the business.

3 Sold $500 worth of merchandise (plus 15 percent HST) on account to J. Simpson, sales invoice No. 614, terms 2/10, n/30.

4 Sold $1,200 worth of merchandise (plus HST) on account to R. Langley, sales invoice No. 615, terms 2/10, n/30.

9 Sold $300 worth of merchandise (plus HST) on account to J. Fellowes, sales invoice No. 616, terms 2/10, n/30.

10 Received cash from J. Simpson in payment of April 3 transaction, sales invoice No. 614, less discount.

20 Sold $2,000 worth of merchandise (plus HST) on account to Phyllis Leung, sales invoice No. 617, terms 2/10, n/30.

22 Received cash payment from R. Langley in payment of April 4 transaction, sales invoice No. 615.

23 Collected cash sales, $1,600 (plus HST).

24 Issued credit memorandum No. 101 to Phyllis Leung for $500 (plus HST) worth of merchandise returned from April 20 sales.

25 Received payment from Roland Doncaster of the amount due from previous month, $907.15.

26 Received cash from Phyllis Leung in payment of April 20 sales invoice No. 617. (Don't forget about the credit memo, HST, and discount.)

28 Collected cash sales, $4,000 (plus necessary HST).

29 Sold merchandise priced at $3,000 (plus HST), on account, to Roland Doncaster, sales invoice No. 618, terms 2/10, n/30.

30 Issued credit memorandum No. 102 to Roland Doncaster for $800 worth of merchandise (plus HST) returned from April 29 transaction, sales invoice No. 618.

Required

1. Journalize the transactions.
2. Record in the accounts receivable ledger and post to the general ledger as needed.
3. Prepare a schedule of accounts receivable as of April 30.

Group B Problems

(The forms you need are on pages 9-16 to 9-38 of the *Study Guide with Working Papers.*)

Multicolumn journal: journalizing and posting to general ledger, recording in accounts receivable subsidiary ledger, and preparing a schedule of accounts receivable

Check Figure

Schedule of Accounts Receivable $3,040.00

9B-1. The following transactions occurred for Max Co. for the month of June:

2001

June 1 Sold grocery merchandise to Joe Kase Co. on account, $800, invoice No. 1.

4 Sold pizza merchandise to Sue Moore Co. on account, $550, invoice No. 2.

8 Sold grocery merchandise to Long Co. on account, $900, invoice No. 3.

10 Issued credit memorandum No. 1 to Joe Kase for $160 worth of grocery merchandise returned because of spoilage.

15 Sold pizza merchandise to Sue Moore Co. on account, $700, invoice No. 4.

19 Sold grocery merchandise to Long Co. on account, $250, invoice No. 5.

Required

1. Journalize the transactions in the appropriate journals.
2. Record in the accounts receivable subsidiary ledger and post to general ledger as appropriate.
3. Prepare a schedule of accounts receivable.

Multicolumn sales journal: use of sales tax; journalizing and posting to general ledger and recording in accounts receivable subsidiary ledger; preparing a schedule of accounts receivable

Check Figure

Schedule of Accounts Receivable $22,600.00

9B-2. In November the following transactions occurred for Ted's Auto Supply (your working papers have balances as of November 1 for certain general ledger and accounts receivable ledger accounts):

2000

Nov. 1 Sold merchandise to R. Volan on account, $4,000, invoice No. 70, plus 5 percent PST.

5 Sold merchandise to J. Seth on account, $1,600, invoice No. 71, plus 5 percent PST.

8 Sold merchandise to Lance Corner on account, $15,000, invoice No. 72, plus 5 percent PST.

10 Issued credit memorandum No. 14 to R. Volan for $2,000 for defective merchandise returned from November 1 transaction. (Be careful to record the reduction in PST payable as well.)

12 Sold merchandise to J. Seth on account, $1,400, invoice No. 73, plus 5 percent PST.

Required

1. Journalize the transactions in the appropriate journals.
2. Record in the accounts receivable subsidiary ledger and post to the general ledger as appropriate.
3. Prepare a schedule of accounts receivable.

Comprehensive problem: recording transactions in sales, cash receipts, and general journals; recording in accounts receivable subsidiary ledger and posting to general ledger; preparing a schedule of accounts receivable

(No GST or PST applied)

9B-3. (In your working papers, all the beginning balances needed are provided for the accounts receivable subsidiary and general ledgers.) The following transactions occurred for Peaker's Sneaker Shop:

2003

May 1 Mark Peaker invested an additional $14,000 in the sneaker store.

3 Sold $2,000 worth of merchandise on account to B. Dale, sales invoice No. 60, terms 1/10, n/30.

4 Sold $900 worth of merchandise on account to Ron Lester, sales invoice No. 61, terms 1/10, n/30.

Check Figure

Schedule of Accounts Receivable $8,000.00

9 Sold $600 worth of merchandise on account to Jim Zon, sales invoice No. 62, terms 1/10, n/30.
10 Received cash from B. Dale in payment of May 3 transaction, sales invoice No. 60, less discount.
20 Sold $4,000 worth of merchandise on account to Pam Pry, sales invoice No. 63, terms 1/10, n/30.
22 Received cash payment from Ron Lester in payment of May 4 transaction, sales invoice No. 61.
23 Collected cash sales, $6,000.
24 Issued credit memorandum No. 1 to Pam Pry for $500 worth of merchandise returned from May 20 sale.
26 Received cash from Pam Pry in payment of May 20 sales invoice No. 63. (Don't forget about the credit memo and discount.)
28 Collected cash sales, $12,000.
30 Sold sneaker rack equipment for $200 cash. (Beware.)
30 Sold $6,000 worth of merchandise on account to Ron Lester, sales invoice No. 64, terms 1/10, n/30.
31 Issued credit memorandum No. 2 to Ron Lester for $800 worth of merchandise returned from May 30 transaction, sales invoice No. 64.

Required

1. Journalize the transactions in the appropriate journals.
2. Record and post as appropriate.
3. Prepare a schedule of accounts receivable.

Comprehensive problem: using sales taxes in recording transactions in sales, cash receipts, and general journals; recording in accounts receivable subsidiary ledger and posting to general ledger; preparing a schedule of accounts receivable

Check Figure

Schedule of Accounts Receivable $2,203.50

9B-4. Bill's Cosmetic Market began operating in April. There are 6 percent PST and 7 percent GST on all cosmetic sales. Bill offers no discounts. The following transactions occurred in April:

2001

April 1 Bill Murray invested $10,000 in the Cosmetic Market from his personal account.
5 From the cash register tapes, lipstick cash sales were $5,000 plus taxes.
5 From the cash register tapes, eye shadow cash sales were $3,000 plus taxes.
8 Sold lipstick on account to Alice Koy Co., $400, sales invoice No. 1, plus taxes.
9 Sold eye shadow on account to Marika Sanchez Co., $900, sales invoice No. 2, plus taxes.
15 Issued credit memorandum No. 1 to Alice Koy Co. for lipstick returned, $200. (Be sure to reduce taxes payable.)
19 Marika Sanchez Co. paid half the amount owed from sales invoice No. 2, dated April 9.
21 Sold lipstick on account to Jeff Tong Co., $600 sales invoice No. 3, plus taxes.
24 Sold eye shadow on account to Rusty Neal Co., $1,000, sales invoice No. 4, plus taxes.
25 Issued credit memorandum No. 2 to Jeff Tong Co. for $300 (plus taxes), for lipstick returned from sales invoice No. 3, dated April 21.
29 Cash sales taken from the cash register tape showed:
1. Lipstick—$4,000 + taxes
2. Eye shadow—$2,000 + taxes
29 Sold lipstick on account to Marika Sanchez Co., $700, sales invoice No. 5 plus taxes.
30 Received payment from Marika Sanchez Co. of sales invoice No. 5, dated April 29.

Required

1. Journalize, record, and post as appropriate.

2. Prepare a schedule of accounts receivable for the end of April.

Comprehensive problem: using HST in recording transactions into sales, cash receipts, and general journals; recording to accounts receivable and posting to general ledger; and preparing a schedule of accounts receivable

Check Figure

Schedule of Accounts Receivable $6,191.19

9B-5. Mary Parker owns Parker's SCUBA Shop. (In your working papers, balances as of April 1 are provided for the accounts receivable and general ledger accounts.) In Mary's province it is necessary to add HST of 15 percent to the sales total to arrive at the final invoice amount. The following transactions occurred in April:

2002

April	1	Mary Parker invested an additional $13,000 in the business.
	3	Sold $800 worth of merchandise (plus HST at 15 percent) on account to J. Simpson, sales invoice No. 614, terms 2/10, n/30.
	4	Sold $1,600 worth of merchandise (plus HST) on account to R. Langley, sales invoice No. 615, terms 2/10, n/30.
	9	Sold $600 worth of merchandise (plus HST) on account to J. Fellowes, sales invoice No. 616, terms 2/10, n/30.
	10	Received cash from J. Simpson in payment of April 3 transaction, sales invoice No. 614, less discount (pre-HST amount).
	20	Sold $3,000 worth of merchandise (plus HST) on account to Phyllis Leung, sales invoice No. 617, terms 2/10, n/30.
	22	Received cash payment from R. Langley in payment of April 4 transaction, sales invoice No. 615.
	23	Collected cash sales, $2,500 (plus HST).
	24	Issued credit memorandum No. 101 to Phyllis Leung for $900 (plus HST) of merchandise returned from April 20 sales on account.
	25	Received payment from Roland Doncaster of the amount due from previous month, $907.15.
	26	Received cash from Phyllis Leung in payment of April 20 sales invoice No. 617. (Don't forget the credit memo, HST, and discount.)
	28	Collected cash sales, $3,200 plus HST.
	29	Sold merchandise priced at $4,000 (plus HST), on account to Roland Doncaster, sales invoice No. 618, terms 2/10, n/30.
	30	Issued credit memorandum No. 102 to Roland Doncaster for $1,000 worth of merchandise (plus HST) returned from April 29 transaction, sales invoice No. 618.

Required

1. Journalize the transactions.

2. Record in the accounts receivable ledger and post to the general ledger as needed.

3. Prepare a schedule of accounts receivable as of April 30.

Group C Problems

(The forms you need are on pages 9-39 to 9-61 of the *Study Guide with Working Papers*.)

Multicolumn journal: journalizing and posting to the general ledger, recording in the accounts receivable ledger, and preparing a schedule of accounts receivable

Check Figure

Schedule of Accounts Receivable $7,655.00

9C-1. The following transactions occurred for Lodge Co. for the month of July:

2001

July	1	Sold upholstery merchandise to Joan Timkins Co. on account, $1,500, invoice No. 115. Terms: net 30 days
	4	Sold carpet merchandise to Chris Cowan Co. on account, $825, invoice No. 116. Terms: net 30 days

8 Sold upholstery merchandise to Cross & Co. on account, $1,950, invoice No. 117. Terms: net 30 days
10 Issued credit memorandum No. 1 to Joan Timkins Co. for $300 worth of merchandise returned because of faulty colouring match.
15 Sold carpet merchandise to Chris Cowan Co. on account, $925, invoice No. 118. Terms: net 30 days
19 Sold upholstery merchandise to Cross & Co. on account, $730, invoice No. 119. Terms: net 30 days
24 Sold carpet merchandise to Joan Timkins Co. on account, $2,025, invoice No. 120. Terms: net 30 days

Required

1. Journalize the transactions in the appropriate journals.
2. Record in the accounts receivable ledger and post to the general ledger as appropriate.
3. Prepare a schedule of accounts receivable.

Multicolumn sales journal: use of sales tax; journalizing and posting to the general ledger and recording in accounts receivable ledger; and preparing a schedule of accounts receivable

Check Figure

Schedule of Accounts Receivable $37,768.50

9C-2. In September the following transactions occurred for Forrest Equipment Supply (your working papers have balances as of September 1 for certain general ledger and accounts receivable ledger accounts):

2002

Sept. 1 Sold merchandise to Ray Fortuna on account, $9,500, invoice No. 703, plus 9 percent PST.
5 Sold merchandise to Wilma Jorge on account, $3,000, invoice No. 704, plus 9 percent PST.
8 Sold merchandise to Cassie Ho on account, $15,800, invoice No. 705, plus 9 percent PST.
10 Issued credit memorandum No. 14 to Ray Fortuna for $1,200 for defective merchandise returned from September 1 transaction. (Be careful to record the reduction in PST payable as well.)
12 Sold merchandise to Wilma Jorge on account, $3,650, invoice No. 706, plus 9 percent PST.

Required

1. Journalize the transactions in the appropriate journals.
2. Record in the accounts receivable ledger and post to the general ledger as appropriate.
3. Prepare a schedule of accounts receivable.

Comprehensive problem: recording transactions into sales, cash receipts, and general journals; recording to accounts receivable and posting to general ledger; preparing a schedule of accounts receivable.

(No PST, GST, or HST)

Check Figure

Schedule of Accounts Receivable $5,884.60

9C-3. (In your working papers, all the beginning balances needed are provided for the accounts receivable and general ledger.) The following transactions occurred for Inner City Sausage Supply Co.:

2000

Sept. 1 Karen Blum, owner, invested an additional $18,000 in the business.
3 Sold $1,850 worth of merchandise on account to Petra's Meat Market, sales invoice No. 460, terms 1/10, n/30.
4 Sold $825 worth of merchandise on account to Chapman's Deli, sales invoice No. 461, terms 1/10, n/30.
8 Sold $930 worth of merchandise on account to Valemont Variety Meats Co., sales invoice No. 462, terms 1/10, n/30.
12 Received cash from Petra's Meat Market in payment of September 3 transaction, sales invoice No. 460, less discount.
21 Sold $1,500 worth of merchandise on account to Discount Meats, sales invoice No. 463, terms 1/10, n/30.

22 Received cash payment from Chapman's Deli in payment of September transaction, sales invoice No. 461.
23 Collected cash sale, $638.
24 Issued credit memorandum No. 101 to Discount Meats for $300 worth of merchandise returned from September 21 sales on account.
26 Received cash from Discount Meats in payment of September 21 sales invoice No. 463. (Don't forget about the credit memo and discount.)
27 Collected cash sales, $813.
28 Sold meat cooling equipment for $900 cash. (Beware.)
29 Sold $1,420 worth of merchandise on account to Chapman's Deli, sales invoice No. 464, terms 1/10, n/30.
30 Issued credit memorandum No. 102 to Chapman's Deli for $420 worth of merchandise returned from September 29 transaction, sales invoice No. 464.

Required

1. Journalize the transactions in the appropriate journals.

2. Record and post as appropriate.

3. Prepare a schedule of accounts receivable.

Comprehensive problem: using sales taxes in recording transactions into sales, cash receipts, and general journals; recording in accounts receivable and posting to general ledger; and preparing a schedule of accounts receivable

Check Figure

Schedule of Accounts Receivable $14,685.50

9C-4. Royce's Communication Sales Co. began operating in August. There are 8 percent PST and 7 percent GST on all sales. Royce's offers no discounts (all terms are net 30 days). The following transactions occurred in August:

2001

Aug. 1 Royce Lamoureux invested $32,000 in Communication Sales Co. from his personal account.
5 From the cash register tapes, cellular cash sales were $5,400 plus taxes.
5 From the cash register tapes, radio cash sales were $8,150 plus taxes.
8 Sold cellular equipment on account to Kelly's Real Estate Co., $4,260, sales invoice No. 201, plus taxes.
9 Sold radio equipment on account to Well's Hotshot Service Co., $3,100, sales invoice No. 202, plus taxes.
15 Issued credit memorandum No. 1 to Kelly's Real Estate Co. for cellular equipment returned, $800. (Be sure to reduce taxes payable.)
19 Well's Hotshot Service Co. paid half the amount owed from sales invoice No. 2, dated August 9.
20 Sold cellular equipment on account to Mountain Explorations Co., $5,770 sales invoice No. 203, plus taxes.
21 Received proceeds of loan from the Business Development Bank of Canada $50,000.
24 Sold radio equipment on account to Walkin's Safety Supply Co., $5,820. Sales invoice No. 204, plus taxes.
25 Issued credit memorandum No. 2 to Mountain Explorations Co. for $1,420, for equipment returned from sales invoice No. 203, dated August 20. Remember to include taxes!
27 Received payment of net amount due from Kelly's Real Estate Co. on sales invoice No. 201 less the credit allowed.
29 Cash sales taken from the cash register tape showed:
(1) Cellular—$8,400 + taxes
(2) Radio—$7,600 + taxes
29 Sold cellular equipment on account to Well's Hotshot Service Co., $4,150 sales invoice No. 205, plus taxes.
30 Received payment from Well's Hotshot Service Co. of sales invoice No. 202, dated August 9.

Required

1. Journalize, record, and post as appropriate.
2. Prepare a schedule of accounts receivable for the end of August.

Comprehensive problem: using HST in recording transactions in sales, cash receipts, and general journals; recording in accounts receivable and posting to the general ledger; and preparing a schedule of accounts receivable

Check Figure

Schedule of Accounts Receivable $13,525.44

9C-5. Martha Worth owns Rarity Collectibles Shop. (In your working papers, balances as of January 1 are provided for the accounts receivable and general ledger accounts.) In this province it is necessary to add HST of 15 percent to the sales total to arrive at the final invoice amount. The following transactions occurred in January:

2002

Jan.	1	Martha Worth invested $34,000 in the business.
	3	Sold $2,600 worth of merchandise (plus HST) on account to Starcraft Reproductions, sales invoice No. 344, terms 2/10, n/30.
	4	Sold $3,200 worth of merchandise (plus HST) on account to Burgess Fancys, sales invoice No. 345, terms 2/10, n/30.
	9	Sold $3,800 worth of merchandise (plus HST) on account to Hard-To-Find Co., sales invoice No. 346, terms 2/10, n/30.
	10	Received cash from Starcraft Reproductions in payment of January 3 transaction, sales invoice No. 344, less discount.
	20	Sold $2,480 worth of merchandise (plus HST) on account to Georgina's Collections, sales invoice No. 347, terms 2/10, n/30.
	22	Received cash payment from Burgess Fancys in payment of January 4 transaction, sales invoice No. 345.
	23	Collected cash sales, $4,125 plus HST.
	24	Issued credit memorandum No. 10 to Georgina's Collections for $500 worth of merchandise (plus HST) returned from January 20 sales on account.
	26	Received cash from Georgina's Collections in payment of January 20 sales invoice No. 347. (Don't forget about the credit memo, HST, and discount.)
	28	Collected cash sales, $4,720 plus HST.
	29	Sold merchandise priced at $5,000 (plus HST), on account to Perfect Sales Co., sales invoice No. 348, terms 2/10, n/30.
	30	Issued credit memorandum No. 11 to Perfect Sales Co. for $1,200 (plus HST) of merchandise returned from January 29 transaction, sales invoice No. 348.

Required

1. Journalize the transactions.
2. Record in the accounts receivable ledger and post to the general ledger as needed.
3. Prepare a schedule of accounts receivable as of January 31.

Real World Applications

(The forms you need are on pages 9-62 and 9-63 of the *Study Guide with Working Papers.*)

9R-1.

Ronald Howard has been hired by Green Company to help reconstruct the sales journal, general journal, and cash receipts journal, which were recently destroyed in a fire. The owner of Green has supplied him with the data shown on page 395. Enter the entries into the reconstructed sales journal, general journal, and cash receipts journal. (Don't worry about dates, invoice numbers, etc.) What written recommendation should Ron make so that reconstruction will not be needed in the future?

Accounts Receivable Subsidiary Ledger

P. Bond

Debit		Credit
Balance	100	150 CRJ
SJ	150	Entitled to 2 percent discount

M. Raff

Debit		Credit
Balance	200	
SJ	100	

J. Smooth

Debit		Credit
Balance	300	1,000 GJ
SJ	2,000	1,000 CRJ ←
SJ	1,000	500 GJ
		Entitled to 1 percent discount

R. Venner

Debit		Credit
Balance	200	400 CRJ
SJ	400	

Partial General Ledger

Cash

Debit		Credit
Balance	12,737	
GJ		

Accounts Receivable

Debit		Credit
Balance	800	1,000
SJ	3,650	500 GJ
		1,550 CRJ

Shelving Equipment

Debit		Credit
Balance	200	200 CRJ

M. Rang, Capital

Debit	Credit	
	1,000	Balance
	5,000	(Additional investment this month)

Sales

Debit	Credit	
	800	Balance
	6,000	CRJ ← 5,000 and 1,000
	3,650	SJ

Sales Discounts

Debit		Credit
CRJ	13	

Sales Returns and Allowances

Debit		Credit
GJ	1,000	
GJ	500	

9R-2.
The bookkeeper of Floore Company records credit sales in a sales journal and returns in a general journal. The bookkeeper did the following:

1. Recorded an $18 credit sale as $180 in the sales journal.
2. Correctly recorded a $40 sale in the sales journal but posted it to B. Blue's account as $400 in the accounts receivable ledger.
3. Made an addition error in determining the balance of J. B. Window Co. in the accounts receivable ledger.
4. Posted a sales return that was recorded in the general journal to the Sales Returns and Allowance account and the Accounts Receivable account but forgot to record it to the B. Katz Co.
5. Added the total of the sales column incorrectly.
6. Posted a sales return to the Accounts Receivable account but not to the Sales Returns and Allowances account. Accounts receivable ledger was recorded correctly.

Could you inform the bookkeeper in writing as to when each error will be discovered?

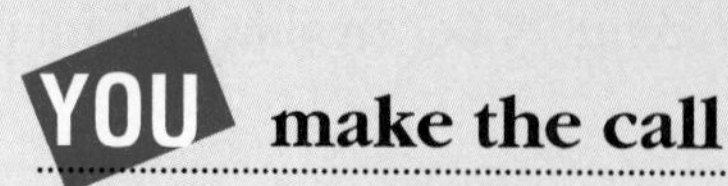

Critical Thinking/Ethical Case

9R-3.
Amy Jak is the National Sales Manager of Rowe Co. In order to get sales up to the projection for the old year, Amy asked the accountant to put the first two weeks of sales in January back into December. Amy told the accountant that this secret would only be between them. Should Amy move the new sales into the old sales year? You make the call. Write down your specific recommendations to Amy.

ACCOUNTING RECALL
A CUMULATIVE APPROACH

THIS EXAMINATION REVIEWS CHAPTERS 1 THROUGH 9.

Your *Study Guide with Working Papers* has forms (page 9-64) to complete this exam, as well as worked-out solutions. The page reference next to each question identifies the page to turn back to if you answer the question incorrectly.

PART I Vocabulary Review

Match each term on the left side with the appropriate definition or phrase in the right-hand column.

Page Ref.		
(353)	1. Accounts receivable subsidiary ledger	A. The results of a cash discount
		B. Records sales on account
(370)	2. Sundry	C. A contra-revenue account
(285)	3. Medical plan payable	D. Clears temporary accounts
(194)	4. Closing	E. In alphabetical order
(229)	5. Deposit in transit	F. Miscellaneous
(349)	6. Sales returns and allowances	G. Records receipt of cash
		H. A liability
(354)	7. Controlling account	I. Deposits not received by the bank
(354)	8. Sales journal	J. Accounts receivable
(370)	9. Cash receipts journal	
(349)	10. Sales discounts	

PART II True or False (Accounting Theory)

(240) 11. Petty cash is a liability.

(355) 12. The controlling account balance at the end of the month will equal the sum of the subsidiary ledger.

(358) 13. Issuing a credit memo results in sales returns and allowances decreasing.

(277) 14. CPP is always an equal deduction every month.

(355) 15. A ✔ means the controlling account has been updated.

Continuing Problem

Tony Freedman will use two specialized journals for recording business transactions in the month of January. To assist you in recording the transactions, the Schedule of Accounts Receivable as of December 31 is shown below and an updated chart of accounts with the current balance listed for each account is provided on page 398.

The partial January transactions are as follows:

Jan.	1	Sold $700 worth of merchandise to Taylor Golf on credit, sales invoice No. 12679; terms are 2/10/n30.
	10	Sold $3,000 worth of merchandise on account to Anthony Pitale, sales invoice No. 12680; terms are 2/10/n30.
	12	Collected $2,000 for cash sales.
	19	Sold $4,000 worth of merchandise on account to Vita Needle, sales invoice No. 12681; terms are 4/10/n30.
	20	Collected balance in full from invoice No. 12680, Anthony Pitale.
	29	Issued credit memorandum to Taylor Golf for $400 worth of merchandise returned, invoice No. 12679.
	29	Collected full payment from Vita Needle, invoice No. 12681.

Schedule of Accounts Receivable
Eldorado Computer Centre
December 31, 2001

Taylor Golf	$2,900.00
Carson Engineering	8,750.00
Total Amount Due	$11,650.00

Assignment

(See pages 9-65 to 9-68 in your *Study Guide with Working Papers.*)

1. Journalize the transactions in the appropriate journals (cash receipts, sales, or general journal).
2. Record in the accounts receivable subsidiary ledger and post to the general ledger as appropriate. A partial general ledger is included in the *Working Papers.*
3. Prepare a schedule of accounts receivable as of January 31, 2002.

ELDORADO COMPUTER CENTRE
CHART OF ACCOUNTS AND CURRENT BALANCES AS OF 12/31/2001

Account #	Account Name	Debit Balance	Credit Balance
1000	Cash	1 367.11	
1010	Petty Cash	100.00	
1020	Accounts Receivable	11 650.00	
1025	Prepaid Rent	1 600.00	
1030	Supplies	450.00	
1040	Merchandise Inventory	7 000.00	
1080	Computer Shop Equipment	3 800.00	
1081	Accumulated Amortization, Computer Shop Equipment		99.00
1090	Office Equipment	1 050.00	
1091	Accumulated Amortization, Office Equipment		20.00
2000	Accounts Payable		1 013.00
2010	Wages Payable		
2020	Income Tax Payable		467.55
2030	CPP Payable		158.24
2040	EI Payable		195.31
3000	T. Freedman, Capital		7 406.00
3010	T. Freedman, Withdrawals	2 015.00	
3020	Income Summary		
4000	Service Revenue		27 250.00
4010	Sales		
4020	Sales Returns and Allowances		
4030	Sales Discounts		
5010	Advertising Expense	480.00	
5020	Rent Expense		
5030	Utilities Expense	486.00	
5040	Phone Expense	315.00	
5050	Supplies Expense		
5060	Insurance Expense		
5070	Postage Expense	25.00	
5080	Amortization Expense, Computer Shop Equipment		
5090	Amortization Expense, Office Equipment		
5100	Miscellaneous Expense	10.00	
5110	Wages Expense	5 885.00	
5120	Payroll Benefits Expense	375.99	
5130	Interest Expense		
5140	Bad Debts Expense		
5600	Purchases		
5610	Purchases Returns and Allowances		
5620	Purchases Discounts		
5630	Freight In		
	Totals	36 609.10	36 609.10

COMPUTER WORKSHOP

COMPUTERIZED ACCOUNTING APPLICATION FOR EXCALIBUR CONSULTING, ACCOUNTS RECEIVABLE (CHAPTER 9)

Recording Transactions in the Sales and Receipts Journals

Before starting on this assignment, read and complete the tasks discussed in Parts A, B, and F of Appendix B: Computerized Accounting at the back of this book and complete the Computerized Accounting Application assignments at the ends of Chapters 3, 4, and 5.

The Sales and Receipts Journals in the *CA-Simply Accounting for Windows* program are designed to work with the Receivables Ledger and General Ledger modules in an integrated fashion. When transactions are recorded in the sales and receipts journals, the program automatically posts the customer's account in the accounts receivable subsidiary ledger, records the journal entry, and posts all accounts affected in the general ledger. However, the type of transaction recorded in the sales and receipts journals in the *CA-Simply Accounting for Windows* computerized system differs from the types of transaction recorded in these journals in a manual accounting system. An explanation of the differences appears in the following chart:

Name of Computerized Journal	Types of Transaction Recorded in Computerized Journal
Sales journal	Sales of merchandise on account
	Sales returns and allowances (credit memos)
	Sales discounts
Receipts journal	Cash receipts from cash and credit customers
General journal	Sundry transactions from all sources

A Customer Aged Detail report (the computerized version of a schedule of accounts receivable) for Excalibur Consulting appears below (terms of 2/10, n/30 are offered to all credit customers of Excalibur Consulting):

Excalibur Consulting – Your Name
Customer Aged Detail As at 11/30/2002 Page 1

			Total	Current	31 to 60	61 to 90	91+
Capitol Systems							
1103	11/10/02	Invoice	1,070.00	1,070.00	–	–	–
Olsen Office Supplies							
1105	11/17/02	Invoice	749.00	749.00	–	–	–
Samson Industries							
1101	11/04/02	Invoice	535.00	535.00	–	–	–
1149	11/27/02	Payment	–535.00	–535.00	–	–	–
1107	11/25/02	Invoice	856.00	856.00	–	–	–
			856.00	856.00	–	–	–
Titan Realty							
1102	11/05/02	Invoice	963.00	963.00	–	–	–
808	11/14/02	Discount	–18.00	–18.00	–	–	–
808	11/14/02	Payment	–945.00	–945.00	–	–	–
1106	11/23/02	Invoice	2,675.00	2,675.00	–	–	–
			2,675.00	2,675.00	–	–	–
			5,350.00	5,350.00	–	–	–

1. Start Windows. Insert your Student Data Files disk into drive A; then double-click on the CA-Simply Accounting icon. The CA-Simply Accounting Select Company dialogue box will appear.
2. Highlight Select an Existing Company; then press **OK**. The CA-Simply Accounting Open Company dialogue box will appear.
3. Enter the following path into the **Open File Name** text box:
   - `a:\excal.asc`
4. Click on the **Open** button; enter 12/31/02 into the **Session** text box; then click on the **OK** button. Click on the **OK** button in response to the message "The date entered is more than one week past your previous session date of 11/30/02." The Company window for Excalibur will appear.
5. Click on the Company Window **Setup** menu; then click on Company Information. The Company Information dialogue box will appear. Insert your name in place of the text Your Name in the **Name** text box. Click on the **OK** button to return to the Company Window.
6. On December 1, 2002, received cheque No. 817 from Titan Realty in the amount of $2,625 in payment of invoice No. 1106 ($2,675) dated November 23, less the 2 percent discount ($50).
7. Open the Receipts Journal dialogue box by double-clicking on the Receipts Journal icon. Click on the arrow button to the right of the **From** text box; click on Titan Realty; then press the TAB key. Enter `817` into the **No.** text box; then press the TAB key. Enter 12/01/02 into the **Date** text box; then press the TAB key. Invoice No. 1106 will be selected; press TAB and the 50.00 Disc. Taken will be highlighted. Titan Realty did take the discount offered; press TAB to accept the discount and press TAB again to accept the Payment Amt (2,625.00). Your screen should look like this:

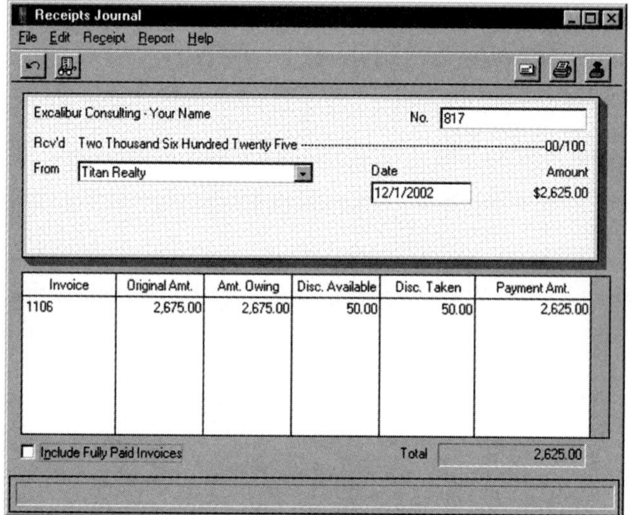

8. Before posting this transaction, you need to verify that the transaction data are correct by reviewing the journal entry. To review the entry, click on the **Receipts Journal Report** menu; then click on Display Receipts Journal Entry. The journal entry representing the data you have recorded in the Receipts Journal dialogue box is displayed. Review the journal entry for accuracy, noting any errors. Note that the program automatically debited the Cash and Consulting Fee Discounts accounts and credited the Accounts Receivable account through its integration feature.
9. Close the Receipts Journal Entry window by double-clicking on the **Control** menu box. If you have made an error, use the following editing techniques to correct it.

Editing a Receipts Journal Entry

- Move to the text box that contains the error by either pressing the TAB key to move forward through each text box or the SHIFT and TAB keys together to move to a previous text box. This will highlight the selected text box information so that you can change it. Alternatively, you can use the mouse to point to a text box and drag through the incorrect information to highlight it.

- Type the correct information; then press the TAB key to enter it.
- If you have associated the transaction with an incorrect customer, re-select the correct customer from the customer list display after clicking on the arrow button to the right of the **From** text box. You will be asked to confirm that you want to discard the current transaction. Click on the **Yes** button to discard the incorrect entry and display the outstanding invoices for the correct customer.
- To discard an entry and start over, double-click on the **Control** menu box. Click on the **Yes** button in response to the question "Are you sure you want to discard this journal entry?"
- Review the journal entry for accuracy after any editing corrections.
- **It is important to note that the only way to edit a journal entry after it is posted is to reverse the entry and enter the correct journal entry**. To correct journal entries posted in error, see Part C of Appendix B at the back of this book.

10. After verifying that the journal entry is correct, click on the Post icon to post this transaction. A blank Receipts Journal dialogue box is displayed, ready for additional Receipts Journal transactions to be recorded. Close the Receipts Journal dialogue box.
11. On December 2, 2002, the company provided consulting services to Slater Systems on account, $1,200 + GST, terms 2/10, n/30, invoice No. 1108. Slater Systems is a new customer and will have to be set up as a new customer of Excalibur Consulting.
12. Double-click on the **Customers** button in the Company Window to view the Customers dialogue box. Double-click on the **Create** button to display the Receivables Ledger dialogue box. Your screen should look like this:

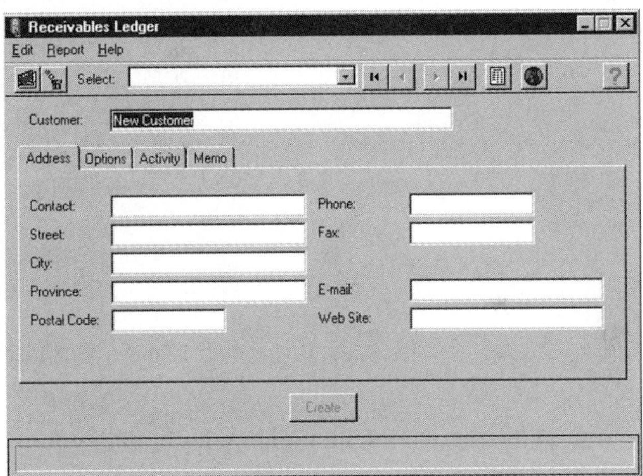

13. Type `Slater Systems` in the Customer field; then press TAB until the flashing insertion point is positioned in the Street field. Enter the following Address information for Slater Systems, using the TAB key to move from field to field:

Street:	11121 Greenview Plaza
City:	Your Town
Province:	Alberta
Postal Code:	T5L 7Z1
Phone:	(403) 467-1581
Fax:	(403) 467-1582

Your screen should look like this:

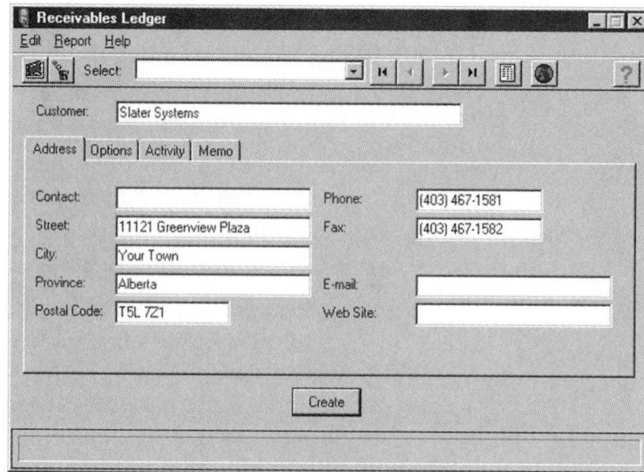

14. Click on the Options tab to view the following dialogue box:

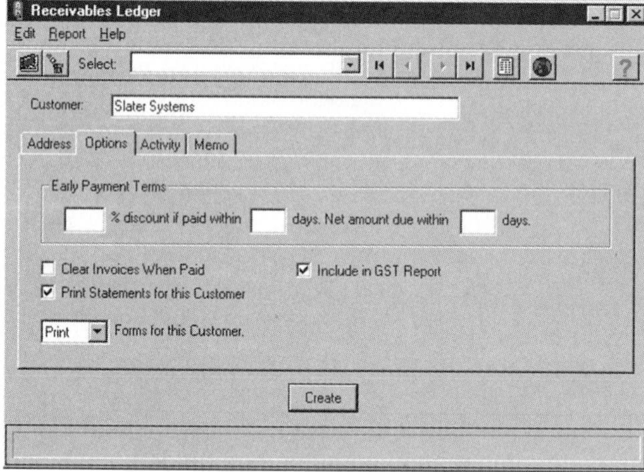

15. The terms under which Excalibur Consulting provides consulting services to Slater Systems are 2/10, n/30. These terms must be entered under Options for Slater Systems. Press the TAB key and the flashing insertion point will be positioned in the % discount field. Enter `2`; then press TAB. Enter `10`; press TAB; then enter `30` and press TAB again. Accept the default settings. Your screen should look like this:

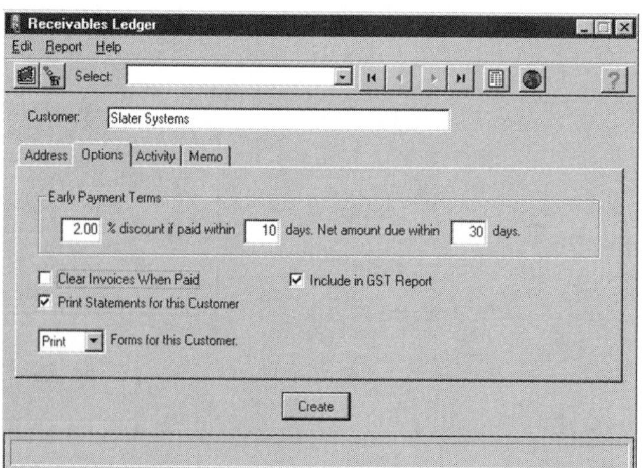

16. Click on the **Create** button and the Slater Systems account is created and the screen is cleared to enter a new customer. Close the Receivables Ledger window by double-clicking on the **Control** menu box. Close the Customer window.

17. Double-click on the **Sales Journal** button to view the Sales Journal—Sales Invoice dialogue box. You will notice that the transaction type automatically comes up as Sale on Account. Since the consulting services were provided to Slater Systems on account, this is acceptable. Click on the arrow button to the right of the **Sold To** text box; click on Slater Systems; then press TAB until the flashing insertion point is positioned in the Invoice field. Note that the program automatically offers invoice No. 1108 as the invoice number for this transaction through the program's automatic invoice numbering feature. Press TAB to accept this invoice number and then enter `12/02/02` in the Date field. Press the TAB key until the flashing insertion point is positioned in the Amount field. Enter `1200`; then press TAB. Press the ENTER key to display the Select GST dialogue box. Select 3-GST @ 7.0%, not included; the flashing insertion point is placed in the **Acct** text box. Press the ENTER key to display the Select Account dialogue box; then select 4005 Consulting Fees. Your screen should look like this:

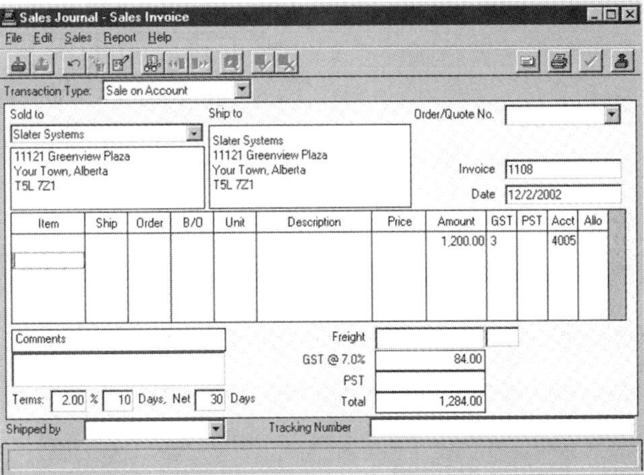

18. Before posting this transaction, you need to verify that the transaction data are correct by reviewing the journal entry. To review the entry, click on the **Sales Journal Report** menu; then click on Display Sales Journal Entry. The journal entry representing the data you have recorded in the Sales Journal dialogue box is displayed. Review the journal entry for accuracy, noting any errors. Note that the program has automatically debited the accounts receivable account and credited the GST charged on sales account through its integration feature.

19. If you have made an error, use the following editing techniques to correct the error.

Editing a Sales Journal Entry

- Move to the text box that contains the error by either pressing the TAB key to move forward through each text box or the SHIFT and TAB keys together to move to a previous text box. This will highlight the selected text box information so that you can change it. Alternatively, you can use the mouse to point to a text box and drag through the incorrect information to highlight it.
- Type the correct information; then press the TAB key to enter it.
- If you have associated the transaction with an incorrect customer, re-select the correct customer from the customer list display after clicking on the arrow button to the right of the **Sold to** text box (customers).
- If you have associated a transaction with an incorrect account, double-click on the incorrect account; then select the correct account from the Select Account dialogue box. This will replace the incorrect account with the correct account.
- To discard an entry and start over, double-click on the **Control** menu box. Click on the **Yes** button in response to the question "Are you sure you want to discard this journal entry?"

- Review the journal entry for accuracy after any editing corrections.
- **It is important to note that the only way to edit a journal entry after it is posted is to reverse the entry and enter the correct journal entry.** To correct sales entries posted in error, see Part C of Appendix B at the back of this book. Note that there is an automated feature which makes this easy.

20. After verifying that the journal entry is correct, click on the **Post** icon to post this transaction. A blank Sales Journal dialogue box is displayed, ready for additional Sales Journal transactions to be recorded. Leave the Sales Journal dialogue box open.

21. On December 4, 2002, provided consulting services of $1,300 + GST as a cash sale. In the Sales Journal, select Sale with Payment as the Transaction Type; select Cash in the Paid by field; then press TAB. Click on the arrow button to the right of the **Sold to** text box; click on <One-time customer>; press TAB until the flashing insertion point is positioned in the Date field. Enter `12/04/02`; then press TAB until the flashing insertion point is positioned in the Amount field. Enter `1300`; then press TAB. Press the ENTER key to display the Select GST dialogue box. Select 3-GST @ 7.0%, not included, then press the ENTER key to display the Select Account dialogue box; then select 4005 Consulting Fees. Your screen should look like this:

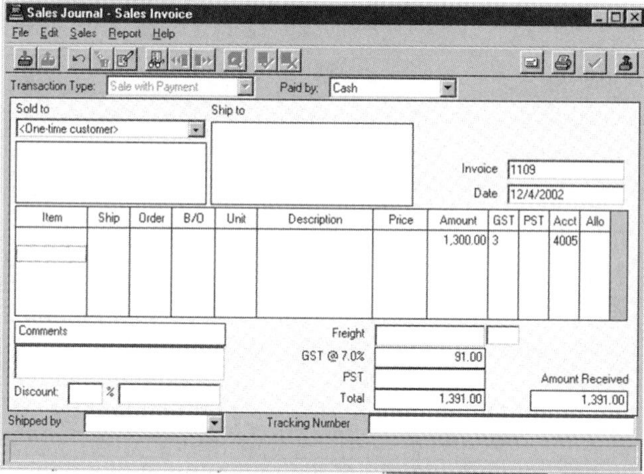

22. Before posting this transaction, you need to verify that the transaction data are correct. Follow the steps outlined previously to view the Sales Journal Entry and to correct any errors. Note that the program has automatically debited the cash account and credited the GST Charged on Sales and Consulting Fees accounts through its integration feature.

23. After verifying that the journal entry is correct, click on the Post icon to post this transaction. Leave the Sales Journal dialogue box open.

24. On December 6, 2002, issued credit memorandum 001 to Slater Systems for overcharge on invoice No. 1108. Select Sale on Account (as Slater Systems has not yet paid invoice No. 1108); then click on the arrow button to the right of the **Sold to** text box; click on Slater Systems; then press TAB until the flashing insertion point is positioned in the Invoice field. Enter `CM001`; press TAB and enter `12/06/02` in the Date field. Press TAB until the flashing insertion point is positioned in the Amount field. Enter `-100` (don't forget the minus sign!); then press TAB. Press ENTER and the Select GST dialogue box will appear. Select 3-GST @ 7%, not included. Press the ENTER key to display the Select Account dialogue box; then select 4010 Consulting Fee Adjustments. Your screen should look like this:

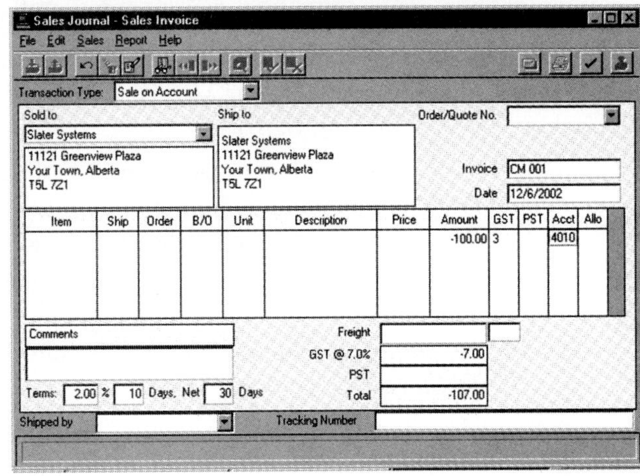

25. Verify that the transaction is correct; then click on the Post icon to post the transaction. Close the Sales Journal dialogue box.

26. Record the following transactions using the General, Sales, and Receipts Journals:

2002

Dec. 6 Purchased office supplies, $300 + GST (cheque No. 9). Record all cash payments in General Journal for now.

7 Paid phone bill, $100 + GST (cheque No. 10).

8 Provided consulting service to Samson Industries on account, $1,400 + GST, terms n/30, invoice No. 1110.

9 Received cheque No. 686 from Capitol Systems for $1,070 in payment of invoice No. 1103, dated Nov. 10.

9 Provided consulting service to Titan Realty on account, $2,000 + GST, terms 2/10, n/30, invoice No. 1111.

11 Received cheque No. 4389 from Slater Systems for $1,155 in payment of invoice No. 1108 ($1,284) dated Dec. 04, less credit memorandum #001 ($107), less 2 percent discount ($22).

12 Purchased additional computer equipment, $1,000 + GST (cheque No. 11).

15 Issued cheque No. 12 for $450 to City Payroll Service Co. for Dec. 15 payroll.

17 Received cheque No. 742 from Olsen Office Supplies for $749 in payment of invoice No. 1105, dated Nov. 17.

19 Received cheque No. 872 from Titan Realty for $2,100 in payment of invoice No. 1111 ($2,140), dated Dec. 9, less 2 percent discount ($40).

20 Issued cheque No. 13 for $300 + GST to Carla's Catering for Christmas party.

21 Provided consulting services of $1,200 + GST as cash sale, invoice No. 1112.

23 Received cheque No. 1208 from Samson Industries for $856 in payment of invoice No. 1107, dated Nov. 25.

23 Paid utility bill, $200 + GST (cheque No. 14).

31 Issued cheque No. 16 for $450 to City Payroll Co. for Dec. 31 payroll.

31 Owner withdrew $1,200 for personal use (cheque No. 15).

31 One month's rent ($1,250) and insurance ($50) have expired.

27. Print the following reports:
    a. Customer Aged report (Detail, Select All)
    b. General Journal (by Posting Date, All Ledger Entries, Start: 12/01/02, Finish 12/31/02).
    c. General Ledger report (Start: 12/01/02; Finish 12/31/02, Select All)

    Review your printed reports. If you have made an error in a posted journal entry, see Appendix B at the back of this book for instructions on on how to correct the error.
28. Click on the **Company Window File** menu; then click on Exit to end the current work session and return to your Windows desktop.
29. Complete the Report Transmittal form included for your use in the *Study Guide with Working Papers*.

Special Journals

10

Purchases and

Cash Payments

The Big Picture

◆

Tony Freedman was delighted to see the difference he made by using the specialized sales and cash receipts journals last month. He has decided to continue his efforts by using two more specialized journals: a purchases journal to track the merchandise Eldorado Computer Centre is buying, and a cash payments journal.

You have learned how specialized journals can benefit the company by easing the posting of transactions. In this chapter you will learn how to use purchases and cash payments journals.

A purchases journal is used to record purchases of merchandise on account, and the cash payments journal is used to record all cash payments. Each creditor you purchase merchandise from will have an individual ledger account showing the volume of business you are giving that creditor on account. The schedule of accounts payable, like the schedule of accounts receivable, will show a detailed list of all creditors and the amount owed to each.

Freedman has two primary objectives for using all of his specialized journals. One is to increase efficiency, and the other is to improve accuracy and detail.

Chapter Objectives

- Calculating cost of goods sold (pp. 408–410)
- Journalizing transactions in a purchases journal (p. 413)
- Posting from a purchases journal to the accounts payable subsidiary ledger and the general ledger (p. 413)
- Recording from the purchases journal to the accounts payable ledger (p. 413)
- Journalizing transactions which include GST/HST, then recording and posting same (p. 425)
- Preparing, journalizing, recording, and posting a debit memorandum, both with and without GST/HST (pp. 415–416 and 426–427)
- Journalizing, recording, and posting transactions using a cash payments journal, both with and without GST/HST (pp. 415–416 and 426–428)
- Preparing a schedule of accounts payable (pp. 418–420)

Chapter 9 focussed on the sellers in merchandising companies. This chapter will look at the buyers. Many of the concepts and rules related to special journals will carry over to this chapter.

LEARNING UNIT 10-1

Chou's Toy Shop: Buyer's View of a Merchandising Company

Purchases

Chou brings merchandise into his toy store for resale to customers. The account that records the cost of this merchandise is called **Purchases**. Suppose that Chou buys $4,000 worth of Barbie dolls on account from Mattel Manufacturing on July 6. The Purchases account records all merchandise bought for resale. Here's how this would be recorded if special journals were not used.

Purchases is a cost.
The rules work just as if they were an expense.

Purchases Dr.	Purchases Cr.	Accounts Payable Dr.	Accounts Payable Cr.
4,000			4,000

This account has a debit balance and is classified as a cost. Purchases represent costs that are directly related to bringing merchandise into the store for resale to customers. The July 6 entry would be analyzed and journalized as follows:

If Chou's purchased a new display case for the store, it would not show up in the Purchases account. The case is considered equipment that is not for resale to customers.

Accounts Affected	Category	↑ ↓	Rules	T-Account Update
Purchases	Expense	↑	Dr.	Purchases: Dr. 4,000 | Cr.
Accounts Payable, Mattel	Liability	↑	Cr.	Accounts Payable: Dr. | Cr. 4,000; Mattel Account: 4,000

July	6	Purchases	4,000 00	
		Accounts Payable, Mattel		4,000 00
		Purchases on account		

Keep in mind that we would have to record a liability to Mattel in the accounts payable subsidiary ledger. We will talk about the subsidiary ledger in Learning Unit 10-2.

Purchases Returns and Allowances

Chou noticed that some of the dolls he received were not as ordered, and he notified the manufacturer of this fact. On July 9, Mattel issued a debit memorandum* indicating that Chou would get a $500 reduction from the original selling price. Chou then agreed to keep the dolls. The account that records a decrease in a buyer's cost is a contra-expense account called **Purchases Returns and Allowances.** This account lowers the cost of purchases.

Purchases Returns and Allowances	
Dr.	Cr.
	500

← Normal balance is a credit.

Let's analyze this reduction to cost and prepare a general journal entry.

Accounts Affected	Category	↑ ↓	Rules	T Account Update
Accounts Payable, Mattel	Liability	↓	Dr.	Accounts Payable: Dr. 500 / Cr. 4,000; Mattel Account: 500 / 4,000
Purchases Returns and Allowances	Expense (Contra)	↓	Cr.	Purchases, Returns & Allowances: Dr. / Cr. 500

			Dr.	Cr.
July	9	Accounts Payable, Mattel	500 00	
		Purchases Returns and Allowances		500 00
		To record debit memorandum		

When posting to the general ledger accounts and recording in the accounts payable subsidiary ledger for Mattel have been completed, the records show that Chou's Toy Shop owes $500 less.

Purchases Discounts

Remember: For Mattel this is a sales discount, while for Chou this is a purchases discount.

Now let's look at the analysis and journal entry when Chou pays Mattel. Mattel offers a 2 percent cash discount if the invoice is paid within 10 days. To take advantage of this cash discount, Chou sent a company cheque to Mattel on July 15. The discount is taken after the allowance.

$4,000
− 500 allowance
$3,500 × 0.02 = $70 purchases discount

Remember: Purchases are debits; purchases discounts are credits.

The account that records this discount is called **Purchases Discounts.** It, too, is a contra-expense account because it lowers the cost of purchases.

Purchases Discounts	
Dr.	Cr.
	70

← Normal balance is a credit.

*Technically, Mattel would issue a *credit* memorandum. This is explained later in the chapter.

Let's analyze and prepare a general journal entry:

Accounts Affected	Category ↑ ↓	Rules	T Account Update
Accounts Payable, Mattel	Liability ↓	Dr.	Accounts Payable: Dr. 500, 3,500 / Cr. 4,000; Mattel Account: Dr. 500, 3,500 / Cr. 4,000
Purchases Discounts	Expense (Contra) ↓	Cr.	Purchases Discounts: Dr. / Cr. 70
Cash	Asset ↓	Cr.	Cash: Dr. / Cr. 3,430

July	15	Accounts Payable, Mattel	3 500 00	
		Purchases Discounts		70 00
		Cash		3 430 00
		Paid Mattel bal. owed		

After the journal entry is posted and recorded to Mattel, the result will show that Chou saved $70 and totally paid what his company owed to Mattel. The actual—or net—cost of his purchase is $3,430, calculated as follows:

Purchases	$4,000
– Purchases Returns and Allowances	500
– Purchases Discounts	70
= Net Purchases	$3,430

F.O.B. **stands for "free on board" the carrier.**

F.O.B. Destination:
Seller pays freight to point of destination.

F.O.B. Shipping Point:
Buyer pays freight from seller's shipping point.

Freight charges are not taken into consideration in calculating net purchases. Still, they are very important. If the seller is responsible for paying the shipping cost until the goods reach their destination, the freight charges are **F.O.B. destination.** For example, if a seller located in Winnipeg sold goods F.O.B. destination to a buyer in Edmonton, the seller would have to pay the cost of shipping the goods to the buyer.

If the buyer is responsible for paying the shipping costs, the freight charges are **F.O.B. shipping point.** In this situation, the seller sometimes will prepay the freight charges as a matter of convenience and will add it to the invoice of the purchaser.

Example

Bill amount ($800 + $80 prepaid freight)	$880
Less 5 percent cash discount (0.05 × $800)	40
Amount to be paid by buyer	$840

Purchases discounts are not taken on freight.

When does title to goods shipped change?

If the seller ships goods F.O.B. shipping point, legal ownership (title) passes to the buyer *when the goods are shipped.* If goods are shipped by the seller F.O.B. destination, title will change *when goods have reached their destination.*

LEARNING UNIT 10-1 REVIEW

AT THIS POINT you should be able to:

- Explain and calculate purchases, purchases returns and allowances, and purchases discounts. (pp. 408 and 409)
- Calculate net purchases. (p. 410)
- Explain why purchases discounts are not taken on freight. (p. 410)
- Compare and contrast F.O.B. destination with F.O.B. shipping point. (p. 410)

SELF-REVIEW QUIZ 10-1

(The forms you need can be found on page 10-1 of the *Study Guide with Working Papers.*)

Which of the following statements are false?

1. Net Purchases = Purchases − Purchases Returns and Allowances − Purchases Discounts.
2. Purchases is a contra-expense.
3. F.O.B. destination means the seller covers the shipping cost and retains title until the goods reach their destination.
4. Purchases discounts are not taken on freight.
5. Purchases Discounts is a contra-expense account.

Quiz Tip:

Buyer

Purchase	Dr.	Expense
PRA	Cr.	Contra-expense
PD	Cr.	Contra-expense

Seller

Sale	Cr.	Revenue
SRA	Dr.	Contra-revenue
SD	Dr.	Contra-revenue

Solution to Self-Review Quiz 10-1

Number 2 is false.

LEARNING UNIT 10-2

Steps Taken in Purchasing Merchandise and Recording Purchases

Merchandising companies must take specific steps when they purchase goods for resale. Let's look at the steps Art's Wholesale Clothing Company took when it ordered goods from Abby Blake Company on April 1.

STEPS TAKEN BY ART'S WHOLESALE WHEN ORDERING GOODS

Step 1: Prepare a Purchase Requisition at Art's Wholesale

Authorized personnel initiate purchase requisitions.

The inventory clerk notes a low inventory level of ladies' jackets for resale, so he sends a **purchase requisition** to the purchasing department. A duplicate copy is sent to the accounting department. A third copy remains with the department that initiated the request, to allow follow-up on any late or missing shipments.

Step 2: Purchasing Department of Art's Wholesale Prepares a Purchase Order

After checking various price lists and suppliers' catalogues, the purchasing department fills out a form called a **purchase order.** This form gives Abby Blake Company the

Purchase Order No. 1
Art's Wholesale Clothing Company
1528 Belle Avenue
Toronto, Ontario M5A 2L4

Purchased From: Abby Blake Company
12 Foster Road
Quebec City, PQ G1M 4H3

Date: April 1, 2001
Shipped VIA: Freight truck
Terms: 2/10, n/60
FOB: Quebec City

Quantity	Description	Unit Price	Total
100	Ladies' Jackets Code 14-0	$50	$5,000

Art's Wholesale
By: Bill Joy

Purchase order number must appear on all invoices.

FIGURE 10-1
Purchase Order

authority to ship the ladies' jackets ordered by Art's Wholesale Clothing Company (see Figure 10-1). Note that purchase orders do not result in any formal entries on the issuer's books. Most accounting software (like *Simply Accounting*) can easily handle the issuance of purchase orders*.

Step 3: Sales Invoice Prepared by Abby Blake Company

Four copies of purchase order: (1) (original) goes to supplier; (2) is sent to accounting department; (3) goes to department that initiated purchase requisition; (4) is filed in purchasing department.

Abby Blake Company receives the purchase order and prepares a sales invoice. The sales invoice for the seller is the **purchase invoice** for the buyer. A sales invoice is shown in Figure 10-2.

The invoice shows that the goods will be shipped F.O.B. Quebec City. This means that Art's Wholesale Clothing Company must pay the shipping costs. The sales invoice shows this freight charge. This means that Abby Blake prepaid the shipping costs as a matter of convenience. Art's Wholesale will repay the freight charges when it pays the invoice.

Step 4: Receiving the Goods

When goods are received, Art's Wholesale inspects the shipment and completes a **receiving report.** The receiving report verifies that the exact merchandise that was ordered was received in good condition.

Sales Invoice No. 228
Abby Blake Company
12 Foster Road
Quebec City, PQ G1M 4H3

Sold to: Art's Wholesale
Clothing Co.
1528 Belle Avenue
Toronto, ON
M5A 2L4

Date: April 3, 2001
Shipped VIA: Freight truck
Terms: 2/10, n/60
Your Order No.:1
FOB: Quebec City

Quantity	Description	Unit Price	Total
100	Ladies' Jackets Code 14-0 Freight	$50	$5,000 50 $5,050

FIGURE 10-2
Sales Invoice

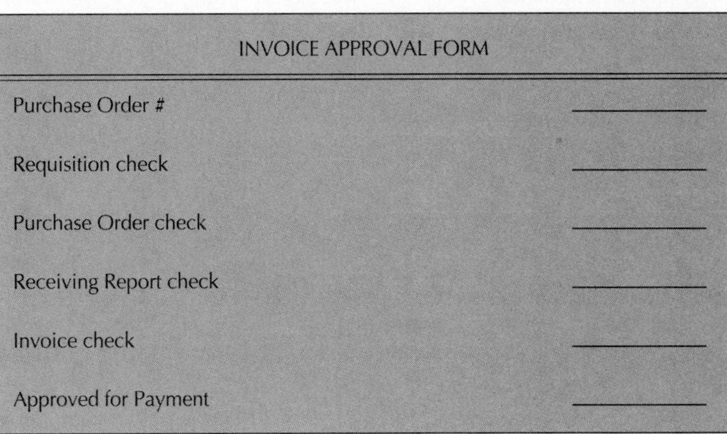
INVOICE APPROVAL FORM

Purchase Order # ________

Requisition check ________

Purchase Order check ________

Receiving Report check ________

Invoice check ________

Approved for Payment ________

FIGURE 10-3
Invoice Approval Form

Step 5: Verifying the Numbers

Before the invoice is approved for recording and payment, the accounting department must check the purchase order, invoice, and receiving report to make sure that all are in agreement and that no steps have been omitted. The form used for checking and approval is an **invoice approval form** (see Figure 10-3 above).

Keep in mind that Art's Wholesale Clothing Company does not record this purchase in its accounting records until the *invoice is approved for recording and payment.* However, Abby Blake Company records this transaction in its records when the sales invoice is prepared.

THE PURCHASES JOURNAL AND ACCOUNTS PAYABLE SUBSIDIARY LEDGER

Let's look at how Art's Wholesale Clothing Company journalizes, posts, and records to the accounts payable subsidiary ledger. We will also look at the **purchases journal,** a multicolumn special journal Art's Wholesale uses to record the buying of merchandise or other items on account, and the **accounts payable subsidiary ledger**, an alphabetical record of the amounts owed to creditors from purchases on account.

For example, on April 3 Art's Wholesale Clothing Company records in its purchases journal the following:

- Date: April 3, 2001
- Account Credited: Abby Blake Company
- Date of Invoice: April 3
- Invoice Number: 228
- Terms: 2/10, n/60
- Accounts payable: $5,050; Purchases: $5,000; Freight-In, $50

See Figure 10-4 for complete purchases journal.

As soon as the information is journalized in the purchases journal (see Figure 10-4), you should:

1. Record in Abby Blake Co. account in the accounts payable subsidiary ledger to indicate that the amount owed is now $5,050. When this is complete, place a ✔ in the PR column of the purchases journal.
2. Post to Freight-In, account No. 514, in the general ledger right away. When this is complete, record 514 in the PR column under Sundry in the purchases journal.

Note that the normal balance in the accounts payable subsidiary ledger is a credit.

The posting and recording rules are similar to those in the previous chapter, but here we are looking at the buyer rather than at the seller.

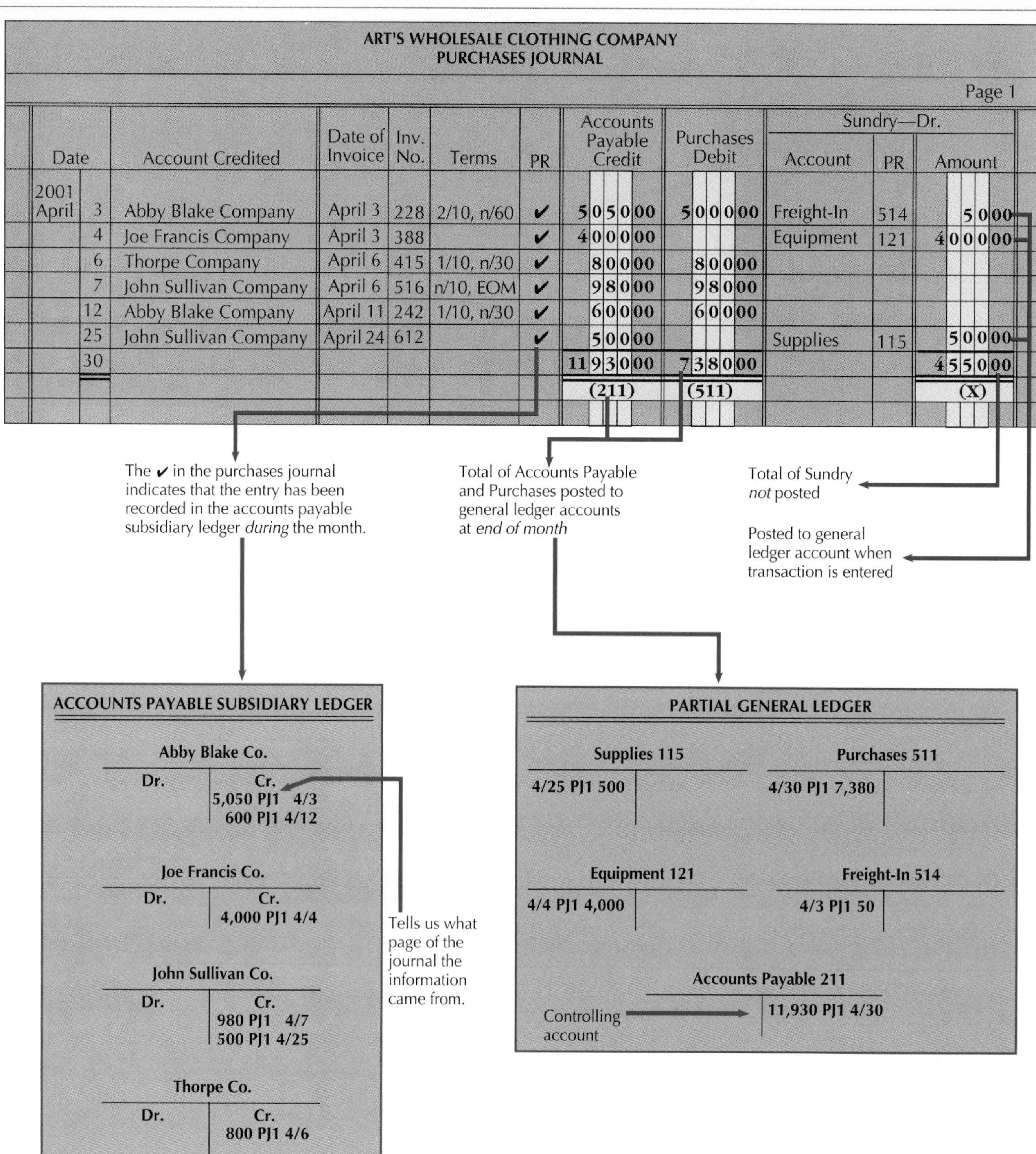

ART'S WHOLESALE CLOTHING COMPANY
PURCHASES JOURNAL

Page 1

Date		Account Credited	Date of Invoice	Inv. No.	Terms	PR	Accounts Payable Credit	Purchases Debit	Sundry—Dr. Account	PR	Amount
2001 April	3	Abby Blake Company	April 3	228	2/10, n/60	✔	5050 00	5000 00	Freight-In	514	50 00
	4	Joe Francis Company	April 3	388		✔	4000 00		Equipment	121	4000 00
	6	Thorpe Company	April 6	415	1/10, n/30	✔	800 00	800 00			
	7	John Sullivan Company	April 6	516	n/10, EOM	✔	980 00	980 00			
	12	Abby Blake Company	April 11	242	1/10, n/30	✔	600 00	600 00			
	25	John Sullivan Company	April 24	612		✔	500 00		Supplies	115	500 00
	30						11930 00	7380 00			4550 00
							(211)	(511)			(X)

FIGURE 10-4 Purchases Journal

THE DEBIT MEMORANDUM

In Chapter 9, Art's Wholesale Clothing Company had to handle returned goods as a seller. It did this by issuing credit memoranda to customers who returned goods or received an allowance on the price. In this chapter, Art's must handle returns as a buyer. It does this by using debit memoranda. A **debit memorandum** is a piece of paper issued by a customer to a seller that indicates that a return or allowance is required.

A debit memo shows that Art's does not owe as much money as was indicated in the company's purchases journal.

Debit Memorandum | No. 1

Art's Wholesale
Clothing Company
1528 Belle Avenue
Toronto, ON M5A 2L4

To: Thorpe Company
3 Access Road
Fredericton, NB E3B 4T3

April 9, 2001

WE DEBIT your account as follows:

Quantity		Unit Cost	Total
20	Men's Hats Code 827—defective brims	$10	$200

FIGURE 10-5
Debit Memorandum

Suppose that on April 6 Art's Wholesale had purchased men's hats for $800 from Thorpe Company (see Figure 10-4). On April 9, 20 hats valued at $200 were found to have defective brims. Art's issued a debit memorandum to Thorpe Company, as shown in Figure 10-5 above. At some point in the future, Thorpe will issue Art's a credit memorandum. Let's look at how Art's Wholesale Clothing Company handles such a transaction in its accounting records.

Journalizing and Posting the Debit Memo

First, let's look at a transaction analysis chart.

Result of debit memo: debits or reduces Accounts Payable. On seller's books, accounts affected would include Sales Returns and Allowances and Accounts Receivable.

Accounts Affected	Category	↑ ↓	Rules
Accounts Payable	Liability	↓	Dr.
Purchases Returns and Allowances	Expense (Contra)	↓	Cr.

Next, let's examine the journal entry for the debit memorandum:

Purchases Returns and Allowances

Dr.	Cr.
–	+

A contra-cost-of-goods-sold account.

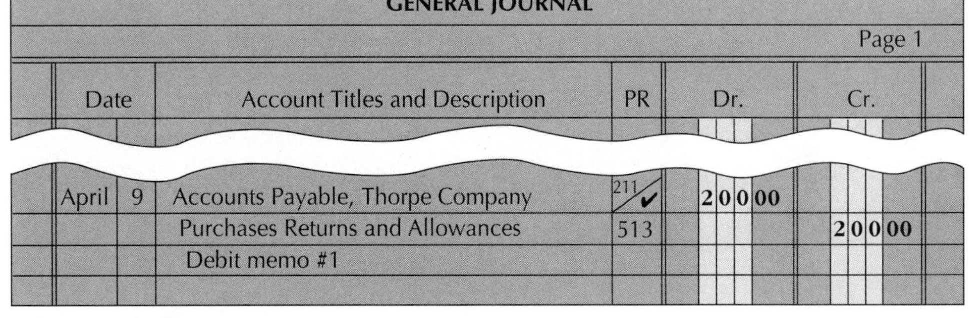
GENERAL JOURNAL

Page 1

Date		Account Titles and Description	PR	Dr.	Cr.
April	9	Accounts Payable, Thorpe Company	211/✔	200 00	
		Purchases Returns and Allowances	513		200 00
		Debit memo #1			

The two postings and one recording are:

1. 211—Post to Accounts Payable as a debit in the general ledger account No. 211. When this is done, place in the PR column the account number, 211, above the diagonal on the same line as Accounts Payable in the journal.
2. ✔—Record to Thorpe Co. in the accounts payable subsidiary ledger to show that Art's doesn't owe Thorpe as much money. When this is done, place a ✔ in the journal in the PR column below the diagonal line on the same line as Accounts Payable in the journal.

3. 513—Post to Purchases Returns and Allowances as a credit in the general ledger (account No. 513). When this is done, place the account number, 513, in the posting reference column of the journal on the same line as Purchases Returns and Allowances. (If equipment was returned that was not merchandise for resale, we would credit Equipment and not Purchases Returns and Allowances.)

LEARNING UNIT 10-2 REVIEW

AT THIS POINT you should be able to:

- Explain the relationship between a purchase requisition, a purchase order, and a purchase invoice. (pp. 411 and 412)
- Explain why a typical invoice approval form may be used. (p. 413)
- Journalize transactions in a purchases journal. (pp. 413–414)
- Explain how to record the accounts payable subsidiary ledger and post to the general ledger from a purchases journal. (p. 414)
- Explain a debit memorandum and be able to journalize an entry resulting from its issuance. (pp. 414–415)

SELF-REVIEW QUIZ 10-2

(The forms you need are on pages 10-2 to 10-4 of the *Study Guide with Working Papers.*)

Journalize the following transactions in the purchases journal or general journal for Munroe Co. Record in the accounts payable subsidiary ledger and post to general ledger accounts as appropriate. Use the same journal headings we used for Art's Wholesale Clothing Company.

2002

May 5 Bought merchandise on account from Flynn Co., invoice No. 512, dated May 4, terms 1/10, n/30, $900.

7 Bought merchandise from John Butler Company, invoice No. 403, dated May 7, terms n/10 EOM, $1,000.

13 Issued debit memo No. 1 to Flynn Co. for merchandise returned, $300, from invoice No. 512.

17 Purchased $400 worth of equipment on account from John Butler Company, invoice No. 413, dated May 16.

Solution to Self-Review Quiz 10-2

MUNROE CO.
PURCHASES JOURNAL

Page 2

Date		Account Credited	Date of Invoice	Inv. No.	Terms	PR	Accounts Payable Credit	Purchases Debit	Sundry—Dr. Account	PR	Amount
2002 May	5	Flynn Co.	May 4	512	1/10, n/30	✔	90000	90000			
	7	John Butler	May 7	403	n/10, EOM	✔	100000	100000			
	17	John Butler	May 16	413		✔	40000		Equip.	121	40000
	31						230000	190000			40000
							(212)	(512)			(X)

MUNROE CO.
GENERAL JOURNAL

Page 1

Date		Account Titles and Description	PR	Dr.	Cr.
2002 May	13	Accounts Payable, Flynn Co.	212/✔	30000	
		Purchases Returns and Allowances	513		30000
		Debit memo #1			

ACCOUNTS PAYABLE SUBSIDIARY LEDGER
JOHN BUTLER COMPANY
18 REED ROAD
WINNIPEG, MB R2B 8G6

Date 2002		Explanation	Post. Ref.	Debit	Credit	CR. Balance
May	7		PJ2		100000	100000
	17		PJ2		40000	140000

FLYNN COMPANY
15 FOSS AVENUE
QUEBEC CITY, PQ G1L 2W4

Date 2002		Explanation	Post. Ref.	Debit	Credit	CR. Balance
May	5		PJ2		90000	90000
	13		GJ1	30000		60000

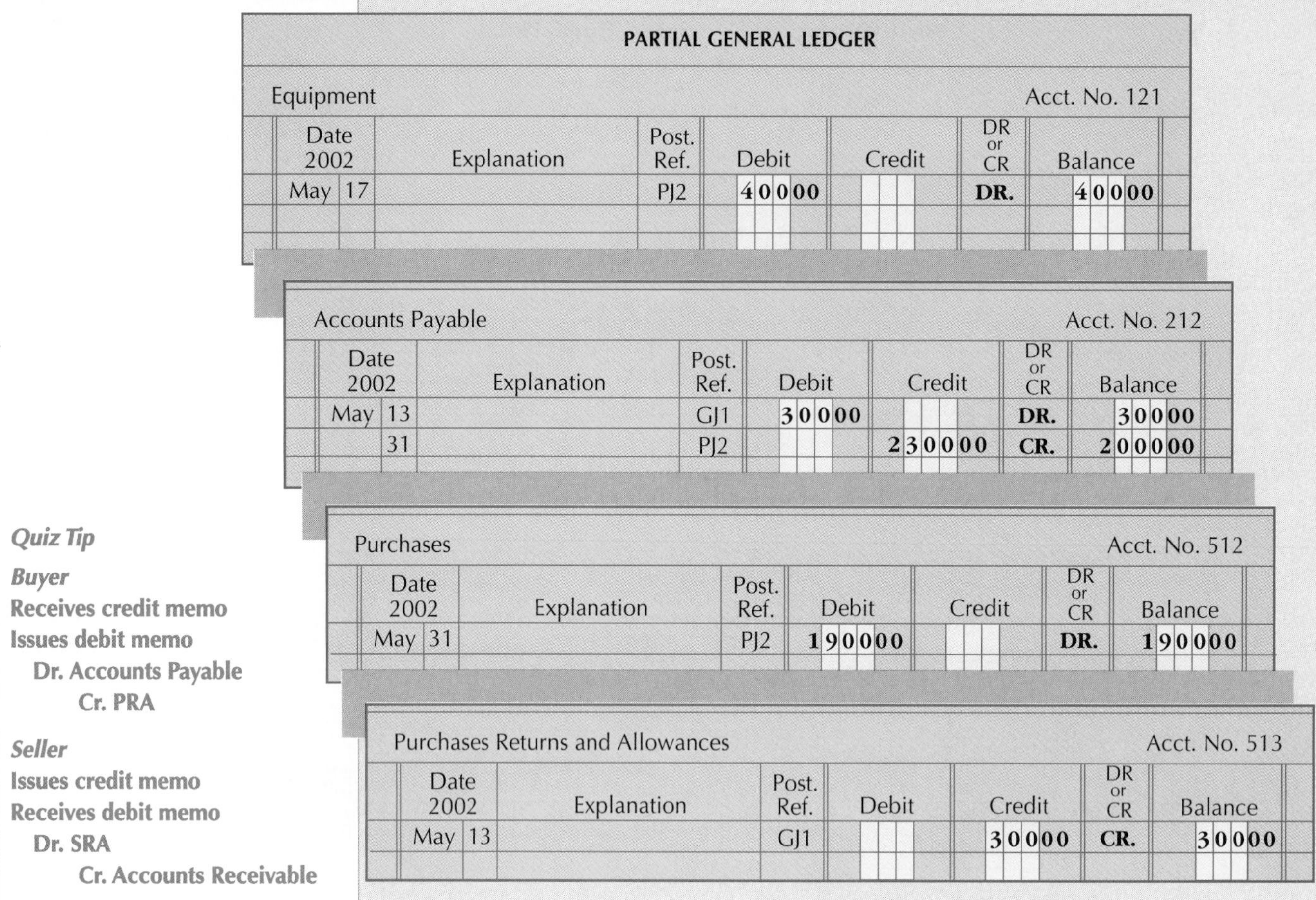

PARTIAL GENERAL LEDGER

Equipment — Acct. No. 121

Date 2002		Explanation	Post. Ref.	Debit	Credit	DR or CR	Balance
May	17		PJ2	400 00		DR.	400 00

Accounts Payable — Acct. No. 212

Date 2002		Explanation	Post. Ref.	Debit	Credit	DR or CR	Balance
May	13		GJ1	300 00		DR.	300 00
	31		PJ2		2300 00	CR.	2000 00

Purchases — Acct. No. 512

Date 2002		Explanation	Post. Ref.	Debit	Credit	DR or CR	Balance
May	31		PJ2	1900 00		DR.	1900 00

Purchases Returns and Allowances — Acct. No. 513

Date 2002		Explanation	Post. Ref.	Debit	Credit	DR or CR	Balance
May	13		GJ1		300 00	CR.	300 00

Quiz Tip

Buyer
Receives credit memo
Issues debit memo
Dr. Accounts Payable
Cr. PRA

Seller
Issues credit memo
Receives debit memo
Dr. SRA
Cr. Accounts Receivable

LEARNING UNIT 10-3

The Cash Payments Journal and Schedule of Accounts Payable

Art's Wholesale Clothing Company will record all payments made by cheque in a **cash payments journal** (also called a *cash disbursements journal*). In many ways, the structure of this journal resembles that of the cash receipts journal discussed in Chapter 9. Now, however, we are looking at the outward flow of cash instead of the inward flow.

Art's Wholesale conducted the following cash transactions in April:

2001

April 2 Issued cheque No. 1 to Pete Blum for insurance paid in advance, $900.

7 Issued cheque No. 2 to Joe Francis Company in payment of its April 3 invoice No. 388.

9 Issued cheque No. 3 to Rick Flo Co. for merchandise purchased for cash, $800.

12 Issued cheque No. 4 to Thorpe Company in payment of its April 6 invoice No. 415 less the return and discount.

28 Issued cheque No. 5, $700, for salaries paid.

The diagram in Figure 10-6 shows the cash payments journal for the end of April along with the recordings in the accounts payable subsidiary ledger and postings to the general ledger. Study the diagram; we will review it in a moment.

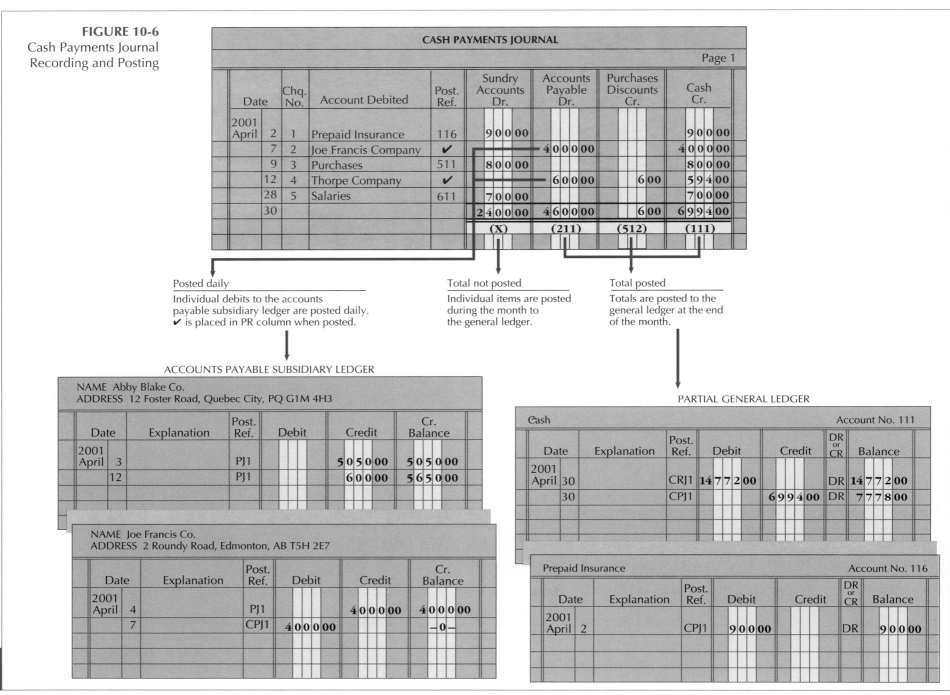

FIGURE 10-6
Cash Payments Journal Recording and Posting

CASH PAYMENTS JOURNAL

Page 1

Date	Chq. No.	Account Debited	Post. Ref.	Sundry Accounts Dr.	Accounts Payable Dr.	Purchases Discounts Cr.	Cash Cr.
2001 April 2	1	Prepaid Insurance	116	900 00			900 00
7	2	Joe Francis Company	✔		4000 00		4000 00
9	3	Purchases	511	800 00			800 00
12	4	Thorpe Company	✔		600 00	6 00	594 00
28	5	Salaries	611	700 00			700 00
30				2400 00	4600 00	6 00	6994 00
				(X)	(211)	(512)	(111)

Posted daily

Individual debits to the accounts payable subsidiary ledger are posted daily. ✔ is placed in PR column when posted.

Total not posted

Individual items are posted during the month to the general ledger.

Total posted

Totals are posted to the general ledger at the end of the month.

ACCOUNTS PAYABLE SUBSIDIARY LEDGER

NAME Abby Blake Co.
ADDRESS 12 Foster Road, Quebec City, PQ G1M 4H3

Date	Explanation	Post. Ref.	Debit	Credit	Cr. Balance
2001 April 3		PJ1		5050 00	5050 00
12		PJ1		600 00	5650 00

NAME Joe Francis Co.
ADDRESS 2 Roundy Road, Edmonton, AB T5H 2E7

Date	Explanation	Post. Ref.	Debit	Credit	Cr. Balance
2001 April 4		PJ1		4000 00	4000 00
7		CPJ1	4000 00		–0–

PARTIAL GENERAL LEDGER

Cash — Account No. 111

Date	Explanation	Post. Ref.	Debit	Credit	DR or CR	Balance
2001 April 30		CRJ1	14772 00		DR	14772 00
30		CPJ1		6994 00	DR	7778 00

Prepaid Insurance — Account No. 116

Date	Explanation	Post. Ref.	Debit	Credit	DR or CR	Balance
2001 April 2		CPJ1	900 00		DR	900 00

FIGURE 10-6 (cont.)

NAME John Sullivan Co.
ADDRESS 18 Print Street, Regina, SK S4P 2A6

Date		Explanation	Post. Ref.	Debit	Credit	Cr. Balance
2001 April	7		PJ1		980 00	980 00
	25		PJ1		500 00	1 480 00

NAME Thorpe Co.
ADDRESS 3 Access Road, Fredericton, NB E3B 4T3

Date		Explanation	Post. Ref.	Debit	Credit	Cr. Balance
2001 April	6		PJ1		800 00	800 00
	9		GJ1	200 00		600 00
	12		CPJ1	600 00		–0–

Note on accounts payable balance: Very occasionally (perhaps because of the return of defective goods after they have been paid for) a debit balance may be called for in accounts payable. Debit balances are opposite to the normal credit balance and are signified by placing the balance in brackets. For example, suppose we get a credit note from Joe Francis Co. for $400 after we have paid off their account completely. Their account would then appear as follows:

NAME Joe Francis Co.
ADDRESS 2 Roundy Road, Edmonton, AB T5H 2E7

Date		Explanation	Post. Ref.	Debit	Credit	Cr. Balance
2001 April	4		PJ1		4 000 00	4 000 00
	7		CPJ1	4 000 00		–0–
	14		GJ4	400 00		(400 00)

Controlling Account

Accounts Payable — Account No. 211

Date		Explanation	Post. Ref.	Debit	Credit	DR or CR	Balance
2001 April	9		GJ1	200 00		DR	200 00
	30		PJ1		11 930 00	CR	11 730 00
	30		CPJ1	4 600 00		CR	7 130 00

Purchases — Account No. 511

Date		Explanation	Post. Ref.	Debit	Credit	DR or CR	Balance
2001 April	9		CPJ1	800 00		DR	800 00
	30		PJ1	7 380 00		DR	8 180 00

Purchases Discounts — Account No. 512

Date		Explanation	Post. Ref.	Debit	Credit	DR or CR	Balance
2001 April	30		CPJ1		6 00	CR	6 00

Salaries Expense — Account No. 611

Date		Explanation	Post. Ref.	Debit	Credit	DR or CR	Balance
2001 April	28		CPJ1	700 00		DR	700 00

Posting and recording rules for this journal are similar to those for the cash receipts journal in Chapter 9.

JOURNALIZING, POSTING, AND RECORDING FROM THE CASH PAYMENTS JOURNAL TO THE ACCOUNTS PAYABLE SUBSIDIARY LEDGER AND THE GENERAL LEDGER

Figure 10-6 shows how Art's Wholesale Clothing Company recorded the payment of cash on April 12 to Thorpe Company. The purchases journal (page 414) shows that Art's purchased $800 worth of merchandise from Thorpe on account on April 6. The amount Art's owes is discounted 1 percent. The amount owed ($800 – $200 returns) is recorded in the accounts payable subsidiary ledger as soon as the entry is made in the cash payments journal. The payment reduces the balance owing to Thorpe to zero. Art's Wholesale Clothing Company receives a $6 purchases discount.

As explained in Chapter 9, Sundry is a miscellaneous accounts column that provides flexibility for reporting infrequent transactions that result in an outflow of cash.

At the end of the month the totals of the Cash, Purchases Discounts, and Accounts Payable accounts are posted to the general ledger. The total of Sundry is *not* posted. The accounts Prepaid Insurance, Purchases, and Salaries Expense are posted to the general ledger at the time the entry is put in the journal.

The cash payments journal of Art's Wholesale Clothing Company can be crossfooted as follows:

Remember, there is no discount on sales tax or freight.

Debit Columns = Credit Columns
Sundry + Accounts Payable = Purchases Discounts + Cash
$2,400 + $4,600 = $6 + $6,994
$7,000 = $7,000

Schedule of Accounts Payable

Now let's prove that the sum of the accounts payable subsidiary ledger at the end of the month is equal to the controlling account, Accounts Payable, at the end of April for Art's Wholesale Clothing Company. To do this, creditors with an ending balance in Art's Wholesale's accounts payable subsidiary ledger must be listed in the schedule of accounts payable (see Figure 10-7). At the end of the month the total owed ($7,130) in Accounts Payable, the **controlling account** in the general ledger, should equal the sum of what is owed the individual creditors who are listed on the schedule of accounts payable. If it doesn't, the journalizing, posting, and recording must be checked to ensure that they are complete. Also, the balance of each account should be checked.

FIGURE 10-7
Schedule of Accounts Payable

ART'S WHOLESALE CLOTHING COMPANY
SCHEDULE OF ACCOUNTS PAYABLE
APRIL 30, 2001

Abby Blake Co.	$5650 00
John Sullivan Co.	1480 00
Total Accounts Payable	$7130 00

Trade Discounts

Trade discounts are not reflected on the books.

Trade discounts are reductions from the purchase price. Usually, they are given to customers who buy items to resell or to use them to produce other saleable goods.

Amount of Trade Discount = List Price – Net Price

Different trade discounts are available to different classes of customers. Often, trade discounts are listed in catalogues that contain the list price and the amount of trade discount available. Such catalogues usually are updated by discount sheets.

Trade discounts have *no relationship* to whether a customer is paying a bill early. Trade discounts and list prices are not shown in the accounts of either the purchaser or the seller. Cash discounts are not taken on the amount of trade discount.

For example, look at the following:

- List price, $800
- 30 percent trade discount
- 5 percent cash discount
- *Thus:* Invoice cost of $560 ($800 − $240) less the cash discount of $28 ($560 × 0.05) results in a final cost of $532 if the cash discount is taken.

The purchaser as well as the seller would record the invoice amount at $560.

LEARNING UNIT 10-3 REVIEW

AT THIS POINT you should be able to:

- Journalize, post, and record transactions utilizing a cash payments journal. (pp. 418–421)
- Prepare a schedule of accounts payable. (p. 421)
- Compare and contrast a cash discount with a trade discount. (p. 421)

SELF-REVIEW QUIZ 10-3

(The forms you need are on pages 10-4 and 10-5 of the *Study Guide with Working Papers.*)

Given the following information, journalize, cross-foot, and when appropriate record and post the transactions of Melissa Company. Use the same headings as used for Art's Wholesale. All purchases discounts are 2/12, n/30. The cash payments journal is page 2.

Accounts Payable Subsidiary Ledger

Name	*Balance*	*Invoice No.*
Bob Finkelstein	$300	488
Al Jeep	200	410

Partial General Ledger

Account No.	*Balance*
Cash 110	$700
Accounts Payable 210	500
Purchases Discounts 511	—
Advertising Expense 610	—

2000

June 1 Issued cheque No. 15 to Al Jeep in payment of its May 25 invoice No. 410 less purchases discount.

8 Issued cheque No. 16 to Moss Advertising Co. to pay advertising bill due, $75, no discount.

9 Issued cheque No. 17 to Bob Finkelstein in payment of its May 28 invoice No. 488 less purchases discounts.

Solution to Self-Review Quiz 10-3

MELISSA COMPANY
CASH PAYMENTS JOURNAL

Page 2

Date		Chq. No.	Account Debited	Post. Ref.	Sundry Accounts Dr.	Accounts Payable Dr.	Purchases Discounts Cr.	Cash Cr.
2000 June	1	15	Al Jeep	✔		200 00	4 00	196 00
	8	16	Advertising Expense	610	75 00			75 00
	9	17	Bob Finkelstein	✔		300 00	6 00	294 00
					75 00	500 00	10 00	565 00
					(X)	(210)	(511)	(110)

$75 + $500 = $10 + $565
$575 = $575

ACCOUNTS PAYABLE SUBSIDIARY LEDGER

NAME Bob Finkelstein
ADDRESS 112 Flying Highway, Montreal, PQ H1K 2H7

Date		Explanation	Post. Ref.	Debit	Credit	Cr. Balance
2000 June	1	Balance	✔			300 00
	9		CPJ2	300 00		–0–

NAME Al Jeep
ADDRESS 118 Wang Road, London, ON N5X 2Y3

Date		Explanation	Post. Ref.	Debit	Credit	Cr. Balance
2000 June	1	Balance	✔			200 00
	1		CPJ2	200 00		–0–

Quiz Tip

The balance of the Accounts Payable subsidiary ledger is zero.

PARTIAL GENERAL LEDGER

Cash — Acct. No. 110

Date 2000		Explanation	Post. Ref.	Debit	Credit	DR or CR	Balance
June	1	Balance	✔			DR	700 00
	30		CPJ2		565 00	DR	135 00

Accounts Payable — Acct. No. 210 ← Controlling account

Date 2000		Explanation	Post. Ref.	Debit	Credit	DR or CR	Balance
June	1	Balance	✔			CR	500 00
	30		CPJ2	500 00			–0–

Purchases Discounts — Acct. No. 511

Date 2000		Explanation	Post. Ref.	Debit	Credit	DR or CR	Balance
June	30		CPJ2		10 00	CR	10 00

Advertising Expense — Acct. No. 610

Date 2000		Explanation	Post. Ref.	Debit	Credit	DR or CR	Balance
June	8		CPJ2	75 00		DR	75 00

LEARNING UNIT 10-4

GST/HST Paid on Purchases

OVERVIEW

In the previous chapter, we learned that GST or HST collected on sales needs to be sent to the government periodically. No surprises here—this is very similar to PST. However, the GST/HST is what we refer to as a value-added tax. Without getting overly technical, each business in effect adds a net tax to the "improvement" in value it adds to the goods and/or services it provides or sells. If a company buys some merchandise (to resell) for $1,000 and actually sells it for $1,500, then the GST/HST is applicable only to the $500 difference.

While that is true, the tax works in the following manner:

Companies remit the net difference between the GST they collect on sales and the GST they pay on purchases.

- First, the business charges the GST at 7 percent on the selling price of $1,500. This would amount to $105 (7% × $1,500) (covered in Chapter 9).
- Second, the business pays the 7 percent GST on the $1,000 for which the merchandise was purchased. This amounts to $70 (7% × $1,000) (covered in this chapter).
- Finally, the tax sent to the federal government is only $35 (7% × $500) because the business gets a credit for the tax it paid on the purchase.

If HST were involved instead of GST, the Summary would look like this:

HST collected	$225
HST paid	150
HST to remit	$75

Summary

GST collected on sale of merchandise: 7% × $1,500.00 =	$105
GST paid on purchase of merchandise: 7% × $1,000.00 =	$70
Net tax to be remitted	$35

Businesses do not keep track of GST/HST separately on each item of inventory they sell, of course. However, the above example makes it plain that companies must keep track of the total GST/HST they pay so they can claim a refund when they calculate the tax they must periodically send to the federal government.

This learning unit details the accounting tasks which must be handled properly to record GST/HST accurately.

Recording purchases with GST/HST

In the above learning units we discussed purchases and cash payments without GST/HST. In Figure 10-1 a typical purchase order is illustrated. Many companies have not changed their purchase orders to include GST/HST since it is now the law for GST/HST to be included even if the purchase order says nothing. Other companies may refer to the fact that the specified price does not include GST/HST. They expect that 7 percent GST or 15 percent HST will be added. Still other companies specify and calculate the tax. These companies would produce a purchase order which would look like the one shown below in Figure 10-8 (assuming GST).

When the supplier fills the purchase order, an invoice will be prepared which includes GST/HST. In Figure 10-2, a sales invoice before GST was illustrated. The same sales invoice incorporating GST is shown in Figure 10-9. Note that GST is charged on the shipping charges as well as the amount charged for the goods.

This invoice is recorded (as others) by the purchaser in a manner similar to that for the original example shown earlier in this chapter (see Figure 10-4). The major change is that now the purchases journal has one additional column—**Prepaid GST.** Figure 10-10 shows how the purchases journal would appear with GST included.

Note: Recording purchases with GST is very similar to recording purchases with no GST—just one extra column is needed.

A more technically correct term for the credit a company receives for the GST/HST it pays is Input Tax Credit. Do not be confused by the use of the word *Credit*; these GST/HST amounts are debits in a formal bookkeeping sense. This is logical, since GST/HST on purchases is considered an asset. However, it is sometimes treated as a contra-liability since it offsets the GST/HST payable on sales made. Some companies record this "asset" in an account which follows GST Collected in the current liabilities section of the chart of accounts.

Purchase Order No. 1
Art's Wholesale Clothing Co.
1528 Belle Avenue
Toronto, Ontario M5A 2L4

Purchased From: Abby Blake Company
12 Foster Road
Quebec City, PQ G1M 4H3

Date: April 1, 2001
Shipped VIA: Freight truck
Terms: 2/10, n/60
FOB: Quebec City

Quantity	Description	Unit Price	Total
100	Ladies' Jackets Code 14-0	$50	$5,000.00
		Add GST	350.00
		Total Price before Shipping	$5,350.00

Purchase order number must appear on all invoices.

Art's Wholesale
By: Bill Joy

FIGURE 10-8
Purchase Order with GST

Sales Invoice No. 228
Abby Blake Company
12 Foster Road
Quebec City, PQ G1M 4H3

Sold to: Art's Wholesale
Clothing Co.
1528 Belle Avenue
Toronto, ON
M5A 2L4

Date: April 3, 2001
Shipped VIA: Freight truck
Terms: 2/10, n/60
Your Order No: 1
FOB: Quebec City

Quantity	Description	Unit Price	Total
100	Ladies' Jackets Code 14-0	$50	$5,000.00
	Freight		50.00
	Sub-total		$5,050.00
	GST		353.50
	Total		$5,403.50
	Business No. 142714982		

FIGURE 10-9
Sales Invoice with GST

Note the following while you review Figure 10-10:

Remember that three provinces (Nova Scotia, New Brunswick, and Newfoundland) charge and collect HST at 15 percent rather than GST at 7 percent and PST at an individual provincial rate. As explained in Chapter 9, the HST replaces both PST and GST in those three provinces.

1. GST/HST is paid on equipment purchases as well as on purchases of goods for resale.
2. A different account (number 125) is used to record GST/HST on purchases than the account used to record sales (recall that account number 212 was used in Chapter 9 for recording GST/HST on sales). While not absolutely required, this procedure can make the preparation of the periodic governmental returns less of a burden.
3. The basic operation of the purchases journal is much the same as before. Cross-footing reveals that the addition of a GST column has not disturbed the equality of debits (7,380 + 4,550 + 835.10 = 12,765.10) and credits (12,765.10).
4. The amounts posted to the accounts payable ledger are posted at the same time and in the same way as previously. The amounts are now higher, of course, as they include GST at 7 percent (or HST at 15 percent).

THE DEBIT MEMORANDUM

A debit memorandum with GST/HST is very similar to a supplier's invoice with GST/HST except that the amounts are opposite in meaning and effect, and often smaller.

As already discussed, from time to time purchased goods are returned to suppliers because of insufficient quality, defective manufacturing, and the like. We have seen an example of a debit memorandum which is prepared when goods are returned (refer to Figure 10-5). When GST/HST is charged on the original purchase, it must also be added to the debit memorandum as shown in Figure 10-11 on page 428.

Recording this debit memorandum is usually done in the general journal, although a specialized journal could be used if a large number of debit memos were common in a given business. Art's Wholesale Clothing Company would record the debit memorandum (illustrated in Figure 10-11) in their general journal (see Figure 10-12).

The four postings are:

1. 211—Post to Accounts Payable as a debit in the general ledger account No. 211. When this is done, place in the PR column the account number, 211, above the diagonal on the same line as Accounts Payable.
2. ✔—Post to Thorpe Co. in the accounts payable ledger to show that we don't owe Thorpe as much money. When this is done place a ✔ in the journal in the PR column below the diagonal line on the same line as Accounts Payable.
3. 513—Post to Purchases Returns and Allowances as a credit in the general ledger (account No. 513). When this is done, place the account number, 513, in the

FIGURE 10-10 Purchases Journal with GST

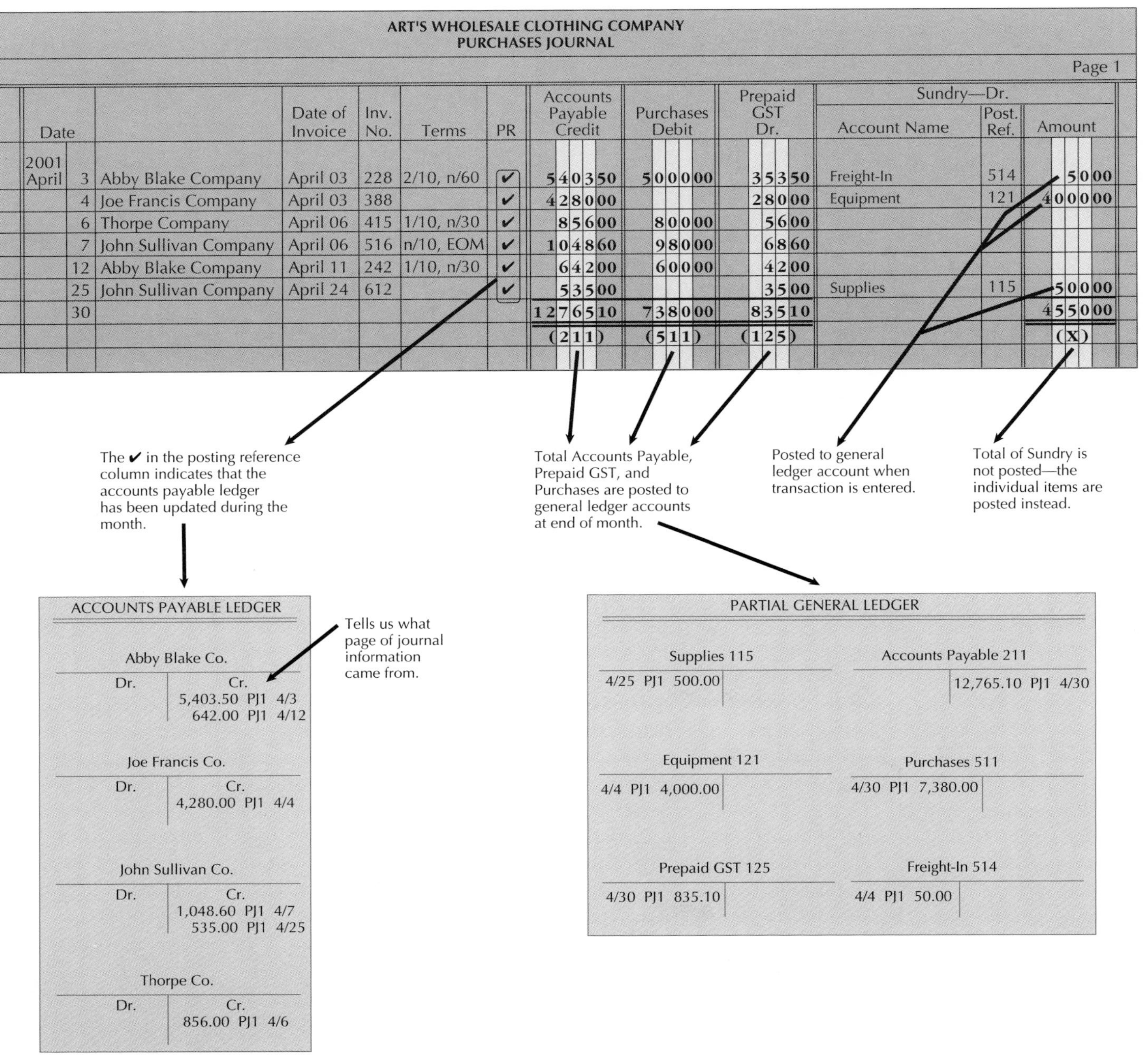

ART'S WHOLESALE CLOTHING COMPANY
PURCHASES JOURNAL

Page 1

Date			Date of Invoice	Inv. No.	Terms	PR	Accounts Payable Credit	Purchases Debit	Prepaid GST Dr.	Sundry—Dr. Account Name	Post. Ref.	Amount
2001 April	3	Abby Blake Company	April 03	228	2/10, n/60	✔	5403 50	5000 00	353 50	Freight-In	514	50 00
	4	Joe Francis Company	April 03	388		✔	4280 00		280 00	Equipment	121	4000 00
	6	Thorpe Company	April 06	415	1/10, n/30	✔	856 00	800 00	56 00			
	7	John Sullivan Company	April 06	516	n/10, EOM	✔	1048 60	980 00	68 60			
	12	Abby Blake Company	April 11	242	1/10, n/30	✔	642 00	600 00	42 00			
	25	John Sullivan Company	April 24	612		✔	535 00		35 00	Supplies	115	500 00
	30						12765 10	7380 00	835 10			4550 00
							(211)	(511)	(125)			(X)

Debit Memorandum Page 1

Art's Wholesale
Clothing Company
1528 Belle Avenue
Toronto, Ontario M5A 2L4

April 9, 2001

To: Thorpe Company
3 Access Road
Fredericton, NB E3B 4T3

WE DEBIT your account as follows:

Quantity		Unit Cost	Total
20	Men's Hats Code 827—defective brims	$10.00	$200.00
	Add GST @ 7%		14.00
	Total Adjustment		$214.00

FIGURE 10-11
Debit Memorandum with GST

GENERAL JOURNAL

Page 1

Date		Account Titles and Description	PR	Dr.	Cr.
2001 April	9	Accounts Payable, Thorpe Company	211/✔	214 00	
		Purchases, Returns and Allowances	513		200 00
		Prepaid GST	125		14 00
		To record debit memo #1			

FIGURE 10-12
Posting the Debit Memo with GST

posting reference column of the journal on the same line as Purchases Returns and Allowances (if equipment was returned that was not merchandise for resale, we would credit Equipment and not Purchases Returns and Allowances).

4. 125—Post to Prepaid GST as a credit. This acts to increase the amount of GST/HST owed to the federal government because it decreases the amount which is claimable to offset the liability recorded in account 212 (see Chapter 9 for details of this account).

The Cash Payments Journal

Note that, even though the CPJ has a column for GST, it is never used when paying a regular supplier. The GST/HST on these purchases is recorded when the original entries are made in the Purchases Journal. Do not record the GST/HST on these purchases twice!

The addition of GST does not alter the fact that Art's Wholesale will record all payments made by cash (or most likely by cheque) in a cash payments journal. However, as you probably suspect, this journal now has a separate column for GST Prepaid, which the original illustration shown in Figure 10-6 did not have.

Trace the following cash disbursements through Figure 10-13 (a revision of Figure 10-6) on pages 429 and 430. The following (revised) transactions affected the cash disbursements journal:

April	2	Issued cheque No. 1 to Pete Blum for insurance paid in advance, $900.
	7	Issued cheque No. 2 to Joe Francis Company in payment of its April 3 invoice No. 388.
	9	Issued cheque No. 3 to Flo Co. for merchandise purchased for cash $800 plus GST $56, total $856.
	12	Issued cheque No. 4 to Thorpe Company in payment of its April 6 invoice No. 414 less the return and discount.
	28	Issued cheque No. 5, $700 salaries paid.

In tracing the cash payments to the payments journal, a few points may be of interest:

1. There is no GST on the insurance payment of $900. Insurance premiums are classified as financial services and no GST is paid on these.

FIGURE 10-13 Cash Payments Journal and Posting with GST

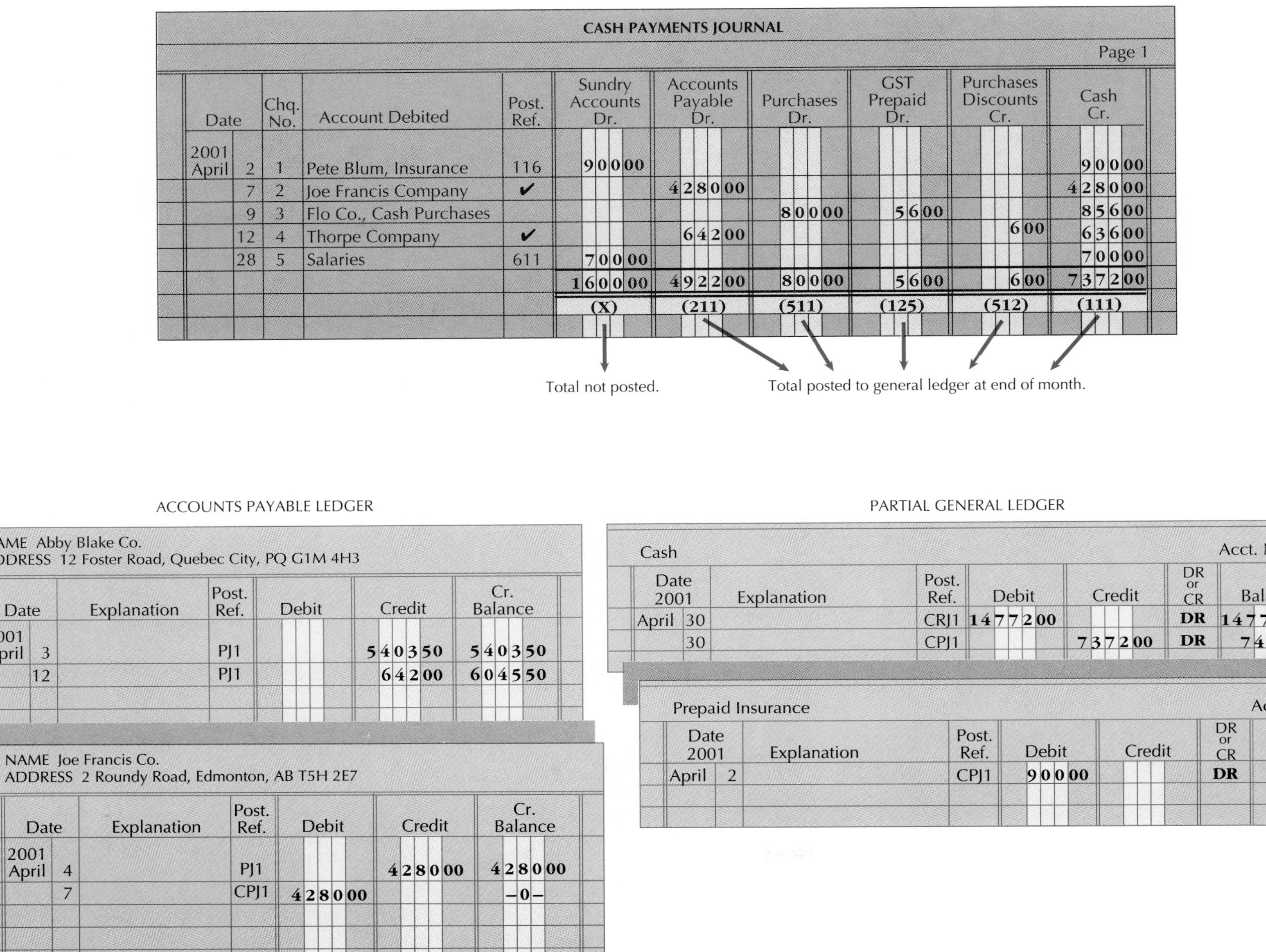

CASH PAYMENTS JOURNAL — Page 1

Date		Chq. No.	Account Debited	Post. Ref.	Sundry Accounts Dr.	Accounts Payable Dr.	Purchases Dr.	GST Prepaid Dr.	Purchases Discounts Cr.	Cash Cr.
2001 April	2	1	Pete Blum, Insurance	116	900 00					900 00
	7	2	Joe Francis Company	✔		4 280 00				4 280 00
	9	3	Flo Co., Cash Purchases				800 00	56 00		856 00
	12	4	Thorpe Company	✔		642 00			6 00	636 00
	28	5	Salaries	611	700 00					700 00
					1 600 00	4 922 00	800 00	56 00	6 00	7 372 00
					(X)	(211)	(511)	(125)	(512)	(111)

Total not posted.
Total posted to general ledger at end of month.

ACCOUNTS PAYABLE LEDGER

NAME Abby Blake Co.
ADDRESS 12 Foster Road, Quebec City, PQ G1M 4H3

Date		Explanation	Post. Ref.	Debit	Credit	Cr. Balance
2001 April	3		PJ1		5 403 50	5 403 50
	12		PJ1		642 00	6 045 50

NAME Joe Francis Co.
ADDRESS 2 Roundy Road, Edmonton, AB T5H 2E7

Date		Explanation	Post. Ref.	Debit	Credit	Cr. Balance
2001 April	4		PJ1		4 280 00	4 280 00
	7		CPJ1	4 280 00		–0–

PARTIAL GENERAL LEDGER

Cash — Acct. No. 111

Date 2001		Explanation	Post. Ref.	Debit	Credit	DR or CR	Balance
April	30		CRJ1	14 772 00		DR	14 772 00
	30		CPJ1		7 372 00	DR	7 400 00

Prepaid Insurance — Acct. No. 116

Date 2001		Explanation	Post. Ref.	Debit	Credit	DR or CR	Balance
April	2		CPJ1	900 00		DR	900 00

FIGURE 10-13 (cont.)

NAME John Sullivan Co..
ADDRESS 18 Print Street, Regina, SK S4P 2A6

Date		Explanation	Post. Ref.	Debit	Credit	Cr. Balance
2001 April	7		PJ1		1 048 60	1 048 60
	25		PJ1		535 00	1 583 60

NAME Thorpe Company
ADDRESS 3 Access Road, Fredericton, NB E3B 4T3

Date		Explanation	Post. Ref.	Debit	Credit	Cr. Balance
2001 April	6		PJ1		856 00	856 00
	9		GJ1	214 00		642 00
	12		CPJ1	642 00		–0–

Note on accounts payable balance: Very occasionally (perhaps because of the return of defective goods after they have been paid for) a debit balance may be called for on accounts payable. Debit balances are opposite to the normal credit balance and are signified by placing the balance in brackets. For example, suppose we get a credit note from Joe Francis Co. for $428.00 after we have paid off their account completely. Their account would then appear as follows:

NAME Joe Francis Co.
ADDRESS 2 Roundy Road, Edmonton, AB T5H 2E7

Date		Explanation	Post. Ref.	Debit	Credit	Cr. Balance
2001 April	4		PJ1		4 280 00	4 280 00
	7		CPJ1	4 280 00		–0–
	14		GJ4	428 00		(428 00)

Controlling account

GST Prepaid — Acct. No. 125

Date 2001		Explanation	Post. Ref.	Debit	Credit	DR or CR	Balance
April	9		GJ1		14 00	CR	14 00
	30		PJ1	835 10		DR	821 10
	30		CPJ1	56 00		DR	877 10

Accounts Payable — Acct. No. 211

Date 2001		Explanation	Post. Ref.	Debit	Credit	DR or CR	Balance
April	9		GJ1	214 00		DR	214 00
	30		PJ1		12 765 10	CR	12 551 10
	30		CPJ1	4 922 00		CR	7 629 10

Purchases — Acct. No. 511

Date 2001		Explanation	Post. Ref.	Debit	Credit	DR or CR	Balance
April	30		PJ1	7 380 00		DR	7 380 00
	30		CPJ1	800 00		DR	8 180 00

Purchases Discounts — Acct. No. 512

Date 2001		Explanation	Post. Ref.	Debit	Credit	DR or CR	Balance
April	30		CPJ1		6 00	CR	6 00

Salaries — Acct. No. 611

Date 2001		Explanation	Post. Ref.	Debit	Credit	DR or CR	Balance
April	30		CPJ1	700 00		DR	700 00

2. Similarly, no GST is paid on salaries of $700 on April 28.
3. GST does not affect the $6 purchase discount allowed when payment is made to the Thorpe Company on April 12. This discount is calculated only on the $600 (net) purchase, not on the $642 which is the total amount payable because of the extra 7 percent GST. The actual amount paid is $636, because the $642 is reduced by $6 because of the allowed purchase discount.

Schedule of Accounts Payable

Notice that it is not difficult to prepare a schedule of accounts payable at month-end from Figure 10-13. This schedule would look like:

Art's Wholesale Clothing Company
Schedule of Accounts Payable
April 30, 2001

Abby Blake Co.	$6,045.50
John Sullivan Co.	1,583.60
Total Accounts Payable	$7,629.10

If you refer again to Figure 10-13, you can see that $7,629.10 is exactly the balance in account 211—Accounts Payable. Hence, the subsidiary ledger accounts are in agreement with the controlling account in the general ledger. As always, if the total of the individual accounts in the accounts payable ledger does not agree with the controlling account, it will be necessary to double-check all postings and the mathematical computations of balances in each supplier's account to find the difference. Also, be sure that any entries made in the general journal are posted to the general ledger accounts.

LEARNING UNIT 10-4 REVIEW

AT THIS POINT you should be able to:

- Describe the nature of the GST/HST. (p. 424)
- Record the GST/HST on purchases. (p. 425)
- Record the GST/HST on returned purchases. (p. 426)
- Record the GST/HST on other cash payments. (p. 428)
- Prepare a schedule of accounts payable at period-end. (p. 431)

SELF-REVIEW QUIZ 10-4

(The forms you need are on pages 10-6 and 10-7 of the *Study Guide with Working Papers.*)

Journalize the following transactions in the purchases journal (page 2) or general journal (page 1) for Munroe Co. Post or record to accounts payable ledger and general ledger accounts as appropriate. Use the same journal headings as we used for Art's Wholesale Clothing Company.

2002

May 5 Bought merchandise on account from Flynn Co., invoice No. 5121, dated May 4, terms 1/10, n/30, $900 plus GST $63. Total $963.

7 Bought merchandise from John Butler Company, invoice No. 403, dated May 7, terms n/10, EOM, $1,000 plus GST $70. Total $1,070.

13 Issued debit memo No. 1 to Flynn Co. for merchandise returned, $300, from invoice No. 512, plus GST $21. Total $321.

17 Purchased $400 worth of equipment on account from John Butler Company, invoice No. 413, dated May 16, plus GST $28. Total $428.

Solution to Self-Review Quiz 10-4

MUNROE CO.
PURCHASES JOURNAL

Page 2

Date		Description	Date of Invoice	Inv. No.	Terms	PR	Accounts Payable Credit	Purchases Debit	GST Prepaid Debit	Sundry—Dr. Account Name	Post. Ref.	Amount
2002 May	5	Flynn Co.	May 4	5121	1/10, n/30	✔	963 00	900 00	63 00			
	7	John Butler Co.	May 7	403	n/10, EOM	✔	1070 00	1000 00	70 00			
	17	John Butler Co.	May 16	413		✔	428 00		28 00	Equipment	121	400 00
	31						2461 00	1900 00	161 00			400 00
							(212)	(512)	(125)			(X)

MUNROE CO.
GENERAL JOURNAL

Page 1

Date		Account Titles and Description	PR	Dr.	Cr.
2002 May	13	Accounts Payable, Flynn Company	212/✔	321 00	
		Purchases Returns and Allowances	513		300 00
		GST Prepaid	125		21 00

ACCOUNTS PAYABLE LEDGER

Name Flynn Co.
Address 7310–34 Avenue, Edmonton, AB T6K 2S1

Date		Explanation	Post Ref.	Debit	Credit	Cr. Balance
2002 May	5		PJ2		963.00	963.00
	13		GJ1	321.00		642.00

Name John Butler Co.
Address 20015 Nottingham Boulevard, Sherwood Park, AB T1R 2S2

Date		Explanation	Post Ref.	Debit	Credit	Cr. Balance
2002 May	7		PJ2		1070.00	1070.00
	17		PJ2		428.00	1498.00

PARTIAL GENERAL LEDGER

Name EQUIPMENT — ACCOUNT NO. 121

Date		Explanation	Post Ref.	Debit	Credit	Dr or Cr	Balance
2002 May	17		PJ2	400.00		DR	400.00

Name GST PREPAID — ACCOUNT NO. 125

Date		Explanation	Post Ref.	Debit	Credit	Dr or Cr	Balance
2002 May	1		PJ2	161.00		Dr	161.00
	13		GJ1		21.00	Dr	140.00

Name ACCOUNTS PAYABLE — ACCOUNT NO. 212

Date		Explanation	Post Ref.	Debit	Credit	Dr or Cr	Balance
2002 May	13		GJ1	321.00		Dr	321.00
	31		PJ2		2461.00	Cr	2140.00

Name PURCHASES — ACCOUNT NO. 512

Date		Explanation	Post Ref.	Debit	Credit	Dr or Cr	Balance
2002 May	31		PJ2	1900.00		Dr	1900.00

Name PURCHASE RETURNS AND ALLOWANCES — ACCOUNT NO. 513

Date		Explanation	Post Ref.	Debit	Credit	Dr or Cr	Balance
2002 May	13		GJ1		300.00	Cr	300.00
			GJ2				

Chapter Review

COMPREHENSIVE DEMONSTRATION PROBLEM WITH SOLUTION TIPS – INCLUDING HST

(The forms you need are on pages 10-8 to 10-10 of the *Study Guide with Working Papers.*)

Record the following transactions in special or general journals. Record and post as appropriate.

Note: All credit sales are 2/10, n/30. All merchandise purchased on account has 3/10, n/30 credit terms.

Solution Tips to Journalizing

	2000		
CRJ	March	1	J. Ling invested $2,000 in the business.
SJ		1	Sold merchandise on account to Balder Co., $500 plus HST, invoice No. 1.
PJ		2	Purchased merchandise on account from Case Co., $600 plus HST, invoice No. 222.
CRJ		4	Sold $2,000 worth of merchandise plus GST for cash.
CPJ		6	Paid Case Co. for previous purchases on account, cheque No. 1.
SJ		8	Sold merchandise on account to Lewis Co., $1,000 plus HST, invoice No. 2.
CRJ		10	Received payment from Balder for invoice No. 1.
GJ		12	Issued a credit memorandum to Lewis Co. for $200 plus HST or faulty merchandise.
CRJ		14	Received payment from Lewis Co.
PJ		16	Purchased merchandise on account from Noone Co., $1,000 plus HST, invoice No. 555.
PJ		17	Purchased equipment on account from Case Co., $300 plus HST, invoice No. 226.
GJ		18	Issued a debit memorandum to Noone Co. for $500 plus HST for defective merchandise.
CPJ		20	Paid salaries, $300, cheque No. 2. (No HST on salaries!)
CPJ		24	Paid Noone balance owed, cheque No. 3.
CPJ		27	Paid Butler Co. $400 plus HST for advertising, cheque No. 4.

Record accounts receivable subsidiary ledger immediately.

J. LING CO.
SALES JOURNAL

Page 1

Date 2000		Inv. No.	Customer's Name	Terms	Post. Ref.	Accounts Receivable Dr.	HST Collected Cr.	Sales Cr.
Mar.	1	1	Balder Company	2/10, N/30	✔	575 00	75 00	500 00
	8	2	Lewis Company	2/10, N/30	✔	1150 00	150 00	1000 00
	31					1725 00	225 00	1500 00
						(112)	(225)	(410)

Total posted at end of month to these accounts

J. LING CO.
CASH RECEIPTS JOURNAL

Page 1

Date 2000		Cash Dr.	Accounts Receivable Cr.	Sales Cr.	HST Collected Cr.	Sales Discounts Dr.	Description of Receipt	Post Ref.	Sundry Cr.
Mar.	1	200000					J. Ling, Capital	310	200000
	4	230000		200000	30000		Cash Sales		
	10	56500	57500			1000	Balder Co.	✔	
	14	90400	92000			1600	Lewis Co.	✔	
	31	576900	149500	200000	30000	2600			200000
		(111)	(112)	(410)	(225)	(430)			(X)

J. LING CO.
PURCHASES JOURNAL

Page 1

Date 2000		Account Credited	Date of Inv.	Inv. No.	Terms	PR	Accounts Payable Cr.	Purchases Dr.	Prepaid HST Dr.	Sundry Dr. Account	Sundry Dr. PR	Sundry Dr. Amount
Mar.	2	Case Co.	Mar. 2	222	3%10, Net 30	✔	69000	60000	9000			
	16	Noone Co.	Mar. 16	555	3%10, Net 30	✔	115000	100000	15000			
	17	Case Co.	Mar. 17	226	3%10, Net 30	✔	34500		4500	Equipment	116	30000
	31						218500	160000	28500			30000
							(210)	(510)	(114)			(X)

J. LING CO.
CASH PAYMENTS JOURNAL

Page 1

Date 2000		Chq. No.	Account Debited	Post Ref.	Sundry Dr.	Accounts Payable Dr.	Prepaid HST Dr.	Purchases Dr.	Purchases Discount Cr.	Cash Cr.
Mar.	6	1	Case Co.	✔		69000			1800	67200
	20	2	Salaries	610	30000					30000
	24	3	Noone Co.	✔		57500			1500	56000
	27	4	Bowler Co.	601	40000		6000			46000
	31				70000	126500	6000		3300	199200
					(X)	(210)	(114)		(530)	(111)

GENERAL JOURNAL					Page 1
Date		Account Titles and Description	PR	Dr.	Cr.
2000 Mar.	12	Sales Returns and Allowances	420	200 00	
		HST Collected	225	30 00	
		Accounts Receivable, Lewis Co.	112/✓		230 00
		Issued credit memo (including HST)	225		
	18	Accounts Payable, Noone Co.	210/✓	575 00	
		Purchases Returns and Allowances	520		500 00
		HST Prepaid	114		75 00
		Issued debit memo			

Record and post immediately to subsidiary and general ledgers.

ACCOUNTS RECEIVABLE SUBSIDIARY LEDGER

Balder Company

Date	PR	Dr.	Cr.	Dr. Bal.
2000 3/1	SJ1	575		575
3/10	CRJ1		575	—

Lewis Company

Date	PR	Dr.	Cr.	Dr. Bal.
2000 3/8	SJ1	1,150		1,150
3/12	GJ1		230	920
3/14	CRJ1		920	0

ACCOUNTS PAYABLE SUBSIDIARY LEDGER

Case Company

Date	PR	Dr.	Cr.	Cr. Bal.
2000 3/2	PJ1		690	690
3/6	CPJ1	690		—
3/17	PJ1		345	345

Noone Company

Date	PR	Dr.	Cr.	Cr. Bal.
2000 3/16	PJ1		1,150	1,150
3/18	GJ1	575		575
3/24	CPJ1	575		0

GENERAL LEDGER

Cash 111

Dr.	Cr.
3/31 CRJ1 5,769	1,992 3/31 CPJ2
Balance 3,777	

Accounts Receivable 112

Dr.	Cr.
3/31 SJ1 1,725	230 3/12 GJ1
	1,495 3/31 CRJ1

HST Prepaid 114

Dr.	Cr.
3/31 PJ1 285	75 3/18 GJ1
3/31 CPJ1 60	
Balance 270	

HST Collected 225

Dr.	Cr.
3/12 GJ 30	225 3/31 SJ1
	300 3/31 CRJ1
	495 Balance

Sales 410

Dr.	Cr.
	1,500 3/31 SJ1
	2,000 3/31 CRJ1
	3,500 Balance

Sales Returns and Allowances 420

Dr.	Cr.
3/12 GJ1 200	

Equipment 116	
3/17 PJ1 300	

Sales Discounts 430	
3/31 CRJ1 26	

Accounts Payable 210	
3/18 GJ1 575	2185 3/31 PJ1
3/31 CPJ1 1265	
	345 Balance

Purchases 510	
3/31 PJ1 1600	

J. Ling, Capital 310	
	2,000 3/1 CRJ1

Purchases Ret. an Allow. 520	
	500 3/18 GJ1

Advertising 601	
3/27 CPJ1 400	

Purchases Discounts 530	
	33 3/31 CPJ1

Salaries Expense 610	
3/20 CPJ1 300	

Summary of Solution Tips

Chapter 9—Seller	*Chapter 10—Buyer*
Sales journal	Purchases journal
Cash receipts journal	Cash payments journal
Accounts receivable subsidiary ledger	Accounts payable subsidiary ledger
Sales (Cr.)	Purchases (Dr.)
Sales Returns and Allowances (Dr.)	Purchase Returns and Allowances (Cr.)
Sales Discounts (Dr.)	Purchases Discounts (Cr.)
Accounts Receivable (Dr.)	Accounts Payable (Cr.)
GST(HST) Collected (Cr.)	GST(HST) Prepaid (Dr.)
Issue a credit memo	Receive a credit memo
or	*or*
Receive a debit memo	Issue a debit memo
Schedule of accounts receivable	Schedule of accounts payable

When Do I Do What? — A Step-by-Step Walk-through of This Comprehensive Demonstration Problem

Transaction *What to Do Step by Step*

2000

March 1 *Money received:* Record in cash receipts journal. Post immediately to J. Ling, Capital, since it is in Sundry. There is no HST on capital transactions.

1 *Sale on account:* Record in sales journal. Record immediately to Balder Co., in accounts receivable subsidiary ledger. Place a ✓ in PR column of sales journal when subsidiary is updated. Total is $575, including HST.

2 *Bought merchandise on account:* Record in purchases journal. Record to Case Co. immediately in the accounts payable subsidiary ledger. Total is $690, including HST.

4 *Money in:* Record in cash receipts journal. No posting needed (put an X in PR column.) Note that total includes $300 of HST.

6 *Money out:* Record in cash payments journal. Save $18 ($600 × 0.03), which is a Purchases Discount. Record immediately to Case Co. in accounts payable subsidiary ledger (the full amount of $690).

8 *Sale on account:* Record in sales journal. Update immediately to Lewis in accounts receivable subsidiary ledger. Total includes HST.

10 *Money in:* Record in cash receipts journal. Since Balder paid within 10 days, they get a $10 discount. Record immediately to Balder in the accounts receivable subsidiary ledger the full amount of $575. Cash is $575 – $10 = $565.

12 *Returns:* Record in general journal. Seller issues credit memo resulting in higher sales returns and customers owing less. All postings and recordings are done immediately. Note the HST amount of $30 ($200 × 0.15).

14 *Money in:* Record in cash receipts journal:

$1,000 – $200 returns = $800
× 0.02
$ 16 discount

Record immediately the $920 ($1,150 – $230) to Lewis in the accounts receivable subsidiary ledger. Cash received is $920 less $16 = $904.

16 *Buy now, pay later:* Record in purchases journal. Record immediately to Noone Co. in the accounts payable subsidiary ledger. Note HST.

17 *Buy now, pay later:* Record in purchases journal under Sundry. This is not merchandise for resale, but HST still applies. Record and post immediately.

18 *Returns:* Record in general journal. Buyer issues a debit memo, reducing their accounts payable because of Purchases Returns and Allowances. Post and record immediately. HST is included at 15 percent.

20 *Salaries:* Record in cash payments journal, Sundry column. There is no HST on salaries.

24 *Money out:* Record in cash payments journal. Save 3 percent ($15), a purchases discount. Record immediately in accounts payable subsidiary ledger, reducing Noone by $575.

27 *Money out:* Record in cash payments journal. (No discount is mentioned.) Debit advertising expense in the Sundry Accounts column and post immediately. Note the HST amount of $60 which is entered in the Prepaid HST column. Total amount paid is $400 + 15 percent, or $460.

At the end of the month: Post totals (except Sundry) of special journal to the general ledger.

Note: In this problem, at the end of the month: (1) Accounts Receivable in the general ledger, the controlling account, has a zero balance, as does each title in the accounts receivable subsidiary ledger. (2) The balance in Accounts Payable (the controlling account) is $345. In the accounts payable subsidiary ledger, Case is owed $345. The sum of the subsidiary ledger accounts does equal the balance in the controlling account at the end of the month.

SUMMARY OF KEY POINTS

Learning Unit 10-1

1. Purchases are merchandise for resale. Purchases are expenses.
2. Purchases Returns and Allowances and Purchases Discounts are contra-expense accounts.
3. "F.O.B. shipping point" means that the purchaser of the goods is responsible for covering the shipping costs. If the terms were "F.O.B. destination," the seller

would be responsible for covering the shipping costs until the goods reached their destination.

4. Purchases discounts are not taken on freight.

Learning Unit 10-2

1. The steps for buying merchandise from a company may include:
   a. The requesting department prepares a purchase requisition.
   b. The purchasing department prepares a purchase order.
   c. The seller receives the order and prepares a sales invoice (a purchase invoice for the buyer).
   d. The buyer receives the goods and prepares a receiving report.
   e. The accounting department verifies and approves the invoice for payment.
2. The purchases journal records the buying of merchandise or other items on account.
3. The accounts payable subsidiary ledger, organized in alphabetical order, is not in the same book as Accounts Payable, the controlling account in the general ledger.
4. At the end of the month the total of all creditors' ending balances in the accounts payable subsidiary ledger should equal the ending balance in Accounts Payable, the controlling account in the general ledger.
5. A debit memorandum (issued by the buyer) indicates that the amount owed from a previous purchase is being reduced because some goods were defective or not up to a specific standard and thus were returned or an allowance was requested. On receiving the debit memorandum, the seller will issue a credit memorandum.

Learning Unit 10-3

1. All payments by cheque are recorded in the cash payments journal.
2. At the end of the month, the schedule of accounts payable, a list of ending amounts owed to individual creditors, should equal the ending balance in Accounts Payable, the controlling account in the general ledger.
3. Trade discounts are deductions off the list price that have nothing to do with early payments (cash discounts). Invoice amounts are recorded after the trade discount is deducted. Cash discounts are not taken on trade discounts.

Learning Unit 10-4

1. GST/HST is paid on most purchases of goods and services in Canada. It is very important for businesses to keep proper track of the GST/HST they pay because they can deduct this from the GST/HST otherwise payable on their own sales.
2. A separate column is added to the purchases journal and to the cash payments journal to record the GST/HST on things purchased either on account or for cash.
3. When a debit note is issued for a purchase return or allowance, the GST/HST is always added to the total. When the debit note is recorded in the general journal, the GST/HST amount is credited to the same account as that used to track the GST/HST amounts paid for the period. This increases the amount owed to the federal government. Other postings are done in the same way as described earlier.

KEY TERMS

Accounts payable subsidiary ledger A book or file that contains in alphabetical order the names of the creditors and the amounts owed from purchases on account (p. 413)

Cash payments journal (cash disbursements journal) A special journal that records all transactions involving payment by cheque (p. 418)

Controlling account The account in the general ledger that summarizes or controls a subsidiary ledger. *Example:* The Accounts Payable account in the general ledger is the controlling account for the accounts payable subsidiary ledger. After postings are complete, it shows the total amount owed from purchases made on account. (p. 421)

Debit memorandum A memo issued by a purchaser to a seller, indicating that some purchases returns and allowances have occurred and therefore the purchaser now owes less money on account (p. 414)

F.O.B. "Free on board," which means without shipping charge to the buyer up to a specified location. The seller bears the cost up to the specified location and the buyer bears the cost from that location to the actual destination. (p. 410)

F.O.B. destination *Seller* pays or is responsible for the cost of freight to destination or purchaser's location (p. 410)

F.O.B. shipping point *Purchaser* pays or is responsible for the shipping costs from seller's shipping point to purchaser's location (p. 410)

Invoice approval form The accounting department uses this form in checking the invoice and finally approving it for recording and payment. (p. 413)

Prepaid GST/HST An asset account used to accumulate the GST/HST paid (or payable) to suppliers on goods or services purchased. It is an asset because it can be deducted from the amount otherwise payable to the federal government. This is sometimes shown with current liabilities (but is still a debit-balance account). (p. 425)

Purchases Merchandise for resale. It is an expense. (p. 408)

Purchases Discounts A contra-expense account in the general ledger that records discounts offered by suppliers of merchandise for prompt payment of purchases by buyers (p. 409)

Purchase invoice The seller's sales invoice, which is sent to the purchaser (p. 412)

Purchases journal A multicolumn special journal that records the buying of merchandise or other items on account (p. 413)

Purchase order A form used in business to place an order for the buying of goods from a seller (p. 411)

Purchase requisition A form used within a business by the requesting department asking the purchasing department of the business to buy specific goods (p. 411)

Purchases Returns and Allowances A contra-expense account in the ledger that records the amount of defective or unacceptable merchandise returned to suppliers and/or price reductions given for defective items sold (p. 409)

Receiving report A business form used to notify purchasing and accounting of the ordered goods received, indicating the quantities and specific condition of the goods (p. 412)

BLUEPRINT OF PURCHASES AND CASH PAYMENTS JOURNALS

Multicolumn Purchases Journal

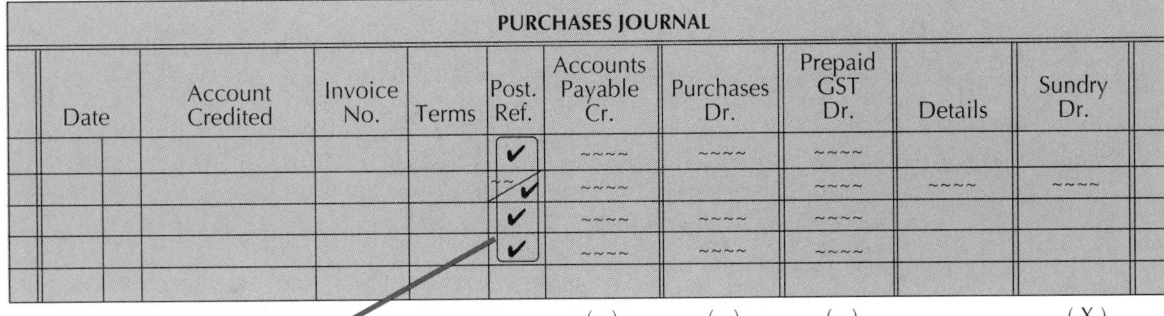

PURCHASES JOURNAL
Date
Account Credited
Invoice No.
Terms
Post. Ref.
Accounts Payable Cr.
Purchases Dr.
Prepaid GST Dr.
Details
Sundry Dr.

( ) ( ) ( ) (X)

During the month the accounts payable ledger is updated as soon as transactions are entered in the journal. A ✔ indicates that posting is completed to the supplier's account in the accounts payable subledger. The number above the slash is the GL account number for the sundry posting.

End-of-month total is posted to Accounts Payable controlling account in the general ledger.

End-of-month totals of both GST and purchases accounts are posted to their respective accounts in the general ledger.

End-of-month total is not posted to the general ledger. Individual amounts are posted as the month progresses.

Recording a Debit Memo with GST in the General Journal

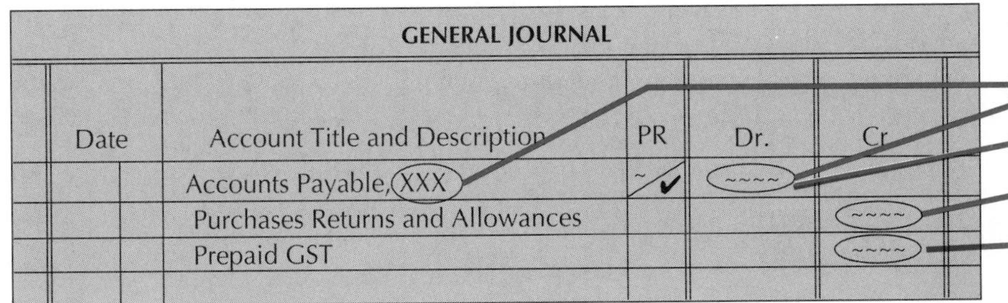

GENERAL JOURNAL
Date
Account Title and Description
PR
Dr.
Cr.
Accounts Payable, XXX
Purchases Returns and Allowances
Prepaid GST

Posted when transaction entered

Four postings:
1. Record to XXX in accounts payable ledger.
2. Post to Accounts Payable in general ledger.
3. Post to Purchases Returns and Allowances in general ledger.
4. Post to asset account in general ledger.

Cash Payments Journal with GST

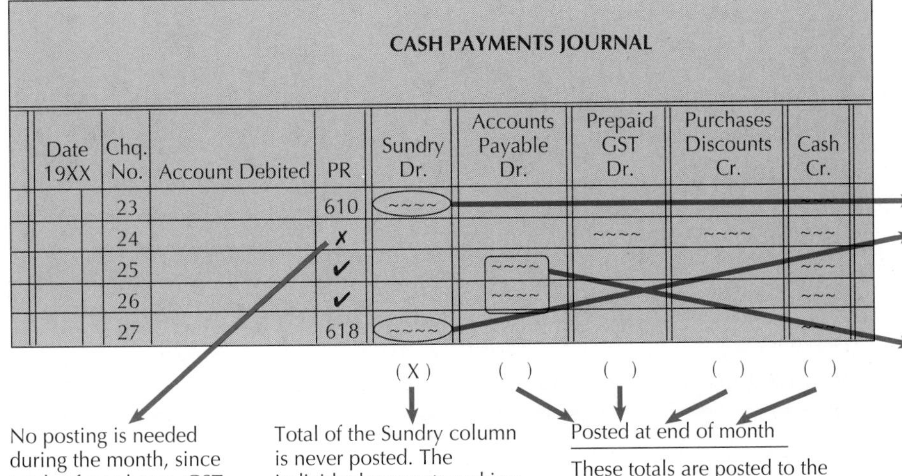

CASH PAYMENTS JOURNAL
Date 19XX
Chq. No.
Account Debited
PR
Sundry Dr.
Accounts Payable Dr.
Prepaid GST Dr.
Purchases Discounts Cr.
Cash Cr.
23
24
25
26
27
610
✗
✔
✔
618

Posted when transaction occurs

Posted to general ledger when transactions are entered, in these cases to accounts 610 and 618.

Posted during the month

These individual amounts are posted during the month to the accounts payable subledger. When posted, a check mark is placed in the PR column of the cash payments journal.

(X) ( ) ( ) ( ) ( )

No posting is needed during the month, since totals of purchases, GST, PST, and cash are posted at end of month.

Total of the Sundry column is never posted. The individual amounts making up the total are posted as the month progresses.

Posted at end of month

These totals are posted to the general ledger accounts at the end of the month.

Questions, Mini Exercises, Exercises, and Problems

Discussion Questions

1. Explain how to calculate net purchases.
2. What is the normal balance of the Purchases Discounts account?
3. What is a contra-expense?
4. Explain the difference between F.O.B. shipping point and F.O.B. destination.
5. F.O.B. destination means that title to the goods will switch to the buyer when goods are shipped. Agree or disagree. Why?
6. What is the normal balance of each creditor in the accounts payable subsidiary ledger?
7. Why doesn't the balance of the controlling account, Accounts Payable, equal the sum of the accounts payable subsidiary ledger balances during the month?
8. What is the relationship between a purchase requisition and a purchase order?
9. What purpose could a typical invoice approval form serve?
10. Explain the difference between merchandise and equipment.
11. Why would the purchaser issue a debit memorandum?
12. Explain the relationship between a purchases journal and a cash payments journal.
13. Explain why a trade discount is not a cash discount.
14. State why it is so important for firms to keep track of the GST/HST they pay each period.
15. Why does GST/HST on a debit note act to increase the net amount of GST/HST payable?

Mini Exercises

(The forms you need are on page 10-11 of the *Study Guide with Working Papers.*)

Overview

1. Complete the following table:

To the Seller		*To the Buyer*
Sales	↔	**a.** ________
Sales returns and allowances	↔	**b.** ________
Sales discounts	↔	**c.** ________
Sales journal	↔	**d.** ________
Cash receipts journal	↔	**e.** ________
Credit memorandum	↔	**f.** ________
Schedule of Accounts Receivable	↔	**g.** ________
Accounts receivable subsidiary ledger	↔	**h.** ________

2. Complete the following table:

Accounts Affected	Category	↑↓	Rules	Temporary or Permanent
Purchases				
Purchases Returns and Allowances				
Purchases Discounts				

Calculating Net Purchases

3. Calculate Net Purchases from the following: Purchases, $6; Purchases Returns and Allowances, $2; Purchases Discounts, $1.

Purchases Journal, General Journal, Recording and Posting

4. For each of the three journal entries below, indicate which of these procedures should be used (more than one number can be used).
   1. Journalize in purchases journal.
   2. Record immediately in subsidiary ledger.
   3. Post totals from purchases journal (except Sundry total) at end of month to general ledger.
   4. Journalize in general journal.
   5. Immediately record in subsidiary ledgers and post to the general ledger.

   a. Bought merchandise on account from Also Co., invoice No. 12, $20.
   b. Bought equipment on account from Jone Co., invoice No. 13, $40.
   c. Issued debit memo No. 1 to Also Co. for merchandise returned, $4, from invoice No. 12.

Recording Transactions in Special Journals

5. Indicate in which of these five journals each transaction described below will be journalized:

   1. SJ **4.** CPJ
   2. PJ **5.** GJ
   3. CRJ

   ____ **a.** Issued credit memo No. 2, $13.
   ____ **b.** Cash sales, $20
   ____ **c.** Received cheque from Blue Co., $50 less 3 percent discount.
   ____ **d.** Bought merchandise on account from Mel Co., $35, 1/10, n/30, invoice No. 20.
   ____ **e.** Cash purchase, $15
   ____ **f.** Issued debit memo to Mel Co., $15 for merchandise returned from invoice No. 20.

6. From the following, prepare a schedule of accounts payable for AVE Co. for May 31, 2003:

Accounts Payable Subsidiary Ledger

Bloss Co.

5/25	CPJ1	10	5/20	PJ1	50

Rowe Co.

			5/7	PJ1	60

General Ledger

Accounts Payable

5/31	CPJ	10	5/31	PJ1	110

Exercises

(The forms you need are on pages 10-12 and 10-13 of the *Study Guide with Working Papers.*)

10-1. From the accompanying purchases journal, record in the accounts payable subsidiary ledger and post to general ledger accounts as appropriate.

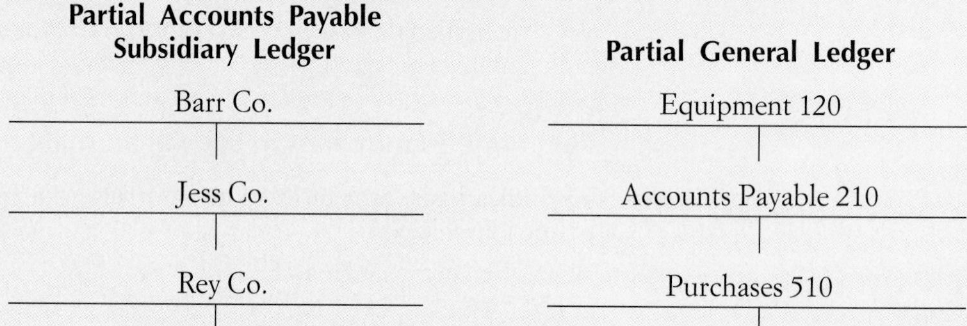

PURCHASES JOURNAL — Page 1

Date		Account Credited	Date of Invoice	Terms	Post. Ref.	Accounts Payable Credit	Purchases Debit	Sundry—Dr. Account	PR	Amount
2002 June	3	Barr Co.	May 3	1/10, n/30		600 00	600 00			
	4	Jess Co.	May 4	n/10, EOM		900 00	900 00			
	8	Rey Co.	May 8			400 00		Equipment		400 00

Recording in the accounts payable subsidiary ledger and posting to the general ledger from a purchases journal

Partial Accounts Payable Subsidiary Ledger

Barr Co.

Jess Co.

Rey Co.

Partial General Ledger

Equipment 120

Accounts Payable 210

Purchases 510

Journalizing, recording, and posting a debit memorandum

10-2. On July 10, 2002, Aster Co. issued debit memorandum No. 1 for $400 to Reel Co. for merchandise returned from invoice No. 312. Your task is to journalize, record, and post this transaction as appropriate. Use the same account numbers as found in the text for Art's Wholesale Clothing Company. The general journal page is page 1.

Journalizing, recording, and posting a cash payments journal

10-3. Journalize, record, and post when appropriate the following transactions into the cash payments journal (page 2) for Morgan's Clothing. Use the same headings as found in the text (page 419). All purchases discounts are 2/10, n/30.

Accounts Payable Subsidiary Ledger

Name	*Balance*	*Invoice No.*
B. Foss	$ 400	488
A. James	1,000	522
J. Ranch	900	562
B. Swanson	100	821

Partial General Ledger

Account	*Balance*
Cash 110	$3,000
Accounts Payable 210	2,400
Purchases Discounts 511	
Advertising Expense 610	

2001

April 1 Issued cheque No. 20 to A. James Company in payment of its March 28 invoice No. 522.

8 Issued cheque No. 21 to Flott Advertising in payment of its advertising bill, $100, no discount.

15 Issued cheque No. 22 to B. Foss in payment of its March 25 invoice No. 488.

Schedule of accounts payable

10-4. From Exercise 10-3, prepare a schedule of accounts payable and verify that the total of the schedule equals the amount in the controlling account.

F.O.B. destination

10-5. Record the following transaction in a transaction analysis chart for the buyer: Bought merchandise for $9,000 on account. Shipping terms were F.O.B. destination. The cost of shipping was $500.

Trade and cash discounts

10-6. Angie Rase bought merchandise with a list price of $4,000. Angie was entitled to a 30 percent trade discount, as well as a 3 percent cash discount. What was Angie's actual cost of buying this merchandise after the cash discount?

Group A Problems

(The forms you need are on pages 10-14 to 10-31 of the *Study Guide with Working Papers*.)

Journalizing, recording, and posting a purchases journal

Check Figure

Total of Purchases Column $2,300.00

10A-1. (GST/HST is not involved in this problem.) Judy Clark recently opened a sporting goods shop. As the bookkeeper of her shop, journalize, record, and post when appropriate the following transactions (account numbers are: Store Supplies, 115; Store Equipment, 121; Accounts Payable, 210; Purchases, 510):

2002

June 4 Bought merchandise on account from Aster Co., invoice No. 442, dated June 4, terms 2/10, n/30; $900.

5 Bought store equipment from Norton Co., invoice No. 502, dated June 5; $4,000.

8 Bought merchandise on account from Rolo Co., invoice No. 401, dated June 7; terms 2/10, n/30; $1,400.

14 Bought store supplies on account from Aster Co., invoice No. 519, dated June 14; $900.

Journalizing, recording, and posting a purchases journal, as well as recording a debit memorandum and preparing a schedule of accounts payable

Check Figure

Total Schedule of Accounts Payable $6,216.70

10A-2. Mabel's Natural Food Store uses a purchases journal (page 10) and a general journal (page 2) to record the following transactions (continued from April):

2000

May 8 Purchased merchandise on account from Aton Co., invoice No. 400, dated May 7, terms 2/10, n/60; $600 plus GST.

10 Purchased merchandise on account from Broward Co., invoice No. 120, dated May 10, terms 2/10, n/60; $1,200 plus GST.

12 Purchased store supplies on account from Midden Co., invoice No. 510, dated May 12, $500 plus GST.

14 Issued debit memo No. 8 to Aton Co. for merchandise returned, $400 (plus GST) from invoice No. 400.

17 Purchased office equipment on account from Relar Co., invoice No. 810, dated May 17, $560 plus GST.

24 Purchased additional store supplies on account from Midden Co., invoice No. 516, dated May 23, terms 2/10, n/30; $650 plus GST.

The food store has decided to use a separate column for the purchases of supplies in the purchases journal, which also has a separate column for GST.

Required

1. Journalize the transactions.
2. Post and record as appropriate.
3. Prepare a schedule of accounts payable.

Accounts Payable Ledger

Name	*Balance*
Aton Co.	$ 428
Broward Co.	642
Midden Co.	1,284
Relar Co.	535

Partial General Ledger

Account	*Number*	*Balance*
Store Supplies	110	$ —
Prepaid GST	112	498
Office Equipment	120	—
Accounts Payable	210	2,889
Purchases	510	16,000
Purchases Returns and Allowances	512	—

Journalizing, recording, and posting a cash payments journal with GST; preparing a schedule of accounts payable

10A-3. Wendy Jones operates a wholesale computer centre. All transactions requiring the payment of cash are recorded in the cash payments journal (page 5). The account balances as of May 1, 2001, are as follows:

Check Figure

Total of Schedule of Accounts Payable $2,033.00

Accounts Payable Ledger

Name	*Balance*	*GST Included*
Alvin Co.	$1,284	$84
Henry Co.	642	42
Soy Co.	856	56
Xon Co.	1,498	98

Partial General Ledger

Account	*Number*	*Balance*
Cash	110	$17,000
Prepaid GST	132	965
Delivery Truck	150	—
Accounts Payable	210	4,280
Computer Purchases	510	—
Computer Purchases Discount	511	—
Rent Expense	610	—
Utilities Expense	620	—

Required

1. Journalize the following transactions.
2. Record in the accounts payable ledger and post to the general ledger as appropriate.
3. Prepare a schedule of accounts payable.

2001

May 1 Paid half the amount owed Henry Co. from previous purchases of computers on account, less a 2 percent purchases discount, cheque No. 21.

3 Bought a delivery truck for $8,000 cash plus GST of $560, cheque No. 22, payable to Bill Ring Co.

6 Bought computer merchandise from Lectro Co., cheque No. 23, $2,900, plus GST.

18 Bought additional computer merchandise from Pulse Co., cheque No. 24, $800, plus GST.

24 Paid Xon Co. the amount owed less a 2 percent purchases discount, cheque No. 25.

28 Paid rent expense to King's Realty Trust, cheque No. 26, $2,000, plus GST.

29 Paid utilities expense to Stone Utility Co., cheque No. 27, $300, plus GST.

30 Paid half the amount owed Soy Co., no discount, cheque No. 28.

Comprehensive review problem with GST (or HST): all special journals and the general journal; schedules of accounts payable and accounts receivable

Reviews Chapters 9 and 10

Check Figures

Total of Schedule of Accounts Receivable $8,132.00 (GST 7%) or $8,740.00 (HST 15%)

Total of Schedule of Accounts Payable $9,630.00 (GST 7%) or $10,350.00 (HST 15%)

10A-4. Abby Ellen owns Abby's Toy House. As her newly hired accountant, your task is to (substituting 15 percent HST for 7 percent GST if your instructor so directs):

1. Journalize the transactions for the month of March.

2. Record in subsidiary ledgers and post to the general ledger as appropriate.

3. Total, rule, and cross-foot the journals.

4. Prepare a schedule of accounts receivable and a schedule of accounts payable.

The following is the partial chart of accounts for Abby's Toy House:

Assets
110 Cash
112 Accounts Receivable
114 Prepaid Rent
116 Prepaid GST/HST
121 Delivery Truck

Liabilities
210 Accounts Payable
218 GST/HST Payable

Owner's Equity
310 A. Ellen, Capital

Revenue
410 Toy Sales
412 Sales Returns and Allowances
414 Sales Discounts

Cost of Goods
510 Toy Purchases
512 Purchases Returns and Allowances
514 Purchases Discounts

Expenses
610 Salaries Expense
612 Cleaning Expense

2001

March 1 Abby Ellen invested $8,000 in the toy store.

1 Paid three months' rent in advance, cheque No. 1, $3,000, plus GST.

1 Purchased merchandise from Earl Miller Company on account, $4,000, plus GST. Invoice No. 410, dated March 1, terms 2/10, n/30

3 Sold merchandise to Bill Burton on account, $1,000, plus GST. Invoice No. 1, terms 2/10, n/30

6 Sold merchandise to Jim Rex on account, $700, plus GST. Invoice No. 2, terms 2/10, n/30

8 Purchased merchandise from Earl Miller Co. on account, $1,200, plus GST. Invoice No. 415, dated March 7, terms 2/10, n/30

9 Sold merchandise to Bill Burton on account, $600, plus GST. Invoice No. 3, terms 2/10, n/30

9 Paid cleaning service $300, plus GST. Cheque No. 2

10 Jim Rex returned merchandise that cost $300 (before GST) to Abby's Toy House. Abby issued credit memorandum No. 1 to Jim Rex for $300, plus GST.

10 Purchased merchandise from Minnie Katz on account, $4,000, plus GST. Invoice No. 311, dated March 10, terms 1/15, n/60

11 Paid Earl Miller Co. invoice No. 410, dated March 1, cheque No. 3.

13 Sold $1,300 (plus GST) worth of toy merchandise for cash.

13 Paid salaries, $600, cheque No. 4.

14 Returned merchandise to Minnie Katz in the amount of $1,000, plus GST. Abby's Toy House issued debit memorandum No. 1 to Minnie Katz.

15 Sold merchandise for cash $4,000, plus GST.

16 Received payment from Jim Rex, invoice No. 2 (less returned merchandise), less discount.

16 Bill Burton paid invoice No. 1.

16 Sold toy merchandise to Amy Rose on account, $4,000, plus GST. Invoice No. 4, terms 2/10, n/30

20 Purchased delivery truck on account from Sam Katz Garage, $3,000, plus GST. Invoice No. 111, dated March 20 (no discount)

22 Sold to Bill Burton merchandise on account, $900, plus GST. Invoice No. 5, terms 2/10, n/30

23 Paid Minnie Katz balance owed, cheque No. 5.

24 Sold toy merchandise on account to Amy Rose, $1,100, plus GST. Invoice No. 6, terms 2/10, n/30

25 Purchased toy merchandise, $600, plus GST. Cheque No. 6

26 Purchased toy merchandise from Woody Smith on account, $4,800, plus GST. Invoice No. 211, dated March 26, terms 2/10, n/30

28 Bill Burton paid invoice No. 5, dated March 22.

28 Amy Rose paid invoice No. 6, dated March 24.

28 Abby invested an additional $5,000 in the business.

28 Purchased merchandise from Earl Miller Co., $1,400, plus GST. Invoice No. 436, dated March 27, terms 2/10, n/30

30 Paid Earl Miller Co. invoice No. 436, cheque No. 7.

30 Sold merchandise to Bonnie Flow Company on account, $3,000, plus GST. Invoice No. 7, terms 2/10, n/30

Group B Problems

(The forms you need are on pages 10-14 to 10-31 of the *Study Guide with Working Papers*.)

Journalizing, recording, and posting a purchases journal

Check Figure

Total of Payables Column $2,200.10

10B-1. (GST/HST is not involved in this problem.) From the following transactions of Judy Clark's sporting goods shop, journalize in the purchases journal and record and post as appropriate:

2002

June 4 Bought merchandise on account from Rolo Co., invoice No. 400, dated June 4, terms 2/10, n/30; $1,800.

5 Bought store equipment from Norton Co., invoice No. 518, dated June 4; $6,000.

8 Bought merchandise on account from Aster Co., invoice No. 411, dated June 8, terms 2/10, n/30; $400.

14 Bought store supplies on account from Aster Co., invoice No. 415, dated June 13, $1,200.

Journalizing, recording, and posting a purchases journal with GST, as well as recording the issuing of a debit memorandum and preparing a schedule of accounts payable

Check Figure
Total of Schedule of Accounts Payable $6,420.00

10B-2. As the accountant of Mabel's Natural Food Store (1) journalize the following transactions in the purchases (page 10) or general (page 2) journal, (2) record and post as appropriate, and (3) prepare a schedule of accounts payable. Beginning balances are in your working papers.

2000
May 8 Purchased merchandise on account from Broward Co., invoice No. 420, dated May 7, terms 2/10, n/60; $500, plus GST.
10 Purchased merchandise on account from Aton Co., invoice No. 400, dated May 10, terms 2/10, n/60; $900, plus GST.
12 Purchased store supplies on account from Midden Co., invoice No. 510, dated May 12, $700, plus GST.
14 Issued debit memo No. 7 to Aton Co. for merchandise returned,.$400, plus GST (from invoice No. 400).
17 Purchased office equipment on account from Relar Co., invoice No. 810, dated May 17, $750, plus GST.
24 Purchased additional store supplies on account from Midden Co., invoice No. 516, dated May 23, $850, plus GST.

Journalizing, recording, and posting a cash payments journal with GST; preparing a schedule of accounts payable

Check Figure
Total of Schedule of Accounts Payable $2,033.00

10B-3. Wendy Jones has hired you as her bookkeeper to record the following transactions in the cash payments journal. She would like you to record and post as appropriate and supply her with a schedule of accounts payable. (Beginning balances are in your workbook and in Problem 10A-3.)

2001
May 1 Bought a delivery truck for $8,000 cash, plus GST; cheque No. 21, payable to Randy Rosse Co.
3 Paid half the amount owed Henry Co. from previous purchases of computer merchandise on account, less a 5 percent purchases discount, cheque No. 22.
6 Bought computer merchandise from Jane Co. for $900 cash, plus GST, cheque No. 23.
18 Bought additional computer merchandise from Jane Co., cheque No. 24, $1,000, plus GST.
24 Paid Xon Co. the amount owed less a 5 percent purchases discount, cheque No. 25.
28 Paid rent expense to Regan Realty Trust, cheque No. 26, $3,000, plus GST.
29 Paid half the amount owed Soy Co., no discount, cheque No. 27.
30 Paid utilities expense to County Utility, cheque No. 28, $425, plus GST.

Comprehensive review problem with GST (or HST): all special journals and the general journal; schedules of accounts payable and accounts receivable

Reviews Chapters 9 and 10

10B-4. As the new accountant for Abby's Toy House, your task is to (substituting 15 percent HST for 7 percent GST if your instructor so directs):

1. Journalize the transactions for the month of March.

2. Record in subsidiary ledgers and post to the general ledger as appropriate.

3. Total, rule, and cross-foot the journals.

4. Prepare a schedule of accounts receivable and a schedule of accounts payable.

(Use the same chart of accounts as in Problem 10A-4. Your workbook has all the forms you need to complete this problem.)

2001
March 1 Abby invested $4,000 in the new toy store.
1 Paid two months' rent in advance, cheque No. 1, $1,000, plus GST.
1 Purchased merchandise from Earl Miller Company, invoice No. 410, dated March 1, terms 2/10, n/30; $6,000, plus GST.
3 Sold merchandise to Bill Burton on account, $1,600, plus GST. Invoice No. 1, terms 2/10, n/30

6 Sold merchandise to Jim Rex on account, $800, plus GST, invoice No. 2, terms 2/10, n/30.
8 Purchased merchandise from Earl Miller Company, $800, plus GST. Invoice No. 415, dated March 7, terms 2/10, n/30
9 Sold merchandise to Bill Burton on account, $700, plus GST. Invoice No. 3, terms 2/10, n/30
9 Paid cleaning service, $400, plus GST. Cheque No. 2
10 Jim Rex returned merchandise that cost $200 (plus GST) to Abby. Abby issued credit memorandum No. 1 to Jim Rex for $200, plus GST.
10 Purchased merchandise from Minnie Katz, $7,000, plus GST. Invoice No. 311, dated March 10, terms 1/15, n/60
11 Paid Earl Miller Co. invoice No. 410, dated March 1, cheque No. 3.
13 Sold $1,500 (plus GST) worth of toy merchandise for cash.
13 Paid salaries, $700, cheque No. 4.
14 Returned merchandise to Minnie Katz in the amount of $500, plus GST. Abby issued debit memorandum No. 1 to Minnie Katz.
15 Sold merchandise for cash, $4,800, plus GST.
16 Received payment from Jim Rex for invoice No. 2 (less returned merchandise) less discount.
16 Bill Burton paid invoice No. 1.
16 Sold toy merchandise to Amy Rose on account, $6,000, plus GST. Invoice No. 4, terms 2/10, n/30
20 Purchased delivery truck on account from Sam Katz Garage, $2,500, plus GST. Invoice No. 111, dated March 20 (no discount)
22 Sold to Bill Burton merchandise on account, $2,000, plus GST. Invoice No. 5, terms 2/10, n/30.
23 Paid Minnie Katz balance owed, cheque No. 5.
24 Sold toy merchandise on account to Amy Rose, $2,000, plus GST. Invoice No. 6, terms 2/10, n/30
25 Purchased toy merchandise, $800, plus GST. Cheque No. 6
26 Purchased toy merchandise from Woody Smith on account, $5,900, plus GST. Invoice No. 211, dated March 25, terms 2/10, n/30
28 Bill Burton paid invoice No. 5, dated March 22.
28 Amy Rose paid invoice No. 6, dated March 24.
28 Abby invested an additional $3,000 in the business.
28 Purchased merchandise from Earl Miller Co., $4,200, plus GST. Invoice No. 436, dated March 27, terms 2/10, n/30
30 Paid Earl Miller Co. invoice No. 436, cheque No. 7.
30 Sold merchandise to Bonnie Flow Company on account, $3,200, plus GST. Invoice No. 7, terms 2/10, n/30

Check Figure

Total of Schedule of Accounts Receivable

$10,593.00 (GST 7%)

or **$11,385.00 (HST 15%)**

Total of Schedule of Accounts Payable

$ 9,844.00 (GST 7%)

or **$10,580.00 (HST 15%)**

Group C Problems

(The forms you need are on pages 10-32 to 10-51 of the *Study Guide with Working Papers.*)

Journalizing, recording, and posting a purchases journal

Check Figure

Total of Purchases Column $2,455.00

10C-1. (GST/HST is not involved in this problem.) Barb Wells recently opened an imported foods store. As the bookkeeper of her store, journalize, record, and post when appropriate the following transactions (account numbers are: Store Supplies, 115; Store Equipment, 141; Accounts Payable, 210; Purchases, 510):

2002

May 4 Bought merchandise on account from Convey Co., invoice No. 751, dated May 3, terms 2/10, n/30; $715.

5 Bought store equipment from Reliable Co., invoice No. 1202, dated May 4; $5,180.

8 Bought merchandise on account from Brendan Co., invoice No. 401, dated May 6; terms 1/10, n/30; $1,740.

14 Bought store supplies on account from Convey Co., invoice No. 823 dated May 14; $785.

Journalizing, recording, and posting a purchases journal with GST, as well as recording the issuing of a debit memorandum and preparing a schedule of accounts payable

Check Figure

Total of Schedule of Accounts Payable $21,411.21

10C-2. Farber's Fabric Co. uses a purchases journal (page 21) and a general journal (page 32) to record the following transactions (continued from July) the GST rate is 7 percent:

2000

August 3 Purchased fabric for resale from European Import Fabrics Co., invoice No. 653, dated August 2, terms net 15 days; $1,362 plus GST.

8 Purchased merchandise on account from Eddyn Co., invoice No. 250, dated August 7, terms 2/10, n/60; $920 plus GST.

10 Purchased merchandise on account from Forward Co., invoice No. 1124, dated August 8, terms 1/10, n/60; $1,626 plus GST.

12 Purchased store supplies on account from Lavoy Co., invoice No. 712, dated August 12, $2,680 plus GST.

14 Issued debit memo No. 8 to Eddyn Co. for merchandise returned, $160 (plus GST), from invoice No. 250.

17 Purchased office equipment on account from Reliant Co., invoice No. 873, dated August 16, $1,610 plus GST.

24 Purchased additional store supplies on account from Lavoy Co., invoice No. 816, dated August 24, terms 2/10, n/30; $725 plus GST.

29 Purchased fabric for resale from European Import Fabrics Co., invoice No. 713, dated August 27, terms net 15 days; $2,740 plus GST.

The fabric store has decided to keep a separate column for the purchases of supplies in the purchases journal and also has a separate column for GST. The account balances as of August 31, 2000, are as follows:

Accounts Payable Ledger

Name	*Balance*
Eddyn Co.	$ 856
European Import	3,267
Forward Co.	1,672
Lavoy Co.	535
Reliant Co.	2,773

Partial General Ledger

Account	*Number*	*Balance*
Store Supplies	130	$ —
Prepaid GST	142	2,873
Office Equipment	180	—
Accounts Payable	220	9,103
Purchases	500	86,340
Purchases Returns and Allowances	510	1,374

Required

1. Journalize the transactions.
2. Post and record as appropriate.
3. Prepare a schedule of accounts payable.

Journalizing, recording, and posting a cash payments journal with GST; preparing a schedule of accounts payable

Check Figure

Total of Schedule of Accounts Payable $2,321.52

10C-3. Jim Stokes owns and operates a wholesale welding supplies company. All transactions requiring the payment of cash are recorded in the cash payments journal (page 45). The account balances as of May 1, 2002, are as follows:

Accounts Payable Ledger

Name	*Balance*	*GST Included*
Dominion Gases Co.	$1,482.20	$ 96.97
Glover Gauges Co.	881.71	57.68
Marker Gloves Co.	1,847.48	120.86
Prism Accessories Co.	3,942.86	257.94
Vertal Rod Co.	2,480.42	162.27

Partial General Ledger

Account	*Number*	*Balance*
Cash	100	$22,941.18
Prepaid GST	145	2,421.14*
Delivery Truck	170	—
Accounts Payable	200	10,634.67
Welding Purchases	500	56,422.29
Welding Purchases Discounts	510	506.20
Rent Expense	670	3,730.00
Utilities Expense	690	1,204.66

*Will not agree with the amounts included in the accounts payable balances.

Required

1. Journalize the following transactions.

2. Record in the accounts payable ledger and post to general ledger as appropriate.

3. Prepare a schedule of accounts payable.

2002

May 1 Paid half the amount owed Dominion Gases Co. from previous purchases on account, less a 2 percent purchases discount, cheque No. 464.

3 Bought a delivery truck for $21,400 cash plus GST of $1,498, cheque No. 465, payable to City Truck Sales Co.

5 Paid the amount owing to Glover Gauges Co, cheque No. 466.

6 Bought welding merchandise (cash purchase) from Vericon Canada Co., cheque No. 467, $1,846, plus GST.

14 Paid the balance due to Prism Accessories Co. after deducting a 5 percent discount as per usual terms for this company, cheque No. 468.

18 Bought additional welding merchandise (cash purchase) from Pulse Co., cheque No. 469, $525 plus GST.

24 Paid Marker Gloves Co. the amount owed less a 2 percent purchases discount, cheque No. 470.

28 Paid rent expense to Abbott Properties Co., cheque No. 471, $1,720 plus GST.

29 Paid utilities expense to Stony Plain Utility Co., cheque No. 472, $364 plus GST.

30 Paid $900.00 to Vertal Rod Co., no discount, cheque No. 473.

Comprehensive review problem with GST (or, optionally, HST): all special journals and the general journal; schedules of accounts payable and accounts receivable

Reviews Chapters 9 and 10

Check Figure

Total of Schedule of Accounts Receivable $7,988.62 (GST 7%) or $8,585.90 (HST 15%)
Total of Schedule of Accounts Payable $29,275.20 (GST 7%) or $31,464.00 (HST 15%)

10C-4. Betty Cardinal runs Cardinal's Book Shop. As her newly hired accountant, your task is to (substituting HST at 15 percent for GST at 7 percent if your instructor so directs):

1. Journalize the transactions for the month of October.
2. Record to subsidiary ledgers and post to the general ledger as appropriate.
3. Total, rule, and cross-foot the journals.
4. Prepare a schedule of accounts receivable and a schedule of accounts payable as of October 31.

The following is the partial chart of accounts for Cardinal's Book Shop:

Assets
110 Cash
120 Accounts Receivable
135 Prepaid Rent
138 Prepaid GST/HST
180 Delivery Truck

Liabilities
210 Accounts Payable
218 GST/HST Payable

Owner's Equity
310 B. Cardinal, Capital

Revenue
410 Book Sales
412 Sales Returns and Allowances
414 Sales Discounts

Cost of goods
510 Book Purchases
512 Purchases Returns and Allowances
514 Purchases Discounts

Expenses
615 Cleaning Expense
650 Salaries Expense

2001

Oct. 1 Betty Cardinal invested $24,000 in the bookstore.

1 Paid three months' rent in advance, cheque No. 121, $2,700 plus GST.

1 Purchased merchandise from Milligan Book Company on account, $4,270 plus GST. Invoice No. 410, dated October 1, terms 2/10, n/30

3 Sold merchandise to First City Library on account, $2,465 plus GST. Invoice No. 781, terms 2/10, n/30

6 Sold merchandise to District College on account, $3,160 plus GST. Invoice No. 782, terms 2/10, n/30

8 Purchased merchandise from Milligan Book Co. on account, $2,940 plus GST. Invoice No. 415, dated October 7, terms 2/10, n/30

9 Sold merchandise to First City Library on account, $1,856 plus GST. Invoice No. 783, terms 2/10, n/30

9 Paid cleaning service $280 plus GST. Cheque No. 122

10 District College returned merchandise that cost $312 (before GST) to Cardinal's Book Shop. Cardinal issued credit memorandum No. 1 to District College for $312 plus GST.

10 Purchased merchandise from Winnipeg Book Supply on account, $1,852 plus GST. Invoice No. 311, dated October 8, terms 1/15, n/60

11 Paid Milligan Book Co. invoice No. 410, dated October 1, cheque No. 123.

13 Sold $1,420 (plus GST) worth of book merchandise for cash.

13 Paid salaries, $920, cheque No. 124.

14 Returned merchandise to Winnipeg Book Supply in the amount of $362 plus GST. Cardinal's Book Shop issued debit memorandum No. 1 to Winnipeg Book Supply.

15 Sold merchandise for cash, $1,047 plus GST.

16 Received payment from District College, invoice No. 782 (less returned merchandise), less discount.

16 First City Library paid invoice No. 781.

16 Sold book merchandise to Rural Bookmobile Co. on account, $2,484 plus GST. Invoice No. 784, terms 2/10, n/30

20 Purchased delivery truck on account from Suburban Auto Sales Co., $18,600 plus GST. Invoice No. 111, dated October 20 (no discount)

22 Sold merchandise to First City Library on account, $2,694 plus GST. Invoice No. 785, terms 2/10, n/30

23 Paid Winnipeg Book Supply balance owed, cheque No. 125.

24 Sold book merchandise on account to Rural Bookmobile Co., $2,412 plus GST. Invoice No. 786, terms 2/10, n/30.

25 Purchased used book merchandise for cash, $3,200 plus GST. Cheque No. 126

26 Purchased book merchandise from Smithsonian Book Co. on account, $5,820 plus GST. Invoice No. 211, dated October 24, terms 2/10, n/30

27 Sold merchandise for cash, $940 plus GST.

28 First City Library paid invoice No. 785, dated October 22.

28 Rural Bookmobile Co. paid invoice No. 786, dated October 24.

28 Betty invested an additional $12,000 in the business.

28 Purchased merchandise from Milligan Book Co., $3,120 plus GST. Invoice No. 436, dated October 27, terms 2/10, n/30

30 Paid Milligan Book Co. invoice No. 436, cheque No. 127.

30 Sold merchandise to Flower & Company on account, $3,126 plus GST. Invoice No. 787, terms 2/10, n/30

REAL WORLD APPLICATIONS

(The forms you need are on pages 10-52 and 10-53 of the *Study Guide with Working Papers.*)

Hint: $R = \frac{I}{PT}$

10R-1.
Angie Co. bought merchandise for $1,000 with credit terms of 2/10, n/30. Because of the bookkeeper's incompetence, the 2 percent cash discount was missed. The bookkeeper told Pete Angie, the owner, not to get excited. After all, it was a $20 discount that was missed—not hundreds of dollars. Act as Mr. Angie's assistant and show the bookkeeper that his $20 represents a sizeable equivalent interest cost. In your calculation assume a 360-day year. Make some written recommendations so that this will not happen again.

10R-2.
Jeff Ryan completed an Accounting I course and was recently hired as the bookkeeper of Spring Co. The special journals shown on page 455 have not been posted, nor are "Dr." and "Cr." used on the column headings. Please assist Jeff by posting to the general ledger and recording in the subsidiary ledger. (Only post or record the amounts, since no chart of accounts is provided.) Make some written recommendations on how a new computer system may lessen the need for posting.

SALES JOURNAL

Account	PR	
Blue Co.		4 8 0 0 00
Jon Co.		5 6 0 0 00
Roff Co.		6 4 0 0 00
Totals		16 8 0 0 00

PURCHASES JOURNAL

Account	PR	
Ralph Co.		4 0 0 0 00
Sos Co.		6 0 0 0 00
Jingle Co.		8 0 0 0 00
Totals		18 0 0 0 00

GENERAL JOURNAL

		Account	PR	Dr.	Cr.
		Sales Returns and Allowances		1 6 0 0 00	
		Accounts Receivable, Jon Co.			1 6 0 0 00
		Customer returned merchandise			
		Accounts Payable, Jingle Co.		8 0 0 00	
		Purchases Returns and Allowances			8 0 0 00
		Returned defective merchandise			

CASH RECEIPTS JOURNAL

Cash Dr.	Sales Discount Dr.	Accounts Receivable Cr.	Sales Cr.	Sundry Account Name	Sundry PR	Sundry Amount Cr.
4 7 0 4 00	9 6 00	4 8 0 0 00		Blue Co.		
1 9 6 0 00	4 0 00	2 0 0 0 00		Jon Co.		
5 0 0 0 00			5 0 0 0 00	Sales		
20 0 0 0 00				Notes Payable		20 0 0 0 00
3 1 3 6 00	6 4 00	3 2 0 0 00		Roff Co.		
4 6 0 0 00			4 6 0 0 00	Sales		
39 4 0 0 00	2 0 0 00	10 0 0 0 00	9 6 0 0 00	Totals		20 0 0 0 00

CASH PAYMENTS JOURNAL

Account	PR	Sundry	Accounts Payable	Purchases Discounts	Cash
Sos Co.			3 0 0 0 00	6 0 00	2 9 4 0 00
Salaries Expense		2 6 0 0 00			2 6 0 0 00
Jingle Co.			4 0 0 0 00	8 0 00	3 9 2 0 00
Salaries Expense		2 6 0 0 00			2 6 0 0 00
Totals		5 2 0 0 00	7 0 0 0 00	1 4 0 00	12 0 6 0 00

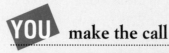

make the call

Critical Thinking/Ethical Case

10R-3.

Spring Co. bought merchandise from All Co. with terms 2/10, n/30. Joanne Ring, the bookkeeper, forgot to pay the bill within the first 10 days. She went to Mel Ryan, Head Accountant, who told her to backdate the cheque so it would look as though the bill was paid within the discount period. Joanne told Mel that she thought they could get away with it. Should Joanne and Mel backdate the cheque to take advantage of the discount? You make the call. Write down your specific recommendations to Joanne.

ACCOUNTING RECALL

A CUMULATIVE APPROACH

THIS EXAMINATION REVIEWS CHAPTERS 1 THROUGH 10.

Your *Study Guide with Working Papers* has forms (page 10-54) to complete this exam, as well as worked-out solutions. The page reference next to each question identifies the page to turn back to if you answer the question incorrectly.

PART I Vocabulary Review

Match each term on the left side with the appropriate definition or phrase on the right.

Page Ref.

(230) 1. Cheques outstanding
(410) 2. F.O.B. destination
(413) 3. Purchases journal
(354) 4. Sales journal
(409) 5. Purchases Discounts
(357) 6. Credit memorandum
(316) 7. PD7A
(414) 8. Debit memorandum
(418) 9. Cash payments journal
(408) 10. Purchases

A. A contra-expense account
B. Issued by a buyer to the seller
C. Special journal that records buying on account
D. Sales on account
E. Seller pays cost of freight
F. Form completed monthly for income tax, CPP, and UI
G. Merchandise for resale
H. Payment by cheque
I. Issued by seller
J. Cheques not yet processed by the bank

PART II True or False (Accounting Theory)

(357) 11. Issuing a credit memo results in the seller's increasing its purchases returns and allowances.
(409) 12. Purchases discounts have a normal balance of a debit.
(280) 13. UI and CPP have different rates.
(414) 14. Each creditor in the accounts payable subsidiary ledger usually has a debit balance.
(239) 15. Petty cash is an asset that will be debited only with establishment or when raising to a higher amount.

Continuing Problem

Tony Freedman was very happy to see the progress made by using the specialized journals. For the other transactions for the month of January (listed below), he will add two additional journals (purchases journal and cash payments journal). To assist you in recording the transactions, the following is an updated schedule of accounts payable as of December 31:

Schedule of Accounts Payable

Alpha Office Co.	$318
City Newspaper	480
Office Depot	50
West Bell Canada	165
Total Accounts Payable	$1,013

The rest of the transactions for the month of January are:

Jan. 1 Paid amount due to Office Depot, $50 (cheque No. 242).

4 Bought merchandise on account from Multi Systems (purchase order No. 4010), $450; terms are 3/10, n/30.

8 Bought office supplies on account from Office Depot (purchase order No. 4011), $250; terms are n/30.

9 Purchased merchandise on account from Computer Connection (purchase order No. 4012), $500; terms are 1/30, n/60.

14 Paid Multi Systems re January 4 purchase, less discount, cheque No. 243.

15 Remitted amount due to Receiver General re December withholdings, $821.10, cheque No. 244.

18 Issued debit memorandum No. 10 to Computer Connection for merchandise returned from purchase order No. 4012, $100.

19 Paid net amount due to Computer Connection, less discount, cheque No. 245.

22 Paid Alpha Office Co. the amount due from the end of December, cheque No. 246.

27 Paid for office supplies, $50, cheque No. 247.

30 Wrote cheque No. 248 to Able Holdings Inc. for February, March, and April rent, $1,200.00.

31 Wrote cheque No. 249 to Automated Payroll Service covering January wages, $6,014.82. Tony has decided to spend his time doing repairs and making sales, rather than on preparing payroll records. This company issues cheques to all employees weekly, but obtains one cheque monthly from Tony's company for wages, benefits, and their own charges.

Assignment

(See pages 10-55 and 10-59 in your *Study Guide with Working Papers*.)

1. Journalize the additional January transactions in the appropriate journals (cash payments, purchase journal, and general journal).
2. Record in the accounts payable subsidiary ledger and post to the general ledger as appropriate. A partial general ledger is included in the *Working Papers*.
3. Prepare a schedule of accounts payable as of January 31, 2002.

COMPUTER WORKSHOP

Computerized Accounting Application for Chapters 9 and 10

PART A: Recording Transactions in the Sales, Receipts, Purchases, and Payments Journals

PART B: Computerized Accounting Instructions for Abby's Toy House (Problem 10A-4)

Before starting on this assignment, read and complete the tasks discussed in Parts A, B, and F of Appendix B at the back of this book and complete the Computerized Accounting Application assignments for Chapter 3, Chapter 4, the Valdez Realty Mini Practice Set (Chapter 5), the Pete's Market Mini Practice Set (Chapter 8), and the Excalibur Consulting workshop (Chapter 9).

PART A: Recording Transactions in the Sales and Receipts Journals, and in the Purchases and Payments Journals

What to record in a computerized sales or receipts journal

The Sales and Receipts Journals in the *CA-Simply Accounting for Windows* program are designed to work with the Receivables and General Ledger modules in an integrated fashion. When transactions are recorded in the sales and receipts journals, the program automatically posts the customer's account in the accounts receivable subsidiary ledger, records the journal entry, and posts all accounts affected in the general ledger. However, the types of transaction recorded in the sales and receipts journals in the *CA-Simply Accounting for Windows* computerized system differ from the types of transaction recorded in these journals in a manual accounting system. An explanation of the differences appears in the following chart:

Name of Computerized Journal	Types of Transaction Recorded in Computerized Journal
Sales journal	Sales of merchandise on account
	Sales returns and allowances (credit memos)
	Sales discounts
Receipts journal	Cash receipts from cash and credit customers
General journal	Miscellaneous transactions from all sources

Computerized schedule of accounts receivable

A Customer Aged Detail report (the computerized version of a schedule of accounts receivable) for The Mars Company appears below (terms of 2/10, n/30 are offered to all credit customers of The Mars Company):

The Mars Company: Customer Aged Detail As at 03/01/02

	Total	*Current*	*31 to 60*	*61 to 90*	*91+*
John Dunbar					
909 02/25/02 Invoice	535.00	535.00	—	—	—
Kevin Tucker					
911 02/26/02 Invoice	749.00	749.00	—	—	—
	1,284.00	1,284.00	—	—	—

What to record in a computerized sales or receipts journal

The purchases and payments journals in the *CA-Simply Accounting for Windows* program are also designed to work with the payables and general ledger modules in an integrated fashion. When transactions are recorded in the purchases and payments journals, the program automatically posts the vendor's account in the accounts payable subsidiary ledger, records the journal entry, and posts all accounts affected in the general ledger. However, the type of transaction recorded in the purchases and payments journals in the *CA-Simply Accounting for Windows* computerized system differ from the types of transaction recorded in these journals in a manual accounting system. An explanation of the differences appears in the following chart:

Name of Computerized Journal	Type of Transaction Recorded in Computerized Journal
Purchases journal	Purchases of merchandise and other items on account
	Purchase returns and allowances (debit memos)
	Purchases discount
Payments journal	Cash payments to credit vendors as well as other miscellaneous cash payments

Computerized schedule of accounts receivable

A Vendor Aged Detail report (the computerized version of a schedule of accounts payable) for The Mars Company appears below:

The Mars Company: Vendor Aged Detail As at 03/01/02

	Total	*Current*	*31 to 60*	*61 to 90*	*91+*
Laurie Snyder					
567 02/27/02 Invoice	428.00	428.00	—	—	—
Pat Young					
789 02/25/02 Invoice	214.00	214.00	—	—	—
	642.00	642.00	—	—	—

Open the company data files.

1. Start Windows; insert your Student Data Files disk into disk drive A; then double-click on the CA-Simply Accounting icon. The CA-Simply Accounting Open File dialogue box will appear.
2. Enter the following path to the **Open file name** text box:
   - `a:\mars.asc` (if you are storing your student data files on the disk in drive A).
3. Click on the **Open** button; enter "03/31/02" into the **Session** text box; then click on the **OK** button. Click on the **OK** button in response to the message "The date entered is more than one week past your previous **Session** date of 03/01/02." The Company Window for Mars will appear.

Add your name to the company name.

4. Click on the Company Window **Setup** menu; then click on Company Information. The Company Information dialogue box will appear. Insert your name in place of the text "Your Name" in the **Name** text box. Click on the **OK** button to return to the Company Window.

How to record a sale on account. Covered in Chapter 9 Workshop.

5. On March 1, 2002, sold merchandise to Kevin Tucker on account, $800 plus GST, invoice No. 913, terms 2/10, n/30. Double-click on the Sales Journal icon to open the Sales Journal dialogue box. Note that the program automatically offers Invoice 913 as the invoice number for this transaction through the program's automatic invoice numbering feature. Click on the arrow button to the right of the **Sold to** text box to display a list of customers; then click on Kevin Tucker. Highlight the **Date** text box; enter 03/01/02; then press the TAB key until the insertion point is positioned in the **Amount** text box. Enter 800; then press the TAB key. The flashing insertion point will move to the **GST** text box. Press the ENTER key to display the Select GST dialogue box; select 3-GST @ 7.0%, not included; then press the TAB key. The flashing

insertion point will move to the **Acct** text box. Press the ENTER key to display the Select Account dialogue box; then select 4110 Sales. Your screen should look like this:

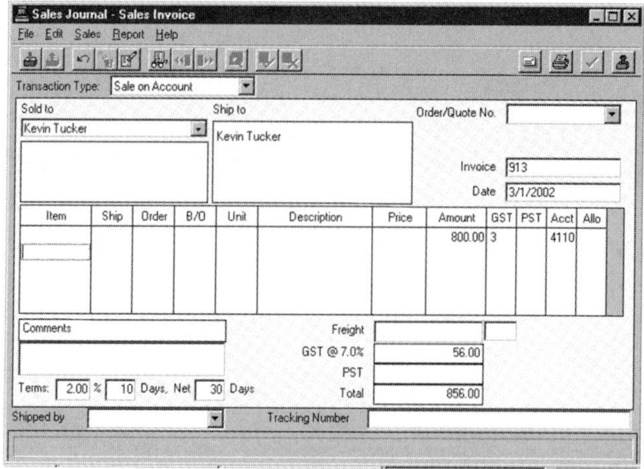

How to review a sales journal entry

6. Before posting this transaction, you need to verify that the transaction data are correct by reviewing the journal entry. To review the entry, click on the Sales Journal **Report** menu; then click on Display Sales Journal Entry. The journal entry representing the data you have recorded in the Sales Journal dialogue box is displayed. Review the journal entry for accuracy, noting any errors. Note that the program has automatically debited the accounts receivable account through its integration feature.

How to edit a sales or purchases journal entry prior to posting

7. Close the Sales Journal Entry window by double-clicking on the **Control** menu box. If you have made an error, use the following editing techniques to correct the error:

Editing a Sales (or Purchases) Journal Entry

- Move to the text box that contains the error by either pressing the TAB key to move forward through each text box or the SHIFT and TAB keys together to move to a previous text box. This will highlight the selected text box information so that you can change it. Alternatively, you can use the mouse to point to a text box and drag through the incorrect information to highlight it.
- Type the correct information; then press the TAB key to enter it.
- If you have associated the transaction with an incorrect customer or vendor, reselect the correct customer or vendor from the customer or vendor list display after clicking on the arrow button to the right of the **Sold to** text box (customers) or **Purchased from** text box (vendors).
- If you have associated a transaction with an incorrect account, double-click on the incorrect account; then select the correct account from the Select Account dialogue box. This will replace the incorrect account with the correct account.
- To discard an entry and start over, double-click on the **Control** menu box. Click on the **Yes** button in response to the question "Are you sure you want to discard this journal entry?"
- Review the journal entry for accuracy after any editing corrections.
- **It is important to note that the only way to edit a journal entry after it is posted is to reverse the entry and enter the correct journal entry,** although the program has a feature which automates this process—see Appendix B near the end of this book for details.

How to post a sales journal entry

8. After verifying that the journal entry is correct, click on the **Post** button to post this transaction. A blank Sales Journal dialogue box is displayed, ready for additional Sales Journal transactions to be recorded.

How to record a credit memo

9. On March 5, 2002, issued credit memorandum No. 14 to Kevin Tucker for returned merchandise that cost $50 plus GST. Click on the arrow button to the right of the **Sold to** text box; then click on Kevin Tucker. Highlight the **Invoice** text box; enter "CM 14"; then press the TAB key. Enter 03/05/02 into the **Date** text box; then press the TAB key until the insertion point is positioned in the **Amount** text box. Enter "– 50" (don't forget the minus sign!); then press the TAB key. The flashing insertion point will move to the GST text box. Press the ENTER key to display the Select GST dialogue box; then select 3-GST @ 7.0%, not included; then press the TAB key. The flashing insertion point will move to the **Acct** text box. Press the ENTER key to display the Select Account dialogue box; then select 4120 Sales Returns and Allowances. Your screen should look like this:

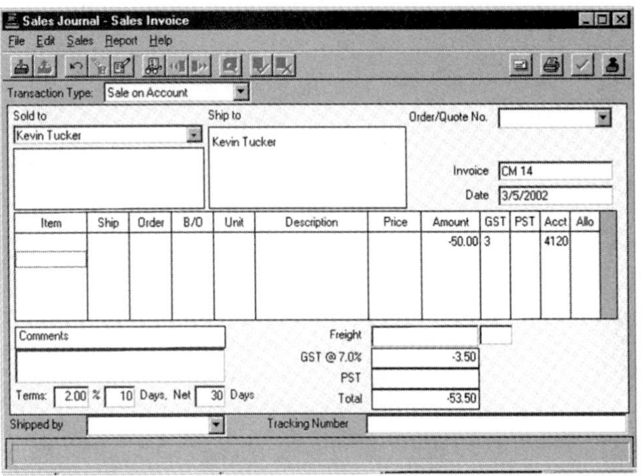

Review the entry.

10. Click on the Sales Journal **Report** menu; then click on Display Sales Journal Entry. Review the journal entry for accuracy, noting any errors. Note that the program has automatically credited the Accounts Receivable account through its integration feature.

11. Close the Sales Journal Entry window; then make any editing corrections required.

Post the entry.

12. After verifying that the journal entry is correct, click on the **Post** button to post this transaction; then close the Sales Journal dialogue box by double-clicking on the **Control** menu box.

13. On March 7, 2002, received cheque No. 1634 from Kevin Tucker in the amount of $787.50 in payment of invoice No. 913 ($856) dated March 1, less credit memorandum No. 14 ($53.50), less 2 percent discount ($15).

How to record a cash receipt with a sales discount covered in Chapter 9 Computer Workshop.

14. Open the Receipts Journal dialogue box by double-clicking on the Receipts Journal icon. Click on the arrow button to the right of the **From** text box; click on Kevin Tucker; then press the TAB key. Enter 1634 into the **No.** text box; then press the TAB key. Enter 03/07/02 into the **Date** text box; then press the TAB key. The 14.00 discount taken for invoice No. 911 will be highlighted. Press the DELETE key; then press the TAB key. The 749.00 amount for invoice No. 911 will be highlighted. Press the DELETE key; then press the TAB key. Kevin Tucker has not yet paid invoice No. 911. The 16.00 discount amount for invoice No. 913 will be highlighted. Press the TAB key five times to accept the 16.00 discount taken, the 840.00 payment amount for invoice No. 913, the –1.00 discount taken, and the –52.50 payment amount for credit memorandum 14. Your screen should look like this (see page 462):

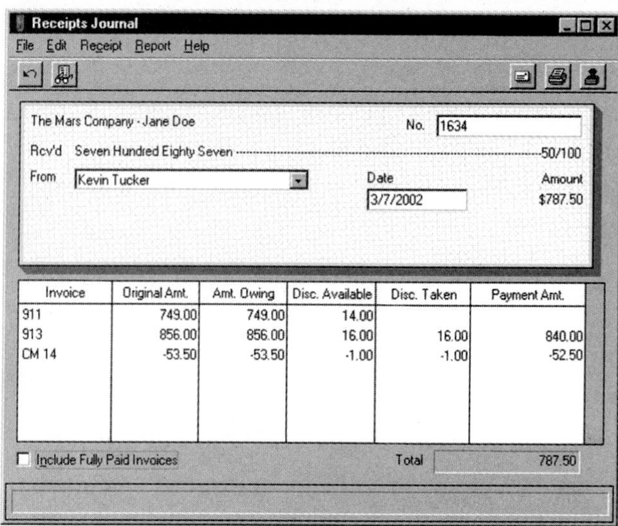

How to review a receipts journal entry

15. Before posting this transaction, you need to verify that the transaction data are correct by reviewing the journal entry. To review the entry, click on the Receipts Journal **Report** menu; then click on Display Receipts Journal Entry. The journal entry representing the data you have recorded in the Receipts Journal dialogue box is displayed. Review the journal entry for accuracy, noting any errors. Note that the program has automatically debited the Cash account and Sales Discounts account and credited the Accounts Receivable account through its integration feature.

How to edit a receipts or payments journal entry prior to posting

16. If you have made an error, use the editing techniques outlined below to correct the error:

Editing a Receipts (or Payments) Journal Entry

- Move to the text box that contains the error by either pressing the TAB key to move forward through each text box or the SHIFT and TAB keys together to move to a previous text box. This will highlight the selected text box information so that you can change it. Alternatively, you can use the mouse to point to a text box and drag through the incorrect information to highlight it.
- Type the correct information; then press the TAB key to enter it.
- If you have associated the transaction with an the incorrect customer or vendor, reselect the correct customer or vendor from the customer or vendor list display after clicking on the arrow button to the right of the **From** text box (customers) or **To the order of** text box (vendors). You will be asked to confirm that you want to discard the current transaction. Click on the **Yes** button to discard the incorrect entry and display the outstanding invoices for the correct customer or vendor.
- To discard an entry and start over, double-click on the **Control** menu box. Click on the **Yes** button in response to the question "Are you sure you want to discard this journal entry?"
- Review the journal entry for accuracy after any editing corrections.
- **It is important to note that the only way to edit a Receipts or Payments journal entry after it is posted is to reverse the entry and enter the correct journal entry**. To correct journal entries posted in error, see Part C of Appendix B at the back of this book.

How to post a receipts journal entry

17. After verifying that the journal entry is correct, click on the **Post** button to post this transaction. A blank Receipts Journal dialogue box is displayed, ready for additional Receipts Journal transactions to be recorded. Close the Receipts Journal dialogue box.

How to record a purchase on account

New to Chapter 10

18. On March 15, 2002, purchased merchandise from Pat Young on account, $275 + GST, invoice No. 796, terms 3/15, n/30. Double-click on the Purchases Journal icon to open the Purchases Journal dialogue box. Click on the arrow button to the right of the **Purchased from** text box; then click on Pat Young. Click on the **Invoice** text box; enter 796; then press the TAB key. Enter 03/15/02 into the **Date** text box; then press the TAB key until the insertion point is positioned in the **G** text box. Press the

ENTER key to display the select GST dialogue box; select 3-GST @ 7.0%, not included; then press the TAB key until the insertion point is positioned in the **Amount** text box. Enter 275; then press the TAB key. The flashing insertion point will move to the **Acct** text box. Press the ENTER key to display the Select Account dialogue box; then select 5100 Purchases. Your screen should look like this:

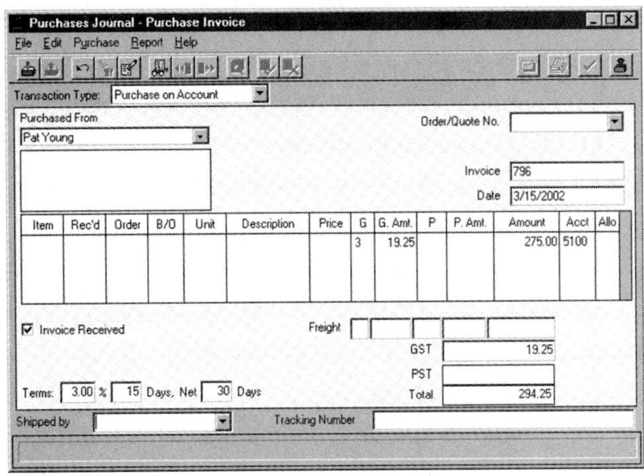

How to review a purchases journal entry

Error correction prior to posting is covered on page 460.

19. Before posting this transaction, you need to verify that the transaction data are correct by reviewing the journal entry. To review the entry, click on the Purchases Journal **Report** menu; then click on Display Purchases Journal Entry. The journal entry representing the data you have recorded in the Purchases Journal dialogue box is displayed. Review the journal entry for accuracy, noting any errors. Note that the program has automatically credited the Accounts Payable account through its integration feature.

20. Close the Purchases Journal Entry window; then make any editing corrections required.

How to post a purchases journal entry

21. After verifying that the journal entry is correct, click on the Post icon to post this transaction. A blank Purchases Journal dialogue box is displayed, ready for additional Purchases Journal transactions to be recorded.

How to record a debit memo

New to Chapter 10

22. On March 17, 2002, returned merchandise to Pat Young originally charged at $75. Issued debit memorandum No. 27. Click on the arrow button to the right of the **Purchased from** text box; then click on Pat Young. Click on the **Invoice** text box; enter `DM 27`; then press the TAB key. Enter `03/17/02` into the **Date** text box; then press the TAB key until the insertion point is positioned in the **G** text box. Press the ENTER key to display the Select GST dialogue box; select 3-GST @ 7.0%, not included; then press the TAB key until the insertion point is positioned in the **Amount** text box. Enter `-75` (don't forget the minus sign!); then press the TAB key. The flashing insertion point will move to the **Acct** text box. Press the ENTER key to display the Select Account dialogue box; then select 5120 Purchases Returns and Allowances. Your screen should look like this:

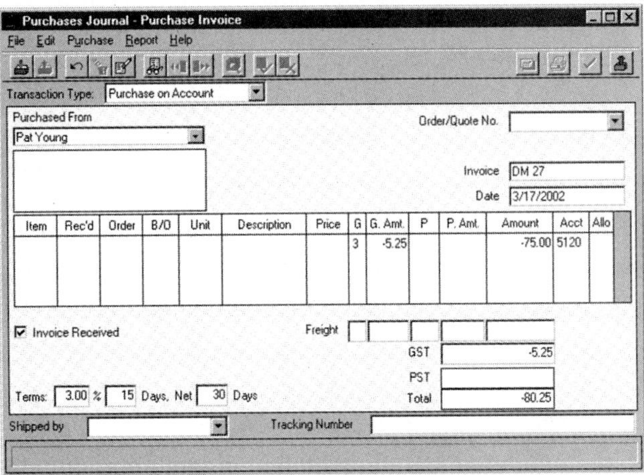

Review the entry.

23. Click on the Purchases Journal **Report** menu; then click on Display Purchases Journal Entry. Review the journal entry for accuracy, noting any errors. Note that the program has automatically debited the Accounts Payable account through its integration feature.

24. Close the Purchases Journal Entry window; then make any editing corrections required.

Post the entry.

25. After verifying that the journal entry is correct, click on the Post icon to post this transaction. A blank Purchases Journal dialogue box is displayed, ready for additional Purchases Journal transactions to be recorded. Close the Purchases Journal.

How to record a purchases discount

26. On March 25, 2002, issued cheque No. 437 to Pat Young in the amount of $208 in payment of invoice No. 796 ($294.25), dated March 15, less debit memorandum No. 27 ($80.25), less 3 percent discount ($6).

How to record a cash payment to a credit vendor

New to Chapter 10

27. Open the Payments Journal dialogue box by double-clicking on the Payments Journal icon. Click on the arrow button to the right of the **To the order of** text box; click on Pat Young; then press the TAB key. Enter `437` into the **No.** text box; then press the TAB key. (The program has offered a default cheque number of 435 which is the next cheque number in the program's automatic cheque numbering sequence. However, since certain cash payments are recorded in the general journal and the cheques used are not recorded in the payments journal, the cheque number needs to be advanced to the next cheque number in The Mars Company's chequebook.) Enter `03/25/02` into the **Date** text box; then press the TAB key. The 112.00 amount for invoice No. 789 will be highlighted. Press the DELETE key; then press the TAB key. The Mars Company is not paying invoice No. 789. The –2.25 discount taken for debit memorandum 27 will be highlighted. Press the TAB key five times to accept –2.25, –78.00, 8.25, and 286.00 in the **Discount Taken and Payment Amt.** text columns. Your screen should look like this:

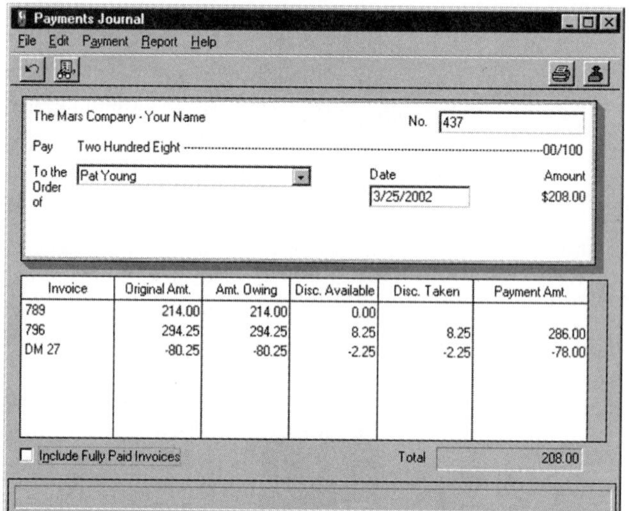

How to review a payments journal entry

Error correction prior to posting is covered on page 462.

28. Before posting this transaction, you need to verify that the transaction data are correct by reviewing the journal entry. To review the entry, click on the Payments Journal **Report** menu; then click on Display Payments Journal Entry. The journal entry representing the data you have recorded in the Payments Journal dialogue box is displayed. Review the journal entry for accuracy, noting any errors. Note that the program has automatically debited the Accounts Payable account and credited the Cash account and the Purchases Discounts account through its integration feature.

29. Close the Payments Journal Entry window; then make any editing corrections required.

How to post a payments journal entry

30. After verifying that the journal entry is correct, click on the Post icon to post this transaction. A blank Payments Journal dialogue box is displayed, ready for additional Payments Journal transactions to be recorded. Close the Payments Journal dialogue box.

How to display and print a Customer Aged Detail report

31. Click on the Company Window **Report** menu; then click on Customer Aged. The Customer Aged Report Options dialogue box will appear, asking you to define the information you want displayed. Click on the **Detail** option button; click on the **Select All** button; then click on the **OK** button. Click on the Customer Aged Detail **File** menu; then click on Print to print the report.

How to display and print a Vendor Aged Detail report

32. Close the Customer Aged Detail window; click on the Company Window **Report** menu; then click on Vendor Aged. The Vendor Aged Report Options dialogue box will appear, asking you to define the information you want displayed. Click on the **Detail** option button; click on the **Select All** button; then click on the **OK** button. Click on the Vendor Aged Detail **File** menu; then click on Print to print the report.

Print reports.

33. Close the Vendor Aged Detail window, then print the following reports:
    a. General journal (By posting date, All ledger entries, Start: 03/01/02, Finish: 03/31/02)
    b. General ledger report (Start: 03/01/02, Finish: 03/31/02, Select All)

    Note that, when you check the **All ledger entries** checkbox in the General Journal Options dialogue box, all transactions recorded in the Sales, Receipts, Purchases, and Payments Journals are reflected in the General Journal report.

    Review your printed reports. If you have made an error in a posted journal entry, see Part C of Appendix B for information on how to correct the error.

Exit from the program.

34. Click on the Company Window **File** menu; then click on Exit to end the current work session and return to your Windows desktop.

Complete the report transmittal.

35. Complete The Mars Company Report Transmittal located in Appendix A of your *Study Guide with Working Papers.*

Part B: Computerized Accounting Instructions for Abby's Toy House (Problem 10A-4)

Note: The date for the computerized version of 10A-4 is 2004.

Open the company data files

1. Start Windows; insert your Student Data Files disk into disk drive A or B; then double-click on the CA-Simply Accounting icon. The CA-Simply Accounting Open File dialogue box will appear.
2. Enter the following path into the **Open file name** text box:
    - `a:\abby.asc` (if you are storing your student data files on the disk in drive A)
3. Click on the **Open** button; enter `03/31/04` into the **Session** text box; then click on the **OK** button. Click on the **OK** button in response to the message "The date entered is more than one week past your previous **Session** date of 03/01/04." The Company Window for Abby will appear.

Add your name to the company name

4. Click on the Company Window **Setup** menu; then click on Company Information. The Company Information dialogue box will appear. Insert your name in place of the text "Your Name" in the **Name** text box. Click on the **OK** button to return to the Company Window.

Record transactions.

5. Record the following transactions, using the General, Sales, Receipts, Purchases, and Payments Journals:

2004		
March	1	Abby Ellen invested $8,000 in the toy store.
	1	Paid three months' rent in advance, cheque No. 1, $3,000 plus GST.
	2	Purchased merchandise from Earl Miller Company on account, $4,000 plus GST, invoice No. 410, terms 2/10, n/30.
	3	Sold merchandise to Bill Burton on account, $1,000 plus GST, invoice No. 1, terms 2/10 n/30.
	6	Sold merchandise to Jim Rex on account, $700 plus GST, invoice No. 2, terms 2/10 n/30.
	9	Purchased merchandise from Earl Miller Co. on account, $1,200 plus GST, invoice No. 415, terms 2/10, n/30.

9 Sold merchandise to Bill Burton on account, $600 plus GST, invoice No. 3, terms 2/10, n/30.
9 Paid cleaning service $300 plus GST, cheque No. 2. Enter this as a purchase with payment transaction. Select <one-time vendor>. Use Mar 09 as invoice date.
10 Jim Rex returned merchandise that cost $300 (plus GST) to Abby's Toy House. Abby issued credit memorandum No. 1 to Jim Rex for $321.
11 Purchased merchandise from Minnie Katz on account, $4,000 plus GST, invoice No. 311, terms 1/15, n/60.
12 Issued cheque No. 3 to Earl Miller Co. in the amount of $4,200 in payment of invoice No. 410 ($4,280), dated March 2, less 2 percent discount ($80).
13 Sold $1,300 + GST worth of toy merchandise for cash. Enter as a sale with payment transaction, invoice No. 4.
13 Paid salaries, $600, cheque No. 4.
14 Returned merchandise to Minnie Katz in the amount of $1,000 plus GST; Abby's Toy House issued debit memorandum No. 1 to Minnie Katz.
15 Sold merchandise for $4,000 cash plus GST, invoice No. 5.
16 Received cheque No. 9823 from Jim Rex in the amount of $420 in payment of invoice No. 2 ($749), dated March 6, less credit memorandum No. 1 ($321), less 2 percent discount ($8).
16 Received cheque No. 4589 from Bill Burton in the amount of $1,070 in payment of invoice No. 1, dated March 3.
16 Sold toy merchandise to Amy Rose on account, $4,000 plus GST, invoice No. 6, terms 2/10, n/30.
21 Purchased delivery truck on account from Sam Katz Garage, $3,000 plus GST, invoice No. 111, (no discount).
22 Sold to Bill Burton merchandise on account, $900 plus GST, invoice No. 7, terms 2/10, n/30.
23 Issued cheque No. 5 to Minnie Katz in the amount of $3,180 in payment of invoice No. 311 ($4,280), dated March 11, less debit memorandum No. 1 ($1,070), less 1 percent discount ($30).
24 Sold toy merchandise on account to Amy Rose, $1,100 plus GST, invoice No. 8, terms 2/10, n/30.
25 Purchased toy merchandise, $600 plus GST, cheque No. 6. Enter as a purchase with payment transaction, invoice No. 1202.
27 Purchased toy merchandise from Woody Smith on account, $4,800 plus GST, invoice No. 211, terms 2/10, n/30.
28 Received cheque No. 4598 from Bill Burton in the amount of $945 in payment of invoice No. 7 ($963), dated March 22, less 2 percent discount ($18).
28 Received cheque No. 3217 from Amy Rose in the amount of $1,155 in payment of invoice No. 8, dated March 24, less 2 percent discount ($22).
28 Abby invested an additional $5,000 in the business.
29 Purchased merchandise from Earl Miller Co., $1,400 plus GST, invoice No. 436, terms 2/10, n/30.
30 Issued cheque No. 7 to the Earl Miller Co. in the amount of $1,470 in payment of invoice No. 436 ($1,498), dated March 29, less 2 percent discount ($28).
30 Sold merchandise to Bonnie Flow Company on account, $3,000 plus GST, invoice No. 9, terms 2/10, n/30.

Print reports.

6. Print the following reports:
   a. Customer Aged report (Detail, Select All)
   b. Vendor Aged report (Detail, Select All)
   c. General journal (By posting date, All ledger entries, Start: 03/01/04, Finish: 03/31/04).
   d. General ledger report (Start: 03/01/04, Finish: 03/31/04, Select All).

   Review your printed reports. If you have made an error in a posted journal entry, see Part C of Appendix B at the back of this book for information on how to correct the error.

Exit from the program.

7. Click on the Company Window **File** menu; then click on Exit to end the current work session and return to your Windows desktop.

Complete the report transmittal.

8. Complete Abby's Toy House Report Transmittal located in Appendix A of your *Study Guide with Working Papers*.

The Synoptic (Combined) Journal

11

The Big Picture

◆

The Eldorado Computer Centre continues to grow in sales and profit. Tony Freedman met one of his objectives by keeping accurate detailed reports in the specialized journals. However, he found the use of so many specialized journals increased his accounting time significantly. It was just not efficient. This month he decided to try a different specialized journal that he hopes will help him accomplish both objectives.

The combined journal replaces the use of all special journals and the general journal. It is similar to an accounting worksheet and can be used in a spreadsheet format on computer. Since Freedman is the only one who handles the day-to-day accounting for the business, he can tailor this journal to his exact business needs.

In this chapter you will learn to use a combined journal. You will also learn the difference between keeping the books using the cash basis of accounting, the modified cash basis, or the accrual basis of accounting. Many businesses will use the cash basis if they operate as a service company offering no credit and handling no inventory. Freedman keeps his books under the accrual system, since he has inventory for resale, offers credit terms to his customers, and makes purchases for the computer centre on credit himself. No system is better than the others. The best choice simply depends on the nature of the business.

Chapter Objectives

- Defining methods of accounting: accrual basis, cash basis, and modified cash basis (pp. 468–469)
- Recording, journalizing, and posting transactions for a synoptic journal of a professional service company using a modified cash basis of accounting (pp. 469–472)
- Recording, journalizing, and posting transactions for a synoptic journal of a merchandising company using the accrual basis of accounting (p. 475–479)

In the first ten chapters of this text, we have used general journals and special journals in recording business transactions. Over the years many students have asked how to set up journals for starting their own small businesses. They have felt that the general journals were too simple and the special journals were too detailed. In dealing with this topic, this chapter is broken down into two units:

- Learning Unit 11-1 Journal for a dentist, Dr. Gail Walensa—a professional service company that uses a modified cash system
- Learning Unit 11-2 Synoptic journal for Art's Wholesale Clothing Company—a merchandising company that uses an accrual approach

From these two presentations, students should be able to take accounting theory and procedures and apply them to their own business record-keeping needs.

Before we start the first unit, however, we need to talk about the difference between the cash basis of accounting and the accrual basis of accounting.

Accrual accounting
- Revenue is recorded when earned.
- Expenses are recorded when incurred.

Cash accounting
- Cash receipts are recorded when received.
- Cash payments are recorded when paid.

In the chapters so far we have been using the **accrual basis of accounting**, which is based on the *matching principle*. The matching principle says that you record revenue when it is earned (not when the money actually comes in), and you record expenses when they are incurred in producing revenue (not when they are paid).

In the **cash basis of accounting**, revenue is recorded when cash is received, and expenses are recorded when they are paid.

Companies choose the accrual basis because they want to show earned revenue along with the expenses that were incurred to earn that revenue. They can do so with the accrual basis but not always with the cash basis. However, service companies sometimes use the cash basis because it is simpler and more convenient, and provides enough information for the decisions they need to make.

Let's look at the difference between the accrual and cash bases with the following example. John Mills earned real estate commissions of $100,000, of which he received $60,000 in cash. Expenses were $25,000, of which $10,000 was paid in cash.

Many service companies will use the cash method if they have no inventories.

Comparison of Cash Basis with Accrual Basis for the Month of July 2001

Cash Basis		*Accrual Basis*	
Revenue (received)	$60,000	Revenue (earned)	$100,000
Expenses (paid)	10,000	Expenses (incurred)	25,000
Net income	$50,000	Net income	$ 75,000

Note that net income differs according to which system is used. Keep in mind that all revenue and expenses will show up eventually if the cash basis is used, but not in this accounting period.

Now let's look at the recordkeeping needs of a dentist, Dr. Gail Walensa, who wants to use a cash-basis system of accounting because of its simplicity and convenience.

LEARNING UNIT 11-1

Synoptic Journal: A Modified Cash System for a Service Company

Dentists can't charge the entire cost of dental equipment to the year in which it was purchased for cash.

Dr. Walensa's accountant has informed her that keeping strictly to a cash-basis system is difficult to do. The reason is that, because of tax regulations, Dr. Walensa's accountant would be distorting financial reports by using a strictly cash system. She feels that the best system for a dentist is a combination of the cash and accrual methods. This combination is known as the **modified-cash-basis** or **hybrid** method. Under this method Dr. Walensa will record professional fees only when cash is received and record expenses only when paid in cash. To satisfy Revenue Canada, an adjustment for amounts accrued at year-end is required before financial statements are prepared (not illustrated here). The following exceptions, however, are an attempt to reflect income clearly and minimize distortion of the financial reports:

Only the supplies *used up* are shown as an expense.

1. Long-lived assets (equipment, building, etc.) are treated the same under cash and accrual accounting. This means that the amount paid for equipment in one year may not be treated as an expense of just that period; Dr. Walensa will be amortizing or allocating the cost of her dental equipment over a period of years.
2. Insurance premiums and purchases of a large amount of supplies are treated the same under cash and accrual accounting. This means that the amount consumed or used up is shown as an expense in the current year and that the amount on hand is carried over into the next accounting period.

These exceptions require adjusting entries (which we saw before under accrual accounting) when the modified cash basis is used.

Two types of personal services might use a modified cash basis. They are:

1. Professional services—lawyers, doctors, dentists, accountants, and so on
2. Business services—real estate, insurance, software support, and so on

CHART OF ACCOUNTS

The chart of accounts for Dr. Walensa is provided in Figure 11-1. Note that, unlike in a chart of accounts on the accrual basis, there are no categories for Accounts Receivable, Accounts Payable, or Salaries Payable (these are added at year-end by the accountant). This chart of accounts does have titles for handling the exceptions (for example, Accumulated Amortization, Prepaid Insurance, etc.). There is no Supplies account under assets, since Dr. Walensa is not buying a large amount of supplies, and thus all can be shown as Dental Supplies Expense without distorting the financial reports.

The transactions that occurred for the month of November are listed on page 470. We will show you the recording of these transactions in the **synoptic journal** (or **combined journal**)—a special journal that will replace the general journal and save journalizing and posting labour. The synoptic journal has the same basic features as the other special journals that we introduced in Chapters 9 and 10. Remember, each business will design the headings of the synoptic journal to fit its individual needs. It is not unusual to find such journals with a total of 24 columns, or even more—although we will be keeping things at a more manageable size in this textbook. Accounts that are used most often are the ones that should have special columns. This will save time when journalizing and posting.

Another important point is that, to keep things simple, GST is not included in the earlier examples in this text, but is covered at the end of Learning Unit 11-2.

FIGURE 11-1
Chart of Accounts

Dr. Walensa
Chart of Accounts

Assets
111 Cash
113 Petty Cash Fund
131 Prepaid Insurance
141 Office Furniture
142 Accumulated Amortization, Office Furniture
151 Dental Equipment
152 Accumulated Amortization, Dental Equipment
161 Auto
162 Accumulated Amortization, Auto

Liabilities
211 Due to Receiver General
212 Other Payroll Deductions Payable
213 Notes Payable

Owner's Equity
311 G. Walensa, Capital
312 G. Walensa, Withdrawals
313 Income Summary

Revenue
411 Professional Fees

Expenses
511 Automobile Expense
512 Rent Expense
513 Salaries Expense
514 Telephone Expense
515 Amortization Expense, Office Furniture
516 Amortization Expense, Dental Equipment
517 Amortization Expense, Auto
518 Miscellaneous Expense
519 Insurance Expense
520 Dental Supplies Expense
521 Payroll Tax Expense

Example of a modified cash system

Transactions for Dr. Walensa

2001

Nov.	1	Paid $700 office rent for November, cheque No. 61.
	1	Received cheques totalling $3,000 from patients for dental work.
	4	Paid telephone bill, $80, cheque No. 62.
	4	Issued cheque No. 63 to Bill Blan Insurance Agency for premium on insurance for three years, $900.
	7	Purchased dental supplies from Roe Suppliers, $450, cheque No. 64.
	8	Received cheques from patients, $1,600.
	8	Calculated current cash balance.
	11	Issued cheque No. 65 to Moe Gas for automobile expenses charged during October, $280.
	11	Dr. Walensa withdrew $500 for personal use, cheque No. 66.
	14	Issued cheque No. 67 to V. P. Suppliers Company for dental supplies charged during October, $650.
	15	Paid office salaries for the period November 1 to November 15, $3,000, cheque No. 68.
	15	Cash receipts from patients totalled $2,800 for the week.
	15	Calculated current cash balance.
	19	Collected $800 from insurance companies for patients' accounts.
	21	Purchased dental supplies from J. Labs, $500, cheque No. 69.
	22	Cash receipts for the week totalled $2,900.
	22	Calculated current cash balance.
	27	Issued cheque No. 70 for charitable contributions, $300.
	27	Purchased dental supplies from J. Labs, $300, cheque No. 71.
	28	Received cheques from patients' insurance companies totalling $3,300.

29 Paid office salaries for the period November 15 to November 30, $2,250, cheque No. 72.
30 Calculated current cash balance and cross-footed journal.

RECORDING TRANSACTIONS IN THE SYNOPTIC JOURNAL

The synoptic journal for Dr. Walensa is shown in Figure 11-2. Note that the bank balance can be calculated at any time. For example, in the explanation column, note the beginning balance of $9,500. On November 8 the current balance was calculated as follows:

Beginning balance	$ 9,500
+ Deposits	4,600
– Cheques written	2,130
Ending balance	$11,970 (Recorded in explanation column)

As we saw with special journals before, this synoptic journal is proved in the following way:

Proving the journal

	Dr.	Cr.
Cash	$14,400	$ 9,910
Sundry	8,010	
Professional Fees		14,400
Dental Supplies Expense	1,900	
	$24,310	$24,310

FIGURE 11-2
The Synoptic Journal

DR. WALENSA
SYNOPTIC JOURNAL

Month: November

Cash Deposits Dr.	Cheques Cr.	Chq. No.	Date 2001		Explanation	Post Ref.	Sundry Dr.	Sundry Cr.	Professional Fees Cr.	Dental Supplies Expense Dr.
					Cash balance *9,500*					
	700 00	61	Nov.	1	Rent Expense	512	700 00			
3 000 00				1	Professional Fees	✗			3 000 00	
	80 00	62		4	Telephone Expense	514	80 00			
	900 00	63		4	Prepaid Insurance	131	900 00			
	450 00	64		7	Roe Supplies	✗				450 00
1 600 00				8	Professional Fees *11,970*	✗			1 600 00	
	280 00	65		11	Auto Expense	511	280 00			
	500 00	66		11	G. Walensa, Withdr.	312	500 00			
	650 00	67		14	V.P. Suppliers	✗				650 00
	3 000 00	68		15	Salaries Expense	513	3 000 00			
2 800 00				15	Professional Fees *10,340*	✗			2 800 00	
800 00				19	Professional Fees	✗			800 00	
	500 00	69		21	J. Labs	✗				500 00
2 900 00				22	Professional Fees *13,540*	✗			2 900 00	
	300 00	70		27	Miscellaneous Expense	518	300 00			
	300 00	71		27	J. Labs	✗				300 00
3 300 00				28	Professional Fees	✗			3 300 00	
	2 250 00	72		29	Salaries Expense *13,990*	513	2 250 00			
14 400 00	9 910 00						8 010 00		14 400 00	1 900 00
(111)	(111)						(X)		(411)	(520)

$24,310 = $24,310

Memorandum records can be used in a modified cash system.

Posting the Synoptic Journal

Since this is a modified cash system, there are no subsidiary ledgers for accounts receivable or accounts payable. Companies using a modified cash basis may keep information about any receivables or payables in an informal memorandum record until cash is received or paid. During the month, items entered into the Sundry column can be updated in the general ledger. At the end of the month the totals of Cash, Professional Fees, and Dental Supplies Expense would be posted to the general ledger. The account numbers are shown at the bottom of the columns of the synoptic journal to show that the totals were posted. The X means that no posting is necessary. The total of the Sundry column is not posted, because the various items making up the total are posted individually.

Recording Payroll Deductions and Employer's Payroll Tax Expense

Back in Chapters 7 and 8 we studied payroll, with the payroll register recording gross pay, deductions, and net pay. From the payroll register a general journal entry is prepared to record the payroll. We also discussed using a general journal to record the employer's payroll tax expense before it is paid (for CPP and EI). The record-keeping involved in paying an employee will be quite similar in a synoptic journal using the cash-basis method, but recording the employer's payroll tax expense will change.

Why? In the cash-basis method of accounting, the owner's share of CPP as well as of EI will not be recorded until paid. Under accrual accounting, we recorded them when incurred, not when paid.

Let's look at the partially completed synoptic journal on page 473 and explain each entry. For simplicity, we are ignoring the remittance requirements and monthly reports that we covered in the payroll chapters.

A. Bill Smith's gross salary of $500 is recorded as a salary expense, and the deductions for income tax, CPP, and EI are listed as liabilities until the employer makes the remittance. Note that the cheque is written for $375 (net pay). The same procedure is followed for Joe Ring.

B. On June 9 the remittance to the Receiver General is assumed made. This means the employer pays the CPP and EI for the employees as well as the matching share along with the income tax deducted from the employees' paycheques.

Note: The payroll tax expense is now being recorded for the employer's share of CPP and EI, since it is now being *paid*. Note that the cheque amount is for $264.80, which includes the following:

Income tax payable	140.00
CPP payable	24.00
Payroll tax expense — CPP	24.00
EI payable	32.00
Payroll tax expense — EI ($32.00 × 1.4)	44.80
	264.80

SYNOPTIC JOURNAL

	Royal Bank							Sundry				Payroll Deductions		
	Deposits Dr.	Cheques Cr.	Chq. No.	Date 2001		Account or Explanation	Post Ref.	Dr.	Cr.	Professional Fees Cr.	Salary Expense Dr.	Income Tax Payable Cr.	CPP Payable Cr.	EI Payable Cr.
(A)		375 00	33	May	5	Bill Smith	✗				500 00	90 00	15 00	20 00
		229 00	34		5	Joe Ring	✗				300 00	50 00	9 00	12 00
(B)		264 80	50	June	9	Receiver General								
						Tax Payable	211	140 00						
						CPP Payable	212	24 00						
						EI Payable	213	32 00						
						Payroll Tax Exp	521	68 80*						

*Calculated as [($24 ×1) + ($32×1.4)]

The end result is to reduce the liabilities owed as well as record the employer's share of CPP and EI as payroll tax expense. When the remittance is actually made to the Receiver General for Canada, the following entry is made in the Synoptic:

	Dr.	*Cr.*
Income tax payable	XXX.XX	
CPP payable	XX.XX	
EI payable	XX.XX	
Payroll tax expense	XX.XX	
Cash		XXX.XX

In summary, sometimes companies will record the expense portion of CPP and EI when the *payroll* is paid, instead of when the remittance is made. If this is the case, then, when the remittance is made, the Synoptic will record this entry:

	Dr.	*Cr.*
Income tax payable	XXX.XX	
CPP payable	XX.XX	
EI payable	XX.XX	
Cash		XXX.XX

LEARNING UNIT 11-1 REVIEW

AT THIS POINT you should be able to:

- Explain the modified cash basis of accounting. (p. 469)
- Journalize transactions in a synoptic journal. (pp. 470–471)
- Calculate the current bank balance of a synoptic journal. (pp. 470–471)
- Prove a synoptic journal. (p. 471)
- Explain how to record payroll as well as payroll tax expense in a synoptic journal. (pp. 472–474)

SELF-REVIEW QUIZ 11-1

(The form you need is on page 11-1 of the *Study Guide with Working Papers.*)

Answer true or false to the following:

1. A modified cash system will have only one exception, long-lived assets, in the adjustment process.
2. A cash-basis system in a chart of accounts usually has titles for Due to Receiver General and Payroll Deductions Payable.
3. Headings of synoptic journals can be modified to meet the needs of the user.
4. The cash balance can be calculated easily in a synoptic journal.
5. Payroll tax expense will be recorded when the remittance is made to the Receiver General.

Solution to Self-Review Quiz 11-1

1. False **2.** False **3.** True **4.** True **5.** True

LEARNING UNIT 11-2

Synoptic Journal for Art's Wholesale Clothing Company

Back in Chapters 9 and 10 we developed the sales journal, cash receipts journal, purchases journal, cash payments journal, and general journal for Art's Wholesale Clothing Company. Many small businesses that are concerned with saving journalizing, recording, and posting labour, however, are not concerned about division of labour (having a different bookkeeper working on each special journal), since they have only one bookkeeper. Such businesses may want the advantages provided by special journals but would like to reduce the number of journals needed. This unit will develop a synoptic journal, a book of original entry, that dispenses with the special journals, yet gains their advantages in journalizing, recording, and posting, for a company that uses an accrual accounting approach. (In order to focus on the basics of the synoptic journal, payroll details are not described at this point.)

Our goal in this unit is to place all the special journals for Art's Wholesale in the following synoptic journal:

SYNOPTIC JOURNAL																
Month: April																Page 1
		Cheque	Post	Sundry		Cash		Accts. Rec.		Accts. Pay.		Sales	Sales Disc.	Purchases	Pur. Disc.	
Date	Explanation	No.	Ref.	Dr.	Cr.	Dr.	Cr.	Dr.	Cr.	Dr.	Cr.	Cr.	Dr.	Dr.	Cr.	

Note that, since Art's business uses *accrual* accounting, we now have columns for accounts receivable and accounts payable.

If Art decided to use the synoptic journal, he and the accountant would go over the chart of accounts. They would be concerned with setting up columns in the synoptic journal for accounts in which transactions would occur frequently. On the basis of their analysis, Art and the accountant agreed to set up the following special columns in a synoptic journal.

- **Cash Dr.** This column records increases in cash.
- **Cash Cr.** This column records decreases in cash.
- **Accounts Receivable Dr.** This column records amounts to be received from sales on account.
- **Accounts Receivable Cr.** This column records amounts paid by customers from past sales on account.
- **Accounts Payable Dr.** This column reflects amounts paid to creditors.
- **Accounts Payable Cr.** This column reflects amounts owed to creditors.
- **Sales Cr.** This column records all sales made for cash or on account.
- **Sales Discounts Dr.** This column records the amounts of discounts taken by customers.
- **Purchases Dr.** All purchases of merchandise for resale are recorded in this column.
- **Purchases Discounts Cr**. This column records the amounts of discounts Art receives by paying for purchases before the discount period expires.
- **Sundry Dr., Cr.** These two columns record transactions that do not occur very frequently. If a transaction occurs and no special columns are set up to record part or all of it, it can be recorded in the Sundry columns.

Figure 11-3 shows the completed synoptic journal for the month of April for Art's Wholesale Clothing Company (we will go over the recordings and postings in a moment).

Checking the accuracy of the synoptic journal

The synoptic journal can be proved as follows:

Account Title	Dr.	Cr.
Sundry	$ 6750 00	$ 8700 00
Cash	14324 00	6994 00
Accounts Receivable	6500 00	4400 00
Accounts Payable	4800 00	11930 00
Sales		8600 00
Sales Discounts	76 00	
Purchases	8180 00	
Purchases Discounts		6 00
Totals	$40630 00	$40630 00

FIGURE 11-3
Synoptic Journal Completed

ART'S WHOLESALE CLOTHING COMPANY
SYNOPTIC JOURNAL

Date		Explanation	Chq. No.	Post Ref.	Sundry Dr.	Sundry Cr.	Cash Dr.	Cash Cr.
2001 Apr.	1	Art Newner, Cap.		311		8000 00	8000 00	
	2	Prepaid Insurance	1	116	900 00			900 00
	3	Hal's Clothing		✔				
	3	Freight-In, Abby Blake		514 / ✔	50 00			
	4	Equip., Joe Francis		121 / ✔	4000 00			
	4	Hal's Clothing		✔			784 00	
	6	Thorpe Co.		✔				
	6	Bevans Co.		✔				
	7	J. Francis Co.	2	✔				4000 00
	7	J. Sullivan Co.		✔				
	9	Purchases	3	✘				800 00
	9	Pur. R&A, Thorpe Co.		514 / ✔		200 00		
	12	Thorpe Co.	4	✔				594 00
	12	Sales R&A, Bevans Co.		412 / ✔	600 00			
	12	Abby Blake Co.		✔				
	15	Cash Sales		✘			900 00	
	16	Bevans Co.		✔			980 00	
	18	Roe Co.		✔				
	22	Roe Co.		✔			1960 00	
	24	Roe Co.		✔				
	25	Supplies, J. Sullivan		115 / ✔	500 00			
	27	Store Equipment		121		500 00	500 00	
	28	Salaries Expense	5	611	700 00			700 00
	28	Mel's Department Store		✔				
	29	Mel's Department Store		✔				
	30	Cash Sales		✘			1200 00	
		Totals			6750 00	8700 00	14324 00	6994 00
					(X)	(X)	(111)	(111)

Recording and Posting the Synoptic Journal

The recording and posting rules we learned for Art's special journals will hold true for the synoptic journal. Here are some key points:

1. **✔** Record in accounts receivable or accounts payable subsidiary ledgers daily.
2. **Sundry** Update the general ledger account on a daily basis. Use the ledger account number as a posting reference.
3. **X** in the Post. Ref. column indicates no posting, since the total is posted at the end of the month. An X below the total means that the total of the column is not posted.

End of Month

SJ1 (Synoptic Journal, page 1) will be placed in the Post. Ref. column of the ledger account, when information from the journal is updated in ledger.

The total of each column (except Sundry) will be posted to the general ledger at the end of the month. Note that the account number from the ledger is placed at the bottom of the column in the synoptic journal, indicating that the total was posted to that account.

Note the following when a synoptic journal is used:

1. Charge *and* cash sales are recorded in the sales column.
2. Purchases returns, sales returns, etc., are recorded in Sundry, since no general journal is used with a synoptic journal.
3. Adjusting and closing entries will be recorded in the Sundry columns.

Month: April

Accounts Receivable		Accounts Payable		Sales	Sales Discounts	Purchases	Purchases Discounts
Dr.	Cr.	Dr.	Cr.	Cr.	Dr.	Dr.	Cr.
800 00				800 00			
			5050 00			5000 00	
			4000 00				
	800 00				16 00		
			800 00			800 00	
1600 00				1600 00			
		4000 00					
			980 00			980 00	
						800 00	
		200 00					
		600 00					6 00
	600 00						
			600 00			600 00	
				900 00			
	1000 00				20 00		
2000 00				2000 00			
	2000 00				40 00		
500 00				500 00			
			500 00				
900 00				900 00			
700 00				700 00			
				1200 00			
6500 00	4400 00	4800 00	11930 00	8600 00	76 00	8180 00	6 00
(113)	(113)	(211)	(211)	(411)	(413)	(511)	(512)

Adjusting and closing entries could be recorded in the Sundry columns of a synoptic journal.

It is possible to use an electronic spreadsheet running on a computer to "build" a synoptic journal in computer form. This idea is workable but of doubtful value since a variety of low cost full-featured accounting programs are available. Many small businesses use *Simply Accounting for Windows* (illustrated throughout this text).

Whether Art's Wholesale uses a synoptic journal or a set of special journals, the schedule of accounts receivable and accounts payable will be the same, as will the trial balance.

To sum up, the synoptic journal is an option for small businesses that do not have many transactions. Lawyers, doctors, dentists, and other professionals may use a synoptic journal, which may be modified in many ways to suit their individual needs.

As the business grows, the volume of transactions may increase, possibly creating the need for more-specialized journals or a computerized set of records rather than just the synoptic journal. For example, if a company adds bookkeepers to its accounting department, management must be prepared to provide a system of dividing the work to be done. This division of labour may play an important part in determining the types of special journals that are needed.

FIGURE 11-4
Synoptic Journal with Sales Tax and GST

SYNOPTIC JOURNAL

Date 2001		Explanation	Chq. No.	Post Ref.	Sundry Dr.	Sundry Cr.	Cash Dr.	Cash Cr.	Accounts Receivable Dr.	Accounts Receivable Cr.
May	1	Bill Jones		✔					116 00	
May	3	Alice Smith		✔					464 00	
May	5	Alice Smith—Pmt. = 2%	376	✔			456 00			464 00
May	7	Birchmount Co.		✔						
May	9	Cooper & Co.		✔						
May	18	Cooper & Co.—Pmt. = 2%		✔				6300 00		
		Month-end totals					456 00	6300 00	580 00	464 00

Recorded immediately to the accounts receivable or accounts payable ledgers.

Totals posted at the end of the month to the general ledger.

Month-end totals

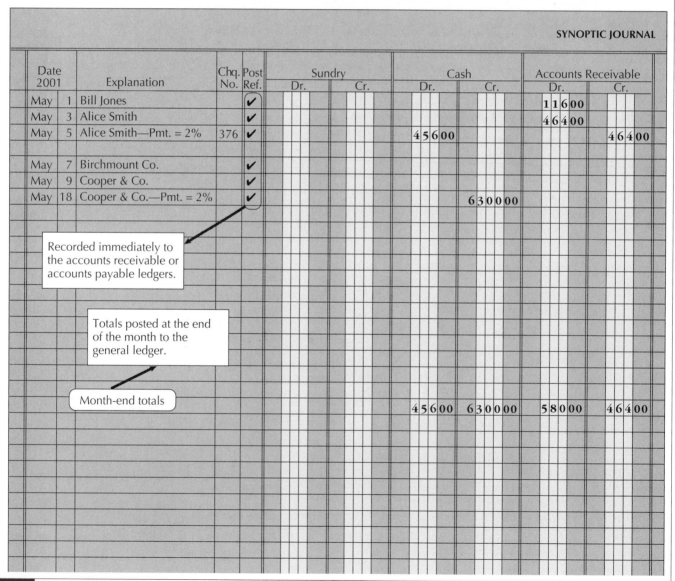

Before stating the objectives of this unit, let's look at a sample of how a synoptic journal might look if it included either Provincial Sales Tax Payable and GST Payable or HST Payable. In Figure 11-4, notice that at the end of the month we will still post to the general ledger the totals of Accounts Receivable, Sales, Sales Tax Payable, and GST Payable. In provinces where HST is used, HST Payable would replace the two columns, Sales Tax Payable and GST Payable. Keep in mind that GST Payable, HST Payable, and Sales Tax Payable are liabilities shown on the balance sheet. Also bear in mind that the principles of recording PST and GST/HST have not changed at all from Chapters 9 and 10 where we covered them in detail. The main difference is that now we are including both collections and remittances in the same journal.

Another point worth stressing is that in the modern business world there is less need to study the large synoptic journal with a lot of intensity. If a large synoptic journal is necessary because of complex transactions (or a large volume of transactions) a computer and some inexpensive software perhaps provide a better solution. Remember that a knowledge of manual bookkeeping and accounting procedures means that a computerized system can be more useful and efficient.

If a retail company has many sales returns and allowances as well as purchases, the synoptic journal heading in Figure 11-4 (starting on page 478) could be designed.

Month: April

Accounts Payable		GST		Sales	Sales Discounts	Purchases	Purchases Discounts	Sales Tax
Dr.	Cr.	Dr.	Cr.	Cr.	Dr.	Dr.	Cr.	Cr.
			7.00	100.00				9.00
			28.00	400.00				36.00
					8.00			
	1,177.00	77.00				1,100.00		
	6,420.00	420.00				6,000.00		
6,420.00							120.00	
6,420.00	7,597.00	497.00	35.00	500.00	8.00	7,100.00	120.00	45.00

LEARNING UNIT 11-2 REVIEW

AT THIS POINT YOU should be able to:

- Journalize transactions in the synoptic journal for a merchandise company. (pp. 477–479)
- Explain how to record and post the synoptic journal. (p. 477)
- Compare special journals (cash payments, receipts, etc.) and the synoptic journal. (p. 479)
- Explain how sales tax and GST/HST could be recorded in a synoptic journal. (p. 479)

SELF-REVIEW QUIZ 11-2

(The form you need is on page 11-1 of the *Study Guide with Working Papers.*)

On the basis of the synoptic journal presented in this unit, classify each statement below as true or false.

1. Synoptic journals are less efficient than other types of special journals.
2. The total of the Cash column is posted daily.
3. The total of the Sundry column is not posted.
4. The total of the Sales column is not posted.
5. All synoptic journals have the same headings.
6. Synoptic journals cannot be proved.
7. Subsidiary ledgers are posted from the cash column.
8. The synoptic journal is used for large companies.
9. A dentist could use a synoptic journal.
10. A lawyer will always use a synoptic journal.

Solution to Self-Review Quiz 11-2

1. False
2. False
3. True
4. False
5. False
6. False
7. False
8. False
9. True
10. False

Chapter Review

Summary of key points

Learning Unit 11-1

1. A company with inventory will not use the cash method.
2. The modified cash system is used because federal and provincial requirements make a strictly cash-basis system difficult to implement without distorting financial reports.
3. The modified cash system will require adjustments for amortization, insurance premiums, and large amounts of supplies purchased. Adjustments often will be recorded in the Sundry columns of the synoptic journal and additional adjustments can be made at year-end.
4. No accounts for accounts payable or accounts receivable are used in the chart of accounts for a modified cash system. Companies use memoranda to keep track of receivables or payables until money is received or paid.
5. The bank balance (cash balance) can be determined at any time when a synoptic journal is used.
6. A synoptic journal can be proved by cross-footing the totals to verify that total debits equal total credits.
7. The payroll tax expense for the employer using a cash-basis system is recorded when the remittance is made. In the cash-basis system no *liability* accounts exist for Due to Receiver General or other payroll taxes payable; you record them when *paid* as part of the remittance to the Receiver General.

Learning Unit 11-2

1. A synoptic journal for Art's Wholesale replaces the individual special journals (SJ, CRJ, PJ, CPJ, GJ).
2. Many small companies use a synoptic journal.
3. A synoptic journal on an accrual basis uses columns for accounts receivable and accounts payable. Subsidiary ledgers will be recorded during the month. The total of the Sundry columns is not posted.
4. Adjusting and closing entries will be recorded in the Sundry columns.

Key terms

Accrual accounting synoptic journal A special journal that combines the features of the sales, cash payments, cash receipts, purchases, and general journals (p. 468)

Accrual basis of accounting An accounting method in which revenue is recorded when earned, and expenses are recorded when incurred (p. 468)

Cash basis of accounting An accounting method in which revenue is recorded when cash is received, and expenses are recorded when they are paid (p. 468)

Modified-cash-basis method (hybrid) The accounting method that records revenue when cash is received, and expenses when they are paid. Adjustments to long-lived assets, as well as insurance premiums and amounts of supplies on hand, are required by provincial and federal laws so that financial reports will not be distorted. (p. 469)

Synoptic (combined) journal A special journal that combines the features of the sales, cash payments, cash receipts, purchases, and sometimes general journals. (p. 469)

Blueprint of a Typical Chart of Accounts for a Lawyer Using a Modified Cash Basis (Including Payroll)

	Assets		
No Accounts Receivable account	Royal Bank	111	
	Petty Cash	112	
	Office Supplies	113	
	Prepaid Insurance	114	
	Office Equipment	115	
	Accumulated Amortization, Office Equipment	116	
	Automobiles	117	
	Accumulated Amortization, Auto	118	
	Liabilities		
No Accounts Payable account	Income Tax Payable	211	
	CPP Payable	212	
	EI Payable	213	
	Bank Loan Payable	214	
	Owner's Equity		
	J. Smith, Capital	311	
	J. Smith, Withdrawals	312	
	Income Summary	313	
Recorded only when cash received →	**Revenue**		
	Professional Fees	411	
	Expenses		
	Amortization Expense, Office Equipment	511	For adjustments so financial reports will not be distorted (511–514)
	Amortization Expense, Auto	512	
	Insurance Expense	513	
	Office Supplies Expense	514	
	Dues	515	
	Postage	516	
	Payroll Tax Expense	517	→ Records the tax expense for the employer when the CPP, EI, and income tax are remitted
	Rent Expense	518	
	Salary Expense	519	
	Telephone Expense	520	
	Miscellaneous Expense	521	

Questions, Mini Exercises, Exercises, and Problems

Discussion Questions

1. All companies with inventory must use the cash basis of accounting. Agree or disagree.
2. Why does the strictly cash basis tend to distort financial reports?
3. List three adjustments that may result when using a modified cash system.
4. Explain how a company can change its method of accounting.

5. A modified cash system has an accounts receivable and an accounts payable ledger. Agree or disagree. Please support your answer.
6. Explain how a cash balance can be calculated during the month when using a synoptic journal.
7. How is a synoptic journal proved?
8. Explain why there are no accounts for Due to Receiver General or other payroll taxes payable in the chart of accounts in the cash basis method.
9. What purpose would an informal memorandum serve when dealing with accounts payable and accounts receivable in a modified cash system?
10. Explain when the Payroll Tax Expense account will be updated in a modified cash system.
11. Explain how using a synoptic journal for an accrual-basis company will aid in reducing the number of special journals needed.
12. "If a company is expanding, a synoptic journal could be efficient." Please respond.

Mini Exercises

(The forms you need are on page 11-1 of the *Study Guide with Working Papers.*)

Accounts Needing Adjustment

1. Which of the following titles may require adjusting entries when using the modified cash basis?

	Yes	*No*
Cash	______	______
Accounts Receivable	______	______
Equipment	______	______
Supplies	______	______
Accounts Payable	______	______
Salaries Payable	______	______
Accumulated Amortization	______	______
Prepaid Insurance	______	______

Payment of Payroll

2. Mel Blanc uses a modified-cash-basis system. His company's payroll records show deductions for income tax $280, CPP $36, and EI $46. Please record the necessary entry in the Sundry columns of the synoptic journal. (Only the Sundry columns are shown.)

Combined Journal Headings

3. Match the following partial list of column headings of Pete Moore's synoptic journal to the statements following the list. Use only one number for each letter.

1. Cash	Cr.
2. Accounts Payable	Cr.
3. Sales Discounts	Dr.
4. Sundry	Dr./Cr.
5. Sales	Cr.

______ **a.** Reflects amounts owed to creditors.
______ **b.** Records the amounts of discounts taken by customers.
______ **c.** Records transactions that do not occur very often.
______ **d.** Records sales made for cash or on account.
______ **e.** Records decreases in cash.

Recording in Subsidiary Ledgers

4. Indicate which of the following transactions would result in a recording in a subsidiary ledger. The company uses a synoptic journal with an accrual accounting approach.

a. Pete Daving invested $20,000 in the business.
b. Sold $300 worth of merchandise to French Co. on account.
c. Cash sales $200
d. Received half the amount owed by French from sales on account in **b**.

Exercises

(The forms you need are on page 11-2 of the *Study Guide with Working Papers*.)

Identifying adjustment titles for a modified cash system

11-1. In a modified cash system, which of the following titles may need adjustments?

- ◆ Cash
- ◆ Supplies
- ◆ Prepaid Insurance
- ◆ Equipment
- ◆ Bank Loan Payable
- ◆ A. Swan, Capital
- ◆ A. Swan, Withdrawals
- ◆ Commission Sales
- ◆ Salary Expense

Posting a synoptic journal using the accrual approach

11-2. Avon Company uses a synoptic journal with the following headings:

Sundry	Dr./Cr.
Accounts Receivable	Dr./Cr.
Accounts Payable	Dr./Cr.
Commission Sales	Cr.
Salary Expense	Dr.
Cash	Dr./Cr.

a. How can the balance of cash be determined at any point in the month?
b. Which column total will not be posted?
c. Do you think Avon Company has subsidiary ledgers? Please explain.
d. Which columns will be used to record the payment of advertising expense?

Preparing a chart of accounts for a modified cash system

11-3. Listed below are the accounts used by Dr. Jonson, who keeps his records on a strictly cash basis. As his accountant, which titles do you think could be added to use a modified cash system? Assume that a large amount of supplies is bought.

Cash; Bank Loan Payable; L. Jonson, Capital; L. Jonson, Withdrawals; Professional Fees; Auto Expense; Rent Expense; Office Furniture Expense; Insurance Expense; Medical Supplies Expense.

Explaining postings of a synoptic journal for a modified cash basis

11-4. Using the headings of the synoptic journal for Dr. Walensa (Figure 11-2), indicate when postings would occur.

2001
May 3 Al Henson invested $4,000 in the dental business.
8 Paid three months' insurance premiums, $1,200.
15 Received cheques from patients, $900.
19 Paid office salaries, $500.

Explaining recordings and postings of a synoptic journal using an accrual approach

11-5. Using the headings of the synoptic journal for Art's Wholesale (Figure 11-3), indicate when recordings and postings would occur.

2001
May 2 Joe Davis invested $12,000 in the business.
5 Bought $600 worth of merchandise for cash.
8 Cash sale, $600
19 Received $400 less a 3 percent discount from Alvie Corp. from past sale on account.

Group A Problems

(The forms you need are on pages 11-3 to 11-11 of the *Study Guide with Working Papers*.)

Journalizing transactions of a modified cash system in a synoptic journal

Check Figure
Cross-footing $18,040

11A-1. Peter Lovejoy, M.D., uses the following chart of accounts:

Chart of Accounts

Assets
111 Alberta Bank
113 Petty Cash
114 Prepaid Insurance
115 Medical Supplies
121 Medical Equipment
122 Accumulated Amortization, Medical Equipment
123 Office Furniture
124 Accumulated Amortization, Office Furniture
125 Auto
126 Accumulated Amortization, Auto

Liabilities
211 Bank Loan Payable

Owner's Equity
311 P. Lovejoy, Capital
312 P. Lovejoy, Withdrawals
313 Income Summary

Revenue
411 Professional Fees

Expenses
511 Rent Expense
512 Donation Expense
513 Salaries Expense
514 Medical Supplies Expense
515 Amortization Expense, Medical Equipment
516 Amortization Expense, Office Furniture
517 Amortization Expense, Automobile
518 Insurance Expense
519 Telephone Expense
610 Cleaning Expense
611 Miscellaneous Expense

The headings of the synoptic journal are as follows:

Page 1

Date	Explanation	Post Ref.	Sundry		Medical Supplies	Dr. Lovejoy, Withdrawals	Cleaning Expense	Prof. Fees	Chq. No.	Alberta Bank	
			Dr.	Cr.	Dr.	Dr.	Dr.	Cr.		Dr.	Cr.

1. Journalize the transactions listed below in the synoptic journal.
2. Prove the synoptic journal.

Transactions

2000

May	1	Dr. Lovejoy deposited $6,000 in the practice.
	3	Paid rent for the month to Foster Realty, $800, cheque No. 1.
	8	Bought medical equipment from Ace Supply Co., $1,500, cheque No. 2.
	12	Bought medical supplies from Lone Co., $700, cheque No. 3.
	15	Received payment for patient services, $2,800.
	18	Bought additional medical supplies from Lone Co., $1,200, cheque No. 4.
	19	Dr. Lovejoy withdrew $600 for personal use, cheque No. 5.
	21	Paid Al's Janitorial Service, $300, cheque No. 6.
	24	Received payment for patient services, $1,900.
	25	Paid for postage stamps, $40 (miscellaneous expense), cheque No. 7.
	27	Paid salaries for month, $1,400, cheque No. 8.
	28	Paid Al's Janitorial Service, $400, cheque No. 9.
	29	Dr. Lovejoy withdrew $400 for personal use, cheque No. 10.

11A-2. The following is the chart of accounts of Dr. Fox, M.D.:

Check Figure

Cross-footing $20,874.60

Journalizing transactions of a modified cash system into a synoptic journal with headings for payroll deductions, as well as recording payroll tax expense

Chart of Accounts

Assets	**Revenue**
111 Bank of Regina	411 Professional Fees
112 Prepaid Insurance	**Expenses**
113 Medical Supplies	511 Rent Expense
122 Accumulated Amortization, Office Equipment	512 Medical Supplies Expense
	513 Salaries Expense
	514 Payroll Tax Expense
Liabilities	515 Telephone Expense
211 Due to Receiver General	516 Amortization Expense, Office Equipment
212 Other Payroll Deductions Payable	517 Insurance Expense
	518 Cleaning Expense
Owner's Equity	519 Miscellaneous Expense
311 Al Fox, Capital	
312 Al Fox, Withdrawals	
313 Income Summary	

The headings of Dr. Fox's synoptic journal are as follows:

Date	Explanation	Post Ref.	Bank of Regina		Chq. No.	Prof. Fees Cr.	Sal. Exp. Dr.	Payroll Deductions			Med. Sup. Dr.	Sundry	
			Dr.	Cr.				Income Tax Payable Cr.	CPP Payable Cr.	EI Payable Cr.		Dr.	Cr.

1. Journalize the transactions listed below in the synoptic journal (beginning balances are provided in the working papers).
2. Prove the synoptic journal.

Transactions

2002

May 1 Received $3,000 for patient services.

3 Issued cheque No. 480 to Lane Drug for medical supplies, $600.
5 Issued cheque No. 481 to A. Realty to pay three months' insurance premiums, $1,200.
9 Received cheque for patient services, $2,000.
12 Issued the following payroll cheques to his staff:

Employee	*Cheque No.*	*Gross Pay*	*IT*	*CPP*	*EI*	*Net Pay*
Abby Slat	482	$ 700	$153	$20	$19	$ 508
Jane Reeves	483	600	114	17	16	453
Bob Swan	484	500	88	14	14	384
		$1,800	$355	$51	$49	$1,345

18 Issued cheque No. 485 to Lane Drug for medical supplies, $400.
25 Dr. Fox withdrew $700 for personal use, cheque No. 486.
28 Dr. Fox made the necessary remittance to the Receiver General from payroll of May 12, cheque No. 487. (Don't forget Dr. Fox's share of CPP and EI.)

Journalizing and proving a synoptic journal; recording transactions using an accrual basis of accounting

11A-3. Debra Clark, a recent graduate of a medical school, has decided to open her own office. Based on the advice of her accountant, she will use a synoptic journal. The following is the chart of accounts for Dr. Clark's office:

Chart of Accounts

Assets	**Revenue**
111 Cash	411 Medical Fees
112 Accounts Receivable	
113 Prepaid Insurance	**Expenses**
121 Office Equipment	511 Telephone Expense
	512 Cleaning Expense
Liabilities	513 Utilities Expense
211 Accounts Payable	
Owner's Equity	
311 D. Clark, Capital	
312 Income Summary	

The headings of Dr. Clark's synoptic journal are:

SYNOPTIC JOURNAL

Month — Page 1

Date	Explanation	Chq. No.	Post Ref.	Sundry Dr.	Sundry Cr.	Cash Dr.	Cash Cr.	Accounts Receivable Dr.	Accounts Receivable Cr.	Accounts Payable Dr.	Accounts Payable Cr.	Office Equip. Dr.	Medical Fees Cr.

Required

Check Figure
Total, Sunday column Dr. $2,060

1. Record the following transactions in the synoptic journal. Complete the Post. Ref. column as if you were recording and posting.
2. Prove the synoptic journal.

2001
July 2 Debra Clark invested $7,000 cash and $4,000 worth of office equipment in the practice.

2 Paid insurance on the office for one year in advance, $1,700, cheque No. 1.
9 Purchased office equipment on account from Smith Stationery Co., $400.
12 Purchased office equipment on account from Vole Stationery Co., $700.
18 Completed vaccination of each schoolchild at Salem Elementary School, $3,000 on account.
18 Received $900 cash for medical fees earned.
19 Performed a complete examination for Alvin Ray's son, $75 on account.
20 Paid Smith Stationery one-half the amount owed from July 9 transaction, cheque No. 2.
26 Paid telephone bill, $90, cheque No. 3.
27 Paid utilities, $170, cheque No. 4.
28 Paid Toby Cleaning Co. for cleaning service performed, $100, cheque No. 5.
29 Paid one-half the amount owed Vole Stationery Company from July 12 transaction, cheque No. 6.

Journalizing, recording, and posting a synoptic journal used to record transactions utilizing the accrual basis of accounting

Check Figure
Total of Sundry column Dr. $2,400

11A-4. (GST at 7 percent and PST at 9 percent [not cumulative] are involved in this problem.) Buzzy Sullivan opened a dry-cleaning store that also sold accessories. The following is the chart of accounts for Buzzy's Cleaning Company.

Chart of Accounts

Assets	**Revenue**
111 Cash	411 Cleaning Sales
112 Accounts Receivable	412 Sales Discounts
113 Prepaid Insurance	413 Accessory Sales
115 Prepaid GST	
121 Cleaning Equipment	**Cost of Goods Sold**
	511 Purchases
Liabilities	512 Purchases Returns and Allowances
211 Accounts Payable	513 Purchases Discounts
212 Bank Loan Payable	
215 GST Collected	**Expenses**
217 PST Payable	611 Utilities Expense
	612 Advertising Expense
Owner's Equity	613 Cleaning Supplies Expense
311 B. Sullivan, Capital	
312 Income Summary	

Here are the transactions for the month of January:

2000
Jan. 2 Buzzy Sullivan invested $8,000 cash in the business.
8 Paid a five-year insurance policy in advance, $1,500 (no taxes), cheque No. 1.
10 Purchased merchandise on account from Role Company, $900, plus GST.
12 Cleaned shirts for cash, $650, plus PST and GST.
15 Cleaned suits on account for Pete Daley, $200, plus PST and GST.
17 Purchased cleaning equipment on account from Ral Co., $900, plus GST.

20	Borrowed $6,000 from National Bank.
21	Cleaned shirts for Pete Daley for $50, plus PST and GST on account.
24	Received entire payment from Pete Daley for January 15 transaction less a 2 percent discount.
25	Purchased merchandise on account from Bomb Co., $250, plus GST.
26	Cleaned slacks on account for Alice Small, $15, plus PST and GST.
27	Paid amount due to Role Company less a 2 percent discount for January 10 transaction, cheque No. 2.
28	Returned $100 worth of cleaning equipment to Ral Company for faulty workmanship. (Remember the GST.)
29	Paid Bomb Company the amount due on the January 25 purchase less a 10 percent discount, cheque No. 3.
30	Cash sales, $800, plus PST and GST.
30	Received amount due from Alice Small on the January 26 transaction, less a 20 percent sales discount.

Required

1. Set up accounts in the general ledger (some accounts may not be used in January).
2. Set up accounts in the accounts payable and accounts receivable ledgers as needed.
3. Journalize the above transactions.
4. Record in the accounts payable and accounts receivable ledgers as appropriate.
5. Post to the general ledger as appropriate.
6. Prove that the sum of the subsidiary ledgers is equal to the controlling account balance.
7. Prove the synoptic journal.

The headings of the synoptic journal of Buzzy's Cleaning Company will be as follows:

BUZZY'S CLEANING COMPANY
SYNOPTIC JOURNAL

Date	Explanation	Chq. No.	Post Ref.	Sundry		Cash		Accts. Rec.		Accts. Pay.		GST		Clean. Revenue	Sales Disc.	Pur.	Pur. Disc.	9% Sales Tax
				Dr.	Cr.	Dr.	Cr.	Dr.	Cr.	Dr.	Cr.	Dr.	Cr.	Cr.	Dr.	Dr.	Cr.	Cr.

Group B Problems

(The forms you need are on pages 11-3 to 11-11 of the *Study Guide with Working Papers*.)

Journalizing transactions of a modified cash system in a synoptic journal

Check Figure
Cross-footing $25,280

11B-1. Using the chart of accounts of Dr. Lovejoy from Problem 11A-1, record the following transactions in the synoptic journal and then prove the journal:

2000		
May	1	Dr. Lovejoy deposited $9,000 in the practice.
	3	Paid rent for the month to Jane Jones Realty, $700, cheque No. 1.
	8	Bought medical supplies from Able Co., $750, cheque No. 2.
	12	Bought medical equipment from Jane's Supply, $4,000, cheque No. 3.

15 Received payment for patient services, $3,000.
18 Bought additional medical supplies from Able Co., $910, cheque No. 4.
19 Dr. Lovejoy withdrew $790 for personal use, cheque No. 5.
21 Paid Ron's Janitorial Service, $500, cheque No. 6.
24 Received payment for patient services, $3,400.
25 Paid for postage stamps, $30 (miscellaneous expense), cheque No. 7.
27 Paid salaries for month, $1,600, cheque No. 8.
28 Paid Ron's Janitorial Service, $300, cheque No. 9.
29 Dr. Lovejoy withdrew $300 for personal use, cheque No. 10.

Journalizing transactions of a modified cash system in a synoptic journal with headings for payroll deductions, and recording payroll tax expenses

Check Figure

Cross-footing $23,617.80

11B-2. Using the chart of accounts for Dr. Fox from Problem 11A-2, record the following transactions in the synoptic journal and then prove the journal. (Beginning balances are in your working papers.)

2002
May 1 Received $4,000 for patient services.
3 Issued cheque No. 563 to Lane Drug for medical supplies, $700.
5 Issued cheque No. 564 to J. Realty to pay three months' insurance premiums, $900.
9 Received payment for patient services, $3,000.
12 Issued the following payroll cheques:

Employee	*Cheque No.*	*Gross Pay*	*IT*	*CPP*	*EI*	*Net Pay*
Abby Slat	565	$ 900	$230	$27	$24	$ 619
Jane Reeves	566	800	189	24	22	565
Bob Swan	567	600	114	17	16	453
		$2,300	$533	$68	$62	$1,637

18 Issued cheque No. 568 to Lane Drug for medical supplies, $900.
25 Dr. Fox withdrew $400 for personal use, cheque No. 569.
28 Dr. Fox sent cheque to Receiver General relating to payroll of May 12, cheque No. 570. (Don't forget Dr. Fox's share of CPP and EI.)

Journalizing, recording, and posting a synoptic journal used to record transactions utilizing the accrual basis of accounting

Check Figure

Total of Sundry column Dr. $1,430

11B-3. Using the chart of accounts of Debra Clark from Problem 11A-3, journalize the following transactions and prove the synoptic journal. Fill in the Post. Ref. column as if you were actually recording and posting to the ledger.

2001
July 2 Debra Clark invested $6,000 cash and $4,000 worth of office equipment in the practice.
2 Paid insurance on the office for one year in advance, $1,200, cheque No. 1.
9 Purchased office equipment on account from Smith Stationery Co., $1,400.
12 Completed physical examinations on each schoolchild at Simcoe Elementary School, $2,000 on account.
18 Received $700 cash for medical fees earned.
19 Performed a complete examination for Alvin Ray's son, $200 on account.
20 Paid Smith Stationery one-half the amount owed from July 9 transaction, cheque No. 2.
26 Paid telephone bill, $95, cheque No. 3.

27 Paid utilities, $60, cheque No. 4.
28 Paid Toby Cleaning Co. for cleaning service performed, $75, cheque No. 5.

11B-4. (GST at 7 percent and PST at 8 percent [not cumulative] are involved in this problem.) Buzzy Sullivan opened a dry-cleaning store that also sold accessories. The chart of accounts and synoptic journal headings for Buzzy's Cleaning Company are given in Problem 11A-4. Here are the transactions for the month of January:

Check Figure

Total of Sundry column Dr. $1,800

2000

Jan. 2 Buzzy Sullivan invested $6,000 cash in the business.
8 Paid for a five-year company insurance policy in advance, $1,200, cheque No. 101 (no GST or PST).
10 Purchased merchandise on account from Role Company, $700, plus GST.
12 Cleaned shirts for cash, $950, plus GST and PST.
15 Cleaned suits on account for Pete Daley, $500, plus GST and PST.
17 Purchased cleaning equipment on account from Ral Co., $600, plus GST.
20 Borrowed $4,000 from National Bank.
21 Cleaned shirts on account for P. Daley, $50, plus GST and PST.
24 Received entire payment from P. Daley, less a 2 percent discount, from January 15 transaction.
25 Purchased merchandise on account from Bomb Company, $90, plus GST.
26 Cleaned silk blouse on account for Alice Small, $20, plus GST and PST.
27 Paid Role Company the amount due (less a 2 percent discount) because of merchandise that was purchased on January 10, cheque No. 102.
28 Returned $200 worth of cleaning equipment to Ral Company for faulty workmanship. (Remember the GST.)
29 Paid Bomb Company the amount due (less a 10 percent discount) on the purchases made on account on January 25, cheque No. 103.
30 Cash sales, $700, plus GST and PST.

Your task is to journalize, record, post, and prove the synoptic journal for the cleaning company. See Problem 11A-4 for detailed requirements.

Group C Problems

(The forms you need are on pages 11-12 to 11-20 of the *Study Guide with Working Papers.*)

Journalizing transactions of a modified cash system into a synoptic journal

11C-1. Using a chart of accounts similar to that for Problem 11A-1, record the following transactions for Carla Walgee, Physiotherapist, in her synoptic journal, and then prove the journal:

Check Figure

Cross-footing $40,135

2002

May 1 Ms. Walgee deposited $18,000 in the practice.
3 Paid rent for the month to Abby Glenn Realty, $800, cheque No. 341.
8 Bought supplies from Perkins Co., $680, cheque No. 342.
12 Bought exercise equipment from Atlas Supply, $6,800, cheque No. 343.

15 Received cash from patients, $4,550.
18 Bought additional supplies from Perkins Co., $920, cheque No. 344.
19 Ms. Walgee withdrew $900 for personal use, cheque No. 345.
21 Paid Rockford Janitorial Service, $420, cheque No. 346.
24 Received payment for patient services, $3,850.
25 Paid for postage stamps, $75 (miscellaneous expense), cheque No. 347.
27 Paid salary to Brenda Curtis for month, $1,820, cheque No. 348.
28 Paid Rockford Janitorial Service, $420, cheque No. 349.
29 Ms. Walgee withdrew another $900 for personal use, cheque No. 350.

Journalizing transactions of a modified cash system in a synoptic journal with headings for payroll deductions, and recording payroll tax expenses.

Check Figure

Cross-footing $41,404.40

11C-2. Using a chart of accounts similar to that for Problem 11A-2, record the following transactions for Sandy Williams, Dentist, in the synoptic journal, and then prove the journal. (Beginning balances are given in your working papers.)

2003
June 1 Received $4,820 from patients.
3 Issued cheque No. 230 to Walkins Drug for dental supplies, $780.
5 Issued cheque No. 231 to Game Agencies to pay six months' insurance premiums, $2,400.
9 Received cheques from patients, $3,910.
12 Issued the following payroll cheques:

Employee	*Cheque No.*	*Gross Pay*	*IT*	*CPP*	*EI*	*Net Pay*
Ted Forth	232	$ 800	$189	$24	$ 22	$ 565
Carol Hahn	233	900	230	27	24	619
Ed Birch	234	700	153	20	19	508
Kim Shaw	235	1,100	306	33	30	731
		$3,500	$878	$104	$95	$2,423

18 Issued cheque No. 236 to Walkins Drug for dental supplies, $1,340.
25 Dr. Williams withdrew $2,400 for personal use, cheque No. 237.
26 Issued the following payroll cheques:

Employee	*Cheque No.*	*Gross Pay*	*IT*	*CPP*	*EI*	*Net Pay*
Ted Forth	238	$ 850	$211	$25	$ 23	$ 591
Carol Hahn	239	900	230	27	24	619
Ed Birch	240	700	153	20	19	508
Kim Shaw	241	1,100	306	33	30	731
		$3,550	$900	$105	$96	$2,449

28 Dr. Williams sent the remittance cheque to the Receiver General for the payrolls of June 12 and 26, cheque No. 242. (Don't forget Dr. Williams's share of CPP and EI.)

Journalizing, recording, and posting a synoptic journal used to record transactions utilizing accrual basis of accounting

11C-3. Using a chart of accounts similar to that for Problem 11A-3, journalize the following transactions for Sammy Wong, Optometrist, and prove the synoptic journal. Fill in the Post. Ref. column as if you were actually recording and posting to the ledger.

2001

April 1 Dr. Wong invested $12,000 cash and $32,000 worth of optical equipment in the practice.
1 Paid insurance premium for one year in advance, $2,870, cheque No. 761.
8 Purchased office equipment on account from Adobe Stationery Co., $4,170.
12 Completed optical examinations on each schoolchild at Eastside Elementary School, $4,120 on account.
18 Received $2,850 cash for professional fees earned.
19 Performed a complete optical examination for Ms. Rachel Flemming, a famous film star, $400 on account.
20 Paid Adobe Stationery one-half the amount owed from April 8 transaction, cheque No. 762.
26 Paid telephone bill, $87, cheque No. 763.
27 Paid utilities, $140, cheque No. 764.
28 Paid Neally Cleaning Co. for services performed, $350, cheque no. 765.
30 Received first payment from Eastside Elementary School, $2,000.

Check Figure

Total of Sundry column Dr. $3,447

Check Figure

Total of Sundry column $8,820

11C-4. (GST at 7 percent and PST at 6 percent [not cumulative] are involved in this problem.) Freda Schragge opened an appliance repair shop that also sold accessories. The chart of accounts for her shop is shown below. Here are the transactions for the month of October:

2000

Oct. 1 Freda Schragge invested $25,000 cash in the business.
8 Paid First City Agency Co. for a three-year insurance policy in advance, $1,120, cheque No. 101 (no GST or PST).
10 Purchased merchandise on account from Colter & Co., $1,680, plus GST.
12 Repaired appliances for five customers for cash, $670, plus GST and PST.
13 Sold accessories for cash, $650, plus GST and PST.
15 Repaired appliances on account for Vince Lombardi, $940, plus GST and PST.
16 Freda withdrew $700 for personal expenses, cheque No. 102.
17 Purchased repair equipment on account from Sattrap Co., $7,000, plus GST.
20 Borrowed $10,000 from National Bank.
21 Repaired appliances on account for Vince Lombardi, $280, plus GST and PST.
22 Sold accessories for cash, $920, plus GST and PST.
24 Received payment from Vince Lombardi for October 15 transaction less a 2 percent discount.
25 Purchased merchandise on account from Apex Company, $840, plus GST.
26 Cleaned stove on account for J. Fresnel, $80, plus GST and PST.
27 Paid Colter & Co. for merchandise purchased on October 10 less a 2 percent discount, cheque No. 103.
28 Returned $200 worth of repair equipment to Sattrap Co. because of faulty workmanship. (Remember the GST.)
29 Paid Apex Company the amount owed (less a 5 percent discount) on the purchases made on account on October 25, cheque No. 104.
30 Repairs made for cash, $620, plus GST and PST.

Chart of Accounts

Assets
111 Cash
112 Accounts Receivable
113 Prepaid Insurance
115 Prepaid GST
121 Repair Equipment

Liabilities
211 Accounts Payable
212 Bank Loan Payable
215 GST Collected
217 PST Payable

Owner's Equity
311 F. Schragge, Capital
312 F. Schragge, Withdrawals
315 Income Summary

Revenue
411 Appliance Sales
412 Sales Discounts
413 Repairs Revenue

Cost of Goods Sold
511 Purchases
512 Purchases Returns and Allowances
513 Purchases Discounts

Expenses
611 Utilities Expense
612 Advertising Expense
613 Supplies Expense

The headings for the synoptic journal should look like this:

FREDA'S APPLIANCE REPAIR AND SALES
SYNOPTIC JOURNAL

Date	Explanation	Chq. No.	Post Ref.	Sundry		Cash		Accts. Rec.		Accts. Pay.		GST Paid/Coll.	Repairs Revenue	Appl. Sales	Sales Disc.	Pur.	Pur. Disc.	Sales Tax Payable
				Dr.	Cr.	Dr.	Cr.	Dr.	Cr.	Dr.	Cr.	(Dr.) or Cr.	Cr.	Cr.	Dr.	Dr.	Cr.	Cr.

Your task is to journalize, record, post, and prove the business's synoptic journal for October 2000.

Real World Applications

(The form you need is on page 11-22 of the *Study Guide with Working Papers.*)

11R-1.
Jeff Smith has been running his business on a strictly cash basis. At a party over the weekend he met an accountant who told him that his business should use a modified cash system. Jeff has brought you his chart of accounts so that you may revise it as well as lay out a synoptic journal. Using the following chart of accounts for Jeff Smith, design a synoptic journal for him. Allow columns for payroll deductions.

Chart of Accounts

Assets
111 Cash
113 Petty Cash

Liabilities
211 Bank Loan Payable

Owner's Equity
311 J. Smith, Capital
312 J. Smith, Withdrawals
313 Income Summary

Revenue
411 Professional Fees

Expenses
511 Insurance Expense
512 Furniture Expense
514 Medical Equipment Expense
515 Medical Supplies Expense
516 Salary Expense
517 Telephone Expense
518 Miscellaneous Expense

11R-2.

Margie Henley is about to open a dry-cleaning shop. She has hired you to design a synoptic journal for her shop. It will definitely be a small business with a limited number of transactions that are not too complicated. After analyzing Margie's company, you develop the following chart of accounts:

1. Cash
2. Accounts Receivable
3. Equipment
4. Accounts Payable
5. Cleaning Sales
6. Wage Expense
7. Supplies Expense
8. Miscellaneous Expense

Margie has asked you to provide her, as soon as possible, with a justification for your design of the parts of the synoptic journal. Be prepared to support the synoptic journal you present to her. Label all headings of the journal in terms of debits and credits. What titles are missing from the chart of accounts?

make the call

Critical Thinking/Ethical Case

11R-3.

Angel Shower, the bookkeeper of Aster Co., also collects the payment of invoices by customers. Angel noticed that Rume Co. paid the April 10 invoice twice. Angel, who is in need of extra cash, does not plan to inform Rume Co. of the double payment. Do you agree with Angel's decision? You make the call. Write down your specific recommendations to Angel.

ACCOUNTING RECALL

A CUMULATIVE APPROACH

THIS EXAMINATION REVIEWS CHAPTERS 1 THROUGH 11.

Your *Study Guide with Working Papers* (page 11-23) has forms to complete this exam, as well as worked-out solutions. The page reference next to each question identifies the page to turn back to if you answer the question incorrectly.

PART I Vocabulary Review

Match each term on the left side with the appropriate definition or phrase in the right-hand column.

Page Ref.		
(469)	1. Hybrid	A. A special journal
(477)	2. Sundry	B. Amounts deducted from employees plus employer's share of CPP and EI

(477) 3. X

(468) 4. Accrual accounting

(477) 5. ✔

(317) 6. Due to Receiver General for Canada

(472) 7. Payroll tax expense

(354) 8. Controlling account

(372) 9. Cross-foot

(469) 10. Synoptic journal

C. Records revenue when cash is received

D. Accounts payable

E. Verification

F. No posting

G. Record to subsidiary

H. Records revenue when earned

I. Miscellaneous

J. CPP + EI (employer's share)

PART II True or False (Accounting Theory)

(353) 11. We post to subsidiary ledgers and record in general ledgers.

(469) 12. Small businesses could use synoptic journals.

(477) 13. Adjusting entries would be recorded in the Sundry columns of a special journal.

(479) 14. Sales Tax Payable has a normal balance of a debit.

(479) 15. The total of Accounts Receivable is posted to the subsidiary ledger.

CONTINUING PROBLEM

Tony Freedman has decided to use a combined journal for the Eldorado Computer Centre, beginning with February 2002.

Assignment

(See pages 11-24 to 11-33 in your *Study Guide with Working Papers.*)

Record the transactions listed below in the synoptic journal of the Eldorado Computer Centre; then post as necessary to the required ledger accounts and prepare a trial balance as of February 28:

Feb. 2 Billed Vita Needle for services performed, invoice No. 12682, $1,300.

5 Paid West Bell Canada the balance owed on the phone bill received in November, $165, cheque No. 250.

6 Received the utility bill for the month, $290, due in 30 days.

10 Collected balance in full from Taylor Golf, $700, sales invoice No. 5000.

11 Paid for advertising with West Bell Canada, $800, cheque No. 251.

14 Sold to Anthony Pitale, goods worth $1,150, sales invoice No. 12683, terms 2/10/n30.

20 Paid insurance premium for the year beginning March 1, 2002, to Willow Agency, cheque No. 252, $1,846. (Dr. Insurance Expense, account No. 5060).

22 Collected $1,700, resale of goods for cash.

25 Paid Universal Sales for supplies, $286, cheque No. 253.

28 Paid Automated Payroll Service for wages and related costs for February, $6,109.00, cheque No. 254.

Preparing a Worksheet for a Merchandising Company

12

The Big Picture

◆

Six months into Eldorado Computer Centre's second year of operation Tony Freedman decides to update his books. He wants to prepare an accurate financial statement to give to the bank. He will make all necessary adjustments to his accounts as he did before. The first step in completing these adjustments is preparing a worksheet that includes merchandise transactions.

The Eldorado Computer Centre has purchased and sold merchandise inventory for computers. To make sure he has had accessories available in stock to increase customer satisfaction, Tony has kept an inventory of many parts and accessories. However, all have not been sold in the first six months of this year.

The worksheet you will prepare for the Eldorado Computer Centre will include new accounts to track the actual inventory Freedman purchased. Some of that inventory became an expense in this time period, and some is still to be sold. Although Freedman tracks purchases of inventory on a monthly basis, accurate value for all inventory cannot be determined until a physical count is completed. This physical count also allows Freedman to see if there has been a problem with theft or breakage of parts.

Freedman updates his inventory as he does the rest of his accounts, at the end of an accounting period. Since his inventory is not that large in quantity or in dollars, he feels an annual update is something he can accomplish without hiring additional people to handle the workload of the business or shutting down operations for a few days.

Chapter Objectives

- ◆ Figuring adjustments for merchandise inventory, unearned rent, supplies used, insurance expired, amortization expense, and salaries accrued (pp. 498–500 and 504–505)
- ◆ Preparing a worksheet for a merchandising company (pp. 503 and 505–508)

In Chapters 9 and 10 we discussed the special journals and subsidiary ledgers of a merchandising company, and in Chapters 7 and 8 we looked at payroll recordkeeping practices and procedures. Now our attention will shift to recording adjustments and completing a worksheet for a merchandising company. Learning Unit 12-1 will introduce two new adjustments that we have not yet discussed, Merchandise Inventory and Unearned Rent. Learning Unit 12-2 will show how to complete the worksheet with these new adjustments.

LEARNING UNIT 12-1

Adjustments for Merchandise Inventory and Unearned Rent

An important item in a merchandising company worksheet and financial records is *Merchandise Inventory*. This means the goods that a company has available to sell to customers. There are several ways of keeping track of the cost of goods sold and quantity of inventory that a company has on hand. In the appendix at the end of this chapter, another system called **perpetual inventory** is discussed. In this system, businesses with large inventories can have current information about inventory on hand and the actual cost of goods sold. Most such companies use a computer to keep track of their inventory records.

In this chapter we will discuss the **periodic inventory system**, in which the balance in inventory is updated only at the end of the accounting period. This system is used by smaller companies which sell a variety of merchandise with low unit prices. The number of companies using this system of accounting for inventory is still significant but is declining. This is because of the increasing availability of computers and software which together encourage the use of the more useful and informative perpetual system.

Let's take as an example the merchandise inventory of Art's Wholesale Clothing Company. Let's assume Art's Wholesale started the year with $19,000 worth of merchandise; this is called **beginning merchandise inventory** or simply **beginning inventory**. During the period, the cost of beginning inventory does not change; instead, all purchases of merchandise are recorded in the Purchases account. During the period $52,000 worth of merchandise was purchased and recorded in the Purchases account.

At the end of the period, the company takes a physical count of the merchandise in stock; this amount is called **ending merchandise inventory** or simply **ending inventory** and is calculated on an inventory sheet as shown in Figure 12-1.

Cost of goods sold

Beginning inventory
\+ Net purchases
− Ending inventory
= Cost of goods sold

This $4,000, which is the ending inventory for this period, will be the beginning inventory for the next period.

When the income statement is prepared, the cost of goods sold section will require two distinct numbers for inventory. The beginning inventory adds to the cost of goods sold, while the ending inventory is subtracted from the cost of goods sold.

FIGURE 12-1
Ending Inventory Sheet

ART'S WHOLESALE CLOTHING COMPANY ENDING INVENTORY SHEET AS OF DECEMBER 31, 2001			
Amount	Explanation	Unit Cost	Total
20	Ladies' Jackets code 14.0	$50	$1,000
10	Men's Hats code 327	10	100
90	Men's Shirts code 423	10	900
100	Ladies' Blouses code 481	20	2,000
			$4,000

Counted by ________ Checked and priced by ________

Remember that the two figures for beginning and ending inventory were calculated months apart. Thus they cannot merely be combined to come up with one inventory figure; that would not be accurate.

Adjustment for Merchandise Inventory

First adjustment transfers amount in beginning inventory from Merchandise Inventory to Income Summary.

Note that Income Summary has no normal balance of debit or credit.

Adjusting the Merchandise Inventory account is a two-step process because we want to keep both beginning inventory and ending inventory amounts separate; we cannot simply combine them. So the first step deals with beginning merchandise inventory.

Given: Beginning Inventory, $19,000 Our first adjustment removes the beginning inventory amount from the asset account (Merchandise Inventory) and transfers it to Income Summary. We do this by crediting Merchandise Inventory for $19,000 and debiting Income Summary for the same amount. This is shown below in T-account form and on a transaction analysis chart:

Merchandise Inventory 114

Dr.	Cr.
Bal. 19,000	Adj. 19,000

Income Summary 313

Dr.	Cr.
Adj. 19,000	

(A)

Accounts Affected	Category	↑ ↓	Rules
Income Summary	Equity	N/A	Dr.
Merchandise Inventory	Asset	↓	Cr.

(The adjusting entries would be first entered on the worksheet and then formally recorded in the general journal, then posted.)

Second adjustment updates inventory account with a figure for ending inventory.

The second step is to enter the amount of ending inventory ($4,000) in the Merchandise Inventory account. This is done to record the amount of goods on hand at the end of the period as an asset, and to subtract this amount from the cost of goods sold (since we have not sold this inventory yet). To do this we debit Merchandise Inventory for $4,000 and credit Income Summary for the same amount. This is shown below in T-account form and on a transaction analysis chart:

Merchandise Inventory 114

Dr.	Cr.
Bal. 19,000 Adj. 4,000	Adj. 19,000

Income Summary 313

Dr.	Cr.
Adj. 19,000	Adj. 4,000

(B)

Accounts Affected	Category	↑ ↓	Rules
Merchandise Inventory	Asset	↑	Dr.
Income Summary	Equity	N/A	Cr.

FIGURE 12-2 Recording Inventory on a partial Balance Sheet and Income Statement

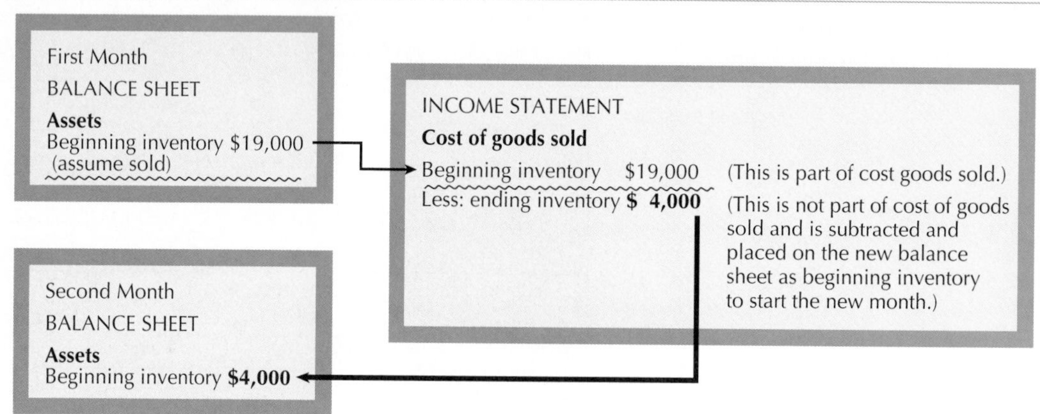

First Month
BALANCE SHEET
Assets
Beginning inventory $19,000
(assume sold)
INCOME STATEMENT
Cost of goods sold
Beginning inventory $19,000
Less: ending inventory $ 4,000
(This is part of cost goods sold.)
(This is not part of cost of goods sold and is subtracted and placed on the new balance sheet as beginning inventory to start the new month.)
Second Month
BALANCE SHEET
Assets
Beginning inventory $4,000

Note: If freight-in were involved, it would have been added to net cost of purchases.

Let's look at how this process or method of recording merchandise inventory is reflected in the balance sheet and income statement (see Figure 12-2). Note that the $19,000 worth of beginning inventory is assumed sold and is shown on the income statement as part of the cost of goods sold. The ending inventory of $4,000 has not been sold and so is subtracted from the cost of goods sold on the income statement. The ending inventory for this period becomes the next period's beginning inventory. When the income statement is prepared, we will need a figure for beginning inventory as well as a figure for ending inventory.

The second adjustment we will discuss in this unit concerns an account that we have never dealt with before, Unearned Rent.

Adjustment for Unearned Rent

A new account we have not seen before is a liability called Unearned Rent. This account records the amount collected for rent before the service has been provided (renting the space). For example, Art's Wholesale is subletting some unneeded space to Jesse Company for $200 per month. Jesse Company sends Art a cheque for $600 for three months' rent paid in advance. This unearned rent ($600) is also often called Rent Received in Advance. Regardless of the actual name, it is a liability on the balance sheet because Art's Wholesale owes Jesse Company three months' worth of occupancy.

Received cash for renting space in future.

Cash	A	↑	Dr.
Unearned Rent	Liab.	↑	Cr.

When Art's Wholesale fulfills a portion of the rental agreement (when Jesse Company has been in the space for a period of time), this liability account will be reduced and the account called Rental Income will be increased, because Art's Wholesale will have earned the rent. Rental Income is another type of revenue for Art's Wholesale, in addition to its revenue earned from sales of merchandise.

The adjustment when rental income is earned

Unearned Rent	Liab.	↓	Dr.
Rental Income	Other Rev.	↑	Cr.

There are other types of unearned revenue besides unearned rent—examples would be subscriptions for magazines, legal fees collected before the work is performed, insurance, and so on. The key point is that revenue, under accrual accounting, is recognized when it is *earned*, whether money is received then or not. Here Art's Wholesale collected cash in advance for a service that it has not performed as yet. Thus a liability called Unearned Rent is the result. Art's Wholesale may have the cash, but no Rental Income is recorded until it is *earned.*

In the next unit we will show how to record the adjustment to Rental Income when the worksheet is completed.

LEARNING UNIT 12-1 REVIEW

AT THIS POINT you should be able to:

- Define the periodic method of inventory accounting. (p. 498)
- Explain why beginning and ending inventory are two separate figures in the cost of goods sold section on the income statement. (pp. 498–499)
- Show how to calculate a figure for ending inventory. (p. 500)
- Explain why unearned rent is a liability account. (p. 500)

SELF-REVIEW QUIZ 12-1

(The form you need is on page 12-1 in the *Study Guide with Working Paper.*)

Given the following, prepare the two adjusting entries for Merchandise Inventory on 12/31/01:

Merchandise Inventory, 01/01/01	$ 6,000
Purchases	9,000
Merchandise Inventory, 12/31/01	5,000
Cost of Goods Sold	10,000
Unearned Magazine Subscriptions	8,000

Solution to Self-Review Quiz 12-1

Dec.	31	Income Summary	6 0 0 0 00	
		Merchandise Inventory		6 0 0 0 00
	31	Merchandise Inventory	5 0 0 0 00	
		Income Summary		5 0 0 0 00
		To record opening and		
		closing inventories		

Quiz Tip

Note that Unearned Magazine Subscriptions is a liability and not involved in the adjustment for Merchandise Inventory.

LEARNING UNIT 12-2

Completing the Worksheet

In this unit we will prepare a worksheet for Art's Wholesale Clothing Company. For convenience, we reproduce the company's chart of accounts in Figure 12-3 (page 502).

Figure 12-4 (page 503) shows the trial balance that was prepared on December 31, 2001, from the general ledger of Art's Wholesale. (***Note:*** It is recorded directly in the first two columns of the worksheet.)

In looking at the trial balance, we see many new titles that have appeared since we completed a trial balance for a service company back in Chapter 5. Let's look specifically at these new titles in the summary in Table 12-1 (page 502).

FIGURE 12-3
Art's Wholesale Clothing Company Chart of Accounts

Chart of Accounts

Assets 100–199
111 Cash
112 Petty Cash
113 Accounts Receivable
114 Merchandise Inventory
115 Supplies
116 Prepaid Insurance
121 Store Equipment
122 Accumulated Amortization, Store Equipment

Liabilities 200–299
211 Accounts Payable
212 Salaries Payable
213 Income Tax Payable
214 CPP Payable
215 EI Payable
218 Unearned Rent
220 Mortgage Payable

Owner's Equity 300–399
311 Art Newner, Capital
312 Art Newner, Withdrawals
313 Income Summary

Revenue 400–499
411 Sales
412 Sales Returns and Allowances
413 Sales Discounts
414 Rental Income

Cost of Goods Sold 500–599
511 Purchases
512 Purchases Discounts
513 Purchases Returns and Allowances
514 Freight-In

Expenses 600–699
611 Salary Expense
612 Payroll Tax Expense
613 Amortization Expense, Store Equipment
614 Supplies Expense
615 Insurance Expense
616 Postage Expense
617 Miscellaneous Expense
618 Interest Expense
619 Cleaning Expense
620 Delivery Expense

TABLE 12-1 SUMMARY OF NEW ACCOUNT TITLES

Title	Category	Report (s) Found on	Normal Balance	Temporary/ Permanent
Petty Cash	Asset	Balance sheet	Dr.	Permanent
Merchandise Inventory* (Beginning)	Asset	Balance sheet prior period	Dr.	Permanent
	Expense	Income statement of current period		
Income Tax Payable	Liability	Balance sheet	Cr.	Permanent
CPP Payable	Liability	Balance sheet	Cr.	Permanent
EI Payable	Liability	Balance sheet	Cr.	Permanent
Unearned Rent**	Liability	Balance sheet	Cr.	Permanent
Mortgage Payable	Liability	Balance sheet	Cr.	Permanent
Sales	Revenue	Income statement	Cr.	Temporary
Sales Return and Allowances	Revenue (contra)	Income statement	Dr.	Temporary
Sales Discounts	Revenue (contra)	Income statement	Dr.	Temporary
Purchases	Expense	Income statement	Dr.	Temporary
Purchases Discounts	Expense (contra)	Income statement	Cr.	Temporary
Purchases Returns and Allowances	Expense (contra)	Income statement	Cr.	Temporary
Freight-In	Expense	Income statement	Dr.	Temporary
Payroll Tax Expense	Expense	Income statement	Dr.	Temporary
Postage Expense	Expense	Income statement	Dr.	Temporary
Interest Expense	Expense	Income statement	Dr.	Temporary

*The ending inventory of the current period is a contra-expense on the income statement and will be an asset on the balance sheet for next period.
**Referred to as Unearned Revenue

FIGURE 12-4
Trial Balance Section of the Worksheet

ART'S WHOLESALE CLOTHING COMPANY
WORKSHEET
FOR THE YEAR ENDED DECEMBER 31, 2001

	Trial Balance	
	Dr.	Cr.
Cash	12920 00	
Petty Cash	100 00	
Accounts Receivable	14500 00	
Merchandise Inventory	19000 00	
Supplies	800 00	
Prepaid Insurance	900 00	
Store Equipment	4000 00	
Accumulated Amortization, Store Equip.		400 00
Accounts Payable		17900 00
Income Tax Payable		1240 00
CPP Payable		260 00
EI Payable		200 00
Unearned Rent		600 00
Mortgage Payable		2320 00
Art Newner, Capital		7905 00
Art Newner, Withdrawals	8600 00	
Income Summary		
Sales		95000 00
Sales Returns and Allowances	950 00	
Sales Discounts	670 00	
Purchases	52000 00	
Purchases Discounts		860 00
Purchases Returns and Allowances		680 00
Freight-In	450 00	
Salary Expense	11700 00	
Payroll Tax Expense	420 00	
Postage Expense	25 00	
Miscellaneous Expense	30 00	
Interest Expense	300 00	
	127365 00	127365 00

Note the following:

1. **Mortgage Payable** is a liability account that records the increases and decreases in the amount of debt owed on a mortgage. We will discuss this more in the next chapter, when financial reports are prepared.
2. **Interest Expense** represents a non-operating expense for Art's Wholesale and thus is categorized as "miscellaneous expense." The interest would be a regular expense if it were incurred for business purposes. We will also be looking at this in the next chapter.
3. **Unearned Revenue** is a liability account that records receipt of payment for goods and services in advance of delivery. Unearned Rent is a particular example of this general type of account.

Adjustments We have already discussed Adjustments A and B (page 499), which make up the two-step process involved in adjusting Merchandise Inventory at the end of the accounting period. Now we will go on to show T accounts and transaction analysis charts for some more adjustments that need to be made at this point in a merchandising firm, just as they do in a service company.

Adjustment C: Rental Income Earned by Art's Wholesale, $200 A month ago, Cash was increased by $600, as was a liability, Unearned Rent. Art's Wholesale received payment in advance but had not earned the rental income. Now, since $200 has been earned, the liability is reduced and Rental Income can be recorded for the $200.

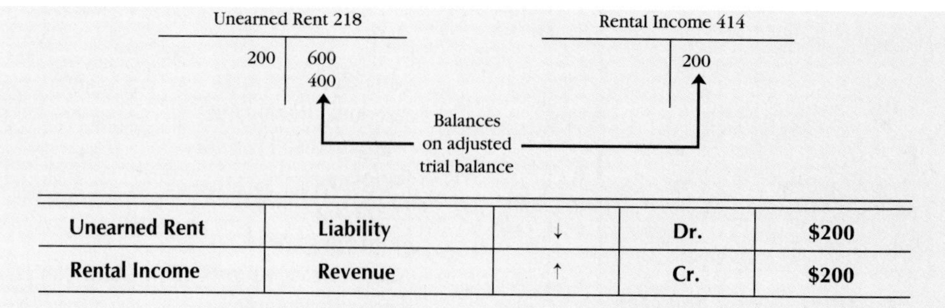

Unearned Rent	**Liability**	↓	**Dr.**	**$200**
Rental Income	**Revenue**	↑	**Cr.**	**$200**

Adjustment D: Supplies on Hand, $300 $500 worth of supplies has been used up; thus there is a need to increase Supplies Expense and decrease the asset Supplies.

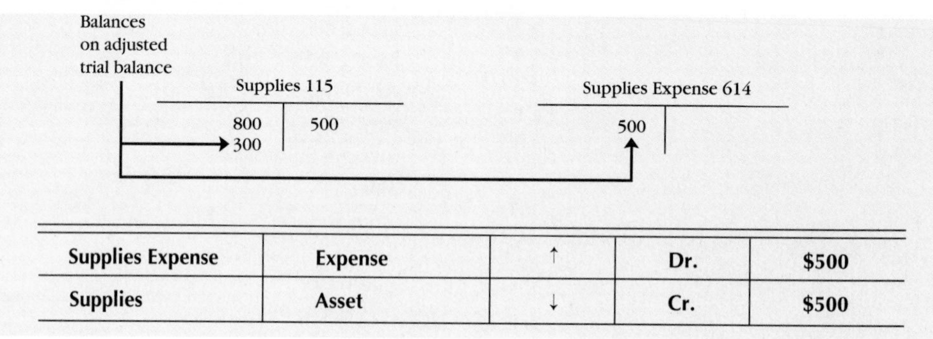

Supplies Expense	**Expense**	↑	**Dr.**	**$500**
Supplies	**Asset**	↓	**Cr.**	**$500**

Adjustment E: Insurance Expired, $300 Since $300 worth of insurance has expired, Insurance Expense is increased by $300 and the asset Prepaid Insurance is decreased by $300.

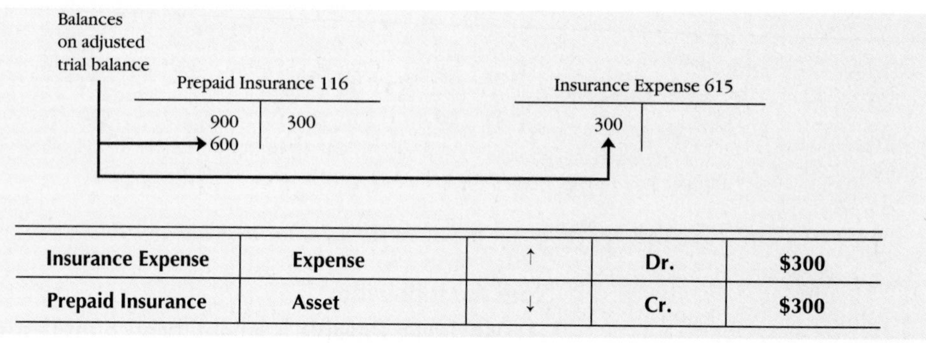

Insurance Expense	**Expense**	↑	**Dr.**	**$300**
Prepaid Insurance	**Asset**	↓	**Cr.**	**$300**

Adjustment F: Amortization Expense, $50 When amortization is taken, Amortization Expense and Accumulated Amortization are both increased by $50. Note that the cost of the store equipment remains the same.

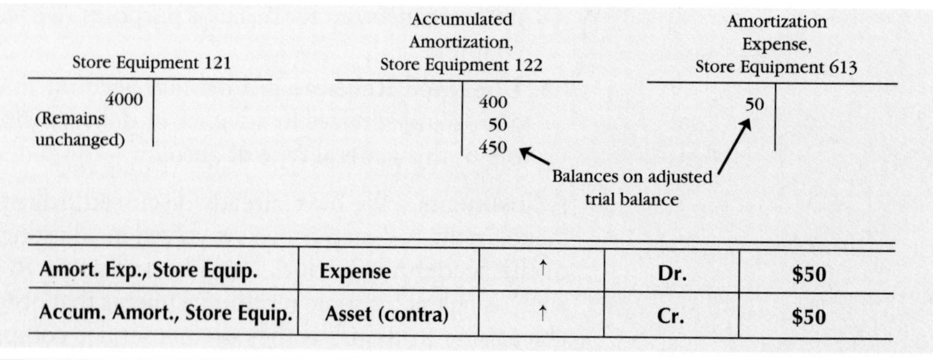

Amort. Exp., Store Equip.	**Expense**	↑	**Dr.**	**$50**
Accum. Amort., Store Equip.	**Asset (contra)**	↑	**Cr.**	**$50**

Adjustment G: Salaries Accrued, $600 The $600 in Salaries Accrued causes an increase in Salaries Expense and Salaries Payable.

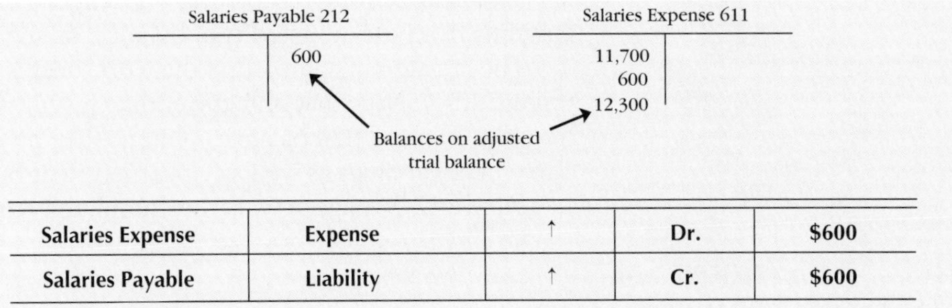

Salaries Expense	**Expense**	↑	**Dr.**	**$600**
Salaries Payable	**Liability**	↑	**Cr.**	**$600**

FIGURE 12-5
Worksheet with Three Sections Completed

Figure 12-5 shows the worksheet with the adjustments and adjusted trial balance columns filled out. Note that the adjustment numbers in Income Summary from

	Trial Balance		Adjustments		Adjusted Trial Balance	
	Dr.	Cr.	Dr.	Cr.	Dr.	Cr.
Cash	12920 00				12920 00	
Petty Cash	100 00				100 00	
Accounts Receivable	14500 00				14500 00	
Merchandise Inventory	19000 00		(B) 4000 00	(A) 19000 00	4000 00	
Supplies	800 00			(D) 500 00	300 00	
Prepaid Insurance	900 00			(E) 300 00	600 00	
Store Equipment	4000 00				4000 00	
Accumulated Amortization, Store Equip.		400 00		(F) 50 00		450 00
Accounts Payable		17900 00				17900 00
Income Tax Payable		1240 00				1240 00
CPP Payable		260 00				260 00
EI Payable		200 00				200 00
Unearned Rent		600 00	(C) 200 00			400 00
Mortgage Payable		2320 00				2320 00
Art Newner, Capital		7905 00				7905 00
Art Newner, Withdrawals	8600 00				8600 00	
Income Summary			(A) 19000 00	(B) 4000 00	19000 00	4000 00
Sales		95000 00				95000 00
Sales Returns and Allowances	950 00				950 00	
Sales Discounts	670 00				670 00	
Purchases	52000 00				52000 00	
Purchases Discounts		860 00				860 00
Purchases Returns and Allowances		680 00				680 00
Freight-In	450 00				450 00	
Salary Expense	11700 00		(G) 600 00		12300 00	
Payroll Tax Expense	420 00				420 00	
Postage Expense	25 00				25 00	
Miscellaneous Expense	30 00				30 00	
Interest Expense	300 00				300 00	
	127365 00	127365 00				
Rental Income				(C) 200 00		200 00
Supplies Expense			(D) 500 00		500 00	
Insurance Expense			(E) 300 00		300 00	
Amortization Expense, Store Equipment			(F) 50 00		50 00	
Salary Payable				(G) 600 00		600 00
			24650 00	24650 00	132015 00	132015 00

beginning and ending inventory are also carried over to the adjusted trial balance and are *not* combined.

The next step in completing the worksheet is to fill out the income statement columns from the adjusted trial balance, as shown in Figure 12-6.

The last step in completing the worksheet is to fill out the balance sheet columns (Figure 12-7). Note that only the ending inventory is carried over to the balance sheet from the adjusted trial balance column. Take time also to look at the placement of the payroll tax liabilities as well as Unearned Rent on the worksheet.

Figure 12-8 (page 508) is the completed worksheet.

FIGURE 12-6
Income Statement Section of the Worksheet

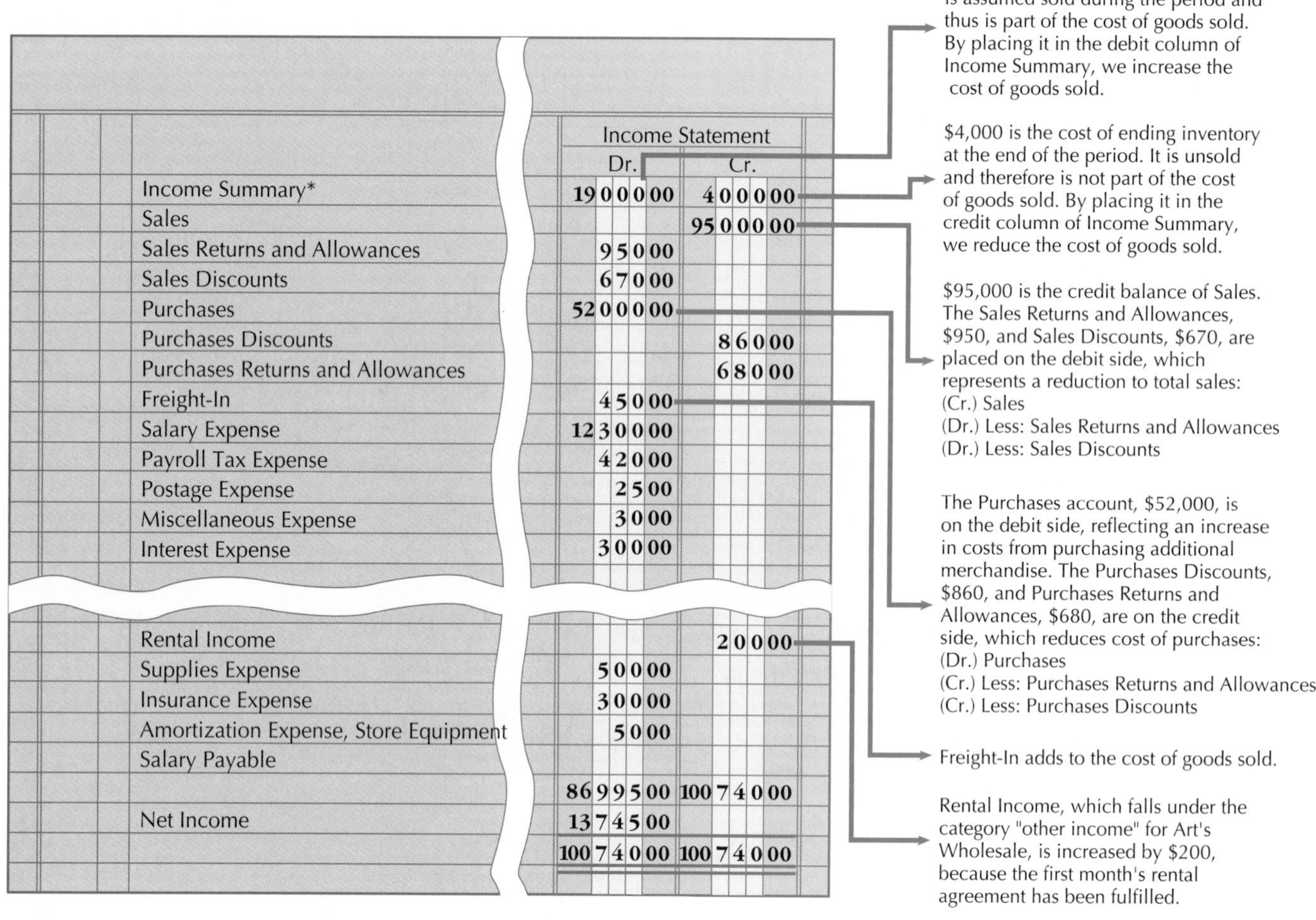

	Income Statement Dr.	Income Statement Cr.
Income Summary*	19,000.00	4,000.00
Sales		95,000.00
Sales Returns and Allowances	950.00	
Sales Discounts	670.00	
Purchases	52,000.00	
Purchases Discounts		860.00
Purchases Returns and Allowances		680.00
Freight-In	450.00	
Salary Expense	12,300.00	
Payroll Tax Expense	420.00	
Postage Expense	25.00	
Miscellaneous Expense	30.00	
Interest Expense	300.00	
Rental Income		200.00
Supplies Expense	500.00	
Insurance Expense	300.00	
Amortization Expense, Store Equipment	50.00	
Salary Payable		
	86,995.00	100,740.00
Net Income	13,745.00	
	100,740.00	100,740.00

$19,000 worth of beginning inventory is assumed sold during the period and thus is part of the cost of goods sold. By placing it in the debit column of Income Summary, we increase the cost of goods sold.
$4,000 is the cost of ending inventory at the end of the period. It is unsold and therefore is not part of the cost of goods sold. By placing it in the credit column of Income Summary, we reduce the cost of goods sold.
$95,000 is the credit balance of Sales. The Sales Returns and Allowances, $950, and Sales Discounts, $670, are placed on the debit side, which represents a reduction to total sales:
(Cr.) Sales
(Dr.) Less: Sales Returns and Allowances
(Dr.) Less: Sales Discounts
The Purchases account, $52,000, is on the debit side, reflecting an increase in costs from purchasing additional merchandise. The Purchases Discounts, $860, and Purchases Returns and Allowances, $680, are on the credit side, which reduces cost of purchases:
(Dr.) Purchases
(Cr.) Less: Purchases Returns and Allowances
(Cr.) Less: Purchases Discounts
Freight-In adds to the cost of goods sold.
Rental Income, which falls under the category "other income" for Art's Wholesale, is increased by $200, because the first month's rental agreement has been fulfilled.

*Remember, we do not combine the $19,000 and $4,000 in Income Summary. When we prepare the cost of goods sold section for the formal financial report, we will need both a beginning and an ending figure for inventory.

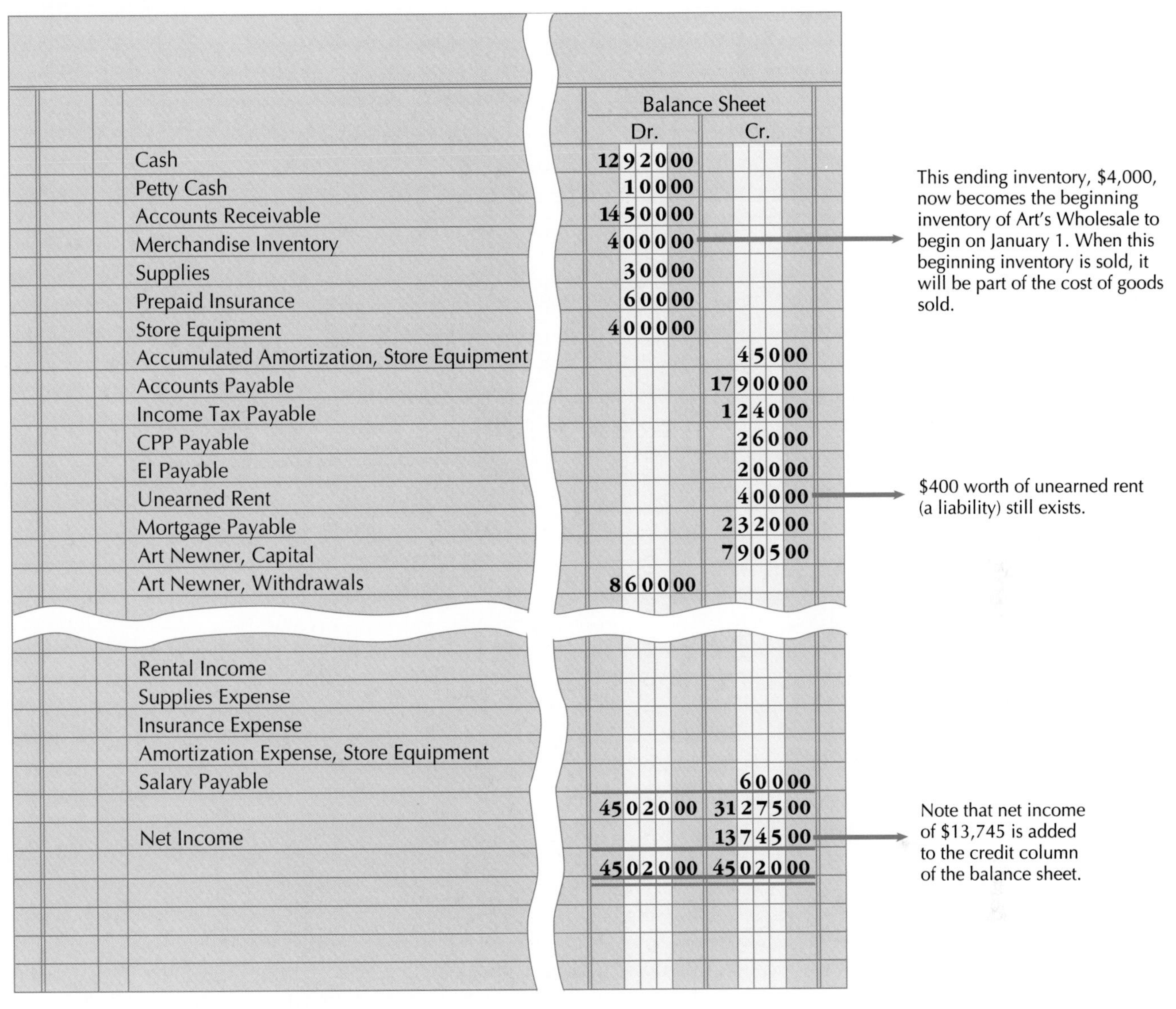

	Balance Sheet	
	Dr.	Cr.
Cash	12920 00	
Petty Cash	100 00	
Accounts Receivable	14500 00	
Merchandise Inventory	4000 00	
Supplies	300 00	
Prepaid Insurance	600 00	
Store Equipment	4000 00	
Accumulated Amortization, Store Equipment		450 00
Accounts Payable		17900 00
Income Tax Payable		1240 00
CPP Payable		260 00
EI Payable		200 00
Unearned Rent		400 00
Mortgage Payable		2320 00
Art Newner, Capital		7905 00
Art Newner, Withdrawals	8600 00	
Rental Income		
Supplies Expense		
Insurance Expense		
Amortization Expense, Store Equipment		
Salary Payable		600 00
	45020 00	31275 00
Net Income		13745 00
	45020 00	45020 00

This ending inventory, $4,000, now becomes the beginning inventory of Art's Wholesale to begin on January 1. When this beginning inventory is sold, it will be part of the cost of goods sold.
$400 worth of unearned rent (a liability) still exists.
Note that net income of $13,745 is added to the credit column of the balance sheet.

FIGURE 12-7
Balance Sheet Section of the Worksheet

FIGURE 12-8 Completed Worksheet

ART'S WHOLESALE CLOTHING COMPANY WORKSHEET FOR YEAR ENDED DECEMBER 31, 2001

	Trial Balance		Adjustments		Adjusted Trial Balance		Income Statement		Balance Sheet	
	Dr.	Cr.	Dr.	Cr.	Dr.	Cr.	Dr.	Cr.	Dr.	Cr.
Cash	12920 00				12920 00				12920 00	
Petty Cash	100 00				100 00				100 00	
Accounts Receivable	14500 00				14500 00				14500 00	
Merchandise Inventory	19000 00		(B) 4000 00	(A) 19000 00	4000 00				4000 00	
Supplies	800 00			(D) 500 00	300 00				300 00	
Prepaid Insurance	900 00			(E) 300 00	600 00				600 00	
Store Equipment	4000 00				4000 00				4000 00	
Accumulated Amortization, Store Equipment		400 00		(F) 50 00		450 00				450 00
Accounts Payable		17900 00				17900 00				17900 00
Income Tax Payable		1240 00				1240 00				1240 00
CPP Payable		260 00				260 00				260 00
EI Payable		200 00				200 00				200 00
Unearned Rent		600 00	(C) 200 00			400 00				400 00
Mortgage Payable		2320 00				2320 00				2320 00
Art Newner, Capital		7905 00				7905 00				7905 00
Art Newner, Withdrawals	8600 00				8600 00				8600 00	
Income Summary			(A) 19000 00	(B) 4000 00	19000 00	4000 00	19000 00	4000 00		
Sales		95000 00				95000 00		95000 00		
Sales Returns and Allowances	950 00				950 00		950 00			
Sales Discounts	670 00				670 00		670 00			
Purchases	52000 00				52000 00		52000 00			
Purchases Discounts		860 00				860 00		860 00		
Purchases Returns and Allowances		680 00				680 00		680 00		
Freight-In	450 00				450 00		450 00			
Salary Expense	11700 00		(G) 600 00		12300 00		12300 00			
Payroll Tax Expense	420 00				420 00		420 00			
Postage Expense	25 00				25 00		25 00			
Miscellaneous Expense	30 00				30 00		30 00			
Interest Expense	300 00				300 00		300 00			
	127365 00	127365 00								
Rental Income				(C) 200 00		200 00		200 00		
Supplies Expense			(D) 500 00		500 00		500 00			
Insurance Expense			(E) 300 00		300 00		300 00			
Amortization Expense, Store Equipment			(F) 50 00		50 00		50 00			
Salaries Payable				(G) 600 00		600 00				600 00
			24650 00	24650 00	132015 00	132015 00	86995 00	100740 00	45020 00	31275 00
Net Income							13745 00			13745 00
							100740 00	100740 00	45020 00	45020 00

LEARNING UNIT 12-2 REVIEW

AT THIS POINT you should be able to:

- Complete adjustments for a merchandising company. (pp. 503–505)
- Complete a worksheet. (pp. 505–508)

SELF-REVIEW QUIZ 12-2

(The form you need is a blank, fold-out worksheet at the end of the *Study Guide with Working Papers.*)

From the trial balance shown here, complete a worksheet for Ray Company. Additional data includes: (a and b) On December 31, 2000, ending inventory was calculated as $200; (c) storage fees earned, $516; (d) rent expired, $100; (e) amortization expense, office equipment, $60; (f) salaries accrued, $200.

RAY COMPANY
TRIAL BALANCE
DECEMBER 31, 2000

Account Titles	Trial Balance Dr.	Trial Balance Cr.
Cash	2486 00	
Merchandise Inventory	824 00	
Prepaid Rent	1152 00	
Prepaid Insurance	60 00	
Office Equipment	2160 00	
Accumulated Amorization, Office Equipment		560 00
Unearned Storage Fees		2516 00
Accounts Payable		100 00
B. Ray, Capital		1932 00
Income Summary	—	—
Sales		11040 00
Sales Returns and Allowances	546 00	
Sales Discounts	216 00	
Purchases	5256 00	
Purchases Returns and Allowances		168 00
Purchases Discounts		102 00
Salaries Expense	2016 00	
Insurance Expense	1392 00	
Utilities Expense	96 00	
Plumbing Expense	214 00	
	16418 00	16418 00

Solution to Self-Review Quiz 12-2

The solution is shown on the following page.

Quiz Tip

The ending inventory of $200 becomes next year's beginning inventory.

RAY COMPANY
WORKSHEET
FOR YEAR ENDED DECEMBER 31, 2000

Account Titles	Trial Balance Dr.	Trial Balance Cr.	Adjustments Dr.	Adjustments Cr.	Adjusted Trial Balance Dr.	Adjusted Trial Balance Cr.	Income Statement Dr.	Income Statement Cr.	Balance Sheet Dr.	Balance Sheet Cr.
Cash	2486 00				2486 00				2486 00	
Merchandise Inventory	824 00		(B) 200 00	(A) 824 00	200 00				200 00	
Prepaid Rent	1152 00			(D) 100 00	1052 00				1052 00	
Prepaid Insurance	60 00				60 00				60 00	
Office Equipment	2160 00				2160 00				2160 00	
Accum. Amort., Store Equipment		560 00		(E) 60 00		620 00				620 00
Unearned Storage Fees		2516 00	(C) 516 00			2000 00				2000 00
Accounts Payable		100 00				100 00				100 00
B. Ray, Capital		1932 00				1932 00				1932 00
Income Summary			(A) 824 00	(B) 200 00	824 00	200 00	824 00	200 00		
Sales		11040 00				11040 00		11040 00		
Sales Returns and Allowances	546 00				546 00		546 00			
Sales Discounts	216 00				216 00		216 00			
Purchases	5256 00				5256 00		5256 00			
Purchases Returns and Allowances		168 00				168 00		168 00		
Purchases Discounts		102 00				102 00		102 00		
Salaries Expense	2016 00		(F) 200 00		2216 00		2216 00			
Insurance Expense	1392 00				1392 00		1392 00			
Utilities Expense	96 00				96 00		96 00			
Plumbing Expense	214 00				214 00		214 00			
	16418 00	16418 00								
Storage Fees Earned				(C) 516 00		516 00		516 00		
Rent Expense			(D) 100 00		100 00		100 00			
Amortization Expense, Equipment			(E) 60 00		60 00		60 00			
Salaries Payable				(F) 200 00		200 00				200 00
			1900 00	1900 00	16878 00	16878 00	10920 00	12026 00	5958 00	4852 00
Net Income							1106 00			1106 00
							12026 00	12026 00	5958 00	5958 00

Chapter Review

Summary of Key Points

Learning Unit 12-1

1. The periodic inventory system updates the record of goods on hand only at the end of the accounting period. This system is used by companies with a variety of merchandise with low unit prices.
2. In the periodic inventory system, additional purchases of merchandise during the accounting period will be recorded in the Purchases account. The amount for beginning inventory will remain unchanged during the accounting period. At the end of the period a new figure for ending inventory will be calculated.
3. Beginning inventory at the end of the accounting period is added to the cost of goods sold, while ending inventory is deducted from the cost of goods sold.
4. The perpetual inventory system keeps a continuous record of inventory. It is used by companies with a low volume of sales and high unit prices, and often utilizes a computer system.
5. Unearned Revenue is a liability account that accumulates revenue that has not been earned yet, although the cash has been received. It represents a liability to the seller until the service or product is performed or delivered.

Learning Unit 12-2

1. Two important adjustments in the accounting for a merchandising company deal with the Merchandise Inventory account and with the Unearned Revenue account (unearned rent).
2. Figures for beginning and ending inventory on the Income Summary line on the worksheet are never combined; they are also carried over separately to the adjusted trial balance and income statement columns of the worksheet. In the balance sheet column, the figure for ending inventory becomes the beginning inventory figure for the new accounting period.
3. When a company delivers goods or services for which it has been paid in advance, an adjustment is made to reduce the liability account Unearned Revenue and to increase a revenue account.

Key Terms

Beginning merchandise inventory (beginning inventory) The cost of goods on hand in a company at the beginning of an accounting period (p. 498)

Ending merchandise inventory (ending inventory) The cost of goods that remain unsold at the end of the accounting period. It is an asset on the balance sheet. (p. 498)

Mortgage Payable A liability account showing the amount owed on a mortgage (p. 503)

Periodic inventory system An inventory system that, at the end of each accounting period, calculates the cost of the unsold goods on hand by taking the cost of each unit times the number of units of each product on hand (p. 498)

Perpetual inventory system An inventory system that keeps continual track of each type of inventory by recording units on hand at the beginning, units sold, and the current balance after each sale or purchase (p. 498)

Unearned Revenue A liability account that records receipt of payment for goods or services in advance of delivery. When the goods or services are delivered, an adjustment is made to reduce Unearned Revenue and increase earned revenue. (The example we used in this chapter is Unearned Rent.) (p. 503)

Blueprint of a Worksheet for a Merchandising Company

WORKSHEET

Account Titles	Adjustments		Adjusted Trial Balance		Income Statement		Balance Sheet	
	Dr.	Cr.	Dr.	Cr.	Dr.	Cr.	Dr.	Cr.
Cash			X				X	
Petty Cash			X				X	
Accounts Receivable			X				X	
Merchandise Inventory	X-E	X-B	X-E				X-E	
Supplies			X				X	
Equipment			X				X	
Accumulated Amortization, Store Equipment				X				X
Accounts Payable				X				X
Income Tax Payable				X				X
CPP Payable				X				X
EI Payable				X				X
Unearned Sales				X				X
Mortgage Payable				X				X
A. Flynn, Capital				X				X
A. Flynn, Withdrawals			X				X	
Income Summary*	X-B	X-E	X-B	X-E	X-B	X-E		
Sales				X		X		
Sales Returns and Allowance			X		X			
Sales Discounts			X		X			
Purchases			X		X			
Purchases Returns and Allowances				X		X		
Purchases Discounts				X		X		
Freight-In			X		X			
Salaries Expense			X		X			
Payroll Tax Expense			X		X			
Insurance Expense			X		X			
Amortization Expense			X		X			
Salaries Payable				X				X
Rental Income				X		X		

*Note that the figures for beginning inventory (X-B) and ending inventory (X-E) are never combined on the Income Summary line of the worksheet. When the formal income statement is prepared, two distinct figures for inventory will be used to explain and calculate cost of goods sold. Beginning inventory adds to cost of goods sold; ending inventory reduces cost of goods sold.

QUESTIONS, MINI EXERCISES, EXERCISES, AND PROBLEMS

Discussion Questions

1. When would a company consider using a periodic inventory system?
2. What is the function of the Purchases account?
3. A low-volume, high-unit-price inventory requires a company to use a periodic inventory system. Accept or reject, and support your answer.
4. Explain why unearned revenue is a liability account.
5. In a periodic system of inventory, the balance of beginning inventory will remain unchanged during the period. True or false?
6. What is the purpose of an inventory sheet?
7. Why do many unearned revenue accounts have to be adjusted?
8. Explain why figures for beginning and ending inventory are not combined on the Income Summary line of the worksheet.

Mini Exercises

(The forms you need are on page 12-2 of the *Study Guide with Working Papers.*)

Adjustment for Merchandise Inventory

1. Given the following, journalize the adjusting entries for merchandise inventory. Note that ending inventory has a balance of $12,000.

Merchandise Inventory 114	
20,000	

Income Summary 313	

Adjustment for Unearned Fees

2. **a.** Given the following, journalize the adjusting entry. By December 31, $300 worth of the unearned dog walking fees were earned.

Unearned Dog Walking Fees 225	
	650 12/1/02

Earned Dog Walking Fees 441	
	4,000 12/1/02

b. What is the category of unearned dog walking fees?

Worksheet

3. Match each of the six items listed below with one of the following locations:
   1. Located on the Income Statement debit column of the worksheet
   2. Located on the Income Statement credit column of the worksheet
   3. Located on the Balance Sheet debit column of the worksheet
   4. Located on the Balance Sheet credit column of the worksheet

   ______ **a.** Ending Merchandise Inventory
   ______ **b.** Unearned Rent
   ______ **c.** Sales Discounts
   ______ **d.** Purchases
   ______ **e.** Rental Income
   ______ **f.** Petty Cash

Merchandise Inventory Adjustment on Worksheet

4. Adjustment column of a worksheet:

Merchandise Inventory
Income Summary

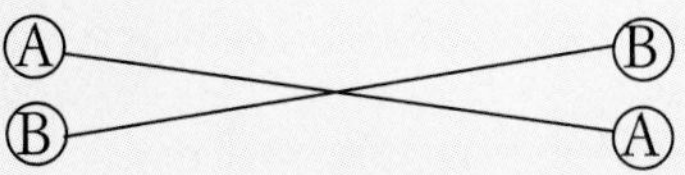

Explain what the letters A and B represent. Why are the letters A and B never combined?

Income Summary on the Worksheet

5.

	Adjustments		Adjusted Trial Balance		Income Statement	
	Dr.	**Cr.**	**Dr.**	**Cr.**	**Dr.**	**Cr.**
Income Summary	A	B	C	D	E	F

Given a figure for Beginning Inventory of $500 and a $700 figure for Ending Inventory, place these numbers on the Income Summary line of this partial worksheet.

Exercises

(The forms you need are on page 12-3 of the *Study Guide with Working Papers.*)

Categorizing account titles

12-1. Indicate the normal balance and category of each of the following accounts:

a. Purchases Returns and Allowances
b. Merchandise Inventory (beginning of period)
c. Freight-In
d. Payroll Tax Expense
e. Purchases Discounts
f. Sales Discount
g. CPP Payable
h. Unearned Revenue

Calculating net sales, cost of goods sold, gross profit, and net income

12-2. From the following, calculate **a.** net sales, **b.** cost of goods sold, **c.** gross profit, and **d.** net income:

Data Sales, $22,000; Sales Discounts, $500; Sales Returns and Allowances, $250; Beginning Inventory, $650; Net Purchases, $13,200; Ending Inventory, $510; Operating Expenses, $3,600.

Unearned revenue

12-3. Allan Co. had the following balances on December 31, 2003:

Cash	
2,100	

Unearned Janitorial Service Revenue	
	600

Janitorial Service Revenue	
	7,200

The accountant for Allan has asked you to make an adjustment, since $400 worth of janitorial services has just been performed for customers who had paid in advance. Construct a transaction analysis chart.

Calculating cost of goods sold

12-4. Lesan Co. purchased merchandise costing $400,000. Calculate the cost of goods sold under the following different situations:

a. Beginning inventory of $40,000 and no ending inventory

b. Beginning inventory of $50,000 and a $60,000 ending inventory

c. No beginning inventory and a $30,000 ending inventory

Preparing a worksheet

12-5. Prepare a worksheet from the following information:

(A and B) Merchandise Inventory—ending	13
(C) Store Supplies on hand	4
(D) Amortization on Store Equipment	4
(E) Accrued Salaries	2

MOORE CO.
TRIAL BALANCE
DECEMBER 31, 2001

	Dr.	Cr.
Cash	8 00	
Accounts Receivable	5 00	
Merchandise Inventory	11 00	
Store Supplies	10 00	
Store Equipment	20 00	
Accumulated Amortization, Store Equipment		6 00
Accounts Payable		5 00
J. Moore, Capital		34 00
Income Summary	—	—
Sales		64 00
Sales Returns and Allowances	9 00	
Purchases	23 00	
Purchases Discounts		3 00
Freight-In	3 00	
Salaries Expense	10 00	
Advertising Expense	13 00	
Totals	112 00	112 00

Group A Problems

(The forms you need are on page 12-4 of the *Study Guide with Working Papers*.)

Calculating net sales, cost of goods sold, gross profit, and net income

12A-1. On the basis of the accounts listed below, calculate:

a. Net sales

b. Cost of goods sold

c. Gross profit

d. Net income

Check Figure

Net Income $2,932

Accounts Payable	$2,200
Operating Expenses	1,490
J. Jensen, Capital	8,200
Purchases	4,250
Freight-In	60
Ending Merchandise Inventory, December 31, 2001	1,240
Sales	9,210

Accounts Receivable	1,389
Cash	656
Purchases Discounts	132
Sales Returns and Allowances	185
Beginning Merchandise Inventory, January 1, 2001	1,560
Purchases Returns and Allowances	247
Sales Discounts	352

Comprehensive problem: Completing a worksheet for a merchandising company

12A-2. From the following trial balance, complete a worksheet for Jim's Hardware.

Check Figure

Net Income $1,982

JIM'S HARDWARE
TRIAL BALANCE
DECEMBER 31, 2000

	Dr.	Cr.
Cash	78600	
Accounts Receivable	115200	
Merchandise Inventory	60000	
Prepaid Insurance	68400	
Store Equipment	216000	
Accumulated Amortization, Store Equipment		66000
Accounts Payable		51600
Jim Spool, Capital		163200
Income Summary	—	—
Sales		1104000
Sales Returns and Allowances	54600	
Sales Discounts	21600	
Purchases	525600	
Purchases Discounts		16800
Purchases Returns and Allowances		10200
Wages Expense	171600	
Rent Expense	79200	
Telephone Expense	11400	
Miscellaneous Expense	9600	
	1411800	1411800

Assumptions

A. **and** B. Ending inventory on December 31 is calculated at $415.
C. Insurance expired, $220
D. Amortization expense on store equipment, $75
E. Accrued wages, $112

Comprehensive problem: Completing a worksheet

Check Figure
Net Income $5,576

12A-3. The owner of Waltz Company has asked you to prepare a worksheet from the following trial balance and additional data:

WALTZ COMPANY
TRIAL BALANCE
DECEMBER 31, 2002

	Dr.	Cr.
Cash	540800	
Petty Cash	24000	
Accounts Receivable	251200	
Beginning Merchandise Inventory, January 1	509200	
Prepaid Rent	61600	
Office Supplies	94400	
Office Equipment	928000	
Accumulated Amortization, Office Equipment		760000
Accounts Payable		596400
K. Waltz, Capital		547600
K. Waltz, Withdrawals	480000	
Income Summary	—	—
Sales		5248400
Sales Returns and Allowances	9600	
Sales Discounts	240000	
Purchases	2931600	
Purchases Discounts		1600
Purchases Returns and Allowances		34800
Office Salaries Expense	740800	
Insurance Expense	240000	
Advertising Expense	80000	
Utilities Expense	57600	
	7188800	7188800

Additional Data

A. **and** B. Ending merchandise inventory on December 31, $2,140
C. Office supplies used up, $345
D. Rent expired, $214
E. Amortization expense on office equipment, $485
F. Office salaries earned but not paid, $280

Comprehensive problem: Completing a worksheet with payroll and unearned revenue

12A-4. From the following trial balance and additional data, complete the worksheet for Ron's Wholesale Clothing Company.

Check Figure
Net Income $349

RON'S WHOLESALE CLOTHING COMPANY
TRIAL BALANCE
DECEMBER 31, 2001

	Dr.	Cr.
Cash	4460.00	
Petty Cash	300.00	
Accounts Receivable	7500.00	
Merchandise Inventory	9000.00	
Supplies	1000.00	
Prepaid Insurance	850.00	
Store Equipment	2500.00	
Accumulated Amortization, Store Equipment		1500.00
Accounts Payable		10635.00
Income Tax Payable		1060.00
CPP Payable		108.00
EI Payable		150.00
Unearned Storage Fees		357.00
Ron Win, Capital		12500.00
Ron Win, Withdrawals	4300.00	
Income Summary	—	—
Sales		45000.00
Sales Returns and Allowances	1475.00	
Sales Discounts	1335.00	
Purchases	26000.00	
Purchases Discounts		550.00
Purchases Returns and Allowances		400.00
Freight-In	225.00	
Salaries Expense	12000.00	
Payroll Tax Expense	420.00	
Interest Expense	895.00	
	72260.00	72260.00

Additional Data

A. **and** B. Ending merchandise inventory on December 31, $7,200
C. Supplies on hand, $380
D. Insurance expired, $560
E. Amortization expense on store equipment, $425
F. Storage fees earned, $154

Group B Problems

(The forms you need are on page 12-4 of the *Study Guide with Working Papers.*)

Calculating net sales, cost of goods sold, gross profit, and net income

12B-1. From the following accounts, calculate **a.** net sales, **b.** cost of goods sold, **c.** gross profit, **d.** net income.

Sales Discounts	$ 452
Purchases Returns and Allowances	64
Beginning Merchandise Inventory, January 1, 2001	79

Sales Returns and Allowances	191
Purchases Discounts	42
Cash	3,895
Accounts Receivable	441
Sales	3,950
Ending Merchandise Inventory, December 31, 2001	75
Freight-In	41
Purchases	1,152
R. Roland, Capital	1,950
Operating Expenses	895
Accounts Payable	129

Check Figure

Net Income $1,321

Comprehensive problem: Completing a worksheet for a merchandising company

12B-2. As the accountant for Jim's Hardware, you have been asked to complete a worksheet from the following trial balance as well as additional data.

Check Figure

Net Income $1,010

JIM'S HARDWARE
TRIAL BALANCE
DECEMBER 31, 2000

	Dr.	Cr.
Cash	96000	
Accounts Receivable	160000	
Merchandise Inventory	73600	
Prepaid Insurance	111200	
Store Equipment	320000	
Accumulated Amortization, Store Equipment		168000
Accounts Payable		140800
J. Spool, Capital		257600
Income Summary	—	—
Sales		1480000
Sales Returns and Allowances	72800	
Sales Discounts	68800	
Purchases	708800	
Purchases Discountss		24000
Purchases Returns and Allowances		24800
Wages Expense	230400	
Rent Expense	184000	
Telephone Expense	55200	
Miscellaneous Expense	14400	
	2095200	2095200

Additional Data

A. **and** B. Cost of ending inventory on December 31, $392

C. Insurance expired, $240

D. Amortization expense on store equipment, $100

E. Accrued wages, $250

Comprehensive problem:
Completing a worksheet

12B-3. From the following, complete a worksheet for Waltz Company.

Check Figure
Net Income $8,010

WALTZ COMPANY TRIAL BALANCE DECEMBER 31, 2002		
	Dr.	Cr.
Cash	380000	
Petty Cash	10000	
Accounts Receivable	340000	
Merchandise Inventory	520400	
Prepaid Rent	120000	
Office Supplies	136000	
Office Equipment	968000	
Accumulated Amortization, Office Equipment		404000
Accounts Payable		796400
K. Waltz, Capital		547600
K. Waltz, Withdrawals	500000	
Income Summary	—	—
Sales		5246200
Sales Returns and Allowances	11600	
Sales Discounts	220000	
Purchases	2929600	
Purchases Discounts		120800
Purchases Returns and Allowances		135000
Office Salaries Expense	740800	
Insurance Expense	220000	
Advertising Expense	80000	
Utilities Expense	73600	
	7250000	7250000

Additional Data

A. **and** B. Ending merchandise inventory on December 31, $2,840
C. Office supplies on hand, $390
D. Rent expired, $300
E. Amortization expense on office equipment, $325
F. Salaries accrued, $295

Comprehensive problem: Completing a worksheet with payroll and unearned revenue

12B-4. From the following trial balance and additional data, complete the worksheet for Ron's Wholesale Clothing Company.

Check Figure

Net Income $4,517

RON'S WHOLESALE CLOTHING COMPANY TRIAL BALANCE DECEMBER 31, 2001		
	Dr.	Cr.
Cash	2600 00	
Petty Cash	30 00	
Accounts Receivable	3000 00	
Beginning Merchandise Inventory, January 1	3600 00	
Supplies	270 00	
Prepaid Insurance	180 00	
Store Equipment	1000 00	
Accumulated Amortization, Store Equipment		496 00
Accounts Payable		4590 00
Income Tax Payable		590 00
CPP Payable		74 00
EI Payable		100 00
Unearned Storage Fees		350 00
Ron Win, Capital		2734 00
Ron Win, Withdrawals	1800 00	
Income Summary	—	—
Sales		19400 00
Sales Returns and Allowances	560 00	
Sales Discounts	480 00	
Purchases	8600 00	
Purchases Discounts		240 00
Purchases Returns and Allowances		160 00
Freight-In	100 00	
Salaries Expense	6000 00	
Payroll Tax Expense	194 00	
Interest Expense	320 00	
	28734 00	28734 00

Additional Data

A. **and** B. Ending merchandise inventory on December 31, $4,800

C. Supplies on hand, $78

D. Insurance expired, $72

E. Amortization expense on store equipment, $95

F. Storage fees earned, $130

Group C Problems

(The forms you need are on page 12-5 of the *Study Guide with Working Papers.*)

Calculating net sales, cost of goods sold, gross profit, and net income

12C-1. On the basis of the accounts listed below, calculate:

a. Net sales

b. Cost of goods sold

c. Gross profit

d. Net income

Check Figure
Net Income $5,405

Accounts Payable	$ 3,800
Operating Expenses	1,150
P. Juarez, Capital	12,460
Purchases	6,785
Freight-In	157
Ending Merchandise Inventory, December 31, 2000	1,670
Sales	13,730
Accounts Receivable	2,675
Cash	1.456
Purchases Discounts	262
Sales Returns and Allowances	315
Beginning Merchandise Inventory, January 1, 2000	1,940
Purchases Returns and Allowances	466
Sales Discounts	376

Comprehensive problem: Completing a worksheet for a merchandising company

12C-2. From the following trial balance and additional data, complete a worksheet for Corocan Tile Company.

Additional Data

A. **and** B. Ending merchandise inventory on October 31, $9,462
C. Supplies on hand, $427.70
D. Insurance expired, $246.72
E. Amortization expense on equipment, $916
F. Advertising bill received, $500 plus GST of $35.00

Check Figure
Net Income $1,566.18

COROCAN TILE COMPANY
TRIAL BALANCE
OCTOBER 31, 2001

	Dr.	Cr.
Cash	1710 40	
Petty Cash	200 00	
Accounts Receivable	4316 70	
Beginning Merchandise Inventory, November 1	13467 00	
Supplies	733 00	
Prepaid Insurance	914 00	
GST Prepaid	748 52	
Tile Cutting Equipment	7820 00	
Accumulated Amortization, Equipment		1466 00
Accounts Payable		16782 40
GST Collected		1673 58
Income Tax Payable		1771 00
CPP Payable		246 20
EI Payable		373 80
Winnie Corocan, Capital		6395 44
Winnie Corocan, Withdrawals	6338 00	
Income Summary	—	—
Sales		69356 28
Sales Returns and Allowances	1388 24	
Sales Discounts	715 42	
Purchases	42772 64	
Purchases Discounts		882 30
Purchase Returns and Allowances		512 86
Freight-In	425 70	
Salaries Expense	15870 00	
Payroll Taxes Expense	1426 00	
Interest Expense	614 24	
	99459 86	99459 86

Comprehensive problem: Completing a worksheet

12C-3. The owner of Chapel Antique Clock Company has asked you to prepare a worksheet from the following trial balance and additional data:

Check Figure
Net Income $5,920.93

CHAPEL ANTIQUE CLOCK COMPANY TRIAL BALANCE MAY 31, 2002		
	Dr.	Cr.
Cash	762.40	
Petty Cash	150.00	
Accounts Receivable	2,715.96	
Beginning Clock Inventory, June 1	10,766.42	
Repair Supplies	624.30	
Prepaid Insurance	753.76	
GST Prepaid	696.14	
Clock Repair Equipment	4,300.00	
Accumulated Amortization, Repair Equipment		1,248.90
Accounts Payable		8,686.92
GST Collected		912.47
Income Tax Payable		1,155.40
CPP Payable		167.70
EI Payable		278.60
Mike Patel, Capital		5,566.09
Mike Patel, Withdrawals	4,380.00	
Income Summary	—	—
Sales		57,245.18
Sales Returns and Allowances	267.10	
Sales Discounts	176.42	
Purchases	31,488.92	
Purchases Discounts		277.44
Purchase Returns and Allowances		512.86
Freight-In	96.31	
Salaries Expense	13,475.00	
Payroll Taxes Expense	1,276.40	
Advertising Expense	721.68	
Rent Expense	2,788.00	
Utilities Expense	612.75	
	76,051.56	76,051.56

Additional Data

A. **and** B. Ending clock inventory on May 31, $11,281.17

C. Supplies used during period, $219.40

D. Insurance expired, $491.16

E. Amortization expense on equipment, $716.16

F. Advertising bill received, $300 plus GST of $21

Comprehensive problem: Completing a worksheet with payroll and unearned revenue

12C-4. From the following trial balance and additional data, complete the worksheet for Gwendolyn's Archery Sales Company.

Check Figure

Net Income $4,648.45

GWENDOLYN'S ARCHERY SALES COMPANY TRIAL BALANCE APRIL 30, 2001		
	Dr.	Cr.
Cash	2467 93	
Petty Cash	75 00	
Accounts Receivable	764 82	
Beginning Merchandise Inventory, May 1	17368 44	
Supplies on Hand	896 26	
Prepaid Insurance	1158 20	
GST Prepaid	1458 76	
Equipment	8975 00	
Accumulated Amortization, Equipment		5762 14
Accounts Payable		21479 50
GST Collected		2444 70
Income Tax Payable		974 70
CPP Payable		132 50
EI Payable		178 32
Gwen Sterling, Capital		11373 06
Gwen Sterling, Withdrawals	8450 00	
Income Summary	—	—
Sales		78422 76
Sales Returns and Allowances	467 13	
Sales Discounts	472 38	
Purchases	56381 58	
Purchases Discounts		782 40
Purchase Returns and Allowances		1328 37
Freight-In	376 82	
Salaries Expense	14762 80	
Payroll Taxes Expense	1566 23	
Advertising Expense	2572 84	
Rent Expense	3720 00	
Utilities Expense	944 26	
	122878 45	122878 45

Additional Data

A. **and** B. Ending merchandise inventory on April 30, $24,718.13

C. Supplies on hand at end of April, $476.39

D. Insurance expired, $622.96

E. Amortization expense on equipment, $817.90

F. Utilities bill received, $110 plus GST of $7.70

REAL WORLD APPLICATIONS

(The forms you need are on page 12-6 of the *Study Guide with Working Papers.*)

12R-1.
Kim Andrews prepared the following income statement on a cash basis for Ed Sloan, M.D.:

ED SLOAN, M.D. INCOME STATEMENT FOR YEAR ENDED DECEMBER 31, 2003	
Professional Fees Earned	5000000
Expenses	1800000
Net Income	3200000

Ed Sloan has requested information from Kim as to what his professional fees earned would be under the accrual-basis system of accounting. Kim has asked you to provide Dr. Sloan with this information, basing it on the following facts that Kim ignored in the original preparation of the financial report:

	2002	*2003*
Accrued Professional Fees	$4,200	$5,300
Unearned Professional Fees	6,200	4,250

12R-2.
Abby Jay is having a difficult time understanding the relationships among sales, cost of goods sold, gross profit, and net income for a merchandising company. As the accounting lab tutor, you have been asked to sit down with Abby and explain how to calculate the missing amounts in each situation listed below. Keep in mind that each situation is a distinct and separate business problem.

	Sales	Beginning Inventory	Purchases	Ending Inventory	Cost of Goods Sold	Gross Profit	Expense	Net Income or Loss
Sit. 1	320,000	200,000	160,000	?	260,000	?	80,000	?
Sit. 2	380,000	140,000	?	180,000	200,000	?	100,000	80,000
Sit. 3	480,000	200,000	?	160,000	?	220,000	140,000	80,000
Sit. 4	?	160,000	280,000	140,000	?	160,000	140,000	?
Sit. 5	440,000	160,000	260,000	?	240,000	?	100,000	?
Sit. 6	280,000	120,000	?	140,000	160,000	?	?	40,000
Sit. 7	?	160,000	200,000	120,000	?	160,000	?	–20,000
Sit. 8	320,000	?	200,000	140,000	?	160,000	?	40,000

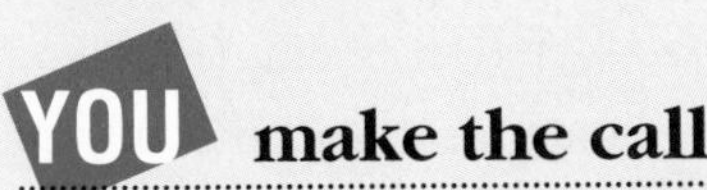

Critical Thinking/Ethical Case

12R-3.
Jim Heary is the custodian of petty cash. Jim, who is short of personal cash, decided to pay his home electrical and telephone bills from petty cash. He plans to pay it back next month. Do you feel Jim should do this? You make the call. Write down your specific recommendations to Jim.

ACCOUNTING RECALL

A CUMULATIVE APPROACH

THIS EXAMINATION REVIEWS CHAPTERS 1 THROUGH 12.

Your *Study Guide with Working Papers* (pages 12-6 and 12-7) has forms to complete this exam, as well as worked-out solutions. The page reference next to each question identifies the page to turn back to if you answer the question incorrectly.

PART I Vocabulary Review

Match each term on the left with the appropriate definition or phrase in the right-hand column.

Page Ref.		
(503)	1. Interest expense	A. A liability
(349)	2. Sales returns and allowances	B. Cost of goods sold
(498)	3. Ending merchandise inventory	C. Continual track
(504)	4. Accumulated amortization	D. Contra-asset
(499)	5. Income summary	E. Non-operating expense
(504)	6. Rental income	F. New figure for capital
(503)	7. Unearned revenue	G. Subtracted from cost of goods sold
(413)	8. Purchases	H. Other income
(176)	9. Closing	I. Contra-revenue account
(498)	10. Perpetual inventory	J. Used in adjusting merchandise inventory

PART II True or False (Accounting Theory)

(500) 11. Unearned rent is an asset.

(499) 12. Beginning and ending inventory are combined on the worksheet.

(499) 13. Ending inventory is added to cost of goods sold.

(318) 14. Due to Receiver General for Canada is a liability that includes only amounts deducted from employees.

(183) 15. The normal balance of Income Summary is a debit.

CONTINUING PROBLEM

Another seven months have passed, and the fiscal year has concluded for Eldorado Computer Centre. Tony Freedman wants to make the necessary adjustments to his company's accounts in order to prepare accurate financial statements.

Assignment

(The worksheet you require is at the end of the *Study Guide with Working Papers.*)

To prepare the necessary adjustments, use the trial balance shown on the next page and the information below.

Complete the ten-column worksheet for the 12 months ended September 30, 2002.

Inventory

Tony took inventory at the end of September and determined that there was $17,400 worth of merchandise left in stock on September 30.

Amortization of Computer Equipment

Computer depreciates at $33 a month—purchased July 5, 2001.

Computer workstations depreciate at $20 per month—purchased September 17, 2001.

Shop benches depreciate at $25 per month—purchased November 5, 2001.

Amortization of Office Equipment

Office Equipment depreciates at $10 per month—purchased July 17, 2001.

Fax machine depreciates at $10 per month—purchased November 20, 2001.

Remember: If any long-term asset is purchased in the first fiteen days of the month, Freedman will record amortization for the full month. If an asset is purchased later than the 15th, he will not record amortization in the month when it was purchased.

Additional Information

Rent for 12 months, at $400 per month, has expired.

Supplies on hand at year-end amounted to $530.

A portion of the insurance paid for in February remains as prepaid insurance at year-end. Remember that the entire premium was debited to Insurance expense.

The balance in Unearned Service Revenue (account 2050) was received from a new customer on June 1, 2002. It represents a prepayment to cover all necessary service on their ten computers for the 12 months ending May 31, 2003.

ELDORADO COMPUTER CENTRE TRIAL BALANCE AS OF 09/30/2002			
Account #	**Account Name**	**Debit Balance**	**Credit Balance**
1000	Cash	2827.49	
1010	Petty Cash	100.00	
1020	Accounts Receivable	21620.00	
1025	Prepaid Rent	5200.00	
1030	Supplies	1860.52	
1035	Prepaid Insurance		
1040	Merchandise Inventory	7000.00	
1080	Computer Shop Equipment	3800.00	
1081	Accumulated Amortization, Computer Shop Equipment		99.00
1090	Office Equipment	1050.00	
1091	Accumulated Amortization, Office Equipment		20.00
2000	Accounts Payable		4362.00
2010	Wages Payable		
2020	Due to Receiver General		
2050	Unearned Service Revenue		4800.00
2060	GST Payable		1149.83
2066	GST Recoverable	818.64	
3000	T. Freedman, Capital		7406.00
3010	T. Freedman, Withdrawals	18735.00	
3020	Income Summary		
4000	Service Revenue		76806.00
4010	Sales		96418.00
4020	Sales Returns and Allowances	378.00	
4030	Sales Discounts	212.00	
4050	Service Contracts Sold		
5010	Advertising Expense	2716.37	
5020	Rent Expense		
5030	Utilities Expense	2482.15	
5040	Phone Expense	1980.04	
5050	Supplies Expense		
5060	Insurance Expense	1846.00	
5070	Postage Expense	176.11	
5080	Amortization Expense, Computer Shop Equipment		
5090	Amortization Expense, Office Equipment		
5100	Miscellaneous Expense	143.12	
5110	Wages Expense	48726.90	
5120	Payroll Benefits Expense	375.99	
5140	Bad Debt Expense		
5600	Purchases	68414.06	
5610	Purchases Returns and Allowances		422.18
5620	Purchases Discounts		145.20
5630	Freight In	1165.82	
	Totals	191628.21	191628.21

Appendices

PERPETUAL INVENTORY

The method of accounting for merchandise inventory that we have been using thus far is characterized by the fact that the inventory account is adjusted only once at the end of the accounting period. Since the inventory account is brought up to date only periodically, this system is named the *periodic inventory method*. Let's now look at the *perpetual inventory method*, an inventory system in which the inventory account is perpetually up to date (or up to date at all times).

In the *perpetual* inventory system we have two key accounts into which we record information every time we buy or sell merchandise. These accounts are the Merchandise Inventory and Cost of Goods Sold accounts.

The Merchandise Inventory account is an asset account and is the same account that was used in the previous discussion of the periodic inventory system. However, in the *periodic* system the balance of the Merchandise Inventory was correct *only* at the end of each accounting period. In the *perpetual* system, we will be recording entries in the Merchandise Inventory account each time our store purchases new merchandise and each time we sell merchandise to a customer.

The other key account is the Cost of Goods Sold account. As we sell merchandise to our customers, we will record entries that remove the cost of the merchandise from the Merchandise Inventory account and transfer that cost to the Cost of Goods Sold account. Thus, the Merchandise Inentory account will show the correct cost for the inventory on hand, and the Cost of Goods Sold account will show the cumulative total cost of all merchandise that has been sold to our customers during the accounting period.

The perpetual method requires more accounting effort but has the important advantage that our key accounts, Merchandise Inventory and Cost of Goods Sold, will always provide *current* information to managers about their investment in inventory and the cost of the merchandise sold to customers.

Example Transactions

Let us imagine a typical college bookstore and look at some sample transactions as this bookstore buys books from publishers and then resells those books to students. We will assume that all transactions are in cash so that we can focus on recording transactions with the perpetual method of accounting for inventory.

2001

March 2 Purchased 10 copies of the textbook for the Math 2301 course at a cost of $29 per book, for a total of $290.

Mar.	2	Merchandise Inventory	290 00	
		Cash		290 00
		To record the purchase		
		of inventory		

The asset account, Merchandise Inventory, has been increased by the cost of the new merchandise we have purchased. Now let's look at a sales transaction.

2001
March 3 Sold a copy of the Math 2301 text for $38.

Date		Account	Debit	Credit
Mar.	3	Cash	38 00	
		Sales Revenue		38 00
		To record revenue		
	3	Cost of Goods Sold	29 00	
		Merchandise Inventory		29 00
		To record the cost of		
		goods sold		

In the perpetual inventory system we record both the retail value of the sale in a transaction entry that records the revenue, and the cost of the sale in a transaction entry which transfers the cost of the item sold to the Cost of Goods Sold account.

When a business is using the perpetual method, it will be necessary to keep a detailed record of the quantity and cost of each item on hand. A subsidiary ledger with an inventory record form for each item in inventory will be created. This is very similar to the way in which we keep a detailed record for each customer in an accounts receivable ledger. On the right below is the inventory record form for our Math 2301 textbook. Note how the form relates to the Merchandise Inventory account.

General Ledger Account

Merchandise Inventory

	Dr		Cr
3/2	$290		
		3/3	$29
Bal	$261		

Inventory Record Form

Math 2301 Text

Date	Purchased	Sold	Balance
3/2	10 @ $29		$290
3/3		1 @ $29	$261

The merchandise inventory ledger will consist of as many inventory record forms as a company has items for sale, and the total of the value of all items on hand will equal the balance of the Merchandise Inventory account.

Let's summarize the journal entries for the perpetual method.

Purchases: Each time we purchase inventory from a supplier we debit the Merchandise Inventory account to increase the balance.

Sales: Each time we sell an item we do *two* entries. One entry records the selling price exactly as we did with the periodic method. The additional entry transfers the cost of the item sold out of the Merchandise Inventory account and into the Cost of Goods Sold account.

The result of these entries is that our Merchandise Inventory, Cost of Goods Sold, and Sales (revenue) accounts are *perpetually* up to date.

Completion of the Accounting Cycle for a Merchandising Company

13

The Big Picture

◆

The Eldorado Computer Centre needs to expand. It currently has 400 square metres of space for repairs, sales, and office activity. Freedman is planning to increase his space and remodel some of the space he currently has. To finance his plan he will take his completed financial reports to the bank and request a line of credit. The bank will review his detailed records to form an opinion on how the business has done and determine the amount of credit the business will be able to repay.

In the last chapter you began the steps to bring the books up to date by completing the adjusting entries for the first year. In this chapter you will record those adjusting entries and prepare the financial reports.

Eldorado Computer Centre's income statement will show more detail than those prepared before, so the bank can see expenses according to the activity of the company. Some expenses can be classified as selling expenses because they relate directly to the sale of the merchandise. Other expenses, including rent and utilities, are administrative expenses, relating to office activity or general expenses of the business.

The balance sheet will also include more detail by breaking down the assets and liabilities into current and long-term categories. Freedman prepares a classified balance sheet for his business to help himself as well as creditors and suppliers understand the business's ability to repay current and long-term debt obligations.

In this chapter you will also review how to close a business year by completing the necessary closing entries and the reversing entries to prepare for the new year. For Eldorado Computer Centre, only the adjusting entries will be recorded and financial statements prepared.

Chapter Objectives

- Preparing financial reports for a merchandising company (pp. 532–536)
- Recording adjusting and closing entries (pp. 539–542)
- Preparing a post-closing trial balance (pp. 542–544)
- Dealing with reversing entries (pp. 545–547)

In Chapter 12 we covered adjustments and completing a worksheet for a merchandising company. In this chapter we will discuss the steps involved in completing the accounting cycle for a merchandising company: preparing financial reports, journalizing and posting adjusting and closing entries, preparing a post-closing trial balance, and reversing entries. First we will deal with preparing financial reports at the close of the accounting cycle.

LEARNING UNIT 13-1

Preparing Financial Reports

As we discussed in Chapter 5, when we were dealing with a service company rather than a merchandising company, the three financial reports can be prepared from the worksheet. Let's begin by looking at how Art's Wholesale Clothing Company prepares the income statement.

THE INCOME STATEMENT

See Chapters 9 and 10 for a review of terms such as net sales, cost of goods sold, and operating expenses.

Art is interested in knowing how well his business performed for the year ended December 31, 2001. What were its net sales? Were there many returns of goods from dissatisfied customers? What was the cost of the goods brought into the store versus the selling price received? How many goods were returned to suppliers? What is the cost of the goods that have not been sold? What was the cost of the freight-in? The income statement in Figure 13-1 is prepared from the income statement columns of the worksheet. (Review it first, and then we will explain each section of the income statement and where on the worksheet the information came from.)

Note that there are no debit or credit columns on the formal income statement—the inside columns on financial reports are used for subtotalling, not for debit and credit.

Note also that the income statement is broken down into several sections. Remembering the sections can help you make sense of the statement and set it up correctly on your own. Basically what it presents is this:

Net Sales
− Cost of Goods Sold
= Gross Profit
− Operating Expenses
= Net Income from Operations
+ Other Income
− Other Expenses
= Net Income

ART'S WHOLESALE CLOTHING COMPANY
PARTIAL WORKSHEET
FOR YEAR ENDED DECEMBER 31, 2001

	Income Statement Dr.	Income Statement Cr.
Income Summary	1900000	400000
Sales		9500000
Sales Returns and Allowances	95000	
Sales Discounts	67000	
Purchases	5200000	
Purchases Discounts		86000
Purchases Returns and Allowances		68000
Freight-In	45000	
Salaries Expense	1230000	
Payroll Tax Expense	42000	
Postage Expense	2500	
Miscellaneous Expense	3000	
Interest Expense	30000	
Rental Income		20000
Supplies Expense	50000	
Insurance Expense	30000	
Amortization Expense, Store Equip.	5000	
Salaries Payable		
	8699500	10074000
Net Income	1374500	
	10074000	10074000

ART'S WHOLESALE CLOTHING COMPANY
INCOME STATEMENT
FOR YEAR ENDED DECEMBER 31, 2001

Revenue				
Gross Sales				$9500000
Less: Sales Ret. and Allow.			$ 95000	
Sales Discounts			67000	162000
Net Sales				9338000
Cost of Goods Sold				
Merchandise Inventory, 1/1/01			1900000	
Purchases		$5200000		
Less: Pur. Discounts	$ 86000			
Pur. Ret. and Allow.	68000	154000		
Net Purchases		5046000		
Add: Freight-In		45000		
Net Cost of Purchases			5091000	
Cost of Goods Available for Sale			6991000	
Less: Merch. Inv., 12/31/01			400000	
Cost of Goods Sold				6591000
Gross Profit				2747000
Operating Expenses				
Salaries Expense			1230000	
Payroll Tax Expense			42000	
Amort. Exp., Store Equip.			5000	
Supplies Expense			50000	
Insurance Expense			30000	
Postage Expense			2500	
Miscellaneous Expense			3000	
Total Operating Expenses				1362500
Net Income from Operations				1384500
Other Income				
Rental Income			20000	
Other Expenses				
Interest Expense			30000	10000
Net Income				$1374500

FIGURE 13-1
Partial Work Sheet and Income Statement

Let's take these sections one at a time and see where the figures come from on the worksheet.

Revenue Section

Sales
− Sales Returns and Allowances
− Sales Discounts
= Net Sales

Net Sales The first major category of the income statement shows net sales. The figure here of $93,380 is *not* found on the worksheet—the accountant must take the individual amounts for gross sales, sales returns and allowances, and sales discounts found on the worksheet and *combine* them to arrive at a figure for net sales. Thus, although the worksheet has the individual components, it is not until the formal income statement that these individual amounts are summarized in one figure for net sales.

Cost of Goods Sold Section

Beginning Inventory
+ Net Cost of Purchases
− Ending Inventory
= Cost of Goods Sold

On the worksheet we separate figures for Merchandise Inventory. The $19,000 represents the beginning inventory of the period, while the $4,000, calculated from an inventory sheet, is the ending inventory. Note on the financial report that the cost of goods sold section uses two separate figures for inventory. Remember that in the periodic system goods brought in during the accounting period are added to the Purchases account, not to the Merchandise Inventory account.

Note that the following numbers are not found on the worksheet but are shown on the formal income statement (they are combined by the accountant in preparing the income statement):

- **Net Purchases:** $50,460 (Purchases − Purchases Discounts − Purchases Returns and Allowances)
- **Net Cost of Purchases:** $50,910 (Net Purchases + Freight-In)
- **Cost of Goods Available for Sale:** $69,910 (Beginning Inventory + Net Cost of Purchases)
- **Cost of Goods Sold:** $65,910 (Cost of Goods Available for Sale − Ending Inventory)

Gross Profit

Net Sales
− Cost of Goods Sold
= Gross Profit

The figure for gross profit ($27,470) is arrived at by subtracting cost of goods sold from net sales ($93,380 − $65,910). The gross profit figure of $27,470 is not found by itself on the worksheet, but, like others we have discussed, is calculated by the accountant from separate figures on the worksheet.

Operating Expenses Section

The total of the operating expenses does not appear on its own on the worksheet; to get this figure of $13,625, the accountant adds up all the expenses on the worksheet that resulted from doing business.

Many companies break expenses down into those directly related to the selling activity of the company (**selling expenses**) and those related to administrative or office activity (**administrative expenses** or **general expenses**). Here's a sample list broken down into these two categories:

Operating Expenses

Selling Expenses	*Administrative Expenses*
Sales Salaries Expense	Rent Expense
Delivery Expense	Office Salaries Expense
Advertising Expense	Utilities Expense

Amortization Expense, Store Equipment	Supplies Expense
Insurance Expense	Amortization Expense, Office Equipment
Total Selling Expenses	Total Administrative Expenses

Other Income (or Other Revenue) Section

This section will record any revenue other than revenue from sales. For example, Art's Wholesale makes a profit from subletting a portion of a building and earning rental income of $200, and that income goes in this section.

Other Expenses Section

This section will record non-operating expenses—those not related to the main operating activities of the business. For example, Art's Wholesale has paid or owes $300 interest on money it has borrowed.

Statement of Owner's Equity

Statement of owner's equity is the same for a merchandising business as for a service firm.

The information used to complete the statement of owner's equity comes from the balance sheet columns of the worksheet. Keep in mind that the capital account in the ledger should be checked to see if any additional investments have occurred during the period. Note in the following diagram that the worksheet aids in this. The ending figure of $13,050 for Art Newner, Capital, will be carried over to the balance sheet, which is the final report we will look at in this chapter.

Any additional investment by the owner would be added to his or her beginning capital amount. The illustration at the right does not show this, however.

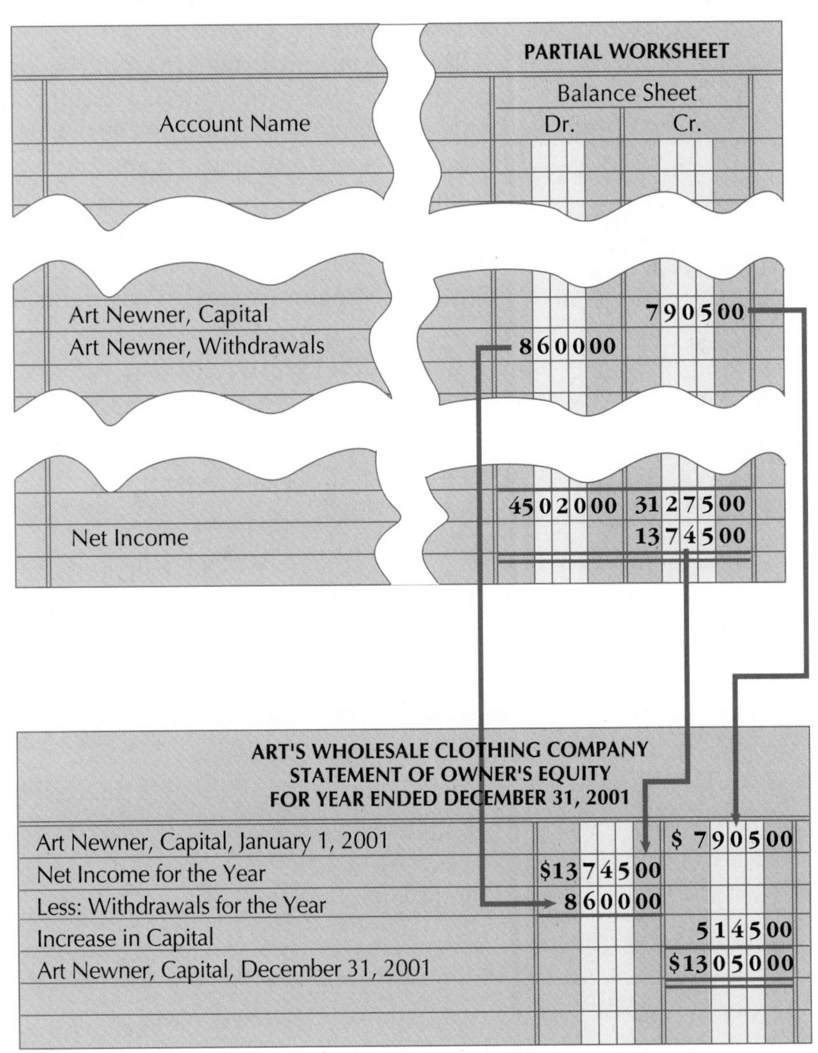

The Balance Sheet

The diagram in Figure 13-2 shows how a worksheet is used to aid in the preparation of the balance sheet. This balance sheet is called a **classified balance sheet** because assets and liabilities are broken down into more detail. Let's look at each of the categories on the classified balance sheet in turn.

Current assets are defined as cash and assets that will be converted into cash or used up during the normal operating cycle of the company or one year, whichever is longer. (Think of the **operating cycle** as the time period it takes a company to buy and sell merchandise and then collect accounts receivable.)

Accountants list current assets in order of how easily they can be converted into cash (this is called *liquidity*). In most cases, Accounts Receivable can be turned into cash more quickly than Merchandise Inventory—for example, it can be quite difficult to sell an outdated computer in a computer store, or to sell last year's model car this year.

Capital assets are long-lived assets used in the production or sale of goods or services. Art's Wholesale has only one capital asset, store equipment; other capital assets could include buildings and land. The assets are usually listed in order of how long they will last; the longest-lived assets are listed first. Land would usually be the first asset listed (and land is never amortized). Note that we still show the cost of the asset less its accumulated amortization.

Current liabilities are the debts or obligations of Art's Wholesale that must be paid within one year or one operating cycle. The order of listing accounts in this section is not always the same—many times companies will list their liabilities in the order in which they expect to pay them off. Note that the current portion of the mortgage, $320 (that portion due within one year), is listed towards the end of the list since that is paid off over the year.

Mortgage payable	$2,320
Current portion	– 320
Long-term	$2,000

The current portion of a long-term liability is the amount of principal to be repaid next year. Do not include any interest to be paid next year.

Long-term liabilities are debts or obligations not due and payable for a comparatively long period, usually for more than one year. For Art's Wholesale there is only one long-term liability—Mortgage Payable. The long-term portion of the mortgage is listed here; the current portion, due within one year, is listed under Current Liabilities.

A classified balance sheet (when examined along with the income statement) can provide management, owners, creditors, and suppliers with more information about the company's ability to pay debts, both current and long-term, as well as provide a more complete financial picture of the firm, than a standard balance sheet would.

Learning Unit 13-1 Review

AT THIS POINT you should be able to:

- Prepare a detailed income statement from the worksheet. (pp. 532–535)
- Explain the difference between selling and administrative expenses. (p. 534)
- Explain which columns of the worksheet are used in preparing a statement of owner's equity. (p. 535)
- Prepare a classified balance sheet from a worksheet. (p. 536–537)
- Explain as well as compare current assets and capital assets. (p. 536)
- Using Mortgage Payable as an example, explain the difference between current and long-term liabilities. (p. 536)

ART'S WHOLESALE CLOTHING COMPANY
WORKSHEET
FOR YEAR ENDED DECEMBER 31, 2001

	Balance Sheet Dr.	Balance Sheet Cr.
Cash	12 920 00	
Petty Cash	100 00	
Accounts Receivable	14 500 00	
Merchandise Inventory	4 000 00	
Supplies	300 00	
Prepaid Insurance	600 00	
Store Equipment	4 000 00	
Accum. Amort., Store Equipment		450 00
Accounts Payable		17 900 00
Income Tax Payable		1 240 00
CPP Payable		260 00
EI Payable		200 00
Unearned Rent		400 00
Mortgage Payable		2 320 00
Art Newner, Capital		7 905 00
Salaries Payable		600 00
	45 020 00	31 275 00
Net Income		13 745 00
	45 020 00	45 020 00

ART'S WHOLESALE CLOTHING COMPANY
CLASSIFIED BALANCE SHEET
FOR YEAR ENDED DECEMBER 31, 2001

Assets		
Current Assets		
Cash	$12 920 00	
Petty Cash	100 00	
Accounts Receivable	14 500 00	
Merchandise Inventory	4 000 00	
Supplies	300 00	
Prepaid Insurance	600 00	
Total Current Assets		$32 420 00
Capital Assets		
Store Equipment	4 000 00	
Less: Accumulated Amortization	450 00	3 550 00
Total Assets		$35 970 00
Liabilities		
Current Liabilities		
Accounts Payable	$17 900 00	
Income Tax Payable	1 240 00	
CPP Payable	260 00	
EI Payable	200 00	
Salary Payable	600 00	
Mortgage Payable (current portion)	320 00	
Unearned Rent	400 00	
Total Current Liabilities		$20 920 00
Long-Term Liabilities		
Mortgage Payable		2 000 00
Total Liabilities		22 920 00
Owner's Equity		
Art Newner, Capital, December 31, 2001		13 050 00
Total Liabilities and Owner's Equity		$35 970 00

Note: The figure of $13,050 for Art Newner, Capital, comes from the statement of owner's equity.

FIGURE 13-2
Partial Worksheet and Balance Sheet

SELF-REVIEW QUIZ 13-1

(The forms you need are on pages 13-2 and 13-3 of the *Study Guide with Working Papers.*)

Using the worksheet from Self-Review Quiz 12-2, prepare in proper form (1) an income statement, (2) a statement of owner's equity, (3) a classified balance sheet for Ray Company.

Quiz Tip

Note that the cost of goods sold has separate figures for beginning inventory and ending inventory.

Solution to Self-Review Quiz 13-1

1.

RAY COMPANY
INCOME STATEMENT
FOR YEAR ENDED DECEMBER 31, 2000

Revenue				
Sales				$11 040 00
Less: Sales Returns and Allowances			$ 546 00	
Sales Discounts			216 00	762 00
Net Sales				10 278 00
Cost of Goods Sold				
Merchandise Inventory, 1/1/00			824 00	
Purchases		$5 256 00		
Less: Pur. Ret. and Allowances	$ 168 00			
Purchases Discounts	102 00	270 00		
Net Purchases			4 986 00	
Cost of Goods Available for Sale			5 810 00	
Less: Merchandise Inv., 12/31/00			200 00	
Cost of Goods Sold				5 610 00
Gross Profit				4 668 00
Operating Expenses				
Salaries Expense		2 216 00		
Insurance Expense		1 392 00		
Utilities Expense		96 00		
Plumbing Expense		214 00		
Rent Expense		100 00		
Amortization Expense, Equipment		60 00		
Total Operating Expenses				4 078 00
Net Income from Operations				$ 590 00
Other Income				
Storage Fees				516 00
Net Income				$ 1 106 00

2.

RAY COMPANY
STATEMENT OF OWNER'S EQUITY
FOR YEAR ENDED DECEMBER 31, 2000

B. Ray, Capital, 1/1/00	$ 1 932 00
Net Income for the Year	1 106 00
B. Ray, Capital, 12/31/00	$ 3 038 00

3.

RAY COMPANY
BALANCE SHEET
DECEMBER 31, 2000

Assets		
Current Assets		
Cash	$2,486 00	
Merchandise Inventory	200 00	
Prepaid Rent	1,052 00	
Prepaid Insurance	60 00	
Total Current Assets		$3,798 00
Capital Assets		
Office Equipment	$2,160 00	
Less: Accumulated Amortization	620 00	1,540 00
Total Assets		$5,338 00
Liabilities		
Current Liabilities		
Accounts Payable	$ 100 00	
Salaries Payable	200 00	
Unearned Storage Fees	2,000 00	
Total Liabilities		$2,300 00
Owner's Equity		
B. Ray, Capital, December 31, 2000		3,038 00
Total Liabilities and Owner's Equity		$5,338 00

LEARNING UNIT 13-2

Journalizing and Posting Adjusting and Closing Entries; Preparing the Post-Closing Trial Balance

JOURNALIZING AND POSTING ADJUSTING ENTRIES

From the worksheet of Art's Wholesale, repeated on page 540 as Figure 13-3 for your convenience, the adjusting entries can be journalized from the adjustments column and posted to the ledger. Keep in mind that the adjustments have been recorded only on the worksheet, not in the journal or in the ledger—at this point the journal does not reflect adjustments, and the ledger still contains only unadjusted amounts.

ART'S WHOLESALE CLOTHING CO. WORKSHEET FOR YEAR ENDED DECEMBER 31, 2001	Trial Balance		Adjustments		Adjusted Trial Balance		Income Statement		Balance Sheet	
	Dr.	Cr.	Dr.	Cr.	Dr.	Cr.	Dr.	Cr.	Dr.	Cr.
Cash	12920 00				12920 00				12920 00	
Petty Cash	100 00				100 00				100 00	
Accounts Receivable	14500 00				14500 00				14500 00	
Merchandise Inventory	19000 00		(B) 4000 00	(A) 19000 00	4000 00				4000 00	
Supplies	800 00			(D) 500 00	300 00				300 00	
Prepaid Insurance	900 00			(E) 300 00	600 00				600 00	
Store Equipment	4000 00				4000 00				4000 00	
Accum. Amort., Store Equipment		400 00		(F) 50 00		450 00				450 00
Accounts Payable		17900 00				17900 00				17900 00
Income Tax Payable		1240 00				1240 00				1240 00
CPP Payable		260 00				260 00				260 00
EI Payable		200 00				200 00				200 00
Unearned Rent		600 00	(C) 200 00			400 00				400 00
Mortgage Payable		2320 00				2320 00				2320 00
Art Newner, Capital		7905 00				7905 00				7905 00
Art Newner, Withdrawals	8600 00				8600 00				8600 00	
Income Summary			(A) 19000 00	(B) 4000 00	19000 00	4000 00	19000 00	4000 00		
Sales		95000 00				95000 00		95000 00		
Sales Returns and Allowances	950 00				950 00		950 00			
Sales Discounts	670 00				670 00		670 00			
Purchases	52000 00				52000 00		52000 00			
Purchases Discounts		860 00				860 00		860 00		
Purchases Returns and Allowances		680 00				680 00		680 00		
Freight-In	450 00				450 00		450 00			
Salary Expense	11700 00		(G) 600 00		12300 00		12300 00			
Payroll Tax Expense	420 00				420 00		420 00			
Postage Expense	25 00				25 00		25 00			
Miscellaneous Expense	30 00				30 00		30 00			
Interest Expense	300 00				300 00		300 00			
	127365 00	127365 00								
Rental Income				(C) 200 00		200 00		200 00		
Supplies Expense			(D) 500 00		500 00		500 00			
Insurance Expense			(E) 300 00		300 00		300 00			
Amortization Expense, Store Equip.			(F) 50 00		50 00		50 00			
Salary Payable				(G) 600 00		600 00				600 00
			24650 00	24650 00	132015 00	132015 00	86995 00	100740 00	45020 00	31275 00
Net Income							13745 00			13745 00
							100740 00	100740 00	45020 00	45020 00

FIGURE 13-3 Completed Worksheet

The journalized and posted adjusting entries are shown below. Note that the liability Unearned Rent is reduced by $200 and Rental Income has increased by $200.

ART'S WHOLESALE CLOTHING CO.
GENERAL JOURNAL

Page 2

Date 2001		Account Titles and Description	Post Ref.	Dr.	Cr.
		Adjusting Entries			
Dec.	31	Income Summary	313	19 000 00	
		Merchandise Inventory	114		19 000 00
		Transferred beginning inventory			
		to Income Summary			
	31	Merchandise Inventory	114	4 000 00	
		Income Summary	313		4 000 00
		Records cost of ending inventory			
	31	Unearned Rent	218	200 00	
		Rental Income	414		200 00
		Rental income earned			
	31	Supplies Expense	614	500 00	
		Supplies	115		500 00
		Supplies consumed			
	31	Insurance Expense	615	300 00	
		Prepaid Insurance	116		300 00
		Insurance expired			
	31	Amortization Exp., Store Equipment	613	50 00	
		Acc. Amortization, Store Equipment	122		50 00
		Amortization on equipment			
	31	Salaries Expense	611	600 00	
		Salaries Payable	212		600 00
		Accrued salary			

Partial Ledger

Merchandise Inventory 114

19,000	19,000
4,000	

Accum. Amort., Store Equipment 122

	400
	50

Income Summary 313

19,000	4,000

Amort. Expense, Store Equipment 613

50	

Supplies 115

800	500

Salaries Payable 212

	600

Rental Income 414

	200

Supplies Expense 614

500	

Prepaid Insurance 116

900	300

Unearned Rent 218

200	600

Salaries Expense 611

11,700	
600	

Insurance Exp. 615

300	

Journalizing and Posting Closing Entries

Back in Chapter 5 we discussed the closing process for a service company. The goals of closing have not changed. They are to clear all temporary accounts in the ledger to zero and update capital in the ledger to its latest balance. A merchandising company will also use the worksheet and the following steps to complete the closing process:

1. Close all balances in the income statement credit column of the worksheet, *except* Income Summary, by debits. Then credit the total to the Income Summary account.
2. Close all balances in the income statement debit column of the worksheet, *except* Income Summary, by credits. Then debit the total to the Income Summary account.
3. Transfer the balance of the Income Summary account to the Capital account.
4. Transfer the balance of the owner's Withdrawal account to the Capital account.

Let's look now at the journalized closing entries in Figure 13-4. When these entries are posted, all the temporary accounts will have zero balances in the ledger, and the Capital account will be updated with a new balance.

Let's take a moment to look at the Income Summary account in T-account form as it would exist after step 2 above:

Income Summary 313

		Dr.	Cr.	
	Adj.	19,000	4,000	Adj.
	Clos.	67,995	96,740	Clos.
		86,995	100,740	
Net income →	Clos.	13,745		

Note that Income Summary before the closing process contains the adjustments for Merchandise Inventory. Sometimes accountants include the inventory adjustments as part of the closing. This is not illustrated in this text; *it is not very important which procedure is used*, just that it is made accurately. The end result is that the net income of $13,745 is closed to the Capital account.

The Post-Closing Trial Balance

The post-closing trial balance (often referred to as an opening trial balance) shown on page 544 is prepared from the general ledger. Note first that all temporary accounts have been closed and thus are not shown on this post-closing trial balance. Note also that the ending inventory figure of the last accounting period, $4,000, becomes the beginning inventory figure on January 1, 2002.

Notice that the adjustments to inventory are not included in these closing entries, although some accountants do include them here.

Quiz Tip

Note in the first closing entry that the four account titles (now listed as debits) were found on the worksheet as credits in the Income Statement column.

ART'S WHOLESALE CLOTHING CO.
GENERAL JOURNAL

Page 2

Date		Account Titles and Description	Post Ref.	Dr.	Cr.
2001		Closing Entries			
Dec.	31	Sales	411	9500000	
		Rental Income	414	20000	
		Purchases Discounts	512	86000	
		Purchases Returns and Allowances	513	68000	
		Income Summary	313		9674000
		To transfer credit account balances			
		on income statement column of			
		worksheet to Income Summary			
	31	Income Summary	313	6799500	
		Sales Returns and Allowances	412		95000
		Sales Discounts	413		67000
		Purchases	511		5200000
		Freight-In	514		45000
		Salaries Expense	611		1230000
		Payroll Tax Expense	612		42000
		Postage Expense	616		2500
		Miscellaneous Expense	617		3000
		Interest Expense	618		30000
		Supplies Expense	614		50000
		Insurance Expense	615		30000
		Amortization Expense, Store Equip.	613		5000
		To transfer all expenses and other			
		debit balances in the income			
		statement column of the worksheet			
		to Income Summary			
	31	Income Summary	313	1374500	
		A. Newner, Capital	311		1374500
		To transfer net income to			
		Capital from Income Summary			
	31	A. Newner, Capital	311	860000	
		A. Newner, Withdrawals	312		860000
		Closes withdrawals to			
		Capital account			

FIGURE 13-4
General Journal

ART'S WHOLESALE CLOTHING COMPANY
POST-CLOSING TRIAL BALANCE
DECEMBER 31, 2001

	Dr.	Cr.
Cash	12920 00	
Petty Cash	100 00	
Accounts Receivable	14500 00	
Merchandise Inventory	4000 00	
Supplies	300 00	
Prepaid Insurance	600 00	
Store Equipment	4000 00	
Accumulated Amortization, Store Equipment		450 00
Accounts Payable		17900 00
Income Tax Payable		1240 00
CPP Payable		260 00
EI Payable		200 00
Salary Payable		600 00
Unearned Rent		400 00
Mortgage Payable		2320 00
Art Newner, Capital		13050 00
	36420 00	36420 00

LEARNING UNIT 13-2 REVIEW

AT THIS POINT you should be able to:

- Journalize and post adjusting entries for a merchandising company. (pp. 539–541)
- Explain the relationship of the worksheet to the adjusting and closing process. (p. 539)
- Complete the closing process for a merchandising company. (p. 542)
- Prepare a post-closing trial balance and explain why ending Merchandise Inventory is not a temporary account. (p. 542)

SELF-REVIEW QUIZ 13-2

(The form you need is on page 13-4 of the *Study Guide with Working Papers.*)

Using the worksheet from Self-Review Quiz 12-2, journalize the closing entries.

Solution to Self-Review Quiz 13-2

Page 2

Date		Account Titles and Description	PR	Dr.	Cr.
		Closing			
Dec.	31	Sales		11,040 00	
		Storage Fees Earned		516 00	
		Purchases Returns and Allowances		168 00	
		Purchases Discounts		102 00	
		Income Summary			11,826 00
	31	Income Summary		10,096 00	
		Sales Returns and Allowances			546 00
		Sales Discounts			216 00
		Purchases			5,256 00
		Salaries Expense			2,216 00
		Insurance Expense			1,392 00
		Utilities Expense			96 00
		Plumbing Expense			214 00
		Rent Expense			100 00
		Amortization Expense, Equipment			60 00
	31	Income Summary		1,106 00	
		B. Ray, Capital			1,106 00

LEARNING UNIT 13-3

Reversing Entries *(Optional Section)*

Reversing entries are not mandatory.

Now that we have completed the accounting cycle for Art's Wholesale Clothing Company, let's look at an optional way of handling some adjusting entries—it is called reversing entries. **Reversing entries** are general journal entries that are the opposite of adjusting entries. Reversing entries help reduce potential errors and simplify the record-keeping process. Let's look at how Art's bookkeeper handles the closing entry for salaries at the end of the year (see Figure 13-5).

Note that the permanent account Salaries Payable carries over to the new accounting period a $600 balance. *Remember:* The $600 was an expense of the prior year.

FIGURE 13-5 Closing Entries

(1)
On December 31, after adjusting entries for $600 of salaries incurred but not paid were journalized and posted

Adjusting Journal Entry

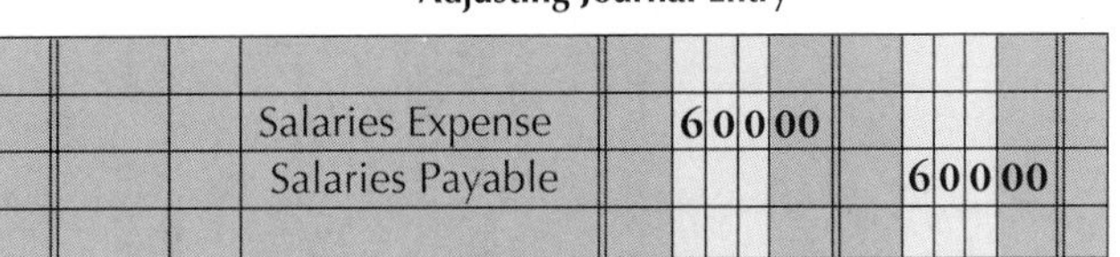

Date		Account	PR	Dr.	Cr.
		Salaries Expense		600 00	
		Salaries Payable			600 00

T Account Update

Salaries Expense		Salaries Payable	
11,700			600
600			

(2)
On January 1, after closing entries have been journalized and posted

Closing Journal Entry (partial)

Date		Account	PR	Dr.	Cr.
		Income Summary		XXX	
		Salaries Expense			12,300 00

Salaries Expense		Salaries Payable	
11,700			600
600	12,300		
Bal. –0–			

On January 8 of the new year, the payroll to be paid is $2,000. If the optional reversing entry is *not* used, the bookkeeper makes the following journal entry:

			Debit	Credit
		Salaries Payable	600 00	
		Salaries Expense	1400 00	
		Cash		2000 00

Salaries Expense	
1,400	

Salaries Payable	
600	600

Cash	
	2,000

To do this, the bookkeeper has to refer to the adjustment on December 31 to determine how much of the salary of $2,000 is indeed a new salary expense and what portion was shown in the old year although not paid then. It is easy to see how errors can result if the bookkeeper pays the payroll but forgets about the adjustment in the previous year. For this reason, reversing entries can help avoid errors.

Figure 13-6 shows the four steps the bookkeeper would take if reversing entries were used. Note that steps 1 and 2 are the same whether the accountant uses reversing entries or not.

FIGURE 13-6
Reversing Entries

(1)
On December 31, adjustment for salary was recorded.

Salaries Expense	
11,700	
600	

Salaries Payable	
	600

(2)
Closing entry on December 31

Salaries Expense	
11,700	12,300
600	

Salaries Payable	
	600

(3)
On January 1 (first day of the following fiscal period), reverse adjusting entry was made for salary on December 31. (This means "flipping" adjustment.)

			Debit	Credit
Jan.	1	Salaries Payable	600 00	
		Salaries Expense		600 00

Salaries Expense	
	600

Salaries Payable	
600	600

By doing this the liability is reduced to zero. We know it will be paid in this new period, but the salaries expense has a credit balance of $600 until the payroll is paid. When the payroll of $2,000 is paid, the following happens:

(4)
Paid payroll, $2,000.

			Debit	Credit
Jan.	1	Salaries Expense	2000 00	
		Cash		2000 00

Salaries Expense	
2,000	600

Cash	
	2,000

Note that the balance of Salaries Expense is indeed only $1,400, the *true* expense in the new year. Reversing results in switching the adjustment on the the first day of the new period. Also note that each of the accounts ends up with the same balance, no matter which method is chosen. However, using a reversing entry for salaries allows the accountant to make the normal entry when it is time to pay salaries.

One should be careful with reversing entries, since not all adjustments can be reversed. Here is a list of the types of adjustments that can be reversed:

1. When there is an increase in an asset account (no previous balance)
   Example: Interest Receivable
   Interest Income
   (Interest earned but not collected: We will cover this in later chapters.)
2. When there is an increase in a liability account (no previous balance)
   Example: Wages Expense
   Wages Payable

Except in the case of businesses in their first year of operation, accounts such as Accumulated Amortization or Inventory will have previous balances and thus will *not* be reversed. As we progress in the course, we will take time to review whether reversing takes place or not.

The increasing use of computers in accounting has changed the role and purpose of reversing entries somewhat. Most accounting software packages allow users to establish recurring entries which can be entered into the accounting records more or less automatically each month. Also, many accounting programs permit a given entry to be automatically reversed in the next period by simply checking a box on a screen.

In this text, we are continuing to illustrate reversing entries as being done manually. Students are encouraged to discover what features are present in the software they are using (or have access to) which modify the nature, purpose, and usefulness of reversing entries.

LEARNING UNIT 13-3 REVIEW

AT THIS POINT you should be able to:

- Explain the purpose of reversing entries. (p. 545)
- Complete a reversing entry. (p. 546)
- Explain when reversing entries can be used. (p. 547)

SELF-REVIEW QUIZ 13-3

(The form you need is on page 13-5 of the *Study Guide with Working Papers*.)
Explain which of the following situations could be reversed:

1.

Supplies Expense	
200	

Supplies	
800	200

2.

Wages Expense	
3,000	
200	

Wages Payable	
	200

3.

Sales	
	4,000
	50

Unearned Sales	
50	200

Solution to Self-Review Quiz 13-3

1. Not reversed—Asset Supplies is decreasing, not increasing.
2. Reversed—Liability is increasing and no previous balance exists.
3. Not reversed—Liability is decreasing and a previous balance exists.

Chapter Review

Summary of key points

Learning Unit 13-1

1. The formal income statement can be prepared from the income statement columns of the worksheet.
2. There are no debit or credit columns on the formal income statement.
3. The cost of goods sold section has a figure for beginning inventory and a separate figure for ending inventory.
4. Operating expenses could be broken down into selling and administrative expenses.
5. The ending figure for capital is not found on the worksheet. It comes from the statement of owner's equity.
6. A classified balance sheet breaks assets down into current and capital. Liabilities are broken down into current and long-term.

Learning Unit 13-2

1. The information for journalizing, adjusting, and closing entries can be obtained from the worksheet.
2. In the closing process, all temporary accounts will be zero and the capital account is brought up to its new balance.
3. Inventory is not a temporary account. The ending inventory, along with other permanent accounts, will be listed in the post-closing trial balance.

Learning Unit 13-3

1. Reversing entries are optional and could aid in reducing potential errors and also simplify the record-keeping process.
2. The reversing entry "flips" the adjustment on the first day of the new fiscal period. Thus, the bookkeeper need not look back at what happened in the old year when recording the current year's transactions.
3. Reversing entries are used only if (a) assets are increasing and have no previous balance, or (b) liabilities are increasing and have no previous balance.

Key terms

Administrative expenses (general expenses) Expenses such as general office expenses that are incurred indirectly in the selling of goods (p. 534)

Capital assets Long-lived assets such as buildings or land that are used in the production or sale of goods or services (p. 536)

Classified balance sheet A balance sheet that categorizes assets as current or capital and groups liabilities as current or long-term (p. 536)

Current assets Assets that can be converted into cash or used within one year or the normal operating cycle of the business, whichever is longer (p. 536)

Current liabilities Obligations that will come due within one year or within the operating cycle, whichever is longer (p. 536)

Long-term liabilities Obligations that are not due or payable for a long time, usually for more than a year (p. 536)

Operating cycle Average time it takes to buy and sell merchandise and then collect accounts receivable (p. 536)

Other expenses These are non-operating expenses that do not relate to the main operating activities of the business; they appear in a separate section on the income statement. One example given in the text is Interest Expense—interest owed on money borrowed by the company. (p. 535)

Other income This includes any revenue other than revenue from sales and appears in a separate section on the income statement. Examples would be Rental Income and Storage Fees. (p. 535)

Reversing entries Year-end optional bookkeeping technique in which certain adjusting entries are reversed or switched on the first day of the new accounting period so that transactions in the new period can be recorded without referring to prior adjusting entries (p. 545)

Selling expenses Expenses directly related to the sale of goods (p. 534)

BLUEPRINT OF FINANCIAL REPORTS

(1) INCOME STATEMENT

Revenue				
Sales				$ XXX
Less: Sales Ret. and Allow.			$ XXX	
Sales Discounts			XXX	XXX
Net Sales				$ XXXX
Cost of Goods Sold				
Merchandise Inventory, 1/1/01			$ XXX	
Purchases		$XXX		
Less: Pur. Ret. and Allow.	$XXX			
Purchases Discounts	XXX	XXX		
Net Purchases		XXX		
Add: Freight-In		XXX		
Net Cost of Purchases			XXX	
Cost of Goods Available for Sale			$XXXX	
Less: Merch. Inv., 12/31/01			XXX	
Cost of Goods Sold				XXXX
Gross Profit				$XXXX
Operating Expenses				
~~			$XXX	
~~			XXX	
~~			XXX	
Total Operating Expenses				XXX
Net Income from Operations				$ XXX
Other Income				
Rental Income			$ XXX	
Storage Fees Income			XXX	
Total Other Income			$ XXX	$ XXX
Other Expenses				
Interest Expense			XXX	XXX
Net Income				$ XXX

(cont.)

(2) STATEMENT OF OWNER'S EQUITY

Beginning Capital		$XXX
Additional Investments		XXX
Total Investment		$XXX
Net Income*	$XXX	
Less: Withdrawals	XXX	
Increase (Decrease) in Capital		XXX
Ending Capital		$XXX

*From the income statement

(3) BALANCE SHEET

Assets			
Current Assets			
Cash		$ XXXX	
Accounts Receivable		XXXX	
Merchandise Inventory		XXXX	
Prepaid Insurance		XXX	
Total Current Assets			$ XXXX
Capital Assets			
Store Equipment	$XXXX		
Less: Accumulated Amortization	XXX	$XXXX	
Office Equipment	$XXXX		
Less: Accumulated Amortization	XXX	XXXX	
Total Capital Assets			XXXX
Total Assets			$XXXX
Liabilities			
Current Liabilities			
Accounts Payable		$XXX	
Salaries Payable		XXX	
Income Taxes Payable		XXX	
Unearned Revenue		XX	
Mortgage Payable (current portion)		XX	
Total Current Liabilities			$ XXX
Long-Term Liabilities			
Mortgage Payable			$ XXX
Total Liabilities			$XXXX
Owner's Equity			
Capital*			XXXX
Total Liabilities and Owner's Equity			$XXXX

* From statement of owner's equity

QUESTIONS, MINI EXERCISES, EXERCISES, AND PROBLEMS

Discussion Questions

1. Which columns of the worksheet aid in the preparation of the income statement?
2. Explain the components of cost of goods sold.
3. Explain how operating expenses can be broken down into different categories.
4. What is the difference between current assets and capital assets?
5. What is an operating cycle?
6. Why journalize adjusting entries after the formal reports have been prepared?
7. Explain the steps in closing for a merchandising company.
8. Temporary accounts could appear on a post-closing trial balance. Agree or disagree.
9. What is the purpose of using reversing entries? Are they mandatory? When should they be used?

Mini Exercises

(The forms you need are on page 13-6 of the *Study Guide with Working Papers.*)

Calculate Net Sales

1. From the following, calculate net sales:

Purchases	$ 50
Gross Sales	100
Sales Returns and Allowances	5
Sales Discounts	2
Operating Expenses	12

Calculate Cost of Goods Sold

2. From the following, calculate cost of goods sold:

Freight-In	$ 5
Beginning Inventory	20
Ending Inventory	15
Net Purchases	50

Calculate Gross Profit and Net Income

3. Using Mini Exercises 1 and 2, calculate:
   a. Gross profit
   b. Net income or net loss

Classification of Accounts

4. Indicate in which of the following four categories each of the ten accounts listed below belongs:
   1. Current assets
   2. Capital assets
   3. Current liabilities
   4. Long-term liabilities

   ____ a. Merchandise Inventory
   ____ b. Unearned Rent
   ____ c. Prepaid Insurance
   ____ d. CPP Payable
   ____ e. Store Equipment
   ____ f. Mortgage Payable (Not Current)
   ____ g. Income Tax Payable
   ____ h. Accumulated Amortization
   ____ i. EI Payable
   ____ j. Petty Cash

Reversing Entries

5.

December 31

Salary Expense

Dr.	Cr.
900	1,200 closing
Adj. 300	

Salaries Payable

Dr.	Cr.
	300 Adj.

a. On January 1 prepare a reversing entry. On January 8, journalize the entry to record the paying of salary expense, $900.

b. What will be the balance in Salary Expense on January 8 (after posting)?

Exercises

(The forms you need are on pages 13-7 and 13-8 of the *Study Guide with Working Papers*.)

Preparing cost of goods sold section

13-1. From the following account information, prepare a cost of goods sold section in proper form: Freight-In, $300; Merchandise Inventory, 12/31/02, $5,000; Purchases Discounts, $900; Merchandise Inventory, 12/1/02, $4,000; Purchases, $58,000; Purchases Returns and Allowances, $1,100.

Categorizing and classifying account titles

13-2. Give the category, the classification, and the report(s) on which each of the following appears (for example: **Cash**—asset, current asset, balance sheet):

a. Salaries Payable
b. Accounts Payable
c. Mortgage Payable
d. Unearned Legal Fees
e. Income Tax Payable
f. Office Equipment
g. Land

Journalizing closing entries

13-3. From the following partial worksheet, journalize the closing entries of December 31 for A. Slow Co.

A. SLOW CO.
WORKSHEET
FOR YEAR ENDED DECEMBER 31, 2001

Account Titles	Income Statement Dr.	Income Statement Cr.	Balance Sheet Dr.	Balance Sheet Cr.
Cash			19300	
Merchandise Inventory			45000	
Prepaid Advertising			56100	
Prepaid Insurance			3000	
Office Equipment			108000	
Accum. Amort., Office Equip.				21000
Accounts Payable				25800
A. Slow, Capital				96600
Income Summary	36200	45000		
Sales		552000		
Sales Returns and Allowances	22300			
Sales Discounts	10800			
Purchases	262800			
Purchases Returns and Allow.		3400		
Purchases Discounts		5100		
Salaries Expense	108300			
Insurance Expense	69600			
Utilities Expense	4800			
Plumbing Expense	5700			
Advertising Expense	1500			
Amort. Expense, Office Equip.	3000			
Salaries Payable				7500
	525000	605500	231400	150900
Net Income	80500			80500
	605500	605500	231400	231400

Preparing a partially completed balance sheet

13-4. From the worksheet in Exercise 3, prepare the assets section of a classified balance sheet.

Reversing entry

13-5. On December 31, 2001, $300 of salaries has been accrued. (Salaries before accrued amount totalled $26,000.) The next payroll to be paid will be on February 3, 2002, for $6,000. Do the following:

a. Journalize and post the adjusting entry (use T accounts).

b. Journalize and post the reversing entry on January 1.

c. Journalize and post the payment of the payroll. Cash has a balance of $15,000 before the payment of payroll on February 3.

Group A Problems

(The forms you need are on pages 13-9 to 13-25 of the *Study Guide with Working Papers.*)

Preparing an income statement from a worksheet

Check Figure

Net Income from operations $761

13A-1. Prepare a formal income statement from the following partial worksheet for Porter's Pants Co.

PORTER'S PANTS CO.
PARTIAL WORKSHEET
FOR YEAR ENDED DECEMBER 31, 2000

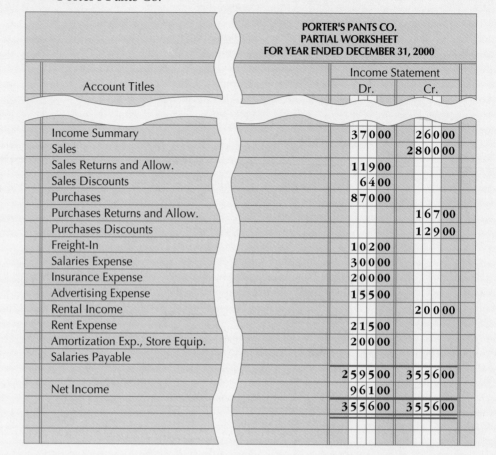

Account Titles	Income Statement Dr.	Income Statement Cr.
Income Summary	370 00	260 00
Sales		2800 00
Sales Returns and Allow.	119 00	
Sales Discounts	64 00	
Purchases	870 00	
Purchases Returns and Allow.		167 00
Purchases Discounts		129 00
Freight-In	102 00	
Salaries Expense	300 00	
Insurance Expense	200 00	
Advertising Expense	155 00	
Rental Income		200 00
Rent Expense	215 00	
Amortization Exp., Store Equip.	200 00	
Salaries Payable		
	2595 00	3556 00
Net Income	961 00	
	3556 00	3556 00

Check Figure

Total Assets $18,340.00

13A-2. Prepare a statement of owner's equity and a classified balance sheet from the partial worksheet for James Company (page 555). ***Note:*** Of the Mortgage Payable, $200 is due within one year.

Completion of worksheet; preparation of financial reports; journalizing adjusting and closing entries

Check Figure

Net Income $4,340.00

13A-3. **a.** Complete the partial worksheet for Jay's Supplies (page 556).

b. Prepare an income statement, a statement of owner's equity, and a classified balance sheet. ***Note:*** The amount of the mortgage due the first year is $800.

c. Journalize the adjusting and closing entries.

Comprehensive problem: worksheet preparation; preparing financial reports; journalizing and posting adjusting and closing entries; preparing a post-closing trial balance; journalizing a reversing entry

Check Figure

Net Income $4,841.00

13A-4. Using the ledger balances and additional data shown on the next two pages, do the following for Callahan Lumber for the year ended December 31, 2001:

1. Prepare the worksheet.
2. Prepare the income statement, statement of owner's equity, and balance sheet.
3. Journalize and post adjusting and closing entries. (Be sure to put beginning balances in the ledger first.)
4. Prepare a post-closing trial balance.
5. Journalize the reversing entry for wages.

Preparing statement of owner's equity and a classified balance sheet from a worksheet

JAMES COMPANY
WORKSHEET
FOR YEAR ENDED DECEMBER 31, 2002

Account Titles	Balance Sheet Dr.	Balance Sheet Cr.
Cash	850 00	
Petty Cash	90 00	
Accounts Receivable	1350 00	
Merchandise Inv.	4000 00	
Supplies	325 00	
Prepaid Insurance	500 00	
Store Equipment	2800 00	
Accum. Amort., Store Eq.		700 00
Automobile	1700 00	
Accum. Amort., Auto		225 00
Accounts Payable		2800 00
Taxes Payable		2400 00
Unearned Rent		8500 00
Mortgage Payable		450 00
H. James, Capital		7400 00
H. James, Withdrawals	100 00	
Salaries Payable		600 00
	19365 00	23075 00
Net Loss	3710 00	
	23075 00	23075 00

Additional Data (for Problem 13A-4)

Account No.		
110	Cash	$1,680
111	Accounts Receivable	960
112	Merchandise Inventory	4,550
113	Lumber Supplies	269
114	Prepaid Insurance	218
121	Lumber Equipment	3,000
122	Accumulated Amortization, Lumber Equipment	490
220	Accounts Payable	1,160
221	Wages Payable	—
330	J. Callahan, Capital	7,352
331	J. Callahan, Withdrawals	3,000
332	Income Summary	—
440	Sales	22,800
441	Sales Returns and Allowances	200
550	Purchases	14,800
551	Purchases Discounts	285
552	Purchases Returns and Allowances	300
660	Wages Expense	2,480
661	Advertising Expense	400
662	Rent Expense	830
663	Amortization Expense, Lumber Equipment	—
664	Lumber Supplies Expense	—
665	Insurance Expense	—

JAY'S SUPPLIES WORKSHEET FOR YEAR ENDED DECEMBER 31, 2001					
	Trial Balance		Adjustments		
Account Titles	Dr.	Cr.	Dr.	Cr.	
Cash	2000 00				
Accounts Receivable	3000 00				
Merchandise Inventory	11000 00		(B) 10400 00	11000 00	(A)
Prepaid Insurance	1880 00			500 00	(E)
Equipment	3400 00				
Accum. Amort., Equipment		1080 00		400 00	(D)
Accounts Payable		5080 00			
Unearned Training Fees		2120 00	(C) 320 00		
Mortgage Payable		1200 00			
P. Jay, Capital		10560 00			
P. Jay, Withdrawals	4280 00				
Income Summary			(A) 11000 00	10400 00	(B)
Sales		95800 00			
Sales Returns and Allowances	3200 00				
Sales Discounts	2600 00				
Purchases	63600 00				
Purchases Returns and Allow.		13600 00			
Purchases Discounts		3200 00			
Freight-In	2680 00				
Advertising Expense	11400 00				
Rent Expense	10000 00				
Salaries Expense	13600 00				
	132640 00	132640 00			
Training Fees Earned				320 00	(C)
Amort. Exp., Equipment			(D) 400 00		
Insurance Expense			(E) 500 00		
			22620 00	22620 00	

Additional Data (for Problem 13A-4)

a. and **b.** Merchandise inventory, December 31	$5,420
c. Lumber supplies on hand, December 31	110
d. Insurance expired	120
e. Amortization for the year	300
f. Accrued wages on December 31	125

Group B Problems

Preparing an income statement from a worksheet

Check Figure

Net Income from operations $845.00

13B-1. From the partial worksheet shown below, prepare a formal income statement.

PORTER'S PANTS CO.
PARTIAL WORKSHEET
FOR YEAR ENDED DECEMBER 31, 2000

Account Titles	Income Statement Dr.	Income Statement Cr.
Income Summary	300 00	295 00
Sales		4100 00
Sales Returns and Allowances	145 00	
Sales Discounts	175 00	
Purchases	2000 00	
Purchases Returns and Allowances		175 00
Purchases Discounts		85 00
Freight-In	50 00	
Salaries Expense	360 00	
Insurance Expense	275 00	
Advertising Expense	165 00	
Rental Income		230 00
Rent Expense	225 00	
Amortization Exp., Store Equipment	115 00	
Salaries Payable		
	3810 00	4885 00
Net Income	1075 00	
	4885 00	4885 00

Preparing a statement of owner's equity and a classified balance sheet from a worksheet

Check Figure

Total Assets $28,294.00

13B-2. From the partial worksheet for James Company shown on page 558, complete:

a. Statement of owner's equity

b. Classified balance sheet

Note: Of the Mortgage Payable, $3,000 is due within one year.

Completing the worksheet; preparing financial reports; journalizing adjusting and closing entries

Check Figure

Net Loss $12,050.00

13B-3. Using the information provided on the partial worksheet for Jay's Supplies shown on page 559, your task is to:

1. Complete the worksheet.
2. Prepare the income statement, statement of owner's equity, and classified balance sheet. The amount of the mortgage due the first year is $800.
3. Journalize the adjusting and closing entries.

JAMES COMPANY
WORKSHEET
FOR YEAR ENDED DECEMBER 31, 2002

Account Titles	Balance Sheet Dr.	Balance Sheet Cr.
Cash	2 500 00	
Petty Cash	50 00	
Accounts Receivable	1 300 00	
Merchandise Inventory	4 250 00	
Supplies	344 00	
Prepaid Insurance	600 00	
Store Equipment	18 000 00	
Accum. Amort., Store Eq.		750 00
Automobile	2 500 00	
Accum. Amort., Auto		500 00
Accounts Payable		3 450 00
Taxes Payable		2 100 00
Unearned Rent		11 000 00
Mortgage Payable		8 000 00
H. James, Capital		10 500 00
H. James, Withdrawals	4 000 00	
Salaries Payable		100 00
	33 544 00	36 400 00
Net Loss	2 856 00	
	36 400 00	36 400 00

Comprehensive problem: worksheet preparation; preparing financial reports, journalizing and posting adjusting and closing entries; preparing a post-closing trial balance; journalizing reversing entry

Check Figure

Net Income $3,480.00

13B-4. From the following ledger balances and additional data on page 559, do the following for Callahan Lumber:

1. Prepare the worksheet.
2. Prepare the income statement, statement of owner's equity, and balance sheet.
3. Journalize and post adjusting and closing entries. (Be sure to put beginning balances in the ledger first.)
4. Prepare a post-closing trial balance.
5. Journalize the reversing entry for wages.

Account No.		
110	Cash	$1,140
111	Accounts Receivable	1,270
112	Merchandise Inventory	5,600
113	Lumber Supplies	260
114	Prepaid Insurance	117
121	Lumber Equipment	2,600
122	Accumulated Amortization, Lumber Equipment	340
220	Accounts Payable	1,330
221	Wages Payable	—
330	J. Callahan, Capital	7,562
331	J. Callahan, Withdrawals	3,500
332	Income Summary	—
440	Sales	23,000

JAY'S SUPPLIES
WORKSHEET
FOR YEAR ENDED DECEMBER 31, 2001

Account Titles	Trial Balance Dr.	Trial Balance Cr.	Adjustments Dr.	Adjustments Cr.
Cash	3000 00			
Accounts Receivable	3000 00			
Merchandise Inventory	11700 00		(B) 8000 00	11700 00 (A)
Prepaid Insurance	1000 00			350 00 (E)
Equipment	5000 00			
Accum. Amort., Equipment		1900 00		500 00 (D)
Accounts Payable		2100 00		
Unearned Training Fees		1450 00	(C) 400 00	
Mortgage Payable		2400 00		
P. Jay, Capital		27750 00		
P. Jay, Withdrawals	4000 00			
Income Summary			(A) 11700 00	8000 00 (B)
Sales		100800 00		
Sales Returns and Allowances	4100 00			
Sales Discounts	2800 00			
Purchases	70000 00			
Purchases Returns and Allow.		2000 00		
Purchases Discounts		1400 00		
Freight-In	2700 00			
Advertising Expense	8000 00			
Rent Expense	8500 00			
Salaries Expense	16000 00			
	139800 00	139800 00		
Training Fees Earned				400 00 (C)
Amortization Exp., Equipment			(D) 500 00	
Insurance Expense			(E) 350 00	
			20950 00	20950 00

441	Sales Returns and Allowances		400
550	Purchases		14,700
551	Purchases Discounts		440
552	Purchases Returns and Allowances	545	
660	Wages Expense	2,390	
661	Advertising Expense	400	
662	Rent Expense	840	
663	Amortization Expense, Lumber Equipment	—	
664	Lumber Supplies Expense	—	
665	Insurance Expense	—	

Additional Data

a. and **b.** Merchandise inventory, December 31	$4,700
c. Lumber supplies on hand, December 31	80
d. Insurance expired	70
e. Amortization for the year	460
f. Accrued wages on December 31	165

Group C Problems

Check Figure

Net Income from operations $6,278.13

13C-1. From the partial worksheet shown below, prepare a formal income statement for Kate's Pie and Kite Shop.

KATE'S PIE AND KITE SHOP
PARTIAL WORKSHEET
FOR THE YEAR ENDED SEPTEMBER 30, 2003

Account Titles	Income Statement Dr.	Income Statement Cr.
Income Summary	4257 82	5477 26
Sales		53568 25
Sales Returns and Allowances	834 50	
Sales Discounts	344 75	
Purchases	21458 34	
Purchases Returns and Allowances		558 30
Purchases Discounts		238 76
Freight-In	471 58	
Rental Income		1800 00
Advertising Expense	1352 50	
Amortization Expense, Equipment	875 00	
Cleaning Expense	2400 00	
Insurance Expenses	368 75	
Rent Expense	7200 00	
Salaries Expense	11458 60	
Utilities Expense	2542 60	
	53564 44	61642 57
Net Income	8078 13	
	61642 57	61642 57

Check Figure

Total Assets $86,242.99

13C-2. Using the information provided on the partial worksheet of Castell Ceramics Co. shown on page 561, complete:

a. Statement of owner's equity

b. Classified balance sheet

Note: Of the Mortgage Payable, $1,800 is due within one year.

Check Figure

Net Income $15,193.86

13C-3. From the partial worksheet of Mikolaski Modern Design Company, shown on page 562, your task is to:

1. Complete the worksheet.
2. Prepare the income statement, statement of owner's equity, and a classified balance sheet. The amount of the mortgage due the first year is $3,600.
3. Journalize the adjusting and closing entries.

CASTELL CERAMICS CO.
PARTIAL WORKSHEET
FOR YEAR ENDED AUGUST 31, 2002

Account Titles	Balance Sheet Dr.	Balance Sheet Cr.
Petty Cash	75 00	
Cash	11538 62	
Accounts Receivable	18976 30	
Merchandise Inventory	22766 28	
Supplies on Hand	1268 75	
Prepaid Insurance	875 40	
Prepaid GST	2137 64	
Cutting Equipment	18760 00	
Accumulated Amortization, Cutting Equipment		7250 00
Delivery Van	21875 00	
Accumulated Amortization, Delivery Van		4780 00
Accounts Payable		27648 36
GST Collected		2874 62
Unearned Rent		1750 00
Chattel Mortgage Payable, Van		15742 37
B. Castell, Capital		42675 98
B. Castell, Withdrawals	14670 00	
Salaries Payable		860 00
Net Income		9361 66
	112942 99	112942 99

13C-4. From the following ledger balances of Brennan Sales Co. as of December 31, 2000, and the additional data on page 563, do the following:

Check Figure

Net Income $3,868.00

1. Prepare the worksheet.
2. Prepare the income statement, statement of owner's equity, and balance sheet.
3. Journalize and post adjusting and closing entries. (Be sure to put beginning balances in the ledger first.)
4. Prepare a post-closing trial balance.
5. Journalize the reversing entry for wages.

Account No.		
1100	Cash	$ 720
1110	Accounts Receivable	1,620
1120	Merchandise Inventory	5,910
1130	Supplies	430
1140	Prepaid Insurance	238
1150	Prepaid GST	647
1210	Equipment	8,500
1220	Accumulated Amortization, Equipment	1,640
2200	Accounts Payable	1,660

MIKOLASKI MODERN DESIGN COMPANY
WORKSHEET
FOR YEAR ENDED NOVEMBER 30, 2001

Account Titles	Trial Balance Dr.	Trial Balance Cr.	Adjustments Dr.	Adjustments Cr.
Cash in Bank	3465 78			
Petty Cash	50 00			
Accounts Receivable	11575 20			
Merchandise Inventory	16479 22		(B) 25672 44	16479 22 (A)
Prepaid Insurance	765 85			257 75 (E)
Prepaid GST	1653 45			
Equipment	21575 00			
Accum. Amortization, Equipment		14762 40		1357 60 (D)
Building	28700 00			
Accum. Amortization, Building		21653 70		647 82 (D)
Accounts Payable		8400 00		
Mortgage Payable		11446 52		
Unearned Rent		2400 00	(C) 800 00	
GST Collected		2167 85		
L. Mikolaski, Capital		32420 22		
L. Mikolaski, Withdrawals	16450 00			
Income Summary			(A) 16479 22	25672 44 (B)
Sales		77327 56		
Sales Discounts and Returns	358 92			
Purchases	42649 04			
Purchases Returns and Allowances		455 72		
Purchases Discounts		576 22		
Freight-In	632 88			
Advertising Expense	1245 00			
Cleaning Expense	2605 60			
Repair Expense	876 20			
Salaries Expense	21575 60			
Utilities Expense	952 45			
	171610 19	171610 19		
Rental Income Earned				800 00 (C)
Amort. Exp., on Equip. and Building			(D) 2005 42	
Insurance Expense			(E) 257 75	
			45214 83	45214 83

2210	Wages Payable	—
2220	GST Collected	897
3300	W. Brennan, Capital	12,012
3310	W. Brennan, Withdrawals	4,700
3320	Income Summary	—
4400	Sales	31,000
4410	Sales Returns and Allowances	630
5500	Purchases	18,400
5510	Purchases Discounts	730
5520	Purchases Returns and Allowances	276
6600	Wages Expense	4,530
6610	Advertising Expense	690
6620	Rent Expense	1,200
6630	Amortization Expense, Equipment	—
6640	Supplies Expense	—
6650	Insurance Expense	—

Additional Data

a. and **b.**	Merchandise inventory, December 31	$4,875
c.	Supplies on hand, December 31	190
d.	Insurance expired	68
e.	Amortization for the year	750
f.	Accrued wages on December 31	395
g.	Advertising bill received — due next year (add Prepaid GST of $14)	200

REAL WORLD APPLICATIONS

13R-1.

Chan Company recently had most of its records destroyed in a fire. The information for 2002 was discovered by the bookkeeper.

CHAN CO.
GENERAL JOURNAL

Page 2

2002 Date		Description	PR	Dr.	Cr.
Dec.	31	Income Summary	312	3 630 00	
		Sales Returns and Allowances	420		140 00
		Sales Discounts	430		30 00
		Purchases	500		2 400 00
		Delivery Expense	600		90 00
		Salaries Expense	610		840 00
		Rent Expense	620		30 00
		Office Supplies Expense	630		50 00
		Advertising Expense	640		10 00
		Amortization Exp., Store Equipment	650		40 00
	31	Sales	410	5 542 00	
		Purchases Discounts	510	120 00	
		Purchases Returns and Allowances	520	100 00	
		Income Summary	312		5 762 00
	31	Income Summary	312	1 732 00	
		J. Chan, Capital	310		1 732 00

Please assist the bookkeeper in reconstructing an income statement for 2002.

13R-2.

Hope Lang, a junior accountant, has the December 31, 2000, trial balance of Gregot Company sitting on her desk. Attached is a memo from her supervisor requesting that a classified balance sheet be prepared. Hope gathers the following data:

1. A physical inventory at December 31 showed $80,000 on hand.
2. The cost of office supplies on hand was $600.
3. Insurance unexpired was $750.
4. Amortization (straight-line) is based on a 25-year life.

Using the following trial balance of Gregot Co., assist Hope with this project. *Hint:* Ending figure for capital is $115,850.

GREGOT COMPANY
TRIAL BALANCE
DECEMBER 31, 2000

	Dr.	Cr.
Cash	1100000	
Accounts Receivable	3800000	
Inventory, January 1	8000000	
Prepaid Insurance	200000	
Office Supplies	100000	
Land	1750000	
Building	5000000	
Accumulated Amortization, Building		1000000
Notes Payable		4000000
Accounts Payable		3000000
G. Gregot, Capital		9840000
G. Gregot, Withdrawals	1300000	
Income Summary	—	
Retail Sales		32900000
Sales Returns and Allowances	2100000	—
Sales Discounts	800000	
Purchases	21550000	
Purchases Returns and Allowances		1160000
Purchases Discounts		400000
Transportation-In	500000	
Advertising Expense	250000	
Wage Expense	5500000	
Utilities Expense	350000	
	52300000	52300000

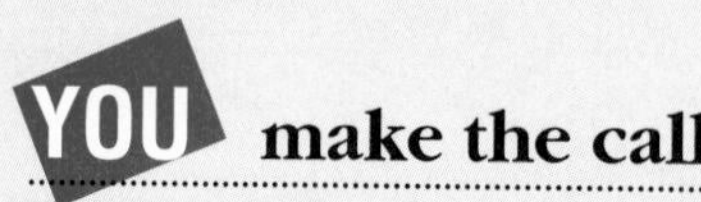

Critical Thinking/Ethical Case

13R-3.

Janet Flynn, owner of Reel Company, plans to apply for a bank loan at Canadian National Bank. Since the company has a lot of debt on its balance sheet, Janet does not plan to show the loan officer the balance sheet. She plans only to bring the income statement. Do you feel this is a sound financial move by Janet? You make the call. Write down your specific recommendations to Janet.

ACCOUNTING RECALL

A CUMULATIVE APPROACH

THIS EXAMINATION REVIEWS CHAPTERS 1 THROUGH 13.

Your *Study Guide with Working Papers* (page 13-46) has forms to complete this exam, as well as worked-out solutions. The page reference next to each question identifies the page to turn back to if you answer the question incorrectly.

PART I Vocabulary Review

Match each term on the left with the appropriate definition or phrase in the right-hand column.

Page Ref.		
(536)	1. Current asset	A. General expenses
(536)	2. Current liabilities	B. Contra-asset
(409)	3. Purchases discounts	C. Converted into cash or used within one year
(542)	4. Income summary	D. Contra-expense
(534)	5. Administrative expenses	E. Land
(134)	6. Accumulated amortization	F. Mortgage payable
(534)	7. Net sales	G. Optional bookkeeping
(536)	8. Capital assets	H. A temporary account used only at period-end
(536)	9. Long-term liability	I. Sales–SRA–SD
(545)	10. Reversing entries	J. Due within one year

PART II True or False (Accounting Theory)

(532) 11. There are debit and credit columns on the formal reports.
(545) 12. Reversing entries are the same as adjusting entries.
(547) 13. All adjustments should be reversed.
(536) 14. Equipment is a current asset.
(534) 15. Administrative expenses are directly incurred in the selling of goods.

Continuing Problem

Using the worksheet in Chapter 12 for Eldorado Computer Centre, journalize and post the adjusting entries and prepare the financial statements. (See pages 13-47 to 13-56 in your *Study Guide with Working Papers*.)

The Corner Dress Shop

This practice set will help you review all the key concepts of the accounting cycle for a merchandising company along with the integration of payroll.

Since you are the bookkeeper of The Corner Dress Shop, we have gathered the following information for you. It will be your task to complete the accounting cycle for March.

The Corner Dress Shop
Post-Closing Trial Balance
February 28, 2001

Cash	1,722.50	
Petty Cash	50.00	
Accounts Receivable	3,011.00	
Merchandise Inventory	5,600.00	
Supplies	624.30	
Prepaid Rent	1,800.00	
GST Prepaid	703.42	
Delivery Truck	21,500.00	
Accumulated Amortization, Truck		8,950.00
Accounts Payable		2,354.00
GST Collected		1,149.27
Income Tax Payable		1909.00
CPP Payable		520.04
EI Payable		583.20
Medical Plan Premiums Payable		112.00
Unearned Rent		800.00
B. Loeb, Capital		18,633.71
Totals	35,011.22	35,011.22

Balances in subsidiary ledgers as of March 1:

*Accounts Receivable**		*Accounts Payable**	
Bing Co.	$2,241.00	Blew Co.	$1,926.00
Gray Co.	—	Jones Co.	428.00
Ronald Co.	770.00	Moe's Garage	—
		Morris Co.	—

*Includes 7 percent GST.

Payroll is paid monthly, and employee claim codes are unchanged.

The payroll register for January and February is provided on page 569. In March, salaries are as follows (all deductions the same unless indicated):

Mel Case	$1,860	New income tax = $225.85.
Jane Holl	2,900	For CPP and EI—use same approach as in Chapter 7.
Jackie Moore	4,300	

Required

1. Set up a general ledger, accounts receivable ledger, and accounts payable ledger, auxiliary petty cash record, and payroll register. (Before beginning, be sure to update ledger accounts on the basis of information given in the post-closing trial balance for February 28.)
2. Journalize all transactions during March.
3. Prepare the payroll register for March.
4. Update the accounts payable and accounts receivable subsidiary ledgers for March.
5. Post to the general ledger.
6. Prepare a trial balance on a worksheet and complete the worksheet as of March 31, 2001.
7. Prepare an income statement, statement of owner's equity, and classified balance sheet.
8. Journalize the adjusting and closing entries.
9. Post the adjusting and closing entries to the ledger.
10. Prepare a post-closing trial balance.

The chart of accounts for The Corner Dress Shop is as follows:

Chart of Accounts

Assets
110 Cash
111 Accounts Receivable
112 Petty Cash
114 Merchandise Inventory
116 Prepaid Rent
117 Supplies
118 GST Prepaid
120 Delivery Truck
121 Accumulated Amortization, Truck

Liabilities
210 Accounts Payable
212 Salaries Payable
214 Income Tax Payable
216 CPP Payable
218 EI Payable
220 Medical Plan Premium Payable
222 Unearned Rent
228 GST Collected

Owner's Equity
310 B. Loeb, Capital
320 B. Loeb, Withdrawals
330 Income Summary

Revenue
410 Sales
412 Sales Returns and Allowances
414 Sales Discounts
416 Rental Income

Cost of Goods Sold
510 Purchases
512 Purchases Returns and Allowances
514 Purchases Discounts

Expenses
610 Sales Salaries Expense
611 Office Salaries Expense
612 Payroll Tax Expense
614 Cleaning Expense
616 Amortization Expense, Truck
618 Rent Expense
620 Postage Expense
622 Supplies Expense
624 Delivery Expense
626 Miscellaneous Expense

PAYROLL REGISTER—JANUARY

Employee	Net Claim Code	Monthly Salary	Cumulative CPP	Income Tax
Mel Case	4	1 800 00	—	208 80
Jane Holl	1	2 900 00	—	605 50
Jackie Moore	3	4 300 00	—	1 094 70
Totals		9 000 00		1 909 00

Deductions				Net Pay	Cheque No.	Expense Accounts	
CPP	EI	Health	Charitable			Office	Sales
48 27	48 60	28 00	20 00	1 446 33		1 800 00	
83 47	78 30	42 00	30 00	2 060 73			2 900 00
128 28	116 10	42 00	40 00	2 878 92			4 300 00
260 02	243 00	112 00	90 00	6 385 98		1 800 00	7 200 00

PAYROLL REGISTER—FEBRUARY

Employee	Net Claim Code	Monthly Salary	Cumulative CPP	Income Tax
Mel Case	4	1 800 00	48 27	208 80
Jane Holl	1	2 900 00	83 47	605 50
Jackie Moore	3	4 300 00	128 28	1 094 70
Totals		9 000 00		1 909 00

Deductions				Net Pay	Cheque No.	Expense Accounts	
CPP	EI	Health	Charitable			Office	Sales
48 27	48 60	28 00	20 00	1 446 33		1 800 00	
83 47	78 30	42 00	30 00	2 060 73			2 900 00
128 28	116 10	42 00	40 00	2 878 92			4 300 00
260 02	243 00	112 00	90 00	6 385 98		1 800 00	7 200 00

Transactions

2001

March 1 Received amount due from Bing, no discount.

2 Purchased merchandise from Morris Company on account, $10,000, plus GST, terms 2/10, n/30.

2 Paid $6 from the petty cash fund for doughnuts, voucher No. 18 (consider this a miscellaneous expense — no GST).

3 Sold merchandise to Ronald Company on account, $7,000, plus GST, invoice No. 51, terms 2/10, n/30.

5 Paid $12.84 from the petty cash fund for postage, voucher No. 19.

6 Sold merchandise to Ronald Company on account, $5,000, plus GST, invoice No. 52, terms 2/10, n/30.

8 Paid $10 from the petty cash fund for first aid emergency, voucher No. 20 (no GST).

9 Purchased merchandise from Morris Company on account, $5,000, plus GST, terms 2/10, n/30.

9 Received amount due from Ronald Co. at February 28 less 2 percent discount.

9 Paid $5 for delivery expense (no GST) from petty cash fund, voucher No. 21.

9 Sold more merchandise to Ronald Company on account, $3,000, plus GST, invoice No. 53, terms 2/10, n/30.

9 Paid cleaning service, $300, plus GST, cheque No. 110.

10 Ronald Company returned merchandise costing $1,000 from invoice No. 52; The Corner Dress Shop issued credit memo No. 10 to Ronald Company for $1,000, plus GST.

11 Purchased merchandise from Jones Company on account, $10,000, plus GST, terms 1/15, n/60.

12 Paid Morris Company invoice dated March 2, cheque No. 111.

13 Sold merchandise for cash, $700, plus GST.

14 Returned merchandise to Jones Company in amount of $2,000; The Corner Dress Shop issued debit memo No. 4 to Jones Company, $2,000, plus GST.

14 Paid $5 from the petty cash fund for delivery expense, voucher No. 22 (no GST).

15 Paid amount due to Receiver General for Canada for February withholdings – cheque No. 112.

15 Sold merchandise for cash, $29,000, plus GST.

15 B. Loeb withdrew $1,000 for her personal use, cheque No. 113.

15 Paid net amount of GST due $445.85, cheque No. 114.

16 Paid amount due to Blew Co. at the end of February, cheque No. 115.

16 Received payment from Ronald Company for invoice No. 52, less discount and less returned merchandise.

16 Ronald Company paid invoice No. 51, $7,490.

16 Sold merchandise to Bing Company on account, $3,200, plus GST, invoice No. 54. terms 2/10, n/30.

21 Purchased another delivery truck on account from Moe's Garage, $17,200, plus GST.

22 Sold merchandise to Ronald Company on account, $4,000, plus GST, invoice No. 55, terms 2/10, n/30.

23 Paid Jones Company the balance owed, cheque No. 116.

24 Sold merchandise to Bing Company, $2,000, plus GST, invoice No. 56, terms 1/10, n/30.

25 Purchased merchandise for cash, $1,000, plus GST, cheque No. 117.

27 Purchased merchandise from Blew Company on account, $6,000, plus GST, terms 2/10, n/30.
27 Paid amount due to Provincial Health Care with respect to February payroll, cheque No. 118.
28 Ronald Company paid invoice No. 55 dated March 22, less discount.
28 Bing Company paid invoice No. 54 dated March 16.
29 Purchased merchandise from Morris Company on account, $9,000, plus GST, terms 2/10, n/30.
30 Sold merchandise to Gray Company on account, $10,000, plus GST, invoice No. 57, terms 2/10, n/30.
30 Issued cheque No. 119 to replenish the petty cash fund.
30 Recorded March payroll in payroll register.
30 Journalized payroll entry (to be paid on March 31). Charitable deductions to be credited to the Accounts Payable account.
30 Journalized employer's payroll tax expense.
31 Paid payroll cheques Nos. 120, 121, and 122.
31 Remitted total March charitable deductions to World Preventable Disease Foundation, cheque No. 123. (Recall that the Accounts Payable account was used to record this amount.)

Additional Data

a. and **b.** Ending merchandise inventory, $4,280.
c. During March, rent expired, $600.
d. Trucks amortized, $480.
e. Rental income earned, $300 (one month's rent from subletting).

Computerized Accounting Application for The Corner Dress Shop Mini Practice Set (Chapter 13)

Inventory Adjusting Entries

Before starting on this assignment, read and complete the tasks discussed in Parts A, B, and F of Appendix B at the end of this book, and complete the Computerized Accounting Application assignments for Chapter 3, Chapter 4, Valdez Realty Mini Practice Set (Chapter 5), Pete's Market Mini Practice Set (Chapter 8), and Chapter 10.

This practice set will help you review all the key concepts of a merchandising company, along with the integration of payroll.

Since you are the bookkeeper of The Corner Dress Shop, we have gathered the following information for you. It will be your task to complete the accounting cycle for March.

The Corner Dress Shop: Trial Balance As at March 1, 2001*

	Debits	Credits
Cash	1,604.56	—
Petty Cash	50.00	—
Accounts Receivable	3,011.00	—
Merchandise Inventory	5,600.00	—
Supplies	624.30	—
Prepaid Rent	1,800.00	—
GST Prepaid	703.42	—
Delivery Truck	21,500.00	—
Accumulated Depreciation, Truck	—	8,950.00
Accounts Payable	—	2,354.00
GST Collected	—	1,149.27
Income Tax Payable	—	1,791.08
CPP Payable	—	520.02
UI Payable	—	583.20
Medical Plan Premiums Payable	—	112.00
Unearned Rent	—	800.00
B. Loeb, Capital	—	18,633.71
Totals	34,893.28	34,893.28

The Corner Dress Shop: Customer Aged Detail as at March 1, 2001

			Total	Current	31 to 60	61 to 90	91 +
Bing Co.							
12	12/31/2000	Invoice	2,241	—	2,241	—	—
Ronald Co.							
310	01/15/2001	Invoice	770	—	770		

*May be somewhat different from manual version due to the precision of the computerized payroll program.

The Corner Dress Shop: Vendor Aged Detail As at March 1, 2001

			Total	Current	31 to 60	61 to 90	91 +
Blew Co.							
510	12/31/2000	Invoice	1,926	—	1,926	—	—
Jones Co.							
914	01/24/2001	Invoice	428	—	428	—	—

The Corner Dress Shop, owned by Betty Loeb, is located at 1 Milgate Road, Whitby, ON L1N 3H8. Her Business Number is 98765 4321 RP. The data set for *CA-Simply Accounting for Windows* packaged with this text uses the tax laws in effect on January 1, 1998. Federal income tax, CPP, and EI are all calculated automatically by the program.

Open the company data files

1. Start Windows; insert your Student Data Files disk into disk drive A or B; then double-click on the CA-Simply Accounting icon. The CA-Simply Accounting Open File dialogue box will appear.
2. Enter the following path into the **Open file name** text box:
   - `a:\dress.asc` (if you are storing your student data files on the disk in drive A)
3. Click on the **Open** button; enter `03/31/01` into the **Session** text box; then click on the **OK** button. Click on the **OK** button in response to the message "The date entered is more than one week past your previous **Session** date of 03/01/01." The Company Window for Dress will appear.

Add your name to the company name

4. Click on the Company Window **Setup** menu; then click on Company Information. The Company Information dialogue box will appear. Insert your name in place of the text "Your Name" in the **Name** text box. Click on the **OK** button to return to the Company Window.

Record March transactions

5. Record the following transactions* using the general, purchases, payments, sales, receipts, and payroll journals:

Transactions

2001

March 1 Received amount due from Bing, no discount.

2 Purchased merchandise from Morris Company on account, $10,000, plus GST, terms 2/10, n/30.

2 Paid $6 from petty cash fund for doughnuts, voucher No. 18 (consider this miscellaneous expense—no GST).

3 Sold merchandise to Ronald Company on account, $7,000, plus GST, invoice No. 51, terms 2/10, n/30.

5 Paid $12.84 (includes $0.84 GST) from the petty cash fund for postage, voucher No. 19.

6 Sold merchandise to Ronald Company on account, $5,000, plus GST, invoice No. 52, terms 2/10, n/30.

8 Paid $10 from the petty cash fund for first aid emergency, voucher No. 20 (no GST).

9 Purchased merchandise from Morris Company on account, $5,000, plus GST, terms 2/10, n/30.

9 Received amount due from Ronald Co. at February 28 less 2 percent discount.

9 Paid $5 for delivery expense (no GST) from petty cash fund, voucher No. 21.

9 Sold more merchandise to Ronald Company on account, $3,000, plus GST, invoice No. 53, terms 2/10, n/30.

9 Paid for cleaning service, $300, plus GST, cheque No. 110.

10 Ronald Company returned merchandise costing $1,000 plus GST from invoice No. 52; The Corner Dress Shop issued credit memo No. 10 to Ronald Company for $1,000, plus GST.

*You will probably find it helpful to print a chart of accounts to aid you in entering transactions.

11 Purchased merchandise from Jones Company on account, $10,000, plus GST, terms 1/15, n/60.
12 Paid Morris Company invoice dated March 2, cheque No. 111.
13 Sold merchandise for cash, $700, plus GST.
14 Returned merchandise to Jones Company in amount of $2,000; The Corner Dress Shop issued debit memo No. 4 to Jones Company, $2,000, plus GST.
14 Paid $5 from the petty cash fund for delivery expense, voucher No. 22 (no GST).
15 Paid amount due to Receiver General for Canada for February withholdings—cheque No. 112.
15 Sold merchandise for cash, $29,000, plus GST.
15 B. Loeb withdrew $1,000 for her personal use, cheque No. 113.
15 Paid net amount of GST due February 28, $445.85, cheque No. 114.
16 Paid amount due to Blew Co. at the end of February, cheque No. 115.
16 Received payment from Ronald Company for invoice No. 52, less discount and less returned merchandise.
16 Ronald Company paid invoice No. 51, $7,490.
16 Sold merchandise to Bing Company on account, $3,200, plus GST, invoice No. 56, terms 2/10, n/30.
21 Purchased another delivery truck on account from Moe's Garage, $17,200, plus GST.
22 Sold merchandise to Ronald Company on account, $4,000, plus GST, invoice No. 57, terms 2/10, n/30.
23 Paid Jones Company the balance owed, cheque No. 116.
24 Sold merchandise to Bing Company, $2,000, plus GST, invoice No. 58, terms 1/10, n/30.
25 Purchased merchandise for cash, $1,000, plus GST, cheque No. 117.
27 Purchased merchandise from Blew Company on account, $6,000, plus GST, terms 2/10, n/30.
27 Paid amount due to Provincial Health Care with respect to February payroll, cheque No. 118.
28 Ronald Company paid invoice No. 57 dated March 22, less discount.
28 Bing Company paid invoice No. 56 dated March 16.
29 Purchased merchandise from Morris Company on account, $9,000, plus GST, terms 2/10, n/30.
30 Sold merchandise to Gray Company on account, $10,000, plus GST, invoice No. 59, terms 2/10, n/30.
30 Issued cheque No. 119 to replenish the petty cash fund.
30 Recorded March payroll in payroll register.
30 Journalized payroll entry (to be paid on March 31).
30 Journalized employer's payroll tax expense.
31 Paid payroll cheques Nos. 120, 121, and 122.
31 Remitted total March charitable deducations to World Preventable Disease Foundation, cheque No. 123.

Additional Data

a. and b. Ending merchandise inventory, $4,280
c. During March, rent expired, $600.
d. Trucks depreciated, $480.
e. Rental income earned, $300 (one month's rent from subletting)

Print reports

6. Print the following reports:

a. General Journal (By posting date, All ledger entries, Start: 03/01/01, Finish: 03/31/01)
b. Trial Balance As at 03/31/01
c. Customer Aged report (Detail, Select All)
d. Vendor Aged report (Detail, Select All)
e. Employee Payroll Register 1 (Select All)
f. Payroll reports as necessary

Review your printed reports. If you have made an error in a posted journal entry, see Part C of Appendix B at the end of this book for information on how to correct the error.

Record March adjusting entries

7. Open the general journal; then record adjusting journal entries on the basis of the following adjustment data:

How to record inventory adjusting entries

a. **and b.** Ending inventory, $4,280. The format of the adjusting entries for inventory in a computerized accounting system, and specifically for The Corner Dress Shop, are as follows:

	Debit	*Credit*
5050 Beginning Inventory	$5,600	
1130 Inventory		$5,600
1130 Inventory	$4,280	
5150 Ending Inventory		$4,280

c. During March, rent expired, $600.
d. Trucks depreciated, $480.
e. Rental income was earned, $300 (one month's rent from subletting).

Print reports

8. After you have posted the adjusting journal entries, close the general journal; then print the following reports:
   a. General Journal (By posting date, All ledger entries, Start: 03/01/01, Finish: 03/31/01).
   b. Trial Balance As at 03/31/01.
   c. General Ledger Report (Start: 03/01/01, Finish: 03/31/01, Select All).
   d. Income Statement (Start: 03/01/01, Finish: 03/31/01).
   e. Balance Sheet As at 03/31/01.

   Review your printed reports. If you have made an error in a posted journal entry, see Part C of Appendix B for information on how to correct the error.

Record entry to close Withdrawals account

9. Open the general journal; then record the closing journal entry for Betty Loeb's Withdrawals account.
10. After you have posted the closing entry for Betty Loeb's Withdrawals account, close the General Journal to return to the Company Window.

Make a backup copy of March accounting records

11. Click on the Company Window **File** menu; click on Save As; then enter the following new file name into the **Save file as** text box:
    - `a:\dressmar.asc` (if you are storing your student data files on the disk in drive A).
12. Click on the **Save** button. Note that the company name in the Company Window has changed from Dress to Dressmar. Click on the Company Window **File** menu again; then click on Save As. Enter the following new file name into the **Save file as** text box:
    - `a:\dress.asc` (if you are storing your student data files on the disk in drive A).
13. Click on the **Save** button. Click on the **Yes** button in response to the question "Replace existing data files with the same name?" Note that the company name in the Company Window has changed back from Dressmar to Dress.
14. You now have two sets of company data files for The Corner Dress Shop on your Student Data Files disk. The current data is stored under the file name dress.asc. The backup data is stored under the file name dressmar.asc.

Advance the Session date

15. Click on the Company Window **Setup** menu; then click on Advance Session Date. Enter `04/01/01` into the **New session date** text box; then click on the **OK** button. Click on the **Yes** button in response to the warning message. The backup you created using the Save As method will serve as the backup suggested in the warning message.

Print a post-closing trial balance

16. Print a post-closing trial balance as at 04/01/01.

Exit from the program

17. Click on the Company Window **File** menu; then click on Exit to end the current work session and return to your Windows desktop.

Accounting for Bad Debts

14

THE BIG PICTURE

After completing the detailed financial reports for Eldorado Computer Centre, Tony Freedman noticed that his accounts receivable was extremely large for the amount of sales his business had done. He decided to take several steps to measure whether he was collecting accounts as he should. First, he looked at his new credit policy to see if he was giving out credit to customers without judging their ability to pay. He decided that his customers were generally creditworthy and that he would need to take a look at his accounts in further detail.

Any business would like to collect on all its debts, but every business that extends credit has to realize that some customers do not, or cannot, pay all or part of their debt. When this happens, the business has an account that becomes uncollectible; this is known as *bad debt*.

In this chapter you will learn how to determine the potential bad debt a business may incur. There are different methods used for making this determination. Some companies prefer to write off bad debt after a certain number of days; others may choose to set an allowance for what they expect to become uncollectible during the year. The allowance for bad debt can be determined by the aging of the accounts receivable or as a percentage of sales on credit. These methods usually require some history of account trends or comparison with another, similar business.

Since Freedman has not been in business that long, he has decided to start by writing off accounts that have not been paid in 90 days. If he continues to see a pattern of growing bad debt, he plans to review his new credit policy and possibly to hire an accounts receivable manager.

Chapter Objectives

- Using the Bad Debts Expense account and the Allowance for Doubtful Accounts account to record bad debts (pp. 577–578)
- Using the income statement approach and the balance sheet approach to estimate the amount of bad debts expense (pp. 580–582)
- Preparing an aging of accounts receivable (p. 582)
- Writing off an account using the Allowance for Doubtful Accounts account (pp. 584–585)
- Using the direct write-off method (pp. 585–586)

All companies that sell goods or services on account will eventually have to face the problem of not being able to collect some of the money owed them. At what point accounts receivable turn into bad debts (or uncollectible accounts), how and what to charge them to, and how to write them off are some of the questions that we will be dealing with in this chapter.

The question of bad debts is important to a company because it affects its credit policy. If a company extends credit too easily, it may end up with too many uncollectible accounts. On the other hand, if the credit policy is too strict, the company will end up losing customers to other firms with easier credit policies—and that could mean a loss in profit just as uncollectible debts do.

In the first learning unit we will look at how bad debts are recorded in the accrual system of accounting.

LEARNING UNIT 14-1

Accrual Accounting and Recording Bad Debts

As we discussed in an earlier chapter, in the accrual system of accounting it is important to match earned revenue with expenses that have been incurred in producing revenue during an accounting period. In other words, in a merchandising firm, for example, it is important to match cost of goods sold with revenue earned by the sale of those goods. One expense that is incurred as a result of sales on credit or on account is bad debts expense. The problem is that, at the time the sale occurs, one doesn't know whether or not it is going to be uncollectible—one may not know this until much later, possibly a year or so. So how can one match sales with expenses (in this case, bad debts expense) on the books?

One way to do this is to estimate at the end of the year what percentage of sales already made will turn out to be bad debts. There are several ways of arriving at the percentage, which we will discuss in a later unit, but for the moment let's say that Abby Ellen Company estimates that 1.6 percent of their sales of $100,000 for the year 2001 will not be collectible; that means that the company expects not to collect $1,600 of the $100,000 owed them from sales.

To handle this situation, we need to introduce two accounts that we haven't dealt with before, Bad Debts Expense and Allowance for Doubtful Accounts. **Bad Debts Expense** is an expense account whose normal balance is a debit; it is a temporary account that is closed to Income Summary at year's end. **Allowance for Doubtful Accounts** is a contra-asset account that accumulates the expected amount of bad debts as of a given date; its normal balance is a credit. It is a permanent account that is *not* closed to Income Summary at the end of the year.

In the case of Abby Ellen Company, which expects to be unable to collect $1,600 of the $100,000 owed them from sales, at the end of the year (2001) an adjustment is made debiting Bad Debts Expense and crediting Allowance for Doubtful Accounts for $1,600. The journal entry is shown below, along with a transaction analysis chart:

Date		Account	Dr.	Cr.
Dec.	31	Bad Debt Expense	1 6 0 0 00	
		Allowance for Doubtful Accounts		1 6 0 0 00
		Record estimate of bad debts		

Will go on income statement as an operating expense and eventually be closed to Income Summary.

Will go on balance sheet as a reduction of Accounts Receivable. The normal balance of the allowance account is a credit. It will not be closed at the end of the period.

1 Accounts Affected	2 Category	3 ↑ ↓	4 Rules
Bad Debts Expense	**Expenses**	↑	**Dr.**
Allowance for Doubtful Accounts	**Asset (Contra)**	↑	**Cr.**

Accounts Receivable
− Allowance for Doubtful Accounts
= Net Realizable Value

Think of the Allowance for Doubtful Accounts as a reservoir that is filled before bad debts occur. When the customers' bills are declared uncollectible, this reservoir will be drained. Abby Ellen Company estimates that, out of its $100,000 of credit sales, $1,600 will prove to be uncollectible, but it does not know at this time which accounts will be uncollectible. The allowance account is subtracted from Accounts Receivable, leaving a **net realizable value** of $98,400. Net realizable value is the amount Abby Ellen Company expects to collect. When an account is written off, the net realizable value doesn't change, because both the Accounts Receivable and the Allowance for Doubtful Accounts are reduced.

We will do write-offs in Learning Unit 14-3. This is only an introductory example.

Figure 14-1 shows a partial balance sheet to see how the Allowance for Doubtful Accounts relates to Accounts Receivable.

Writing off an account
Note: Bad Debts Expense is not involved.

ABBY ELLEN COMPANY PARTIAL BALANCE SHEET DECEMBER 31, 2001		
Assets		
Current Assets		
Cash		$ 51 4 0 0 00
Accounts Receivable	$100 0 0 0 00	
Less: Allowance for Doubtful Accounts	1 6 0 0 00	98 4 0 0 00
Merchandise Inventory		200 0 0 0 00
Total Current Assets		$349 8 0 0 00

FIGURE 14-1
Partial Balance Sheet

At some point a customer's bill must be written off as uncollectible. Let's look at how Abby Ellen Company would write off the account of Jones Moore on June 5, 2002. (The sale was made in 2001.)

Writing off an account deemed uncollectible

Remember, at the end of year 2001 Abby made an adjusting entry increasing Bad Debts Expense (debit) and filling the Allowance for Doubtful Accounts (credit) with the estimate of accounts receivable that would not be collectible.

Now, on June 5, 2002, Jones Moore's account is deemed to be uncollectible in the amount of $200, and the following journal entry is recorded to write off this account:

			Dr.	Cr.
2002 June	5	Allowance For Doubtful Accounts	200 00	
		Accounts Receivable, J. Moore		200 00
		Writing off J. Moore account		

The bad debts expense was recorded in the old year when credit sales were earned.

Note that we did *not* debit the account Bad Debts Expense, since the estimate for this account was made on December 31, 2001 (and applies to that year, not to 2002). When that estimate was made, we did not know which customers' accounts would turn out to be uncollectible, and thus we recorded the estimate in the Allowance for Doubtful Accounts. Now that the debt is identified as uncollectible, we *reduce* or drain the allowance account and reduce the controlling account Accounts Receivable, and also update the accounts receivable ledger. Note that the subsidiary ledger will be credited just as the controlling account is.

LEARNING UNIT 14-1 REVIEW

AT THIS POINT you should be able to:

- Define and explain the purpose of Bad Debts Expense and Allowance for Doubtful Accounts. (pp. 577–578)
- Explain why the subsidiary ledger account cannot be updated at the time the Bad Debts Expense is estimated. (p. 577)
- Prepare an adjusting entry for Bad Debts Expense. (p. 578)
- Prepare a partial balance sheet showing the relationship between the Allowance for Doubtful Accounts and Accounts Receivable. (p. 577)
- Explain net realizable value. (p. 578)
- Prepare a journal entry to write off a customer's debt in a year following the sale. (p. 579)

SELF-REVIEW QUIZ 14-1

(The form you need is on page 14-1 of the *Study Guide with Working Papers.*)

Respond true or false to the following:

1. The Bad Debts Expense account should be updated only when the customer's debt is declared to be uncollectible.
2. The Allowance for Doubtful Accounts is a contra-asset account on the balance sheet.
3. Bad Debts Expense is part of cost of goods sold.
4. Net realizable value equals Accounts Receivable less Allowance for Doubtful Accounts.
5. When a customer's debt is written off as uncollectible, the account Allowance for Doubtful Accounts is credited.

Quiz Tip

The Allowance account fills with a credit and drains with a debit.

Solutions to Self-Review Quiz 14-1

1. False **2.** True **3.** False **4.** True **5.** False

LEARNING UNIT 14-2

The Allowance Method: Two Approaches to Estimating the Amount of Bad Debts Expense

As we said earlier, at the end of the year a company estimates what percentage of the sales that occurred that year will turn out to be uncollectible accounts, or bad debts. How is this estimate arrived at? In this unit we will look at two approaches to making an annual estimate of Bad Debts Expense. Figure 14-2 presents an overview. Don't memorize it; we will be covering it step by step.

THE INCOME STATEMENT APPROACH

Bad debts expense is based on a percentage of the dollar volume of net credit sales on the income statement.

Abby Ellen Company uses the **income statement approach** at the end of the year to calculate how much bad debts expense will be associated with this year's sales. On the basis of the past several years, the company has averaged bad debts expense of 1 percent of net credit sales. From the following facts, let's prepare an adjusting entry to record the bad debts expense that is based on a percentage of net credit sales.

2004	*Dr.*	*Cr.*
Sales (all credit)		$95,000
Sales Returns and Allowances	$10,000	
Sales Discounts	5,000	
Accounts Receivable	7,000	
Allowance for Doubtful Accounts		100

Analysis:

	Sales	$95,000
−	SRA	10,000
−	SD	5,000
	Net Credit Sales	$80,000

1 Accounts Affected	2 Category	3 ↑ ↓	4 Rules
Bad Debts Expense	**Operating Expenses**	↑	**Dr.**
Allowance for Doubtful Accounts	**Asset (Contra)**	↑	**Cr.**

Dec.	31	Bad Debts Expense	800 00	
		Allowance for Doubtful Accounts		800 00
		Record estimate of bad debts		
		(0.01 × $80,000)		

When posted, the allowance account is as follows:

Allowance for Doubtful Accounts

Dr.	Cr.
	100 → Balance *before* adjustment
	800 → Adjustment
	900 → New balance

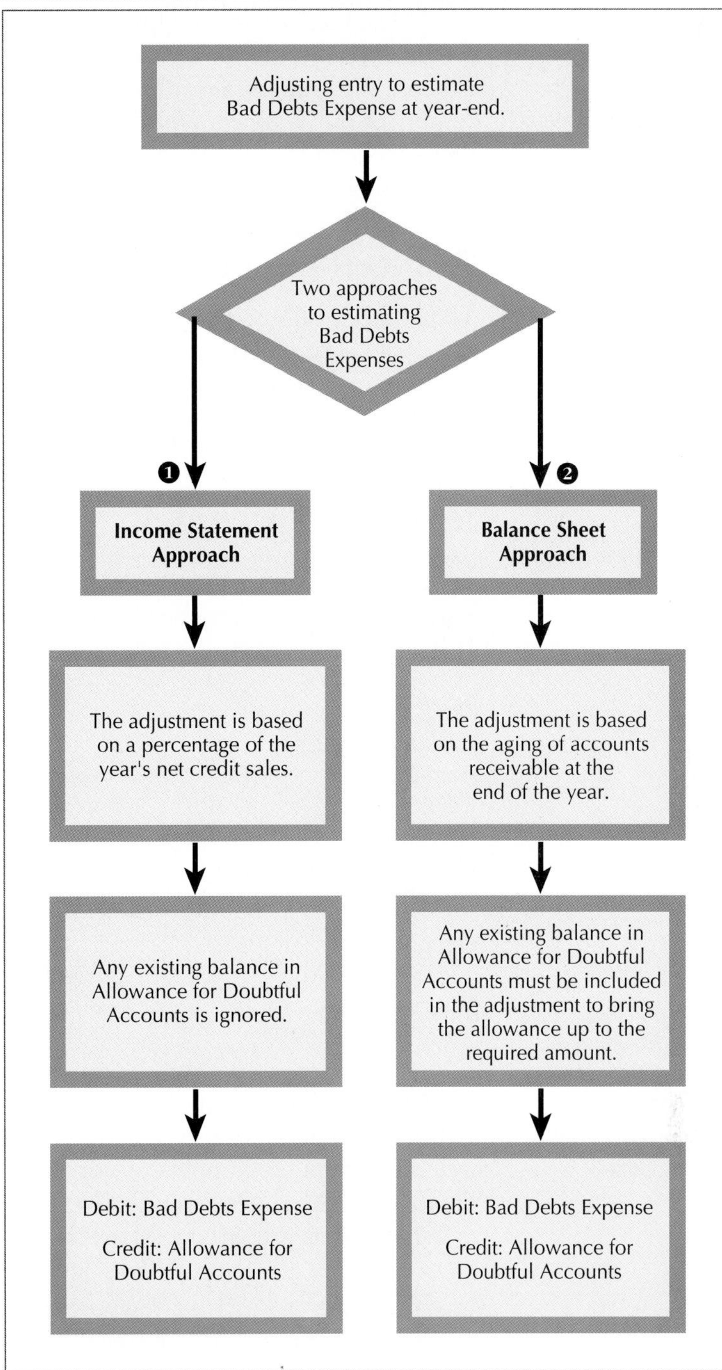

FIGURE 14-2
Two Approaches to Estimating Amount of Bad Debts Expense

Beginning balance in allowance account represents potential bad debts from previous periods.

Why? The balance in the Allowance for Doubtful Accounts is ignored, since this approach calculates the amount of bad debts expense *for the year* based on a percentage of net credit sales. This approach emphasizes the matching requirements of the income statement. The $100 in the allowance account represents a carryover of potential bad debts from prior years. Thus, the total of $900 represents total potential uncollectible accounts of several periods of sales. If, over the years, the estimate for bad debts expense has been inaccurate, an adjusting entry can be made in the current year's bad debts expense. If this happens, the company may re-evaluate its percentage, and use a higher or lower percentage as necessary.

THE BALANCE SHEET APPROACH

In the income statement approach, the estimate for the bad debts expense used a percentage of net credit sales from the income statement as the basis for the adjusting entry. The **balance sheet approach**, on the other hand, uses accounts receivable on the balance sheet as its basis in preparing the adjusting entry to estimate bad debts expense. *Keep in mind that the adjusting entry will take into consideration the existing balance in the Allowance for Doubtful Accounts.* (In the income statement approach the balance in the allowance account was ignored.)

Let's look now at one balance sheet approach—the aging of the accounts receivable.

AGING THE ACCOUNTS RECEIVABLE

Aging **classifies uncollected amounts for individual customers according to days past due.**

The longer a bill has been due and not paid, the more likely it is that it is not going to be paid. Therefore, one way of estimating the amount of bad debts for the year just past is to look at Accounts Receivable and analyze it according to how many days past due the accounts are. This is called **aging the accounts receivable**. Table 14-1 shows an analysis that the Abby Ellen Company did on December 31, 2004.

TABLE 14-1 AGING OF ACCOUNTS RECEIVABLE

Name of Customer	Total Balance	Not Yet Due	Days Past Due 1–30	31–60	61–90	Over 90
Sarah Elliot	$ 100	$ 100				
Joshua Karras	30			$ 30		
Alan Ledbury	160	160				
John Sullivan	180				$160	$ 20
Sheri Missan	80	80				
Others	6,450	3,260	$2,000	840	40	310
Totals	$7,000	$3,600	$2,000	$870	$200	$330
Percentage of total (rounded to nearest whole number)	100%	51% ($3,600 / $7,000)	29% ($2,000 / $7,000)	12% ($870 / $7,000)	3% ($200 / $7,000)	5% ($330 / $7,000)

Today, with the computer, an analysis of Accounts Receivable can be completed quickly.

Note that 29 percent of the total receivables for Abby Ellen is past due from 1 to 30 days. (This analysis will also provide feedback to the credit department as to how well the current credit policy is working.) Now let's look at how the company will estimate what allowance is required to meet probable bad debts. The schedule shown in Table 14-2 is prepared to assist the company in calculating the needed balance.

TABLE 14-2 BALANCE REQUIRED TO MEET PROBABLE BAD DEBTS AND ADJUSTING ENTRY

	Amount	Estimated Percentage Considered to be Bad Debts Expense	Amount Needed in Allowance for Doubtful Accounts to Cover Estimated Bad Debts Expense
Not yet due	**$3,600**	**3**	**($3,600 × 0.03) $108**
Days past due			
1–30	2,000	4	80
31–60	870	10	87
61–90	200	20	40
Over 90	330	50	165
Total accounts receivable	$7,000		
		Total balance required in Allowance for Doubtful Accounts	$480
		Less current balance	−100
		Adjusting entry	$380

In this schedule, Abby Ellen Company has applied a sliding scale of percentages (3, 4, 10, 20, 50), based on *previous experience*, to the total amount of receivables due in each time period. For example, of the $200 overdue by 61-90 days, 20 percent or $40 will probably never be paid. Looking at this schedule reveals that Abby Ellen Company needs $480 to cover estimated bad debts. *Presently* the balance in the allowance account is $100. Thus, to reach a balance of $480, we must adjust the balance of the account by the following adjusting journal entry:

The balance in the Allowance for Doubtful Accounts is not ignored.

2004 Dec.	31	Bad Debts Expense	380 00	
		Allowance for Doubtful Accounts		380 00
		Record estimate of bad debts		

Bad Debts Expense

Dr.	Cr.
380	

Allowance for Doubtful Accounts

Dr.	Cr.
	100 Beginning Balance
	380 Adjustment
	480 New balance in account

Some companies that feel aging is too time-consuming may estimate bad debts on the basis of a percentage of total Accounts Receivable.

The desired balance of $480 is now reached. If the Allowance had a *debit* balance of $100 before the adjustment, the amount of the adjusting entry would be $580 credit to Allowance for Doubtful Accounts to arrive at the $480 balance. Once again, the adjustment *must* consider the *existing balance* in the allowance account before the adjusting entry is prepared.

LEARNING UNIT 14-2 REVIEW

AT THIS POINT you should be able to:

- Explain the two approaches to estimating Bad Debts Expense. (pp. 580–583)
- Explain why the balance in Allowance for Doubtful Accounts is ignored when an adjusting entry for bad debts is prepared in the income statement approach. (p. 581)
- Show how to prepare an aging of accounts receivable. (p. 582)
- Explain how the aging of accounts receivable is used to arrive at the balance required in Allowance for Doubtful Accounts. (p. 583)

SELF-REVIEW QUIZ 14-2

(The form you need is on page 14-1 of the *Study Guide with Working Papers.*)

From the following, prepare an adjusting journal entry for bad debts expense for (1) the income statement approach and (2) the balance sheet approach.

Allowance for Doubtful Accounts

Dr.	Cr.
	400

Income Statement Approach

Net Sales: $160,000
1% of Net Sales

Balance Sheet Approach		*Percentage Considered Bad Debts*
Not yet due	$4,000	4
Days past due		
1–30	3,000	5
31–60	400	10
Over 60	5,000	30

Solution to Self-Review Quiz 14-2

(1)	Dec.	31	Bad Debts Expense	1600 00	
			Allowance for Doubtful Accounts		1600 00
			(0.01 × $160,000)		
(2)		31	Bad Debts Expense	1450 00	
			Allowance for Doubtful Accounts		1450 00
			$4,000 × 0.04 = $ 160		
			3,000 × 0.05 = 150		
			400 × 0.10 = 40		
			5,000 × 0.30 = 1,500		
			$1,850		

Quiz Tip

Note allowance adjusted:

$1,850 – $400 = $1,450

LEARNING UNIT 14-3

Writing off Uncollectible Accounts

This unit will look at two ways to write off uncollectible accounts, one using the Allowance for Doubtful Accounts, the other using the direct write-off method.

WRITING OFF AN ACCOUNT USING THE ALLOWANCE FOR DOUBTFUL ACCOUNTS

Let's assume that on March 18, 2007, the Abby Ellen Company determines that the account of Jill Sullivan for $900 is uncollectible. (The sale to Jill Sullivan was back in 2006.) This means that this Accounts Receivable amount should no longer be considered an asset and should be written off. The following journal entry reduces Allowance for Doubtful Accounts and reduces the Accounts Receivable controlling account as well as the accounts receivable subsidiary ledger.

2007 Mar.	18	Allowance for Doubtful Accounts		900 00	
		Accounts Receivable, Jill Sullivan			900 00
		Wrote off Sullivan account			

Note the following key points:

1. This journal entry does *not* affect any expenses. Remember, Bad Debts Expense is *not* affected when an account is finally written off under this method. The estimate for bad debts expense was recorded in the previous year before the bad debt actually occurred.
2. If more than one customer is written off, a compound entry can be used, debiting Allowance for Doubtful Accounts for the total and crediting each individual account.
3. The net realizable value of Accounts Receivable is unchanged. Let's prove this:

	Balances before the Write-off		*Balances after the Write-off*
Accounts Receivable	$12,000	$900 write-off →	$11,100
Less: Allowance for Doubtful Accounts	2,000	$900 drain →	1,100
Estimated realizable value (what to expect to collect)	$10,000	No change →	$10,000

Let's look now at what would happen on the books of Abby Ellen Company if Jill Sullivan in the future should pay part or all of the debt.

Let's assume that Jill Sullivan is able to pay off half of her debt and sends a cheque to Abby Ellen Company on February 1, 2008. (Keep in mind the fact that her account was written off on March 18, 2007, and the original sale was made in 2006.) To record this, Abby Ellen Company reverses in part the entry that was made to write off the account in the amount expected to be recovered and records the amount received from Jill. The following are the journal entries to record the recovery of $450 out of the original amount of $900:

Reinstates the account

Records the amount received

Date		Account	PR	Dr.	Cr.
2008 Feb.	1	Accounts Receivable, Jill Sullivan		450 00	
		Allowances for Doubtful Accounts			450 00
		Restores collectible portion			
	1	Cash		450 00	
		Accounts Receivable, Jill Sullivan			450 00
		Records payment received			

The reason we record both a debit and a credit to Accounts Receivable is that it provides a clear picture of the transactions involving Jill Sullivan. If the company is considering giving credit again to Jill Sullivan, these previous records could be of assistance in determining how much credit, if any, should be extended. Note how the first entry reinstates the account and the second entry records the cash received. In fact, the second entry would be made in the Cash Receipts journal.

Let's look now at another method of handling bad debts expense, the direct write-off method.

The Direct Write-Off Method

The direct write-off method does not fulfill the matching principle.

When a company cannot reasonably estimate its bad debts expense, it may use the **direct write-off method**. Using this method, an account that is determined to be uncollectible would be directly written off to this year's Bad Debts Expense account without regard to when the original sale was made. In this method, the Allowance for Doubtful Accounts is not used, since no adjustment is needed at the end of the year to estimate bad debts expense. Let's replay the Jill Sullivan write-off as well as the recovery so that we can make comparisons between the Allowance for Doubtful Accounts method and the direct write-off method. In the recovery, we will see a new account title, Bad Debts Recovered. Think of it as a revenue account found in the Other Income section of an income statement.

Writing off Jill Sullivan on March 18, 2007: Note that Allowance For Doubtful Accounts is not used.

Date		Account	Dr.	Cr.
2007 Mar.	18	Bad Debts Expense	900 00	
		Accounts Receivable, Jill Sullivan		900 00
		Wrote off account		

Recovery of half the amount owed by Jill Sullivan on February 1, 2008: Note that Bad Debts Recovered replaces Allowance for Doubtful Accounts.

On the balance sheet, Accounts Receivable is recorded at gross. No allowance account or realizable amount is used.

Date		Account	Dr.	Cr.
2008 Feb.	1	Accounts Receivable, Jill Sullivan	450 00	
		Bad Debts Recovered		450 00
		Restores collectible portion		
	1	Cash	450 00	
		Accounts Receivable, Jill Sullivan		450 00
		Records payment received		

Bad Debts Recovered	Other Revenue	↑	Cr.

In the direct write-off method, when the amount is written off, Allowance for Doubtful Accounts is not used. Rather, the debit is to Bad Debts Expense. On the recovery in years following the sale, instead of crediting Allowance for Doubtful Accounts, the direct method credits **Bad Debts Recovered** (an account in the Other Revenue category). This in effect increases the revenue and puts the Accounts Receivable back on the books. If recovery is made in the same year (let's say on May 1), you just reverse the entry you made to write off the account:

Date		Account	Dr.	Cr.
2007 May	1	Accounts Receivable, Jill Sullivan	450 00	
		Bad Debts Expense		450 00

Insight into Income Tax Regulations

For tax purposes, the law permits the bad debt reserve method of deducting bad debts. Since the direct write-off method does vary from generally accepted accounting principles, tax law follows the *CICA Handbook* and allows the deduction of an annual reserve.

LEARNING UNIT 14-3 REVIEW

AT THIS POINT you should be able to:

- Write off an account using the Allowance for Doubtful Accounts method. (pp. 584–585)
- Explain why net realizable value is unchanged after a write-off is complete. (p. 585)
- Prepare journal entries to recover entire or partial amounts that were once declared uncollectible. (p. 585)
- Explain the direct write-off method and prepare appropriate journal entries for write-off and recovery. (pp. 585–586)

SELF-REVIEW QUIZ 14-3

(The form you need is on page 14-1 of the *Study Guide with Working Papers.*)

Respond true or false to the following:

1. When an account is written off using the Allowance for Doubtful Accounts method in a period following the sale, the result is a debit to Bad Debts Expense and a credit to Accounts Receivable.
2. The direct write-off method will sometimes use the Allowance for Doubtful Accounts account.
3. When an account is written off (using the Allowance for Doubtful Accounts method), net realizable value is unchanged.
4. Bad Debts Recovered is an asset.
5. A debit balance in Allowance for Doubtful Accounts indicates that the estimate for Bad Debts Expense was too low.

Solutions to Self-Review Quiz 14-3

1. False **2.** False **3.** True **4.** False **5.** True

Chapter Review

Summary of Key Points

Learning Unit 14-1

1. If accrual accounting is used, bad debts expense should be recognized in the year in which the sale was made, even though the actual write-off may not yet have taken place.
2. Bad debts expense is an expense found on the income statement.
3. The Allowance for Doubtful Accounts is a contra-asset account found on the balance sheet that accumulates the amount of estimated uncollectibles before they are actually written off.
4. Net realizable value equals Accounts Receivable minus Allowance for Doubtful Accounts.
5. When an account is written off, the Allowance for Doubtful Accounts is debited and Accounts Receivable is credited (along with the subsidiary ledger account).

Learning Unit 14-2

1. The two approaches to estimating bad debts expense are the income statement approach and the balance sheet approach.
2. The income statement approach estimates bad debts expense on the basis of a percentage of net sales. (Some companies use credit sales; some use total sales.) The balance is ignored in Allowance for Doubtful Accounts when the bad debts expense is estimated from sales of the period.
3. The balance sheet approach estimates the balance required in Allowance for Doubtful Accounts by aging the accounts receivable. The balance in the allowance account will have to be adjusted, based on the anticipated default rate determined by the aging of the receivables.

Learning Unit 14-3

After the write-off, net realizable value is unchanged.

1. When an account is written off (using the allowance account) in years following the sale, the result is to debit Allowance for Doubtful Accounts and credit Accounts Receivable. Do not debit Bad Debts Expense, as it has already been debited in the year in which the sale was made.
2. When an uncollectible account has been written off and is now recovered, the entry reverses the original write-off by debiting Accounts Receivable and crediting Allowance for Doubtful Accounts. Then the cash received is debited to the Cash account and credited to Accounts Receivable.
3. The direct write-off method will recognize the bad debts expense only when the customer account is declared uncollectible. The direct method does *not* use the Allowance for Doubtful Accounts account, since no estimate is made for bad debts. This method does not follow the matching principle in accrual accounting.
4. Bad Debts Recovered is classified as Other Revenue when a customer account is reinstated after being written off in the direct method.

BLUEPRINT SUMMARY OF RECORDING BAD DEBTS EXPENSE, WRITE-OFFS, AND RECOVERY

Situation	Allowance for Doubtful Accounts Method						Direct Write-off Method		
	A. Income Statement Approach			*B. Balance Sheet Approach*					
Adjusting entry is made to record estimated uncollectible accounts.	Bad Debts Expense	XX		Bad Debts Expense	XX		None		
	Allowance for Doubtful Accounts		XX	Allowance for Doubtful Accounts		XX			
	Based on percent of net sales			Aging of Accounts Receivable					
	Balance in allowance account			determines amount needed					
	is ignored.			in allowance account.					
				Balance in allowance account					
				is adjusted.					
Receivable is determined to be uncollectible.	Allowance for Doubtful Accounts	XX		Allowance for Doubtful Accounts	XX		Bad Debts Expense	XX	
	Accounts Receivable		XX	Accounts Receivable		XX	Accounts Receivable		XX
Bad debts are recovered.	Accounts Receivable	XX		Accounts Receivable	XX		Accounts Receivable	XX	
	Allowance for Doubtful Accounts		XX	Allowance for Doubtful Accounts		XX	Bad Debts Recovered*		XX
	Cash	XX		Cash	XX		Cash	XX	
	Accounts Receivable		XX	Accounts Receivable		XX	Accounts Receivable		XX
Bal. sheet updated.	Shows net realizable value.			Shows net realizable value.			Does not show net realizable value.		

*Used if recovery is not in the same year as the write off.

Key terms

Aging of accounts receivable The procedure of classifying accounts of individual customers by age group, where age is the number of days elapsed since due date (p. 582)

Allowance for Doubtful Accounts A contra-asset account that is subtracted from the Accounts Receivable. This account accumulates the *expected* amount of uncollectibles as of a given date. (p. 577)

Bad Debts Expense The operating expense account that estimates the amount of credit sales in a given accounting period that will probably not be collectible when the allowance method is used. For the direct write-off method, this account would be the actual amount written off. (p. 577)

Bad Debts Recovered When an account receivable has been written off and is recovered, this account, which is in the Other Revenue category, is credited in the direct write-off method if the recovery is in a year *following* the write-off. (p. 586)

Balance sheet approach A method used to calculate the amount *required* in Allowance for Doubtful Accounts to cover expected uncollectibles. This method is based on the Accounts Receivable account and the aging process. The adjustment to Allowance for Doubtful Accounts will bring the new balance of that account to the new required level. (p. 582)

Direct write-off method The method of writing off uncollectibles when it is determined that an account is uncollectible, thus not using the Allowance for Doubtful Accounts account. This method does not follow the matching principle of accrual accounting. (p. 585)

Income statement approach A method that estimates the amount of bad debts expense that will result on the basis of a percentage of net credit sales for the period. The amount of the expected bad debts is added to the existing balance of Allowance for Doubtful Accounts. (p. 580)

Net realizable value The amount (Accounts Receivable – Allowance for Doubtful Accounts) that is expected to be collected. (p. 578)

Questions, mini exercises, exercises, and problems

Discussion Questions

1. Explain the matching principle in relationship to recording bad debts expense.
2. What is the purpose of the Allowance for Doubtful Accounts account?
3. What is net realizable value?
4. When an Account Receivable is written off, Bad Debts Expense must be debited. True or false? Please discuss.
5. Explain why Allowance for Doubtful Accounts is a contra-asset account.
6. Recording bad debts expense is a closing entry. True or false? Defend your position.
7. The income statement approach used to estimate bad debts is based on Accounts Receivable on the balance sheet. Accept or reject. Why?
8. In which approach is the balance of Allowance for Doubtful Accounts considered when the estimate of bad debts expense is made? Please explain.
9. Why would a company age its accounts receivable?
10. Using the Allowance for Doubtful Accounts method, what journal entries would be made to write off an account as well as to record later the recovery of the receivable?

11. Why doesn't net realizable value change when an account is written off using the allowance account?
12. What is the purpose of using the direct write-off method?
13. Explain the purpose of the Bad Debts Recovered account.

Mini Exercises

(The forms you need are on pages 14-2 and 14-3 of the *Study Guide with Working Papers.*)

Categorizing Accounts

1. a. Complete the following transactional analysis chart:

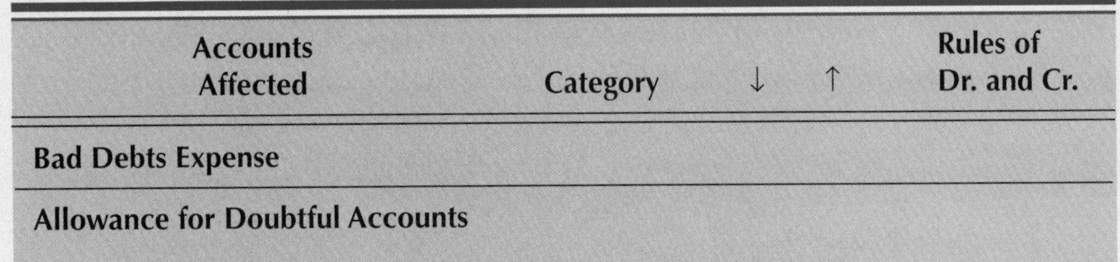

Accounts Affected	Category	↓	↑	Rules of Dr. and Cr.
Bad Debts Expense				
Allowance for Doubtful Accounts				

b. Which financial statement will each title be recorded on?

c. Which account is temporary? Which account is permanent?

Allowance Method

2. Complete the table:

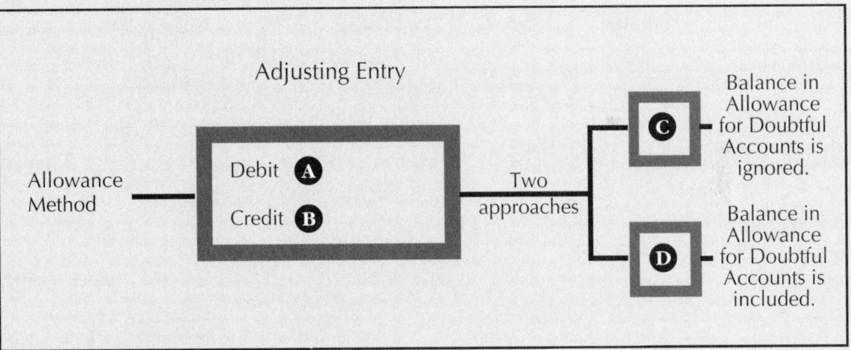

Journalize Adjusting Entries for Income Statement and Balance Sheet Approaches

3. Given that the balance in the Allowance for Doubtful Accounts is $100 credit, prepare adjusting entries for bad debts based on the following assumptions:
   a. Bad debts are to be 5 percent of net credit sales or $400.
   b. Bad debts should be $400, on the basis of the aging of Accounts Receivable.

Writing off Uncollectible Accounts, and Reinstatement—Allowance Method

4. Journalize entries for the following situations (assume allowance method):

Situation 1: Wrote off Bill Allen as a bad debt two years after the sale for $50.

Situation 2: Reinstated Bill Allen who sent in his past due amount.

Writing off an Uncollectible Account and Reinstatement—Direct Write-Off Method

5. Journalize entries for the following situation (assume direct write-off method).

Situation 1: Wrote off Bill Allen as a bad debt two years after the sale of $50.

Situation 2: Reinstated Bill Allen who sent in his past due amount two years after it had been written off.

Exercises

(The forms you need are on pages 14-4 and 14-5 of the *Study Guide with Working Papers.*)

Preparing a partial balance sheet with Allowance for Doubtful Accounts

14-1. Jetson Co. has requested that you prepare a partial balance sheet on December 31, 2000, from the following: Cash, $105,000; Petty Cash, $60; Accounts Receivable, $60,000; Bad Debts Expense, $40,000; Allowance for Doubtful Accounts, $12,000; Merchandise Inventory, $18,000.

Calculating bad debts expense with income statement approach

14-2. Given the information in the T accounts below, journalize the adjusting entry on December 31, 2000, for bad debts expense, which is estimated to be 4 percent of net sales. The income statement approach is used.

Accounts Receivable	
30,000	

Sales	
	110,000

Sales Returns and Allowances	
500	

Allowance for Sales Discount	
9,500	

Doubtful Accounts	
	5,000

Calculating bad debts expense by balance sheet approach

14-3. Assuming that in exercise 2 the balance sheet approach is used, prepare a journalized adjusting entry for bad debts expense. Aging of accounts receivable indicates that an $8,000 balance in the allowance account will be needed to cover bad debts.

Journalizing adjustment for bad debts, as well as reinstatement by Allowance method; comparison with direct write-off method

14-4. The Austin Co., which uses an Allowance for Doubtful Accounts, had the following transactions in 2001 and 2002.

2001
Dec. 31 Recorded Bad Debts Expense of $12,000.

2002
Apr. 3 Wrote off Angie Ring account of $4,000 as uncollectible.
June 4 Wrote off Mike Catuc account of $3,000 as uncollectible.

2003
Aug. 5 Recovered $500 from Mike Catuc.

a. Journalize the transactions. (They use the income statement approach in estimating bad debts.)

b. Journalize how Austin Co. would record the Mike Catuc bad debt situation if the direct write-off method were used.

Journalizing adjustments for bad debts expense on the basis of (1) percentage of sales, (2) aging of Accounts Receivable with balance of Allowance for Doubtful Accounts, a debit balance

14-5. Rowe Company had credit sales of $200,000 during 2002. The balance in the Allowance for Doubtful Accounts is a $1,000 debit balance. Journalize the bad debts expense for December 31, using each of the following methods:

a. Bad debts expense is estimated at 0.5 percent of credit sales.

b. The aging of Accounts Receivable indicates that $2,200 will be required in the allowance account to cover bad debts expense.

Group A Problems

(The forms you need are on pages 14-6 to 14-10 of the *Study Guide with Working Papers.*)

The income statement approach: journalizing bad debts expense and writing accounts off

Check Figure

Aug. 24
Dr. Allowance for Doubtful Accounts
Cr. Accounts Receivable, Jill Neuman

14A-1. The Palter Co. has requested that you prepare journal entries from the following (this company uses the Allowance for Doubtful Accounts method based on the income statement approach).

2000
Dec. 31 Recorded Bad Debts Expense of $11,000.

2001
Jan. 7 Wrote off Gene Smore's account of $800 as uncollectible.
Mar. 5 Wrote off Paul Jane's account of $600 as uncollectible.
July 8 Recovered $300 from Paul Jane.
Aug. 19 Wrote off Bob Seager's account of $1,300 as uncollectible.
24 Wrote off Jill Neuman's account of $750 as uncollectible.
Nov. 19 Recovered $400 from Bob Seager.

The balance sheet approach: aging analysis and journalizing of bad debts expense

Check Figure

Net Realizable Value $146,650

14A-2. Given the additional data in the table below:

a. Prepare on December 31, 2001, the adjusting journal entry for bad debts expense.

b. Prepare a partial balance sheet on December 31, 2001, showing how net realizable value is calculated.

c. If the balance in Allowance for Doubtful Accounts was a $300 debit balance, journalize the adjusting entry for bad debts expense on December 31, 2001.

Balances: Cash, $30,000; Accounts Receivable, $152,000; Allowance for Doubtful Accounts, $300; Inventory, $12,000.

Additional Data

Alvie Co.
December 31, 2001

	Amount	*Estimated Percentage Considered to Be Bad Debts Expense*	*Estimated Amount Needed in Allowance for Doubtful Accounts*
Not yet due	$130,000	1	________
0–60	9,000	5	________
61–180	8,000	20	________
Over six months	5,000	40	________
	$152,000		

The direct write-off method

Check Figure

Dec. 7
Dr. Bad Debts Expense
Cr. Accounts Receivable, J. Miller

14A-3. T. J. Rack Company uses the direct write-off method for recording Bad Debts Expense. At the beginning of 2002, Accounts Receivable has a $119,000 balance. Journalize the following transactions for T. J. Rack:

2002
Mar. 13 Wrote off S. Rose's account for $1,800.
Apr. 14 Wrote off P. Soy's account for $750.

2003
Nov. 8 P. Soy paid bad debt of $750 that was written off April 14, 2002.
Dec. 7 Wrote off J. Miller's account as uncollectible, $285.
12 Wrote off D. Lovejoy's account for $375 due from sales made on account in 2001.

Journalizing and posting adjustments for bad debts expense and write-offs and recovery based on balance sheet approach; preparation of partial balance sheet

Check Figure

Total Current Assets $272,360

14A-4. Simon Company completed the following transactions:

2001		
Jan.	9	Sold merchandise on account to Ray's Supply, $1,500.
	15	Wrote off the account of Pete Runnels as uncollectible because of his death, $600.
Mar.	17	Received $400 from Roland Co., whose account had been written off in 2000. The account was reinstated and the collection recorded.
Apr.	9	Received 10 percent of the $4,000 owed by Lane Drug. The remainder was written off as uncollectible.
June	15	The account of Mel's Garage was reinstated for $1,200. The account was written off three years ago.
Oct.	18	Prepared a compound entry to write the following accounts off as uncollectible: Jane's Diner, $200; Keen Auto, $400; Ralph's Hardware, $600.
Nov.	12	Sold merchandise on account to J. B. Rug, $1,900.
Dec.	31	On the basis of an aging of Accounts Receivable it was estimated that $7,000 will be uncollectible out of a total of $160,000 in Accounts Receivable.
	31	Closed Bad Debts Expense to Income Summary.

Additional Data

	Account No.	*Balance*
Allowance for Doubtful Accounts	114	$4,100
Income Summary	312	—
Bad Debts Expense	612	—

Required

1. Journalize the transactions.

2. Post to Allowance for Doubtful Accounts, Income Summary, or Bad Debts Expense as needed. (Be sure to record beginning balance in the allowance account in your workbook.)

3. Prepare a current assets section of the balance sheet. Ending balances needed: Cash, $13,000; Accounts Receivable, $160,000; Office Supplies, $2,110; Merchandise Inventory, $103,000; Prepaid Rent, $1,250.

Group B Problems

(The forms you need are on pages 14-6 to 14-10 of the *Study Guide with Working Papers.*)

The income statement approach: journalizing bad debts expense and writing accounts off

Check Figure

Aug. 24
Dr. Allowance for Doubtful Accounts
Cr. Accounts Receivable, Jim O'Reilly

14B-1. The Palter Co. has requested that you prepare journal entries from the following (this company uses the Allowance for Doubtful Accounts method based on the income statement approach).

2000		
Dec.	31	Recorded bad debts expense of $14,800.
2001		
Jan.	7	Wrote off Woody Tree's account of $1,200 as uncollectible.
Mar.	5	Wrote off Jim Lantz's account of $600 as uncollectible.
July	8	Recovered $600 from Jim Lantz.
Aug.	19	Wrote off Mabel Hest's account of $750 as uncollectible.
	24	Wrote off Jim O'Reilly's account of $950 as uncollectible.
Nov.	19	Recovered $500 from Mabel Hest.

The balance sheet approach: aging analysis and journalizing of bad debts expense

Check Figure

Net Realizable Value $166,000

14B-2. Given the information below, and assuming the following balances: Cash, $42,000; Accounts Receivable, $173,000; Allowance for Doubtful Accounts, $400; Inventory, $12,000:

a. Prepare on December 31, 2001, the adjusting journal entry for bad debts expense.

b. Prepare a partial balance sheet on December 31, 2001, showing how net realizable value is calculated.

c. If the balance in Allowance for Doubtful Accounts was a $400 debit balance, journalize the adjusting entry for bad debts expense on December 31, 2001.

Additional Information

Alvie Co.
December 31, 2001

	Amount	*Estimated Percentage Considered to Be Bad Debts Expense*	*Estimated Amount Needed in Allowance for Doubtful Accounts*
Not yet due	$150,000	2	________
0–60	10,000	6	________
61–180	9,000	20	________
Over six months	4,000	40	________
	$173,000		

The direct write-off method

Check Figure

Dec. 7
Dr. Bad Debts Expense
Cr. Accounts Receivable, Joe Francis

14B-3. T. J. Rack Company uses the direct write-off method for recording bad debts expense. At the beginning of 2002, Accounts Receivable has an $88,000 balance. Journalize the following transactions for T. J. Rack:

2002
Mar. 13 Wrote off Jill Diamond's account for $1,950.
Apr. 14 Wrote off Buffy Hall's account for $900.

2003
Nov. 8 Buffy Hall paid debt of $900 that was written off April 14, 2002.
Dec. 7 Wrote off Joe Francis's account as uncollectible, $880.
12 Wrote off Joe Martin's account for $410 from sales made on account in 2001.

Journalizing and posting adjustments for bad debts expense and write-offs and recovery based on balance sheet approach; partial balance sheet prepared

Check Figure

Total Current Assets $284,200

14B-4. Simon Company completed the following transactions:

2001
Jan. 9 Sold merchandise on account to Lowe's Supply, $1,900.
15 Wrote off the account of Kevin Reese as uncollectible because of his death, $700.
Mar. 17 Received $300 from J. James, whose account had been written off in 2000. The account was reinstated and the collection recorded.
Apr. 9 Received 20 percent of the $5,000 owed by Long Drug. The remainder was written off as uncollectible.
June 15 The account of Morse's Garage was reinstated for $3,100. The account was written off three years ago.
Oct. 18 Prepared a compound entry to write the following accounts off as uncollectible: Sal's Diner, $800; Ring Auto, $1,300; Neel's Hardware, $800.
Nov. 12 Sold merchandise on account to Able Roy, $1,950.
Dec. 31 On the basis of an aging of Accounts Receivable, it was estimated that $8,000 would be uncollectible out of a total of $170,000 in Accounts Receivable.
31 Closed Bad Debts Expense to Income Summary.

Additional Data

	Account No.	Balance
Allowance for Doubtful Accounts	114	$3,300
Income Summary	312	—
Bad Debts Expense	612	—

1. Journalize the transactions.
2. Post to Allowance for Doubtful Accounts, Income Summary, or Bad Debts Expense as needed.
3. Prepare a current assets section of the balance sheet. Ending balances needed: Cash, $24,000; Accounts Receivable, $170,000; Office Supplies, $3,000; Merchandise Inventory, $94,000; Prepaid Rent, $1,200.

Group C Problems

The income statement approach: journalizing bad debts expense and writing accounts off

Check Figure

Aug. 24
Dr. Allowance for Doubtful Accounts
Cr. Accounts Receivable, Ellen Watt

(The forms you need are on pages 14-11 to 14-15 of the *Study Guide with Working Papers.*)

14C-1. The Samsom Co. has requested that you prepare journal entries from the following (this company uses the Allowance for Doubtful Accounts method based on the income statement approach).

2000
Dec. 31 Recorded bad debts expense of $9,200.

2001
Jan. 7 Wrote off Helen Jamison's account of $850 as uncollectible.
Mar. 5 Wrote off Rob Hart's account of $400 as uncollectible.
July 8 Recovered $200 from Rob Hart.
Aug. 19 Wrote off Brian Brisk's account of $1,640 as uncollectible.
24 Wrote off Ellen Watt's account of $525 as uncollectible.
Nov. 19 Recovered $700 from Brian Brisk.

The balance sheet approach: aging analysis and journalizing of bad debts expense

Check Figure

Net Realizable Value $102,200

14C-2. Given the additional information presented below:

a. Prepare on December 31, 2002, the adjusting journal entry for bad debts expense.

b. Prepare a partial balance sheet on December 31, 2002, showing how net realizable value is calculated.

c. If the balance in Allowance for Doubtful Accounts was a $500 debit balance, journalize the adjusting entry for bad debts expense on December 31, 2002.

Additional Information

Dominion Company
December 31, 2002

	Amount	Estimated Percentage Considered to Be Bad Debts Expense	Estimated Amount Needed in Allowance for Doubtful Accounts
Not yet due	$76,000	1	______
0–30	12,000	2	______
31–60	8,000	6	______
61–180	4,000	13	______
Over six months	6,000	30	______
	$106,000		

Balances: Cash, $16,400; Accounts Receivable, $106,000; Allowance for Doubtful Accounts, $700; Inventory, $53,700.

The direct write-off method

Check Figure

Dec. 5
Dr. Bad Debts Expense
Cr. Accounts Receivable, S. Lowe

14C-3. Camping Equipment Company uses the direct write-off method for recording bad debts expense. At the beginning of 2003, Accounts Receivable has an $86,700 balance. Journalize the following transactions for the company:

2003
Mar. 23 Wrote off F. Robichaud's account for $1,280.
Jun. 9 Wrote off K. Cheung's account for $915.

2004
Aug. 15 K. Cheung paid bad debt of $915 that was written off June 9, 2003.
Dec. 5 Wrote off S. Lowe's account as uncollectible, $418.
18 Wrote off R. Patel's account for $316 due from sales made on account in 2002.

Journalizing and posting adjustments for bad debts expense and write-offs and recovery based on balance sheet approach; partial balance sheet prepared

Check Figure

Total Current Assets $265,022

14C-4. Prospecting Supply Company completed the following transactions:

2001
Jan. 8 Sold merchandise on account to May Expeditions, $4,160.
Feb. 19 Wrote off the account of Avery Fischer as uncollectible because of his death, $624.
Mar. 14 Received $600 from Maximum Co., whose account had been written off in 2000. The account was reinstated and the collection recorded.
Apr. 5 Received 25 percent of the $6,400 owed by Airborne Surveys. The remainder was written off as uncollectible.
July 18 The account of Hallicrafter Explorations was reinstated for $3,000 (amount received). The account was written off three years ago.
Oct. 28 Prepared a compound entry to write the following accounts off as uncollectible: Corbett Co., $275; Quark Co., $654; Lonely Expeditions, $247.
Nov. 17 Sold merchandise on account to Partridge Surveys, $4,280.
Dec. 31 Based on an aging of Accounts Receivable, it was estimated that $6,850 would be uncollectible out of a total of $142,000 in Accounts Receivable.
31 Closed bad debts expense to Income Summary.

Additional Data as of 01/01/2001:

	Account No.	*Balance*
Allowance for Doubtful Accounts	1124	$6,150
Income Summary	3100	—
Bad Debts Expense	6125	—

Required

1. Journalize the transactions.

2. Post to Allowance for Doubtful Accounts, Income Summary, or Bad Debts Expense as needed. (Be sure to record beginning balance in the allowance account in your workbook.)

3. Prepare a current assets section of the balance sheet. Ending balances needed: Cash, $16,742; Accounts Receivable, $142,000; Office Supplies, $2,630; Merchandise Inventory, $107,000; Prepaid Rent, $3,500; and your calculated balance for Allowance for Doubtful Accounts.

Real World Applications

(The forms you need are on page 14-16 of the *Study Guide with Working Papers.*)

14R-1.

Joan Rivers, the newly hired bookkeeper of Lyon Company, has until 5 p.m. today to prepare an analysis on December 31, 2001, of Accounts Receivable by age as well as record the entry for bad debts expense. Assist Joan, who has found the following invoices and balances scattered on her desk. Terms of all sales are n/30.

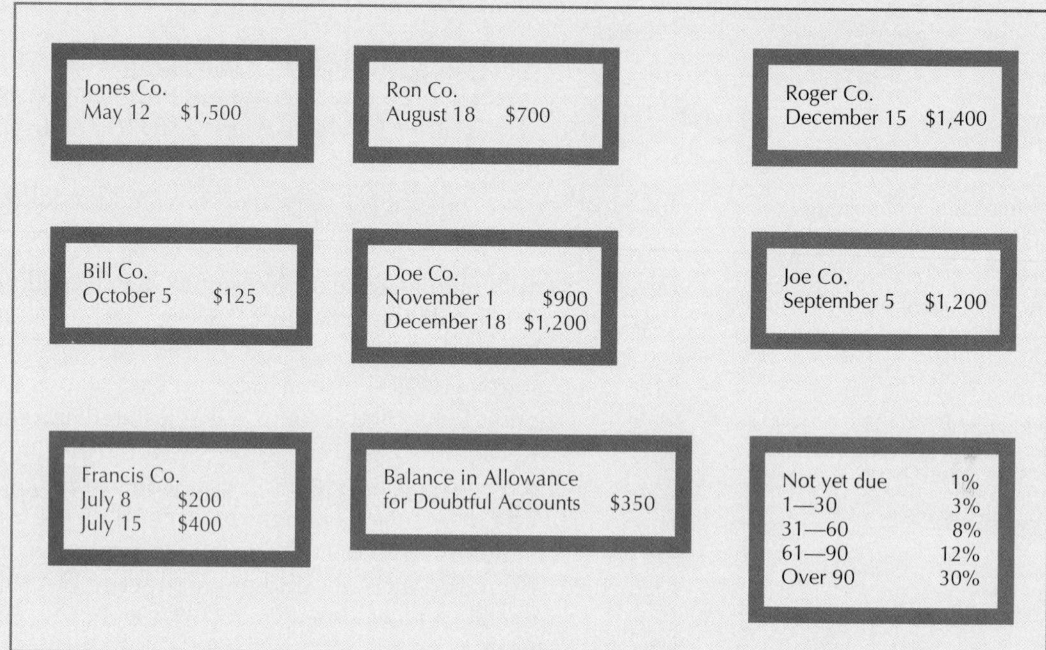

Jones Co.
May 12 $1,500
Ron Co.
August 18 $700
Roger Co.
December 15 $1,400
Bill Co.
October 5 $125
Doe Co.
November 1 $900
December 18 $1,200
Joe Co.
September 5 $1,200
Francis Co.
July 8 $200
July 15 $400
Balance in Allowance
for Doubtful Accounts $350
Not yet due 1%
1—30 3%
31—60 8%
61—90 12%
Over 90 30%

14R-2.

TO: *Al Jones* *September 30, 2001*

FROM: *Peter Flynn, President*

RE: *Bad Debts*

At a party last night, a friend of mine told me that we should not be using the direct write-off method. He told me that it doesn't fulfill the matching principle of accounting. Give me your arguments to support or reject this information.

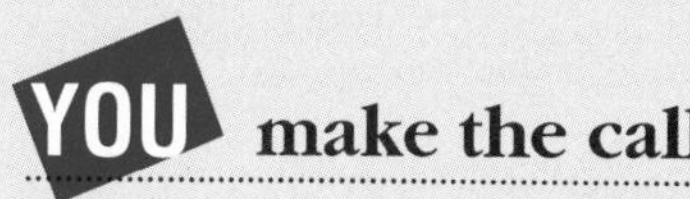

Critical Thinking/Ethical Case

14R-3.

Pete Sazich, the accountant for Moore Company, feels that all bad debts will be eliminated if credit transactions are done by credit card. He also feels that the cost of credit card charges should be added on to the price of the goods. Pete feels that in the future the allowance method will be totally eliminated. You make the call. Write a letter stating your opinion regarding this matter to Pete's boss.

ACCOUNTING RECALL

A CUMULATIVE APPROACH

THIS EXAMINATION REVIEWS CHAPTERS 1 THROUGH 14.

Your *Study Guide with Working Papers* has forms to complete this exam, as well as worked-out solutions. The page reference next to each question identifies the page to turn back to if you answer the question incorrectly.

PART I Vocabulary Review

Match each term on the left side with the appropriate definition or phrase in the right-hand column.

Page Ref.		
(582)	1. Aging of accounts receivable	A. In alphabetical order
(586)	2. Bad debts recovered	B. Balance in allowance account will have to be adjusted
(498)	3. Ending merchandise inventory	C. Operating expense
(577)	4. Allowance for doubtful accounts	D. Does not use allowance for doubtful accounts
(536)	5. Capital asset	E. Classifying of account balances by age
(353)	6. Subsidiary ledgers	F. Land
(578)	7. Net realizable value	G. Contra-asset account
(585)	8. Direct write-off method	H. Other revenue
(582)	9. Balance sheet approach	I. Subtracted from cost of goods sold
(577)	10. Bad debt expense	J. Accounts receivable less allowance for doubtful accounts

PART II True or False (Accounting Theory)

(581) 11. In the income statement approach, any existing balance in Allowance for Doubtful Accounts is ignored.

(580) 12. The income statement approach is based on aging of accounts receivable.

(585) 13. Allowance for Doubtful Accounts is used in the direct write-off method.

(577) 14. Allowance for Doubtful Accounts is listed on the income statement.

(577) 15. A debit to the allowance account will increase it.

CONTINUING PROBLEM

At the end of the fiscal year, the Eldorado Computer Centre has a $21,620 balance in Accounts Receivable. Here is a current schedule of Accounts Receivable:

Eldorado Computer Centre
Schedule of Accounts Receivable
September 30, 2002

Taylor Golf	$ 6,270
Vita Needle	10,610
Accu Pac	1,450
Fortune Consulting	3,290
Total	$21,620

Assignment

(See page 14-18 in your *Study Guide with Working Papers.*)

Although Accu Pac's account is not 90 days past due, Freedman has determined that it is necessary to provide for one half of that balance because the business has closed. Of the remaining balances, 5 percent may become bad debts at some future point.

Calculate the necessary allowance at the end of the company's fiscal year; then make the necessary journal entry to record it. Please use a new account, #1022—Allowance for Doubtful Accounts.

State what changes would have been made to the annual financial statements that would have been prepared based on the information given in the Chapter 12 Continuing Problem if the entries covering bad debts transactions had been made at that time.

Suppose that later in the year (assume November 30, 2002) it was obvious that the entire Accu Pac account was uncollectible and must be completely written off. Show the journal entry you would make to record this event. What effect would this have on the net income for the fiscal year ending September 30, 2003?

Accounting for Merchandise Inventory

15

The Big Picture

◆

With plans to handle all business entries on computer, the Eldorado Computer Centre is in the process of evaluating several accounting software packages. Before implementing a new accounting method, Tony Freedman wants to take a closer look at how he evaluates his merchandise inventory.

For the first year of the business, Freedman used an inventory method that created an adjustment at the end of the accounting period to bring his books up to date. Using that method did not give him an accurate picture of what he actually had in stock as items were sold. To remedy the situation he decided to track his inventory using the perpetual system, which updates the inventory account as items are sold. He realizes that this new method will not track stolen or damaged items that cannot be sold—so periodically he will need to do a physical count.

In this chapter you will also learn that there are different methods used to track the value of the inventory. Each method will give you a different dollar value for the cost of inventory sold and the amount of inventory still on hand. You must decide which method is best for your type of business. The Eldorado Computer Centre has previously used the First-In, First-Out method to track its inventory. This method assumes that the merchandise first bought by the computer centre is sold first. Freedman uses this method because it reflects his type of business. In the constantly changing computer business, merchandise becomes outdated quickly; therefore it is necessary to sell the oldest merchandise first, before it cannot be sold at all.

Chapter Objectives

- Understanding and journalizing transactions using the perpetual inventory system, and explaining the difference between the perpetual and periodic inventory systems (pp. 602–606)
- Maintaining a subsidiary ledger for inventory (pp. 607–609)
- Understanding periodic methods of determining the value of the ending inventory (pp. 611–616)
- Estimating ending inventory using the retail method and the gross profit method, and understanding how the ending inventory amount affects financial reports (pp. 618–620)

Have you ever thought of the perfect present for someone at Christmas time only to find that everyone else in the world had the same idea, and the stores were out of stock? In recent years such gifts have included Lion King, Barney, Power Rangers, home computers, video games, and so on. Having the right quantities of inventory is crucial to a retail business. It's bad to run out of stock and miss out on sales revenue, especially at Christmas, but it's also harmful to have too much of an item. A store must consider the cost of carrying inventory, and it must also worry about product obsolescence or the possibility that a fad will run its course before all the products are sold. A good example would be your local computer store. Models change so quickly that an inventory of old models could mean losing sales to competitors.

In Chapter 12 we discussed the periodic inventory system. A major weakness of the periodic system is that inventory is checked and counted only at the end of the accounting period, and managers do not know the actual amount of inventory on hand or the actual cost of goods sold until the end of the accounting period. In businesses with large inventories, managers need to have *current* information about how much of their capital is tied up in inventory and they need to have *current* information about the profitability of their sales of merchandise. The *perpetual* system of accounting for merchandise inventory will provide this information on a transaction-by-transaction basis. Managers will know the balance of inventory and the profitability of sales as soon as each sale is completed. The perpetual system requires extra time and effort in order to gain these benefits but, fortunately, computers can handle much of the detail. In this chapter we will look at how the perpetual inventory system can be used in a merchandising business. We will also compare the perpetual system with the periodic system.

In the last part of the chapter we will discuss how to assign costs to inventory using the *periodic inventory system*—since many businesses with small inventories still use this system.

LEARNING UNIT 15-1

Perpetual Inventory System

In the **perpetual inventory system** we have two key accounts: Merchandise Inventory and Cost of Goods Sold.

The Merchandise Inventory account is an asset account which will reveal the current balance of inventory at all times (perpetually). This is the same account as was used in the previous discussion of the periodic inventory system, but in the periodic system the balance of the Merchandise Inventory account was correct *only* at the end of each accounting period. In the perpetual system, entries will be recorded in the Merchandise Inventory account each time the store purchases new merchandise and each time the store sells merchandise to a customer.

The other key account is the Cost of Goods Sold account. As merchandise is sold to customers, an entry will be recorded that will remove the cost of the merchandise from the Merchandise Inventory account and transfer that cost to the Cost of Goods Sold account. Thus, the Merchandise Inventory account will show the correct cost for the inventory on hand, and the Cost of Goods Sold account will show the cumulative total cost of all merchandise that has been sold to customers during the accounting period.

With the perpetual inventory system, the key accounts, Merchandise Inventory and Cost of Goods Sold, will always provide current information to managers about their investment in inventory and the cost of the merchandise sold to customers.

Accounts Affected	Category	↑ ↓	Rules
Merchandise Inventory	Asset	↓	Cr.
Cost of Goods Sold	Expense	↑	Dr.

You have been hired to work for a software retail business called *Painless Bytes.* A best seller for *Painless Bytes* is an accounting software package called *A-I-B* (Always In Balance). Let's record some transactions relating to buying and selling A-I-B software. Since most businesses buy their merchandise inventory on account, we will use Accounts Payable in the transactions.

2001
June 2 Purchased 10 packages of A-I-B software at a cost of $25 per package for a total of $250.

				Debit	Credit
June	2	Merchandise Inventory		250 00	
		Accounts Payable			250 00
		To record the purchase of inventory			

Note that the asset account, Merchandise Inventory, has been increased by the cost of the new merchandise we have purchased. Now let's look at a sales transaction.

2001
June 3 Sold three software packages for cash to a customer at $50 each for a total of $150.

				Debit	Credit
June	3	Cash		150 00	
		Sales Revenue			150 00
		To record sale of 3 packages of A-I-B			
June	3	Cost of Goods Sold		75 00	
		Merchandise Inventory			75 00
		To record the cost of goods sold			

Note that in the perpetual inventory system we record both the retail value of the sale (3 units at $50) in the Sales Revenue account and the cost of the sale (3 units at $25) in the Cost of Goods Sold account with two related transactions. But what if the customer returns one of the packages? Assuming that the returned package is still in new condition, here is what we would record:

2001
June 5 Allowed the customer to return one package for a cash refund, $50.

June	5	Sales Returns and Allowances	50 00	
		Cash		50 00
		To record the return of one		
		package A-I-B		

June	5	Merchandise Inventory	25 00	
		Cost of Goods Sold		25 00
		To record return of one package		
		A-I-B at cost		

In this transaction we must record the reduction in revenue of $50 and we must also record that we now have returned one package of software to our inventory by adding the $25 cost of that unit back to the Merchandise Inventory account.

Once in a while a business may have to return some inventory that came in damaged or for some other reason. Painless Bytes would prepare a debit memo. Let's see how this transaction is handled in a perpetual inventory system.

2001
June 6 Returned one damaged A-I-B software package from the June 2 purchase

June	6	Accounts Payable	25 00	
		Merchandise Inventory		25 00
		To record return of damaged A-I-B		
		package to vendor		

This transaction reduced what we owe our vendor by $25, the cost of the package, and we reduced the asset account—Merchandise Inventory—because we returned the item to the vendor. ***Note:*** We do not use a Purchases Returns and Allowances account when we are recording in a perpetual inventory system. The asset account Merchandise Inventory is directly reduced by the amount we returned to our vendor.

Now let's look at how these transactions relate to the accounts and to the financial statements. In the T accounts that follow, you can see that the Merchandise Inventory account shows the correct balance for the seven software packages remaining in inventory, and that the Cost of Goods Sold account shows

GENERAL LEDGER ACCOUNTS

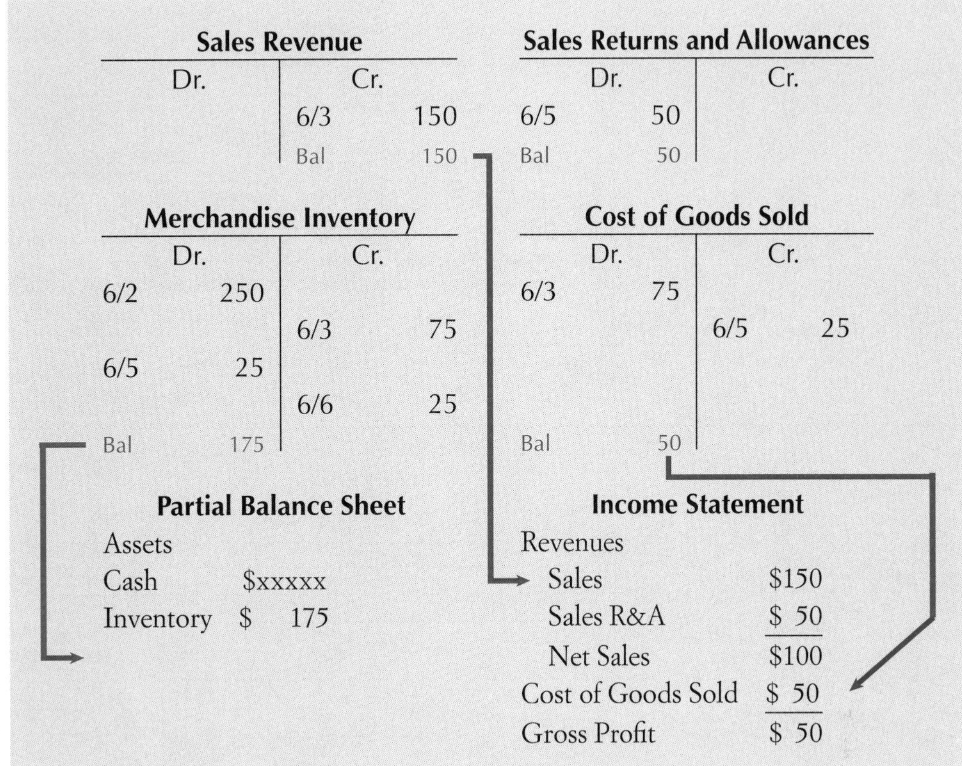

the correct amount for the cost of the two software packages actually sold. Asset accounts such as Merchandise Inventory are shown on the balance sheet, and the Sales and Cost of Goods Sold accounts appear on the income statement. Remember that we calculate gross profit when we subtract Cost of Goods Sold from Sales. In fact, we know the gross profit on each sale just as soon as the sale is completed.

COMPARISON OF THE PERPETUAL AND PERIODIC INVENTORY SYSTEMS

In our discussion of the perpetual inventory system, we noted that the primary benefit from this system is that the value of merchandise inventory is known after every purchase and sale. Also, the cost of goods sold is known after every sale. The Merchandise Inventory account becomes an active account. Cost of Goods Sold is now an account in the general ledger rather than just a item on the income statement. The *periodic inventory system* does not give accurate or up-to-date information about merchandise inventory or cost of goods sold until after an ending inventory is taken.

The taking of a physical inventory at least once a year is not eliminated by a business that uses the perpetual inventory system. An inventory must be taken at least once a year to detect any inventory recording errors, shoplifting, or damage to the merchandise inventory.

The comparison of the recording of transactions in the two systems is revealed in the chart at the top of the next page. The chart shows that, in a perpetual inventory system, the Purchases, Purchases Returns and Allowances, and Freight-In accounts *do not* exist. Inventory and Cost of Goods Sold are updated immediately.

Comparison of Perpetual and Periodic Systems

Transaction	Perpetual System	Dr.	Cr.	Periodic System	Dr.	Cr.
(A) Sold merchandise that cost $8,000 on account for $20,000.	Acc. Receiv.	20,000.00		Acc. Receiv.	20,000.00	
	Sales		20,000.00	Sales		20,000.00
	Cost of Goods Sold	8,000.00				
	Merch. Inventory		8,000.00			
(B) Purchased $900 worth of merchandise on account.	Merch. Inventory	900.00		Purchases	900.00	
	Acc. Payable		900.00	Acc. Payable		900.00
(C) Paid $50 freight charges.	Merch. Inventory	50.00		Freight-In	50.00	
	Cash		50.00	Cash		50.00
(D) Customer returned $200 worth of merchandise. Cost of this merchandise was $100.	Sales Ret. & Allow.	200.00		Sales Ret. & Allow.	200.00	
	Accounts Receiv.		200.00	Accts. Receiv.		200.00
	Merchandise Inv.	100.00				
	Cost of Goods Sold		100.00			
(E) Returned $400 worth of merchandise previously bought on account because of defects.	Acc. Payable	400.00		Acc. Payable	400.00	
	Merch. Inv.		400.00	Pur. Ret. and Allow		400.00

LEARNING UNIT 15-1 REVIEW

AT THIS POINT you should be able to:

- Explain the perpetual inventory system. (p. 602)
- Journalize transactions for a perpetual inventory system. (pp. 603–604)
- Explain the difference between the perpetual and periodic inventory systems. (pp. 605–606)

SELF-REVIEW QUIZ 15-1

(The blank forms you need are on page 15-2 of the *Study Guide with Working Papers.*)

Journalize the following transactions for a firm that uses a perpetual inventory system:

a. Bought $200 worth of merchandise on account.
b. Sold on account $100 worth of merchandise that cost $50.
c. Allowed a customer to return for cash $30 worth of inventory. Cost was $15.
d. Permission was obtained from vendor to return $30 worth of inventory.

Solutions to Self-Review Quiz 15-1

a.

Account	Debit	Credit
Merchandise Inventory	200 00	
Accounts Payable		200 00

b.

Account	Debit	Credit
Accounts Receivable	100 00	
Sales		100 00

Account	Debit	Credit
Cost of Goods Sold	50 00	
Merchandise Inventory		50 00

c.

Account	Debit	Credit
Sales Returns and Allowances	30 00	
Cash		30 00

Account	Debit	Credit
Merchandise Inventory	15 00	
Cost of Goods Sold		15 00

d.

Account	Debit	Credit
Accounts Payable	30 00	
Merchandise Inventory		30 00

LEARNING UNIT 15-2

Using a Subsidiary Ledger for Inventory

Suppose that the business Painless Bytes sells many different kinds of software packages. How can Painless Bytes keep track of the costs and balances of a variety of inventory items? How do stores such as Wal-Mart keep track of the thousands of items which they keep in inventory? The answer is found in the use of a subsidiary ledger for inventory and the use of computers to maintain the subsidiary ledger.

Recall from Chapters 9 and 10 that, when we had a large number of accounts receivable or accounts payable accounts, we used subsidiary ledgers to maintain the details for each customer or vendor. This same accounting procedure can be used to keep track of inventory. The Merchandise Inventory account becomes a controlling account keeping track of the total balance of inventory, while the details are kept in separate inventory records in a subsidiary ledger for inventory. Let's first show the existing Merchandise Inventory account with a subsidiary ledger and with the transactions from Learning Unit 15-1. On the left is the inventory account in T form and on the right is an inventory record form for the A-I-B product.

GENERAL LEDGER ACCOUNT

Merchandise Inventory			
Dr.		Cr.	
6/2	250		
		6/3	75
6/5	25		
		6/6	25
Bal	175		

SUBSIDIARY LEDGER RECORDS

A-I-B Software

Date	Purchased	Sold	Balance
6/2	10 @ $25		$250
6/3		3 @ $25	$175
6/5		(1) @ $25	$200
6/6	(1) @ $25		$175

Notice that the inventory record form on the right contains the detail about the quantity and per unit cost for the transactions posted to the general ledger account on the left. Notice, too, that the return of 6/5 is recorded in the inventory record as a negative sale and that the ending balances agree. The debit memo transaction of 6/6 is entered as a negative purchase and again the ending balances agree. Try using your calculator to see if you can also calculate the running balance shown in the inventory record.

In this next transaction, Painless Bytes adds R&C (Rows and Columns), a spreadsheet software package, to the line of software that they sell.

June 6 Purchased 7 packages of R&C software on account at a cost of $225 per package and a total of $1,575.

			Debit	Credit
June	6	Merchandise Inventory	1 575 00	
		Accounts Payable		1 575 00
		To record the purchase of inventory		

Note that the Merchandise Inventory account has again been increased by the cost of the new merchandise we have purchased. Since we now have two products in inventory, our inventory ledger will have a new inventory record form for the R&C product. Check out the way our inventory records relate to the Merchandise Inventory account.

GENERAL LEDGER ACCOUNT

Merchandise Inventory			
Dr.		Cr.	
6/2	250		
		6/3	75
6/5	25		
6/6	1,575	6/6	25
Bal	1,750		

SUBSIDIARY LEDGER RECORDS

Product #1: A-I-B Software

Date	Purchased	Sold	Balance
6/2	10 @ $25		$ 250
6/3		3 @ $25	$ 175
6/5		(1) @ $25	$ 200
6/6	(1) @ $25		$ 175

Product #2: R&C Software

Date	Purchased	Sold	Balance
6/6	7 @ $225		$1,575

Does the total of the balances of the two inventory records agree with the Merchandise Inventory account?

Now let's try another sales transaction.

2001
June 9 Sold two A-I-B packages at $50 each and three R&C packages at $295 each for a total of $985

				Debit	Credit
June	9	Cash		985 00	
		Sales Revenue			985 00
		Sold 2 A-I-B and 3 R&C			
June	9	Cost of Goods Sold		725 00	
		Merchandise Inventory			725 00
		To record the cost of goods sold			

Again, we record both the total sales price of the transaction and the cost of the merchandise sold. Do you know how we arrived at the cost of goods sold figure of $725? A quick look at the inventory record forms will show us how we know the cost of goods sold.

GENERAL LEDGER ACCOUNT

Merchandise Inventory

Dr.		Cr.	
6/2	250		
		6/3	75
6/4	25		
6/6	1,575	6/6	25
		6/9	725
Bal	1,025		

SUBSIDIARY LEDGER RECORDS

Product #1: A-I-B Software

Date	Purchased	Sold	Balance
6/2	10 @ $25		$ 250
6/3		3 @ $ 25	$ 175
6/4		(1) @ $195	$ 200
6/5	(1) @ $25		$ 175
6/9		2 @ $ 25	$ 125

Product #2: R&C Software

Date	Purchased	Sold	Balance
6/6	7 @ $225		$1,575
6/9		3 @ $225	$ 900

We obtained the cost of goods sold total when we posted the quantities sold to each of the inventory records. Two units of A-I-B at $25 each plus three units of R&C at $225 each equals a total cost of $725. Notice that the ending balances of the two products will total to the same amount as the balance shown in the Merchandise Inventory account.

In summary, a business with a variety of products in inventory will use an inventory subsidiary ledger with an individual record for each different product. These records will keep the detail about the quantity and cost of inventory on hand and will allow us to calculate the cost of goods sold on each sale.

Computerized accounting systems can handle a perpetual inventory system with ease. You have no doubt seen such systems in operation when the clerk at your local store used a laser scanner or a bar code to enter your purchases into the cash register. The transaction put into the cash register will record the sale and

Inventory Control									
Item VX113						Maximum 22			
Description Digital Clock						Reorder Level 12			
Location Storeroom 1						Reorder Quantity 10			
	Received			Sold			Balance		
Date	Units	Cost per Unit	Total	Units	Cost per Unit	Total	Units	Cost per Unit	Total
2001 Jan. 1	Balance		FWD				14	50	$ 700
12				2	50	100	12	50	600
19	10	60	600				12	50	
							10	60	1,200
25				8	50	400	4	50	
							10	60	800

FIGURE 15-1
An Inventory Record

update the cost of goods sold and inventory. Computerized systems keep track of inventory by many different methods. When figuring the value of the inventory, they could use average cost; first-in, first-out (FIFO); or last-in, first-out (LIFO). The example in Figure 15-1 uses the first-in, first-out (FIFO) method in determining the cost of the merchandise for each sale.

LEARNING UNIT 15-2 REVIEW

AT THIS POINT you should be able to:

- Understand how a subsidiary ledger for inventory works with a controlling account for inventory. (pp. 607–608)
- Journalize and post transactions that affect the general ledger Merchandise Inventory account as well as the individual inventory records in the Merchandise Inventory subsidiary ledger. (pp. 608–609)

SELF-REVIEW QUIZ 15-2

(The forms you need are on pages 15-2 and 15-3 of the *Study Guide with Working Papers.*)

Journalize and post the following transactions for a firm that uses a subsidiary ledger for Merchandise Inventory. Post only to the accounts that you have.

a. Bought 3 X-Products at $3 each on account.
b. Sold one of the X-Products we purchased above for cash, $6.
c. Bought 4 more X-Products at $3 and 5 Z-Products at $10 on account.
d. Sold for cash 2 more X-Products at $6 each and 3 Z-Products at $20 each.

Solutions to Self-Review Quiz 15-2

a.

Merchandise Inventory	114/✔	9 00	
Accounts Payable			9 00

b.

	PR	Dr.	Cr.
Cash		6 00	
Sales			6 00
Cost of Goods Sold		3 00	
Merchandise Inventory	114 / ✔		3 00

c.

	PR	Dr.	Cr.
Merchandise Inventory	114 / ✔	62 00	
Accounts Payable			62 00

d.

	PR	Dr.	Cr.
Cash		72 00	
Sales			72 00
Cost of Goods Sold		36 00	
Merchandise Inventory	114 / ✔		36 00

GENERAL LEDGER ACCOUNT

Merchandise Inventory

	Dr.		Cr.
a.	9	b.	3
c.	62	d.	36
Bal.	32		

SUBSIDIARY LEDGER RECORDS

Product #1: X Product

Date	Purchased	Sold	Balance
a.	3 @ $3		9
b.		1 @ $3	6
c.	4 @ $3		18
d.		2 @ $3	12

Product #2: Z Product

Date	Purchased	Sold	Balance
c.	5 @ $10		50
d.		3 @ $10	20

LEARNING UNIT 15-3

Methods of Determining the Value of the Ending Inventory When Using the Periodic Inventory System

For a small business or any business using the **periodic inventory system,** the method used to assign costs to ending inventory will have a direct effect on the company's cost of goods sold and gross profit. Look at the table on the next page, and note that the ending inventory does in fact have an effect on the gross profit.

If all inventory brought into a store had the same cost, it would be simple to calculate the ending inventory, and we would not have to have this discussion. Unfortunately, things are not that easy; often the very same products are purchased

	Situation A		Situation B		Situation C		Situation D	
Net Sales		$50,000		$50,000		$50,000		$50,000
Beginning Inventory	$ 4,000		$ 4,000		$ 4,000		$ 4,000	
Net Purchases	20,000		20,000		20,000		20,000	
Cost of Goods Available for Sale	24,000		24,000		24,000		24,000	
Ending Inventory	5,000		6,000		7,000		8,000	
Cost of Goods Sold		19,000		18,000		17,000		16,000
Gross Profit		$31,000		$32,000		$33,000		$34,000

and brought into the store at different costs during the same accounting period. Over the years, four generally accepted methods have been developed to assign a cost to ending inventory. The reason these methods are needed is that often inventory is brought in at different times. The result is that the inventory is made up of many past purchases at *different* prices. Think of the inventory methods as a way of tracing costs. These methods are: (1) specific invoice; (2) first-in, first-out; (3) last-in, first-out; and (4) weighted average. Each is based on an assumed flow of costs, not on the actual physical movement of goods sold in a store.

We will now look at how the four inventory cost assumptions are applied within the periodic inventory system. The following situation occurred at Jones Hardware. Jones Hardware sells rakes. The job before us is to come up with the value of the ending inventory and cost of goods sold using the four methods we have listed. The following table provides us with all the information needed to accomplish our task.

Goods Available for Sale

		Units	Cost	Total
January 1	Beginning Inventory	10	@ $10 =	$100
March 15	Purchases	9	@ 12 =	108
August 18	Purchases	20	@ 13 =	260
November 15	Purchases	5	@ 15 =	75
		44		$543

Actual inventory on December 31 revealed that 12 rakes remained in stock.

SPECIFIC INVOICE METHOD

In the **specific invoice method,** the cost of ending inventory is assigned by identifying each item in that inventory by a specific purchase price and invoice number, and maybe even by serial number.

For our example of this method, let's assume that Jones Hardware knew that six of the rakes not sold were from the March 15 invoice and the other six were from the August 18 purchase. Thus $150 was assigned as the actual cost of ending inventory. If the total cost of goods available for sale is $543, and we subtract the actual cost of ending inventory ($150), this method provides a figure of $393 for cost of goods sold.

Specific Invoice Method

	Goods Available for Sale					Calculating Cost of Ending Inventory			
	Units		Cost		Total	Units		Cost	Total
January 1 Beginning Inventory	10	@	$10	=	$100				
March 15 Purchased	9	@	12	=	108	6	@	$12	$ 72
August 18 Purchased	20	@	13	=	260	6	@	13	78
November 15 Purchased	5	@	15	=	75				
	44				$543	12			$150

Cost of Goods Available for Sale	$543
Less: Cost of Ending Inventory	150
= Cost of Goods Sold	$393

Let's look at the pros and cons of this method.

Specific Invoice Method: A Reference Guide

Pros

1. Simple to use if company has small amount of high-cost goods—for example, autos, jewels, boats, antiques, etc.
2. Flow of goods and flow of cost are the same.
3. Costs are matched with the sales they helped to produce.

Cons

1. Difficult to use for goods with large unit volume and small unit prices—for example, nails at a hardware store, packages of toothpaste at a drugstore
2. Difficult to use for decision-making purposes—ordinarily an impractical approach since companies usually deal with high-cost unique items

First-In, First-Out Method (FIFO)

In the **FIFO method,** we assume that the oldest goods are sold first. Therefore, the items in the ending inventory will be valued at the costs shown on the most recent invoices.

First-In, First-Out Method

	Goods Available for Sale					Calculating Cost of Ending Inventory				
	Units		Cost		Total	Units		Cost		Total
January 1 Beginning Inventory	10	@	$10	=	$100					
March 15 Purchased	9	@	12	=	108					
August 18 Purchased	20	@	13	=	260	7	@	$13	=	$ 91
November 15 Purchased	5	@	15	=	75	5	@	15	=	75
	44				$543	12				$166

Cost of Goods Available for Sale	$543
Less: Cost of Ending Inventory	166
= Cost of Goods Sold	$377

In our Jones Hardware example, the ending inventory of 12 rakes on hand is assigned a cost from the last two purchase invoices of rakes (purchases made on November 15 and part of the purchases made on August 18), totalling $166. If you are having difficulty with this, think of the inventory as being taken from the bottom layer first, then the next one up. If our ending inventory is valued at $166, then our cost of goods sold must be $377.

The following are the pros and cons of this method.

FIFO METHOD: A REFERENCE GUIDE

Pros

1. The cost flow tends to follow the physical flow (most businesses try to sell the old goods first—for example, perishables such as fruit or vegetables).
2. The figure for ending inventory is made up of current costs on the balance sheet (since inventory left over is assumed to be from goods last brought into the store).

Cons

1. During periods of inflation this method will produce higher income on the income statement—thus more taxes to be paid. (We will discuss this later in the chapter.)
2. Recent costs are not matched with recent sales, since we assume *old* goods are sold first.

LAST-IN, FIRST-OUT METHOD (LIFO)

Under the **LIFO method**, it is assumed that the goods *most recently acquired* are sold first. Therefore, the items in the ending inventory will be valued at the invoice costs shown from the top of the list down.

For the Jones Hardware this assumption means that the 12 rakes not sold were assigned costs from the 10 listed in beginning inventory and 2 from the March 15 invoice. The ending inventory totals $124 and the cost of goods sold would be $419.

LAST-IN, FIRST-OUT METHOD

	Goods Available for Sale			Calculating Cost of Ending Inventory		
	Units	Cost	Total	Units	Cost	Total
January 1 Beginning Inventory	10	@ $10 =	$100	10	@ $10 =	$100
March 15 Purchased	9	@ 12 =	108	2	@ 12 =	24
August 18 Purchased	20	@ 13 =	260			
November 15 Purchased	5	@ 15 =	75			
	44		$543	12		$124

Cost of Goods Available for Sale	$543
Less: Cost of Ending Inventory	124
= Cost of Goods Sold	$419

These are the pros and cons of this method.

LIFO METHOD: A REFERENCE GUIDE

Pros	Cons
1. Cost of goods sold is recorded at or near current costs, since costs of *latest* goods acquired are used.	**1.** Ending inventory is valued at very old prices.
2. Matches current costs with current selling prices.	**2.** Doesn't match physical flow of goods (but can still be used to calculate flow of costs).
3. During periods of inflation this method produces the lowest net income. (The lower cost of ending inventory means a higher cost of goods sold, with a higher cost of goods sold, gross profit and ultimately net income are smaller.)	**3.** It is illegal in Canada to use this method for tax purposes. Therefore, a second valuation must be made for tax purposes.

WEIGHTED-AVERAGE METHOD

The **weighted-average method** calculates an average unit cost by dividing the *total cost* of goods available for sale by the *total units* of goods available for sale. In this example, the total cost of goods available for sale was $543 and the total units available for sale was 44. Taking the $543 and dividing that number by the 44 total units for the period would give a $12.34 weighted average per unit.

In this illustration, Jones Hardware assumes that the 12 units left on hand are *average* units and therefore assigns an *average* cost figure of $12.34 to each of the 12 rakes left in inventory. Thus we have a fair approximation of the cost of the ending inventory at $148.08 and of the amount of cost of goods sold, $394.92.

WEIGHTED-AVERAGE METHOD

	Goods Available for Sale				
	Units		**Cost**		**Total**
January 1 Beginning Inventory	10	@	$10	=	$100
March 15 Purchased	9	@	12	=	108
August 18 Purchased	20	@	13	=	260
November 15 Purchased	5	@	15	=	75
	44				$543

$\frac{\$543}{44}$ = $12.34 weighted-average cost per unit

12 rakes × $12.34 = $148.08

Cost of Goods Available for Sale	$543.00
Less: Cost of Ending Inventory	148.08
= Cost of Goods Sold	$394.92

The pros and cons of this method are as follows:

WEIGHTED-AVERAGE METHOD: A REFERENCE GUIDE

Pros	Cons
1. Weighted-average takes into account the number of units purchased at each amount, not a simple average of the various unit costs. It is good for products sold in large volume, such as grains and fuels.	1. Current prices have no more significance than prices of goods bought months earlier.
2. Accountant assigns an equal unit cost to each unit of inventory; thus, when the income statement is prepared, net income will not fluctuate as much as with other methods.	2. Compared with other methods, the most recent costs are *not* matched with current sales. This is important in financial reporting so as to provide an accurate picture of the company.
	3. Cost of ending inventory is not as up to date as it could be using another method.

Remember that all four methods are acceptable accounting procedures. Management needs to select the method best suited to their business and be consistent in their application of that method.

WHEN CAN AN INVENTORY METHOD BE CHANGED

In accounting there is a principle of **consistency,** which means that, once a business selects a particular accounting method, it should follow it consistently from one year to the next without switching to another method. In the previous part of this chapter, we saw four methods of inventory valuation causing four different results for a business in terms of cost of goods sold and, ultimately, net income. Therefore, if a company kept switching from LIFO to FIFO each year, significant changes would result in the profit it reported. The financial reports would become undependable. If the company maintains the same method, readers of the financial reports can make meaningful comparisons of the cost of ending inventory, cost of goods sold, etc., from year to year.

The principle of consistency doesn't mean that a company can *never* change from one method of inventory valuation to another. If a change is decided upon, however, the company should fully disclose, in a footnote on the financial report, the change, the effects of the change on profit and inventory valuation, and the justification for the change. This is called the **full disclosure principle** in accounting.

ITEMS THAT SHOULD BE INCLUDED IN THE COST OF INVENTORY

Goods in Transit

On the date inventory is taken, goods in transit should be added to inventory if the ownership of the inventory has been transferred to the buyer. For example, if the merchandise was purchased *F.O.B. shipping point,* the buyer becomes the owner of the merchandise when the merchandise is placed on the carrier at the shipping point. On the other hand, if the buyer purchases the merchandise *F.O.B. destination,* the seller has ownership of the merchandise until the merchandise reaches the destination, and it should not be included in the cost of the buyer's inventory.

Merchandise on Consignment

Consignment means that a business (the **consignor**) is selling its merchandise through an agent (the **consignee**) who doesn't own the merchandise but has possession of it. Consigned merchandise belongs to the consignor and should not be included in the consignee's inventory cost.

Damaged or Obsolete Merchandise

If the merchandise is not saleable, it should *not* be added to the cost of the inventory. For merchandise that is saleable but at a lower cost, the value of that inventory should be estimated at a conservative figure and added to the cost of the inventory.

LEARNING UNIT 15-3 REVIEW

AT THIS POINT you should be able to:

- Calculate cost of ending inventory and cost of goods sold by specific invoice: first-in, first-out; last-in, first-out; and weighted-average methods. (pp. 612–615)
- Explain the pros and cons of each method used to calculate cost of ending inventory and cost of goods sold. (pp. 613–616)
- Explain the principles of consistency and full disclosure. (p. 616)
- Explain how merchandise in transit, merchandise on consignment, and damaged or obsolete merchandise are counted in calculating inventory. (pp. 616–617)

SELF-REVIEW QUIZ 15-3

(The forms you need are on page 15-4 of the *Study Guide with Working Papers.*)

1. From the information given below, calculate the cost of inventory as well as the cost of goods sold, using the (a) specific invoice, (b) weighted-average, (c) first-in, first-out, and (d) last-in, first-out methods.

	Goods Available for Sale			Additional Fact:
	Units	Cost	Total	Inventory Not Sold
January 1 Beginning Inventory	40	@ $ 8 =	$ 320	
April 1 Purchased	20	@ 9 =	180	40 from January 1
May 1 Purchased	20	@ 10 =	200	4 from May 1
October 1 Purchased	20	@ 12 =	240	4 from October 1
December 1 Purchased	20	@ 13 =	260	
	120		$1,200	

2. Respond true or false to the following:
   - **a.** It is possible for a company to change from LIFO to FIFO if the company follows specific guidelines.
   - **b.** Goods in transit (shipped F.O.B. shipping point) will not be included as part of the inventory for the purchaser.
   - **c.** Damaged goods are always added to the cost of inventory.

Solution to Self-Review Quiz 15-3

1. a. Total cost of goods available for sale — $1,200

Less ending inventory based on specific invoices:		
40 units from Jan. 1 purchased at $8	$320	
4 units from May 1 purchased at $10	40	
4 units from Oct. 1 purchased at $12	48	
48 units in ending inventory		408
Cost of goods sold		$ 792

b. $1,200 ÷ 120 units = $10 weighted-average cost per unit

Total cost of goods available for sale		$1,200
Less ending inventory priced on weighted-average basis: 48 units at $10.00		480
Cost of goods sold		$ 720

c.

Total cost of goods available for sale		$1,200
Less ending inventory priced on FIFO:		
20 units from Dec. 1 at $13	$260	
20 units from Oct. 1 at $12	240	
8 units from May 1 at $10	80	
48 units in ending inventory		580
Cost of goods sold		$ 620

d.

Total cost of goods available for sale		$1,200
Less ending inventory priced on LIFO:		
40 units from Jan. 1 at $8	$320	
8 units from April 1 purchased at $9	72	
48 units in ending inventory		392
Cost of goods sold		$ 808

2. a. True **b.** False **c.** False

LEARNING UNIT 15-4
Estimating Ending Inventory

The actual taking of a physical inventory is time-consuming and expensive. Because of the time and expense involved, most businesses take a physical inventory only once a year. For the business using the periodic inventory system, it may become necessary to have an inventory cost figure more often. This is especially true when a business makes interim financial reports. This business may find that estimating the inventory rather than taking a physical inventory is accurate enough. Another reason to estimate the ending inventory is in case of a fire when the inventory may be destroyed. The business would need an inventory cost figure when it submits a claim of loss to the insurance company.

Two common and recognized ways to estimate ending inventory are the *retail method* and the *gross profit method.*

LOWER-OF-COST-OR-MARKET PRINCIPLE

Market doesn't mean what goods will sell for. It stands for *replacement cost.*

So far, we have estimated the value of ending inventory by looking at the cost that was paid to bring it into the store. Over the years a traditional conservative principle in accounting has been to price inventory at the **lower of cost or market**. The objective is to place all items on the balance sheet at a conservative figure. *Market* means what it *would have* cost to purchase or replace the goods on that inventory date. By choosing the lower of the two figures, we place a conservative figure for inventory on the balance sheet. In the USA, the procedure for determining the lower of cost and market can be quite complex. Here in Canada, the rule is actually fairly simple: use cost (LIFO, FIFO, or whatever) or market—whichever is the lower. Sometimes companies must make a decision as to whether to apply the rule to the whole of inventory, classes of inventory, or each item in inventory. As long as this decision is made carefully and the results applied in the same way from year to year, the financial results are not materially distorted.

RETAIL METHOD

To use the **retail method**, a business must have the following information available:

1. Beginning inventory at cost and at retail (selling price)
2. Cost of net purchases at both cost and at retail
3. The net sales at retail

Let's look at the calculation below to see how French Company estimates ending inventory at cost by the retail method.

French completed the following steps to arrive at ending inventory cost of $3,600.

Step 1: Calculate cost of merchandise available for sale at cost and retail.

Step 2: Calculate the cost ratio (cost of goods available for sale at cost divided by cost of goods available for sale at retail). It cost French Company .60 or 60 cents for each $1 of sales of the merchandise.

Step 3: Deduct net sales from retail value of merchandise available for sale to arrive at an estimated ending inventory at retail.

Step 4: Multiply cost ratio (.60 in this case) times ending inventory at retail to arrive at ending inventory at cost of $3600.

Keep in mind that at year-end French will take a physical inventory.

THE RETAIL INVENTORY METHOD

			Cost	Retail
	Goods Available for Sale:			
	Beginning Inventory		$ 4,100	$ 6,900
	Net Purchases		7,900	13,100
Step 1 ⟶	Cost of Goods Available for Sale		$12,000	$20,000
Step 2 ⟶	Cost Ratio (relationship between cost and retail)	$\frac{\$12,000}{\$20,000} = .60$		
Step 3 ⟶	Net Sales at Retail			14,000
⟶	Inventory at Retail			$ 6,000
Step 4 ⟶	Ending Inventory at Cost, $6,000 × .60		$ 3,600	

GROSS PROFIT METHOD

Another method of estimating ending inventory without taking a physical count is the **gross profit method**. This method develops a relationship among sales, cost of goods sold, and gross profit in estimating the cost of ending inventory.

To use this method, a company would have to keep track of the following:

1. Average gross profit rate
2. Net sales, beginning inventory, net purchases

The steps Moose Company takes to estimate its ending inventory are shown in the accompanying presentation. We assume a normal gross profit rate of 30 percent of net sales. If 30 cents on a dollar is profit, 70 cents on a dollar is cost.

THE GROSS PROFIT METHOD

	Goods Available for Sale:		
	Inventory, January 1, 2001		$10,000
	Net Purchases		4,000
Step 1 →	Cost of Goods Available for Sale		$14,000
	Less: Estimated Cost of Goods Sold:		
	Net Sales at Retail	$6,000	
Step 2 →	Cost percentage (100% − 30%)	.70	
	Estimated Cost of Goods Sold		4,200
Step 3 →	Estimated Inventory, January 31, 2001		$ 9,800

Step 1: Moose determines cost of goods available for sale (beginning inventory plus net purchases).

Step 2: Moose estimates cost of goods sold by multiplying cost percentage (70 percent) times net sales.

Step 3: Moose subtracts cost of goods sold from cost of goods available for sale to arrive at an estimated inventory of $9,800.

This method, besides helping prepare financial reports, can help determine the amount of inventory on hand following a fire or can verify at year's end the accuracy of the physical inventory.

Before concluding this unit, let's look at how an error made in calculating ending inventory will affect financial reports.

HOW INCORRECT CALCULATION OF ENDING INVENTORY AFFECTS FINANCIAL REPORTS

As we have stated before, assigning costs to ending inventory can have an effect on cost of goods sold, gross profit, net income, and current assets, as well as owner's capital. Let's look at the diagram below to see, if a mistake is in fact made, what items on the income statement will be affected and what the mistake's impact will be over time.

	Correct				**Incorrect**			
	2001		**2002**		**2001**		**2002**	
Sales		$200		$300		$200		$300
Cost of Goods Sold:								
Beginning Inventory	$ 30	correct →	$ 70		$ 30	incorrect →	$ 60	
Purchases	95		85		95		85	
Goods Available for Sale	125		155		125		145	
Ending Inventory	−70	55	−100	55	−60	65	−100	45
Gross Profit		$145		$245		$135		$255

SUMMARY:

	Correct	**Incorrect**	**Difference**
Year 2001, Gross Profit	$145	$135	−$10
Year 2002, Gross Profit	245	255	+ 10
Total effect of mistake after two periods			0

Note that, when the incorrect figure of $60 is used for ending inventory in 2001, it causes cost of goods sold to be $65 instead of $55 and profit to be $135 instead of $145. In other words, when ending inventory is understated ($60 instead of $70), cost of goods sold is overstated and profit is understated.

As we look next at 2002, we see that the incorrect ending inventory of 2001 is carried over as the beginning inventory of 2002. The understatement of beginning inventory in 2002 of $60 (instead of $70) causes cost of goods sold to be understated and gross profit to be overstated.

Thus, at the end of 2002, the error will be self-correcting.

To review, look at the table that follows and prove it to yourself by going back over the previous explanation.

Ending inventory works in the same direction as profit. Beginning inventory is inversely related.

If the item is	Overstated	Understated
Beginning Inventory	Profit is Understated	Profit is Overstated
Ending Inventory	Profit is Overstated	Profit is Understated

Keep in mind that, since ending inventory is recorded as a current asset on the balance sheet, any mistake will cause the assets to be under- or overstated. The statement of owner's equity will also be affected, since we have seen that the net income will be over- and understated.

LEARNING UNIT 15-4 REVIEW

AT THIS POINT you should be able to:

- Calculate ending inventory by the retail method. (p. 619)
- Calculate ending inventory by the gross profit method. (pp. 619–620)
- Explain how understating or overstating ending inventory will affect financial reports. (pp. 620–621)

SELF-REVIEW QUIZ 15-4

(The forms you need are on page 15-5 of the *Study Guide with Working Papers.*)

1. Alon Company needs to estimate its month-end inventory. From the following, estimate the cost of ending inventory on September 30 by the retail method.

	Cost	Retail
Beginning Inventory	$ 8,000	$10,000
Net Purchases	40,000	60,000
Net Sales		30,000

(Carry out the cost ratio to nearest hundredth percent.)

2. Respond true or false to the following:
   a. The retail inventory method is an estimate.
   b. The cost ratio in the gross profit method represents only sales, not costs.
   c. The first step in the gross profit method is to determine cost of goods available for sale.
   d. If ending inventory is overstated, net income will be overstated.
   e. If beginning inventory is overstated, net income will be overstated.

Solution to Self-Review Quiz 15-4

	Cost	Retail
1. Beginning Inventory	$ 8,000	$10,000
Net Purchases	40,000	60,000
Cost of Goods Available for Sale	$48,000	70,000
Cost Ratio, $48,000/$70,000 = 68.57%		
Net Sales at Retail		30,000
Inventory at Retail		$40,000
Ending Inventory at Cost, $40,000 × .6857	$27,428	

2. a. True **b.** False **c.** True **d.** True **e.** False.

"Not again!" moaned Sally. "Didn't we just take an inventory of the stockroom last month? My sister works at Wal-Mart, and they only take inventory once a year!"

"Yes, we did. And now we're doing it again," said Fred patiently. "We have a very different business than Wal-Mart—we have to make sure that we get enough cream cheese and milk—but not too much, or it will spoil. And I don't want to run out of Coffee Coolatta™ mix again. That special rush shipping costs extra."

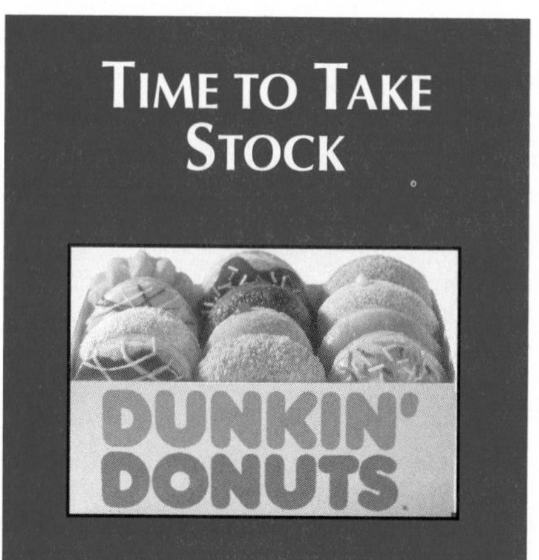

"I'm selling lots of Coolatta, 'specially the hazelnut," said Sally. "It's my favourite, too. We can't run out of it!" With that, she sped to the stockroom and started work on the inventory.

The popularity of the new Coffee Coolatta™ had taken Dunkin' Donuts by surprise. The test marketing in 2000 had been successful, but the roll-out had surpassed all expectations. Shop owners reported that their regular morning coffee and doughnut customers were returning in the afternoon for a Coolatta—and often another doughnut. Fears that the Coolatta would just replace hot coffee sales were unfounded. Instead, Coolatta sales accounted for 30 percent of all coffee sales in just six months. Hot coffee sales were unaffected.

The necessity of managing physical inventory is clear in a business that sells prepared food and drinks. In terms of physical flow, perishable inventory must be FIFO; the first inventory in is the first used, so that nothing is allowed to get stale or spoiled. If a Dunkin' Donuts shop uses the FIFO method for accounting, the cost follows the physical flow. While every Dunkin' Donuts shop owner uses the FIFO method for physical flow, not every shop owner chooses the FIFO method of accounting. Some prefer LIFO for financial accounting, because with this method the cost of goods sold is matched to current selling prices.

Dunkin' Donuts currently uses a periodic inventory system. It is encouraging the use of new computerized cash registers because they will create a perpetual inventory system. But a physical count of inventory will still be needed—because spoilage and shrinkage are always possible.

Discussion Questions

1. Learning Unit 15-4 discusses the retail inventory method. Why does Fred insist on a physical count?
2. The different benefits LIFO and FIFO offer Fred are discussed above. Why might Fred choose a weighted-average method of accounting for inventory costs?
3. The price of coffee is subject to rapid changes, depending on growing conditions in Brazil, Colombia, Kenya, and other parts of the world. What effect might this changeability have on the method of financial accounting a Dunkin' Donuts shop owner chooses?

Chapter Review

Summary of key points

Learning Unit 15-1

1. In the perpetual inventory method, we have two key accounts that are kept up to date at all times. These accounts are Merchandise Inventory and Cost of Goods Sold.
2. Each purchase of merchandise is recorded by a debit to the Merchandise Inventory account.
3. Each sale requires two entries. One entry records the revenue or selling price of the merchandise and the other entry transfers the cost of the items sold from the Merchandise Inventory account to the Cost of Goods Sold account.
4. Sales returns also require two entries, one to record the reduction in revenue in a Sales Returns and Allowances account and the other entry to move the cost of the items returned back to the Merchandise Inventory account from the Cost of Goods Sold account.
5. When the business returns merchandise to the vendor because of damage or for some other reason, the Merchandise Inventory account is credited because we no longer have the merchandise to sell.
6. The comparison of the perpetual inventory system and the periodic inventory system reveals that the Purchases, Purchases Returns and Allowances, and Freight-In accounts do not exist in the perpetual inventory system. The accounts Merchandise Inventory and Cost of Goods Sold become active accounts in the perpetual inventory system.

Learning Unit 15-2

1. If there are many items in inventory, a subsidiary inventory ledger will be used to keep track of the details of quantities and costs for each item in inventory.
2. An inventory record form will be used for each item in the inventory. This form has columns for recording the quantities and costs of units purchased and units sold, and it provides a running balance of inventory on hand.
3. When selling an item, the inventory record form provides the cost information for the debit to Cost of Goods Sold and the credit to Merchandise Inventory.
4. The total cost represented by all of the inventory record forms will equal the balance of the Merchandise Inventory account in the general ledger.

Learning Unit 15-3

1. In assigning a cost to ending inventory, the flow of goods may *not* follow the actual flow of costs.
2. The specific invoice method identifies each item in inventory with a specific invoice in assigning a cost of ending inventory. It matches costs exactly with revenues.
3. FIFO assumes that the old goods are sold first. Since ending inventory is valued at the most recent costs, FIFO provides the most realistic figure for ending merchandise inventory.

4. LIFO assumes that the newest goods are sold first. It provides the most realistic figure for cost of goods sold.
5. The weighted-average method provides an average unit cost of all inventory. Weighted-average inventory value generally falls somewhere between LIFO and FIFO.
6. Accounting principles require that we be consistent in the use of the inventory method that is adopted.
7. Goods in transit should be added to the value of the inventory. Merchandise on consignment and damaged or obsolete merchandise should not be included in the value of the inventory.

Learning Unit 15-4

1. Taking a physical inventory is costly and time-consuming.
2. If a business needs to take an inventory more often than once a year, the retail method or gross profit method is used to prepare interim financial reports or in submitting a claim for insurance purposes.
3. The ending inventory amount has an effect on the financial reports, and a mistake will cause the assets to be under- or overstated. Net income will also be under- or overstated by this mistake.

KEY TERMS

Consignee A company or person to whom merchandise is consigned but who doesn't have ownership (p. 617)

Consignment Sales of goods through an agent who has possession but not ownership (p. 617)

Consignor The one who consigns merchandise to the consignee (p. 617)

Consistency The accounting principle that requires companies to follow the same accounting methods or procedures from period to period (p. 616)

FIFO (First-In, First-Out) method Valuing of inventory assuming that the company sells the first goods received in the store first (p. 613)

Full disclosure principle The accounting principle that requires companies to disclose fully on their financial reports changes in accounting procedures and methods, along with the effects of the changes and justification for the changes (p. 616)

Gross Profit method A method used to determine the value of the ending inventory using a predetermined gross profit rate. This method can be used to determine the value of ending inventory if a loss from fire occurs. (p. 619)

LIFO (Last-In, Last-Out) method Valuing of inventory with the assumption that the last goods received in the store are the first to be sold (p. 614)

Periodic inventory system An inventory system that does not keep continuous records of the inventory of merchandise on hand (p. 611)

Perpetual inventory system The inventory system of a company that keeps a continuous (perpetual) record of inventory on hand and of the cost of goods sold (p. 602)

Retail method A method used to determine the value of the ending inventory using a cost to retail ratio. This method is often used for interim financial reports. (p. 619)

Specific invoice method Valuing of inventory where each item is identified with a specific invoice (p. 612)

Weighted-average method Valuing of inventory where each item is assigned the same unit cost. This unit cost is found by dividing cost of goods available for sale by the total number of units for sale (p. 615)

QUESTIONS, MINI EXERCISES, EXERCISES, AND PROBLEMS

Discussion Questions

1. Why would a manager prefer the perpetual inventory system over the periodic system of inventory?
2. What are the two key accounts in the perpetual inventory system?

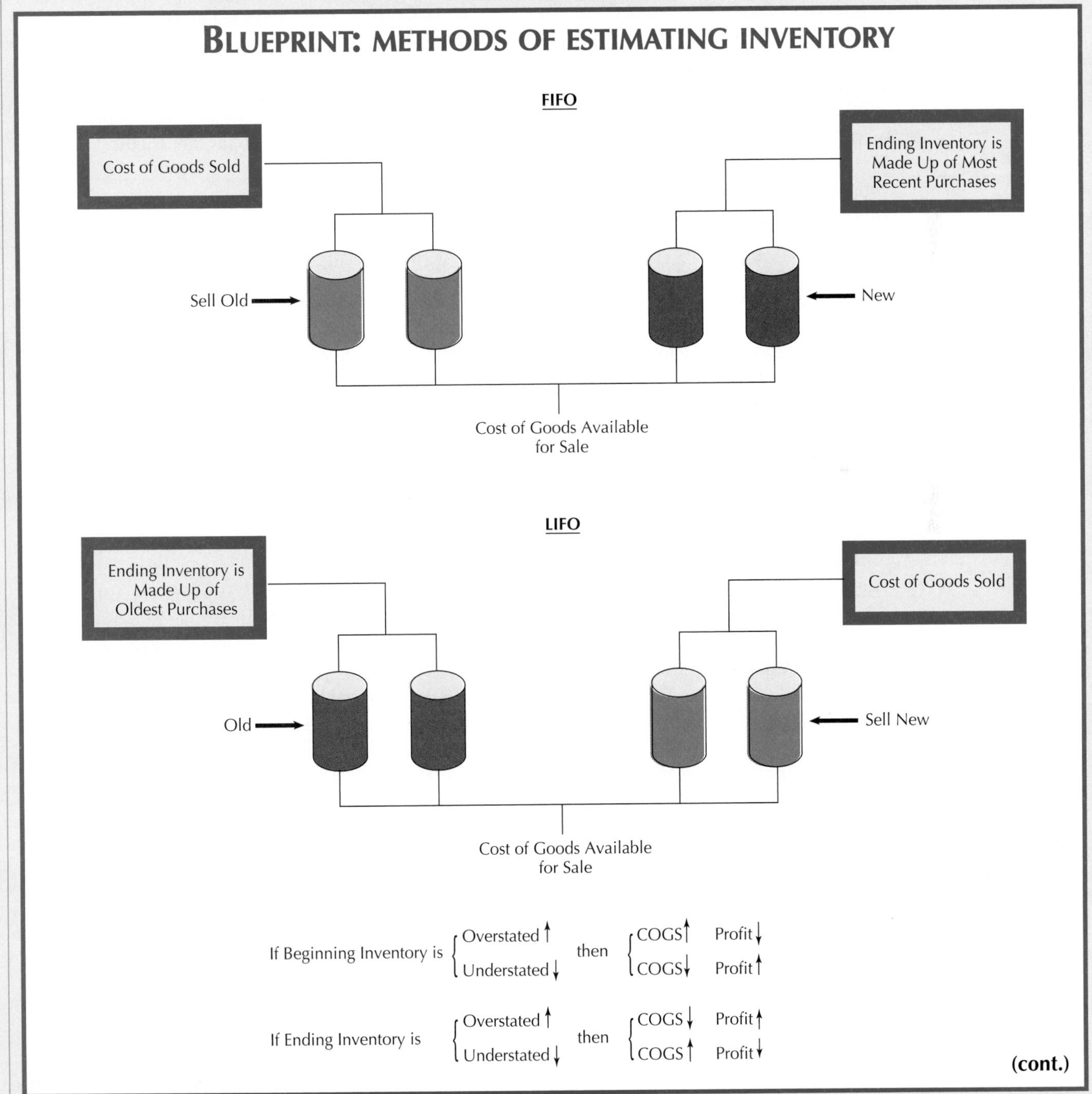

BLUEPRINT: METHODS OF ESTIMATING INVENTORY (cont.)

SUMMARY OF PROS AND CONS OF INVENTORY VALUATION METHODS

	Pros	Cons
Specific Invoice Method	**1.** Simple to use if company has small amount of high-cost goods—for example, autos, jewels, boats, antiques, etc. **2.** Flow of goods and flow of cost are the same. **3.** Costs are matched with the sales they helped to produce.	**1.** Difficult to use for goods with large unit volumes and small unit prices—for example, nails at a hardware store, packages of toothpaste at a drugstore **2.** Difficult to use for decision-making purposes—ordinarily an impractical approach
	Pros	**Cons**
Weighted-Average Method	**1.** Weighted-average takes into account the number of units purchased at each amount, not a simple average cost. It is good for products sold in large volume, such as grains and fuels. **2.** Accountant assigns an equal unit cost to each unit of inventory; thus, when the income statement is prepared, net income will not fluctuate as much as with other methods.	**1.** Current prices have no more significance than prices of goods bought months earlier. **2.** Compared with other methods, the most recent costs are *not* matched with current sales. **3.** Cost of ending inventory is not as up to date as it could be using another method.
	Pros	**Cons**
First-In, First-Out (FIFO) Method	**1.** The cost flow tends to follow the physical flow (most businesses try to sell the old goods first—for example, perishables such as fruit or vegetables). **2.** The figure for ending inventory is made up of current costs on the balance sheet (since inventory left over is assumed to be from goods last brought into the store).	**1.** During inflation, this method will produce higher income on the income statement—thus more taxes to be paid. **2.** Recent costs are not matched with recent sales, since we assume *old* goods are sold first.
	Pros	**Cons**
Last-In, First-Out (LIFO) Method	**1.** Cost of goods sold is stated at or near current costs, since costs of the *latest* goods acquired are used. **2.** Matches current costs with current selling prices. **3.** During inflation, this method produces the lowest net income. (The lower cost of ending inventory means a higher cost of goods sold; with a higher cost of goods sold, gross profit and ultimately net income are smaller.)	**1.** Ending inventory is valued at very old prices. **2.** Doesn't match physical flow of goods (but can still be used to calculate flow of costs). **3.** It is illegal to use this method for tax purposes. Therefore a second valuation must be made for tax purposes.

3. In the perpetual system, what account is debited to record the cost of merchandise purchased?
4. Why are there two entries required to record each sale in the perpetual inventory system?
5. Explain the relationship between the merchandise inventory account and the subsidiary inventory ledger.
6. Must the flow of cost in inventory match the physical movement of merchandise? Please explain.
7. What are the four methods of inventory valuation? Explain each.
8. During inflation, which inventory method will provide the lowest income on the income statement?
9. Which inventory method provides the most current valuation of inventory on the balance sheet? Please explain.
10. Explain why goods in transit (F.O.B. shipping point) to buyer and goods issued on consignment are added to inventory valuations.
11. When ending inventory is understated, what effect will this have on cost of goods sold and net income?
12. Why would a company use the retail method to determine the value of the ending inventory? Why would they use the gross profit method?

Mini Exercises

(The blank forms you need are on pages 15-6 and 15-7 of the *Study Guide with Working Papers.*)

Transaction Analysis

1. Complete the following transaction analysis:

Accounts Affected	Category	↑ ↓	Rules
Merchandise Inventory		↓	
Cost of Goods Sold		↑	

Journal Entries

Use the perpetual inventory system.

2. Journalize the following transaction in correct form:

2000
March 1 Sold merchandise on account, $500. The merchandise cost $300.

3. Journalize the following transaction in correct form:

2000
March 15 A customer returned merchandise for a cash refund of $250. The item cost the seller $125.

4. Journalize the following transaction in correct form:

2000
March 20 The business returned to the vendor a damaged inventory item that cost $150.

Estimating Inventory Value

5. From the following information, calculate the cost of ending inventory and cost of goods sold using (1) FIFO, (2) LIFO, and (3) Weighted-Average.

		Units	Cost
January 1	Beginning Inventory	5	$1
March 6	Purchased	3	2
August 9	Purchased	2	3
December 10	Purchased	4	4

The ending inventory reveals six items unsold.

Retail Inventory Method

6. Complete the following using the retail inventory method. (Round the cost ratio to the nearest whole percent.)

	Cost	Retail
Goods available for sale		
Beginning inventory	$50	$100
Net purchases	70	90
Cost of goods available for sale	A	B
Cost ratio	C	
Net sales at retail		140
Inventory at retail		D
Ending inventory	E	

Gross Profit Method

7. Complete the following using the gross profit method. Assume a normal gross profit rate of 40 percent of Net Sales.

Goods available for sale		
Inventory January 1, 2002		$50
Net purchases		10
Cost of goods available for sale		A
Less: Estimated cost of goods sold		
Net sales at retail	$40	
Cost percentage	B	
Estimated cost of goods sold		C
Estimated inventory January 31, 2002		D

Exercises

(The blank forms you need are on pages 15-8 to 15-11 of the *Study Guide with Working Papers.*)

Journalizing perpetual entries

15-1. The DMM Electric Company uses the perpetual inventory system. Record these transactions in a two-column journal.

2001
Feb. 3 Purchased 10 model 77DX light fixtures on account from Dealer's Electric at total cost of $230, terms n/30.
5 Sold 3 model U67 light fixtures for cash for $84 total. The cost of these three fixtures amounted to $54.

6 The customer returned 1 model U67 light fixture and was given a $28 cash refund.
10 A debit memo for $23 was issued to Dealer's Electric for 1 model 77DX light fixture that came in damaged in the shipment of February 3.

Perpetual inventory—subsidiary ledgers

15-2. The RJM Company uses the perpetual inventory system with a subsidiary ledger for inventory. Enter the following information into the inventory record form for product U47. Be sure to keep the balance on hand up to date.

2000
Nov. 5 Purchased 5 units at a cost of $10 each. (There were no units on hand prior to this purchase.)
6 Sold 3 units for $16 each. (*Hint:* The inventory record form contains only information about the cost of a product, not the selling price!)
7 Sold 1 unit for $15.50.
10 Purchased 12 additional units at a cost of $10 each.

Journalizing perpetual entries

15-3. Journalize and post the above transactions for RJM Company using a two-column journal.

FIFO—perpetual method

15-4. CVR Sales uses the FIFO method with the perpetual inventory system. Enter the following information into the inventory record form for product 44BX. Be sure to keep the balance on hand up to date.

2001
Oct 1 Balance on hand—3 units at a cost of $21 each
2 Purchased 5 units at a cost of $23 each.
5 Sold 2 units for $31 each. (*Remember:* Use cost and not selling price in the inventory record.)
6 Sold 5 units for $31 each.
8 Purchased 6 units at a cost of $24 each.

Periodic method

15-5. The Loyola Company uses the periodic inventory system. Calculate the cost of ending inventory and cost of goods sold using the (a) FIFO, (b) LIFO, and (c) weighted-average methods. Loyola sells only one product called SM57.

		Units	**Cost per unit**
Jan. 1	Beginning inventory	50	$ 9
Mar. 18	Purchased	12	10
Aug. 19	Purchased	40	12
Nov. 8	Purchased	48	13

Ending inventory is 52 units.

Shipping goods

15-6. From the following facts, calculate the correct cost of inventory for Ray Company. The facts:

- Cost of inventory on shelf, $4,000, which includes $300 worth of goods received on consignment
- Goods in transit en route to Ray Company shipped F.O.B. shipping point, $22,000
- Goods in transit en route to Ray shipped F.O.B. destination, $300. Ray has $600 worth of goods on consignment in Alice's Dress Shop.

Retail inventory

15-7. Miles Company's May 1 inventory had a cost of $58,000 and a retail value of $72,000. During May, net purchases cost $255,000 with a retail value of $405,000. Net sales at retail for Miles Company during May were $225,000. Calculate the ending inventory at cost using the retail inventory method. (Round the cost ratio to the nearest hundredth percent.)

Gross profit method

15-8. Amy Company on January 1 had inventory costing $30,000, and during January had net purchases of $67,000. Over recent years, Amy Company's gross profit has averaged 40 percent on sales. Given that the company has net sales of $106,000, calculate an estimated cost of ending inventory using the gross profit method.

Group A Problems

(The blank forms you need are on pages 15-12 to 15-18 of the *Study Guide with Working Papers.*)

Journalizing perpetual inventory

15A-1. The Wren Company uses the perpetual inventory system. Record these transactions in a two-column journal. All credit sales are n/30.

Check Figure
March 13
Dr. Cost of goods sold $290
Cr. Merchandise inventory $290

2003

March
5 Purchased merchandise on account totalling $1,750. Terms n/30
6 Sold merchandise on account to Tommy Dorsey for $85. This merchandise cost $63.
8 Returned $100 worth of defective merchandise purchased March 5.
9 Sold $125 worth of merchandise for cash. This merchandise cost $98.
9 Allowed a return for credit of merchandise sold for $7 on March 6. The cost of the returned merchandise was $5. (*Hint:* Don't forget to return the cost of the merchandise to the Merchandise Inventory account.)
10 Purchased $800 worth of merchandise on account from BG Supply. Terms n/30
12 Received payment from Tommy Dorsey for the March 6 sale less the return.
13 Sold $380 worth of merchandise for cash. The cost was $290.

Journalizing perpetual inventory

15A-2. Mr. E. L. Best owns an electronics supply company called Best Electronics. His company uses the perpetual inventory system with a subsidiary inventory ledger to maintain control over an inventory of thousands of electronic parts. Here are the quantities and costs for three of the parts in his inventory:

Check Figure
KT88 Ending balance $192.50

Part #	Quantity on hand	Cost per unit
KT88	3	$17.50
EL34	22	16.40
12AX7	5	8.70

Your job is to:

1. Enter the above beginning balances in the inventory record forms; beginning inventory is $456.80.
2. Journalize and post the following transactions.

2001

Oct
10 Purchased the following on account:

Part #	Quantity	Cost per unit
KT88	24	$17.50
12AX7	36	8.70

(*Hint:* Be sure to update each inventory record.)

11 Sold four number KT88 units for cash at a selling price of $27.50 each. (*Hint:* Remember to record both the revenue and the cost. The cost data will be found in the inventory record form for this part number. Don't forget to update the form.)

13 Sold the following for cash:

Part #	Quantity	Sales price per unit
KT88	12	$27.50
EL34	8	25.00
12AX7	14	12.90

15 A customer brought back one KT88 unit bought two days ago because it did not work.
16 Best Electronics sent back to the vendor the faulty KT88 unit that the customer had brought back.

Perpetual inventory – FIFO

15A-3. Agree Company uses a perpetual inventory system on the FIFO basis. From the information given below, prepare an inventory control sheet. Assume on January 1, 2002, a beginning inventory of 660 units at a cost of $7 each.

Check Figure

Ending balance $18,600

RECEIVED			*SOLD*	
Date	*Quantity*	*Cost per unit*	*Date*	*Quantity*
Apr. 15	280	$ 6	Mar. 8	620
Nov. 12	1,420	10	Oct. 5	240
Dec. 31	600	11	Nov. 30	300

Periodic inventory

15A-4. Ashley Company, using the periodic inventory system, began the year with 250 units of product B in inventory with a unit cost of $15. The following additional purchases of the product were made:

Check Figure

(b) LIFO Cost of goods sold $23,050

Apr. 1	300 units @ $18 each
July 5	400 units @ 20 each
Aug. 15	500 units @ 22 each
Nov. 20	150 units @ 24 each

At year-end, Ashley Company had 525 units of its product unsold. Your task is to calculate the cost of ending inventory as well as cost of goods sold by (a) FIFO, (b) LIFO, (c) weighted-average. (Round weighted-average to nearest cent.)

Retail inventory method

15A-5. Marge Company uses the retail method to estimate cost of ending inventory for its monthly interim reports. From the following facts, estimate Marge's ending inventory at cost for the end of January. (Round the cost ratio to the nearest tenth of 1 percent.)

Check Figure

Ending inventory at cost $20,748

January 1 inventory at cost	$ 17,200
January 1 inventory at retail	33,000
Net purchases at cost	114,200
Net purchases at retail	197,000
Net sales at retail	193,600

Gross profit method

15A-6. Over the past four years, the gross profit rate for Hall Company was 30 percent. Last week a fire destroyed all of Hall's inventory. Luckily, all the records for Hall were in a fireproof safe and indicated the following facts:

Check Figure

Estimated inventory $22,698

Inventory (January 1, 2003)	$ 34,000
Sales	125,400
Sales Returns	1,940
Purchases	76,400
Purchases Returns and Allowances	1,280

Please estimate the cost of inventory that was destroyed in the fire.

Group B Problems

(The blank forms you need are on pages 15-12 to 15-18 of the *Study Guide with Working Papers*.)

Journalizing perpetual inventory

15B-1. The Wren Company uses the perpetual inventory system. Record these transactions in a two-column journal. All credit sales are n/30.

Check Figure

March 23

Dr. Cost of goods sold $320

Cr. Merchandise inventory $320

2003

March 15 Purchased merchandise on account totalling $1,450. Terms n/30

16 Sold merchandise on account to Bobby Hackett for $92. This merchandise cost $71.

18 Returned $120 worth of defective merchandise purchased March 15.

19 Sold $230 worth of merchandise for cash. This merchandise cost $175.

19 Allowed a return for credit of $14 worth of merchandise sold on March 16. The cost of the returned merchandise was $11. (*Hint:* Don't forget to return the cost of the merchandise to the Merchandise Inventory account.)

20 Purchased $900 worth of merchandise on account from JT Supply. Terms n/30

22 Received payment from Bobby Hackett for the March 16 sale less the return.

23 Sold $410 worth of merchandise for cash. The cost was $320.

Journalizing perpetual inventory

Check Figure

12AU7 Ending balance $117

15B-2. Mr. E. L. Best owns an electronics supply company called Best Electronics. His company uses the perpetual inventory system with a subsidiary inventory ledger to maintain control over an inventory of thousands of electronic parts. Here are the quantities and costs for three of the parts in his inventory:

Part #	Quantity on hand	Cost per unit
6L6	4	$12.50
EL84	18	9.40
12AU7	3	7.80

Your job is to:

1. Enter the above beginning balances in the inventory record forms; beginning inventory is $242.60.
2. Journalize and post the following transactions.

2001

Oct. 10 Purchased the following on account:

Part #	Quantity	Cost per unit
6L6	18	$12.50
12AU7	28	7.80

(*Hint:* Be sure to update each inventory record.)

11 Sold four number 12AU7 units for cash at a selling price of $18.50 each. (*Hint:* Remember to record both the revenue and the cost. The cost data will be found in the inventory record form for this part number. Don't forget to update the form.)

13 Sold the following for cash:

Part #	Quantity	Sales price per unit
6L6	10	$18.50
EL84	9	14.00
12AU7	12	11.80

15 A customer brought back one 6L6 that was bought two days ago because it did not work.

16 Best Electronics returned to the vendor the faulty part that was returned yesterday.

Perpetual inventory—FIFO

Check Figure

Ending Balance $11,720

15B-3. Agree Company uses a perpetual inventory system on the FIFO basis. From the information given below, prepare an inventory control sheet. Assume a beginning inventory of 600 units at a cost of $8 each.

RECEIVED			*SOLD*	
Date	*Quantity*	*Cost per unit*	*Date*	*Quantity*
Apr. 15	240	$ 7	Mar. 8	480
Nov. 12	1,420	11	Nov 30	1,260
Dec. 31	500	12		

FIFO, LIFO, weighted-average

Check Figure

(b) LIFO Cost of Goods Sold $39,020

15B-4. On January 1, 2001, Ashley Company, which uses the periodic inventory system, began with 200 units of product B in inventory with a unit cost of $24. The following additional purchases of the product were made:

Apr. 1	210 units @ $28 each
Jul. 5	500 units @ 32 each
Aug. 15	450 units @ 38 each
Nov. 20	200 units @ 44 each

At year-end, Ashley Company had 500 units of its product unsold. Your task is to calculate cost of ending inventory as well as cost of goods sold by (a) FIFO, (b) LIFO, (c) weighted-average. (Round weighted-average to nearest cent.)

Retail inventory method

Check Figure

Ending inventory at cost $46,864

15B-5. Marge Company uses the retail method to estimate cost of ending inventory for its monthly interim reports. From the facts given below, estimate Marge's ending inventory at cost for the end of January. (Round the cost ratio to the nearest hundredth percent.)

January 1 inventory at cost	$ 34,200
January 1 inventory at retail	69,800
Net purchases at cost	241,600
Net purchases at retail	407,000
Net sales at retail	396,000

Gross profit method

Check Figure

Estimated inventory $11,700

15B-6. Over the past four years, the gross profit rate for Hall Company was 32 percent. Last week a fire destroyed all of Hall's inventory. Luckily, all the records for Hall were in a fireproof safe and indicated the following facts:

Inventory (January 1, 2003)	$ 7,600
Sales	139,200
Sales Returns	2,450
Purchases	98,900
Purchases Returns and Allowances	1,800

Using the gross profit method, estimate the cost of the inventory that was destroyed in the fire.

Group C Problems

(The forms you need are on pages 15-19 to 15-25 of the *Study Guide with Working Papers.*)

Journalizing perpetual inventory

Check Figure

March 24

Dr. Cost of Goods Sold $455

Cr. Merchandise Inventory $455

15C-1. The James Company uses the perpetual inventory system. Record these transactions in a two-column journal. All credit sales are n/30.

2002		
March	15	Purchased merchandise on account totalling $1,948. Terms n/30
	16	Sold merchandise on account to Denise Chan for $125. This merchandise cost $87.
	18	Returned $250 worth of defective merchandise purchased March 15.
	19	Sold $350 worth of merchandise for cash. This merchandise cost $220.
	19	Allowed a return for credit of merchandise sold for $20 on March 17. The cost of the returned merchandise was $14. (*Hint:* Don't forget to return the cost of the merchandise to the Merchandise Inventory account.)
	20	Purchased $1,220 worth of merchandise on account from Mercury Sales Co. Terms n/30
	22	Received payment from Denise Chan for the March 17 sale less the return.
	24	Sold $625 worth of merchandise for cash. The cost was $455.

Journalizing perpetual inventory

Check Figure

XGY23 Ending Balance $70.62

15C-2. Ann Engle owns a lighting supply company called Engle Lighting Co. Her company uses the perpetual inventory system with a subsidiary inventory ledger to maintain control over an inventory of thousands of lighting parts. Here are the quantities and costs for three of the parts in the company's inventory:

Part #	Quantity on hand	Cost per unit
PL45	6	$10.80
KG149	24	7.16
XGY23	5	6.42

Your job is to:

1. Enter the above beginning balances in the inventory record forms; beginning inventory is $268.74.
2. Journalize and post the following transactions.

2001

March 10 Purchased the following on account:

Part #	Quantity	Cost per unit
PL45	3	$10.80
XGY23	16	6.42

(*Hint:* Be sure to update each inventory record.)

12 Sold six number PL45 units for cash at a selling price of $16.20 each. (*Hint:* Remember to record both the revenue and the cost. The cost data will be found in the inventory record form for this part number. Don't forget to update the form.)

14 Sold the following for cash:

Part #	Quantity	Sales price per unit
PL45	3	$16.20
KG149	4	12.80
XGY23	10	10.25

16 A customer brought back two PL45 parts that were bought two days ago because they did not work. A cash refund was made.

17 Engle Lighting returned to the vendor the faulty parts that were refunded yesterday.

FIFO, LIFO, weighted-average

Check Figure

LIFO Cost of Goods Sold $33,147.40

15C-3. Robbins Company began the year with 425 units of product B in inventory with a unit cost of $16.20. The following additional purchases of the product were made:

Apr. 15	340 units @ $18.46 each
Jul. 25	425 units @ 21.12 each
Aug. 5	550 units @ 24.86 each
Nov. 26	275 units @ 27.10 each

At year-end, Robbins Company had 600 units of its product unsold. Your task is to calculate the cost of ending inventory as well as cost of goods sold by (a) FIFO, (b) LIFO, (c) weighted-average. (Round weighted-average to nearest cent.)

Retail inventory method

Check Figure

Ending Inventory at cost $32,670

15C-4. Pound Company uses the retail method to estimate cost of ending inventory for its monthly interim reports. From the following facts, estimate Pound's ending inventory at cost for the end of March. (Round the cost ratio to the nearest tenth of 1 percent.)

March 1 inventory at cost	$ 42,600
March 1 inventory at retail	78,200
Net purchases at cost	184,760
Net purchases at retail	337,400
Net sales at retail	356,200

Gross profit method

Check Figure

Estimated Inventory $35,080

15C-5. Over the past five years, the gross profit rate for Genesis Company was 35 percent. Last week a fire destroyed all of their inventory. Luckily, all the records for Hall were in a fireproof safe and indicated the following facts:

Inventory (January 1, 2001)	$ 47,000
Sales	141,200
Sales Returns	2,200
Purchases	79,600
Purchases Returns and Allowances	1,170

Estimate the cost of the inventory that was destroyed in the fire.

Perpetual inventory—FIFO

Check Figure

Ending Balance $17,840

15C-6. Sawyer Company uses a perpetual inventory system on the FIFO basis. From the information given below, prepare an inventory control sheet. Assume on January 1, 2001, a beginning inventory of 600 units at a cost of $10 each.

RECEIVED			*SOLD*	
Date	*Quantity*	*Cost per unit*	*Date*	*Quantity*
Apr. 15	260	$ 9	Mar. 8	420
Nov. 12	1,400	13	Oct. 5	260
Dec. 31	600	15	Nov. 20	900

REAL WORLD APPLICATIONS

(The forms you need are on page 15-26 of the *Study Guide with Working Papers.*)

15R-1.

To: Tom Hoover

From: Jennifer Ring

Re: Inventory Mistakes

The following mistakes have been found on our financial reports:

a. The beginning inventory was reported as $300 when it should have been $100.

b. The figure of $800 for ending inventory was understated by $200.

c. Purchases account of $18,000 was understated by $1,100.

d. Sales were overstated by $2,000.

Indicate what effect these mistakes will separately have on (1) cost of goods sold, (2) gross profit, and (3) owner's equity. Explain your answers.

make the call

Critical Thinking/Ethical Case

15R-2.

Lyon Co. has used a perpetual inventory system for six months. The company president has issued a memo stating that the new computer system has failed to deliver acceptable standards in servicing his customers—too many goods out of stock. Fran, Lyon's accountant, blames the Computer Department and tells the president to fire the head of that department. The President wants to return immediately to a periodic inventory system. You make the call. Write down your recommendations to the president.

ACCOUNTING RECALL

A CUMULATIVE APPROACH

THIS EXAMINATION REVIEWS CHAPTERS 1 THROUGH 15.

Your *Study Guide with Working Papers*, page 15-27, has forms to complete this exam, as well as worked-out solutions. The page reference next to each question identifies the page to turn back to if you answer the question incorrectly.

PART 1 Vocabulary Review

Match each term on the left with the appropriate definition or phrase on the right.

Page Ref.

(602)	1. Perpetual inventory system	A. Contra-cost-of-goods-sold
(239)	2. Petty cash	B. Subtracted from cost of goods sold
(577)	3. Allowance for Doubtful Accounts	C. Uses a cost ratio
		D. Related to how selling price moves
(614)	4. LIFO	E. Last goods sold first
(619)	5. Retail method	F. Contra-asset
(618)	6. Lower of cost or market	G. Ledger balance rarely changes
(409)	7. Purchases discounts	H. Accounts payable
(421)	8. Controlling account	I. Continuous inventory of merchandise
(617)	9. Consignee	J. Doesn't have ownership
(498)	10. Ending inventory	

PART II True or False (Accounting Theory)

(621) 11. If ending inventory is overstated, then cost of goods sold is overstated.

(613) 12. FIFO assumes that the old goods are sold first.

(349) 13. Sales Returns and Allowances is a contra-cost-of-goods-sold account.

(612) 14. Net sales less cost of goods sold equals gross profit.

(529) 15. In the periodic system, the Purchases account is not used.

Continuing Problem

Assume that the Eldorado Computer Centre had 300 pieces of merchandise inventory as of March 31, 2003. The inventory was purchased with prices as follows:

Lot	Price each piece	Number of pieces	Total cost
1st lot	$1.00	100	$100
2nd lot	$1.75	100	$175
3rd lot	$2.00	80	$160
4th lot	$2.50	100	$250
5th lot	$1.65	100	$165

Lot numbers represent oldest to newest.

Assignment

(See page 15-28 in your *Study Guide with Working Papers.*)

Using the FIFO, LIFO, and weighted-average methods, calculate the dollar value of the Eldorado Computer Centre's ending (partial) inventory.

COMPUTER WORKSHOP

Computerized Accounting Application for Chapter 15

Perpetual Inventory System

Before starting on this assignment, read and complete the tasks discussed in Parts A, B, and F of Appendix B at the end of this book and complete the Computerized Accounting Application assignments for all the previous chapters which have Computer Workshops.

One of the most powerful features of a computerized accounting system is its ability to maintain perpetual inventory records easily and accurately. In the earlier Computer Workshops, this feature was not demonstrated as you focussed on the tasks associated with maintaining a periodic inventory system. *Simply Accounting* has the ability to maintain perpetual inventory records through its Inventory module. *Simply Accounting* uses the weighted-average method as its inventory cost flow assumption.

In this Computer Workshop you will be working with the data files for a company called The Paint Place. The Paint Place uses the General, Payables, Receivables, and Inventory modules of Simply Accounting to maintain its accounting and perpetual inventory records. The Paint Place extends terms of 2/10, n/30 to all of its credit customers. An Inventory Synopsis (a computerized schedule of the current status of the perpetual inventory records) for The Paint Place appears below:

Computerized perpetual inventory schedule

The Paint Place
Inventory Synopsis 03/01/02

Number	Description	Unit	Price	Quantity	Cost	Value	Margin (%)
1	Latex Flat	Gallon	16.95	642	7.47	4,795.74	55.93
2	Latex Semi-gloss	Gallon	16.95	1,066	7.47	7,963.02	55.93
3	Latex High-gloss	Gallon	16.95	600	7.47	4,482.00	55.93
4	Oil High-gloss	Gallon	17.95	801	8.97	7,184.97	50.03
5	Oil Semi-gloss	Gallon	17.95	502	8.97	4,502.94	50.03
						28,928.67	

Open the company data files

1. Click on the **Start** button. Point to Programs; point to Simply Accounting; then click on Simply Accounting in the final menu presented. The Simply Accounting Open File dialogue box will appear.
2. Insert your Student Data Files disk into disk drive A. Enter the following path into the **File name** text box: `A:\student\paint.asc`
3. Click on the **Open** button; enter 03/31/02 into the **Session** text box; then click on the **OK** button. Click on the **OK** button in response to the message "The date entered is more than one week past your previous **Session** date of 03/01/02." The Company Window for The Paint Place will appear. Note that the two journals associated with the Inventory module (Transfers and Adjustments) are available. The Transfers and Adjustments Journals are used to record non-routine types of transactions that affect inventory quantities and values such as adjustments to the perpetual inventory records for items that have been damaged or become obsolete. Routine perpetual inventory transactions such as the sale or purchase of an inventory item are recorded in the Sales and Purchases Journals dialogue boxes.

Add your name to the company name.

4. Click on the Company Window **Setup** menu; then click on Company Information. The Company Information dialogue box will appear. Insert your name in place of the text "Your Name" in the **Name** text box. Click on the **OK** button to return to the Company Window.

How to record a sale on account

5. On March 1, 2002, sold 5 gallons of Oil High-gloss (Item #4) at $17.95 per gallon + GST to Elaine Anderson on account, invoice No. 5468, $96.03, terms 2/10, n/30.

   Double-click on the Sales icon to open the Sales Journal dialogue box. Note that the program automatically offers Invoice 5468 as the invoice number for this transaction through the program's automatic invoice numbering feature. Click on the arrow button to the right of the **Sold to** text box to display a list of customers; then click on Elaine Anderson. Highlight the **Date** text box; enter `03/01/02`; then press the TAB key. The insertion point will be positioned in the **Item** text box. Press the ENTER key to display the Select Inventory item dialogue box; then highlight Item #4 Oil High-gloss, and click on the **Select** button. Note that the program automatically enters the Unit, Description, default sales Price, and sales Acct (4010 Sales) associated with this inventory item (Item #4). If the item is being sold at a price other than the default sales price shown, the Price offered by the program can be modified. For example, the item may be on sale, or a volume discount may be offered to the customer.

6. The flashing insertion point appears in the **Ship** text box. Enter 5; then press the TAB key. The program will automatically multiply the Qty times the Price and enter the result in the **Amount** text box. Press the TAB key until the flashing insertion point is positioned in the GST field. Press the ENTER key to display the Select GST dialogue box; then highlight 3-GST @ 7.0%, not included, and click on the **Select** button. Your screen should look like this:

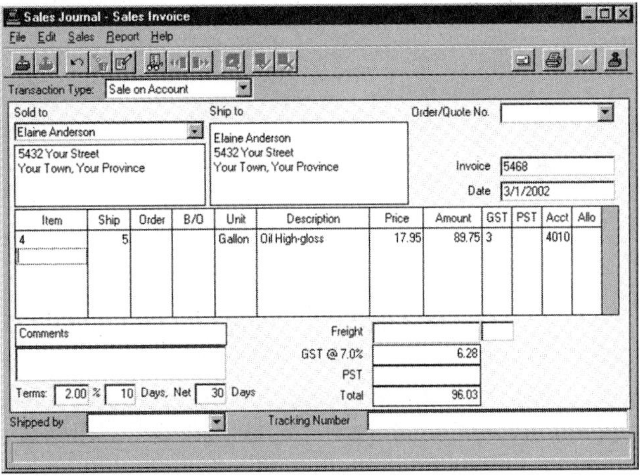

How to review a sales journal entry

7. Before posting this transaction, you need to verify that the transaction data are correct by reviewing the journal entry. To review the entry, click on the Sales Journal **Report** menu; then click on Display Sales Journal Entry. The journal entry representing the data you have recorded in the Sales Journal dialogue box is displayed. Review the journal entry for accuracy, noting any errors. Note that the program has automatically created a compound journal entry, recording the retail value of the sale and the cost of the sale through its perpetual inventory integration feature. Close the Sales Journal Entry window; then make any editing corrections required.

How to post a sales journal entry

8. After verifying that the journal entry is correct, click on the Post icon to post this transaction. A blank Sales Journal dialogue box is displayed, ready for additional Sales Journal transactions to be recorded. Close the Sales Journal dialogue box.

How to record a purchase on account

9. On March 2, 1997, received invoice No. 6892 from Wholesale Paints in the amount of $1,504 + GST for the purchase of 200 gallons of Latex High-gloss (Item #3) at $7.52 per gallon, terms 2/10, n/30.

   Double-click on the Purchases icon to open the Purchases Journal dialogue box. Click on the arrow button to the right of the **Purchased From** text box; then click on Wholesale Paints. Click on the **Invoice** text box; enter 6892; then press the TAB key. Enter `03/02/02` into the **Date** text box; then press the TAB key. The insertion point will be positioned in the **Item** text box. Press the ENTER key to display the Select Inventory item dialogue box; then highlight Item #3 Latex High-gloss, and click on the **Select** button. Note that the program automatically enters the Unit, Description, Price (current weighted-average cost per unit), and Acct (1300 Merchandise Inventory) associated with this inventory item (Item #3). For some purchases, the default Price offered by the program will need to be modified to agree with the per unit price stated on the vendor's invoice. For example, the price of the item being purchased may be increased or decreased, or a volume discount may be extended by the vendor.

10. The flashing insertion point appears in the **Rec'd** text box. Enter `200`; then press the TAB key until the insertion point is positioned in the Price field. Change the Price to 7.52 (don't forget to change the Price!); then press the TAB key. The program will automatically multiply the number of items in the **Rec'd** text box times the Price and enter the result in the **Amount** text box. Your screen should look like this:

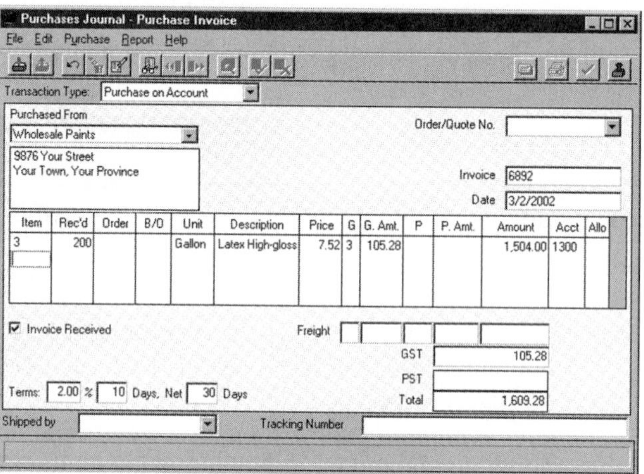

How to review a sales journal entry

11. Before posting this transaction, you need to verify that the transaction data are correct by reviewing the journal entry. To review the entry, click on the Purchases Journal **Report** menu; then click on Display Purchases Journal Entry. The journal entry representing the data you have recorded in the Purchases Journal dialogue box is displayed. Review the journal entry for accuracy, noting any errors.

12. Close the Purchases Journal Entry window; then make any editing corrections required.

How to post a sales journal entry

13. After verifying that the journal entry is correct, click on the Post icon to post this transaction. A blank Purchases Journal dialogue box is displayed, ready for additional Purchases Journal transactions to be recorded. Close the Purchases Journal dialogue box.

How to record a purchase on account

14. Record the following additional transactions:

2002

March 3 Received invoice No. CC675 from Painter's Supply in the amount of $906 + GST for the purchase of 100 gallons of Oil High-gloss (Item #4) at $9.06 per gallon + GST (don't forget to change the Price!), terms 2/10, n/30.

4 Sold 5 gallons of Oil High-gloss paint (Item #4) at $17.95 per gallon + GST to Jake Kerns on account, invoice No. 5469, $96.03, terms 2/10, n/30.
6 Received cheque No. 8723 from Wes Young in the amount of $3,445.50 in payment of invoice No. 5466 ($3,521.32), dated February 28, less 2 percent discount ($65.82).
7 Issued cheque No. 2345 to Vantage Tints in the amount of $1,160.98 in payment of invoice No. E5658 ($1,194.47), dated February 28, less 3 percent discount ($33.49).
14 Sold 10 gallons of Latex Semi-gloss (Item #2) at $16.95 per gallon + GST to Elaine Anderson on account, $181.37, invoice No. 5470, terms 2/10, n/30.
16 Received invoice No. 6943 from Wholesale Paints in the amount of $1,213.38 for the purchase of 150 gallons of Latex Semi-gloss (Item #2) at $7.56 per gallon + GST (don't forget to change the Price!), terms 2/10, n/30.
19 Received invoice No. CC691 from Painter's Supply in the amount of $1,732.06 for the purchase of 175 gallons of Oil Semi-gloss (Item #5) at $9.25 per gallon + GST (don't forget to change the Price!), terms 2/10, n/30.
21 Sold 10 gallons of Latex Semi-gloss (Item #2) at $16.95 per gallon + GST to Jake Kerns on account, $181.37, invoice No. 5471, terms 2/10, n/30.
24 Sold 25 gallons of Oil Semi-gloss paint (Item #5) at $17.95 per gallon + GST to Elaine Anderson on account, $480.16, invoice No. 5472, terms 2/10, n/30.
25 Received invoice No. CC787 from Painter's Supply in the amount of $497.55 for the purchase of 50 gallons of Oil Semi-gloss (Item #5) at $9.30 per gallon + GST (don't forget to change the Price!), terms 2/10, n/30.
31 Sold 25 gallons of Oil Semi-gloss (Item #5) at $17.95 per gallon + GST to Jake Kerns on account, $480.16, invoice No. 5473, terms 2/10, n/30.

How to display an inventory activity detail report

15. Click on the Company Window **Reports** menu; point to Inventory and Services; then click on **Transaction**. Click on the **Detail** option button, click on the **Select All** button; leave the **Inventory by Asset** option button checked; change the **Start** date to 03/01/02; leave the **Finish** date set at 03/31/02; then check the check boxes for **Purchases, Sales, Transfers, Adjustments,** and **Balance forward.** Your screen will look like this:

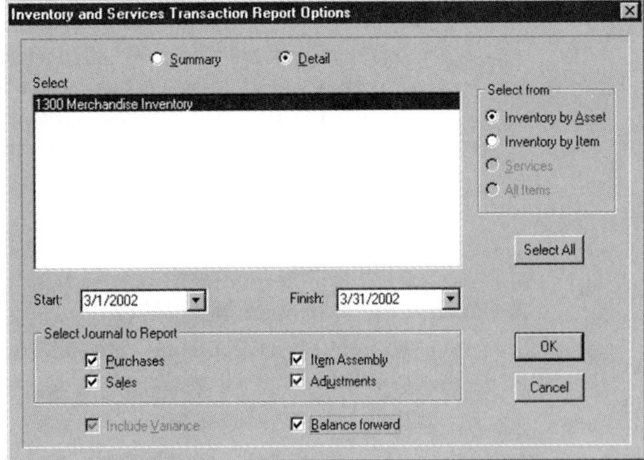

16. Click on the **OK** button. Your screen will look like this:

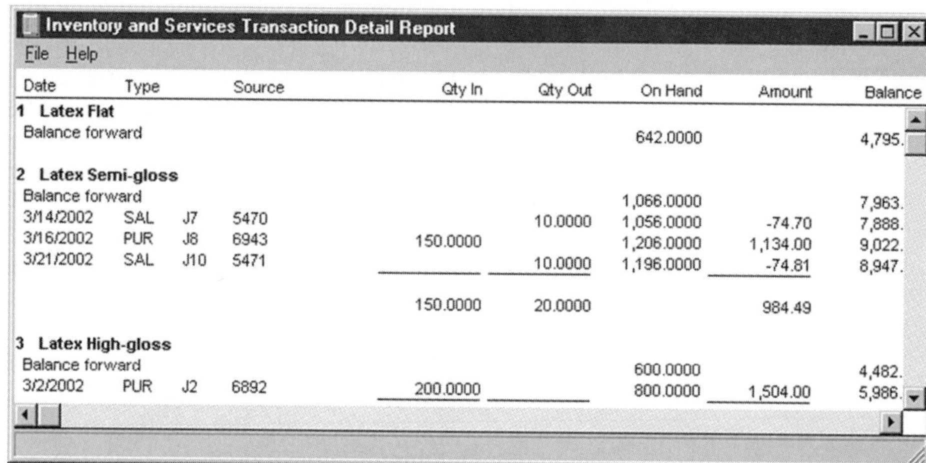

Date	Type		Source	Qty In	Qty Out	On Hand	Amount	Balance
1 Latex Flat								
Balance forward						642.0000		4,795.
2 Latex Semi-gloss								
Balance forward						1,066.0000		7,963.
3/14/2002	SAL	J7	5470		10.0000	1,056.0000	-74.70	7,888.
3/16/2002	PUR	J8	6943	150.0000		1,206.0000	1,134.00	9,022.
3/21/2002	SAL	J10	5471		10.0000	1,196.0000	-74.81	8,947.
				150.0000	20.0000		984.49	
3 Latex High-gloss								
Balance forward						600.0000		4,482.
3/2/2002	PUR	J2	6892	200.0000		800.0000	1,504.00	5,986.

How to access invoice lookup

17. Move the mouse pointer opposite the 03/16/02 purchase of Latex Semi-gloss. The mouse pointer will appear as a magnifying glass and the **Status** bar will indicate that you can "Double-click to display Invoice Lookup." Double-click with your mouse. Your screen will look like this:

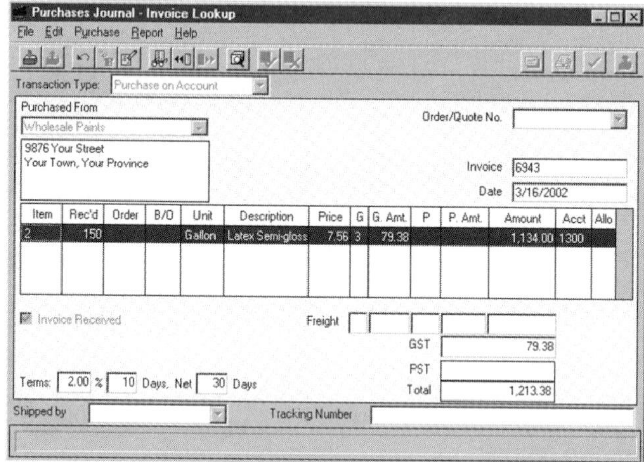

Important information about automatic journal entry reversals

18. The program has drilled-down to show the details of this transaction in the Purchases Journal dialogue box. In addition to viewing the details of the transaction from this dialogue box, you can also use *Simply Accounting*'s automatic reversing feature for incorrect journal entries from this dialogue box. Instead of using the procedures described in Part C of Appendix B for correcting a posted transaction, certain types of journal entries can be reversed automatically by drilling-down to the detail of the journal entry and deleting the entry. This feature is available for reversing purchase and sales invoices, and is especially useful for companies that use a perpetual inventory system because the program automatically updates the inventory item records for the reversal. If you find an error in a purchases or sales journal entry, you can reverse the entry by drilling-down to the invoice and removing each detail line on the invoice. The program will automatically create and post the reversing entry, inserting the letters ADJ in front of the original invoice number. The accounting records will be in the same position as if the original transaction had not been posted in the first place, but a complete record of the original entry and the reversing entry will appear in the journal you are working with and in the General Journal. You can then re-enter the journal entry correctly.

How to automatically reverse a purchases journal entry

19. Let's try it! We are going to assume that the purchase of 150 gallons of Latex Semi-gloss at $7.56 per gallon + GST from Wholesale Paints on March 16 was recorded incorrectly. The price should be $7.65 per gallon + GST. Click on the **Purchase** menu in the Purchases Journal–Invoice Lookup window; then click on Adjust Invoice. Click on the Description of the item; click on the **Edit** menu in the Purchases Journal–Adjust Invoice window; then click on Remove Line. Click on the **Yes** button in response to the question, "Are you sure you want to delete the item?"

20. Click on the Post icon; then click on the **Yes** button in response to the statement, "Are you sure you want to reverse this invoice? All original inventory quantities will be reversed, new quantities on the invoice will not be recorded; you must use the Adjustments journal to record the new quantities."

How to re-enter a purchases journal entry

21. A blank Purchases Journal dialogue box will appear. Enter and post the following transaction:

March 16 Received invoice No. 6943 from Wholesale Paints in the amount of $1,227.83 for the purchase of 150 gallons of Latex Semi-gloss (Item #2) at $7.65 per gallon + GST (don't forget to change the Price!), terms 2/10, n/30.

How to view the updated Inventory Activity Detail Report

22. Close the Purchases Journal dialogue box. Click on the Company Window **Reports** menu; point to Inventory and Services; then click on **Transaction**. The Inventory and Services Transaction Detail Report will appear, showing the reversed entry and the correct entry. Note that the program did not adjust the sale on 03/21/02 to reflect the new weighted-average cost for the Latex Semi-gloss inventory item. To update the accounting records to reflect the correct weighted-average cost for this sale, you need to reverse and then re-record the sale.

How to automatically reverse a sales journal entry

23. Move the mouse pointer opposite the 03/21/02 sale of Latex Semi-gloss. The mouse pointer will appear as a magnifying glass and the **Status** bar will indicate that you can "Double-click to display Invoice Lookup." Double-click with your mouse. The program has drilled-down to show the details of this transaction in the Sales Journal dialogue box.

24. Click on the Sales menu in the Sales Journal–Invoice Lookup window; then click on Adjust Invoice. Click on the Description of the item; click on the **Edit** menu in the Sales Journal–Adjust Invoice window; then click on Remove Line. Click on the **Yes** button in response to the question, "Are you sure you want to delete the item?"

25. Click on the Post icon; then click on the **Yes** button in response to the statement, "Are you sure you want to reverse this invoice? All original inventory quantities will be reversed, new quantities on the invoice will not be recorded; you must use the Adjustments journal to record the new quantities."

How to re-enter a sales journal entry

26. A blank Sales Journal dialogue box will appear. Enter and post the following transaction:

March 21 Sold 10 gallons of Latex Semi-gloss (Item #2) at $16.95 per gallon + GST to Jake Kerns on account, $181.37, invoice No. 5471, terms 2/10, n/30.

How to print an Inventory Activity Detail Report

27. Close the Sales Journal dialogue box. Click on the Company Window **Reports** menu; point to Inventory and Services; then click on **Transaction**. The Inventory and Services Transaction Detail Report will appear, showing the two entries that you have reversed and corrected. The sale on 03/21/02 to Jake Kerns will reflect the correct weighted-average cost amount based on the corrected purchase from Wholesale Paints. Click on the Inventory and Services Transaction Detail Report **File** menu; then click on Print to print the report. Close the Inventory and Services Transaction Detail Report window.

How to display and print an Inventory Synopsis

28. Click on the Company Window **Reports** menu; point to Inventory and Services; then click on Inventory in the final menu presented. Click on the **Select All** button; leave the **Inventory by Assets** and **Item Synopsis** option buttons checked; then click on the **OK** button. Your screen will look like the one below.

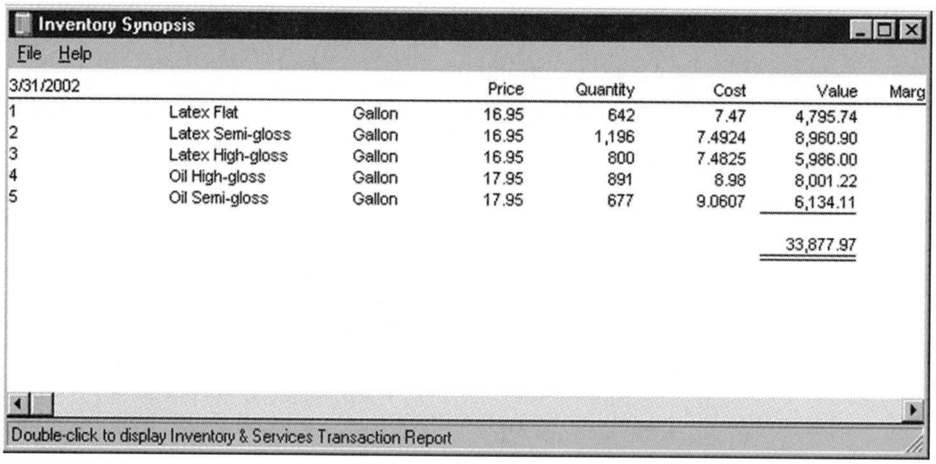

Inventory Synopsis

File Help

3/31/2002			Price	Quantity	Cost	Value	Marg
1	Latex Flat	Gallon	16.95	642	7.47	4,795.74	
2	Latex Semi-gloss	Gallon	16.95	1,196	7.4924	8,960.90	
3	Latex High-gloss	Gallon	16.95	800	7.4825	5,986.00	
4	Oil High-gloss	Gallon	17.95	891	8.98	8,001.22	
5	Oil Semi-gloss	Gallon	17.95	677	9.0607	6,134.11	
						33,877.97	

Double-click to display Inventory & Services Transaction Report

Print reports

29. Click on the Inventory Synopsis **File** menu; then click on Print to print the report. Note that the weighted-average cost of the inventory items has changed, based on the transactions you have recorded.

30. Close the Inventory Synopsis window; then print the following reports:

A. General Journal (By posting date, All ledger entries, Start: 03/01/02, Finish: 03/31/02)

B. Trial Balance As at 03/31/02

C. Customer Aged report As at 03/31/02 (Detail, Select All)

D. Vendor Aged report As at 03/31/02 (Detail, Select All)

E. Income Statement (Start: 01/01/02, Finish: 03/31/02)

F. Balance Sheet As at 03/31/02

Exit from the program

31. Click on the Company Window **File** menu; then click on Exit to end the current work session and return to your Windows desktop.

Complete the report transmittal

32. Complete The Paint Place Report Transmittal located in Appendix A of your *Study Guide with Working Papers.*

How Companies Record Credit Card Sales in Their Special Journals

Recording Bank Credit Cards

Example: Credit Card Sales of $100 on MasterCard

It is interesting to note that for bank credit cards (MasterCard, Visa, and so on) the sales are recorded in the seller's Cash Receipts Journal, since the slips are converted into cash immediately. Bank credit card sales are not treated as accounts receivable. The fee the bank charges (about 2 percent to 5 percent) is deducted, and the bank credits the depositor's account immediately for the net amount. The end result for the seller is:

Accounts Affected	Category	↑ ↓	Rule
Cash	Asset	↑	Dr. $97
Credit Card Expense	Expenses	↑	Dr. 3
Sales	Revenue	↑	Cr. 100

CASH RECEIPTS JOURNAL

Date 2001	Cash Dr.	Credit Card Expense Dr.	Accounts Receivable Cr.	Sales Credited	Sales Tax Payable Cr.	Sundry Account Name	Sundry Post Ref.	Sundry Amount Cr.
	97 00	3 00		100 00				

It is the responsibility of the credit card company to sustain any losses (bad debts) from customers' nonpayment. If the bank waits to take the discount until the end of the month, the seller makes an entry in the cash payment journal to record the credit card expense; the end result would be credit card expense up and cash balance down. Usually, the bank would send the charge on the monthly bank statement. *Remember: bank credit cards are not treated as accounts receivable.*

Recording Private Company Credit Cards

Private companies such as American Express and Diners Club are considered by most sellers as accounts receivable. The seller periodically summarizes the sales slips and submits them to the private credit card company for payment (these are usually paid within two weeks). Let's look at two situations to show how a company would handle its accounting procedures for these credit sales transactions.

Situation 1: On May 4, Morris Company sold merchandise on account $53.50 to Bill Blank. Bill used American Express. Assume Morris Company has low dollar volume and few transactions.

Note in Figure A-1 how the sale of $50 + GST is recorded in the sales journal. Keep in mind that Morris is treating American Express, not Bill Blank, as the accounts receivable. In Figure A-2 we see that payment is received on June 8 from American Express and results in:

1. Cash increasing by $50.82
2. Credit card expense rising by $2.68
3. Accounts receivable being reduced by the $53.50 originally owed by American Express

SALES JOURNAL

Date 2001		Invoice	Description of Accounts Receivable	Post Ref.	Accounts Receivable Dr.	GST Payable Cr.	Sales Cr.
May	4	692	American Express		53 50	3 50	50 00
			(Bill Blank)				

FIGURE A-1

CASH RECEIPTS JOURNAL

Date 2001		Cash Dr.	Sales Discounts Dr.	Credit Card Expense Dr.	Accounts Receivable Cr.	Sales Tax Payable Cr.	Sundry Account Name	Sundry Post Ref.	Sundry Amount Cr.
June	8	50 82		2 68	53 50		American Express		
							(Bill Blank)		

FIGURE A-2

Situation 2: On March 31, Blue Company summarized its credit card sales for American Express. Payment was received on April 13 from American Express. Assume Blue Company has high dollar volume and many transactions.

Note in Figure A-3 that each credit company has its own column set up. There is an account set up for each in the ledger as well; the posting to the ledger would be done at the end of the month. With high volume and the need to record many transactions, the use of these additional columns (versus Figure A-1) will result in increased efficiency. Figure A-4 shows the receipt of money from American Express less the credit card expense charge.

These new titles are found in the general ledger. Subsidiary ledgers are not needed, since a file is kept of all copies submitted for payment.

BLUE COMPANY SALES JOURNAL

Date 2001		Invoice	Description of Accounts Receivable	Post Ref.	Accounts Receivable Dr.	Credit Cards: American Express Dr.	Credit Cards: Diners Club Dr.	G.S.T. Payable Cr.	Credit Card Sales Cr.	Sales Cr.
Mar.	31		Summary of			121 980 00		7 980 00	114 000 00	
			American Express							
						(112)	(113)		(401)	

FIGURE A-3

Accounts Receivable American Express 112	
Total of column posted from sales journal at end of month	

Accounts Receivable Diners Club 113	
Total of column posted from sales journal at end of month	

Credit Card Sales 401	
	Total of column posted from sales journal at end of month

BLUE COMPANY CASH RECEIPTS JOURNAL

Date 2001		Cash Dr.	Sales Discounts Dr.	Credit Card Expense Dr.	Credit Card Accounts Rec.: Accounts Receivable Cr.	Credit Card Accounts Rec.: American Express Cr.	Diners Club Cr.	Sales Cr.	G.S.T. Payable Cr.	Sundry: Account Name	Sundry: Post Ref.	Sundry: Amount Cr.
April	13	114 661 20		7 318 80		121 980 00				Summary of		
										American		
										Express payments		
				(510)								

FIGURE A-4

Credit Card Expense 510	
Total of columns posted from cash receipt journal at end of month	

Computerized Accounting

B

PART *A*
An Introduction

Accounting procedures are essentially the same whether they are performed manually or on a computer. The following is a list of the accounting cycle steps in a manual accounting system as compared with the steps in a computerized accounting system.

Steps of the Accounting Cycle

Manual Accounting System	Computerized Accounting System
1. Business transactions occur and generate source documents.	1. Business transactions occur and generate source documents.
2. Analyze and record business transactions in a journal.	2. Analyze and record business transactions in a computerized journal.
3. Post or transfer information from journal to ledger.	3. Computer automatically posts information from journal to ledger.
4. Prepare a trial balance.	4. Trial balance is prepared automatically.
5. Prepare a worksheet.	5. No worksheet is necessary.
6. Prepare financial statements.	6. Financial statements are prepared automatically.
7. Journalize and post adjusting entries.	7. Record adjusting entries in a computerized journal; posting is automated.
	8. Printing of journals is optional.
8. Journalize and post closing entries.	9. Closing procedures are completed automatically.
9. Prepare a post-closing trial balance.	10. Post-closing trial balance is prepared automatically.

The accounting cycle comparison shows that the accountant's task of initially analyzing business transactions in terms of debits and credits (both routine business transactions and adjusting entries) is required in both manual and computerized accounting systems. However, in a computerized accounting system, the "drudge" work of posting transactions, creating and completing worksheets and financial statements, and performing the closing procedures is all handled automatically by the computerized accounting system.

In addition, computerized accounting systems can perform accounting procedures at greater speeds and with greater accuracy than can be achieved in a manual accounting system. It is important to recognize, however, that the computer is only a tool that can accept and process information supplied by the accountant. Each business transaction and adjusting entry must first be correctly analyzed and recorded in a computerized journal; otherwise, the financial statements generated by the computerized accounting system will contain errors and will not be useful to the business. Before a business can begin to use a computerized accounting system, and specifically the *Simply Accounting* system, it must have the following items in place:

1. A computer system
2. Computer software
   a. Operating system software
   b. Applications software
      (1) Accounting applications software
      (2) *Simply Accounting*

COMPUTER SYSTEM

A computer system consists of several electronic components that together have the ability to accept user-supplied data; input, store, and execute programmed instructions; and output results according to user specifications. The physical computer and its related devices are the hardware, while the stored program that supplies the instructions is called the software.

To understand how a computer system works, we must first look at a conceptual computer that demonstrates the major components and functions of a computer system. The conceptual computer shown in Figure B-1 has four major elements—input devices, processing/internal memory unit, secondary storage devices, and output devices. The illustration also shows the flow of data into the computer and of processed information out of the computer.

Input devices are used to feed data and instructions into the computer. Once the data and instructions are entered, the computer must be able to store them internally and then process the data based on the instructions. Storage and processing occur in the processing/internal memory unit.

There are two main types of internal computer memory: random-access memory (RAM) and read-only memory (ROM). RAM is the largest portion of the memory but still has limited capacity; consequently, secondary storage devices are needed. In addition, RAM is temporary—anything stored in RAM is erased when power to the computer is interrupted. Therefore, data stored in RAM must be saved to a secondary storage medium through the use of a secondary storage device before the power is turned off. ROM is permanent memory and consists of those instruction sets necessary to start the computer and receive initial messages from input devices.

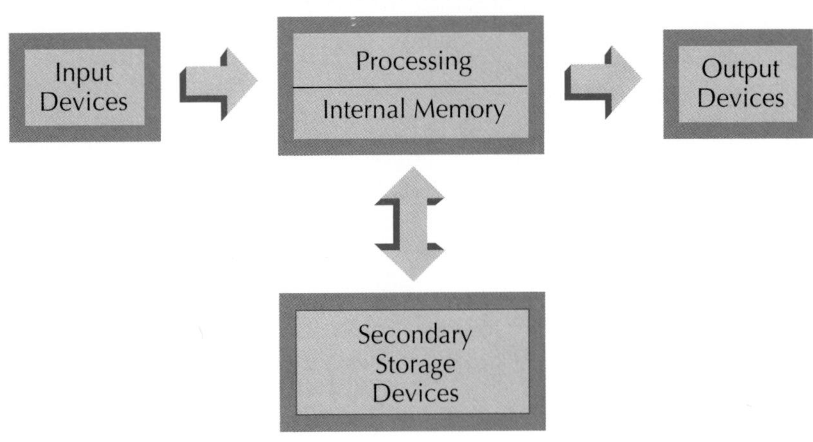

FIGURE B-1
Conceptual Computer

FIGURE B-2
Typical Configuration of a Microcomputer System

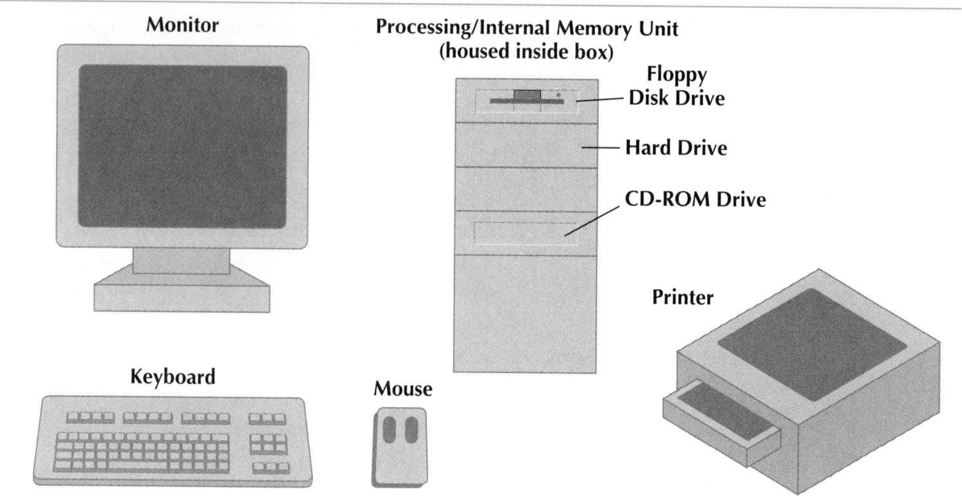

ROM takes up only a small portion of the total internal memory capacity of a computer system.

Finally, the results of processing must be made available to computer users through output devices. These components form a collection of devices referred to as computer hardware because they have physical substance.

In a typical microcomputer system (see Figure B-2), a keyboard and mouse are used for input and a printer and monitor are used for output. The processing/internal memory unit is housed inside a box along with secondary storage devices, usually consisting of a hard drive unit, one or more floppy disk drives, and a CD-ROM drive. There are other popular secondary storage devices as well, such as ZIP and Jaz drives and disks, and many others which are just now appearing in the marketplace. Most of these new disk drives feature removable disks—sort of a super large capacity floppy disk.

Computer hardware can do nothing without a computer program. Computer programs are supplied on floppy disks or CD-ROMs, which are secondary storage media used in floppy disk or CD-ROM drives. Figure B-3 shows an example of a floppy disk and of a CD-ROM.

To operate a particular computer program, you must first load the program into the system's internal memory (RAM) through the use of a floppy disk or CD-ROM drive or by accessing the program that has been installed and stored on the system's hard drive. Once a program is accessed by RAM, the computer can execute the program instructions and process data as directed by the user through the keyboard or mouse. At the end of a processing session, the results may be viewed on the monitor, printed on the printer, and/or stored permanently on the hard drive, on a floppy disk, or on some other removable medium.

Computer Software

The computer can do nothing without a computer program. Computer programs control the input, processing, storage, and output operations of a computer. Computer

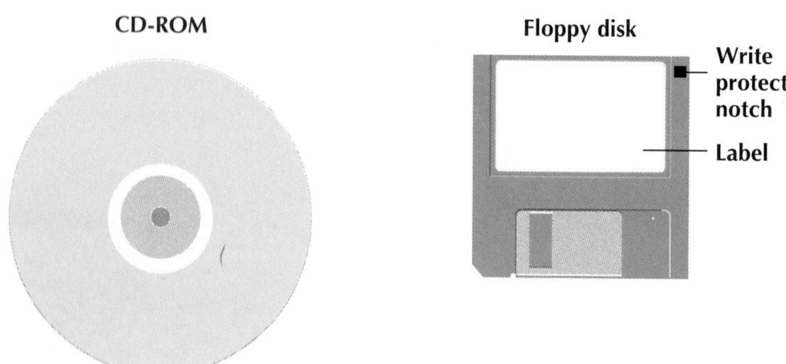

FIGURE B-3
Storage Media

programmers write the instructions that tell the computer to execute certain procedures and process data. There are two broad categories of computer software: operating-system software and applications software.

Operating System Software

Operating system software provides the link between the computer hardware, applications software, and the computer user. It consists of programs that start up the computer, retrieve applications programs, and allow the computer operator to store and retrieve data. Operating system software controls access to input and output devices and access to applications programs. There are several popular operating systems for microcomputers. They include Windows 98 (and previous versions), DOS, DOS combined with Windows 3.XX, OS/2, the Macintosh operating system, and UNIX.

Applications Software

Applications software refers to programs designed for a specific use. Five of the most common types of business applications software are database management, spreadsheets, word processing, communications, and graphics. Spreadsheet software allows the manipulation of data and has the ability to project answers to "what if" questions. For example, a spreadsheet program could project a company's profit next year if sales increased by 10 percent and expenses increased by 6 percent. Word processing software enables the user to write and print letters, memos, and other documents. Graphics software displays data visually in the form of graphic images. Communications software allows your computer to "talk" to other computers, but to accomplish communications you need additional hardware: a modem to transmit and receive data over telephone lines. Database management software stores, retrieves, sorts, and updates an organized body of information. Most computerized accounting systems are designed as database management software. Accounting information is data that must be organized and stored in a common base of data. This allows the entry of data and the retrieval of information in an organized and systematic way.

Applications software is frequently linked with a particular operating system. Database management, spreadsheet, word processing, graphics, communication, accounting, and other software applications are available in versions that work with most of the popular operating systems. For example, if your computer system is using Windows 98 you would purchase the Windows 98 version of a word processing program. Usually, programs written for previous operating systems (such as Windows 95) will work well in newer versions like Windows 98. If you were using a Macintosh computer and operating system, you would purchase the Macintosh version of a spreadsheet program.

Accounting Applications Software Most computerized accounting software is organized into modules. Each module is designed to process a particular type of accounting data, such as accounts receivable, accounts payable, or payroll. Each module is also designed to work in conjunction with the other modules. When modules are designed to work together in this manner, they are referred to as integrated software. In an integrated accounting system, each module handles a different function but also communicates with the other modules. For example, to record a sale on account, you would make an entry into the accounts receivable module. The integration feature automatically records this entry in the sales journal, updates the customer's account in the accounts receivable subsidiary ledger, and posts all accounts affected in the general ledger. Thus, in an integrated accounting system, transaction data are entered only once. All of the other accounting procedures required to bring the accounting records up-to-date are performed automatically through the integration function.

Version 7 of *Simply Accounting* no longer uses the terms "Ready" and "Not Ready."

Simply Accounting *Simply Accounting* has been selected for use in this text to demonstrate and help you learn how to use a computerized accounting system. It is easy to use, fully integrated, and is also available in versions that work with different operating systems. *Simply Accounting* includes six modules: General, Receivables, Payables, Inventory, Payroll, and Project. Two modes of operation are available in *Simply Accounting:* Ready and Not Ready. The Not Ready mode is used when you are converting a manual accounting system to a computerized accounting system. The Ready mode is used for regular accounting purposes. The educational version is the complete commercial program package and is available in many college bookstores at a very reasonable price. Most colleges will have this software available for use in their computer labs.

WORKING WITH *SIMPLY ACCOUNTING*®

Before you begin to work with *Simply Accounting*, you need to be familiar with your computer hardware and the Windows 98 operating system. When you are running Windows 98, your work takes place on the desktop. Think of this area as resembling the surface of a desk. There are physical objects on your real desk and there are windows and icons on the Windows 98 desktop.

A mouse is an essential input device for all Windows 98 applications. A mouse is a pointing device which produces different shapes on your monitor as you move the mouse on your desk. According to the nature of the current action, the mouse pointer may appear as a small arrow head, an hourglass, or a hand. There are five basic mouse techniques:

- Click — To quickly press and release the left mouse button
- Double-click — To click the left mouse button twice in rapid succession
- Drag — To hold down the left mouse button while you move the mouse
- Point — To position the mouse pointer over an object without clicking a button
- Right-click — To press and release the right mouse button quickly

The Windows 98 Desktop

Figure B-4 shows a typical opening Windows 98 screen. Your desktop may be different, just as your real desk is arranged differently from those of your colleagues. Windows 95 screens are quite similar to those in Windows 98.

- **Desktop icons:** Graphic representations of drives, files, and other resources. The desktop icons that display will vary depending on your computer setup.
- **Taskbar:** Contains the **Start** button and other buttons representing open applications.
- **Start button:** Clicking on the Start button displays the start menu and lets you start applications.

FIGURE B-4
Windows 98 Desktop

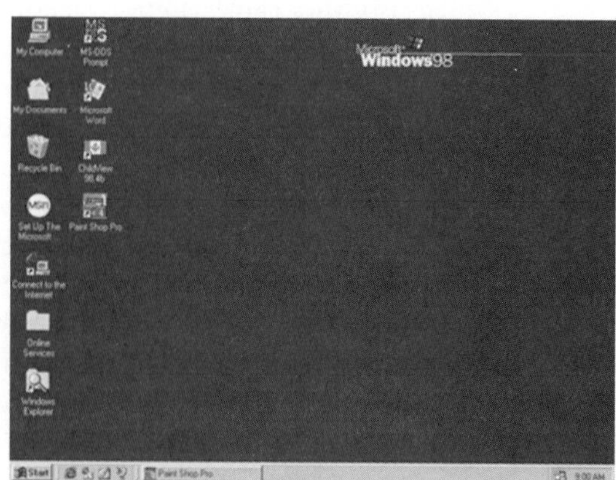

Applications Window (the Company Window)

As you work with *Simply Accounting*, two kinds of windows will appear on your desktop: the application window (called the Company Window—see Figure B-5), and windows contained within the Company Window (called dialogue boxes). An application window contains a running application. The name of the application and the application's menu bar will appear at the top of the application window. Regardless of the windows that are open on your desktop, most windows have certain elements in common.

FIGURE B-5
Simply Accounting Application (Company) Window

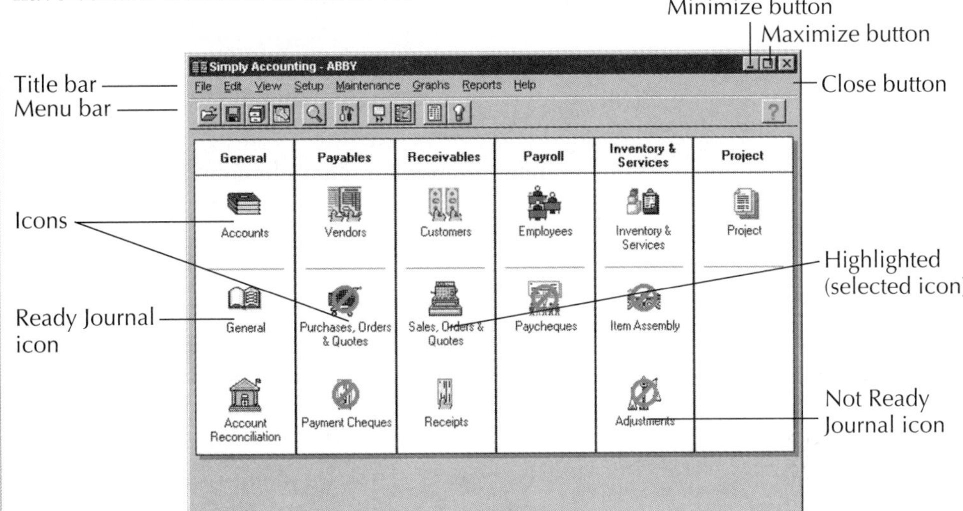

- **Minimize button:** Clicking on this button minimizes a window and displays it as a task button on the taskbar.
- **Maximize button:** Clicking on this button enlarges the window so that it fills the entire desktop. After you enlarge a window, the maximize button is replaced by a **Restore button** (a double box, not shown) that returns the window to the size it was before it was maximized.
- **Close button:** Clicking on this button will close the window.
- **Title bar:** Displays the name of the application.
- **Menu bar:** This window element lists the available menus for the window.
- **Icons:** The Company Window displays the icons that represent a company's accounting books—the full set of Ledgers and Journals that you use to record accounting transactions. The top row contains the Ledgers: the bottom two rows contain the Journals aligned vertically with their related Ledgers.
- **Highlighted (selected) icon:** The active icon in the Company Window.
- **Not Ready Journal icon:** A Journal icon is shown with a no-entry symbol if its status is Not Ready.
- **Ready Journal icon:** A Journal icon is shown without a no-entry symbol if its status is Ready.
- **Status bar:** A line of text at the bottom of many windows that gives more information about a field, button, or menu item. If you are unsure of what to enter in a field or what a button is for, point to it with your mouse and read the status bar.

Dialogue Boxes

A dialogue box appears when additional information is needed to execute a command. There are different ways to supply that information; consequently, there are different types of dialogue boxes. Most dialogue boxes (see Figure B-6) contain options you can select. After you specify options, you can choose a command button to carry out a command. Other dialogue boxes (see Figure B-7) may display additional information, warnings, or messages indicating why a requested task cannot be accomplished.

FIGURE B-6
Dialogue Box 1

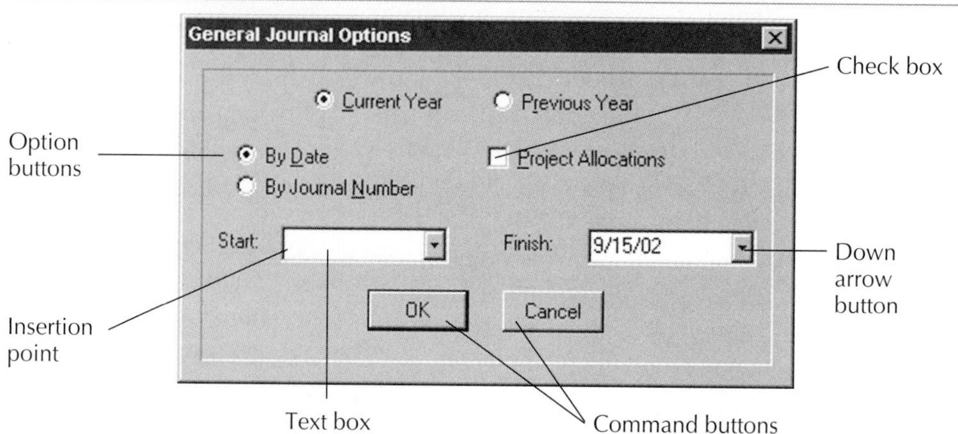

- **Insertion point:** This element shows where you are in the dialogue box. It marks the place where text will appear when you begin typing.
- **Check box:** A small square that represents an option. When you select an option (click on the empty check box), the check box contains a ✔; when you turn off the option (click on the check box to remove the ✔), it is blank.
- **Option buttons:** A small circle that represents an option. When you select (click on the button) an option from a group, that button contains a large black dot; the remaining buttons in the group are blank. Option buttons represent mutually exclusive options. You can select only one option button at a time.
- **Text box:** When you move to an empty text box, an insertion point appears at the far left-hand side of the box. The text you type starts at the insertion point. If the box you move to already contains text, this text is selected (highlighted), and any text you type replaces it. You can also delete the selected text by pressing the DELETE or BACKSPACE key.
- **Command buttons:** Choose (click on) a command button to initiate an immediate action such as carrying out or cancelling a command. The **OK, Cancel, Yes, No,** and **Post** buttons are common command buttons.
- **Down arrow button:** Click on this button to display a list of choices.

FIGURE B-7
Dialogue Box 2

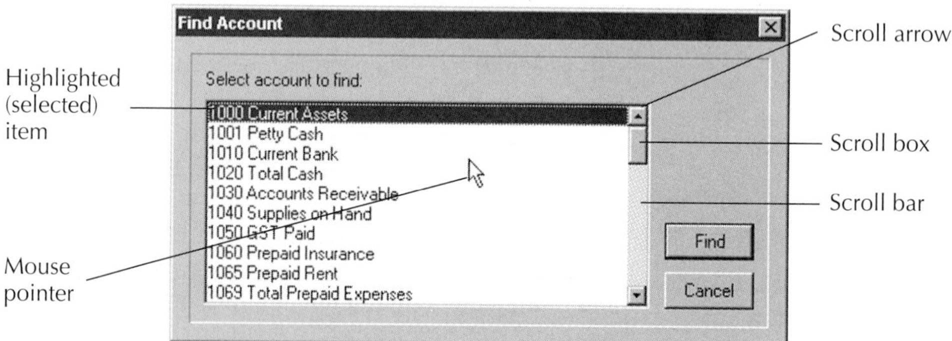

- **Highlighted (selected) item:** To highlight or select an item in a displayed list, click on the item.
- **Scroll bar:** A bar that may appear at the bottom and/or right side of a window or dialogue box if there is more text than can be displayed within the window.
- **Scroll arrow:** A small arrow at the end of a scroll bar that you click on to move to the next item in the list. The top and left arrows scroll to the previous item; the bottom and right arrows scroll to the next item.
- **Scroll box:** A small box in a scroll bar. You can use the mouse to drag the scroll box left or right, or up or down. The scroll box indicates the relative position in the list.
- **Mouse pointer:** The mouse pointer is shown as a small arrow head in this example.

Using Menus

Commands are listed on menus, as shown in Figure B-8. Each application has its own menus which are listed on the **Application** menu bar. To display a complete menu, click on the *menu title*. When a menu is displayed, choose a command by clicking on it or by typing the *underlined letter* to execute the command. You can also bypass the menu entirely if you know the *keyboard equivalent* shown to the right of the command when the menu is displayed.

A *dimmed command* indicates that a command is not currently executable; some additional action has to be taken for the command to become available. Some commands are followed by *ellipses* (. . .) to indicate that more information is required to execute the command. The additional information can be entered into a dialogue box, which will appear immediately after the command has been selected.

FIGURE B-8
Sample Menu

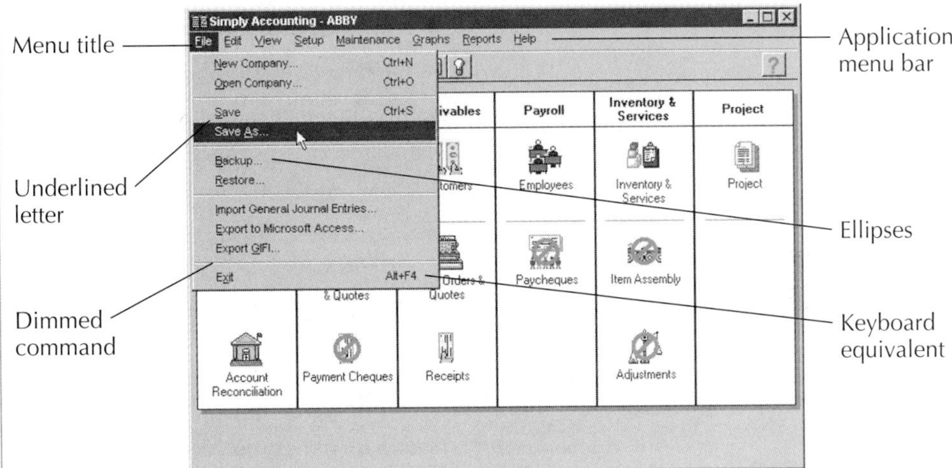

Working in the Windows 98 Environment

You can use a combination of mouse and keyboard techniques to navigate within the Windows 98 environment. For example, you can click on an item to select it, and then press the ENTER key to choose it, or you can just double-click on the item. Simply Accounting is designed for a mouse, but it also provides keyboard equivalents for almost every command. It may seem confusing at first that there are several different ways to do the same thing. You will find this flexibility useful. For example, if your hands are already on the keyboard, it may be faster to use the keyboard equivalent of a mouse command. Alternatively, if your hand is already on the mouse, it may be faster to use a mouse technique to carry out a command. When a procedure in an assignment says to select or choose an item, generally use whichever method you prefer. Alternative procedures are often provided as well. It is not necessary to memorize any particular technique; just be flexible and willing to experiment. As you gain experience with the program, you will develop personal preferences, and the various techniques will become second nature.

Windows 98 Tour

Windows 98 includes a highly recommended tour to acquaint new users with mouse techniques and the Windows 98 operating environment. Use the following instructions to access the Windows Tour on your computer system:

1. Click on the Start button; then click on Run.
2. Type `tour.exe` into the **Open** text box; then click on the **OK** button.
3. Follow the instructions on your screen to complete the tour.

PART *B*

Installing *Simply Accounting*/Creating a Student Data Files Disk

This section of the appendix discusses several basic operations that you need to complete to install the *Simply Accounting* program (should you need to) and create a Student Data Files disk for use in completing the computer workshop assignments in this text.

SYSTEM REQUIREMENTS

The recommended minimum software and hardware your computer system needs to run both Windows and Simply Accounting successfully are:

- Microsoft Windows 3.1 or 3.11, Windows 95, or Windows 98
- A personal computer with an 80486/33 processor
- A hard disk with free disk space of approximately 20 MB
- One 3.5-inch high density floppy disk drive
- A CD-ROM drive (the Simply Accounting program is also available on 3.5-inch high density floppy disks, but a CD-ROM is preferred).
- 8 MB of RAM
- A VGA, or similar high-resolution monitor that is supported by Windows
- A printer that is supported by Windows
- A mouse that is supported by Windows

CD-ROM CONTENTS

The *Simply Accounting* installation and program files for use in completing the computer workshops are on the CD-ROM that accompanies the software, if you purchased it. Student data files are on the diskette which accompanies this book.

Installation Procedures

To install *Simply Accounting* on your hard disk, follow the detailed instructions which accompany your software, or the shorter version shown here:

1. Start Windows.
2. Make sure that no other programs are running on your system.
3. Insert the CD-ROM in your CD-ROM drive. (The installation may commence automatically; if so, skip to point 6 below.)
4. Click on the Start button; then click on Run.
5. Type `d:setup` and press the ENTER key. For d, substitute the letter used by your CD-ROM drive.
6. Follow the step-by-step instructions as they appear on the screen. Enter your name and your school's name as the Company when requested. Enter the serial number from the box your software came in, when requested. Install all of the *Simply Accounting* components. Read the ReadMe text file; then click on the Close button.
7. Put your CD-ROM away for safekeeping.

Installing *Simply Accounting* on a Network

Simply Accounting can be used in a network environment as long as each student uses a separate Student Data Files disk to store his or her data files. It is assumed that all network installation steps will be carried out by competent technicians, so no details are provided here.

Students should consult with their instructor and/or network administrator for specific procedures regarding program installation and any special printing procedures required for proper network operation.

Creating a Student Data Files Disk

The Student Data Files for use in completing the computer workshops are on the diskette that accompanies this text. You need to copy these files to another 3.5-inch high density floppy disk. You will need another blank, formatted 3.5-inch high density floppy disk labelled "Student Data Files Disk, Working Copy."

1. Insert the original diskette into drive A.
2. Double-click on the My Computer icon on your Windows 98 desktop. The My Computer window will appear.
3. In the My Computer window, right-click on the icon for your 3.5-inch floppy disk drive. Several more choices will be displayed.
4. Click on the Copy Disk menu choice; then select 3.5-inch floppy A in both the Copy From and Copy To windows. Click on Start, and follow the on-screen instructions.
5. When the copy process is finished, close all open windows and store the original diskette safely away. Use the copy you just made for all assignments in the text.

PART C
Correcting a Posted Transaction

Once a transaction is posted in *Simply Accounting*, the journal entry will be permanently reflected in the accounting records. This feature of *Simply Accounting* is designed to ensure that a good audit trail of all transactions is constantly maintained within the program. Consequently, the only way to correct a posted transaction is to reverse the original entry. After this is accomplished, the accounting records will be in the same position as if the transaction had not been posted in the first place, but a complete record of the original entry and the reversing entry will be maintained by the program. After the reversing entry is posted, enter the correct journal entry.

The term *reversing entry* as it is used here should not be confused with the optional way of handling certain adjusting entries. The optional reversing entry procedure for adjusting entries is designed to help prevent errors. Reversing an incorrect entry in a computerized accounting system is a required procedure designed to correct an error that has already occurred.

Beginning with Version 5.0 of the program, *Simply Accounting* added a very useful feature which can be used to automate this process when dealing with:

- A sales invoice (in Accounts Receivable)
- A purchases invoice (in Accounts Payable)
- A payroll cheque (in Payroll)

In each case, the program asks the user to identify the incorrect transaction by document number, then enter a corrected transaction. It then automatically posts a reversing entry to offset the previous (incorrect) one, and posts the corrected transaction (which you have to enter, of course). The program takes over most of the technical details such as accurately reversing the previous amounts, adding appropriate new document numbers (such as invoice numbers), etc. In this appendix, we suggest using this new feature, and we illustrate its use where appropriate. It is still possible to follow the "old style" reversal/re-entry steps, of course, but that seems like a waste of time, and all students should attempt to follow the new procedures if they make an error. Note that this new procedure cannot be used in the general ledger or to amend receipts from customers, or cheques to vendors.

The following procedures for reversing an incorrect journal entry and re-entering the correct journal entry are not intended to be exhaustive, but to give you the general idea of how to correct transactions posted in error. It is impossible to predict the particular error or combination of errors you might make in an assignment.

Correcting an entry made in the General Journal dialogue box: Use the General Journal.

You will need to have a printed copy of a General Journal report listing the entry you intend to reverse on hand as you work through the following reversing and correcting procedures.

1. Open the General Journal; enter the word "Reverse" into the **Source** text box; press the TAB key; enter the **Session** date into the **Session** text box; press the TAB key; enter an explanation for the transaction into the **Comment** text box; then press the TAB key.
2. Refer to your printed copy of the General Journal Report. With the flashing insertion point positioned in the **Account** text box press the ENTER key to bring up the Select Account dialogue box. Double-click on the account that you credited in the incorrect journal entry; enter the amount used in the credit portion of the incorrect journal entry into the **Debits** text box; then press the TAB key.
3. *If you are reversing a compound journal entry, skip this step and go to step 4.* With the flashing insertion point positioned in the **Account** text box, press the ENTER key to bring up the Select Account dialogue box. Double-click on the account that you debited in the incorrect journal entry; then press the TAB key to accept the default **Credits** amount.
4. If you are reversing a compound journal entry, press the ENTER key with the flashing insertion point positioned in the **Account** text box to bring up the Select Account dialogue box. Double-click on the first account that you debited in the incorrect compound journal entry. The program will offer a default Credits amount and the Credits amount will remain highlighted. Override the default Credits amount by entering the amount used in the debit portion of the incorrect compound journal entry. Press the TAB key; then press the ENTER key to bring up the Select Account dialogue box. Double-click on the second account that you debited in the incorrect compound journal entry. The program will offer a default Credits amount; press the TAB key to accept the default **Credits** amount.
5. Click on the General Journal Report menu; then click on Display General Journal Entry. Verify that the reversing entry is the exact opposite of your incorrect journal entry. Accounts and amounts originally debited should be credited, and accounts and amounts originally credited should be debited.
6. Close the General Journal Entry Display window. Make editing corrections if necessary.
7. Click on the Post icon to post the entry. At this point, the accounts are as if no entry at all has been made.
8. Re-enter the journal entry correctly. Enter the word `Correct` in the **Source** text box to indicate that it is a correcting entry; enter the **Session** date into the **Date** text box.

NOTE: *Simply Accounting* will not accept duplicate invoice or cheque numbers in the Sales, Receipts, Purchases, Payments, or Payroll Journals. This feature of the program is designed to prevent the error of entering invoices and cheques twice. Consequently, invoice and cheque numbers must be modified when reversing and correcting entries are entered. Insert the letter R after the invoice or cheque number to indicate a reversing entry. Insert the letter C after the invoice or cheque number to indicate a correcting entry.

Correcting an Incorrect Payroll Cheque: Use the Payroll Journal Adjust Cheque Feature.

An employee was promised a $200 per month raise for the current month, but this memo was lost and a cheque was prepared at his previous salary level. It is necessary to cancel the first cheque and recalculate a new one based on the updated information. Note that the procedure detailed below can be used to correct a wide variety of payroll errors.

1. Double-click on the Paycheques icon to open the Payroll journal.
2. Click on the Adjust Cheque icon (it is the fourth from the left in the toolbar). A screen appears with the title "Select Entry to Adjust." Highlight the transaction you need to correct; then click on Select. Details of that previous payroll cheque are retrieved and displayed. These details would match exactly the journal entry created when this employee's data was processed.
3. Note the Advisory which appears in a box on the screen, warning that you may need to recalculate taxes when finished. Close that advisory for now.
4. Enter the new salary amount in the Salary field.
5. Click on the **Recalculate Taxes** icon in the toolbar. (It is the one on the right which looks a bit like a calculator.)
6. Click on the Post icon.

That's it! If you care to examine the formal records, you will discover that the old payroll entry was reversed, and a corrected one was added.

Reversing and Correcting Entries Made in Special Journals

You must know for certain which dialogue box you originally used (Sales Journal, Receipts Journal, Purchases Journal, or Payments Journal) to record a transaction prior to attempting to use the reversing procedures described in the following sections for special journals. If you are uncertain about which dialogue box you used to record the journal entry you wish to reverse and correct, print Sales Journal, Receipts Journal, Purchases Journal, and Payments Journal reports. To print any of the available journals, follow these instructions:

1. Click on the **Reports** option shown on the Company Window task bar.
2. From the choices displayed, click on Journal Entries.*
3. There are several choices presented, but the list should include Sales, Receipts, Purchases, and Payments. Click the one you wish to print (assume Sales, for illustration) and a dialogue box appears where you can specify the range of dates you wish to cover. Insert the desired Start and Finish dates (you can often use the drop-down lists to choose available relevant dates); then click on **OK**.
4. The journal appears and it can be printed in the normal way.

Review each report to determine which report contains the journal entry you wish to reverse; then use the chart at the top of page 660 to determine which set of instructions following the chart to use to reverse the journal entry and enter the correct entry.

---

*This choice will read Transaction Details if you have chosen to display Non-accounting Terms.

If the journal entry you wish to correct appears on the:	Use these instructions to reverse the entry and enter the correct entry:
Sales Journal	Correcting an Entry Made in the Sales Journal Dialogue Box: Use the Sales Journal.
Receipts Journal	Reversing an Entry Made in the Receipts Journal: Use the Sales Journal.
Purchases Journal	Correcting an Entry Made in the Purchases Journal: Use the Purchases Journal.
Payments Journal	Reversing an Entry Made in the Payments Journal: Use the Purchases Journal.

Correcting an Entry Made in the Sales Journal Dialogue Box: Use the Sales Journal.

Simply Accounting has a useful feature which allows the user to "automatically" correct errors made when recording sales in the Sales Journal. The procedure outlined below should be used to correct quickly and easily errors made when recording sales invoices:

1. Open the Sales Journal and select the appropriate Transaction Type. It will usually be a Sale on Account, but a Sale with Payment can be corrected just as easily.
2. Click the Adjust Invoice icon in the toolbar section. (It is generally the fifth one from the left.) The Adjust an Invoice screen appears; it looks like this:

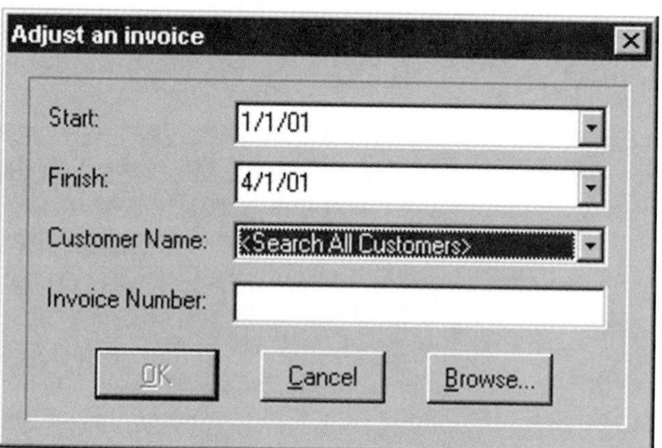

3. Ensure that the Start/Finish dates are acceptable; then choose the customer name in the appropriate field. If you did not recall the customer name, you could locate it by clicking on the **Browse** button.
4. Next, choose the invoice number you wish to correct from the list presented. The program displays the invoice details as they were originally recorded.
5. Make whatever corrections are required to the displayed invoice. Ensure that the new total is in agreement with the corrected amount and that all necessary details are in order.
6. Post the revised invoice by clicking on the Post icon.

Congratulations! You have just done the following tasks:

- Created and posted an adjusting sales journal entry which is the exact opposite of the original entry. This effectively "wipes out" the original invoice.
- Created and posted a "new" invoice with the correct amounts. This enters the revised invoice in place of the orginal, incorrect one.

Note that the program automatically attends to details such as the suitable references for both the reversing and the revised sales journal entries.

Reversing an Entry Made in the Receipts Journal Dialogue Box: Use the Sales Journal.

1. Open the Sales Journal; click on the arrow button to the right of the **Sold to** text box; select the customer from the list displayed; then press the TAB key until the **Invoice** text box is highlighted.
2. Enter the customer's cheque number used in the incorrect entry into the **Invoice** text box, followed by the letter R to show that you are reversing this entry; then press the TAB key.
3. Enter the **Session** date into the **Date** text box; then press the TAB key until the flashing insertion point is positioned in the **Amount** text box.
4. Enter the amount debited to the Cash account in the incorrect journal entry into the **Amount** text box; then press the TAB key.
5. Enter the Cash account number into the **Acct** text box; then press the TAB key.
6. If necessary, enter the amount debited to the Sales Discounts account in the incorrect journal entry into the **Amount** text box; then press the TAB key.
7. Enter the Sales Discounts account number into the **Acct** text box; then press the TAB key.
8. Click on the **Sales Journal Report** menu; then click on Display Sales Journal Entry. The entry should debit the Accounts Receivable account and credit the Cash account (and the Sales Discounts account, if necessary) for the amount of the entry you are reversing. Verify that the entry is correct.
9. Close the Sales Journal Entry window. Make editing corrections if necessary.
10. Click on the Post icon to post the entry.
11. Re-enter the customer's payment correctly, using the Receipts Journal dialogue box. Insert the letter C after the customer's cheque number to show that this is a correcting entry; enter the **Session** date into the **Date** text box. Enter amounts as necessary into the **Disc Taken** and **Payment Amt** text boxes to record the correct amount received from the customer.

Correcting an Entry Made in the Purchases Journal Dialogue Box: Use the Purchases Journal.

Just as with the Sales Journal, *Simply Accounting* provides a useful feature which allows users to "automatically" correct errors made when recording purchases from vendors. The procedure outlined below will quickly and easily correct any errors which may have occurred when recording purchase invoices:

1. Open the Purchases Journal and select the appropriate Transaction Type. It will normally be a Purchase on Account, but a Purchase with Payment can be corrected in the same way.
2. Click the Adjust Invoice icon in the toolbar section. (It is generally the fifth one from the left.) The Adjust an invoice screen appears; it looks like this:

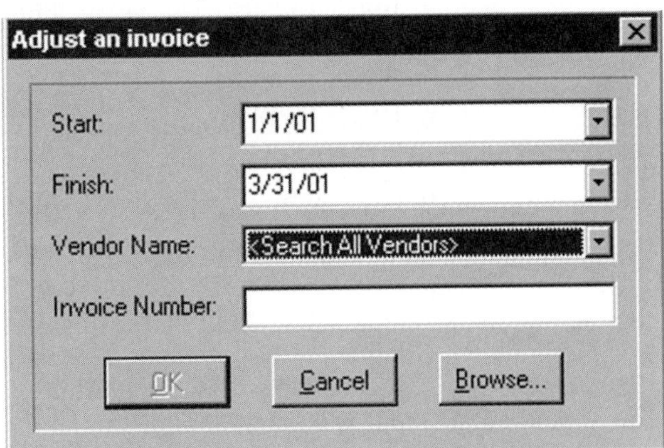

3. Ensure that the Start and Finish dates include the date of the invoice you are correcting; then choose the name of the affected vendor in the appropriate field. (You could use **Browse** to locate the name if you are not certain of it.)
4. Next, choose the invoice number you need to correct from the list presented. The program responds by displaying all the details of the previously-recorded invoice.
5. Make whatever corrections are needed to the displayed invoice. Ensure that the new total agrees with the corrected amount and that all relevant details are acceptable.
6. Post the corrected invoice by clicking on the Post icon.

Congratulations! You have just accomplished the following two tasks:

- ◆ Created and posted a purchases journal entry which is the exact opposite of the original entry. This effectively "wipes out" the original invoice.
- ◆ Created and posted a revised invoice with the corrections made. This enters the new invoice in place of the original, incorrect one.

Note that the program automatically attends to details such as suitable references for the reversing and revised purchase journal entries.

Reversing an Entry Made in the Payments Journal Dialogue Box: Use the Purchases Journal.

1. Open the Purchases Journal; click on the arrow button to the right of the **Purchased from** text box; select the vendor from the list displayed; then press the TAB key until the flashing insertion point is positioned in the **Invoice** text box.
2. Enter the cheque number used in the incorrect entry into the **Invoice** text box, followed by the letter R to show that you are reversing this entry; then press the TAB key.
3. Enter the **Session** date into the **Date** text box; then press the TAB key until the insertion point is positioned in the **Amount** text box.
4. Enter the amount credited to the Cash account in the incorrect journal entry into the **Amount** text box; then press the TAB key.
5. Enter the Cash account number into the **Acct** text box; then press the TAB key.
6. If necessary, enter the amount credited to the Purchases Discount account in the incorrect journal entry into the **Amount** text box; then press the TAB key.
7. Enter the Purchases Discount account number into the **Acct** text box; then press the TAB key.
8. Click on the **Purchases Journal Report** menu; then click on Display Purchases Journal Entry. The entry should debit the Cash account (and the Purchases Discount account, if necessary) and credit the Accounts Payable account for the amount of the entry you are reversing. Verify that the entry is correct.
9. Close the Purchases Journal Entry window. Make editing corrections if necessary.
10. Click on the Post icon to post the entry.
11. Re-enter the payment issued to the vendor correctly, using the Payments Journal dialogue box. Insert the letter C after the cheque number to show that this is a correcting entry; enter the **Session** date into the **Date** text box. Enter amounts as necessary into the **Disc Taken** and **Payment Amt** text boxes to record the correct amount of the payment issued to the vendor.

PART *D*

How to Repeat or Start Over on an Assignment

You always have the option to repeat an assignment for additional practice or start over on an assignment. To repeat or start over on an assignment, make a new Student Data Files disk using the procedures listed in the Creating a Student Data Files Disk section of this appendix (page 657). Relabel your first Student Data Files disk "Student Data Files #1" and label your new copy "Student Data Files #2." Store your disk labelled "Student Data Files #1" in a safe place; then use the disk labelled "Student Data Files #2" to repeat the assignment or start over on the assignment.

After you have repeated or started over on an assignment, you can continue to use the disk labelled "Student Data Files #2" to complete the remaining assignments in this text.

PART *E*

How and When to Use the Backup Copy of a Company's Data Files

At certain times in the assignments you are asked to make a backup copy of a company's data files. There are several reasons why you might wish to access the backup copy of a company's data files. For example, you may not have printed a required report in an assignment before advancing the **Session** date to a new month, or you may want to start an assignment over at the point where the backup copy was made rather than at the beginning of an assignment.

To use the backup copy of a company's data files complete the following procedures. The backup data files for Valdez Realty for June are used to explain the process in the following procedures.

1. Click on the **Start** button. Point to Programs; point to *Simply Accounting*; then click on Simply Accounting in the final menu presented. The *Simply Accounting* Open File dialogue box will appear.
2. Insert your Student Data Files disk into disk drive A. Enter the following path into the **File name** text box: `A:\student\valdjune.asc`.
3. Click on the **Open** button; leave the **Session Date** set at 06/30/03; then click on the **OK** button. The Company Window for Valdjune will appear on your screen. If you only need to print reports for Valdez Realty for June, print those reports now; click on the **Company Window File** menu; then click on Exit to end the current work session and return to your Windows desktop. If you want to start the Valdez Realty assignment over at the point where you made the June backup copy (i.e., you completed the June transactions and adjusting entries correctly, but made an error in the June closing process and/or made errors in the July transactions) continue with the following instructions.
4. Click on the Company Window File menu; click on Save As; then enter the following new file name into the **File name** text box: `A:\student\valdez.asc`.
5. Click on the **Save** button. Click on the **OK** button in response to the question "Replace existing file?" Note that the company name in the Company Window has changed from Valdjune to Valdez.
6. Continue with the Valdez Realty Mini Practice Set, starting with instruction #17 under Part A: The June Accounting Cycle.

If you want to use the backup copy of a company's data files in a situation other than that described above, substitute the desired backup file name for valdjune. asc and the desired current data file name for valdez. asc into the procedures described above.

PART *F*

Print and Display Settings in Simply Accounting for Windows

When you install *Simply Accounting*, the program automatically installs the default printer established in Windows as the default printer for *Simply Accounting*. If you have not yet installed a default printer in Windows, you will need to do so prior to attempting to print any reports from the *Simply Accounting* program. Refer to your Windows manual for information on installing a printer. You do not need to re-install *Simply Accounting for Windows*. The next time you access *Simply Accounting*, the Windows default printer will automatically be established as the default printer for *Simply Accounting*.

The installation process for the Windows default printer does not ensure that the default printer and display settings within *Simply Accounting* will work to your satisfaction; consequently, you must test and if necessary adjust your printer and display settings before you complete any of the assignments in the text. Once the print and display settings are adjusted, they will become the default printer and display settings for each set of company data files. You need only make these adjustments once.

HOW TO TEST AND ADJUST THE DEFAULT PRINTER AND DISPLAY SETTINGS FOR SIMPLY ACCOUNTING

1. Click on the **Start** button. Point to Programs; point to Simply Accounting; then click on Simply Accounting in the final menu presented. The Simply Accounting **Open File** dialogue box will appear.
2. Insert your Student Data Files disk into disk drive A. Enter the following path into the **File name** text box: `A:\student\printest.asc`
3. Click on the **Open** button. The program will respond with a request for the **Session** date. Leave the **Using Date for this Session** text box set at 04/01/01; then click on the **OK** button. The Company Window will appear.
4. Click on the Company Window **Setup** menu; then click on Settings. The Settings dialogue box will appear.
5. Click on the Display tab; then adjust the display features based on the following definitions and suggestions:
   - **Display Font:** Click on the arrow button to the right of the **Display Font** text box to display a list of available fonts. Select the font you want to see on the screen when you display reports.
   - **Size:** Click on the arrow button to the right of the **Size** text box to display a list of available type sizes. Select the type size you want to see on the screen when you display reports.

   NOTE: It is suggested that you adjust the display settings to agree with **Display Font** and **Size** used for the screen illustrations in the text. These settings are:
   - **Display Font:** Arial
   - **Size:** 8
6. Click on the **OK** button to return to the Company Window. These display settings will become the new display settings for all sets of company data files.
7. Click on the Company Window **Reports** menu; point to Financials; then click on Trial Balance. The Trial Balance Options dialogue box will appear. Leave the **As at** date set at 04/01/01; then click on the **OK** button. The Trial Balance Report window will appear.
8. The scroll bar can be used to advance the display to view other portions of the report.

9. Click on the Trial Balance **File** menu; then click on Print to print the Trial Balance.
10. Click on the **Close** button to close the Trial Balance window and return to the Company Window.
11. Review your printed Trial Balance report. If the font, type size, and/or margins are not satisfactory, continue with the following instructions. If the font, type size, and margins are satisfactory, click on the Company Window File menu; then click on Exit to end your current work session and return to your Windows desktop.
12. To adjust the printer settings, click on the Company Window **Setup** menu; then click on Reports and Forms. The Reports and Forms dialogue box will appear.
13. Click on the Reports and Graphics tab; then adjust the printer settings as necessary, based on the following definitions:
    - **Printer:** Click on the arrow button to the right of the **Printer** text box to display a list of available printers. These are the printers you set up in Windows. If you want to use a printer that is not on the list, you must install the new printer in Windows. Select the printer you want to use.
    - **Font:** Click on the arrow button to the right of the **Font** text box to display a list of available fonts. Select the font you want to use.
    - **Size:** Click on the arrow button to the right of the **Size** text box to display a list of available type sizes. Select the type size you want to use. The larger the type size selected, the larger the type will appear on your printed reports. If no type size options appear, make sure that you have selected a font in the **Font** text box; then select the type size for the font you have selected.
    - **Top Margin:** Enter the amount you want the top margin of the text to be lowered or raised if your reports are being printed too high or too low on the page. The amount should be expressed in inches and decimal fractions of an inch (up to two decimal places). Positive amounts lower the top margin; negative amounts raise it.
    - **Left Margin:** Enter the amount you want the left margin of the text to be moved to the right or left if your reports are being printed too far to the left or right. The amount should be expressed in inches and decimal fractions of an inch (up to two decimal places). Positive amounts move the left margin to the right, negative amounts move it to the left.
14. After you have established the desired printer settings, click on the **OK** button to return to the Company Window. These printer settings will become the new printer settings for all sets of company data files.
15. To test your adjusted printer settings, click on the Company Window **Reports** menu; point to Financials; then click on Trial Balance. The Trial Balance Options dialogue box will appear. Leave the **As at** date set at 04/01/01; then click on the **OK** button.
16. Click on the Trial Balance **File** menu; then click on Print to print the Trial Balance.
17. Click on the **Close** button to close the Trial Balance window and return to the Company Window.
18. Review your printed Trial Balance report. If the font, type size, and/or margins are still not satisfactory, go back to instruction #12 and make new adjustments. If the font, type size, and margins are satisfactory, click on the Company Window **File** menu; then click on Exit to end your current work session and return to your Windows desktop.

Index